1

Finding the Lost Battalion:
Beyond the Rumors, Myths
And Legends of America's
Famous WW1 Epic

By: Robert J. Laplander

American
Expeditionary
Foundation

www.amexfound.com

Lulu Press
www.lulu.com

Laplander, Robert John
Finding the Lost Battalion: Beyond the Rumors, Myths and Legends
of America's Famous WW1 Epic / Robert J. Laplander
Includes biographical references, photos, maps and index.

ISBN 1411676564

1. World War, 1914-1918. 2. Argonne, Battle of the, France, 1918. 3.
United States Army Division, 77th – History. 4. United States Army
Regimental histories.   I. Title

Laplander, Robert John 1966 -

Original Copyright © 2006 by Robert J. Laplander.
2nd Edition January, 2007 by Robert J. Laplander.
Presented by: The American Expeditionary Foundation, Waterford,
Wisconsin, U.S.A. www.amexfound.com
Printed by Lulu Press. www.lulu.com
Lulu Press ID # 176869

This book is respectfully dedicated
to the memory of
Charles White Whittlesey
January 20, 1884 – November 26, 1921
and to the men that served under him.

Contents:

The marker above the Pocket along the Binarville-La Viergette Road as it appears today
(Taylor V. Beattie)

Preface and Author's
Note to the 2nd Edition

In the year or so since the original version of *Finding the Lost Battalion* was released, I am pleased to note that it has been quite well received by the public. As I had imagined when I originally began the project, nearly a decade ago now, what had arguably been the single greatest story to come out of America's participation in the First World War still had the power to capture the imagination. It was a damned good story then, as now, and during this passed year I have been the recipient of hundreds of letters, phone calls, and e-mails concerning this work, as well as my on-going research into the Lost Battalion. It has been my pleasure to have made acquaintance with even more families of Lost Battalion men, and to continue to gather information, records, and stories of not only the events both on l'Homme Mort and in the Charlevaux Ravine, but those events surrounding each of those episodes as well. I am honored to be the man of this era charged with the responsibility of gathering and holding whatever there is out there to be discovered about the Lost Battalion in one lifetime, in order that further generations will never forget this magnificent episode. I find myself in good past company (please see the chapter *Creating a Legend*, as well as *Appendix B*), and accept the responsibility earnestly and whole heartedly. Therefore, I here introduce this second edition of *Finding the Lost Battalion*. It is essentially the same as the First Edition, save that I have taken the opportunity to correct some misspellings and a few of the men's names that were wrong, as well as one or two minor details. Also, that I may express here my deepest appreciation to my many readers for trusting me to tell them such an incredible story.

Thank you. And you may rest assured that my research will continue, and that this is not the last you will hear from me on the subject of the Lost Battalion!

A great many of the sources referenced for this book remain wholly unique to it alone, as quite a number of them have never before been seen by the general public. These are the basis for the details that set this work apart from all other books about the Lost Battalion. Additionally, when the original manuscript for this volume was initially completed, it was nearly double the length of the eventual 'finished product'. Therefore, in an effort to keep the book to a reasonable length, I found it necessary to par down the manuscript and 'compress' events into a reasonable space. In doing this, I unfortunately had to sacrifice some of the individual soldier's reflections in order to focus more thoroughly on the correction of the many long-standing errors and myths to the true story, and to accurately describe how the whole Lost Battalion situation came about in the first place. While nothing would have pleased me more than to have been able to include every scrap of information that I uncovered in my initial 8+ years of research into the Lost Battalion, this has simply not been possible. That said, I nevertheless believe that I have successfully struck an equitable balance of 'informational fact' and 'individual grit' that offers as complete a picture of the events described as could be in a 'popular' book of a reasonable length. I trust that I will have met the reader's expectations.

(Please note that in February, 2007 the author put out a second book on the Lost Battalion containing many additional facts and stories left out of this work, entitled 'The Lost Battalion: Return to the Charlevaux', available at www.lulu.com.)

There were many individuals that helped me over the many years that I have been working on this volume; far too many, in fact, to be able to list them all here. However, my deep and heartfelt thanks continue to go out to those people listed below, without whom this book would not be what it is, most especially (but not limited to), Ken 'Wichita' Miller, for all the maps, illustrations, patience and friendship, as well as to the following: John Hicks, John Larney, Tom Baldwin, Frances Bingham, Leo and Glenn Jammaron, Jim Downs, Thomas O. Bell, Jeannie Hughes, Carmen Calbi Jr., Robert Von Pentz, Ruth Eager Moran, Brett Reynolds, Rick Lytle, Becky Henn Richard Amick, Joyce and Bob Bromm, Patricia Nirmaire, Julie Girard, Thomas Kilkenny, Alfred DiGiancomo, Rita Comeau, Don Wilkinson, Brian Quinn, James Wickman, George and David Gaedeke, Susan Carr, Angelo Levi, Maricarol Miller, Jeff Wilfahrt, April Young, Billie Hendricks, Willy Drinkwater, Julie Nelson, Marshall P. Hoke, Zachary Allen, Orvin Peterson, Samuel Steele, Robert Collins, Joseph Pagliaro, Robert Conner, John Lanning, Marc Goncher, Chris Yoder, Tony Cepaglia, Rhonda Walker, Martha Young, Gene Holderman, Tommy Bragg, Boyd Leuenberger, Laurie Esch and the Esch family, Kathy Morgan, Dan Olson, George Ryan, Kevin McDonough, Marvin Edwards, Richard Tuite, David Gehris, Victor and Joanne Fritch, Marylou Weber, John Culleeny, Mark Erickson, Larry Butler, Steve Clay, George Ross, Andrew Berkowitz, George Weinmann, Perry Haberman, Eric Fangman, Jack Fosmark, Lonnie Collins, Paul Kendall, Ed Gombar, Chester Marcus, Lowell and Darlene McFarland, Francis Kopel, William Whittlesey, Steve Whittlesey, Penny Leak, Kurt Johnson, Steve Stone, Eric Christian, Alan Tobin, Don and Matt Rademacher, Earl Roth, Steve Ray, and Glenn Hyatt.

I am also deeply grateful to the following staff of the Williams College Archives Department for their help in setting up the appointment for me to see the Charles White Whittlesey collection and Thomas Johnson papers, and then in helping us go through it all: Head of the department, Ms. Sylvia Kendrick Brown; her chief assistant, Ms. Linda Hall; and the two students who 'gave their all' in hauling all the stuff up from where it is stored, Ms. Nicole Theriault and Ms. Amy Rupert.

I wish to thank the following citizens of Florence, Wisconsin for all their help in my search up there: Mrs. Sheila Dagastino and Mrs. Debra DeMuri of the Florence County Historical Society, who spent a good deal of time showing me Whittlesey's old 'haunts' and relating what stories remain of the boy that became the man; Mrs. Lucille "Toots" Lawrentz, who shared pictures and descriptions of the old Whittlesey home (and who could still Charleston better than me – at well over twice my age); Mrs. Lucille McMullen; the right Reverend Andy Swartz, for setting me on the right path in Florence and for his words of wisdom and guidance; the right Reverend Doug Johnson, current clergyman at the 1st Presbyterian Church, where the Whittlesey family congregated, for inviting me in and showing me where the family still exists up there; and finally to Evelyn Riedel of Townsend, Wisconsin, my driving partner and Wisconsin research analyst.

Any research into the AEF really needs to center on the National Archives and Records Administration (NARA), College Park facility. I therefore wish to express appreciation not only to the extremely efficient and helpful staff at NARA, but most especially to probably the single most knowledgeable man on their staff, as far as WWI is concerned, Mr. Mitchell Yockelson. Not only did he take time out of his busy day (and I'm not kidding; this guy is beyond busy) to show enough interest to personally see that I got what I needed, but then also spent several dozen of his precious minutes talking over this project with me. His level of professionalism is truly impressive. Mitch, I thank you from the bottom of my very being…

And, to the 'unsung heroes' of my project; my Lost Battalion Research Team. In the U.S., this team included the following: John Cotter, who with his son, Sean, runs the official Lost Battalion website and has been a tremendous help, and friend, throughout the years in contacting Lost Battalion family members, as well as researching in France twice; Paul Infranco, whose website, *Longwood's Journey*, is quite simply amazing. Paul is also probably the single most knowledgeable person around on the lore of Camp Upton; Mike and Jenny Jetzer, Mike is my official Lost Battalion photographer and kept the project supplied in the computer equipment we needed. Jenny proofread the manuscript, helped me out tremendously on the ground in France, and has probably been the single biggest supporter of the project all along; Lieutenant Colonel Taylor V. Beattie, who not only wrote the forward to this book, but helped gather prospective for it while in France from the standpoint of a combat experienced officer of comparable rank to Major Whittlesey; Dave Zajicek, whose knowledge of WWI detail is astounding and who helped me with research at the National Archives; Deb Sedona, who helped tremendously with computer research; Bill Bethia, who helped with the layout work on the book, answered a million computer questions and is my oldest friend.

And in France: Gilles Lagin and Alexandre Herreman. Gilles, who has become without a doubt my closest friend in France, runs the U.S. Marine Corps Museum at Belleau Wood and that is his greatest passion. No one knows more about what the Marines did in France than does Gilles. Period. He is also an expert at navigating the sometimes dangerous battlefields of his country and knows of the nooks and crannies from the war that have escaped popular notice. He, along with the trusty Alexandre Herreman, another eminent battlefield expert, has made many trips to the Argonne when I could not be there and needed further research done on the ground. I can never repay the work they have done for me, especially Gilles, or adequately express my thanks and appreciation. I gladly give it anyway, however inadequate, and I strongly urge everyone to visit Gilles' ultra-fantastic U.S. Marine Corps Belleau Wood Museum if you are ever in France. I further encourage you to look him up and hire him as your battlefield guide. You will *not* be disappointed; Frederic Castier, who is *the* man to go to concerning anything the American army did in France during both WWI and WWII and has helped me out in so many ways that I cannot begin to count them. His dedication to preserving the battlefields and memories of those Americans who fought on his country's soil in both those World Wars is nothing short of incredible. Thank you Fred, for all that you do.

To those who lent help or offered support in those flagging moments, or with the hundred and one other details someone on a quest is so apt to overlook, I also here offer my hearty thanks to... My mother, Rose, for giving me the greatest two gifts I have ever gotten: life, and a true love of reading. She told me very early on that as long as I could read I could go anywhere, do anything, and be anybody that I wanted. She was right. I have been all over the world and all through history and never had to leave my house to do it until just recently. And, for the last decade or so, I have frequently spent great deals of time in a narrow, muddy ravine in the northeastern part of France of nearly 90 years ago. I never could have accomplished this project without her initial caring and love. Thanks for everything mom; Mssr. Jerome Boulanger, a ranger with the French Office of National Forests who works in the Binarville area. He and his maps came in handy at the right place and at the right time to several muddy and lost woods-walkers; Paule et Jerome Patte, of the Hotel le St. Paul, Verdun, France, who put up with boisterous, hungry, non-French speaking Americans *very* early in the morning and muddy, grumbling Americans very late at night – all with a smile; Mssr. Damien George, His Honor the Mayor of Fleville, France, and chief forest ranger of the general area, for leading us into places along the line we never would have otherwise found; Mssr. Jean-Christophe

Keller, for going the 'extra mile' during filming; Mr. Craig Rahanian, superintendent of the massive Muese-Argonne Cemetery at Romagne, France, for helping us through the cemetery; Jan Collins, who shared with me letters and diary extracts of her aunt, a one-time nurse 'over there' who had worked at one of the camps where many of the Lost Battalion wounded were brought; Joyline Hornburg, RN, BSN, Milwaukee, WI, for answering all my hundreds of inane medical questions; Ms. Toni B. Wulff, Ph.D. Associate Professor of French at Mt. Mary College, Milwaukee, WI, for the translations; Mr. Thiemo Kuehner of Fox Point, WI, for bailing me out with some very difficult German translations that nobody else would touch; Barry Abrahams, Warren Whitby, and Dave Stieghan, for pointing me in the right direction of certain articles and information when I needed them; David and Trisha Hornburg and Tamara Evans, for the never-ending (and continuing) support with the details of life *outside* the battalion; Kevin Kaleck and Randy Avery, for proofreading parts of the manuscript; Mike Hanlon and Roger Jones, for helping me get a copy of the 1921 movie; Mike Monte, a writer by profession, for his interest and good advice; Sue Fisher, for even more good advice; The staff of the Minnesota History Center, for their professionalism and help in locating what I needed; Green Door Antiques of Bellflower CA - you know what for; The Great War Association, The Great War Preservation Society, The Western Front Association, and The American Expeditionary Foundation; Ray Pirus, for asking the questions that made me think; Jim Liesenfelder, for always encouraging me to do what I dreamed I could do, no matter how far fetched it might seem; Tony Antonucci, the 'New York lion'; Lisa 'Tater' Horngren, for comforting words and a pat on the back - followed by a shove in a correct direction; and Laura Rinaldi, for thinking so much of me and my project.

And to the most important member of my team - my long-suffering and unbelievably patient and tolerant wife, Trinie. She has, for these many years, been forced to share her home and husband with the ghosts of 1,000 or so long dead men; sifted through hundreds of pages of dusty and (to her) boring files; heard countless retellings of the same story over and over again (until she can recite it word for word herself); been dragged all over this country repeatedly and France twice, enduring heat, humidity, rain and Argonne mud, brush and brambles; edited and corrected and then re-edited and re-corrected the same manuscript over and over again (and taught me to type in the process); not seen her kitchen table for over two and a half years (and then lost her dining room table for six months after that); generally had to put up with the erratic behavior of someone obsessed with a project that occupied his thoughts at virtually all times… and then actually hung around to see the final outcome. You must really, really, really love me. Thanks. I love you too, even more than ever.

Finally, and most especially, to the men of the Lost Battalion themselves; for their tremendous sacrifices, made so very long ago for the sake of freedom.

Well done.

Rest in peace.

Robert J. Laplander
1:07 p.m.
August 21st, 2007
Tichigan, Wisconsin

Foreword

By
Lt. Col. Taylor Voorhis Beattie
U.S. Army, Special Forces

"When an individual shows courage under stress,
we feel a thrill at his achievement,
but when a group of men flash out in the splendor of manliness
we feel a lasting glow that is both pride
and renewed faith in our fellow man"

Lt. Col. Charles Whittlesey
November 11, 1920 (I)

Deep within the Argonne forest, in the Ardennes region of France, there is a small, gloomy ravine where the sun does not shine, nor do the birds sing. The warming rays of the sun are blocked by the thick interlaced canopy above and the birds seem to avoid the place altogether. It is deathly quite in there, the ground smells of rotting vegetation and fertile soil with a hint of sulfur wafting from the marshy ground surrounding a diminutive brook that has meandered through the area since before the birth of man. The place smells, feels, and looks like purgatory, or some sort of middle earth suspended in time, conjuring the misery that permeated the place for five dreadful days over eighty years ago in early October 1918. It has been clear to me for some time now that the small ravine buried in the Argonne Forest, is haunted; haunted by the ghosts of the "Lost Battalion".

"If ye break faith with us who die we shall not sleep…" (II)

That is not to say that the ravine is a frightening place, or that the ghosts of the brave men of the Lost Battalion do not enjoy the company of the visitors. Quite the contrary; I have always felt welcome in the ravine and would gladly spend the night there with the spirits of these fine young men. And that is what is so troubling about the ravine… They were young men, cut down in their prime, miles from home and family, doing what patriots do best - sacrificing all that they ever have, or will be, for the liberty of others. I have been to the ravine many times, as pilgrims like I often return again and again to be in the company of these spirits, all the while searching for clues to understand their story. The place and the spirits residing within beckon to me, and with each visit I leave with my own spirit unsettled as new questions emerge to tickle my curiosity, tug at my soldier's intuition and stretch my imagination. The imagination of a professional soldier - a witness to the horrors of war and genocide in the former Yugoslavia, the Middle East and portions of Central Africa; contemporary examples of man's inhumanity to man. In spite of this, I still struggle to comprehend the level of misery that defined the small ravine in 1918.

My particular questions concerning the saga of the Lost Battalion have always centered not so much on the *how* it happened, but the *why*. As a Special Forces Officer, I am at the core a combat leader; a light Infantryman with some understanding of tactical maneuver. Why had Charles Whittlesey, the commander of the composite unit, led his command into this position? Why were they all bunched up in a small perimeter that only allowed a portion of his available combat power to be effective in any direction? Why had Charles Whittlesey then taken his own life three years following the siege of the ravine? And perhaps tangentially related, the most bothersome question of all; was all of this necessary? Indeed, when wandering through the ravine the words of Shakespeare's 'Henry V' echo through my thoughts:

"When all those legs and arms and heads chopped off in battle, shall join together at the latter day, and cry 'all we died at such a place' some swearing, some crying for a surgeon, some upon their wives left poor behind them, some upon their debts they owe, some upon their children rawly left. I am afeard there are few die well that die in battle…"

My first visit to the Charlevaux Ravine was in February of 1994. It was President's weekend, my family and I were stationed in Stuttgart Germany, and it was a long weekend. We had no specific plans, so when an Army buddy, Ron Bowman, suggested our families' travel together to see the U.S. World War I battlefields in France, the notion seemed as good as any. Not that I had any particular interest in the First World War, but as a soldier I am drawn to the quieted battlefields of yesterday. Through some sort of allied military understanding, we were able to secure accommodation at the French officer's club, *Circle des Officers*, in Verdun for the weekend and there settled into our pleasant, large rooms, shared drinks in the bar, and had a good dinner in the officer's mess.

The following day we toured the Great War sites of Verdun. We saw the Forts Douaumont and Vaux, as well as the "Trench of the Bayonets"; where French soldiers standing at the parapets in their trench were buried alive by an artillery round. Today their rifle muzzles peek skyward from the dirt and their owners remain buried for eternity grasping their weapons in anticipation of a Boche attack. Just down the road, at the eerie Douaumont Ossuary, we squatted down to peek through windows at the piles of skulls and bones collected from adjacent battlefields and interred within. On Sunday, we drove out to the Meuse-Argonne Battlefield where the Americans fought. We visited the impressive U.S. Monument at Montfaucon, marking center sector of the battlefield. Later, we stopped by the U.S. cemetery at Romagne, where over fourteen thousand American soldiers killed in the region now rest. The place was erected in 1921 as "a sacred rendezvous of a grateful people with its immortal dead" according to the inscription on the chapel wall. Our last stop on that Sunday before heading home was to the site of the "Lost Battalion" near Charlevaux Mill…

A simple stone marker marked the spot along the winding Apremont road. The stone lists the units of the composite battalion, and an arrow directs your gaze down into the ravine. Ron read the story of the Lost Battalion out of the *American Battlefields of Europe*, as Katy, the kids, and I scrambled down the steep slope, noting the remains of individual fighting positions on the way down to the brook at the bottom. On the floor of the ravine there were numerous shell craters, filled now with water half frozen over from the cold. Spirits of the Lost Battalion not withstanding, the temperature dropped ten degrees between the road above and the bottom of the ravine. At the brook, I dipped my hand into the frigid water to retrieve a hunk of metal, dark against the light brown sand. I held the heavy shell fragment in my hand with the notion that during the time of my grandfather's youth, this piece of metal broke away from an exploding shell; the fragments from which killed or scared the hell out of American soldiers shivering from fear and cold in their "funk holes" hacked into the slope above. For five dreadful days these men were surrounded and harassed from all directions - out of water, food, ideas, and luck. Grown men sobbed as they listened to wounded comrades moaning pitifully beyond help in adjacent funk holes. Some of these would die in the night succumbing to their wounds, aggravated by cold, hunger, and thirst. Each morning, Major Whittlesey would designate burial parties to bury the dead in the funk holes where they lay. Later in the day German mortar and artillery rounds would rain in, blowing the dead from their new graves to rejoin the living in adjacent holes. In my mind's eye I captured a fleeting glimpse of it all and something touched my soul down there in that Pocket deep within the bowels of the Argonne Forest. Shell fragment in hand, I scrambled back up the slope past those scars in the hillside, changed forever and haunted by a desire to learn - and then tell - their story.

This is the book that I wanted to write. Shortly following publication of the article "Ghosts of the Lost Battalion" (*Military History*, August 2002), I came into contact with Robert Laplander. We developed a collegial relationship via email and telephone, which eventually led to an opportunity to meet at the Pocket in the Argonne later that year and walk the ground, exchanging information and perspectives. Rob had taken my inclinations to write a book on the Lost Battalion and put them into action, as he had been working on his for quite some years by then. He had already gathered an incredible amount of information concerning the force in the ravine and had tirelessly chased down every source of knowledge concerning the Lost Battalion that he could find, including me. I knew immediately that this was the man that was intended to write their story and that I should join his extensive network and research team.

I am glad that I did. This is without a doubt the most comprehensive book that has yet been written on the Lost Battalion. Not only does Rob painstakingly trace to movements of the force through the battle, using mostly previously unseen archival resources, but he provides a fine dialogue and postulates why things happened and when. His inclusion of the event from the German perspective is also a welcome addition to the story and one that helps us to understand that it was as much an epic for them as it was for Major Whittlesey and his men. Never before had the brutal truth of the Lost Battalion been told, so when Rob asked me to write the Foreword for this book I jumped at the opportunity to be part of the effort to remember these fine men.

Now, as I settle down to compose this Foreword, it is with a sense of irony. I have returned to Stuttgart Germany on temporary duty to assist in a military exercise. It is the evening of the 11th of November 2004, and it has been ten years since I first stumbled down the steep slope of the ravine, past the scars of those funk holes. Nine years from this day, I sent the leaders from my company to France with Ron Bowman to visit the site of the Lost Battalion and to lay a wreath during the Veterans Day ceremonies at the U.S. cemetery in Romagne. I had planned that trip for a year and was pulled away at the last minute to attend a NATO planning conference for the impending Peace Enforcement operation in the Balkans; ironically the birthplace of the Great War. Within weeks I would be taking the men that I sent to France with Ron into Tuzla, Bosnia-Herzegovina for a four-month mission, to insert ourselves between the belligerents of their horrible civil war on a peace enforcement mission. But first, I had desperately wanted the leaders in my company to see the site of the Lost Battalion in order to connect with the spirits within, not just so that they would understand the great sacrifices and privations that had been endured by Americans of their grandfather's generation, but also to know that if necessary they could endure the same to see the mission through...

Here, sitting in my Stuttgart hotel room, it occurs to me that 86 years have passed since the last shots rang out in the Great War, the seminal event of the 20th century. This 'war that would end all wars' was in reality the genesis of 20th century conflict - World War II, the Cold War, and all of the little brush fire wars that sprouted from the same. Earlier today, all over France they recognized the ending of the Great War in numerous ceremonies in small villages all over the country. Some of these ceremonies occurred around crumbling monuments, erected to commemorate the liberation of these villages by American forces. I know this because in past years I have been privileged to attend a number of these ceremonies and have stood at attention in front of these American monuments. These French inhabitants, the descendants of those who were liberated by the Americans, remember and mark the day annually.

Sadly, the feats of the American soldiers to whom these crumbling monuments had been erected have been forgotten back in these United States. Those veterans of the AEF who returned to the U.S. got on with life and living. They survived the depression, raising and nurturing those who Tom Brokaw would call the "greatest generation". And yet, these veterans of the Great War - knowing first hand the horrors of war - sent their sons and daughters to the second round of the bloody argument for the destiny of the 20th Century. But destiny plays no favorites from generation to generation, as a wholly new generation of American Heroes and Patriots has again answered the call, moved to the sound of the guns and have made the supreme sacrifice in our 21st Century War on Terror.

"If ye break faith with us who die we shall not sleep…" (II)

Thanks to Robert Laplander's dedication and relentless search for anything related to the Lost Battalion, the men and feats of that honorable band of men will never be forgotten. While ultimately we will never know exactly what happened in the ravine, I am convinced that Rob has gotten us as close as we can get to providing the answers to questions which I fear rested heavily on Charles Whittlesey's mind as he mounted the rail of a steamer bound for Cuba, peered down into the black waters below and stepped out to join the members of 'his' Lost Battalion…

Lieutenant Colonel Taylor V. Beattie
U.S. Army Special Forces
Stuttgart, Germany
11 November 2004

(I) From "A Tribute" written for *History and Rhymes of the Lost Battalion*, by Buck Private McCollum.
(II) From "In Flanders Fields" by Lt. Col. John McCrae

About This Book

The book you are about to read is the culmination of the first eight years worth of my research into the Lost Battalion, which is ongoing, conducted through seven states of the U.S. and on two different continents. It is by no means the complete story, but instead as complete a story as can be told up to this time and in a reasonable amount of space. In writing this, I have made every attempt at separating the rumors, myths, and legends from the facts in order to present as accurate a story as possible. I have presented, in some instances, different versions of the same story in an effort to sift the facts and thus recreate what really happened. In other places, I have used several similar descriptions of an event or action to recreate it from several viewpoints. I have also used the actual men's words where appropriate, though I have paraphrased some quotes in an effort to cut out unnecessary or long-winded descriptions. Where there were multiple descriptions left behind by the same man, I have sometimes combined them to provide as clear and accurate a picture as possible. Contrarily, I have usually unchanged their words, leaving most of their grammar intact so as to preserve the 'flavor' of what they said. Additionally, nearly all of the dialog used here is what was really said, as near as can be established from reliable written or otherwise recorded sources left by the men that were there at the time. The men of the 77th were, for the large part, pretty rough and tumble, and this was well reflected in their language. Please note then that in places the language – as well as descriptions of some scenes and events – do get rather graphic. The longer actual quotes I have used that have been taken from writings/recordings left behind by the men themselves, I have put in Italics within double quotation marks. Shorter quotes, or actual conversational dialog, I have left in plain text with double quotation marks. Any recreated dialog is only given to illustrate a point and has been placed in italics with single quotes and is very likely what was said anyway.

I have included background information on the 77th Division as a whole as well, but what information I have included I felt was necessary in order for the average reader to understand the character and makeup of the division and the 308th Infantry Regiment in particular, as well as the great offensive in which they participated. All of this had a direct bearing on the men's actions in the Charlevaux Ravine, and most particularly on Charles Whittlesey's. If this was the 1920's or 30's, most of this information might be familiar, but it is far less likely to be known from this distance of time. These prepatory chapters I have attempted to keep as brief as possible however, merely providing descriptive 'windows' through which to view the divisional training, arrival in France, and first battles up to the Muese-Argonne attack, so as not to bog the reader down in sidebar details. So too the first chapter, which gives a very short description of the heady world atmosphere prior to America's entry into the war, as seen through the eyes of a future casualty of the Lost Battalion.

For the reader that may not understand some of the terms of combat, or how some of the more obscure aspects of warfare of the time worked, the following descriptions should help illustrate those occurrences referred to in the text.

World War I has been called the 'battle of the guns' with good reason. Artillery played a large part during the war, accountable for about eight out of every ten wounds and roughly the same in deaths. Since hostilities opened in 1914, artillery had been used to 'soften up' an enemy position before the infantry would move over in waves in assault. The French term for the delivery of a rain of shells onto a predetermined zone or target was 'barrage'. A 'fixed barrage' was the artillery 'ranging', or aiming their fire onto a specific target, position, or area, and simply pounding it with shellfire unmercifully, or else the dropping a 'wall' of shellfire designed to block either an avenue of attack or retreat. As the war progressed, these barrages became not only standard, but also longer and fiercer in intensity as well. The weight of the barrage at the start of the Muese-Argonne Offensive was about one million shells on the first day alone.

The alter ego of the 'fixed barrage', was the 'rolling', or 'creeping' barrage. This specific form of shellfire called for extremely delicate timing and co-operation on the part of both the infantry and the artillery. It began with a fixed barrage falling on a definite target. At a prearranged time, the artillery fire would 'lift' or 'roll/creep' forward a certain distance, firing as it went, to eventually settle on a further fixed point. At that moment, the infantry would swarm 'over the top' and out of their own trenches and attack the freshly shelled enemy positions, while the shellfire prepared new positions ahead to be attacked. At yet another prearranged appropriate time, the process would be repeated. Used successfully, it was a tried and true form of movement.

However, the system was not without its flaws. If the artillery advanced its fire too quickly, or the infantry for whatever reason failed to keep up, then the infantry would be forced to watch as their protective 'screen' of fire moved away from them - with no way to recall it. Conversely, if the infantry advanced too quickly, or the artillery batteries did not all advance their fire together, disaster would befall the unfortunate men stuck under the curtain of shells. Thus, timing was *everything* during the rolling barrage.

There was also the 'box barrage'. In a box barrage, the fall of artillery shot was arranged in such a way that the wall of shells was positioned to fall *around* a specified locality on three sides, leaving only the side facing the attacking force open. In this way, the attackers could rush against their enemy who was 'boxed in' with no place to fall back to, and thus had no choice but to either fight it out or surrender.

Another common practice during the war was 'Infantry Contact Patrol' used by the Army Air Service to obtain direct observation or liaison of the forces on the ground with those in the air through a series of colored flares, or more commonly, white cloth 'panels' of different sizes and shapes (depending on the ground units' individual needs or strengths). These panels were laid out on the ground in a variety of patterns, each pattern meaning a different thing; the same being true about the number and color of flares fired. When spotted from the air, the flyer thus knew either where the infantry unit was or what it wanted, and then passed the information on along the correct channels necessary. The panels could also be arranged to indicate which unit a plane was flying over, thus identifying the actual position of the battle lines during an attack - extremely important in the midst of battle, where the front lines shifted often.

However, the infantry were sometimes reluctant to answer the airmen's calls for panels or flares (especially flares) for fear of giving their position away to any German airmen that may also be in the vicinity, or an enemy that may be on higher ground around them. (Airplanes were also frequently used as a means to first locate a position and then call down an artillery barrage onto it.) Though this frustrated the high command, one might easily understand the reluctance of the infantry to 'announce' themselves as it were, to whoever may be watching. Several methods were tried to 'cure' the problem, but it remained a thorn in the air corps' side throughout the war.

Perhaps the biggest problem in the First World War though was the lack of any 'real time' two-way portable communication. Field telephones depended on heavy, yet fragile, wire that was more often than not cut by shellfire as quickly as it was laid down, and 'wireless' (radio) was in its infancy, with no voice communication possible, only the slow

Morse code. Additionally, wireless sets, and their accompanying batteries, were heavy and cumbersome for field use, and not very reliable. Therefore, with 'real time' communications rarely possible between advancing units and the rear (including the artillery), the 'runner system' of hand delivering written messages was a very common practice. Contact was maintained through a 'chain' of runner posts, which an advancing headquarters unit established as it moved forward, usually setting them two to three hundred meters apart. These posts generally consisted of two or three men. A message would be given to a man at post #1, who would run it to post #2 and hand it off to a man there, then taking his position while the second man, message in hand, headed out for post #3 to hand it off and take a place there, and so on down the line until the message eventually arrived at its intended destination. Messages that needed to go to the head of an attack ran the gamut in reverse. While not the speediest of methods, it did have the advantage of having an observant man able to answer questions as the bearer of the missive.

The alternative to the runner was the carrier pigeon, used when the distance was great or when time was of the essence. Special pigeon handlers in the headquarters units carried these in wooden backpack style coops (8 birds to a coop), and they were used with quite a bit of success. Yet the greatest drawback with the birds was their unreliability. They tended, for whatever bird-like reasons, to sometimes go astray, thus leaving the message sender in the lurch.

The U.S. entered the war woefully unprepared as far as useful combat gear went. Consequently, the government bought a lot of French and British equipment, particularly weapons. The automatic rifle (or 'light machine-gun') used by the 77th Division, and frequently mentioned herein, was a French model called the 'Chauchat'. Nicknamed the 'Sho-Sho' (and occasionally referred to as the 'Shit-Shit') by the troops, the French model was chambered for an 8mm rimmed rifle cartridge and had a nasty habit of jamming after only a few rounds had been fired. This was primarily due to the open sided half-moon clip that fed it, which allowed dirt and debris to get into the mechanism. It was not a particularly hardy weapon (the company that made it, the Gladiator Corporation, had been a bicycle manufacturer before the war), but it was fairly hard hitting. Doughboys joked that the best way to clear a jam in the Chauchat was to throw it away – and sometimes they were not joking. The heavy machine-gun used the most was the air cooled French Model 1914 Hotchkiss, also in 8mm and fed from straight 24 round clips packed in wooden crates that had to be hand carried everywhere. It was an extremely heavy weapon (gun and tripod weighed in at a hefty 110 pounds), but was unfailingly reliable. Both remained in service with the 77th Division until mid October 1918.

On a following page will be found a flow chart table of organization of the 77th Division so that the reader may understand the breakdown of a common National (draft) Army 'boxed' Infantry Division in the First World War. Also contained on the chart is a 'code key' to the code supposed to have been used by the 154th Brigade, though few actually used it. Certainly, Charles Whittlesey rarely did and this is reflected in the messages he sent, examples of which pepper the text, written just as he wrote them and which were copied from the originals. Please note that I have taken the liberty of shortening some military unit designations in the text of the book. For instance, 1st Battalion, 308th Infantry Regiment becomes 1st/308th for brevity; Battalion has sometimes been shortened to 'Bn'; maps and diagrams are spaced throughout the text in order for the reader to follow, as easily as possible, the progress that the 77th Division, and in particular the 308th, made through the Argonne Forest to October 8, 1918. Most places and map coordinates mentioned in the text are already marked on these maps, and those that are not are explained if the need be. The drive through the Argonne was very confusing at times so be warned – there are many names and places that come and go with relative rapidity. One will also note that the French had a habit of referring to their roads at the time by their beginning and ending destination points, instead of actual road names. For instance, the Binarville-La Viergette road thus ran between the town of Binarville and a little crossroads in the forest called La Viergette. Photo sections have been placed at the end of the two most central parts of the book to help the reader 'picture' some of the people and places mentioned in the text as well.

Some of the terms also used here fell out of use with the armistice in 1918 and therefore may not be readily known to the average reader. For instance, the 'American Expeditionary Force', which was what the U.S. forces in Europe were designated, has been shortened to the more common AEF, and U.S. troops are referred to by the then commonly used term 'Doughboys' (the arguments as to just why rage to this day). Also, U.S. troops had a tendency to favor several French phrases, not the least important of which was *'Poste d'Command* (Command Post), which has been shortened to the commonly used PC, as well as the derogatory term 'Boche' for Germans. While I have also used several other terms that the Doughboys used to describe the Germans, their use here is not meant to offend, but merely because they are what the men themselves used, and the Germans were, after all, the enemy. One term included is the very common 'Dutch', which was a Doughboy bastardization of the German word *'Duetch'*, which was German for the word 'German', and had nothing whatsoever to do with Dutch people at all.

At the end of certain paragraphs, or sections within chapters, the reader will find specific source note numbers. These correspond to the numbered sources in Appendix B. Also, at the end of each chapter are additional source numbers for other sources used in creating the chapter. The author wishes to apologize for the relative generalities of the sources indicated. Please contact the author direct concerning questions regarding those sources used. Photographs used are credited either to the provider direct or to the source (as indicated by a source number) from which they came. Those photos with no provenance are from the author's personal collection. And finally, at the end of the book, before the appendixes, is given a description of the Charlevaux Ravine and the surrounding area as it is today. This chapter was actually written in the Pocket during two different visits, both at high summer and again in early October. For what they are worth, I have given my own humble impressions of it. However, I can tell you this now; even some 87 years later, it is still a sacrosanct and most hallowed piece of ground.

Epic in the Argonne:
An Introduction to the Story
Of the Lost Battalion

"Go to Hell!"
Part of the legend.

Rumors, myths, and legends. The "Lost Battalion" of the First World War has been surrounded with these ever since the little band of survivors from that beleaguered force walked out of what has since become known as the 'Pocket' in the Charlevaux Ravine on the afternoon of October 8, 1918. There, on a lonely hillside in the French northeastern Argonne Forest, they had made history. For five days and nights, approximately 680 men of the U.S. 154th Infantry Brigade, 77th 'Metropolitan' Division, American Expeditionary Force, had desperately stood their ground and fought off repeated attacks by troops of the German 254th and 122nd Infantry Regiments, who had them surrounded in the narrow ravine. For five days and nights, machine-gun, sniper, grenade, and trench mortar fire tore into the little U.S. force, under the able command of then Major Charles W. Whittlesey, a New York lawyer in civilian life, and Captain George G. McMurtry, a one time Teddy Roosevelt 'Rough Rider' and Wall Street millionaire. For five days and nights the little command, a combination of New York street toughs and replacements from the woodlands of the Middle-Western states, tenaciously clung to the chilled, rain soaked, autumn mud of that French hillside. Without food, water, medical supplies, or blankets, they steadfastly refused to give up through attack after attack. Their own artillery unknowingly bombed them. Re-supply, dropped to them from the air, failed to fall within their grasp, but instead drifted into the enemy lines and fed the very soldiers that tried so desperately to destroy them. Ammunition ran so low that they were finally forced to go through the pockets of their dead comrades for cartridges, and strip the enemy dead of their weapons and ammunition too. Those very same dead remained scattered where they fell, horribly mangled and unburied. No one had strength enough left to bury them. Out of horrific necessity, the bodies of those dead were then stripped of their bloody bandages for re-use on others' wounds. Then, finally, the consummate insult; a request for him to surrender his force was sent to Major Whittlesey by the Germans via a captured Doughboy, followed by the Major's supposed response of "Go to hell!" Ultimately, when the request was simply ignored (which is what really happened), the Germans then launched the final deadly assault, which came with flame-throwers and very nearly broke the little command.

In the end, Major Whittlesey and his filthy, ragged, band of men prevailed and were relieved by the remaining elements of the 308th Infantry that had been left behind, and the 307th Infantry; units that had practically destroyed themselves in trying to break through to him. Casualties in the Pocket had been high. Of the 680 or so troops that went in (the actual number has never been firmly established), only 194 were able to walk out, with the rest being either killed, captured, wounded, missing, or simply too weak to walk. By that time, however, Charles Whittlesey was a hero in the press back home, and the 'Lost Battalion' was already on its way into the history books. He was promoted to Lieutenant Colonel on the very day of the relief, and - along with two other of his officers - awarded the Medal of Honor; the highest award that the United States can give and the first man in the 'Great War' to get it, in December 1918. Two flyers of the 50th Aero Squadron, who had gone out looking for the beleaguered force and died in the attempt also later won the Medal of Honor, as did two other members of the 308th that had worked to get Major Whittlesey and his men out of the Pocket. Additionally, a score of his men won the Distinguished Service Cross for gallantry during those five harrowing days, usually based on their Major's recommendation. They all came home to a heroes welcome in May, 1919 where General John J. Pershing, in charge of the American Expeditionary Force in France, called Charles Whittlesey one of the three outstanding heroes of the war (along with Sam Woodfill and Alvin York), and the 'Lost Battalion' episode one of the greatest stories of courage and determination in the AEF. No higher praise could have been sought nor given.

But there was a price to it. Charles Whittlesey wasn't the same after the events in the Charlevaux Ravine. He came home a different man. By all accounts always a calm and gentle soul before hand, he nevertheless apparently could not bear the thought of what had happened 'over there', and afterwards was given to uncharacteristic outbursts of temper. The memory of those five days and nights dragged unmercifully on him, and he would spend days in deep, dark depressions. He often had horrible and repeated nightmares and a deep, wracking cough had him in a tight fist much of the time. His health was failing him. Only wanting to be left alone, the newspapers constantly hounded him, and he received a never ending string of invitations to speak at various social functions - always about the incident in the Charlevaux Ravine - few of which he felt he could turn down. Telling friends his fondest wish was to forget the whole war, he nevertheless could not help but visit the veteran's hospitals and war invalid wards, and let himself be wrangled into chairing the Red Cross Roll Call. He was also made Colonel of the 308th Infantry Reserve, a post he did not feel he deserved but yet did not feel he could turn down. Hardly a day passed without someone who had served under him coming to see him at his office, always with a hard luck story in the immediate economical dip of the post war period, hoping that their old commander – the 'Iron Hero' of the 'Lost Battalion' – could help. There was little he could do, but he apparently could not let anyone out the door without giving them money should they ask, marking himself among many as a 'soft touch'.

There also seems little chance that he could not have heard the rumors circulating behind his back within military circles. That had it not been for the press coverage that the incident received, he would have been court-marshaled; that he had made a mistake; that the entrapment of his command had been his own fault; that it had been his own ambitions of glory that had led them there; that he did not get out when he had the chance; that the blood of all those dead and wounded men was on his own hands...

Many of those who spoke against him pointed out as supposed "evidence" of his irresponsible behavior while in command an incident that had occurred a few days before the one in the Charlevaux Ravine. Between the evening of September 28, 1918, the third day of the massive assault on the Argonne Forest, and the morning of September 30, Major Whittlesey and approximately four companies of his battalion had inadvertently gotten out in front of the main force and became surrounded out on a bleak hillside called l'Homme Mort, "without liaison in any direction", as he himself put it. Therefore, they said, he had gotten his command into the same kind of trouble not just once, but actually *twice*. Could that then be the actions of a man deserving of the Medal of Honor - our country's highest award - they asked?

Most of the whispered rumors came from jealous regular army men, men who would likely go their entire career without ever even *seeing* a Medal of Honor, let alone winning one. And now here was Charles Whittlesey, an 'emergency officer' (meaning an officer provided by the draft), winning one for what they termed 'a blunder of his own making'. Never mind that he had advanced into the Charlevaux Ravine under competent and direct orders from above. Never mind that he had done just what he had been ordered to do, even when no other unit commander apparently had been able to. Never mind that for a man whom the war itself had thrust into a position of leadership – a position that in peace he would have been wholly unqualified for – he had managed his affairs remarkably well. None of that mattered to those with an axe to grind or a bruised ego in that heady atmosphere of the immediate post war period. Charles Whittlesey could not possibly have deserved that medal when he had managed to get so many men killed and wounded in such preposterous circumstances of his own making.

Or so they said.

In the end, it all proved to be too much for the sensitive, beleaguered ex-officer; the whispers, the never-ending nightmares, the markedly failing health, the constant reminders. Would the war never end for him? Until finally he had had enough and decided to take matters into his own hands. Three years after the end of the war, he booked passage on a ship bound for Cuba, not telling anyone of his plans. On the first night of the voyage, he sat drinking with other passengers in the saloon after having had dinner at the captain's table. They all knew who he was and they discussed the war - and for once he spoke openly and freely about it. Then all at once, just after 11:00 p.m., he excused himself, headed out the door and leaped over the side of the ship and into oblivion. No one saw him go. Later, in his stateroom, carefully arranged letters to his relatives, friends, and co-workers were found with instructions to the captain as to what he wanted done with his luggage - but his service revolver was never found. None of the letters gave an explanation, but none was really needed.

Charles White Whittlesey, lawyer, ex-officer, and reluctant war hero had finally found his peace.

Perhaps the beginning of the great myth began that night that Charles Whittlesey ended his pain, for ever since it seems he has been nearly canonized for his actions there in the Charlevaux Ravine. And precisely because of that adoration, few today realize that he was a man like any other, and had his warts and scars as everyone else does. After all, we like our heroes larger than life. But he was, in the end, just a man. It is without doubt that he did his best, which was, by and large, a good job. In fact, he was the only one *to* do such a good job. But does he really deserve all the praise that has been heaped in his direction all these years? Perhaps, but only then with the caveat that he be remembered as an ordinary man first and a hero second, for without that first point, the second could not have been. Such was the nature of Charles Whittlesey's character. And thus the story of the 'Lost Battalion' then becomes, in essence, the story of Charles Whittlesey's character itself, for without the one the other could not have stood.

Certainly the legend began even before the action there in the Charlevaux Ravine, though few would realize it. The situation that the 1st Battalion, 308th had found itself in out on l'Homme Mort can actually be traced back to as the beginning of the problems that Major Whittlesey and his men were to have, even though the incident has been largely ignored all these years. Why then is it important to know about? Mainly because it illustrates to a high degree Charles Whittlesey's intense devotion to duty and his dedication to follow his given orders to the letter, even when what would seem to be common sense indicated a different path and his own sense of reasoning told him otherwise. We see prime demonstrations of his thought process and views which help us understand why he did the things he did and acted the way he acted in the later, more famous, second Pocket. Charles Whittlesey was a creature of habit and had a tendency to repeat what many have termed as his 'mistakes' – which were, in all actuality, directions of action taken for good, sound military reasons. Therefore, it is difficult to truly understand what happened to his command in the Charlevaux Ravine October 2 - 8, without having first examined the 'preview' of that incident which occurred out on l'Homme Mort September 28 - 30. To study the first Pocket then, is to understand the second Pocket - and by extension Charles Whittlesey - to a much greater degree.

The press certainly locked on to the story of the second Pocket with a tenacity that few other events had garnered during the 19 months that the U.S. was involved in the First World War (meanwhile pretty much ignoring what had happened on l'Homme Mort and thus inadvertently combining facts from both Pockets into one). And though the whole time the army did its best to keep the situation quiet, they ultimately failed in their efforts. In their eyes, it was just simply another day's business at the front. It was not the first time that a body of men had been trapped for a short period of time, since it had happened to Major Whittlesey's command once already, and there had also been a whole platoon working to get the Major out of the Charlevaux Ravine that had similarly been surrounded - and nearly completely wiped out in the process. Yet neither of those episodes apparently had the 'drama' of the one in the Charlevaux Ravine.

For Major-General Robert Alexander though, commanding the 77th Division, it was something of an embarrassment. Reporters haunted his headquarters hoping for a break in the story and asking numerous questions which, though he was loathe to, he had no choice but to answer. First Army Headquarters launched an investigation into the matter even while Major Whittlesey and his men were still trapped which, luckily, the press never got wind of. At the time, the Colonel who had dictated the orders to Major Whittlesey to advance into the Charlevaux Ravine received the lion's share of the blame for the whole thing, even though he was in no way responsible for the orders that put the beleaguered command in the ravine. That Colonel had merely passed on those orders, issued largely by General Alexander himself, to a subordinate officer. Later, after the war, General Alexander was big enough to stand up and take the blame for the whole thing, but by that time it was too late; the Colonel's career was in ruins, sides had already been drawn up, and a verdict on Major Whittlesey already reached – the public loved him, and many in the Regular Army officer corps resented him. Above all, the press had gotten their story, however wrong the facts may have been, created an unwitting hero and had sold a lot of newspapers in the bargain.

It was easy for Charles Whittlesey's naysayers to deride his actions in the Charlevaux Ravine, then as now. After all, they had not been there, and one can rarely determine his own actions in a difficult situation such as the one the men in that muddy ravine had faced, as one can never know all the facts, having not been there to assess the situation for ones self. Such was the case with Charles Whittlesey and the Lost Battalion. His situation was a unique one and it was only through a set series of circumstances, occurring in just the right order, that his predicament came to be. Had any one of those circumstances played out different, there is little doubt but that there would be no need for this book to be written. But those circumstances did happen, and in the correct order, with the end result being Major Whittlesey and his command becoming surrounded. Then too, had the Majors unbending character been different from what it was, they may never have found themselves in the situations that they did either. In the end however, second-guessing can do no real good, for it is fair to say that no one but Charles Whittlesey himself had the right to judge his actions in the Charlevaux Ravine. After all, he was the only one in possession of all the facts and the only one responsible for the decisions made there. Some have said that, in a way, he did pass that judgement. There was plenty of talk after he died that he took his own life out of 'guilt, over what was termed as 'his own mistake'.

Yet the fact of the matter remains that, love him or hate him, he had become an American war hero and if this were the 1920's or 30's, everyone would recognize the name. Today, few do. Nonetheless, the story has remained one of valor and undeniable determination and was initially kept alive by veterans of the conflict that could appreciate it and could perhaps somewhat understand Charles Whittlesey's motives, if not his actions. In the 30's, as some of the pain of the war started to fade, occasionally a newspaper somewhere would print a story about it, or one of the Battalion men would die and the obituary would never fail to mention that he had been a member of the venerable, old outfit – whether he actually was or not (more on this later). Then, when books began to be written about the war in a big way during the late fifties and throughout the sixties, they never failed to mention two things: Sergeant York, and the Lost Battalion. Thus did the legend of the Lost Battalion grow. And while it did, over the years, so too have the many mistakes and errors that were at first incorrectly associated with the story come to be accepted as fact. Two motion pictures have been made on the subject, one in 1921 and another 80 years later in 2001, and a first serious effort at chronicling the siege in the Charlevaux appeared in the form of a 1938 book called, *The Lost Battalion* by authors Thomas Johnson and Fletcher Pratt. There have also been numerous magazine articles and monographs written on the event. Within a widely varying degree, all these labors have told the story within a certain parameter of accuracy. None however have been able to tell the complete story and none the whole story truthfully, for a variety of reasons. All contained a certain amount of myth.

In this book, I have tried to separate fact from rumor, distill the truth from the legend, and present as accurate and complete a story of the adventure of the 308th Infantry in the Argonne as possible. However, before the complete story unfolds, let us look at some of the details of the legend of the Lost Battalion which are not altogether true but which have, to one degree or another, generally come to be accepted as fact. The name itself is a good starting point.

The name 'Lost Battalion' is a complete misnomer. In the first place, they were never actually 'lost' in the sense that they were un-locateable (except to the 50th Aero Squadron it seems, but that will be explained). The 77th Division Headquarters knew exactly where they were as Major Whittlesey had been able to send several messages back by carrier pigeon indicating his position in the ravine with the proper map co-ordinates. Indeed, the Major sent constant messages indicating his proper location all throughout the day of October 2nd, the day they walked into the Pocket, and on the 3rd and 4th as well. This itself goes far in refuting another oft-repeated claim; that Charles Whittlesey sent back the wrong coordinates and thus caused undo problems for himself. In the case of the Lost Battalion, the term 'lost' referred to their general situation. At one point during their siege, Brigadier General Evan Johnson, the commander of the 154th Brigade, of whom the 308th was a part, actually feared that Major Whittlesey's command had all been killed, captured, or wiped out – 'lost', if you will. The French forces on Major Whittlesey's left apparently also believed this. The term 'Lost Battalion' itself was first coined by a newspaper man back home sending a request to his correspondent at the front for more information on certain stories which the correspondent had 'fished' to the editor, including one about the trapped command. The actual cable the editor returned read "Send more on lost battalion". It seemed a fitting enough name at the time, as it looked as though Major Whittlesey's command was indeed either wiped out, or about to be, and in any case few civilians knew exactly what a battalion was anyway. It just *sounded* important. So we see that they were not at all 'lost' in the classic sense. This then brings us to the 'battalion' part of the name Lost Battalion.

No one actually there at the front knew with any exactitude how many men Major Whittlesey had up with him, including the major himself it seems. One reason for this was the high rate of attrition during the previous seven days of the massive Argonne drive. Also, as we shall see, there was terrible dispersion of units in the denseness of the forest, and therefore a lot of mixing of troops from different companies and battalions. What Major Whittlesey had there in the Charlevaux Ravine was what would become known in a later war, as a 'composite unit' – a unit made up of men from many different outfits within the 308th. Basically, there were companies, or more accurately portions of companies, A, B, and C of the 1st Battalion, 308th Infantry and E, G, and H of 2nd Battalion, 308th Infantry; roughly a shot up platoon each from companies C and D of the 306th Machine Gun Battalion (totaling 9 guns); and, from the morning of October 3 on, the majority of Company K of the 3rd Battalion, 307th Infantry. In addition, there were a handful of men from companies D and F of the 308th, as well as a few 'strays' that had been earlier assigned to Major Whittlesey; two men from Company I of the 3rd Battalion/308th, five medical men (all enlisted medics, none a real doctor), and two artillery enlisted men and their officer from Battery D/305th Field Artillery Regiment. So as we see, there were actually parts of many different battalions under Major Whittlesey's command, not just one. Additionally, the nearest anyone has ever come to making an accurate count of the men the Major had under him has been a total of 679 'effectives' and the eight 'supportives', for a total of 687. A First World War battalion at full strength could actually bring to bear about 1,000 rifles, less support troops such as cooks and wagoneers and such. Therefore, if the seven companies of infantry and two platoons of machine gunners up with Major Whittlesey in the Charlevaux Ravine had been up to anything near full strength, which they were *far* from, then their total would have been in the neighborhood of 1800 or 1900 guns, or about two full battalions worth. And since what Major Whittlesey actually had in the ravine probably totaled less than 700 then, he was well below even single battalion strength.

In any case, most veterans of the beleaguered command did not like the name Lost Battalion anyway. "Hell, we weren't lost," they would say, "The goddamned Krauts knew where we were the whole fucking time!"

And that just about says it all.

Major Whittlesey also did not 'rush forward in a burst of ego', thus causing the entrapment of his command, for Charles Whittlesey was not a glory hunter at all, but in fact quite the contrary. In this instance, as he had all throughout the Argonne drive, he advanced into the Charlevaux Ravine under competent and direct orders from his superiors, doing exactly what he was ordered to do. What's more, he did not like those orders one bit and *twice* tried to get them changed, fearing that exactly what did happen, would. Even at the time, not many knew that 1st Battalion of the 308th had already been cut off for those three days of September 28 – 30, and it was with the thoughts of this first cut off - which had really been a close call - still fresh in his mind that Major Whittlesey lodged those protests against his ordered advance toward the Charlevaux Ravine. Those protests were, of course, largely ignored and that is what, in part, placed him and his men in their precarious position in the first place – not, after all, the Major's own ambitions.

Another untruth of the story, and this one was very popular and well known for many years, concerned Major Whittlesey receiving the surrender letter from the Germans. Supposedly, the major was so enraged by the demand, that he stood up, letter in hand, turned toward the German lines (and being surrounded, one wonders exactly which way that would be) and shouted that the Germans could, "Go to Hell!" Another version has him wrapping the letter in a rock and throwing it back up the hill at the Germans at the same time. While it does make for a good addition to the story, it simply did not happen, and while there has been much speculation as to exactly what *did* happen, there are enough eyewitness accounts to corroborate the Major's later claim that he never actually said that to take it to the bank that he did not. Nor was it in Charles Whittlesey's nature to say something like that in the first place; in fact the moniker tagged on him by the press, "Go to Hell Whittlesey", bothered him to no end. Actually, General Alexander inadvertently had a hand in starting this particular tale by telling a reporter offhandedly that this was *in essence* what his battalion commander had said. As Charles Whittlesey himself, in his official report on the matter, later stated simply, "No reply seemed necessary."

Nor was the Lost Battalion 'saved' by the carrier pigeon, Cher Ami, either as is frequently thought. Released at the height of an inadvertent barrage of friendly shell fire on the second day in the Pocket (October 4) with a pleading message to lift that fire, the bird actually got back to his loft at general headquarters *after* the artillery had already been alerted to its mistake and was already slacking off their bombardment. Nor had the Lost Battalion been 'found' by the 50th Aero Squadron. In truth, the 50th had much trouble pinpointing where the men were in order to attempt a drop of supplies – the first aerial resupplyment in history, as a matter of fact. And it was only through inexperience that the resupply failed.

Finally, we come to the much-debated matter of who was to blame for the predicament. This matter will be discussed at length later in the book, so for now let us just say as stated before, that it was a peculiar set of circumstances that led the Lost Battalion into the Charlevaux Ravine. No one person or event can take full blame for the incident. This includes the disastrous American artillery barrage of October 4, said to have been the fault of incorrect map coordinates on Major Whittlesey's part, which is also not true. Other numerous attempts have been made repeatedly to put the blame on the 'Negro regiment', the 368th Infantry, working on the 308th's left, for leaving that flank exposed and thus providing an 'open door', if you will, for the Germans to infiltrate in behind the 308th through. However, when one considers the facts of the matter concerning the 368th, one cannot help but come to the conclusion that it was only their fault in part and then indirectly. Certainly they cannot be held accountable for the entire episode, which has often been the case, if for the simple fact that they were no longer in the line by October 2, the day Major Whittlesey lead his men into the Pocket. So too of the French, who took over the area the 368th had occupied once they had been relieved the morning of October 1. And though General Alexander, whose orders sent Major Whittlesey into the ravine, did try to shoulder responsibility for the whole mess, even he cannot be blamed totally. He too had orders from above to follow. Therefore, the blame is wide and varied, and its full analysis for now will have to wait.

By sifting through the rumors, myths and legends that have surrounded the Lost Battalion for so many years, I hope to have brought to light the truth of one of the greatest tales to come out of that terrible tragedy of the early 20th century, the First World War. Unfortunately, as we now embark into the 21st century and the heroes and stories of that war fade into history and shrink in the shadow of a Second World War, all too often the sacrifices made by the Doughboys of 1917-1918 are overlooked by a generation that can, thankfully, never know their brand of warfare. This is a catastrophe and a grave mistake, as no man's sacrifice in war for the sake of freedom should ever be overlooked. The men - the heroes - of the Lost Battalion are all gone now, yet their spirit lives on through their story. They were a special band of men, led by special officers, one in particular. They exemplified all the best qualities of America and set a shining example of determination and fortitude in the face of incredible odds, trial and adversities. Their deeds on that cold, muddy hillside in France so long ago should never be forgotten and all Americans can look to their conduct with pride.

This then, as near as I can tell it, is their story.

Part 1:
Goodbye Broadway, Hello France

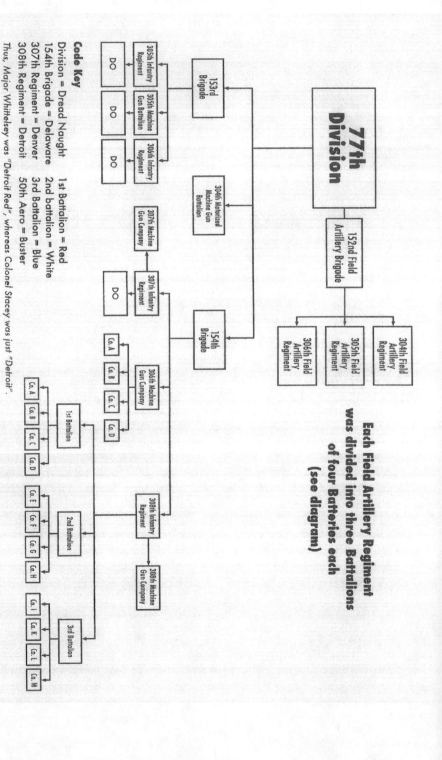

77th Division

152nd Field Artillery Brigade
- 304th Field Artillery Regiment
- 305th Field Artillery Regiment
- 306th Field Artillery Regiment

Each Field Artillery Regiment was divided into three Battalions of four Batteries each (see diagram)

153rd Brigade
- 305th Infantry Regiment — DO
- 305th Machine Gun Battalion — DO
- 306th Infantry Regiment — DO

304th Motorized Machine Gun Battalion

154th Brigade

307th Infantry Regiment
- 307th Machine Gun Company
- DO

308th Infantry Regiment
- 306th Machine Gun Company
  - Co. A
  - Co. B
  - Co. C
  - Co. D
- 308th Machine Gun Company
- 1st Battalion
  - Co. A
  - Co. B
  - Co. C
  - Co. D
- 2nd Battalion
  - Co. E
  - Co. F
  - Co. G
  - Co. H
- 3rd Battalion
  - Co. I
  - Co. K
  - Co. L
  - Co. M

Code Key

Division = Dread Naught
154th Brigade = Delaware
307th Regiment = Denver
308th Regiment = Detroit

1st Battalion = Red
2nd battalion = White
3rd Battalion = Blue
50th Aero = Buster

Division = Dread Naught
1st Battalion = Red
154th Brigade = Delaware   2nd battalion = White
307th Regiment = Denver   3rd Battalion = White
308th Regiment = Detroit   50th Aero = Buster

Thus, *Major Whittelsey was "Detroit Red", whereas Colonel Stacey was just "Detroit".*

The War Nobody Wanted

"It is a terrible thing to lead this great and peaceful nation into war…"

President Woodrow Wilson

War burst forth across Europe in early August 1914. It was a war that nobody had particularly wanted, but which became reality nonetheless. In the beginning, no one thought it would last long, each side believing it would be home – victorious – before that famous first Christmas. Instead, it raged for four years and four months and touched every corner of the earth in some way. Before the guns at last fell silent on November 11, 1918, the war had consumed billions of dollars, taken 13 million lives, and left behind, as noted author John Keegan put it in his book, *The First World War*, "A legacy of political rancor and racial hatred so intense, that no explanation of the causes of the Second World War can stand without reference to those roots." Yet today it remains strangely ignored, even though its effects are still felt geographically, politically and in the family photo albums of those many men who did not return. Forgotten statues and commemorative plaques abound in overlooked corners of city parks and town squares the world over in honor of the fallen. Forgotten too are many of the stories of heroism and valor that had their foundations in the muddy trenches and forests of France and Belgium; stories once well known and popular, their facts now blurred by time and overshadowed by the stories of a Second, larger, World War.

The political history behind the causes of the First World War is beyond the scope of this volume, and would serve little purpose to the story about to unfold. An assassin's bullet, multi-nation mutual protection treaties, and the unwillingness of the youngest of the European nations – Germany – to back down at the moment of crisis, all played their part in the events that led to war in the summer of 1914. By Christmas, the basic players had drawn up sides, and what had started as a simple murder in Sarajevo had escalated into a global conflict. Before 1914, battles had once been fought in which casualties were counted in the thousands. Very quickly within the new arena of conflict however, they were being counted in the tens of thousands, and then before long, in the hundreds of thousands. The magazine rifle, rapid fire machine-gun, and artillery in heretofore unheard of calibers and numbers insured that each side's weight of fire was devastating. It was a 20th century war, being fought with 20th century weapons, but with outdated 19th century tactics. Where the great armies came together, a stark battle line was formed, commonly referred to as the 'front'. Running from Nieuport, up on the Belgian coast, all the way down to the Swiss frontier, the 'Western Front' was a ribbon of utter destruction, an average of 3 to 4 miles wide and four hundred and eighty miles long. Within it, a unique brand of warfare was waged, which the world, thankfully, is unlikely to ever see again.

As for America, the country stood by and watched events unfold in Europe with mild interest, but little more. Most all agreed that the country should stay out of it, not the least of which were the great numbers of German immigrants residing within the United States. That began to change on May 7, 1915, when the Cunard liner *Lusitania* was sunk by a German submarine off Kinsale Head on the Irish Coast, taking the lives of 1,152 souls – 102 of them Americans. The press in the U.S. went wild and there were calls for vengeance against Germany. Heretofore, the 'war in Europe' had been looked at as just that - a war in Europe, affecting only Europe. United States interest in the European conflict was limited to commerce. U.S. factories sold both finished goods as well as raw materials to England and France at fantastic rates. Other than that, 'let them duke it out amongst themselves over there' was the general feeling.

The sinking of the *Lusitania*, however, brought change. Suddenly war fever raged; the country was divided, half wanting war, the other half not. Germany needed to be "taught a lesson", those in favor of military action said, and the U.S. were "just the ones to do it". Yet "I didn't raise my boy to be a soldier" was a response, heard repeatedly. President Woodrow Wilson settled it by declaring America was "too proud to fight", and secured a guarantee from Germany that she would restrict her actions on the seas and torpedo no unidentified ship. He also called on all Americans to be neutral in thought, as well as word and action.

However, there were already plenty of American boys in the war fighting for 'European freedom from tyranny', despite President Wilson's request. Some had left home and went north to Canada and joined the Imperial Forces, though to do so, one had to give up his American citizenship and swear allegiance to King and Crown. Arch Whitehouse, a 19-year-old kid from New Jersey, worked his way over to England on a horse transport, served in the British cavalry, and eventually wound up a crack gunner in the Royal Flying Corps. James Norman Hall, of Iowa, served with the British Infantry. Others traveled to France and joined the French Foreign Legion, which made no citizenship demands. Many of these men who first served the French on the ground later transferred to the air service, forming the Lafayette Escadrille – an elite air fighting squadron manned exclusively by Americans, like Victor Chapman and William Thaw. And there were several that would later wind up in the Lost Battalion that had received their baptism of fire in Foreign Service long before the U.S. was involved in the war. Among those was a man originally from Minnesota who was to be a much-loved central figure of that 'beleaguered force'. His name was Marshall Peabody. (8, 16, 35)

Marshall Grant Peabody was already 31 years old when the war broke out in 1914. A single man, he had been living in New York City for several years, working on Wall Street, and serves as an excellent example of the sort of men that jumped into the war well before America got involved. 'Marsh', as he was known to friends and family, moved within the finer circles of New York society, but by all accounts was far from being afflicted by any snobbish attitudes. Today, he might be ranked as upper middle class; well bred, but down to earth. He was a handsome, tall, athletic man, very powerfully built, and a dedicated American.

To that end, Peabody was also a member of the New York National Guard, attached to Squadron 'C' of the 7th NYNG Cavalry Regiment. However the National Guard at the time was sometimes not much more than a social club, and this was especially true of cavalry regiments, which were considered the 'elite' of military service organizations. They sometimes hosted parties in their armory's squad buildings, most of which were fully equipped with bar facilities, and duty weekends were usually more akin to social get-togethers. The regiments were also quite frequently associated with local sporting organizations, and the NYNG's association was with the New York Athletic Club, where Peabody was one of the prime stars. Successful and popular, Marshall Peabody led a good life.

Despite all that though, by the fall of 1914 Peabody was bored, business on Wall Street was as he described "down" and there was a war on. He therefore decided it was time for a break and set out for France to seek the war and adventure, not yet sure how that would come about but trusting to luck to guide him there. In mid September 1914, he set out for Montreal, paid $60.00 for a ticket on a freighter to England and landing in France on October 10, wrote:

"At Dieppe we saw some French soldiers in their archaic uniforms of red and blue that you can see for a mile... Finally we got to Paris at 10:00pm and it had a very forsaken appearance. There were few lights and hardly any people in the streets. Most of the hotels and all of the restaurants near the station were closed..."

His opinion of the 'City of Lights' quickly changed though, for the next day he discovered:

"Paris is wonderful! In spite of all the effects of the war I have been intoxicated with the atmosphere of this place and am delighted with it... I have never seen anything so beautiful as... the Place de Concord, the Seine with its wonderful bridges and trees, and the Louvre with its gardens and exquisite statues. Everything is so artistic... (but) there is another side. Many funerals go by and the streets are full of women in black, so that you do not forget the terrible tragedy going on not many miles away. Antwerp has fallen, and I am afraid the end of the war is a long way off..."

He stayed in Paris, enamored with Parisian life and practiced his French until the end of the month when he set out for Calais, determined to find the adventure for which he had come. What he found instead were military zones off limits to civilians, trains packed with troops heading for the front, and hundreds of wounded streaming to the rear. He returned to Paris within 24 hours, moved by what he had seen and seriously considered the possibility of joining the British army.

Instead, on November 17, Peabody paid a visit to the American Red Cross station in nearby Neuilly and offered his assistance to the American Ambulance Service. He was accepted as a driver and began his training immediately. Being an international service, and therefore a-political, the American Red Cross was permitted to operate its ambulance service where it wished in impartiality, despite the fact that America was still a neutral in the conflict. He was in good company. Two of his compatriots were Elliot Cowdin (an ex-Roosevelt 'Rough Rider' of the Spanish-American War) and Choteau Johnson, both of whom would later distinguish themselves in the French Air Service.

He trained for several weeks far behind the battle zone in Belgium until, in early December 1914, he was assigned to a Belgian field hospital near Furnes, servicing the Belgian 1st Division. Here, he found his war:

"Hubbard and I went to the trenches... We joined the troops in a farmhouse... and when it was quite dark... moved out with them to relieve the boys... the men moved quietly along the muddy roads in the continual rain... When we had gone about ½ mile, we stopped and waited while the old troops gradually came out of the trenches and the new ones went in. This was a difficult operation as the fields were a sea of mud and water and all so dark... We waited some time and finally went with the doctor to a small farm house about a ½ mile behind the second line of trenches where we hid our car behind the ruins of an old wind mill... and spent the night on some straw in the farmhouse... outside it was cold, raining, and windy...The guns were booming from both sides...Nearby all of the little houses as far as the eye could reach were ruins and hardly a person could be seen... The country was flat, desolate, and a sea of mud, and the fields were literally filled with round holes where the shells had burst... In the distance we could see Dixmude, held by the Germans, and with careful observation I could occasionally

pick a flash from their batteries. The whistle of the shells could be heard and the crack as they burst over the trenches…"

Here, he and his pals did their work, carting the wreckage of war back to their field hospital through the horror of the Belgian landscape. It did not take long before he had finally seen enough. In January 1915, he was granted an indefinite leave of absence and went back to Paris, and by February was back in New York. There he made note of some of the things of warfare he had learned.

"Now that the trenches are near together a general advance is impossible. One way to advance is for artillery to concentrate on a certain spot, and then with a large number of troops try to break through and attack from the rear. But what a chance! Impossible to attack against trenches ordinarily. Men wiped out before reaching them. Machine guns, when in position, mow men down like wheat. But they are easily destroyed when discovered and should have no fixed position with the unit, but must be placed in most favorable firing positions, usually a number together."

This last is interesting, because when the 7th Cavalry Regiment of the NYNG was federalized right after America entered the war in 1917, they were redesignated as a portion of the 306th Machine Gun Battalion, 77th Division. In it, Marshall Peabody was to become a Lieutenant in charge of a platoon of D Company, and thus end up with Major Whittlesey's force in the Pocket of the Charlevaux Ravine. (181, 226)

Meanwhile, things politically progressed and America moved on toward what now appears to have been the inevitable. Despite all President Wilson's best efforts throughout 1916, the war clouds continued brewing over American skies, and nothing it seemed could stop them. In late January 1917, Wilson, in an effort to show no partiality, made the suggestion of "peace without victory" to the belligerents of both sides and offered to mediate such a peace. Both, however, simply ignored the proposal as ludicrous. Then, on January 31, Germany upped the anti by recommencing her unrestricted submarine warfare program, sinking anything she felt like - including several U.S. ships. President Wilson then made it clear that the country would stand for little more when finally, on February 3, the U.S. officially broke off diplomatic relations with Germany.

The storm really broke however on March 1, 1917, when Washington announced it had intercepted a secret telegram meant for the Mexican government and sent by the German consulate to the U.S., Herr Zimmermann, on February 28. In it, the German government offered to give the Mexicans back their 'lost' territories of New Mexico, Arizona, and Texas at the conclusion of a successful war with the U.S., if the Mexican government would declare war against the U.S. on the side of the Central Powers and let the Germans invade from across their border. Meanwhile, over the course of the month, several more U.S. ships fell victim to German U-boats.

It was the last straw - the country had had enough. President Wilson, elected to a second term of office on the platform of 'He Kept Us Out of War', now faced the inevitable and on April 2 asked Congress to vote a state of war between the U.S. and Germany and her allies. The Senate passed the vote on April 4, and the House of Representatives finalized the war resolution on April 6 and Wilson signed the declaration later that day. The United States had officially entered the 'Great War'.

She was woefully unprepared for it though. With a standing regular army of only 107,000, a National Guard of 130,000, and a Marine Corps of only 15,000, she ranked

17th on the world list of military powers. The only real military action that the country had participated in since the end of the Civil War, some 60 years earlier, had been the short lived Spanish-American War of 1898 and a somewhat dubious expedition across the border with Mexico chasing the bandito Pancho Villa in 1916. It was painfully apparent then that drastic measures needed to be taken in light of the size of the armies then fighting in France. The popular call went out for "a million men by May", and soon, volunteers were streaming into the recruiting offices. However, the government knew full well that once that first burst of patriotic enthusiasm had passed, the U.S. Army would still be found profoundly lacking. A drafted 'National Army' had to be raised.

Here was one of the only spots where America had planned ahead a little and an officer corps to lead that National Army was already in basic preparations. US Army General Leonard Wood had long ago realized that there was little chance that the U.S. was to remain neutral for the duration of the war. And knowing also that the only way America could field an army large enough for the battlefields of France would be through a national draft, he had correctly assumed that there would be a tremendous need for officers to lead them. To that end, he had set up 'business men's training camps', which were used to train the 'upper classes' of society as officers for the National Army. Though General Wood and his accomplices were forced to fight hard to get the idea off the ground in the first place, the first camp, held in 1915 and lasting 30 days, was a huge success. The program was then expanded in 1916 to several camps around the country, though it has since become known by the name of the most popular and successful of the camps, the one at Plattsburg, New York. It was a tremendously radical idea in 1916. No one had ever thought that competent officers could be made out of raw civilians in as little as 90 days, 'upper class' men or not. However, the 'Plattsburg Program' had proven that it could achieve its goals, in theory anyway, and steps were taken to expand the program even further in 1917.

The 'upper class' men attending the actual camp at Plattsburg, New York were the social elite of primarily New York business society; slightly older than the norm and serious toward their goals. Businessmen from Wall Street, bankers, corporate stock traders, and lawyers were well represented. Even the mayor of New York came out to get involved until city duties forced him back to his desk. Most of these men knew each other outside of camp, at least socially, and were therefore somewhat aquatinted with each other's personalities. This would prove a very valuable asset later on, when the effects of war showed where the flaws (and there were flaws) in the Plattsburg Program were. But it was a start; something America desperately needed. (7, 35, 19)

Therefore, with an officer corps for a National Army now in place, at least in theory, it was time to build an army. Training camp sights were picked out and started to go up, while tent cities were springing up all over. America, always a hotbed of industry, was beginning to wake up and flex her formidable industrial muscles, gearing up for total war. The first 'Liberty Loan' was organized, and congress passed war bills for the millions needed to build the machines of war and a mighty army. George M. Cohen hit the pot of gold with the song 'Over There'; "And we won't come back 'till it's over, Over There!" was on everyone's lips. General John J. "Black Jack" Pershing, recently returned from leading the 'adventure' down on the border with Mexico, was named to lead the American Expeditionary Force (the AEF) in France and landed 'Over There' at St. Nazaire in June with the first elements of the 1st U.S. Division. All that was needed now for the new AEF were the men…

Therefore, on May 18, President Wilson signed and put into effect the national draft act, initially calling on all men between 21 and 31 to register and then on July 10 federalized the National Guard. On July 13, the first draft call was made to the 687,000 men who were to be the vanguard of an eventual 4,000,000 U.S. 'Doughboys' all tolled (two million of whom would actually see service overseas) and by July 20, the initial National Draft List had been completed. There were nearly ten million men listed, and suddenly the war that nobody had wanted in the first place was touching home. (35, 16)

The 'Metropolitan Division'
and 'Galloping Charlie'

"Yaphank? Where the hell is Yaphank?"

A commonly heard expression among new recruits to the 77th Division.

As names for towns go, it was not the most readily recognizable one, but it certainly earned its place in history. Yaphank, N.Y. was located in Suffolk County, out on Long Island, about 60 miles from New York City as the crow flies. Situated somewhere near the midway point between Patchogue on the south shore and Port Jefferson on the sound, the town rested comfortably along a line of the Long Island Railroad. It was a quiet little antebellum community in the spring and early summer of 1917, and may have been allowed by time and progress to remain so for two or three more decades had war not visited the United States in April of that year.

But come it did, and not long after President Wilson made the fateful, if inevitable, decision to enter the war in Europe that spring, members from the Cantonment Division of the national draft board met to discuss exactly where to train the vastly expanded army that would be needed to fight 'over there'. It was eventually decided to create 16 new cantonments, built in different parts of the country, to handle the flood of drafted men who would soon be arriving to fill the planned for new National Army Divisions. On June 21, 1917, the Army Construction Quartermaster, Major O.K. Meyers, along with Colonel F.H. Lawton (Army Department of the East), and Major M.J. Whitson (of the Cantonment Division), arrived on Long Island to choose the spot for the training ground of the planned for New York area division. After some little deliberation, they finally settled on a spot about a half-mile from the town of Yaphank. It was an area of sandy soil and pine trees, about 50 to the acre, in all totaling about 19,000 acres of undeveloped land.

Field surveys began on June 23, and construction began as early as June 25. A tent city quickly sprang up to house the army of rough and rowdy laborers that soon began to flood the area, and by the height of construction there would be between 9,000 and 15,000 men working on any given day, all eager to spend money in the local shops, saloons, hotels, and restaurants. Town folk little realized that it was only the beginning of what was yet to come. The war had arrived in Yaphank.

Slowly, through the long, hot summer, the site began to take shape under the watchful eye of Major Meyer, who the army had given the additional unenviable task of overseeing the whole blamed project. (Causing town folk sometimes refer to it as "O.K.'s Mess".) In the end, it was a veritable city, large enough to feed, train, and entertain 40,000 recruits, officers, and staff for as long it took to prepare such a body of men for the largest war the world had ever seen. It was also meant to keep training men for as long as that war lasted, if necessary. Therefore, no amenity was to be spared, including the most modern of barrack blocks, fully equipped with electric light and indoor plumbing; a complete and modern road, rail, and telephone system; theaters; recreation, and drill halls; houses of worship for all the different major faiths; laundry and tailoring facilities; 200 target rifle range; full artillery range; and enough warehouse space to hold everything needed for a division of 26,000 men. In all, upon completion there were some 1,400 buildings on premises.

Finally, the site was given a name—Camp Upton, after the brilliant Civil War figure, Major-General Emory Upton, whose major accomplishment in life had been a book titled *The Military Policy of the United States*, published some 20 years after he had committed suicide. In it, he railed against America's constant unpreparedness for war and urged a national military system similar to what the Germans (Prussians, when the book was actually written) had in place. In Europe, it was commonplace for every young man to be required by law to serve a certain period in his early manhood in the active military, and thereafter, for the rest of his life, to be engaged in some form of reserve duty. The program was still in place in WWI, not only in Germany, but in France as well. At the time, Upton's ideas had been ignored by all but the most far-sighted. Now, in 1917, he was being recognized as a far thinker by those, like General Leonard Wood, who had railed against America's current state of unpreparedness since the war had broken out in 1914. But the honor was a hollow one so many years later.

On August 4, the war department created the 77th Division with the stroke of a pen. It was to train at the new cantonment of Camp Upton, and its men were to be drafted from the teeming metropolis of New York City, while its officers would come from the Plattsburg Officers Training Camp then in session. Therefore, for the most part the division was all metropolitan New York, hence the nickname it eventually decided upon for itself—the "Metropolitan Division." It has also been called "New York's Own," but this is to confuse it with that erstwhile body of New York National Guardsmen, the 'Fighting 69th' infantry regiment that served with the 42nd "Rainbow" Division during the war, and had already claimed that name. (I) It was also to be referred to as the "Statue of Liberty," or sometimes just plain "Liberty" Division, after the divisional emblem it had picked for itself while still at Upton, the outline of the Statue of Liberty. Nothing could have been more appropriate for a division from New York, but it was first known as the Metropolitan Division and under that moniker, it was to gain fame.

On August 13, the Divisional Headquarters was organized and established, its core personnel culled from ranking Regular Army men. Major-General J. Franklin Bell, then commanding the Army's Department of the East, was warned that he would soon be given command of the new 77th Division. Bell immediately began preparations for the transfer, very much looking forward to the opportunity. He was a well-experienced, fair, and decent officer, had graduated West Point in 1878, and had begun his career in the Regular Army out on the plains as a lieutenant with the 7th Cavalry (of General Custer fame). By 1917, as the Army's commander of the eastern department, he was responsible for the oversight of the Plattsburg Officers Training Camp and was no doubt the best man for the job of leading a division officered by men whom he himself helped train.

On the same date, August 13, two days before their graduation, the recruit officers at Plattsburg received their first duty assignments, most finding themselves assigned to Camp Upton, with orders to report following a two-week furlough. One of those officers ordered to Upton was a tall, thin 33-year-old New York City lawyer who would graduate the Plattsburg Camp with such high honors as to skip the ranks of 1st and 2nd Lieutenant and instead head the Captain's list. His name was Charles Whittlesey. (28, 41, 109,116, 152, 308, 344, 352)

Charles White Whittlesey was born on a snowy January 20, 1884, in the small town of Florence, Wisconsin, just a stone's throw from the Michigan border. He was the second of Frank Russell and Anna Elizabeth Whittlesey's six children. Frank Russell Whittlesey came from a long line with a reputation for steadfastness of character and hard line values. The Whittlesey name in America is traceable as far back as colonial days and, before that, to native England (there was a Whittlesey on the *Mayflower*, in fact). The clan was generally known as a Yale-schooled family, and followed a personal creed of dedication to God and country that stressed leadership in civil practices as well as military service. Senators, congressmen, community leaders of all kinds, as well as military heroes, had all sprung from the Whittlesey line.

Frank Whittlesey left his native Connecticut along with his brothers, Charles and William, for the northern mid-west sometime in the 1870's and he wound up in what is now the area of Florence County, Wisconsin, still Indian country at that time. Frank's brother Charles was an accomplished surveyor and it is he that is largely responsible, even today, for the divisions of land in most of what are now Florence County and its surrounding environs, while Frank apparently did much to foster good relations with the local tribes and bought up land. William started a sawmill and before too long the town of Florence had its beginnings there in the vast expanses of woodland that stretched virtually unbroken into Canada. (In fact nearly all the original buildings in Florence were built from 'Whittlesey Wood'.) It was the huge mining boom in the area however that provided Frank with his main source of income. Hired by the Stanley Electric Corporation as a purchasing agent, he brought electricity to the mining industry of northern Wisconsin and the upper peninsula of Michigan. It was during one of his business travels north that Frank met Anna (Annie) Elizabeth Gibbs, and on October 5, 1881, married her in her hometown of Menomonee, Michigan. Quickly, Frank settled his new bride just across the state line in Florence.

There was definitely a 'right' side and 'wrong' side of the tracks in Florence, and the Whittlesey's were just as definitely on the 'right' side. Decorous invitations survive to this day that show them being invited to all the prestigious gatherings in town, and Annie to be a popular hostess of her own events. Frank built them a large, beautifully crafted two-story house on a hill at the end of Lake Street, with a rambling slope just out the front door and a fantastic view overlooking Pike Lake and the surrounding woods—just a stone's throw from the courthouse, the mining office and the church of their choice (The First Presbyterian). The first of the couple's children arrived in 1882, and was named Frank Russell, Jr., but unfortunately did not survive long. The second child, who followed in January 1884, they named Charles White Whittlesey, for Frank Sr.'s brother. In August 1885, a daughter, Annie Elizabeth, was born. The only girl the couple would have, she was absolutely adored by both her parents as well as young Charles. In July of 1887, came brother Russell; in February 1892 brother Elisha; and finally, in July 1893, brother Melzar, the last of the children.

Charles, as the oldest of the surviving Whittlesey siblings, had certain expectations to live up to as he grew. Learning was paramount (for with knowledge came power), as was earning a place for one's self in society through hard work and honest dealing. While there is little doubt that he learned to revere hard work from a very young age, he was far from a hardy boy. He was thin and frail from the very first. Yet what he lacked in physique, Charles more than made up for in a strong and active mind. He discovered books early on and seemed always to have his nose buried in them, all the while developing a tremendous love for nature and the outdoors. Not that he was a boring child mind you, as he had also gained something of a reputation in town as a bit of a mischief-maker. Stories, now seldom told, relate how Charles and the town sheriff's son, a youth by the name of Pemberton, would sneak around town at night. Yet no amount of youthful exuberance could cloud the atmosphere of that time and place - an atmosphere that demanded of its young people courtesy and respect of their elders, lessons he must have taken to heart for he was forever unfailingly courteous. He had been taught the Golden Rule and definitely learned to live by it. The Whittlesey's were also of a strongly religious nature, attending the First Presbyterian Church; Germanic, Norwegian, and English in its congregation and strict in its values. This early exposure to a dutiful family belief, stern congregational value system and its insistence in a definite right and wrong, as well as an association with ordinary rank and file people of different views, ethnic backgrounds, and personalities was to have an impact on young Charles and would stay with him all his life.

Another event that would prove to have a heavy bearing on his life, perhaps more so than any other until the events of October 1918, was the untimely death of his little sister Annie, in June of 1894. Just two months shy of her 9th birthday, Annie fell ill with what was then listed as black diphtheria. Within a week, she was dead. Little Russell, also horribly stricken by the same illness, pulled through. The family was devastated, particularly Anna, who remained almost inconsolable. Indeed, even in letters written years after the event, it is apparent that her heart remained forever broken by the loss. After a service at the church, the little girl's body was carried the short distance down Lake Street and laid to rest next to the grave of Frank Jr. on the hillside in front of the Whittlesey house. (Later, a beautiful baptismal font of carefully carved and polished oak would be crafted in little Annie Whittlesey's honor, bearing her name and the year of her death. It is still used to this day.)

Compounding the darkness of the event, the family had been making final preparations to move half way across the country. Frank had accepted a position as production manager at the new General Electric Corporation, which had recently acquired Stanley Electric, and the resulting transfer was to send the family back to his beloved New England. There, plans had been made to settle in Pittsfield, Massachusetts. (By 1914, Pittsfield would claim fame as the 'High Voltage Capital of the World'.) In August 1894, the family left Wisconsin for good.

Once settled in the East, 10-year-old Charles found in the Berkshire country a land almost the same as that which he had left behind in northern Wisconsin. The trees and hills now surrounding him somehow seemed fondly familiar to the tall timbers and kettles of the countryside he had loved that had encompassed Florence, making him feel almost at home. What was more, the studious Midwesterner also quickly found that not only did he fit into the New England surroundings particularly easily, but that his temperament blended excellently with those around him and the lifestyle they lived. The Midwestern values sat suitably with New Englanders he now found friends among, and New England values sat equally well with him until, ultimately, the combination of the two systems - in conjunction with his own strong personality - was to prove a formidable mélange.

Charles the youngster - quiet, thoughtful, polite and honest almost to a fault - was very well liked for his forthright nature and quick wit. Though at first painfully shy, he nevertheless made friends relatively easily, if at an arm's length, and soon was accepted, almost as if he had been a New Englander from the start. Before too long then, Pittsfield truly became home and when later asked where he was from, he was more apt to answer "Pittsfield, Massachusetts," rather than be drawn into the long and painful explanation concerning the move from Florence.

Charles attended Pittsfield High School, graduating with high marks before then attending Williams College in nearby Williamsburg, Massachusetts. Williams is an old and well-respected "society" college in the New England area, and young Charles slid easily into the early 20th Century college lifestyle. He was by now six feet two inches tall, much taller than most of his classmates, most of it legs. However, he was horribly nearsighted. Therefore, his one concession within the college lifestyle was that, while at Williams, he was said to have never once been seen with a ball in his hands of any kind. It made no difference, for Charles was still more inclined to studious pursuits. As in high school, he remained quiet and polite and carried himself well. He took a great liking to poetry and literature, the classics quickly becoming his favorites. He continued the association with nature that had bred its way into him in Wisconsin, discovering bird watching. Though he considered hunting and fishing "cruel forms of amusement," he was far from being a vegetarian. And at college, as before, he still found long, quiet walks in the surrounding

Berkshire Hills - alone - a quite wonderful escape from the world at large.

Despite his propensity for spending quality time alone, he was a popular and very well liked fellow on campus. He was known to be involved with several forms of roguishness and youthful behavior of a college nature, particularly those that required intricate planning or leadership. His many and varied friends found him engaging and amusing in conversation during all-night bull sessions and an enticing storyteller. His sense of humor was dry, witty, and cutting, and his laughter infectious. Tall and impeccable in dress, his Williams graduation photo shows a handsome young man of 21 who still looked closer to 16. He was known irregularly as Charley, and more often by the college sobriquets of "Chick," a popular nickname for Charles of the time, and "Count," for the aristocratic manner of speech he had adopted and for the way he carried himself. If anything, Charles Whittlesey was determined to be a gentleman.

It was also while at Williams that young Charles began to take a real interest in the situation of the world he was about to enter. He began to think analytically about things and form his own opinions concerning social matters. The idealism of youth led him to write, in 1904, that the purpose of a college education, as he saw it, was "learning to judge correctly, to think clearly, to see and to know the truth, and to attain the faculty of pure delight in the beautiful." It is easy to see his literary likes and their influence on him within these ideas and the extent to which he exercised his mind. It was thoughts such as this, as well as his general popularity, which led him to be a member of one of the more exclusive fraternities on campus, the Delti-Psi House. There he roomed with a good friend, John Sheddon, and also for a time with a man who was to become famous in another way, and whose ideas helped shape Charles' political thinking—Max Eastman.

By the time he met Charles Whittlesey, Eastman was already a confirmed Socialist. Whittlesey embraced the socialistic ideas that Eastman and others taught him, believing that socialism could be the only vehicle through which a wider cooperation of peoples of all types could come about. With no worldly knowledge to base this on, only the arguments of the idea, it was therefore unfeasible for a young Charles to realize that the prime impossibility in the practical application of socialism in a society is due simply to human nature. Eventually though, Whittlesey was to realize the folly of this line of thinking and turn to a sort of modified form of liberal democracy, also allowing for the presence of God (something that, in light of his upbringing, it is unlikely he ever denied anyway). And he never did give up in believing in the basic goodness of human beings and their willingness to work together toward a greater good, though the later war in Europe and his experiences in it would sorely test that belief.

As he absorbed ideas from Eastman, his college career also gathered steam. In his senior year, the revered Gargoyle Society invited him to join, and he made editor in chief of the Williams College yearbook, the *Gulielmensian*. He was already editor of the *Williams Literary Monthly*, as well as the *Williams Record*, both of which he contributed to on a regular basis. The honor was presented to him of writing an essay concerning the literary enterprises of his class, that of 1905, for the class book. Graduating near the top that year, Whittlesey's classmates showed their love and respect for him by voting him the "Third Brightest Man of the Graduating Class of 1905."

Following graduation, Whittlesey resisted the urge to descend into a life of frivolity among the Greenwich Village Cafés that seemed then to swallow so many of his young fellow socialists. He instead decided to make use of the education he had received and try to do some good in the world. Breaking family tradition, he went to Harvard and began to study law. No doubt it was here that his political views underwent their first modifications as he settled down to serious studies and began to really learn something of the world. Harvard was tough, and there was little time for the sort of social gadfly lifestyle he had enjoyed at Williams. And while he remained in contact with his Williams friends, most notably a young fellow named Belvidere Brooks, he made new ones while at Harvard as well. Among them was his dearest friend for life, a fellow law student, John Bayard Pruyn. He also held one Max Berking in very high esteem, but generally had little time for social pursuits while at Harvard. This included women.

In recent years, the question has been raised as to whether Charles Whittlesey was, in fact, a closet homosexual. For whatever reason, this debate seems to matter greatly in some circles, where this theory is cited as a contributing factor to Whittlesey's eventual suicide and has led to considerable controversy. The main evidence behind the dispute seems to be two-fold. First, Whittlesey never married, nor apparently had any serious relationship with a woman that is known of. This has lead many to believe that he lacked interest in the opposite sex. Second, is one of the opening lines of his suicide note to John Pruyn, in which he states, "I'm a misfit by training and by nature..." There is also the text of a letter sent from France to his friend Max Berking that could—if one wished—be interpreted in a suggestive manner. These have evidently been taken as some sort of admission of a closet homosexuality that he was unable to come to terms with; a condition which then, some argue, helped lead to his suicide.

Under closer scrutiny, neither point really stands up to the light, especially the second, which seems a great stretch. With concern for the first, while Whittlesey apparently found little time throughout his life for women, he was no prude. Charles was known to occasionally date women, and in fact was out on a date the night before he left on the trip during which he took his life, with a woman he had both known and 'kept company' with for years. The woman, John Pruyn's sister-in-law Marguerite Babcock, turns up time and again in connection with Whittlesey, but so far no solidly conclusive evidence of a serious relationship between the two has ever been revealed. As far as is known, no other woman ever captured his fancy, or if one did, he never let on that he had pursued the attraction. Moreover, the time in which he might have had his greatest interest in pursuing women - his college years - had been totally devoted to study, though it was during that time that he first met Miss Babcock and began whatever sort of relationship he might have had with her. However, by nearly all accounts, Charles Whittlesey was a private person where his personal life was concerned. And, those who knew him always maintained that he was a confirmed bachelor throughout his life. Some speculate that the death of his beloved sister had such an adverse effect on him that he was reluctant to place himself in a position close enough to a woman that would then one day allow that sort of pain back into his life. Whatever the truth behind this much-discussed side mystery about the Lost Battalion's commander, it remains one of the unsolved rumors of his life and will likely remain so.

Whittlesey graduated from Harvard University with his law degree in 1908 and almost immediately went to work as an assistant with Murray, Prentice & Howland at 37 Wall Street, New York City dealing in banking law (mainly contractual and regulatory matters). He was, according to his contemporaries, a better than average lawyer, notably characteristic in the courtroom for his ability to "destroy the arguments" of his opposite numbers. It was not by accident that he was successful at this. He was never unprepared, being an exceptionally precise and strict man to the point of being anal-retentive about exactitudes within a case. In fact, he was particularly adept at preparation law, with an innate ability to go over a case and point out the flaws and weaknesses of both sides of the argument, arriving at the truth, even when that truth was not to his side's favor. This provided him with the necessary edge in the courtroom, where he frequently non-plussed his opponents with irrefutable, calm argument, rarely spoken in anything but the lowest and even measured of voices and with a tone of undeniable finality. By all accounts, he was also unfailingly fair and honest, and not only on the job. No man could ever accuse Charles Whittlesey of lying, cheating, or unfair tactics in any way, shape, or form. In fact, just prior to his death, when he lied to his friend John Pruyn in saying that he was going to visit his mother in Pittsfield for the weekend (when in reality he boarded the ship from which he took his own life), Pruyn later made the statement that it was, "the only lie Charley ever told."

Whittlesey did, however, have a tendency to downplay his own accomplishments, preferring to remain out of the limelight and comfortable in the little niche in life he was carving out for himself. He coveted neither vast wealth nor great power, and maintained his ease with persons of all classes and experiences—a trait which no doubt stemmed from his early years in Wisconsin where he associated everyday with the rank and file miners and lumberjacks. Success to Whittlesey was measured by his own sense of self worth as he had been taught years before in Florence.

He continued to vote the Socialist ticket and read almost continuously. He especially enjoyed spending time with friends at the William's Club in New York City, with the occasional trip back to Pittsfield to see his parents. In 1911, he left Murray, Prentice & Howland to start his own firm in partnership with Pruyn. They set up shop at 2 Rector Street in the City and began to take cases. Nothing could be finer for a man of Whittlesey's ilk than to be in business with a friend, doing something that he enjoyed. He did not want for money, he had an untroubled mind, and life seemed at its comfortable best for Charles Whittlesey. Then, war broke out in 1914.

War to Whittlesey, the Socialist, was an unnecessary and abhorrent thing for two main reasons. First, war, in his mind, was socially reprehensible, morally unacceptable, and an unthinkable proposition for the country that he loved. He was totally behind Democrat President Woodrow Wilson's America being "too proud to fight" rhetoric (even though he had voted for the socialist nominee, Eugene V. Debs, in the 1912 election). And in keeping with basic Socialist doctrine, he firmly believed that any nation that did not want war, would then find no reason to engage in one. Second, war meant destruction—of life, land, and resources—and destruction offended the sensitive side of his nature. Dismayed by apparent human folly, he was horrified by the casualty counts coming back from the Western Front all through 1915 and into 1916, and he began to feel angry and worried for the human race. Whittlesey was not a loud or boisterous man; he usually remained calm and low of voice at virtually all times. It took a lot to get his blood up and for him to loosen the tight grip he had on the reigns of his sensibilities, but the war did just that. Additionally he found, much to his dismay, that his political party of choice was engaging in what he considered equally reprehensible behavior.

By 1916, it was obvious that war was going to come to the United States. Indeed, since the sinking of the Lusitania in 1915, any that had cared to look could have been seen it coming. Whittlesey, thoughtful as he was, realized war was coming, and knew he had to make a decision concerning where he stood. On the one hand, he was a Socialist and should back the party doctrine. But, the party, at the time, was doing everything it could to force its opinions onto the majority, including the backing of strikes and the use of sabotage, and of force in its anti-war stance. This flew in the face of everything it stood for, contradicting its own doctrines, and Whittlesey found himself becoming increasingly disillusioned by the party.

On the other hand, Whittlesey was greatly concerned about America's preparedness for the coming war. Few, especially the party, were willing to entertain the idea of being prepared to fight when all there was to prepare against was as yet unprovoked outside aggression. But, the war was coming, and though Whittlesey may have been a pacifist, to leave the personal freedoms guaranteed to all by the Constitution and the Bill of Rights unprotected would mean the collapse of the American way of life. No, there had to be an active defense ready for what was coming.

In the end, the Socialist Party made the decision for him when, toward the end of 1915, it is said that while reading of the party's tactics of coercion in pressing its ideas forward on the majority, Whittlesey suddenly tired of it all, tossed the paper aside, and exclaimed, "To hell with that crowd!"

Still, his apparent 'divorce' from the party did not mean that he had dropped all his original political philosophies. The only thing that really changed was that he no longer believed that the Socialists could lead humanity down a better path of life while war loomed. He was still, and always would be, a Socialist at heart, except now he apparently began to modify his views to bring more balance to them in light of the times. Above all, however, he was an American, and firmly believed that it was the sworn duty of every real American to defend his country's interests and way of life. Now Whittlesey saw those interests and that way of life about to be threatened, and anything that he could do to preserve that would be the right thing.

That summer of 1916 brought General Woods' 'businessmen's camps', the Plattsburg Officers Training courses, to his attention. While Whittlesey was certainly no lover of the military, he conceded that they had their place in the grand scheme of things and decided that here was the correct avenue of action. Therefore, he signed up for the 30-day course, leaving Pruyn to handle the office, and became Private Charles W. Whittlesey, U.S. Army Reserve.

This first brush with the military was short for Whittlesey and uneventful. He served in Company L, 7th Training Regiment, and his duty lasted from July 12 to August 8. His completion certificate, signed by commanding officer 1st Lieutenant Harry L. Hodges, lists his service as "honest and faithful." Yet while a fine start, he was in reality no closer to being a soldier than before he went. The real difference was that the Army had had a chance to assess his abilities, give him an initial taste of military duty, and put him on the list for call-up in case of national emergency. General Wood and his crowd had already deemed the Plattsburg camps a success in 1915. Now, in 1916, the turnout had been magnificent, and the stripe of man who had showed up was just the sort that was needed for a National Army Officer Corps.

Men of the stripe that included the 32-year-old Charles Whittlesey, who had by now filled out his lanky 6' 2" frame and tipped the scales at around 185 pounds. Most of his great length of body was made up of legs as his uniforms, now held in the Whittlesey Collection at Williams College, can attest. (II) Slightly balding with a receding hairline in that last summer of peace, Whittlesey kept his sandy brown hair neatly close cut. His features were not unkind—long aristocratic nose, alert (though horribly near-sighted), gentle blue eyes behind round steel framed-glasses, a slight puffiness to the cheeks that spoke of a good life, and a handsome smile that seemed to slowly steal across his face with the good humor that brought it. More often than not impeccably dressed and groomed, he was, not surprisingly, an exceptionally neat and organized man. His manner was one of quiet confidence and peace; it took a lot to get Whittlesey's hair up, but once it was up, he was not one to mince words and his tone could be like acid. He was not one to ordinarily use foul or vulgar language though, the occasional 'hell' or 'damn' being the most common exceptions. Otherwise, he spoke in a quiet, continental manner. It was not, "Wouldn't it be better if…" it was "Would it not be wise should…" or "Would we not be better off if…"; "Can't we…" became "Can we not…". He generally gave the initial impression of a schoolmaster, or perhaps a college professor and his long legs were rarely rushed into motion by lateness for some appointment or matter he had forgotten.

His vocal range, however, was of an uneven timbre. Usually he spoke in a natural, even tone within the lower portions of the mid-range scale that gave him a distinction of self-assurance and solid positiveness. In court, his voice was cause for attention; such was the authority of the instrument, which naturally brought people's focus to what he had to say. At the Williams Club, his dry wit combined with the relaxed atmosphere gave the mid-range tone a somewhat richer sound, warm and full, and his laugh a deeper ring. It was only when he became excited that his voice betrayed its frailties. Then, the raised volume caused the voice to shift into a higher measure within the mid-range scale, becoming a thin, reedy sounding instrument and slightly nasal. At those times the Wisconsin twang crept back in and some said that it became impossible to take him seriously at all. There was simply not enough 'meanness' in his bearing to compensate for the very thinness of his voice.

No one who met Charles Whittlesey disliked him, though many found him hard to know. Thus, he had many acquaintances and casual friends but few real intimate ones. John Pruyn, Bell Brooks, and Max Berking remained perhaps his closest friends before the war. George McMurtry, whom he would serve with in the Army, he later considered a friend, but it was a different situation with McMurtry. With him, Whittlesey had shared the great circumstance in the Charlevaux Ravine, and this had left a dark scar across what might otherwise have been an even greater friendship. Whittlesey also remained close with his family, visited Pittsfield fairly often, and was further hurt by the death of his younger brother Russell some years before the war. Another brother, Elisha, had gone to France with Section 133 of the American Field Service as a camion (truck) driver and Charles read with interest and no little worry the letters that he sent home from the front. Little did either realize that Elisha was operating in some of the same areas that Charles would the very next year. (III)

After the 1916 camp ended, the next few months (the last of peace for the United States) passed very quickly. Whittlesey continued at his law practice as the war clouds gathered. Eventually, the final slaps of Germany's unrestricted submarine campaign and the Zimmerman telegram put an end to the waiting. It was not long before Whittlesey received his call-up notice in the mail.

Whittlesey reported for the complete 90-day officers training course at Plattsburg barracks on May 14, 1917. He gave his address as 136 East 44th St. in New York City, was listed as 33 years old and 6 feet, 1 inch tall. He had retained his uniforms and accouterments from the 1916 camp, was assigned his bunk, stowed away his civilian clothes, and settled in. It almost seemed like he had not been gone, except this time the mood was different. Gone was the flippant, summer camp atmosphere of the previous year. There was a purpose in the air now, and Whittlesey steeled himself for whatever may come. As always, he was resolved to do his best; only his best would suffice in any case. Officer training at the spring 1917 Plattsburg Camp was tough, the Army's theory being that one could not lead troops if one could not do all - and more - than was expected of them. Besides, this was something that had never been done before. Civilian men were expected to learn in 90 days what typically took Regular Army officers years to learn, and many, in fact, thought it could not be done. The corporeal aspects alone turned out to be too much for some. Most officer candidates were in their 30s and 40s, had spent a great amount of their working life behind a desk, and were not used to so much heavy physical activity. Drill, calisthenics, rifle practice, exercises in tactics and theory, and endless hikes and marches did many in. There was also plenty of classroom work to go along with the physical activity. Military courtesy, military law, battlefield tactical training, logistics problems - all designed to stretch the mind and teach the candidate to act and react immediately. Hours usually lasted from 5:00 a.m. until well after dark, sometimes as late as 10:00 or 11:00 p.m. The men who would be officers were expected to do it right, the first time, every time. There could be no second chances. Lives would be on the line.

Fortunately, nearly all the officer candidates there at Plattsburg knew one another. A large percentage was lawyers who either had worked together at the same firms, or had faced each other in the courtroom. Many had been at college together as well, so there was a certain familiarity among the men, and this helped the camaraderie enormously. It was assumed, correctly as it turned out, that most of these men would be going to the same division and this too helped buck up flagging spirits during hard times, as they knew that they would still be able to associate with each other later on.

By all accounts, Whittlesey performed his duties most admirably while at Plattsburg—we could expect nothing else from a perfectionist. He was, this time, a private in the 7th Company of the 2nd Provisional Training Regiment. His only apparent flaw, as far as the Army was concerned, appears to have been a tendency toward independence of thought. In instances where most officers would simply obey and go along with what was ordered, Whittlesey frequently wanted to know "why". But this was no lack of faith in the system. Instead, it was simply a means of understanding the 'bigger picture'. If he was to lead men, he apparently felt it in his best interest to be as informed as possible (and rightly so). His discharge papers from Plattsburg that August 1917, have his commanding officer, Captain John B. Barnes, noting his service as again "honest and faithful" and his character as "excellent." And his exceptionally high degree of proficiency in performance of his duties and dedication as an officer did not go unnoticed by the powers that be either. Upon his graduation, he skipped the ranks of 2nd and 1st Lieutenant, and was placed at the very head of the list of those awarded the rank of Captain, U.S. Army Officer Reserve Corps.

Whittlesey, along with a majority of his comrades from Plattsburg, were ordered to Camp Upton on September 5 where he was made commanding officer of the Headquarters Company of the 308th Infantry. His familiarity with paperwork probably had a lot to do with the assignment, but there is also the possibility his superiors figured that in the Headquarters Company the questioning Captain Whittlesey could stir up little trouble. In any case, he soon gained a reputation among his men as a stern disciplinarian. He had a job to do, and there was no doubt it would be done and done right; he would see to that. However, with his thick glasses and long legs he became an easy, natural target, and stupid nicknames in reference to his physical frailties abounded. Only two, however, seemed to stick for any length of time, "The Stork" and "Galloping Charlie", though never to his face.

If Whittlesey was not particularly imposingly mean in stature or demeanor, he could (and apparently did) assign those who displeased him seemingly unending menial duties as punishment that would nearly kill the offender with boredom. Yet as time went on, the men realized that although he was strict, he was eminently fair and understanding, and before long, the nicknames were used less and less. While he generally appeared as aristocratic and uppity to the rank and file at first, they quickly came to see that he had at least a basic grasp of the problems they faced, and for that they appreciated him. No man wanted to be in trouble with Whittlesey, and no man wanted to let him down either. It was a sort of mutual acceptance, because in return he went to great lengths to care for his men, perhaps too much at times. Walter Baldwin, who was later to rise to the rank of Battalion Sergeant-Major under Whittlesey in the 1st Battalion/308th put it very plainly when he said, "We knew that if he was bossing the job, it would be done right."

One aspect of military life that sat very well with Whittlesey was the distinction between right and wrong, which ran very close to his own personal beliefs. These were similar to the Army's philosophy where there are only two ways of doing things—the wrong way and the Army way. His extremely high sense of moral conduct therefore made him a very efficient officer and his command an extremely reliable one in the eyes of the Army. However, his own views eventually were again forced to undergo yet another modification. While he did not necessarily let up on discipline per se, he did come to realize that sometimes less-important 'rules' occasionally needed to be bent for the greater good. Conversely, the all-important 'orders' were things not to be trifled with, sometimes coming through for reasons not always readily clear at the time. It was this distinction that would prove so very important during the Charlevaux episode.

He also gained the men's respect in a great way during the 'Liberty Loan scam' foisted on the men while at Upton. The 'establishment' decided that Upton would be a prime location to solicit Liberty Bonds (war bonds), and called on all regiments to participate.

They put pressure on officers to not only make an example by purchasing a few themselves, but to heavily urge their men to do so as well. In the 306th Regiment, for example, the officers fell in behind the program fully, and the regiment topped out by buying more than any other in the division. Whittlesey though bristled, his sense of right and wrong unbalanced by the coercion. "These men are already doing enough as it is," he said and refused to put pressure on his men in the Headquarters Company/308th. He was called on the carpet for his refusal but steadfastly defended his action, using his best lawyer approach in his usual calm, self-assured, low-voiced way. How could the men be expected to contribute, he argued, when most were poor to begin with, were horribly underpaid, had families to support in many cases, and were already on their way to laying down their lives in a foreign land for freedom? What more could possibly be asked of them? In the end, his plain deal appeal must have worked, for the matter was eventually dropped. While the high command of the 308th had a newfound respect for him, they were nonetheless a tad non-plussed by his actions.

This was indicative of how Whittlesey thought about and treated his men. It was a long time before the men found out about the Liberty Bond incident, and it was to be a slow road to his being accepted as OK in their eyes, but he eventually was. If he was only respected in the beginning of their training, he was very nearly loved by the time they got to France. As for his fellow officers, according to "The History of the 308th Infantry Regiment", Whittlesey was "respected and beloved more than any man in the regiment.

He spent as much off time as he had available to him at his favorite haunt, the Williams Club in the City (a special retreat for Williams alumnae and their guests). Here, just as before he was in the army, along with his fellow officers and friends he could relax and let the cloak of command slip from off his shoulders and just be Charley Whittlesey once again, rather than 'Captain Whittlesey'. There were several of his college friends in the regiment with him, most notably Belvidere Brooks, and there was no shortage of good conversation and camaraderie. He and Brooks would often brag about and compare tales of men under their respective command and it was times at ease like that when Whittlesey's sharp sense of humor would kick in. Captain Wardlaw Miles, later historian for the 308th, said, "After a little necessary preparation, he would get telling some of his fool stories and half the club would end up sitting at that table."

There, he felt at home and the worry of war was a thousand miles away. (7, 19, 29, 51, 65, 69, 72, 76, 78, 109, 116, 152, 218, 234, 236, 239, 245, 246, 258, 264, 274, 311, 312, 313, 346, 347, 349, 350, 353, 357, 358, 359)

On August 15, staff officers began to arrive at Camp Upton to begin the monumental task of organizing the brand new division, and on the 18th, General Bell assumed command and moved into the new commanders' quarters up on Headquarters Hill, which dominated Upton from the center of camp. While work continued on the camp, the 77th Headquarters staff continued organization until, in early September, the future officers of the division began to arrive.

The new officers were assigned quarters in Section J of the camp, and then barracks to house their new charges, once they arrived. Non-commissioned officers of the Regular Army arrived about the same time and were parceled out to the new officers, and assigned as drill instructors. A million details had to be taken care of — uniforms and boots ordered to be on hand, rifles and combat gear gathered and ready for distribution, barracks supplies needed to be readily available, and kitchens and hospitals set up and stocked. The list seemed never ending. However, by the time the first draft of men arrived, the officer staff was at least as ready for them as the camp was.

It was not until September 10 that the first group of men received orders to proceed to Camp Upton. That morning, 2,000 gathered at the dock of the 34th Street ferry to be taken over to Long Island and the waiting trains as the first draftees of the 77th Division. A description of a party of men who arrived several weeks later, by an anonymous writer in the History of the 305th Infantry, provides a pretty fair assessment of the situation: (308, 352)

"It was a Wednesday afternoon, about three p.m. and raining like mad when our train pulled into a place called Camp Upton. They had a band of music at the station playing 'The Star Spangled Banner' to get us to feel like fighting. It did — the way they played it! A few roughnecks from the regulars received us. The sergeant gave the command: "Column of two's. Forward, MARCH!" But we bums stood like a bunch of dopes, for we didn't know what a column of two's meant..." (113)

Army life for a draftee civilian in the First World War, as in all wars, was somewhat of a shock at first. Typically, a new recruit at Upton arrived on the ferry, took the train into town, and a bus to the camp. (The bus was eliminated once the camp rail spur was laid in October.) Upon arrival, he was taken to a casuals barracks run by a Receiving Captain with a staff of tough, old sweat sergeants. Here, initial paperwork was taken care of, including the all-important qualification card, which listed all the recruit's civilian skills and talents, important for later assigning a man to where he would do the most good, sometimes with dubious consequences.

"Well, the cards were a lovely color, and beautifully theoretical; and they did provide some amusement. Questioned as to his age, one man answered "Twenty-seven." When asked when he would be twenty-eight, he scratched his head, utterly baffled, and ventured: "Either May or December." (113)

Each man was given a haircut, assigned a bunk, and told not to switch with anyone, as the bunk assignments were initially the only way to tell who was there and who was not. Over the next few days the recruit was given a standard physical, a myriad of shots, and was instructed in the rudiments of military courtesy. (This last was not always very well taken by civilian men used to doing whatever they wanted. Hence, the casuals barracks captain and his staff were usually very tough men.) It generally took about a week to complete a casual period before the recruit was assigned to his permanent company.

Once in his permanent company, a recruit was introduced to the company commander and his staff including, most importantly, his drill sergeants, before being assigned a bunk in a barracks building. There was very little freedom or privacy in basic training, and usually someone around with stripes on his arm or bars on his shoulders barking out orders who did not know the meaning of the term "normal tone of voice." Additionally, life was especially hard on the few "apple knockers" (non-city men) in the division. Most of the regiment was made up of poor men from New York's Lower East Side, mainly immigrants and street toughs. Sometimes dealing with these boys from "The City" could be a trial of nerves, but more usually it was a trial of brawn, as all types of ruffian were well represented among those men, including members of the city's toughest gangs from Harlem and Hell's Kitchen, who had called truce long enough to fight the Kaiser before they went back to killing each other. To the relatively innocent apple-knockers from up state, the city boys could be a very rude awakening.

Personalities also abounded in the 77th, with many occupations represented, from bankers, barbers, draftsmen, teamsters, school teachers, mechanics, blacksmiths, shop keepers, salesmen, carpenters, tailors, policemen, printers, musicians, drifters, burglars, ne'r do wells, bums... the list was endless. Probably the most famous within the ranks was a young sergeant, Irving Berlin, who was to write the Broadway musical "Yip Yip Yaphank" and the popular song "Oh, How I Hate to Get Up in the Morning", based on his experiences at Camp Upton. And the 77th was unique in another way too. When Congress passed the draft registration act, it allowed unnaturalized aliens to be included within the national draft. This led to the phenomenon where there were at least 20 different nationalities represented within the divisions' ranks. While this may truly be representative of what America is - the melting pot of the world - this did cause at least two major problems.

First, many aliens were of European origin, and had come to American in order to escape the militarism that plagued 19th and early 20th century Europe, and they simply did not want to fight. Many were already successful in civilian life, such as Jack Herschkowitz who originally came from Romania. He and his brother had built a rather successful dried food business by 1917. "I didn't feel like going," he told author Henry Berry in an interview for the book, *Make the Kaiser Dance*, in the mid-1970s. "Who wants to get killed? So I first tried to get out of it. But, once I was there, I did it right." And do it right he did, for Herschkowitz later won the Distinguished Service Cross in combat.

Others did not want to fight for ethnic reasons. There were more than a few men in the 77th of German origin and some did not want to take the chance of fighting someone who could be their relative. For example, Louis Max Probst of the 308th, who would later wind up in the Lost Battalion, had a brother serving in the German army. Others, while not supporting the German cause, nevertheless did not feel it right to fight against their country of birth. There were religious reasons too. Many took the commandment of "Thou shalt not kill" to heart and refused to be trained to do so. Some of these men were made stretcher-bearers and the like, while the more ardent of these conscientious objectors were placed under arrest and put in the guardhouse until a decision could be made on them.

The second, and more intrinsic problem, was one of language. With so many different nationalities and immigrants within the divisional ranks, it soon became clear that there were many that simply could not yet speak English. In the 308th Infantry in particular this problem was manifest, as there was said to be in the neighborhood of 42 different languages and dialects among its recruits. This led to some perplexing situations. The following incidents from the 306th Regiment are indicative of what was happening all over the division in those first days:

"...It was a week before Captain Marshall discovered that Gregory, who had faithfully reported 'Present' at every formation... never had appeared at Camp Upton at all, and that Gregowski, who had been marked absent... was laboring under the impression that they had Americanized his name. But then roll call always caused more confusion than comprehension.

"Tomaso?"
"Here!"
"Tortoni?"
"Here!" this from the same individual.
"Who are you, Tomaso or Tortoni?"
"No spigh Ingleesh..." (90)

When one new company officer took over his new command, he found the 'skyline' of the men somewhat askew. He then proceeded to arrange the men by height from tallest on the left, gently sloping to shortest on the right. Satisfied at the fine sight before him, he gave the command "Right by squads!" and was mystified when some men turned the wrong way, some executed the wrong maneuver, and some did nothing at all; this from a company that had drilled just fine a short time before. Then, one squad leader quietly informed the new officer that the squads had been arranged by nationality. When the order was given, each squad leader had surreptitiously turned his head to his squad and translated the order into the proper language. Successful drill was the obvious result.

The squads were quickly returned to their original formations. (4, 35, 308, 352)

Yet it was problems such as these that helped weld the regiments of the 77th into close-knit and efficient organizations. Once the men had a laugh at the expense of the unfortunate non-English speaking subject, then the business of teaching that man the language began (which is a very 'New York' way of doing things). Then too, there was the fierce pride in and rivalry between the regiments. Each felt it could not stand to have anything wrong within its ranks, and definitely not have it show should there be a problem. Language was only a catalyst to that fire. God help the outsider from, say, the 305th that was caught hazing a 308th man about his language problems. Such a thing could lead to bloodshed. Each regiment, wanting to prove itself above the others, strove to make sure its men could march, shoot, look, and of course speak, at the very least, as well as the others, and preferably much better. Within the regiment, there was rivalry between companies as well. However, that was more akin to brotherly ribbing than anything else. Brigades and battalions were theoretical combat formations, not generally understood by the common soldier, and therefore of little significance. But the regiment, with its traditions and customs, was a different story. This spirit of rivalry between the regiments would later cause some problems for the 77th on the battlefield, which only time and a new commanding general could fix. However, the high spirits and unit loyalty within those regiments was to prove invaluable under fire, and the 77th had that in spades right from the beginning. Each regiment also took a great deal of pride in their foreign charges, considering themselves truly representative of what America stood for. (Again, this was particularly true of the 308th, then becoming something of a darling to the newspapers, who were occasionally referring to them now as 'New York's Own'.) There was very little *real* discrimination based on race or creed, despite the wide variety of derogatory language commonly used within the ranks. Part of the fantastic tradition of the division holds that during a lull in the fighting in the later weeks of the Muese-Argonne offensive, some 200 immigrants of the 77th were officially sworn in as U.S. citizens, right there in the Argonne Forest.

By the beginning of October 1917, enough men had arrived and been outfitted for General Bell to launch the 16-week intensive basic training program developed by the Army War Department, and the drill sergeants really set to the business of making soldiers. (IV) To begin with, the training centered greatly on drill, which builds the cohesiveness of a unit by teaching interdependence between individual soldiers of that unit. This in turn builds discipline and a sense of order in that individual soldier, who ceases to see himself so much as an individual, but more as a part of the larger unit. The soldier also learns to follow instructions and to trust his leaders to make the correct decisions regarding his actions. To that end, the recruits of the 77th drilled, drilled, and then drilled some more. They drilled in the dusty sunshine; they drilled in the muddy rain. They drilled with arms, they drilled without arms, they drilled by squads, companies, battalions, regiments, brigades, and finally as a division. It was not long before the citizen soldiers found themselves becoming proficient at close-order drill, open-rank drill, and bringing the weapon to right shoulder arms in the first three paces off the mark. The 30-inch step became their natural gait and their fingernails gleamed from lightly brushing the side seam of the wool uniform breeches as the arms swung easily back and forth.

Going hand-in-hand with drill was physical conditioning. Hours of sit-ups, push-ups, 3-, 5-, and 10-mile runs, chin-ups, and squat-thrusts soon began to tell on the men. Those who had never done a day of physical labor in their lives, those whose job was at a desk, the lazy, the weak, all began to realize the benefits of exercise. Muscles began to appear where none had been before. Fat began to melt away. Uniforms suddenly began to fill out and actually fit, and the men in them looked and felt good. They were toughening up and reveling in it.

There was boxing for sport and fitness, where quickly the champs emerged and became instantly popular. Hand-to-hand combat classes were given, featuring jujitsu. This ancient Japanese personal combat technique fascinated all, and gave a fine feeling of powerful comfort once learned. Baseball was played quite a bit in the off hours. In fact the famous baseball hero of the day, Eddie Grant, was in the officer ranks of the 307th.

French and British instructors were also assigned to the camp, men who had actually seen combat in the trenches of France and Flanders. The 302nd Engineers constructed a mock combat zone, complete with trenches, barbed wire, and sandbags and classes began in earnest concerning practical trench warfare. The trainee Doughboys charged up and over the top in mock bayonet charges; learned trench clearing drill and trench consolidation; went out on trench raids at night and patrols through the barbed wire hell of the fake no-man's-land; all under the eye of the watchful French and British instructors. The rumbling of a real tank could be heard in the background, sent from England to train with, while live ammo was fired over the men's heads as they crawled around wire entanglements 'for effect'.

School of the Bayonet was held. At first, the enemy were stacked hay bails that later became stuffed dummies hung by ropes on huge wooden frames. The commands of thrust, parry, jab, and slash brought instant action and a hearty yell in what the British instructor called the "spirit of the bayonet." Gas masks were brought out and the instruction in their use could not be emphasized enough. The different types of poison gas then in use by the enemy were discussed and the effects of Mustard, Phosgene, and Chlorine were explained in stomach-turning detail. The instruction in gas discipline culminated in a trip to the gas shack, where the men applied all they knew in a real, if non-lethal, gas environment. Everyone got to try it. Those who had not paid attention in class were soon found out.

Grenade training was also given, first with fake and later with live grenades. The sergeants noted those with an especially good arm. So too did they note the best shots when rifle training was given on the 200-target rifle range built for practical experience by the divisions' 302nd Engineer Regiment. The 77th was equipped with the .30 caliber M1917 American Enfield rifle, commonly referred to as the "Eddystone." This rifle was the workhorse of the National Army, and by war's end nearly 75 percent of the Doughboys overseas were armed with Eddystones, despite the commonly held misconception that the main U.S. rifle used in WWI was the M1903 Springfield rifle. And, in spite of the fact that virtually all of the city boys had never even *seen* a real rifle before they were in the Army, the standard of marksmanship was relatively high.

By October 31, the second officers training camp at Plattsburg for 1917 had been eliminated and the men participating went to the 77th as 'casuals' (unassigned replacements). By December 20 the camp, under a sea of mud, was declared officially finished, and Major Meyers handed over complete control to General Bell (and then promptly left on a well-earned furlough). Christmas leave was granted for half the camp, while the other half got leave for New Year's. A beautiful 30-foot lighted Christmas tree adorned 'Headquarters Hill' that year.

As training proceeded, discipline continued to grow. The holidays had been a sure sign of that. Earlier in training, when a man had wanted to go home and visit the city, he just went - pass or no pass. Now, a man understood the need for the pass and the necessity that his superiors knew where he was, for rumors of overseas departure were starting to float; something that no one now wanted to miss. Leave itself had also taken on a new meaning. Now when in town, these striding soldiers were looked on with some bit of reverence by their fellow New Yorkers. The uniform was a symbol that spoke saying, "I am not an ordinary man—I am a 77th Division man," and the men walked the streets, heads high. Those with newly won stripes on their arm displayed them prominently and enjoyed a pride they had never before known. New York wondered, "Can these be the same ragged men who shambled off to camp just a few months before?" Indeed they were, but now a well-disciplined lot, tough and ready for anything.

On Washington's Birthday, the four regiments of the division turned out and paraded down 5th Avenue through a light snowfall. They were the first National Army Division to

51

parade its colors in New York City. The crowds that greeted them were huge as New York came out to see "her division"—the Metropolitan Division—strut its stuff. The parade was a great success and everybody went away feeling as though the 77th could win the war all by itself. The press ate it up as well, and General Bell's staff (the General had left for an inspection tour of France at the end of December)—realizing that good press was essential for the morale of the division as well as the populace—invited them out to the camp. Impressed by what all had been done since they had last been allowed out there in September, they too went away with a tremendous feeling of pride.

In March, the rumors of departure for France began to be more insistent, however each day that the rumor mill claimed would be "the day," consistently came and went without pause. Then, at the end of the month, word came that the Germans had pushed to within 30 miles of Paris in a new drive, and it seemed a desperate situation for the Allies. The rumor mills really picked up steam, but preparations had already been under way for more than a month. Huge lots of equipment of all types had been arriving daily, and quartermaster sergeants were seen packing and sealing crates that not only bore the divisional emblem of the Statue of Liberty, but also the address of AEF - American Expeditionary Force. The beloved campaign hats were ordered laid aside for all time, and overseas caps (the hated "cootie catchers") were issued, along with long spiral puttees in place of the smart canvas leggings. Blue denim overseas bags were issued out and ordered packed. Long packs were rolled and gear assembled. Worn equipment was traded in for new. Last leave was granted for tearful good-byes and the telephone lines buzzed. It was like electricity in the air—the day could not be far off! Then it finally came in the first few days of April and each regiment was warned to be ready to sail within 36 hours. Suddenly, there was not enough time and everyone seemed endlessly busy.

Everyone except Major-General Bell, that is. He had returned home from France in early March to find his division well on its way to being ready for overseas duty, which he was enthusiastic about leading. However, a physical examination he had taken soon after his arrival back in the United States left the doctors believing that he was simply not up to the task of leading a division in combat. Sadly, Bell was forced to agree with them, and turned over temporary command of the division to Brigadier General Evan M. Johnson, commander of the 154th Brigade, at the end of March, who would then take them to France. General Bell then went back to his post at the head of the Army Department of the East, where he died in 1919.

After eight months of preparation, the Metropolitan Division was finally on its way to war. (8, 28, 45, 87, 90, 101, 109, 116, 308, 344, 349, 352)

I. The 308th Infantry also laid claim to the title however, and it *was* sometimes referred to in the newspapers to some extent as such. This has occasionally caused some confusion over the years.
II. Whittlesey was acutely aware of his great length. Once later, while under fire and seeking cover with a fellow officer in a funk hole, he exclaimed in no small measure of unintentional ironic humor, "Why did not God standardize me?"
III. Elisha was eventually gassed and sent home in October 1917. He died a year or so after Charles from gas related complications after being bed-ridden at the home in Pittsfield for a long spell.
IV. It is interesting to note that changes were to occur within this basic training system in the United States over the course of the next year. As the demand for soldiers overseas grew through 1918, the 16-week course seemed to get lost in the shuffle, until eventually soldiers began to arrive at the front with little or no real training. Within the 77th Division, however, we get a chance to see the full benefit of the 16-week program.

Ancillary sources used in this chapter include: 93, 94, 98, 100, 103, 117

From Camp Upton
to the Vesle

"I may be gone for a long, long time…"
A popular song of the day.

In front of a barracks at Camp Upton, New York, April 6, 1918:

"At five o'clock the next morning the company fell in facing east, where the sun was just beginning to light the clouds… Then came the captain's harsh command, that searched the waiting line and swung it into action; we stepped out slowly, at last… on our way to France." (45)

So wrote Corporal Louis Ranlett of Company B/308th as the regiment began their journey to war. Ranlett, a Harvard man, had been one of the officer-minded attendees of the cancelled 2nd Plattsburg camp of 1917, but now accepted his new station in life as enlisted man with capitulation.

In the 36 hours or so since it had been warned to prepare for overseas departure, the 308th Infantry Regiment had come close to chaos as it prepared itself to go to war. Then, just a few short hours after Corporal Ranlett and his pals set out, the 308th had already made the train ride to waiting ferries that then deposited the men and all their gear at the docks in Brooklyn. There awaited the huge transport ships that would take the regiment 'over there', each battalion assigned to a different ship. First Battalion, commanded by Major Nelson, along with Captain Whittlesey and the headquarters detachment, went on the Red Star Liner 'Lapland'; 2nd Bn., under Major Kenneth P. Budd, went aboard the 'Cretic'; 3rd Bn., under Major Chinner, boarded the 'Justicia'. Commanding the whole of the 308th from aboard the 'Lapland' was their regimental commander, Colonel Nathan K. Averill - an old cavalry officer much admired by his men.

Loading took a few more hours, and the men weaved their way around piles of equipment stacked within a monstrous warehouse like a line of ants, each headed toward the small openings in the sides of the enormous ships. Then up the gangplank, checked in with the officer at the end, shouting just to be heard. Each man was given a deck, bunk, and mess assignment card, and issued a cork life belt. "Once we get underway, keep this on at all times. Got it?" Then the trip took them into the bowels of the ship to find their assigned places. The men were surprised at the lack of space within such a large ship. The passageways were narrow and it was a struggle to get through them with the bulging packs strapped to their backs. Corporal Ranlett found his assigned space on N Deck - the very last deck at the very bottom of the ship. It was disconcerting, to say the least.

"My chief want, after once seeing my sleeping quarters, was to get all the air I could, while I could. Four double flights of stairs brought me to the lowest open deck, which I found covered with great numbers of soldiers, just milling around…. I quickly found a way to the top of the pilot house, which, being the highest accessible point, afforded an excellent view." (45)

Below him, Ranlett saw the whole of the ship covered in khaki clad figures. It seemed, he feared, that rails of the decks might at any moment collapse due to the multitude of bodies pressing against them. Derrick nets swung up and were attacked by workers unloading the blue denim barracks bags and carting them away while coal barges unloaded their payload into the waiting scuppers of the immense ship.

Eventually, a loud note burst forth from a steam whistle somewhere and all the men were sent below as the great engines were started. All knew it would not be long now. A few lucky ones managed to find space on the jammed, open lower decks, but most found themselves confined within the depths of the ship jockeying for position around the many portholes for one last look at home. The departure of the Division was supposed to be a secret, but if there had been any secrecy in the first place, it quickly faded. It was just after five o'clock - quitting time for New York City - when the trio of ships turned down the river and got underway. Everyone who saw them knew what the huge transports signified. Passing ferries blew their whistles and the throngs of homeward bound civilians aboard them cheered loudly. From windows all along the river-way, white towels waved and white faces peered intently. Slowly the ships moved along, heading out toward the unknown. It began to grow dark. The Statue of Liberty - the emblem of the Division - slipped quietly by in the fading light. The departing soldiers slowly started to drift away to spaces within the ship as a deep silence began to envelop the scene. Ranlett remembered:

"...I was held spellbound by the wonder of the fact that here I was, actually going to war... What was before me now? The long expanse of gray water, ever widening and blackening, symbolized the unknown future that stretched ahead... The stars came out. My friend and I looked at each other, said nothing, and went below." (45)

On the afternoon of April 8, the ships pulled into Halifax Harbor, Nova Scotia. There they remained for the next 24 hours, taking on more coal and additional supplies, and waiting for the rest of the convoy for the trip over to England to arrive. The Doughboys practiced lifeboat drill in the harbor while waiting; everyone enjoyed dropping the little boats in the harbor and rowing around aimlessly for a few hours. At sunset of the next day, all ships swung out to sea. As the 308th passed by, a band on one of the British battlewagons belted out, *Over There* and *The Star Spangled Banner*, while a little further on a U.S. Marines Corps band aboard the transport *Olympic* ragged, *There'll be a Hot Time in the Old Town Tonight*. Led by the U.S. scout cruiser *St. Louis*, nine camouflaged transports steamed out to sea, skirted by a multitude of British and American battleships, cruisers, and sub chasers. They were on their way.

The crossing was uneventful, the weather fair and the sea calm all the way across. On April 19, the coast of Ireland was spotted. At that, many of the men with shamrock-shaped hearts leaned against the rail, peering hard through a tear in the eye for a glimpse of the "auld sod." Then, the cliffs of Wales came into view, the escort cruisers dropped away, and the ships pulled up the River Mersey. There, they dropped anchor for the night. The next morning, the transports docked at Liverpool, the men debarked, and as the *History of the 308th* put it, "Soon hob-nailed boots were planted again on terra firma."

The 308th was rapidly unloaded and marched out of the docks, headed for British Rest Camp No. 2 at Dover, which they reached late on the 20th. The next morning, half the regiment boarded cross channel steamers. Under escort of two ships of the Dover Patrol and a Royal Navy blimp, they crossed over to France and landed at Calais, the first National Army troops to set foot in that war-torn country. The morning after that, the rest of the regiment arrived and all were marched out to another British rest camp on the other side of Calais. Here they traded their Eddystones in for British Enfields and were issued steel helmets and gas masks. Says Corporal Ranlett upon receiving his gas mask:

"Three British soldiers stood outside and spoke to each man as he passed... "You are now to draw gas masks. Pay strict attention to what the next man says"... The sergeant in charge of the group in which I took my lesson left a parting word of cheer for us. "These are all good masks. Every one of 'em's seen service. The fellows who 'ad 'em all went west some way or t'other, and now they've been fixed up for you'uns." (45)

By the end of the week, the men of the 308th were again on the move. Rumor held that they were immediately going into the line to stem the tide of the German surprise offensive that had exploded into Allied lines on the morning of March 21. But, it was not to be. The regiment still had some training ahead. After a seemingly unending ride, they detrained just outside of Zutkerque, a little village about 60 kilometers from the famous battered town of Ypres, Belgium. They were in the British back areas now and brigaded with the Kings 39th Division for intensive advanced combat training. In the distance, one could hear guns booming at the front. (7, 45, 87, 101, 103, 109, 116)

On May 10, Major-General George B. Duncan arrived to take over command of the division from Brigadier General Johnson, who then went back to command of the 154th Brigade. General Duncan, who would command the division until August, was a West-Pointer, class of 1886, and was the only officer in the entire U.S. Army to have seen action on all of the fronts of the Spanish-American War. His service with the 77th was not to be particularly eventful, even though it was under him that the division saw its first real action during the war.

Brigadier General Evan Malbone Johnson, on the other hand, had a long and particularly distinguished career in the Army. Born in 1861 into a line that stretched back to the settlement of the American colonies, he began his military career by enlisting in the 10th Infantry as a private in June 1882. He served in nearly every branch of the service, was in the Spanish-American War, and did a long stretch in the Philippines. There, he wore many hats, from provincial military governor, to the leader of numerous expeditions against insurgent factions. Johnson had fought against the Apache Indians of Arizona and New Mexico, had been a professor of Military Science and Tactics at Mount Union College, served as editor of the *Infantry Journal,* and held down a host of other duties and posts far too numerous to mention here. By July 1917, however, he was a Colonel in the 5th Infantry, when he was promoted to Brigadier General and given command of the 154th Brigade of the newly formed 77th Division, a post he held until October 30, 1918, when he would be transferred to the 79th Division. He was truly a good soldier, knew nearly every job in the service as if it were his own, and rarely did things the same way twice. Instead, he usually preferred to find a better or more efficient way to do whatever it was that needed doing. General Johnson was also not one to spend lives in battle foolishly and was a great believer in common sense - not necessarily a good thing in war, which sometimes demands that things be done that defy common sense. Tall and thin, hard-bitten and rather consumptive looking, he was well respected by his men and his peers as one of only a handful of officers in the Army with an apparently innate understanding of battle. He was much happier in command of the 154th than he had been at the head of the division, although bringing the 77th to France was yet another proud moment in a long and eventful career. He will figure greatly in the Lost Battalion episode. (7, 87, 109, 116)

According to the *History of the 308th,* the men of the 77th made quite an impression on the British during training. Few words can equal the praise laid at their feet by Sir Phillip Gibbs, who later wrote of them:

"Physically they were splendid...taller than any of our regiments (apart from the Guards)... and had a fine easy swing of body as they came marching along... Better dressed than our Tommies... there was a

dandy cut about this American uniform, and their cloth was of good quality... I was struck by the exceptionally high level of individual intelligence among the rank and file... The American private soldier seemed to me less repressed by discipline than our men... had more original points of view, expressed himself with more independence of thought, and had a greater sense of his own personal value and dignity." (109)

The Doughboy officers held their British counterparts in high esteem as well, but there the mutual respect ended. The NCOs and enlisted of the two divisions found little to like in each other, and there were some tense moments as many harsh words, and more than a few blows passed between the two groups. However, all feelings of rancor were put aside once the British instructors settled down to the business of teaching the Doughboys how to stay alive in the trenches. Then the Americans shut up, listened, and learned with rapt attention.

The British, believing that practical experience is the best experience, were before long conducting 'Cooks Tours' for a day or two stretch up in the front lines for the Officers and NCO's of the 308th. Here was the real thing! Here was gained the first experience of shellfire - which at first terrified the Americans, as it does all men - and here was gained the first combat-related injury in the regiment when Lieutenant Paul R. Knight of Company D was lightly wounded in the arm by shrapnel. It was far from the last bit of German 'scrap steel' that he was to receive.

On May 13, the regiment boarded trains under orders to move in with the British 2nd Division farther down the line, in the Arras sector. Here Captain Whittlesey, acting as Regimental Operations Officer for the 308th, got his first real job overseas - that of finding billeting for three battalions of infantry. Not an easy job, but one he performed with the admirable quality that was to mark nearly everything he did in the Army.

Training continued there, preparing the Doughboys for the coming attractions. Long-range enemy artillery searched the area regularly, causing the first regimental battle death, Private Stanley Belen of Company I, who was killed at La Bazique Farm, where the 3rd/308th were billeted. On June 4, orders came through directing that the regiment be taken apart and distributed by company within the British 2nd Division, who had orders to move up to the first line positions south of Arras. Captain Whittlesey then had his second important assignment of his young command - that of drawing up orders sending men into battle for the first time.

In reality, the plan was for the British to simply amalgamate U.S. troops into their own units as replacements, something that the French and the British pushed General Pershing for the entire length of the war, convinced that the United States could never command its own army in Europe. General Pershing, however, would have none of it. Instead, he insisted that only a united American force, under American control, would do justice not only to America, but to the cause as well. Grudgingly, the French and British agreed. Therefore, with slightly over 24 hours left before the time that the 308th was to move out and merge into the British 2nd Division, an order came through countermanding the previous one. The 308th stayed its own unit; Pershing got his way.

On June 6, as the U.S. Marines were spilling buckets of blood in the wheat fields before Belleau Wood further to the south, the 77th Division got orders to proceed to British stores and exchange their Brit equipment for the U.S. stuff they had turned in weeks before. Then, again with Eddystones in hand, the division lit out toward Alsace-Lorraine to the Baccarat sector, at the foot of the Vosges Mountains. It turned out to be the place they had been waiting so long to see, for here they would assume a section of the line all to themselves, although under the watchful eyes of the French 61st Division.

The Baccarat sector was supposed to be a quiet one, and indeed not much had been going on there in the last couple years, making it particularly well suited for the gentle breaking in of fresh troops. Units of the 42nd "Rainbow" Division were the current proprietors of the sector when, on the night of June 18, the 308th set out for the front lines to relieve them:

"Yesterday was New York "Old Home Day" on the roads of Lorraine. We marched out from Baccarat on our hunt for new trouble, and met on the way the 77th Division, all National Army troops from New York City. It was a wonderful encounter. As the two columns passed each other... in the bright moonlight, there were songs of New York, friendly greetings and badinage, sometimes good humored, sometimes with a sting to it... More often it would be somebody going along the lines shouting "Anybody there from Greenwich Village?" or "Any of you guys from Tremont?"... The answer was almost sure to be "Yes."... A man went the whole line calling for some one man: "Is John Kelly there?" the answer from our side being invariably, "Which one of them do you want?"... (48)

So wrote Father Francis Duffy of that venerable old unit, the "Fighting 69th" of the New York National Guard, now federalized into the 42nd Division as the 165th Infantry. "Good lads," he continued about the 308th. "God bless them, I hope their wish comes true."

Two signs greeted the incoming National Army Doughboys telling them that their wishes had indeed come true. Over part of the road coming in was stretched a huge French camouflage net and hung from it a large board, bearing the ominous message "Zone Dangereuse." Then, once the front lines were actually occupied on the night of June 21-22, odd bits of wood were seen to be held up by the Germans at several points in the trenches across no-man's-land that read, "Goodbye 42nd! We're sorry to see you go! Welcome 77th! We'll give you Hell!" So much for secrecy.

The official German welcome came forty-eight hours later, at 3:00 a.m. on the morning of June 24, when the Germans of the 35th Landwehr Division, reinforced by a battalion of storm troops, struck the first agonizing blow against the 308th. The 1st Battalion was in the front lines under Major Nelson, when all at once a storm of German artillery suddenly began to rain down in the form of a box barrage, well centered and well aimed. Mixed in among the high explosive (HE) and shrapnel shells came that most terrifying of weapons: poison gas. Corporal Ranlett, whose Company B occupied the middle of the regimental sub-sector, describes the weird scene inside his dugout:

"Gas boys, gas!"... We bounced off our helmets, dove into our masks, which had been close tied under our chins for the last four days, and then fumbled on the floor again for the suddenly discarded headgear. The masks shut us off from everything even more than the terrific sound which still eddied about us (and) we drew in around the one candle... At the edge of the little circle of light ranged a row of huge staring eyes in black pointed faces, from the snouts of which a shaking pipe led down into the darkness... mud colored helmets... hid the foreheads... conversation was reduced to a mere series of gurgles..." (45)

Then came the German attack. Storm troops brought flame-throwers, and in some spots there was savage and terrifying bayonet and hand-to-hand fighting in the eerie pre-dawn darkness, with the Doughboys out numbered 3 to 1. The scene from Battalion Headquarters, described with a stark drama by Captain Wardlaw Miles in the *History of the 308th Infantry* gives a good picture of the situation as the attack and the shelling slowly eradicate communications:

"One by one the wires began to go out. First died the one to French Headquarters, and soon only two were left, one forward to an observing post in Chamois, and the other back to Regimental Headquarters. The operator in Chamois stuck to his post throughout, and as daylight dawned, reported no attack in that sub-sector. The message went through to Regimental H.Q. and then this line died. Major Nelson turned to two men of the Signal Platoon and commanded them to go out and repair the line.

"Out there?" asked one of them quizzically.

"Certainly out there! The infantry is out there, isn't it?"

...Shortly after daylight, the only remaining telephone line... died, and an impenetrable curtain of ignorance descended over the happenings at the front... At last a 'C' company runner staggers into Battalion Headquarters... white-faced, mud covered... his uniform torn. "Trenches all gone. Men all gone. Everything all gone..." (109)

In the Regimental subsector, Company A, on the left, fared the best; its greatest loss was deemed to be the company's field kitchen, which was blown to smithereens. Company B, in the middle, held its own while receiving a few casualties, some contact related and a good dose of gas. It was Company C on the right, however, that really took it in the neck. One platoon suffered over 50 percent casualties, with about 20 men disappearing over to the other side of the lines - "guests" of the Kaiser for the duration. In another platoon, only five unwounded and three wounded made it back.

By 5:00 a.m., the attack was over.

It had been a valuable learning experience, but the only serious action the regiment was to see during its five-week stay in the Baccarat sector. Not that the rest of their stay was any cakewalk. The shelling of the back areas and trench lines continued, and there were a few more casualties. Major Nelson was nailed by a shrapnel ball at the end of June; not too seriously, but bad enough to be sent to the hospital. Captain Whittlesey then took over the 1st Battalion for a short time (an advance look at what was to be, one could say). Then, in mid-July, Lieutenant Colonel Fred Smith, assistant regimental commander, took over 1st Battalion and brought them again into the front lines. They were still there on August 1 when the 37th Division came into the sector and relieved the 77th, which then began a two-day journey that would bring them to what would always be remembered by its men as "The Hell-hole Valley of the Vesle." (7, 34, 35, 45, 48, 87, 91, 109, 116, 121)

"Lorraine was only a boxing match. But the Vesle; now that was a *real* fist fight," was how one veteran officer described the fighting the division did there. The Vesle front was where the 77th Division finally learned to work as a team toward one common goal. The soldiers of the different regiments here came to regard each other almost as brothers while engaged in the crucible of combat, and command of the division was to pass to the man who would lead them through their toughest fight of the war, the Muese-Argonne Offensive. If the 77th could be said to have entered the sector as a recruit division, it certainly exited the area a veteran one—a tired but proud, close-knit organization, tough as nails.

The River Vesle is certainly not much to behold, and barely deserves the name of "river." It is a muddy, meandering waterway, with an average width of about 30 feet and an average depth of some 10 feet. In the area of operations of the 77th Division, it ran on a general north-west/south-east course, through mostly open country, between banks an average of five feet in height. A narrow gauge railroad followed the path of the river for a time, connecting several small towns in the area. On either side of the river and rail line are found sloping gradients that create the river's valley, giving way to a not altogether unpleasant atmosphere. That is, until the Germans came.

The Valley of the Vesle was along the line to which the Germans had drawn their forces back after the beating that they had taken around Chateau Thierry earlier that summer. They had established themselves north of the river, laid miles of coiled barbed wire into the river itself to prevent anyone getting the bright idea of crossing it, brought their artillery up in quantity, and dug in deep. Nearby Bazoches and Fismes, two important rail towns in the area, were in German hands. Farther north, deep behind the enemy's lines, was a loop of the River Aisne. Already firmly entrenched in the line when the 77th moved up were the 17th, 29th, and 216th divisions of the Regular German Army, and the crack 4th Prussian Guard Division - none of whom had any intentions of going anywhere.

The 77th quickly moved in and took over the sector occupied by the French 62nd and American 4th Divisions, who had chased the Germans back beyond the river itself. On the left was another French division, while to the right was the U.S. 28th Division. On the night of August 10-11, the first relief of the front lines was attempted, but met by such intense shellfire from the enemy that the operation could not be brought about and the Doughboys were forced to dig in for the first time.

'Digging in' was something new to the men of the 77th, but it would be a mainstay from this point until the end of the war. The shelling was so intense that "funk holes," the forerunner of World War Two's foxhole (basically any hole that could be dug fast enough and deep enough to shelter a man), became a common sight on the Vesle front. "Everything is bomb proof until it is hit" was a not-too-funny joke on the Vesle heard a million times. Additionally, the funk holes did not protect at all from gas. Being heavier than air, gas had a tendency to linger in the low spots for days. And the Germans were throwing plenty of gas shells around as well as regular ones. Barely an inch of ground could be found that had not been pounded or gassed by enemy artillery. However, for every German shell that fell within the American lines, two were sent back in answer. At least that is what the infantry were told, though few actually believed it.

Basically, the 77th's action on the Vesle front fell into two phases. The first phase involved them hammering away at the German positions north of the Vesle (and the Germans hammering away at them) for about four weeks, with no real gain of ground, yet much loss of personnel. The second phase commenced when the division took part in a serious offensive action that finally drove the Germans back to the Aisne River. During both phases, the 3rd Battalion of the 308th took the brunt of the punishment for that regiment, while 2nd Battalion provided support (and got kicked about pretty badly itself) and 1st Battalion, beaten up first at Baccarat, generally stood in reserve.

During the first phase, there was much nasty hand-to-hand night combat as the soldiers of both sides fought over bridges, got into each other's lines, and just generally raised havoc whenever, and wherever, they could. Typical of what the Vesle fighting was like in this phase, is this account from the *History of the 77th Division*:

"A patrol of one officer and two men stumbled over a perfectly innocent looking shell hole on the night of August 15th, and found in it two Germans with auto rifles, hand grenades, and two other rifles stacked against the sides of the hole. It was a well-hidden snipers post. A hand to hand struggle ensued; one German was wounded, and the other escaped. Ten minutes later, the light artillery was filling the region with gas and high explosive, for it was thought that other shell holes in the vicinity were undoubtedly being used for the same purpose. Such were the encounters in the valley of the Vesle. It was not a struggle of masses; it was the tussle of man with man." (116)

It was a hot summer, and clean water was at a premium due to gas infestation of most water supplies. The 302nd Engineers had their hands full digging new wells, as well as trying to repair the few bridges spanning the Vesle while under fire. Meanwhile, the 308th continued to slam away at the door of the German defenses and casualties mounted. For the purposes of this book, simple bits and pieces stand out to illustrate the fighting:

On August 15, the 2nd/308th was at the front, heavily engaged with the enemy. Along the road connecting Ville-Savoie with Chery-Chartreuve was Cemenocal Cave, and within this cave were members of 2nd Battalion headquarters platoon. Through a terrific artillery barrage going on outside, a message from the 308th's Regimental Operations Officer, Captain Whittlesey, at Regimental P.C. in Chery-Chartrueve, came through, ordering up a squad of men with a 37mm gun, the famous "one-pounder," from the Regimental

Headquarters Company to support the hard-pressed men of 2nd Battalion out on the line.

Company H, which had started out the fight on the Vesle with 196 men, was down to six lonely souls, gas accounting for many of the rest. The remainder of 2nd/308th did not fare much better, and the medics were hard pressed to keep up. Major Budd, in charge of 2nd/308th since Upton, clumped down the short flight of stairs into the cave with those losses burning in his mind. The cave was slightly below ground level; good for safety, bad for gas. Major Budd was already suffering from some gas poisoning himself, the filter of his mask obviously nearing the end of its useful life, and he glanced at the message from Whittlesey. The Captain had just been there that afternoon seeing if there was anything he could do and Budd had mentioned the 37mm gun. There had been no doubt that it would show up.

Outside, buried in the din of explosions that filled the late afternoon, there was a peculiar warbling sound, which grew closer. Gas shells do not scream and then explode with a roar like shrapnel or high explosive shells do. Rather, they warble and then bang, breaking open to spread sickness and death.

Perhaps some in the cave noticed, perhaps not. In any case, the next few moments saw two gas shells sail down toward the mouth of the cave and burst near the opening. In seconds, the cave filled with gas and men scrambling to get their masks on as they rushed for the door. The next day, the regimental surgeon sent Major Budd, under protest, to Evacuation Hospital #11 at Brizeaux-Forestiere to be treated for gas poisoning. He is lucky though; his case was not that severe and he rejoined the 308th in time for the jump-off into the Muese-Argonne Campaign the following month.

On August 17, the 308th lost its regimental commander, the much-loved Colonel Averill, when he was relieved of his command and sent to a new one within the 3rd Division. Colonel Austin F. Prescott, a Regular Army old salt with hash marks down to the ground, and the crusty disposition to go with them, took his place. Colonel Prescott came over from the 302nd Ammunition Train, and was thus not particularly qualified for command of a combat regiment (he could not even read an operations map), nor was he particularly well liked. Word had it that well placed friends had gotten him a combat command to further his career. Almost from the start he clashed with his junior officers, including his questioning Operations Officer Captain Whittlesey.

At 10:00 p.m. on August 21, at the mouth of Cemenocal Cave, a group of battalion officers and enlisted men of 1st/308th PC waited to set up shop in the cave following the relief of 3rd Battalion from the area. As usual, the German artillery was falling at a rapid rate. No sooner had Lt. Graham, liaison officer of the 305th Field Artillery Regiment, expounded his view that standing out in the open during an artillery barrage was probably not the best of ideas, when a familiar scream cut the air. It got louder and yet louder and finally ended in a dull thump as a dud shell plopped to the ground near the opening of the cave. Too close! Another scream began to rip the air close by. Captain Breckenridge, temporary 1st Battalion commander, shouted, "Look out!" and there was a mad dash for the cave by everyone. Lieutenant Graham and another officer stepped aside to let the enlisted men in first, just as the scream ended in the bright flash and tremendous roar of a bursting high explosive shell, which fell directly in the middle of the group. Killed instantly were Lt. Graham; Lt. Lederle, the 3rd Battalion adjutant; Lt. Lusk, gas officer for the 3rd Battalion; two enlisted men whom they never found enough of to identify; and the officer who stepped aside with Graham, Captain Belvidere Brooks, former officer commanding Company D and close friend and college pal of Charles Whittlesey.

What Whittlesey thought about Brooks' death, the first real friend he lost to the war, is difficult to know. After the war, whenever he gave speeches concerning his exploits in France and Bell Brooks' name came up, he would only smile and gave praise to a "courageous and gallant man." In any case, Whittlesey was otherwise occupied that very day, and it is unlikely that he heard about the incident until some time later. When the 3rd Battalion Intelligence Officer rang up Chery-Chartrueve earlier that day to request more replacement runners be sent, he was calmly told, "Call up again; I can't talk to you now," by Captain Lindley, the then Regimental Intelligence Officer. A series of shells had just torn through the roof of the house that held the 308th Regimental P.C., including several gas shells, and all was chaos. Most of the men in the house were either badly wounded or badly gassed and ended up in the hospital. Lieutenant Meredith Wood, Regimental Signal Officer, was cited in General Orders for rescuing several men from the turmoil and getting himself gassed in the process, bad enough to put him in the hospital until mid-October.

Another one who was gassed, and apparently rather severely, was Charles Whittlesey - who never reported the fact. Just why he did not is easy to figure; they would have taken him off the line, just as they had done with Ken Budd a few days earlier. That, to Whittlesey's high sense of duty, would have been unacceptable. It was unfortunate that he did not receive the treatment he required at the time for the poison that had infected his lungs. Later we shall see just how unfortunate, for the incident was to have a dramatic and far-reaching effect on his life. (35, 48, 58, 91, 93, 109, 116, 121, 246)

On August 27, a massive raid was launched on the ruined town of Bazoches with the intention of taking the high ground beyond it away from the enemy and thus relieving some of the intensive shellfire that the 77th had been forced to endure thus far. The artillery, the trench mortar battalion, the machine-gunners, and the infantry - everyone took part. Exactly how successful the raid was is of some debate. Some sources claim that it was a great success overall, while others denounce it as a dismal failure. Certainly General Robert Alexander, who arrived the day of the raid to take command of the division, thought the latter. In his memoirs he states, "The attempted occupation of Bazoches (as conducted) was, in my opinion, especially unfortunate," and he refers to the attack as "tactically unsound and… had been directed against an objective which the enemy could make valueless at will." He goes on to say, "In a word, conditions along the front line were not at all satisfactory." (2)

It is true that morale was low in the division at the time, due in large part to the heavy casualties and seemingly unending shellfire. However, a glance through the lists of commendations handed out to men for individual acts of heroism and bravery reads like a book in itself, illustrating that even if morale was low overall, the level of individual spirit and tenacity of the men was not. But perhaps the most important thing about that August 27 raid was that it was conceivably the first time that the individual regiments of the division acted together in a true spirit of cooperation. This new spirit of cooperation that slowly gripped the division was largely fostered and encouraged to grow by the new divisional commander, Major-General Robert Alexander, who had taken command of the 77th on the afternoon of the Bazoches raid. In referring again to conditions on the day he took command, he says:

"When I reached the Chateau de Fere shortly after noon of the 27th, I found the acting division commander (General Duncan) pacing the floor of his office in a state of great perturbation. I asked him what the trouble was; he told me his losses had been "terrible" and gave the details of his attack of that morning. I then told him that I was there to take over the command, and made the mental reservation that as long as I was responsible for the division, we would try no more such experiments…" (2)

If General Alexander had thrown in the white horse and armor, what a perfect tale it could be! In all seriousness, Robert Alexander is an anomaly. On the one hand, he was to do great things for and with the division; on the other, he was to be the cause of a great many of its troubles. Still, of all the commanders that the 77th had during the time from its formation until the time of its demobilization, he is arguably the only one who could have successfully led the division under the trying circumstances of the second phase of the Vesle offensive and to success in the Argonne. Due in large part to his stern and at times unorthodox leadership, the 77th Division learned not only how to function as a single unit, but became the AEF division that racked up the most kilometers of advance against the enemy, out of all of Pershing's divisions. There was a high price to it though, and that is perhaps the most debatable point concerning his leadership. That was brought up several times after the war and in part kept him from being remembered as one of its great generals.

The other factor that may have perhaps prevented this was Alexander's apparently abrasive and distracting personality. Because of this, few of his peers in the 1st Corps (of which the 77th was a part during the Muese-Argonne drive) seemed to have cared much for him at all. Some who associated with him during the Charlevaux episode, for instance, have indicated Alexander's ostensive attempts at 'shifting the blame' from himself during the affair - usually in the direction of Brigadier General Johnson; someone with whom Alexander lost no love whatsoever. Further, he apparently did so with a haughty, self important air about himself. This abrasiveness also later displayed itself to both Colonel Eugene Houghton, who would very soon command the 307th, as well as the future commander of the 308th during the Charlevaux event, Colonel Cromwell Stacey. Indeed, even other, more junior, officers seemed to have little use for their division commander as well, something that will be further illustrated later on.

Yet by contrast, Alexander seems to have been very well thought of by most enlisted men that came into contact with him. Both of these conflicting views may be explained by his wide and varied background.

Born in October of 1863 in Baltimore, Maryland, Robert Alexander's father was a Justice on the Court of Appeals for Maryland State, and a member of the Circuit Court of Baltimore City. Like his father, Robert too became a lawyer. However, after passing his Bar exam, he instead enlisted in the army's 4th Infantry Regiment in April 1886 as a private and eventually wound up in command of a regiment on the Mexican border with Pershing by 1916. In fact, Alexander served in virtually every campaign the U.S. was involved in, was cited three times for gallantry and held nearly every rank from private on up to Major-General during his long career. Unlike many of his fellow commanders however, Alexander was not a graduate of the military academy at West Point; he had instead attended the Army War College at Ft. Leavenworth, Kansas. Though he was held in high esteem by his true friends, some of his fellow officers at the time thought that because of this he could never stand on a level field with those who had attended the military academy. Alexander recognized and resented this, and worked twice as hard to prove himself worthy of all he accomplished. Thus, it appeared to many that he had a chip on his shoulder, and he has since been described as a glory seeker and a self-serving individualist. This may in fact be true to some degree but, unlike many officers, this particular background allowed him to see things from both sides, officer as well as enlisted. He recognized that the enlisted man was the one who was going to get dirty; after all, as a private he had gotten dirty himself. He also believed that the enlisted could not *do* if the officer would not *lead*, thus, he did not abide incompetence in his officers of any rank, which he described as "weakness". However, Alexander also expected his enlisted to recognize their place and accept it. Simply put, since he had *made* himself, if others found that they were not where they wanted to be, they too could change things for themselves. However, in the mean time, the job was *yours*; do it. This made Alexander seem very hard, when in reality it was just good soldiering.

Since Alexander had risen from the ranks, he was commonly known as a "private's soldier", much in the same vein as General Grant had been in the Civil War. He had an innate ability to instill in his men pride in themselves, their unit, and their country. He was not adverse to a couple hands of poker with the men (provided higher ups were not within seeing distance), a trademark cigar stuck in his big, ruddy Scots face, and he never forgot a loyal man.

In France, he was first given the 41st (Depot) Division, which he whipped into the best depot division in the AEF. Pershing, so impressed, placed Alexander in command of the 63rd Infantry Brigade/32nd Division as a reward, with whom Alexander saw action in the Second Battle of the Marne. It was there that he learned what it took to fight in this new theater of 20th Century warfare. He remained with the 32nd until promoted to Major-General on August 26 and was given command of the 77th Division the next day. He dove right into his new command with a typical rabid enthusiasm. (I)

Yet neither a new commander nor a better divisional attitude was enough to make up for losses within the 77th Division. Almost a month of combat had brought officer material to a premium and all the regiments down on men, with few outside replacements in the offing. Brigadier General Johnson, commander of the 154th Brigade, was gassed, along with his diminutive adjutant, Major Bradley Martin, on September 5 and temporarily sent down. Colonel Smedberg of the 305th Infantry then stepped in to take control of the brigade in the Brigadier's absence. The loss of so many officers at Cemenocal cave had also been a tremendous blow, and even one of General Alexander's aids, Captain Klotz, had been wounded.

So when Captain Lucien Breckenridge, who himself had only temporary command of the 1st/308th, was wounded at the end of the month, it was decided that Captain Whittlesey was to be pulled out of Regimental Headquarters Company, promoted to Major with seniority dating back to August 13 and would once again be given command of the 1st Battalion, this time for good. Though he had not the experience necessary to lead a battalion into combat, Colonel Eugene Houghton, the then Divisional Machine Gun officer (who would soon himself take command of the 307th Regiment), personally recommended Whittlesey for his Majority. "He was the only one in the regiment who could tell me anything," Houghton would later remark. Thus, Charles Whittlesey gained command of the 1st Battalion and took the first steps on the road toward the Charlevaux Ravine. (2, 103, 109, 116, 161, 152, 153, 154, 161, 246)

With the dawn of August 30, the 152nd Field Artillery Brigade again began to lay a destructive barrage on the town Bazoches and its surrounding environs in preparation for a major push in the area. The barrage continued, without let up, right through September 4. However, as early as September 2, forward observation posts were reporting fires and explosions within the enemy back areas, and columns of troops moving northward. The next day, the area towns of Paars, Perles, Vauxcerem, and Blanzy, all deep within the German lines, were seen to be showing columns of dense smoke. No doubt about it, the enemy had had enough and was finally pulling back.

So began the second phase of the fight on the Vesle - the chase to the River Aisne. The 77th crossed the Vesle on September 4 and began to move out over the flat lands and ravines, in hot pursuit of the retreating enemy. Pushing out ahead of its flanking units and dragging them along, the division was finally stopped by stiff resistance on the heights above Haute-Maisons. French cavalry rushed out ahead, but were stopped as well. A slow slamming maneuver was now begun; hammer with artillery and move the infantry ahead, hammer with artillery and move the infantry ahead. In this way, with great effort the enemy was pushed back to the Aisne. All that was needed was one final big push, and it may well have been the close of action on that front.

However, that was not to be - for the 77th Division anyway. On the morning of September 13, with all the preparations made for an attack, the order of relief came. The

Italian 'Garibaldi' Division was to take over the front along the Aisne; the 77th was needed elsewhere. Therefore, after a solid month with no break from combat, what was left of the division marched out of the lines and set out for yet another unknown destination in which to meet the enemy. Among those marching ragged Doughboys, the 308th's new 1st Battalion commander, Major Charles Whittlesey, lead his men along the first steps of a journey that would weave them into the fabric of history. (2, 35, 91, 98, 109, 116)

(I) The official reason for General Duncan's relief from command of the 77th was supposed to have been on medical grounds. Most available evidence however indicates that it likely had more to do with General Pershing's displeasure over the performance of the division on the Vesle, as well as perhaps the AEF commander's personal dislike for the outspoken Duncan. General Duncan himself was livid over the decision and threatened to go to a civilian doctor, get himself cleared physically, resign his commission and then reenlist as a private, in order to prove his fitness. Pershing, apparently sensing a public affairs scandal in the works if he did not quiet the officious General, eventually relented and shipped Duncan off to the newly formed 82nd Division, with whom he did good work in October helping to relieve the 77th 'problem' in the Charlevaux ravine. Such was the 'Peyton Place' of AEF high command.

Ancillary sources used in this chapter include: 3, 8, 20, 24, 30, 87, 93, 94, 95, 07, 100, 104, 105, 106, 113, 114, 117, 119, 121, 347, 349, 350, 352, 353, 357, 358, 359, 364, 366

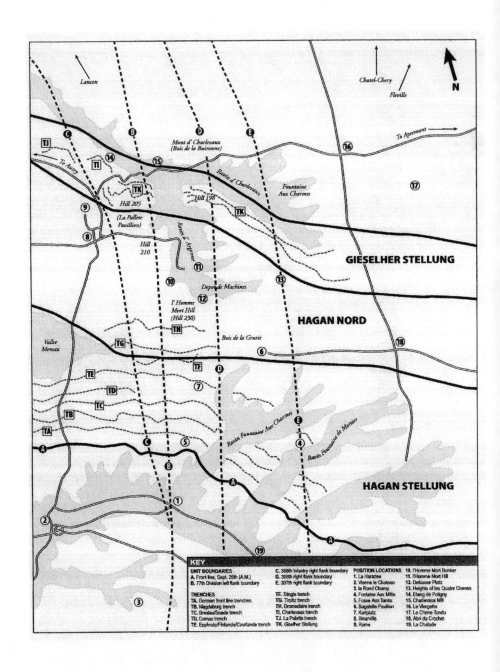

Lancon

Chatel-Chery

Fleville

N

To Apremont

C

B

D

E

TJ

14

TI

15

Mont d' Charlevaux
(Bois de la Buironne)

Ravin d' Charlevaux

Fountaine
Aux Charmes

16

17

To Autry

TK

Hill 205

Hill 198

TK

9

(La Pallete
Pavillion)

8

Hill
210

Ravin d' Argonne

TI

GIESELHER STELLUNG

10

Depot de Machines

13

12

l' Homme
Mort Hill
(Hill 230)

HAGAN NORD

TH

Vallee
Moreau

TG

Bois de la Grurie

18

TF

6

TE

TD

TC

D

7

5

TB

E

TA

Ravin Fountaine Aux Charmes

4

Ravin Fountaine de Morter

A

C

B

HAGAN STELLUNG

A

1

2

A

19

3

KEY

UNIT BOUNDARIES
A. Front line, Sept. 26th (A.M.)
B. 77th Division left flank boundary

C. 368th Infantry right flank boundary
D. 308th right flank boundary
E. 307th right flank boundary

TRENCHES
TA. German front line trenches
TB. Magdeburg trench
TC. Breslau/Suede trench
TD. Damas trench
TE. Euphrato/Finlande/Courlande trench

TF. Tringle trench
TG. Tirpitz trench
TH. Dromadaire trench
TI. Charlevaux trench
TJ. La Palette trench
TK. Gieselher Stellung

POSITION LOCATIONS
1. La Harazee
2. Vienne le Chateau
3. le Rond Champ
4. Fontaine Aux Mitte
5. Fosse Aux Tanks
6. Bagatelle Pavilion
7. Karlplatz
8. Binarville
9. Rome

10. l'Homme Mort Bunker
11. l'Homme Mort Hill
12. Defouer Platz
13. Heights of les Quatre Chenes
14. Etang de Poligny
15. Charlevaux Mill
16. Le Viergette
17. Le Chene Tondu
18. Abri du Crochet
19. La Chalade

"Up In the Argonne"

"Who ever called it 'Sunny France' must have been kidding…"

Pvt. Charles Minder, Company B/306th M.G. Battalion

The offensive in the Muese-Argonne district, to which the 77th Division was now heading, would be the largest land battle that the U.S. Army would ever participate in until the great battles fought during World War II, some 23 years later. It eventually played out into two main phases and wound up costing the AEF the greatest number of casualties that it would see as well. In the roughly six weeks that the U.S. Army spent fighting the offensive, casualties for all divisions involved totaled some 26,277 killed and missing and 95,786 wounded. The 77th Division alone suffered officially 2,375 killed and missing and 7,302 wounded. During the course of the operation, 1.2 million Doughboys faced approximately 40 enemy divisions. In the end, it was the AEF's crowning achievement, and victory, of the war.

The ground over which the great offensive was fought stretched from the heights just astride the Muese River in the east, above the city of Verdun, to the heights along the Aisne River, western border of the Argonne Forest, hence, the official title of "Muese-Argonne Offensive". This name, however, has often been bastardized through the years down to "The Argonne Offensive," or more simply "The Argonne," (and even 'The Oregon') neither of which is correct when referring to the battle as a whole. Many men who are said to have been killed or wounded "up in the Argonne" were, in fact, never anywhere near the Argonne Forest itself, but merely involved in the Muese-Argonne Offensive. Additionally, the woodland area surrounding the Argonne Forest is often referred to as part of the forest itself, when in fact it is merely part of the *region* of the Argonne.

In truth, the 77th Division was the only division to actually fight through the forest proper. (The 28th and later the 82nd Division's, fighting on the right of the 77th, only pushed through its eastern third.) With the possible exception of a position a few kilometers to the east of the forest called Montfaucon, the forest turned out to be the toughest nut to crack of the whole offensive and definitely took a fierce bunch to clear it. Perhaps it was something along those lines that was in the minds of the men who decided to assign the forest to the 77th, a division of mainly street toughs from New York City. It certainly was not for their forestry skills! (8, 30, 35, 42)

The Muese-Argonne Offensive was to be an all-American attack along a front some 24 miles in length. The initial, or "jump-off," line stretched from the town of La Harazee in the west, inclusive, near the base of the Argonne Forest, over to a point on the west bank of the Muese River, exclusive. Basically, its long-range (final phase) objective was the capture of the northern towns of Sedan and Mezieres in order to secure the large rail junctions located within them. Without access to the Lille-Metz railway line through the region, the Germans would be denied major rail transport to supply their armies in Belgium and Northern France. This, it was thought, would force the enemy to begin a withdrawal from those occupied territories that the Allies could then follow up on. During the summer of 1918, Marshal Foch, overall Allied supreme commander, had let General Pershing choose where he would make his great attack, his choices being either side of the Aisne

River, bordering the western side of the Argonne Forest. Pershing chose the attack zone east of the Aisne, arguing that the ground there offered the only real chance of breakthrough along the whole of the Western Front.

The French 4th Army, therefore, remained in place where it was west of the Argonne Forest, with plans to attack in unison along side the U.S. forces. The U.S. troops would then displace the French 2nd Army then in place east of the Aisne. Meanwhile, east of the Muese River above Verdun, the French also butted the flank of Pershing's great 1st American Army. Farther to the northwest, in Belgian Flanders and the northern parts of France, the British under Field Marshal Douglas Haig had plans to launch a consolidated offensive in conjunction with the French and American forces. Thus a major, coordinated Allied effort would be launched along nearly the whole of the Western Front, so designed as to place the Allied armies in perfect stance to launch the war-winning offensive planned for the spring of 1919.

Therefore, by late August, Marshal Foch had begun placing extravagant demands on Pershing to move his troops into place so that the attack could begin no later than mid-September, well before the French winter set in, making the going difficult. This might have been possible were it not for the fact that Pershing's forces were then busily preparing for another battle 60 miles to the south around the St. Mihiel salient, which Foch was aware of but had little faith in.

The salient at St. Mihiel had been a thorn in the French's side since September 1914 when the Germans had seized the area. The battle launched there on September 12, 1918, aimed to eradicate that thorn, and 400,000 Americans, along with 48,000 French, cleaned up on 75,000 Germans. Resistance was light, relatively speaking, as the Germans were taken almost completely by surprise. By September 14, the offensive was essentially over, a tremendous Allied victory and a great learning experience. However, had Foch allowed Pershing to follow up the victory with further attacks against the retreating enemy—who were themselves convinced that the Americans would indeed continue—the war might have then been brought to a speedier conclusion. (23)

Instead, once the St. Mihiel salient appeared to have been secured, Pershing and his staff turned their attention to the next gargantuan task. Nine initial assault divisions, plus their supporting artillery, supplies, food, weapons, ammunition, and reserves - well over 600,000 men - needed to find their way to the Muese-Argonne battle line no later than the morning of September 25, the final deadline Marshal Foch had set for the start of the great offensive. Charged with the monumental task of getting it all there was a young, capable U.S. Major who would make quite a name for himself in a later war named George C. Marshall. Major Marshall surveyed the situation and found, much to his distress, only three narrow, badly shelled, muddy roads leading up to the jump-off lines for the whole 24-mile front, coming from only three widely spaced rail heads of useable size. Chaos loomed inevitable. Nevertheless, Marshall drew up his plan and submitted it, which General Pershing approved as a "good piece of work", much to Marshall's own surprise. Enacted though, that "good piece of work" began to fall apart almost immediately, which was *not* to Marshall's own surprise.

Even before the St. Mihiel salient was given the final pronouncement of secure, many U.S. troops that had been engaged there began the journey north. More troops were traveling south, coming in from the Vesle, Marne, and other sectors as well. Almost immediately, the three narrow, muddy roads became horribly overwhelmed and tremendous traffic jams ensued. Adding to the difficulties, nearly all movement had to be done at night to keep the Germans from catching on. This led to unending delays as units were entangled and lost trying to find their route in the pitch-black, unfamiliar French countryside.

Compounding the problem was an unusually heavy and incessant early fall rain, which had started on the evening of September 8, and had rarely stopped since. This turned already atrocious roads into impossible quagmires. Motor trucks became buried beyond the axles and turned over. Overworked horses collapsed and died, with no way to move them off the roadway. Men already spent from miles of marching through the French countryside found themselves forced to hoof it through thick mud, knee-deep in some places, adding to their exhaustion. At every halt, the used up Doughboys instantly dropped off to sleep. It became a moving nightmare of mud, fatigue and never-ending rain.

Therefore, though it may sound as if the 308th did not have a particularly hard time getting to the Argonne sector, little can we today realize the pain involved in the simple statement "The men of the 308th Infantry left the Vesle sector at 2:00 a.m. on the morning of September 16th". The move, hurried and hard pressed, was truly a journey through hell for the battle weary 77th Division men.

However first, they had to actually get going. Units of the Italian 8th (Garibaldi) Division had arrived to take over the positions that the 308th was going to vacate and the diary of Private Paul Sluck, Machine Gun Company/308th Infantry, makes mention of the fact:

"Relieved 5AM by Italians. Stayed in old dugouts all night. Made flapjacks. Some job. Pulled out at 8PM. Hiked in pouring rain all night. 20 kilos." (230)

The entry for the next day, the 17th, notes "Arrived Vezilly 9:30AM. All tired out. Lost pack and all my personal stuff…" Pvt. Sluck was not the only one who began the move poorly though, as the situation as described by Major Whittlesey points out:

"We were supposed to start around midnight when the relief was complete. However, during the afternoon, two Italian battalions sent up officers and they squabbled with each other as to which was going to make the relief. I hurried to Regimental Headquarters of the 307th, (our own Headquarters had gone south) to get the news straightened out; but to my horror, when it came night up pops both of the Wop battalions…! So finally I sent off my battalion… stuck one Italian battalion in place, and spent the rest of the night trying to lodge the other. It was a pretty discouraged Wop commander, when we finally had to go away…" (109)

Major Budd, back from the hospital and again commanding the 2nd Battalion, had a similar experience with two other Italian officers arguing until almost full dawn over who was going to relieve his battalion. Eventually having had enough, Budd finally rounded up his men and simply marched out, leaving the two Italians still haggling.

By 10:00 a.m. on the 17th, most of the 308th had joined Private Sluck and Machine Gun Company/308th in the fields surrounding the little hamlet of Vezilly. Here again quoting Major Whittlesey, "We had the bliss of getting up pup tents and really sleeping like Christians and getting clean." In the rivers and streams of the area, the men washed the mud of the Vesle and the Aisne from their bodies and equipment, ate reasonably well, and rested up for a couple days in the rainy weather. Here, the Regimental Personnel Officer for the 308th was also able to take accurate count of the numbers of men in each company without the added distraction of machine-gun fire and shellfire constantly forcing him to revise his numbers. It was disturbing news. The regiment was short nearly 1,400 men, with some of the companies being down to only a single officer. Before replacements could be brought in however, the regiment was on the move again. By the 22nd, the three battalions of the 308th had arrived in the Argonne district towns; the 1st was at a forest crossroads called La Croix Gentin; the 2nd near the famous old town of St. Menehold; and the 3rd near the slightly larger burg of Florent. They were packed into barns, houses, and in tents under trees - anywhere to stay hidden - and given orders to sit tight and not show themselves outside during daylight hours. The roads, packed with traveling troops by night, were deserted by day. It continued to rain off and on.

By the evening of the 25th (the jump-off had been pushed back one morning to the 26th to accommodate late arriving units), the order of battle along the 24-mile front of the U.S. 1st Army ran as follows: On the right of the 1st Army Sector, which had the Muese River as its eastern border, General Bullard commanded the 3rd Corps which consisted of (from right to left in line) the 33rd Division, the 80th Division, and the 4th Division. To the west of 3rd Corps was the 5th Corps, commanded by General Cameron, and which contained (R to L) the 79th Division, the 37th Division, and the 91st Division. On the left of the Zone of Advance was the 1st Corps, commanded by General Liggett. His corps (R to L) contained the 35th Division, the 28th Division, and, on the extreme left flank of the U.S. 1st Army Sector, the 77th Division. There were also three other divisions kept on hand as Corps reserve - the 3rd, 32nd, and the majority of the 92nd (Colored) - and three others in Army reserve, the 1st, 29th, and 82nd.

Before the Muese-Argonne Offensive ended, virtually every combat division of the AEF would see at least some action somewhere in that great war zone, much of it difficult and bitter. However, the single most difficult attack zone of the whole line was undoubtedly that 7-kilometer portion on the extreme left faced by the 77th Division and known as the 'Foret de Argonne' - the Argonne Forest. (2, 5, 9, 16, 18, 35, 39, 42, 43, 48, 51, 109, 116)

Since Roman times, the wooded mountainous mass known as the *Foret de Argonne* has been justly regarded as the bulwark of defense for that portion of France northwest of Verdun. For centuries, armies have fought around it, considering its dense, dark interior virtually impenetrable and much preferring the relatively easy avenues of advance up the valleys of the Aisne and Aire rivers, which border it to the west and east respectively. The forest's heart is a tangled, twisted mass that extends from the open foot-lands south of St. Menehold, all the way up beyond the town of Grand Pre in the north, a distance of some 39 kilometers. Along its eastern edge, Varrenes, Montblainville, and St. Juvin lie in its shadow, while some 12 kilometers to the west can be found Binarville, Lancon, and Grand Ham. That heart and the surrounding copses of woodland (*Bois* in French) for at least double that distance form the Region of the Argonne, the largest woodland expanse from the Mediterranean to the Rhine River. It remains to this day a magnificent example of nature in control of space.

Few places are less suited for the style of combat practiced in the First World War than the Argonne Forest. It is a deep, dark, forbidding jungle, made up of large trees and young second growth over a dense, tangled carpet of thick undergrowth and even thicker bushes, cut through by a multitude of small streams and ravines of various sizes. The ravines edge off in steep ridges and limestone rock outcroppings, perfect spots for defensive positions. It is a rolling, rocky wilderness that harkens back to medieval times in its almost primal nature. Often, in its deep recesses, solid footing gives way to sodden marshland without indication or warning and just as quickly changes back again. In many spots, visibility is virtually nonexistent due to the heavy growth. Few real roads approached it, and even fewer traversed it, further making it seem an impregnable fortress.

Initially the U.S. attack plan did not call for the forest barrier to be taken by direct frontal assault. Instead, the forest (which as we shall see was actually a great German stronghold), was to be pinched off on each side by the two great armies bordering it, the French in the west and the Americans in the east. These would eventually join above the forest at the town of Grand Pre, thus cutting enemy supply lines down into the forest itself. The surrounded enemy within would then either be only too ready to surrender, or unable to fight for any great period of time. Meanwhile, the 77th would attack in force and keep constant pressure on the third side of the triangle against what was hoped to be the retreating enemy. Additionally, the division, together with troops from the 28th Division working along the eastern 1/3rd of the forest, was detailed to eradicate the enemy artillery positions that had been placed on the eastern heights of the forest. Positioned to drop their fire directly on a major intended avenue of advance, the Aire River Valley, if left to their devices then that route would be closed off. (3, 5, 91, 131)

The Germans had, early in the war, invaded the great forest from the north, trickling down into its recesses, taking up good defensive positions, and digging and wiring their way in wherever possible. They were well aware of the great defensive potentials of the forest, as were the French, and therefore it had been a hotly contested section of the line from 1914 until early 1916, when both sides admitted neither was likely to win there and the line went mostly static. During that time, the French 3rd Army had lost a staggering amount of men in trying to push the Germans out; by late 1915, 3rd Army commander, General Sarrail, was forced to admit in his diary:

"Since the 8th of January (1915) I have lost in the Argonne 1,200 officers and 82,000 men – almost half of the army's effective strength…" (18)

Bloody attacks that had been launched, rebuffed, and countered by both sides in the first years of the war left a bleak no-man's-land of destroyed ground in front of the southern base of the forest. Bracketed as it was on the northern (German) and southern (French) sides by a labyrinth of wrecked trenches and deep dugouts, the intervening space had become an uninhabitable wasteland blasted almost beyond recognition. Save for Verdun and Passchendale, nowhere else on the Western Front had the war left such an indelible mark. Captain Walter Kerr-Rainsford, commanding Company L of the 307th Infantry, upon first seeing it, described the area as:

"A bleak, cruel country of white clay and rock and blasted skeletons of trees, gashed into (by) innumerable trenches, and seared with rusted acres of wire, rising steeply into claw like ridges, and descending into haunted ravines, white as leprosy in the midst of that green forest. A country that had died long ago, and in pain…" (103)

By late 1915, the French 2nd Army had moved in to take over for the broken 3rd and within the first few months of 1916, the sector came to be regarded by both sides as a quiet one. It now became an area where battle-weary soldiers could be transferred to rest after serving stints in more hotly contested parts of the line. It was also where older or second-rate troops could be given responsibility for a section of the line (the risk of attack being almost nil) thus freeing up more able-bodied men to serve elsewhere. A sort of 'live and let live' feeling descended upon the area. Although things would occasionally heat up and a few artillery shells might fall about, some small, local battles or occasional machine-gun duels break out, this feeling continued to prevail on both sides of the trenches into 1918. The diary of one Lieutenant Capart, a member of the little army of Belgium, records a visit to the line in the Argonne after things had 'cooled off' a bit:

"We went this afternoon to see one of our friends, a lieutenant of infantry, in the neighboring sector. Bringing along a bottle of champagne, we drank it with him in his listening post, twenty-five yards from the enemy. Naturally, the bottle was hurled by a skillful hand into the trench of our neighbors to the front.

The reply was not long in coming: three 77's which, by the gods, were placed well enough, but which, luckily, did no damage.

These imbecile Boches always lack the proper spirit." (6)

To the French, who had paid so dear a price simply for the tangled mess of overgrown first-line trenches of the Argonne sector in the first place, the American plan to invade the forest was, quite literally, mad. Outwardly, to the Americans of the 77th, whom they helped during the build-up in front of the forest that late September, the French wished nothing but luck. Privately, they had already begun to mourn the loss of what they felt would be a great number of fine troops. Five companies of the French 120th Infantry Regiment remained in the first line positions to be taken over by the 308th right up to the last minute to guard against the Germans tumbling on to the secret build up. Then, relieved by a line of khaki clad troops in the wee hours of D-Day, September 26, the horizon blue clad French slowly filed out, many with tears streaming down their faces for the terrible tragedy they were sure was about to befall the Americans relieving them. (9, 10)

As previously stated, three main roads led up to the area across which the Muese-Argonne battle would be fought and over which all supplies for the battle would flow, one of which lead directly into the base of the forest itself. While getting to the forest was one thing, getting through it was another entirely. To say that few roads traversed the forest is a bit of an understatement. What roads there were, were not much more than wagon paths or cow tracks. The exceptions were three roads that cut through the forest from the town of Binarville on its western border, and extended eastward to different points (of which more to follow). All three were in German hands when the 77th Division arrived to take up their places for the jump-off into battle, and each made an excellent reference point within the forest as well as admirable objectives. (It was virtually impossible to judge a line in the forest with no landmarks to navigate from.) These roads would provide not only a means of moving up at regular intervals for the artillery, which obviously could not drag their guns through the dense forest itself, but also an avenue for the bringing up of supplies and taking out wounded. Provided, that is, that these roads could be wrested from German control.

As it stood by the time the 77th had begun to mass for the attack, the Germans maintained control of slightly over 22 of the forest's 39 kilometers, and its complete width within that area. This ground had been in their possession for nearly four years, and they had scarcely wasted a moment of that time in building up their defenses. Augmenting the natural defenses with man-made ones ensured that the Argonne was a veritable fortress, provided with all the comforts of home, while maintaining a solid military footing.

Militarily, the defensive network of the Argonne Forest is really quite simple. The Germans had incorporated all that they had learned about defense in-depth, which they preferred to call "elastic defense," in conjunction with sheer firepower, and created two 'prepositions' grouped into an initial defensive line, followed by three main defensive lines. Directly across the blighted nightmare of no-man's-land that separated the two armies was a dilapidated line of trench networking, shell holes, and listening posts - the front line - which served as not much more than an advanced warning system. This line, some 500 meters deep, had seen the brunt of the fighting that had occurred in the area and was similar to the French front line directly across from it, also virtually destroyed. Any major attack would quickly overrun the front lines and give the Germans plenty of warning as to what was coming.

Slightly further on were the real battle lines of this initial pre-position—three firmly held and wired trench complexes. Here was where any attacks made in the last four years had terminated and been turned back, and the devastation of the landscape gradually became less beyond the final line of trenches. The Germans called all these lines and machine-gun posts of this first pre-position the 'Hagan Stellung' and it extended for a depth of some 2 kilometers or so. (*Stellung*, or the plural *Stellungen*, being the German term for a fortified defensive line.) It was not meant that an enemy should get past the Hagan Stellung. If, however, that should be the case, the unfortunate enemy would then find himself facing a second pre-position, known as the 'Hagan Stellung-Nord'.

The Hagan Stellung-Nord was basically a machine-gun-covered, presighted artillery target extending over the broken woodland and into the forest proper just beyond the initial Hagan Stellung for, again, some 2 kilometers in depth. Here, the Germans were very well entrenched and there was little devastation, in sharp contrast to the initial pre-position. Together, the Hagan and Hagan Nord formed what was known as the 'Etzel Stellungen'; however, it was within Hagan Nord where things would really begin to get hot for the attacker.

The German artillery had long ago plotted every advance, ravine, cut, natural alley, and draw within the head of the Hagan Stellung-Nord on artillery firing maps. They had their guns sighted almost to the yard there; nothing had been left out. Should an enemy find himself unfortunate enough to be occupying that ground, he would soon be blasted to nothing by the massive weight of the artillery fire being accurately poured upon him. In conjunction with this artillery zone was a machine-gun zone that extended well into the depths of the forest. The gun positions had been placed to deadly effect, and there were hundreds of them. Many positions were spread out, which enticed an enemy to advance into clear, overlapping fields of fire from an expertly camouflaged complex system of trenches, firing nests, and dugouts, all of which were well connected by a myriad of tunnels and cleverly concealed crawl trenches. (This allowed a relatively small force to maintain the façade of a large presence.) Above, in the treetops, men in unseen lookout stations kept watch of the forest ahead and any possible line of approach and sniped at anyone getting through.

Barbed wire added to the mire; hundreds of miles of it strung everywhere, in some places so thick that it could hardly be seen through and to a height that quite frequently reached over a man's head, yards deep. The natural defenses also played their part, camouflaging the wire and some trenches with an effective cover that prevented a man from seeing either until he was right on top of them, at which point it was too late.

It was also within the Etzel Stellungen that 'pavilions' appeared. The Germans, situating for the long stay, had built fine rustic log structures in which to comfortably house the troops. In fact, some pavilions were as nice as some hotels back in Germany, incorporating comfortable beds, fully stocked kitchens (serving hot meals in fine mess halls on white linen tablecloths), saloons, bars, and libraries, and even a full size regulation bowling alley in one. Some rooms were fitted with curtains and paneling of beaded oak, the floors covered with fine carpets. There were beer gardens at several locations, one or two motion picture theaters, barbershops, and (the crowning achievement) a full size concrete swimming pool. Miles of stoutly crafted wooden walkways connected the buildings. The Germans installed power plants on the rivers running within their possession, making electricity and hot and cold water available. Dug into the hills that some of the pavilions occupied were dormitories capable of holding a hundred-plus troops, all in comfortable, well-heated spaces. With little threat of attack from the French, life within the pavilions seemed, at first glance, pretty soft indeed.

Yet, the pavilions were military emplacements and were structured as such. Surrounding each was a system of trenches well fortified with machine-guns, angled for interlocking fields of fire and efficiently wired in. Each pavilion complex had also been given a name, which stuck for life within the memories of the Doughboys who had fought to take them—Bagatelle, LaPalette, and St. Hubert's were among the toughest. Additionally, a narrow gauge rail system tracked all over the forest. One could go virtually anywhere within the forest and not be forced to walk but a short distance. A very sophisticated telephone system also connected all various pavilions, rail stops, and lookout posts with each unit's command headquarters, thereby ensuring that troops could be called and carried to any spot, at any given time, relatively quickly. It was this elaborate and well thought out defensive system that proved to be the main difficulty of the U.S. attack, and was the reason that the Germans managed to hang on so long with a much smaller force than their attackers had.

Beyond the Etzel Stellungen were the three main defensive lines of the greater Hindenburg line (the main defensive battle line, or *Haupt-Widerstands-Lienie* in German.) The Germans had given each of these Stellungen the name of a Wagnerian witch, the first being the Giselher Stellung. It consisted of a strong, complex system of trenches, sniper and machine-gun nests, wire belts, and dugouts. Its standout features within the Argonne Forest were the protective screen of the Etzel Stellungen ahead of it, and the natural defenses of the forest itself. East of the forest, the ruins of the Cathedral of Montfaucon, up on its grim promontory, proved the crowning strongpoint of the Giselher along the Muese-Argonne line, the responsibility of which fortunately fell outside the 77th's zone of advance.

A few kilometers beyond the Giselher was the Kriemhilde Stellung, which ran along the heights of Romagne, a ridgeline of whaleback hills that form the strongest natural barrier line in France. If the Giselher were to fold, all troops remaining had orders to fall back and join the men garrisoned in the Kriemhilde. Here the line closely resembled the Giselher, plus. No tactic of defense had been spared. If the mood of the Giselher was one of testy, self-assured vigil, then the mood of the Kriemhilde could be classed as one of grim determination. Therefore, Pershing and his staff considered the Kriemhilde the real obstacle to be overcome in order to gain a true breakthrough in the Muese-Argonne.

Then, a couple more kilometers back from Kriemhilde, lay the unfinished Freya Stellung, the last ditch barrier. It is unclear whether extreme confidence in the first two Stellungen or poor economic circumstances back in Germany caused the Germans to allow the Freya to remain uncompleted, but available evidence would seem to point to the latter. In any case, the German High Command was certain of one thing: if the Allies made it as far as the Freya, then there was not much that could be done to stop them.

Not so incredibly, considering the strength of the line, the positions of the Giselher within the Argonne Forest were actually rather lightly held. There were never at any time actually enough troops on hand to man all the various defensive positions contained therein. While sufficient reserves were held farther back at Kriemhilde to provide for any emergency, Allied intelligence had it figured that they could not be brought successfully to bear in sufficient numbers for two days at least. Thus, Pershing's staff had developed the reasonable hypothesis that the entire first phase of the offensive - a drive through the Giselher Stellung to the Kriemhilde and beyond - could be brought to a successful conclusion within a 72-hour time frame, when plans for the second phase, the drive to the Muese, could begin.

This plan, however, failed to take into account the dedication of those troops manning the Argonne Forest and in reserve at Kriemhilde, whom American intelligence had classed mostly as second- and third-rate units. It was true that these units were perhaps not first-rate, however, reasoning among those troops was that it was either a very determined enemy, or a very demented one, who would dare their position within the forest. In either case, they were resolved not to give up their pavilions without one hell of a fight. And though the Stellungen ultimately failed to prove themselves as impenetrable as the Germans had hoped, they certainly were no cakewalk, leaving a lasting impression on those who faced them and survived. Years after the war, one grizzled old veteran of the fighting in the Argonne forest said of the Giselher, Kriemhilde, and Freya, "What bitches they were! Any goddamn kraut that didn't have a machine-gun, had a cannon. If I live to be a hundred, I'll never forget..." (51)

Facing the 77th in the Argonne Forest were German troops from two separate divisions; the 76th Reserve Division, and the 2nd Landwehr Division (or, LwD for short). The rough dividing line between the two generally followed a line running just east of the eastern ridge of the Ravin d'Argonne, a wicked north/south slice which cut through the western side of the forest for a time. Immediately to the west of the line, the 76th Reserve would arrive late the night of September 25 in answer to an early German call for reinforcements in the area and put its 1st battalion/254th Infantry Regiment in the front line on its left and its 2nd battalion on its right. The 76th RD had been recruited from the Grand Duchy of Hesse in 1915 and spent all its active time until early 1918 on the Eastern Front. Having endured heavy casualties during its years of fighting there, it was generally relegated to defensive duties upon its transfer to the Western Front, while yet again suffering considerable losses during its time in the sector around Verdun. Refitted with fresh, young troops by September 1918, it was stationed around Lancon when it received orders to begin moving into the Argonne early in the morning of September 25th. The 254th Infantry Regiment was commanded by Major Manfred Hunicken. The commanding officer of the 76th Reserve Division was a man with the imposing title and name of General Freiherr Quadt-Wykradt-Huchtenbruck. West of the 76th was the 9th Landwehr Division, which displaced west along the line when the 76th came in. The 9th had its 83rd Regiment next to the 254th, and its 116th Regiment next to the 83rd. Also from Hesse, the 9th LwD had been in the Argonne since the beginning of the war and knew the area well. (They, however, would not face the 77th Division.)

East of the dividing line was the 2nd Landwehr Division, a sort of 'national guard' type outfit composed mainly of over age, inactive reservists from the Grand Duchy of Wurttemberg, and classed by American intelligence as a fourth-rate division. That, however, was to dismiss its long service in the Argonne, where it had been stationed since September 1914, enduring all the hard fighting against the French in those early years. It now had its 122nd, 120th, and 125th Regiments in line west to east. The 122nd had its 2nd and 3rd battalions in line left to right, Rittmiester-Frieherr Wiedenbach (who would also eventually act as operations officer for the regiment) and Lt. Col. Von Biela commanding, respectively. Lieutenant Colonel Schmidt commanded the whole of the 122nd. All three of these divisions then fell under the control of 1st Reserve Corps, commanded by General Karl Wellmann, and from there under the umbrella of General Von Kliest's Army Group Argonnen, which controlled the area running from just west of the Aisne, to just east of the Aire Rivers. Finally, ultimate command passed to district commander General Max C. W. Von Gallwitz, commander of the Von Gallwitz Group of Armies, sometimes known as Composite Army Group 'C'. (5, 30, 42, 120-129, 364-371)

On the Allied side, the French dispositions west of the 77th Division consisted of the 4th Army under General Gouraud, the 38th Corps of which butted the 77th's left flank. Within the 38th's command was the 1st Dismounted Cavalry Division (or D.C.D), west of the Aisne River, and a liaison force under 1st D.C.D control called 'Groupement Durand' (so named after its commander, French Colonel Rene Durand of the 1st D.C.D.). This liaison force occupied the intervening space between, and provided a link for, the French and American armies. Groupement Durand itself was initially composed of the 368th Infantry Regiment of the U.S. 92nd Division - an outfit comprised of African American soldiers (then called Negro soldiers) which the U.S. high command, in an incredibly reprehensible act of racism, provided little if any training and then foisted upon the French - the French 11th Cuirassiers a Pied (or C.a.P). Within its zone of advance, the Negro troops of the 368th occupied the east sector, while the 11th C.a.P took the west.

The 11th C.a.P's mission within Groupement Durand was to provide a liaison between the 368th and the main body of the French attack force west of the Aisne River, the French 1st D.C.D. (left arm of the pincer movement that was to cut off the Argonne). They would also act as right flank attack force for them along the eastern bank of the Aisne. However, the zone of advance occupied by the 11th between the French 1st D.C.D and the 368th gradually began to narrow soon after the jump-off line as their left boundary swung to the east following the path of the Aisne River. Thus it was figured that the 11th would eventually be pinched out just beyond the town of Binarville and the 368th would assume responsibility for the whole area.

The 368th Infantry was immediately to the right of the 11th C.a.P., and their mission within Groupement Durand was three fold. First, they were charged with protecting the French right flank attack force east of the Aisne River, (the 11th C.a.P) while providing liaison between them and the 77th Division on there immediate right. Second, they were to prevent any separation of the French 4th Army on their left from the American 1st Army on their right caused by any enemy counter-attack emanating from the northeast (the greater Argonne Forest). To accomplish this, they were to constantly advance on the enemy in their sector and keep intense pressure against him, and in the event of an enemy withdrawal, to pursue with aggressiveness. Third, they were to be prepared to send an attack force against Binarville in conjunction with the 11th C.a.P once that town had been reached, a prime objective within Durand's attack zone. After that, they would take over the whole front of the liaison area when the French 11th was finally pulled out. (10, 91, 92, 133, 146)

Finally, east of Durand's right flank, came the 77th Division—left flank of the whole American 1st Army, with the 308th Infantry on their far left flank as hinge of the great attack. The 308th, in turn, had placed two platoons from its Company I to liaison with the black troops of the 368th.

Behind the U.S. line, there was also to be plenty of artillery fire support. As had the infantry, the 152nd Field Artillery Brigade of the 77th had spent the better part of the week before the Muese-Argonne jump-off traveling. A German mine exploded at a point close to the front under the only stone based road leading into the forest from the division's rail head at the town of Les Islettes had only added to the delay, and it was not until the night of the 23rd-24th that some of the batteries had gotten into position. Once in place, the forty-eight 75mm guns of the 304th and 305th (light) Field Artillery Regiments, and the twenty-four 155mm guns of the 306th (heavy) F.A.R., were forced to lay (sight) their guns by astronomical calculation, as no ranging shots were allowed. It was imperative to avoid as much as possible the Germans tumbling onto what was actually afoot. To complete the ruse, trees screening the field pieces were left up but carefully sawed three-quarters through with ropes attached to pull them down only at the opening barrage. Overhead, huge camouflage nets stretched across some of the more open areas while for many nights even before the arrival of the 152nd, ammunition had poured up the wrecked roads and been piled in dumps near where the guns were likely to be placed.

In addition to its own divisional artillery units, the 77th Division also had at its disposal, for the opening of the offensive, several batteries of French manned 75mm guns, the entire French 39th Field Artillery Battery with 155s, and 4 batteries of U.S. Coastal Artillery (16 railroad-mounted 8" guns placed well to the rear). Once the initial firing of preparation for the jump-off was over, however, most of the French artillery was to be pulled out for use elsewhere. The French 247th F.A. (75s) and elements of the U.S. 37th Division's artillery batteries (both 75s and 155s) provided covering fire for Groupement Durand. It was obvious, even to the most casual observer, that the weight of fire was going to be tremendous.

The artillery was there, of course, to pave the way for the infantry. Getting them through the enormous belt of wire ahead was the first order of business. Engineers who were going over the top with the assault companies were brought forward (in French uniforms for secrecy) and shown the lanes through the French wire, while the 152nd F.A. was given definite initial fire assignments to cut lanes, some 10 to 12 meters wide, in the enemy wire ahead. Of the three artillery regiments making up the 152nd, the 304th had been assigned to the 153rd Infantry Brigade on the eastern side of the divisional sector, the

305th to the 154th Brigade on the western side of the sector, and the 306th was equally divided between the two. If the artillery failed the infantry in any way for the initial jump-off, it was in its inability to fully cut the lanes in the wire, only about half of which were actually blown open. However, enemy troops were driven from their forward entrenchments by the heavy barrage and thus the infantry's difficulties were eased in that respect. (91, 92, 93, 97, 98, 100, 107, 109, 114, 116, 117)

It was also decided that the Muese-Argonne attack would be afforded plenty of air support, and each division was assigned one U.S. air squadron to be used for reconnaissance, artillery observation, and most importantly, infantry contact patrol. The 50th Aero (Observation) Squadron supported the 77th Division. The 50th Aero had organized at Kelly Field at San Antonio, Texas, in August 1917, sailed for England in January 1918, and under the command of 1st Lt. Daniel P. Morse Jr., its DH-4 "Liberty" planes had done good work for both the 82nd and 90th Divisions throughout the battle of St. Mihiel, only losing one crewman. By September 18, the squadron was in reserve and packing to move upon receipt of orders for duty in the Muese-Argonne Offensive. At 9:00 a.m. of the 23rd, most of the squadron set out in trucks borrowed from another squadron over the slippery, mud-choked roads for the outskirts of a town called Remicourt, situated below and in the shadow of the Argonne. There they would share a field with the 1st and 12th Aero Squadrons. The planes followed the next day when the weather finally broke a little.

During the move, the pilots were forbidden to fly anywhere near the lines on their way to Remicourt. The 50th had gained somewhat of a reputation for tenacity with the Germans during St. Mihiel and they had come to know the squadron's 'Old Dutch Cleanser Girl' insignia well (chosen to play upon the squadron slogan "Cleaning up on the Boche"). With care then, Lt. Morse and his men moved into their new digs quickly and quietly, and no one but the French, on their own aerodrome at nearby Duacourt, were the wiser. Soon, French area maps were spread out on the tables of the squadron mess.

On the morning of September 25, 1st Lieutenants Mitchell H. Brown, pilot, and Woodville J. Rodgers, observer, made the first reconnaissance flights from Remicourt over the lines above the Argonne Forrest in one of two French Salmson A2A planes borrowed from Duacourt (to preserve the secrecy). Painted on the lower left-hand wings of these planes was the outline of the Statue of Liberty, done to show the men of the 77th, now gathering forces for the move into the trenches, that their air cover had arrived. Throughout the day, the two borrowed planes made several trips back and forth over the lines as different pilots and observers familiarized themselves with the ground over which they would soon be operating. (I) Later that day, 10 of the 50th's pilots got in a Fiat truck and scouted out a suitable emergency landing field as close to the battle area as was deemed wise, just in case. About 2 kilometers north of the little ruined village of Clermont-en-Argonne, just to the east of the Clermont-Varrenes road, they found what they wanted, marked it on the maps, and headed for home. The 50th Observation Squadron was now ready to do battle. (47, 48, 89, 110, 241, 249, 277)

The first of the much-needed replacements for the 77th Division, a small batch of officers, arrived in the Argonne billet areas on the 22nd, and after them, the enlisted started to flow in right up to the afternoon of the 25th. "At one of our halts we saw tired Doughboys lying all about by the side of the road, their packs still strapped to their backs, sleeping," wrote one officer of the 304th Artillery Regiment. "Replacement troops they were, sent in to fill up the depleted ranks of our own infantry. Most of them had never been in the lines before."

These men came mostly from the 40th "Sunshine" Division, big, healthy, strapping boys, and they were definitely a welcome sight. The 40th had originally been a National

Guard division, with its men coming from California, Arizona, Colorado, Utah, Nevada, and New Mexico, and most of the original men of the regiments had served on the Mexican border in 1916. However, once the National Guard units had been federalized as the 40th Division in September 1917, almost immediately the Army had started feeding these experienced men into other units that were to form the base elements of the new National Army divisions. The 40th then became a training division for drafted National Army men, based at Camp Kearney in California, feeding its trainees into overseas divisions in two large drafts - one in the winter of 1917 and another in the early summer of 1918. Then, in August 1918, together with a large contingent of men from Camp Lewis in Washington State, the division finally sailed for France. There it was designated a depot division and continued to serve as a vehicle to feed replacements into the combat divisions - some 27,000 of them by the end of the war. (100, 115, 109, 116, 355)

Now, the 40th Division was feeding replacements into the 77th, the large majority of which were draftees from Montana, Minnesota, and Washington State. One of the incoming replacements, Private Sidney Smith, drafted out of Virginia City, Montana where he had been farming when the United States got involved in the war, described being "thrown in" with the New Yorkers like this:

"We walked to a place called Bourges (sic). That's where they was gathering up men for the 77th Division. It had just made a forced stand at the Chateau Thierry sector and at Vesle and a lot of the division had been killed and taken prisoner. They throwed us western men in there to fill up the division. I was put in the 308th Infantry, Company H. And it wasn't any time before we was part of the 77th and going over the top..." (256)

Unfortunately, the replacements from the 40th sent to the 77th's regiments were soon found to be not all that they had initially seemed. The first disappointment was that despite the draft that had arrived on the 22nd, there were few officers or NCOs among them, both of which were sorely needed. Private John W. Nell, who arrived as one of these replacements on the morning of the 23rd, was put into Company G/308th and later wrote:

"The company commander was a first lieutenant and the only commissioned officer in the company. We only had one sergeant in the company and about four or five corporals. There were 236 men in the company, when there should have been 250. The officers who were expected to come up as replacements in the 77th Division for some reason never arrived in time." (40)

Actually, there had already been a very small draft of officers transferred in on September 14, and these inexperienced men accounted for a great majority of the officers then in charge by the time Private Nell arrived. Among them were 1st Lt. Thomas G. Pool of Beaumont, Texas (assigned to Company K/307th), and 1st Lt. James V. Leak of Memphis, Texas (who went to Company E/308th). Settled into his new command, Leak wrote home to his mother on September 25th:

"The 40th Division was made a training division (sic) and had a surplus of officers so I was transferred, much to my delight. My new company has made quite a name for itself and the Germans (Jerrys) have a wholesome respect for them. We have just received replacements and they too came from my old division but from another regiment to what I was in..." (236)

Leak and Pool would meet up again 3 weeks later, but under far less hospitable circumstances.

The second disappointment occurred was when it became evident that some replacement troops had not received the type of training that was needed to have them ready for combat once they reached France. Private Ralph E. John was drafted into the Army from McIntosh, South Dakota, and went to the 40th Division at Camp Lewis in Washington state where:

"...I was sent to be sworn into the army and to receive my first training. This was very limited. We were outfitted with the full clothing and equipment of an infantryman, and had only a little drilling during the five weeks at this camp... Camp Kearny, California was the next stop... Up to the time I reached this camp, I had had only two days training with the army rifle... (But) In those days there was no delay and... off we went at the end of two weeks (for the) final stop at Camp Mills in New Jersey... and on to a big boat for the hop across the pond." (220)

By the time Pvt. John reached the Argonne on the morning of September 25, he had been in the Army a little shy of five months. By the standards of the already combat experienced veterans of the 77th, he was far from being a competent soldier. He was looked upon by them as more of a liability than anything else due to that inexperience. However, although his combat training had been meager ("I had never even seen a gas mask until the next day when we started to the front lines"), at least Private John had had some training. Again Pvt. Nell of Company G:

"While the rifle ammunition was being passed out, they found three boys without rifles... The lieutenant asked "Where are your rifles; did you lose them?" The answer was "No Sir, we never had any issued to us."... "(Well) take your ammunition anyway, for you will be able to pick up rifles shortly after we go over the top... keep your eyes open and grab the first one to fall." I knew these boys from Camp Kearney... Many of (them) did not know how to load a rifle without getting it jammed, had never shot an army rifle, and had never been taught anything about hand or rifle grenades. Many of them were drafted in June, 1918... they were kept in quarantine fourteen days in Washington then shipped to Camp Kearney. There they were again kept in quarantine fourteen days and the latter part of July shipped by rail to Camp Mills, Long Island. They were at Camp Mills just forty-eight hours before being sent overseas." (40)

It is true that many of the 40th Division replacements were at a distinct disadvantage at the start of the Argonne drive when compared to the battle-hardened New York enlisted veterans they were placed beside, who regarded the men from the heartland of America with derision. However, the pressure of a learn or die situation forced many of them to become adept at what the New York men were already past masters of - combat survival - and many surviving original officers of the regiment later remarked with praise on the eagerness, innate ability, and general sturdiness of the 40th Division men with great enthusiasm, those that lived anyway. And, although they were taciturn about it, many New Yorkers did lend a hand in giving the green troops at least a little knowledge before the storm broke, in order to delay as long as possible what nearly all the old hands were secretly sure was inevitable.

It was these sort of replacements then that flowed into the 77th, some 4,500 of them before it was all over, with 1,250 of them going to the 308th. (An incredible amount, which well illustrates the kind of casualties the regiment had suffered on the Vesle.) And so the ranks of the 'Metropolitan Division' were filled out with men from America's heartland. It was that last little bit of spice needed to complete the melting pot that was the 308th Infantry Regiment. (II) (109, 115, 116, 207, 236, 238)

For the week leading up to the battle, in order for the 77th's officers to have some idea of what lay ahead, it was decided to send small groups up to the trenches to be used for the jump-off, on scouting missions. Every precaution was taken, including providing the visitors with competent French guides, as well as French uniforms to avoid the enemy possibly seeing the Americans and guessing what might be going on. In turn, artillery officers and observers, combat engineers that were to be in the assault waves, and infantry officers alike, were taken out on the 'Cooks Tours' and shown the finer points of the areas they were to either be responsible for, or to attack across. Major Whittlesey, having gotten the lay of the land, took his officers up in turn on the nights of the 23rd and 24th to the jump-off area assigned to the 308th and managed to find a smattering of humor in the affair:

"They gave us French helmets and overcoats — Whiting, Schenck, Lewis and me — and we hiked the ten kilometers north to the trenches. You should have seen the Frenchmen laugh when we passed — for all the overcoats were the same size — and on Ed Lewis and me they did not look just alike — and that was funny anyhow. And you should have seen the place the French were holding! At Harazee it was on the north slope up from a little river. We went down the long decline to the bottom of the valley, and across the river through just the tiniest remains of a town that looked like as though it had been destroyed in the middle ages. The trench system looked as though it was a relic from an earlier war..." (109)

It would have been a true miracle if the U.S. Army had managed to move over half a million men, all their equipment, and all their supplies into the battle area wholly undetected. All the secrecy fooled the Germans, but only partly. They took it on faith that *something* was going on and had even managed to capture a couple of replacement Doughboys on the night of the 25th (who didn't even know where they were let alone what was about to happen), but never dreamed the extent of the attack that was coming. While French aircraft tried to prevent the German observation planes from combing the area, several had been able to get through. Upon return to their aerodromes, their reports were mostly innocuous. They did point to some doings of one sort or another yet, miraculously, the huge contingent of American troops somehow went undetected. Similarly, forward observers in the German first line trenches were reporting suspicious movements across no–man's-land, and somewhat more activity than usual in the French trenches. German telephone monitors had taken notice that there seemed to be a lot of new wire being run, but were disappointed when all they heard on it was apparently general, innocuous French transmissions. (By this point Pershing had forbade everyone along the Muese-Argonne sector from speaking anything but French on the telephone system. It was, in fact, a court martial offence not to do so.) Yet, the Germans were getting nervous. (91, 109)

On the night of the 22nd, the uncommon happened. A strong German combat patrol attacked a French outpost position in what was to be the zone of advance of the 308th. Several American officers, in the section doing a reconnaissance tour, managed to beetle back without a problem, and the enemy was beaten off after a very stiff fight. Still, it had been a close shave. On the night of the 23rd, the same thing happened again, a little farther down the line, with the same results. A harassing artillery barrage, including gas, swept the little crossroads of La Croix Gentin, where 1st/308th was holed up, on the afternoon of the same day. Then, in the early morning hours of the 24th, the Germans fired a huge pre-planted mine under the road leading up from Les Islettes and sent three waves of infantry in attack against various parts of the Argonne line. French artillery responded to keep up appearances. Private Charles Minder, a Camp Upton man serving with a Hotchkiss crew in Company B/306th Machine Gun Bn., wrote his mother:

"An artillery outfit must have moved in about fifty yards away from us during the night (sic) and started firing this morning. It lasted for about half an hour. We were told that this was a quiet front. It was, but no more!

We found out that the Germans sent three waves over this morning, and that the French troops, who are in the lines, drove them back each time. When I heard our own artillery (sic) so close to us, I knew we must be a mile at least behind the line. We were scared stiff. We thought sure we would be in for a shelling from the Germans. They always try to locate an artillery outfit, and then they start a duel with each other. I figure that the shells always seem to fall about fifty yards short, and it was just about fifty yards that we were in front of them this morning." (37)

About mid-morning of the 25th, gas shells started coming in around the section of forest near where the 2nd/308th was bivouacked, giving some of the 40th Division replacements over there a first taste of what was to come. That afternoon, German patrols were again probing French forward positions, but by this time the Boche had not long to wait before finding out exactly what lay in store for them.

For a short time, the sun showed its face on the 24th and raised hopes of fair weather for the jump-off, but the incessant rain returned on the afternoon of the 25th as plans for the attack moved forward. Maps were handed out for study on the afternoon of the 24th, but marking those that were to be carried into the front lines was strictly forbidden; an order that was rarely followed. Carefully blacked out billets, containing earnest officers and NCO's gathered around maps of every shape and size of their assigned area, dotted the dark of that night. Eyes strained in the dim light of candles, trying to find the best route across to the enemy first line beyond the artillery cut lanes in the wire, the safest route that would cost the least amount of lives. Still, little was known of the German defenses. The masses of paper that seem to float every army during wartime came in piles now, and orders flew between the various PC's at an alarming speed and quantity. Then, on the afternoon of the 24th, the final orders from the division were handed down as Field Order No. 43, parts of which read:

1. Situation: The enemy holds the front from the Muese to the Aisne River with 5 divisions. The allied armies will attack on the front between the Muese and the Suippes Rivers. The 1st American Army attacks on the front between the Muese and the Aisne Rivers. The 1st Army Corps, with the 35th, 28th, and 77th Divisions in line from right to left in the order named, attacks from Vauquois to La Harazee, both inclusive. The first Army Corps will be assisted in reducing the Forest d'Argonne by the 5th Army Corps on its right and by the 38th French Corps on its left.

The tactical situation was laid out in other portions of the long order:

9. Tactical Disposition: (a) Attacking force will be disposed as follows: 2 companies in advance – 2 mopping up platoons – 2 companies in support. The use of the new hand and rifle phosphorous grenade will be studied for (a) blinding machine guns and (b) for dispersing small bodies of troops waiting for the advance. They will also cover, to a great extent, the necessary cutting of wire in rear of the enemies front lines.

(b) The advance companies of the lead battalion will move forward in small groups of squad columns, preceded by one or two scouts per group. These scouts will be accompanied by engineers in such quantity as the battalion commander deems necessary.

(c) The support companies will move forward in column of half sections and platoons, staggered with deploying distance between each section and platoon. The second line battalion will move forward in sections and platoon columns, staggered, 500 yards in rear of the leading battalion. This distance will not be taken up until the enemies first line has been crossed by both battalions.

Paragraphs of Section 10 of the order called for a 37mm guns to travel with the Battalion Headquarters platoons, and also made provisions for machine-gun units to be assigned to the attacking and support battalions. Additionally, there were provisions made for a reserve battalion, a reserve machine-gun unit, and for three Stokes Mortars to follow the support companies of the lead attack battalion. Section 2 of the order dealt with the actual execution of the attack, and the artillery's responsibilities:

The artillery preparation for the attack will begin at H minus 3 hours. Troops will be in position at H minus 4 hours, and at H hour the front line battalion will go over the top and spring to the attack, following the advance barrage at 500 meters. Rate of march, 100 meters in 5 minutes. Barrage will conform to this rate. Should, however, the resistance in our front be slight, the infantry must call for a lengthening barrage and pursue the enemy with aggression and rapidity... (116, 131, 144)

To the west, in the French zone of attack, the barrage was set to begin at 11:30 p.m. of the 25th, in order to draw attention away from the American zone. Then, at precisely 2:30 a.m. on the 26th, the barrage of the enemy wire and first line would begin in the American sector. This would fall for three solid hours. Then, 20 minutes before 'H hour' (the moment of attack), the artillery fire was to double in intensity to a "prepatory bombardment" for 20 minutes. Then, exactly at 'H Hour' (5:50 a.m.), after all the lanes in the wire ahead had ostensibly been cut and the enemy first line rendered useless, the 75s were to throw over a rolling barrage 500 meters ahead of the Doughboys going over the top. The 155s, meanwhile, were to provide a standing barrage 500 meters ahead of the 75s. At 'H' plus 25 minutes, all the artillery were to advance their fire by 100 meters, and from then on, further increase at 100 meter leaps every five minutes, with the infantry to follow, to the limit of the gun's range. This scenario was then to be repeated as needed over the next 72 hours, the length of time allotted for the 1st phase of the battle to run its course.

For the infantry to enact their portion of the plan, and to cover the rather large section of front that was assigned to the 77th Division, (slightly over 7 kilometers), it had been decided to depose all four of the division's infantry regiments in line abreast, descending in numerical order from left to right. It was a lot of ground to cover, nearly 2 kilometers per regiment, and the brigade commanders were not very happy with having to place all the regiments in line at once, as it left nothing in reserve. It was necessary, therefore, to simply create reserves from within the regiments themselves, each placing a battalion on line, another in support, and the final one in reserve. The lead assault units were also to take pioneer infantry (combat engineers) into battle with them, in addition to the divisional engineers already assigned them. These would facilitate speedy passage beyond obstacles of any kind, be they wire, wide trenches, or what have you. An artillery liaison officer and two aids were also assigned to each assault battalion to call down any needed additional barrages, and to act as advanced observers. (93)

First Phase Objectives laid down for the 77th's advance through the Argonne Forest ran as follows. The 1st Corps Objective was a line along Abri St. Louis—Barricade Pavilion—St. Hubert Pavilion, with the nose 500 meters north on a line Bagatelle Pavilion—Tranchee' de la Tringle. This was about a 4-kilometer advance beyond the line of departure. The 1st American Army Objective was a line Pont a' l'Aune—Fontaine du Ton, with the nose 800 meters northwest of Moulin de l'Homme Mort, about 6 kilometers from jump-off and on a line just before the Giselher Stellung. The Combined Army Objective (first phase line) was to be a general line 500 meters north of the prescribed 1st Army Objective. In other words, the Giselher Stellung itself, a distance of some 7 to 10 kilometers on average, over the whole of the 77th's front.

Dispositions for the division were thus: On the right of the 77th's zone of advance was the 153rd Brigade, on the left the 154th. On the eastern flank, along side the 28th Division, the 153rd placed the 305th Infantry, while to the 305th's left, was the 306th, with its 2nd Battalion in divisional reserve acting as liaison group to the 154th Brigade. In the 154th Brigade's zone of advance, the 307th Infantry, Lt. Col. E.A. Houghton commanding, took its place on the right, next to the 306th. Lead battalion was the 3rd, under Major Carl F. McKinney, with its companies I and M forward (left to right), and K, and L behind them respectively. Evenly placed among the four companies of the lead battalion were Company E/302nd Engineers and 3 platoons of the 2nd Bn./53rd Pioneer Infantry. In support, 500 meters behind them, were 2nd/307th under Captain (acting Major) John H. Prentice with Company A of the 306th M.G. Bn. dispersed among it. The 1st/307th, under Major Peter P. Gardiner, along with Machine Gun Company/307th, was held back as divisional reserve.

To the left of the 307th, and forming the left flank unit for the whole American advance along the Muese-Argonne Offensive as well as the 77th Division, was the 308th Infantry, Col. Austin F. Prescott commanding. Lead battalion going into the Offensive was the 1st, commanded by Major Charles W. Whittlesey. The Major had placed his Company D forward on the left, third and forth platoons in the lead, and Company A forward on the right, first and third platoons leading. Providing support directly behind Company D was Company C, and directly behind Company A was Company B. Company F/302nd Engineers and 3 platoons of 1st Bn./53rd Pioneers completed Major Whittlesey's assault force. Providing support 500 meters behind 1st Battalion was 2nd/308th under Major Kenneth P. Budd, with companies H and E (left to right) in the lead followed by companies G and F respectively. Company D/306th M.G. Bn. rounded out the 2nd's combat assignments. Finally, bringing up the rear in Brigade Reserve was the 3rd/308th under Major McNeill. In the 3rd/308th, Company I had been detached as a liaison force. Its first and second platoons and half of Company C/306th M.G. Bn. were to form liaison with the 307th on the right; third and forth platoons and the other half of Company C/306th M.G. with the French on the left through Groupement Durand. The remainder of 3rd would hold the rear along with Company B/ 306th M.G. Bn., while Machine Gun Company/308th remained at the disposal of the brigade commander.

With everything and everyone as set as they would ever be, on the afternoon of September 25, all 77th Division field and staff officers assembled at General Alexander's PC in the Bois des Petits Batis (near the town of La Harazee) for their final instructions before the jump-off. It was a tense meeting, with the general giving a sobering yet strangely uplifting talk. All went away feeling that they were on the verge of something great, but one has to wonder if they were at all aware of the history that was about to be made among them. (5, 10, 32, 48, 91, 109, 116, 120, 128, 131, 132, 133, 142)

During that day, the Doughboys in the individual companies were given instructions to drop packs, as they would be leaving nearly everything behind. With the thinking that the first phase would be complete within the 72 hours allotted, at which time fresh troops could take over the line if need be, a full regular load of equipment would be unnecessary. (III) Therefore, each man left behind his overcoat, poncho, rain slicker, blankets and shelter tent half in favor of basic combat gear, though there is evidence to suggest that at least some of the combat experienced Upton men held on to their raincoats or overcoats. 102, 109, 349)

Combat gear consisted of rifle, bayonet, steel helmet, gas mask, short combat pack containing two days iron rations of four boxes of hard bread and two cans of corned beef, mess kit, entrenching tool, and cartridge belt with full load of 100 rounds of ammunition, full water canteen (1 qt.) and first aid pouch. Some of this equipment, though, was running pretty scarce with the replacements, particularly entrenching tools. Some had even shown up in the forest with their bayonets wrapped only in newspaper. Each man was also to carry two extra cloth bandoleers of ammunition (60 rounds each) in addition to his full cartridge belt and on top of this, some men were picked to carry ammunition for the Stokes Mortars in special canvas aprons, four shells to a man at nearly 11 pounds each. Explosive hand and rifle grenades, as well as gas and incendiary grenades were also to be carried. Private Minder, of Company B/ 306th MG Bn., recorded:

"At six thirty, the Sergeant came along and told us to make up our packs and a separate roll of the

shelter halves and blanket. This is called the short pack. It makes it lighter, and when we are told to leave it behind, it's a sign that we are going to be on the move for a while." (37)

Private John W. Nell, Company G/308th remembered:

"About nine o'clock the company commander blew his whistle, and a command was given to fall in. He gave us orders to break camp, roll up our packs, and leave nothing out but our mess kits and water canteen. We were to be sure our canteens were full of water. Pointing to a large oak tree that stood out in front to our right, he said "Men, just as fast as you can get your packs rolled, bring them up and pile them against that tree. Put your raincoats and overcoats in the same pile, and if you have an extra pair of shoes, put them by the other tree... Assemble back here as fast as you can... I want you men to be ready by the time I get back." Off he went. Everyone was wondering what had happened all of a sudden, as we had been told we would be at that location about a week. We packed up very quickly and soon were assembled again."

They soon found out:

"Speaking in a heavy, choking voice, he said... "We are to move out of here by twelve midnight into the front line trenches which are just two miles from here. Our orders are to go over the top at six o'clock in the morning, and when we climb out of the trenches, I want every man to do his duty. If one of your buddies, or friends, or even relatives if you have any in this company, gets shot or wounded, do not stop to help him or apply first aid, as every fighting man is needed. Now, I want to impress on your minds and you to remember, anyone caught lagging behind will be considered a straggler and a yellow coward... a straggler is shown no sympathy in time of war. This area is known as the Muese-Argonne Woods, Alsace-Lorraine sector (sic)." (40)

Nor were Private Nell and Company G the only ones getting a pep talk that day. Private Lee Charles McCollum was another of the 40th Division replacements with about six months service time under his belt that had been assigned to Company A, 1st/308th. McCollum, from Seattle Washington, had originally been rejected when he tried to join the army in 1917. In 1918 however, he was accepted as a substitute for another man and was sent to Camp Lewis for initial training. He had a flare for poetry and writing, which after the war he turned to good use, recording some of his experiences during those hectic days of 1918. Here he relates how all the replacements in his company, who had arrived only the night before, were gathered together at the Croix Gentin crossroads before the commanding officer just before the move up to the front lines:

"By now we knew that we were a part of the 77th Division... Company 'A', 308th Infantry regiment... About four o'clock that afternoon, we were called into a small clearing where Captain Whiting (who in reality was still a lieutenant) and his staff... waited. Captain Whiting seemed very young, but we liked him instantly... (Then) in short, terse language he spoke briefly of what lay ahead of us. The job we had to do. He told us how they of the 77th, only a few short months before, had been in our same position, and he knew how we felt. He gave us minute instructions about what to do when we would first go "over the top". We listened intently... then our new officers and non-coms took over... they gave us more instructions... Night had come again (and) the rain had stopped." (32)

As the afternoon wore on into evening, and the evening into night, tension increased as units prepared to move out. For men like Private Nell, who knew when they were to begin the move up, there was at least a fixed point on which to concentrate. For others, who had not been told when they would set out, the wait seemed interminable. That morning of the 25th, Private James Larney, Major Whittlesey's signalman (the man who carried the airplane signaling panels) in 1st platoon, Headquarters Company/308th, began a new diary. His old one had earlier been confiscated by higher ups; keeping a diary at the front was strictly against the rules for security reasons, though many men kept one in secret anyway. This new diary, along with some of Larney's later remembrances, would become some of the most poignant records of not only the later incident in the Charlevaux Ravine, but of the movements of the 308th through the Argonne as well.

Larney was one of the originals to the 77th Division from the Camp Upton days. He was older than most of the other men in the 308th, being 27 at the time, and was a trained civil engineer with an especially good eye for detail. He describes with frank directness spending that Thursday morning of the 25th by first going to mass and communion, and writing to the folks back home, then making up his battle pack in the afternoon. "(Sgt.) Evans delivered a new panel code to me today," he wrote that evening. "He says we are to make a 30 mile drive. This drive to end the war. Beaucoup guns in the forest here…" Later, as they waited with everyone else to move up, reality started to set in and he wrote:

"Baldwin, Monson, Flannery, Fernes, and Herschkowitz, and myself sitting around my candle talking it over considered our chances, hoping for the best and all agreeing quite frankly that we are in the hands of God, wherever we are, come what may… Waiting to go over the top 'with the best of luck' for fathers, mothers, and other dear ones' sake. Please God, I come through as well as for my own. I have made my peace with God, hold no grudges, hereby putting them all aside if I had any and offer up whatever happens in sacrifice and reparation for my past offences. The light is going out. The Lord be with us all." (152, 218)

In the forested area around Croix Gentin later that night, where the 1st/308th was bivouacked, the darkness was near total, except for occasional flashes of lightning. The rain had stopped, at least for the time being, but it was very damp. In addition, it was unseasonably cold. The Doughboys shivered as last minute details were attended to, not the least of which was the issue of rations. Some units had not received their issue of battle rations yet, and Major Whittlesey and his staff spent a desperate eleventh hour in trying to track them down. In the end, despite all their efforts, several combat squads still went forward without the 'iron rats' they were supposed to have. This turned out to be a phenomenon that was to repeat itself with maddening regularity at all points of the line, throughout the battle. Then, the final straw of ludicrousness—an issue of equipment handed out at the last minute, some of which baffled the men. Major Whittlesey later wrote:

"They issued us bombs, and at the last second, after dark of the night when we were to pull out — with no candles available and every one set to go — they tried to issue some new-fangled rifle grenade affair. Very complicated, with a tail." (109)

The failure to plan ahead in some instances led to some strange situations indeed. One unit received flare pistols of one caliber but cartridges of another, while Private Sidney Smith of Company H/308th recalled that he and some of his buddies went over "bare handed," despite being "loaded down with ammunition and grenades." Captain Walter K. Rainsford, leading Company L of the 307th, later recorded the antics that befell him and his men on their way to the front as an ordinance officer tried to issue out different pyrotechnic and incendiary devices to many a bewildered Doughboy who had never received training for such devices:

"As the battalion filed out at dusk of the 25th, an officer stood at the roadside explaining their various purposes and methods of functioning, and expounding, like a patent medicine artist at a fair, their many sterling qualities.

"This one will call down a friendly barrage in your front; you better take a couple. This one will indicate

your position to a passing airplane, works equally well by day or night, every soldier should have one (wait till the plane circles about and drops six white stars). This will burn through flesh and bone and provide a high quality of illumination for night attacks (may be thrown by hand or from the rifle). And here is one (with apologies for the fact that it weighs ten pounds) that will destroy man and beast within a radius of forty yards..." and so on, until his voice was lost in the darkness." (103)

As the long night drew on, German artillery started throwing stray shots around, much the same as the last few nights, while slowly the great move forward to the jump-off line began. About 7:00 p.m. companies D and A, lead assault units of the 308th, received the order to sling packs and set out for the French first line. Lee McCollum remembered:

"The door swings open silently, and our Lieutenant walks into the candle-lit cabin... "Gather round here boys, the lieutenant wants a word with you." We needed no second invitation and crowded around the lieutenant and the sergeant, waiting... Then the lieutenant spoke. "This is it boys... listen closely..." Our bodies moved nearer in one tense, nerve tightened line. "As you leave this cabin, you are to..." the lieutenant continued with detailed instructions... As he departed, the sergeant said "Fifteen minutes to go... make a last check of your equipment..." Instinctively, all of us who were rookies grouped together... The sergeant and corporals checked us all quickly and carefully. Satisfied that everything was in order, the sergeant, who kept glancing at his watch, said "All set boys... Let's go." We formed a single file, semi circle line ready to march. Someone extinguished the two candles. The sergeant opened the door to the darkness of night... the line was moving. We were on our way to the trenches." (32)

Nerves on edge, men silently filed out through the darkness all along the battle line. Private Sidney Smith, back in Company H, held apprehensions as well as 2nd Battalion moved out about 9:00 p.m. for the jump-off trenches:

"When it got good and dark, we started out to the front. We didn't know where we was going. I could see down in a draw, there was a couple of them French blacks handling ammunition, two to each shell, for this big gun. I said to the fella with me, "Webb, I think we're going someplace." He said, "Oh, no. They wouldn't put us greenhorns up front..." (256)

It was cold and appallingly damp. The paths leading to the front, covered with the frosty fall leaves, were soon churned into slippery, muddy lines weaving through the trees. The men of the 1st/308th had an average of a mile and a half to trek up to the jump-off trenches; others had even more. There, in the incredible darkness, with literally thousands of men jockeying for position, accidents were bound to happen. There were several. In Company A, a man slipped down into one of the many old, abandoned trenches that cut the area and snapped his leg like a twig. Behind, two machine-gun men of Company C/306th MG Bn. carrying the enormously heavy Hotchkiss machine-gun, tripod, and ammunition, slipped off some of the muddy duck-boarding lining one of the paths and did the same thing. (109, 116)

Private McCollum had been handed two mussette bags full of hand grenades soon after leaving the shelter of the cabin his company had occupied. Not long after they had started, a young replacement near him in line complained about the clumsy stretcher he was forced to cart about and McCollum offered to exchange burdens. Gratefully the other man accepted. About an hour into the trip up, as they were making their way along an old, moss-lined trench, an explosion ripped the air ahead. Someone had banged a bag full of grenades against a rock sticking out from the side of the trench, knocked the charging fuse of one, and blown himself and several others to kingdom come. Private John, a short distance back, initially thought they were being attacked and brought his rifle to bear, terrified to have to fight in the inky blackness. Private McCollum too was petrified, until

86

word came back of what had happened. Rushing forward McCollum loaded up one of the wounded on his stretcher and started back, now considering himself a very lucky man. (He returned later that night - in plenty of time for the start of the attack.) Back in Company G, a similar accident occurred when a grenade unknowingly fell from a bag. The forth man in line ahead of Private John Nell accidentally kicked the lethal weapon and charged the fuse. The resulting explosion killed the first man and wounded the next three, but miraculously, Nell escaped harm. The mess was cleaned up and slowly the men continued their journey through the cold, dark, forest night. (32, 40, 220)

Once the front line trenches were reached, there was more waiting to endure. Immediately, only the necessary number of troops stayed in the trenches to keep everything looking as natural as possible to any snooping Germans right up until the end. Others tucked down in old, dilapidated, shallow dugouts underground, accessed by narrow, staired passageways. The rest took shelter in the narrow communication trenches that stretched backward and hugged the walls as the horizon blue clad French soldiers of the 120th filed out with pressed handshakes in the dark and perhaps a whispered "Bon chance!" Then the French artillery started up to the west around 11:30 p.m. and filled the air with the shriek of passing shells and the terrible, low rumble from the resulting explosions to the left front.

Down in the dugouts, an attempt was made to keep smoking to a minimum, though largely in vain. Most, above or below, sat in the cold, muddy darkness and stared off blankly into the night, coolly smoking and trying not to think about what lay ahead. And they shivered. There was hoarfrost on the logs of revetment holding the old trenches together. Breath shown in light, silvery clouds as again the temperature dipped into the mid-40s Fahrenheit. Orders were for no talking, but the order was hardly necessary. First, there was a tense, stark reality in the air that precluded small talk; the "thing" seemed too big for words. Second, whenever possible, a new recruit had been assigned to stay near one of the seasoned veterans of the regiment (in hopes he might learn something that would keep him from getting his head blown off immediately), and the veterans were little disposed to talk to the greenhorns anyway. Most tried desperately to avoid looking directly into the faces of their terrified charges. They did not want the responsibility in the first place and certainly did not want the specter of some scared, half-trained Doughboy face haunting them for the rest of their lives, if the seemingly inevitable should happen. (IV)

The engineer men peered nervously out over the edge of those horrible ditches as the flashes of artillery fire to the west occasionally lit up their waxy faces and wide eyes, shrouded under the dew-coated brim of their steel helmets. Somewhere out there was the Boche wire that they would have to find their way through. Deep in the trenches, cigarette after cigarette glowed under cupped hands that shook, not always from the cold. Stomachs churned and nervous boys vomited quietly off to the sides. No one paid them any mind. A never ending procession of men stood up and urinated against the corner of the trench or dugout and steam rose up, adding the stench of warm piss to the stale, cold, damp smell of the earth in that dilapidated little corner of war-torn France. A thick fog rolled in, covering everything with a frosty, dewy blanket as the hour for the start of the U.S. barrage approached.

It was about to hit the fan, "up in the Argonne."

(I) Later on, after the war, men who had fought through the tangle of the Argonne would consistently relate how they saw lots of "French" aircraft flying overhead, but never any of their own. Indeed, in my research for this book, again and again this same statement was made. However, after reviewing the record of the 50th Aero Squadron, who flew daily missions over the forest, almost hourly in fact (weather permitting, of course), it is safe to assume that the infantry mistook their airplanes for French ones. In the first place, few in the infantry had any idea of the difference between French aircraft markings and those of the U.S. Air Service, or the different types of aircraft flown by the two. Second, we may also assume that these two French aircraft piloted by American pilots on

September 25 over the men's heads repeatedly would be the primary aerial memory that stayed with many of the men, since later on they had much more to worry about than watching passing airplanes. Even during the Charlevaux Ravine episode, several men would later claim that no aircraft other than French ones ever flew over them, which is simply ridiculous. The myth of 'French planes only' was further perpetuated when Captain Nelson Holderman (who commanded Company K/307th in the Pocket and won the Medal of Honor there), in a monograph for the Army Infantry School at Ft. Benning in the early 1920's, also stated that "French" aircraft repeatedly flew over them, one even directing a barrage onto the surrounded force. Contrary to all of this however, I have been unable, in eight years of diligent research, to find *any* evidence that *any* French aircraft, piloted by French pilots, *ever* flew over the zone of advance of the 77th Division before October 10...

(II) It should not be taken, however, that all men that transferred in from the 40th were in such sorry shape militarily. It was primarily those who had been drafted into service relatively recently and had only been funneled through the 40th. Most, though not all, of the men that had originally sailed with the 40th had at least some marginal training. Nor was it as uncommon as it first would seem for men to be sent into combat in the latter part of the war with such limited training, as had their late arriving troops. The urgent need for replacements to cover combat casualties, coupled with the Army's planned expansion of the AEF in Europe, was causing corners to be cut. Over 2 million men would be on French soil by the end of the year—an incredible number when one considers that the United States had entered the war with only about 250,000 ready troops. The U.S. Army lacked adequate training facilities to handle the increased flood of draftees, and what facilities there were had already been stretched to capacity. Therefore, the later National Army troops did not benefit from the same comprehensive training the early draft divisions had received. For instance, Corporal Richard Pierce, a draftee toward the end of the war, did not receive any rifle instruction at all until he arrived in France, whereupon he was given *five minutes* worth. At least he got some. Not so with Private Willie Gaskin, Company B, 56th Pioneer Infantry. "Never had a day's training," he wrote "and was on the fighting front within 59 days after leaving Smithfield (North Carolina)..." (50) Even General Pershing admits in his memoirs to being aware of the problem and sending a cable back to the states in mid-September 1918 concerning it. This, however, did no good for the men about to be thrown into battle in the Argonne.

Much has been made of this lack of training, rifle training in particular, as American soldiers of the time were ordinarily well known in France for their skill as marksmen. The truth of the matter, as far as the replacements sent to the 77th was concerned, is that a large percentage of these draftee men had grown up around guns. Being mainly from the Northwest and Midwest, most already knew how to handle them reasonably well, in some cases even better than the instructors that might have trained them. Therefore, what these men generally lacked was not rifle skills so much as skill with the Army magazine-fed weapon. A fairly well known story from the 308th at this point in the preparations for the battle has Major Whittlesey of the 1st/308th coming across a young replacement to his battalion sitting under a bush exclaiming, "How the hell do you make the bullets go in this thing?" The Major then drops to one knee and shows the inexperienced man the secret. While the story may be true in the stricter sense, it has likely been taken out of context. What Whittlesey probably did was simply show the man how to load a full stripper of five rounds into the magazine, whereas heretofore the soldier had been loading a single shot at a time. What many replacements did lack, however, was knowledge of both automatic weapons and hand grenades—things that they would quickly learn in the school of battle.

(III) The sad truth is that the Army had horribly miscalculated. Instead of taking 72 hours to reach the first phase line in the Argonne Forest, it would take 8 days. This was a situation that, as we will see, the army had unfortunately not prepared itself to deal with and one for which the men were to suffer greatly.

(IV) As much as was possible, the replacements had been given the menial tasks in the companies, such as bearing stretchers, toting grenades, carrying extra rifle and machine-gun ammunition, being cooks helpers, company or battalion runners, etc... That said, there were still a considerable number of them forced to man the line, since the casualties on the Vesle had hit the ranks of the riflemen in the companies so hard.

Ancillary sources used in this chapter include: 3, 4, 9, 10, 14, 16, 18, 20, 22, 30, 31, 33, 34, 36, 39, 43, 95, 102, 106, 11, 138, 139, 142, 144, Various 152-216, 223, 228, 257, 260, 266, 277, 288, 289, 349, 364, 367, 368, 369, 370, 371

Part 2:
Into the Den of the Lion

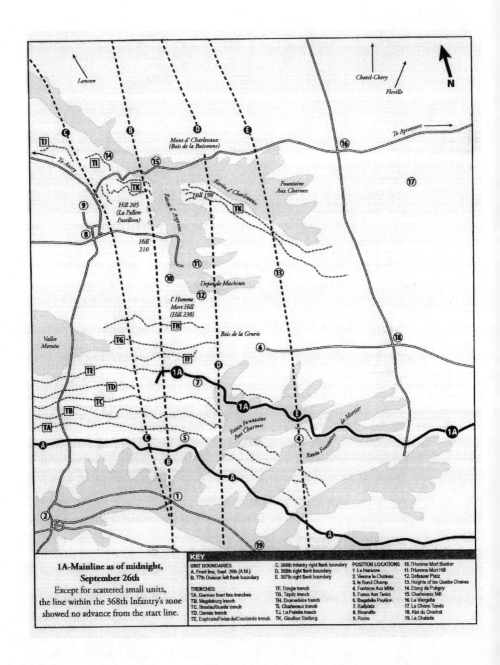

Lancon

Chatel-Chery

Fleville

N

Mont d' Charlevaux
(Bois de la Buironne)

To Apremont

To Autry

Fountaine
Aux Charmes

Ravin d' Charlevaux

Hill 205
(La Pallete
Pavilion)

Hill 198

Ravin d' Argonne

Hill
210

Depot de Machines

l' Homme
Mort Hill
(Hill 230)

Bois de la Grurie

Vallee
Moreau

Ravin Fountaine
Aux Charmes

Ravin Fountaine de Mortier

**1A-Mainline as of midnight,
September 26th**

Except for scattered small units,
the line within the 368th Infantry's zone
showed no advance from the start line.

KEY

UNIT BOUNDARIES
A. Front line, Sept. 26th (A.M.)
B. 77th Division left flank boundary

C. 368th Infantry right flank boundary
D. 308th right flank boundary
E. 307th right flank boundary

TRENCHES
TA. German front line trenches
TB. Magdsburg trench
TC. Breslau/Suede trench
TD. Damas trench
TE. Euphrate/Finlande/Courlande trench

TF. Tringle trench
TG. Tirpitz trench
TH. Dromedoire trench
TI. Charlevaux trench
TJ. La Palette trench
TK. Giselher Stellung

POSITION LOCATIONS
1. La Harazee
2. Vienna la Chateau
3. le Rond Champ
4. Fontaine Aux Mitte
5. Fosse Aux Tanks
6. Bagatello Pavilion
7. Karlplatz
8. Binorville
9. Rome

10. l'Homme Mort Bunker
11. l'Homme Mort Hill
12. Defsauer Platz
13. Heights of les Quatre Chenes
14. Etang de Poligny
15. Charlevaux Mill
16. Le Viergotte
17. Le Chene Tondu
18. Abri du Crochet
19. La Chalade

September 26, 1918

"It seemed…that our army, with all its improvisations, might accomplish what it so ardently hoped…"
Thomas Johnson, AEF reporter.

Over an unfamiliar route, swimming through a blanket of fog and darkness on his way back to the 308th Regimental PC, came a runner with a message from Lt. Arthur McKeogh, Major Whittlesey's adjutant in the 1st Battalion:

From: 1st Bn. Hq. 308 Inf.
Sept. 26 '18 2.20am
To: C.O. 308 Inf.
1 – Bn. Hq. temporarily established at 95. – 70.65.
2 – All companies are present(ly) going into position. We have no report from companies yet and liaison established, but runners from companies are still in the rear to be collected and shown this P.C. Have left 12 relay posts, No. 1 at Regimental Hq.
3 – Everything quiet. Relief effected without event.
4 – Delay experienced thro fault of French companies forward in getting thro complicated trench system.

By order Maj. Whittlesey
Lt. A. McKeogh
1st Bn. Adjt. (246)

Ten minutes later, at precisely 2:30 a.m., the half sawed through trees screening the artillery pieces of the 152nd Field Artillery Brigade were pulled down. Then, all along the battle line from La Harazee in the west to the Muese River in the east, some 3,928 field guns began to throw a storm of shells into the German wire and back areas ahead. Awakened by the roar some 25 kilometers behind the battle line, General Von Gallwitz recorded in his journal later that morning that the windows of his quarters reverberated from the concussion of the fire. In fact, all totaled, the actual weight of ammunition fired into the German lines solely by U.S. batteries over the next three hours alone is said to have been greater than that used by the whole Union Army during the entire Civil War.

Of the 2,700 American-manned guns pounding the German lines in the pre-dawn darkness, over 200 were massed against the 7.5-kilometer front of the 77th Division facing the dank, mist shrouded Argonne Forrest. Most of the firing was blind, however, as forward artillery observers up with the troops in the trenches peered intently into the darkness, which had been made nearly impenetrable by the thick morning fog mixed with the artillery smoke, and saw - nothing. (109, 116, 140)

Behind the screen of fire, Major Whittlesey and his men of the 1st/308th hunkered down in the muddy, wet trenches with bayonets fixed anticipating the signal to move forward. The men from down below in the dugouts had slowly filed out into the trenches above once the shelling started. There was certainly no need for secrecy anymore. It was a relief to be out of the claustrophobic conditions underground, even if the forward and communication trenches were crowded now. One well-placed Hun shell would have done untold damage had there been any falling. However, there were few. The German artillerymen no doubt sought shelter in their own dugouts once the Allied shells had started coming in on them. Dominating the scene now was that terrific barrage of the Allied guns, which tore over the Doughboy's heads on its way to Hunland. In a letter to his mother later that day, Pvt. Charles F. Minder of Company B/306th Machine Gun Battalion gave some indication as to the extent of the noise that the barrage was putting up:

"It (the barrage) started on the minute, and you can bet there was no sleeping after that! The noise was terrific; I thought my eardrums were going to burst a couple times during the night. If it was as bad as that for us, it must have been ten times as bad for the Germans..." (37)

Most men for the rest of their lives remembered that opening barrage as particularly hell raising. It seems strange then to read a line from Lt. McKeogh's next message back to the Regimental PC, timed at 5:15 a.m., where he says, "Artillery preparation has not been of the world beating class." He no doubt changed his tune 15 minutes later though, when at 5:30 a.m. the artillery fire increased in intensity. The "prepatory bombardment" had begun and the Doughboys instinctively ducked their heads and pressed closer to the damp, frozen earth as the increased waves of sound and light washed back over them. Everyone tensed. The wait was almost over. Lee McCollum, over in A Company, vividly describes the scene that shortly followed:

"When we spoke at all it was in whispers — which was pointless, because our heavy guns were beating out a roaring barrage. Finally the sergeant said, "Get ready fellows, this is it! We are going over." He stood there in that heavy morning mist as rigidly as though he were carved of stone, hand high at an oblique, tense angle; while in the other hand he held a small whistle poised to his lips... then he looked over down the line sharply at us... half nodded his head, blew the shrill sounding whistle, motioning us to 'come on' with his hand, and started to crawl over the top of the trench..." (32)

It was 5:55 a.m.; the rolling barrage had lifted forward the 100 yards prescribed in orders and the assault waves of the 1st/308th went surging up and over the top. Private John remembered:

"With a parting word and warning of instruction to each man by an officer standing in the trench, up and over the top we went. It was an odd feeling. It didn't seem like fear, nor even dread, but more just a feeling of wonderment at what we might see or learn as we pushed out into no-mans land. I never saw so much barbed wire in my life..." (220)

In a forest full of misty darkness, Company A left the jump-off trenches split into two sections of two platoons each. On the left was 1st Lt. (acting Captain) Clinton L. Whiting with 1st and 2nd platoons, 1st Platoon in the lead. On the right was 2nd Lt. Ransom S. Pattison with 3rd and 4th platoons, his 3rd Platoon leading. Filled with apprehension, the men crawled out into the muddy darkness, hardened to hurl forward at the remnants of the German 2nd Landwehr Division and "Fully expecting to be met with a fusillade of enemy bullets," according to McCollum. "(But) nothing happened to us." Company D, over on the extreme left flank, also left their trenches in two dual platoon sections; 1st Lt. (acting Captain) Paul R. Knight ahead with 2nd and 3rd platoons, 3rd leading on the left; and 1st Lt. Edward W. Akers with 1st and 4th platoons, 1st leading on the right.

What they found once they got under way came as a shock. Instead of the strong storm of enemy resistance the men had expected, the scene that met the Metropolitan Division that morning was a terrain of near impossibility. The foggy pre-dawn had coated everything in a thick, frosty blanket of darkness, causing men to advance only a few yards from the edge of the trenches and stop for fear of losing their fellows. Officers and NCOs behind urged the men on, only to see them disappear in the blankness ahead, before they then attempted to follow. Stumbling ahead, men fell into unseen shell holes, and became entangled in hidden wire while struggling in vain to find the concealed lanes through the belts ahead. Almost immediately, a few enemy machine-guns that had by some miracle survived the bombardment started firing blindly into the dark fog, and the German artillery began to throw shells into the advancing wave. A blanket of apprehension slowly began to spread over the Doughboys along with the fog. (132, 137, 218, 257, 273)

Back with Major Whittlesey's 1st Battalion PC, 1st Lt. Edward N. Lewis gives perhaps the most moving account of the initial advance into the unknown, which he chose to tell in the third person.

"...The Major (Whittlesey) said, "Let's go!" He boosted the Lieutenant (Lewis) to the parapet and was in turn pulled up by hand to take his perch on the edge of the weirdest panorama of mist and mystery that mortal imagination could conjure up. No mans' land, which should have beckoned straight into the heart of the Argonne, was shrouded in a thick white fog. It seemed to close in from all sides on that little infantry company, isolating it entirely from the colossal allied advance, and nullifying in one chilly breath all the carefully planned instructions in regard to liaison; the vital necessity to keeping in touch.

Beyond and through the fog the flashes of bursting shells flickered. The ear was confused by the muffled echoes of friendly artillery. The eye was confused by the haze, which kept from vision all objects more than 100 feet away, and curiously distorted the few stumps and posts that clung to the sides of the slope at their feet. It was almost as though the infantry was asked to go over the top blindfolded. Even more depressing than the lack of vision, however, was the dank breath of the Argonne, saturated, until by dawn the air had passed mellowness, with the odor of stagnant, muddy pools hiding beneath treacherous carpets of tangled wire grass, and bringing to the nostrils of the new crusaders a reminder of the awful slaughter which had left another carpet on this mutilated soil in those historic days when a barrier of horizon blue poilus had hurled back the Crown Princes' army.

A dark blotch down the steep slope... proved to be an abandoned French trench, thirty feet deep, filled with coils of rusty wire, and spanned by a single log – all that remained of a footbridge. Reconnoitering to the right and left failed to reveal any other means of advance... thus this particular battalion headquarters went into action... Company 'B' followed more slowly, platoon by platoon, squad by squad, (until) the log began to shrink; chipped by the gougings of many hobnails... According to the artillery plan, the rolling barrage... was to advance every five minutes in 100 meter bounds. Hence, during the 45 minutes that one infantry company was making the first 50 meters in the Argonne drive, the protection of supporting artillery (had) jumped ahead nearly 1000 meters..." (266)

Lewis was far from alone in his assessment of the deplorable conditions of that morning. All along the divisional line, the New Yorkers and their new Midwestern compatriots were first forced to battle the darkened forest itself before they could even begin to concentrate on the destruction of the enemy. Walter Kerr-Rainsford, the 45-year-old Plattsburg Captain commanding Company L/307th, to the right of the 308th, later recorded:

"Orders had been given before leaving camp for a very open order advance, and there was no chance of getting word to the troops to change formation no matter what the weather was. So, at 5.50 am I climbed out with the nearest platoon into the darkness and impenetrable fog mixed with powder smoke, started them forward by compass, and went to look — or feel — for the others. I didn't find them again until afternoon.

Our artillery was supposed to have blown a passage through the heaviest wire between some craters marked on the map near the head of the Ravin Sec, but there didn't seem much chance of finding it by sense of touch. I found myself with my striker and two runners adrift in a blind world of whiteness and noise, groping over something like the surface of the moon. One literally could not see two yards, and every where the ground rose into bare pinnacles and ridges, or descended into bottomless chasms, half filled with rusty tangles of wire. Deep, half-ruined trenches appeared without system or sequence, usually impossible of crossing. Bare splintered trees, occasional derelict skeletons of men, thickets of gorse, and everywhere the piles of rusted wire…I remember trying to light a pipe, but the tobacco was so saturated with powder smoke and gas that it was impossible…" (103)

As had been found over in the 308th's zone of advance, at least half of the lanes in the wire that Rainsford and his men were looking for did not exist. Fortunately, some 200 pairs of long handled French wire cutters had been issued out to the assault companies of the brigade just before the move to the jump-off trenches. Now, the engineers found themselves forced to carve a way through the wire themselves; an incredibly difficult prospect in the blindness around them. They also carried with them pre-assembled 20-foot bents of light footbridge. Used for crossing not only wire but also trenches and shell holes, the method worked exceptionally well, as did rolls of 2-ply chicken wire netting 30 feet long and 8 feet wide, rolled out forward over dense wire fields. Yet, despite all the foot bridging and chicken wire, it remained slow going as the fog effectively prevented anyone from finding openings in the wire.

Besides the fog and wire, other debilitating factors hampered Doughboy efforts as well. Following orders, the artillery batteries had gone ahead and fired smoke dispensing shells into the wire line ahead, so as to shield U.S. troop movements the closer they got to the enemy, though the fog had made this completely unnecessary. Many of the attacking men, fearing it was gas, immediately donned the hot, sweaty gas masks (usually referred to derisively as "slobber catchers"), which were always uncomfortable and difficult to fight in. In fact gas was being used that morning—the Argonne Forest being number one on the 1st Army's list of "Priority Targets—Gas."

Adding to this problem, the German artillery, which had gotten cranked back up once the U.S. barrage had passed, was sending over gas of their own along with high explosive and shrapnel shells. Private Smith, back in Company H, along with a number of other replacements, made the same mistakes that many inexperienced men did concerning gas. "We lay close to the ground," he later said, "in the lowest places we could to keep out of the mustard gas and the like." They soon found out, disastrously, that since gas is heavier than air, it settled in those low spots and hung there - sometimes for days.

Five hundred meters behind the 1st/308th came the men of the 2nd Battalion, struggling along with a similar set of problems. Initially Major Budd's nervous men, bathed in the glow of the already falling opening barrage, had a somewhat rougher time moving into the crowded 2nd line trenches. Their slow going caused, at 3:00 a.m., Colonel Prescott to send forward a sharply worded note, admonishing Budd for not having checked in as yet, and demanding frequent updates. (109, 116, 131, 132)

Additionally, the initial jump-off for 2nd Battalion had not gone off exactly according to plan in spots either. Pvt. Nell of Company G, who sat waiting in the trench with his officer, remembered:

"We sat there talking and watching the time, and at 5:45 the lieutenant looked at his watch and with a long breath and a sigh said, "Well, it's only fifteen minutes more." For the next quarter hour we sat there speechless… a heavy fog had settled down and it was so dark we could not see each other… At 5:55 he murmured "Five minutes more."

We both stood there silent, choked with fear. The barrage was quieting down (actually, it was lifting forward – author). At 6:00 he calmly said "All right men. Let's go."

We both climbed out together, but could not see each other. He stumbled and fell. We were the only ones who had climbed out. We could hardly see for the thick, heavy fog and could hardly move without getting our feet tangled in the barbed wire. He whispered "Lets go back in the trench for a while and maybe the fog will begin to lift." We got back in the trench and stayed until ten minutes after six. Then the lieutenant spoke in a grave voice "All right men; everybody out on top; let's go!"

It was just as dark as ever..." (40)

Once under way, the 2nd Battalion unfortunately was to face the brunt of what German shellfire there was, in that they followed behind the struggling 1st Battalion by 500 meters. Thus, by the time the Boche had found the range of the 1st Battalion, it was more likely the 2nd that was occupying the spot. Therefore, it was they who paid a higher price in shellfire casualties in the first hours of the attack. Private Jacob Rangitsch, a replacement drafted out of Columbus, Montana, had only been in the service seven weeks before he found himself advancing into the Argonne with Company E. Now, out in the fog, he looked around to left and right and found himself among strangers. The pal who he had begun the advance with had almost immediately been hit by shrapnel and gone down, and the other men whom he knew were lost somewhere out in the confusion of the forest as well. Finally, he found another familiar face, a neighbor farmer also from Montana. Together they pushed ahead — but not for long. Rangitsch remembered:

"The shells were still dropping like streaks of lightning... (We) went a little ways farther (and my) comrade was hit by a piece of shrapnel that cut off a piece of his chin bone..." (225)

The man's cheek and chin had fallen away "like a door on a hinge" and, against orders which instructed him to pass up the wounded and continue the advance under all costs, Rangitsch stopped to help. He carefully folded the torn flesh and bone back into place on the man's face, applied an emergency dressing, and started him off in the direction of the rear area and help. Turning, he then continued his own advance toward hell. (182, 225)

Likewise, the dispersion that was plaguing Major Whittlesey's lead battalion was also wreaking havoc in Major Budd's 2nd Battalion. The only fortunate thing in Budd's favor as far as the advance was concerned lay in the fact that the lanes were already open in the wire once they reached it - provided they could find them. However, Company H, according to Pvt. Sidney Smith, faced an even more difficult problem:

"When we first went over the top, it was in the wrong place. It was some mistake that the officers had made. I remember the men in front of me running back. They were all bunched up. There was a lot of shooting and I and my partner crawled into a ditch. Our officers ordered us to double time back... When we come back to the front, there was barbed wire tangled in every way and hard wire cables with knife blades tied in them going through there. And the way the machine guns was playing through there, and with all that tangled wire, there's times there I thought we was all going to get shot down..." (256)

Part of the trouble that morning was not so much the officers in charge of directing the men's movements through the fog, as it was a most fascinating phenomenon. Extraordinarily, in some cases compasses failed when old metal shrapnel fragments imbedded in the ground from earlier battles interfered with their magnetic field! (Indeed, 85 years later, the author experienced this phenomenon while retracing Major Whittlesey's route into the Argonne.) In many instances, company commanders could do little else but start their unit off on what they believed to be the right course and hope for the best, only to find—too late—that what they thought was the correct direction, was not. (109)

Major Whittlesey himself blew the initial whistle that started his men forward, and then went over the top with a pistol in one hand and a massive pair of French wire cutters in the other. He exuded a positive, enthusiastic attitude that quickly spread to those around him in the 1st Battalion PC Platoon, dissipating some of the fear they all felt—this in spite of physical ailments that plagued him. At the start of the attack, the major was suffering from a nasty case of dysentery, was in possession of a cold so severe he could scarcely talk above a whisper, and had a rattling cough that had been keeping him awake (souvenirs from the gas on the Vesle). Around 7:00 a.m., he sent his first message of the day back to Regimental PC, which incredibly made it in good time. It stated, "Progressing favorably with little opposition. Do not know distance have progressed." Colonel Prescott passed the message back to General Johnson at the 154th Brigade PC immediately. Whittlesey, meanwhile, plowed on. (109, 246)

All units had been given instructions ahead of time for the attack to be made in a company size, open order advance, heading due north. This style of advance meant a wide spacing between men - 10 meters per man on the average - of a steadily advancing skirmish line. The lead assault line would average 200 men across a four-platoon/two-company front equaling, in the case of the 1st/308th, a little over a kilometer in length. Behind this line was a gap of about 50 meters, followed by the line of the support platoons of each company in the assault battalion. Following that, after a gap of some 500 meters, came the initial skirmish line of the lead companies of the support battalion. Fifty meters behind them, came their own support companies. Under moderately difficult conditions, this would have been a feasible plan. The Argonne, however, was beyond moderately difficult. (349)

Initial dispersion of units due to the difficulties of terrain and weather conditions continued unabated all morning, ruining the advance plan. With no way for commanders to retract the initial orders and issue corrections, it was obvious that the situation could only continue to steadily worsen. While units trudged forward as best they could, the "line" was never really one at all. It became something more akin to moving pockets of men attempting to drive an enemy out of a particular area, while making every effort to stay in contact with its neighbors and coordinate an advance. Some units, or fragments thereof, found themselves trailing far behind or worse, well out in front of the neighboring units in the area, with no flank protection. Lieutenant McKeogh of 1st/308th neatly summed the situation up when he said, "We went through such rank growth that there was always the danger of losing the man ahead, although he was almost within arm's length...You were prisoner of untamed nature." The all-important liaison was therefore uppermost in unit commanders' minds most of the time, though in practice was more often than not hit or miss. At Division PC, however, it was expected that once full daylight came, visual liaison could be established, making the going much easier as the advance moved relentlessly forward. (34, 42, 48, 109, 116, 257)

At 8:30 a.m. General Johnson, anxious for word of what was happening in his brigade zone, telephoned Colonel Prescott and asked, "Colonel, do you know where your front line is?"

Prescott, who truly was still in the dark, was forced to admit as much.

"No, General. I do not."

"You must send up and get information as to where that front line is, Colonel!" Johnson said. "If your battalion commander cannot send back reports, you must relieve him and put in someone who can."

General Johnson as yet did not recognize the conditions under which the attack had gone over... (131)

The dispersion continued nearly unabated, as the advance ground on relatively unopposed. Lost somewhere out in the foggy wilderness, a steady drain of man power on the 1st Battalion occurred as Lt. McKeogh set up his runner chain and sent messages back in an effort to maintain some semblance of contact with the Regimental PC. To compensate for this loss of personnel, Major Whittlesey began collecting whomever he ran across to replace those men spent in other duties - a practice that only added to the dispersion problem, but one that was to be habitually repeated by Whittlesey all through the Argonne fighting. Meanwhile, 2nd Battalion units, though they were supposed to be 500 meters to the rear of 1st Battalion and moving in support, instead found themselves intermingling with the rear units of the 1st, despite orders to avoid doing so.

Both Whittlesey and Budd had anticipated, to one degree or another, nearly all the problems they were now encountering. Dissatisfied with the stacked battalion plan of attack prescribed by Division, before jump-off they had discussed what they might do should events tangle the respective commands in such a situation as they now faced. Nevertheless, there was no hard and fast answer. In any event, little could be done because, intermingling of battalions notwithstanding, serious problems of communication continued. Runners sent out with messages for other companies, or merely with instructions to find other companies, failed in their tasks. An example would be Private McCollum of A Company, who was given a message to run to the B Company commander. He left at 7:00 a.m., but did not even *find* B Company until well after 11:00 a.m. At 9:30 a.m., Major Whittlesey had Lt. McKeogh send back a message to Regimental PC detailing all that had happened since the initial message and with their current position - but that message would not arrive until 1:15 p.m. The first message Prescott got with any really useful information from anywhere near the head of the attack was from Major Budd at 8:45 a.m. - and that message had been sent at 7:10 a.m. (32, 109)

Therefore, Colonel Prescott sent the assistant regimental commander, Lt. Col. Frederick E. Smith, and the regimental intelligence officer, Captain Bradley Delehanty, to check progress and report back. Lieutenant Colonel Smith, who had first joined the 308th during its days in the Lorraine sector, was very well thought of in the regiment and much admired for his courage and friendly, easygoing nature. He hailed from Portland, Oregon, had served his country well through a long regular army career and was most noted in the 308th for his acceptance of the emergency officers with whom he served. As a commander, he was keenly interested in the welfare of the men whom he commanded and made it a point to watch out for them as best as he could in every way possible. Seemingly impervious to the nerves most men showed under fire (a trait he shared with Charles Whittlesey), Smith, along with Delehanty, wandered the battle zone most of the morning before reluctantly returning to the Regimental PC with their report. Reluctantly, because Smith would have much rather preferred to have been with the men in command of a combat section, not sitting idly by at Regimental PC. According to Lt. Ed Lewis:

"...Two shapes loomed up ahead through the mist. "Halt! Who's there?" the lieutenant shouted. "Colonel Smith," came the reply. "Where's the Major?"... No messages from the Major had reached regimental headquarters (yet)...His (the Lt. Colonels) wrapped puttees were in shreds and miniature red rivulets on his shins showed he had traveled rough-shod over wire entanglements and brambles to catch up with the first line of the attack. He and the captain and their bulging map cases disappeared as they retraced their steps toward the north..." (266)

Doggedly, the attack continued to progress in Smith's wake... (109, 266)

For the Germans defending the Argonne, the day had begun with an edge. On the night of the 25th, an observation patrol of the 8th Company/2nd Bn/122nd Landwehr Regiment had been sent out to scout no man's land beyond the front lines in the area unknowingly facing the U.S. 308th Infantry. German intelligence was sure that something big was in the works, based on what little information they had been able to get from the few prisoners taken within the last two days. These, though, turned out to be inexperienced

Doughboy replacements that had wandered off to 'see the front' and had gotten lost. They did not really tell anything, simply because they did not know anything. Therefore, it was an experienced man of the 8th, Sergeant Schatzle, who took responsibility for the observation patrol and spent the better part of two hours probing the area ahead before being recalled for a report. Back at their headquarters camp near the Madame Fountain Valley, the commander of the patrol, 2nd Lt. Richter, reported that, "the enemy was totally calm." No sooner had he made his report though than the French artillery started up from the southwest with a vengeance.

The front line positions of the regiments (divided into two-sector zones of action) were being held by 2nd Lt. Nast and his 12th Company, 3rd/122nd. He had placed a separate section of his company within each sector and further divided these units into patrols, with strict orders to keep close watch on the lines ahead and report any movement at all. High command had alerted all front line positions just that morning that an enemy attack was expected. Lieutenant Nast's headquarters, called Mont Hauser Camp, meanwhile had the 8th Company, led by 2nd Lt. Ulshofer, behind them in support. Lieutenant Nast was waiting impatiently in his headquarters dugout for news from the front when a runner came in from an outpost to the west and announced that the attack had likely begun. By then, however, the falling shells had already told that tale, and the news was old.

West of the 122nd, the first battalion and machine-gun companies of the 254th Infantry Regiment/76th (Reserve) Division, had arrived the night before and taken up positions between the 2nd and 9th Landwehr Divisions, while the 2nd/254th moved down from the rear, soon to take up position between the 1st/254th and the 122nd Regiment of the 2nd LwD. The 83rd Regiment of the 9th LwD had helped the 254th to get into place within Raw Nerves Valley. There they mostly faced the zone occupied by the Negro U.S. 368th Infantry and by the time the French artillery started to drop on them late the night of the 25th, they had a muster roll of 22 officers and 720 men, all well hunkered down for a siege.

At around 6:00 a.m., shells started to drop directly on the positions held by Lt. Nast's men of the 12th Company. Shortly thereafter, Allied soldiers came crashing through the fog and smoke toward them. Before long, groups of attackers had pushed beyond German outposts and into the valleys of the Fontaine Aux Charmes and the Mortar Fountain Stream. Nast's men held them off in a fighting retreat as per orders to protect the western flank of the regiment and to give heavy mortar companies time to get the range on the attacking groups.

Behind the 12th Company line, heavy U.S. artillery fire fell upon 8th Company, waiting to be used as "shock reserves," with devastating results. There, the headquarters dugout was directly hit causing 17 casualties and effectively ending the company's usefulness. Word was received soon after that support reserves were already well on the way to being in place, in the form of sections from the 11th, 7th, and 5th Companies.

Lieutenant Nast, meanwhile, waited for reports from the front line. He had heard only sporadic bits and pieces since the great barrage had started to fall into his positions and he was concerned that his patrols might have all been wiped out. Unable to venture forward himself to obtain the information he needed due to intense artillery fire, he paced impatiently and cursed with regularity. Finally, around 7:15 a.m., a report arrived; the "French" were on both sides of the Fontaine Aux Charmes stream, and one of his lieutenants on outpost duty was wounded. By 8:30 a.m., the support companies had arrived and taken up positions and were engaging the enemy at all points immediately. Nevertheless, at 8:40 a.m. the enemy that had earlier broken through his line arrived at Mont Hauser, thus forcing Lt. Nast to retreat with the remainder of his company to the rear.

Meanwhile the 11th Company, commanded by 2nd Lt. Ihle, rushed into the line as reinforcements and a counterattack was staged near 9:00 a.m. close to the center of the regimental front. It first appeared to be a success. However, by 10:00 a.m., the Allied soldiers were back pressing the line. The question then arose: Could these really be Frenchmen attacking the "impregnable" Argonne with such tenacity and disregard for casualties after all these years of quietus? The answer was not long in coming when a patrol of the 5th Company brought in the first live prisoner around that time, and one from the 7th company, a dead one. The cat was then out of the bag.

They were Americans. (120, 122, 128, 367, 371)

Taking off from Remicourt aerodrome that morning, the 50th Observation Squadron found the ground shrouded from their view by the fog and mist. The pilot, 1st Lt. Maurice F. Graham, did first reconnaissance with 1st Lt. H.H. Ashley as observer at first light. After staying out an hour and 20 minutes, their report on conditions over the battle area was not very encouraging. Nonetheless, the first effort at infantry contact patrol was attempted soon after Graham and Ashley's return by 1st Lt. David C. Beebe, pilot, and 1st Lt. Howard C. French, observer. Flying down to within 400 feet of the ground, the two aviators spent an hour and 35 minutes in the air calling for infantry signals, saw nothing of the troops they were to report on, and finally gave up and went home. Two further recon patrols were sent out at intervals later in the morning before another attempt was made at a contact patrol, which did no better than the first. It would not be until early afternoon that Lt. Morse's flyers would do any good at all. (110, 249)

The 1st/308th continued to push out ahead. By midmorning, it was moving more easily through areas where the fog had started to break up some and the smoke mostly dissipated. American and French shelling had virtually ended by 7:30 a.m., with only specific targets being worked over from that point. The German shelling was starting to come in heavier however, but it gave the impression of being ragged and disorganized. Then, overhead, the German observation planes started to buzz down, making the Doughboys nervous that they might be spotting for the Hun artillery, which they were. Then the enemy artillery barrages were increasingly on target from that point on. Doughboys took to raising their rifles and taking potshots through the mist at the Hun aircraft, but to no real effect.

About 9:00 a.m., a watery sun poked through a few gaps in the clouds, but there was no real warmth in it. It was also about that time that 1st/308th reached the first of the major German trench lines they were to encounter in the Hagan Stellung, the Ludwig, within the 2nd line of the German's 1st pre-position. Crashing forward against defending machine-gun fire, Company A men jumped down into it and encountered a small rear guard of a larger force left behind to retard the American's progress as long as possible. A short firefight ensued, described by Pvt. John:

"All of us dropped as close to the ground as we could. There were a lot of them that didn't get close enough to the ground. As soon as Jerry stopped shooting, we crawled around until we found the door leading to the machine gun nest. I threw a hand grenade in and just as it hit the door, it exploded. There were six of them. Three looked as if they were around seventy years of age and had great long whiskers. But the other three looked very young…" (220)

Four live men of the 7th Company, 2nd/122nd were taken prisoner, the leader of which, 2nd Lt. Bezner, was shot in the chest and later died of his wound. The prisoners elicited much interest. Private McCollum and his replacement buddies in A Company stared at the first enemy soldiers they were to see in the war with great curiosity before the prisoners and their guards were sent to look for Major Whittlesey's Headquarters

Company.

Once they found the 1st Battalion PC, the Major questioned the Germans briefly using Private Robert Manson as interpreter. Two were surly and hard looking men who told him little. However, one man cried incessantly, much to the disapproval of his comrades. Private Larney's diary records of the incident:

"We questioned them on size and number of their troops. We brought in one 48 years old crying bitterly, and he continued to cry and wipe his eyes with a dirty handkerchief. He thought we were going to kill him... He took out his cheap billfold and offered Manson all his money if we would not hurt him. He assured him that we would do him no harm." (218)

Soon, Major Whittlesey sent the prisoners back with their small guard detail and the attack continued. Company D, on the left, was encountering similar pockets of men and took in a few prisoners, as did Company B, who captured a live machine-gunner; something akin to rain in the desert thanks to the good work of the 'gangs'. (145)

Experience on the Vesle had taught the New Yorkers the 'gang method' of attack against static machine-gun positions. Now, here in the Argonne, they made full use of all they had learned. Ltieutenant McKeogh described the gang thus:

"The gang is a development of modern warfare. Numbering from eight to twelve, these men are trained specialists who have simulated attacks upon machine gun positions in practice. The gang is an elastic collection of perhaps two scouts, an automatic rifleman with two ammunition carriers, two or three bombers, a rifle grenadier and a couple of bayonet men. Each man has his job. The bombers are particularly effective, because rifle fire — a grazing fire — is not of much avail against the protections of a nest; it is more vulnerable to bombs dropped from above... The automatic rifleman, sometimes called a light machine gunner, can bore and bore like a steel drill on one spot, until eventually his lead breaks through..." (34)

The method that the gangs used differed as each situation dictated but, with persistence, a gang could usually silence a nest in 30 to 45 minutes. Occasionally, there would be another nest, unseen, off on a flank lending enfilading fire. In such a situation, a well-practiced gang could splinter itself and deal with the additional threat as well. And there were to be plenty of opportunities for the gangs to become practiced in the days ahead.

Behind the assault companies, support companies too were facing their own enemy encounters. It was about this time that Pvt. Sidney Smith, in Company H, came across his first dead German:

"...We started to move forward and we came up to this hole, like a grave, and there was the first dead German I seen, some old man in his 60's. I come up there with my gun, ready to shoot down the trench and that old man was sitting there and somebody had shot him right between the eyes." (256)

With increasing daylight, and the resultant burning off of fog, the company commanders slowly began to tie the knots together a little and move forward in larger, more effective, units. Ahead, commanders in company's A and D got what troops they had organized into platoon sections and started filtering out down into Ludwig's system of communication, fire, and support trenches that fanned out around them. Companies B and C continued above, over the broken ground, bringing up the rear with shells falling around them and bullets singing through the air. Company A men, traveling below, came to the end of a trench line and climbed into the face of a rattling machine-gun, well hidden in the wooded edge of a small clearing. It was there that the company lost 2nd Lt. Ransom S. Pattison, the first officer of the 308th to be killed in the offensive. Meanwhile Company D, on the left, was getting away more easily, the Germans apparently having shifted some of their fighting force from that flank toward the center to meet the attacks. And on 1st/308th's extreme right, where a fragile liaison made with 3rd/307th was collapsing due to enemy fire, even an engineer section played a small combat roll. Inadvertently lost out in front of the 307th, a platoon of the "bridge builders" from Company F/302nd Engineers fought off a German machine-gun patrol, captured seven of them, and earned eight divisional citations in the process.

By just after 10:00 a.m., 1st Battalion scouts were at the Tranchee' de Courlande, specifically the Karlplatz trench section. Karlplatz, near the far edge of the Hagan Stellung, was a marvelous complex of defense and dugouts. It comprised several nicely built and furnished concrete and log huts half-sunk into the ground, interlocking and well constructed trenches that had yet to see war, plenty of machine-gun posts, and still more wire. The Doughboys managed to drive German machine-gunners out by about 10:30 a.m. and found that they were now only about 600 meters from the Corps objective. Here, Major Whittlesey finally conceded that the dispersion of his forces was simply too much and with daylight finally broken and the objective in sight, he brought the advance to a temporary halt. The order went out for company officers to organize a line of defense and begin gathering in stray troops.

Men flopped down where they stood and while they rummaged their packs for something to eat, the Major took the opportunity to affect liaison with his flanks. He had already reestablished contact with Major Budd and 2nd Battalion earlier that morning. They in turn had had contact with 3rd Battalion. The 2nd Battalion had also had some contact with the 368th Infantry, on the left flank, about 7:15 a.m. Therefore, in spite of the dispersion, liaison forward in the attack seemed to be progressing rather well.

Not so with Regimental PC behind, however. General Johnson's inquiries of Colonel Prescott concerning the progress of the attack continued throughout the morning, but there was little that Prescott could tell the General. Contact with Major Whittlesey's battalion had been sporadic. Though messages were coming through from all three of his battalions, many of them were taking up to two hours to get back over the horrible terrain, and Colonel Prescott could not tell if his messages were getting forward any sooner than that. Nevertheless, General Johnson telephoned Colonel Prescott with further advance orders around 11:00 a.m., which the Colonel dutifully passed forward, but with little confidence that the message would reach Major Whittlesey in time.

At the attack head, halted in the advance sector, Whittlesey sent word for Major Budd to bring the 2nd Battalion, such as it was, up adjacent on the left, which Budd did over the midday, though with some difficulty. (In truth, it was the only way to hold the line, as neither battalion had enough available troops for the task.) Here, the two battalions accepted a shared responsibility for portions of the front line for the time being, while they continued gathering the stragglers and discussing the morning's events. As they were near the Corps objective for the day, Major Whittlesey made note of the Karlplatz, with an eye to setting up forward Battalion PC there if the opportunity should present itself. (32, 91, 96, 109, 116, 135, 154)

The 308th had gone an average of just under 2 kilometers, an incredible achievement when one considers the truly atrocious conditions under which they were forced to make the attack. The men, while remaining in high spirits, were tiring quickly, though. The task just of moving through the horrible landscape, to say nothing of the nervous strain and shellfire, was beginning to tell. The reorganization could not have come at a better time. Near 11:30 a.m., Colonel Prescott's message for a continued advance showed up. A standing barrage would fall slightly north of the Corps objective at half past noon and then move forward at 1:00 p.m. The 1st Battalion was to follow it, with 2nd in close support, again under strict orders not to intermingle. There was to be no new objective once the

Corps objective was passed. Instead, they were to plow on as fast and as far as possible toward the Combined Army Objective. The reorganization and repositioning of troops continued then until slightly after 1:00 p.m., when the 1st Battalion stepped off behind the advancing barrage for the second time that day. (32, 105)

Immediately after the second jump-off of the day, Company D took their first serious casualties of the day when a shower of machine-gun and sniper fire befell them as they crawled out over the top of the Karlplatz trench system. The rest break had obviously benefited the Germans as well. Despite the confusion behind their lines, they had taken the opportunity to assemble a tactical force in the edge of a swampy area ahead of the 308th. Slowly the Doughboys again forced their way forward. Shortly into D Company's attack, Lt. Akers, on the left, moved his lead platoon further left in an effort to flank some of the German gunners, leaving his support platoon to hold the line. On the right, Lt. Knight swung his lead platoon out yet further right and did likewise. Slowly, the two D Company sections pushed around on either side of the resisted area in an attempt to cut off the Germans, though all the while totally out of touch with each other. It was a maneuver that took real skill and leadership. (32, 96, 105)

At the same time Company A, right of D, met its own share of machine-gun resistance. On their far right flank, Pvt. McCollum remembered:

"...Here, the underbrush was so dense that our only means of advance was by paths cut ...by the Germans and their prisoners. We were coming down the hillside through a small open space in the woods...suddenly, our advance was stopped...We were approaching [a] sweeping cross fire of machine guns...within a few minutes all around us lay the dead and wounded. We retreated, then advanced again...through uncut underbrush where the machine guns were. Locating them...we took these positions..." (32)

Meanwhile, it took D Company nearly the remainder of the afternoon for its two combat forces to link up again, having surrounded and eliminated several machine-gun nests within their combat zone. They were lucky, in that they had only suffered a handful of casualties; three dead and perhaps a dozen wounded. Company A had, so far, suffered eight dead, 23 wounded, and one missing for the day.

By late afternoon, though 1st Battalion had its assault platoons on a fairly straight line again, the attack had broken down into a number of small, local actions; poorly coordinated or controlled. Behind, 2nd Battalion was also doing a lot of "Indian fighting" in the cataclysmic surroundings and therefore the afternoon attack failed to gain any real ground. In the fading light, the clouds rolled in anew and blocked what sun there had been, which simply added to the dismal scene. (105, 109, 136)

It was about 1:30 p.m. when a field message emanating from Division HQ was sent to 1st/307th, acting as division reserve, directing elements of the battalion to pass to General Johnson's command for use "protecting the left flank of the division." The move would place them behind and left of the 308th. As the 1st/307th companies set out, no one knew for sure what the move was all about, only that it didn't sound good. It was not until much later that anyone came to realize that it signaled that the first of a series of problems concerning Groupement Durand had begun.

On the morning of the attack, the right section of Groupement Durand, the 'Negro' 368th Infantry, had its 2nd Battalion in the assault position. Following 500 meters behind in support was 3rd Battalion, who were additionally charged with maintaining liaison between the 2nd/368th and 1st/308th with the help of two platoons sent from Company I/308th. The 1st/368th remained in reserve. Occupying the left section of Groupement Durand, the French 11th Cuirassiers a Pied had a wider zone of attack and therefore placed both their 2nd and 3rd battalions in line (l to r), while holding their 1st battalion in support. Their immediate objective was to capture of the town of Servon and occupy a general line eastward to the regimental boundary line with the 368th. The 368th would, in turn, advance on an even line with the 11th and extend that line further east to the divisional dividing line with the 77th. In the 308th's zone of advance, this would put them on a line about even with Tranchee de Courlande - thought to be an entirely achievable objective. Contrarily, it did not go as planned.

Groupement Durand went over the top and into the wall of foggy darkness that morning at 5:25 a.m. across an open area virtually devoid of any cover. In the advance zone of the 368th, the French 1st Dismounted Cavalry Division (which had immediate local control over Groupement Durand) had allotted only a single French artillery regiment, the 247th, along with a few elements of the U.S. 62nd Artillery Brigade for prepatory fire. Therefore, as the black Doughboys streamed out across the devastated No Man's Land they found to their horror that virtually none of the wire shielding the enemy positions had even been damaged, let alone destroyed, despite the six-hour preceding barrage. Further, the 1st D.C.D. had supplied no heavy wire cutters, and existing lanes in the wire belts were well covered by enemy machine-guns. Once the Doughboys were known by the enemy to be out in the open, the German counter artillery fire started, heavy and accurate. Unit integrity within the 368th collapsed, and there was massive dispersion as the men advancing into the hailstorm of enemy fire desperately sought cover of any kind, or fell back of their own accord. In one section, officers turned the retreating men back to battle at pistol point. In another, men surged forward three separate times. However, with little artillery to support them, they battled across the machine gun-swept open ground west of the great Argonne to little gain.

There were few options open to them, and company commanders found themselves forced to advance what troops they still had available to them down existing communication trenches and paths, fighting tooth and nail against enemy rear guard action every foot of the way. Thus compelled by the extreme circumstances to travel apart from one another, lateral communication between companies instantly disintegrated. In the confusion, the battalion split into three separate and isolated groups—Company G moving on the left, Company F moving up the center, and companies E and H moving on the right.

Company G charged forward and battled desperately against the withering enemy fire, but by dusk had only managed an advance of about half a kilometer. There, in an isolated trench, they set outposts and gained liaison with the 1st Battalion (support) of the 11th C.a.P, whose 3rd Battalion (assault) had, by dark, taken Servon. The 1st/11th refused the French right flank back down to meet with Company G and covered the gap, but on Company G's right, there was only open air.

In the center, Company F had gained the enemy first line trenches with relatively little difficulty, but once there was met with heavy machine-gun fire and immediately split into two dual platoon sections. One group, moving on the right, went up a long German communication trench and forced their way forward about a kilometer by late morning. There they were stopped by terrible machine-gun fire. They battled throughout the midday there, managing to put a scout section forward about another 400 meters, but the whole section was eventually driven back by heavy artillery fire, bit by bit, throughout the long afternoon. By dusk, they had fallen back to a point some 300 meters behind their original jump-off trenches. The other section of Company F had advanced up the same communication trench to roughly the same point as the first section, then turned left and were driven back by much the same artillery fire as the other section, though not quite as far. They took position for the night in an open area just in front of the jump-off trenches. Neither section had communication with each other, or with any other units.

On the right, companies E and H pushed forward separately and took fire all morning. However, by midday they had managed to reach the objective line along Tranchee de Courlande and dug in for a short reorganization. At 1:15 p.m., what remained of the two companies were back on the move, following a narrow gauge rail line forward about another half kilometer. By 2:30 p.m., however, contact with the Company I/308th liaison team to their right, which had never been anything more than sporadic anyway, had been completely lost in the intense fighting. Further reconnaissance revealed no liaison available in any direction - only plenty of enemy. Yet, they continued to battle until nightfall, making no further progress. They were still with no liaison when, almost surrounded by heavy enemy resistance and with massive artillery fire raining down, what remained of them finally fell back as well. They too took up positions behind the original line of departure of that morning not far from, but out of touch with, that portion of Company F located back there as well. With isolated and broken companies scattered all over, there was no real line within the 368th's zone of advance throughout the long night. The regiment suffered casualties of 450 killed, wounded, and gassed for virtually no gain. The day had been a disaster.

Therefore General Alexander, getting disturbing contact reports all morning and recognizing that liaison to the left flank was spotty at best, had hedged his bets by starting elements of the 1st/307th over about 1:30 p.m. to cover the left rear flank. The gamble, as it turned out, paid off. By the close of active operations for the day, there was a cleft directly adjacent to the left flank between the 308th and the 368th that was just about two kilometers wide and almost an equal distance deep. The trouble over there had begun. (10, 46, 91, 92, 139, 146, 367, 370, 374)

In the positions against which companies E and H/368th had been pressing all day, the German 122nd had placed its 10th Company, under 2nd Lt. Hopf, in a forward line position with the 6th Company, under 2nd Lt. Grimminger, in assault reserve. These two companies were to work in collaboration with a section of the 1st/254th, on the regimental west flank, on a security mission. The point of juncture of the two regiments was weak and convoluted, as the 254th was still unsure of its new positions and were receiving support on their right by the 83rd/9th LwD. However, with the two companies of the 122nd in assistance on the 254th's left, security of the joint might then be assured.

The Germans, who had not seen such brazen impudence of fire for many years in the region, marveled at the 368th's initial attacks. The black soldiers came out of the high grass before the wire "as if there were no longer any Germans there," wrote one Landwehr officer, and fell to the attack with a vengeance. Lieutenant Hopf ordered up a machine-gun to deal with the superior numbers of the enemy coming at him, while Lt. Grimminger prepared his own assault and machine-gun units for action. German artillery broke up the attacking Doughboy formations while the 10th's machine-guns arrived and set to. Attacks continued and were repulsed all day. On the 10th's right flank, some 20 to 30 attacking Doughboys did manage to make some headway and break into the Charlotte Valley just beyond the Tranchee de Courlande in the late afternoon. However, assault units of Lt. Grimminger's 6th Company drove them back with grenade launchers and the sector was secure once again, though Grimminger himself was severely wounded in the battle.

That evening, a company of the 254th arrived to take over the positions occupied by the 10th and 6th Companies/122nd. A Doughboy force attacked one last time just as this relief was coming off, "firing and screaming like madmen," according to one German witness. However, they were repulsed, ultimately and bloodily, for a final time. That night the Germans searched the black soldiers' bodies left within the wire for intelligence. Only the confusion of the two different regiments trying to keep that flank secure, the general surprise and intensity of the overall attack, and poor communications between the 122nd and 254th, prevented the Germans from realizing that the entire eastern flank between them and the Americans on their left was wide open for a time that night. (120, 123, 128)

About 3:00 p.m., General Johnson at 154th Brigade Headquarters finally received some solid information from Colonel Prescott concerning the attack, in the form of a field message timed at 2:00 p.m.

At: 272.0 – 295.3

Two companies leading battalion on Corps objective evidently meeting some resistance. Machine guns. Have discovered some machine gun nests in rear of first line. Am mopping them up with the 2nd battalion. Expect to advance 1st battalion during the next hour. Found companies and battalions out of touch with each other and not keeping up liaison on right and left. This I am correcting. Will keep you fully informed as to my position. Will move the front line as soon as I clear out machine guns.

Prescott (131)

It is interesting to note Colonel Prescott's remarks concerning the lack of contact between the companies and battalions, since there is ample evidence to suggest otherwise by that hour of the afternoon. (Liaison, however, was definitely a different story.) More interesting, though, is his apparently personal direction of the attack, when the coordinates of the message show him nowhere near the front line. Nor has there ever been any evidence found which suggests that he ever left his PC that day.

Shortly before 4:00 p.m., General Johnson transmitted instructions to his two regiments for the occupation of the line Fontaine du Ton—Depot de Machines—Moulin de l'Homme Mort, the 1st Army Objective line, which was already to have been reached. However, the 308th was still a considerable distance short of that line, and with the day rapidly drawing to a close, there was little to no chance that they would achieve that particular objective before nightfall.

Also about 4:00 p.m., Major Whittlesey finally received word concerning Groupement Durand and conditions on the left flank. A runner arrived at 1st Battalion PC stating that Company I/308th men had reestablished contact with them, and that units of the 368th were in the process of pulling back due to heavy resistance and intense shellfire. This would leave a gap on the left and few things will upset a commander more than an exposed flank. Major Whittlesey was well aware of the nasty German habit of infiltrating in small groups and then, when the odds were stacked well in their favor, attacking. That was an old Hun trick the regiment learned during the days on the Vesle and the heavily wooded ground now surrounding the 77th Division lent itself perfectly to that sort of tactic. (The results could be devastating and being cut off from the main force became a distinct possibility.)

However, exactly how wide the gap was remained unknown. It is likely that Whittlesey already realized that his flank had conceivably been open all day anyway, since there had been only sporadic liaison from that direction. Last solid contact with the 368th by the 308th attack force had been by a patrol of 2nd Battalion about 7:00 a.m., which had apparently run into some of the 368th's wandering troops. If the dispersion Majors Whittlesey and Budd's units had experienced was any guide to what might be happening over on the left, then that would almost certainly be the situation.

With that the case then, it was probably only the weather, the element of surprise coupled with confusion among the enemy's troops and the intensity of the attack itself that had likely saved the 308th from flank troubles thus far. There had likely been no infiltration yet because there were not enough Germans left, or because they were simply not organized enough, to do the infiltrating. The situation was not yet critical then, no matter how wide the gap. It did, however, definitely have the potential to develop into something precarious, if not attended to in good time. Therefore, it would have been with no small measure of relief to Major Whittlesey when he learned, from the Company I men, of the arrival of the elements of 1st/307th sent over by General Alexander, even though they were only covering the left rear and not the whole left flank gap.

Then, at about 5:30 p.m., the 308th Regimental PC received word from Division that during the night, a squadron of dismounted American cavalry was to move up as protection for the left flank. Whether they actually arrived is unknown. No records have been found either confirming or discounting the action, but it seems extremely unlikely. In any case, by this time, General Johnson had already ordered the Company I/308th liaison platoons, along with a section of Company C/306th M.G. Bn., to turn back and refuse the regiment's left flank. This they had done, extending to the southwest for some 300 meters from Tranchee de Courlande, into the 368th's area of operations, down to Tranchee de Suede. Then, once the 1st/307th elements had shown up and extended the line from there back to the original jump-off line, long-range patrols sent out by Company I made contact that afternoon with retreating elements of the 368th and a runner was sent out to Major Whittlesey with the information. With these units in place, Division felt the left flank secure for the night. Another attempt at securing the ground within the 368th's advance sector would be made tomorrow. Meanwhile, for Major Whittlesey, the situation on the left flank was not any kind of emergency - yet. (132, 135, 138, 139, 146)

Also that afternoon, Division passed down a message from General Pershing himself that illustrated, without any shadow of a doubt, his desire that everyone continue to push on, fight hard, and that there were to be no unnecessary delays. The message read, in part:

Division and Brigade Commanders will place themselves as far up toward the front of advance of their respective units as may be necessary to direct movements with energy and rapidity in any attack. The enemy is in retreat or holding lightly in places, and the advance elements of several divisions are already on the First Army Objective and there should be NO delay or hesitation in going forward. Detachments of sufficient size will be left behind to engage isolated strong points which will be turned and not permitted to hold up or delay the advance of the entire brigade or division. All officers will push their units forward with all possible energy. Corps and Division Commanders will not hesitate to relieve on the spot any officer of whatever rank who fails to show in this emergency those qualities of leadership required to accomplish the task which confronts us... (43, 131)

Close examination of this order is very revealing. First, "holding lightly in places" is a relative statement. It was true that stronger resistance had been expected, but what they had encountered thus far had certainly been no cakewalk. (If the enemy were holding lightly or in retreat, it certainly did not look that way to Company A/308th anyway.) The Germans were stunned, to be sure, and were falling back to more secure places of the line (elastic defense), but "retreat" seems hardly the correct word. Nevertheless, the picture painted by the wording of Pershing's message provided General Alexander with the 'whip' to drive his division on. Most particularly, the statement about "NO delay or hesitation in going forward," was just the ammunition he needed to give the 77th's drive the relentless characteristic he felt necessary for success.

By early evening, a runner had found Major Whittlesey and passed the message that most of Company A had reached the objective line and were holed up, alone, out in a swamp ahead, virtually surrounded on three sides. (Company D was then still out of touch.) The actual objective line ran straight through this swamp and it was doubtful whether any attacker could actually manage to obtain and hold an offensive position in such inhospitable terrain for long. Therefore, Colonel Prescott would simply have to be satisfied with the 308th drawing a 'line in the sand' just before the objective line; if not actually *there*, as per orders, at least still close enough to count, considering the circumstances. In any case, if Company A stayed where they were, they would eventually end up surrounded and cut off and so they must be pulled back.

Therefore, Major Whittlesey decided to call a halt to operations for the night. After floundering around for a bit in the fading light, 1st Battalion PC found their way back to the same dugout the Major had earmarked earlier in the Karlplatz system. Set up there, the Major then dispatched a runner back to Regimental PC and sent word up to Company A, telling them to pull back out of the swamp to a line about 300 meters ahead of the Karlplatz. There the outpost line dug in.

Major Budd arrived at Karlplatz sometime around 5:30 p.m. with companies E, F, and G on line, as well as Whittlesey's lost company D and also began regrouping. He pulled his battalion back up and around to Tranchee de Courlande, again occupying the same spot as earlier on Whittlesey's left, and then joined Major Whittlesey in the Karlplatz bunker with the 2nd Bn. PC. With darkness settling in, Major Budd sent squads out from Company F to patrol the area ahead, while 1st Battalion's A and D held the line. They encountered heavy undergrowth and, much to their surprise began to take fire from enemy machine-guns they discovered within 45 meters of Major Whittlesey's outpost positions! These the men had cleaned out in about 15 minutes. They were learning fast.

As night fell, so did the temperatures and it started to rain once again - hard. No food had come up all day, and no fires were allowed. Men began to suffer without blankets, overcoats, or shelter halves. Lieutenant Arthur McKeogh, Major Whittlesey's adjutant, described it "as if the body was wrapped in iced towels." Men dug in on the outpost line found their funk holes quickly filling with muddy water and were forced to crawl out and try to sleep fully exposed on the open ground. Machine-gunners of the 306th MG Bn., and those who thought themselves lucky to have been in a position to occupy the old German trenches, soon encountered a similar situation. For Majors Whittlesey and Budd and their small command staff, who were occupying one of the nicer abandoned German dugouts, things were a little better. "We found mineral water in bottles," Whittlesey later wrote, trying to find the bright side, "so it might have been worse." The shelling that had started again in the afternoon continued throughout the night. Not that much sleep would have been possible anyway. It was far too cold and wet, and there was plenty of sporadic rifle and machine-gun fire all around to remind them that they were not alone. (40, 105, 109,116, 220)

At 10:00 p.m., 1st Army H.Q. issued orders calling for a continued advance to the Combined Army Objective (the Giselher Stellung), to commence with a barrage at 5:30 a.m. the next morning. Division then passed down the orders, which reached the 308th PC at about 2:15 a.m. of the 27th. General Johnson decided there was no need for a change in unit disposition, so Majors Whittlesey and Budd prepared themselves for another day of dispersion. They were fully aware that their zone of attack was too wide and dense for a single battalion front, even if General Johnson was not as yet. Out on the line, men stared out into the rainy darkness around them, hopeful that tomorrow would be easier than today but probably knowing in their hearts that it would not. (131)

To the east of the 308th, the 307th had faced a similar day. No liaison had ever been properly reestablished with the 308th to the west since right after the jump-off that morning. Nor had any been reestablished with the 306th to their east for that matter either, though not through any lack of effort. The atrocious weather and horrible dispersion that had plagued the 308th had also wreaked havoc within the 307th's zone of advance, as evidenced by this message from Captain E.L. Grant, commanding Company H/307th:

26th September, '18   9.30am

Presume I am at 295.9 – 270.3. Have touch with only one platoon. Am trying to get liaison with 308th on the left, also to the front. Have just found 'K' company, that is, Lt. Pool is here with nine men. (The) Rest are lost.

Grant (103)

It was in a deep trench near Fontaine la Mitte, to the right of the 2nd/307th's sector, that Captain Grant and his men found what they thought they were looking for, fully a kilometer east of where they were supposed to be. Likewise, the problem of intermingling units that the 308th had faced also plagued the 307th, so much so that the 2nd and 3rd battalions eventually merged that day under the command of Major Carl McKinney and Captain Crawford Blagden, though the arrangement was strictly unofficial.

The 307th also met somewhat more determined resistance than had the 308th. Once out of the morning fog and beyond the wire, their afternoon advance pushed forward until only about 2:00 p.m. Then, they were stopped cold by intense machine-gun, trench mortar, and sniper fire from the southern slope of a ravine that stretched from Tranchee des Fontaines, on to Ravin de la Fontaine aux Charmes. They battled in this area for the rest of the afternoon, but to no avail. This placed their outpost line at a point some 200 meters behind the 308th on their left, and some 600 meters ahead of the 306th on their right. Two companies of 2nd/307th then formed back on the right flank in the direction of the 306th and remained there throughout the night. Meanwhile, regular liaison was finally reestablished with the 308th on the left later that night. A basic skirmish line was set up in the dark, fairly straight and solid, of men from both regiments. The advance of the 307th this first day of the offensive had gone only fair and as night fell, they too turned to the task of negating the effects of the massive dispersion that had plagued them all day. Late that night, Captain Walter Kerr-Rainsford, commanding Company L on the far left of the 307th's sector, found himself and the man supposedly guiding him to battalion headquarters lost in the maze of trenches, until:

"...By one o'clock (a.m.), in a 15 foot (deep) trench with unscalable walls and a stream along its bottom, I knew where nothing was, except the guide, my company headquarters, and half a platoon. It rained all night and we slept in the stream..."

And so the 307th passed the night. (103, 138, 139)

The attack had gotten off to a good start; there was no doubt about that. The line had advanced everywhere along the U.S. front. Some 5,000 prisoners had been captured and resistance, as well as casualties, had been lighter than anticipated. The only real dark spot, as far as General Pershing was concerned, had been his army's inability to take the German strongpoint at Montfaucon (considered the strongest point of the Giselher Stellung line in the area) on the first day as he had predicted they would.

As far as General Alexander was concerned, the situation within his zone of attack was perhaps not quite as bright as he would have liked, but it was tolerable. The 77th Division was lagging behind all the rest of the divisions of the offensive, and while this irked him, their performance as a containing force, applying constant and steady pressure against a well-entrenched enemy, had been more than satisfactory. True, there was still the problem of the 368th Infantry, west of the 77th Division. They had not held up their end of the attack and had left the left flank open, which might have resulted in disaster were it not for the element of surprise enjoyed by the attacking Doughboys that first day. They had been damned lucky over there. It had been better off their right flank. Most of the 28th Division had made good and steady progress, all except for their left flank regiment, which was also lagging behind, dragging through the eastern edge of the Argonne. These facts eased

Alexander's ego somewhat concerning the minimal progress of his own division. Nevertheless, one with an axe to grind might say that Alexander's flanks could be the cause of any slow down to those units to his left or right, and there were several with axes to grind with his name on them, as previously discussed.

Yet only 15 hours or so into the planned 72 of the battle, the Germans still had not poured many reinforcements into the area. The 77th had not only reached Corps Objective, but had done so while remaining in relatively good shape and good spirits. Now there they sat, poised and ready to catch up with the rest of the advance line the next day. So there could really be no legitimate complaint about the 77th's first day's progress. (2, 5, 16, 22, 30, 42, 43, 48)

Not so with General Max C.W. Von Gallwitz, in command of German Composite Army Group C, who later wrote:

"I believe myself justified in stating that our front between the Argonne [Forest] and the Muese [River] was broken through on September 26th, as the Americans in several places had penetrated to the extent of seven kilometers. (This was a maximum. The average was four; less in the Argonne itself. – author) Of my Army Group only two weak divisions, holding together a front of fourteen kilometers, were located near the Muese. The principle penetrations were made in Bois de Cheppy, near Very, Cuisy, and Sivry…" (30)

Truth be told, the Germans had almost lost their hold in the Muese-Argonne sector. Almost.
But that was just the first day.

Ancillary sources used in this chapter include: 50, 87, 90, 93, 94, 95, 97-101, 113, 117, 119, 140, 142, 144, Various 152-215, 227, 230, 233, 235, 246, 252

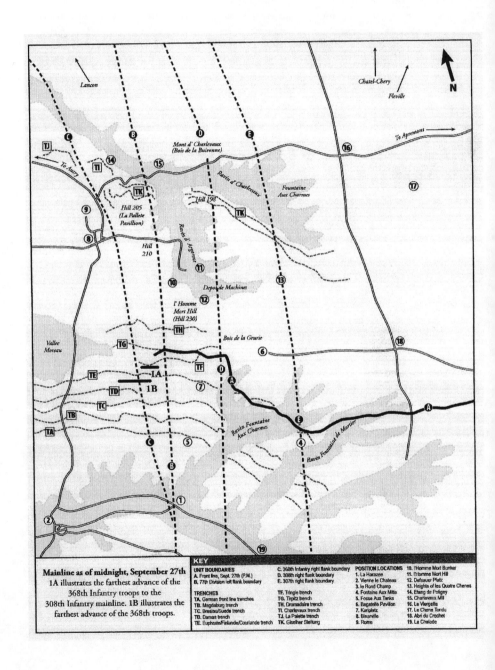

Mainline as of midnight, September 27th

1A illustrates the farthest advance of the 368th Infantry troops to the 308th Infantry mainline. 1B illustrates the farthest advance of the 368th troops.

September 27, 1918

"…Already in the evening the danger was averted by bringing up reserves. On the 27th and 28th we had no more worries…"

German General Max C.W. Von Gallwitz, commanding Composite Army Group C, Argonne Forest.

By the night of the 26th, the Germans had nothing but machine-guns in some places of the Muese-Argonne line with which to stop the oncoming tide of American troops. At one point in the Aire Valley, only a single depleted German infantry regiment, the 20th, blocked the way. However, despite the very thinness of their line, the German plan of elastic defense had paid off well. The long, wet night of September 26-27 bought them the time they needed for their stunned troops to pull back to the relatively stronger positions deeper within the Etzel Stellung and time for reinforcements to start down from the Kriemhilde. The German general staff, though at first taken by surprise by the sheer magnitude of the attack, nevertheless managed to keep relatively cool through all that was taking place. The front sent them reports hourly and they in turn methodically issued orders designed to stem the hemorrhage of American troops pouring through the ruptured lines. (I)

At this critical juncture, had the American forces engaged in a night attack—and the plan had been given some consideration at one point—it is entirely possible that the Combined First Army Objective could have been reached by dawn of the 27th. It is doubtful if the Doughboys could have pulled off such an attack in the Argonne Forest however, considering the atrocious weather conditions and equally deplorable terrain. Thus, the American advance unknowingly paused for the night at a strategic strait that gave the Germans the time they needed to reinforce their already formidable defensive positions. Therefore, the German official communiqué for the morning of the 27th read in part:

…The great American and French attempt to break through, with its extensive objectives, failed on the first day of the battle as a result of the stubborn opposition of our troops. New battles are imminent…

"Failed" was far from the correct word, to be sure. It is a debatable point as to whether it was a stubborn enemy that had stopped the U.S. forces from reaching farther ahead than they had that first day, and not perhaps the difficulties of the terrain and the conditions under which the attack had been launched. One thing was not debatable though: If there had been any weakness in the German line ahead that the American troops might have exploited that first night in the zone of the 1st Corps, it was gone by the morning of the second day. (30, 122)

The 1st Corps orders for the 27th directed that the battle be jump-started again at 6:00 a.m., after a half-hour artillery barrage had fallen 100 meters ahead of the line that had held through the night. The order also contained an ominous line that, at the time, seemed appropriate enough considering the situation. It stated that the advance was to be "pushed (forward) without reference to troops to the right or left." This wording, which would return in slightly different forms repeatedly in the days to come, had been inserted into the order for a particular reason.

The valley of the Aire River, east of the Argonne Forest, was one of the main avenues of attack intended for breaking through to the all-important Kriemhilde Stellung. The key to the Aire Valley, however, was not thought to be the taking of the Argonne Forest so much as that of Butte de Montfaucon, east of the valley. This high, commanding hill was within the 5th Corps zone of attack. From up on its heights, the Germans had a clear view of the eastern edge of the valley. Combined with the heights along the eastern edge of the Argonne, around a promontory called le Chene Tondu (within the zone of the 28th Division), which looked down on the valley from the west, this effectively blocked use of the Aire Valley from any advance.

General Pershing had relied on taking Montfaucon hill and the ruins of the town and cathedral there, on the first day of the offensive and had every confidence that his army was fully capable of the feat. Marshal Foch however thought this plan sheer madness, since Montfaucon was considered the single strongest position along the whole of the Hindenburg Line in the Muese-Argonne sector. Frontal assault through Montfaucon Woods and then up its long, bare slopes was simply suicide. Both men, as it turned out, were wrong, but neither by much.

General Pershing's plan was to pinch off Montfaucon in a similar way as with the Argonne Forest. The 91st Division would attack left, the 37th Division would attack near the center, and the 79th Division would attack center right, with the 4th Division, a part of 3rd Corps, providing right flank support to the 79th. Unleashed however, the plan faltered that first day. The 91st, most of the 37th, and the 4th pushed out ahead, reached their objectives and there they stopped, marking time as per orders and waited for the rest of the attack force to catch up. The 79th however, a division of 60 percent green replacements, had met withering machine-gun and artillery fire along the slopes of the hill. Darkness found them still below and looking up at the ruins. Adding to the disaster, several units from the three advanced divisions had fallen back some as well.

Simply put, had those units in advanced positions (the 91st, the 37th, and the 4th) been allowed to press forward rather than simply marking time on the Corps Objectives that first day, Pershing's staff felt it entirely conceivable that the Germans may have abandoned Montfaucon altogether. The likelihood of being surrounded by the three Doughboy divisions in such a scenario would perhaps have been too much for the relatively weak defenders. After all, it was principally the formidable position itself that was keeping the Doughboys out. However, it had not played out as such the first day and therefore 1st Army needed to figure a way to prevent such a wonderful opportunity from slipping through their fingers again. Hence, the line in the general order passed down through Corps on to each division stating that the advance be "pushed forward without reference to troops to the right or left".(5, 35, 116, 142)

Obviously, the intent of the order—in light of what had happened at Montfaucon—was to keep divisions from slowing their attack should a neighboring *division* not be doing so well. In other words, do not wait for a neighboring *division* to advance on a line even with you. Instead, push forward and continue the attack, regardless of the progress of flanking divisions. On the other hand, the order might also have been interpreted in a more literal sense to mean do not wait for a neighboring *unit* (such as brigade, regiment, or even company) to advance on a line even with you, but push ahead. The word "troops" is never clearly defined. Therefore, it appeared to give those outside the 1st Army general staff— divisional, brigade, and regimental commanders—apparent carte blanche to press forward with a unit's attack at all costs, regardless of the unit's size or, more importantly, its situation. This was the interpretation of the order that Generals Alexander and Johnson of the 77th Division apparently assumed defined the challenging situation that their commands faced in the tremendously difficult Argonne.

This leads to the quandary. The order left little room for interpretation with the lower level officers who would actually be doing the attacking and thus be in the best position to understand the conditions surrounding an attack. They were not to be consulted on the matter but simply be given their orders and then expected to carry them out, regardless of the situation or consequences. At first glance, this may seem an obvious recipe for disaster, but the reasoning behind the order is actually militarily sound in this case.

Few emergency officers of the AEF were believed to possess the experience or depth of military thought necessary to see the battle in the abstract way that the high command did. Correctly, their primary concerns encompassed their command, what transpired immediately around and in it, and those actions immediately concerning it. What effect their own actions, or lack thereof, might have on other units or the battle as a whole, remained pretty much beyond their scope, for the most part. Consequently, if left to make their own decisions in tight situations they might, say, withdraw or stall their drive in the face of violent resistance in an effort to save lives within their units and the resulting aftereffects be damned. That withdrawal or stall might, in turn, have its effect on a neighboring unit and cause a withdrawal or stall there. The effect could ripple on down the line, ending in the loss of the all-important momentum to the overall offensive, similar to what had occurred in limited form before Montfaucon (although there it had been an ordered halt that had caused the problem). Therefore, these new orders had now been modified to allow continued assault under almost any circumstance, regardless of how ill advised that continuation might seem in the minds of the lower level officers in command. (II)

This was a dangerous precedent (albeit a very necessary one) that in the coming days would have further reaching effects than anyone realized. For even though the order was rarely to be followed to the letter, when it was it would provide for both great success - and tragedy.

The rain came down relentlessly all that first night, only slacking off some in the early morning hours of the 27th. So too did the German shellfire. Gas was mixed in with the shrapnel, but fortunately, the rain had negated much of its effects. Otherwise, the troubled outpost Doughboys, sleeping beside their muddy funk holes might have found the situation much more intolerable, having to attempt sleep in the hated gas masks. Farther behind, where men were taking up positions within the old German quarters, it was a little better. Back in the Battalion PC at Karlplatz, Signalman Private Jim Larney, sleeping on the floor of the same dugout as Major Whittlesey, was at least out of the rain. He wrote in his diary that night, "no blankets, real cold, no rest... someone stole my chunk of bread," while outside the machine-guns kept up a sporadic, nervous chatter all night long. (218)

On the exposed left flank, the two platoons of Company I/308th and elements of Company C/ 306th M.G. Bn. struggled to maintain refusal of the open flank there. It was not an easy job in the dark, rainy, unfamiliar territory, so the left flank remained something of a mess most of the night. While right flank liaison to the 307th was firmer, it also contained plenty of room for doubt as to where exactly the solid line ran.

Company commanders in 1st and 2nd/308th got little sleep that night. Most spent those hours at attempted reorganization of their fractured, scattered companies and tried to scare up some rations. Sergeants and corporals worked hard, ensuring their men were well set into position and had plenty of ammunition. The two battalion commanders themselves worked harder than anyone else did. Major Budd wanted to have his command settle in for the night something as it had been for the initial attack, but the murky pre-dawn found him still trying to tie up loose ends and scrounge rations. His night patrols, probing into the line ahead, reported that there would probably be a good bit of resistance for the second day's attack if the scattered machine-gun fire throughout the night and ghostly movements in the far brush were any indication. Major Whittlesey's scouts were reporting much the same, but Whittlesey, sick and sleepless, faced yet another, more immediate problem in those morning pre-attack hours. (109, 132, 133, 146)

Sometime, well before daylight of the 27th, Major Whittlesey received a message from Colonel Prescott directing him to send 20 of his 1st Battalion men back to be detailed as runners to fill the depleted ranks of Regimental Headquarters. Colonel Prescott's original runners had long since gone that first day, as had much of his staff, disappearing into the fog. Conversely, few outside runners had been able to reach the Regimental PC with incoming messages or condition reports in the dirty weather and confusion, so there had been no natural re-supply of men. Regimental was therefore basically blind of front-line information. Colonel Prescott apparently figured that men from the point of the drive (1st Battalion) would be in the best position to not only provide current battle information, but would also be most familiar with the battlefield as well, making them more efficient runners. Rest for the near exhausted men apparently never figured into his equation.

When he received the message, Major Whittlesey was apparently beside himself. His men were worn out and hungry from the horrendous first day of the advance. It was cold and raining like hell, and now the Regimental Commander wanted them to burn up what little strength they had left as runners. This time, he felt the Colonel had gone too far and according to Lost Battalion and Charles Whittlesey historian Fletcher Pratt, the fever-wracked and exhausted Major did something completely out of the ordinary for him. He refused the order.

Major Whittlesey next called Colonel Prescott from the advanced telephone head and reportedly told the Colonel that since he was then in Brigade Reserve he was under no obligation to follow such an outrageous order. Exactly why Major Whittlesey claimed this that night remains something of a mystery, as does the exact, full content of the call. (No log of the phone call was apparently taken, or if it was it remains to be found.) One possible explanation could be that he had already called General Johnson and discussed the situation with him before calling Colonel Prescott, at which time the General most probably placed the Major's command temporarily under those orders, to be lifted only come morning advance time. Both Generals Johnson and Alexander would have been the only ones with the power to place Major Whittlesey and his command in such a position. However, there is no evidence to suggest that Major Whittlesey and General Alexander ever knew, met, or even spoke to each other before October 8, following the episode in the Charlevaux Ravine. Therefore, it had to be General Johnson. If that is the case then (and it more than likely is), the order was evidently never put to paper. Major Whittlesey certainly would not have lied about such a thing, and General Johnson, having worked with Whittlesey on the Vesle already, knew the Major to be both a fair-minded and dependable officer. He would probably have been predisposed to listen to the Major's case then. On the other hand, already by this time the Brigadier was starting to become well aware of some of Colonel Prescott's deficiencies and reportedly was never too fond of him anyway. Whatever the arrangements made that night, they had the desired consequences; the Major got to keep his men and Colonel Prescott was forced to scrounge runners from some other quarter. While it was not the first clash that Whittlesey and the unpopular Prescott had, it would be the last. (274)

In his memoirs, General Alexander stated that although 1st Army ordered renewal of the attack for the morning of the 27th, he himself had no exaggerated expectations of a great advance that day within his own divisional sector. If true (and the general's memoir is full of questionable statements), he was not to be disappointed by the 308th. The morning dawned murky and dirty again and a blanket of mist hung in the air over a thick carpet of fog that rolled around the shivering, muddy Doughboys huddled in their holes. At 5:30

a.m., the barrage started flying overhead and everyone in the 1st and 2nd/308th set themselves to move forward. However, even as shells screamed over into 'Hunland', no final orders authorizing the advance had yet come up from Colonel Prescott at Regimental PC and as the barrage dragged on toward its lifting time, Major Whittlesey grew more concerned. He could not move without final orders authorizing him to do so and if they did not come up soon, the barrage would get away from them. Runners sent out returned empty handed. The signalmen's telephone lines were a mess; German shells overnight had pounded the area and cut most of them. Slowly the clock edged forward. Finally, Whittlesey and Budd were forced to simply stand by their respective commands the second morning of the offensive and impotently watch the barrage walk away at 6:00 a.m. Their orders had miscarried. It did not portend of a good day. (131, 132)

It was full light, 8:40 a.m. - two and a half hours after his regiment was to have stepped off into the Argonne once again - before Colonel Prescott finally got around to sending out word to General Johnson concerning his lack of forward progress:

Unable to get orders to C.O. 1st Bn in time to follow barrage this A.M., also unable to get 2nd Bn together until 7:30 A.M... I believe an advance can be made now without serious loss if troops on right and left come up so as to protect flanks... Will have telephone here very soon.
Prescott (131)

Although it is never exactly explained why in this deceptively short field message, we may surmise that Colonel Prescott's inability to get orders up to Major Whittlesey in time for the jump-off that morning may likely be due in part to situational ignorance. For despite the façade that he tried hard to present to General Johnson in his last dispatch of the evening before, it appears that Colonel Prescott actually had little substantive perception of most of his command's actual whereabouts through that night. This may or may not have been his fault, however. The incredible dispersion of the 1st and 2nd battalions in terrain that would have challenged any combat leader, experienced or not, and the lack of firm communications that dispersion brought, no doubt had a great deal to do with that apparent situational ignorance. Add those problems to the fact that the Colonel was not even a combat infantry leader and there is little wonder why he apparently was incapable of performing the duties of directing his regiment during the advance, or of knowing their exact whereabouts. Further, while it was true that 2nd Battalion still had some stragglers wandering in even as the sky began to lighten in the east (Company G had been particularly hard hit by dispersion the afternoon before) the dispersion of the support battalion hardly seems reason enough to hold up the lead battalion's initial advance.

A better explanation for the delay is found in Colonel Prescott's next sentence, stating his belief that "an advance might now be made without serious loss if troops on right and left come up so as to protect flanks". The statement is ominous; he is obviously nervous about making an attack without flank support, thus illustrating the "incorrect thinking" that the morning's advance orders ("push forward without reference to troops to the right or left") apparently sought to eradicate altogether. Colonel Prescott would have had no way of knowing that the order had originated as a divisional redress. General Johnson was certainly not going to tell him - if that was what Johnson himself believed in the first place, which later events seem to indicate was not the case anyway. Be that as it may, the 308th was not that far advanced of the 307th on the right to begin with, and even if the 368th was nowhere to be found on the left, that was no reason to simply ignore orders and not move forward as instructed. Therefore, Colonel Prescott was in dereliction of duty.

Something along those lines probably crossed General Johnson's mind when Colonel Prescott's message crossed his desk at Brigade PC about 10:40 a.m. that morning. Reading it, the Brigadier became incensed. It was inconceivable that Colonel Prescott would risk losing the initiative that the 308th had so desperately won the day before, here at the critical juncture of the second day's advance! That advance was then almost *five hours* overdue when General Johnson fired off a message back to Colonel Prescott at 10:45 a.m.:

If you have not moved, do so at once and comply with your orders. The battalion on your right moved at 6 a.m. today. Report at once whether you have moved and your action. Also position of advanced troops. (131)

It was shortly thereafter, about 11:00 a.m., when General Alexander called to check progress of the attack in the 154th Brigade sector and General Johnson reluctantly was forced to give up the tragic information.

"Do I understand that Prescott has not advanced?" General Alexander asked sternly.

Johnson was compelled to admit as much.

"Yes sir. That is correct."

"Then if he has not advanced, you are to relieve him at once from his command and send him here under arrest!" Alexander fumed and the line went dead.

But who would take Prescott's place? (131)

Actually, Colonel Prescott's replacement was already waiting at Division Headquarters; an old salt, career Army Colonel just transferred in from the 3rd Division, Colonel Cromwell Stacey. Stacey was the son of a Civil War colonel and he and his sister grew up in army camps during the middle of the Indian campaigns, where a close friend of the family was General William Tecumseh Sherman. Therefore, it was not surprising then that Cromwell would begin a career in the military at his earliest convenience, becoming a U.S. Marine Corps drummer boy at 16 in 1892, serving aboard the U.S. flagship *San Francisco* with the Coast Guard during the Nicaraguan Revolution. By 1898, he was a well-experienced 18-year-old 2nd Lieutenant in the U.S. Army Regulars and served throughout the Spanish-American War with the Puerto Rican Expedition, seeing some of the hottest action of the war. His next tour of duty took him throughout the Philippine Insurrection era of 1899 through 1914 where, as a Captain of the prestigious Scouts, he earned fame and notoriety among his contemporaries as the Army's "Scout of Scouts," as well as a Silver Star for bravery. He finished his time in the Philippines as president of several tribal wards and a company commander in the 2nd Battalion/21st Infantry.

From 1914 to the American entry into the World War in 1917, he served first as a Captain of Infantry and then as unassigned inspector/instructor to the Arizona and Illinois National Guards. When General Leonard Wood started his officers training camps, Stacey became examining officer and senior instructor for the camp held at Fort Sheridan, Illinois. For his exceptional work, General Wood - a close, personal friend of Stacey - promoted him to Lt. Col. at the outbreak of war. In December 1917, Wood assigned him as assistant regimental commander of the 30th Infantry Regiment, to be part of the 3rd Division, which was then forming for overseas duty at Camp Green, North Carolina. It was with the 30th that he went to France, arriving there on March 10, 1918.

Upon arrival in France, Lt. Col. Stacey attended and graduated the 2nd Corps school at Chatillon-sur-Siene, and was then attached to the French 161st Infantry as an observer to obtain practical experience. With them, he spent two weeks up in the Lorraine sector in May. In June, he fought through the battle of Chateau-Thierry, actually commanding the bulk of the 30th through combat while his Regimental Commander took charge of the divisional reserves. At the end of the month he was given a field rank of full Colonel, though retained his status as Regimental Sub-Commander. The 3rd Division would gain true fame in July 1918 for stopping the Germans at the Marne River during their fifth, and last, drive toward Paris, thus gaining them the unit designation "Rock of the Marne" division. During the battle, Colonel Stacey earned the Croix de Guerre with Palm for bravery under fire for rescuing a horribly wounded private from certain death, greatly risking his own life in the process. He commanded from the front line, never from the rear, and had the respect of everyone in his regiment for that.

After the battle, Stacey was hospitalized for a short time with Mustard gas burns and poisoning; he had taken his mask off during a gas attack so that his men could clearly hear his orders. At the end of July, he was given full command of the 30th, taking it in battle along the Vesle River and around the town of Fismes before the 77th Division showed up. While under his command, the 30th participated in the reduction of the St. Mihiel salient, where they performed admirably and Stacey again saw all the action from the head of the attack. Happy and popular in his post with a unit that he had helped form and bring to France then, he was surprised and much chagrinned when on September 22 he received orders transferring him to the 77th Division to take over a regiment there. Colonel Stacey and the 3rd Division's overall commander, Major General Beaumont Buck, had seriously clashed over some of Stacey's 'policies', not the least of which were several comments the Colonel had made about the division commander's handling of his regiment in the battle before the Marne. General Buck, outraged out of proportion to Colonel Stacey's comments (which might arguably have had a ring of truth to them), had the errant Colonel transferred, in apparent retaliation. (III)

About midday on September 27 therefore, after a hard trip, Colonel Stacey arrived on the doorstep of 77th Division Headquarters. There he met with General Alexander, who informed him that he would be placed in command of the 307th Infantry at the earliest opportunity. (Colonel Houghton, remember, was actually the regimental machine-gun officer and only temporarily in charge of the 307th.) However, by that time, the regiment was already actively engaged, and General Alexander said that he wanted things to stabilize some before he sent the Colonel forward to assume command. Stacey, for his part, settled in to wait for his turn at bat with his new regiment. The wait would not be long. That afternoon, with Colonel Prescott relieved of his command for dereliction of duty, General Alexander gave Colonel Stacey command of the 308th instead and left Colonel Houghton in command of the 307th permanently. Therefore, at about 2:00 p.m. that afternoon, Stacey again gathered his things together and then set out for the 308th's advanced Regimental PC. (238, 347)

The delay in the jump-off that morning gave Majors Whittlesey and Budd a chance to make thorough inquiries of the individual company commanders concerning the replacements that each battalion had earlier received. The results were far from encouraging. A large proportion of casualties taken thus far were 40th Division men, which was not at all surprising considering the lack of training some had. On the other hand, the replacements that had managed to survive that first day had proven themselves strong stuff, just the kind of fighters the regiment needed in the hell of the Argonne. They stuck together in small groups, largely ignoring the New York men as being neither like them nor interesting, and took to the woods fighting business as easily as could be expected from men who had emanated from the Midwest and Northwest - both largely areas of woodland. It was second nature to be out in the forest for a majority of them, and the New York men quickly gained a new respect for the "hayseeds" and "apple knockers" who had so recently invaded their venerated ranks.

The 40th Division boys, in turn, found themselves admiring the sheer tenacity of the New Yorkers in battle. These men, whose only previous experience with trees had in many cases been a visit to Central Park on Sunday, had forced themselves to adapt to the unfamiliar surroundings, with an attitude of "If those guys can do it, I sure as hell can!" (which is a very 'New York' way of thinking). The New Yorkers, as could be expected, largely kept to themselves as well. Nevertheless, some in the two groups did manage to put cultural and geographic differences aside and a few friendships formed.

However, the attrition of the replacements still bothered Major Whittlesey a great deal, more than even he himself admitted at the time. As the battle wore on and fatigue, hunger, and just plain inexperience caused casualties to mount, so too did the Major's own nervous strain of watching that happen lead him to go to relatively abnormal lengths as a commander in an effort to save lives. Privately, he and Major Budd together expressed outrage and concern at the criminal lack of training the replacements had received, but this was of little consequence. Even Colonel Stacey, soon to take over the 308th and to be Whittlesey's commander during the hardest part of the battle, later expressed a great measure of affront that these men had gone into battle not even knowing the basics of how a hand grenade operated. It was only Major Whittlesey's strong sense of professionalism that kept him from voicing his opinions more resolutely and in front of those who should have known better. Again, the Major's grasp of the 'big picture' meant that he also understood the need for those replacements, trained or untrained. That understanding rendered the outrage he felt impotent, thus creating an emotional quandary that a man as sensitive and dedicated as Charles Whittlesey would be hard pressed to reconcile. (1, 26, Various 52-86, 109, 116, Various 152-215, 351)

There had also been no ration detail overnight, nor had the rolling kitchens made it up, and so hunger raised its ugly head that morning. Despite the efforts of Whittlesey and Budd to find food, many men who had moved into the jump-off trenches on the night of the 25th without any rations in the first place went into the battle on the 27th hungry again. Likewise, no clean water made it up to the lines, forcing canteens to be filled by what rain water had been caught overnight or with water from shell and funk holes, which was at best only muddy and at worst gas contaminated. (95)

Around 12:30 p.m., a drizzly, irritating rain began to fall again, increasing the close, earthy odor of the forest. Morosely, men sank deeper into shallow funk holes in the sodden ground, waiting out the stall of the advance. German shells tore down through the haze, and machine-guns chattered occasionally out ahead as patrolling scouts probed enemy positions. Private Nell, in Company G said:

"...Most everyone was wet and stiff from the cold and hunger... we were to move out to a new objective this day. The fog was heavy and the shells dropping now and then close by could be seen through the mist, bursting a pinkish red and with a terrific crack and roar. The machine guns on both sides were popping..." (40)

The 307th had been underway for something close to eight hours already when, about 2:00 p.m., General Johnson received a message from Colonel Prescott, timed at 1:43 p.m. and reading:

Troops now moving to advance. Will be at telephone in person as soon as get things well started — say in about 40 minutes.

Prescott (131)

It was just after 1:30 p.m. in the steadily increasing rain shower when once more the men of the 1st and 2nd/308th climbed up from the muddy protection of their funk holes and out from under trees and bushes and began to move into the heavy woodland before them. To Private John, in Company A, it felt as though he was reliving a nightmare from which he could not wake up. A detached sense of his surroundings (a by-product of exhaustion) seemed to have him in a firm grip, while all around him he again watched his comrade's fall. There was nothing he could do for them—orders still held to continue on and either let those from behind gather the wounded, or let them fend for themselves. Twenty-four years later, the memory still haunted him as he wrote:

"…Marching on and on, I didn't think anything of stepping over dead bodies of men with whom I had started out or wading through a pool of blood… To think back, I can just see them drop; to look at them and hear what they said and their requests for help. But we had to go on and leave them lay for others to aid when they could work up to them. I don't know who felt worse…" (220)

With great difficulty, they passed into the swampy woodland ahead where ran the line of the 1st Corps Objective of the previous day, then out of the marshy bog and onto dryer ground beyond. Once in the underbrush across the swamp, enemy machine-guns waited. The advancing Doughboys began to take serious fire from seemingly all sides. Major Whittlesey's men scrambled for what cover they could get, some failing and dropping as others found respite. Private Smith in Company H remembered:

"Our officers started us out, one following the other, and ordered us not to get bunched up, not to get closer than five feet, so we wouldn't all get killed. We passed over one knocked out German machine gun, and then another one off to the left side opened up, and another one in front of us, and one off down to the side. They was a shell hole there with water in it, and I hit that…" (256)

Officers and NCO's immediately crawled off through the wet leaves looking for ways of performing flanking maneuvers on the German nests. Lieutenant Arthur McKeogh, Major Whittlesey's diminutive little adjutant, best describes the 'gang method' used by the Doughboys to take out the many machine-guns they met:

"…Worming his way towards the sound… the officer studies each bush, each irregularity of the ground… (he) notices little white "bites" suddenly appearing low on the bark of the trees. Then he spots it! That big bush ahead… Leaves do not turn their paler underside to the light. Here there are many such, indicating that fresh cut boughs have been inserted at an un-natural angle in the bush… big rocks piled a little too regularly… a thick tree trunk lying flat. Just in front of the bush the forest is a little thinner, offering something approximating a field of fire. The forepart of the gun takes shape — the slender muzzle… its "flash screen"… the fat, round "jacket"… The officer notes surrounding objects… then he crawls back to his men.

With minuteness he tells his non-coms where it is. "Sergeant, you take their left — Corporal, I'll go with you to the right. Let's go." One by one… the men crawl out along the lines of a 'V'. As they draw nearer, the nest breaks into a frenzy of fire. A courageous German dashes out from the rear… to throw… hand grenades… For the first time, American bullets are spent. The Boche drops… The auto rifles get into the action… a bomb drops at the edge of the nest. Another seems to have exploded right on top of it!… They've stopped firing now. Is it a trick? No… through the trees at the rear two gray-green figures are darting… "Get 'em!"… a dozen Yanks plunge after them… The officer looks at his watch… nearly an hour has elapsed… that seemed like ten minutes. Four of his men have been killed; six wounded. Four Germans are dead; one badly wounded.…

"Sergeant, let's get going". (34)

Slowly they beat their way past machine-guns and came into the first German trench systems of the Hagan Stellung Nord. Similar to those they had encountered the day before, these were much more complex. Dugouts, well-concealed fire steps, and concrete machine-gun platforms seemed everywhere. What the forest did not conceal, it camouflaged. Barbed and chicken wire nets were slung between trees several feet high, which were now grown over by brush and vines and undetectable until a man ran headlong into it, thinking it only more brush to drive through. On the other side of the net was usually at least one machine-gun - the spider guarding its web. Here was where the men of the 308th also experienced the rare hell of hand-to-hand combat for the first time. The Germans, under orders to hold at all costs, did just that. The fighting progressively took on a more vicious, relentless and brutal face. Trench knives, brass knuckles, shovels and hand grenades were the weapons of the day as the Doughboys and Germans met man-to-man in the trenches and woods, while the shells rained down around them all.

They had only managed to battle forward about 150 meters north into the forest beyond the swamp before Major Whittlesey decided that to make any real headway at all, the sudden influx of Major Budd's men in 2nd Battalion was needed. He sent word back ordering Budd to swing his men around to the left and come up on an even line again. (Major Whittlesey, as lead battalion commander, had the authority to use his support battalion in such a way if he felt the situation warranted it.) Major Budd, who was actually the most experienced battalion commander in the 308th, easily recognized the need for this himself and in compliance readily moved his men into place quickly. (132, 134, 136)

Major Kenneth Pepperell Budd is the forgotten battalion commander of the whole Lost Battalion saga, overshadowed by his later successor, George McMurtry. A quiet, intensely private, unassuming and rather tall, bald and cadaverous looking man in his late 30s by the time he served in the Army, he possessed a seemingly permanent and highly intense stare, which made many who were required to deal with him uncomfortable. There is, however, evidence based on his record that he was perhaps one of the finest officers of the 308th and one with whom other officers genuinely liked to work.

A Harvard graduate, Ken Budd had been a successful dry goods merchant before attending the Plattsburg camps of 1916 and 1917. He was made an assistant instructor in 1917 due to his innate abilities as an officer and teacher. Then, demonstrative of his abilities, upon graduation he was offered the rank of Major straightaway but turned it down, not yet feeling himself personally qualified for the responsibilities of the rank. At his own request, he was promoted Captain instead. However, due to his outstanding record at Plattsburg and tremendous efforts in organization within the new 77th Division, which he had been assigned to in August, he could not long avoid eventual promotion. Therefore, on January 1st, 1918 Captain Budd was promoted to Major and given command of the 2nd Battalion/308th Infantry. It was Ken Budd then who had taken 2nd Battalion over to France and through their first battles in the Baccarat sector and then on to the 'fist-fight on the Vesle', where he was gassed severely. Fortunately, he returned to his command just prior to their move up into the Argonne, apparently little worse for the wear. (72, 84, 347)

Just how much input Major Budd actually had in the decisions that Major Whittlesey faced in the Argonne can only be guessed, but it is easy to imagine Whittlesey co-conspiring with the more accomplished battalion commander, as he was no doubt well aware of the intrinsic value of Budd's greater field experience. Whittlesey also respected Budd as an officer of high intellect, something that obviously meant a lot to him. For his own part, it appears Budd recognized Whittlesey's innate 'commanding respect' (something all good leaders intrinsically possess) and saw the Major as a thoughtful and intelligent combat officer who would see the job done. In any case, it was becoming increasingly clear to both officers that second day, that the German plan of defense had evolved into interlocking fields of machine-gun fire, echeloned in depth the farther the Doughboys advanced. Both officers also agreed that only men - and lots of them - acting in complete unison could overcome those difficult obstacles.

The arrival of Major Budd's men on the advance line however was both a blessing and a curse. A blessing because the sudden swarms of American infantry unnerved the Germans, working them up until they could not resist the temptation to fire and thus giving away their most cleverly hidden positions for the Doughboys to capture or eliminate. A curse because the specter of dispersion began to rear its ugly head once again as it had the day before. Units mixed into one another as they tried to find an accessible route through the heavy underbrush, while at the same time trying to minimize casualties and fight off an enemy now only too willing to close with the bayonet. Therefore, instead of two distinct battalions moving in unison, what Major Whittlesey instead actually got was a 'swarm' of men from both battalions moving along as best they could. (34, 91, 132, 133, 136)

What happened to Company D is indicative of what the other units faced and provides a good illustration of what the bloody advance entailed. After untangling itself from some 2nd Battalion units, Company D checked course, shifted, and again moved out straight ahead. Second and third platoons under Lt. Akers were on the left; first and fourth platoons under Lt. Knight were on the right. Immediately after cutting their way through a mass of German barbed wire well out in front of the main line, the company was hit in the face with withering machine-gun fire from multiple nests. Disregarding the resistance, they continued to push forward through the chilly rain against nest after nest for the next four hours with brutal tenacity. During the course of the afternoon's fighting, liaison between the left and right was lost. Yet, the two forces continued to advance, inches at a time, independent of each other.

On the right, all of the Chauchat auto rifles under Lt. Knight jammed, leaving the two platoons' gangs to rely on rifle and grenade alone. On the left, Lt. Akers's men pushed on through a particularly dense portion of the forest, wreathed in wire, doggedly slamming away at the enemy until it was too dark to advance anymore. They settled down for the night in improvised trenches, near the last nest they had cleaned out, where Lt. Akers first set listening posts before sending out liaison parties to try to locate Lt. Knight's group. Just as the last of the light was fading from the forest, the right group finally came up even with the left and the line was indeed a line again. Enemy observers must have been up ahead though, as the position was accurately and thoroughly shelled several times that night, killing one man and wounding several. Attacks from German patrols also continued sporadically throughout the night; terrifying things in the rain-swept dark of the woods. Most outposts managed to successfully fend off the attackers, but it was a long night. (105)

Company A, meanwhile, drew up on a corduroy road deep in the woods that afternoon. Few paths or roads were marked on the Allied maps of the forest, but intelligence had warned of this. While the company lay down in the mud on its edge, Lt. Whiting sent runners and scouts out to gather in strays and ordered Sgt. Herman Anderson to grab two men and scout the enemy's front across the road. One of the men Sergeant Anderson picked to accompany him was Pvt. L.C. McCollum. With the Germans a bare 100 feet directly in front of them, the trio dashed across the road. Said McCollum later:

"We made a quick jump into the open space of the road, ran across it, and threw ourselves into a shallow ditch along side it. And none too soon! German machine gunners opened up on us with everything they had. I thought we were "goners"… The brush and weeds were cut off from the top of the ditch by the machine gun bullets as cleanly as though some farmer had been over it with a scythe…" (32)

The trio crawled along the road's edge, continuing the patrol until Sergeant Anderson had seen enough. He then led Pvt. McCollum and his pal back across the road at a safer place and again to the waiting arms of their comrades. However, the patrol had left McCollum, a poet in his own right, scared almost beyond words.

By then, most stragglers had been gathered in and Lt. Whiting moved the company across the road and back into battle with the waiting Germans on the other side. In the brush ahead, they slowly began to work around the enemy machine-guns again. (96)

Off to Company A's left, Company G of 2nd Battalion also drew up on the same road farther down, also commenced a short reorganization and also wrestled with their own machine-gun problems. Here, Pvt. Nell went out to flank a German machine-gun that was working over the area pretty thoroughly. Moving down a ditch on his own side of the log road, he encountered the bodies of eight men who had tried to take out the nest before him. Farther on, he came to the most chilling spectacle:

"...Crawling down the ditch, I saw a boy on his knees looking straight ahead. I thought I would have a partner to help. I crawled up close behind him and whispered, "Do you see him; have you got him located?" No move or answer. I whispered it again, with no answer. I crawled around and looked him in the face. I saw he was dead, his eyes open. About eight feet in front of him there lay another dead man. I knew then I would be next..." (40)

When Pvt. Nell finally crawled close enough to the Boche nest to toss in a hand grenade, he discovered that the Germans had "fled out the back way" and the position abandoned. With a tremendous sigh of relief, he signaled the all clear to the rest of the company and laboriously they continued their advance as well. The next nest was not abandoned... (40)

By now it was obvious to the Germans that the 368th, left of the 308th, held intentions for the town of Binarville, a rather sleepy little hamlet whose importance centered on the fact that it was the crossroads for two main, stone-based roads that ran through the Argonne region. The first and most important of these ran from the larger town of Apremont in the east, to the town of Servon in the west, which by the afternoon of the 27th had fallen into French hands. The second was a route that led down from the northern town of Autry, through Binarville and beyond to the area that had once been the German front lines, since overrun. Thus, by capturing Binarville the Allies could partially hobble the German supply and communication systems between the central Argonne Forest and the eastern sector of the Champagne front by denying an important east/west point of access. It also would mean the capture of a solid based main supply road running along a north/south course that the attacking Allied forces could use to move their own men and material up to the local front more rapidly.

Predictably, the Germans had put steps in place to prevent the town's capture. The land that lays on the approach to Binarville and around it—open and rolling farmland, broken by sporadic tangles of woodland—had been heavily entrenched and well supplied with both men and material. There was very little cover for attacking troops, machine-guns were everywhere and German artillery had been fixed to almost pin point accuracy, due to the availability of direct observation to the fall of shot. It was these defenses that had raised havoc with the 368th's assault forces that first disastrous day of the attack. Now, they were to try it again. (10)

The 368th Infantry received its orders for advance at 3:45 a.m. that morning. Taking into account the disaster the first day had been, they were ordered to place both their 2nd and 3rd battalions (right to left) in the battle line for the second day's attack, scheduled to come off at 5:15 a.m. The 2nd Battalion companies were scattered and disorganized, however, and it was unable to advance at the prescribed time. It spent the morning trying to reassemble itself as a battalion and reconnoiter the planned avenues of advance. Only Company G on the left, operating within the zone that the 3rd Battalion was to take over, managed any headway at all that morning.

There, Company M of the 3rd Battalion, in assault and followed by Company I, backed Company G/2nd in an attack that jumped off at about 9:00 a.m. They made steady progress all morning, despite fierce enemy resistance from the disorganized German 254th. By noon, they were in the Tranchee de l'Euphrate. Company G was then withdrawn for afternoon attacks to be made in the eastern zone, and 3rd/368th totally took over the front line in the western zone. At 5:30 p.m., the 3rd attacked across their whole zone of advance with companies K, I, and M in line (l to r). By 7:00 p.m., companies I and K had reached Tranchee Tirpitz and settled down for the night after a gain of about a kilometer. Company M managed to push another 350 meters beyond that, punch a hole in the 254th's lines, and gain limited access to the Vallee Moreau before they were finally fought to a standstill. On a line slightly behind them, Company K made liaison with the French 11th C.a.P. to the left late that night, but Company M could not find anyone from 2nd/368th out on the right at all. (46, 92, 137)

Colonel Prescott had just telephoned in Major Whittlesey's advance line coordinates to Brigade PC when, just before 4:00 p.m., the message from General Johnson arrived that relieved him of his command of the 308th and placed Lt. Col. Smith in charge until Colonel Stacey could make it up to the advanced Regimental PC. Colonel Prescott was to proceed immediately to Division PC. There were also orders for Major Whittlesey to curb his advance; the product of a long, argumentative, and acrimonious conversation General Johnson and General Alexander had had around 2:30 p.m. concerning the state of affairs within the 154th Brigade. (V) Although the 308th had only managed to push forward some 400 brutal meters since they had gone over the top that afternoon, they nevertheless had again outdistanced the 307th in that short time. Consequently, General Johnson had gotten permission for them to halt, dig in, re-organize and wait for the 307th to come abreast of their line; certainly an interesting example of interpretation concerning the units moving "without regard to troops to the right or left" line of the attack order for the day. The merged 1st and 2nd/308th had by then reached the Tranchee Tirpitz across a relatively even 800-meter section of the front and had outposts thrown out about 2-300 meters ahead. Lieutenant Colonel Smith sent the order to Major Whittlesey, which arrived in about 20 minutes. The Majors answer went back to Regimental at 4:30 p.m.:

At: 94.9 – 72.7
To: CO 308 Inf.
Just received order from you to dig in here in front of what I think is Terpitz (sic) trench. We were held up here by severe MG and grenade fire. Only one severe and two or three minor casualties.
Do not have the location of D Co. yet. A Co. is here in part. (246)

As the 1st and 2nd battalions dug in and began a general reorganization, they also sent out liaison patrols. To the east, where it was known that the 307th had fallen behind, General Johnson had made arrangements (actually on General Alexander's urging) to send two companies of 3rd/308th to cover the gap and clean up some enemy machine-guns reported to be laying down harassing fire there. To the west, where 2nd Battalion units had met fierce resistance on the left flank, no word had again been heard from the 368th all day. (10, 92, 136, 138, 139, 154)

After departing from the zone of the 1st/254th early that morning, the German 6th Company/122nd took up positions across from the point about where the 308th and the 368th came together, with the 10th Company/122nd falling back into support. The French 247th F.A. gave them both hell that afternoon as the Doughboys of the 368th plowed into them and messages arrived at the 254th's PC stating that the Americans had punched a hole through the line near where the new partition between the 122nd and the 254th was. Fortunately for the Germans, two machine-gun sections there, laying down crossfire, had virtually wiped out an entire American attack company at that point. The western section of 6th Company shifted fire against that flank to assist, but it was not until elements of the 8th Company arrived that evening that the 500-meter gap was closed and the black Doughboys were finally driven to a standstill. It had been a close call.

Meanwhile, across the line of advance on the U.S. side, it had not been until 4:30 p.m. that Company G, on the left of 2nd/368th's eastern advance zone, had moved forward in attack with Company F in support to the right of, but well behind, the area being hammered by Company M. Almost immediately the intense enemy machine-gun fire they met separated the two companies. By dark, Company G had managed to battle forward to Tranchee Tirpitz but was stopped there by virtually unapproachable enemy fire. They settled down for the night with no liaison to their own regimental units on their left and separated by some 300 meters of lateral distance (the zone of companies H and E/368th) from the 77th Division on their right. Company F, meanwhile, had pushed its way into a shallow valley just north of Tranchee Tirpitz and hung on grimly. By 10:00 p.m. however, they had been forced back to an isolated position behind Tirpitz itself, with no liaison in any direction.

Just west of the divisional dividing line to the 77th, Company H attacked about noon, with Company E in support, and met with heavy enemy fire. Again, the assault platoons fragmented as they battled their way forward and by early evening, it was all over. Only two tired, battered platoons of Company H managed to scratch as far forward as Tranchee de la Tringle. The remainder of companies H and E had only gained as far as Tranchee de Courlande. The two solitary front line platoons remained isolated for the night with no liaison to the left flank of the 308th, then some 300 meters ahead and to the right, nor with the rest of 2nd/368th (Company G), some 300 meters ahead and to the left. Only the most tenuous of runner lines connected them with the remainder of their own battalion elements, some 300 meters behind. There, Company E, itself 600 meters behind the 308th's line, also attempted throughout the night to locate someone from the 77th Division, but never did. So once again, there was at least a 300-meter long gap in the 308th's left flank. Though later that night two liaison platoons from Company I/308th did manage to find remaining elements of Company H/368th at Tranchee de Courlande, the hole ahead never really filled. (91, 92, 120, 123, 128)

Over on the right, the 307th had another bad day. When they jumped off at 6:00 a.m., disposition of the troops had not changed. Again, 3rd Battalion led the attack with 2nd Battalion in close support. Colonel Houghton sent a message to Major McKinney (actually in command of the assault force) reading in part, "I have a direct order to reach intermediary objective today at 295.3-274.8, 296.6-274.7…." Those coordinates would put the 307th against a ridge on the other side of a place on the map called Depot de Machines, which was a German rail and supply dump located within a narrow ravine that cut east/west across their regimental front. It was also slightly over two and a half kilometers of machine-gun and grenade swept Argonne jungle ahead of their present position. A tough nut to crack, no doubt!

Nevertheless, the 307th went over the top at 6:00 a.m., following a largely ineffective artillery barrage, threw themselves forward at the waiting Germans and met with a wall of fire. Fighting in this portion of the line was then confined mostly to trying to work up the ridges of the Ravine of the Fountaine aux Charmes, a bastard of a ditch with steeply sloped and wooded sides, running some 180 feet deep. The Germans naturally had covered all the high ground and approaches carefully, particularly toward their right flank, with enfilading machine-gun fire and barbed wire that had been cleverly strung to funnel attacking troops indirectly into their waiting muzzles. However, the Doughboys of the 307th knew that trick already and instead used their long-handled wire cutters to clip their way forward, paying no attention to the traps. Consequently, the German machine-gunners changed tactics and caught the 307th men at the bottom of the ravine with guns and trench mortars well hidden on the high ridges across. The Doughboys pulled back, and Major McKinney called in an artillery barrage at about 2:00 p.m., mixed with trench mortar fire, while a reorganization of the heavily dispersed troops commenced. At 4:00 p.m., the now merged 2nd and 3rd battalions renewed the attack. This attack ended in failure too, with nothing but casualties gained and barely any ground at all won.

A final push for the day was planned for first 6:45 p.m., then at the last minute changed to 7:45 p.m. to enable a fierce 15-minute artillery barrage to be arranged to break up the strong enemy defenses that the scouts reported were out ahead. Again, the subsequent attack raged forward in the dark but ultimately resulted in no change to the disposition of the 307th's front at all - only to the casualty lists. Halted, they remained throughout the night on a line stretching from Ravin de la Fontaine aux Charmes in the west (where they hooked up with two companies of 3rd/308th), to the Tranchee des Fontaines in the east. Here, they formed liaison with the 153rd Brigade, which had not advanced much either. They gathered in their stray troops one more time, and settled down into muddy funk holes to endure another long, cold Argonne night, as unending shellfire again screeched down through the dark. (103, 138, 139)

Around 4:00 p.m., even as the 307th was futilely pounding their heads savagely against the German positions north of Fontaine aux Charmes, a message arrived at 2nd/308th's PC informing Major Budd that Colonel Prescott had been relieved of command. Major Budd was to come rearward and assist Lieutenant Colonel Smith in taking charge of the regiment. However, while the message was in route, General Alexander had changed his mind, deciding to give the 308th to Colonel Stacey instead and keeping Colonel Houghton permanently at the head of the 307th. Lieutenant Colonel Smith, then, would only need to take charge of the 308th temporarily until Colonel Stacey, who had set out a short time before the message went, arrived at the advanced Regimental PC. Then, Smith would assist the new commander in taking over, so Budd would not be needed after all. However, by that time, the message had gone out, so a second runner was dispatched with a message countermanding the first order. This second message found Major Budd about 10 minutes after the first one. He was relieved to know that he would able to stay at the head of 2nd Battalion after all—at least for the time being. (109, 131, 132, 136)

Colonel Stacey, meanwhile, set out with a guide about 2:00 p.m. from Division PC. So confusing were conditions on the battlefield that afternoon that it took them until suppertime to reach General Johnson's PC. After a short conference with the Brigadier, Stacey snatched a quick meal and about four hours sleep before setting out with a guide to his new advanced Regimental PC. Along the way, he got a first-hand look at the terrain his new regiment had been forced to fight through; a rather overwhelming sight and not at all what he had expected. That was nothing compared to what he found waiting for him at his new command. It both shocked and dismayed him and Stacey later wrote:

"When I arrived at the PC, I found Lt. Col. Smith in command (with) no staff, no system of runners and no maps. It was necessary for me to select an adjutant, an operations officer, an intelligence officer, a gas officer, and secure an artillery liaison officer... I organized a system of runners and after several hours of energetic search was able to locate the positions of the companies of my regiment... and establish communications with them. During all this time the regiment was engaged with the Germans, and we were exposed to heavy shellfire and gas.

I found that the regiment was absolutely unprepared for this advance. I lacked rifle ammunition, clothing, hand grenades, rifle grenades, heavy wire cutters, Stokes mortar ammunition, and ammunition for my 37mm cannons. The regiment was terribly disorganized... I had many men killed in the Argonne... who had been drafted late in June... about three weeks recruit drill in a training camp, and the remainder of the time on the road... many of these men had never fired a single cartridge out of their guns..." (238)

Obviously, Colonel Stacey was displeased with his new charge right from the start. Nor were his impressions to improve much over the next eight days that he was in command of the 308th. In fact, they were to worsen. True, he had good officers under him; Lt. Col. Smith and Major Whittlesey were, in particular, exceptional men, as was Major Budd. There were also several very good platoon leaders and company commanders as well and for the most part the NCOs could readily be counted on to get a job done. However, that was hardly enough to compensate for all the deficiencies the Colonel perceived within the regiment as a whole. Moreover, this was only scratching the surface. To begin with, he had not had to watch the grinding erosion that the regiment had endured for the past two days and, as described above, he initially had his hands full just getting organized. Then, on the afternoon of the 28th, just when his authority finally began to find a voice, he would be forced almost immediately to deal with the episode of the 1st Battalion being cut off in the 'Small Pocket'. This certainly was an inauspicious beginning to a new command assignment. More importantly, it marked the first steps down the path of the most damaging eight days of Cromwell Stacey's career.

Major Whittlesey's last message for the day went back to Regimental PC at 5:35 p.m.:

From: CO 1st Bn
To: CO 308 Inf
Can you not get us up grenades and food early tomorrow morning?
We are being fired at by artillery from our left front and front.
Aim poor. (246)

Although some artillery was still falling, all the heavy action was basically already over by about 5:00 p.m. and the troops of 1st and 2nd/ 308th were dug in either along a line parallel with that of the Tranchee Tirpitz, or had found places to stash themselves within the trench line itself. There, they tried to get comfortable, but the misty chilly rain had not really stopped all day and no one had been dry for two days now. No food had come up for supper, 'iron rats' were about gone and again the only water the men had was either rainwater or muddy water from the cleanest looking puddle they might have passed during the day. Besides grenades, ammunition was also running low. Carrying parties went out to fetch more ammo from nearby dumps brought up during the day and to see what food could be scared up. Brutal exhaustion was creeping over everyone now along with the evening shadows. (136, 218)

It was to be another long and nerve-wracking night, with the artillery of both sides continuing overhead at intervals and occasional bursts of machine-gun fire ringing out in the light of the many flares sent up by the Germans. Chauchat gunners and the men of the 306th M.G Bn., who set up their outposts carefully ahead and to the flanks, popped off nervously at sounds that refused to identify themselves. Patrols went out in all directions and liaison parties moved off the flanks into the heavy darkness. Private Charles Minder, behind the 308th in Company B of the 306th MG Bn., described moving up in reserve closer to the front line in the wake of the day's actions:

"...We picked up the equipment and started to march, up and down hills, thru barbed wire entanglements, into trenches, and up on top again. They were the German trenches only yesterday morning. I never saw such a labyrinth of trenches since I've been in France. For miles and miles, nothing but trench after trench, with heavy doors between the communication trenches, and miles and miles of barbed wire all over. At some places it was absolutely impossible to walk on top at all. We walked until nine o'clock. Shells started dropping all around us — word was sent along the line that we could sleep..." (37)

About the time that Pvt. Minder was finally bedding down, General Johnson handed down 154th Brigade's attack orders for September 28. The advance within the 308th's zone would resume, promptly this time, at 6:00 a.m., preceded by the usual half-hour artillery barrage. The right flank of the brigade would advance through an identical assault made by the 307th. To the left, Groupement Durand (largely meaning the 368th Infantry) stated its intention to advance their line as well. The 3rd/308th would remain behind in brigade reserve and clear out remaining enemy pockets of resistance around the eastern Fontaine aux Charmes. Major Whittlesey received the orders at Karlplatz around 9:30 p.m., where he and Major Budd had retired and set up a combined Battalion PC once again. Plenty of time to prepare this time. They were now some 39 hours into the allotted 72 of the offensive and overall the advance of the 27th had gained little ground for the 77th Division, though the fighting had been extremely intense. (VI) Hopefully though, the advance on the 28th would fair better. In fact, it was imperative that it did so, for loss of momentum might give the enemy the time he needed to bring up fresh troops—just as the Doughboys were tiring. (116, 131, 132)

Which is exactly what was happening. Around midnight, a message came through to the division message center, this one from Captain Bradley Delehanty, the 308th's Regimental Intelligence Officer:

2 German prisoners have just been turned over to the M.P. our corps. 7th Co., 254th Inf. Regiment, 76 Div. Captured at 1.30pm Sept. 27... place of capture approximately 95.5 – 72.4 Reserve div, they say, came in last night. (145)

The map coordinates given put the place of capture well within the operational zone of the 308th Infantry, in fact some 800 meters east of the borderline with the 368th. The 7th Company was in the 2nd Battalion of the 254th. With the 1st/254th already known to be on line against the 368th, it was clear then that German reinforcements were beginning to arrive. This was the first indication to 77th Division Headquarters that anyone other than the 122nd/2nd LwD was out there ahead of the 308th.

Very early in the morning of September 28, Major Whittlesey, Major Budd, and probably 1st Battalion adjutant, Lt. McKeogh (the 2nd Battalion adjutant had already been killed) made their way back through the rain toward the advanced Regimental PC to meet with their new regimental commander. What they all thought of Colonel Stacey is not recorded, but in light of later actions, it is safe to assume that the Colonel did not leave a very favorable first impression on anyone. (Which likely had more to do with the burden he had seemingly been saddled with than with his own personality; Stacey has actually been described as a very likable chap.) The results of the first meeting at least seemed encouraging in one way however, in that Colonel Stacey seemed to agree with the combined battalion movement that Majors Whittlesey and Budd had been using for the past two days. The Colonel, ever the old experienced scout, would have easily recognized that there was little else that could be done in light of the width of the front his new regiment faced and the tremendously difficult terrain they were forced to attack through. When details for the morning attack had been hammered out and Colonel Stacey thoroughly briefed by his battalion commanders of the situation in each of their areas of responsibility, the officers were dismissed to attend to their business. Outside the PC, Major Whittlesey scrawled for a time in his field message book and calling for runners, handed out the messages with instructions for delivery. Ahead in the forest, the light of German flares glowed confidently through the trees and cast an eerie glow upon the rainy darkness. (109, 246)

From: CO 1st Bn 308   At: Rgtl. Hqrs
Date: 28 Sept   Hour: 3 AM
To: Co. B CO   Copy To: A Co.
  The Regt. Will attack at 6 AM following a barrage lasting from 5.30 to 6. 1st Bn advance Batt. You will lead on right followed by Co. A. E and C Cos. will be in support behind you.
  You will proceed slowly and with caution in order that G Co. may catch up in your rear.
  F and D companys (sic) are well over on your left followed by H Co.
  At 9 AM you will halt and reform, get in touch with me, and await further orders.
  A Co. will conform to the above order.
  I will advance with C Co.
  If this order reaches you send messenger you received it.

Whittlesey Major 308 (246)

  With the messages heading out to their companies, plans for the 'morrow were laid and all was in readiness for the 308th's third day of advance. Ahead of them lay full forest and the slopes of a hill rising some 200 meters high. That hill was to provide a foretaste of things to come and was called l'Homme Mort - "The Dead Man."

(I) But the General Staff *was* worried nonetheless. The attack by the Americans was quickly followed by simultaneous offensives by the French in the Champagne region and the British in Belgian Flanders and Northern France. Everywhere the German lines were erupting and as the hours of those first critical days passed, it became more and more clear to the German Generals in command of the Imperial Forces, Ludendorff and Hindenburg, that the war was now very likely lost. (It is said that once the full impact of the offensive became clear to Ludendorff that he had a stroke and was incapacitated for two days or so.) Germany had gambled her last reserves in the spring and summer offensives, designed to win the war before American might could be brought to play, and she had lost the bet. Now, there were no more reserve troops with which to stem the flood of khaki and horizon blue flowing through their lines and the best that they could now hope for was to stave off the enemy until an 'honorable' peace could be reached with the allies. All of this was quite unknown to the men in trenches however, who were still determined to beat back their enemies at any cost, as usual.

(II) Yet to Major Charles Whittlesey, orders in general contained little room for personal interpretation in any case and were meant to be followed to the letter. The only possible exception would be, as he had demonstrated before, if an order perhaps placed unreasonable demands on his men or placed them in inordinate harm's way *unnecessarily*. Yet, he would still carry that order out if there seemed a worthwhile goal to be achieved by it. This shows that Charles Whittlesey was, ironically, probably one of the few 'civilian officers' of the 308th with the ability to actually see the battle in a larger sense. The trained attorney had the wherewithal to look the facts in the face and the skills to constantly anticipate strategy ahead of his opponent. At the same time, war was an abhorrent abomination to Whittlesey. The quicker it was finished, the better, and he trusted his superiors to make the correct judgment calls and issue orders that would bring about that end as timely and efficiently as possible.

  It appears then that it was only as the battle progressed and Whittlesey was forced to recognize the true attrition around him, that he began to question orders that appeared to have been poorly thought out. The start of this questioning might arguably even be traced back to the period immediately following the episode of the first 'Small Pocket'. Afterward, Whittlesey appears to have lost a great deal of his faith in his superiors. While he still carried out those orders that he questioned to the best of his ability, he was then much more likely to let it be known to those doing the ordering that he did not necessarily agree with those orders. At first glance, this may not seem like much of a problem. But, in the Army at that time, for a man of Whittlesey's rank, responsibility, and position to show his official displeasure to formal orders caused for a great deal of consternation.

(III) Again, we see another prime example of how the AEF upper level command sometimes worked. Apparently, Colonel Stacey's comments had a lot to back them up, while other sources claim that Stacey was simply 'getting too big for his britches'. Still other corners claim that Stacey's star shown too bright for General Buck and that, in conjunction with Stacey's comments, proved more than Buck's ego could handle. This could very well be the case, as Colonel Stacey had a lot of military success, coupled with just the right amount of political aplomb, to back him up. In any case, Buck himself was later reassigned from command of the 3rd Division by General Pershing - but that is a whole other story for another day.

(IV) This action marks a turning point in the conduct of battle within the forward zone of the 308th. From that afternoon on, attacks were generally begun with the 1st Battalion forward as ordered, but the 2nd Battalion would be brought up at first opportunity. Initially, Major Whittlesey's decision to use 2nd Battalion in this way was a reaction to the extreme difficulties of advancing across a front that was, as previously stated, actually too wide and too dense for a single battalion alone. Then, later, as casualties rapidly reduced the effectiveness of either of the battalions to work alone, it became a real necessity. Yet, it was a decision for which Whittlesey would later take a great amount of heat, even though a comparable system had been in effect over in the 307th's zone of advance with their forward 2nd and 3rd Battalions almost since the start of the offensive.

(V) Transcripts of this conversation, found buried in the files of the 77th Division, accurately illustrate two things: First that, while General Alexander admittedly was under intense pressure from above to continue the advance at all costs, it is fairly obvious that he did not yet clearly understand the tremendously difficult conditions along his front. Second, that while there was a certain amount of respect between these two men in deference to each other's accomplishments, there was certainly no love lost at all between them.

(VI) By evening of the 27th, Montfaucon had fallen and the U.S. line had been advanced almost everywhere - except in the Argonne Forest. By contrast, west of the forest the French were slowly forcing their way up the difficult Aisne valley, while east of the forest the majority of the 28th Division was doing the same in the equally difficult Aire valley, all of which was according to the original plan to try and 'pinch out' the greater Argonne. The plan however still required the 77th and the western most regiment of the 28th, which was working along the eastern edge of the forest, to maintain a steady drive against the German troops therein to help 'drive them out'. It is difficult to say which force (either of the flankers or those driving through the forest) was feeling the strain more though.

Ancillary sources used in this chapter include:17, 24, 30, 34, 36, 42, 43, 50, Various 87-119, 144, Various 152-216, 220, 222, 223, 224, 225, 227, 230, 233, 235, 236, 240, 243, 257, 258, 266, 347, 360, 370

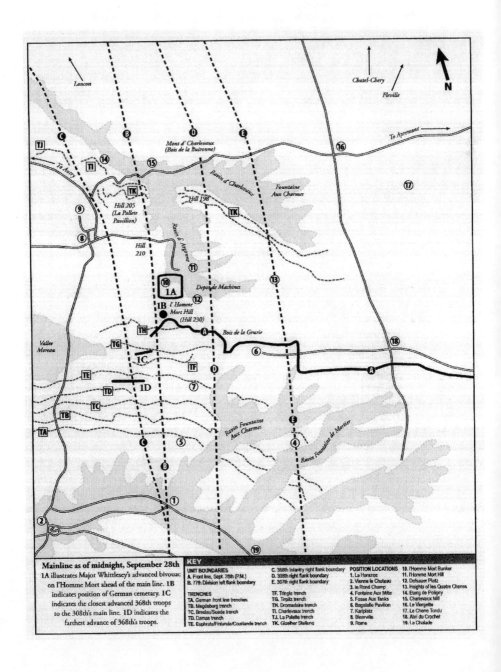

Mainline as of midnight, September 28th

1A illustrates Major Whittlesey's advanced bivouac on l'Homme Mort ahead of the main line. 1B indicates position of German cemetery. 1C indicates the closest advanced 368th troops to the 308th's main line. 1D indicates the farthest advance of 368th's troops.

KEY

UNIT BOUNDARIES
A. Front line, Sept. 28th (P.M.)
B. 77th Division left flank boundary
C. 368th Infantry right flank boundary
D. 308th right flank boundary
E. 307th right flank boundary

TRENCHES
TA. German front line trenches
TB. Magdeburg trench
TC. Breslau/Suede trench
TD. Damas trench
TE. Euphrate/Finlande/Courlande trench
TF. Tringle trench
TG. Tirpitz trench
TH. Dromadaire trench
TI. Charlevaux trench
TJ. La Palette trench
TK. Giselher Stellung

POSITION LOCATIONS
1. La Harazee
2. Vienne le Chateau
3. le Rond Champ
4. Fontaine Aux Mitte
5. Fosse Aux Tanks
6. Bagatelle Pavilion
7. Karlplatz
8. Binarville
9. Rome
10. l'Homme Mort Bunker
11. l'Homme Mort Hill
12. Defsauer Platz
13. Heights of les Quatre Chenes
14. Etang de Poligny
15. Charlevaux Mill
16. Le Viergette
17. Le Chene Tondu
18. Abri du Crochet
19. La Chalade

Map labels: Lancon, Chatel-Chery, Fleville, To Apremont, Mont d' Charlevaux (Bois de la Buironne), Ravin d' Charlevaux, Fountaine Aux Charmes, To Autry, Hill 205 (La Pallete Pavillion), Hill 198, Hill 210, Ravin à Argonne, Deposde Machines, l' Homme Mort Hill (Hill 230), Bois de la Grurie, Vallee Moreau, Ravin Fountaine Aux Charmes, Ravin Fountaine de Mortier, N

September 28, 1918

"…We went forward for three days, but we went too far, see? Then Whittlesey finds out we can't go forward or backward. Oh, those Germans were everywhere!"
Private Jack Herschkowitz, HQ Company, 1st/308th.

Very early on the morning of September 28, 77th Division HQ issued General Order #27 by authority of Major General Robert Alexander. It was not a particularly long or eye-catching order, save for one specific part, which read:

> *It has (further) come within the knowledge of the division commander that in the case of the operations of the 27th inst., a body of troops which had gained important territory was withdrawn therefrom by some unauthorized person in the rear directing them to retire. This incident, well established in itself, is now in process of investigation for the purpose of determining the individual responsible for giving such an order.*
>
> *It is again impressed upon every officer and man of this command that ground once captured must under no circumstances be given up in the absence of direct, positive and formal orders to do so emanating from these headquarters. Troops occupying ground must be supported against counter attack and all gains held. It is a favorite trick of the Boche to spread confusion among our troops by calling out "Retire" or "Fall back". If, in action, any such command is heard officers and men may be sure it is given by an enemy. Whoever gives such a command is a traitor and it is the duty of any officer or man who is loyal to his country and who hears such an order given to shoot the offender upon the spot. WE ARE NOT GOING BACK BUT FORWARD!* (116, 131)

Taken literally, the meaning of the order is clear—there was to be no retirement of any kind, for any reason whatsoever, unless specifically by command of General Alexander himself. If there was, and it occurred without the general's express order, the individual giving the order was libel to be shot. Quite succinct and to the point, to say the least. When examined outside the arena of war, however, the order is found flawed on at least two major points and may not have been quite as clear to those receiving it, as it seems at first glance. First, any order forbidding any retirement, of any kind, could not be followed in all circumstances. In fact, officers of the 308th later said of G.O. #27 that, "there was always something along those lines coming down from the brass" in an effort to "bolster the offensive spirit." Most also stated that such orders were rarely paid much attention. Second, and more importantly, the order was utterly illegal. General Alexander had not the authority, nor legal recourse, to issue an order that gives *carte blanch* to wonton murder of American troops, under unexamined circumstances. Yet, General Alexander never shrank from the responsibility of issuing the order though. Indeed, he defended it for years after the war as a correct course of action taken to spur his command on towards victory.

Following the *context* of the order however, was a different story. When taken in that light, the order then becomes more practicable: ground once occupied should not be given up without orders from GHQ, *in every situation possible*. Commanders under General Alexander faced some important questions concerning the order then:

1. Did General Alexander in fact mean the order to be taken literally? Judging from the wording of the text, and taken in the strictest sense, yes.

2. Would it then be possible to expect a normal, levelheaded officer to follow such a bold order to the letter? The answer can only be, yes and no. No, because certainly some common sense must be applied. Yes, because in the eyes of the army it was a general order and simply must be obeyed. This then brings us to the third question.

3. Did that last portion of the order mean that a unit in an impossible situation was to be completely slaughtered - or nearly so - while it waited for "direct, positive, and formal orders" to fall back (not wholly unlike what Major Whittlesey and his command would go through in the Charlevaux Ravine in just a few days)? Taken in the light of the basic combat principles of the time, one of which states, "Do not hesitate to sacrifice the command if the result is worth the cost," then apparently yes, since General Alexander definitely considered it, "worth the cost."(I)

The reality is, of course, that the order was not followed in all instances. In fact, many officers later claimed to have never even seen the order. Yet, it was certainly distributed on the morning of the 28th down to at least company level. Again, quoting Private James Larney, it is "a fact" that the order was received in the 1st/308th. He does add, however, "(but) I never thought of it or heard it mentioned in the Lost Battalion." Nonetheless, coupled then with the order of the previous day stating that the offensive be "pushed (forward) without reference to troops to the right or left," a most dangerous precedent was being set. (245)

The main importance of this order lies in the fact that perhaps this one order more than any other order has caused the greatest amount of controversy concerning Major Whittlesey's combat decisions. The claim has often been made that his fear of retribution for failure to follow this particular general order is part of what led him not only into both Pockets, but held him in the second one when he might well have gotten out with fewer casualties. This would be a hard position to disclaim were it not for knowledge of Charles Whittlesey's character and, perhaps more importantly, Jim Larney's above statement. Since he was by Major Whittlesey's side for virtually the entire battle, he would be in perhaps the best position to know how the Major perceived the order. It was not the fear of getting a bullet in his head from one of his men, or the fear of General Alexander's wrath then that dictated Charles Whittlesey's decisions and actions; it was simply his sense of duty.

It is also claimed that the order gave Whittlesey the official 'permission' he needed to 'rush out ahead' in an effort to seek 'glory and honors'. That line of thought proposes to ignore all the previous orders issued urging further and more rapid advances, any one of which also gave the same supposed 'permission'. It also does not take into account Charles Whittlesey's character, which is, as previously described, one that follows orders not out of a need to feed glory, but out of a desire to fulfill his given duty. Major Whittlesey further had the presence of mind to see what greater good the successful accomplishment of those orders might bring. (258, 274)

A few minutes after 5:00 a.m., Lt. Col. Smith telephoned General Johnson at brigade with a message sent in by Major Whittlesey earlier that morning which read:

We must have stretchers and bearers. Lt. Knight (D. Co) has 10 wounded he knows of and others he has not found yet. Has 10 men available for fighting. Schenck (C. Co) has 30 men for fighting. Please get bearers and litters to rear post. (246)

If these dispositions are taken as any indication, then dispersion had once again done some dirty work in at least part of Major Whittlesey's command the afternoon before. D Company may well have had only "10 men for fighting" when the Major wrote the message, but certainly a portion of the remainder were simply lost and would later show up. C Company's given total would reflect this as well. In fact, the problem was endemic of all the line units. (G Company in particular would again fail to gather all its men in time to make the jump-off, thereby delaying its initial advance until about 7:00 a.m.) Yet, the casualty rate was indeed heavy and Major Whittlesey's plea for stretchers and litter bearers was not just a request; it was a definite necessity. Many of the remainder that had not been dispersed during the fighting had been hit and their numbers were almost equal to those who had been wandering. Company strengths, never full to begin with, were already fast approaching the appallingly low levels that they had reached on the Vesle only weeks before. Nor was the weather cooperating. The rain and mist had only stopped just before dawn. German artillery fire also continued most of the night. Between the two, again no one had gotten much sleep. Thankfully, some rations had come up early that morning, but there had still not been nearly enough for everyone and hunger was beginning to constitute an emphatic problem. Therefore, 48 hours into the planned 72, the 308th was definitely beginning to feel the strain.

Yet at just after 6:00 a.m., following the usual half-hour artillery barrage, most of the regiment still managed to get underway. As with the previous two days, the clouds obscured the rising sun and fog shrouded the battlefield as the two battalions slowly moved forward into the forest behind the line of bursting shells. Incredibly, resistance was light at first. Scouts pushing out ahead came upon craters with bloody remains in them—signs that the trench mortars, which had themselves fired most of the night, had done much good. Farther and farther the scouts advanced, returning with reports of an occasional machine-gun or enemy squad seen hightailing it in the opposite direction and lots of general movement from the Boche, but well behind their line. It was all too easy, and the Doughboys knew it. What was going on? (131, 136, 143)

From the German perspective, the situation in the Argonne that morning was much more severe than the Americans realized. The Hagan Stellung line had collapsed; not an entirely unacceptable situation had it not appeared that the Hagan Nord was merely slowing down the U.S. forces—not stopping them. There were other problems as well. The western flank of the Aire Valley was threatened by the U.S. 28th Division and needed reinforcement badly, while east of the forest, repeated and savage attacks of the 368th were worrying the 254th to no end. Therefore, Army Group Argonnen saw an urgent need to realign their forces to better effect. Accordingly, 2nd Landwehr piecemealed out the 122nd's entire 1st Battalion, supported by its 9th and 11th companies, and sent them into the Aire Valley to assist in repulsing attacks being made over there against the town of Montblainville on the forest's eastern flank. The 6th Company/254th meanwhile, now situating itself to the immediate west of the 122nd, was in need of some guiding in its new, unfamiliar territory. Therefore, the 10th Company/122nd received orders to go back into the assault line with them. Further 122nd company sections, along with a few from the 120th Regiment, were also sent out on the western flank to shore up the vulnerable joint between the 254th and the 122nd. A near breakthrough there the previous afternoon had shaken the 254th troops. Unknowledgeable of the area, they badly needing reinforcement by men who knew the ground.

It was 8:25 a.m., before the German situation really gained focus in American eyes. That is when General Alexander's PC received a telephone call from General Johnson at 154th Brigade PC. The Brigadier had been questioning prisoners of the 2nd/254th that Major Whittlesey's men had captured the day before when one had let it slip that all units in the Argonne had received orders for a gradual retirement from within the Hagan Nord into more secure positions approaching the Giselher Stellung 'Haupt-Widerstands-Lienie', yet some 800 meters to their rear. The general retirement had actually begun at 1:00 a.m. on the morning of the 28th and was to continue all day, while strong combat patrols covered the withdrawal with grenade, trench mortar, and plenty of machine-gun fire.

Therefore, as the 308th's Doughboys relentlessly came on, the leading line companies of the 254th and 122nd were drawing themselves back into positions within the wide and deep north/south running Ravin d'Argonne to the north, primarily consolidating across the ravine bottom and on both of its heights. To the east, the main body of the 122nd concentrated up in the heights called Le Quatre Chenes, primarily facing the 307th Infantry and the 308th's far right flank. Meanwhile, the rest of the 2nd/254th, which had just moved ahead out of support positions, also backed up and butted the 122nd right flank on the ravine's eastern ridge. They then extended down across the ravine bottom and up into defensive positions along its western heights east of Binarville, occupying two hills there, labeled on Allied maps as Hill 210 and Hill 205, the latter having the La Palette Pavilion crowning its crest and therefore more popularly known as La Palette Hill.

Therefore, as the 308th again drove hard ahead that morning, what they unknowingly found was an enemy in retreat; the first ordered general retreat since the Allies had begun their offensive. Its meaning was not lost to the German line troops, nor to the 77th Division's command structure. If the Germans really were on the run, General Alexander surmised, then it was now time to really put the whip to his division. (10, 123, 128, 307)

By about 8:30 a.m., Majors Whittlesey and Budd's men had incredibly progressed forward nearly a kilometer through a rain of enemy shells. Ahead of them in the trees lay the apron of a gentle valley yawning between two long slopes and a narrow gauge railway line, running north and south across the 308th's attack path. It was along the sides of this railway where they finally encountered the first serious resistance of the day. The Germans had arranged machine-gun nests during the night to cover their withdrawal, and were well prepared by morning. Company B, out front acting as a scout company and swinging to the right with a platoon of E in its wake, ran into them first. A general fight ensued and, again, 1st and 2nd battalions closed up together and extended a thick line. Company A, also out front, swung left and situated itself at a junction of the north/south RR line where a spur line ran east/west farther to the south. There it sat while C, in support, moved passed them and continued to advance. The mortar crews, traveling with Battalion PC (which itself was attached to C), began to shell the German machine-gun positions to some effect, while portions of Company F scooted toward the far-left flank and H kept steady pressure in between the two. Toward the right flank, D and G backed B on the left and portions of E on the right. Everything was finally working as it should have. Though resistance steadily increased, thankfully the terrible dispersion that had plagued the preceding two days seemed to be under control.

Major Whittlesey brought his PC to a halt at a crossroads of wagon paths to the left of the railroad tracks behind Company C and about 300 meters southwest of Company B's position, got out his maps and set up shop. A kilometer or so ahead, on the other side of the hill to the left called l'Homme Mort, was the Moulin de l'Homme Mort (Dead Man's Mill) a complex of concrete hutments and machine-gun posts that was the day's aiming point. Between them and the mill were sure to be 'plenty of things German' though, and the maps that Whittlesey and Budd were armed with proved almost useless as far as enemy positions were concerned. American and French intelligence knew little of what lay this deep into the Argonne. The mill itself was shown (as it had been pre-war built) situated within the Ravin d'Argonne; a wide, deep north/south cut that l'Homme Mort formed part of the western ridge of immediately ahead. They now faced the start of that ravine, a crevice that would effectively divide the 308th's zone of advance in two.

Major Budd had moved up and swung his own PC ahead and to the right, not far from Major Whittlesey's, and sent reports over of meeting resistance from beyond a wagon path and across a hollow. That would be the Depot des Machines, a large, heavily defended German railhead, ammunition and local supply dump that *was* shown on the map. The Depot was located within a ravine that spurred east from the head of the Ravin d'Argonne around the foot of l'Homme Mort and some 400 meters northeast from their present position. Scouts came back reporting it well protected by heavy belts of barbed wire and simply crawling with Germans. The 308th's current position faced just the angle from off the Ravin d'Argonne where it turned to the western end of the ravine that contained the Depot. The majority of it lay within the 307th's zone of advance and beyond. Fortunately, good liaison was in effect with the 307th to the right for a change, as by that time they had managed to come up on nearly an even line with the 308th. Perhaps a combined effort then could carry the Depot, if all went well. (34, 91, 101, 105, 109, 116, 132, 133, 144)

Pondering the situation ahead, Major Whittlesey shot a message down the runner chain back to Colonel Stacey at Regimental PC:

At: 94.9 – 73.6 Hour: 9Am
To: CO 308 Inf.
The 2nd Bn. is here. 1st Bn is now held up by stiff resistance (MG and trench mortar) A Co. (17 men) is at junction of RR and sent runners. E at 94.9 – 73.7. One platoon D Co. extends along the road to the N.E. C Co. is on the left with 3 platoons and one of D Co. F Co. (2nd Bn) is extending the left flank. Major Budd is following the rest of 2nd Bn. and is sending report. He has started to reorganize and will await orders here before advancing. Believes there is heavy opposition in front. At least he has suffered considerable losses; and many of the men have not eaten in 48 hrs.
We need rations badly for 200 men.
Have not heard from B Co. (246)

Colonel Stacey, settling in and beginning to assert his command now after a long, difficult night, got the message in good time. The enemy mortar fire the Major was suffering most likely came from the mill complex on the other side of l'Homme Mort. To that end, the Colonel sent a request back to General Johnson that an artillery barrage be dropped in ahead of Major Whittlesey's men. As the mill position was the day's objective, General Johnson decided to drop a barrage onto both the steep far slope of the hill and the mill complex itself, in order to 'pave the way in' for the Majors men, so to speak. The barrage would begin at 11:30 a.m. and last until noon. Afterward, a general line attack would be made. Sending the orders out to Stacey, the Brigadier also sent a similar set of orders out to Colonel Houghton at the 307th, who were themselves also currently stalled under heavy mortar and machine-gun fire before the approaches to Depot des Machines. (131, 138, 139, 238)

When word reached Majors Whittlesey and Budd about the coming barrage, they pulled their men back several hundred meters and began making plans even as the shells started flying overhead. Charging directly down the ravine, though the easiest route, would only make them sitting targets for the Germans still up on the heights on either side (low though they were). Instead, once the barrage lifted they would begin up the ravine on either side, keeping to the high ground of its bordering ridges, 2nd Battalion on the east, 1st Battalion on the west. The 2nd Battalion, with B Company in assault and companies E and G in support, would attack north across the east/west Depot des Machines ravine, just east of the angle and in conjunction with the left flank of the 307th. They then would work their way toward the heights of Les Quatre Chenes beyond. Meanwhile 1st Battalion, with Company A in assault and supported by companies C and H, would start up l'Homme Mort and force an effort over the hill. In contrast to a full liaison group, a single man would not present much of a target and therefore they would maintain liaison across the ravine between the two echelons through individual runners. By early evening, both battalions should have reached the Moulin de l'Homme Mort complex, where they would reunite, take it, and establish a general line across the wide Ravin d'Argonne from crest to crest. There they could reorganize and pass the night waiting for fresh orders.

Shortly before the barrage was scheduled to begin however, ration and water carrying parties finally began to arrive, as Major Whittlesey had requested. With great relief, most men forgot the danger ahead for a few minutes. For many, it was their first meal since the morning of the jump-off and for some, their last. Still, there were those who missed out, particularly the ones out-posting the attack pause farther afield, and many of the scouts and runners busy plying their trade. Unfortunately, for those men, it would be some time before rations were to appear again. (91, 109, 116, 131)

The artillery arrived right on time and laid down a beautiful barrage far out ahead until just after noon. Soon thereafter, men began to move forward in two large, spread ranks, combing out into the forest. The 1st Battalion slowly moved up l'Homme Mort along the left side of the railroad tracks and as they passed the railroad junction, the command also picked up a small contingent from companies F and D. Mixed in were a couple of machine-guns and their crews from Company D/306th MG Bn. The majority of the rest of F Company remained behind on the left flank extending the line in support, while the rest of D extended along the railroad as a containment force. The 2nd Battalion set off toward Depot des Machines with the remainder of the Company D/306th MG Bn. Hotchkiss guns throwing a barrage of indirect fire over their heads toward the Depot ravine ahead. Scouts followed the railroad tracks around its flank.

Company B, drawn back and lodged along the rail line slightly behind A's former position, had started out that morning at a great disadvantage with only two platoons in line. The others they had given up as runners and ammunition carriers for the Stokes mortar men the day before. Therefore, a platoon of Company E, commanded by 2nd Lt. Stevens, was now assigned to them to flesh out their ranks. The now-merged company pushed out into the woods immediately ahead, acting as a scout force for the rest of the 2nd Battalion. It soon began to draw heavy enemy fire from their left and front.

The assault continued until about 1:30 p.m. to no good end before Major Budd finally halted the 2nd Battalion advance. As the men dug in temporarily, he sent gangs out to reconnoiter the left while a runner went back to bring forward the remainder of E, left behind as a reserve force dug in at the spot where the two battalions had split. In command of Company E that day was probably the best-liked and most well respected company commander in the whole of the 308th, Captain George G. McMurtry. (92, 136)

George Gibson McMurtry Jr. was born in Pittsburgh, Pennsylvania, on November 6th, 1876. His father, George Sr., was an Irish immigrant who had come to America virtually penniless and eventually wound up owning his own steel mill. Therefore, George Jr. was instilled at an early age with a strong work ethic and an innate understanding of the common man. These two traits were to stand him in good stead all his life, and help make him popular with his soldiers. Short and stocky, with a generous mop of black hair and a ruddy complexion, he was by all accounts a gregarious, likable chap but possessed a hot Irish temper and fists of iron. When angered, his steely gaze could set wood aflame and a stream of vitriolic oaths of seemingly impossible violence would emit from his throat, his face turned a bright crimson. Fortunately, this was not often. (II)

He was enrolled at Harvard, Class of 1899, when the Spanish-American War broke out in 1898. Seeing a terrific chance for adventure, the 22-year-old McMurtry left college and enlisted in June into the 1st Regiment, U.S. Volunteer Cavalry: Theodore Roosevelt's famous 'Rough Riders'. With them, while in Troop D, commanded by Captain R.B. Huston he participated in Teddy's now famous charge up Kettle Hill on the San Juan Heights. However, overseas he caught a mild case of 'jungle fever', returned home and was mustered out of the service that October. He returned to Harvard immediately and worked hard enough to graduate with his class that next year. Immediately thereafter, he headed for New York City, and by 1900, was a full partner in the brokerage firm of 'Benjamin and

McMurtry'. By age 30, he was a self-made millionaire.

McMurtry was 40 years old already when he attended the Plattsburg Camp in 1917. Nevertheless, through typical hard work and diligence he quickly moved up the ranks from lieutenant to captain in charge of his own company at Camp Upton. In truth, a large measure of his success was probably due to his maturity and his positive attitude, as well as the transfer of enthusiastic energy that he managed to radiate to his men. Having already experienced the details of service life as a member of the 'Rough Riders', his experience at Upton was almost one of reliving youth; something that at his age he probably regarded as a Godsend. He loved what he was doing and wanted his men to see it his way and love it too. Therefore, he personally attended to many details that most company commanders were apt to leave to their subordinates. He drilled his men hard, had them keep their barracks and persons spotless and did his best to ensure that his unit, Company E, was the best on the rifle range. This naturally instilled a great deal of pride within the unit.

He was an extremely tough company commander, but eminently fair and trusting, almost to a fault. He steadfastly refused to believe that a man under his command could commit any indiscretion. Were one of his company accused of some misdeed, he would fight tooth and nail; "Oh I don't believe that at all! You must be mistaken. He's quite incapable of that sort of thing." And should it finally be proven beyond all shadow of a doubt that the man was actually guilty of the misdeed, McMurtry would immediately look for a defense for the commission of the act. "Well, if you're sure of it, then it must be so. But I'm quite sure that he had a perfectly good reason." He would then insist upon taking care of the matter himself. His punishments, though severe, were always meted out with a lecture so that the guilty party knew without doubt just why he was being punished and therefore would not take it personally. McMurtry was no fool though and was a keen judge of character. Malcontents, slackers, and ne'er-do-well's were quickly sent packing. By the same token, if any of his men directly lied to him, or caused undo harm to the company's reputation, that man would often find himself on his way to another company, usually before the hour was up.

His popularity with his men also stemmed from his compassion to their problems. While it helped that he felt himself to be just like any one of his men, more importantly *they* saw him as, deep down, one of them, despite his status before the war. He had a ready, easy smile and a genuine affection for his men and his work that he made no effort whatsoever to hide. He was as apt to clap the lowest buck private on the back in good humor as he was a fellow officer. Moreover, McMurtry also had a tendency to take the failures of his company to heart, which, in and of itself, was heartbreaking for his men to see. Therefore, they tried harder than other units to please their commander, so as not to break the big, generous heart at their lead. None of this is to say that McMurtry was 'walked on' or considered amiable by the men he commanded however. On the contrary; it was well understood by everyone who was the leader and who were the led, and no doubt his status as a 'hero' of the Spanish-American War held some of his men in awe.

In addition to his soldiers, McMurtry was tremendously popular within the group of officers that made up the 308th. He had known a good deal of them in civilian life as business contacts and nearly all felt honored to be able to call him friend as well as serve with him. Many of his fellow officers remarked later that one of the finest sights at Camp Upton was seeing McMurtry proudly leading his Company E in formation marching; always out front, his chest bursting with pride like a father.

McMurtry was particularly noted for his trademarks of speech, his most famous being the saying "Practically OK". Nothing was ever, "fine and dandy", "wonderful", or "fabulous" with McMurtry; it was always, "Practically OK". Moreover, nothing was going to happen, "right away", or he was never, "positive"; the correct correlating response to either was, "Surest thing you know". And, more often than not, he would announce his arrival at some official function by striding through the door with the exclamation, "Okay I'm here. What's the dope?"

Now, in France, Captain McMurtry was leading "his boys" into death and destruction, watching them get killed and maimed. However, it apparently did not bother him as much as one would think. He was, after all, a realist and a war veteran. His company was a company of war, and it was expected that it would take casualties. He had watched it already in 1898 and again on the Vesle in 1918 and had long ago prepared himself for it. Now, he simply accepted it. While some men returned home broken by the war mentally or emotionally, by all accounts it appears to have little affected George McMurtry, despite the many men he saw killed and the wounds he himself was to later receive in the Pocket with the Lost Battalion. (12, 29, 48, 51, 52, 72, 79, 101, 109, 152, 153, 219, 238, 246, 257, 343, 347, 350, 357, 358, 359, 361)

In looking at the map of the area they were now in, Major Whittlesey would have had a good general idea of the 1st Battalion's situation as it moved forward that afternoon, even in light of his map's technical deficiencies. To the west of l'Homme Mort (militarily known as Hill 230) was more broken forest and then farmland. Through that open land, ran the regimental dividing line that his left flank had actually been operating across on and off for the last two days looking for liaison with the 368th. Further west of the line was more farmland and the broken ground within the zone of Groupement Durand before the little town of Binarville. Heading due north, as his command now was, the heavily forested opposite slope of l'Homme Mort came down into the Ravin d'Argonne at a point where it opened up some and the Binarville-Moulin de l'Homme Mort road ran at its foot to the mill. The mill complex itself was situated on the right side of the ravine some 200 meters north of l'Homme Mort, astride a wagon road, a rail line and a small pond and was overlooked by the heights of Les Quatre Chenes to the east. The ravine itself continued on a southern course, around to the east of l'Homme Mort, gradually narrowing; that particular section of the ravine was commonly referred to as the 'Ravin Moulin de l'Homme Mort'. The ravine then continued relatively straight for about 400 meters before it made a sharp eastward angle to form the 'Ravin Depot des Machines'. And it was there that 2nd/308th was busy getting its teeth kicked in along the southwestern grade of the Depot ravine. (365, 368, 370)

Once they had arrived, soon after 2:00 p.m., Major Budd placed Captain McMurtry and the rest of Company E to the rear of the advance zone, reuniting him with Lt. Stevens's unit and hooking him up with the remnant of Company B. The gang of B sent out to find the machine-gun that had been giving them fits on the left had since returned to report that it had disappeared. With that flank apparently secured, the command slowly began to advance. It soon came upon a dense wire belt near the crest of the ridge looking into the ravine. Breathless scouts that had been following a rail spur line as it ran into the ravine came back to report of major Hun activity there and a fair sized rail and goods yard.

Quickly, Major Budd dispersed the 2nd Battalion for battle, spread out in skirmish lines with the left along a rail line from that flank and the right hooked with the 307th, which was fighting its way through terrible tangles of barbed wire overgrown with weeds. The area was very properly defended. To the east, at the point of juncture with the 307th, enemy machine-guns opened up and were doing sizable damage. Captain McMurtry sent out a Chauchat team to see what could be done about silencing it, while from behind, long-range Hotchkiss fire continued to skim in just over the heads of the Doughboys. Out ahead, the two platoons of Company B ran into fire from directly in front and hunkered down to deal with it. Not realizing that they had halted, Captain McMurtry kept E moving and soon had them running up into B from the rear. He pulled the reins back, but it was too late and was going to take some time to straighten out. The enemy shellfire, meanwhile, started coming in heavier. Mixed in with it, men caught the heavy scent of mustard gas. Masks on, they continued to try to work their way around the nests. It was almost 2:30 p.m. (101, 109)

Meanwhile, with the 1st Battalion moving steadily up l'Homme Mort and the 2nd Battalion now properly engaged and presumably well on its way to battling through to the objective line, Major Budd took his PC over and joined it with Major Whittlesey's. Whether this was by Whittlesey's order or on Budd's own initiative is unclear. In either case, Captain McMurtry, experienced combat officer that he was, seemingly had things well in hand on the right (McMurtry's entangled situation was most likely unknown to both Budd and Whittlesey at that moment). With the attack progressing well, combining the two PCs would not have seemed a bad idea. Major Budd would have felt no qualms about combining with Major Whittlesey and then moving out behind the 1st Battalion toward the objective, which is in fact what they were to do. Hindsight, of course, says different, for this decision left the 2nd Battalion basically leaderless at a critical juncture that afternoon.

The 1st Battalion began the advance up the gentle up slope of l'Homme Mort with Company A again out front. It was there on that gloomy hillside that Lt. Clint Whiting, last surviving officer of A, was hit. Unheeding of the danger, he had stayed out front of the company directing a gang's fire against a machine-gun hidden in some marshy area, in an eerie similarity to the afternoon of the 26th. (Seriously wounded, he would eventually die in later in October.) Company 1st Sergeant Herman J. Bergasse immediately stepped forward and silenced the nest, which actually contained two guns. Sergeant Bergasse later got the Distinguished Service Cross for the action but, in the meantime, found himself temporarily in command of Company A - or what was left of it. (32, 96, 137)

Fighting past the narrow gauge rail line and on up the hill, Major Whittlesey's scouts slugged it out heatedly with a determined German machine-gun crew near a small clearing. When the smoke cleared, they pushed on ahead and came upon an unpretentious German cemetery surrounded by a low wooden fence. Off to one side was a small hut, nearly indistinguishable from the forest around it. Saplings had been bent over in front of the little building making it barely noticeable, save for the beaten footpath leading to the doorway. One of the scouts that helped clear the area was Pvt. Nell:

"That afternoon we passed by a two room log cabin… and a little cemetery out to one side. We circled around this place and just as we got to the back of it, a machine gun opened up on us, the bullets hitting all around… We all dropped to the ground, but our platoon leader stopped and looked at a piece of paper, which I suppose was a map… the commander put the paper back in his pocket, looked at us and said, 'Get up, and stay up. What are you dropping to the ground for? You men must be scared to stand up?' We kept on advancing in spite of the machine gun fire…" (40)

Off in the distance to their right, a pitched battled echoed as the Combined Battalion PC, moving 200 meters behind the main line, came through the area at about a quarter to five that afternoon. Lead elements were out combing the hillside ahead and there was plenty of small arms fire. Major Whittlesey's 1st Battalion adjutant, Lt. McKeogh, placed a three-man runner post dug in near the north edge of the cemetery as they paused for a time. The distance he was dropping his posts from each other had been steadily diminishing over the past two days, from an average of 300 meters in between posts at the start to now closer to 150 meters. In many cases, posts were even closer; 100 meters or less, due to the denseness of the damned foliage. Little did the lieutenant know, but it was not the last he would see of the area. (34, 109, 116, 271)

By about 3:30 p.m., the 2nd Battalion advance was already faltering. Private Halligan, an accomplished battalion runner in Company E, was the first to notice the serious trouble when he spotted four Germans off the *left* flank moving around farther back than they should have been. Heading off at top speed to report the news to Captain McMurtry, Pvt. Halligan took a hit along the way, but made it with the information nonetheless. Lieutenant Stevens took another gang from Company E off into the bushes to reconnoiter the area just as combat teams that Major Budd had earlier sent out to the right were returning to Captain McMurtry with the news that there were Huns all over the place on that flank. Fire was coming from the heights of the crest across the Depot ravine, as well as from within the Ravin Moulin de l'Homme Mort ahead and left. Intense mortar fire was dropping in everywhere and despite all good efforts, they had not been able to get anywhere near to crossing the Depot ravine. Things looked bad, and they were about to get much worse.

Lieutenant Stevens and the platoon of Company E had just completed their reconnaissance search for Private Halligan's Germans on the left. Having found nothing, they were moving back into place when the trouble really started. Captain McMurtry was still back with the majority of E, to the rear of B, when someone again saw Germans moving, this time by the far *right* flank. Almost at the same instant, a German machine-gun opened up and tore into the right rear of Company E. A cry ripped the air: "We're flanked!" Men began to drop and American rifles turned, pouring general fire toward the right and right rear. A messenger tore through the woods for Lt. Stevens, who turned a Chauchat team back with the hopes of taking out the machine-gun from the rear, while the rest of Company E pushed hard against the flank, trying to keep the enemy at bay.

This was serious trouble. A wedge of Germans had apparently pushed their way between the left of the 307th and the right of the 308th and appeared to be attempting to turn the 2nd Battalion's right flank. Worse, the 307th, farther afield to the east, seemed to be faltering as well and there was simply not enough left of 2nd/308th to extend the line farther in that direction. Similarly, since they had not been able to keep up with the relatively rapid progress made by the 1st Battalion going up l'Homme Mort on the other side of the ravine ahead, fire was coming in from the left too. (Liaison between the two had broken down about the time the German had been spotted on the left.) That meant that if Pvt. Halligan's Germans were there in any strong numbers, both flanks were seriously threatened. There seemed little choice then: 2nd Battalion would have to fall back… (101, 103, 109)

The 307th had, in fact, managed remarkably well this day compared with the previous. Jump-off had been accomplished at around 6:45 a.m. behind a rolling barrage and forward progress was rapid from the get-go. At first, companies I and M, from left to right (with L and K behind), formed the advance line and slowly plodded off into the wilderness behind the raining shells, with the 2nd Battalion following in close support about 400 meters back. They already knew that the terrain would be difficult from the previous days' advance. Therefore, bracing themselves for the storm of fire they expected, they plowing forward and were pleasantly surprised to find that the enemy retreat had given them the break they needed to push across and up the opposite slope of the Ravin Fountaine aux Charmes. By about 11:00 a.m. they had reached the Bagatelle Pavilion, about a kilometer ahead. Bagatelle however was all that the pavilions in the forest could be, containing both electric lights, hot water, and, similar to what the left column of 308th had found, a small Boche cemetery, this one surrounded by a low, stone wall. It was also cleverly laid out and rear-guard elements of the German 122nd and 120th made sure that the fight at Bagatelle was exceptionally sharp. Ultimately, however, the pavilion fell into U.S. hands. By noon, lead elements of the regiment had paused to catch their breath and scrounge German rations from within the pavilion, while the remainder of the two merged battalions caught up in the rear.

They moved off again behind a midday barrage and soon caught up with the 308th's right flank. Trenches and rail line were encountered across the front again as the troops slowly and relentlessly pressed forward. Toward mid-afternoon, scouts encountered some heavy belts of wire and reconnoitered a German railhead, which turned out to be the Depot des Machines. The 2nd Battalion of the 308th was then attacking the southwest edge and angle of the position. The 307th's Company I attacked in force near the middle of the Depot, as Company L came up from support and tried to turn around their east flank. Neither attack was successful, though Captain Rainsford's men in L did manage to swing the line a bit farther north on the right. Then the Germans counterattacked and drove some infiltrators through between the 307th and 308th at the liaison point. Company I was slightly beaten back by the enemy mortar and machine-gun fire, which the 2nd/308th mistook for a withdrawal and so themselves began to slowly sink to the rear as well. Company K turned to assist, but it was too late. With liaison gone, infiltrators firing machine-guns into their left and the attack by Company L failing on their right, Company I now actually did pull back. By early evening, the 3rd/307th was a scattered unit, retired almost 600 meters behind the leading unit of the 308th's right flank and all liaison to the west was gone. (91, 99, 103, 104, 119, 139, 235)

With Germans infiltrating on both flanks, there seemed little choice but for the 2nd/308th to pull back. Yet, any action such as that would be a direct violation of G.O. #27. Even Captain McMurtry, as ranking officer of the unit at that moment, hardly had the authority to order the maneuver. In this instance however, it is eminently clear (and so it was in Company I/307th to the right) that there was no time to wait for such an order to be first requested, then received, approved, then received back, and then acted upon. A field decision needed to be made *now* and for all intents and purposes it appears that Captain McMurtry made it, though without any official authorization from 77th Division PC to do so. (However, if McMurtry, or any other officer for that matter, had made the official request, or if it was approved, no record of it has yet been found anywhere.) It is unlikely that such a movement would have been authorized anyway, for not only would that mean a set back to the all important forward momentum, but it would also leave Major Whittlesey and the 1st Battalion in just such a position as they were to soon find themselves; well ahead of the main body of the 308th, with only a thin runner line connecting them to the rear. An order for continued assault would almost certainly have been the answer to any request to pull back. Yet, the decision to evacuate the slope of the Depot ravine was made, although precisely by who remains a mystery. In any case, a gradual withdrawal started back to the line of the railroad track. It was just after 4:30 p.m.

As they drew back through the shelling, Captain McMurtry stood at the forefront with pistol in hand blazing away, since Lt. Stevens had been badly wounded by that time and carried back. This left Lt. James V. Leak, the 40th Division replacement officer from Texas, as the last Company E officer standing, other than Captain McMurtry himself. During the movement rearward, a ration party came up, attempting to get food to the men who had earlier missed out. However, they were forced by a sudden and intense mortar attack to abandon their precious cargo and take shelter in a trench with some Company E men. Slowly, all around them they watched as the battered 2nd Battalion made its way back, in direct violation of General Order # 27, over the ground it had just crossed two hours earlier as the precious food was blown away. (91, 101, 103, 109)

Conversation was kept to a minimum as Major Whittlesey and the combined battalion PC passed the cleared German cemetery and crossed up to and over the crest of l'Homme Mort that afternoon. The officer-less Company A was still out ahead, while scouts snaked through the underbrush, occasionally coming back with a report. It was unusual for a battalion commander to move so far ahead, just about 200 meters behind the main assault company, but it was good for control in the dense terrain of the forest. The scouts could easily find him, and he could know quickly any situation that might develop and act accordingly. Though the shelling had slacked off considerably, light trench mortar shells were still dropping through the trees in a random pattern. The men could hear the Germans moving about freely in the woods in front of them, but could hardly see them through the thick brush. It was nerve-wracking work in the lessening light of the murky day. As the Doughboys pushed up the hill, machine-guns rattled and rifles cracked up toward the crest, to the right and left. Word came back of serious resistance near the top.

The Major had most likely listened to the noise of the pitched battle that the 2nd Battalion had been having to his right rear and no doubt had wondered what troubles they had found. Liaison had been sporadic since the two units had split apart and the Major had recently sent another scout team out to try to make contact and investigate, but they were not back yet. None of the patrols sent west that afternoon had yet returned either, so Whittlesey still had no solid information to go on from that direction as well. But at least there was a solid link with the rear. Lieutenant McKeogh had been establishing his runner posts about every 100 meters now, for safety, until by the time they had reached the northern slope of the hill in the failing light of that afternoon, he had 12 in place stretching back to advanced Regimental PC (now situated at Karlplatz). As thunder echoed across the hillside, the men shook their heads and swore. It was a racing certainty that it would rain again sometime during the night. (32, 40, 91, 218, 220, 271)

The scout team that Major Whittlesey sent out that afternoon consisted of Sergeant Robert Hitlin of Company F and two privates, whose names are lost to the sands of time. Their orders were to proceed across the shallow valley to the east, find Captain McMurtry and report the situation back to Major Whittlesey as quickly as possible. Almost as soon as Sgt. Hitlin and the two junior men started through the woods into the Ravin Moulin de l'Homme Mort, machine-guns opened up on them from seemingly all sides. It was obvious that the Huns still had control immediately to the right of the 1st Battalion's current position. Yet by making best use of the tangled mess around them for cover, Sgt. Hitlin and his men slowly started working their way across.

By early evening, when all had been quiet for some time, they felt that they had to be close to where the 2nd Battalion had been engaged, but instead found only a large German camp down in a ravine. Pushing on, in an attempt to make contact with anyone in khaki now, the sergeant and his two men were spotted and fired at by another two machine-guns buried deep in the trees opposite a small clearing they were crossing. Sergeant Hitlin and one private managed to make it across, but the other private took a hit halfway and went down. Up in a flash, Hitlin dashed out into the open, slapped a field dressing on the wound in record time and carried the private back to cover. Quickly and quietly, the three men worked deeper into the brush and hid themselves from the enemy patrol that came out looking for them. They were obviously surrounded and realized they would have to wait for nightfall before they could attempt to move again. (109, 116, 237)

Major Whittlesey called a halt in the increasing forest shadows and the men began digging in. It had been the devil's own day and everyone was exhausted. They had made it to the north foot of l'Homme Mort, but without ease. Coming up to the crest of the hill, on top, and then coming down the opposite slope, there had been a fine fight against a German outpost line, with plenty of grenades, machine-gun fire and stiff resistance of every kind. Still, they had suffered few casualties. Once they broke through to the opposite foot of the hill, scouts came back with encouraging reports. Straight ahead and to the right, some 150 to 200 meters into the wide Ravin d'Argonne and against the slope of the heights of Les Quatre Chenes, sat the Moulin de l'Homme Mort next to its little millpond and a complex of bunkers and cabins on the slope above it. A thick screen of trees camouflaged it from view. (32, 40, 220)

They were in sight of the objective. However, there were other points to consider as the two battalion commanders discussed their situation. Sergeant Hitlin and his men had not yet returned from the east. Without the 2nd Battalion, which was yet nowhere in sight, any attack forward would have to wait for tomorrow for lack of support. Nor had any further orders come up yet from anyone at Regimental. It was about 5:20 p.m. Not much choice but to stay put for the night—if not actually on the objective, at least close enough to readily reach it, once they had the right number of troops. Dark was falling rapidly, along with a steady light rain again, as he sent word for company commanders to gather in a small clearing at the bottom of the hill for disposition orders.

They were currently parked on a northern slope where they would be open to enemy shellfire. That was bad. On the other hand, their current position offered plenty of comfortable shelter. Tucked into a wash of the northern slope of the hill they had just crossed was a fine concrete bunker with a log pavilion above and behind it, further into the cutting. Here Major Whittlesey put combined Battalion PC and had the wounded moved into part of the bunker and the huts above it. Across from that bunker, on the opposite side of the wash, were more light buildings. Running past the cutting and wrapping around the foot of the hill in an easterly direction was a portion of rail line, which followed a road that lead in from Binarville, to their west. Dug into the slope of the hill, on the south side of the rail line, was a series of log cabin-like structures that had been leveled by the afternoon barrage. The rail line continued around the hill southward to the Depot des Machines. Near the top edge of the hill, before it began its steep northern decent toward the clearing they now stood in, ran a narrow, muddy path running east/west with a proper entrenchment along a high bank on its southern edge. Here, the Germans had made a stiff stand. There was plenty of wire up there and the men had had a devil of a time fighting through it. Below the hill, in front of the dugout complex in the wash, was the clearing. It was about a quarter the size of a football field and bordered on the north by the Binarville-Moulin de l'Homme Mort road. Another muddy road slowly angled off and away from the Binarville road and ran past the mill before continuing on down the floor of the Ravin d'Argonne, with its steep slopes of underbrush and young timber towering above on each side. A rail line ran parallel to the road and down the ravine as well. A stream bubbled its way from the millpond and under the Binarville road before taking a more easterly path around the foot of the hill. (109, 367, 370, 371)

It had gotten strangely quiet around them as Majors Whittlesey and Budd waited for their officers with resignation. There was no denying the situation. No word had been received from 2nd Battalion on the right all afternoon. In fact, it had been ominously quiet over there for some time. Obviously they were not on an even line with the 1st Battalion, indicating that they remained somewhere behind and probably disorganized. This presumably left the 1st Battalion's right flank open for an unknown distance. Similarly, there had been no word from the 368th on the left and knowing how far back *they* had been for the last two days, it seemed a racing certainty that they too were nowhere near even with the 1st/308th, meaning that the left flank was likely wide open as well. The Germans were sure to probe both areas and, left or right, infiltration was infiltration. The 1st Battalion was then at great risk of being cut off from the rear and surrounded; an unsettling thought if there ever was one.

Still, things might not be as bad as they first seemed. After all, there had been no infiltration through the left flank as yet during the battle and it had been open for three days now. Additionally, division was definitely aware of the 368th's deficiencies and had been making compensations for them. There was no reason to believe that they would not continue to do so. Then too, the hold up on the right was likely just temporary and any open areas to the east would quickly be filled in during the attack that was sure to come at first light next morning. Liaison might even come up yet tonight. Therefore, if the 1st Battalion could manage this one night alone, everything would likely be fine in the morning.

It is easy to imagine Major Whittlesey looking up at his company commanders gathered around him in the failing light of that little clearing, the drizzling rain dripping off his helmet and speckling his wire frame glasses, as he laid things out in his usual calm, low voiced way.

They would dig in; disposition in a narrow hollow square would be roughly 350 meters by 250 meters or so. Company C along the north side, F along the east, H along the south, and A along the west. Combined battalion headquarters would be in the concrete bunker near the northern edge of the perimeter with the First Aid. Outposts would be set accordingly, but kept in tight. Heavy machine-guns would be arranged to guard both flanks accordingly. Companies A and F, which were the weakest, would be widely spaced and the position would not very wide in depth because of that. Therefore, to provide them plenty of protection and allow for some slight 'overlap' on the corners, auto rifle teams would be interspersed along the northern and southern sides at regular intervals. The few trench mortar men would stay put around Battalion PC with orders that no mortar would fire unless absolutely necessary. There would also be no shooting unless attacked. Given their very exposed position, they had to presume that both flanks were open and they could not, therefore, risk a big fight. However, he advised his officers not to apprise their men of the situation that night, in order to avoid greater panic. He did however remind them to warn their men to be very much on guard because the Boche was already known to be fond of infiltrating in small groups and then striking when the odds were decidedly in their favor. There would also be regular, shallow, patrols run out all night, but kept to the short space between the battalion and the German's 'front yard', the mill complex just head of their position. (32, 40, 109, 271, 367, 370, 371)

With dispositions set, Major Whittlesey's next concern was to send word to the rear of their present situation. He scribbled out a message and gave it to Lt. McKeogh to start down the runner chain, giving position coordinates and asking for food, water, and ammunition for the Chauchat auto rifles. "We have also suffered considerably from lack of drinking water...The men are tired but in good spirits..." it read in part. (246)

With that message heading back, Lt. McKeogh decided it might be a good idea to fly a message out by pigeon as well. That he thought to do this is a pretty good indication of the high degree of concern over their situation he must have felt, as well as just how tenuous he thought the runner line might actually be. (And who would likely know better?) Certainly, the situation warranted it, for they had never found themselves in quite such a precarious position as this one was. It is also likely that Major Whittlesey, despite the calm façade he presented to the men, probably felt this way too, but never let on. Instead, he remained outwardly convinced that all would be well with morning. Lieutenant McKeogh released his bird anyway:

Our position for the night is now being organized at 100 yards south of l'Homme Mort (294.7 – 274.5). 2 Co's 1st Bn and 2 Co's 2nd Bn and 1st and 2nd Bn Hqs are here. The 4 Co's on right of ravine we have not heard from yet except that they were advancing beyond parallel 274 three hours ago. (246)

It was sometime after 5:30 p.m. when the 1st Battalion handler, Private Omer Richards, rolled the thin message paper up, stuffed it into the tiny tube attached to the pigeon's leg and tossed the bird into the air - which immediately started for the German lines. The message would not be found until noon of the 30th, when the pigeon landed in the loft of the French liaison officers assigned to the 306th Infantry, well over to the east and far too

144

late to be of any good. (144)

Meanwhile, the night's darkness and rain proved just what Sergeant Hitlin and his hunkered down patrol was waiting for. Since there seemed little chance that he and his two men would be able to find the 2nd Battalion's position in the darkness, the sergeant had decided to haul ass back to Major Whittlesey's position and report all they had seen that day. There did not seem to be anyone on the right except Germans and that, Sgt. Hitlin knew, was bad news that the Major would want to know immediately. With less worry about sound now that intermittent machine-gun and rifle fire was popping off from all different directions along with the falling rain, the three men set off through the cold, black night.

Possessed with a gifted sense of direction, Sgt. Hitlin led right back to the beginning of the trail leading up the hill near the Hun cemetery. As they stumbled through the darkness, feeling their way forward, it dawned on Hitlin that they had come across no runner posts yet. All at once, they were hailed - in German! Momentarily stunned, they froze. Then, recovering their wits, all three quickly dove for cover in the brush as rifle fire sang out after them.

They had quickly become separated as they tore pell-mell through the dark night and Sergeant Hitlin found himself alone, hiding in the brush. After things had calmed down some, the slightly unnerved sergeant carefully began a reconnaissance of the area. He *had* to be in the right spot; even in the darkness, he could recognize some physical features of the land he had taken note of earlier. Carefully and quietly, he continued his search over the hillside and found nothing but Germans. Lots of them. Slowly, he came to the disturbing conclusion that Major Whittlesey and the rest of the men up on the hill had been cut off from the rear sometime during the evening and were quite possibly surrounded. (109, 116)

As full darkness fell so too did a heavy, cold rain. Company I/307th pulled back to a quarry located in a smaller ravine that ran north/south into the Depot ravine. There, they began scraping out their funk holes, taking up secure positions tucked into the hillside with no liaison in any direction. Company L withdrew eastward 600 yards away from the ravine, buried its dead on a flat in the wet darkness, and set outposts in a full circle around the position it occupied on a slope. Captain Rainsford did not risk sending out liaison parties; he was already convinced that they were out ahead of the main force and alone in enemy territory. The remainder of the 307th's companies simply camped where darkness and rain had stopped them. All, that is, except Company E, which had failed to keep up and was extended in a long Cossack line off the right flank back to the 306th.

Throughout the night, all forward units of the 307th, each believing itself to be alone, kept a nervous vigil. Occasional shells dropped, machine-guns and rifles sang out from nervous fingers and flares and star shells burst overhead and slowly wound to the ground. It was all too much like a nightmare for the men concerned and one hell of a long night. (138, 139)

Meanwhile, a ration detail had also been sent back down the runner line from the 1st/308th's bivouac on l'Homme Mort just before 9:00 p.m. to bring up much-needed food. Below the north slope of the hillside, the men who tried to get water from the stream found themselves under sniper fire. There were a few wounded because of it and thus the men had only the mixed blessing of rainwater again. The wounded were carried to the little log hut above the concrete dugout, where battalion medics had set up shop. Some of the Company C men, manning the northern edge of the position, got lucky and took up residence within the ruins of the bombed out huts along the hillside. Throughout the night, they took turns manning the holes of the perimeter line, the outposts and going on patrol. On top of the hill, along the southern edge of the perimeter and along both flank sides, men talked in half whispers in the light rain and huddled together in their holes to try to generate a little warmth. They could hear movement in the pitch-black bushes around them, but no one could say for sure whether it was their own patrols or the Germans. Thank God there was little shelling to worry about. Only occasional rifle fire and the bark of a distant machine-gun cut the air, but none seemed close enough to matter. Nevertheless, the glow of a cigarette or the flash of a match made an excellent aiming point. Therefore, the usual no smoking order went out. Not that it was much needed in the rain. (32, 34, 109, 237, 271)

The rain continued to be a mixed blessing to the 2nd/308th men dug in back on the main divisional line as well. Since one can only drink muddy or gas-infected water for so long before the body reacts violently to it, patrols going out and ration details headed for the rear left canteens, mess kits and upturned helmets sitting out. German shelling had eased quite a bit in the rain and ahead all was relatively quiet. A strange sort of resignation set in along the line on both sides, the obvious result of the relentlessly shitty weather and exhaustion.

On the main line, following the unplanned rearward exit of 2nd Battalion that afternoon, a 400-meter-wide lateral hole had been left open in the 308th's line between the further advanced 1st Battalion and the 2nd to the rear. Nothing had been heard from Major Whittlesey for several hours. Did he not recognize that 1st Battalion was alone out there? Even if he did, it was increasingly unlikely that the Major would risk a mass movement of his command back down l'Homme Mort through the ink-black forest at night, especially without formal orders to do so and as far as anyone knew (including Captain McMurtry), no such withdrawal order had been sent up - or was likely to be.

Therefore, the hole in the main line needed to be covered to prevent enemy infiltration. It would be a simple enough task; merely set a line of men along a compass bearing headed due west to the general area of the divisional boundary line. The remains of Company F were already out on that flank to connect with anyway. It would necessarily be a very thin line though, because 2nd Battalion did not have many men at its disposal, but the line would advance and reach Major Whittlesey the next morning anyway. Therefore it would be all right; for one night anyway.

Once the pull back on the right had been completed and the positions there solidly established then, it was likely Captain McMurtry that extended the line westward, using Company G to cover the ground left open by the advanced 1st Battalion. The 2nd Battalion then was at least 400 meters or so to the rear of Major Whittlesey's right flank and consolidated on a line running parallel to a railroad track extending from the divisional left boundary over to the Boyau des Cuistots, a major north/south communication trench that the Boche would not be using anytime soon. Liaison to the 307th was uncertain in the dark. To the 368th in the west, liaison between them and 2nd/308th was still nonexistent and few knew the exact position of their line. (91, 109, 132, 133)

However, by 8:00 p.m. that night, two aviators of the 50th Aero Squadron, Lt. Forrest McCook and Lt. 'Mickey' Lockwood, knew the 368th's true line positions though. Flying to a mere 500 feet at times, they had given up on locating the 77th's line in the dense forest that afternoon. Instead, they had turned their attentions to finding the scattered 368th, when they were downed by enemy machine-gun fire somewhere over the Groupement Durand area. They came down among the French, who turned them over to some 368th Doughboys and the two flyers then scouted the situation by foot and field telephone. By nightfall, they had the full scoop and telephoned their PC at Remicourt with the information. (110, 249)

The 368th had been a broken regiment when daylight came on the 28th. Its companies, scattered all to hell and back in the wire and devastation two and a half kilometers south of Binarville, had little liaison with each other, let alone with the 308th, and plenty of casualties. The French 1st D.C.D decided that reinforcement was needed and sent Machine Gun Company/368th and two platoons of the 351st Machine Gun Battalion to be divided equally between the 2nd and 3rd/368th for the day's fresh assaults. In the right zone, where 2nd Battalion was licking its wounds, the news raised little hope. Company F, which had gotten farthest forward and almost ruptured the German 254th's lines the afternoon previous, had limped back from its positions in front of Tranchee Tirpitz about 5:00 a.m., arriving at Tranchee de Finlande about 11:00 a.m.. Along the way, it managed to gather in the squads it had lost the previous day, but casualties had reduced the company by almost half now. Companies E, G, and H also assembled in and around Tranchee de Finlande throughout the morning, but no attacks were attempted as the disorganized units tried to straighten themselves out.

At 12:30 p.m., attack orders were issued calling for the 2nd Battalion to protect the right flank of the 3rd in an afternoon attack, which had as its objective the little flattened town of Binarville. Again, it was Company F in the middle that made it the farthest, reaching a position in the Vallee Moreau about 200 meters ahead of Tranchee Tirpitz before being halted about 5:30 p.m. in the face of intense machine-gun fire. Once more, they remained isolated all night in an exposed position with no liaison. On the left, Company H also reached Tranchee Tirpitz, turned west and attacked down the Vallee Moreau in an effort to protect the 3rd Battalion's right flank as ordered. They met with heavy machine-gun and artillery fire and by 6:00 p.m. had fallen back to the Tranchee de Damas, 500 meters farther south of Tranchee de Finlande, where they had started.

On the right, Company E advanced north all afternoon through intense shelling and machine-gun fire following a narrow gauge rail line and communication trench, until by 4:00 p.m. they had made it to Tranchee Tirpitz. However there, German rear guards (of the 1st/254th) had a score to settle with the black Doughboys of E from the previous day and launched a furious grenade and machine-gun assault. Rumor had it among the Germans that Company E had captured several 254th men, tortured and finally executed them; the story apparently begun by a self-proclaimed "lone survivor" who managed to crawl back to the German lines, though horribly wounded. Therefore nothing was spared against the black troops and they were forced back as far as the Tranchee de Finlande in some of the most vicious and brutal fighting yet seen in the area. They finally ended the night in a narrow valley behind Finlande, isolated, without any liaison and at least a kilometer behind the 308th's left flank.

The left section of the 368th, the 3rd Battalion, had no more luck that day than their 2nd had. All their morning attacks had fragmented and failed by 2:30 p.m. just south of the Vallee Moreau. Drawn back, a second effort was made about 5:30 p.m., which also never made it past the valley. Though companies of the battalion held a relatively even line just south of Moreau all night, they had no firm liaison in either direction.

Had the 368th been able to get into Binarville that day as planned, Groupement Durand had assigned to them a French cavalry regiment, the 10th Dragoons, to exploit the breakthrough. However, by the time the 3rd Battalion's afternoon attack had floundered and the 2nd had scattered to the wind, the French decided drastic measures were needed in Groupement Durand's area. Orders were issued for the 1st/368th, then in reserve, to move forward and relieve the 2nd/368th overnight while a battalion of the French 9th C.a.P would relieve the 3rd/368th. The Dragoon detachment would then act as liaison between the 9th and 11th C.a.P., while 1st/368th had strict orders to reestablish contact with the 308th on September 29. With these arrangements made, another attack on Binarville was scheduled for dawn. (46, 92)

Sometime during the evening, 154th Brigade PC sent orders for liaison elements of

Company I/308th to head for the Tranchee du Dromadaire, a trench line roughly corresponding with the line occupied by the 308th's leading elements (Major Whittlesey excluded). They set out for, but did not reach, the trench until early the next morning. Instead, they had remained holed up for the night in the vicinity of Tranchee du Courlande due to the extreme dark and rain. Their mission had not been to protect the left flank overnight anyway, but instead to position themselves to cover it during the attack scheduled for the next day; an attack, which was scheduled to come off in full accordance with the "pushed (forward) without reference to troops to right or left" order. There was, therefore, no front line liaison of the left flank at all during the night of the 28th between the 368th and the main body (2nd Battalion) of the 308th. Instead, a 600-meter gap existed between them and the established 308th front line, with an additional 400 meters or so between there and Major Whittlesey's forward position.

Therefore, the situation that night ended with 2nd/308th holding the line with refused flanks, the majority of 3rd/308th down near Regimental PC in the dark and the whole of the 368th either scattered or held up in the rear. Major Whittlesey's 1st/308th consequently had absolutely no flank support whatsoever for some 450 meters on the right and for at least a full kilometer on the left. There they unwittingly remained - an island of U.S. khaki in a sea of German field gray. (10, 91, 92, 131, 146)

Stealthily, with his nerves taking a beating at every turn, Sergeant Hitlin slowly worked his way back through the pouring rain, past the German encampments behind l'Homme Mort. It seemed as if 'hundreds' of Germans had magically appeared in the last few hours, and he tried hard to make mental notes of as many positions as possible. Pre-dawn found him struggling into the Company I/308th element ensconced in front of the Tranchee du Courlande. From there, he was quickly guided back to the Regimental PC, which had that day moved up to Karlplatz. There before Colonel Stacey, Lt. Col. Smith, the 308th's Regimental Adjutant, Lt. Conn, and Captain Bradley Delehanty, the Regimental Intelligence Officer, Sgt. Hitlin told his tale. It was the first information to come in concerning the 1st Battalion since Lt. McKeogh's last runner message. Sent around 6:00 p.m., it that had only arrived a short time ago. They all stood listening, incredulous, as Sgt. Hitlin relayed his assurance that Major Whittlesey and 1st Battalion were indeed cut off. Between 9 and 10 p.m., he had encountered German patrols all along the l'Homme Mort hillside, he said. The area behind and right of Major Whittlesey's position was literally crawling with them. It was about 1 a.m. as they pulled out a map for Hitlin to better describe his direction and the hazards he had encountered.

Later, as Colonel Stacey, Lt. Col. Smith, and Captain Delehanty set about making preparations to try and relieve Major Whittlesey and 1st/308th, Sergeant Hitlin probably curled up in a dry corner near the coke stove and got the first real good sleep he had in four days. He earned it, would earn it again the next day and was completely unaware that his actions of the last 18 hours or so had also earned him the Distinguished Service Cross. (109)

Around that same time, Captain McMurtry managed a trip back to Karlplatz through the rainy dark and made his own report of conditions along the main line to Colonel Stacey. It could not have been good news to the new Regimental Commander, particularly as a Regular Army man. His 1st Battalion was now apparently stranded out in enemy lines due in part to an unauthorized troop movement on his right flank by his own 2nd Battalion and in part to the incompetence of the 368th Infantry on his left. Compounding that problem, both the assault and support battalion commanders were stranded out there together, leaving the remainder of 2nd Battalion leaderless. There was also no actual liaison between 2nd/308th and those elements on the 307th's left flank, which no one seemed to know the exact position of, nor with the 368th, which appeared to be in much the same shape and place it had been for the last two days. Therefore, Colonel Stacey had to be wondering just what in hell he had been saddled with.

However, there was little anyone could do about it until light. Until then, Colonel Stacey had Lt. Col. Smith, now designated as temporary 2nd Battalion commander, start laying out plans to attempt a reconnaissance of the situation and organize an ammunition carrying party up to Major Whittlesey at dawn. He himself worked on plans for a continued attack on September 29 that would bring the main line up to the Major's position. There still seemed no need to panic. The open areas surrounding Major Whittlesey would no doubt be filled in during the morning attack and he and his command would be once again fully connected with the rest of the regiment. Colonel Stacey never recorded any questions he may have had concerning the actions of 2nd Battalion's officers and just who started the withdrawal that led to all this, but certainly he must have had some. (109, 238)

General Johnson sure did when he was informed of the situation that night over the telephone however. He fumed at Colonel Stacey, "Any ground gained must be held... If I find anybody ordering a withdrawal from ground once held, I will see that he leaves the service!" This statement by General Johnson not only reinforced General Alexander's original order (this time in a legal way), but it probably carried more weight within the 308th and 307th since the Brigadier was closer within the chain of command to those charged with carrying out the order. (131, 144)

Captain McMurtry, now satisfied that there was nothing more that could be done, decided to call it a night. The rain had chilled him thoroughly. He borrowed an overcoat from a Red Cross man, which he shared in half-hour intervals with three enlisted men and tried to get some sleep. Then, just before dawn, he set off tiredly for the railroad line again. (109)

At 11:00 p.m., 1st Corps issued its orders for the next day's attack. The advance was to begin following the usual half-hour artillery barrage that would commence at 5:30 a.m. Orders also reiterated that the attack would again be pushed forward "without reference to troops to the right or left" and had unchanged objectives. Succinct enough, as neither corps nor division felt a need to expand on the order, this despite the fact that it invited just the sort of troubles that Major Whittlesey and 1st Battalion now found themselves in. However, details of Major Whittlesey's predicament remained largely unknown and would remain so to most; incredibly, even to General Alexander to some degree. Therefore, that particular link in the chain of events leading Major Whittlesey and his men toward the pending incident in the Charlevaux Ravine remained forged and then forgotten. (91, 131)

(I) 'Rules of Engagement' type ideas have been around as long as war itself and have shifted in focus and purpose as each war demanded. However, the AEF in the First World War truly abounded in such twaddle. Literally *hundreds* of documents meant to help civilian soldiers do their jobs better were printed up during the war, some helpful, others much less so. *"Questions For A Battalion Commander To Ask Himself Prior To Taking Over And While Occupying A Portion Of The Front Line"*, *"Questions A Platoon Leader Should Ask Himself On Taking Over A Trench And At Frequent Intervals Thereafter"*, *"Effective Liaison Between Neighboring Units"*, and *"Signaling Instructions For Ground Personnel To Contact Airplanes"* were some of the more 'questionable' manuals issued. Additionally, officers in training were usually taught a set of basic principals under which they should try to conduct their portion of the war. These principals changed slightly in wording and content between the arms of the services as needed, so there was really no 'set' form to them. Nevertheless, they all usually conveyed the same ideas. I found what I believe to be the clearest and most concise set of these ideas in the manual used by the U.S. Marines, *"The Naval Landing Force Manual"* (1918 edition) (11) and it is those principals that I have used as a gauge during the preparations of this book and in my analysis of the orders issued down to Major Whittlesey. They are:
1. Avoid combats that offer no chance of victory or other valuable results.
2. Make every effort for the success of the general plan and avoid spectacular plays that have no bearing on the general result.
3. Have a definite plan and carry it out vigorously. Do not vacillate.
4. Do not attempt complicated maneuvers.
5. Keep the command in hand; avoid undue extension and dispersion.

6. Study the ground and direct the advance in such a way as to take advantage of all available cover and thereby diminish losses.
7. Never deploy until the purpose and proper direction are known.
8. Deploy enough men only for the immediate task in hand; hold out the rest and avoid undue haste in committing them to the action.
9. Flanks must be protected either by reserves, fortifications, or the terrain.
10. In a decisive action gain and maintain fire superiority.
11. Keep up reconnaissance.
12. Use the reserves, but not until needed or a very favorable opportunity for its use presents itself. Keep some reserves as long as practicable.
13. Do not hesitate to sacrifice the command if the result is worth the cost.
14. Spare the command all unnecessary hardships and exertion.

(II) George McMurtry Sr. was an orphaned Irishman from Belfast. He married one Clara Lathrop and came to America in 1870, listing his occupation as 'bookkeeper'. By all accounts, he was a tremendously hard working and ambitious man and must have truly been so, for by the time George Jr. was born, the family already owned and operated several tin plating mills and had virtually built the town of Vandergrift, Pennsylvania, where those mills were located. In fact, one of the local fire stations in Vandergrift is still named for George Sr.

Ancillary sources used in this chapter include: 30, 33, 40, 96, 105, 108, 120, 122, 123, 126, 142, 144, 145, Various 152-216, 218, 219, 224, 227, 230, 245, 246, 252, 264, 272, 374

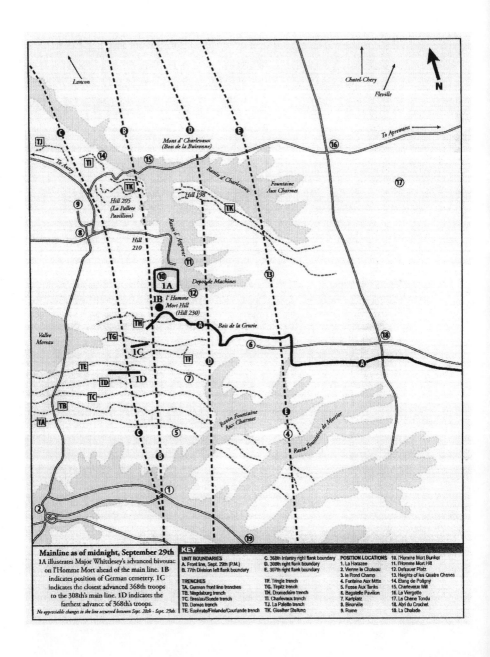

September 29, 1918

"...Stiff and full of rheumatic pains and generally miserable, and to cap the climax we discover that
Jerry has cut us off and we are surrounded. They have broken our line of communication."
From the diary of Private James F. Larney, HQ Company, 1st/308th.

At no time in the so called 'Small Pocket' was there any immediate and clearly defined point at which it was realized by the few officers in Major Whittlesey's command that the 1st Battalion was indeed cut off on the l'Homme Mort hillside. Instead, it was a gradual realization that came over the course of a long morning and slowly gripped them. For their part, the officers simply accepted the situation, if a bit apprehensively, and sat tight to wait it out. The affect was even less emotional on the enlisted men. Most never realized how close a call it was out on that hillside simply because the vast majority were never told of the situation in the first place. By all accounts, Major Whittlesey kept it that way in order to prevent panic or dispersion by men determined to find a way out. Their officers merely told them to sit tight, not wander off, keep quiet, and stay on guard. Some actually thought it was a rest break and wondered aloud about food. (32)

Major Whittlesey played a large part in keeping everyone calm. He was feeling better; the hard living of the previous days of advance having seemingly cured him of most of his initial ailments, except for the disturbing cough which was aggravated by the wet weather. He set a fine example, shaving every day in whatever water he could find, keeping his uniform as clean as he could, and maintaining an optimistic attitude. His only lament, made singularly to his officers and never in front of the men, was the inability to bathe. Calm, cool, and controlled, he stalked all over the hillside that rainy evening of the 28th, talking with the men, praising their efforts and listening intently to their patrol reports periodically through the night. He never seemed to sleep and yet they always found him the same—alert and on the ball. (109, 246)

Looking back, this Small Pocket experience is really an eerie foreshadowing of what would happen in the Charlevaux Ravine in just a few days to come. Here was the first true demonstration of the dedication to orders and vital optimism that made Charles Whittlesey who he was. The whole time on that bleak hillside, he remained sure that the encirclement, if that was truly what it was, would be nothing more than a temporary stall and that the remainder of the regiment would be coming up from the rear at any time. Only once, days later, did he refer to the situation on l'Homme Mort as being "cut off"; instead usually referring to the Small Pocket by saying that they had merely been "without liaison in all directions." His messages out from l'Homme Mort, carried by pigeon, were clear and concise and indicate little, if any, signs of real worry. On the contrary, he showed a remarkable measure of control over the situation and a genuine reluctance to abandon the position in favor of pulling back. He might relatively easily have accomplished this as well early on September 29 by using his men in force, had he received orders to do so. However, he did not receive any orders to withdraw from l'Homme Mort. Therefore, he remained, despite the ever-increasing level of danger around him and the very real possibility of his small units' complete annihilation. The 'close call' of the Small Pocket was not lost on Major Whittlesey either (nor on any of the officers there with him). In fact, it appears to have weighed heavily on his mind over the next two days as his command's story took a much grimmer turn. (109)

As for the Germans, who were in the midst of their general withdrawal to the Giselher Stellung when 1st/308th battled up and settled onto that hillside for the night, they had obviously failed to fully grasp the exact nature of the situation until it was far too late to make full use of it. If they had, Major Whittlesey and his battalion might never have reached their destiny in the Charlevaux Ravine. However, the numbers of the enemy that had infiltrated around the 1st/308th were actually relatively small (despite Doughboy reports of "hundreds of Germans" surrounding them); too small to do much real damage. Due to the withdrawal, only German rear guards (primarily from 6th Company/254th and 10th Company/122nd) were left in the immediate area to deal with the Doughboy threat. The obvious German reinforcements, just down at Depot des Machines, were otherwise occupied with keeping the 2nd/308th and the 3rd/307th at bay. Then too, the general disorganization caused by the savage fighting around Depot des Machines on Major Whittlesey's right, coupled with Groupement Durand's relentless attacks toward the important crossroads town of Binarville to his left, further deflected German attention. Not only had this created a window of opportunity that had allowed 1st/308th to pierce into German withdrawal territory and take up position deeper than the Germans would have liked, it also deflected attention from the position itself just long enough for the rest of the 308th to close up. By the time the Germans had finished pulling back and had gotten organized then, it was too late to take advantage of the unique situation on l'Homme Mort.

That was a mistake by the Germans which would not be repeated. (10, 123, 128, 307)

A hard rain fell continuously throughout the night and by morning misery had again found a home in the forest. Anyone in 1st/308th that managed any sleep had done so only through sheer exhaustion. The sun was far from up when the rain at last began to taper off into a steady, irritating drizzle that would continue sporadically throughout the day. The air was thick and musty with the cold, heavy smell of the wet forest. Smaller funk holes and outpost rifle pits again had standing water in them, while larger funk holes and the entrenchments atop l'Homme Mort were bogs of frigid slime. Chilled to the bone, with uniforms soaked through, the men on outpost duty hugged the muddy earth beneath them. Shivering almost uncontrollably without overcoats or blankets and, peering hard through the icy ground fog around them, they watched for signs of enemy movement. Their teeth chattered violently and they could make out their breath coming in silvery puffs in the dim, dreary light of the pre-dawn forest. The shallow patrols came in, reported and sloshed back out again. The effort of movement at least provided some warmth.

There had been no replies to earlier messages sent back to the Regimental PC, nor had the 9:00p.m. ration detail sent out yet returned. This was odd and Lt. McKeogh, emerging from the concrete bunker and traipsing quietly into the cold, dark clearing was concerned. There, in the gloaming, he shivered, peered again into the near-pitch black forest to the south for the hundredth time since the previous night and wondered silently: Perhaps the runners had gotten lost out in the underbrush and dirty weather and had decided to hold up until light. Then again, perhaps not. Perhaps they had instead found themselves waking up as 'guests of the Kaiser', or even worse, not waking up at all. This woods fighting was truly a bitched up mess. Peering into the darkness up the hill, Lt. McKeogh then carefully lit a cigarette inside his helmet and, making up his mind, called softly for one of the battalion runners. Whipping out his field message book, the lieutenant dashed off another request to regimental for food and supplies, handed the note to the boy and watched as he loped through the drizzle up the hill toward the runner line to the south. By the light of the cigarette cupped carefully in his hand, he looked at his wristwatch. It was just before a chilly

4:00 a.m.

A short time later, muffled machine-gun fire ripped the air from above the hill, first one burst, then another. Odd, as it had been a very quiet night. Before long, the runner that Lt. McKeogh had sent came crashing back down the hill. Panting hard, he reported that he had been challenged in German and then fired at by a machine-gun somewhere not far along the message chain. Majors Whittlesey and Budd emerged from the bunker as well now and the runner retold his story. The three officers exchanged apprehensive glances in the gloom. They were all well aware that they had no machine-guns out that far behind. Maybe there were elements of the 2nd Battalion pushing up back there, but that would not explain the challenge in German and the particular sound of a German Maxim's rapid stutter fire, as opposed to the steady 'chug' of a Hotchkiss. As if to lend confirmation, from the wet darkness another muffled anvil chorus of machine-gun fire, distinctively German, came from beyond the hill.

Quickly, Major Whittlesey had Lt. McKeogh assemble a three-man scout patrol and send them out with instructions to find out what was going on with the line of communication beyond the hilltop. The three officers watched as the patrol tramped through the mud, into the trees, and up the hill. There was nothing to do but wait. It was now about 4:45 a.m.

The dawn was just beginning to lighten the woods in the east when the two battalion commanders started making rounds to each company commander's funk hole or dugout asking for reports from the overnight patrols. The news was disturbing. There seemed to be plenty of suspicious movement in the woods, particularly beyond the far outposts to the rear and left. Everyone was well aware that the Germans were just across the open area and road to the north, still occupying the mill complex within the Ravin d'Argonne (though in what numbers no one was really sure), as well as likely still down in the Ravin Moulin de l'Homme Mort on the right. No one had any illusions as to the situation off to the far left either. However, gunfire to the *rear* of the position? Disquieting, to say the least. Certainly Majors Whittlesey and Budd both must have had some intimation of what was going on by this point, but if so they never let on. Instead, they left definite instructions, reminiscent of the night before: Recall any patrols and hold them in and do not send any more out until further notice. Everyone would sit tight and keep quiet. Troops would re-enforce positions if need be, and keep a sharp eye. They were to make sure that their auto-rifle men had good, clear fields of fire at the outposts and plenty of surface protection. No one was to engage the enemy if it could be avoided.

Then, through the waterlogged woods, came the distinct, sporadic stutter of German machine-gun fire again, except now the chorus was steadier and seemed to have increased. It was possible to discern at least two separate guns firing intermittently and men in position along the line atop the hill looked at each other uneasily. Reports of movement out in the brush along the left side of the bivouac were being whispered around. Then, shortly after, below the hill the brush at the south edge of the little clearing rustled again and Lt. McKeogh turned toward it, expecting to see the scouting party back. Instead, two different men came ahead, one helping another limp along with a bloody bandage around his leg. As a medic rushed forward, the lieutenant got their story. They were from one of the runner posts—number 11, at the cemetery—and had earlier been shot at by a German machine-gun that appeared to be playing along the line of communication. It looked at first as if the fire was coming from well behind the outpost line. The third man on the post had been killed outright and the post behind them, number 10, had been attacked, although neither man could say to what end.

Off in the distance, the morning U.S. artillery barrage started and the sounds of the cannon fire rolled over the hill and echoed down the ravine. Just as Lt. McKeogh finished getting the runners' story, Majors Whittlesey and Budd returned to the PC area from their inspection of the bivouac. A short conference ensued. Lieutenant McKeogh told the two commanders that he believed the runner line was cut. Evidence was on his side: Sergeant Hitlin and his scouts had never returned from yesterday's liaison mission, nor had the patrol sent out earlier that morning and that had been well over an hour ago. No messages had come up, nor rations or ammunition, despite the messages and the carrying party sent back the previous night. With reports of machine-gun fire and movement to the rear, coupled with the runners' stories, it certainly looked dire. If there were infiltrators along the line of communication, it would be imperative to quickly clean them out and have supplies brought forward. Otherwise, the command would likely be in a very bad way very soon, since they lacked for just about everything.

Therefore, it was beyond time to find out what, if anything, was going on with the all important communication line. Shortly after 6.30a.m., Major Whittlesey sent Lt. McKeogh, the only officer who could be spared, to the rear with a small combat force, under orders to check things out along the runner line, repair it if it was indeed broken, and report back his findings. Lieutenant McKeogh assembled his gangs, mostly automatic riflemen and runners. If there were machine-guns back there, the gangs would need plenty of grenades so he took most of what was left with him, along with a good supply of 8mm ammo for the Chauchats. Filing up the hill and down the narrow trail past the outpost line, they pushed out through the wet brush of the dank morning in a squad column, headed toward the cemetery and were quickly lost from view. Immediately, (about 6.45a.m.) Major Whittlesey sent another strong scouting party off under Battalion Sergeant Major Benjamin F. Gaedeke, a dependable New York boy, to reconnoiter the immediate vicinity. Then, to the east he sent off a strong patrol of Company F scouts with instructions to establish liaison with 2nd Battalion, if indeed they were forward again by this time and could be contacted. As they all disappeared into the brush up the hill, the Major then called for a bird and one of the 2nd Battalion pigeon handlers, Private Palmer Kyllo, a 40th Division man from Minnesota, came trotting up. Major Whittlesey will never be noted for his neat handwriting, but this message is relatively clear.

From: CO 1st Bn 30   At: 94.8 – 74.5
Date: 29 Sept   Hour: 7.02am
To: CO 308 Inf.
    Our runner posts seem to have broken down during the night as we have received no word from you. Have sent adjutant 1st Bn to re-establish route. It was OK till 9pm yesterday.
    We have not heard from patrols & 4 Cos of this regt. on East of ravine. Have just sent another patrol of our best men to find them.
    Will await orders here for the time being. In any event will either stay here or advance. (246)

In this first message of the day, Major Whittlesey appears to be covering all bases, wanting regimental to know what was happening and his intentions, while all the time preparing for what might come either way. He states that the runner chain "seem(s) to have broken down during the night," but then apparently resigns himself to the fact in the next line by stating, "Have sent adjutant 1st Bn to re-establish route". This last seems to indicate that the Major probably already realized the exact nature of the situation, but still believed that it would only be temporary. Perhaps the beginning of an infiltration, but certainly not an actual severance of all liaison. His last two lines are significant in that he makes it clear that he has absolutely no intention of falling back.

It is a fact that Charles Whittlesey, like most combat commanders at that time, preferred to send his messages by foot whenever possible. After all, a bird could not answer questions concerning terrain or conditions and a man rarely, if ever, flew off in the wrong direction! The day before, in fact, a message had been passed down from Brigade demanding to know why the pigeons were not being used more and issuing standing orders to do so. Here, however, Major Whittlesey obviously had no choice and handed the message to Pvt. Kyllo, who wrapped it into the tiny metal tube attached to the pigeon's leg and gave the bird a toss upward. As the pigeon headed for the U.S. lines through the misty morning, German rifles cracked in the woods around them surprisingly close. The enemy knew what the pigeons were for and used them as well. Unlike its predecessor of the evening before however, this bird actually went straight to the home loft at 77th Division PC, where the message center then passed it down to Regimental. Colonel Stacey however, was already well aware of the situation up ahead, even more so than was Major Whittlesey thanks to the important information that Sgt. Hitlin had already brought in earlier that morning. By the time the bird had landed in the loft, it was about 7:20a.m. and an attempt had already been made to break through to Major Whittlesey... and Lt. Col. Smith was dead. (10, 32, 34, 40, 96, 109, 137, 218, 224, 271, 320, 321)

At the first peek of dawn, Colonel Stacey ordered Lt. Col. Smith to assemble a combat team of 10 men from Company B, 15 runners and two officers, and set out for the 1st Battalion position, with Sgt. Hitlin guiding the column. Lieutenant Bradley Delehanty, the Regimental Intelligence Officer, was one of the officers, while the other was Lt. Karl Wilhelm of Company E, returning to the regiment from hospital after having been badly gassed on the Vesle in August. With them, they carried a copious supply of ammunition and hand grenades, but not enough hands remained to bring up any appreciable amount of food. Figuring they would only need to re-supply Major Whittlesey's force to hold out until 2nd/308th could come up on an even line sometime that day, food and water could wait. The military objective must come first.

They set out in the pre-dawn darkness and were able to move rather rapidly through the tangle, dropping runners evenly and heading up what they believed to be the correct pathway leading to the 1st Battalion position. At a fork in the path, however, not far from the cemetery, Sgt. Hitlin apparently took the wrong branch. They unknowingly found themselves moving off in the direction toward the left rear flank of the 1st Battalion position and well below the hill. Lieutenant Colonel Smith, at the head of the column with Sgt. Hitlin, had gone only about 50 meters up the narrow path when he spotted movement in a thick tangle ahead off to one side. Even as he shouted for the men to take cover, the first stream of lead ripped through the air and into his leg. Going down, Smith managed to crawl into the brush at the side of the trail, blazing away at the unseen machine-gun ahead with his .45 automatic as the rest of the force scattered into the brush and also returned fire. Though painful, his wound did not appear to be too bad, and Smith shouted for the little command to head back down the trail while he provided what cover fire he could. Once he saw that most of the party had taken up a better position, he began to plan a next move to flank the enemy gun. However, the chatter of a machine-gun from a different direction snapped his concentration. It caught Lt. Col. Smith in the side and he went down again. This time the wound was serious.

Smith, who had thought himself alone, now felt other hands attempting to dress the fresh wound. Looking around he found that one of the ammunition carriers, Pvt. David Cipis of Company F, had crawled forward and was trying to put a field dressing over the badly bleeding wound in the Lt. Colonel's torn side. Cipis, who had been just behind Smith, was carrying two bags of hand grenades, which he dropped to one side of the trail in his haste to get under cover. Spotting the two discarded bags, Lt. Col. Smith shrugged off the private's efforts to bandage him; there would be plenty of time for that later. Ordering Cipis to stay put he dashed out across the trail, grabbed both the bags, and kept right on going, diving into the brush on the other side with a thick trail of blood in the mud behind him. The enemy guns hammered away in his wake but he was not hit, their aim no doubt thrown off by the very daring of the act. While those behind laid down covering fire and watched, Smith, with a grenade in each hand, painfully began moving forward through the underbrush to reconnoiter the Boche positions in what Pvt. Cipis later recalled as "the single most courageous act I had ever witnessed." Nevertheless, Lt. Col. Smith's star was fated. There was a break in the brush in front of him, and the brave officer popped up to catch a quick glimpse of what lay ahead. A short distance away, a German gun gave a brief stutter and Smith went down, this time with a slug through the head. (Fred Smith received a posthumous Medal of Honor after the war for his actions on that forgotten little trail deep within the Argonne Forest. Few hardly deserved it more.)

After a short, sharp, and decidedly one-sided firefight with the Boche machine-guns - which fell in the Germans' favor - Lieutenants Delehanty and Wilhelm gathered in the rescue party and reversed back down the trail. After returning to Regimental PC, the two troubled, dirty officers explained the battle and Lt. Col. Smith's loss to Colonel Stacey. They had been unable to recover Smith's body, and this upset them both greatly as the Lieutenant Colonel had been a well-loved man within the regiment. A dark cloud of depression settled in over Karlplatz that Colonel Stacey, though he did not share as deeply as the others, nonetheless well respected. He too had seen his share of comrades killed during his long service career.

General Alexander, when informed of Lt. Col. Smith's loss later that day, was especially aggrieved. The young Smith had served under him the previous summer in the 41st (Depot) Division and it was Alexander who had given him a combat assignment (at Smith's request) in reward for his excellent service. General Alexander truly liked and respected Lt. Col. Smith and in his later memoirs, he took a cheap shot at Colonel Stacey for sending him out on the assignment to break through to Major Whittlesey saying, "The task was not compatible with his rank, but his Regimental Commander designated him to perform it." This is an unfair judgment, as Smith voluntarily took on the task in an effort to assist his new regimental commander in any way he could. Additionally, there were few officers then available to Colonel Stacey. In any case, Lt. Col. Smith both liked and respected Major Whittlesey and certainly would have wanted to see the Major's situation as stable as possible. (2, 109, 116, 350, 351, 353, 360)

Lieutenant Arthur McKeogh was, by this stage of the battle, an expert at clearing out Boche machine-gun nests. With a force of five Chauchat auto rifle teams and a small band of men, he set out early that morning down the trail from the 1st Battalion bivouac confidant that they could quickly clear away any that may have interrupted the line of communication. Said McKeogh later:

"...The Major gave me fifteen or twenty men with grenades to wipe out what we thought was a single machine gun nest on the left...but when we got close to it, we found that there were three nests and at least three machine guns in each nest..." (271)

Lieutenant McKeogh also took eight fresh runners with which to re-man the broken line. The little combat patrol quietly spread out into the early morning forest looking for trouble. At the head and tail of the column, he placed Chauchats, at intervals dropping off one of the auto-riflemen and a loader in a strategic location to insure that they would have a solid escape route back to the bivouac if need be. One of these teams contained Private Emil Peterson of Company H:

"...Next morning a buddy, with a French Chauchat machine gun and myself were taken by an officer, along with some other buddies, to the rear and right and posted part ways down a hill. We were told to hold the Germans from cutting in on our runners or our company... later on a company (sic) would soon come to

relieve us..." (224)

Carefully the column moved ahead, watchful in all directions. The cold drizzle fell in drops from the tree limbs and tapped on their steel helmets. The weak morning light was penetrating the trees, so it was easier to see through the gloom. There was no excuse for being caught unaware. Lieutenant McKeogh was in line ahead with his .45 in his right hand, immediately behind the point, a Chauchat crew leading the way. The bivouac area was post # 13. Post #12 was some 150 meters away down to the south, north of the cemetery. Post #11, the one that had been abandoned, was just near the northern edge of the cemetery. Post #10, about 150 meters further south of that, was the one the post #11 men said had been attacked in conjunction with their own and more than likely was under German control. Beyond that, it was anyone's guess who had control. That meant that, with at least two of the runner posts in Boche hands (post #12 appeared to be holding), there would be a gap of about 300 meters in the line of communication behind the bivouac. Three hundred meters was a lot of ground in those woods, and the Germans could put a great many men in a gap that large. What's more, if the gap extended back even further, or was allowed to progress forward, the trouble could only worsen. And judging by the sounds of the machine-guns waking up and chattering in the brush all around them, that was precisely what was happening. (What Lt. McKeogh and his team did not yet realize was that they had entered German-held territory the minute they stepped out beyond the 1st Battalion perimeter.) (34, 271, 237)

It was about 7:30a.m. and the column was still creeping forward, nearly at the spot where he had left post #12 the afternoon before, when shots rang out from behind them in the direction of the auto-rifle drop-off post on the right rear. Lieutenant McKeogh, acutely aware that they did not know exactly where the machine-guns around them were firing from, was alarmed. It would not do for them to be cut off from the main force! Reversing the column, they hustled back to the post where they found Pvt. Peterson and his buddy crouched down within the brush alongside the trail they had been instructed to cover. Private Peterson:

"...As we were sitting in the brush, one on each side of the trail which led down the hill, hiding behind some small bushes, I asked my buddy how his French Cho-chat (sic) was working. He started looking it over and found he could not fire it at all.

We had not been there very long when I saw five Germans move out of the brush, about a hundred and fifty feet away. While the leader stood with an overcoat on looking through field glasses, the others were busy putting up a machine gun, pointing the barrel over us and to the top of the hill. Looking back up the hill I saw a company, who I thought were coming to relieve us, coming towards us. (This was the patrol that Whittlesey had sent out under Sgt. Mjr. Gaedeke – Author) They did not see the Germans and would have made an easy target for the machine gun...I fired two or three shots at the German machine gunners, and soon an American officer came running towards me (McKeogh – Author) shouting "Sentry! Sentry! That may be some of our own boys!" But when he got up to me and also saw they were Germans, together we ran over to the German machine gun firing our guns as we ran. We captured their gun and also some of the gunners. The rest ran away in the bushes. The company (sic) now spread out and a battle was on..." (44, 224)

When the smoke cleared, they found a German NCO was dead at the gun and a German private that was wounded, but the rest had scattered. The Doughboys had taken a few wounds as well. Sergeant-Major Gaedeke and his patrol now came along as well, picked up the two Germans and their gun and headed back to the Battalion PC with the Doughboy wounded in tow. Majors Whittlesey and Budd would want both the Boche searched for intelligence and the live one questioned. McKeogh sent Pvt. Peterson and his buddy on a patrol of the area up the hill, to the right and rear of the bivouac, where there was sporadic small arms and machine-gun fire popping all over the place now. Then, turning with his band of marauders, the lieutenant set out again in search of more trouble.

They did not take long to find it. Moving was easier through the brush now. The assault on the machine-gun previous seemed to have scattered the concentration of the other German machine-gun crews. It was then around 8:45a.m. when Lt. McKeogh and his band finally reached post #12 and found the last remaining runner stationed there, Private George W. Quinn of Company D. "Three Boche just came up the path about fifteen minutes ago lieutenant," Pvt. Quinn reported. "I don't think they knew we were here, 'cause they were strolling along just as they might be in back of their lines, talking excitedly over a piece of paper one of them was reading. They stopped before they came upon me, tore up the paper and then turned around and went down the hill. I would have taken a crack at 'em if someone would have been with me." (58)

However, Lt. McKeogh was only half-listening and merely nodded absently while peering hard in the distance. Something had caught his eye moving through the brush ahead. Slowly, he began to make out the shape of German 'coal scuttle' helmets moving through the brush. Eyes wide, he was about to give the order to disperse the men when Pvt. Quinn suddenly swung his rifle over his shoulder and fired behind. Instantly there was a yowl of pain, followed by the sound of bodies crashing through the brush. The runner had dropped a German and two others were tearing through the woods toward the hill. Instantly Lt. McKeogh and the rest dropped to the ground and listened for more movement but heard only wet forest silence, scattered machine-gun chatter and small arms fire and the familiar boom of artillery in the distance. Some others crawled over to the fallen German, but he was dead by the time they got to him. Instantly, they went through his pockets and knapsack looking for food. Finding none, Lt. McKeogh searched the corpse for intelligence. Sending a man back to the bivouac with the body, he then turned his attention back to the woods around them.

It was pretty obvious that there were bound to be plenty more Germans out there. The main bivouac position was most definitely cut off from the rear, but exactly how far did the damage to the line of communication extend? Lieutenant McKeogh now decided to disperse his men in a combat formation in the woods rather than in a column moving down the trail. His mission had obviously changed from one of repair to the line of communication to one of reconnaissance of that line instead; it was time to find out exactly how much ground they had lost overnight. However, before they had a chance to set out, the lieutenant's attention was again drawn to the right rear as shots rang out close by along the hill immediately south of the bivouac. (271)

There, Pvt. Peterson and his buddy had been moving forward and closing up on Lt. McKeogh's position, completing their reconnaissance of the area up the hill as ordered and firing at stray Germans as they went. It seemed as though there were Germans everywhere. Private Peterson was just to the southwest of the Company A outpost line moving and through the brush when, out of the corner of his eye, he spotted movement. Peterson later wrote:

"I was to the left… firing at the Germans below the hill… I turned around and saw a German with a long barreled pistol in his hand trailing me, and while he was going around some bushes I stepped behind a tree and pointed my rifle to the other end, from which he would emerge…" (224)

Private McCollum was in one of the funk holes of the Company A line and was also a witness to the situation. He tells the story from another angle:

"…A German soldier was seen by one of our outposts. He was coming directly toward our lines and

moving stealthily and cautiously. We all lay quiet, waiting for him to come through our lines and then capture him. He passed through without any interference…" (32)

However, there was not only one German trailing Pvt. Peterson. Soon, a second one appeared, following a short distance behind the first. As Lee McCollum stated, they let them both into the position, but after that it was just too much for the nervous Doughboys. Private Sidney Smith was also manning the outpost line, on the southwest shoulder and later remembered:

"…This German… came running right in to where I sat. This fella with me, Sidney Mann from Northern Montana, he hollered two or three times for the German to halt, but the German was bound to go on, so Sidney Mann shot him through…" (256)

Peterson:
"…As he emerged from out of the brush, with the pistol still in his hand, I fired at him…" (224)

McCollum:
"…When an excited soldier, standing a considerable distance from him pulled his rifle to his shoulder and shot him…" (32)

Peterson:
"He fell, mortally wounded… waved his pistol and shouted 'Kamerad, Americano!'" (224)

McCollum:
"The shell tore deep into the flesh of the German's hip." (32)

Smith:
"The German went down." (256)

Who actually got the German trailing Pvt. Peterson, an officer, and who killed the other one, a sergeant, is really anybody's guess. From Peterson's and McCollum's descriptions, it is likely that Peterson was the one who dropped the officer, at which point the sergeant took off running and Pvt. Mann shot him. In any case, Pvt. Peterson ran over to the German he apparently shot, who was bleeding into the grass, moaning and calling out. He then ran back to get Lt. McKeogh, telling him he had nailed a Boche officer. McKeogh hustled back to the spot along with Private Jack Herschkowitz, a Company C runner who could speak German. Finding the officer writhing on the ground, Lt. McKeogh examined the gunshot. Seeing how badly wounded the German, a Reserve Lieutenant of the 254th Regiment named Korthaus, was the lieutenant knew he would likely not last long. He therefore asked Pvt. Herschkowitz to ask him how many guns there were at the cemetery and how they were disposed. Private Herschkowitz and the gasping German rapidly exchanged words.

"He says there are about 70 Germans out in little sniping parties in this part of the woods (Private Smith, who was crouching there too, puts the number at 90), but he doesn't know about the cemetery guns, sir." Pvt. Herschkowitz translated. McKeogh then asked the German to turn over his maps. When the German refused, according to Pvt. Smith, the lieutenant had Pvt. Herschkowitz tell him that he would get no medical attention unless he did. The officer then quickly produced his maps and papers, swearing through clenched teeth. The lieutenant studied the documents for a short time, then stood upright and ordered two men from a nearby funk hole to take the German back to the Battalion PC for Major Whittlesey to talk to before he died. Absently, he handed the maps and papers to one of the men to deliver and then turned his men back down the hill and continued on. In the distance to the south, another machine-gun fired. (4, 123, 256, 271, 356)

Back at the concrete bunker, north of the bivouac position, Major Whittlesey scrawled again in his pigeon message book. Around him, sporadic rifle and machine-gun fire crackled as the sun rose higher behind a solid gray bank of clouds overhead. The Germans were waking up to the fact that their enemy was lodged out there on l'Homme Mort. Major Whittlesey wrote:

Hour: 9am
To: CO 308 Inf.
Our runner post 10 has been broken by German M.G. The 2nd Bn. in support is sending 5 Chauchat teams to re-establish this post and strengthen the 5 advance posts; but it is impossible for us to maintain liaison over a long stretch to the rear as the nature of the terrain (woods) makes it impossible to prevent German M.G. from filtering back. Request that line of communication be maintained by unit from the rear that we may advance. Our patrols indicate German camp occupied in valley to our East. We are now reconnoitering to find the number of Germans there. Not in touch yet with the 4 companies of this regt on the right of the valley to our East. (246)

The bird disappeared from view in the correct direction. The support from 2nd Battalion was obviously Lt. McKeogh's combat force, which was composed mainly of men from companies F and H. The patrol mentioned is the one Sgt. Mjr. Gaedeke had earlier lead, which had since returned with the bodies of the two Germans from the machine-gun nest that had been attacked by Lt. McKeogh and Pvt. Peterson, a wounded private and a dead NCO. Apparently what the runner post men from post #11 had said earlier that morning accounts for Major Whittlesey's knowledge concerning the severity of the break. The "German camp occupied in valley to our East" is likely an obvious reference to the Ravin Moulin de l'Homme Mort, or perhaps even the Depot des Machines. There is also a hint of nervousness to the tone of this message, for with no support, not even one so slender as a communication/supply line, the position they occupied would soon be rendered untenable. Every moment they sat there, the enemy gained a stronger hold around them, while they used up what little supplies they had. Then, once the Germans really had them locked in, it would not be difficult to simply turn a score of machine-guns in their direction and let fly, or simply shell the little command into the dust. With the bivouac situated both on the top and the northern slope of the hill, facing the direction of the enemy—admittedly a poor location in which to have stopped and taken position—German artillery would have little problem completely annihilating them.

However, by asking if the line of communication could possibly be held open from the rear, Major Whittlesey made a reasonable request with an eye to eradicating any chance of that untenability by simply advancing. To do so, he would need all his men pushing forward. But since his numbers were small to begin with, having only the two depleted Battalion H.Q. companies and about four shot-up companies worth of riflemen on the hill, he consequently felt that no manpower could readily be spared for the runner line. The request is also in keeping with the standing order that advance should continue under almost any circumstance, with disregard for security of the flanks. But did that debatable flank doctrine extend to include the areas to the rear? Perhaps so, since portions of 3rd Battalion were then doing mop up work in those rear areas already taken while the assault battalions carried on. In that case, he should really not be waiting for 3rd Battalion, or anyone else for that matter, to come up and fill the communication line but should instead advance regardless.

There was also G.O. #27 to consider, something that must certainly have crossed the Major's mind, not only reminding him of his duty (as if that were necessary) but also virtually stripping him of any decision over his situation he might have had in the first place. With no communication, he could not request nor receive orders to abandon the hillside if the situation turned hopeless. Nor did he apparently feel willing or able to make the call himself, such as had happened the day before in front of Depot des Machines within 2nd Battalion. That would have gone against not only his standing orders, but also his own moral code. Advance was the only real way out of the already downward spiraling situation out on that hillside then.

The men sent back to the Battalion PC area by Lt. McKeogh with Pvt. Peterson's wounded German officer and the accompanying dead German sergeant arrived shortly after the 9:00 a.m. pigeon message had gone out. Major Whittlesey had the wounded officer carefully laid out. The medics got to work on him while he summoned Pvt. Robert Manson, the 1st Battalion interpreter. The German (Lt. Korthaus) was slipping away fast; he had lost too much blood, and the medic pronounced there was nothing he could do. Private Manson worked equally quickly. A short exchange followed and the officer garbled out with gasping breath a few disjointed details concerning German troop dispositions and what they could expect to face farther up the Ravin d'Argonne before finally sputtering, "You will meet serious resistance ahead... My company is only seventy men out sniping... up ahead..." and that was the last Manson got out of him before the man died. (109, 271, 356)

Major Whittlesey had the German officer's now lifeless body again searched for intelligence and one of the men who had brought the Hun in then absently handed the Major the maps and papers that Lt. McKeogh had sent back. When Whittlesey and Budd unfolded one of the maps, they got the greatest shock of the war. Here was a map with virtually all the trenches and machine-gun emplacements in their zone of advance marked on it! Obviously, the officer, new to the area, had carried the map so he did not get lost. Unfolding one of the French/U.S. maps that the battalion commanders carried, they compared the two. The German map showed many other things that were not shown on the U.S. map as well as the trenches and gun emplacements; most importantly, it contained details of the Giselher Stellung ahead and its approaches within the Ravin d'Argonne. This was certainly a magnificent find! Excitedly, the two started making notes and sketch marking their own maps as Pvt. Manson interpreted the written notations and place names. Now armed with the information concerning enemy dispositions, as well as the gold mine of information on the maps, any future advance up the Ravin d'Argonne ahead did not as appear as grim as it had when first viewed on the detail deficient Allied maps. Now, if they could just get moving again. (109, 132, 137, 271)

Advancing through the underbrush, Lt. McKeogh and his men managed to locate and clean out one of the machine-gun nests that had bothered them earlier and were now again moving forward toward the cemetery. Cautious as they were in their approach though, it was simply not possible to move through the forest without stirring up some noise. This put everyone's nerves even more on edge. There was already plenty of rifle and machine-gun fire coming from the hill behind them. The last thing that the small reconnaissance force wanted was to draw an inordinate amount of attention to themselves. About the time that Whittlesey and Budd were excitedly examining the dead German officer's maps, Lt. McKeogh and his men were just coming up to the low log railing surrounding the graves of the cemetery. Suddenly, a German voice loudly called out to them and instantly the Doughboys dropped to the ground. Private Sidney Smith, advancing on the right flank of the group, remembered:

"An interpreter was with us (Private Louis Calmenson, of Company 'F' - Author). We went up a ridge and a bunch of Germans came up close. They came right in ahead of us, and I lay down on a path on this ridge as flat as I could get. One of the Germans was talking, and the Sergeant asked the interpreter

what he'd said. "He's telling them to keep down."..." (256)

Peering through the brush, Lt. McKeogh could see several German helmets moving diagonally across from them among the grave markers in the little yard. His automatic was already in his hand, where it had been nearly the whole morning, when the Germans called out again something that ended with the word "Kamerad." Lieutenant McKeogh later remembered:

> *"I thought to myself, "Well this is cheering. We'll take this bunch prisoners and suffer no casualties." So I scurried back along the line...to find...(Herschkowitz). We drew up closer to the rustic railing around the cemetery. "Tell them to come out at once, unarmed, into the open," I instructed Herschkowitz. There followed a long palaver that taxed my patience. There had been a number of "Kamerads" interchanged, and that was the extent of my lingual understanding.*
> *"Damn it! What's he saying?" I demanded finally.*
> *"Why lieutenant, he says they've got us surrounded. They expect us to surrender — to do the Kamerad to them!" Herschkowitz replied."* (271)

Incredulous, Lt. McKeogh listened as Privates Herschkowitz and Clamenson tried in vain to convince the Germans that it was they who should surrender, but to no avail.
"Tell them, 'Kamerad Hell!'" Lt. McKeogh finally said.
Private Herschkowitz delivered the message with great glee. What happened then, down on the right, stuck in Private Smith's mind for the rest of his life:

> *"...There was a cemetery down below us with a fence around it and the Germans got down in there and planted a machine gun. Our interpreter (Private Calmenson) suddenly went walking down in there, and I didn't know what he was doing. He went to talking to them and they talked back and forth in German a time or two. He just got right up and stood up and walked down to this cemetery and he set his gun down against the fence and talked to them..."* (256)

According to his citation in General Orders #2 of January 10, 1919, Private Calmenson "volunteered to ascertain the location of an enemy machine gun", and "with utter disregard for his own safety... advanced alone with his hands up, as though he intended to surrender, to engage in conversation with a German who came out to meet him. Detecting his purpose, the German fired, wounding Private Calmenson severely." The citation goes on to say that Calmenson shot the German with his pistol and, though terribly wounded, managed to crawl back to his company with the location of the nest. However, according to Pvt. Smith the story is somewhat different: (109)

> *"...They turned the machine gun on him, and I could hear his cloths rip. He went down like a rag. Then our sergeant started over there and they turned the machine gun on him too. They shot him in the head with an explosive bullet (sic), and I heard him scream when his head got blowed up...You know, to this day I don't know why the interpreter walked over there. I think the Germans must have said they would give up, and that he went over to take them prisoner. Instead they shot him..."* (256)

After that, a fusillade of rifle and machine-gun fire pelted the Doughboys from two different directions. Lieutenant McKeogh sent a man to take back to the bivouac the horribly wounded sergeant. (Despite Pvt. Calmenson's citation, the sergeant was actually the one that had managed to crawl back to his squad) The rest of his men answered the Germans with pistol, rifle, and Chauchat but it was no match. Two of the five Chauchat auto-rifles jammed hopelessly and it took almost 20 minutes for the men to pull back to more secure positions in the brush out of the terrible crossfire in which the Germans had caught them. What Lt. McKeogh needed was time to recon the German positions. It sounded as if they might have two or three of the heavy machine-guns chugging away, but without a closer look there was no way to be sure. Placing two of the remaining three working Chauchats out on either flank to the rear, he grabbed a couple grenade men and the remaining auto-rifle team and prepared to set out against the guns in a makeshift gang formation. There were only two ways out now; back up the hill to the bivouac or to the rear towards the division main line. Going back up the hill would accomplish nothing, so it was to the rear that Lt. McKeogh now set his sights on.

Then, a Hun voice called out 50 yards to their rear, from within the brush along the hillside. The voice at the gun in the cemetery, which had been silent for a time, answered back and all at once two machine-guns along the hillside, two on the flanks and one ahead in the cemetery opened up at the same time. Once again, the Germans had the little team bracketed by enfilading fire. The Germans in the nest ahead started to lob rifle grenades in on the Doughboys. Fortunately, their range was slightly on the short side in the heavy brush. McKeogh grabbed several of the French offensive grenades that the team had with them, crawled forward a bit and, finding a suitable opening through the trees, tossed them in the direction of the Boche nest. To what end, it was impossible to say with any certainty, but they seemed to have done some good as one of the machine-guns went silent. Although they were not losing any ground, the Doughboys were not gaining any either and casualties within the little force were beginning to mount. (237, 271)

Back at the bivouac, where men worked at improving the mud-filled funk holes they dug the previous night, the relative quiet of the morning was now really beginning to break. Strong, savage firefights were sparking up "at all points of the compass" as the Germans tested the strength and borders of the Doughboy force with rifle and light machine-gun fire and potato masher grenades, which had a short wooden handle that made throwing them onto a specific target relatively easy. Below the hill, intense sniper fire raked the open edges of the clearing from the direction of Moulin de l'Homme Mort. Getting water from the stream was now out of the question as snipers in the brush between the bivouac and the mill cut down every Doughboy who tried. A light trench mortar from somewhere within the Ravin d'Argonne in the direction of the mill started lobbing shells into the position too. Fortunately, for the Doughboys though, their aim was so bad that few found their mark. Nevertheless, casualties were starting to mount and the two 2nd Battalion medical men up with the surrounded force, Privates Louis Rickler and Samuel Chester (both of Company E), had little to offer in the way of assistance other than basic first aid. Still, Major Whittlesey would not risk using his Stokes mortar and tip his hand to the Germans about their true strength or give a corrective point upon which the enemy mortar fire could center and thus improve their accuracy. Instead, the Doughboys simply sat, fought back like furies and watched their ammunition supply drop as a pall of apprehension slowly began to steal across the hillside.

Through it all, Majors Whittlesey and Budd stalked all over the bivouac, going from funk hole to funk hole lending moral support and encouragement and assisting company commanders in directing return fire. Little had been heard from Lt. McKeogh as yet, other than the basics sent back with the wounded. It was almost noon now and the firing from behind the hill pretty much told the story anyway. They could also hear the sounds of battle further in the distance to the east where the 2nd Battalion was obviously trying to break through and that at least lent some encouragement. But if 2nd Battalion did not step up their advance, the hammering that 1st was taking would only continue to no good end. From the west however, there was still only that morose silence; the same as the last 3 days. Either the 368th was not moving, or they were so far back that the sound of battle was lost over the tremendous distance. Either way, it did not bode well for the rear left flank again.

Another general patrol under Sgt. Mjr. Gaedeke went out on a short leash around the bivouac again while Sergeant Anderson of Company A took a general patrol to the west to attempt liaison with anyone from the 368th, or to at least get some idea of how bad the break in the line was over there. There was also the morning Company F patrol, still somewhere out to the east that had not been heard from as yet. Nobody was about to say it aloud, but things were starting to look bad. (32, 40, 91, 96, 109, 137, 164, 172, 174, 209)

Similarly, Lt. McKeogh had heard nothing from Major Whittlesey, though he was certain that the Major could hear his fire. Shortly after noon, the lieutenant called Pvt. Quinn forward, pulled out his field message book and quickly scribbled out a note for the Major. The Germans were strongly lodged around the cemetery and they had not been able to get any further. If Major Whittlesey would send the Stokes mortar team forward, they might be able to drop in a few shells to help break them up. He gave Pvt. Quinn the message, who thrust it in the breast pocket of his tunic and disappeared through the thick underbrush, headed up the hill. When there was neither answering message nor Stokes team within the hour, Lt. McKeogh assumed that the private had either gotten lost, killed, or captured and so sent another man out with a similar message before turning his attention back to the fighting again. It was proving to be a long day for the little combat patrol... (58, 170, 231)(III)

It was 12:30 p.m. or so when Sgt. Mjr. Gaedeke and his patrol returned with news that, as far as they could ascertain, 1st Battalion had no liaison in any direction and no immediate chance of it. They were definitely surrounded. Under these circumstances, with no contact from Lt. McKeogh and hearing the startling amount of firing in the rear, Major Whittlesey sent yet another combat team out, this one under the command of Lt. William 'Red' Cullen of Company H. Lieutenant Cullen's instructions were specific; help clean up the German machine-guns in the rear if possible and tell Lt. McKeogh to try and break through to the rear any way that he could and let them know what was happening, on the off chance that the birds were not getting through. (109, 237, 271)

The Major then called for another pigeon and whipped out his message book again. Things had now gone from bad to worse.

Hour: 1.09pm
To: CO 308 Inf.
Our line of communication with the rear is still cut at 12.30pm by German M. Guns. We are going to clean out one of these guns now. From a wounded German officer prisoner we learn there is a German company of 70 operating in our rear to close the gap we made yesterday. We can of course clean up this country to the rear by working our companies back over the ground we came. But we understand our mission is to advance, and to maintain our strength here; and it is very slow trying to clean up this rear area from here by small details, when this trickling back of the M. Guns can be repeated by the enemy indefinitely. Can this line of communication not be kept open by a unit from the rear?

We have been unable to send back details for rations and ammunition; both of which we need badly.

We are not yet in touch with the 4 Cos of this Regt. To the east of the ravine East of here as none of our patrols have yet returned.

The closing up of the 1st and 2nd Bns was necessitated by yesterdays operation, and the splitting of the echelons by the ravine East of here. Major Budd collaborates in these reports. (246)

Here again, Major Whittlesey reiterates his request that the line of communication be maintained from the rear. Again, this is actually nothing more than a good illustration of what he and Major Budd had already figured out; that only swarms of men were going to drive the Germans from their forest positions. Major Whittlesey did not have swarms of men to maintain both his front and rear; he only had enough for one or the other, so if he was to advance as per orders, then he must receive support. Perhaps the most significant part of this particular message is the last lines, giving explanation for some of the moves of the previous day. Explaining the closing up of the two battalions is no doubt a precursor for the next line, clarifying why the two echelons had split in the first place. However, Colonel Stacey already knew of and approved the 1st and 2nd battalions working together. Further, being a Regular Army officer, he also no doubt already deduced that the split was actually caused by something much more tangible than just the topography, whether Major Whittlesey himself realized it or not - inexperience.

Any commander with any appreciable knowledge of movement during the First World War knew that to split his force in the face of a massed and well-entrenched enemy, no matter what the terrain, rarely resulted in anything more than a divided force and infiltration between the separated parts, especially without strong support from behind. That is exactly what had happened, not only between 1st and 2nd battalions, but also between the 308th's left flank and the 368th as well. Additionally, while the terrain in this case (the Ravin Moulin de l'Homme Mort) was certainly difficult to maintain liaison across, it might have been fully carried by more experienced men under more experienced direct leadership, both of which were lacking in the 308th. In spite of what they may have accomplished on the Vesle, neither Major Whittlesey nor Major Budd actually had the combat experience needed to deal with the situation that had presented itself on the 28th. Bear in mind that in peacetime, neither would likely be any farther along in rank than 1st Lieutenant, or perhaps Captain at the most. Additionally, there were simply too many replacements in the regiment, a certain portion of which had arrived virtually untrained. However, in combat drastic steps are often taken and the next in line fills the job, top or bottom, and experience be damned.

Finally, once again the orders themselves, considered by division to be both necessary and reasonable to continue the rapid advance needed to win the battle, also played their part in the disastrous position 1st Battalion faced as well. Had they not been moving under orders to advance "without regard to troops to the right or left", or had G.O. #27 not robbed Major Whittlesey of his power to make the decision to pull back on the afternoon of the 28th, as had 2nd Battalion (and as he probably should have), it is entirely likely that the situation out on l'Homme Mort would have been avoided.

The patrol Major Whittlesey ordered to make contact with Lt. McKeogh set out just as the irritating drizzle seemed to be abating for the time being. It was nearly 2:00 p.m. when they finally found the lieutenant and his men in skirmish on the other side of the cemetery. They had met the second runner Lt. McKeogh had sent back to the bivouac with the message for Major Whittlesey, still alive despite harassment from the increasing number of German patrols and brought him back with them. Private John "Jack" Monson, a runner from Company A, gave Lt. McKeogh the message that Major Whittlesey had sent. As there did not seem much hope of the small Doughboy contingent clearing a way to the rear, McKeogh decided to send everyone back, select two runners, and with them try to make his way back to Regimental PC any way they could. Gathering ammo for his pistol from the officer that had led the relief force in (Lt. William 'Red' Cullen of Company H), Lt. McKeogh selected Privates Monson and Herschkowitz to accompany him. It was around 2:30 p.m. when the three men crawled off through the bushes to the south and the combat patrol turned around and headed back toward the bivouac. (4, 237, 271)

Throughout the day, following a half-hour's worth of artillery preparation, there were repeated attempts being made to break through to the command on the far slope of l'Homme Mort by 2nd Battalion, but to little effect. Each patrol quickly discovered that the Germans appeared to have put a great many machine-guns within the intervening space and had things locked up tight as a drum. Each attack was beaten back, each patrol scattered, killed, or captured. Meanwhile, Majors Whittlesey and Budd were not simply sitting idly by. They could hear the efforts being made from the direction of the main line and were sending out small combat patrols to try to link up, but also to no good end. Each patrol sent out was forced back in, killed, or captured as well. In Company A, Pvt. McCollum lay watchful in his funk hole:

"Things were beginning to look serious, in spite of the fact that there had been no (real) fighting and none of our lives lost. There was a sense of impending danger as we lay waiting. I overheard two officers talking about Lieutenant McKeogh and wondering if he "got through okay." He had been sent back to headquarters to advise what was taking place..." (32)

Private McCollum and his hole mate, Private Art Kidwell, suspected what was up, but wisely kept it to themselves.

In truth, by this time (mid-afternoon) had Major Whittlesey received orders to withdraw to a more secure position, he probably would not have been able to do so without heavy casualties. To tip his hand by attempting movement of his force would have simply given the Germans emplaced there around him a visible target within their own assault zone, no matter how many (or few) troops the Germans actually had there around them. This is not to say that the bivouac was an untenable position as yet. Quite the contrary; though surrounded, the position was still very tenable, provided they stayed put and defended themselves. There was only just some light, inaccurate trench mortar activity and a certain amount of small arms and machine-gun fire that, though growing increasingly savage, was still within a tolerable range. At the moment then, they were fairing rather well, all things considered.

However, that, Major Whittlesey knew, was going to change as time passed, because the more serious problem then facing his force was their dangerously low grenade and ammunition supplies. If the enemy launched a series of strong attacks against the position—and it was simply a matter of time before they would—then it would not be long before they would be out of ammunition and then be overrun. A great many of the new replacements, particularly the men who had picked up the Chauchats when their original owners had been killed or wounded, had the nasty habit of "point and spray"; not really aiming the weapon as much as pointing it in the general direction of the enemy and letting as much lead fly as possible. This was incredibly wasteful of ammunition, but as one former Doughboy replacement put it, "The thing made an excellent hose." Those same nervous Doughboys were equally wild with general rifle fire, as an unseen enemy continually rattled through the thick brush all around them. (29, 51, 109, 116)

To the west of the 1st/308th bivouac during most of that day, the 368th made no actual forward movement. The 1st/368th had only managed to move up from reserve during the night and their relief of 2nd/368th was still a long way off. It was not until midmorning that they finally had combat patrols probing forward looking for advanced troops of the 2nd. And with the 2nd's units scattered as they were, it was slow going. Company F, the furthest forward, was the first to retire, dragging what was left of itself back to Tranchee de Finlande soon after full daylight. By about 11:00 a.m., most of 1st was in the Tranchee Tirpitz, but it was still not until around 3:30 p.m. that the rest of the broken 2nd had limped back into reserve well behind the original jump-off trenches.

Meanwhile, the 1st/9th C.a.P had not managed its relief of the 3rd/368th by dawn as ordered either. Instead, it took until nearly 4:30 p.m. to complete the move. The relieved 3rd/368th, in not nearly as bad of shape as the 2nd, then took up support positions within Tranchee de Breslau and Tranchee de Magdebourg, behind the 9th and 368th line units.

The French 1st D.C.D. then announced that another try was to be made by

168

Groupement Durand to take Binarville on the 30th. However, before the attack could be attempted, the enemy needed to be driven from his positions within the Tranchee du Dromadaire. Still an average of half a kilometer ahead, it would make an excellent jump-off point. Therefore an attack on Tranchee du Dromadaire then was scheduled for 6:00 p.m., and once captured it was to be strongly organized against the inevitable counter attack and held at all costs. The 2nd and 3rd/11th C.a.P would attack on the far left, with the 1st/9th C.a.P. attacking right of them toward the middle. Meanwhile, elements of the 3rd/308th had established an extension of their line into the Tranchee du Dromadaire on the far right that morning by 5:00 a.m., crossing the divisional dividing line a short distance into the territory of the 368th and refusing their left flank. Therefore, once the French forces attacked and took their objective, this would leave a narrow corridor of enemy-held territory between the 9th C.a.P., on the left, and the 308th to the right. The inexperienced 1st/368th, facing that corridor, would not participate in the attack but would instead remain at Tirpitz and prepare itself for the attack of the 30th. If all went well, the enemy would likely pull out of that narrow alley of their own accord and thus give the 1st/368th a veritable 'walk in' the next morning.

For once, all went according to plan. After a short artillery barrage by the French 247th and some 155's from the 77th Division's 306th F.A., the assault battalions pushed forward and by late that evening, the French were in Tranchee du Dromadaire. All that remained now was for the 1st/368th to bring up its section of the line into Dromadaire the next morning. The attack on Binarville was set for noon of the 30th. (I) (10, 92, 146)

The pre-dawn of the 29th had meanwhile found the units of the 2nd and 3rd/307th waking up on hillsides and in valleys to find they were not quite as alone in the world as each had imagined itself the night before. Companies I and F had been forced to move their positions during the night due to concentrated artillery fire. In the misty murk of that morning, F found itself on the far left of the 307th's line. They sent out a patrol under Sergeant Lenahan and Corporal Engelhard, two experienced men, to attempt liaison with whomever they could find and before too long they ran into advanced elements of 2nd/308th in well-hidden funk holes near the down slope from Depot des Machines. The redoubtable Captain Rainsford and Company L eventually found elements of four other 307th companies located within a 500-meter radius of their position and slowly the 2nd and 3rd/307th began to straighten themselves out and shake off the night.

Word passed forward that rations had come up. Elements of the 3rd/307th pulled back to the high-walled German cemetery they had overrun the day before, collected their share, and sat among the Boche graves to eat their first real meal in almost four days. To the 2nd Battalion, who held the line, rations were passed forward and they too stretched out in the morning mist to eat. It was almost too good to be true.

Promptly at 6:00 a.m., after a half-hour artillery barrage had paved the way, the 307th's morning advance started. They fought like badgers against the Depot slopes until about 8:15 a.m., when they were finally and firmly held up by intense machine-gun fire. At 8:40 a.m., Colonel Houghton called General Johnson requesting an artillery barrage be dropped on the Depot des Machines ravine, to begin at 10:00 a.m. and last for 30 minutes. In the intervening space of time, company commanders of the 2nd Battalion pulled their men back 500 meters and reorganized for the attack while the 3rd Battalion closed in with them again.

The barrage came off without a hitch, lifted promptly at 10:30 a.m., and the Doughboys surged out into the wreckage ahead in an open order advance. Retribution from the Germans was swift and severe. Company I, on the left front, sent in Chauchat teams to attempt to force the slope ahead with a frontal assault and only got a stream of casualties to the rear as a result. Meanwhile, that portion of Company F off to the far left next to elements of 2nd/308th, joined them and pushed against the angle where the east/west Depot ravine bent north, just southeast of l'Homme Mort hill. There they learned that a portion of 1st/308th was cut off somewhere on the other side of the hill and repeatedly pushed into the forest, only to be met by determined resistance and be pushed back. The attack looked to be failing once again.

Soon however, combined Battalion PC, located in a little log hut halfway between the Depot ravine and the German cemetery to the rear, received a surprise. A message arrived from Lt. Weston Jenkins of Company E, over on the right flank, stating simply that he was in close contact with the enemy, progressing on the right, and had companies M and H supporting him. Lieutenant Jenkins and his company had spent a nerve-wracking night on the right flank in a long, thin line of Cossack posts stretched southeast to the errant 306th until finally, with the battle fully underway, regimental decided his companies' services would be better used in an advance position ("without reference to troops to the right or left" indeed). Gleefully abandoning the open flank, Company E pushed forward all day and by 3:30 p.m., Colonel Houghton was reporting to General Johnson, "Have gotten two companies across the ridge at 74.35. Two companies on that point, but pretty heavy fighting at Depot des Machines..." By 5:30 p.m. however, Lt. Jenkins and his men were forced to halt for the night by heavy machine-gun fire with their outposts facing nearly due west and north, while the remainder of the 307th's regimental line faced north. They had almost, but not quite, turned the enemy's east flank at the Depot ravine for the 154th Brigade. Organized then along a line again further in advance of the 306th, Company E refused their right flank back to the southeast for about 200 meters, but the two regiments never did connect. Consequently, a wide gap existed in the divisional line between the 306th and 307th throughout the night.

On the left however, combined 2nd and 3rd/307th and 2nd/308th actually had outpost liaison that night and slept in a firm, muddy line under the shadow of that "bitch of a ditch" they had been unable to beat, the Ravin de Depot des Machines. They had made no real gain however. Therefore, tomorrow promised to be another day of grim effort. (17, 99, 103, 104, 119, 134, 138, 139)

On their hands and knees, Lt. McKeogh, Pvt. Herschkowitz, and Pvt. Monson crawled off through the thick underbrush, heading south. They could see scarcely 10 yards in any direction through the dense foliage. McKeogh kept track of their heading by compass, his .45 automatic still ready in his free hand. All around, they could hear signs of German habitation and occasionally were able to get a glimpse through the tangle of brush of enemy troops. It was nerve-wracking work and they knew that every moment they spent out in the cold, wet woods was borrowed time.

They had been traveling but a short while when rifle fire rang out a little distance in the front of them. Instantly, the three froze in the dirt, thinking that they had been spotted, but no more fire was forthcoming. Then, the brush ahead rustled and crackled and a big German, crouched forward tensely, emerged, paused, and stalked off through the trees. By the sounds of it, there were more behind him. McKeogh turned his head to the two runners lying by his side and without making a sound mouthed, "Don't fire." Luckily, they had not been spotted.

As they lay waiting in the brush, the lieutenant realized it was going to be a long shot that all three men would get back to the Regimental PC together. Silently, he motioned the other two men up to his side. Putting his lips close to each man's ear, he whispered the Major's message to each of them and had them each repeat it back to him. He then scooped a little hole out of the sodden ground under his chin, ripped up the message and several others he had been carrying in his map case, and buried the lot. Again whispering into each man's ear, he impressed upon him the importance of at least one of them getting back to regimental. That meant no fighting unless absolutely necessary. In case of a sticky spot, they were to separate and each try to make his way back independently. Each nodded, understanding. Then, another German clumped past through the brush. Immobile and silent, they waited in the dim afternoon. (4, 109, 271)

It was nearing 3:15 p.m. when Sergeant Anderson and the Company A patrol returned to the bivouac on l'Homme Mort from their reconnaissance to the southwest and reported to Major Whittlesey. They had gone over two kilometers out in a wide arc, and had reached what they thought was Tranchee du Dromadaire (obviously well to the west of where the elements of the 308th were). They had met absolutely no American forces anywhere along the way. Near the spot where the little force had finally decided to turn around and head back, they did find odd bits of U.S. gear and so assumed that this was the farthest that the 368th scouts had managed to reach at some point and been driven back by Germans. Of those, there were plenty to be found all around them, every step of the way.

Things were not looking up. Save for the lucky few who had managed to make the resupply the afternoon before, or store away some of what little they had, again nobody ate. Water from the stream was out of the question as the sniper fire was too bad. All day long, they had beaten off repeated squad-sized attacks from nearly all points of the compass as the Germans tested the strength of the Doughboy lines. The order went out to conserve ammunition, which was running very low now, as were grenades. Within the dim recesses of the forest, shadowy forms flitted and as the afternoon wore on, all eyes strained into the brush, while tensed nerves jumped at the sporadic enemy trench mortar shells bursting around them. A terrible tension filled the air, for rumor had it that the Germans were going to attack them in force. (Everybody knew that the Huns always counter-attacked to retake lost ground.) The attack was expected at dusk. The few officers tried to quiet the gossips, but that strange sense of impending doom still hung over the bivouac like the thick clouds above. Obviously, this was no rest break. (29, 34, 109, 246, 271)

Major Whittlesey called for another bird and scrawled out another message that merely reiterated what the previous three had said, but with some added detail of patrols:

Hour: 4pm
To: CO 308 Inf.
A patrol which we sent to get in touch with units on our left has just returned, having crossed the R.R. track S.W. of here, and reached a point approximately 294 – 273.5. Germans, including 2 officers, were seen at this point, and others along the way. No Americans were met.
We have killed a German officer who was scouting here (94.8 – 74.5) this morning; also killed one other German, and taken a wounded prisoner. We have seen about 20 others passing through the woods near here. From the officer we have taken some valuable maps.
We have not been able to keep open our lines of communication, owing to German Mach. Guns which have filtered thru in our rear or come in from the West; and we shall not be able to do so without abandoning part of our position, which we hesitate to do, as we understand our mission to be to advance.
We have sent three pigeon messages today asking that our lines of communication be kept open by units from our rear, that we may get food and ammunition, and advance. (246)

About 20 minutes later, the pigeon landed safely at Rondchamp (the town where the 77th's message center was) at Mobile Pigeon Loft #11. At about that same time, the Company F patrol Major Whittlesey had sent east that morning sloshed back into the bivouac. Though they had tried all day, they had been unable to make contact with any friendly forces. The cordon around the American command there on the hill was just too tight for the smaller force to break through. Whether the rest of 2nd Battalion behind had been able to make any real headway or not, was still anyone's guess.

Frustrating as the lack of solid information was, Major Whittlesey focused on the paramount: hold on, do not lose faith in the forces to the rear and continue to keep everyone calm. Slowly, the two battalion commanders again worked their way from hole to hole, always reassuring the nervous men and conferencing with what company officers remained. Since ammunition was running very low, strict fire discipline was again reiterated. (34, 40, 91, 109, 132, 133, 224, 246, 256)

The 2nd/308th had gone into battle behind the morning barrage in good order. With elements of 3rd Battalion solidly entrenched in Dromadaire, 2nd's line had run at daybreak straight east from just across the divisional dividing line to the railroad junction near where Major Whittlesey had his PC set up the day before. From there, it angled north about 300 meters toward the Depot ravine before again swinging east to the 307th, which it was not in firm contact with at attack time. By 8:30 a.m., the 308th's advance was held up by stiff machine-gun fire, particularly at the angle of the ravine, and General Johnson was making preparations for the 10:00 a.m. barrage in front of the 307th, which he decided to extend westward to help cover that troublesome angle as well. General Johnson telephoned Colonel Stacey about 9:20 a.m. to inform him of the coming barrage, and the Colonel told the Brigadier that he deemed it inadvisable to advance at that time due to the condition of his left flank.

"The Negroes have fallen back behind Dromadaire, General, perhaps even farther, and that is why I don't want to advance," the Colonel warned.

"I have sent to your left flank my reserve, Colonel," General Johnson said, meaning the elements of the 3rd/308th that had taken the short section of Dromadaire early that morning. "Why can't you move Smith's troops a little to the left so I can put artillery fire on the railroad track and angle?"

"Sir, Lieutenant Colonel Smith was killed by machine-gun fire this morning trying to get up to my advance battalion, which appears to be cut off from communication," Colonel Stacey said. "He was shot in the head."

There was a short silence on the line then, "Colonel, do your best to clear up that angle before 10:00 a.m., then stand fast. Try to get a connection organized and set up by 10:30 a.m., when Houghton's advance will take place. Establish your liaison group between regiments at point 95.6-73.6 and wait until Houghton catches up and then make the advance with him." This was yet another interesting example of units "moving without reference to troops to the right or left", for if General Alexander was selective with the orders' incorporation in respect to gaining any and all objectives indiscriminately, then General Johnson was equally selective in using it only when he deemed it necessary.

By the time the barrage went over, General Alexander, at General Johnson's request, had authorized the 1st/307th for use as a containment force on the left flank again. General Johnson had them down just north of La Harazee at a place called Fosse aux Tanks. If the 368th could not mount a successful attack against Dromadaire Trench, then they would be in place to meet the gap up to the 3rd/308th elements already at Dromadaire. Major Whittlesey's situation would still remain beyond touch, but that should be corrected during the afternoon attacks of 2nd Battalion.

By noon, the left of the 307th and the right of the 308th were firmly liaisoned together and getting their teeth kicked in on the Depot ravine slopes again. By 3:30 p.m., Colonel Stacey had sent back a runner message that the advanced PC of the 308th was under heavy artillery and machine-gun fire and that his telephone lines had been cut. On the left, enemy machine-gunners were operating as far back as where the 1st/307th was sitting at Fosse aux Tanks. German Red Cross litter bearers had been spotted back there as well. With the 368th still unentrenched to any degree of firmness, the left flank was fairly exploding with enemy troops. General Johnson then ordered elements of the 1st/307th to fan out in a protective outpost line to cover the hole. As for Major Whittlesey's 1st Battalion, "As far as I know," the Brigadier told General Alexander over the phone at about 3:00 p.m., "advance elements on the left are at point 74.6." (2, 109, 131, 132, 133, 144, 238)

As the light faded, Lt. McKeogh led his two men through the brush once again. It was not long before they came upon the target the Germans had been shooting at earlier. A crumpled figure in khaki lay in the bushes ahead, apparently a doughboy that had strayed from the protection of the bivouac, or perhaps one of the runners who had been holed up all day and had made a poor choice for an exit time. All three men looked at him, but none recognized the man. After another half an hour of painful crawling through the brush, the three men hit upon a broad clearing that cut across their course, running north and south. Down the center was a path. A path meant real progress rather than slow pain, but at greater risk. Deciding it was worth it, all three slid down the little trail, keeping to one side. Shortly, out of a side trail about 50 yards ahead, turned two Germans. Doughboys and Germans alike froze in complete surprise for the barest of seconds, then the lead German drew his revolver and pointing it at McKeogh, yelled something that ended in "Kamerad". Pvt. Monson yelled, "Kamerad hell!" and all three dived into the brush again with Boche bullets kicking up mud at their heels.

They ran a short way, fanned out in the undergrowth, and laid down as the Germans followed. Lieutenant McKeogh found a spot behind a tree with a low bough parallel to the ground and rested his right arm across it, pistol extended. A German pushed through the brush directly in front of him, their eyes meeting at slightly less than 10 feet away, and both fired. McKeogh got off four shots, but it was the first one that counted. He drilled the German right between the eyes, but not before one of the Boche bullets had torn into his right wrist and exited some three inches up his forearm. Around him, he heard Privates Monson and Herschkowitz firing at the second Hun, who took off through the brush. Then, silence.

The two privates quietly made their way over to the injured lieutenant, and all three found a better hiding place deeper in the brush. Private Monson dressed McKeogh's wound which, while slight and clean, had nevertheless caused his arm to swell alarmingly. At the same time, the lieutenant ordered Herschkowitz to go and search the Hun he had shot (a task that revolted Herschkowitz, even 60 years later when he talked of it). Then, huddled in the wet brush, the three shivering men decided the safest course was to wait for full dark before setting out. McKeogh found a piece of stale bread in the bottom of his gas mask bag, which he shared with the other two and carefully he and Pvt. Monson shared a smoke. Private Herschkowitz, who unknown to the others was suffering terribly with the Spanish Flu, dozed off. To the rhythm of machine-guns in the distance, they waited for nightfall.

Once darkness had taken hold, the three stiffly set out again. About 8:00 p.m., they again came to a clear path. Sticking close to one side as before, they carefully moved forward. They had made about 10 minutes fast progress when a voice called out authoritatively from within the dark ahead, "Bist du Deutsch?" ("Are you German?") Instantly, they flattened on the ground. The voice called out again and then there was the click of the safety lock on a rifle snapping in the darkness. The owner of the voice fired and several more rifles on each side then joined in. The bullets whined off harmlessly to the north and the three quickly rolled into the bushes as any noise they made was covered by the wild rifle fire. They had unknowingly stumbled directly into the outpost line of a German camp! Lieutenant McKeogh whispered softly that they would stay put until things again settled down and then promptly dozed off. Around midnight, Pvt. Monson woke him by gently pounding on his thigh. All was quiet again and they set off.

McKeogh, again leading by compass, tried to skirt the German funk holes of the encampment, but instead mistakenly led them right into the middle of it. Out of the darkness ahead came another demand in German, this time much closer. It was time for action; Major Whittlesey's message had to get back somehow. The safety lock of a rifle snapped again just as Lt. McKeogh yelled, "Separate!" into the inky darkness and the three men took off in different directions, followed by a fusillade of rifle fire. McKeogh made for a hole in the ground through an opening in the trees he could just make out ahead, his heart pumping furiously despite his tiredness. Like a long-jumper, he leapt the last few feet to the hole with his legs stretched out in front of him, intending to slide the rim of the hole and come to rest in a sitting position. Instead, he landed in the hole with a muffled 'crump' on something soft. It was a German soldier! Next to him, he could see the silhouette of a second man slowly rise. The lieutenant thought fast. He knew practically not a word of German but managed to fish up, "Was ist los?" ("What is wrong?"), while the darkness bought him the time that he needed. The German next to him apparently could not see the dirty American well enough to identify him as such, for he answered back, "Was ist *los*?" with much surprise. Now just waking up to the fact that he was still armed, Lt. McKeogh sharply reached out his wounded right arm and placed the muzzle of the .45 firmly against the German's left breast and fired twice. He then drew back, crooked the pistol between his knees and put two slugs into the back of the man wriggling under him. The body went slack and he put one more into the man on his right, who had fallen back against the side of the hole and was fishing for something in his belt (probably a knife). Then he was up and out of the hole in a flash.

All around, there was a tremendous rifle fusillade and shouts and cries went up as all three Doughboys tore through the dark. Private Monson found a spur line of narrow gauge railroad track and followed along it in the brush at its edge. Suddenly, a German came hustling down it, and Monson drew back into the brush. As the German came abreast, he dropped him with a pistol shot to the side of the head before again tearing off through the brush. Lieutenant McKeogh sprawled out under another bush some distance from the funk hole in which he had killed the two Germans and waited. Private Herschkowitz carefully found a safe spot and waited as well.

Around 2:00 a.m., a driving rainstorm pelted the countryside, and at about 4:00 a.m. Lt. McKeogh set off again, circling around to the west before settling on a southerly course. Several more times he narrowly avoided patrolling Germans along his way. It was almost a full, gray dawn when he came to a wagon road. He was shy of taking it at first, but all the firing seemed to be behind him now. His pistol swung listlessly by his side and for the first time in over 24 hours he put it back in the holster. Then, he tucked his wounded arm up into the sling of his gas mask bag and walked right down the middle of the road in the rain in an exhausted daze.

Hearing voices ahead brought him around some and he quickly ducked into the brush at the side of the road. Drawing his pistol again, he leveled the automatic over a branch with his left hand and as the voices came closer, McKeogh could hardly believe his ears when he realized that the words were English! Stepping out onto the road once again, the mud-covered lieutenant saw a small group of Doughboys standing around the lip of a funk hole. They were men of Company I/308th. He had made his way back as far as Tirpitz trench. "My God, but am I ever glad to see you fellows!" Lt. McKeogh exclaimed as he walked up, startling the men. "Say something to me in American, will you? All I've heard for the last twenty-four hours is that goddamn Hienie shit!"

They led the exhausted lieutenant back to the Regimental PC, where he reported to Colonel Stacey, who was just sitting down to breakfast and gave his report while a medic cleaned and dressed his wounded arm. Plans were already being acted upon to rescue Major Whittlesey, Major Budd and their men, Colonel Stacey said. It was then that Lt. McKeogh learned that Lt. Col. Smith was dead, a fact that saddened and infuriated him. He answered as many questions as he could concerning the Hun force behind 1st Battalion while devouring a mountain of flapjacks placed before him. Colonel Stacey intended to send him to lead a combat rescue force back up l'Homme Mort, but was vetoed by the combat surgeon on duty at the time. Instead, someone from the 77th was needed to go back to the United States as an experienced combat instructor, and the wounded Lt. McKeogh was informed he had just volunteered. Therefore, clean and dry, he was headed to the coast to catch a transport home within 24 hours.

As Lt. McKeogh was tearing into his plate of flapjacks, first J.J. Monson and then Jack Herschkowitz both arrived at the Regimental PC, both exhausted but otherwise unwounded. Private Monson had headed west and run into Company I men as well, but outside of his adventure along the railway had managed a mostly uneventful trip back. Private Herschkowitz had gone so far west he ran into a French unit, who were kind enough to lead the flu ridden Doughboy back to the 308th's lines. He arrived at the Regimental PC with a raging fever of 105, made his report and then promptly dropped to the floor. The medics carted him off to the hospital almost dead, and there he remained for the rest of the war, battling the Spanish Influenza into 1919. All three men received the Distinguished Service Cross for their adventures. (IV) (4, 34, 91, 271, 320, 321, 325, 338)

By 7:30 p.m. on September 29, the 154th Brigade attacks were all but over. The 308th and 307th regiments had been driven away from the slopes of the Depot ravine and were again held up on a general line 300 meters or so south, almost where they had started from. Except for a small advance element of the 307th in a very tenuous position, barely across the ravine on the far right, there had been virtually no gain at all for much blood spilled. Later that night, General Johnson telephoned to General Alexander, "They (the enemy) are holding that ravine in considerable force as far as machine-guns go and are evidently trying to stop us along that line. I am trying to maneuver them out by going round in their rear. Boche got in between the lines of the left and rear of the 308th and cut out a section... leading forward. Had trouble there." (131, 136, 139)

Out on l'Homme Mort, Major Whittlesey and his men knew nothing of all this, only that they were cold, wet, hungry, and surrounded. The day had been a bad one and if things continued along the same path, tomorrow would prove worse still. Tension among the officers and NCO's who knew the situation was thick enough to cut. Troops were almost completely out of food and water and fast running out of ammunition. On the other hand, by some miracle, though there had been lots of light wounds, there had been only a few serious casualties and even fewer killed. Nor had the expected dusk attack occurred. Now, however, the rumor mill was predicting an early morning attack. One thing was certain; if it did come, they would definitely have a difficult time beating it off in their present depleted condition. Then, it started raining, again... (40, 109, 209)

Concerning the issue of hunger, Pvt. McCollum, in Company A, had thought he heard the low howling of a dog the previous night and had mentioned it to his 'hole mate', Pvt. Art Kidwell, who thought he was nuts. Then, while on patrol that next morning, they found the body of a German police dog in the bushes just beyond the outpost line, shot through the head. Corporal Domenico Levi, also of A and one of the few seriously wounded in the Small Pocket, used to tell a story in later years about a dog being killed and eaten when his unit was surrounded in the Argonne. He never said if he partook, but being one of the wounded, it would seem hardly likely - hungry or not. (32, 174)

(I) The French were definitely having their share of problems in the zone of Groupement Durand, largely because of the problems that the 368th Infantry were having. And while this is true, that unit has, nevertheless, since become an all encompassing 'scapegoat' for *all* the problems that were encountered in their general region; and most especially the Lost Battalion episode. It was a popular misconception after the war, when the story of the Lost Battalion first became legend, that it was solely the fault of the 368th—the "Negro Regiment", as they were described in the popular press of the time—that Major Whittlesey and his men were surrounded. Observers charged that by failing to keep the left flank secure, they left an 'open door' through which the enemy was able to flank and thus hem in the 308th. In most cases, the misconception persists to this day. However, it is only true to a point. While the 368th Infantry did fail to keep up in the west, leaving the 308th's left flank open from the start of the offensive, something which contributed directly to the first entrapment Major Whittlesey and his men were to face out on the hill of l'Homme Mort (since known as the 'Small Pocket') it only indirectly contributed to the Pocket in the Charlevaux Ravine—the officially recognized 'Lost Battalion' episode. Nor was it necessarily within the 368th Infantry's control to fully prevent this either. The positions against which the 368th was thrusting itself were tremendously difficult objectives. Further, as it lay outside the borders of the greater Argonne Forest, the ground over which they were forced to attack was much more open than that of the 308th and therefore the Germans had the area wired and machine-gun swept to a greater degree than normal. And being mostly open country, there was also little cover offered an attacker from the heavy and accurate shellfire continually raking the area. At the same time, the 368th had received far too little of their own in the way of artillery support for their attacks. All these difficulties meant the attack zone would have been difficult for any regiment to carry, let alone one with the inherent difficulties that the 368th Infantry had, of which there were several.

The initial problem was one of policy. The U.S. Army in the First World War was a very segregated organization, as many at the time believed that Negro troops were inferior fighters (despite much evidence to the contrary from the Civil War). Therefore, most black units serving in the AEF usually found themselves far behind the lines in the Service of Supply, not in combat. Those Negro units that actually found themselves assigned to front line service, usually piecemealed out to the French (as was the 368th), found that their combat training was minimal at best, and their equipment was usually substandard. Then too, the average Negro soldier was uneducated, a fact many whites pointed to as a serious deficiency for a fighting man; this despite plenty of evidence that there were plenty of uneducated whites in the Army as well. Yet, despite the lack of support from outside, as well as within, the AEF, black soldiers continued to request combat assignments. Therefore, any failing of the 368th did not occur because the Negro troops lacked offensive spirit; but because they merely lacked the necessary 'tools' of modern war. In other words, they were simply not well prepared in many respects to face what they did in the Muese-Argonne Offensive.

The 368th in particular further faced another, even bigger and unique problem of their own west of the 77th, one concerning their right boundary line with the 308th. While the boundary in the west, between the 368th and the French 11th C.a.P, was roughly defined as the Binarville-Vienne la Chateau road, the eastern boundary that separated the 368th and the 308th was merely lines on a map and nothing so realistically tangible as a road. This perhaps would not have been so disturbing were it not for the fact that those map lines representing the two individual regimental boundaries, while coinciding at the jump-off line, almost immediately thereafter began to slowly angle away from each other. By the time they reached above Binarville, some 4 kilometers or so distant from the start line (and where the 368th would eventually be withdrawn), they were separated by just over 800 meters. What led to this unfortunate misalignment of attack paths is unclear. What is clear, however, is that it was considered the 368th's responsibility as liaison force between the French and American armies to fully occupy and control the space. This ever-increasing space then forced the 368th to constantly realign its forces as the attack progressed. (In the event, the 308th's left flank was usually operating over this line anyway.) Coupled with their inability to maintain general steady progress over the difficult ground of their attack zone, failure was virtually guaranteed from the start. Once news of that eventual failure made its way back to the United States, those with a racial axe to grind took the story and ran with it. Thus, when the story of the episode in the Charlevaux Ravine really gained steam, so too did one of the supposed 'reasons' behind the 308th's predicament, gleaned from the few meager details of the first entrapment that had filtered through and inadvertently gotten mixed in with the second, or Charlevaux, entrapment details. The 368th failed on the 308th's left flank not because individual black soldiers were inferior fighters, but because the task assigned them was beyond their capabilities *as a regiment*, due to an archaic racial policy that left them ill-equipped for their duties.

Yet, their inability to maintain the integrity of the left flank set into motion three sets of events that all *indirectly contributed* to the episode in the Charlevaux Ravine. First, was the initial entrapment on l'Homme Mort, largely caused by their failures. Second, was their own later withdrawal from the line due to those failures, which then forced the French 9th and 11th Cuirassiers a Pied to try and 'pick up the slack' and rush to catch up the 308th's line (something that we can see starting as early as September 29 - see text). This in turn contributed (though again, it must be stressed, *indirectly*) to the third; Major Whittlesey becomes trapped the second, more famous, time. This later entrapment is due in part to a left flank insecurity, caused by the French being forced to deal with an enemy that has had time to reorganize and regroup. And this problem, we have seen, was originally initiated by the 368th's failures. Thus, we can trace an *indirect* link to the famous Pocket in the Charlevaux Ravine from a more direct link to the Small Pocket on l'Homme Mort.

However, a portion of the blame for the initial entrapment also falls on the 2nd/308th for their actions on the afternoon of September 28th. By falling away from Major Whittlesey's right flank that day (in direct violation of General Alexander's G.O. #27 remember), they left a second, though narrower, door open for a distance of about half a kilometer. While nearly all available evidence points to the encircling infiltration around the Small Pocket coming mostly from the left flank, it is entirely likely, in fact probable, that the methodical Germans had infiltrated from both flanks, connecting along the trail by the cemetery where Sergeant Hitlin first found them. There were certainly still plenty of Germans in the Depot des Machines ravine to the east of l'Homme Mort to affect such an action from that side, and they still had a certain amount of control over the Ravin Moulin de l'Homme Mort along the east side of the hill as well, even though their major withdrawal back to the Giselher Stellung was then well under way.

(II) In his citation for the Distinguished Service Cross, Sgt. Mjr. Gaedeke is erroneously given credit for bringing down this German officer, which, as earlier described, he did not do. The confusion is probably due to the four Germans all being brought back to the Battalion PC within a relatively short period of each other. Since the wounded German officer was carried to the PC soon after Sgt. Mjr. Gaedeke brought in the dead German NCO from the earlier McKeogh/Peterson adventure at the machine-gun nest, it is not hard to see how the confusion could have happened. It is also possible that the Sergeant Major was given credit for the action in order to ease the pain of his loss on his family, for Battalion Sergeant Major Benjamin Gaedeke was killed five days later in the Charlevaux Ravine.

(III) The final experience of Private George W. Quinn makes an interesting aside, as it was not until after the war that anyone found out what had actually happened to him. In midyear 1919, *Colliers Magazine* ran a story written by Lt. McKeogh chronicling his experiences with the 308th in which he mentioned Pvt. Quinn's disappearance. Not long after, the *Colliers* offices forwarded a letter to him from a Jack S. Grady, formally Captain, Company E/805th Pioneer Infantry. In the letter, Grady explained how he and his men had by chance found George Quinn's body there in the forest while out on a grave registration detail in late January 1919, exactly four months to the day that the runner had disappeared. Surrounding him were three German corpses and judging from the positioning of the bodies, it had been deduced that Pvt. Quinn had been able to kill all three before succumbing to a mortal wound inflicted by one of his attackers.

Four months is a long time to lie out in any forest, not to mention the jungle of the Argonne and it was a small miracle that Pvt. Quinn's body was ever located in the tangle in the first place. (Eerily, Pvt. Charles Minder of Company B/306th MG Bn. wrote his mother the very day Quinn disappeared stating, "Some of the wounded fellows are going to have a tough time getting found where they fell in this wilderness today. They might never get found...") In the runners pockets, they found Lt. McKeogh's message to Major Whittlesey, as well as an unfinished letter to his mother and one to his aunt, though none were clearly legible. When the Army, now in possession of the facts, tried to notify Mrs. Caroline Quinn with confirmation of her son's death, in February 1919, the message came back as undeliverable; Mrs. Quinn had since moved.

Lt. McKeogh, now emotionally drawn to the whole episode, then wrote a poem entitled, "Runner Quinn" which he had published in the August 16, 1919 edition of the *Saturday Evening Post*. Mrs. Quinn saw the poem and contacted the *Post* requesting an address to write to Lt. McKeogh. Sadly, it was the first news that she had had concerning her son since his last letter to her, which had been dated June 2, 1918—over 14 months ago. The *Post* then informed Lt. McKeogh, who quickly exchanged letters with Mrs. Quinn and her sister and was able to provide the grieving mother with details of her son's final days. Today, Pvt. George W. Quinn's remains rest in the Muese-Argonne American Cemetery at Romagne sous Montfaucon, France. His stone mistakenly lists him as having died September 28.

(IV) J.J. Monson survived the war only to die alone and poor and living on the streets of New York. Like so many of the wars' heroes after the initial glow of victory wore off, he was cast aside and forgotten about. Aimless in the wars' aftermath and haunted by all he had seen, he began to drink. By 1921, he was a full-blown alcoholic when, by chance, he was given a shot at a real job - provided he could clean up. Checking himself into Belleview Hospital for treatment, it was there that he died. Nobody there thought much of his death until a couple of days after when they were gathering up his few personal effects and found his medals and discharge papers in a small box he had brought with him. With this information in hand, someone at the hospital cared enough to contact his sister, who immediately claimed the body and began a subscription effort to raise money for a proper funeral. She had been just in time too; Monson was due to have been buried in Potters Field under only a numbered stone the day after she claimed him. The newspapers carried the sad story and the public rallied a hero's burial for the man, which he was then given. Charles Whittlesey, by then a Lt. Col. in the 308th Organized Reserves, gave the eulogy and carried Monson's medals on a pillow behind the casket as it was carried from the church, despite being extremely ill at the time. Arthur McKeogh went home and returned to the newspaper publishing business that he had left to go to war. He wrote two books on the 77th Division, not playing up his accomplishments at all in either one, but neither sold very well. Stupidly, he was also looked on as a subversive, along with author Lawrence Stallings (with whom he was a close friend) in the early 1920's by the FBI for his involvement in several veterans' organizations. He died suddenly in 1929. Jack Herschkowitz lived the rest of his life out peacefully in New York City, lasting well into the 1970s. It is believed that he gave his last real interview concerning his experiences in the Argonne to author Henry Berry for his excellent book, *Make the Kaiser Dance*. He was the last of the three Small Pocket heroes to die.

Ancillary sources used in this chapter include: 92, 123, 128, 131, 133, 142, 145, 152, 153, 179, 200, 218, 219, 231, 235, 245, 370, 371, 367

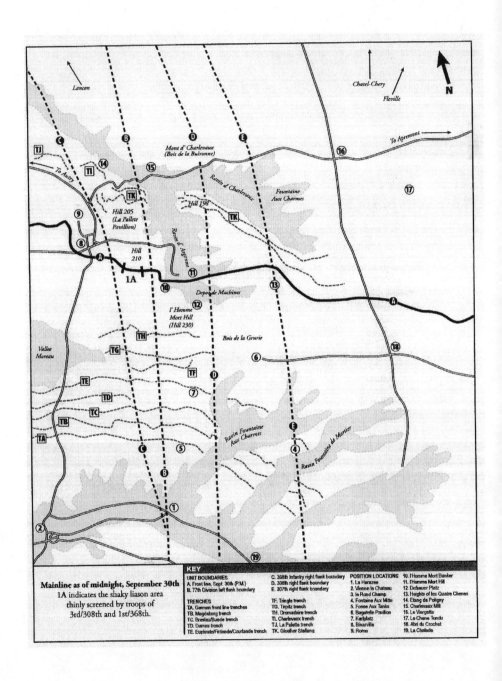

Mainline as of midnight, September 30th

1A indicates the shaky liason area
thinly screened by troops of
3rd/308th and 1st/368th.

KEY

UNIT BOUNDARIES
A. Front line, Sept. 30th (P.M.)
B. 77th Division left flank boundary

C. 368th Infantry right flank boundary
D. 308th right flank boundary
E. 307th right flank boundary

TRENCHES
TA. German front line trenches
TB. Magdaburg trench
TC. Breslau/Suede trench
TD. Damus trench
TE. Euphrate/Finlande/Courlande trench

TF. Tringle trench
TG. Tirpitz trench
TH. Dromadaire trench
TI. Charlevaux trench
TJ. La Palette trench
TK. Giselher Stallung

POSITION LOCATIONS
1. La Harazee
2. Vienne le Chateau
3. le Rond Champ
4. Fonbaine Aux Mitte
5. Fosse Aux Tanks
6. Baguetelle Pavilion
7. Karlplatz
8. Binarville
9. Rome

10. l'Homme Mort Bunker
11. l'Homme Mort Hill
12. Defsauer Platz
13. Heights of les Quatre Chenes
14. Etang de Poligny
15. Charlevaux Mill
16. Le Viergette
17. Le Chene Tondu
18. Abri du Crochet
19. La Chalade

September 30, 1918
"...a night of utter wretchedness..."
Diary of Pvt. Jim Larney.

On the evening of the 29th, end of the fourth day of battle in the Muese-Argonne, General Pershing found himself reluctantly forced to concede that the 72-hour time frame for the 1st Phase of the offensive was now just a dream. Only certain divisions had reached the 1st phase objective (the 77th Division was not one of them), and much of the all-important momentum of the drive had been lost in the rain and mud of the second and third days. True, Montfaucon had been taken on the second day and that was a great triumph. However, individual units all across the line were tiring and there were heavy losses, requiring yet more replacements. Plus, logistics were still a nightmare, as the three roads leading up to the front remained hideously jammed with men and material. Thus, after a little persuasion by his staff, General Pershing agreed to a short halt in the assault to reorganize and prepare his forces. Consequently, at 11:00 p.m. on September 29, the 1st Army order issued for September 30 stated that due to the severity of fighting, loss of flank liaison between units, intermingling of troops and difficulties of supply and evacuation of wounded from captured areas, the entire front was to organize for defense. Positions were to be consolidated and reorganized in depth with strong reconnaissance patrols sent out to the front to maintain contact with the enemy. Everyone was to generally prepare for a fresh renewal of the main attack.

Therefore, no general line attack was to occur on the morning of the 30th within the 1st Corps zone. Instead, the exhausted Doughboys watched the forest lighten without the aid of artillery flashes for the first time since the 26th. Corps orders were issued at about 9:30 a.m. calling for an attempt to stabilize the line and reorganize all divisional forces as best possible. This included cleaning up back areas of stray enemy troops and substantiating supply lines, and throughout the morning carrying parties were sent back to supply dumps to return with huge quantities of rifle, machine-gun, and Stokes ammunition. Some food and water was brought up and the rolling kitchens came as far as the captured and repaired roads would take them. Within the Argonne Forest, men from the 302nd Engineer Regiment of the 77th repaired and began to make use of those sections of the narrow gauge rail network that had fallen into U.S. hands. Field dressing stations and ambulance stops, reorganized and repositioned better to suit the frontal area which they served, also made use of the rail network, as did supply units. All this preparation was done with an eye toward resumption of the general line attack, scheduled to begin again at dawn of October 1. (8, 16, 22, 43, 116, 117, 130, 131)

In the wee hours of the morning of the 30th, General Alexander and his aids paid a visit to General Johnson at his advanced Regimental PC. Their purpose was to gather details concerning the dispositions within the zone of the 308th, particularly the 1st Battalion's situation and General Johnson's plans for its relief. (This was brought about by the last word General Johnson had sent through the night before, concerning the section of the 308th that had been "cut out".) General Johnson told General Alexander that he had already passed orders down to Colonel Stacey directing reorganization of his forces, which were currently spread thin along the main line after the beating they had taken on the 29th. They were in the midst of preparations for an assault to be made the afternoon of the 30th specifically aimed at forcing the main line up to and around Major Whittlesey's position. Meanwhile, Company K of the 3rd Battalion had been sent up to Captain McMurtry, who was now in temporary command of the 2nd Battalion since Lt. Col. Smith's death. Their objective was to try and break through to 1st Battalion with supplies at the earliest practical time. They were even then preparing to send out a strong patrol in hopes of perhaps slipping past the German outposts behind the 1st Battalion in pre-dawn darkness. Other elements of 3rd Battalion remained firmly established in Tranchee du Dromadaire, waiting to connect with the 368th if the planned assault over there came to fruition, while the remainder continued 'mopping up' in the 308th's rear areas. During this time, the 1st/307th was yet sitting down near Fosse aux Tanks guarding the rear of the left flank, where the 368th had still not neared. General Alexander then wanted to know if General Johnson had any more recent contact with either Major Whittlesey or Major Budd. Not since the last pigeon message of the afternoon before, the Brigadier told him. However, with the Germans pulling back, apparently to a point even beyond the 1st Battalion's position, according to the prisoners that he had interrogated the other day, General Johnson had every confidence that they would be able to break through to Major Whittlesey's force very soon. (2, 131, 144)

It was while General Alexander was at 154th Brigade PC that Major General Ballou (commanding the 92nd Division) and Brigadier General Hay (commanding the 184th Brigade) showed up, inquiring as to the situation and the 368th's effectiveness thus far. It was a decidedly short meeting. "Not good enough," were the words both Alexander and Johnson used and neither spared them any details while the two 92nd Generals listened in stony silence. The circumstances along the left flank - the wide gap and lost liaison that General Johnson believed responsible for Major Whittlesey's then 'unfortunate' predicament - were all laid out with thorough candor (though the problems that 2nd/308th had on Major Whittlesey's right were apparently never mentioned). "They were given (the) information with the utmost frankness," General Alexander later wrote, "and the interview closed without further remark." (2, 46)

Major Whittlesey's men woke up in their funk holes stiff and sore (those who had slept anyway). Lots of movement around the bivouac all night had kept the outpost men's nerves stretched near the breaking point. Therefore, the dim, gray morning found them sleepless and strained. There had been little in the way of enemy fire or actual enemy contact though and that had been at least somewhat of a blessing. Certainly no one among the Doughboys had been popping off unnecessarily; there was not enough ammunition left for that sort of nonsense. (The machine-guns and auto rifles were running particularly low.) Gone almost completely now were any hand grenades; the 'all around' attacks of the day before having virtually used up what few had been left in the first place.

Nerves that were already shaken by hunger and cold stretched further as the usual Argonne morning fog rolled in and once again blanked everything. No patrols sent out that night had been successful either in getting off the hill or in making contact with anyone friendly; only the enemy seemed to be out there and he was moving around a lot. The patrols themselves had been nothing short of nightmares out in the pitch-dark, rain-swept forest. Yet outside of a couple very small firefights, most had avoided any problems. Nevertheless, each returned patrol was forced to reluctantly repeat the same old story; the Germans appeared to be consolidating their positions around the Doughboy contingent, as far as they could tell in the dank blankness and it certainly looked as if neither side was going anywhere any time soon.

Most of the rest of the men had not been out of their funk holes for going on two days now, except to relieve themselves if the risk looked low enough. The effects of that idleness, coupled with the previous days' hardships, were now beginning to show. Seriously cramped muscles, swollen, achy feet and rheumatoid joints were causing many great pains. Sickness too was setting in. The temperature had insisted on remaining relentlessly and unseasonably low and the incessant rain only added to the misery. With no shelter halves, overcoats, ponchos, or blankets to combat the elements - nothing except wool uniforms that had been almost continuously wet for almost five days - exposure was beginning to grip many in its tight, chilled fist. Colds, deep rattling coughs that presaged pneumonia, in some cases the 'flu and terrible diarrhea were starting to seriously set in. Nearly all of the men were filthy, as they were unable to wash or clean their teeth in almost a week, there was little water for shaving, many were infested with body lice, and rare was the man without at least a light case of gas poisoning. (I) But of all the pains, hunger had to be the worst. Theirs was not just a gnawing appetite, but a deep, raw pain emanating from low within one's stomach. Some men had not eaten since well before they landed on l'Homme Mort and were worse off than those who had managed a meal or two since. A few had not eaten since the start of the offensive five days before. Until the Small Pocket, water had controlled hunger somewhat, clean or not, as had cigarettes. Yet with the only local source of water, the little creek below the hill, under deadly and accurate sniper fire, getting water was almost impossible, and the last packages of smokes had long been emptied. (34, 109, 218)

Major Whittlesey, who seemed to not sleep at all, was up and out well before the sun making his rounds, stalking to each Company PC position fully upright through the ground fog with his peculiar, long-legged gait, hands behind his back, apparently oblivious to any danger. At each position, he made inquires as to the previous night's actions, company strength and conditions before perhaps correcting fields of fire, suggesting a better positioning of men, offering a few words of encouragement and moving on. *'Do not worry, 2nd Battalion is right behind us. They shall be up today, no doubt. Plenty of food, water and ammunition are on the way!'* His words were always welcome and rarely, if ever, sounded hollow. The Major himself seemed to believe every positive thing he said and that lent great credence to his statements. If he had any loose nerves concerning their predicament on that bleak hillside, it did not show to any of the men. (109, 152, 153)

However, with ammunition and supplies nearly gone, their fate seemed precarious at best, a fact that even Major Whittlesey could not ignore for long. Unquestionably, he was more than a little concerned, borne out by the messages he sent to the rear the day before. They had also taken considerable casualties over the past four days, something that would haunt any combat commander. In fact, earlier in the battle a Company I liaison leader operating on their left flank, Sergeant Carmen Calbi, had caught Major Whittlesey alone in the Karlplatz dugout crying. Obviously then, there were some nerves to the man after all. However, out on l'Homme Mort, the Major went to great lengths to foster the impression of a pillar of stone. He continually set examples from which the men were able to take great strength and courage, despite the shabby physical state that all endured. (109, 143, 159, 209)

Perhaps the most noticeable of these examples was that he never walked around hunched over while under fire. Instead, Major Whittlesey nearly always remained erect, hands usually clasped behind his back and seemingly totally calm, only very occasionally ducking down, even during the heaviest of barrages. Lieutenant McKeogh later remembered him as being "absolutely indifferent" to shellfire and "seemingly oblivious of the danger". This was a sentiment that Private James Larney echoed. "Whittlesey *never* ducked under shellfire, but instead always walked upright," he later wrote. Certainly, like anyone, the Major could, of course, be surprised by occasional close shell bursts (usually just the first one), but he never panicked under fire, at least not outwardly. (II) (34, 218)

181

Internally however, it is very likely that Major Whittlesey was in constant turmoil. By all accounts, he had a very sensitive nature and was no doubt touched to the very quick by the terrible cataclysm around him of bursting shells, devastated countryside and maimed and destroyed human life. The killing of anything was abhorrent to him, as would be no less his participation in it. He undoubtedly hated the role he was now compelled to play and the terrible pain and suffering of the men under him that he was forced to witness (and in many cases provide the orders leading to). He had likely wished himself out of the position many times and at almost any cost. Yet, it was his deep sense of right and wrong that prevailed upon him to remain and see 'The Cause' through; a Cause he thoroughly believed in. Indeed, it was that same overruling perceptional belief in the justice of 'The Cause', and the greater good that it would eventually bring, that had brought him to take part in the war to begin with. It also bade him now to go to great lengths to try to keep the spirits of his men (the very men forced to risk the most for that Cause) as high as possible so that their burden might be lighter should they be forced to face their final moments. (246, 258, 274)

By just after 6:30 a.m. on September 30, everything was still surprisingly quiet along the ragged outpost line of the bivouac. They had heard no earlier artillery barrage preliminary to a U.S. assault as had happened each of the previous mornings of the offensive. This was cause for concern. What had happened in the south? Was there to be no attack? Or was the artillery simply fearful of firing into the surrounded battalion's lines, thus forcing the infantry to attack 'barebacked'? If so, it was the quietest attack any had ever heard, for there was virtually no gunfire to speak of down to the south. Nor had the rumored morning counter-attack by the Boche materialized, but it could just be that the methodical Germans were merely waiting for the morning fog to burn off before they came over. On the other hand, there had been no preparatory trench mortar fire either, as all had feared there would be. One of the damn things had opened up for a while yesterday and dumped in more than a few rounds, startling the daylights out of everyone with their sharp whine and loud crack when they exploded. Their aim had been off though and they had really hurt no one, but if the Huns got the thing working properly, it would not take them long to wipe out the little force on the hill. So too with their heavy artillery. All the German troops would have to do is pull back a little from the Doughboy perimeter and theirs would be a clear field of fire. Yet the most likely immediate threat was deemed to be the all around assault for which Major Whittlesey's Doughboys were as ready as they could be. Most all knew however that the worsening ammunition situation would soon render their position untenable. Therefore, the cool morning of September 30 found the men waiting in the fog nervously for the enemy.

It came as a great surprise then, when just after 6:30 a.m., a small, stray patrol of four men and an NCO in khaki snaked up the hill from the south, dragging with them two German prisoners. They pushed through the brush, asking for the Battalion PC and were passed through the outpost line and taken down to the bunker. Nobody recognized them as 1st Battalion men and immediately rumors started to fly from hole to hole. Majors Whittlesey and Budd, as startled by the turn of events as any, immediately questioned the patrol leader, Corporal (acting Sergeant) Legers; who were they, where had they come from and how the devil had they gotten through the German cordon? Sergeant Legers, a serious and dedicated soldier, presented his two prisoners. They were a 2nd Battalion scout patrol he said, sent out at dawn to try and break through to the command stranded forward of the 308th's main line. They had only encountered light resistance at a machine-gun nest, which they had then properly dispatched, taking these prisoners in the bargain. Was this the position of the 1st Battalion, they asked? (109, 116, 132, 136, 144)

On the main line, 2nd/308th had sat in their muddy funk holes all throughout an

182

uneventful night filled mostly with morose silence. There had not even been the usual light show of German flares to provide any minor entertainment. Machine-gun and rifle fire had remained very sporadic. Both sides, it seemed, had hit a solid wall of exhaustion. Even the few German artillery shells, which had started coming over just before midnight, were scattered and desultory. Around 2:00 a.m., it started to downpour. By the time it stopped later that morning, the cloudy, cool autumn fog it left behind greeted carrying parties coming up with food, clean water and ammunition in bundles. Liaison parties from Company I went out to firm up the connection with the 307th on the right and look for somebody out on the left, but everyone already knew that there was nothing that way except open air and Germans.

Major Whittlesey's pigeon messages of the previous day had made it pretty clear that his command was rapidly running out of supplies. It would not take the Germans long to capture them if the ammo ran out; that or kill them all. This disconcerting thought spurred Colonel Stacey to spend considerable time over night organizing a plan to get the rest of his regiment up to the Major's line. The plan was not to be so much a 'rescue effort' as a planned, proper advance to a further advanced unit. General Johnson also had a hand in Colonel Stacey's scheme, for to facilitate bringing the main line up to Major Whittlesey's he had given the Colonel the 3rd Battalion's Company K, under 1st Lt. John S. Taylor, to flesh out the 2nd Battalion's depleted ranks. Colonel Stacey then gave Lt. Taylor orders to spearhead directly to the 1st Battalion during the day's coming attacks. In the meantime, he decided it might be prudent to attempt to get some sort of line through to Major Whittlesey to make sure he was still there and in relatively good shape, as no word from the hillside had come through since the previous afternoon. While a company might not be able to break through, Colonel Stacey figured, a smaller patrol might, similar to how Lt. McKeogh and his two men had gotten out on the night of the 29th. Darkness would help, but not the pitch black of midnight. That would only result in a lost patrol. Just before first light would be better. A small patrol of 2nd Battalion scouts would try and blaze a trail up to the Major and let him know what was happening, the Colonel decided. They would return for the rest of Company K, which could make its advance with the afternoon attack along a known trail. In the meantime, 2nd Battalion would reorganize and prepare for the afternoon push, as per orders, and then bring the main line up to the objective line beyond Major Whittlesey's position. If all went according to plan, by late afternoon there would be 2nd Battalion men manning the line and Major Whittlesey's 1st Battalion could stand down for the night to a well-deserved rest and meal farther back. Assuming, of course, that the Germans cooperated with the plan. And since they were in the midst of a general retirement, that should be the case (although they certainly did not seem to be in retirement the previous afternoon around Depot des Machines).

At 4:30 a.m., the first small patrol went out; four men armed mainly with grenades lead by an acting Sergeant Legers. They slinked through the lines in a northwesterly direction, headed for l'Homme Mort through the chilly fog. Moving swiftly through the heavy brush, they were making good progress when, near the cemetery behind l'Homme Mort, they ran into a short stutter of machine-gun fire. There in the half-light of morning, they quietly worked around the German nest and took it out, snatching up two prisoners of the 6th Company, 254th in the process. Using the two prisoners as guides, they swiftly made it up to the bivouacked 1st Battalion without further incident. Standing at the edge of the clearing with the incredulous Majors Whittlesey and Budd, the patrol related that they had seen relatively few other German troops out there on the hillside.

Major Whittlesey would then likely have figured that the movement throughout the night could only mean that the Germans were actually pulling back and not consolidating after all. If that were the case, all would be well. Therefore, he quickly organized some patrols and sent them to find out exactly what was going on around and behind the position. By about 7:00 a.m., preliminary reports were coming in; it certainly appeared as if most of the Germans had indeed pulled out overnight. There were still several machine-gun nests out there and plenty of sniping going on, and the mill complex was still fairly well occupied, but outside of that it looked as if they had caught a break. Only the Boche artillery, which was again starting to fall in heavy behind them, appeared to be of any real difficulty. The Germans apparently were pulling back deeper into the actual line of the Giselher Stellung, which Majors Whittlesey and Budd now knew the true positions of, thanks to the information and maps obtained from the German officer killed the day before.

Therefore, about 8:00 a.m. Major Whittlesey sent Sgt. Legers and his scout patrol back down the way they had come, taking with them the small gaggle of German prisoners that had been collected over the last two days. Several 1st Battalion men also went along to reestablish the runner line. With him, Sgt. Legers carried a rather long message from Major Whittlesey for Colonel Stacey, pointing out some of the difficulties surrounding the position and some of the details of the previous 15 hours. The basic content of the message is probably best made clear by Major Whittlesey's last desperate line: "We need food and water very badly." (32, 91, 109, 132, 133, 144)

Meanwhile, two other separate patrols had been sent out from the 2nd Battalion lines to reconnoiter and try to break through to Major Whittlesey as well. The first of these, 16 men of Company B under 2nd Lt. Harold Rogers, left at 5:30 a.m. They headed due north toward the western edge of the Ravin Moulin de l'Homme Mort (the eastern slope of l'Homme Mort), unknowingly closely following almost the same course that Sgt. Legers had taken. The second was a 16-man Company K force under Lt. Taylor, which made off northwest for l'Homme Mort itself. Even if enemy machine-gun resistance was fading farther up l'Homme Mort, as appeared to be the case, it was still holding on the main line and enemy artillery was beginning to come in at a good clip. Both patrols, larger than Legers' small four man job, were now visible by the light of dawn and were quickly spotted and driven back in within an hour, having never gotten anywhere near the 1st Battalion's position.(III)

Throughout the morning, further strong, probing patrols continued to test the German lines at intervals as well, while the majority of the 2nd Battalion kept up reorganization efforts, but none were able to get through. Sergeant Legers came back in around 8:45 a.m. with the message from Major Whittlesey, announcing that the command was still in relatively good shape and that an established (if insecure) route up to him had been laid. Everyone at the advanced Regimental PC breathed a small sigh of relief. Without delay, Colonel Stacey began organizing small carrying parties, sending them up l'Homme Mort at wide intervals with food, water, and ammunition. They went with orders to attract as little attention as possible. The Colonel was aware that the Germans were supposedly in retreat, but it would be better to err on the side of caution, as Major Whittlesey was not 'out of the woods' yet, so to speak. Before the hour was up, he was on the phone to General Johnson with the news. (2, 91, 109, 136, 144)

By about noon, General Alexander felt confident enough that his division had reorganized about as much as it was ever likely to. He therefore requested that 1st Corps let him go ahead with his afternoon attack. Having already lost the better part of a day on the drive within the zone of the 308th on the 27th, he was anxious to push on. (Interestingly, while he was aware of Major Whittlesey's situation, it does not appear that it was one of General Alexander's motivating factors behind continuing the drive so quickly.) Corps granted approval, delighted with the feisty young General's fire. Therefore, about 3:30 p.m. Division PC sent orders to General Johnson for the afternoon attacks to get under way. By a little after 4:00 p.m., the American barrage in 2nd/308th's zone had begun. The shelling was concentrated mainly on the angle of the Ravin Moulin de l'Homme Mort, where it turned east down to the Ravin de Depot des Machines, along the southeastern slope of l'Homme Mort hill. This was deemed to be probably the weakest spot of the line and near where a small log bunker, named Defsauer Platz on German maps, stood. The barrage went out for 30 minutes, even as German shells came in. This caused one Company D man to later remark, "Our artillery during the meantime seemed to be trying to outdo the Germans in the amount of shells thrown over. We found they were quite successful in doing so..." (2, 31, 105, 131)

Once the shelling lifted, the waterlogged Doughboys slowly rose from their muddy funk holes and plodded forward. Shelling from the German side continued to build in tempo and intensity. Machine-gun fire sang out, light but accurate. Company B was out front acting as assault company on the left, still under orders to get through to Major Whittlesey and 1st Battalion's right flank. Company D was in close rear support, still being lead by the redoubtable 1st Lt. (acting Captain) Paul R. Knight. Fanning out against the angle, they proceeded down into the gentle ravine that had split the assault battalion's two days ago, fighting hard for every forward inch. The Germans may have been pulling back, but it seemed as if they had left behind a whole lot of scrap steel flying around! Company E, to the right of the angle and now being led by 1st Lt. (acting Captain) Karl Wilhelm (Captain McMurtry had the 2nd Battalion's command temporarily), was headed to cross the ravine just right of the angle, with Company G in close support. What remained of Company F was still over on the far left and the borrowed Company K aimed a path directly up l'Homme Mort with as many stray 2nd Battalion men as it could gather.

Once across and up to the ravine edge, things changed. The line troops met with resistance, but it was not like what they had faced in the previous days. The Germans seemed reluctant to engage fully, yet the Doughboys were still having a devil of a time making forward progress. An enemy machine-gun would open up out ahead, causing the advance in its vicinity to halt as a gang was sent out to get it. What the gang found once they had laboriously worked their way forward however, was that the gun had disappeared. Slowly the advance would continue, only to have the same thing happen again. It was a dirty game of cat and mouse that ate up a lot of time. Occasionally however, the gun would remain and a real battle would take place. The problem was, the Doughboys were never sure which scenario they might face at each gun and so caution was the word and the advance slow because of it.

Still, 2nd Battalion continued to push the line as the afternoon light dissolved. Enemy artillery and machine-gun fire started to slack off with the diminishing light and progress improved. There was no division of echelons this time; instead, a solid line of men progressed forward, stretched across the Ravin Moulin de l'Homme Mort and all along the slope of l'Homme Mort itself, following up the German rear guards that gave up the ghost and recommenced their retreat into the Giselher Stellung positions. Off to the right, word was received from the 307th that they had a few men across the ravine now and scouts working up into the heights south of Le Quatre Chenes, in the direction of a hill marked on the map as Hill 198. It looked to General Johnson as if all was going to work out that afternoon.

The German units that were slowly giving way across the angle at Ravin Moulin de l'Homme Mort in front of Company B/308th's assaults, were sections of the 6th and 8th Companies/122nd, under Rittmiester (Cavalry Captain) Von Wiedenbach. Slowly, as the Doughboys relentlessly pushed against his line, the Rittmiester began to draw his meager company line sections back toward the Ravin d'Argonne, covering the retreat of the main force. Meanwhile, other sections of those companies set to the task of installing machine-guns and trench mortars in pre-prepared positions farther afield within the ravine, under direction of a Lt. Col. Von Biela. At the same time, the force along the southern slope of l'Homme Mort (elements of the 6th Company/254th under the command of the able Lt. Max Mann, and the 10th Company/122nd under Lt. Ulshofer), was slowly pulling back, but in some disorder. Most of their comrades had pulled back overnight as ordered and Lt. Mann's immediate superior, Hauptman (Captain) Herman Petri (the 2nd Battalion/254th's commander) had designated them to act as "sacrificial forces". They were to be left behind to slow the American advance as much as possible until the main body of the German force had taken up their better positions farther within the ravine. This they were doing admirably against the attacking Company K/308th, all the while trying to figure a way out for themselves. They had already lost one machine-gun and its attendants earlier that morning and were not anxious to lose any more.

Ultimately out numbered, the Germans were slowly pushed back farther and farther as the afternoon faded toward evening. Finally, at a little after 6:00 p.m., exhausted and depleted, they simply gave up. Packing up what remained of their equipment, they pulled back around to the west of l'Homme Mort, the direction from which they had infiltrated two days earlier. And with that, the extraordinary opportunity that there had been to crush the U.S. force out on the hillside was gone; robbed by the ordered retreat to the Giselher positions. It had been a long, trying day. (2, 91, 96, 101, 105, 109, 116, 123, 128, 307)

While the rain eventually ceased, the ground fog that had persisted all morning kept the flyers of the 50th Aero Squadron grounded once again during the 77th's reorganization period. The squadron had however, so far put forth a great effort flying repeated missions daily (indeed, almost hourly) throughout the battle, striving to obtain line information for 77th Division PC. However, it had been largely unsuccessful. The troops on the ground were reluctant to shoot off flares for fear of giving their position away to enemy artillery. And though they put them out, they further worried that their signal panels would be seen by enemy flyers as well. This, as it turned out, was a superfluous concern. The 50th's observers themselves had a tremendously difficult time locating the relatively small ground panels in the denseness of the forest as it was, and they at least had some idea of where to look, as opposed to any random German flyers. Consequently, much of the time the 50th's pilots were forced to fly at nearly tree top level so that observers could obtain line information by direct observation and identification of uniforms. This was an incredibly dangerous approach that drew dreadful amounts of enemy fire, resulting in several narrow escapes.

Once the battle had resumed that afternoon of the 30th however, pilot Lt. Maurice Graham took off with observer Lt. James McCurdy on a contact patrol. The big DeHavilland DH-4, with its big Liberty engine, also carried with it several little packages of newspapers, chocolate, and cigarettes wrapped up together to be dropped to the advancing troops. This was essentially a YMCA expansion on something else the flyers had already been doing for the last few days—dropping propaganda leaflets over the German lines urging them to surrender (a duty that the men thoroughly disliked). Above the lines that afternoon, the flyers received little in return to their calls for line signals and once again a 50th plane dipped below the thousand-foot mark before anything could be made out in the great tangle of forest. Enemy rifle and machine-gun fire rattled up at them as they raced across the treetops. Peering hard through the foliage and smoke of the battle (they would later report it as a "smoke barrage"), Lt. McCurdy was just barely able make out the uniforms below, mark a general track of the front line on his map and toss out the packages while the plane suffered for it.

This patrol and the others on the afternoon of the 30th, was indicative of the ever-increasing difficulties faced by the 50th's flyers in completing their assigned duties. The deeper the 77th's Doughboys drove into the dense tangles of the Argonne, the more difficult line sighting became, until it was an all but impossible task in the featureless green and brown vegetation. Adding fog, mist, or smoke on top of that, virtually outstripped the navigational technology of the time. Given a specific area to look into, or fly supporting cover over, then became a definite problem. This leads one to wonder if the 50th might have done any good at all given a mission to first locate Major Whittlesey's isolated battalion on l'Homme Mort and then to drop him the supplies he so desperately required had the Small Pocket went on longer. There is no evidence that they were ever given such a mission however. Judging simply by their later efforts over the Charlevaux Ravine, a larger and much more open spot than l'Homme Mort, one is forced to admit that they would not have been successful, no matter how much good work they had done thus far. Yet in this instance, they were never notified to be on the look out for Major Whittlesey's command, but instead were sent out on routine missions to find the line (a line that had not moved since around 5:00 p.m. of the 28th) and so one can only speculate. (110, 241, 249, 276)

All throughout that day of the 30th, small relief parties of men continued moving up and down the thin runner line to 1st Battalion's position, carrying food, water, and ammunition up to the beleaguered men. They were careful and thus encountered few Germans as they moved along the route that had been reestablished that morning. Major Whittlesey also had scouting parties out in considerable force. In fact, the Major himself even went out a couple times with them to get a good look at what they would face over the next day or two. Much of the exploring settled around the Ravin d'Argonne ahead and the slopes to the west, which was listed on the maps as Hill 210. The mill complex to the east still remained in enemy hands, making scouting of that side of the ravine and the heights of Le Quatre Chenes above it, virtually impossible. Before long though, coupled with the good map information from Lt. Korthaus (the dead German 254th officer), the Major and his command had a fairly clear idea of what lay ahead and could spend some thought on the best way to go about a further attack. Yet, while the Germans were obviously pulling back, there was little Major Whittlesey could do just then. His best bet was still to stay put and wait for the rest of the 308th to come up even with him. And with no orders for either advance or retreat yet in hand, it was his only real option. In any case, the men could definitely use the short respite from combat vigilance and the comfort that food and water had brought. Private McCollum remembers the first food he had in three days:

"The next day our ration details came in. Boy were they a welcome sight! We went at that food like a pack of wolves… the ration details packed in everything they could carry, which in itself was no small job over that distance and ground…" (32)

The sick and wounded were also sent back down the line, a few at a time. As the day wore on and it became even clearer that the danger was dropping, more supplies continued to slowly flow up. A few isolated firefights broke out with patrols to the north from time to time, but they were sporadic and no one paid them much attention. There was some enemy shellfire to the rear and toward the head of the ravine to the right of the position, but none on the 1st Battalion's bivouac. The sniper fire was actually the worst threat, yet men still crawled out above ground, stretched and tried to work the kinks out of bodies that had been folded into narrow, muddy holes for two days and nights. Private Nell later recalled how he and his buddy had to help each other out of the hole they shared and how his hands had cramped up so badly that he could not grip his rifle. Others tried to shave and clean up some, now that a little water was at hand. Still others dug their holes deeper, not taking any chances. There seemed to be a weird, watchful calm in the air, made even stranger by the circumstances surrounding it. The day progressed relatively quietly until by 4:15 p.m. Major Whittlesey was back at the bivouac, having made a personal reconnaissance, and sent back a message to Colonel Stacey concerning his situation:

At: 94.8 – 74.5

Rations, ammunition, and water have come up and everyone is feeling greatly improved. The men would be in excellent shape if it were not that they have been exposed to the cold and wet for five days without overcoats, slickers, blankets/shelter halves (per division orders). As it is they are doing well.

The runner system was reestablished early this morning, as the Germans are believed to have drawn out from our rear during the night.

I have just returned from reconnoitering the open country to our North looking for a better position. The hill in the open a mile north of here is wired and would provide an excellent position, though from what the German officer we captured yesterday told us before he died I believe we might have to fight to take it.

Our present position is quite good: field of fire is fair. (Would be excellent if it was not wooded.) The slopes are advantages, as while gas would hang a long time in the woods, probably it would work down into the ravine on our East rather than hang on long here.

We have runners here from our companies on the East (i.e. B&D)

Artillery fire from our own guns fell near us on the Northwest this noon. No casualties today, Everything quiet. I have established an OP at the corner of the opening 294.7 – 274.5 (246)

Then, off in the distance to the south and east, at about 5:30 p.m., they heard the rest of the regiment coming on in considerable force. The renewed 2nd Battalion push up l'Homme Mort and down the mill ravine made good initial progress until German shells flying over the heads of the 1st Battalion men began to fall at a rapid rate. Pounded unmercifully by the storm of artillery, by just before 6:00 p.m., the 2nd Battalion had been driven back. It seemed to be the last the Germans could muster however, for enemy troops were soon thereafter seen high tailing it northwestward. At 6:30 p.m., Captain McMurtry slammed 2nd Battalion forward again and finally broke through the line. Company B rolled down the ravine in good shape and made the Moulin de l'Homme Mort - Binarville road just about the time that Lt. Taylor was leading Company K down the north slope of l'Homme Mort hill and into the open area next to Major Whittlesey's PC, heavily loaded down with more food, water, and ammunition. By 7:00 p.m. or so, the line back down the hillside was pronounced safe and secure and the 307th had drawn up on an even line farther to the east and made liaison with the 308th's advanced line. Private McCollum remembered the relief he felt:

"Our scouts, who had been out many times during the day, were returning from their last trip, and they reported that everything was clear now. The tight circle of German opposition had loosened up, and we could proceed again… I shall always feel that our leaders did a brilliant job of handling a difficult situation during the three days just past (sic). We will never know how many of us owe our lives to their strategy of having us lie quietly in that forest, rather than attacking or exposing ourselves to a superior force (sic)." (32) (40, 91, 109, 224, 238, 256)

In truth, there never was a superior force surrounding the 1st Battalion on l'Homme Mort. If Major Whittlesey had received orders to do so early the day before, he could easily have fought his way out and back down to the main line. The reason he stayed, of course, was because he never received such orders and it was therefore his duty to remain where he was. Doing this proved the final catalyst to breaking the Hagen Stellungen in the 154th Brigades attack zone. He and his command first pierced that line and got stranded, thus necessitating their rescue, which then forced the remainder of the brigade to fight through to him and, *voila*, the line was broken. This act put its own succession of events into play, however. It helped drive the Germans deeper into the positions within the Giselher Stellung from which they would reek terrible havoc not only with the 308th in general, but

Major Whittlesey's command in particular over the next eight days. Thus was brought into play perhaps the strongest of events leading to the Lost Battalion episode in the Charlevaux Ravine—that of repetition. There are strikingly similar characteristics between the Small Pocket on l'Homme Mort and the bigger one at Charlevaux, which include the events leading up to both. It had been a hell of a fight even getting to l'Homme Mort and there was no doubt that it had been a close call out there on that hillside. That fact was obviously not lost on Private McCollum, as evidenced by the above quote. Nor was it lost on Charles Whittlesey, as we shall see. (32, 122, 367)

The companies of the 307th had remained throughout that uneventful night entrenched in those positions to which they had drawn back during the afternoon before, in front of Depot des Machines. With the dawn of the new day, they set about reorganization in earnest, gathering and redirecting the 2nd and 3rd battalions in depth, as per the divisional orders. They also continued to send out strong patrols throughout the foggy morning and by afternoon scouts were reporting signs that the enemy seemed to be either pulling back, or had largely gone underground. The latter could only spell doom as it meant rooting the Germans out of well-concealed and highly defensible positions that would likely be linked by underground passages, a particularly vicious and nerve-wracking method of fighting. Word came down from General Johnson that a simultaneous attack with the 2nd/308th was to come off at 4:30 p.m. against the Depot positions. Leading it was to be a 30-minute artillery barrage of preparation against the slopes of the ravine, across the base of l'Homme Mort and surrounding the angle and valley between the two. (17, 91, 99, 104, 119)

There was a wrinkle though: "On the left, the 308th reported their forward battalion in the neighborhood of the cross-roads of the Boyau des Cuistsots (sic); but it was cut off from the rest of the regiment…" wrote Captain Rainsford. With that serious situation then to consider, General Johnson had therefore ordered a change of dispositions. Instead, the 307th's battalions would be reorganized in line, with 2nd on the right and 3rd on the left. There could be no doubt this time; the Depot ravine *had* to be taken at all costs and the line carried forward beyond. The 1st/308th, stranded out on l'Homme Mort, depended on it. All the while, the German artillery got cranked up again and soundly shelled the reorganizing battalions. (103)

They were well into position when the U.S. barrage started to roar overhead promptly at 4:00 p.m. Captain Rainsford and Company L, occupying the far left flank, right next to the 308th, described the start of it, which resulted in an unfortunate miss-fire:

"…It was known to a sufficient number of officers just where the barrage line was to fall; and there the greater part of it was to fall, but not all. A company of the second line (sic) had just posted its right platoon with its head resting on a group of birch trees, when the barrage came down three hundred yards in front, all save one gun, which made hit after hit on the birch trees…" (103)

The errant company caught in the bursts was Company F, left flank unit of the 2nd Battalion and, therefore, directly at the junction of 2nd and 3rd battalions. To their right was Company E, which already had small elements of its men outposted forward across the ravine since the night previous and which now found itself *ahead* of the artillery barrage. There they faced their own share of problems. With German machine-guns pouring fire into them from left, right, and front and with their own artillery blocking any escape path to the rear, those men of E lived the longest, and deadliest, 30 minutes of their lives. Immediately to the left of Company F was Company I, right flank unit to 3rd Battalion. The scene there, in the middle of those two attacking battalions as they moved out, is described here by Sgt. Jean Grosjean, of Company F:

189

"No sooner had we left than "I" company on our left was subject to intense high explosive and trench mortar fire, holding them in. On the side of this hill Sergeant Jack Shreck, while receiving a message... was killed, Sergeant Lenahan taking charge of the left flank. "I" company was forced to withdraw. We changed our course and kept going until held up by machine gun fire." (235)

Despite these problems, the 307th threw itself forward into the battle with reckless abandon. The two battalions quickly overwhelmed the now mostly deserted ravine, storming the southern slope and down into the midst of the Depot. Here, large stores of material were found abandoned, a few prisoners taken and a multitude of narrow-gauge rail cars captured when, from up on the slopes ahead, machine-gun fire began to pour down onto the Doughboys. The Germans had them cold. It was savage and brutal fighting as the 307th men forced their way up the slope to try and dispatch the enemy machine-guns dug in at the top of the ridge. Gas shells rained down, filling the ravine with deadly fumes and blocking the line of retreat while the machine-guns on the crest spat lead.

But the 77th's artillery had done good work, for there were a number of shell holes on the northern slope offering a measure of protection as the Doughboys clawed their way to the top and fought against the machine-guns there. Another passage from Sgt. Grosjean states that "Riker, with other men, crossing (the) ravine and fired on by machine-guns, killing Riker and wounding Corporal Engelback, Dilato and seven others." It was bloody stuff, particularly there in the center where I and E bracketed Company F. On the far left flank, Company L made solid liaison with Company B/308th, which was then pushing against the angle of the ravine. Together they moved forward with vigor. (17, 91, 99, 103, 104, 119)

Yet despite the rising casualty total (and a temporary faltering of the 308th due to shellfire), at around 5:30 p.m. an excited General Johnson telephoned General Alexander.

"Houghton just told me that a wounded man just brought in states that before he was wounded, troops were across the railroad," he said.

It was the sort of report that General Alexander had been waiting two days to hear. "That must have been about five o'clock?" he asked.

General Johnson, obviously too pleased to answer, continued, "Their objective is to go forward to 74.6 for tonight. When they are going to reach that point though I don't know."

"Hold on to the left until the others on the right can swing up to it," General Alexander said. "They are to go forward as long as they can until their objective is reached. Has Depot des Machines been taken?"

"Yes, that is where we crossed," the Brigadier answered.

General Alexander already had reports that the 153rd Brigade was doing well too, and that the 28th Division, far off to the right, had promised to come up on an even line just as soon as they could. With Colonel Stacey confident that the 2nd/308th would be up and moving again shortly (in fact they already were), it looked as though things might finally come together after the previous two days of setbacks. Even to the far left, in the zone of Groupement Durand (specifically in the zone of the 368th), things at last seemed to be improving as well. The black troops were said to have pushed well beyond the town of Binarville by that time. Perhaps, then, the Boche really were in retreat as 1st Corps thought. (91, 92, 131, 144)

On the left, nearly a kilometer of forest lay in enemy hands between the 368th and the 308th when day broke that morning. Around 8:00 a.m. Sept. 30, the 1st/368th sent out their first long-range reconnaissance patrols of the morning from Tranchee Tirpitz toward the direction of Tranchee du Dromadaire. They met no resistance. The Germans had indeed evacuated the boxed-in position as hoped. Therefore, the Doughboys wasted no time moving forward and by 9:00 a.m., Groupement Durand was reporting to 77th Division PC that Dromadaire was in their hands. By 11:00 a.m., the 1st/368th had established itself in the line with companies A, B, and C, left to right, and with Company D remaining behind in support within Tranchee Tirpitz. Firm liaison was established between Company A/368th and the French 9th C.a.P to the left, but none was yet available with the 308th on the right. That, however, was a detail that they would correct through the course of the afternoon's attack.

Orders issued the evening of the 29th had called for the 1st/368th to be prepared to attack Binarville and its environs in conjunction with the 9th and 11th C.a.P regiments at high noon of the 30th. But unknown to the 368th as they moved into position in Tranchee du Dromadaire, the French 1st D.C.D changed the attack orders. Instead, the new directive ordered the two French regiments to move against Binarville on their own, while the 1st/368th remained behind at Tranchee Tirpitz in support with orders to gain firm liaison with the left flank of the 308th. A message to the 77th Division PC that morning claimed that the change in orders was due to the black troops retreating in a panicked flight in battle. (These new orders, unfortunately, did not arrive at 1st/368th PC until well into the evening, by which time the battle had long since ceased.)

To support the noon attack in Groupement Durand's area, a request had been made by the French for not only American artillery, but also for indirect heavy machine-gun fire on specified targets. 77th Division provided for both requests. The 305th and 306th Field Artillery units each detached a gun farther forward for the purpose, with elements of Company C/306th M.G. Bn. and Machine Gun Company/308th providing the heavy machine-gun fire. At noon, a Franco-American artillery barrage paved the way for the two French regiments to advance against the areas west of Binarville. Success quickly greeted their efforts and by 2:00 p.m., the French troops were at the enemy entrenchments just south of town. Observing the commencement of the attack by the French and believing their general instructions of the night before still stood (though there had been no detailed attack orders issued that morning, as was usually the case), the officers commanding the 368th went ahead and jumped off themselves at 2:00 p.m. in a general advance against the town of Binarville proper. It was hard and vicious fighting, but by about 4:00 p.m. Company A/368th, along with support troops from the 9th C.a.P, had advanced north around the west end of Binarville and then turned east in an attempt to drive against the German line above the town. They slammed forward, overrunning a little ruined collection of buildings just on the northern edge of town known as Rome Farm, and continued to push. They were finally stopped by heavy artillery and machine-gun fire at a fork where the Binarville-La Virgette and Binarville-Autry roads came together before running south into the top of Binarville itself.

Company A was now manning an off-kilter, lateral line across some apple orchards looking northeast with a horizontal line of 9th C.a.P men extending back to the French main line. They faced an area heavily infested with German entrenchments and troops at the foot of the slopes of Hill 205, also known as Butte de LaPalette. Here, long-range machine-gun and trench mortar fire began to pour down on the black Doughboys from up on the hill. They could advance no farther. Meanwhile, companies B and C/368th, with French support troops, had entered Binarville itself at about the same time and were organizing within against the inevitable German counter attack. They did not stay long in possession of the town however, as German artillery fire from the heights of Mont d'Charlevaux, ahead to the northeast, grew so intense it forced them to withdraw to the line of enemy entrenchments about 300 meters south of the town. Company A, along the north/south line northeast of town, was also eventually forced by this fire to shorten its line to a point about 200 meters south of the fork in the road. They then sent the majority of their force back to the old enemy entrenchments south of town, leaving only about 100 men in a shaky outpost line extending southward from their new line back. Binarville was technically in Allied hands, but uninhabitable due to enemy shelling. By 7:00 p.m. then, the line in the eastern sector of Groupement Durand had come to rest for the night under the shadow of Hill 205.

Hill 205 was essentially an armed encampment, rising above Binarville to the northeast and lying in that desperate strip of ever-increasing space between the attack paths of the 308th and the 368th. Atop the hill was the LaPalette Pavilion, heavily fortified, firmly entrenched, and well wired against any assault up its slopes. Its various entrenchments were scattered all along the slopes of the hill, facing south, east and west as well as along the top. They were bristling with machine-guns and the Germans had only recently placed trench mortars up there as well, a fact that would soon become known to both the French and the Americans. Importantly for the 308th, Hill 205 sat at the southwestern point of junction where the Ravin d'Argonne (running north/south) terminated at the Ravin de Charlevaux (running east/west, just north of the hill) some 2 kilometers yet north of the 308th's current position on l'Homme Mort. At the armed base of Hill 205, within the Ravin d'Argonne, ran a stretch of the Giselher Stellung main trench line. The line ran up the western ravine slope through a wide wash in the hillside and continued to the top, where it wrapped around the pavilion there on its eastern, western, and southern sides. At the bottom of the ravine, the Giselher trench stopped at a swampy, heavily wired, impassable area that was about 75 meters wide. Beyond that, it once again continued up the eastern slope of the ravine and then onto the top of Hill 198, directly east across the ravine from Hill 205, where it continued unbroken along the crest. Thus, fire could be poured down on top of any attacker moving within the Ravin d'Argonne from up on the heights of both ridges. This arrangement effectively barred entrance to, and across, the Charlevaux Ravine and up the Mont d'Charlevaux beyond it, from the outlet of the Ravin d'Argonne. (This, however, was the 308th's intended attack path.)

For the French, the armed stud of hill meant a barred path to the northeast of Binarville. It also indirectly provided for a difficult path to the northwest of town as well, between Binarville and the town of Lancon. There, two strong trench lines of the Giselher, the Tranchee de LaPalette and the Tranchee de Charlevaux, ran just northwest of the hill and were tied into and fed by the LaPalette defensive system and its reserve of man power. Heavy belts of wire stood out before both trench lines, in the broken, wooded country around them. Thus, any unit moving in large formation against them could be easily held off with artillery and then simply machine-gunned into the ground. Further, an attacker endeavoring to force the draw directly up the hill from the south/southwest, or to simply bypass the hill by heading due north around its base, would find either way blocked by the formidable Hill 205 defenses as well. It was Groupement Durand, under the control of the French 1st D.C.D., which had the majority of the hill within its boundaries of advance and the task of eliminating the obstacle then fell on that unit now primarily facing it - the beleaguered 368th Infantry. (10, 46, 91, 92, 146, 252)

Finally forced to abandon Binarville, the German 1st/254th found themselves falling rapidly back to the Giselher Stellung main line. The 2nd/254th were already establishing themselves firmly within the La Palette Pavilion up on Hill 205 and down along the western ridge of the Ravin d'Argonne. The 122nd Regiment of the 2nd Landwehr still had the Moulin de l'Homme Mort as well as most of the eastern ridge of the ravine and the heights of Le Quatre Chenes, back to Hill 198. But, for how long? The *Americanernest* that the combined 122nd/254th force had had bottled up on l'Homme Mort had been reconnected with their own troops that afternoon when the Depot des Machines had fallen. And beyond even that, other American troops were already working in small numbers (sure to increase) onto the heights of Le Quatre Chenes.

With 2nd/254th and the 122nd already then pulling back to within the Ravin d'Argonne, the 1st/254th itself now drew back around the western slope of Hill 205 and regrouped. The black Doughboys and the French had given them a thorough licking that day, but they knew that they had given nearly as much as they had taken. Dragging themselves back, together with the 83rd Regiment of the 9th Landwehr on their right, they extended into the trenches and bunkers behind the broken woods and wire north of Binarville.

The German retreat, begun two days earlier, was now as complete as they ever wanted it. Trench mortars were being placed to best effect on the east and west sides of Hill 205 and machine-guns located to cover all the approaches up the Ravin d'Argonne, along the Giselher advanced positions. The artillery, back behind Mont d'Charlevaux, had been alerted and given coordinates for the all-too-obvious intended attack path of the Americans. Established along the Haupt-Widerstands-Lienie of the Giselher Stellung then, the German forces regrouped and dug in their heels for a siege. (120, 122, 123, 124 126, 128, 307)

At 7:00 p.m., General Johnson triumphantly messaged General Alexander, "I report that Colonel Houghton gained his objective, occupies the general line 74.5 and is organizing for an advance tomorrow. He has sent out strong patrols to the front." The Doughboys of the 307th had indeed completely broken up the German defenses on their front and now their outposts were advanced by half a kilometer north of the Depot des Machines ravine. Here were the heights of le Quatre Chenes, which run before Hill 198 to the north and terminate on the slope of the Ravin d'Argonne to the west. Up there, the tired, dirty men of the 307th found, as Captain Rainsford put it:

"German bungalows, with their elaborate white birch balconies, and their comfort of cots, blankets, and stoves, of strange pink bread tasting of malt, and of apple jam..." (103)

On the right flank, they had outrun liaison with the 306th again and therefore that flank lay wide open. (Fortunately, the 306th was able to advance a liaison party forward late that night and come up even the next day.) On the left, their flank now sat in the narrow valley between the ridge behind the Depot ravine on their right and l'Homme Mort on their left, where by 6:30 p.m. the main body of 2nd/308th was already through to Major Whittlesey and his men out on that lonely hillside. There, along a line through the woods, firm liaison had been established across a series of outposts. (91, 109)

Lieutenant Taylor and his Company K/308th men had brought seemingly tons of the much-needed supplies with them; Taylor later noting in his diary, "Starved and no water for three days, the poor fellows!" Rifle, Chauchat, and Hotchkiss ammunition, French rifle grenades and their launching cups, hand grenades... quickly the 1st Battalion men filled their rifle belts and grabbed as many grenades as they were allowed, determined never to run low again. Lieutenant Delehanty, the Regimental Intelligence Officer, and Lt. Conn, the Regimental Operations Officer, had come up with Lt. Taylor to investigate the situation and make a report to Colonel Stacey. Quietly, they talked with the tired looking Major Whittlesey off to one side and told him that the Colonel wanted to talk to him in person as soon as he could. They also brought with them orders to send Major Budd back to Brigade, finally to be on his way to the Staff College at Langres. Captain McMurtry was to take command of the 2nd Battalion as of this date, as he was the most experienced man then available and his beloved Company E was to go to Lt. Karl Wilhelm, a dependable and efficient young man from Buffalo and one of the original Plattsburg officers. Major Budd shook hands all around in the falling darkness, looked everyone in the face with his peculiar stare one last time, grabbed what gear he had, and tramped off up the hill and down the runner line for the last time.

By 8:00 p.m. most of the men who had held the line out on l'Homme Mort had been relieved by fresher 2nd Battalion and Company K men. Pulling back to positions further south of the hill, they then took up a support role for the night. Company D slid over to the left along with Company A, now fully reformed as one unit again. Company F stalked out ahead, but some of its men, those that had been in the hillside bivouac for the two days, remained behind. (In fact, some would not get back together with the company until after the Charlevaux incident, eight days in the future. Others never would see their company again - or anything else for that matter.) There were great gaps in some of the companies now. The casualties over the last few days had taken a toll and now more than a few men from 3rd Battalion were being sent up to fill in some of the empty spaces, along with a few from some of the other machine-gun units in the brigade that went over to Company's C and D/306th M.G. Bn. Captain McMurtry came up to see Major Whittlesey and broke the news of Fred Smith's death, which had been a terrible blow to the regiment. The Captain was very bucked at the news that he was to take command of 2nd Battalion and would soon wear gold oak leaves of Major on his shoulders. There in the falling darkness, he efficiently directed the relief of Major Whittlesey's men by his own. The ordeal was over, and finally Whittlesey could allow himself to breathe a heavy sigh of relief. (96, 101, 109, 132, 134, 137, 143)

With the situation then seemingly well in Captain McMurtry's hands, a short while later the Major and a guide set out down the runner line through the pitch-black night to the advanced Regimental PC, to make his own personal report to Colonel Stacey and get his morning's attack orders. What passed between the Colonel and Major Whittlesey that night neither ever recorded, the Major later simply noting only:

"I'll never forget going into the Headquarters dugout and getting warm for the first time, and seeing Frank Weld's (Stacey's adjutant -author) genial face. Cocoa, cigars, then back to the battalion again, which I found with great difficulty in the darkness. Orders were to advance at daybreak…" (109)

Now well established on a line roughly corresponding with the foot of l'Homme Mort, the 308th that night found that the 368th was about even with them along a line that they had taken up in the old enemy entrenchments just south of Binarville. For the first time in the five long and harrowing days since the beginning of the offensive, the door that had been left open between the two regiments was finally closed. That did not mean that the door was yet locked, however. There was, by then, about a 600-meter gap existing between the two regimental borders, the last 200 meters or so only thinly occupied by the scarce liaison forces provided by elements of Company I/308th and a few stray elements of the 1st/368th. Therefore, by late that afternoon the 92nd's 184th Brigade decided to move a battalion of the 367th Infantry up into the gap over night to plug the hole firmly. However, at about 8:30 p.m. the French 1st D.C.D countered the order, deciding not to move any more American troops into the area. It was expected that within another 24 hours of further advance, the front of Groupement Durand would have narrowed enough for a single regiment alone to cover, due to the eastward dive taken by the 1st D.C.D's right flank following the Aisne River. The regiment the French chose to take over the area was not the 368th, but instead the 9th C.a.P. Therefore, at about 10:00 p.m. the 1st/368th received orders from the 1st D.C.D. to hold its positions overnight and begin a general withdrawal the next morning, at which time two battalions of the 9th would move in and take over their front. (10, 91, 92, 109)

However, the left of the 9th C.a.P, west of Binarville, had actually gotten even farther afield than had the 368th. By 7:15 p.m., they had reached a point between and about 200 meters in front of the Tranchee de LaPalette and the Tranchee de Charlevaux, almost 2 kilometers west of where the Ravin d'Argonne terminated at the Charlevaux Ravine. There they were stopped and driven back some 400 meters by intense rifle and machine-gun fire and requested an artillery barrage on what they thought was Tranchee de Charlevaux; but they actually gave the coordinates of Tranchee La Palette instead. However, the 77th Division's liaison officer over at 1st D.C.D PC, Captain Klotz, realized this and, believing (as did the French) that elements of the 77th were "in Charlevaux", erred on the side of caution and rang up General Alexander's staff. (Klotz had actually heard the name mentioned in a briefing about the next days planned objective for the 308th just that afternoon.) The mistake was quickly cleared up and before long French shells were flying, correctly, into the Tranchee de LaPalette. However, already there were proving to be breakdowns in the chain of liaison with the French to the left, even with the addition of Groupement Durand on an even line between the two armies. This was something that would not bode well for the future of the 308th. (2, 10, 131, 140, 144, 146)

(I) Probably the worst of the sicknesses that the men suffered through though, and one that would later have consequences for many after the war as well, was gas poisoning. The Germans used a lot of gas against the Doughboys in the Argonne, primarily Mustard and Phosgene. Both were quite equally effective. Phosgene was a vesicant, which caused death basically by over stimulation of the water glands in the lungs, until a man literally drowned internally. It generally had the smell of new mown hay, or of rotting bananas. Mustard gas (the Germans' primary gas of choice), had the smell of strong mustard seed and was really not a gas at all, but a liquid that was sent over in shells that vaporized it into the air when they exploded. Mustard gas killed by burning; when inhaled or swallowed it seared everything inside on its way down. Additionally, if one brushed up against trees, bushes or even ground that Mustard gas had settled onto, the residue would then cling to the mans skin or uniform and cause burns to the epidermis. (Stories abound of men taking off their service coat and peeling a layer of skin off with it.) Both kinds of gas had similar effects in other ways too. Even a little bit of gas inhaled - and most men that served on or near the front at one time or another inhaled a little gas - brought on diarrhea and traces of gas in the air or on the ground had the nasty effect of drying out ones fingertips near the cuticle until they split open and bled. The gas then got into the dried cracks and sometimes caused infection. Enough in the eyes could cause blindness. Inhaled gas usually also produced a heavy, dry chest-deep cough as well and made the nose run incessantly. The wet weather only increased its effects and therefore gassed men were sometimes difficult for others to listen to as they snuffled and gasped for breath. Gas masks were carried by everyone and were supposed to prevent the worst of the gasses effect; those of inhalation. However the masks were only effective if they fit snuggly around a mans face, and a mask could not fit snuggly if a man did not shave everyday. Therefore, AEF regulations insisted that a man shave daily, but in the hell of the Argonne, where water was at a premium, this was clearly not possible.

(II) One might wonder about Charles Whittlesey's state of mind as he wandered around fully upright in the midst of shell and machine-gun fire, but the truth is that he probably realized what many experienced combat troops already knew; the sound of gunfire was very often worse than the gunfire itself. (It is entirely probable that Whittlesey learned this from his brother Elisha, who had driven an ambulance with the French the year before.) It might also be guessed that Major Whittlesey was presumably something of a fatalist anyway. If there was a bullet out there with his name on it, he was going to get it and no amount of ducking or hiding would change that. Most experienced combat men knew that the best soldiers accepted that they were already dead the minute their boot first hit the battlefield. By accepting death, it then could be faced fearlessly, and their job could be successfully accomplished. Again, while Charles Whittlesey was not the most experienced combat officer, he probably accepted this common sense idea very early on nonetheless.

(III) Another grim patrol out that dismal morning had a particularly doleful mission; to attempt the recovery of the body of Lt. Col. Smith. Led by Sergeant Hitlin and the 308th's chief spiritual advisor and friend to all, Father James Halligan, the dozen-man patrol ranged the area of the firefight of the day before, but to no avail. It seemed that the Boche had taken the body. Still, Father Halligan would not let the men give up. All day, they continued the search, taking sniper fire and dodging shells, only stopping at nightfall. They suffered several casualties in the search and did not find Lt. Col. Smith's body until the afternoon of October 1. He had actually been dragged by the Germans into some dense bushes to a point a hundred yards from where he had been killed where the body had been thoroughly searched, the Germans even going so far as to take his boots. When they did find it, the Lieutenant Colonel would finally be laid to rest in the little churchyard at La Harazee on the rainy afternoon of October 2.

(IV) Major Budd had originally been ordered to report there on the 24th, but since there had been no one to take his place at the head of 2nd Battalion and lead them into combat, the order had been quietly shelved. It is interesting however to note how fast he was sent away following relief of the Small Pocket. More so, when one considers how few officers there were in 2nd Battalion at that time and that there was certainly not any one any more experienced to take command of the 2nd Battalion than there had been at the start of the offensive. This begs the question then, was Major Budd being sent away as a sort of 'punishment' for leaving his command leaderless on the afternoon of September 28th, when he tagged along with Major Whittlesey on up l'Homme Mort? It may well be, since Major Budd was the only original battalion commander from the Upton days and it seems unlikely that he would be replaced - by a Captain, no less - at such a critical time in the battle and when there was such a desperate shortage of officers in the regiment. One might wonder if General Alexander had a hand in this, but there has so far been no paper trail concerning the transfer (outside of the original order sending him off on the 24th) or any speculation left behind by any of the officers involved that has so far come to light.

(V) This decision has been much debated over the years but seems to have been ultimately made because, in French eyes, the situation appeared much worse than it really was. They believed that the main line of the 77th Division had actually pushed farther forward during the afternoon attack than it had and was by then in the Ravin de Charlevaux, yet some two kilometers farther north of their present line. This made the 368th seem laggard once again, when in fact they actually had liaison (albeit slim liaison, but liaison nonetheless) with the 308th's left flank running along a line extended through the woods from just in front of Binarville on over to the bunker at l'Homme Mort. It was actually advanced scout elements of the 305th Infantry, well over on the 77th's right flank and dragging behind, which were in the Charlevaux Ravine already. Over in their sector, the track of the ravine dived farther to the south by over a kilometer's depth from where it ran in the area of the 308th. Consequently, the 184th's order to bring elements of the 367th into the line was viewed as simply a desperate attempt to cover up yet another disastrous situation. Appearing to have once again failed in their mission to bring liaison between the two great armies, this countered heavily in the French decision to relieve them. There has also been some speculation that some prejudice on the part of the French also played a part in the 368th's withdrawal, and it may well have. Colonel Durand himself is said to have made comments to that effect some time after the 368th was withdrawn, but these statements are clouded in misquote and speculation. Not so with statements made by General Robert Bullard, who commanded the 92nd Division for a time; in an article in *The Literary Digest* for June 27th, 1925, he levels serious condemnation on the Negro soldiers' performance. In any case, the 368th's agony in the Argonne was all but over by the night of September 30.

Ancillary sources used in this chapter include: 20, 29, 30, 35, 37, 87, 89, 90, 93, 94 97, 98, 105, 112, 113, 114, 118, Various 152-216, 218, 219, 220

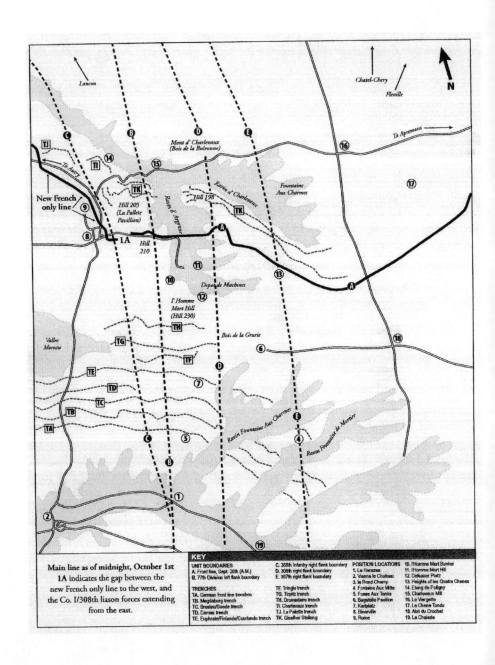

Lancon

Chatel-Chery

Fleville

N

To Apremont →

To Autry

New French only line

Mons d' Charlevaux
(Bois de la Buironne)

Ravin d' Charlevaux

Fountaine Aux Charmes

Hill 198

Ravin d' Argonne

Hill 205
(La Pallete
Pavilion)

1A   Hill
210

Depot de Machines

l' Homme
Mort Hill
(Hill 230)

Vallee
Moreau

Bois de la Grurie

Ravin Fountaine Aux Charmes

Ravin Fountaine de Mortier

Main line as of midnight, October 1st

1A indicates the gap between the
new French only line to the west, and
the Co. I/308th liason forces extending
from the east.

KEY

UNIT BOUNDARIES
A. Front line, Sept. 26th (A.M.)
B. 77th Division left flank boundary

C. 368th Infantry right flank boundary
D. 308th right flank boundary
E. 307th right flank boundary

TRENCHES
TA. German front line trenches
TB. Magdaburg trench
TC. Breslau/Suede trench
TD. Damas trench
TE. Euphrate/Finlande/Courlande trench

TF. Tringle trench
TG. Tirpitz trench
TH. Dromedaire trench
TI. Charlevaux trench
TJ. La Palette trench
TK. Giselher Stellung

POSITION LOCATIONS
1. La Harazee
2. Vienna le Chateau
3. le Rond Champ
4. Fontaine Aux Mitte
5. Fosse Aux Tanks
6. Bagstelle Pavilion
7. Karlplatz
8. Binarville
9. Rome

10. l'Homme Mort Bunker
11. l'Homme Mort Hill
12. Defsauer Platz
13. Heights of les Quatre Chenes
14. Etang de Poligny
15. Charlevaux Mill
16. Le Viergette
17. Le Chene Tondu
18. Abri du Crochet
19. La Chalade

October 1, 1918

"Mistakes from which we do not learn, we are destined to repeat."
An old saying - seldom heeded.

For once, there was food for breakfast. Carrying parties continually made trips back and forth all night long to bring supplies up to the starved Doughboys of 1st Battalion and now there was hardtack and canned corned beef in quantity for everyone. Strong hands even carried a few Dixies of hot stuff up from the rolling kitchens behind and then returned carrying the wounded back out to an ambulance station doing relay to La Croix Gentin, where the 1st Corps had set up a field dressing station. It was a long and rough trip back; the enemy had not been quiet throughout the night and sporadic and inaccurate German shellfire continued to drop harassingly behind the main U.S. line well toward dawn. Patrols from 2nd Battalion sent out found stray snipers both ahead and wandering the back areas as well, which resulted in some intense moments in the dark of the forest.

Well before dawn, 1st Battalion company and platoon commanders started to gather their men together and get things situated to head back up to the jump off positions at the foot of l'Homme Mort. They were again to lead the attack in, with 2nd Battalion again in support, and it did not take very long for them to move the kilometer or so back up and get parked into their assigned spots. This was in sharp contrast to the way the tired men had dragged back down l'Homme Mort the evening before; some proper rest and a good meal had obviously done a world of good. Scouts were already moving into the head of the Ravin d'Argonne when the bulk of 1st Battalion arrived, exploring the area given a cursory look-see the day before. The all too familiar opening barrage of yet another general U.S. line advance was set to go over soon after 6:00 a.m. of yet another frosty, damp morning. Yet while cold and damp, at least for once it was, thankfully, not raining.

Major Whittlesey's orders for that first day of October 1918, stated that the 308th was to advance straight north up the Ravin d'Argonne to a point where it terminated at the east/west running Ravin d'Charlevaux. Once there at the junction the regiment was to move across the Charlevaux brook, take the Moulin d'Charlevaux (Charlevaux Mill) beyond, which was slightly west of north from the junction point and sat next to a little millpond, and then extend a general line eastward along the Binarville-La Viergette road. The road itself was situated behind the mill and ran east/west along a bench-like cutting carved out of the limestone about half way up the northern slope of the Charlevaux Ravine, which is the southern side of the Mont d'Charlevaux. There, they were to ensure liaison to both flanks and then prepare for a further ordered advance. Intelligence also had it that a narrow gauge rail line ran parallel to the road farther up toward the top of Mont d'Charlevaux as well, and once the 308th had reached the road, scouts were to be sent out to confirm or deny this. (I)

Reaching the objective was a tall order. To get there, the advance would be one of slightly over two kilometers of machine-gun swept Argonne woods, heading up a difficult and tactically tricky ravine to maneuver. Perhaps the most difficult part however, would be crossing out of the north/south Ravin d'Argonne and into the east/west Ravin d'Charlevaux; there at the junction of the two ravines was a bottleneck, where the hills to the right and left provided for effective enfilading fire down onto the approaches. (131, 256)

Nevertheless, it was an important stretch of real estate for two main reasons. First, because as previously discussed, the Germans used this road as a main supply route from the larger town of Apremont to cross the forest to their positions in its western reaches. Therefore, taking control of the road would seriously hobble the German effort in the western Argonne. Similarly, it would also provide a much-needed American supply route as well, as the east/west running road cut all the way across the 77th's area of operations, leading from a curve in the road just south of the Charlevaux Mill, where it came up from Binarville. (The town itself was now in allied hands and was to be fitted out as a large supply dump by the French.)

Second, because it would provide a very necessary method of movement and placement for the artillery. While the 306th's big 155mm guns were capable of tossing shells tremendous distances and were therefore not required to change positions quite as often, this was not true of the 304th and 305th. Their smaller 75mm guns had a considerably shorter range due to an inefficient angle of fire and that forced them to move much more frequently. With the road in U.S. hands then, the artillery would be able to move at will and with relative ease into new positions farther forward in the future. (39)

The food, clean water and break in the weather found the 1st Battalion Doughboys then taking position along the forested line not doing too badly. "Their spirits were up", according to the war diary of Captain Leo Stromee, the commanding officer of Company C. Leo Stromee, of San Bernadino California, was the former commander of Company K/160th/40th Division, a unit that had originally been part of the California National Guard and he had arrived in the 308th with the small officer draft of September 14. With the Cal. N.G., he had earned his captaincy the hard way, coming up through the ranks, and served down on the border in 1916. He was an efficient, hard working soldier and turned out to be one of the few replacement officers of whom Major Whittlesey took serious note. Indeed, he had proven himself an able commander during the episode on l'Homme Mort. Now, he stood quietly in the frosty morning air watching as his boys prepared for the morning's 'coming attractions'. Most had been up early scrounging around for more rations to stuff into their haversacks and extra ammunition so platoon leaders had not a terribly difficult time in initially rousing them for the move up to the advance start line. Said Pvt. Smith of Company H: (144, 233, 355)

"...We was now on a hill, and we come around to where the Germans had had there supplies... some fella came up there with a bottle of beer and he said "I got this stuff off a dead German", and handed it around. It was the best stuff we ever tasted..." (256)

Just before 5:30 a.m., two new replacement officers arrived at the l'Homme Mort bunker and reported to Major Whittlesey, who still maintained a combined Battalion PC there with Captain McMurtry, and they were a welcome sight. Officer blood had run thick in the Argonne ever since Lt. Pattison of Company A had been the first 308th officer to be killed in combat there. Even a short glance at the 308th's casualty lists today show Lt.'s Bebell of Company G and Greenstein of D, as well as Briggs of E, among the names on the 28th alone. Lt. Akers of D was now gone, as were Lt.'s Whiting of A (whose wounds would prove fatal in October 1919), as well as Murphy and Stevens of E, while Lt. Cronkhite, a replacement officer from Yakima County Washington serving in

C, was soon to take a serious hit and end his own short 9 day tour of duty with the 308th. Some officers never even had a fighting chance. Lieutenant David Thalumm, Battalion adjutant under Major Budd, had only lasted half a day; posted to 2nd Battalion on the morning of the 28th, he was wounded before noon and sent down just after – and he had been the replacement for Budd's original adjutant, who had already been killed on the 27th. By that morning of October 1 then, as those two new men reported to Major Whittlesey, sixteen officers had already been listed in regimental records as having been killed or evacuated for wounds or sickness, with the real test in the forest yet to begin.

Therefore, the new officers were definitely a welcome sight, especially since one of the new officers was not really new at all. Lieutenant Charles W. Turner was returning to the regiment after having been wounded on the Vesle with Company D in August, and now Major Whittlesey sent him back there once again, to assist Lt. Knight. The other was as green as they came; Lt. William T. Scott, who the Major detailed to take command of Company A, now down to a mere 129 men and being led by the Company 1st Sergeant, Herman 'Meat-Nose' Bergasse. Major Whittlesey instructed the new lieutenant to work closely with Sgt. Bergasse until he had some time in under fire and to pay careful attention to his surroundings, hopeful he would last a little longer than some of the others had. (II) (109, 136, 137, 143)

Nor did the lieutenant long wait for his baptism of fire. Not long thereafter, the Major, orders in hand, called his remaining officers together in the little clearing before the l'Homme Mort bunker to hand out individual company advance instructions. It was then just after 6:00 a.m., and the barrage was already going over when Pvt. Nell remembered:

> "They gathered in a circle, about five or six officers present at the time. I stepped up in the circle by the side of Major Whittlesey, thinking he might want to send a message back to regimental headquarters.
>
> Major Whittlesey gave each officer his order, then the sergeant (Bergasse of 'A') spoke and said, "I have some men out on relay. I will go and get them."
>
> The Major said, "Never mind. Take charge and lead out as an officer." Then… he gave out the battle orders. When he finished, he stepped backwards two or three steps, looked around and said, "Leaders, get your men up!" (40)

The plan of advance was actually a modified form of what had proved such a disaster on the afternoon of the 28th. Two bodies of 1st Battalion troops would again attempt to work the ravine ridges, but this time there would be complete liaison across the width of the ravine, with each body of troops operating there as well. The dividing line between the right and left bodies of troops ran roughly down the middle of the ravine bottom and followed a muddy road and narrow gauge rail line there. One body of troops was to work along the western ridge and slope of the ravine, to develop the areas on the hill that Major Whittlesey and his scouts had reconnoitered the evening before, and to probe positions before Hill 205. They would also extend liaison to the French on the left. Meanwhile, the second body would work its way along the eastern ridge and slope of the ravine (the heights of Le Quatre Chenes) in liaison with the 307th to their right. Captain McMurtry's 2nd Battalion would follow 300 meters behind, itself split in two as well and support the left and right accordingly.

This was just the situation that Major Whittlesey had hoped to avoid by the "splitting of the echelons" when they had come to the Ravin Moulin de l'Homme Mort on the 28th. And we may reasonably assume that the Major was still probably quite unsure about this 'boxing' of any of his men in between two high, armed ridges and justifiably so. Working a rather large body of men down a deep and wide forested ravine provided for many tactical difficulties to their commander, more so to one as relatively inexperienced as Charles Whittlesey; a fact he had as much as admitted in his last message of the previous night. It would be very easy to loose liaison between units working above and down in the ravine and have one or the other inadvertently get out ahead of the main body and become surrounded. (The situation might arguably be slightly worse if the force along a ridge became separated, as it meant the force in the bottom had first to fight up hill just to get to a position from which to attempt rescue of the force above. Unfortunately, as it turned out, both scenarios would be faced.) However if communications were kept tight there should be no problems and considering that the Major had extended company lines the entire width of the ravine, including the slopes, there was no reason why they should not be. Insurance to this was the 'mirrored' lines of the 2nd Battalion, whose dispositions originally matched the 1st's. This meant that there were plenty of troops working atop both ridges, providing plenty of mutual fire support between there and the bottom of the ravine. Additionally, machine-gunners of Company D/306th M.G. Bn. were traveling in the 2nd Battalion closer to the head of the advance than was usual. Therefore, heavy firepower could be called forward quicker if it was needed. There were also a few gun teams from Company C/306th M.G. Bn., working the flanks of the 1st Battalion's advance as well which, as it turned out, came in quite handy. Therefore, while Major Whittlesey's fears of moving down a tactically difficult ravine were justified, his dispositions nevertheless were well organized and carefully thought-out. He was obviously taking no chances. (91, 109, 134)

Since everyone had been up early because there was finally something to eat, there had been plenty of time to straighten out the ranks. Therefore, most companies were again with their parent battalions for the attack. Leading on the left was Company A, supported by Company D; leading on the right was C, supported by B. Moving down the middle of the ravine along the road and rail line between D and B was Major Whittlesey's 1st Battalion PC. Captain McMurtry's 2nd Battalion followed them by 300 meters, Company F leading on the left with G in their support and company E leading on the right with H as their support and 2nd Battalion PC between G and H. (91)

On paper, the disposition looks tight, strong and solid, but in reality, it was a thin line. Casualties and sickness over the previous five-day's fighting had slowly whittled the two battalions down and there would be a greater distance between men because of it. Most hard hit had been Companies A and D, who had been at the head of the attack since the beginning. Yet Major Whittlesey continued to use them in such a demanding role as point to the advance thinking no doubt that whoever was left would know their job well and would be unlikely to make a mistake. To 'train' other companies to take the lead would likely cost in time and lives.

However, the front of the 77th Division had now also narrowed slightly, giving some relief to the stretched front. This was due to a shift in the right flank divisional dividing line between the 77th and the 28th Divisions, which had gradually swung westward as the 28th's right flank followed the Aire Valley. This had in turn progressively compressed the 77th's regimental fronts as they moved forward. For the 308th, this meant that in the attack of October 1 their right flank would run well up along the eastern ridge of the Ravin d'Argonne and their left would coincide with a second class road and narrow gauge rail line running north/south atop the west ridge (Hill 210) of the ravine, about a kilometer east of Binarville. Their front was now just barely over a kilometer wide, which would provide considerable relief in the dense wilderness. However, overlooking their main axis of advance – up the Ravin d'Argonne itself – were the emplacements of the LaPalette Pavilion atop Hill 205 to the left front and the trenches of the Giselher Stellung Haupt-Widerstands-Lienie along the crest of Hill 198 to the right front. Both were by far the most forbidding positions Major Whittlesey's Doughboys had yet come upon. The line atop Hill 198, a double trench line well wired in, was bisected by the regimental dividing line shared with the 307th, across whose entire front the dire slopes of Hill 198 loomed. On the other side of the ravine, just east of the summit of the grim promontory of Hill 205, ran the 308th's left flank line which then gave them only the eastern slope of the hill that emptied into the Ravin d'Argonne. This in turn left the majority of that formidable hill position, the southern and western slopes, actually within the strip of mostly uncovered territory between Groupement Durand's eastern boundary and the 308th's western. And with the 368th now being withdrawn, responsibility of the area would then fall to the 9th C.a.P, who would in turn accept it without complaint and quickly extend a thin line of outposts across the mostly vacant zone. But first they all had to get up there. (10, 91)

The 308th moved off down the ravine at just before 7:00 a.m., a little behind the barrage. The first order of business was to make sure the l'Homme Mort mill complex was cleaned out, which took very little time at all for Captain Stromee's Company C to accomplish. As the Germans had finished most of their evacuation overnight, there was virtually no resistance at first. Yet the cautious Doughboys moved slowly and carefully. The slopes of the ravine were steep and thick with foliage, giving plenty of possible cover for enemy machine-guns and snipers, and no one was taking any chances. Major Whittlesey's first message of the day went back at 7:15 a.m., reading:

1st. Bn advanced at 7AM. Patrols have gone to East, West by South, North, and Northeast – the first to see that the ravine is clear. (246)

Companies A and C continued to push on further into the heavily wooded ravine, slowly and carefully fanned out and meeting no real resistance, only occasional sniper fire. Both were actually acting more as 'scout' companies rather than as 'assault' units, for most of the 1st Battalion scouts were long since gone. It seemed incredible that they could move up the ravine with such ease, particularly when the Giselher Stellung line, as evidenced by the German officer's map they had seen, was only just about 2 kilometers ahead. Surely it should have better protection than so far encountered? Major Whittlesey, moving up the ravine along the muddy road at the bottom, no doubt would have eyed the high hills on either side of him with distrust. The memory of the afternoon of the 28th probably tugged at him and kept his mind whispering, 'Must keep the men spread out and moving and keep the liaison patrols out…' It had been this way going up l'Homme Mort at first too – little resistance that had slowly increased and eroded flank liaison off to the east with 2nd Battalion. 'Advance independent of units to the left and right' as per orders then? Not likely! At 8:00 a.m., he sent back his second message, stating:

C and A companies are now working up West of the ravine 94.8 – 74.7. No opposition yet. (246)

And then, at 9:00 a.m.,

We are going cautiously up North side of ravine (read: western ridge) giving scouts time to develop the hills and the valley to the east. A Co. is on the hill North. (246)

By 9:30 a.m., still with no real resistance to speak of ahead, 2nd Battalion had managed to form a solid line of liaison with the French along the Binarville-Moulin de l'Homme Mort road. Though they were still taking shellfire, the 9th C.a.P right flank force had moved forward again at dawn and now held Binarville solidly. Early reports had their left flank advanced almost two kilometers ahead of the town and the French line thus ran on a sharp angle, extending north west from the liaison point with the 77th, then between Binarville and Hill 205 before ending at a point either just in front of, or just beyond, the Tranchee de LaPalette (records are unclear which). Yet further west, the 11th C.a.P held a more even line but took heavy fire from the direction of Autry on their left and had their right flank liaisoned with and resting on the same point as the 9th's left. But by nightfall, the left of the 11th's line would advance north from that point until near dead even with Lancon, yet some two kilometers distant, while the 9th would still be lost somewhere in the tangled strip to the right of Binarville before Hill 205. (91, 101, 105, 108, 146)

It was somewhere on Hill 210 to the north, after about a half kilometer advance and at about 10:00 a.m., where Company A ran into the 308th's first serious resistance of the day, and from then on the battle broke all over the ravine and on both ridges. Part of the company was moving along through the brush of the ridge when they ran into a machine-gun nest located ahead and near the bottom of a shallow wash. Lieutenant Scott, seeing the only chance was to move deeper into the brush along the ridge, gave the order to fan out into the foliage. Private McCollum was up front during this advance:

"…We were given orders to cut a path through the underbrush…much to our surprise, we (were not) fired upon. We came to a bend in the ravine (and) could see why we had come through without being molested. In a little clearing in front of us was what remained of a large building… One of our shells had made a direct hit on the roof… Hardly had we reached this opening when we were strafed with machine gun and sniper fire. There was no place for us to go except straight up the hillside… Quickly we climbed to a ridge and safety near the crest of the hill…" (32)

A runner went back to find Major Whittlesey with the news of enemy contact, but the machine-guns echoing across the ravine had already told the story. He sent orders forward for C Company to swing a couple gangs around forward to try and flank the machine-guns from the northeast. At the same time, he dispatched Lt. Dobson, of the H.Q. Company, out with his Stokes mortar crew to hook up with A. They were to move up the ridge to the top, through a large apple orchard south of the position and then hit the guns with mortar and Chauchat fire from there. At 10:10 a.m., the Major sent back to Colonel Stacey: (32, 131, 144)

We are held up by MG fire from the west. Are starting C and A companies around the slopes to the east and south. They will open with MG's on them from here. (246)

Ahead of A, at the end of the orchard, were two concrete bunkers skirted by a wire field nearly a hundred feet deep. A few Stokes shells in that direction brought no enemy response and cautiously the men moved forward, cut there way through the wire, crossed an old trench and set up on the low roofs of the bunkers. Then, all hell broke loose.

German observers in a tower located atop Hill 205 must have seen them, for artillery started falling in directly on target. Lieutenant Scott, not yet with the company even six hours, was wounded (the wound would prove fatal), as was Company 1st Sergeant Bergasse. Sergeant Finnegan then took over and got the men pulled back into the old trench. That turned out to be a mistake as the Germans then trapped them in it with a well-placed box barrage, while machine-guns opened up from the direction of the bunkers. The Stokes' answered back, buying time, and A began to beat a retreat back through the wire, taking casualties the whole way. Sergeant Finnegan was killed there and after that the company split into two distinct sections in their mad efforts to get out of the orchard. One group fell back to the rear into a shallow ditch in the brush on the hillside under acting Sergeant Jimmy East, while the other, under Sergeant Herman Anderson, headed back to the ravine to report the situation to Major Whittlesey. (32)

Just before noon, the Major received a message from Colonel Stacey with instructions to continue with the attack, once he had reaffirmed his flank liaison after having reached the Binarville-La Viergette road. Apparently, the earlier rapid advance of the battalion had raised hopes of easily obtaining the day's objective. Colonel Stacey, meanwhile, was in the process of moving his advanced regimental headquarters into a bunker marked on the German map as 'Defsauer Platz' from his previous advanced position at Karlplatz. Defsauer Platz was at the western end of the Depot des Machines Ravine, where it turned north to head to the right of l'Homme Mort and only about 500 meters from the l'Homme Mort bunker, which was quickly being fitted out as a first aid station and combat support depot. (131, 238)

Major Whittlesey sent back a message at noon acknowledging receipt of Colonel Stacey's instructions and informing him that l'Homme Mort was indeed now clear of Germans. He went on to relate, *"Just met French liaison officer who reports French at road 7 kilos north of Binarville."* (This was only partly true however; while there were elements of the French forces much farther advanced than the 308th, they were not yet anything like 7 kilometers out.) What the French officer had not apparently mentioned to the Major however, was that the French forces actually *at* Binarville itself were then halted by fire from Hill 205 and its environs, as the 308th would soon be. Major Whittlesey further indicated that his scouts had run into troops from the 307th out on the right up on the heights of Le Quatre Chenes operating within the 308th's regimental boundaries, so flank liaison in that direction was not yet a problem. He also reported Lt. Dobson shot, indicating that he must have been by this time well aware of Company A's difficulties. Then, forty-five minutes later, he sent back a more detailed message: (10, 131, 144, 246)

At: 94.8 – 75.1
Hour: 12:45pm
Held up in this ravine by MG fire from hills on both east and west. Am forcing the attack. Another scout reports advance elements of 307 in the hills just east of the ravine (i.e. considerably off their course) and halted by MG fire. Lines of communication will be difficult to maintain thru this valley unless Boche pulls out or is searched thoroughly. (246)

Shadows of the recently relieved situation on l'Homme Mort echo in the last sentence of this message, indicating that the Major was definitely erring on the side of caution now. Similar to his pigeon messages out from the l'Homme Mort hillside, Whittlesey appeared to want his 'back watched'. Experiences of the last five days left him little doubt that eventually Captain McMurtry would need to close up 2nd Battalion with the 1st, thus leaving the rear areas virtually wide open again. The 3rd Battalion, in brigade reserve, would be the obvious choice to correct this, but they were not under Colonel Stacey's control, instead being in brigade reserve under General Johnson. This deprived the Colonel of fully a third of his fighting force in a terrain and situation that verily screamed for as many men as could be mustered to the line, at a time when the battalions were well down in strength. However, with none other available to him, it was a long shot that General Johnson would be likely to commit his only reserves. Colonel Stacey - and by extension then Major Whittlesey - would just have to make do. (109, 116)

Lieutenant's Knight and Turner with their Company D, following A in support, meanwhile had come upon the dugout with the collapsed roof A had earlier seen. They too had moved across the orchard, but only after being forced to veer off further to the west following an hour-long machine-gun assault there. Elements of Company D/306th M.G. Bn. came up with their heavy Hotchkiss gear, took position, and broke the stalemate but it was too late. Once again, D discovered it was out of touch with the main body of the regiment, as well as with company A. Then, at a cutting further ahead, they found a German camp and a general fight broke out with the company taking considerable casualties. Relentlessly, D continued to hammer at the German positions all through the late morning and into the afternoon, while unknown to them, A had pulled back out of the wire, beyond the orchard and back into the ravine. And with that, D was alone on the west ridge. (105)

In the ravine, the pace of the fighting was increasing steadily as German resistance stiffened the closer the 308th drew toward the Giselher Stellung line - by that time in the morning less than 600-700 meters away to the north. There seemed to be machine-guns everywhere and enemy trench mortar shells were now coming into the Doughboy positions with relative precision, along with regular shellfire and gas. They were coming up on more wire again as well, weed grown and thus well camouflaged, which was taking a lot of time to work through. Adding to the difficulties was the track of the ravine itself, now shifting slightly westward and slowly narrowing into a bottleneck as it neared the bases of Hills 205 and 198. That bottleneck made for perfect defensive enfilading machine-gun and sniper fire from up on both ridges bracketing it, while the ravine floor was well wired at the narrowest points. Washes found at intervals along the sides of the ravine proved to hold well-concealed machine-gun nests too, while marshy swamp covered large spots along the eastern side of the ravine floor, making advance against guns on that side particularly difficult. Therefore, though they kept the pressure on all morning, the Doughboy advance slowly ground to a halt by about 11:00 a.m. (29, 30, 91, 109, 116)

From the German perspective that morning, Lt. Mann and his 6th Company/254th, along with Lt. Hopf and his 10th Company/122nd held out on the strong defensive line in the Ravin d'Argonne that they had withdrawn into. (This was the line that that had actually been in preparation since the afternoon of the 30th.) Once it had become apparent that the Americans had advanced in force and were then in the process of taking l'Homme Mort come hell or high water, there had been little choice in the matter. Though the *Americanernest* on the l'Homme Mort hillside had offered them a wonderful chance to kill or capture a great number of their enemy had they been reinforced to do so, their general orders still called for their withdrawal. Therefore, little had been done, since Lieutenants Hopf and Mann's men had been acting as rear guard all along - not in assault. It had been at 5:15 p.m. that afternoon of the 30th then that the two lieutenants had sent messages back to their respective regimental commands that the Americans had broken the line and they themselves were beginning to pull back. Four strong thrusts of American troops against the 6th Company/254th had further convinced Lt. Mann that it was the correct course of action.

Now, on the morning of October 1, both units had thoroughly regrouped and had many light machine-guns set up in the pre-prepared positions that dotted both slopes and ridges of the ravine and were well supported with troops from other companies of their respective regiments. Here they were having a dandy time chopping at the Americans then pushing up the narrowing valley and along its heights, particularly on the eastern side. Second Lieutenant Gobel, commanding a section of 5th Company/122nd and who took over the position on the immediate eastern side of the Ravin d'Argonne from Lt. Hopf and the 10th, wrote, "It was predictable that the enemy would begin their big October 1st offensive with even more energy, since the terrain was so favorable to them, so I tried to procure as much ammunition as possible." And with good cause too, for the troops of the 307th and the eastern most companies of the 308th ahead of the German positions began their assaults hard and fast, forcing the defenders to call for all the support that could be spared to be immediately sent into the area. However, with such good defensive positions for their automatic weapons, combined with the trench mortars that were now throwing their deadly loads down onto the American's, it appeared that they had the Doughboy advance stopped cold and could hold it there indefinitely, if they chose. As was usually the case in the Argonne, the machine-guns were making up for the deficiencies in German manpower.

With both the situation over on Hill 198 as well as within the ravine itself seemingly well in hand then, it seemed safe enough to man the trenches of the LaPalette Pavilion and the Haupt-Widerstands-Lienie on the eastern side of Hill 205 with only a skeleton crew - if the need were to arise. And the need, as it turned out, was indeed great. That morning Major Manfred Hunicken, commanding the 254th, decided to send most of his troops hustling over to the western side of the hill to counter the repeated French assaults emanating from Binarville against the Giselher Stellung line and the 253rd stationed over there. Only Lt. Mann and his 6th Company, backed by stray parts of another infantry company and a machine-gun company, would be left on the eastern side of Hill 205 to cover the junction of the two ravines (the north/south Ravine d'Argonne and the east/west Charlevaux Ravine), in case the Americans should somehow miraculously manage to get that far. However, considering the terrain and the amount of support from the 122nd to his east, that looked to be increasingly unlikely.

Yet Lt. Gobel, then in position up on Hill 198, disagreed with this action as it would leave the line that his company was manning in the trenches along the ridge of Hill 198 spread far too thin for security, whether they had the Americans stopped cold or not. He had already been forced to send half of his company east to help out at the joint with the 120th where the American attack had begun fiercely. However, with Lt. Hopf and his 10th Company equally occupied ahead and to his left, there would be problems should the Americans actually pass along the bottom of the Ravin d'Argonne. To that end, Lt. Gobel that afternoon made his way over to see Major Hunicken at the 254th's PC to ask that some kind of support be given his thinly stretched company. The Major, then busily warding off the French assaults being made against his own understrength command, nevertheless heard the young lieutenant out and ultimately agreed to send someone as soon as he was able. Leaving with about as much satisfaction as he was ever likely to get, Lt. Gobel made his way back to his company area, where he found that they had just fended off a major assault by the American forces before them. Obviously, the enemy had much more in the way of reserves than did the hard-pressed 5th Company. Casualties had been heavy; another assault like that before his own reserves could come up might seriously threaten that portion of the line, Lt. Gobel knew. With that in mind, and wanting to buy time until the promised support arrived from the 254th, Lt. Gobel called for a barrage, with gas, that helped keep the attacking Doughboys at bay for the rest of the day. Near 6:00 p.m., just when it seemed as if the situation had been forgotten, a section of the 3rd Machine Gun Company/ 254th (about 40 men) arrived, along with a few heavy machine-guns. Taking up a position slightly west and forward of Lt. Gobel's 5th Company section atop Hill 198, they staked out fields of fire and dug in.

Meanwhile, yet farther east, other bits of the 122nd waited patiently through a storm of American shells that rained down on them that morning to meet the heavy attack that followed. As the first wave of 307th's Doughboys came up at them out of the fog and smoke, the German outpost machine-gunners began firing and continued to do so until their barrels grew too hot to touch. Eventually, slowly the figures in khaki were forced back away from the main line atop Hill 198. In charge of the 5th Company section sent over from the western edge of the ridgeline to help out was Offizierstellvertreter Ruopp, who was directing his machine-guns into the best possible positions he could find. There was a minor road running a roughly north/south track through his defensive zone, with a wagon path crossing it roughly on an east/west course, and these presented some unique problems. At about 9:45 a.m., the first of the Doughboy troops, about 50 of them, hit Officer Ruopp's main line hard and the young officer soon found himself wounded and a prisoner, along with several of his men and a light machine-gun. Dangerously, liaison between the 122nd troops and those of the 120th, to the east of them, was broken. In a short time however, the 5th Company counterattacked and swiftly repelled the 307th's men, recaptured the machine-gun and a couple of their troops and had liaison back with the 120th. Officer Ruopp, however, remained a prisoner.

More support troops were called for and a section of the 8th Company/122nd under Lt. Ulshofer, then in reserve, came up with two heavy machine-guns, which were quickly set up and readied for action. The first was placed so as to cover the line of a barely discernable wagon path running along in front of the 122nd, near the top of Hill 198 in front of the main German trench line up there (the Giselher Stellung). The second gun was placed further behind and to the east to cover a small clearing near the back crest of the hill, beyond a second trench line used for quick access along the main line and usually referred to as an 'ammunition trench'. This gun was there just in case there should be a break through and to lend long-range fire. More troops were then called for; the request being made to the Regimental Commander, Lieutenant Colonel Schmidt, for permission to draw the line in tighter from the west towards the east in preparation for an expected heavy American counter attack to come that afternoon. Since the 254th and the 5th Company/122nd seemed to have the Doughboys attacking up the Ravin d'Argonne bottled up pretty good on a line well forward by almost ¾'s of a kilometer, then those troops manning the line east of the ravine could most probably indeed be drawn farther east without fear. Word had also come through that men from the 254th (the group that Lt. Gobel had requested) were on the way over and would soon help insure that the termination of the Hill 198 line at the ravine would be well in hand. Consequently, with little danger from that corner, Lt. Col. Schmidt indeed sent permission for his men to move eastward in order to counter any major threat that presented itself that afternoon if need be and, most importantly, the next day too. Now situated with enough well placed troops to counter any almost threat, much to the Doughboy's painful reticence, the German line held stiffly throughout the rest of the day and promised to do so tomorrow as well. However by swinging most of the troops away from the 'high shoulder' of Hill 198 further to the east and leaving only a small machine-gun force to cover the gap left by those departing troops, no matter how temporarily, the Germans were setting a dangerous precedence that would come back to haunt them. (120, 123, 124, 128, 307)

Sergeant Anderson and his little band of Company A men reached Major Whittlesey's position in the bottom of the ravine around a quarter after one that afternoon with news of the beating the company had taken. There were a lot of casualties and the rest of the company was still up on the hill to the west. Where was D Company, which was to provide A support, the Major wanted to know. Nobody knew. Therefore, to Captain McMurtry behind in support, he dashed off a quick message from his position in the ravine bottom at 94.9 – 75.1: (32, 105)

Please send one company immediately to support A Co. which is encountering considerable trouble on the left about 94.5 – 75.1. D Co. which was to have supported A seems to be off its course. (246)

Captain McMurtry dispatched Company F for the job. They were to have been supporting D in any case and were therefore the closest at hand. And yet, more trouble continued to present itself as the ravine narrowed and the right sector grew swampier.

The Germans were well organized and well hidden on the slopes and hills above, making searching them out a very labor-intensive process. More and more, C Company was forced to draw itself up the eastern slope toward the top to take care of sniping enemy machine-guns and sharp shooters from above (or the 'high flank') as the marshy ravine bottom prevented taking them in the 'low flank'. This left gaps in the line across the bottom, where the coverage through the mire there was already difficult to begin with. (29, 105, 109)

It was extremely important to maintain good order and keep all the units connected together and as the day progressed toward the afternoon Major Whittlesey could see that the Boche dispositions were making that all but impossible, even in the narrowness of the ravine. Earlier premonitions were proving correct; what was again needed was simply more men. With the debacle of the afternoon of the 28th no doubt still fresh in his mind, Major Whittlesey sat down to scribble another message to Captain McMurtry. He was at 94.7 – 75.0 on the map now, and it was just 2:00 p.m.

The Boche is sniping from hills to East and rear of us and is holding us up with MG fire. Will you not have one company follow up C Co. in close support on the east of the ravine? They have reached approximately parallel 75.1. Or better still will you not come up with this runner and talk things over? (246)

Captain McMurtry followed the runner back and he and Major Whittlesey set up a combined Battalion PC in a shallow shell-hole near some dense brush at the bottom of the ravine and Sergeant Cahill brought up his advanced telephone head. Once that was done, they then set out for the left to scout the situation there. Runners had been sent to find out just where Company D was but so far, they had not had any success in finding them. At Company A's location on the hill above the west slope, they found most of the company reassembled again, now under the leadership of a single NCO, Sgt. Herman Anderson, and the line spread thin. Major Whittlesey gave orders to continue the attack once word came through and then moved on. Company A, which had began the assault on September 26 with 244 men, was now down to a mere 110, of which only about three-quarters were actually manning the line. (137, 245)

Major Whittlesey and Captain McMurtry found the line open elsewhere too. With C Company high enough up on the east ridge to run into 307th men - no matter how far those men were off course - and A and D well up on the west ridge, there was necessarily gaps across the ravine that needed covering. Seeing that, the two commanders quickly decided to send G Company forward into the ravine to extend across the middle. Company H, on the right, diverted to provide close support to G. With the remainder of A up on the hill, D somewhere out there too, and F moving into position along the west slope for their support, the left of the ravine and the center would be covered. Since C was up on the hill to the east, their support company B, was sent to cover the slope and Captain McMurtry sent Company E up to support B. Therefore, once again, the two battalions were forced to close up and act as one by circumstances that later Major Whittlesey detractors would ignore in their efforts to decry his actions. It took some time to move everyone into position, but the Major was finally able to send the order out to try another advance down the ravine about 3:00 p.m., American shells again lead their way forward. (91, 101, 109, 245)

The advance of the 307th on this day was one of confused, extreme violence. They initiated their assault on the German positions ahead from their even line with the 308th in the hills beyond the Depot des Machines. By nightfall, they found themselves occupying a line only about 400 meters north of where they had started from, though again widely scattered and with much blood having been spilled in the Argonne mud. The attack began badly, with a half-hour artillery barrage starting at 5:30 a.m. intended to break down some of the wire before the attacking troops. In the event, the barrage had very little effect at all. (A mortar barrage on the same positions that had been going on most of the night had produced paltry results as well.) Nevertheless, the attack went over at 6:00 a.m., with assault 2nd Battalion leading 3rd in support. The 307th Doughboys, exhausted and stiff from a long, sleepless, cold night in shallow, water-filled funk holes, advanced into the hills without optimism. It was a dismal morning, with no sun shining through a solid cloudbank and a light frost on the barbed wire. They pushed hard against solid machine-gun resistance and slowly started an advance against the wide belt of rusty wire ahead. A secondary road on a general east/west course, with a wagon path crossing it near the middle of the 307th's attack path, cut in front of them. Some German machine-gun teams seemed to have the area well covered and quickly broke up the small Doughboy formations coming at them out of the dense tangle and wire. Quickly, parts of 3rd Battalion closed up with 2nd; the need for men on the line of the 307th was just as acute as with the 308th. Companies E and H slipped into the line while in Company F: (103)

"Lieutenant Gilbert reported back to battalion headquarters to get orders. All the while Jerry threw over a heavy mustard gas barrage on our back area. Lt. Gilbert was gassed and sent back to the hospital. Because of this the company consolidated with 'I' company under the command of Lieutenant's Lord and Perry. 'K' company then took over our position..." (235)

Company K slipped up on the right flank of the 307th's zone of advance, a flank that was as wide open as was ever the 308th's left, with little bands of enemy infiltrators coming through for them to deal with. In command of Company K that morning were two 40th Division replacements to the regiment, Captain Nelson M. Holderman of California and Lt. Thomas Pool of Texas. (103, 235)

Captain Nelson Miles Holderman - 'Neb' to his family and close friends - had only been with Company K a short time but was already an experienced officer, well liked and respected by the men (something rather unusual for a replacement officer). Born November 10, 1885 in Trumbell, Nebraska, Nelson Holderman had come to the 307th already a Captain. He had earned his bars with Company L of the old 7th California National Guard on the Mexican border in 1916, in which he had enlisted as a private and risen through the ranks. He was truly a soldier's soldier, honestly loving every aspect of the job - even the mud, discomforts and long marches. His uniform was home and a badge of honor to him all in one. Those who served with him always remembered him as an ambitious and conscientious officer, always ready for a good fight and never known to have turned down a patrol where adventure might be forthcoming. Young and handsome, he was about 5' 7" and went at about 150 pounds of solid, athletic muscle, with dark, straw blond hair and pale blue/gray eyes. He had a great sense of humor, but it was very dry and mature. He arrived in France in the same draft of 40th Division officers as Lieutenants Pool and Leak on September 14, and was first sent to command Company G of the 307th for a short ten days before being given Company K on September 24. There, much to his delight, he found several men from his old 40th Division company assigned.

Those replacements that Captain Holderman had known from the 7th California had quickly passed the word among the New Yorkers of Company K that the Captain was 'top notch'. It did not take long for them to agree either. They called him "Cap", and they became his world in turn. He was an excellent shot with rifle and pistol alike and did his best to look after his men during the trying days of the offensive, asking in return only that they fight at least as hard as he did. That in and of itself was a tall order, but one which few ever let him down on. By the same token, cowards and fools he did not suffer, and quickly had them relegated to positions within the company that did not bring them into contact with the 'hard' fighting men who needed to depend on the next man. Dashing, daring, brave, foolhardy, Nelson Holderman cut the figure of an excellent soldier. He was completely unflappable in battle. (103, 109, 115, 195, 350, 355)

That same officer draft had brought Lt. Thomas G. Pool to Company K as well, who himself was an equally respected officer on par with Captain Holderman but in a diametrically different way. Lieutenant Pool gained the men's respect through his serious nature and hard fighting capabilities alone. He was not their buddy; he was their commander and took the job to heart. His serious and mature manner naturally brought the nickname 'Tom Fool', but very few ever used it, particularly as the battle progressed and they saw how good a leader he really was. He had an easy-going character that belied his earnestness in battle, where he possessed an innate ability for combat on a local level. Tall and thin, he took men for what they were and counted on them to do their best. As he was the only other officer left in Company K besides Captain Holderman, he therefore stood on an even field with the Captain, who treated him as such, even though he still only wore the bars of a 1st Lieutenant. Together, they were a good combination. (115, 245, 338, 355)

By about a quarter to noon, the 307th's advance was at a standstill, and Major McKinney and Captain Blagden pulled their men back 300 meters and called in another short artillery barrage. Then, with no time for any real reorganization, McKinney and Blagden took the men immediately back into battle once the barrage had lifted at 12:10 p.m., in hopes of attaining an element of surprise. It was not to be. Although the Doughboys made it far enough forward to see clearly through the trees up to the crest of Hill 198 (only about a 20 to 30 meter rise before them at that point but still some 200 meters ahead), the 30 meters of wire belt before them had them stopped cold. The artillery had again done little good. (103)

Lone scouts did manage to pierce points of the German line however, later reporting themselves as having crossed the Ravin d'Charlevaux and reached the Binarville-La Virgette Road, but it is considerably doubtful that they had actually gone that far. (In the east, the 305th was reporting the same, however the ravine dipped to the south there making the move less spectacular than it sounds.) Meanwhile, German infiltrators were breaking through into U.S. lines as well, filtering back into rear areas to raise a little hell before disappearing back to their side of the lines in the confusing, tangled woodland mess. And all day scouts moving along the 307th's left flank continued to go off course, and come down toward the Ravin d'Argonne and into the 308th zone of advance. All in all then, the 307th's afternoon attack largely devolved into uncoordinated confusion, broken up by heavy German resistance. By early evening it was over and palpably a dismal failure. The troops pulled back some, dug new funk holes in the sodden ground and reorganized, while reports went back to Brigade and Division, some of which placed the main line at the wrong coordinates in the evening rain. Evidence shows that only the far right flank of the 307th had its main line position running anywhere close to the crest of Hill 198. Other parts of the line were reported there as well, but were in grave error. (III) By nightfall, the farthest forward of the 307th's troops were actually no further ahead than along the south slope of the hill looking toward the top, and these were nothing more than outposts at best. Nobody except the Germans were actually up there. Dispositions showed the 307th had Company H butted against the 308th with fair liaison; Company was E right of H; the combined Company F/I right of E; and Captain Rainsford's Company L, backed up by Captain Holderman's K, on the right flank with shaky liaison to the 306th. Company G took support between the line companies and Depot des Machines. Nobody slept well that night as the rain again came down. (91, 103, 113, 235)

That evening, after all allied attacks had been successfully beaten off on each unit's front, over on the German side of the lines both Lt. Col. Schmidt of the 122nd and Major Hunicken of the 254th, in looking at the success of the day saw little need to change the disposition or general orders for their troops. Since all had worked so well that day, there should be no reason to expect that to change on the next. The well placed automatic weapons, the fluid movements of available troops and the very terrain itself made it seem as if an American advance any further up the Ravin d'Argonne would be virtually impossible. Therefore, the main body of troops of the 254th that were then holding the French at bay along the western slopes of Hill 205 stayed put, supporting elements of the 253rd there. Meanwhile, the skeleton force of the 6th Company, along with strays from another infantry company and a machine-gun company, manned the Giselher trenches and eastern slopes of Hill 205, facing into the Ravin d'Argonne. These were excellent and strong positions, well placed to deadly effect and taking them would be no easy task, no matter how thinly manned they might be; particularly since Major Hunicken had also called up division and requested a company of pioneer infantry be sent down as reinforcement.

Between Hills 205 and 198, where the ravine's sides narrowed considerably between the heights to the left and right of it, along the ravine bottom there were no manned defenses at all – nor were they needed. This was, quite literally, an impassable zone, covered by a swampy section of the forest floor, a stand of pines and thick, 10 meter high tangles of wire woven into the brambles and rush grass there for a depth of over 30 meters. There was a few angled pathways that led across the area, reasonably dry, but almost impossible to find without knowledge of their location. In any case, machine-gun positions placed on either crest-end opposite and along both slopes well covered any approach to the wired area in between them. Therefore, the zone offered either death by Maxim bullet or death by swamp.

Across the ravine, up on the shoulder of Hill 198, the lone understrength 3rd M.G. Company/254th arrived late that afternoon and took up decent defensive positions along the hillside, slightly farther down from the trenches on top, which they had been told were already manned. However, as far as they knew they were alone out there on that slope, with no real support from any direction and not very happy about it at all. (The company consisted of mostly older men, unused to such strenuous military activity.) They had brought no communications equipment with them and there seemed to be a restrained tension in the air that unnerved them. Above, and now slid east of them, the 5th and portions of 8th Companies/122nd manned their portion of the line in considerable force, though as stated, there was no contact between the two different regimental units, though the 8th and 5th both knew that the 3rd M.G. Company/254th had arrived. The 10th, 12th, and 7th Companies/122nd had also slipped into the line and were taking up position at various points too, but the 3rd M.G. Company/254th remained largely alone out there on the shoulder of the hill. East of, and working in conjunction with the 122nd, was the 120th. Before them, on the eastern slopes of the Ravin d'Argonne and in the heights of le Quatre Chene, they faced the eastern most units of the American 308th and most of the 307th regiments, in muddy positions beyond the 30-meter belt of thick, rusty wire that lay before them. From their solid, well built trenches up on the crest, through the trees the German troops keeping watch ahead could see wet American corpses hanging limply in that wire as their flares punctured the rainy night sky. From the other side of the wire, outposts of the 307th could also see the gruesome spectacles hanging there as well and shivered in fear, disgust, and discomfort in their shabby, mud-filled holes in the rain. German shells were still dropping into the ravine, but at least the rain was keeping the gas down again and providing a little water. (120, 123, 128, 367, 368, 371, 374)

General Alexander returned to his PC that afternoon from an inspection trip to the front not the most heartened by what all he had seen in some places of the line, especially after the good day of advance previous. The left zone of the 154th Brigade in particular had the General concerned. There, they desperately needed to get the advance up and out of the Ravin d'Argonne and past Hill 205. The enemy artillery pouring down on the 154th was thought to be hidden up behind the crest of Mont d'Charlevaux, and it needed to be stopped to prevent a general stall of the attack in that zone of advance. A stalled mass movement in war is extremely difficult to get moving again, the General knew, and would also give the enemy the time he needed to reorganize and strengthen his positions. Therefore, when General Alexander telephoned General Liggett, commanding officer of the 1st Corps, at his PC with his report that evening, the division commander was already guessing what the Corps chief would probably have to say about the situation.

Instead of General Liggett personally though (Liggett was away just then), General Alexander got Colonel Malin Craig, General Liggett's Chief of Staff for the 1st Corps. Colonel Craig heard General Alexander out patiently as the division commander apparently started weaving excuses for his division's lack of general progress. Then the Colonel began a litany of his own concerning the advance through the Argonne. General Pershing himself, while generally pleased with the performance of the 77th Division thus far, wanted still more action; faster and farther advance. Colonel Craig explained that since the 72-hour plan had been scrapped, General Liggett believed it was now absolutely imperative that the 77th keep up with the rest of the main line – which it was not doing. The right flank of the division was wrapped up under Le Chene Tondu (as was the left flank of the 28th Division as well; almost certainly a point of contention with General Alexander, but he apparently said nothing), while the left flank was mired in the ravine in front of Hill 205 under the guns of La Palette Pavilion. The French however, were already almost to Lancon in the west, some 5 kilometers ahead of the 77th's left flank, and the rest of the U.S. line had also outrun them off to the east. The 77th was lagging and needed to catch up; of that there could be no doubt whatsoever. (2, 131, 144)

Colonel Craig then laid out an attack plan concocted for the morning of October 2, which variously has been credited to the 1st Corps staff, General Liggett personally and even to Colonel Craig himself. In the east, the 28th would make a concerted effort against Le Chene Tondu in conjunction with the 77th's 305th Infantry in order to break the stalemate there. To the west, the French would strike the southern and western positions of Hill 205 at the same time that their forces continued the press on Lancon. Meanwhile, the 308th would attack against the southeastern positions of the hill from along the Ravin d'Argonne. The combined effort would be enough to carry the left of the 154th Brigade past the hill to the objective beyond, where they could work up the slopes of Mont d'Charlevaux on the 3rd, yet on the other side of the Ravin d'Charlevaux and eliminate the enemy artillery up there. That would be all that was needed to bring the all-important left 'hinge' flank of the 1st Army forward. Probably in anticipation of the question he could guess would already be on General Alexander's mind, Colonel Craig added that General Pershing himself had stated, "The attack should not concern itself with its flanks or losses, but should instead push ahead as far and as rapidly as possible." "Flanks", General Alexander was further told, "will be taken care of by our own people". There was to be no holding back (as if there had been so far). (2, 109, 116, 131, 144)

General Alexander listened in obedient silence. Later he would simply state, "That the 77th would advance when an advance was possible I felt was a certainty; that our flanks would always be secure I felt at liberty to doubt." And that doubt was definitely justifiable, considering what had been happening not only with the division's interior lines for the last six days, but along the divisional dividing line to the west as well. Case and point: the incident concerning Major Whittlesey's command out on the l'Homme Mort hillside two days ago. Close call, that. Then there was that whole difficulty of the divisional dividing lines between the 77th and the French. With those two situations alone in mind, General Alexander had little more reason to believe that his left flank would be secure than he would General Pershing himself would come and shine his boots for him. (2, 116)

On the other hand, General Alexander was more than aware that the offensive needed to move forward if it was to be completed before the hard part of winter set in. A winter spent in the Argonne would not put anyone in the proper position for the final, war-winning offensive planned for the spring of 1919 and that was something General Pershing would never stand for. As the youngest division commander in France, Robert Alexander already felt he had something to prove and history would not be kind to the man in command of the division that held up the greatest offensive of the war. Nor would General Pershing for that matter, so the pressure on General Alexander was beginning to mount. (IV) (2, 16, 35, 43)

In the end of course, General Alexander knew that it was not his place, nor was he about to show any apparent 'weakness' to question, the orders he was given although he did apparently make at least one left handed comment again concerning the security of his flanks. Colonel Craig apparently once again reiterated, in no uncertain terms, that he need not pay attention to his flanks. If everyone was doing their job, then the flanks would be well covered. General Liggett had said that the 77th should push ahead, fast and far. With that, General Alexander now had his orders. (31)

After hanging up the phone, Alexander spent little time considering any orders for his 154th Brigade as a whole. As they had made little progress within their zone on that day of October 1, their divisional orders and objectives for the 2nd would basically repeat, except for the instructions to the 308th to carry out the 1st Corps plan for a coordinated attack on Hill 205 with the French. The troop dispositions and actual details of the attack he left up to General Johnson, whom he naturally trusted to be in a better position to know the local situation.

General Alexander then telephoned General Johnson. There was never any love lost between these two men while in the Argonne to begin with (both of there egos, it is said, often got in the way), and so in light of what had been transpiring on his left since the start of the advance, those orders did not sit very well with General Johnson. In the end, he let General Alexander know as much too. Without security on the flanks, he warned, they would be inviting infiltration in a country and terrain that had lent itself to just such activity once already. His interior lines fairly begged for attention. Liaison between the 308th and the 307th was shaky at best in the heavily wooded zone of advance and to the right the 153rd Brigade had had its own fair share of trouble keeping up to the 154th. As for the left flank, the French might very well be up as far as Lancon, but locally they were barely beyond Binarville and their line thinned the closer it stretched toward the 308th. That was across that damn strip of territory with Hill 205 right in the middle of it. While the 308th had some troops operating in part of that area off their flank, as did the French, it was still an uncertain sector. General Johnson also may well have reiterated the predicament that Major Whittlesey had just been relieved from the day previous in further detail; in fact almost certainly did so. But in the event, the orders did not take into consideration any possibility of a repeat of such a circumstance and so the point was a moot one, as far as General Alexander was concerned anyway.

Nor was General Alexander, now under the gun from 1st Corps, in the mood to argue. The 154th brigade would advance, General Johnson was told, and it would do so with expedience. The problem of Hill 205 would be solved by the simultaneous attack with the French, whom General Alexander said he had a hard time believing were as disorganized as General Johnson implied. (Or at least he made it seem that he did at the time. Only later would he admit that he knew full well that they were not where he had insisted they were.) After all, they had a liaison line stretched almost three kilometers back from Lancon, didn't they? Then there was definitely a line extended over to the 308th – General Johnson had even admitted as much (though here again, General Alexander conveniently overlooked that General Johnson had also admitted that the line was tentative at best). As for security of the interior lines, if each individual unit were doing its job, then they should not be a problem. The orders were clear then; attack, regardless of flanks or losses. (V) (2, 10, 91, 131, 144)

In the end, a certainly frustrated General Johnson was forced to face that he now had his orders, questionable though they were. What to do? He was well aware now of the difficult situation along his front. To advance with a total lack of concern for losses could be justified by the hour, on one hand. After all, this was war and the objective must come first. However, to ignore the flanks, when experience of the previous six days of advance seemed to council otherwise, seemed madness. Therefore after some serious thought and study General Johnson, always the tactician, finally struck upon a plan concerning his brigade, particularly the 308th, that he deemed had at least a better than average chance of success, considering all factors. According to Colonel Stacey's reports, there was less resistance along the eastern ridge of the ravine than on the western side, in front of Hill 205. Not much less, but perhaps just enough to make a difference. If a smaller containing force were left on the west ridge to keep the Germans busy in conjunction with the French, as per orders, then a strong push along that eastern ridge by a larger main force might get them past the bottleneck, opening a way for the rest of the regiment to slam through. By then sending a portion of the attacking force back to link up with that 'containing force' along the western ridge, they would have the eastern side of the hill firmly surrounded. If they could maintain that line through the enemy front, then they could begin a roll up around the Germans' eastern flank, link with the French beyond and completely 'pinch out' that damned hill. With the left of the brigade front well sewn up, then perhaps the 307th (who should be right on the 308th's right flank, if General Alexander was right) would push forward and get to the artillery up over Mont d'Charlevaux. Therefore, the plan, if it worked, had a lot going for it.

Colonel Stacey received General Johnson's call at Defsauer Platz about 4:00 p.m., and listened in strained compliance as the Brigadier dictated the next morning's attack order to him. No change in general orders and they were to push on without regard to flanks or losses. Then General Johnson laid out the new plan to maneuver around the difficulty of Hill 205. Colonel Stacey obediently took down the order as General Johnson read it out, but he did it with considerable disquiet. In the light of the French failure to break past Hill 205 and all that the 308th had learned of the German defenses within the Ravin d'Argonne during the attacks of the last 10 hours or so, the success of such a plan - if indeed it succeeded - seemed likely to put the 1st and 2nd Battalions in a difficult position at best. They would be about a kilometer further ahead of their current line, yet beyond Hill 205 and across a wide and difficult ravine, dominated front and rear by high slopes, extended upon an exposed road position along the hillside behind the Charlevaux Mill; hard to get to, but even harder to defend and maintain a firm contact/supply line with. Additionally, any such breakthrough along an enemy line like that which the 308th was now facing was likely be a very slender and tenuous one that would have to be carefully tended overnight. It seemed unlikely that such a breakthrough would succeed until late in the day, judging from the tenacity with which the enemy was defending the approaches to the Charlevaux Ravine. Therefore, the end result would likely be Major Whittlesey's command in an extremely tentative position, well to the front and very likely surrounded on three sides by the enemy. (10, 29, 91, 116, 131, 144, 238, 246)

Further, Colonel Stacey was well aware of the actual condition of his flanks, despite the 'official' line from Division PC. He was positive that the French on his left were not locally in firm contact with his advance battalion, and might not have even been up on the same line as his support battalion; it did not matter if they were said to be nearing Lancon, farther west. That was divisional speculation and the Colonel was dealing in local reality. Additionally, he was fairly sure that liaison with the 307th was conditional at best, and was confidant that they had been purposely mis-reporting their true main line positions, instead reporting the outpost line as such. Therefore he might very well wind up with another l'Homme Mort situation on his hands only up in the Ravin d'Charlevaux instead, a much more indefensible and difficult place to be stuck than the bleak hillside of before. Obviously then, as far as Colonel Stacey was concerned anyway, General Johnson had no real appreciation of the actual situation facing the 308th.

Finally, the Colonel found a voice and went straight to the heart of the matter, pointing out of the Charlevaux Ravine, "My scouts find that position will be untenable, General."

There was a short silence on the other end of the phone.

"Are you questioning my orders Colonel?" General Johnson asked.

"No sir," Colonel Stacey replied. "But if you send them up there you will have to give me the orders in writing, and I will also write a statement to the effect that if you order me to send those men up there I will do so, but I will not be responsible."

There was then another short silence, after which General Johnson said that a runner would come up with the orders, and then hung up. (238)

But a lot of what Colonel Stacey had said actually made sense to General Johnson. The Colonel, he knew, was a good officer and a good leader. His record told that tale. While he was simply looking out for the best interests of his men as all good leaders are apt to, he was obviously not exaggerating the situation either. His insubordination to a direct order in time of war was proof; no regular army officer would risk his career in such a way unless there was a damn good reason for it. And of all people, General Johnson knew, Colonel Stacey would be in the prime position to know his local situation best. Therefore, after a short time of reflection, the Brigadier called General Alexander back and explained his conversation with Colonel Stacey and his own shakily corroborating opinion. The reply he got was short and to the point; he had been given his orders and was therefore expected to carry them out. The attack *would* go over as originally ordered. (29, 131 144)

Around 4:00 a.m. on that chilly morning of October 1, companies B and C of the 1st/368th had begun to withdraw from their positions south of Binarville and were headed back for the Tranchee de Damas. Along the way, they picked up Company D, which had remained in support at Tranchee Tirpitz and about 7:00 a.m., Company A withdrew from the line above Binarville and also made their way back. The 368th Regiment had suffered fairly heavily, with about 400 killed, wounded and gassed since the 26th and by midmorning it was all over for them in the sector as the 9th C.a.P moved in and relieved their positions. Initially there was some talk of the French 1st D.C.D being pulled out of the line and the whole 92nd Division moving in to take over, but French 4th Army shot the idea down in short order. They no longer trusted in the 92nd's abilities and there was too much at stake to risk them another chance.

There was general fighting across the narrow Durand front all day, but to no good end. On the 9th's left, their flank moved forward in good stead while their right flank remained mired before Hill 205 and the northern environs of Binarville. The French were beginning to realize just what the 368th had been up against as the Germans poured fire on them all day. At 1:00 p.m., the French sent a message to General Alexander mentioning that heavy machine-gun fire had them stopped, but that the liaison post earlier established with the 2nd/308th through the 3rd/308th liaison troops was still holding. Then there was no word for a long, long time.

That afternoon the French 11th C.a.P attacked steadily west of Binarville and by evening, they had crossed the Bois de Plemont in force and were almost in Lancon, but facing great resistance. The troops of the 9th C.a.P made it up even to them with their left flank, but their right flank still had not managed to move past Hill 205. They attacked the positions of the hill repeatedly and doggedly all day, but as the afternoon fell into night, the exhausted soldiers pulled back into Binarville and set up a defensive perimeter just north of town limits. By dark, the 9th's line then ran almost due south from its connection with the 11th (just before Lancon), skirted around Tranchee de LaPalette, followed the Binarville-Autry road south into town and then curved around it, dissolving into nothing a little further back. In Binarville itself the French held a firm line, building reserves in anticipation for another large attack against Hill 205, Tranchee La Palette and Tranchee de Charlevaux scheduled for the morning of October 2.

Then finally, at 9:45 p.m., word was received from Lt. De La Chapelle, the 9th's liaison officer to the 77th Division PC. The lieutenant reported that there appeared to be about a 500-meter horizontal cleft between his own regiment and the left flank of the 308th. Liaison with the 308th had broken and disappeared sometime late that afternoon and the gap opened up between the two regiments was due east from Binarville. Therefore, once again through the night Major Whittlesey's left flank was as open as the sea before the defenses of Hill 205, only thinly screened by the small liaison elements of Company I/308th. (10, 46, 91, 92, 146)

It was just after 5:00 p.m., when the 308th's attack finally ground to a halt for the day. Major Whittlesey and Captain McMurtry went back to the bunker at l'Homme Mort and re-established their combined Battalion PC there. The outpost line, meanwhile, had advanced about three-quarters of a kilometer up the ravine and had set up a shaky perimeter across it. It had been a tough day; by far the toughest they had yet seen since the 26th. Above it threatened to rain again, while below the ground still had not dried out from the last round of showers the night before. A flatcar came clattering up the narrow gauge line at the bottom of the ravine, pushed by hand. Lots of rations, water, ammunition and grenades, but still no overcoats, blankets or shelter halves. Enemy artillery and trench mortars continued dropping into the ravine sporadically, along with gas shells. Everyone put on their masks again and continued to dig, slipping the masks up at intervals to nibble some hardtack or corn willy. It was a wonder some of the men had any appetite left at all, after the day they had just had. (91, 109, 116, 218)

In the bunker, Major Whittlesey wrote out a final, long message for the day, which Colonel Stacey received just before 7:00 p.m. or so. In it, the Major gave his company dispositions and an explanation of the afternoon's assault, which ultimately had gotten him no further than he had been at 10:00 a.m. *"Had a reversal on the left flank,"* he began, *"Lt. Scott commanding Co A was wounded while attacking machine guns on hill 94.5-75.2. Company was shelled by artillery and badly shaken."* When Company D, sent up to support A on the ridge, had disappeared, F Company had gone up in support as well and this is where they all remained, extended from the ridge top eastward, down into the ravine. On the right, Captain Stromee's C Company had made contact with the 307th to the east, but to do it they had to extend a line back to the southeast to reach them. (This gave evidence to the theory that the 307th was not as far forward as Colonel Houghton reported them.) Company G, on C's left flank down in the ravine bottom, had not been able to drive as far up the middle as C had along the slope either, so they needed to have C extend a line back to them as well. They in turn had firm contact with D and F, against the opposite slope. Company B had spread out in support of the thinly stretched C, with E in strong support behind them. Company H, meanwhile, was at the combined Battalion PC advance post, in support behind G in the muddy middle of the ravine bottom. It was a fairly strong line, with only the left flank looking a bit weak. It is interesting to also note that Major Whittlesey stated directly in his message, *"Have a mixed liaison post with the French on left. Line extending N.E."* This post was composed mainly of Company I/308th men still connected with 2nd/308th men at 5:00 p.m., when the Major wrote his message, but it would be all but gone by 9:00 p.m. (91, 246)

Major Whittlesey also made clear his impressions of the terrain over which he was now forced to attack:

> *Resistance of the Germans is stiffer here than we have met elsewhere and it is very difficult trying to manage two sides of the ravine at the same time. I personally was in the ravine when 'G' company attacked as I assumed the ravine to be the point of the chief difficulty with machine guns. This ravine is difficult. The sides are very steep; the bottom is marshy, and any solution to the problem involving an operation on both sides by one unit will be difficult. (246)*

By "one unit" we can safely assume the Major is referring to the basically merged 1st and 2nd battalions, both now understrength and badly in need of additional support. He seems to be again fishing around for that additional body of men actually needed to watch the ravine behind him as he attacked. But if he was, Colonel Stacey had no other troops to commit, as previously discussed. And while most of this information Major Whittlesey was passing along Colonel Stacey did not yet actually know, judging from the messages he had been sending back all day, the Colonel had already formed a pretty good idea of what the Major was going through up in the ravine. Therefore, about 4:30 p.m., Colonel Stacey had sent a message up to the Major containing General Johnson's 'right flank maneuver' instructions, on the off chance that it might relieve some of the pressure on the companies working the west ridge and coming up against the machine-guns on Hill 205. The message read:

> *You will press on to your objective at all costs. Attack along the hills east of the ravine, leaving two companies as a containing force on the supposedly more difficult western side of the ravine; one company to be detached from the force on the east when it has reached its objective to return and assist from the rear on an attack on the western side of the ravine. (131, 144, 246)*

However, Major Whittlesey had only gotten this message some time after 5:00 p.m., by which time the days' actions were mostly over and his tired troops were already digging in under the advancing darkness and light mist. Therefore, he had obviously had no time to try the maneuver and accordingly he ends his last message of the day back to Colonel Stacey by stating, *"Instructions about flanking just received. This will be done tomorrow. Will attack this point more deliberately."* (246)

Tomorrow then looked like it was going to be a long day.

It was around 10:00 p.m. that night when Colonel Stacey's adjutant, Captain Francis Weld, came up the runner line from Defsauer and walked into the l'Homme Mort bunker with the actual orders that the Colonel had cut for the battalion commanders to execute during the next morning's attack. There he found Major Whittlesey, Captain

McMurtry, Lieutenant William Cullen of 'H', Captain Stromee of 'C' and a couple of new lieutenants just arrived, all huddled around a small coke stove, talking about the difficult advance up the ravine that day. The mood, by all accounts, was rather morose. Frank Weld, however, was a genial man, known to most of them from the Camp Upton days and so he was greeted warmly. Yet, even he seemed grave and distracted on this occasion and after a few pleasantries, he uncomfortably produced and read the short attack order for the 308th in all its disquieting detail:

The advance will be resumed on October 2nd at 6.00am. Your objective is the line 294.5-276.6. You will take your objective and hold it at any cost until support arrives.

This basic order was followed with a repeat of the order for the right flank maneuver that the Colonel had issued that afternoon. Handing the paper to Major Whittlesey, there was a short, strained silence once Captain Weld had finished, with the officers casting sideways glances at each other in the shadowy light of the oil lanterns. The orders were virtually unchanged from that morning; this despite some measure of hope that the final afternoon reports of the veritable bloodbath that the day had been, might just alter the minds of those concocting advance orders for the next day. A vain hope as it turned out, for the co-ordinates given as the objective line would deposit them at the Charlevaux Mill, slightly more than a kilometer yet ahead of the current line. With Hill 205 undoubtedly remaining in German hands (since the orders specifically called for its bypass, not its immediate eradication), they would then be sitting ducks to fire from that direction, as well as the artillery from up over Mont d'Charlevaux ahead, while they waited to move forward again. Worse still, the position would most likely leave them without flank support, if the French actions to the west that day, not to mention those of the 307th to the east, were any indication of things. Any fool could see that the position described was nigh on untenable. The order then represented nothing less than operational suicide.

It was Lt. 'Red' Cullen that finally broke the silence. Never one to mince words or ordinarily hide his feelings anyway, he now looked up at Captain Weld and, with just a hint of the flippant menace in his voice he usually reserved for subordinates, said, "Then it will be the same thing. We'll be cut off again." Captain Weld, after another short silence there in the half-light, finally said dryly, and to no one in particular, "That possibility has been considered, but the attack has been ordered nevertheless."

It seemed inconceivable that they were to simply repeat again the same attack that had resulted in so little gain that day. True, there was the right flank maneuver to consider, but that only added to the dilemma by virtually insuring their advance into an untenable position. There simply had to be another way. (29, 51, 109, 116, 161, 184)

A chilly night fog was rolling in when, sometime around 10:30 p.m., Major Whittlesey made the trek back down the runner line through the dark to Defsauer Platz hanging on to the back of the cartridge belt of each runner leading him and with Captain McMurtry holding the back of his coat. Once there, the Major wasted little time in telling Colonel Stacey that, in his opinion, the order was definitely not a good idea. Expanding on what he had stated in his last message that afternoon; any attack up the ravine would likely have both battalions decimated in no time at all, the right flanking maneuver notwithstanding. Colonel Stacey agreed to a point that it was a difficult assignment, but stated that he was quite confidant that the Major and his men would be able to achieve the objective. No doubt, it would be the determined attack against Hill 205 and the La Palette Pavilion that would indeed provide the distraction that was needed to have his men work along the east ridge (Hill 198) and break through the line. Major Whittlesey countered that companies C and G had already been up against the wire and slope of that damned hill and beaten back down. The slope was just too well wired and literally stuffed with machine-gun nests. The Germans held every possible advantage.

Colonel Stacey, being a regular army officer, was not used to having his subordinates question his orders. (Nor was he used to giving out such questionable orders as these for that matter, but that was beside the point.) '*Nonsense!*' the Colonel irritably replied. Why, the 307th had had men up on Hill 198 just that day (technically true). He was losing patience now (something becoming more and more frequent in the last couple days) and heatedly told Major Whittlesey that his command would attack as ordered, obtain their objective as ordered, and do it regardless of losses as ordered. What about flank support, the Major wanted to know. Without it, they would be sitting ducks out there, if and when they made it across the Charlevaux Ravine. Colonel Stacey simply reiterated what he himself had been told; that the Major's flanks would be well covered by "our own people on the right and the French on the left", and so not to worry about his flanks. The French, in fact, were already well ahead of the 308th to the west. "Perhaps beyond Binarville, but not locally", Major Whittlesey replied, to which Colonel Stacey, his nerves now having had enough, burned bright again. Reiterating the orders loudly and firmly, he then dismissed Major Whittlesey and Captain McMurtry with infinite finality. The orders, such as they were, would stand. (29, 238, 246)

Outside of Defsauer, a kilometer to the north, German flares sailed up through the night and machine-guns rattled in the distance as a concerned Major Whittlesey started back through the fog towards the l'Homme Mort bunker, with Captain McMurtry again following behind him. Just then, silently out of the ground fog to one side, there appeared Sergeant Charlie Cahill of the Signal Platoon, Headquarters Company/308th. He had just gotten back from over at the Depot des Machines that very afternoon, where he had been trying to scrounge some much-needed communication wire for his field telephone set. Now he quickly caught up to Major Whittlesey and with a salute in the dark, stopped him momentarily. His breath showing silvery clouds, Sgt. Cahill asked how much wire the Major thought they would need for the attack tomorrow, in order to bring the field telephone right up to the advance Battalion PC once on the objective.

"You haven't got enough wire to reach where I'm going," Major Whittlesey said, and turning, disappeared into the fog toward l'Homme Mort… (29)

(I) Previously, this rail line has been reported as never found by the 308th, but this is not true. As we shall soon see, they indeed reached this rail line, which was farther up Mont d'Charlevaux than the 77th Division command believed. The myth was started by Johnson and Pratt's 1938 book, *The Lost Battalion* (see bibliography). However, the author has photos in his collection of the section of line near the Charlevaux Mill and the bed of the rail line referred to in the 308th's orders can still be discerned up in the forest on Mont d'Charlevaux, though one must know what to look for and be willing to hike to find it.

(II) The lists for the enlisted casualties, such as they are, read even longer and are horribly incomplete. Many wounded men never reported the hits they took unless they were of a most severe nature, or until after a particular action was over, so as not to leave their comrades short handed. Sometimes it would be days before they would, or could, report to a medical officer and even then some would only want to be patched up quickly so they could get back to their company. The enlisted medics at the first aid stations were usually the ones to treat the more lightly wounded men and they sometimes did not bother to report them. In many instances, men who were only lightly gassed never reported it either, especially those who had suffered through the hell of the Vesle where gas poisoning was common. By October 1 then, while there are 288 *reported* enlisted wounded in the 308th's records, the actual number should probably be half again as high as that at the very least. There were also many men who simply 'disappeared' into the forest, and that also quite often went unreported. Many officers figured that most had simply gotten lost in the tangled wilderness and had been picked up by another company and would likely turn up again in a day or so. (Whittlesey himself was notorious for gathering in 'strays' and keeping them as scouts and runners with the Battalion PC.) This was, indeed, usually the case. In fact, despite the fantastic opportunity for it, there was very little actual "straggling" in the Argonne, which is a fine testament to the fortitude of the men that fought there. Usually any straggling had more to do with men taking a short 'break' from combat during a slower time to make a quick trip to search out a field kitchen. Once they had found a little food, the men would then head right back to their unit. If anyone asked – and few ever did – they might simply say they had been 'lost in the woods'. Some, however, never did turn up, their bodies only found months - and in some cases years - later. In some companies, officers were also the only ones who kept track of the men and when they went down the list of who was there and who was not went with them.

(III) The main body of 307th troops actually held positions about 500 to 600 meters north of the Depot des Machines that night, but certainly no more than that. This 'creative' way of reporting his line position was apparently something of a regular habit with Colonel Houghton and caused Colonel Stacey considerable difficulty with General Johnson, who would then use Houghton's apparent 'success' as a whip to drive the 'lagging' Stacey on. Though there have never been any telephone logs that the author has found to support it, legend has it that Stacey and Houghton had at least one heated telephone conversation during the battle concerning this issue.

(IV) General Pershing had in fact already reassigned a number of divisional officers that had failed to show the proper 'offensive spirit' in those first days of the offensive and in the coming days and weeks there would be more to follow. Reassignments from combat usually spelled the end for a Regular Army career that had taken a lifetime to build. On the other hand, success made for fast promotion during the war and for that reason alone many of the higher ranking officers tried hard to please Pershing, who had himself been promoted well ahead of many of his contemporaries to lead the AEF, due in large part to his many and varied abilities. All that aside, Pershing demanded action and if he did not get it, it did not matter how well connected an officer was, how many years he had in, or whether Pershing liked the man personally or not – inaction or failure under fire meant reassignment, or even demotion.

(V) Here it is very interesting to again point out the tremendously selective use of the order concerning 'units moving without regard to troops to the right or left' by General Alexander. We have already seen previous examples of General Johnson being ordered by him to hold up the advance of the 308th in order to let the 307th catch up the interior lines of the 154th Brigade, apparently for reasons relating to security of the advancing main line. However, in this instance, he insists that the interior lines - be they either brigade or regimental apparently - will be fine on their own, despite the actions of flanking forces and plenty of evidence to the contrary. Also note here that the ante has just been bumped up as well; the attack is now to progress regardless of flanks *or losses*.

Ancillary sources used in this chapter include: 21, 25, 29, 30, 34, 49, 51, 148, 149, 150, Various 152-216, 250-254, 257, 260-262, 268, 269, 272, 273, 278-280, 282, 283, 285, 286, 292, 296-306, 309, 310, 314-319, 323, 326-330, 338

"The Hell-hole Valley of the Vesle"
(38)

The main bunker at Karlplatz
(109)

The cemetery below the slope of l'Homme Mort

A section of Depot des Machines looking east

The Moulin de l'Homme Mort

Brigadier General Evan M. Johnson (Highlighted)
(38)

Major General
Robert Alexander
(116)

The bunker in the wash on the north slope on l'Homme Mort, April 1919 (Gilles Lagin)
Inset: The bunker as it appears today (Taylor V. Beattie)

Lt. Arthur McKeogh
(344)

Pvt. John Monson
(344)

Pvt. Jack Hershkowitz
(344)

Col. Cromwell Stacey

Lt. Col. Fred Smith
(26)

Major Ken P. Budd
(109)

Looking northeast to the heights of Le Quatre Chenes from the clearing before the bunker on l'Homme Mort - October 2002 (Taylor V. Beattie)

Looking north up the wagon road at the bottom of the Ravin d'Argonne – October 2002 (Taylor V. Beattie)

Part 3:
A Little Corner of Hell

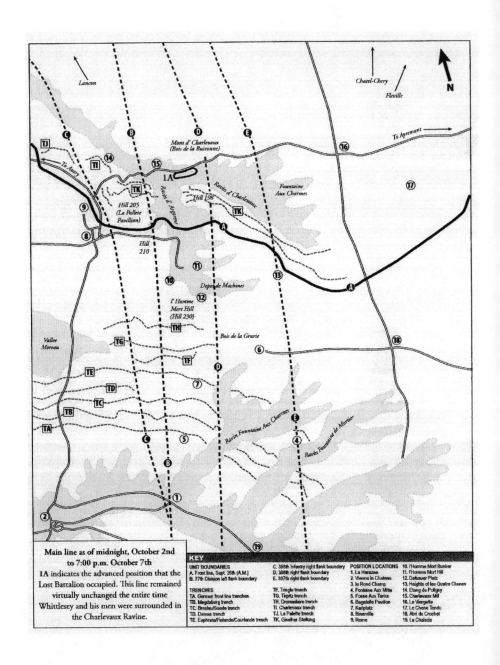

Main line as of midnight, October 2nd to 7:00 p.m. October 7th

1A indicates the advanced position that the Lost Battalion occupied. This line remained virtually unchanged the entire time Whittlesey and his men were surrounded in the Charlevaux Ravine.

KEY

UNIT BOUNDARIES
A. Front line, Sept. 26th (A.M.)
B. 77th Division left flank boundary

TRENCHES
TA. German front line trenches
TB. Magdaburg trench
TC. Breslau/Suede trench
TD. Damas trench
TE. Euphrate/Finlande/Courlande trench

C. 368th Infantry right flank boundary
D. 306th right flank boundary
E. 307th right flank boundary

TF. Tringle trench
TG. Tirpitz trench
TH. Dromadaire trench
TI. Charlevaux trench
TJ. La Palette trench
TK. Giselher Stellung

POSITION LOCATIONS
1. La Harazee
2. Vienne le Chateau
3. le Rond Champ
4. Fontaine Aux Mitte
5. Fosse Aux Tanks
6. Bagatelle Pavilion
7. Karlplatz
8. Binarville
9. Rome

10. l'Homme Mort Bunker
11. l'Homme Mort Hill
12. Defzauer Platz
13. Heights of les Quatre Chenes
14. Etang de Poligny
15. Charlevaux Mill
16. Le Viergette
17. Le Chene Tondu
18. Abri du Crochet
19. La Chalade

228

October 2, 1918 - A.M.

"But it will be the same thing. We'll be cut off again…"
Lt. William Cullen, Company H.

Major Whittlesey and Captain McMurtry silently slogged back up the ravine through the cold, misty night, while the German artillery continued further up the ravine sending back muffled explosions and brilliant flashes of light. Back at the bunker, each commander set out to gather strength reports from their company commanders to make as accurate a determination as possible about what kind of numbers they had to work with. Casualties had not been light on the 1st day of October and the numbers they found were less than encouraging. While nearly all units had lost men in the vicious attacks up the ravine that day, 2nd Battalion had obviously faired better than had 1st, to no one's surprise. Hardest hit again had been Company A, now with its total strength hovering right around 100, but no one seemed to know who was gone and who remained in the company. As near as the two battalion commanders could gather, the enemy had killed or wounded some 80 men between the two battalions on October 1 alone. At that rate, the regiment would be used up in no time. Near 12:30 a.m. then, Major Whittlesey sent a short, terse note back to Colonel Stacey: (137)

At: 94.7 – 75.1
List of casualties of 1st battalion not obtainable tonight. 'A' Company 1st Sgt. – only man familiar with roll of Company – wounded. I put a corporal of 'A' Company on the post this afternoon and he has gone down to the first aid station tonight (corps La Croix) with a stretcher bearer detail to obtain this information, and will have it for me the first thing in the morning. (246)

Sometime in the early morning hours of October 2, Lt. Henry J. Williamson, one of the platoon leaders in Company D, came over at Major Whittlesey's request to help out. The Major immediately sent him to the officer-less Company A, which was to be pulled off the assault line and amalgamated with Company G. Major Whittlesey's plan was to use the remaining A men mainly as runners and stretcher-bearers throughout the attacks of the 2nd. Therefore, posting Lt. Williamson with A might at least keep the intrepid officer's career with the company from being anything as short as Lt. Scott's had been with them. (32, 109, 137)

The temperature had again dropped that night, dipping into the mid 40's Fahrenheit. Shivering sergeants went around shaking awake what few men had slept, shortly before 5:00 a.m., to ready themselves for the attack. Captain Rainsford, over in Company L/307th wrote: (136)

"Captain Blagden came into the old German dug out where I had been sleeping to tell me that we were to attack behind a rolling barrage… at six (sic), and I remember that my teeth were chattering so with cold that I could hardly answer him… (The men) rose, shaking with cold, from the half frozen mud… and stumbled numbly forward through a forest white with frost." (103)

No hot rations had made it up for the 308th that Wednesday morning, however a large dump of iron rations had been left to one side of the railroad track about half way up to the outpost line from l'Homme Mort sometime overnight. A good supply of ammunition and clean water was also left. Small parties of men went to it and brought tins of hardtack and corned willy up to the line. Monotonous fare, but there was little bitching about it. The men were glad to have anything for a second breakfast in a row. More carrying parties went out to fetch ammunition and grenades. Now, if they could just get overcoats or blankets. (29, 109, 116)

When final orders came up around 5:00 a.m., they found that the main objective, despite Major Whittlesey's protestations, still remained the Binarville-La Viergette road. The renewed attack up "that damned ravine" was scheduled to come off at 7:00 a.m., behind the usual half-hour's worth of artillery expenditure. Companies D and F were designated by Major Whittlesey and Captain McMurtry to remain along the western ridge as the 'containing force'. The rest of the two battalions would make the flanking maneuver over Hill 198 - provided they could get up and over it, that is. The captured map information showed a double trench line ran up there (the Haupt-Wilderstande-Linie), and it was a sure bet then that the Germans would have it well defended. Whittlesey's scouts had found wire there yesterday - lots of it - but had not been able to get beyond that. Obviously, there would be machine-guns covering that point of termination of the Ravin d'Argonne from the crest above. But, how many would there be covering the slopes up the hill? An ugly mystery to be sure. (I) (109, 131)

It was what was beyond Hill 198 that obviously worried Major Whittlesey more though, for there ran the Charlevaux Ravine, a narrow slit between two steep slopes: Hill 198 to the south and Mont d'Charlevaux to the north. If they got down in there with no flank support (and he was obviously sure that such would be the situation if and when they made it that far) then the Germans would have little trouble bottling them up again, just like on the night of the 28th. Only this time there would be little mystery as to what would happen to them, as the Charlevaux Ravine looked a much better containment area than the bleak l'Homme Mort hillside.

Still, for his attack dispositions that morning, Major Whittlesey moved little from where they had come to rest the night before. The only differences were that he slipped what remained of Company A down to the middle of the ravine with G (a stray A platoon still out on patrol somewhere near the left flank would join later), and that he also sent elements of companies C and D of the 306th M.G. Bn. forward to provide heavy fire support to the main attack force. Judging by the resistance of the day before, they would be needed. Already situated on the west ridge, Major Whittlesey left companies D and F there as the containing force, commanded by Lieutenants Knight and Kiefer respectively. Lieutenant Paul R. Knight was a popular and respected officer in the 308th from the Camp Upton days and had been with the 102nd Engineer Regiment of the New York National Guard before the war, giving him a slight edge on some of the Plattsburg men. Short and muscular with dark, sandy hair, he was a serious leader and just short of his captaincy at the time. Earlier, he had the dubious honor of being the first 308th officer wounded in the war, when he was hit slightly by shrapnel while training with the British and had been hit again on the Vesle. Now, standing in the beginnings of a light rain in the mud, listening to Major Whittlesey's orders, little did he realize that he was not yet done collecting his share of German scrap steel. (91, 105, 109)

The Major reminded the two officers of the plan: they would stay behind and keep pressure on the German gunners while the rest of the two battalions broke through the line on the right. Once on the objective, Captain McMurtry would send back companies E and H to link a line with them forward, probably later in the afternoon, but certainly with first light the next morning at the very latest. If the French forces attacking the other side of Hill 205 kept up a steady advance, then the two forces should be able to link up behind the hill early the next morning.

It was about 6:20 a.m. when Major Whittlesey and Captain McMurtry moved down into the clearing before the bunker to brief their officers again, same as the morning before. The men on the line ahead were finishing up breakfast. All at once, heads raised and tired eyes peered into the rain-soaked sky at the familiar, freight train like sound of the barrage as it started rushing overhead into the Boche lines. As with the German shells, most of which were still dropping well behind the Doughboy line, the resulting explosions were muffled by the wet forested ravine and sent a dream-like echo washing back over them all. It seemed a desultory barrage, ragged and weak (even an operations report for that morning would call it "of little effect"); a barrage that filled no one with confidence. As slowly the minutes ticked by, the men readied themselves. It was just before 7:00 a.m. when the shellfire lifted forward and the 308th again surged out into the ravine in a loose, open order advance. (20, 29, 91, 131, 218, 245)

The assault units had not slept far from the German lines, so it did not take long before they came to contact with the enemy, first with rifle volleys and then with machine-gun fire. Ahead and above on La Palette, a trench mortar opened up and began to dump in its shells fairly square onto the advancing companies while the Hun heavy artillery worked over the areas just vacated by the 308th. Their aim was still just a touch off. The mist held on in a thin, white blanket covering the bottom of the ravine, powder smoke mixing in with it and increasing the density. Sergeant Cahill showed up on the advance line from Defsauer Platz with his field telephone gear again, at the end of what wire he had scrounged from the Depot des Machines. He and Private Ralph Prescott set up a telephone head in the same spot near some bushes at the bottom of the ravine that they had the afternoon before. (245)

In the bottom of the ravine, Major Whittlesey had the A/G Company combination going down the center, paying out runners as it went from the head of the attack back to Defsauer Platz. "Thirty of us were taken out of Company 'G' and placed at runner posts along a narrow gauge railway track," Private Ben Doctor later wrote. "We were still there when the boys got out of the Pocket..." These men the Major placed under the command of Sergeant David Jolley, a capable Upton man in Company G and one of the last actual sergeants left standing from the Vesle days. Moving behind G/A in support was Company H. Between these two was the combined Battalion PC. Moving along the east ridge and slope, Company C would again take the lead, with B in support and E right behind them. It looked a solid line on the east, and therefore the right flank maneuver plan appeared to stand at least a fair chance of success. (91, 44)

As the opening minutes of the attack ticked by, German rifle and machine-gun fire increased from the ridges down onto the Doughboys advancing up the bottom of the ravine, as it did against those slamming away above it. Companies D and F, swarmed out and down the far slope of the hill that Major Whittlesey had so boldly scouted on the afternoon of the 30th (Hill 210). They found themselves doing just what General Johnson had hoped would be the case; drawing heavy fire from the La Palette Pavilion up on Hill 205. West of them, came the sounds of battle too, as Company I and the French 9th C.a.P slammed forward from Binarville, and further west, beyond even them, the 11th C.a.P and the French 71st Division forced their way up toward Autry. Meanwhile, in the Ravin d'Argonne, the German artillery started to get the range better and shells fell across the line taken up by the support companies traversing the slopes. On the right, it was slow going through the marshy ravine bottom. There seemed to be little progress. No reports had come from the ridge above yet, but firing could be heard in the hills. (10, 91, 105, 109)

At 8:40 a.m., Major Whittlesey sent back a report from the ravine bottom, sparse and to the point:

Advance started as ordered. No reports from right yet, but grenade fire up the ravine shows they are advancing. On the left having trouble. Lt. Kiefer commanding 'F' Company just wounded. They are dropping heavy artillery (shrapnel) fire on our support. (246)

The loss of yet another officer was a hard blow to the command. That left only Lt. Paul Knight and Lt. Turner as the principal officers on the left. Lieutenant Knight saw this and ordered half of F to close up on his rear, effectively merging the two companies into one. The F sections would be support for what remained of the broken D, now, like A, reduced to only about 100 men. The other half of the company extended on the left of D, making an effective, if thin, line over to Company I. (105, 137, 143, 146)

They only had to keep the Huns occupied long enough for the right echelon of the regiment to pass on that flank. There was no time to lose either. Colonel Stacey would soon be wanting to know if the flanking maneuver had been tried yet and Major Whittlesey considered the circumstances. Though he had little desire to attempt it, attempt it he must; those were the orders. If they had to try and punch through the line, better to attempt it now in the morning with fresh troops than in the afternoon with tired ones. Therefore, the Major sent orders out for renewed aggressiveness against the Hill 205 positions and the Giselher Stellung line. The regiment surged forward. (29, 246)

On the left, the Doughboys came down through the wilderness of the shallow northern slope of Hill 210 like furies. From behind, a 2nd Battalion Stokes mortar traveling with Company F threw shell after shell into the Giselher trench line ahead, but to little effect. The tree cover was too thick for accuracy. The heavy Hotchkiss gear (most of Company C/306th M.G. Bn.) chugged out rounds at a rapid rate, sawing through branches in the way, but the Germans fought back viciously, gave no ground, and then counterattacked. As the Doughboys came on, they were caught in an enfilading machine-gun crossfire, sweeping from atop Hill 205 and from the nests along its slope. The wave of khaki stopped as if slamming into a brick wall, fell to the ground, took what cover it could and slowly began to return fire. At the same time, the line of Doughboys moving up the ravine floor hit square at the Giselher line on their left front. Here, too, machine-gun and rifle volleys drove the khaki line to ground, this time the enfilade coming not only from their immediate front and the heights of Hill 205, but from Hill 198 on the right as well. Trying to flank the refused Giselher line by the right down the ravine bottom was useless. The Germans had wired it well all the way across the marsh for a depth of at least 20 meters. To try and cut through that mess would expose the men directly to the enfilading fire from both of the heights, without any cover at all, and cost a great many lives. Therefore, the left echelon was effectively stopped. Meanwhile, on the right, the advance was slogging through the marshy bottom and working against the wire leading to the ridgeline of Hill 198. It was a desperate bid to find a way through and attempt the flanking maneuver, but they too were making little more progress there than was anyone anywhere else in the ravine. (10, 91, 105, 137, 245, 246)

Major Whittlesey, in Battalion PC moving well up front between companies G and H, had little trouble getting all this information in good time, but it soon became obvious that the 308th's attack was stalling. The Germans were counter attacking all along the 308th's front and holding them firmly in place. There were also liaison reports coming in that the initial attack on the right by the 307th had been halted at the wire before Hill 198 as well. Therefore, with no apparent flank support to his east, Major Whittlesey was obviously reluctant to press the attack and carry on with the right flanking maneuver, despite the order to "advance without regard to flanks or losses." While it might yet be possible to pull it off, with the memory of September 28 still looming fresh. Coupled with the serious misgivings about the Charlevaux position that he had in the first place, it seemed too much like asking for the same problem again. On the other hand, any attack "north straight ahead up the ravine," as called for in yesterday's orders, would bring the command under the fire of the two opposite ridges. They would be wiped out in no time. While he understood that 'orders were orders' (few understood better in fact), the situation here seemed to go beyond that dictum and cross into the realm of operational suicide. Therefore, slightly before 10:00 a.m. the Major scribbled out a quick, carefully worded, note to the Colonel:

At: ravine bottom
Advance held up by machine gun fire from west along line 294.8 – 275.5.
Westward and north straight ahead progress impossible without aid from both flanks. (246)

Notice that Major Whittlesey does not discount the possibility of success using General Johnson's flanking maneuver eastward. On the contrary, he merely points out his inability to move up the middle and on the left. Then, he simply sidesteps the whole issue of the maneuver to the right by not mentioning it. This he perhaps did in the vain hope that without flank support from the 307th (which Colonel Stacey had to, by that time, be well aware of), it might then be deemed as an inadvisable action, as it should have been.

But there was another component of the plan that was obviously especially unappealing to Major Whittlesey as well; separation of his command. The havoc of dispersion in the first days of the battle, as well as the effect of the "splitting of the echelons" on the afternoon of the 28th, were lessons well learned. But, here, the orders were calling for him to divide his force again, albeit for a seemingly good reason, and this dragged heavily against the grain. Arriving across the Charlevaux Ravine without flank support was bad enough. But to then add to the difficulties by having his command situated in two different places, and only connected to the rear by a thin runner line, seemed to beg even more trouble from an already unstable situation.(II)

Therefore, Major Whittlesey dispatched a runner to take his message back to Sgt. Cahill at the telephone head, who in turn called it in to Colonel Stacey at Defsauer Platz. It was 10:10 a.m., and the advance up the ravine had hit an impasse. (29, 91, 245, 246)

By this time, so too had Colonel Cromwell Stacey's nerves. His adventures on the Marne the summer before had left him weakened and shaky, and he still had a rattling cough from the gassing he suffered there. Then, there had been the sudden transfer from his regiment, which had left him despondent; the very regiment he had helped form, bring across, and lead through its first trying battles. He had been happy with seasoned men he was proud to lead into battle and from whom he had the highest respect. Here, in the 308th, it had been a battle just to get the regiment to function as a unit, let alone fight, so disorganized had it been when he arrived. Additionally, no one here knew, nor cared, who he was.

There was also the incessant wrangling he felt he was forced to do with General Johnson at every turn. The Brigadier insisted on results, which on its own was only to be expected, but he also wanted *constant* and repeated updates, something that the Colonel felt he had little time to deal with in the middle of a battle. While he certainly respected General Johnson and was well aware that he was only doing what had to be done, with orders of his own to follow, it nevertheless seemed that the General did not fully appreciate the extreme circumstances under which the Colonel was forced to make his attacks, nor the inexperience of the soldiers making those attacks. Yet, what appalled Colonel Stacey the most, was the ostensibly reckless manner with which the Brigadier seemed to gamble with the lives of the men in his regiment in such questionable attacks as the one up the Ravin d'Argonne.

Finally, Colonel Stacey had recently received bad news from home from his sister, Delia. His mother, with whom he had always been particularly close, had taken gravely ill and it did not appear that she would be long of this world. Stacey then was in the absolute last place he wanted to be: Literally sick and tired; stuck in France in a regiment he did not particularly care for (or that particularly cared for him); in the midst of a battle he felt was being seriously mishandled; surrounded by infuriating officers who issued questionable orders, and other officers who questioned those he issued (most particularly Major Whittlesey); and with the lives of thousands of inexperienced and largely untrained soldiers resting on his shoulders, Colonel Cromwell Stacey's nerves were beginning to rapidly unravel...

Reading the message from Major Whittlesey handed to him by the telephone operator at about 10:15 a.m., Colonel Stacey could not have been very surprised, but in fact more likely had suspected that this would probably be the outcome of the morning attack. Yet, what bothered him was not that Major Whittlesey had been stopped, so much as that he had yet to try the flanking maneuver that had ordered. *And* the Major specifically mentioned wanting flank support, when the divisional orders just as specifically instructed him to push on regardless of flank support - which he was not doing. *Damn him!* This meant that Colonel Stacey's next move would be a particularly troubling one. General Johnson had already been hounding him for progress reports of the advance that morning. Now, the tired Colonel braced himself to call the Brigadier with the news of the stall in his sector, and the reasons for it. (238)

There was also trouble within Major Whittlesey's command as well, though he himself did not yet know it. Company D had rolled out of their holes and gotten moving in relatively good shape that morning, considering that the company was already down to just about half strength and those remaining were not in very good shape. Together with Company F, they plowed forward to meet whatever the Boche had in store for them along their difficult, steep side of the ravine. They advanced only a short distance, which brought them down the reverse slope of Hill 210 into a deep, narrow wash that cut between the hill behind them and the approaches of Hill 205 ahead of them, and drained to the right down into the main ravine. Crossing it would be tricky, but it had to be done. Doing so meant that the right lead platoon section, under Lt. Knight, would have to advance off the slope and onto the floor of the main ravine. Meanwhile, Lt. Turner would take the left platoon section down the slope of the wash itself; all under the watchful eyes of the German troops within the La Palette pavilion and the Hill 205 positions, a bare 300 meters ahead and to their left. Lieutenant Knight later wrote:

"To advance along the bottom of the ravine would (have been) suicide, as there was nothing then to prevent the enemy from surrounding us entirely. (However) at 8.15am we had advanced but a short distance along the hill on the right (the left slope of the ravine – author) when the expected resistance was met. The Germans could see us as we went across the ravine and occupied positions just above us. It was impossible to see them though they were just above us, but they must have had a wonderful view of us, for they showered us with hand grenades..." (105)

Left of Lt. Knight, Lt. Turner's troops stormed down the slope into the wash where they were stopped cold. Digging in, they began to pour fire onto the German positions ahead and hammered away steadily for an hour, but it was no contest. The Germans held every advantage. Meanwhile, to Lt. Turner's right, with his own casualties piling up Lt. Knight was forced to realize that there was no way that his company would be able to hold onto the position, even with Company F's assistance. He was also again out of touch with the now combined Battalion PC (nor had any runners left that knew the way anyhow; they had all been already killed or wounded). Therefore, Lt. Knight was unable to get word of his precarious situation to Major Whittlesey or Captain McMurtry. Yet, something had to be done and, orders or not, it was clear what that was; Knight gave the command for a general withdrawal. It was either that, or face complete annihilation.

Seeing the withdrawal, the Germans launched a counterattack and quickly gained a foothold of their own almost directly between the two platoon sections, and with a push, they fractured the American line. Unknowingly separated from Lt. Turner on his left, Lt. Knight continued to pull his force back. In the confusion, it was not until the withdrawal was complete that anyone realized what had happened, and by then it was too late to rectify the situation: Lt. Turner and the 14 men of the left platoon section (about all that then constituted the 2nd platoon out of D's four) had been cut off and surrounded by the enemy down within the wash, about 300 meters or so ahead of the fresh Company D main line. It was then nearly 10:00 a.m., and about the time that Major Whittlesey was sending the message of the stall back to Colonel Stacey. (10, 91, 105, 109, 123)

The morning had been unkind to the 307th, east of Colonel Stacey's line, too. From a line just about even with the 308th, Colonel Houghton had sent his men into battle with the 2nd Battalion as assault and the 3rd as support. The men of the 2nd Battalion had watched the morning artillery barrage with a dubious eye. Most of the shells seemed to be tearing down through the mist and into the German positions just *beyond* the belt of wire they had been up against the previous day, leaving the wire itself untouched. Stokes' mortar fire laid down helped little as well.

They moved out from just beyond a narrow wagon road, cutting across a flat, heavily wooded ridge top at 7:00 a.m. through the dense, rain-soaked undergrowth. Proceeding down a muddy slope and into a shallow ravine, they then came up against the belt at the foot of Hill 198. Hun trench mortar shells were sending geysers of dirt and steel in all directions as sprinting Doughboys rushed forward and went to work with wire cutters. Potato masher grenades tumbled through the air and machine-gun and rifle fire swept the brush around them. The Americans answered with Eddystone and Hotchkiss fire; Company A/306th MG Bn. men rammed 8mm ammunition through their machine-guns as fast as it was eaten up. The medics, too, were kept very busy.

Doggedly, the 2nd Battalion pushed the line until it again became clear that a single, under strength battalion could not do the job. Major McKinney sent Captain Blagden back to bring forward the 3rd Battalion and the 2nd then slid right and gave them the left flank of the regimental front. Company L was now on the far left, with Company H to their right, connecting with 2nd Battalion. Bisecting the incoming 3rd's front was the wagon road from atop the hill where it turned sharply south and headed down the slope. It ran between companies L and H, and made inter-battalion communication a difficult endeavor. Captain Rainsford illustrates the point in this field message he sent that morning: (103, 134, 235)

Am on this line (295.95-275.45) and Boche is putting minnenwerfers on us. MG's still in position and one is at bend of road ahead. Have tried to flank him every way, but he is covered by other guns and is hard to see in this brush. Can't locate (my) guns close enough to get them with Stokes and think artillery had better be put on them. But if so let us know in time to withdraw as it has a habit of hitting us… (103)

No artillery was forthcoming and soon, the shallow ditches on either side of the road were filling with the bodies of dead and dying runners. Additionally, liaison with the 308th to the left, never good to begin with, was lost completely as the 3rd filled the line. On the far right flank, only a tenuous line stretched back to the lagging 306th, from the 2nd Battalion. The state of affairs along the 307th's front was perhaps best described in these excerpts from a rather detailed situation report that Colonel Houghton sent back to General Johnson at about 9:20 a.m. that morning: (90)

M and K companies in support... have liaison together... H Company under heavy machine gun fire from north, also from east. Heavy machine gun fire from left seems to indicate that L Company has also met opposition. Am sending patrols northeast to develop situation there. Grant is getting in touch with Rainsford, who is attacking on the left, to help develop what is in front of him. I am giving H Company one platoon as they need it to extend. From volume of machine gun and rifle fire, also from the fact that the 77's are fairly close, I should report that our artillery was ineffective this morning... I may be able to work around the right though and fight it out with patrols. (131, 139)

Only on the left, where Captain Rainsford pushed with Company L, was any 'give' to the line felt at all. By mid-morning, with help from Captain Grant's Company H, Rainsford's men had pierced the wire in a couple small spots and managed to infiltrate a few men up the slope. The Captain soon realized, however, that with no communication to the 308th on his left, and only little to his right across the wagon road, his position offered nothing in the way of a real success. With no additional troops available to exploit the break, the rest of Company L could hardly hold on. Resistance from the German force above then seemed to stiffen considerably, until Captain Rainsford decided, around 10:00 a.m., that his best bet would be to pull his few men back down the slope through the gaps and regroup. Better that than to remain out front alone and risk getting cut off from around exposed flanks. By 10:30 a.m. then, he and his men were pulled back into almost their original positions and the Germans were repairing the gaps in the wire that they had left behind - all that there was to show for the company's morning efforts. (91, 103, 138)

However, Captain Rainsford's thrust up Hill 198 *had* had some effect, though not the effect that either he or the American command structure ever realized they might have been looking for in the first place. Once his Company L men had begun to seriously batter at the wire east of the 308th, and then actually make headway in spots, the Germans massed everything they could spare to bar the Doughboy's way there, and ultimately drive them back. However, it had been a close call, since the previous six days of defense, counterattack, and retreat had left the Germans in as sorry - if not sorrier - shape than their American counterparts. Little sleep, exposure to the elements, short rations, and constant movement, all by troops who had previously existed in primarily soft conditions, had taken a heavy toll. However, the main difficulty was that the Germans had even less in the way of reserves than the U.S. 77th Division had. German divisions, and as such their ancillary units, were half the size of American divisions to begin with (as were all military units of all the other European countries, except Russia). On top of that, by this point in the battle most German divisions were down to half strength of even that, meaning that a German company, which began the battle with a mere 120 men (as opposed to the 244 in a U.S. company), was now likely averaging between 60 or 70 men, 80 at the most. Reserves, similarly to the U.S. divisions in the offensive, were being created internally; one meager battalion (4 companies and a machine-gun company) from each regiment was held back. This further weakened their line. (121, 122)

With such a distinct disadvantage in numbers, only two things saved the German army in the Argonne then: the formidable terrain and the defenses they had set up there (along with their complete knowledge of them), combined with their ability to rapidly shift troops along the line to where they were needed most. They mostly held the American 154th Brigade at bay east of the Ravin d'Argonne with the 5th, 6th 7th, 10th, and 12th companies of the 122nd, generally in that order. (The 8th Company was then providing reserves.) Next to them, to the east, was the 120th. However, all along there was considerable

236

confusion in the German trenches along the ridge and much moving of units to and fro, mostly in order to counter the most serious of threats being made at different points along the line.

While the 7th, 10th, and 12th companies/122nd were busy slamming away at the rest of the 307th, Captain Rainsford's somewhat off-course men of Company L/307th (they were actually attacking slightly within the 308th's right flank zone of advance at one point) initiated their assault from what they thought was their own left flank. This caused a minor German panic. Ahead of them was the under strength 6th Company under Lt. Fritz. When he saw the Americans before him making headway into his wire, he immediately requested assistance from his neighbors on either side. The 7th Company, to the east, was busily occupied with its own problems, but the 5th to his west, under Lt. Gobel, was only sporadically being engaged against the 308th, which was struggling to go anywhere at all. Well supported ahead and slightly west by the machine-gun section from the 254th that had arrived the day before, they could be spared then to lend aid and quickly hustled down the trench line east to Lt. Fritz's area. There they helped to drive Captain Rainsford's Company L/307th men back from the brink of full penetration of the line by a thrust made forward from just west of 6th Company. The 5th Company then filed back toward their own positions once the American attack died off late that morning. Both German commanders were pleased by the success of the arrangement and the knowledge that it could be repeated again if need be for any afternoon attack the Americans might make. (120, 123, 124, 128)

West of the ridgeline of Hill 198, General Freiherr Quandt-Wykradt-Huchtenbruck's 76th Reserve Division was desperately fending off French attacks against the southwestern and western sides of Hill 205. At the same time, they were trying to keep the Americans at bay within the Ravin d'Argonne and off the southeastern side of the hill. His artillery (the 56th Reserve Field Artillery Regiment) was flailing both armies murderously, particularly the Americans struggling up the ravine east of Hill 205. He seemed, at least for the moment, to be holding all of his enemies in check. This was much to his credit, as off the western flank of his portion of the line, the German front had already been severely bent back on itself and the French were knocking on the door of Lancon with their rifle butts. Additionally, to the east of the Argonne Forest, the Americans were already well beyond Montfaucon and pushing up the Aire Valley, an incredible achievement. Along the front of the 76th Reserve Division of Hesse however, though there had been some give, there had been no breakthrough. (123)

This was primarily due to the division's excellent Chief of Staff, Hauptmann Friedrich Wilhelm Von Sybel, who as C.o.S. was also chief Operations Officer for the 76th. Over the past few days, he had seen to it that the line of the 76th had been handled as efficiently as possible, utilizing his few troops to the best advantage, even during the unavoidable initial pull back. Once the German army had been forced back in the Argonne to the Haupt-Widerstands-Lienie, he had recognized Hill 205 and the La Palette Pavilion as the single most important defensive positions in his area of operations, and had made every effort to exploit them to his advantage. (Such was a similar case with the Operations Officer for the 122nd Regiment, Hauptmann Von Wiedenbach, who had surmised that the ridge of Hill 198 was his regiment's key defensive point.) Basically, facing the French in the open areas west of the hill, Hauptmann Von Sybel had garrisoned the 253rd regiment. Their orders were clear; they might let the enemy take Binarville if need be, but they were to allow them no progress beyond the ruined town. Next, he had made the hill and pavilion itself the responsibility of Major Hunicken's 254th. Their job was equally clear; if the hill fell to the enemy, the last major holdout portion of the Giselher Stellung would be lost and the way left wide open to the Kriemhilde Stellung in the 76th's sector. Therefore, the hill must be held and the 254th should dedicate itself to destruction before withdrawal. Since the threat from the Americans was not considered as great as from the French, he had allowed Major Hunicken to shift the bulk of his troops to the western side of the hill. Anyway, it would be an easy enough proposition to move them back if need be. Finally, he kept the 252nd regiment in divisional reserve, moving them back and forth where needed, as with his remaining reserves: a battalion of divisional pioneer infantry, the 376th, and two companies of detached pioneer infantry, the 76th, and 77th. Communications between the 254th and the 122nd across the Ravin d'Argonne were good, as was cooperation. Along with a line well fitted with trench mortars and machine-guns, the system of defense seemed almost insurmountable.

Hauptmann Von Sybel however, was accomplishing the great task of organizing the divisional lines in the sector only by proxy. The task should really have belonged to the 1st Reserve Corps Operations Officer, Major Becker, except that Becker had recently been transferred to an Army Group staff job. His replacement, Major Von Ditfurth, had only just arrived and did not yet know the sector clearly. Therefore the job fell naturally to the divisional men under him (though with Major Von Ditfurth well informed of all movements) and Hauptmann Von Sybel, along with the 76th's Divisional Intelligence Officer, Hauptmann Rienhard Bickel, had so far accomplished it with extreme competency. Sitting tight between the 118th Regiment of the 9th Landwehr to the west and the 122nd/2nd Landwehr to the east, all seemed as secure as could be. (120, 121, 123, 124)

Yet, Hauptmann Von Sybel and Hauptmann Bickel were worried, mostly because the Americans simply would not stop attacking and seemed to be a bottomless pit of manpower. Being aware of their own disappearing numbers, how long could they expect to hold out then? Not since the beginning of the war had they seen such large individual units or such recklessness in attack. The Americans simply kept coming, long after the French or Russians would have turned away, and they seemed willing to accept that casualties were part of the game. Additionally, aerial photographs showed massive amounts of American artillery behind the lines slowly being moved up, almost by the hour. That could only presage a massive assault to come against this last holdout portion of the Giselher Stellung. On the other hand, several ragged prisoners taken in the last day or two commented on the sorry state of some of their companies and that the U.S. high command had made a mistake and underestimated both the projected length of the battle as well as the amount of supplies needed. High casualties, lack of rapid food and ammunition resupply, general unpreparedness… Perhaps that might be the 'edge' then that their own under-strength companies needed to succeed over the Americans.

Still, they needed to be as well prepared as they could be, no matter what the state of the American army. The morning attack that the Doughboys launched had been strong in spots, after a couple days of relative ease in the general area during the draw back. Only the distraction of a small American force, which they had kept from harassing their draw-back efforts by briefly surrounding, had been the real action this far up the ravine. In any case, they must now be fully prepared everywhere to face the coming assault on the Stellung line, leaving nothing to chance. The thinnest portion currently was that over on the shoulder of Hill 198. Major Hunicken had earlier sent an understrength 254th machine-gun section from his 3rd Company to cover the seam there between the 76th and the 2nd Landwehr, working in conjunction with a company of the 122nd. Though the U.S. attacks so far that day had not really been focussed in that area, one never knew what might happen. Therefore, Hauptmann Von Sybel called Major Hunicken and asked him to send a few sniper parties into the area, to further bolster support. The Major agreed, and sent one or two parties of four or five men each fanning out into strategic positions. By late morning, everything seemed pretty much as in order to thwart any assaults made into the area as could be at the time. (122, 123, 128)

Meanwhile, General Johnson was in the process of packing to move his Brigade PC farther forward when Colonel Stacey called him with the morning's bad news. The General took it better than the Colonel had expected. Stacey explained his regiment's position as Johnson listened in stony silence and then simply hung up. A mud-stained runner, sent by Colonel Houghton, had been standing next to the Brigadier only minutes earlier with details of an identical stall that the 307th was then facing. With neither regiment moving, there was nothing to do but face the inevitable and call General Alexander with the bad news. Ringing up Division PC only to find the division commander out at the moment, General Johnson no doubt breathed a small sigh of relief and then left a short message containing only the bare facts that the assault in the 154th Brigade's sector had stalled and then set out for his new forward PC.

General Alexander got General Johnson's message at about 10:30 a.m. and, by all accounts, promptly hit the roof. A similar message had just been received from General Whittenmeyer commanding the 153rd Brigade as well, and therefore things, at least in General Alexander's eyes, could not have been worse. He knew that there had already been reports coming in to 1st Corps PC that morning stating that the advance was grinding to a standstill all up and down the Corps line after but a few hours of attack and that General Pershing was livid over it. In the zone immediately surrounding the 77th, while the 28th Division had begun to move up the Aire Valley with their right flank, their left flank nevertheless remained mired in the eastern third of the Argonne at a place called Le Chene Tondu. Compounding this problem, as evidenced by this most recent report, the 77th's own 153rd Brigade was not faring any better. In fact, while dismally on an even line with that laggard left flank of the 28th Division, they were also actually to the *rear* of their neighboring 154th by at least a half a kilometer. That was bad enough. But now to discover that in the zone of the 154th Brigade things were only mildly better, only worsened the situation. Latest word was that the French on the 154th's left had finally made it as far as Lancon with their left flank, outdistancing the 77th's left flank by at least *4 kilometers*. This fact, coupled with the holdup on the division's right, now made the whole of the 77th look slack. (This, even though the French *right flank* was still floundering in the mud above Binarville under the machine-gun fire of Hill 205 and also still a short distance *behind* the left of the 308th - something that General Alexander was fully aware of.) Therefore, with the units on either side of the 77th pulling ahead of them, all reasons and local facts and difficulties would be swept aside, and General Alexander knew full well that he would have a lot of explaining to do if things did not get moving again. After all, General Pershing was already sending out orders that fairly smoked on the paper, urging his commanders to drive their divisions on faster and farther, and which seemingly promised demotion and humiliation to those who did not hold up their end of the great attack. (Nor was the AEF commander indifferent to replacing laggard division commanders, as previously discussed.) (10, 91, 131, 144)

Perhaps then it was some measure of vanity that made General Alexander's next move what it was. There is, after all, ample evidence that the General was very 'aware' of himself.(III) Certainly he knew that it was his duty to move his division forward by any means at his disposal, and casualties be damned where there was a larger picture involved. Some perhaps may also accuse him of over-action in this next move, but in reality the situation *needed* a strong, aggressive division commander to drive men through the hell of the Argonne. And despite any criticism or faultfinding over the execution of his next decision (and there would be plenty of both in the post war years), General Alexander never once doubted that what he did next was the *correct* course of action. Indeed, he defended it until his death.

His move? General Alexander, lied.

Telephoning General Johnson's PC he fumed, "Where is General Johnson?"

The man who had unsuspectingly answered the phone was Captain Medley G. Whelpley, the 152nd Field Artillery Brigade Liaison Officer assigned to General Johnson's 154th Infantry Brigade.

"Sir, the General is on his way to the new Brigade PC at Fontaine aux Charmes and should arrive there shortly."

"What is the 154th doing?" General Alexander asked, and Captain Whelpley explained that last he knew the brigade had moved forward behind the artillery barrage and had been halted, in liaison with the 153rd Brigade behind on the right and with the French well to the rear on the left.

Nonplussed, Alexander replied, "You tell General Johnson that the 154th Brigade is holding back the French on the left and holding back everything on the right, and that the 154th Brigade must push forward to their objective today! By 'must' I mean 'must' and by 'today' I mean 'today' and not next week. You report heavy machine-gun fire, but your casualties do not substantiate this. Remember that when you are making these reports. I have not yet received the casualty reports that I asked for last night."

Captain Whelpley, as tactfully as he could, allowed that the reports had been ordered turned in upon receipt of the General's request and that everything that could be done to expedite the reports, was being done. However, the General needed to understand that it was "very difficult for the front line companies to get in reports of that character, especially at night."

It was the wrong thing to say to Alexander at the wrong time.

"If the company commanders cannot make reports any more quickly than this then there is something wrong with the control of their companies!" the irritated division commander said, and the line went dead. (2, 93, 131, 144, 150)

As explained, General Alexander knew full well that neither the French nor the 153rd were being held up by the actions of the 154th. They might be in the future however, if that brigade remained stalled. For that reason alone, there could be no holdup in the offensive by any unit anywhere along his portion of the line, as far as he was concerned. Later on General Alexander would state that he "coincided with the belief expressed by both army and corps headquarters that the enemy was in retreat". It was true that the Germans had been in retreat to the Giselher Stellung in days previous, but that was obviously as far as they had gone; a fact born out by the heavy fighting his units were now encountering. He would further claim that he believed that his flanks would be well taken care of by his "own people." Again, there is ample evidence to suggest he should have known otherwise. Whether he actually believed any of what he later said or not is open to some debate. It would appear inconceivable that a division commander, who made almost daily trips to his front, after seven days of hard fighting could be that far out of touch with the local realities of his assault battalions. On the other hand, General Alexander would certainly not be the first General in the A.E.F. to twist facts in order to spur a subordinate into action. After all, this was war, results were what counted and ethics be damned. Whatever the truth, General Alexander was determined to get the 154th Brigade up and moving forward as quickly as possible - any way that he could.(IV) (2)

It was just after 11:00 a.m. when General Johnson got to his new PC and was handed General Alexander's message, which he no doubt read in grim silence. It was inconceivable to him that the 154th could be holding up the line; Colonel Stacey's last reports put the French at least 500-600 meters off to the rear of the left flank of his advance elements. And as for the right flank of the brigade, Colonel Houghton would have definitely made mention of it if the 153rd had had any momentum, and he had last reported them *behind* his right flank. Could the 153rd then have actually broken out far enough ahead to be held up by some sort of immobility of the 154th? Even when the standing orders called for "advance without regard to flanks"? Only if there had been a major turnaround in action during the short, half-hour ride up the Fontaine aux Charmes could that be possible, which seemed highly unlikely. General Johnson was therefore positive that the 153rd was facing just as much resistance as was the 154th, if not more, and simply could not be held up by his brigade.

Yet, whether he believed what General Alexander had stated (and he did not; not in the least) was beside the point. The central point was that the division commander obviously expected the 154th to attack. There could be no explanations, excuses, or failures. Bound then by duty, it was his job to see that the General's wishes were carried out. Knowing that it was not going to be an easy call, when General Johnson next telephoned General Alexander it was going on 11:10 a.m. The Brigadier reported a long litany of details concerning the morning attack, some good, some bad. Ultimately, however, he was forced to admit that the brigade had come to a definite standstill in the face of determined German counter resistance. (131, 144)

There was no pause, nor hesitation, on Alexander's part.

"General, that will not do. If that line does not move, I will have to get somebody up there to command it! That line has got to move," General Alexander began, before continuing with orders for an afternoon attack.

"You have the command reorganized for an advance. Your orders are at 12:30 p.m. there will be an artillery preparation of 20 minutes put down in front of the line. Move forward at 12:50 p.m. at the rate of 100 yards in 5 minutes to point on the map... (Here Alexander paused and checked his map before continuing.) It may be designated generally as a point on a parallel with 276.2, where it will stand 10 minutes and then raise. Infantry is to follow the barrage as closely as possible as far as the first objective, the road and railroad, which generally speaking runs generally 276.5. At that place they will halt and establish liaison right and left, reorganize and prepare for further advance under orders, which will be later given." he concluded, also stating that the French had already taken Lancon and were on a line 279.0, according to their aerial reports.

General Johnson answered back, laconically, "If you can tell me how in a dense forest an aeroplane can see his men, I will be much obliged. If you can tell me how shellfire can be effective when it cannot be directed, I will be much obliged." It was obvious that he did not believe the French; not in the least.

"General, that line has got to move," General Alexander interrupted. "You can let your Colonels know that that line has got to move. If that line does not move, they will! Push it along! Everything to the right and left is ahead of you; the French are in Lancon and the 153rd Brigade is in advance of the 154th's position. You are to advance your position - *regardless of your flanks or losses* - and if you can not do it I will get someone who can! Is that clear, General?"

General Johnson, no doubt seething inside, acknowledged in the affirmative and General Alexander hung up. (131, 144, 238, 246)

It was about 11:20 a.m. when the Brigadier placed his next call, to Colonel Stacey at Defsauer Platz, and prepared himself for some sort of argument or apprehension such as he had received the afternoon before when he had issued the orders sending the 308th into the Charlevaux Ravin in the first place. He was somewhat surprised then, when instead all he got was simple, tired acknowledgment. Colonel Stacey merely listened, there apparently being no point in arguing, and then made some left-handed inquiry concerning his flanks one last time, since he was sure that Major Whittlesey would ask. The Colonel also asked again for the order in writing. General Johnson merely echoed General Alexander's words, apprehensively assuring the Colonel that his regiment's flanks would be "well cared for" by his "own people" and said he'd send a runner out with the order right away. With everything apparently set in the 308th's zone then, General Johnson hung up and then called Colonel Houghton over at the 307th with the orders for the afternoon attack there. (131, 238)

"Colonel, I have given all the coordinates to the artillery," the Brigadier began, and laid out the fire and movement instructions. "The movement will be coordinated between your regiment and that of the 308th, which will advance at the same time and under the same conditions," the General continued. "The movement forward will commence by the infantry at 12:50 p.m. The men must creep up close to the barrage, Colonel, and the moment it ceases, you must leap forward and follow it. They will advance as far as the road and railroad 276.5, halt, reorganize, get liaison right and left and await further orders."

Colonel Houghton was much more matter of fact about the orders than had been Colonel Stacey, however. Never a man to mince words, he told General Johnson in no uncertain terms about the position his regiment was then engaged against. The German line ahead, he explained, was so heavily wired in and so accurately defended with intense trench mortar, machine-gun, and artillery fire, that he seriously doubted his regiment's ability to drive through it in their present understrength, exhausted state. And Colonel Houghton was definitely one man in the 154th Brigade who knew what he was talking about. (131, 139, 144)

Eugene M. Houghton could have been the model for the classic turn of the century adventurer. Born in Racine, Wisconsin, he had already scouted for gold in the Yukon, explored parts of the Canadian wilderness, and done a turn as a soldier of fortune in the Philippines (where he had picked up a case of recurrent Malaria), all before the Great War had broken out. By 1914, he was in Minnesota working as a lumberjack when hostilities began. Unable to remain out of it, 1915 found him enlisted in the Canadian army as a private, where he was among one of the first Canadian drafts to sail for France. He spent the next three years in front line service with the British forces in Belgium, going over the top on at least 17 occasions (including the fantastic Canadian assault up Vimy Ridge). A high attrition rate meant that he quickly rose through the ranks to officer status. By the time America got into the fighting and he transferred over to the AEF, Houghton was one of the last survivors of his original Canadian unit. He had been wounded at least twice (some sources say as many as four times) and had been decorated with the British Military Medal for valor.

His transfer to the AEF came through just as the 77th Division arrived in Belgium to train with the British. Immediately assigned to the division, he became Divisional Machine Gun Officer, staying at the post through the fighting at Baccarat and onto the Vesle, where he was given the 307th to command just before the advance to the Aisne. He was a serious, muscular, 'tough customer', of medium height with brown hair and cropped mustache, piercing brown eyes, usually described as "fidgety" and very powerful of personality. What he said he meant, and few there were that would risk arguing with him; the main exception being his own personal and totally dedicated 'batman' who had followed him over from the Canadian army, a diminutive Chinese named Lee, with whom he joked almost constantly, especially during his occasional Malaria attacks. ("I don't know who's more yellow today; me or you!" he would say, to which Lee would only stare wisely into Houghton's sweaty, hued face and predict an early death.) (2, 60, 103, 238, 245, 358, 359, 360)

When he talked to Colonel Houghton that day, the clock was just passing 11:30 a.m. and General Johnson, who had just finished getting his ass chewed by General Alexander, was in no mood to argue. He was also very much aware that Colonel Houghton's personality was not as fragile as that of Colonel Stacey, who lately had been exhibiting some of the classic signs of the then-unnamed malady, to be later known as "battle fatigue." The Colonel had his orders, General Johnson said shortly to Houghton, and would be expected to carry them out. There would be no holdups or excuses tolerated! Colonel Houghton, realizing he would get nowhere fast with the Brigadier, made no further comment other than to also inquire about his flanks, as had Colonel Stacey. When told that he should not have any problems on his right since the 153rd was well up past his line, there simply came a muttered string of almost unintelligible curses. Then the line went dead in General Johnson's ear before he could even mention the lie about the French. (138, 139)

By that time, the French 71st Division (under whose aegis the area west actually fell) was indeed on a line about even with Lancon and did have possession of the town - on their left at least. On their right, it was a much different story. There, the French 9th C.a.P that morning had no direct liaison with the 308th Infantry on their right, only some sporadic local bits and pieces directly with 77th Division PC through General Alexander's French agent to the 9th's Binarville PC, one Lt. Andre De Coppett. It was a tangled mess in front of Hill 205 between the 9th and the 308th. Binarville itself was still under considerable shellfire, the French line was barely 200 meters north of town and no one on either side was entirely sure where the dividing line between the two great armies ran, only that it was east of the town limits. Not that it mattered much, since wherever it ran, Hill 205 was sure to be in its path and it did not look like anyone would be taking that formidable position anytime soon.

That morning, the 9th C.a.P. had orders to bring its right up beyond Hill 205 in a joint effort with the left of the U.S. 77th Division, aimed at flanking the heavily fortified hill position. East of Hill 205, an American force was to move forward down the Ravin d'Argonne with orders to obtain the objective of reaching the Binarville-Moulin de Charlevaux road at the Charlevaux Mill itself. There, they would form liaison with an advanced right element of the 9th C.a.P. That advanced right element was to be initially a single French infantry company, meant to punch a narrow hole in the German line at a strategic point, through which reinforcements could be moved. Moving behind the main line, they were to work their way forward fast along the road heading north out of Binarville to the fork where one road ran left to Autry and the other right toward the Moulin de Charlevaux. Crossing the line and taking the road on the right toward the Mill, the company would then push down the hill and through the forest, working forward and cutting a narrow seam between the Tranchee de Charlevaux on their left and Hill 205 on their right. Thus, they would flank both the nasty German positions, something a larger force could not accomplish but that the smaller force stood a good chance of pulling off. Once beyond, a short distance down the ravine, they would meet up with the Americans either at the Charlevaux Mill, or at least along the road. More French troops would then follow, pouring through the gap that the assault company had driven and the line would mushroom into the German back area. With the line extended on both sides, the Germans would be surrounded within their difficult hilltop position on the wrong side of the main battle line. The 9th's right flank would then be poised to make a push around the Etang de Poligny (The Pond of Poligny; a small water obstacle that presented the French with its own set of problems) while the Americans simultaneously pushed up the Mont de Charlevaux.

The assault company of the 9th C.a.P. started out early that morning behind a magnificent barrage, which had been fleshed out by U.S. machine-gunners and heavy artillery. It passed beyond Rome Farm just above Binarville before turning toward the line and advancing. German resistance was stiff as they cut their way through a wide belt of thick barbed wire near the fork in the road and began to push along the narrow, muddy Binarville-Moulin de Charlevaux road, sticking to the woods on the left of the roadway. They took fire from both sides, as the Germans operating in the Tranchee de Charlevaux on their left, thought them to be a flanking element of the main body of French troops that were attacking across their whole front, sent to try and push up the road and around the east end of the trench. No matter, however, as men from the German 253rd took up positions around the trench to stop them from behind another barbed wire belt.

More fire came from a narrow, short enemy trench on an even line with the Tranchee de Charlevaux. A short distance beyond, the road made a sharp hairpin loop that cut directly behind a second, stronger trench line on Hill 205. On the map, the attacking French force saw that the loop merely followed a contour of the sharp slope leading down into the Charlevaux Ravine, then only some 300-400 meters ahead. Once down there, it was but a sharp turn to the east and a drive up the ravine bottom for about half a kilometer to the mill and the waiting Americans. So close, yet so far! It would be suicide to attempt to follow the road—the road loop was under direct enemy observation and they would be cut to pieces in minutes. No, they must move through the woods of the slope, straight ahead into the ravine.

But the woods were full of barbed wire and they stalled, forced to drop to the ground and begin carving a way through. Meanwhile, enemy trench mortars from Hill 205 opened up, got the range good and quick, and began to plaster the French troops. Under the murderous barrage, confusion reined as the one lone officer of the company tried desperately to keep his men calm and focused, while the leaden sky above the meager tree cover rained shrapnel - and then suddenly stopped. Then machine-guns opened up on them, first from behind, then from the sides, and then from the front. *Merde! (Shit!)* They were surrounded. (10, 92, 146)

To borrow an old pilot's descriptive term, the dawn had again brought 'pissy' flying weather that day; more clouds, more mist, more rain. Still, through the drizzle, Lieutenant Morse's men managed to drag a few of the big DH-4 Liberty's into the air. Infantry contact patrols had actually improved some over the past couple days, as the 50th had sent forward a series of observers, acting as liaison agents, into the trenches. Their job was to try and impress upon the infantry commanders the great necessity of firing their flares and showing their panels when they were called for. And the program was actually bearing fruit. In the zone of the 308th Infantry though, ground contact remained sporadic at best since no liaison men from the squadron had ever made it up to Major Whittlesey's position in the Ravin d'Argonne. In fact, that left zone between the 77th Division and the French as a whole remained a difficult area for the flyers. It was beginning to require an inordinate amount of attention, and only occasionally would they get an answering rocket or see a panel down in the dank forest. Additionally, the area was literally crawling with the enemy, particularly upon a high piece of ground at the southwest corner of a junction where two ravines crossed paths, marked on their maps simply as "La Palette." The closer the infantry advanced to that damned hill, the heavier the ground fire and the greater the risk of getting knocked down, since they were forced to fly so low to spot the line by direct sight.(V)

It was early that morning that Lt. Morse himself was out flying around that piece of ground in the misty fog looking for the line, with Lt. Stewart Bird as observer. Below, the battle was raging through the forest, exploding shells tearing the air, smoke and mist shrouding the area. Where was the line? Who knew? Suddenly, there was a sharp 'whap', and a big hole appeared in the right-hand lower wing of the plane. Lt. Morse, startled, immediately and gently pulled the plane around in a wide turn and headed back for Remicourt. The mission had been a wash; they had seen not a single panel or rocket, despite repeated calls for the line. On the other hand, they did have a German shell pass right through their wing.

Damned Boche. (110, 249)

Second Lieutenant Sherman W. Eager trudged through the mud down the bottom of the Ravin d'Argonne at Major Whittlesey's side, struggling to keep pace with the Major's long-legged gait. Lieutenant Eager was a new officer, one of three that had come up from Division PC the night before. He had reported to the Combined Battalion PC dugout at l'Homme Mort about 10:30 p.m.; just in time to hear Captain Weld deliver the disquieting advance orders for the morning of the 2nd. Entering the service in Indianapolis, Lt. Eager was of medium height and build, and possessed a fine intellectual character and great spirit of adventure. He was bumming around Australia when America declared war and immediately returned home and applied for the Officer Training Course at Fort Benjamin Harrison in Indiana. However, at 29 he was rejected at the time as too old! When a second call for recruits went out in August 1917, he again volunteered and this time was accepted. By February 1918, he was the Regimental Intelligence Officer for the 366th Infantry/92nd Division, and with them he sailed for France that June. After seeing some initial, minor action that summer in the Vosges sector he, along with two other officers of the regiment, received orders at the end of September sending them to the 77th Division, then engaged in the Argonne.

Arriving at Defsauer Platz on the evening of October 1, Colonel Stacey decided to take one of the three new officers, a Lt. Heitman, and place him in charge of the 37mm 'one pounder' outfit. Lieutenant Eager and the other officer, 2nd Lt. Victor Harrington, after a bite to eat, were assigned a guide to take them forward to Major Whittlesey's PC on l'Homme Mort. Lieutenant Eager later vividly described the trip up to Defsauer Platz and then on to l'Homme Mort:

"Going out through this woods, and it was dark by this time, there were a lot of big shell holes, and we would fall in the shell holes and stumble along and the guide took us from number 1 to number 2; then another one picked us up and took us from number 3 and number 4… we went through about 10 posts and we got up to the 10th and the men on duty up there were about asleep. We got them woke up… and reached Major Whittlesey and Captain McMurtry…about 10.30 at night on October 1st, 1918… at that time they were in some small buildings along the foot of this hill, and I could hear the German shells going over and landing on the hill just above us… I didn't realize until the next morning how dangerous it was at this place and that they were on the wrong side of the hill, but the next morning I found out…" (234)

Early that next morning, Major Whittlesey assigned Lt. Eager to Company G and sent Lt. Harrington over to Company E just before the jump-off. By noon, the two green officers had experienced their first Argonne fight. With the advance at a stand still, Major Whittlesey was up among Company G's ranks, inspecting the situation and doling out words of encouragement, when Lt. Eager hailed him.

"Doesn't this outfit ever eat?" the new lieutenant asked, only half jokingly.

Major Whittlesey looked up and smiled only briefly.

"Oh, there will be food up after while," he said.

(It would be six more days before Eager would get his meal.) (161, 184, 234)

Just then, a runner trotted up with a message for the Major from Sergeant Cahill's telephone head at the advanced combined Battalion PC. Major Whittlesey scanned the message and Lt. Eager saw his jaw visibly stiffen. It was orders from Colonel Stacey for the afternoon assault, written out in Cahill's careful, delicate script. They were to attack anyway, despite all Major Whittlesey had reported of the conditions that morning… (234)

To: C.O. 1st Bn 308
Time: 11.35am
The commanding general is dissatisfied with your rate of progress.
Therefore the advance of infantry will commence at 12.50 – At 12.30 an artillery barrage will start and will last 20 minutes, then it will move forward every 5 minutes until 276.2 is reached.
There it will stand 10 minutes and then stop.

The infantry attack will be pushed forward until it reaches the line of the road and railroad generally along 276.5 where the command will halt, reorganize, establish liaison right and left, and be ready for orders for a further advance.

This does not change the plan as given you by Detroit 1. You still leave two companies on your left as a containing force and push forward on your right with the remainder of your force, that is the remainder of 1 & 2 Bns.

The general says that you are to advance behind the barrage regardless of losses. He states there will be a general advance along the line.

Our planes have gone over and I don't think you will be bothered by Boche planes.

Detroit 1 (131, 238, 246)

Looking up from the message, with obvious disquiet cutting deeply across his face, Major Whittlesey glanced in Lt. Eager's direction and gestured with the message in his hand. "Walk along with me back to this as I wish to talk to you along the way," he said calmly and turned toward the rear. (234)

Now, Lt. Eager was squelching through the mud at Major Whittlesey's side on the way back to the telephone station, with Private Jim Larney, the 1st Battalion signalman, following. Bullets zinged around them and shells, exploding farther up the ravine, sent showers of dirt and debris falling back through the leaves of the trees as Lt. Eager struggled to keep up with the Major (when uptight, Charles Whittlesey's walk was many people's run). The Major seemed to hardly notice the war around him however. In a still and calm, but distracted voice, he presented innocuous questions to the green officer. Was he married? How long had he been in the service? Seen much action? What had he done before the war? For all the concern the Major showed for his surroundings, Lt. Eager thought, he and Major Whittlesey might have been taking a stroll down some country road back home. (234)

Presently, they arrived at the combined Battalion PC, really nothing more than a shell hole scrapped clean in the sodden ground under a convenient large bush near the middle of the ravine, and Major Whittlesey asked Sergeant Cahill if he would please ring up the Regimental PC. Captain McMurtry was already squatting nearby, in fact had been inspecting support company positions behind when the message had first come through and had already seen it. He stood up now and exchanged a hard, concerned look with Major Whittlesey, while Private Prescott fiddled with the wires and Sergeant Cahill put through the call. Neither said anything.

The operator on duty at Defsauer Platz who answered the call that midday was Private Robert Marchant. Sergeant Cahill, observing strict telephone protocol, asked Pvt. Marchant for Colonel Stacey by his code name, "Detroit 1," saying "Detroit-Red" was on the line and then handed the phone to Major Whittlesey. Colonel Stacey broke away from a discussion he was having with Father Halligan to take the handset from Pvt. Marchant and he and the Major then had a spirited, rapid conversation. Major Whittlesey obviously recognized that this was his last opportunity to get the orders changed, as Captain McMurtry, Sgt. Cahill, Pvt. Prescott, Lt. Eager, and Pvt. Larney looked on in the sodden forest ravine. On the other end, in the Defsauer Platz bunker Colonel Stacey, exasperated at having the same argument over virtually the same orders as the day before, instantly burned bright. Could Major Whittlesey not see that there was nothing he could do to get the orders changed? He had already tried and was in no mood to debate the point with him yet again! As Pvt. Marchant and Father Halligan listened, the short argument took on an eerie similarity to the one that the two officers had had the previous night.

Finally, in exasperation, Major Whittlesey pronounced, "It will only lead to the same thing again. We'll be cut off!"

Colonel Stacey replied irritably, "You're just getting panicky. Proceed with the attack as ordered Major."

There was a short pause, and then Major Whittlesey said sharply, "Alright, I'll attack; but whether you'll hear from me again I don't know!"

Tossing the handset to Sgt. Cahill, he beckoned to Captain McMurtry and Lt. Eager and, turning, stalked back up toward the main line through the mud.

It was just passing noon. (29, 218, 234, 238, 245, 246)

(I) That Major Whittlesey only left two companies along the western ridge of Hill 210, facing Hill 205, to work in conjunction with the French is indicative of two things. First, it is obvious that he had little faith in the likely success of French efforts in that direction and therefore putting more of what little manpower he had over there simply seemed a waste. (Indeed, by all accounts no one had any faith in French success over there.) After all, there was already going to be, besides D and F, the majority of Company I from the 3rd Battalion over there, which had been doing liaison duty to the French in the area. (Since the 307th had come up on the right, there had no longer been a need for the Company I liaison men over there and they had been redirected over to the left.) That made three U.S. companies over there to assist in that debacle. Second, and more importantly, Major Whittlesey was very aware that his men would face a difficult task moving against Hill 198, and with his company strengths already depleted by the last six days' fighting, both of the battalions were going to need all the hands they could spare to bring the right flank maneuver to fruition. One can see how difficult a position the Major was in then, having to send D and F into a battle that had little apparent chance of success, and then sending the rest of his men against a position that he obviously believed would require more men than he had.

(II) Yet, the fact of the matter was that there were no other real options for breaking the Giselher Stellung at that point except by a direct, frontal assault enhanced by local variations, especially since the artillery was still of little *real* use in the dense forest. And the flanking maneuver was a good local variation, with a better than average chance for success, whether Major Whittlesey liked it or not. However, without flank support, it would necessarily leave the attacking force in a virtually untenable position, something Colonel Stacey himself had already recognized and had emphasized to General Johnson on the afternoon of the 1st. And, as we have seen, Major Whittlesey had argued this point with Stacey over that night as well. Unfortunately, the point was made totally moot by the general attack order to "advance without regard to flanks or losses"; a blanket order that does not take into account local variations of battle, such as faced here.

(III) One of Major Whittlesey's officers, Lt. Sherman W. Eager, later commented that he was of the opinion that "General Alexander would have lined all his men up and shot every one of them if he thought it would have gotten him a promotion." Quite the damning statement, to be sure! General Alexander was also fully aware by that point that the Doughboys of the 77th were very tired (in truth exhausted was more the word) and the units severely beaten up. Most companies in the assault battalions were down to just over a hundred men each now, and none had a full compliment of officers. The task before them then, particularly in the 308th's zone on the left, seemed almost Herculean.

(IV) Shortly after this call was placed to General Johnson's PC, General Alexander also called General Whittenmeyer's PC and gave him an earful too, making much the same extravagant claims about the 153rd holding up *its* flanks. This was just as much claptrap over there as it was in the 154th's zone. The 153rd was holding back neither the left flank of the 28th Division, nor the right of the 154th Brigade – the German defenses were, and nothing more or less. Nor was it a lack of effective leadership by the line officers, or a lack of effort on the part of the individual Doughboys, as is sometimes rumored to have been the case.

(V) To illustrate the sort of problems the flyers faced: in one unnamed infantry battalion, it was discovered that instructions had been given to them to use their signal flares only at night, as they could not be seen during the day - something that was not true at all. Therefore, they had simply never fired any since no calls had come after dark. This situation was quickly corrected and from then on that particular battalion commander took great delight in firing off his Very lights whenever called for, rather than just dragging them around uselessly. And, as explained before, many of the men claimed never to have seen any American planes, only "French" ones; another situation that the liaison men had constantly to try and clear up. With problems such as these being corrected, cooperation with the flyers was improving, however it never would reach the truly effective point that it probably could have.

Ancillary sources used in this chapter include: 21, 25, 29, 30, 47, 49, 51, 148, 150, Various 152-216, 250-254, 257, 260, 261, 262, 268, 269, 272, 273, 278-283, 285, 286, 292, 296-306, 309, 310, 314-319, 323, 326-330, 338. Additionally: 37, 40, 220, 267

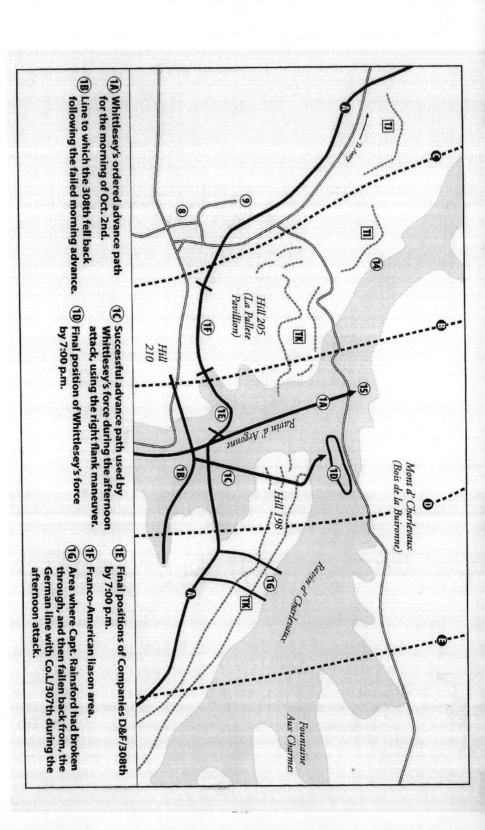

1A Whittlesey's ordered advance path for the morning of Oct. 2nd.

1B Line to which the 308th fell back following the failed morning advance.

1C Successful advance path used by Whittlesey's force during the afternoon attack, using the right flank maneuver.

1D Final position of Whittlesey's force by 7:00 p.m.

1E Final positions of Companies D&F/308th by 7:00 p.m.

1F Franco-American liason area.

1G Area where Capt. Rainsford had broken through, and then fallen back from, the German line with Co.L/307th during the afternoon attack.

Larv 91.

Hill 205 (La Pallote Pavillion)

Hill 210

Ravin d' Argonne

Mont d' Charlevaux (Bois de la Buironne)

Hill 198

Ravin d' Charleuux

Fountaine Aux Charmes

October 2, 1918 - P.M.

"Alright, I'll attack…"

Major Charles Whittlesey, about noon, October 2.

As the wet day slowly passed into an equally sloppy afternoon, the men of the 308th munched their meager lunch, reclined in their muddy holes and waited for the attack that was sure to be ordered. The scouts had been busy that midday, and when Major Whittlesey got back up near the head of the line they brought news that they may have found the way up Hill 198 on the right. Several hidden breaks in the wire ahead had lead them to up narrow paths leading across the marsh and up toward a wide wash in the hill running up the slope at a slight angle. The wash was just deep enough and wide enough to allow a reasonable body of troops to pass along with some measure of protection from the La Palette machine-guns. (29)

On the right, both companies C and B had pulled back into a wide cutting that spurred off to the east into Hill 198 from the ravine and were there bandaging wounded, chewing on iron rations and cleaning the mud from their weapons. Companies D and F were doing much the same on the left, worrying about Lt. Turner and his platoon still out ahead, while other companies, scattered in holes across the ravine, hunkered down and eyed the sky apprehensively. German artillery was falling again, along with the irritating light mist when messages from Major Whittlesey and Captain McMurtry began to arrive at company PC's: (29. 91)

From: CO 1st Bn. 308
Hour: 12.15p
The barrage will start at 12.30. You are to advance at 12.50 (when barrage ends). Push forward behind the barrage regardless of losses. This is to be part of a general advance. (246)

Further messages to company commanders followed providing more specific instructions. So did the two battalion commanders, quickly traipsing through the mud to meet personally with some officers, particularly the ones at the head of the attack, to impress upon them the seriousness of the situation. Neither commander wanted them working in the dark, but instead wanted them to understand clearly and precisely what they were to do and the risks involved. (This is not to say that either man expressed his own personal opinion. Instead, they just passed instructions, short and precise.) But, all too quickly, what little time they had for the task slipped away. Shells were already going over by the time each returned to his respective PC location. (29, 246)

Lieutenant Eager remembered the barrage actually starting at 12:20 p.m., and for the second time that day the men of the 308th listened to the rush of American shells passing overhead. If the barrage that lead the morning attack had seemed meager, then the afternoon stunt was positively dismal and lent no sense of security whatsoever. German shelling had been slow and lackluster around lunchtime, but that quickly changed as the U.S. barrage continued and more German shells now came down into the ravine, including gas. The men again donned the hated masks and continued to wait. At 12:40 p.m., from behind the Hotchkiss guns from Company C & D/306th, MG Bn. threw over a 10-minute machine-gun barrage ahead before repositioning themselves within the support companies to move forward with the attack. The ammunition they expended would be remembered with regret in days to come. Finally, at almost exactly 12:50 p.m., the barrage rolled forward and, tiredly, the Doughboys rose from the mud of the Ravin d'Argonne once again to push against the Giselher Stellung line.

Company B, supported by Company H, formed lines of advance moving north out of the cutting they were occupying and on up Hill 198, facing a dense 20-meter wire belt that had lain rusting in the forest for four years. Slowly, they began to carve lanes through it as occasional machine-gun bursts and trench mortar shells slashed the forest around them. Captain McMurtry and forward 2nd Battalion PC followed closely behind H. To their left, Company C, supported by Company E, drove up the marshy ravine bottom and along the eastern slope through the dropping shells, coming into contact with the enemy and looking for the paths across. There was good liaison between the two moving echelons and with the rear, where the combined companies G and A, along with the forward 1st Battalion PC, set out from the cutting along the ravine bottom and slope behind Company E. They also made incredibly slow and careful progress. (29, 91, 134, 234)

On the left, meanwhile, Lieutenant Knight, with what remained of companies D and F, along with one platoon of A for use as runners, extended across Hill 210 both ways (east and west) and down the slope toward the ravine bottom before moving out ahead. Their immediate concern was the relief of that section of their men surrounded in the wash with Lt. Turner. If they could rescue them, there would be a natural break in the Boche line to exploit. As they aggressively pushed forward that afternoon, amid a hail of enemy artillery fire and gas, they were stopped in the forest murk by murderous rifle fire and grenade activity before they had even reached to the edge of the wash. Between Lt. Knight's and Lt. Turner's men, the Germans had a double line dug in, extending all along the slope and down into the ravine. One side busied itself fighting off Lt. Knight and his attack force, while the other poured rifle and machine-gun fire and grenades down onto Lt. Turner's tiny, beleaguered command. They were now completely surrounded in the wash. Down in there, a grim drama was unfolding, the outcome of which did not look good.

Lieutenant Turner must have realized almost immediately that morning what was happening when he saw Germans working along the heights behind him and down on his right, where the wash emptied into the ravine. But, by then, it would have been too late to do anything about it. Instead, they dug into a small, hollow, oblong circle at the bottom and there the little force stayed the remainder of the morning, valiantly beating off attacks from the heights on three sides and up the wash's opening. Their rescue then was in Paul Knight's hands. Then, sometime after 1:00 p.m., came the sounds of a push from behind them that probably brought renewed hope and Lt. Turner's remaining men hunkered down deeper in their desperately scrapped funk holes and continued to fight like cornered badgers. Lieutenant Knight was coming... (91, 105, 109)

Meanwhile, on the right of the ravine, the men worked slowly out into the thick brush while harassing enemy artillery fire burst around them, not finding much flesh but still scaring the hell out of them. Resistance was light at first, compared with the previous attack. It was machine-gun and sniper fire mostly, with most of the fire along Hill 198 seeming to come from across the valley within the La Palette positions, but it was hard to tell. The brush was dense and the enemy gunners had a hard time drawing a bead on the Doughboys from that distance because of it, making it seem as if bullets were flying in from all directions. Nevertheless, there was a slow but steady drain of men. Cries for "First Aid" ripped the air as they took hits and either sat down behind trees to wait for care, or were carried back. As usual, there were a great many low wounds, particularly around the legs and feet. This forced the rest of the men to try to stay upright as much as possible rather than going to ground. If the enemy was shooting low, better to get it in the leg than in the head.(I)

At 1:00 p.m., Major Whittlesey sent back a message to the telephone head for Colonel Stacey, telling him that the advance had started on time and giving his dispositions. In the distance to the east, the sounds of the 307th battling forward, against heavier resistance than faced the 308th, echoed back through the forest. But if there were any sounds of battle coming from the French west of Hill 205, they were lost in the sounds made by companies D and F as they pounded against the German line surrounding Lt. Turner and his 2nd platoon. (29, 91, 238, 246)

There were plenty of sounds in the French part of the line west of the 308th to be heard, if one was really listening. In fact, the French attacks had scarcely ceased all day as the 9th C.a.P. tried desperately to bring its right flank up even with its left, or at least get a line extended down the Ravin d'Charlevaux to link up with the American units who were supposed to already be there. By 10:00 a.m., with the fair-sized town of Lancon in their hands, they had established a general main line running southwest from the town, its left flank resting on the banks of the River Aisne not far from Autry. But from a point just east of the Lancon town limits, however, the right flank still took a serious dive south. There, it passed down to run between the Tranchee de La Palette (frequently disputed, but at that particular hour in French hands) and the Tranchee de Charlevaux (still in German hands). From there it then followed the Binarville-Autry road to a point, at that hour, pushed up to about 400 meters north of Binarville itself. From there, the line then turned east for a very short distance before essentially disappearing in the tangle and machine-gun fire before Hill 205 and the La Palette Pavilion.

It was along this broken section of line that the real pressure was building and little progress being made. The German resistance was fierce and steadily increased as the day wore on, the enemy giving little ground and exacting a big price for what little he did give. About midday, the 9th's PC received word that the assault company sent out from the right flank that morning to work through the lines and down the Charlevaux Ravine was cut off somewhere beyond the Tranchee de Charlevaux. The rest of the battalion could not get through to them. The hole they had opened in the German lines had been quickly sewn shut by the methodical enemy before any supporting troops had been able to push through. This news was followed by a couple desperate pigeon messages out from the surrounded company, which left little doubt but that they could not hold out much longer. Repeated and costly assaults were made to rescue them, but all failed. The French were gutsy fighters and willing to take casualties to reach their buddies, but there was just too much artillery raining down from Mont d'Charlevaux, too much machine-gun and mortar fire from La Palette, and not enough ground cover left to mask their movements. Progress appeared impossible and moving the line up to the beleaguered company began to seem hopeless.

Then, late that afternoon, came a massive German counterattack that slammed forward everywhere along the French line, forcing them to fall back over well-earned ground taken in the last two days of bitter struggle. On the left, Lancon and Tranchee de La Palette were temporarily wrestled from their hands. They were also driven back to poorer positions before the Binarville-Autry road before they managed a rally, made another stand and brought the German assault machine to a halt.

Farther down the line on the right, meanwhile, the surrounded French company finally became overwhelmed, as the cloud covered sun was sinking in the west. By that late hour, what the lone French lieutenant in command brought into captivity with him was little more than a skeleton of what he had brought through the line earlier that morning.

And of the French line along the right flank in general? It gave slightly overall, surrendering about half of its meager gains of the day which, above Binarville, brought the outpost line down to about 300 meters north of town. Elsewhere, the loss had been about equal. Over all then, the French were forced to discouragingly admit defeat for the day. By 9:00 p.m., it was all over and a tense, tired silence settling on the French zone of attack like a wet blanket. There was some liaison made late that night with elements of the 308th, though. Along the shell-battered Binarville-Moulin de l'Homme Mort road, messages began to drift back and forth. The Americans had a force situated up in the Ravin d'Charlevaux as expected. Where was the French element that they were meant to link up with, if you please? (5, 10, 91, 92, 133, 146)

It was 1:25 p.m. that afternoon when the runner Major Whittlesey had sent back to Sergeant Cahill's telephone head arrived with a message to be called in to Colonel Stacey:

At: 294.5 – 275.3
Battalion has made 300 yds. Shrapnel is falling on the ravine to our left rear and is on the woods around us. Some sniping and MG fire. (246)

The machine-gun fire was indeed getting heavier, as was the sniper fire; some 50 to 60 men had fallen due to it already, reducing even further the effectiveness of the assault forces. Still, slowly, progress *was* being made. By shortly after 2:00 p.m., companies C and E had found the breaks in the wire and the paths across the marshy part of the ravine. They were then moving slowly across it toward the wash on Hill 198. Machine-guns from Hill 205 now divided their time between companies C and E and companies D and F. More machine-gun fire initially came down from up on Hill 198 as well and then, strangely, faded. Major Whittlesey and his PC, on the move across the marsh behind his assault companies, sent back another message:

At: 294.5 – 275.5
Line is still pushing on. Is near trench at 275.7. 'C' Co. seems to have suffered severely from snipers and MG fire. Shrapnel apparently ineffective. M. Guns seem to be retiring. (246)

However, those guns were not retiring as Major Whittlesey thought. Instead, they were slowly being taken out. The first to go had been the one facing Company C, which took a direct hit from an American shell, killing all hands manning it but still leaving plenty of sniper fire. Then, on the right, where Company B had managed to push through the wire belt and had been slowly working the slope in a company advance line, they ran into another of the three remaining machine-guns. This was one of the guns that the little band of 3rd Company/254th men had up on the ridge with them, and it quickly forced the Doughboys to ground. The lieutenant in charge of the Company B movement was an able Upton officer, 2nd Lt. Harry Rogers. Pinned down by the unseen enemy, Lt. Rogers sent a small band of men out to scout the Hun position. They were back shortly, pretty sure they knew where the epicenter of the fire was and the lieutenant quickly detailed one of his best Upton NCOs, Sergeant Thomas Owens, to take a gang out and eliminate the trouble spot. Meanwhile, the remainder of the company, concealed behind trees and brush, drew the German's attention forward. As the company began to put down slow, deliberate fire, Sgt. Owens and his men made a wide swing far over to the right. With luck, there would not be another enfilading nest anywhere close by. It was about 2:00 p.m.

The operation came off almost too easily. Coming up behind the enemy nest with a few grenades and the bayonet, the fight was decidedly short and one sided. The few Germans in there were quick to throw down their weapons and come out of cover with their hands high in the air. Fearful of a trap, Sergeant Owens's men inched cautiously up to disarm them and were surprised to discover that the nest was actually a deep dug-out, from which they pulled two more machine-guns and another batch of the enemy, among them a young, English speaking lieutenant.

They had been on that hillside, the enemy lieutenant said, for better than 36 hours (a lie, but it must have certainly seemed that long), without contact from any of their own troops, left or right. No, there were no reserves close by that he was aware of; they were at least 300 meters back last he knew. Their orders had been to hold, but once the barrage had let up and they saw the forest swarming with Doughboys, he had known that it was but a matter of time before it would be all over. He had six killed and one missing since coming into this position and now had only 23 privates and 4 NCOs left, all standing in a forlorn group in the woods with their hands laced against the backs of their heads. Most were glad to get out of the war, he said. Germany no longer had a hope of victory. Why could the politicians not see that? (29, 91, 109, 144, 145, 246)

Lieutenant Rogers and a small gang of runners quickly came up once the firing stopped. It had taken about 40 minutes to shut the nest down. Rogers ate up a little more time talking to the German lieutenant before detailing Sgt. Owens and four men to take the prisoners back to Regimental PC (just then moving up from Defsauer Platz to the bunker at l'Homme Mort). It was 3:25 p.m. when Lt. Rogers then sat down and sent Major Whittlesey word of his successful capture of prisoners and that he was pushing on to the objective. Sergeant Owens' party and the Germans disappeared through the brush down the hill, later to meet Pvt. Charles Minder and his Company B/306th MG Bn. gun team on the trail back, who later wrote: (246)

"Infantrymen came along… with German prisoners. They were an awful looking bunch. The infantry fellows asked us, "How the hell do you get out of this jungle? We've been walking around all day trying to get these Heinies back. If we don't find headquarters soon we'll have to kill them." He looked at them with a brutal stare and they trembled. They were scared to death…" (37)

Captain McMurtry, meanwhile, had moved ahead and latched his advanced PC onto Major Whittlesey's now and both then moved to the right flank of Company C, whose left flank was slowly fighting its way up the wash. Sniper fire was still popping and long-range machine-gun fire from across the ravine was kicking up leaves and trimming branches all around them. Unit integrity had diminished some but was still miles ahead of what it had been in the first days in the Argonne. The Major sent runners out to gather company positions, but few had come back yet. He also had small liaison teams out to the flanks, particularly the right flank where he could still hear the 307th slugging it out. None had yet returned however. By 3:15 p.m., the again combined Battalion PC reached a small German slit trench part way up the slope. Major Whittlesey sent another report back, reading: (29, 109)

At: 294.7-275.9/ small trench
Units are pretty well mixed up in front but are pressing on. 'H' Co. has taken 2 M. Guns. I just passed another w/ abandoned German in gully on a path. Can't find the exact location of the companies. I am with 'C' Co. M. Guns still around us in hoards but decreasing. (246)

The "hoards" of machine-guns was in reference to the two just taken out by Lt. Roger's men, (which the Major was not yet aware of) and the one that Company H had captured, as well as the intense amounts of sniper fire. With the last gun already destroyed, this being the one Major Whittlesey passed "abandoned" in the gully, and with all the men of the 3rd M.G. Company/254th then captured, the fire would necessarily be on the decrease. All except the artillery fire, which was coming in hot, heavy, and accurate now, thanks in large part to a German observation tower somewhere up ahead on Hill 198.

By 3:30 p.m., Lt. Rogers' message about the prisoners reached combined Battalion PC and the runner that brought it gave details of Company B's position. They already had scouts pushed up to the top of the hill by that time and apparently were even making tentative probes into the narrow ravine beyond, though those scouts had yet to return. About that same time, a Company C runner also came tearing down the hill to the little slit trench with word that their scouts had crossed a major trench line atop the hill and were on a narrow road behind it - with nary a German in sight. *With Lieutenant Schenck's compliments, sir; the Major should really come and see for himself, if you please, sir.'* Soon, a couple more runners came down the hill with similar messages. (29, 109, 246)

Major Whittlesey quickly scribbled another message back to Colonel Stacey with the barest of details concerning the position of his advance companies, but nothing about what they thought they had found. No sense in raising the Colonel's hopes if this was just some little ammunition trench and not the Haupt-Widerstands-Lienie. Indeed, the Major would definitely need to see for himself. It was all simply too easy, and he and Captain McMurtry knew it. The only troops garrisoned in the main line of the Giselher Stellung – the main line in the area - were a meager batch of machine-gunners? It did not seem likely. Handing the message off to a runner to start down Sgt. Jolley's chain of company A and G men, he and McMurtry then gathered their headquarters men together and started up the hill. To the east, fighting within the zone of the 307th seemed to be settling down and except for the constant thud of the artillery and the sounds of battle emanating from the west side and floor of the ravine, it was getting eerily quiet on the wooded hillside. (29)

Falling back after the morning attack, Captain Rainsford and Company L/307th had settled two of his battered platoons into a short stretch of dilapidated, muddy trench just opposite Hill 198. The rest of his men were dispatched to the road farther back, from where they had started out that morning. He was not pleased with the day's events so far, nor the job yet before them. All it would have taken was a few more men and a little more time to rip the line wide open during that first attack. Now, knowing that they were going to be ordered to try the hill again, his plan in sending men back was to create at least some small form of reserves for himself through which he might sustain a longer campaign if they got through the wire again. That might buy the time necessary to get someone else up there too, but just who that 'someone' would be, he was uncertain. Sitting there in the muddy trench awaiting further orders he still had no real communication from the rear, only sporadic bits from the unit on his right (which he could not even see through the trees) and nothing from the 308th to the left.

It was somewhat of a surprise then, when from the left rear a liaison runner came crashing through the brush at about 11:30 a.m. Finding Captain Rainsford, the mud encrusted figure saluted, stating he was from the 308th, sent out by Major Whittlesey to locate the 307th and that Company L was the first unit he had come to. He also stated that he had to make a wide circle *back* in order to find them. Rainsford simply stared at the man. Could the 308th really have gotten that far ahead of his line that morning, so that the runner actually had to circle *back* to find them? Truthfully, the move up and positioning had been so hurried that morning, and the action so confusing, that the lost liaison with the 308th had passed by his attention with little notice. Until they had dented the German line that is. Now, if the 308th really was up as far on his left as this runner was claiming, and if they were going to attack again that afternoon (as they surely would), here was a golden opportunity to get liaison with Major Whittlesey's force. Then if Company L managed to get through the wire again, together with the Major's right flank unit, they might be able to really exploit the break. The question then was exactly how far ahead was the 308th?

Captain Rainsford pulled out his map. "Show me," he said to the muddy figure before him. But neither he nor the 308th runner could figure out the route that the man had taken, until after much debate the Captain finally decided that the man had obviously gotten lost and found Company L more by luck than by skill. He also decided that the 308th could not possibly be as far forward as the man figured, although the runner very well could have been right *at one time*. Hill 198 actually tracks to the south as it extends east and therefore if the Major were advancing up its slopes in his own sector, he would necessarily be ahead of Company L. But, even if the 308th had elements along the slope when the runner left (thus necessitating the circular route rearward), Captain Rainsford figured that the attack over there had probably failed as well and that those troops had already been pulled back, for it was near 11:30 a.m.

Then, just a little after noon, a second runner came from Colonel Houghton's PC in the rear with General Johnson's orders for renewal of the attack that afternoon. It was to be a simultaneous, brigade-wide attack, and Captain Rainsford took the order to be more evidence that Major Whittlesey's 1st/308th could not be much farther forward than the 3rd/307th was. If they were, it would only seem logical to delay any *brigade* attack until such time as a *regimental* attack had brought the 307th up on an even line with the 308th (orders to "attack regardless of flanks" notwithstanding apparently).

No matter; the attack was ordered, so attack they would. Looking at his wristwatch, Captain Rainsford saw that there was little time to prepare and immediately began setting his remaining two battered platoons in position for an open order advance. Then, at the last minute, his doubts got the better of him and he changed his mind, firmly deciding that the 308th was nowhere near Company L's line and in the event of any breakthrough he was likely be alone again. In that case, he decided that he wanted all the men he could muster after all and would just have to rely on his right flank company (Captain Grant's Company H) for assistance. He was sending a runner back to bring up the remaining two platoons from the rear when the barrage started to go over at 12:30 p.m. (103, 138, 139)

Again, the shells were mostly missing the wire ahead and falling instead on the German positions. Nonetheless, following his orders to the letter, Captain Rainsford moved his men up to within 40 yards of the line of falling shells, laid them down in the mud and waited, with front row seats for the awesome display of destruction. When the barrage lifted, they leapt forward, crossed to the wire, and again quickly began cutting. German machine-gun fire immediately ripped at the surrounding foliage, and U.S. Chauchats answered back. At the same time, off to the right, he could hear Company M, which had slid into the line east of him during the break, battle forward and east of the wagon road companies E and H of 2nd Battalion slamming forward as well.

Once again, only to the west in Company L's sector was there any real ground gained. There, Captain Rainsford's men made it beyond the wire in several spots, though on a wider scale this time than they had in the morning and were driving hard against that flank. Slowly, inch by relentless inch, they began to feel the line shift. The runner reappeared with the last two platoons from the rear and Rainsford put them to good use. The sudden influx of men against the shell-stunned enemy proved just the ticket. From out of a dugout on the far left came a group of Germans who quickly surrendered, and the Captain sent them back under a small guard. Then, in a wide wheeling movement, his left flank slowly swung around and passed up and across another wire belt, into a deep double trench line atop the ridge. Company L's left flank was squarely through the German line. It was just after 2:30 p.m.

But Captain Rainsford knew that he was through on only a narrow front. While a window of opportunity beckoned, it would not stay open for long without reinforcement; his line was much too thin and they were already beginning to fend off attacks from three sides now. The enemy numbers seemed to have increased to the west of him and they were taking some casualties because of it. With additional help, they might begin a roll-up of the German line from west to east that would definitely pay handsome dividends. His support was supposed to have been Company I, but they were out of touch; decimated, and attached to F over in 2nd Battalion's sector, all of whose companies were currently engaged in their own fights and could not help. Captain Holderman's Company K, which had then been detailed to back both L and M, currently had its hands full supporting Company M, who was having massive troubles getting through the wire and moving up the slope farther to the right; they could not help either. Therefore, it would be Major Whittlesey's 308th men that would be the natural selection for the assistance he needed. To that end, the Captain sent out his Lt. Rogers (no relation to the one in the 308th) to look for them off to the west. He also sent a runner back to Regimental PC with the message that he was through the line, pushing around the regimental left flank, and desperately needed support.

Another half-hour's time found the left flank of the company well over the hill and looking down the opposite slope into the Charlevaux Ravine, facing almost due east and with the right flank nearly separated from the rest of the battalion by the wire. Individual scouts had penetrated across the Charlevaux Ravine as far as the Binarville-La Virgette road and came back reporting massive amounts of enemy troops beyond. Lieutenant Rogers and his men returned as well, with many wounded in tow, reporting no contact with the 308th, only with more Germans. To the right, all the battle sounds were still well down below the hill. To the left, his men were pouring fire into the Germans. Then he discovered that there was now no liaison through the wire to the rear. Company L was isolated and losing men too quickly, and slowly the long thin line began to collapse in on itself from the left flank (now on top of the hill) downward, as the Germans began outflanking their flankers. Time had run out for the formal request to be made and for reinforcement to get up there and Captain Rainsford, looking around, sensed that narrow window of opportunity closing. (103)

It was just about 3:15 p.m. when a runner found the Captain with a message from Captain Blagden. Crawford Blagden was a hale and hearty, bluff man with an active and ambitious mind. A ruddy New Yorker, ex Harvard footballer, and graduate of Plattsburg, he was assisting Major McKinney in commanding the unofficial combination of 2nd and 3rd/307th, he had been coming up to check Captain Rainsford's progress when he was accosted by a Company L runner. All was not well, the runner related, and the company looked to be all but cut off; something Captain Blagden had already figured. That situation must be corrected. Except for a slight turning on the far right by the 2nd Battalion, which was swiftly being beaten back, Captain Rainsford's men had been the only ones to get through. There were simply no 307th troops available to follow them up. And the Germans, having lost a stretch of trench line, were sure to counter attack en masse to take it back; they always did and the hurt, under strength, and virtually surrounded Company L would be decimated. For Captain Rainsford to stay would be suicide. Therefore, Captain Blagden sent a message forward that while echoing Rainsford's earlier orders to "organize for defense once the German line is broken," ended now with the sentence, "You can't fight the war alone…" (7, 103, 138, 139)

With no support available and the Assistant Battalion Commander's apparent, if unofficial, blessing in that ending sentence, Captain Rainsford finally decided that he had little choice but to pull back once again and "organize for defense" in a better defendable position. Considering the hurt state of his company (he had taken about 30 percent casualties from an already well under strength total in this afternoon attack alone), the position he now chose was back beyond the wire on the ridge opposite Hill 198; virtually where he had started from. Any closer would still leave him out ahead of the rest of the battalion main line. Gathering his men then, he pulled them back down the slope, fighting a violent rear guard action as he did so and closing that window of opportunity firmly behind him. By about 3:45 p.m., most had gotten down. By quarter after four, his broken company was back in their original funk holes, stunned and shaken by the serious battering they had taken and the lost opportunity. Then, just as they were settling in, a runner found the Captain with a message from a small platoon's worth of men (those that he had written off as unreachable casualties) who were still holding out along the far side of the hill well behind the wire, asking what they were to do next. Captain Rainsford, shaken by his extreme *faux pa*, sent them word to pull back immediately.

That was just about the same time Major Whittlesey and Captain McMurtry were climbing up with their Headquarters men to the German trench line atop Hill 198, half a kilometer or so to the west... (29, 91, 103)

"I would like night to fall or relief to arrive..." was the thought of Lieutenant Hopf of the 10th Company/122nd as the American shells rained down on his positions that noon hour. Before either was to come however, an afternoon of deadly earnest was again in the offing. "After a half hour of artillery preparation," he continued, "the enemy attacked once more." Grenade and machine-gun fire echoed dully through the wet leaves as a mist began to blanket the scene. Then came the American troops, cutting through the wire calmly and snaking up the hillside on their bellies. The 8th Company machine-gun near the wagon road was the first one to go, in a cloud of grenade smoke. Soon after, there was a band of U.S. troops approaching the top of the hill in the area of the 7th Company. The 7th fell back and again put out a request for support. Lieutenant Hopf rushed to the scene with a small contingent of his 10th Company. There he found a breech in the line around the west flank of the 7th company. Hand-to-hand combat ensued among the wet foliage. "One American showed exemplary courage," Hopf's report of the situation continues, "by planting himself, bayonet in hand, 5 meters from where I was in the midst of my men. A revolver bullet brought him down. The enemy (was suffering) very heavy losses..." (120, 128)

Yet, the American force kept pushing up the hill. The 7th and 10th Company men were managing to keep the advancing force in khaki contained, but just barely. They were ever so slowly inching their way up and over the hill. It was only a matter of time before the American commander would have his reserves up and through the wire, and then there would be no stopping them. The line would be broken! The second 8th Company machine-gun on top of the hill was still in operation ("One man was always behind the machine-gun with his finger on the trigger," said Hopf), but it was doing little good now. There was no artillery fire from behind, nor any mortar fire; the artillery had been shifted to the Aire Valley to cover the break there. The situation looked grim.

Then, the 5th Company again showed up from the western shoulder of the hillside, moving down and then up and out of the Haupt-Widerstands-Lienie to pour fire in on the Americans atop the hill from behind, completely surprising them. The 7th and 5th companies, along with Lt. Hopf's men, now outnumbered the Doughboy force to be sure. As Lt. Hopf remarked, "My first thought was: 'Things will go quickly now, says the sparrow just when the cat is sneaking up the ladder'." The American line shifted and began to return fire, but it was obvious that they had no hope without reserves - and none were coming. Before too long then, the Doughboy line began to slowly retire down the hill and through the gaps they had carved in the wire, the German troops following and firing all the way. Action along the line to the east had long since ceased. It was late in the afternoon when the last of the Doughboys pulled out. A small band of them, fighting aggressively with auto rifles and grenades, made their way back to American lines, dragging their wounded with them in the fading light. Then a muddy silence fell across the scene.

Orders from the rear came up that the line must be held at all costs and the German officers exhaustedly arranged their men to meet any further attack that might come.

Evening attacks were not uncommon for the Americans, and there was still some desultory artillery fire coming in. Seeing this, Lt. Gobel and his 5th Company remained firm on the 7th's right flank instead of returning to their place in line farther west, since they might very well be needed yet that evening. Once full darkness fell they could return to their place in safety, because everyone knew that the Americans did not attack or move around much at the front in the dark. (120, 126, 128)

Major Whittlesey, Captain McMurtry and the combined Battalion PC reached the crest of Hill 198 to find a wide belt of wire and a double trench line, well overgrown with brush and weeds. Lieutenant Schenck, with a small group of his Company C men, stood upright on a narrow road beyond to greet them. The main trench was definitely no ammunition trench (though the second was) but it was a proper fighting trench, well revetted and fire stepped, with a drainage sump along one side of the bottom and many trench mounts and firing platforms firmly secured in place for both heavy and light machine-guns. There appeared to be little in the way of artillery damage and scouts had already started to carve a path through the waist high wire. Major Whittlesey picked his way across and down into the trench line with Captain McMurtry right behind him. A few stray shots from La Palette sang in their direction. Some enemy light artillery also fell, but both were mostly un-aimed and more of a nuisance than anything. The Major immediately sent patrols down the trench in either direction, but both were back in no time. To the west the trench line continued to where the slope of the hill dropped down into the Ravin d'Argonne and there ended near a tangle of wire at a path leading down to the ravine floor. To the east, the trench continued seemingly forever, though the scouts had not gone down more than a couple hundred meters. There were no Germans anywhere and as far as they could tell the whole damned trench and hillside was theirs. (29, 109, 234, 236, 245, 246)

Nor was there but little sound from the 307th on the far right. Either they had broken through the line as well and reached their objective over there, or they had been licked and fallen back. The former would be good news for the 308th, meaning that Major Whittlesey's fears of no flank support in that direction would remain unfounded and they would be all right, at least in that direction. The latter, however, was unthinkable; orders forbade it…

To the west, it was impossible to tell exactly how things were going, as he had no way to get liaison to the French. Nor did they currently have liaison with companies D and F, for that matter. If the French were actually moving beyond the slopes of Hill 205, as was the plan, the only way Major Whittlesey would be able to find that out for sure would be to get into the Charlevaux Ravine and send out patrols in that direction. It was a fifty-fifty chance. They had been having a difficult time over there, as had the 308th on their own side. Yet, in reality, Major Whittlesey obviously had little faith that they would actually break past the damned hill and meet any of his patrols along the Binarville-La Viergette road on the other side. As with the 307th on the right, if they were there, so much the better; if not, there would be trouble. In any case, the Majors orders were perfectly clear and he knew what he had to do next - continue through the break they had just made and cross into the Charlevaux Ravine beyond.

He had, however, only a small token force on the hill with him at the time and would need to collect some more troops before moving on. Crossing over the main trench line, a second belt of wire, then the second, smaller ammunition trench and the wagon road beyond, he stopped where the slope started to drop sharply into the valley below. Before him stretched the Ravin d'Charlevaux and, by peering hard, he could just make out through the trees the objective ribbon of road running along the south slope of Mont d'Charlevaux. They were nearly there; the flanking maneuver was going to work. Now, since they were actually in sight of the objective, it was time to let Colonel Stacey know. Most of Company

258

B and some small elements of C were already out there developing the opposite slope of the ravine as he sat down and scribbled out the details. The message is timed at 3:30 p.m., even though it was actually about 10 minutes later than that:

At: 294.8-276.15

Have just reached crest of hill with small group of 'C' company. Sounds in the rear indicate others are close up. (I got too much in front by mistake.) Am sending scouts to locate other companies as they come up. The artillery observation tower is on the crest in front of here. 50 degrees east negative. (III) (246)

The last lines were apparently added at the suggestion of the artillery liaison officer up with the 308th, 1st Lt. J.P. Teichmoeller of Battery D/305th F.A. Regiment. Lieutenant Teichmoeller had left Wittenburg College, where he had been studying to become a minister, to attend the first 1917 Plattsburg Camp and had only recently been assigned liaison duties with Major Whittlesey, as the original 305th liaison officer had been killed. As liaison officer, he and his two assistants, Privates Thomas G. Sadler and Charles E. Jeffries, were charged with locating pockets of strong resistance and targets of opportunity holding up the infantry and then sending out for fire missions against them whenever possible. So far, however, artillery liaison in the Argonne had been poor, due to the nature of the terrain and the fact that the artillery units still had little time to register their fall of shot. Many of the 308th men looked upon the lieutenant and his assistants with some measure of disdain. But perhaps with this information, the steady thump of German artillery that continued to drop onto the ravine and slope behind could be curbed some. (93)

Soon after Major Whittlesey's runner disappeared rearward with the message, another came scrambling up the slope from within the Charlevaux Ravine, where there was some measure of rifle fire, with one from Lt. Rogers of Company B:

Am at 294.70-276.25 and sending scouts to railroad. 'H' is near. Will wait here before moving on. (246)

Those coordinates put B down the slope and well across the Charlevaux Ravine already. Major Whittlesey sent another message back to Colonel Stacey with the information, adding that he planned to join B once he had collected a few more men. He then sent a similar message out to Lt. Rogers. If things sound confused, with Major Whittlesey seeming to have little actual idea of exactly where all his companies were, it is because that was exactly the case. With the battalions cleanly through the German main line, the objective practically in sight and facing virtually no resistance, forward units were naturally moving ahead very fast, in fact too fast for the Major to keep track of by the limited communication system of runner relays. Company commanders however, had things well under control so there was virtually no dispersion at this point, only an exuberant advance, particularly by Lt. Rogers at the lead who was a good officer but a bit of a maverick. With this last message from across the ravine, Major Whittlesey realized the lieutenant would have to be reined in, otherwise he would probably wind up well past the objective and over the other side of Mont d'Charlevaux! Therefore, he sent Captain McMurtry and a bunch of scouts to move down and across the valley to get the lay of the land, in order to figure dispositions for the evening, and to make contact with the high-spirited Lt. Rogers. It was just after 4:00 p.m. when they set out, while from behind more men were already starting to stream up the quieting hill. (29, 106, 246)

On the west ridge, Lt. Knight's attack was by that same time drawing to a close. He and his men had failed to break through the cordon surrounding Lt. Turner's men in the wash, try as they may, and had slowly been forced to fall back to the positions they had dug during the midday break. There, the beaten D crawled into a support position, scattered out along the side of Hill 210 while F, spread out below them, took over outpost positions. It was a thin line. As the exhausted men flopped to the ground, carrying parties went out to fetch ammunition, food and water and runners to look for the combined Battalion PC with news of Lt. Turner's predicament, which looked dark indeed. They returned well after nightfall, having not been able to find anyone from either Battalion PC, but instead bringing back word that the flanking maneuver had indeed worked. The main force had broken past the enemy line and was on the objective. Turner's predicament had had a positive effect in at least one regard then; the enemy had certainly been kept busy, thus drawing attention away from the right flank, now hadn't they? And since no linking force from the Major had yet made its way back, they must have taken up the position late.

If there was any moon that night, it was hidden behind a thick cloud cover as Lt. Knight began to arrange for the attempted link-up with companies E and H that Major Whittlesey would be sending back the next morning then. With the additional troops of those two companies they would then be in a much better position to affect Lt. Turner's rescue, something that the lieutenant should know. (Provided, that is, that they were still there to be rescued.)

Lieutenant Knight then asked for a volunteer to try and carry a message out to Lt. Turner. A patrol would draw fire, but a single man working under the cover of darkness stood a better than average chance, particularly since a light, local, rain shower had started falling again, that would help mask sound. Ultimately, it was Pvt. William Sipple who agreed to try and Lt. Knight quickly scribbled out a note and sent him on his way. Private Sipple was back just a few hours later though, seriously wounded, having been unable to get to the stranded men's position and reporting that he had heard the Germans seemingly celebrating about something. (105, 109, 131)

Shortly after 4:00 p.m., General Johnson received a long report from Colonel Stacey, reading in part that the 308th had:

...(The 1st/308th has) captured two machine guns, passed one abandoned gun and captured 28 prisoners, one of whom is an officer... There is a great deal of machine gun fire to the front and flanks. This is decreasing at present. The 308th is almost to its objective. The 307th is held up in the center by continuous barbed wire 30 feet deep and is working around the flank to take the Boche in the rear. That was the conditions at 3.30pm, the hour the messengers were sent from the front elements. I do not know the exact conditions at this moment, namely 4.00pm. (131)

General Johnson then rang up General Alexander's PC with the news that it looked like they would reach objective yet that day, and got the division Chief of Staff, Colonel John R.R. Hannay. He repeated Colonel Stacey's report and then added, "I wish you would state this to the General, Hannay. He told me that if I could not do the work he would get someone that would. I want you to tell him just the conditions, which I know to be fact. On my left, the French are fighting on a line just in rear of my troops. I know this from a Corps observer who has just left them. On my right, the 153rd Brigade is on a line 275.5. My brigade is, or has been, away ahead of everything on my right or left. If he will look at the map he will see it. Relatively the French should be on a line 275.0, but they are actually back of my line. The 153rd Brigade should be relatively on a line 277.0 but they are also actually in my rear. So these elements are not only relatively, but actually behind my troops. I want him to understand absolutely these conditions. The information was just given me by a Corps observer who has just left this office and I know what I'm talking about. I have been ahead from the beginning, I am ahead, and I don't think I deserve the criticism you gave."

General Johnson listened as Colonel Hannay relayed the message word for word to General Alexander, who had declined to come to the phone.

"General Alexander says, 'Congratulations,'" Colonel Hannay said.

It had to be a tense moment.

"No, I do not consider it a matter for congratulation, but I wished to put him absolutely in possession of the facts," General Johnson replied.

Colonel Hannay then said that he understood the Brigadier's position and agreed with him, adding, "Just do your best."

"Well I am much obliged to you Hannay," General Johnson said. "But I am, have been, and will continue to do my duty to the best of my ability. And anytime he feels that I am not doing this, he is perfectly free to say so and relieve me," Johnson finished, and hung up. (131, 144, 148, 150, 238)

By about 4:30 p.m., Captain McMurtry was back and he and Major Whittlesey were planning dispositions. Down the steep back slope of Hill 198, a path lead through the brambles, brush, and trees to a small flat spot at the foot of 198, among a stand of pines and scrub oak. The path then continued ahead to the meandering Charlevaux Brook, where a rustic, almost quaint, footbridge crossed it and went to the left of a marshy strip beyond the creek before terminating at a muddy wagon path running east and west along the foot of the Mont d'Charlevaux slope. Near the spot where the path emptied onto the wagon road, the hillside bulged out into the ravine, and a few meters east of the bulge, a light spring trickled from the foot of the hill, spilling under the wagon road and into the brook. Looking down the ravine to the east, there was little to see between the two high, steep, wooded banks of Hill 198 and Mont d'Charlevaux, except the brook snaking down the ravine bottom, flanked on either side by many meters of marshy ground, and choked with dense trees and underbrush. Looking to the west, the ravine widened to a valley proper and was much more open. A clearing of trampled grass, barely a dozen meters to the left of the footbridge, appeared to be a German drill field of sorts, flanked on all sides by tall rush grass, but few trees. Some 200 meters yet further down, the Ravin d'Argonne terminated on the left at a wide spot in the Charlevaux between a narrow gap made by the flanking Hill 198 and 205 embankments. Opposite from the gap and still another 400 to 500 meters west, was the Moulin d'Charlevaux with the Binarville-La Viergette road running around near it, the original objective for the day.

The face of the slope going up Mont d'Charlevaux, across the ravine straight ahead from where Major Whittlesey stood on Hill 198, was very steep and covered by trees and thick brush. Perhaps 75 meters up from the narrow wagon path at the bottom, the Binarville-La Viergette road ran east/west; a gravel-topped, single lane running along a shelf-like cutting carved out of the limestone hillside. The white streak left by the wall along the north side of the road gave the impression of a great ugly scar gashed across the small mountain. That wall extended another 12 meters high on average where, above it and set somewhat further back, was a German trench line protected by several machine-gun positions. It was against this slope, between the main road above and the wagon road at the bottom that Major Whittlesey and Captain McMurtry proposed to dig in for the night. (29, 109, 148, 245, 246)

The spot held several advantages, not the least of which was its reverse slope from the German artillery behind the mountain itself, which made it virtually impervious to the enemy's shellfire. (This, in sharp contrast to the position Major Whittlesey had taken up on the l'Homme Mort hillside.) For any German shells to fall onto the hillside itself, the gun's trajectory would have to be ridiculously high. A second attractive feature was the availability of plenty of water from the brook and spring for the parched Doughboys. As far as they were concerned, both battalion commanders agreed that the spot was close enough to the "road and railroad" specified in the orders. To actually go up and occupy a line on the road, or even further yet above it onto the hillside, would leave them in an extremely exposed position unnecessarily. But the hillside toward the bottom however, if not actually following the letter of the order at least followed the general spirit of it, while at the same time providing much good cover. It would have to do then.

Above, an American airplane wheeled overhead briefly and called for the line. From slightly behind, somebody in the 2nd Battalion Headquarters Company dragged out a Very pistol and sent up a shot. Then, from the 307th's zone farther down to the east, two more of the colored balls cut the air well above the trees, but considerably to the rear of the 308th. It was nearing a quarter to five when the troops started filing past Major Whittlesey and down the hillside into the ravine and the Major dashed off another message to Colonel Stacey. After sending a runner off with it, he then led the combined Battalion PC moving down the slope and toward the small clearing in front of the footbridge:

To: CO 308
We are just sending the companies across the marsh (creek and woods) to dig in along the road. Will have outposts well in front. H Co. on left flank, then B, C, E, others will extend to right as they come in. M. Guns will be placed in left flank immediately. (246)

If there had been any doubt in Major Whittlesey's mind before concerning the left flank, it appears to have solidified into complete pessimism now, as evidenced by the last line of the message. With darkness fast approaching, he obviously realized it was now going to be too late to connect back with companies D and F behind any more that day. And he had still had no liaison (or word of any kind for that matter) from the French on the other side of Hill 205. To extend straight out on the left then would be to send men into enemy territory with virtually no hope of meeting any friendly troops at all. Again, visions of that exposed left flank of the 28th must have danced through his head as he made his way down the hill, so similar were the two situations.

Half way down the slope, looking across the ravine off over the open left, the Major spotted two figures in coal scuttle helmets and overcoats standing on the road looking back across at them, hands in pockets. Whittlesey watched them for a moment and then pointed them out to a nearby Doughboy, Private Carl Rainwater, a 1st Battalion scout replacement from Montana. Private Rainwater squeezed off two quick shots, but it was a long shot – at least 300 meters – and he missed, to no one's surprise. The two Germans quickly disappeared behind the brush along the road. They were the first enemy anyone had actually seen since Lt. Rogers had cleaned those Germans out of the dugout earlier, though they had certainly been shot at by plenty of them. It was about 5:15 p.m. (29, 135, 246)

At the bottom of the hill, he sent shallow patrols out to the east and west again and called for what officers were then available to gather round. Now, says Lt. Eager, Major Whittlesey finally let his pessimism show:

"Whittlesey called his officers together down there and he said that "The coordinates of the position we (are) supposed to take up is at the bottom of the hill over there, (and) if we cross over we won't be able to come back." (But) he said "That is our position and that is what we are ordered (so) we will cross over"... (234)

Not everyone agreed that it was such a good idea. Lieutenant Cullen, the redheaded leader of Company H, is said to have taken exception to the plan and made his feelings known there in front of everybody, though exactly what he said is in some debate.(III) Major Whittlesey apparently agreed with him, but again reiterated that 'orders were orders'. When Lt. Cullen again looked to argue the point, the Major coolly and pointedly told the lieutenant to get moving and the argument died a quick death. Turning to Captain McMurtry, he sent him over the bridge first with his 2nd Battalion PC and a small group of scouts to coordinate things. With the light fading fast, the other officers started their men across the footbridge in two's and three's at a dead run for safety. Then, over on La Palette, a machine-gun on the eastern side turned its attention on what was happening down in the Charlevaux Ravine, as did one near the Charlevaux Mill, and sprays of long-range lead peppered the area. There was no doubt about it now; the Germans knew full well that the Doughboys were on the move into the ravine. Bullets splashed the water around their feet as the men rambled through the tall grass and across the narrow plank bridge. A few went down and had to be snatched up by the next men coming over, however most made it in fine stead. To Private George Newcom of Company G, a former cattle rancher from Oakley, Kansas, it looked just like a heard of cattle moving at times and he could not suppress a small smile. (29, 44, 109, 245)

Companies B and C were almost all over by the time the mass move started, as was a portion of H. Once himself across, Captain McMurtry directed each company officer to a position, along with the steady flow of men, until all had made it across in the rapidly gathering darkness. Last over the bridge and into what over the next six days would become world-famous as "The Pocket," was Major Whittlesey himself and his 1st Battalion PC. That was at about 6:30 p.m.

Dispositions were quickly straightened out and men rapidly started to dig in. On the far left, wrapping its way east around the outward bulge in the hill just across the footbridge was Company H, under 1st Lt. William Cullen and 1st Lt. Maurice V. Griffin. The strongest of all the companies of 2nd Battalion, it was also lead by one of the battalion's most experienced leaders in Cullen. Refusing that flank a few meters distant of Company H's perimeter boundary was a line of six tripod-mounted Hotchkiss guns from Company D/306th MG Bn. under 2nd Lt.'s Marshall G. Peabody and Maurice P. Revnes. Their line stretched from just below the road, down the hill and a short way into the ravine, before turning the flank back.

This was the important flank, where Major Whittlesey felt the prospect of attack was strongest, for two reasons. First was its proximity not only to the concentration of enemy troops around Hill 205, but to those at the Charlevaux Mill as well, now only a bare 700 meters or so west of the position. Second was his complete lack of faith that the French would be able to break past Hill 205 on their side and make the link with his command any time soon. There was no sign of them as the Doughboys came into the ravine, had been no sign of them all day and there was no reason to believe that it would be different anytime soon. There would also be a large gap left there by the absence of contact with companies D and F as well, since it was too late now to send a line back to them. This, even though it had been the left flank that had been the main conduit that had led to the grief back on l'Homme Mort; a fact that must have tugged on Whittlesey's conscience more than a little. Therefore, with the conditions here troublingly similar, what precautions that could be taken, were. This the Major did by arming that flank to the teeth with Hotchkiss guns and delegating it to someone like Lt. Cullen. (29, 148, 149, 150)

Another New York lawyer and Plattsburg man, Lt. William "Red" Cullen is difficult to write about in that he was apparently not all that well thought of in the regiment. Not many of the men that served with or under him later cared to talk or write about him much, outside of only hints and left-handed comments that allude to his character, as they perceived it. And drawing off those conclusions, it would appear that he apparently had an alienating, abrasive personality and possessed a very high opinion of himself. Yet, despite this attitude (or perhaps because of it), he was a very good and efficient officer and had done an exceptional job in the first entrapment, where he led several important patrols and helped keep the men calm. While he talked a good game and certainly looked the part -

closely cropped red hair, powerful build, square jaw, steely-eyed stare, low booming voice, and rolling gait - some nonetheless have implied that his accomplishments had more to do with his own apparent reluctance to face danger than to any innate heroic persona. Instead, it seems (according to some of his contemporaries) that he was more apt to send his men into the tight spots and then collect the kudos himself later. Whatever the truth, Major Whittlesey could obviously count on him for at least two reasons. First, he had been a combat leader almost since the beginning, seeing fighting both on the Vesle and ever since the jump off into the Argonne (though he had originally been the Regimental Supply Officer). That made him one of the most experienced company commanders left in the regiment. Second, his façade of inviolability – if that is what it truly was – would not likely allow him to let his commander down, or lose face in front of him. Therefore, the left flank was definitely in good hands. (109, 152, 153, 245, 347)

Cullen's assistant in leading Company H, Lt. Maurice V. Griffin, was a 40th Division replacement officer from Denver. He was a slight, diminutive man of 5'6" or so, with a very boyish, innocent looking face. Yet, despite his looks, he was proving to be a good and tough officer. Born in North Carolina, Griffin had been on the border with the Colorado National Guard and had worked for the Mountain States Telephone and Telegraph Company before the war. He was also one of the few officers in the Pocket that was married. (106, 347)

Right of Company H, Major Whittlesey placed what remained of Company B, under the maverick Lt. Harry Rogers. For whatever reason, B seemed to have been top heavy with replacements and had suffered fairly heavily during the previous two-day's fighting. But, the experienced Lt. Rogers, a Missourian that had been a Sergeant in the 6th Infantry until accepting a commission in July of 1918, had molded what remained into an efficient fighting force. Nonetheless, one of its Minnesota men, Private Clyde Hintz, later admitted an initial foolish act once they reached the Charlevaux. "We got in the Pocket in the evening," he wrote, "and in order to avoid getting hit by machine gun bullets, I laid in the swamp near the Pocket and got wet. It was very cold. Later, I crawled over to the rest and dug a hole…" It was also under Company B's position that, coming out of the side of the hill just above the wagon road, the small natural spring bubbled and men flocked over to it to fill their canteens as they worked in the failing light. (44, 347)

Right of Company B was placed 1st Battalion's strong Company C, under Captain Leo Stromee, 2nd Lt. Gordon L. Schenck, and 2nd Lt. Leo W. Trainor. Although Captain Stromee (whom we have already met) was actually in charge of the company, it should rightly have been Lt. Schenck leading it. Gordon Lockwood Schenck was another original Plattsburg officer and a particular favorite of Major Whittlesey. Tall, handsome and muscular, Lt. Schenck came from an old Brooklyn family, had graduated from Yale in the Class of 1913, was a much more experienced combat veteran than was Captain Stromee and an excellent platoon commander. In fact, prior to the move into the Argonne, Major Whittlesey had recommended that the young officer be given command of the company, but the recommendation had come too late to be acted upon before the battle. Nevertheless, he now accepted his subaltern role willingly and gave all assistance he could to Captain Stromee. Lieutenant Trainor was another of the Midwestern replacement officers, hale and hearty, but otherwise unremarkable. (54, 109, 347)

As they settled onto the hillside, part of Company C was still out patrolling, (as were some elements of Company B). Major Whittlesey would continue to rely heavily on C to provide patrols in the days to come; one reason he initially kept them as close to the combined Battalion PC as he did, which he located just to C's right. Here, he and Captain McMurtry shared a rather large command hole, initially dug a short distance down from the edge of the road near the middle of the Pocket. The two commanders then divided the Pocket in two – Major Whittlesey taking everything from the command hole right, and

Captain McMurtry everything from the hole left. What remained of the two battalion headquarters platoons and their rather large collection of scouts and runners (including more than a smattering of men from companies D, F and I), were dug into the hillside just below and around the command hole.

To the right of the PC position, came the under strength Company G, being commanded by 2nd Lt. Frederick Buhler and the brand new Lt. Eager. Occupying the upper right hand corner of the Company G position were those remnants of Company A attached to G, commanded by 2nd Lt. Williamson and a mere 18 men strong. A short time later, an under strength platoon of Company A men that had been out on the left flank liaisoned to Company D came tramping down the back-slope of Hill 198 into the Charlevaux Ravine, just after sundown. The Major immediately sent them back out to reinforce the runner line. He was taking no chances this time and wanted as solid of a line as he could get, even if it meant diminishing his command in the ravine a little further. Among those sent back was Private Lee McCollum, unaware that it would be five days before he would see his buddies in the Pocket again. (29, 32, 148, 149, 150)

Finally, right of the G/A position was the last company in line, Company E, Captain McMurtry's old company. The second strongest in 2nd Battalion, just behind Company H, they were lead by the highly experienced 1st Lt. Karl Wilhelm, from Buffalo, New York, and another Plattsburg man, Texas's 1st Lt. James V. Leak, and the brand new 2nd Lt. Victor A. Harrington. A dozen meters or so outside E's perimeter, 2nd Lt. Alfred R. Noon set up two Hotchkiss guns from Company C/306th MG Bn. and one from Company D. There did not seem much to fear from the ravine off this flank, tree-choked as it was and extending east for who knew how far. The only position of possible concern might have been a precipice jutting out from Hill 198, relatively close at that point, which looked down on the flank from just beyond the brook to the rear. It was a perfect place to conceal a machine-gun or sharp shooters, who might then pour fire down almost point blank. However, it was to the rear, and the 307th was supposed to be out there on the right seemingly making that flank secure. Therefore, nobody initially paid the little cliff much attention. (29, 101, 134)

Major Whittlesey spaced out what auto rifles they had left, and there were not many, just below the lip of the road to fire forward in case of attack. Latrines were dug at the bottom under convenient bushes and orders went out to use them (something the Doughboys could be very lax about at times). What wounded there were, the medics laid out in a long shallow hole scraped out near the foot of the hill, below and to the left of where the combined Battalion PC was. The more seriously wounded were immediately taken out of the ravine and back down the runner line as darkness came. Meanwhile, the more lightly wounded were taken care of by the five medics then with the command: Privates Saul Marshallcowitz, James M. Bragg, "Baron" Irving Sirota, John "Jack" D. Gehris, and George "Sailor" Walker. These more lightly wounded men could wait and make the trip back tomorrow. Fortunately, they were few. (29, 54, 109, 118, 206)

A check with company commanders as their men passed over the bridge showed Major Whittlesey and Captain McMurtry that they had taken more casualties coming over the hill than they had originally thought. Surviving records show 87 wounded being treated by regimental surgeons that day. However, as previously stated, the records can be terribly misleading and the number was almost definitely much higher. Nevertheless, that amount alone would be a serious blow to the already under strength battalions, chewed up as they were by the previous six days fighting. Instead of two battalions totaling some 1,800 rifles, by the time Major Whittlesey and Captain McMurtry walked those portions of six 308th companies and nine 306th machine-guns with their crews into the Charlevaux Ravine, they had slightly over 700 effectives total. Even figuring in the losses to the command represented by the missing companies D and F (about 230 to 250 men between the two), this still leaves a pitifully low number of effectives. Both commanders, however, were to remain unsure of their actual strength. (The numbers are explained in greater depth in Appendix A.) (143, 246)

It was well past 6:30 p.m., and while dispositions were straightening out, when Major Whittlesey sent his last message for the night which was quickly carried back down the runner line to the telephone head and immediately called in to Colonel Stacey. It was the message that everyone had been waiting to hear:

At: 294.6-276.2

308 has reached objective. C Co. now at 294.7-276.25; B Co. is at 294.8-276.5 sending scouts to railroad. Have had 90 casualties total. Will reorganize here for the night and await further orders. (131, 246)

It was the first really good news of his new command and Colonel Stacey immediately sat down and scrawled out a message back to Major Whittlesey, telling of rations that had been brought up and giving him advance warning of the morning attack. It was just after 7:30 p.m. then and he next called General Johnson with the news, who was delighted and offered his congratulations. Finally, something firmly positive to report to General Alexander! General Johnson in turn immediately telephoned the gruff Division Commander. "The 308th has five companies up on their right across the river (sic) and dug in with patrols on the hill beyond," he told General Alexander. "At 4:30 p.m., the two left companies (L and M) of the 307th were approaching the road. A full report has not yet been received. They were sent to turn out a position but have not yet been heard from."(IV)

This was the only truly good news General Alexander had received from anywhere on his divisional front all day. To the far right, General Whittenmeyer's 153rd Brigade had barely moved and was still some distance to the rear of the 154th, which itself had not really moved either, outside of Major Whittlesey's command. Major Whittlesey was, therefore, the only battalion commander in the 77th Division who had followed his orders and reached his objective. The division commander now congratulated General Johnson heartily for it.

Sensing opportunity to regain some of the all-important flank support, General Johnson continued, "Tomorrow morning I am going to wait until my right (the 307th) is up and until the 153rd, which is behind me, approaches my position before I move. I want to get set, reorganized and get rations and things up to the men and then move out. I don't want to move my brigade until the brigade on my right comes up… I am now trying to get up rations to feed the men up there." (131, 144)

General Johnson's statement was tantamount to telling his Division Commander that he knew that the General had lied about the positions of the brigade lines when he had issued the afternoon attack orders earlier that day, but it made no difference. What was done, was done. If the statement bothered General Alexander, he did not let on. His lie had obviously had the effect that he had intended as the objective had been reached, though on a much smaller scale than he figured. Small or not though, it was a step in the right direction and could be exploited, if they used the opportunity well. That was all that really mattered.

"Have your men had food up today?" General Alexander asked.

"Haven't had any hot meals for the last three days, General." Johnson replied.

"They have solidified alcohol now, haven't they? It was issued to the supply officers." Alexander continued, and the two then hammered out details for getting supplies up the Ravin d'Argonne by the rail network.

"They are using horses now to pull the cars," General Alexander said. "We will have locomotives tomorrow."

Looking at the map one could see that General Johnson was right about his internal flanks; the Major *had* to have support. If the command up in the Charlevaux Ravine were supported quickly enough, and then managed to push back beyond the Binarville-La Viergette road the next day, the potential for exploitation of the break they had affected that afternoon would be enormous. With the 307th so close up and threatening rupture of the line in their zone, certainly no later than the next day, a roll up of the German line from west to east might begin. This could then carry over to the lagging 153rd Brigade and in turn on over to the 28th Division sector. The whole damned Argonne line might break wide open! From there it was simply a matter of time until the whole German line collapsed on the 1st Corps front. Therefore, yes, there was no doubt but that Major Whittlesey must be supported! (2, 131, 144, 148, 150)

Thoughts such as these must have been running through General Alexander's mind as he contemplated Major Whittlesey's position in the Charlevaux Ravine. The greatest gap, of course, was on the Major's left, between the French positions above Binarville and his own advanced position in the Charlevaux Ravine. But this could more realistically be defined as two separate gaps. General Alexander asked Brigadier Johnson what troops he had on the left and what preparations he had made to cover the Major's flank there. General Johnson told him about Lt. Knight and his companies D and F, now digging into the main line along the western ridge of the Ravin d'Argonne, then approximately 700 meters behind Major Whittlesey's left flank. He then detailed the plan for the Major to send two of his companies back over the hill to link up with them once he had reached the objective line. This move would then complete a U.S. line along the eastern side of Hill 205 and would effectively close the first portion of the gap, that off Major Whittlesey's immediate left flank, between the main line and the objective line position. This was something that the Major should be accomplishing very soon yet, if in fact he had not done so already.

As for liaison between the French at Binarville and the 308th's main line - the second portion of the gap - it had never really been more than sporadic at any time for the last week in any case. This gap was now perhaps 600 meters wide, extending between the left flank of the 308th main line, and the French right flank just outside Binarville. The unit currently covering the gap, as best as they could in conjunction with the French, was elements of Company I of the 3rd Battalion, but they were stretched far too thin in the duty. With Major Whittlesey's and Captain McMurtrey's forces stretched equally as thin as they already would be in closing the first gap up to the Charlevaux position, there would not be the manpower available then to connect firmly over to the French. This meant that the left flank would be open *behind* the current *main line.*

General Alexander then asked what troops General Johnson had available in Brigade Reserve. The remainder of the 3rd/308th were his reserves, the Brigadier said, currently doing mop-up work in the rear.

"Well, you had better move them up and use them to plug that gap between the French and your regiment then, General," the Division Commander said. This would then put them in a splendid position not only of protection overnight, but also to extend the line around Hill 205 when Major Whittlesey pushed the rest of the way up Mont d'Charlevaux the next day, necessarily dragging companies D and F with him. Once the French came up over on their side and linked with Whittlesey's force above Hill 205, the 3rd Battalion would then be in an excellent position to mop-up the pinched out hill from the rear.

However, this was a double-edged sword, for it would effectively use up the only reserve of manpower that General Johnson had available to him. The only thing left after that would be the divisional reserves, which only General Alexander could commit to battle. Nevertheless, General Johnson could see the necessity of the current hour and agreed to move elements of the 3rd up to the left to close the gap. By late that evening then, companies I, L, and M had moved up to l'Homme Mort, along with elements of the 308th MG Company. There they prepared to move up to the main line, connect with companies D and F on the right and then spread west, down the Binarville-Moulin de l'Homme Mort road and connect with the French just outside of Binarville on the left. By the time they had received their orders and gotten everything together for the move however, it was well after dark and General Johnson decided to have them wait for dawn near l'Homme Mort, rather than risk them wandering around in the dark looking for a French flank that might, in reality, be anywhere. It did not seem immediately necessary to make contact with the French that very night anyway, since there was very little danger of an infiltration some 700 meters *around* and *behind* Major Whittlesey's left flank, into an area obviously crawling with U.S. troops. Besides, the Germans rarely attacked at night. If a counter-attack would come, it would be in the morning, by which time contact with the French would have been made. (2, 131, 135, 144, 146, 148, 150, 159, 246)

Now, General Johnson has taken a lot of heat over the years for his non-positioning of the 3rd Battalion that night and then their repositioning the next day along the Binarville-Moulin de l'Homme Mort road; all of which is completely unfair. Part of the legend of the story implies that, by not moving the 3rd Battalion into a position to guard Major Whittlesey's left flank, the Germans were then able to filter their troops in behind him. The issue has also quite often been misconstrued to lead one to believe that the gap General Alexander actually wanted General Johnson to place the 3rd Battalion within existed between Major Whittlesey and the French, and not between the French and the 308th's main line. This was an idea General Alexander himself went far in promoting, even going so far as to directly state in his memoirs (as well as in a deposition given during an official Army investigation of the affair) that he had wanted General Johnson to move the 3rd/308th "into the gap on the left between the French and Whittlesey's left flank". Further, he stated that he was never able to understand why the Brigadier had not done so. This is a clear perversion of the facts, based on two accounts. (2, 109, 116)

First, it does not take into consideration the D/F-E/H arrangement, which General Alexander was definitely aware of and which would make a 3rd Battalion extension of the line from the French right flank, all the way up to Major Whittlesey's left, quite unnecessary. Unless, however, by "Whittlesey's left flank" he had meant the left flank of the D/F portion of the line. Basically in command of both the 1st and 2nd battalions, Major Whittlesey's far left could technically be termed as D/F's left and not the left flank in the ravine, should one so chose to interpret things as such. If that is indeed what the Division Commander meant, then that is exactly what General Johnson did, although maybe not in as speedy a manner as General Alexander had wanted.

That being said, the flip side of the equation would to be to consider the Major's left flank as that one in the Charlevaux Ravine. If this is the case, then extending the 3rd Battalion from the French right all the way up to the Major's left flank in the ravine would obviously be absurd. However, it appears as though that is just what General Alexander intended – or at least would have had everyone believe was his intention.

In retrospect, we have the general's own words to refute this weird point of intention: "Well, you had better move them up and use them to plug that gap between the French and your regiment then, General." *"Your regiment"* are the key words here, pretty clearly referring to the gap between the French and the 308th's main line, which would be where D/F waited for E and H. Might General Alexander have meant to reference the 1st and 2nd/308th up in the Charlevaux Ravine however (thus excluding D and F all together)? Possibly. But why would he, given that General Johnson had only just briefed him on the actual situation? (2, 109, 116)

In the end, it certainly appears as though General Alexander did not fully appreciate the situation on his division's left, misconstrued it, and then later convinced himself that he had not done so. Whatever General Alexander might actually have meant, one thing remains clear; he firmly seems to have believed that General Johnson had not done what he had intended him to with the 3rd/308th that night, and that this helped lead to Major Whittlesey's later predicament. And since General Johnson died soon after the war and was not around to defend his actions, the blame that General Alexander, and others, have tossed his way, however unfairly, has stuck for all these years. But it is completely unwarranted, for General Johnson *did* place the 3rd Battalion off Major Whittlesey's left, that left being D/F out on the west ridge of the Ravin d'Argonne; the only "left" that made any sense at all. That there was no firm contact attempted between D/F and the French that night seems then to only add to the controversy, even though it would make no difference at all in what would happen over that night.

"What about Whittlesey's right?" Alexander next asked. (Since the 307th had not made it up, the Major's right flank was as open as the sea, as was then the area roughly between the Ravin d'Argonne bottom and the 307th's left flank, a distance of almost half a kilometer.) Colonel Houghton's own 3rd Battalion was close on the left though, wasn't it, the Division Commander asked. General Johnson allowed that it was, had almost made it up themselves as a matter of fact. Then why not have them move up to Major Whittlesey's position, through the gap in the line he had snaked through earlier and extend back from the 308th's advanced right flank to connect with the 307th's main line left flank, Alexander suggested. A fine idea, but that would leave the 307th short-handed at a critical time in the battle, General Johnson argued. If they were going to be able to break through that wire the next day, then they would need every man that they could muster to do so. General Alexander agreed that, if needed, he would send up the 1st/307th, currently in Divisional Reserve at Depot des Machines, to help the mauled 2nd/307th man the line. Fresh blood would definitely help, General Johnson knew, in both positions. By morning then, everything would be in place to exploit the break in the line. It was finally all coming together.

General Johnson then called Colonel Stacey who, despite the success in his sector, was sounding more tired and cranky than ever. He told the Colonel he had ordered up his 3rd Battalion and would have them extended along the Binarville-Moulin de l'Homme Mort road by morning. Colonel Stacey was heartened to finally have the missing portion of his regiment back at his disposal. Had there been word from Lt. Knight as to whether the liaison between he and Major Whittlesey had been made, General Johnson wanted to know. None as yet, the Colonel answered, but it was still relatively early.

Colonel Houghton however, only listened in stony silence to the order to advance his 3rd Battalion up to Major Whittlesey's right, and then asked about his own exposed flanks. With his 3rd Battalion gone, that would seriously weaken his line at a time when more men were needed, not less.

"Never mind that," General Johnson said. "I'm sending you your 1st Battalion to make up for it. Send your 3rd forward, tonight." Then the line went dead. (2, 29, 51, 109, 116, 131, 138, 139, 144, 246)

The 3rd/307th, then in support on the heights of Le Quatre Chenes, was fortunate in one sense. They had just finished a hot meal brought up to them from the rolling kitchens when word came through for the men to ready themselves to move out in support of the 308th's advanced right flank. The 2nd Battalion, manning the line, grumbled, as they would now have to wait for their chance at a hot meal until the 1st Battalion could come up and take their place, morning at least, by which time it would be time to attack again. As a guide up the Ravin d'Argonne, 2nd Lieutenant Bernard Currier came over from the 307th Regimental PC, along with a small squad of 3 or 4 enlisted runners, to pick up the 3rd Battalion, arriving at about 9:00 p.m. Squad leaders for the 3rd/307th went around shaking the exhausted, full-bellied men awake and lining them up in company columns as a light mist began to fall in the chilly darkness. A few elements of the 1st Battalion were just beginning their march up into the Le Quatre Chenes heights as the 3rd filed obliquely down from the heights toward the Moulin de l'Homme Mort at about midnight, each man with a finger hooked into the back of the cartridge belt of the man in front of him. It was slow going as company commanders tried to keep their columns straight once down in the muddy, pitch-black ravine.

Just behind Lt. Currier and a guide was Company K, led by Captain Nelson Holderman and Lt. Tom Pool. Lieutenant Pool took the lead of the company while Captain Holderman brought up the rear. Following K was I, now augmented by the wrecked F and substituted for Captain Rainsford's ailing L that had suffered badly in the day's fighting and was still on the 307th's left flank. Major McKinney and a small squad from his Battalion H.Q. Company traveled at the rear of I/F. Slowly they set out as the mist thickened. At a side cutting northeast of the l'Homme Mort bunker, the column picked up Company M, commanded by 1st Lt. Andrew F. Shelata, and slipped them in line between companies K and I/F before continuing on their way.

"Guide by the slope" the orders of movement had said, "following along Major Whittlesey's route." Simple enough orders, but it was a tough journey in darkness so thick that one literally could not see his hand in front of his face. The long column frequently came to unexplained stops and starts in the mostly deserted ravine, with the men bunching up and then jerking forward again, fingers losing the belt of the man in front. More often than not, they then only found each other again by slamming into one other. As the night wore on toward 1:00 a.m., some men reported to their company commanders hearing German voices coming from the heights of the slope to their right... (29, 51, 131, 144, 138, 139, 148)

By late that night, Lt. Hopf had combined forces with Lt. Fritz's 6th Company and, as the only 1st Lieutenant still on the German firing line, had begun to reorganize things along the line to better advantage. He also sent some men out on liaison duty along the Hill 198 ridge to contact the machine-gun company of the 254th on the western end of the hill and return with a full report of conditions over there. Lieutenant Gobel and his few men had already some time ago slipped back down the line, but only a short distance. There they remained easily in reach if there were further problems for their neighbors to the east. Lieutenant Hopf felt this was safe since the 254th had the ravine farther over well covered with their machine-guns. However, Hopf's liaison party returned shortly with disturbing news; there was no one out there along the hill to the west at all. About that time, word also filtered in from behind of Americans working in the area just east of the Charlevaux Mill. How could this be? They had beaten the Doughboy troops back down the hill earlier and, as far as the lieutenant knew, there had been no further attacks anywhere along the line afterwards. Therefore, Lt. Hopf immediately sent word back to his battalion commander of what he knew and quickly was informed that communications with the 254th across the Ravin d'Argonne had broken down. The situation was cloudy, but apparently there had been a break in the main line, through which an enemy force had been able to slip. Just where or how severe the break had been was not yet definitely known, but there were indeed an unknown number of American troops apparently established somewhere in the Charlevaux Ravine. Scouts should be sent out at the earliest opportunity to investigate.

In the dark, Lt. Hopf hesitated for only a few minutes. First thing was to contact Lt. Gobel and see what he knew. This he did, but Lt. Gobel knew nothing. Sending scouts out through the forest in the dark would be largely a waste, since there was little they might see in the pitch darkness. Hearing, though, was a different story, since the dark would not affect that. Orders being orders then, he gathered up several scouts and sent them out in different directions to hear what they could hear. The first ones returned in the small hours of the morning—there were Americans on the move up the Ravin d'Argonne.

At the same time, over on Hill 205, the Germans of the 254th were already dealing with the disturbing situation. There had been a break in the line, but where or how badly had yet to be discovered. Their first evidence of the break came early, from two 252nd Regiment men stationed at the Charlevaux Mill complex who had been traversing the Binarville-La Viergette road late that afternoon. Glancing across the Charlevaux Ravine beside them, they had been more than a little surprised to see a large body of American troops moving down the slope into the ravine from the top of Hill 198. Alarmed, they stood in astonishment and watched the proceedings until fired upon, at which time they beetled back to the Mill and reported what they had seen to their commanding officer. A call was placed to La Palette, but the news was old and a couple long range machine-guns and a trench mortar had already opened up on the American force, which was lodging itself into the side of Mont d'Charlevaux on the northern side of the brook, across the ravine.

The 76th Division headquarters was quickly informed of the situation and Hauptmann Von Sybel immediately called for scouts to be sent out to find out what had happened. They were back shortly, telephoning with news that the machine-gun force that was supposed to be out on Hill 198 was not there and that there appeared to be American troops pouring over the hill through a gap in the wire - lots of them. Hauptmann Von Sybel immediately called Major Ditfurth to inform him of the situation and Major Ditfurth gave orders for a reconfiguration of the division's dispositions. A break in the line, especially the last portion of the Giselher still holding out, was a serious thing! There would surely be more Americans coming, if not tonight then first thing in the morning. Therefore, the 252nd was to take over the line before the French. The 253rd was to slide down and take over the western side of Hill 205, and the 254th was to assume responsibility for the whole of the eastern side, as well as extending across the ravine bottom and occupying the now apparently empty shoulder of Hill 198. The 254th then would be the ones primarily charged with stopping any further American drive into the Charlevaux Ravine. Communications with the 122nd Regiment, currently broken, were to be reestablished as soon as possible. The break most likely had come at the seam where the two regiments joined and if this was so, it must be repaired at once. (51, 120, 123, 124, 128)

Hauptmann Von Sybel also had a short meeting with the Commanding General of the German division, General Quadt-Wykradt-Huchtenbruck, who was livid and insistent on discovering the strength and disposition of the American force and how they had gotten through. Beating a hasty retreat from the angry general's PC at Grand Pre, Hauptmann Von Sybel rounded up Hauptmann Bickel and the two made off for La Palette at top speed. Once there, they gathered up a small party of scouts and Hauptmann Von Sybel headed them out through the dark across the Ravin d'Argonne, toward the PC of the 122nd, to gather what information they could along the way. They found out little in the darkness and Hauptmann Bickel, also sent to the 122nd's PC, returned later, equally empty-handed, having lost his way. Yet, Hauptmann Von Sybel kept his patrols out roaming Hill 198 and its environs, determined to find the answers. But it was what he and Hauptmann Bickel found waiting for them when they returned to the 254th PC that more than made up for these disastrous forays - a live, unwounded prisoner from the force in the ravine. He had been brought in by some 252nd men out on patrol along the Binarville-La Viergette road, captured but a few hours ago.

Hauptmann Bickel, who could speak English fairly well, sat down with the prisoner, a moody, dejected Private named Hutt, and began to question him.

"How many men have you there in the ravine?"

No answer.

"We already know from others we have captured that you are the 308th Jaeger

Regiment and your commander is the Major Whitsley. Are you of the 1st or 2nd battalion?"

The prisoner smiled icily, said one word and then shut up completely.

"Both."

Hauptmann Von Sybel quickly calculated the answer that Bickel translated for him. Two battalions of American infantry would be somewhere in the neighborhood of 1,500 rifles. Allowing for casualties, they might figure 1,100, maybe 1,200. That is, if the prisoner was telling the truth and if he actually knew what he was talking about; he was nothing but a private after all. Still, it would be better to err on the side of safety. If the prisoner was correct, that was more than the whole of the 254th Regiment by that time. With that in mind then, Hauptmann Von Sybel called up General Quadt-Wykradt-Huchtenbruck back at Grand Pre and asked that he be allowed to commit some of the division's reserves into the area, perhaps one of the pioneer companies. The General, aware that not only had his line been pierced, but that the divisional bakery (on the opposite side of Mont d'Charlevaux) was in the direct path of the renegade American force, conceded. By midnight then, Hauptmann Von Sybel had elements of the 376th Pioneer Reserve Battalion on their way. He further sent orders for them to be well supplied with light machine-guns and grenades and for the 76th Pioneer Company to be on stand by, ready to move to close the break that Hauptmann Von Sybel was beginning to suspect was a large one.

As it turns out, they would indeed be needed. (29, 51, 123, 124, 307)

On the American side, activity in the Charlevaux Ravine had continued through the evening. The Germans reminded everyone that they knew the Americans were there until well after dark. Sniper and machine-gun fire continued to zip down from the direction of Hill 205 and the Charlevaux Mill position and even a few potato masher grenades came sailing down onto the Doughboys from the hill above the front of the night bivouac. The digging was tough in the rooted, rocky ground of the hillside under fire and was made especially more so by a shortage of digging implements. Many veterans of the regiment had lost their digging tools during the previous week's fighting, while most replacements never had had one. Consequently, men waited their turn for what tools there were. Private John Nell in G had only an old hoe head he had picked up somewhere along the way to dig with and shared it out, while Private Julius Langer of Company H had even less:

"I was alone in the hole I dug. I had only a mess kit spoon and a bayonet to dig with, but it is wonderful how fast one can dig when bullets are whistling around. There was dirt flying in all directions for a few minutes and it was everybody for themselves." (44)

Others were getting hit as they dug in, too. The first officers wounded in the Pocket, 2nd Lt.'s Fred Buhler, commanding Company G, and the new Lt. Victor Harrington of E, got theirs just after dark as later described by Lt. Eager:

"The lieutenant in charge of G Company... had dug him out a nice fox hole and he was sitting down there and it looked like he was safe and Lt. Harrington, who went up there with me, and I were standing there talking to him. He was sitting down in his foxhole with rock piled up in front of him, which he had dug out in digging his foxhole and it looked like good protection. While we were standing there a German grenade thrown from above the road on top of the hill... came down there and landed right on the rocks and just cut his face all to pieces. Lieutenant Harrington got a slug (sic) through the shoulder out of it too (but) I did not get a scratch although I was standing just as close as any of them... I took over the company (G) from then on, being the ranking officer..." (161, 234)

Despite the wounds being absorbed, Major Whittlesey and Captain McMurtry had actually put together a good defensive position. There was plenty of heavy firepower to the flanks, particularly on the all-important left, from the Hotchkiss guns and a good line of firepower to the front in the Chauchat line. Both commanders inspected the machine-gun positions thoroughly, checking angles and traverses of fire, making suggestions, giving direction. The auto-riflemen, just up under the lip of the road, dug in good and deep and put the half moon shaped ammo clips for the weapons on the edges of their holes within easy reach. Riflemen occupied the spaces between the auto-rifles. A few scouts had managed to get above the road ahead where they were carefully keeping watch, but no permanent positions could be taken up there, due to the close proximity of the Germans. Within the fire line, the three strongest companies at either end and in the middle of the position gave good protection for the weaker companies between them. There was plenty of natural cover all around, as the hillside was well overgrown with brush and heavily wooded. All along the sides of the wagon road below, stood plenty of weeds and bushes before the wooded and rush grass-choked marsh of the Charlevaux Brook. Above all, the reverse slope was virtually invulnerable to heavy shellfire from the front.

The perimeter itself, from outpost to outpost, was almost exactly 400 meters long, but the great majority of the command was along a line about 350 meters. Outposts in shallow funk holes occupied the remainder of the space on the flanks. From the lip of the road above, to the edge of the wagon road at the bottom, there was an average of 75 meters, slightly more on the flanks. This gave the Pocket that the command occupied an unusual elliptical shape following the contour of the hillside with a slight curve at the middle. From the front and the flanks, it offered plenty of protection. From the rear, however, there was little protection, merely a few outposts and an auto-rifle or two. Nor was it reasonable at that time for Whittlesey to expect that it would be needed, even if, deep down, his guts might have said different.

If there were flaws to the position they now occupied, they were just these: First, Major Whittlesey allowed the men to dig in very close together. Most holes, as evidenced even today, were rarely any more than 2 or 3 meters apart, and many were closer than that. Additionally, there was usually more than one man in a hole, frequently two or three or even four. Being so tightly packed, the layout presented enemy snipers and machine-gunners with a target-rich environment from which movement could easily be pinpointed, even in the thick brush. It also virtually guaranteed that any grenades or shelling by trench mortar would find plenty of Doughboy flesh. (29, 51, 116, 148, 150)

Second, and much more importantly, Major Whittlesey made the fatal error of not sending anyone back to connect up with companies D and F that night, instead deciding to wait until morning. If Charles Whittlesey was at fault in any way for the predicament he and his command were about to endure, it was for this one grave mistake. This left an open flank, wide open; a situation that would ultimately prove to be the gateway to the infiltration that he had so feared. Yet, strangely, both of these decisions are justifiable.

In the first place, with plenty of room to spread out to the east, at first glance it seems to make little sense for Major Whittlesey to bunch his men up so, yet with a closer look it is easy to see why he did it. To begin with, the Major appears to have thought that he had less men up with him than he actually did, and this would have lead him to the conclusion that his perimeter must be much smaller than it really needed to be. Another factor, by this stage of the battle, were the Major's nerves, which had already taken a beating. Initially he had entered the battle physically run down, with a "cold" that was more likely after-effects of the gas he had taken on the Vesle. Adding to this, he had already watched considerable suffering during the previous seven days fighting; suffering that orders he had provided, had created. Whether he realized it or not then, he was grouping his men together in an apparent subconscious effort to assert as much local control as he could over them, taking upon himself the added responsibility of 'saving' the remainder of men that had thus far survived, through direct supervision. (Unrecognized in World War I, Major Whittlesey's actions are now well-known, classic signs of war neurosis, especially among inexperienced combat leaders who often garner a more active conscious; and conscious Whittlesey had in spades.)

Concerning his decision in regard to his left flank, two points can be deduced for the Major's action, or rather inaction. First, the order had been repeatedly drummed into his head not to concern himself with his flanks and that they would be "taken care of by our own people." This might have meant, to Major Whittlesey, that Colonel Stacey would be watching his rear areas for him while he advanced far out ahead as per orders, whether those orders called for a connecting line to be thrown back or not. And, if Colonel Stacey *was* watching things, then he would know that the connection had not been made that night and make allowances for it. This meant that if everyone was doing their job, then the line back on the left would not really matter all that much. (And, considering the recent situation on l'Homme Mort, someone had damn well better be watching the back areas!) Besides, Major Whittlesey already did have a connection back through his runner line, which was now triple strength since the addition of the late arriving Company A platoon that he had sent back, and was generally along the path that the connection line would have taken anyway. Perhaps it was not quite as solid a line as companies E and H would have formed, but it was still a line, and at triple strength, it would likely be enough to hold, overnight anyway.

Second, it is possible (indeed likely) that Major Whittlesey simply did not want to risk his exhausted men getting lost, killed, or captured while trying to make the link over unfamiliar ground, in the pitch darkness and well within the midst of the enemy. And even if he did make the link back to Lt. Knight's command that night, that line of two understrength companies would likely not have been nearly strong enough to stop a determined German assault from Hill 205 the next morning anyway; an assault that was all but guaranteed to come, since the Germans would desperately want to close the hole that had been punched in their line. Thus, it might have appeared to Major Whittlesey as being nothing more than a potentially wasted effort in the darkness, and one that would probably be costly in lives. This line of thought also dovetails very well with the reasoning of the Major trying to protect his remaining troops as much as possible.

Either way, not making the connection back would prove the biggest mistake that Major Whittlesey could have made, for it afforded the enemy an 'open-door invitation' to reestablish their presence up on Hill 198 *behind* the advanced Doughboy position. (246)

Yet, this is not to say that the Major and his force were not looking for liaison in both directions that evening. Quite the contrary; one of the first things Major Whittlesey and Captain McMurtry did, once the command was relatively settled, was to send out basic scout patrols and liaison parties to the flanks. Ahead, they sent a small group across the road and up the hill, who were back within a relatively short time. Private Harry Melvin, a 2nd Battalion scout from Company F that was one of the party, tells:

"...As we were out scouting, a sergeant and another private and myself, while crawling around we got to a steep bluff. Looking over we noticed, 40 or 50 feet below us, a lot of Germans around a fire. In crawling around in the dark we... crossed the road on the hillside and got past their outposts and were now looking at the main bunch. They were walking around talking, but I could not hear what they said..." (44)

The patrol also reported seeing other Germans elsewhere. Meanwhile, a liaison patrol sent out down the ravine to find the 307th on the right was also back soon thereafter, reporting no 307th for at least three-quarters of a kilometer to the east but also plenty of Germans. With Mont d'Charlevaux and the ravine to the right crawling with the enemy, and Hill 205 still quite well occupied on the left, it was obvious that the flanks had not kept up. This could make things hot indeed for the next day, but, then again, that was nothing new. (29, 51, 148, 149, 150, 246)

To the west, along the road above, Captain McMurtry had only sent out a two-man crew, not wanting to risk a large group on the fool's errand of trying to find what both commanders knew was not out there to find in the first place - the French. Privates Thomas Hutt and George Newcom, both of Company G, set out through the brush of the hillside below the funk holes at the edge of the road just after dark. "Keep under cover of the road," had been Captain McMurtry's parting words of warning, "and be careful." They snaked along, Newcom leading with Hutt about 5 yards behind. They saw nothing but brush in the near darkness for about 500 meters. Then, all at once, they picked up sound and movement coming from up on the road to their right. Private Newcom, ahead and plowing through a particularly dense stand of brush, froze and heard Pvt. Hutt call out from behind, "What outfit is that up there?" Turning quietly, he saw Hutt framed through an opening in the brush, looking up toward the road. Carefully dropping to the ground and peering hard at the road through the gloom, Newcom's heart tripped as he saw *nine* Germans with a light machine-gun, who all had their weapons pointed straight at Hutt.

Private Newcom raised his rifle and drew a bead, but it was obvious he could not get them all before one opened up on Hutt. One of the Germans called for Hutt to come up to the road. Swearing heartily, he raised both hands and his rifle above his head and scrambled the few meters up the hill. The Germans led him off down the road westward, going through his pockets as they did so. Newcom lay quiet for a while until he was sure the Germans were gone, and then beat it back to the Pocket, reporting to Captain McMurtry what all had happened.

Neither Major Whittlesey nor the Captain were little surprised to find no one friendly was out on the flanks however. Yet while that was a disconcerting fact, at least there was still the solid runner line back to assure that communication remained open. In any case, nothing more could be done that night. Tomorrow, in the pre-dawn, they would send the two companies back to link with Lt. Knight on the west ridge of the Ravin d'Argonne and thus complete their left flank. Then, they would wait for word from Colonel Stacey as to what he wanted done next. The smart money was on "attack," but that was for tomorrow. (20, 51, 109, 116, 148, 150)

After setting outposts and guards and sending shallow patrols out into the ravine, which was occasionally being lit up unnervingly by German parachute flares, Major Whittlesey and Captain McMurtry retired to the command funk hole. With full darkness, all the firing and grenade dropping into the Pocket by the Germans had stopped and everything had mostly settled down. Only a few occasional shots rang out down the ravine, along with some machine-gun bursts from behind on the left. Far over in the French zone, well off to the left, there was still plenty of real action. Off to the right however, the ravine was dead silent. Down below the hill from the command hole, the few wounded groaned and tried to sleep in spite of the pain. Most of the Pocket, however, was eerily quiet.

Then, about 10:30 p.m., a crouching figure loomed from the murky night and saluted from the edge of the command hole. It was 2nd Battalion Sergeant-Major Clarence R. Roesch, reporting that Private William Powers, a signal man in the 2nd Platoon/Headquarters Company, had just reported hearing German voices coming from up on the hill "back the way we came, sir." A sleepy Major Whittlesey irritably allowed that Private Powers was most likely having nightmares and he should forget about it and go back to sleep.

But Pvt. Powers *had* heard right; there *were* Germans up on the hill behind them, and Major Whittlesey likely would not have argued him in court about it. Yet while the very fact that the Germans were there did not necessarily mean that any kind of *encirclement* was in progress, it was still unlikely that the Major slept very well himself that night. (29, 51, 245)

(I) It was a common practice of German machine-gunners to shoot low. The point was to hit a man in the legs and drive him to the ground. Then, once he was on the ground, the gunners would continue to shoot into the area where he had fallen, at the same angle of fire, and thus the wounded man would likely be hit in the head or upper chest, taking him out of it for good. Rarely was German machine-gun fire ever more than 12 to 18 inches above ground level. An added advantage of this low angle of fire was that the gunners provided a much horizontally narrower target themselves.

(II) A most interesting line in this message is the one concerning Whittlesey being "too much in front by mistake". In reality, it was likely no mistake at all, for the Major had been well up front virtually the whole battle. Usually the only units ahead of him and the Headquarters Company were the advance (scout) platoons of companies A and D. In fact, Lt. McKeogh later remembered seeing Whittlesey himself, on the first day of the offensive, carving a lane through a barbed wire field for the 1st Battalion scouts to drive through. He was definitely not a Battalion Commander who led from the rear, as earlier evidenced by his own personal scouting of the positions ahead of them from the Small Pocket on the afternoon of September 30th. And while it was unusual for a Battalion Commander to be so far forward, it made for exceptional control of the units. It is likely that Whittlesey realized that his inexperience as a combat leader would demand that he use any means available to better 'balance the scales', as it were, and being ahead, just behind the advance units, did just that. It also gave the men around him an exceptionally high level of confidence in their immediate command structure to see their Battalion Commander taking the same risks as they were. Is it any wonder then that the men under him thought so very much of him?

(III) Lieutenant Cullen always after alleged that he told the Major in no uncertain terms that he thought it was not at all a good idea to go into the ravine. Others have alleged that Cullen never said a word to the Major as they were going into the ravine and that it was Cullen's own active imagination that had created his version of the story. Shortly we will explore 'Red' Cullen's character, as suggested by some who served with him. His actual character aside however, a preponderance of the evidence points to Cullen indeed having said something to the Major at this point, but just what it really was is not clearly known.

(IV) It was not an altogether true statement that anyone from the 307th was actually "approaching the road"— obviously the Binarville-La Viergette road—even though a couple scouts of Company L had earlier been there. The original message Colonel Houghton sent to General Johnson merely stated that they had found "a weak spot in the belt" on his left where "some" men had "filtered through" up the hill and into the Charlevaux beyond. This was no doubt where Company L had been through and then fallen back. Perhaps then, Captain Rainsford had mentioned his scouts making it up to the road in a message to Colonel Houghton, who might then have passed the information on to General Johnson at some point. However, Colonel Houghton himself would know nothing of the actual circumstances surrounding the retirement of Company L for another nine years, until told of them during an interview by author Thomas Johnson for his 1938 book, *The Lost Battalion*. In any case, weak spot or not, Colonel Houghton had further indicated to General Johnson in the original message that he thought it would take "a good deal of preparation to get through the wire ahead." Therefore, it looks as if General Johnson might have been trying to paint a little bit better picture of the situation to ease some of the tension with General Alexander. And, why not? Major Whittlesey was already on the road, so the 307th getting there as well would not have seemed much of a stretch. In any case, no one could have predicted what was going to happen over the next five days in that ravine.

Ancillary sources used in this chapter include: 21, 25, 29, 30, 47, 49, 51, Various 152-216, 250-254, 257, 260, 261, 262, 268, 269, 272, 273, 278-283, 285, 286, 292, 296-306, 309, 310, 314-319, 323, 326-330, 338.
Additionally: 218, 219, 220, 223, 224, 236, 240

Initial German dispositions

Mont d' Charlevaux
(Bois de la Bairomme)

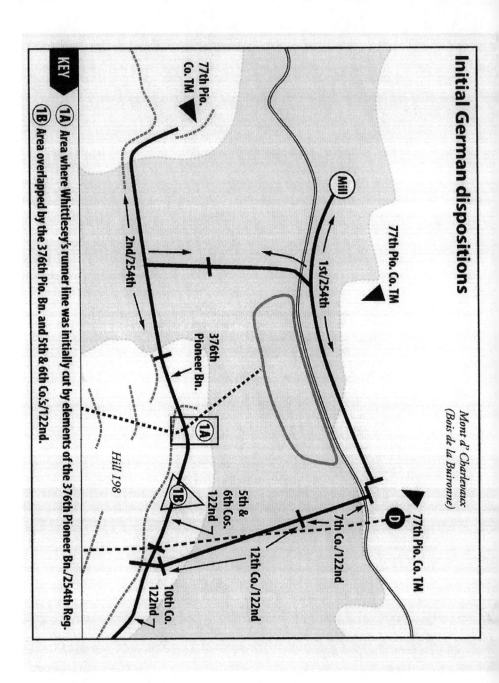

KEY

1A Area where Whittlesey's runner line was initially cut by elements of the 376th Pioneer Bn./254th Reg.

1B Area overlapped by the 376th Pio. Bn. and 5th & 6th Co.s/122nd.

77th Pio. Co. TM

2nd/254th

376th Pioneer Bn.

Hill 198

Mill

1st/254th

77th Pio. Co. TM

5th & 6th Cos. 122nd

7th Co./122nd

12th Co./122nd

10th Co. 122nd

77th Pio. Co. TM

October 3, 1918 - A.M.

"...They are having a tough time down the valley a little way..."
Pvt. Charles Minder, Company B, 306th M.G. Battalion, in a letter to his mother.

With difficulty, the 3rd/307th continued its slow progress up the Ravin d'Argonne through the misty night toward the Charlevaux position. There were frequent, unexplained halts and pauses in the pitch darkness and then guarded scrambling to maintain contact as Lt. Currier and his guides struggled to keep the column moving. They had not been underway long when, during one of the pauses, Captain Holderman realized that his company would likely need morning rations. He sent a squad of seven men and a sergeant hustling back to Depot des Machines to quickly fetch some, giving them detailed instructions on where they would be able to catch up with the main body of Company K. After seeing the ration party back off down the ravine, the Captain made sure the rear of K had solid contact behind with M's commander, Lt. Andrew Shelata, before passing himself up the line and letting Lt. Pool know that rations would be coming. Then, jerkily, the column started forward again.

They had not progressed much farther when, sometime just before 2:00 a.m., there was another, extended halt. The lead guide had gotten out too far ahead and Lt. Currier went out to look for him. Exhausted and grumbling quietly, the troops in line began to fall out and flop down on either side of the trail. Seeing this, Captain Holderman and Lt. Pool began to traipse silently up and down the line, whispering the K men back on their feet, knowing it would be too easy to break contact in the inky darkness if the men were allowed to get too comfortable. Still griping, they stood back up and leaned against each other as a way to both rest and still maintain contact.

Behind Company K, Lt. Shelata's Company M men began to fall out as well. Even Lt. Shelata himself, never a strong man to begin with and now fatigued nearly to the point of total collapse by the rough Argonne fighting, dropped exhaustedly to a knee. It was a numbing night, and it felt good to stop for a moment. The light rain tapped soothingly on everyone's helmet and dripped silently to the ground. Relaxation began to drape itself over the scene like a blanket. The halt stretched on toward the half-hour mark, and slowly the tired lieutenant's eyes closed. Up ahead, the guide was found, contact reestablished, and the gentle rustling sound of men's boots swishing quietly through the wet leaves washed dimly into the darkness as Company K moved off down the ravine. (103, 138, 139, 235)

At about 2:00 a.m., three mud-covered men, dragging a wounded comrade, came sliding through the weeds toward the company D positions along the west ridge of the Ravin d'Argonne. Immediately, they were recognized as men from the company and passed through the outpost line. Leading was Corporal Carmine Fellito and with him were Privates Everett Holcomb, Arthur Fetting, and a wounded Earl Hawkins. They were all that remained of Lt. Turner's stranded platoon, an exhausted Cpl. Fellito told Lt. Knight. The rest of the platoon had been wiped out - killed down to a man. The four survivors had been lucky enough to escape in the dark. Hell, the goddamned Hienies could even be heard in a dugout close by the wash partying over their success. Lieutenant Knight stood silent for a moment and then asked what else had the corporal seen of the enemy defenses? Plenty, and he related all as Lt. Knight began revising his plan of attack for the coming dawn. His Company D stood at just something over 90 bedraggled men now, and F was not much stronger, with the real test yet to come. (105)

Lieutenant Shelata awoke in the darkness of the ravine. Though only a few minutes had passed, the rustling sound was gone, as was the Company K man that had been in front of him. Panicked, Lt. Shelata did nothing for a moment, debating a course of action in the darkness. The column should realize its mistake soon and send someone back. Then again, perhaps he should proceed forward and try to catch up. Finally, he decided he must move. "Guide by the slope" the orders had read. How hard could it be to walk a straight line up to the rest of the column?

Except the ground along the eastern side of the Ravin d'Argonne is covered in marshy swamp, and this forced the Company K column to swing out more toward the middle of the ravine before again shifting northward. Lieutenant Shelata discovered this by stumbling into the marsh himself. However, after angling his column westward around the swamp he never again really turned back north, instead cutting across the ravine and eventually winding up somewhere facing the western slope. Hopelessly lost now, Company M floundered around near the base of the slope for a short time drawing enemy fire until, despondently, the errant lieutenant finally called a halt. Too tired to care anymore as to the outcome of their predicament, he posted guards and had the men dig in to wait for the first morning light.

Behind, the I/F combination had steered off course as well, following M across the ravine. Somewhere near the middle, they somehow veered off to the right from M's tail however and wound up tangled in the wire and swampy mess at the ravine bottom, also totally lost, while Lt. Shelata's men thrashed aimlessly about in the darkness somewhere off to their left. By the time the combined companies' two officers, Lieutenants Lord and Perry, realized the mistake, it was too late. Then they too halted and also dug in off the western slope, just left of the swamp up on dryer ground. Major McKinney, who had been traveling with them, fumed impotently in the misty darkness. (103, 138, 139, 235)

Around 2:50 a.m., word came to the head of the Company K line from the rear to "about face and march back." Certainly an odd request. Thinking that perhaps one of the other companies had some sort of trouble, Holderman halted the line and had Lt. Pool trot back to investigate. There, he discovered the trailing companies were gone. A 10-minute search failed to turn up anything. Finally, the lieutenant decided it was fruitless to continue searching the pitch darkness. Returning to the head of the column, he informed each man in line to take orders only from the head from then on and to maintain sharp contact with the man in front of him. Some of the men in return again told him that they thought they could hear German voices in the darkness to the right. Lieutenant Pool whispered for each man to remain as silent as possible and then proceeded forward again. Telling Captain Holderman what he had found, they held a short conference. (29, 51, 103, 109, 138, 139)

Alone, the company did not figure to do much good. The preceding days of battle in the Argonne had been hard on Company K and they were now barely over 100 men, with the ration detail gone. Any line they might form off Major Whittlesey's right flank would be a very thin one then and seem hardly worth it. Yet, there was little choice but to keep going. They had no contingency orders for such a situation, meaning that the original orders still stood and Major McKinney had made it pretty damned clear that they needed to get up to the 1st/308th's right flank quickly. If they had indeed broken through, then they would definitely need some sort of flank support, no matter how small the contingent. In any case, the other companies could not be far behind and were almost certain to follow along, worst case being only when they could see where they were going. There being no real choice, Captain Holderman and Lt. Pool got Company K slowly moving forward through the darkness again.

By about 3:30 a.m., the column had reached one of Major Whittlesey's advanced runner posts; this one in a little clearing at the head of a path that lead through the cutting up Hill 198. There, they got directions to where 1st/308th was. "Up and over the hill to the valley on the other side. There's a trench line along the crest and another runner post the other side of that. Can't miss it," the runner told them. Captain Holderman dismissed Lt. Currier and his guides, who quickly disappeared into the darkness of the ravine in the direction of l'Homme Mort and then commandeered one of the runners as guide. The runner led them north up the hill, past two other posts until finding the post on the crest of the hill. Here again, they received more directions: "At the foot of the hill is an open field; on the edge is the next post. Across the field is a bridge, over the brook. Beyond that, through the strip of woods and up against the far slope of the valley, you'll find the Major."

With great difficulty, Company K moved forward down the steep slope in complete darkness. No clear idea of what they were coming down onto led to several nasty falls along the way. Fortunately, no one was really injured and, oddly enough, the crashing of bodies falling down the hill drew no enemy fire. Once everyone was down, Captain Holderman gathered them together in a little clearing at the base of the hill and sent Lt. Pool out with a scout to find the next post, while the Sergeants took a head count. Including the two officers, there were 108 Company K men present, most without rations and counting on the party sent back earlier to catch up to them with something for breakfast.

Lieutenant Pool and the scout were back within a short time, reporting that they could find neither a field, bridge, nor brook in the darkness and that there was no one where they figured the next runner post should be. While the ravine they were facing seemed to open up to the left, to the right it was too dark to see exactly what it looked like. Nor could they see how far it was across. Yet, Major Whittlesey's position could not be too much farther forward, if what the last runner had said was correct. They could press on. However, in the dark without any guidance, they were likely to end up as lost as the other two companies, or perhaps even shot at by their own troops, or the enemy.

Captain Holderman hardly considered the situation. It was madness to wander aimlessly around in the forest. Better to sit tight, get what sleep they could, and send out scouts to locate the 1st/308th at first light. True, they were not following orders to the letter by failing to make the connection with them that night, but they were situated in a position of close support, which would have to be good enough. Lieutenant Pool agreed.

It was coming up on 4:00 a.m. and quiet as a tomb in the forest when Captain Holderman gave the order for the men to dig in, outposted the position, and sent a nine-man reconnaissance patrol out on a short leash to make sure the surrounding area was secure.

They never returned. (29, 51, 103, 138, 139, 149, 188, 195)

Meanwhile, Captain Holderman's ration party had made it relatively quickly back to Depot without getting lost, loaded up with iron rations and then started back down the ravine. It was just about 3:30 a.m. or so in the dank quiet of the rainy darkness. Private Peter Koshiol was one of those men the Captain had sent back and later recalled:

"Towards morning we started back to our company. Everything was so quiet we thought the war was over. (Then) as we came to a railroad cut, the Germans started firing... We finally got to the Pocket carrying rations on the fifth day. Here we located the balance of our company, but there was not many left..." (44)

Fended off by the Germans, the little band of men returned to Depot and reported the news to Captain Blagden, who passed it on to Colonel Houghton. The Colonel knew this could be serious trouble. Obviously, the extension of the line back from the Charlevaux Ravine had not been completed; otherwise, the ration party would have found it and not the Germans. It almost sounded like the Boche had somehow worked in around behind the 3rd Battalion as it had passed forward and then blocked them from completing the line back. However, there had been no firing heard. Indeed, the forest was eerily quiet. Strange. Had there been any other word from anyone in 3rd Battalion since they left? None, other than the ration detail, Captain Blagden told him, and Colonel Houghton grabbed the telephone. (131, 144, 238)

General Johnson heard out the Colonel's report with growing concern. He had just gotten off the phone with Colonel Stacey, who had similar concerns about the line up to the position within the Charlevaux from the left side. Stacey had sent a message up to Major Whittlesey at 7:00 p.m. the evening before concerning rations and ammunition - two things the Major had been asking for - and had gotten no answer back, which was very unusual for Whittlesey. Nor had anyone from the Major's command come for the rations or ammo requested and it was quickly running on toward dawn now. In addition, the Colonel had received word from Lt. Knight on the west ridge a short time ago about a platoon of his men that had been cut off ahead of the main line. Sometime after 2:00 a.m., four men had crawled back into the outpost line from the surrounded platoon's position to say that the remainder of the platoon, including Lt. Turner, had been wiped out and that the Germans were firmly in control up there. Most importantly however, Lt. Knight reported that Major Whittlesey had never sent back either of the two connecting companies he was supposed to, or word of why he had not or when they might be coming up.

General Johnson considered all this for only a short time before he called General Alexander, but there must have already been a sinking feeling grabbing at his stomach even as he reached for his telephone. He was not yet sure, the Brigadier told the Division Commander, but it appeared that as of that time (around 5:00 a.m. or so) that the communication line up to Major Whittlesey's advanced position in the Charlevaux Ravine might have been severed, and that almost certainly neither of his flanks had been covered as intended... (109, 116, 131, 144, 238)

The first of the German patrols that Lt. Hopf of the 10th Company/122nd had sent out early that morning was back at around 4:00 a.m. with a full disturbing report; there was no contact to be had with the 254th on the western end of Hill 198. Instead, were signs that the machine-gun company that had been out there had been captured. German gear littered the general area that they had been occupying and a couple of the patrols reported seeing American message posts at regular intervals stretching back down the hill toward their own lines. Other scout patrols, sent behind into the Charlevaux Ravine, were reporting a definite American presence in relatively large numbers, at least company size, but strangely not making any move toward extending their occupied area. There could be no doubt that they had every intention of expansion, however, since the patrols had also observed Doughboy reinforcements moving up the Ravin d'Argonne and into the Charlevaux in the early morning hours. Strange, since the Americans rarely moved at night.

Not long after Lt. Hopf sent his report back to the 2nd Division PC, he received word from Hauptmann Von Wiedenbach that the gap in the line west of him was in the process of being closed by reinforcements of the 254th from over on Hill 205. Hours before, his patrols had reported, much to his own horror, that the break had been nearly 800 meters wide.(I) After that, they had all sweated the chilly night out in fear that the Americans in the ravine might try and drive the gap wider. Especially so Lt. Gobel and his 5th Company on the end, whose numbers were well down at this stage of the battle. Lieutenant Hopf himself had, by that hour of the morning, only 60 men in his own company, and there were scarcely fewer in the other companies along the line as well. Therefore, if the Americans made a determined effort from front and back at driving the gap wider, there would be little that anyone could do to stop them. It was a huge relief to hear that the break was finally closing and reinforcements had arrived.

Soon thereafter, it was with some measure of shock that the lieutenant received another message from Hauptmann Von Wiedenbach, ordering that he clear out the Doughboy force in the Charlevaux Ravine; clearly an impossible task with the limited numbers he had. With every reason to expect another American attack on the line that morning, gaining the reinforcements he would need for such an operation from among the line companies was out of the question. Therefore, as tactfully as he could, he refused the order and waited for the reply that might just be a relief of command. Instead, he received another shock when fresh disposition orders came from the Divisional PC around 6:00 a.m. and fresh patrols from the 254th came to them from out of the west.

The orders now called for the 7th and 12th companies to move down into the Charlevaux Ravine off the eastern flank of the American force, thus blocking the enemy from advancing farther down and linking with any of his forces that might make it through the lines. The 7th Company was to take a position extending from above the Binarville-La Viergette road down to about the middle of the Charlevaux Ravine, keeping well back from the Americans in order to avoid detection. The 12th Company was to continue the line from the 7th left flank back up to the main line on Hill 198, where they were to loosely make contact with the right flank of the 10th Company, which would remain in place on the main line. Immediately, the troops began stringing new wire, miles of it, atop the hillside sloping down into the Charlevaux Ravine. From the 10th's flank westward remained the 6th and 5th companies, also watching the main line ahead and also stringing new wire between them and the ravine. However, the only orders changing their disposition were ones directing that every other machine-gun in the main line be taken back to strategic positions and reversed to pour fire down into the Charlevaux Ravine, along with reinforcements from the 8th Company's machine-gun section. The remainder of the 8th was to extend the 10th Company flank eastward to connect with the 9th Company/120th Regiment and then face south to meet the American assaults there. Thus, the disposition of the 122nd Regiment was set to annihilate the troublesome Americans in the Charlevaux Ravine from the eastern side of the area they occupied, while still maintaining the main line.

As dawn approached, 2nd Lt.'s Ulrich (7th Company), Fehrle (10th Company), and Baum (12th Company) sent out patrols to guide their men into position. With those operations well underway, Lt. Ulrich took a patrol of men around on a wide swing to the north and west across the Charlevaux Ravine to try and reestablish contact with the 254th, since he was unaware whether the gap west of the 122nd on Hill 198 had actually been closed. Arriving at the Charlevaux Mill later that morning, he was heartened to learn that the gap had indeed been closed by some pioneers of the 254th hours earlier. They and the regiment's 1st and 2nd Battalions had the American force sewn up from the three remaining sides - north, west, and south. Lieutenant Ulrich immediately made a telephone call to the 122nd PC, surprised that the phone was working again. (Major Whittlesey's men had cut the lines as they had passed through the trenches on Hill 198 the afternoon before.) Ulrich informed them of the 254th's progress since the confusion of the pre-dawn hours and he, in turn, was informed of the 122nd's successful deployment east of the American presence in the ravine. This he passed along to the 254th's Operations Officer and then, with a smile at the "cat in the bag" scenario he sensed, gathered up his patrol and headed back toward the 7th Company positions.

Across the Ravin d'Argonne from the 122nd, the first of the German pioneer infantry that Hauptmann Von Sybel had ordered showed up by truck long before the watery sun made its first rainy 'appearance' that morning. Along with them came copious amounts of grenades, ammunition, and light machine-guns. It had become apparent as the pre-dawn hours slowly passed, from the sporadic reports confusingly filtering into his temporary PC at La Palette, that the break in the line was a wide one and that the Doughboy contingent that had broken past the Giselher must be crushed quickly. If not, they would collect reinforcements quickly. Therefore, he and Hauptmann Bickel organized patrols among the new men and sent them out in the direction of Hill 198 with several light machine-guns, loads of grenades and orders to close the gap in the line. Once accomplished, they were to complete liaison with the 122nd Regiment further east and then form a strong line to the western end of the hill, defensive in nature to the south and offensive in nature to the north. There was a group of Americans in the Charlevaux Ravine beyond, and they would no doubt be waiting for their reinforcements to follow the path that they had blazed through the line, come the anticipated morning attack. The American contingent must not be allowed to reinforce. Once everything was in place, they were to be destroyed. Clear that the pioneers understood the importance of the situation, both Von Sybel and Bickel watched them stalk carefully off through the darkness toward the Ravin d'Argonne in the direction of Hill 198. In fact, there had already been a report of American reinforcements moving in the direction of the Charlevaux, and both officers silently prayed their preparations would not be too late. (51, 120, 126, 128)

Elsewhere, the changeover of German regiments had begun in the area of the 76th Division, as prescribed by Major Ditfurth. The 1st Battalion/254th PC had moved down and taken position at the Charlevaux Mill, while the 252nd had moved out to relieve the 253rd, then moving onto the western side of Hill 205. The 1st/254th spread out up onto Mont d'Charlevaux, above the Binarville-La Viergette road (where they met up with troops from the 7th/122nd farther to the east) and then down to around the middle of the Charlevaux Ravine. They carefully and quietly pressed in as close to the companies of Americans as they dared, dug in, and waited. Moving into position, they had snatched up a couple of lone outposts from the fringe of the American bivouac, making prisoners of the ragged Doughboys and sending them back for interrogation. It all seemed too easy and many were secretly sure that something raw was afoot. They remained confident, however, that they could make quick work of the impudent band of Americans.

The 2nd/254th also moved quickly and quietly into position, extending the line from the 1st Battalion ahead, on over around the base of Hill 205 and then up onto the shoulder of Hill 198, where they made liaison with the 376th Pioneers then digging in up there. All along this line, the Germans primarily concerned themselves with establishing protected machine-gun positions with good fields of fire into the ravine and stocking them with as much ammunition as they could before daylight hit. Soon after the morning had foggily established itself, scouts came in to inform the 2nd/254th commander, Hauptmann Petri, that there was a band of Americans on the move southwestward down in the Charlevaux, heading right into the 2nd Battalion's gun positions. The 2nd Battalion, which had just completed its initial arrangements and was already sending its first ranging fire into the nest of Americans, made ready to meet this first onslaught.

The 3rd/254th, meanwhile, moved into position all along Hill 205 facing the enemy line to the south and occupied the La Palette Pavilion. Down a wash in the west side of the ridge, ahead of the hill, the Giselher line snaked down from the hilltop to the ravine floor. There, from a concrete bunker, the troops surveyed the ravine from ground level, while observers in La Palette did the same from above. A team from the 77th Pioneer Company, *Minnenwerfer* (trench mortar) Section, had set up their gun along the backside of the hill and had been shelling the French to the northwest. Now, they redirected their fire to drop into the Charlevaux Ravine instead, just as the American's big guns began their morning barrage. That falling artillery announced that the American morning assault could not be far off.

As dawn crept closer, the 76th Division's 376th Pioneer troops, about 60 of them, had carefully crept away from Hauptmann Von Sybel and up the slopes of Hill 198. They had come across the ravine bottom following a carefully laid maze of lane through the wire, their groups at wide intervals, without arousing any undue suspicion. The main American line was some 600 meters to the south, so movement should have been relatively safe. However, things in the immediate area were confusing, what with Americans in the ravine ahead and reportedly on the move up the ravine from the south as well. Therefore, one could not be too careful. Up the Hill 198 slope, a few steps at a time. Stop; listen... nothing; proceed. Then, on up to near the top. It was unnervingly quiet in the pre-dawn forest to the men of war; only occasional shots and rattles of machine-gun fire in the distance announced that there was anything akin to their war-torn world. Moving in small parties of four to six men each and grouped around the man carrying the light machine-gun, they kept careful watch in all directions. It seemed incredible that the Americans had not outposted the break they had perpetrated in the Stellung, and everyone was sure that there would be automatic rifle fire coming at them with every step. Then... there was the trench outlet, apparently abandoned. All men immediately and silently went to ground. Eye contact in the dim light and the wave of the leader's hand - *'Scouts, out!'* Dimly rustling footsteps proceed through the leaves ahead. Waiting... surely here, if they were to meet the American outposts at all, was where it would likely be. A scout comes back. All seemed clear.

Quietly moving forward, a firebase was set up around the end of the trench and some men carefully made their way down along it, using a familiar drill designed to make use of the trench's kinks and traverses to make sure it is clear. Other teams moved above ground, fanning out to cover a wide area. The trench, incredibly, was found clear; the ground above was not. One of the flanking scout parties, moving along the base of the hill down in the Charlevaux Ravine ahead of the main force, finally met one of the expected American outposts there in the dark, near the edge of a wide field, and quickly dispatched them. Some time later, a flanking party of the main force, moving up on Hill 198 itself came upon more of the runner posts. There was a short fight and three Americans were captured outright, while another, wounded, would be found and brought in later. Several other of the enemy were killed and their bodies searched for intelligence materials, stripped of their boots and left. Two managed an escape however, rifles thrown aside, running hell bent for leather toward the Charlevaux Ravine. American message posts strung out in a long line were familiar things. Now though, the communication line from the nest of Americans - the *Americanernest* - down in the Charlevaux Ravine was broken.

Before long, a solid German line was firmly reestablished in the trench where the break had been, with machine-guns mounted and pointed alternately north and south. Carrying parties went out to fetch more ammunition and yet wire was strung strategically, since there was too much light to move about in the open and string it generally. Noise was no longer a factor, since the Americans would soon be made very aware that the 254th had arrived. Liaison reached the men of the 122nd farther down to the east, which was now mostly under the command of a Lt. Hopf, a connection was solidly made there (even overlapped a little) and the lieutenant was informed that the breech has been effectively closed. Through the liaison, the leader of the 376th Pioneers, in turn, learned that the 122nd had corralled the eastern end of the ravine. Then came a runner with the news that the western and northern sides of the Charlevaux had been covered as well. With the 376th and the 122nd troops strung out along the southern side then, the ravine was as tight as Major Ditfurth and Hauptmann Von Sybel had hoped it would be just a few short hours before.

It was no later than about 10:00 a.m., and the Americans in the Charlevaux Ravine were completely surrounded. (29, 51, 123, 124)

The sun was barely coming up behind the solid gray above, and Doughboy privates Otto Volz and Herbert Tiederman of the 308th Headquarters Company were on outpost duty off the left flank, when they thought they heard rustling in the brush ahead of them. Crouching in the tall grass, they listened intently as the sounds drew closer, accompanied by mutterings, unmistakably German and unhappy. At the last moment, the two Doughboys stood up suddenly, raising their rifles. "We found a young German," Tiederman later remembered, "about 17 or 18 years old, who upon seeing us held up his hands and called 'Kamerad, Kamerad.'" They quickly disarmed him and searched him (Pvt. Volz acquiring a fine Luger pistol in the bargain) and then turned him back toward the bivouac area. The Major would want to talk to the little Hun.

Major Whittlesey and Captain McMurtry were not at the command hole when they brought the German in. However, Private Jim Larney was, as was Corporal Walter Baldwin, who had charge of the runners, Private Bob Manson, the Major's preferred interpreter, and a host of other Headquarters Company men. Private Manson greeted the prisoner genially and offered him his half-sack of Bull Durham, which the youngster greedily accepted and emptied into an enormous pipe, passing back the empty sack with a wicked smile. A few questions were asked, mostly innocuous small talk, while they waited for the Major; name, rank, and unit. The real questioning began when Major Whittlesey and Captain McMurtry returned from sending out a patrol forward across the road and up the hill ahead and making an early morning check up of positions. (29, 51, 218, 245)

He was Musketeer Ernst Brahn of the 376th Pioneer Battalion/254th Regiment, from Hesse, and had come up to LaPalette last night in trucks, along with some 70 others. In fact, the whole battalion should be in line by now, though he had seen but a few infantrymen when he first arrived. Their orders were to hold the advance of the Americans in the Charlevaux Ravine and then grind them down into the dust. Most of his comrades were of the opinion that it would not be that difficult. (123, 135, 145)

Major Whittlesey relied on his lawyer skills to get what information he could from the German, but it was obvious that the boy actually knew little. In any case, he found it difficult to create the steady banter so necessary to preventing his witness from spinning a connected web of lies, due to the necessity of Pvt. Manson as interpreter. Still, with what he got, the Major's thoughts ran deep. If what the prisoner said was true, then there would be a veritable herd of German troops right between his position and Lt. Knight's back on the west ridge of the Ravin d'Argonne before long, and his left flank was yet still an 'open door'. That must be remedied.

The Major sat down and scrawled a quick message to Lt. Knight, instructing him to extend his forces, post haste, along the axis of advance that the main force had followed into the Charlevaux the previous day. Companies E and H were being sent back and would meet them. While he was writing this, a runner approached him from Captain Holderman's Company K, some 300 meters just the other side of the ravine. They had been sent, the runner said, to extend the Major's right flank. That was good news and Whittlesey sent the runner back to Captain Holderman with instructions to come forward and then gave the message for Lt. Knight to another runner, who disappeared back over the brook toward the slope of Hill 198 (and was never heard from again). It was about 6:20 a.m. and French artillery and machine-gun fire was tuning up on the other side of Hill 205. (149, 246)

The patrol that the Major had sent out forward just a short time earlier now came back, reporting they had spotted a number of Germans up ahead, thrown a few shots in their direction and taken some light machine-gun fire in return. Damn... Germans ahead was one thing, but Germans ahead *and* to the left rear was another. Obviously, despite all the racket that had come from over there last night, the French were nowhere near even with the 308th's position in the ravine. If they were even close, or anything of a threat to the Germans on Hill 205 for that matter, then why had the 70 enemy Pioneers from the 254th been brought up to face the 308th instead of the French? Worse still, neither early morning liaison team had come back yet, and they had been gone well over an hour. Shades of the morning of the 29th probably flitted through Major Whittlesey's mind, even as long-range machine-gun fire from over on Hill 205 started to pepper the left flank of the position irritatingly. Exchanging knowing looks with Captain McMurtry, the Major then called for another runner… "Ask Lt. Wilhelm to report to me." (29, 51, 135, 148, 149, 150)

Company's I/F/307th awoke just before first watery light to find themselves in the midst of a weedy wire field and taking fire from German gunners up on Hill 205. Company M awoke to find itself dug in only a short distance from I/F, along the western slope of the ravine and drawing enemy machine-gun fire from the Haupt-Widerstands-Lienie on the ravine floor just ahead, but defiladed from the majority of it by a hillside spur. After checking his map and gathering his mud-stained men, Lt. Shelata pulled closer to I/F. There, a furious Major McKinney grouped everyone together again to move down the ravine in the wan morning light to catch up Company K. They had not gone far however, when they began to take heavy shell and machine-gun fire and were driven to ground. Sending a message back to Colonel Houghton at 6:10 a.m. telling of their initial failure, Major McKinney started the troop back to the Depot des Machines. Once there, almost beside himself with rage over the disastrous operation, he interrogated Lt. Shelata briefly and then placed him under arrest for dereliction of duty. Then came the call to Houghton and the reluctant recitation of all the night's happenings. Perhaps Company K had made it up, McKinney speculated, as scouts sent out that morning had not found any evidence of them. The Regimental Commander replied that it was entirely likely. Either that or they had been wiped out. Early indications were that the 308th force, which they had been sent to assist, had been cut off from communications. If K had indeed made it up there, they would have no way of knowing. Colonel Houghton then ordered the party, or parties, responsible for the disaster that night arrested and sent to him as soon as possible. (Lieutenant Shelata was later court-marshaled over the incident.) In the meantime, the Colonel ordered Major McKinney to take what remained of 3rd Battalion and get them some hot food and rest - they were going into support for the time being. He then immediately called General Johnson. (103, 138, 139, 235)

Meanwhile, at dawn, General Johnson had Colonel Stacey send a liaison force from Company I/308th forward and then west, out along the Binarville-Moulin de l'Homme Mort road toward the town, looking for the French left flank. At the same time, M/308th made its way up to the point where D and F had established their line, formed liaison, and extended back to L/308th and the remainder of I, which together had curved a line down the road toward Binarville.

Company I's liaison platoons fanned out in the dreary morning and worked carefully for nearly a kilometer down the road without finding any French. To their right front, above Binarville, there was artillery and machine-gun fire in the distance, but where they were moving it was strangely quiet. Who had control over the area? They had not quite made it to town when, at a fork in the road almost buried in barbed wire, they were assaulted by a heavy machine-gun hidden in the brush off to one side. Quickly skirting the gun (their mission was for liaison, not avoidable offensive action), they continued north overland and eventually came out into an apple orchard just north of town and a little east of the Binarville-La Viergette road. There, they stumbled onto a 9th C.a.P. outpost, well hidden and occupied by three very unconcerned Frenchmen, who promised to take 'le bon soldat Americans' to their company PC - right after breakfast. Runners were sent out to draw the rest of the troops of the 3rd Battalion section forward and by mid-morning, a link had been made. The second, further gap behind Major Whittlesey's left had been closed, for all the good it did. (10, 131, 146, 159, 238)

At about 6:30 a.m., Captain Holderman and a guide came over the little footbridge and met with Major Whittlesey. The Captain, experienced soldier that he was, was not pleased with all he saw in the misty morning light. First, he had not realized in the dark just what a steep hill he and his men had come down earlier that morning. If they should have to fight back up it for any reason, they would definitely be in for a tough time. Second, the ravine was far too narrow and the hills around it held too much of a commanding view over it for him to feel comfortable about taking up a position extending the 308th's right flank in it. Neither of the other two companies behind him had shown up yet and alone he would not have enough men to extend back the distance they had come during the night.

Nevertheless, the Captain introduced himself and presented his orders for the extension of the right flank to Major Whittlesey and Captain McMurtry, reporting that he and his lieutenant, who was back minding the men, had only 97 soldiers with them, but that the other two companies behind should be along any time. Somehow, they had been separated in the dark. He said this with apparently little conviction though, realizing that they should not have been all that far behind. Every minute that they remained unaccounted for in the rapidly progressing daylight, diminished their chances of showing up at all.

Nevertheless, Captain McMurtry said, with an intense note of relief in his voice, "Oh, then we're alright." It was a sentiment no doubt shared by Major Whittlesey. Both realized just how precarious the position in the ravine actually was. They were, once again, a small khaki force in a large sea of field gray with only a thin runner line stretching back, like a lifeline. Then, there were Major Whittlesey's missing liaison teams, as well as Captain Holderman's lost patrol, both of which would be enough to give any commander pause. Therefore, support in any form would be warmly welcomed.

Additionally, to Major Whittlesey and Captain McMurtry, Company K/307th's arrival also signaled two other very important and positive things. First, the triple-strength runner line they had left behind was still intact and operational, indicating full contact with the rear, no matter what was happening on the other three sides. (This despite what Captain Holderman reported about at least the last runner post being abandoned.) Second, the 307th was making every effort to come up on the right and help exploit the break in the line that the 308th had affected. This would seem to indicate that General Johnson was fully aware of the situation and that they should not be alone in the ravine very long. It would also appear to suggest that Colonel Stacey was indeed keeping an eye on the rear areas. And with the force in the Charlevaux about to make the connection back to companies D and F on the left, all would then be in good order and Major Whittlesey's fears for a repeat of the night of the 28th-29th would be dispelled.

Around them, the five medics were preparing some men to carry a few more of the wounded back down the runner line and out of the Pocket, while others worked on deepening their holes or the latrines. "Have your company report here," Major Whittlesey told Captain Holderman. However, according to Jim Larney, Captain Holderman balked at first. While his right flank extension orders seemed to put him at Major Whittlesey's disposal once he arrived there, he definitely did not favor the position in the ravine, especially without the support he had started with. Moving farther into the ravine only seemed to invite trouble then. He, therefore, demanded to be shown the Major's orders, stating that without seeing specific orders to hold such a position he would not take it up and instead take his company back out the way he came. The Major was apparently a bit peeved at this; arguing with a junior officer was not something he tolerated easily. Nonetheless, he quietly produced the orders, which of course stated that once he had broken the line, he was to hold and extend liaison left and right and then Captain Holderman accepted that he had no choice.

"Where do you want me?" he said flatly, looking up and the Major told him to take up the right flank, which Lt. Wilhelm's Company E would soon vacate as it moved out, along with H, to meet up with D and F behind. Captain McMurtry then mentioned that he thought, under the circumstances, sending H out along with E might not be such a good idea. Company H was the strongest company present. If the Germans were out in force off the left, as evidenced by the prisoner, that flank would need as much protection as it could get. The threat on the right, on the other hand, was significantly less and could be covered by the relatively small K/307th once E had gone. Major Whittlesey, seeing the logic, agreed; Company E would go back alone. Once they brought the line forward, then H could extend back some if needed, perhaps across the ravine. (29, 51, 109, 148, 149, 150, 245)

It was 6:45 a.m., and Captain Holderman was heading back over the bridge to bring Company K forward when Lt. Wilhelm arrived. Company E was a good choice for the mission rearward. It was Captain McMurtry's old company, fearless and strong and Major Whittlesey had great faith in Lt. Karl Wilhelm, the quick-witted, intelligent Upton officer from Buffalo at its helm. In addition, the company also had both Lieutenant's Leak and Harrington to support Lt. Wilhelm, meaning that it would have plenty of control in any tight spots. After a brief review of the plan, the Major sent Lt. Wilhelm and his men on their way. They headed off southward in the direction of Charlevaux Brook, crossed the bridge, turned slightly right and disappeared into the early autumn foliage. As Company E left, the helmets of Company K men could be seen bobbing toward the bridge through the brush off the base of Hill 198. Major Whittlesey then sat down and scrawled his first message of the day to Colonel Stacey and handed it off to a runner. It was 6:50 a.m. (20, 29, 101, 148, 149, 150)

At: 294.7-276.3
Have sent order to D and F Co's to advance rapidly to join us. Am sending E and H down west side of ravine to assist this movement. Will await orders here. McMurtry is with me and we are working together. (246)

By 7:30 a.m., Captain Holderman's men had firmly settled into the funk holes Company E men had dug the night before, with Chauchat gunners setting up shop near the road. A machine-gun over on La Palette, which had dropped shots on the K men coming in and the E men going out, continued to play across the left flank. Then, overhead, an enemy plane wheeled briefly before turning northwest and disappearing over Mont d'Charlevaux. Everyone knew what it meant; the plane was obviously spotting for the artillery. Sure enough, shortly thereafter a few shells started to come into the position from the north, falling farther out into the ravine and sending up tremendous geysers of dirty water and mud that showered the men. The shellfire actually meant little however; it would have taken an extraordinary piece of gunnery to land a shell on the reverse slope of the hill the command now occupied. Still, the men dug furiously, though the ground was pretty tough, very rocky and full of roots. The psychological effect of surface cover should never be denied, even if they were only in the ravine temporarily. Said Pvt. Arnold Morem, of Company E:

"...In the Pocket, I was sitting in the hole, trying to dig it deeper and to enlarge it somewhat, when a sniper's bullet hit the bank just along side of me. That ended the needed improvements for the time being..." (44)

While all this was going on, a runner came down the hill into the position with a message for Major Whittlesey that Colonel Stacey had sent out the previous night at 7:00 p.m., reading:

Plenty of rations at your PC of last night. Send for them if you want them. Believe railroad will prevent details from getting lost. Am making every effort to get up blankets, overcoats and slickers. Be prepared to move forward at 0700, but do not advance until you receive the order from me. At daylight try and establish liaison with troops on right and left. Why not try one pounders on observation tower? Will try and have overcoats at ration dump by midnight. Two companies reserve 3rd battalion are now at your PC of last night.

Detroit 1 (131)

Major Whittlesey read the message over a second time no doubt with a sinking feeling. The message had taken over 12 hours to reach him. Orders for a fresh advance had not come up yet and he had no 'one pounders' up with him; they had been left back at the l'Homme Mort dugout, the forest being too thick and one pounders too heavy and unwieldy to bring along. Obviously then, the Colonel was *still* failing to fully grasp the situation. Major Whittlesey then decided to try one more time to drill it home to him and quickly scribbled into his field message book. He handed the result to a runner, upon whose body the message would only much later be found, by 302nd Ammunition Train men bringing ammo up along the old runner line, long after the Major and his men had been relieved:

At: 294.6-276.2
Hour: 7.40am
Have just received your message of last night about rations. Don't dare send back for them if we are to advance. Can't you send them to us? Also overcoats and blankets if possible. Have sent only E company back to join D and F as I feared too much dispersion if we must advance again. Casualties yesterday (estimated in B,E,G,H and C Co.'s, the ones now here) 8 killed, 80 wounded. (246)

Major Whittlesey and Captain McMurtry now mulled over the time it had taken Colonel Stacey's message to get through. Both seemed to agree it was most likely due to man failure than to anything else. Either a runner had gotten lost, or had simply gotten scared and decided to hole up and wait for a bit of light. That was a common practice in the forest at night. But, might it not be something more? They had already been sending out patrols that morning, trying to get a clearer picture of their situation and many were starting to report back in now. Those reports spoke of Germans off both flanks and ahead in fair numbers - but that was to be expected, since they were occupying a position that was advanced well into the Hun lines. However, from the south (where everyone's attention would soon focus) a patrol had brought in a wounded man, Private Harvey M. Farncomb of Company D. He had been hit in the ankle crossing the bridge the afternoon before, passed out and laid in the marsh all night. He told of seeing some Germans moving in the brush around the back of the bivouac and hearing German voices in the dark. Additionally, Both the Major and Captain McMurtry, as well as Captain Holderman, had heard suspicious noises coming from Hill 198 in the pre-dawn hours that had caused them all much internal disquiet, though none were yet ready to admit it out loud. Pals of the Pioneer from the 376th they had captured earlier that morning perhaps? Perhaps… (29, 44, 109, 116, 131, 144)

Then, shortly after Colonel Stacey's message had come in and Major Whittlesey's had gone out, the Major had a couple of the company commanders approach him while their men ate a breakfast of cold corn willy and hard tack. The officers reported that some of the men had not gotten any reserve rations from the dump the day before. In fact, there were about two companies worth that had come into the Pocket completely *sans* food. That meant that, if the runner line actually was working as poorly as it seemed, Major Whittlesey's line concerning rations in his last message ("Can't you send them to us?") would only bring results long after those men had gone into battle hungry once again. And there had already had been far too much of that sort of nonsense in the offensive as far as both Battalion Commanders were concerned. Since no advance orders had come up yet (and might not, depending again on the runner line's operating capacities), ration parties would definitely have to be sent back after all. Therefore, Captain McMurtry quickly assembled a small carrying party, about 15 men and medic Pvt. Saul Marshallcowitz, who was sent along to bring up more medical supplies. Major Whittlesey, meanwhile, wrote out a formal request for the correct number of rations. He handed the message off to the leader of the detail, 1st Sgt. Harold Kaplan, and sent them off with instructions not to follow along the runner line, but instead to try and catch up behind Lt. Wilhelm and Company E, who had left only a short time before and were headed along a slightly different route. (29, 51, 109, 116, 148, 149, 150, 245)

Captain Holderman came up just after the ration party left with still more disturbing news. A runner he sent out just before they moved into the Pocket that morning with a message reporting his position and situation to Major McKinney, had since found his way back in, stating that he had been unable to get through. He reported Germans roaming all around up on Hill 198 and a complete absence of any manned runner posts. The Major took the news uneasily. Combined with Captain Holderman and Lt. Pool's report of the empty runner post of last night, and the slowness of Colonel Stacey's message in arriving, the situation behind them darkened considerably. Further, adding the report by Pvt. Farncomb of Germans seen in the brush around them and Private Powers' mentioning of "voices on the hill behind" last night (as well as his, McMurtry's and Holderman's experiences), there would certainly seem to be some serious questions concerning the communication line. (149)

Yet, Major Whittlesey was apparently not yet ready to entertain the thought that it might be another encirclement. After all, they were in a very advanced position and obviously with no flank support. That would certainly place Germans behind their immediate right, since the 307th was not yet up on an even line with them. Perhaps Captain Holderman's runner had simply strayed off course. And, any Germans back on Hill 198 might likely be just small, wandering bands of infiltrators, similar to the Pioneer that they had captured that morning and something that the division had been having a devil of a time with during the whole battle thus far. Besides, Company K's very presence seemed to indicate things were all right along the runner line, did it not? (This, even though they had still not seen anything of the companies that had been behind them.) At least, up until about 4:00 a.m. anyway, Captain Holderman noted. But what was the line condition now, some four hours later?

Major Whittlesey decided to test the line. Captain Holderman needed to get word back of where he was anyway and so the Major sent a message to that effect, which Colonel Stacey could then pass along to Colonel Houghton. If the runner came back, they would know without a doubt that the line was broken. If not, they could reasonably assume that the line was secure and their position relatively safe from infiltration from the rear. Standing there, he scribbled briefly again in his message book, tore it out, and handed it to a runner, telling him to be especially watchful. (29, 51, 135, 148, 149, 150)

At: 294.6-276.3
Hour: 8.20am

Capt. Holderman with K Co. attached to 2nd Bn. 307 is here with his Co. They were sent to get in touch with 308th and last night came up our runner line from our advanced telephone station. Mr. Holderman says that at 21.00 last night the two advance companies of 307 (G&H) were at 295.4-276.45 (246)

Just as the runner trotted off through the brush, headed across the brook and up the hill, it occurred to Captain McMurtry that Major Whittlesey had not included the Headquarters Company men or machine-gunners up with them in his earlier ration request. Writing out his own message, in the Major's message book, he quickly sent a runner off with it to try and catch up with the ration party:

From: CO 2nd Bn 308 Inf   At: 294.7-276.3 Hqts 1st & 2nd Bns.
Hour: 8.42am   To: Lt. Taylor. Co K 308 Advance Tele Station
Do not forget to send following rations for the Bn Hqts. + MG's"
1st Bn. Hqts – 32
2nd Bn Hqts – 43
MG Detachs – 50

G.G. McMurtry (II) (246)

By now, the shelling into the Charlevaux Ravine was getting more than a little annoying and they were picking up a few light shrapnel wounds because of it. Major Whittlesey had a short conference about it with Lt. Teichmoeller, the artillery liaison officer, and the lieutenant agreed that it was only a matter of time before German spotters got the range good. In that case, there would really be problems. Therefore, something needed to be done quickly. However, if the runner line was so damaged as to take 12 hours for a message to get through, sending a runner back would simply be a waste. They needed action much more quickly. That left the messenger pigeons, which had worked fairly well from l'Homme Mort, despite the Major's general lack of faith in them. Writing out a quick note in one of the little pigeon message books, Whittlesey called for Private Omar Richards, the 1st Battalion pigeon handler, and watched as Pvt. Richards clipped the little aluminum tube to the bird's leg and tossed it in the air. (III) (29, 51, 109, 116, 148, 149, 150)

At: 294.6-276.3
Hour: 8.50am
We are being shelled by German artillery. Can we not have artillery support? Fire is coming from North-West. (246)

Then, Lt. Teichmoeller also sent out a pigeon (one of Pvt. Tollefson's), soon after Major Whittlesey's had gone, with a message of his own, calling for counter fire:

From: J.P. Teichmoeller, Liaison Off. 305 FA   At: 294.8-275.6
Hour: 9am   To: CO 305th FA
We are being shelled at this point. Cadence – 1 per minute. Caliber – Minen 77 HE. Fire – Northwest. Give us artillery; work quickly.

Teichmoeller (131, 246)

Importantly, the coordinates in the two messages differ greatly. Much has been made out of Major Whittlesey's apparent "mistakes" in sending back his location coordinates. The allegation has often been that, by sending back messages with the wrong position for his command, he not only brought down an American barrage on the afternoon of October 4 directly upon them, but also caused the misdrops of supplies perpetrated later by the 50th Aero Squadron. This is perhaps the single most persistent of the myths surrounding the Lost Battalion and another that is, again, totally unfounded. There was an initial attempt to clear up the question of the coordinates made by authors Thomas Johnson and Fletcher Pratt in their 1938 book, *The Lost Battalion*. However, they inaccurately positioned the Pocket on the maps illustrating their book, and this inaccuracy thus placed Major Whittlesey's position some 75 meters south of their true location on the hillside. (IV) (365, 369, 370, 371, 372, 374)

However, Major Whittlesey was actually very accurate in his calculations all through the Argonne and was conscientious in his reporting of them as correctly and quickly as he could. Therefore, he was in no way the cause of the problems that beset the Lost Battalion due to any inaccuracies of calculation on his part. Lieutenant Teichmoeller's message, on the other hand, would have farther-reaching and more disastrous consequences.

Neither Major Whittlesey nor Lt. Teichmoeller's birds flew to the Regimental PC, there being no loft there. Instead, both birds landed at divisional mobile loft #9, near the town of Florent, where the messages were logged into the message center at 10:55 a.m., but were not immediately acted upon. Nor is this necessarily a bad thing, as a comparison of the map coordinates on the two makes clear. Lieutenant Teichmoeller's message gave coordinates of a vertical line of 294.8, which is altogether fitting as it places him just right of the centerline of the Pocket. Then, however, he gave a horizontal line of 275.6, which is actually a line across the other side of Hill 198; some *800 meters south* of his true line in the Charlevaux Ravine. Just how he figured those coordinates is unknown, but a good guess would be that he inadvertently transposed the numbers 5 and 6. Though still some 100 meters or so too far north of his actual line under the road, a horizontal of 276.5 would certainly put him closer to his correct position. (The Binarville-La Viergette road may, in that general area, be coordinated as being at 276.4.) He may also have thought himself actually slightly farther north, since navigation in the Argonne was such a difficult thing for one with little experience. Moreover, Lt. Teichmoeller, as explained, was a new liaison officer with the 308th, having only been with them about two days.

By contrast, all of Major Whittlesey's messages out of the Pocket give the same horizontal line of 276.3, which is basically the line of the wagon road running along the bottom of the Pocket, give or take 10 meters. For all his vertical coordinates, the Major gave one of two lines, either 294.6 or 294.7. The farthest left flank line of the Pocket was just shy of 294.6 (actually at about 294.55), while 294.7 would have put him a bit left of the center, or just about between his command hole and where a large majority of the wounded were to later be laid out, down toward the bottom. Both were positions that Major Whittlesey spent a great deal of time in. All of these coordinates have been double checked by the author, both on the map and then actually in the Argonne and the Pocket, using both modern methods as well as period methods. It was found that Major Whittlesey's positioning had been extremely accurate, right to within about 10 to 12 meters, which would not have been enough to cause any real problems for his command, provided the coordinates were followed. (V) (29, 51, 131, 135, 144, 148, 149, 150, 246, 369, 374)

Major Whittlesey listened to the gunfire that morning, which was now getting heavier. That, however, was to be expected, since they were actually out ahead of the advance and the Germans were very close indeed. Yet, the firing in the distance behind them should not have been that far back - not if the way was indeed as open as it had been the afternoon before. As both pigeons winged off to the south, Major Whittlesey and Captain McMurtry organized some more strong patrols to go out about 9:10 a.m. On the left flank, a squad from Lt. "Red" Cullen's Company H fanned out into the brush to size up the situation to the west. To the right, Captain Holderman sent a squad out on a similar mission east. With Lt. Wilhelm and Company E already to the southwest (from where sounds of a pitched battle now began to filter back, much closer than the rest, indicating that Lt. Wilhelm had found trouble), all the bases were covered, since they already knew what lay ahead.

Within half an hour however, the flank patrols were back and reporting both directions blocked by small parties of heavily armed Germans operating not far off in the brush, making liaison impossible without actually fighting a way through. Then, just before 10:00 a.m., what remained of Company E came limping back over the footbridge. (29, 51, 148, 149, 150)

Setting out across the Charlevaux Brook that morning, Lt. Wilhelm had decided to take Company E over the slope of Hill 198 at an oblique angle around the end of the hill, rather than directly over the ridge and down the runner line. Doing so, he could then run a straighter course over to companies D and F. Lieutenant Knight would likely be running a similar oblique course across the Ravin d'Argonne toward Hill 198 from his end, and this would make the task of linking up with them that much easier. The resulting firefight with the waiting Germans that followed however, was a confusing, vicious melee from which it was lucky that anyone survived. The following description is a reconstruction based upon several different written accounts, including Karl Wilhelm's own recollections. (20, 101, 109, 116)

Lieutenant Wilhelm took his time moving down and across the ravine that morning. He was in no hurry, being well aware of the danger posed by the exposed left flank and having been briefed by Major Whittlesey before he set out with the information provided by the recently captured prisoner. He moved E slowly through the brush so as not to alert any Germans that might be about that the Americans in the ravine were on the move. Before they had progressed very far, the ration party that Captain McMurtry had sent out caught up with them and Lt. Wilhelm amalgamated them into the column. More rifles meant more security.

They had only gone perhaps a half kilometer, and were still fanned out on the hillside some 30 meters below the crest when Lt. Wilhelm, out front with his scouts, was startled by a voice clearly calling down from up above, on top of the hill.

"Americans?" the voice questioned.

The Doughboys froze in their tracks. There was no Teutonic accent; perhaps it was men from D or F.

"Yeah," a little New York Greek, Private Alfio Iraci, called back.

"What company?" the voice wanted to know.

Three or four men answered back, "E Company, 308th."

Then there was silence.

The silence made Lt. Wilhelm suspicious. He sent a scout up the hill to investigate while the rest of the company nervously held position. When the scout did not come back after a few minutes, the lieutenant himself took a couple scouts with him and started up the hill. They had crawled only a short distance ahead when they heard voices, speaking low and in German. Lieutenant Wilhelm turned questioningly to Mechanic-Private Louis Probst, who was German by birth and actually had a brother then serving in the German army. Probst listened intently to the voices for a moment and then called out excitedly, "He's giving them our range!"

The little party reversed back down the hill, not bothering at cover now. Lieutenant Wilhelm was just giving the order to move out when all hell broke loose. From above, rifle and machine-gun fire tore down into the under strength company, potato masher grenades sailed through the air and men ducked into whatever cover was at hand. The lieutenant tried to get the men moving forward across the slope again; there could be no falling back, as the link with Lt. Knight needed to be made. Barely had they begun to move though, when another machine-gun opened up from that direction. A squad tried to flank it left up the hill, but then another opened up. And then another.

Low on grenades, they were effectively cut off from any forward advance on at least two sides within the first few minutes. Down the slope and to the rear seemed clear though, perhaps a wider swing down instead of up would work. Men retraced their steps, but were cut off when another gun, below them on the slope, opened up. It was the single worst concentration of machine-gun fire any of them had ever seen. Company E now had between five and seven machine-guns ripping into their ranks from three sides, while from across the ravine snipers working from brush below the road off the left flank of the Pocket picked off the wounded trying to crawl to cover. Lieutenant Leak took a glancing gunshot wound to the head that pierced his helmet and creased his scalp, but he stayed on his feet. Lieutenant Harrington was hit again and went down, but he was up giving orders in the time it took to hastily wrap the field dressing on his leg. Private Irwin Hurd, an original Upton man, also took a wound, one from which he would not get back up.

Too many others never got up again either. Private Henry Miller snaked through the brush, took careful aim, and plugged a nearby sniper. Turning his head to a buddy next to him he smiled saying, "I got him!" just as a machine-gun opened up. (Other reports have this action later off the left flank in the Pocket; however, eyewitnesses put him here with Lt. Wilhelm's group.) His posthumous Distinguished Service Cross citation for his careful shot begins, "For extraordinary heroism…" Private Iraci went down, as did a Minnesota replacement, Private Oscar Swenson.

Lieutenant Wilhelm quickly assessed that if they stayed put, the company would be quickly annihilated. Grabbing Lieutenants Leak and Harrington, he shouted for them to take the majority of the men (including the wounded) and try and work their way back to the Pocket any way they could. He would take the remainder of the company and try to fight through and link with D and F. Fifty-one men had set out behind Lt. Wilhelm that morning (less the ration party). With only a handful left, the lieutenant now set out to try and complete his orders. However, it did not take long for the plan to fall apart. Said Karl Wilhelm later:

"I took ten men and worked for a hundred and fifty yards to see if there was a possible chance for the company advancing between the machine gun firing from the foot of the hill and the infantry company above us… After five of these men had been shot, I determined that this was not feasible and started back toward the remainder of the company, only to find that the Germans had swung down in between myself and the rest of the company. We were cut off… The only thing left for us was to head straight up the hill… We had (only) advanced 5 or 6 yards (when) we found that there were Germans all around us. They were shouting to one another and evidently had some idea we were in the vicinity, so we crawled into thick underbrush and lay there all during that day.

A little path… evidently lead to a German gun position… for during the day the Germans were passing… so close we could hear what they said. After dark, we decided it would be much safer to work back in smaller groups… in the general direction of the American lines. It took us from 8.00pm to 12.00am that night to go an eighth of a mile.

Directly in front of us were three stretches of barbed wire 30 yards across, protected by machine guns… We started working through this wire, our progress being necessarily slow as every time a flare went up we would have to stand perfectly rigid until it had died out. They fired frequently with machine guns, searching the wire for any enemy that might be there… As luck would have it, we got through safely… to our own posts." (20)

It was slightly after 3:00 a.m. on the morning of October 4 when they finally managed to crawl through American lines. Lieutenant Wilhelm had been slightly wounded in the hand and, out of the original force he set out with, he had only Sergeant William Callahan, a corporal and two privates with him. That was all. (20, 54, 101, 109, 116, 135, 154, 184, 236)

The wounded Lieutenants Leak and Harrington came limping back into the position with about 18 men in tow just before 10:00 a.m. From then on, everything started to rapidly go horribly wrong. They reported to Major Whittlesey the lashing they had taken, that Lt. Wilhelm was still out trying to work his way through, and that they had been ordered back with the wounded any way possible. This, along with the 9:30 a.m. reports from Lt. Cullen's and Captain Holderman's patrols, did not sit well with Major Whittlesey or Captain McMurtry. All signs seemed to indicate that there were many more Germans working their flanks than anticipated. Worse, there had still been no orders up from Colonel Stacey, meaning that their only option was to sit where they were while the enemy strengthened his positions off both flanks and ahead. While there was firing in the distance that told the story of the 307th in the east, as well as with Lt. Knight in the west, it did not sound like they were having much success. To the immediate rear, behind Hill 198, there was only sporadic rifle and machine-gun fire, which *might* have been an indication of a clear path back down to the Ravin d'Argonne. However, with no orders to fall back, the only option was to remain in the ravine and wait. Again, shades of the 28th-30th loomed...

Back on the western ridge, Lt. Knight had Company D up front again, supported by F, ready to extend the line westward as the sun began to pinken the cloudy, pre-dawn sky. The runner Major Whittlesey had sent out to find the lieutenant with the line extension instructions that morning had never made it and therefore Lt. Knight remained ignorant of the Major's intentions. There had been no sign of E and H the previous afternoon and he had expected to see them already this morning. However, when there was still no sign of them by early dawn, he figured something must have gone wrong in the ravine ahead. Major Whittlesey had made it absolutely clear the afternoon before how important the link on the left would be and would not have deviated from the plan without there being a definite, and most likely dire, cause. (105, 109)

General Johnson had hoped to rest his 308th battalions that morning until the 307th came up abreast, and then rest both of the regiments until the 153rd Brigade came abreast. However, the events of the overnight had changed all that. Learning from Colonel Stacey that there was definitely no flank support to either side of Major Whittlesey, and apparently no communication either, the Brigadier changed gears and set everyone in both regiments for a general line advance, aimed at driving the flanks ahead into the Charlevaux Ravine. H-hour was set for 7:00 a.m., following a 20-minute artillery preparation. (131)

At 7:00 a.m., Lt. Knight led his combined company force into battle against the enemy line with the modified plan in mind of a simple drive forward at a slightly oblique angle to try and force the link up to Major Whittlesey himself, without E and H companies. The loss of Lt. Turner and his platoon had hurt the company physically, but had also spurred the men to try to exact some measure of revenge and split the line ahead. As they threw themselves forward that morning, they could hear the heavy machine-gun fire of the attack being executed against Lt. Wilhelm and Company E. They had no inkling of the drama being played out on that opposite slope of Hill 198, only that someone over there was really getting pasted. All morning they pushed, making little headway. By 11:00 a.m., they had again been stopped near where they had been the previous afternoon by the heavy machine-gun and artillery fire. Once again, they fell back to their night positions. Lieutenant Knight then took a couple scouts and went out to try and figure a way around the enemy blockade ahead, while what remained of the two companies chewed on corn willy and hardtack in their muddy funks. A fresh grimness settled in. If they could not get to Major Whittlesey, then that meant that Major Whittlesey could not get to them either. (105, 116)

Hardly had Lieutenants Leak and Harrington finished telling of their adventure, when there was a sharp whistle followed by a tremendous explosion that threw everyone to the ground. A second, and then a third, followed it closely. In no time, Major Whittlesey and several others were back on their feet, waiting for the next rounds to fall, in order to determine the angle of fire. Their artillery obviously doing no good, the Germans had now opened up with a heavy trench mortar - *Minnenwerfer* - from somewhere behind the Pocket and were throwing shells into the American perimeter with good accuracy. Actually, this mortar had thrown a few ranging shells farther out into the ravine the evening before as well, but not enough to do any real damage or raise anyone's hackles. Now however, in light of the accuracy of the rounds, this turn of events was alarming. While the Boche artillery shells then falling well out into the ravine had little hope of hitting anything, a well ranged trench mortar operating from *behind* could cause untold harm to the little command. (29, 51, 135, 148, 149, 150)

Another round crashed in, falling almost square on the left flank into a group of funk holes and sent a couple bodies flying through the air. There were screams and shouts as men who had been caught out in the brush were running fast for cover. Among them was Private Lowell Hollingshead of Company H, a, young, impressionable 18-year-old replacement from Mt. Sterling, Ohio. He quickly jumped down into his shallow hole and began to dig furiously. "Holly," as he was known to his army pals, had joined up in January, trained at Camp Jackson, South Carolina, where he had made Corporal and sailed to France in June with an artillery salvage and supply unit. However, bored with the job by the end of summer and craving action, he requested transfer to a line outfit, thinking that in light of his experience he would go to an artillery unit. Instead, he was assigned to Company H/308th Infantry just prior to the Muese-Argonne jump-off and there was broken down to Private, due to his inexperience with the infantry. It was a rude awakening from his boredom, to say the least.

Now, nine days later, the young man stared in horrified awe as a German trench mortar shell decapitated a man not 10 feet in front of him, the body remaining jerkily on its feet for several seconds before collapsing. Off to one side, he saw another man have both legs blown off and fall to the ground, screaming for his mother until he quickly bled out. Terrified, Holly gave up digging and cowered in the bottom of his hole as low as he could, little realizing the important part he was to later play in the great drama just beginning to unfold. Another shell landed near the command hole and Thomas Cavallo, a little Italian private from New York in the Headquarters Company, was nearly torn in half. Farther down the hill Private Harvey Farncomb, the 1st Battalion scout who had been hit in the ankle crossing the bridge the evening before and laid out all night, now got himself buried by a shell - and a shoulder wound to go along with his ankle. (142, 143, 163, 222, 351)

Something needed to be done, and quickly. Field glasses up, Major Whittlesey spotted the offending mortar in position (from its smoke), grabbed a scout, pointed out the direction, and sent him to investigate. He was back within about 15 minutes; the gun was not far off, only about half a kilometer to the southwest, below La Palette and up from the foot of Hill 205. The catch was at least one machine-gun was guarding it, of course, and there was probably more than one...

Major Whittlesey sat down with his field message book again. It was 10:10 a.m. and he thought for a moment before deciding that the maverick Lt. Harry Rogers and his Company B were the ones for the job. They had done good work the day before against the machine-guns coming into the Pocket, and were close at hand. He figured they could also be spared at the moment. Lieutenant Rogers, however, was a bit rambunctious and the Major needed all the officers he could keep. Better rein him in a bit.

To: Company Commander B co. 308
The man who accompanies this note has located a German trench mortar protected by a MG 40 yds

west of us. Send a platoon with him with 2 Chauchats and 4 rifle trombones (rifle grenade launching cups) *to get the bird. Don't go yourself. Acknowledge receipt by signing and returning this message.* (246)

It was returned duly signed on the bottom "Rogers" within a few minutes. Shortly thereafter, U.S. helmets again bobbed off at a trot over the bridge and through the brush to the southwest; the 20 men that Lt. Rogers had sent out were under the command of acting Sergeants Albert Copsey and Marten Lokken.

Company G men, meanwhile, were reporting that they were hearing much activity coming from the road ahead. All of a sudden, from up there a machine-gun opened up and began showering the hillside with lead, causing the men dug in just under the lip of the road to draw back down the hill some. Then, a few of the potato masher grenades favored by the Germans came down. Their explosions tore small divots out of the hillside. At virtually the same time, another machine-gun opened up against the command from across the brook at the foot of Hill 198, just west of the footbridge. German troops were also plainly seen up near the crest of Hill 198 and on the right flank, a machine-gun opened up from the little cliff behind Captain Holderman's position. The eastward patrol sent out that morning came limping back in about that time, dragging with it several casualties; they had been machine-gunned and grenaded by a German crew farther out on that flank. Yet Major Whittlesey still held his cool, turning his attention instead to the gunfire echoing back from the southwest: Lt. Rogers' men had apparently found the trouble they had gone out seeking. (29, 51, 109, 116, 135, 148, 149, 150, 234, 246, 348, 363)

It was about 10:30 a.m. when the suspected trouble with the runner line was first definitely reported by Private John "Shano" Collins, a Company A man that Major Whittlesey had sent back the evening before to double up the line. Private Collins came tearing up to Major Whittlesey, tugging at the Major's arm with a half salute just as he was engaged with the trench mortar affair. His position, just on the crest of Hill 198, had been machine-gunned a short time earlier, the frightened private said, and he had been very lucky to get away. The other two men on his post had been killed he thought. One, however, Private Adlare LeMay, had not been. He later wrote: (29)

"I laid on the hillside two days wounded, although conscious and saw the Germans across the ravine moving around and once in a while could hear them talking. Two other wounded Americans a short distance back of me who could talk German were calling to the Germans to come and remove them, which they finally did. They also found me, because when I woke up there were Germans all around me and I was in a different location." (44)

Private Collins had only escaped death by having been bent double picking something up when the gun had opened up. In addition, he had heard moans and cries from the post behind his and was fairly certain that at least one of those men was either killed or wounded. Right behind Pvt. Collins was another runner, Private Robert "Ernie" Pou of Company E:

"A runner (Pvt. Collins - author) *from the next post dashed up and said that the Germans had captured or killed the other runners of his post. Before he could finish telling us about it, a bunch of Germans popped up all around us. He and another runner threw up their hands and surrendered. (Here Pvt. Pou is mistaken, for Pvt. Collins was not one of the men captured - author) The other runner* (Pvt. Collins) *and myself jumped into the brush, but not before we were fired at several times. We worked our way back through the thick brush opposite the bridge, which spanned the creek. Across the creek and not far from the end of the bridge, lay four stretcher bearers and the wounded they had been carrying, all dead."* (44)

Then, Private Fred Evermann, a Company B man and the one who had been sent out with Major Whittlesey's earlier "test" message, reported back, right on the heels of Privates Collins and Pou:

"...I found the third relay post, but found no runners and (so) I returned to the Major. I believe this was the first notice the Major had that our communication was cut off to the rear (sic). From then on we were under constant shellfire and continual raking of our flanks with machine gun fire..." (44)

The two Battalion Commanders took in all this information with grave concern. It was time to face facts: More Germans had filtered into the rear areas than either one of them would have liked to imagine and the runner line was most definitely severed. The very thing that Major Whittlesey had twice warned Colonel Stacey about was now being realized. But to what extent this time? It was certainly a question that Major Whittlesey had been sure the evening before, at the foot of the hill just as they were walking into the position, that he would be asking himself. Now there could be no more doubt, and here in the Charlevaux the command was in even worse shape than they had been on l'Homme Mort. Both commanders were well aware of the ration situation and the ammunition situation was certainly no better. In this narrow ravine, Major Whittlesey was even more under strength than he had been the previous time (relatively speaking), and already the casualties were mounting from the trench mortar rounds and the small, nibbling three-sided attacks they were facing. If the Germans had rolled up the runner line, then how long would it be before the fourth side came under attack? Under those circumstances - completely surrounded - how long could they hold out?

First things first, however, The runner line was cut, but was it by just a wandering band of marauding Germans or was it by an enemy actually back in force up on Hill 198? Either way, it was imperative that the runner line be reestablished as quickly as possible; a patrol must see to it. Another concern was the machine-gun just across the brook, which needed to be taken out before it did too much more damage. But who to send? Major Whittlesey reasoned that Company K/307th was supposed to have extended the right flank back anyway, had just come down the line a short time ago and were therefore somewhat familiar with the path back. If it were only a small band of the enemy, they would make short shrift of them; if it was more, they had the numbers with which to fight. He also decided to send along an additional 20 scouts from 2nd/308th to use as support and to fill in the runner line at the breaks. Captain McMurtry agreed, and Major Whittlesey sent a runner to fetch Captain Holderman and Lt. Pool. (29, 51, 148, 149, 150)

Though Captain Holderman glowed at the prospect of the fight, the pragmatic Lt. Pool instead eyed the ridge behind with much more apprehension. He told Major Whittlesey that, in his opinion, they did not have enough men for such an operation without the rest of the 307th's 3rd Battalion, as had been intended. The Major apparently disagreed, again reiterated his orders and reminded Lt. Pool of the twenty 308th scouts also going along. That line *needed* to be reestablished. There was a moment's pause, and then a salute as Captain Holderman and Lt. Pool headed back through the brush for the right flank to get their men ready. (VI) (29, 51, 149, 219, 245)

At 10:45 a.m., Major Whittlesey called for a pigeon. One of the trench mortar shells had already wounded Private Tollefson by this time. A wide piece of shell had smacked him across the forehead, but luckily had done no real damage. He had not gone down to the collection point for the wounded at the base of the hill however, but had instead remained in his hole and been bandaged by his buddy, Private Herbert Tiederman. Thus, Major Whittlesey was actually unaware he had been hurt. Private Bill Cavanaugh, Tollefson's 'second,' now hustled over with the basket, grabbed the pigeon message book from its little pocket in the cover flap, and handed it to the Major, who scribbled out another message to Colonel Stacey. His location coordinates are exactly as on the 8:50 a.m. pigeon message, 294.6-276.3. (44, 143)

Our runner posts are broken, one runner captured. Germans in small numbers are working to our left rear about 294.6-276.2. Have sent Co. K 307 to occupy this hill and open the line. Patrols to east ran into Germans at 295.1-276.3 (6 Boches). Have located German mortar at 294.05-276.3 and have sent platoon to get it. Have taken a prisoner who says his company of 70 men were brought in here last night to 294.4-276.2 from rear by motor trucks. He saw only a few infantry men here when he came in. German MG constantly firing on valley in our rear from hill 294.1-276.0. E Co. (sent to meet D&F) met heavy resistance, at least 20 casualties. 2 squads under Lt. Leak have just fallen back here. (246)

Comparing all these coordinates to both a period German map and French map of the area reveals several things. First, where the German prisoner said he was dropped off out of the motor truck appears to be the truth. There was a good second-class road running right along the spot, making it an eminently plausible place for him to have been situated, not too far from where he had been captured. Also, the break in the runner line that Major Whittlesey sent Company K out to repair, he reports to be just south of the second trench line on Hill 198. This fits well with what the three runners came back and reported. (VII) The German map also shows a small spur trench up on Hill 205 at La Palette Pavilion where a machine-gun would be, although it was a long distance, nearly 500 meters, to fire. Still it would be plenty harassing. The only mistake Major Whittlesey makes in his reporting is in his placement of the trench mortar. Far from being "40 yards away" as he messaged to Lt. Rogers, the mortar was actually about 200 meters away, at the end of a trench half way up Hill 205 and some 30 meters south and 20 east of where the Major reported it. As we have seen, this was also well covered by machine-guns. (368)

As Major Whittlesey's message was winging its way back, Captain Holderman and Lt. Pool were taking their combat force across the ravine. Attacked by machine-gun fire almost immediately upon reaching the brook, the two officers nevertheless sent the men crawling across it well east of the bridge in single file, something Captain Holderman later succinctly described as, "infiltration under harassing fire." It took a long time and they attracted a lot of attention doing it. As the crossing continued, a German voice called out loudly from the road north of the Pocket to the troops on the crest of Hill 198, apparently that the Americans in the ravine were on the move again and there were several answers back from across the ravine. Climbing up the steep slope of Hill 198, the two officers set their squads accordingly. Coming up near the crest, they braced themselves for heavy action and were surprised when they met nothing. The Germans had pulled southward of the crest, deeper into the prepared positions on the northern side of the Haupt-Widerstands-Lienie. (149)

With the 2nd/308th scouts fanning out before them and with strong combat sections guarding the flanks, they started moving backward through the trees toward the 2nd German trench line. It was around noon when they came to a wire belt that had, by the looks of it, not been there the night before. Lieutenant Pool, at the head, formed the men into a wedge, with he and his four sergeants up front, and carefully began cutting their way through, expecting at every moment to be attacked. Once through, they went only a short distance beyond before coming upon a second belt. And it was there that the machine-guns were waiting... (109, 135, 149, 195)

Near 11:20 a.m., a runner jogged his way northward up the bottom of the Ravin d'Argonne along the trail heading toward Hill 198. He was sent from Sgt. Cahill's telephone head to try to break a way through to Major Whittlesey with a message from Colonel Stacey:

Heavy artillery fire will be put down parallel (2)75.5 and to the North of it. This will be furnished at 12 noon. (131)

A shot came from somewhere, the runner dropped and the message went undelivered; a message that would have done Major Whittlesey no good whatsoever anyway. When that fire came at noon, it fell much too far back to be of any help to the men in the Charlevaux Ravine (the coordinates are 1,000 meters south of the Charlevaux position), coming down instead in the vicinity of troops just back of the main line. They, in turn, pulled farther back and desperately reported the short firing. (131, 143, 144)

The main importance behind this particular never-delivered message is that it shows that Lt. Teichmoeller's mistaken coordinates had definitely found their way to the 152nd Field Artillery Brigade's Headquarters and been acted upon, despite many claims to the contrary over the years. It was a first step in a chain of mistakes regarding those coordinates that would soon have calamitous results.

By about 11:30 a.m., a watery sun had broken through the clouds and the pigeon with Major Whittlesey's 10:45 a.m. message was just landing at loft #66, on the French side of the airfield at Colombey La Belle (*well* off course). It was also at that time that Sergeants Copsey and Lokken, and what remained of their tired, dirty, and beaten men, came dragging back into the Pocket to report their failure to take out the machine-guns guarding the trench mortar. Only four of the 20 that had set out were unwounded, and they had been forced to leave behind their dead. Among them was Pvt. Earl Jepson, the first man to be drafted out of Douglas County, Nevada. Sadly, Pvt. Jepson's father was the chief of the Douglas County draft board and had therefore been compelled to send his son off to war. It had been a hard and fruitless fight, the two sergeants reported. They were too few, and the trench mortar had been far too heavily protected. The Major heard out their report and then sent the exhausted men back to their position on the hillside, as the trench mortar shells continued to fall and machine-guns chewed at the positions perimeter. (29, 51, 82, 135, 144, 348, 363)

If that mortar was left to its own devices, there would be hard times ahead. With any luck however, Captain Holderman's efforts would yield better results. With a way cleared to the rear and D and F brought up, perhaps Lt. Knight's men could attack the mortar from one direction while some men from the Pocket attacked from another. As had been proven repeatedly in the last eight days, numbers, which the Major obviously could not then spare, were the key to advance in the mighty Argonne.

The trench mortar shells stopped dropping around noon however, as did the infrequent artillery shells and machine-gun fire. The methodical Germans had apparently suspended operations for lunch. Yet, all around the Pocket, sporadic small-arms fire continued. A few Germans showed themselves briefly on Hill 198 to the rear, as well as on the road to the front and there was a lot of yelling back and forth across the ravine. Private John of Company A recalled:

"My buddy and I were lying in our little… foxhole, keeping watch of the Germans coming in behind us. They were hollering as they were passing through an open space in the timber. I told him that the next time one came out, I was going to cut loose. We weren't the only ones who had the same idea. My gun barrel got so hot I couldn't touch it with my bare hands. They didn't scare us as much as they thought they would…" (220)

Doughboys carefully worked at improving their holes but kept a wary eye out at the calls and responses. Already, several long, thin, almost trench-like holes were being dug. Cover, in the form of leaves and branches, was gathered up. Many decided their best bet was to dig in under fallen logs or at the base of a tree, such as Private Emil Peterson in Company H:

"(On) the hillside where we dig our fox holes, which is now known as the Pocket of the Lost Battalion, when we got there I picked out a place close to a tree and we all dug in with spades, bayonets, sticks and anything we could dig with. Each day I dug my hole a little deeper, until it was about four feet deep. " (224)

"Regular caves they had," Pvt. Powers later noted of some men. One private, digging toward the left flank, hit a chalk pocket, leaving a wide apron of white before the hole in the hillside that, as noted by Lt. Cullen, made an excellent aiming point for the trench mortar. Figuring "the deeper the hole, the higher the rank," the Germans manning the mortar later dumped round upon round on it, virtually demolishing the hole and nearly burying the digger alive until he was finally forced to abandoned the spot. (29, 51, 109)

Below, the four remaining medics also dug deeper, making a long hole near the base of the hill where the wounded were laid out. Their numbers were growing as the fire all around the Pocket steadily increased. Supplies of bandages and the like had already been diminished by the high casualty rate of the previous afternoon, so it was hoped that Pvt. Marshallcowitz had gotten through and might yet be back soon. The medics reported to Major Whittlesey that without that resupply, they could not hope to remain effective and there were several seriously wounded who desperately needed evacuation or they would likely die. Men like Private Everett Bickers, a replacement from Eureka, Montana in Company C, who had a machine-gun bullet tear through both thighs that had left horrible, gaping wounds. Another of the early wounded was Pvt. Nick Kurtz, a Minnesotan in Company H, who had taken a serious sniper shot to the forearm. Private Sydney Smith recalls the attention he gave to a wounded comrade who had been shot: (44, 80, 206)

"When I got to him, the bullet had come straight down his rifle barrel and took both the sights off and hit him right in the temple. He was still alive and every time he would breathe, a bubble of blood would raise on the side of his head. I couldn't get him up out of the mud and water; he'd have had the cloths shot off him in a little bit. I had to just let him lay there in the mud all that time… But he was still laying there alive when they came through there days later and took us out of there." (256)

From behind, the steady thump of artillery kept up its dull, constant beat all morning as usual. Then, all at once, the throb of explosions grew louder and closer and all eyes turned to the rear. Work paused. A barrage was falling on the opposite side of Hill 198, and the distinctive cough of Chauchats and the chug of Hotchkiss guns soon followed from that direction. Attack! But from *directly* behind them? The men looked at each other questioningly. Around them, enemy machine-guns only snapped out an unconnected and disjointed chatter. The trench mortar had fallen silent, and overall, it was relatively quiet in the Pocket, while a real battle was going on just to the rear. Just how far ahead of the main line were they anyway? The air now began to fill with a strange and unsettled tension and the men that had been out on that l'Homme Mort hillside (and there were quite a few in the Pocket here now) looked at each other. *'Aw, fuck… not again…'* The Hotchkiss gunners and Chauchat men now held their fire when they could. Ammunition was relatively limited already, and those who had been there remembered well what the situation had been like by the morning of the 30th.

As what was left of Lt. Rogers' men wandered back into their positions, the last cans of corn willy and hard tack were being opened for lunch and shared out with those who had not gotten resupplied before the advance. (29, 51, 109, 116, 135)

And that was the last of the food.

By noon, Hauptmann Von Sybel's plans for the elimination of the *Americanernest* were well on their way to fruition. All morning, he had handed out orders for a constant harassment of the Americans to be carried out. He had first called for a barrage line of mortar shells to be dropped out into the ravine, just to the south of the American line, designed to keep the trapped Americans in and to keep out any relief that might possibly force a way through a restored line up on Hill 198. (Despite all the positives that had so far happened, his confidence in the Pioneers was far from complete.) Harassment orders included sporadic firefights, lots of random machine-gun barrages, much yelling and hollering back and forth between troops to unnerve the enemy and plenty of grenade tossing. The machine-gun fire was particularly useful, for even if it did not find flesh, it had a way of stripping foliage away and destroying morale. Moreover, it was imperative to test the Americans and find the weaknesses in their defenses. Sporadic and random small attacks were then of equal importance. The weather was certainly cooperating, providing the misty fog needed to hide and move in the ravine until as late as 10:00 a.m. and the harassing troops were frequently rewarded with a yelp or cry for their efforts. Apparently, the Americans had yet to learn the importance of deep holes to hide in.

Additionally, there were reports from Major Hunicken of fierce enemy contact with a strong band of Doughboys attempting to drive rearward earlier that morning. They had tried coming up the shoulder of Hill 198, apparently expecting to find the route they had driven through the evening before still open. They had walked into a well-laid trap of machine-gunners from his 2nd Battalion and according to reports and the bodies left behind in the brush, the American force had been cut to pieces. Not long after, the enemy attempted to attack the trench mortar on the back of Hill 205, an attack that had met with equal disaster, again thanks to the regiment's skilled machine-gunners. So far then, all was playing out rather well.

Reports were also coming in concerning the actual strength of the American contingent. Far from being just a single company or two, it was beginning to look like the prisoner captured the previous evening had been telling the truth; there were something near two battalions in the ravine. This was alarming news, since that number would well outstrip the number of troops in all of the units combined then surrounding them. Few reserves were to be had since half of the single reserve battalion of the 254th, the 1st, had already been thrown into battle against the Charlevaux Ravine. Therefore, the German forces surrounding the ravine were very likely outnumbered, and badly at that. (VIII)

However, the German troops had the initiative on their side, as well as the 'edge' of knowing the ground well. Therefore, Hauptmann Von Sybel passed out orders for an afternoon attack, specifically designed to incapacitate and then destroy the Americans in the Charlevaux. It was to be a coordinated effort between the two regiments, so timed and executed that, by nightfall, they should see the American troops either surrendering or about ready to collapse. Each individual unit was to make a headlong attack in the strongest force from all sides simultaneously, thus giving the enemy no respite and no room to breathe. There was to be no let up until the enemy had cried out, "Enough!" Should the attack fail to completely incapacitate the Doughboy force in the Charlevaux initially, the assault would be resumed the next day. Then a decision would surely be made - surrender, or death.

It was extremely important to both Hauptmann Bickel and Hauptmann Von Sybel that they destroy the American force as quickly as possible. The American commander obviously did not realize the extremely fine position he and his men were in just then, they surmised. For if he did, he would have definitely made some sort of authentic offensive move, not just penny ante pushes in one or two directions. He also had no way of knowing the superiority he possessed in numbers. If he wished, he could simply reverse his force and fight his way back through to his own lines with very little difficulty. In fact, by staying put, he was making it clear that he considered his numbers inferior to those of his enemy. While this was the time to strike hard, instead the American was waiting for a reinforcement that he really did not need.

Another contributing positive factor to Hauptmann's Von Sybel and Bickel's extreme confidence in the attack was that, despite their belief that they were outnumbered, they also believed that the possibility of resupply or reinforcement to the beleaguered force in the ravine was remote. Several patrols sent out earlier that morning from the ravine, ostensibly to fetch food or ammunition, or even to guide relief troops up, had already been killed or captured, just as had been their message line men earlier that morning. In addition, a strong attack from their rear elements, back on the main line of battle in the Ravin d'Argonne, had also been successfully repelled that morning, despite a heavy opening artillery barrage that had verily drenched the German lines with shrapnel. Therefore, there was no way in or out of that ravine for those Americans, except by the grant of Hauptmann Von Sybel or their own deaths. In fact, even at that hour a small force from the *Americanernest* was attempting another breakout - and failing miserably. (51, 123, 128, 149, 307)

(I) This was not quite true. The break in the line was not nearly as wide as that, but instead was just about 500 meters, a portion of which actually ran into the 307th's attack zone as well; it was certainly no more than that. It is very likely that the Germans were counting in the western shoulder of Hill 198, extending down into the Ravin d'Argonne, into this figure. The 308th's entire front was only slightly under 900 meters at that point, from the liaison point with the French beyond the western ridge before Hill 205, on over to the liaison point with the 307th, in the Heights of Le Quatre Chenes above the eastern ridge.

(II) Nobody, however, appears to have thought to include Captain Holderman's Company K. By midday then, having had no resupply from the party the Captain had sent out the night before, they would jump into the same boat of hunger as everyone else. Neither did Company K bring a medic into the Pocket with them as some have suggested.

(III) Private Palmer Kyllo, the 2nd Battalion handler who had sent most of the pigeons out from l'Homme Mort, had been killed soon after the Small Pocket was relieved. His place had since been taken by a young boy from Hayfield Minnesota, Private Theodore Tollefson. Each handler carried a wicker coop on his back that held eight birds. However, Tollefson's coop had been dropped during the fight coming up Hill 198 the day before, the door had come open and all his pigeons had escaped. This left only Pvt. Richards' coop of eight birds left for the two battalions. Privates Richards and Tollefson had decided therefore to split the pigeons up, each taking four in case one or the other of them was killed or wounded. Once they settled into the Pocket that night, they had transferred half into Pvt. Tollefson's coop. Following this initial message, which Major Whittlesey sent out on one of Pvt. Richard's birds, he would use Pvt. Tollefson's four before he would use the others, though exactly why is unclear. Private William Cavanaugh, another Minnesotan, was the other 2nd Battalion handler, assistant to Pvt. Tollefson. Interestingly, it is Pvt. Cavanaugh who is thought to have actually sent out at least two of Pvt. Richards' birds with messages, as well as at least one of Pvt. Tollefson's.

(IV) For evidence of this, see Johnson and Pratt's *The Lost Battalion* and refer to the many photos of the relief map therein. This relief map was constructed by Tom Johnson's wife out of clay, using a U.S. Army topographical map of the area (Army map, "1:20,000 Binarville") and then photographed from above. Later, the photographs were marked with the positions. Unfortunately, Johnson mistook the wagon road at the bottom of the Pocket for the Binarville-La Viergette road above it, and thus placed the Pocket *south* of the *wagon road*, skewing the map calculations by some 75 meters. This then causes some general confusion between the text and the illustrations. Perhaps the main reason for the mistake though, is that Tom Johnson, though an AEF reporter during the war and one of the first to interview Major Whittlesey following the episode, was writing about a time span of a half of a day that he had spent in the Charlevaux Ravine, *20 years* before. Further, unless one is very careful in examining copies of the army maps of the time, it can be very easy to get confused by the many different German wagon roads, secondary roads and footpaths marked on some of those maps. Johnson and Pratt also consistently refer to the Binarville-La Viergette road in the book as "the old Roman road", which it is not. The road that they are referencing is actually further east, around Apremont. They additionally referred to the Binarville-La Viergette road as being constructed on a bed made of "huge lime stone bricks", which it is not. The road is actually little more than two *very* narrow lanes, running along a sort of 'shelf' carved out of the side of the lime stone interiored Mont d'Charlevaux. Naturally then, there *is* exposed limestone in some spots along under the lip of the road, and most especially above it along its northern side, but no 'construction' with lime stone bricks by any means. It probably looks much the same today as it did in 1918, except that it has a solid blacktop covering now, as opposed to the mud and open limestone surface that Major Whittlesey's men knew.

(V) The only exception to these will be a message that Whittlesey sends at 7:40 a.m. October 3, in which he gives the line as 276.2, and this is a moot point anyway since the runner delivering it is killed on his way and so no one ever sees it. This one differing coordinate may also actually be an error in handwriting analysis, as the only surviving example of the message is the carbon copy in Major Whittlesey's field message book, pale and hard to read after these many years. The only other coordinate the Major will ever give for the Pocket is when he sends out the emergency message to stop the U.S. artillery barrage on the afternoon of October 4, giving a horizontal of 276.4, which is generally the line of the Binarville-La Viergette road, running above the Pocket. Even in that instance, he states that they are *"along the road parallel 276.4"*, not actually on it.

(VI) It has always been thought that at that point Lt. Pool simply acquiesced and K went on their way. Instead, again according to Pvt. Jim Larney, who talked to Tom Pool at a Lost Battalion reunion several years later, there was, "much more to it than that." Pool apparently began arguing his point much more strenuously until finally Major Whittlesey, with the tensions of the situation beginning to mount, cast a stony eye on the lieutenant and growled irritably, "You have your orders, lieutenant. Now, proceed." It is important for the reader to keep in mind that, despite the oft-repeated statements about the great 'camaraderie' of the Lost Battalion, these were real people with individual thoughts, ideas and personalities, some good; some bad. Not *everyone* loved Whittlesey or McMurtry (or anyone else in the command structure, for that matter) and certainly not everyone agreed with his ideas of adherence to the orders, or their true purpose in the Charlevaux Ravine.

(VII) Remember that Pvt. Collins at post #3 (going back out from the Pocket), just south of the 2nd trench line up on Hill 198, reported hearing moans and cries from the post behind him, #4, which was slightly west and about 75 meters south down the cutting leading up from the floor of the Ravin d'Argonne. Private Evermann had reported post #3 abandoned by the time he got there. This was about the time Pvt. Collins came tearing up to Pvt. Pou at post #2, just north of the 2nd trench line near 198's crest. Of course, #1, at the bottom of the hill just before the bridge, had already been found abandoned by Company K the night before, something reiterated by Pvt. Pou, who had discovered the bodies of a couple stretcher-bearers and the former wounded they had been carrying, near there. This makes it likely that posts #5 and #4 (#5 being at the southern bottom of Hill 198 and just behind the line being set by the Germans) were taken out by German troops emanating from the first trench line. Posts #3 and #2, on either side of the 2nd trench, were taken out by enemy troops coming from that line. Post #1 was eradicated between 2:30 and 3:00 a.m. by an advance patrol of Pioneers from the 376th. This is the post that Lieutenant Pool found empty not long after, probably about 3:30-3:45 a.m. or so. This makes the break in the communication line nearly three-quarters of a kilometer long with Major Whittlesey's reported sever point near the middle.

(VIII) This was actually untrue, at least in the beginning. Von Sybel was routinely convinced that the force in the ravine was twice as strong as it really was. The number of German troops then surrounding Whittlesey's men at midday of the 3rd, including those troops watching the line up on Hill 198, was a conservative total of around 800-900. However, eliminating those troops not directly involved in the dealings in the Charlevaux - those specifically detailed with watching the main line - brings the total down to around 600-650. By that time, however, Whittlesey's numbers had already dropped some from their original total of about 687 (see Appendix A). Therefore, the two opposing forces were about equal in strength by that noon hour. By the end of the first 48 hours of the siege however, there would be a marked difference in the numbers, as we will see, and the Germans gained a definite edge, though they would never realize it. Even by the end, they still believed that they were out numbered, which is definitely not true. Another myth about the siege is that Whittlesey's force was held in place by a 'much smaller' contingent than he himself had in the ravine, but, again, American casualty figures that will be given later in this text will belie that. These figures have been compared against known German casualty lists for the same period, which show German casualties to be something less than half of the American total, from an almost equal strength to begin with.

Ancillary sources used in this chapter include: 21, 25, 29, 30, 47, 49, 51, Various 152-216, 250-254, 257, 260, 261, 262, 268, 269, 272, 273, 278-283, 285, 286, 292, 296-306, 309, 310, 314-319, 323, 326-330, 338. Additionally: 2, 33, 35, 42, 48, 81, 87, 347, 355, 360

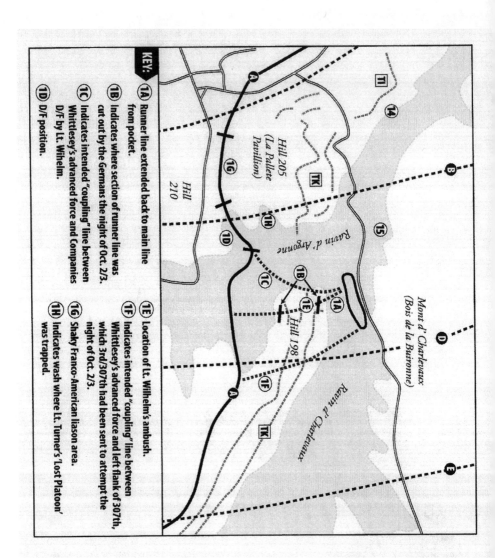

KEY:

1A Runner line extended back to main line from pocket.

1B Indicates where section of runner line was cut out by the Germans the night of Oct. 2/3.

1C Indicates intended "coupling" line between Whittlesey's advanced force and Companies D/F by Lt. Wilhelm.

1D D/F position.

1E Location of Lt. Wilhelm's ambush.

1F Indicates intended "coupling" line between Whittlesey's advanced force and left flank of 307th, which 3rd/307th had been sent to attempt the night of Oct. 2/3.

1G Shaky Franco-American liason area.

1H Indicates wash where Lt. Turner's 'Lost Platoon' was trapped.

306

October 3, 1918 - P.M.

"…Our mission is to hold this position at all costs…"
Major Charles Whittlesey, about noon of October 3.

Following the reported failure of the morning attack that had been meant to drive the line up to Major Whittlesey's position (for fail it had), General Alexander called up General Johnson wanting a full report of the actual situation in the 154th's zone of advance. The Division Commander was already in something of a tizzy over the phone call he had received from General Johnson earlier that morning anyway, when the Brigadier had initially reported that contact with the Major's advanced position may have been broken. It was not necessarily the lack of contact with Major Whittlesey that had General Alexander bugged however, so much as it was General Johnson's apparent disregard for the instructions that General Alexander felt he had clearly given him. (In fact, General Alexander would later admit of the situation in the Charlevaux Ravine that, "it did not, at the time, make a very deep impression on me.") The D/F – E/H linking arrangement apparently forgotten, the Division Commander demanded to know why those elements of the 3rd/308th had not been used to plug the gap "between the French and the 308th" as he had instructed. (In other words, why had they not been extended from the French to contact with Major Whittlesey's direct left flank?) Additionally, if conditions along the ravine extending to the Major's right were so terrible as well, then how was it that Company K/307th had been able to make it up with apparently no problems? And, if one company could advance up, then why had the rest of the 3rd/307th not followed them? Or the rest of the 308th, for that matter?

General Johnson told his commander the truth as he knew it; that the remainder of the 3rd/307th had fallen back under heavy machine-gun fire after having been separated from K during the trip up in the dark. The officer responsible was already under arrest at Colonel Houghton's PC. Apparently, it was only after Company K had gotten forward that the enemy had filtered in and severed contact with the Charlevaux Ravine. Colonel Houghton was then making plans to drive his line up, but the 306th was well in his rear and he believed that fact would make it very difficult to advance without exposing his brigade's right flank to enemy infiltration. In fact, that situation was starting to develop, as evidenced by a message from Captain Blagden. The Captain had told the Colonel that, after polling his company commanders, he thought any major attack made by the 2nd Battalion companies in their present condition was bound to fail. They were low on ammunition and personnel, the men were exhausted by the advance and terrible weather, no one had had a hot meal in three or four days and the enemy was already taking advantage of the fact that the 3rd Battalion had gone, seriously weakening the line. With the 306th so far back, they had not had enough men to refuse their own flank back far enough, Colonel Houghton had said, and the Huns had moved a couple machine-guns down off the right and were wreaking some little havoc over there. Further, the Captain commanding Company L, which had only recently been pulled back into support, was reporting evidence of infiltrators as far back as *a kilometer* behind the line. Though the 1st/307th had mostly arrived at Depot des Machines by then and were in the process of relieving the hurting 2nd from the line, it would be nightfall before the relief would be complete. In the meantime, Colonel Houghton also reported that Captain Blagden was planning one more attempt; what he called a "holding attack", with one company along the line behind a Stokes mortar barrage. A second company would then try a 'hook' attack around to the left, where Company L had gotten some men through the wire yesterday. However, overall he had little confidence it would do much. (2, 29, 51, 90, 103, 109, 131, 138, 139, 144, 235)

As for Colonel Stacey, General Johnson continued, one of the 307th's company commanders had sent a message back to him stating that a sergeant from Major Whittlesey's Company E had just come into their lines. Germans had ambushed him on the link-up mission with D/F, which the Major had sent them on early that morning. The company had been scattered by heavy machine-gun fire on the slope of Hill 198. He had no real idea what had happened to the rest; indeed, he had been lucky himself to get through. Therefore, the link back had been attempted, but thwarted by enemy activity (a fact that General Alexander apparently now heard - and would then forget once again).

As for what remained of Major Whittlesey and Captain McMurtry's battalions and the three companies of 3rd/308th up on the line, Colonel Stacey was preparing to send out a post-noon assault meant to drive the line up to the objective, just before Captain Blagden would launch his own assault. Artillery fire was set to begin at 12:00 p.m. sharp and the onus would mostly be on Lt. Knight to break through. There was a solid line to the French now, made by companies I, L, and M, and therefore he could afford to take D and F both, along with a strong force of the remaining machine-gunners, into combat and make the assault unhampered by concern for his flank. By 11:30 a.m., Lt. Knight had told Colonel Stacey that he believed he might have the answer to breaking past those stubborn defenses there before Hills 205 and 198. If he could draw the enemy's fire with a feint attack around from the right with one company section closer in toward the ravine, then he could strike a real blow on an oblique from the left with a second section. That *should* drive the enemy back and allow a third section to drive up the ravine bottom toward Major Whittlesey's flank. Company D would lead out and make the draw, while F and a detail of heavy machine-gunners from Company C/306th MG Bn. would follow behind and hook left, straight into the enemy's belly. If all went well, they would be on the Major's line by nightfall. (103, 105, 131, 144, 238)

General Alexander merely told General Johnson to keep him informed and hung up.

That morning, the French had not attacked in the strength anyone had expected, nor in relation to the large amount of noise echoing from their sector (which was in fact mostly German artillery). A late German counter-attack the day before had driven them back slightly. Now, in the early afternoon of October 3, the enemy shellfire once again forced them back, but this time even further, into the entrenchments south of Binarville. This move broke the liaison with the 308th that had been reestablished again only that morning. Therefore, Lt. Knight and his men went into their attack that afternoon with a hole not only to their front, but one well to their left rear again as well, though they did not know it at first. Fortunately, the Germans did not throw troops into the mix against the French at Binarville (not many anyway), only artillery. So, when the fire slacked off enough very late that afternoon, the French simply reoccupied what remained of the village under orders to establish a solid base from which to launch a major attack the next day.

While the French were being driven from Binarville again, artillery for the attack up the Ravin d'Argonne went over precisely at noon, and Lt. Knight wasted no time in getting under way. His companies were soon well engaged, the "draw and hook" maneuver *mostly* worked, and by late afternoon they had cleared the wash where the bodies of some of Lt. Turner's men were found. (Charles Turner himself remains listed as 'Missing in Action' to this day however.) By mid-afternoon, they had beaten the enemy off the high ground around the wash and pushed them back into tighter defensive positions around Hill 205. Yet the Giselher Stellung main line held. Then, about 3:00 p.m., the Germans counterattacked and came pouring down from the hill. They hit Company M, in support behind D and F, from the west side, which savagely fought to keep them from the back of Lt. Knight's assault force, then trying to push down the ravine. In the Pocket ahead, Major Whittlesey's men lifted their heads at these grinding sounds of battle and wondered silently how far ahead they were that there was such a terrific din *behind* them. (10, 91, 92, 105, 146)

The exhausted Doughboys of D and F did all that they could that afternoon, but by nightfall the attack had stalled out in virtually the exact same place that Lt. Turner had been surrounded. There, Lt. Knight accepted the situation and dug his few men in, almost within 'spitting distance' of the Germans. He had perhaps 70, maybe 80, men left in each company now. Settling in and setting outposts, a trench mortar situated somewhere up within the La Palette position just would not give up and made the night a constant misery of continual shellfire right up until morning, causing the men to change positions frequently and thus depriving them of sleep. Additionally, German patrols continually hunted and probed the Doughboy line all night by the light of parachute flares and Very lights. Farther ahead, they could be heard stringing more new wire along the ravine bottom between Hills 205 and 198 and up on the eastern ridge. They also listened to a score of machine-guns keep up an almost constant harassment, - on both sides of Hill 198, Lt. Knight noted. He had been called to Sgt. Cahill's telephone station earlier that night to talk direct to Colonel Stacey. The next day, he was told, they were to try again to drive the line beyond the ravine to reach the Major and the rest of the two battalions up with him — if there was anyone left to reach. (105, 144)

Up on Hill 198 that afternoon, Captain Holderman and Lt. Pool's men wasted no time hitting the dirt once the German machine-guns started chattering. A single one up front might not have been so bad, but there were others on the flanks, and sniper fire ringing out as well. The sheer amount of enemy troops and wire that had appeared overnight alarmed both officers; the hillside seemed to be covered with both and there appeared to be no way around any of it. Casualties were building. Nonetheless, Captain Holderman urged the men on, positive that the communication line was indeed cut and that they had to get through - some how, some way - and slowly they started carving through the second belt of wire. Yet soon, the enemy's plan became painfully evident. Snipers were slowly corralling the flanks into a tighter circle, ever working their way around toward the back of the command with the obvious intention of cutting them off not only from the 77th's lines, but from the Charlevaux Ravine bivouac as well. Thus isolated, annihilation by machine-gun fire would be the next step. Seeing this, Captain Holderman finally shouted out the order to fall back, and Lt. Pool organized the men into a reverse combat group, fighting a rear guard action to get out and swearing all the way. (149)

They came staggering back across the brook about 1:00 p.m. with many wounded in tow. Major Whittlesey, watching them come in, sent the able-bodied back to the right flank and the wounded to the medics. After hearing Captain Holderman's report, he held council with Captains McMurtry and Holderman, Lieutenants Pool and Cullen, and both Battalion Sergeant-Majors (Ben Gaedeke and Clarence Roesch) in the command hole, all speaking in low tones. Private Larney, Corporal Baldwin, and others of the Headquarters Company strained to listen from a near distance. There was no doubt about it; the Germans had infiltrated a large number of troops through one or the other of the flanks during the night again, set up numerous machine-guns and much new wire between the Charlevaux bivouac and the main line. They had then severed the communications line and now had no intentions of being pushed back out. The combination command was definitely and decisively cut off from the rear, just as both Lieutenant Cullen and Major Whittlesey had predicted it would be. (135, 148, 149, 150, 245)

It was a conclusion none of them wanted to come to, particularly Major Whittlesey, as evidenced by his apparent refusal to initially see the almost overwhelming preponderance of evidence pointing in that direction most of the morning. Yet, contrary to what has usually been written, though there was deep concern among the command's senior officers, once word of their situation got around there was no great immediate panic. After all, the Major had recognized that there was a better than average chance that the morning might bring such a situation and had already somewhat prepared his officers for it with the little speech he had given before crossing the bridge the evening before. Overall, the situation was merely viewed at first as little more than business as usual in the Argonne, though perhaps with a bit more apprehension than normal (surrounded was surrounded after all).

Therefore, while the trench mortar shells once again started to drop down into the position irregularly and the enemy machine-guns chewed raggedly along its fringes, the four head officers considered their situation carefully. Though the runner line was gone, they still had several pigeons. They could at least get word of their plight out. Then too, Captain Holderman's report of the 307th's progress of the day before had been encouraging, and the 308th could not be too far back. D and F companies might be working their way forward even now or, at the very least, soon. Ammunition was low, however with fire discipline they could definitely make it last until relief came. As for food, they had been without it many times before since the drive had started. The most serious issue was the wounded, but since there was no solution to their problem just now, they would simply have to tough it out a little bit longer.

Then, abruptly, the discussion turned to any immediate remedy to the situation that they themselves might be able to facilitate. The idea was presented (never allowed by whom, but most likely by the prudent Lt. Pool) that perhaps a pull back to the main line might not be such a bad idea. They certainly had the manpower to break through. However, before serious thought could be given this idea, Major Whittlesey noted that to attempt such a measure would leave the wounded to bring up the rear, some of whom by this time could not walk. They would then be forced to move through a battle zone as their flanks collapsed behind the forward moving 'point' of the attack; thus, some of the wounded would likely be stranded and the end units hard hit. Put the wounded in the middle then, some one suggested, protected on all sides. A possibility, except then the rapid forward progress so imperative in a risky breakthrough such as proposed would likely be lost.

The discussion went on in this vein for few more minutes until, in the end, Major Whittlesey firmly and with finality pointed out that any such move would be in direct violation of their standing orders. Since no new orders had come up countermanding the original orders of the afternoon of October 2, to hold the position and await fresh assault instructions, the Major maintained that those original orders still held. (Perhaps G.O. #27 flashed through his mind here as well, but that is doubtful.) Then the question of just how fresh orders were to get up if communications were cut off was presented. No matter. They would break through from behind soon enough, just as they had done before. Until then, however, the command in the ravine had their orders and was bound by duty to carry them out. (29, 51, 135, 148, 149, 150, 245)

There was a short, tense silence in the hole, everybody listening to the sounds of strong fighting filtering over from the other side of Hill 198. Finally, Captain McMurtry reached into his tunic pocket, pulled out a field message book, and started to scribble. Tearing the page out, he handed it over to Major Whittlesey, who read it and nodded.

"That should just about cover it, George," he said, pulled out his own message book and started to copy:

310

To all officers: Our mission is to hold this position at all costs. No falling back. Have this understood by every man in your command. (246)

Calling over Cpl. Baldwin, he handed him the messages and ordered them delivered to all officers in the Pocket. Corporal Baldwin and his runners fanned out and by 1:30 p.m., officers were crawling from hole to hole, filling their men in on the situation. Before the hour was up, everyone in the ravine was aware that they were cut off and were going to sit tight and await relief. This was in sharp contrast to the 'secret' that the first cut off had been. Perhaps the Major was not quite as confidant in relief as he made it out to the others, which is quite possible, or perhaps he simply wanted everyone to be ready for what he figured might be the enemy's next move, which could only be the inevitable counter-attack.

At 2:00 p.m., General Alexander was summoned to a late afternoon 1st Army staff meeting to discuss kick starting the stalling Muese-Argonne operations. He had hoped to be able to give a good accounting of his division's progress and he did not want to have to report that a portion of his front line force - the portion actually up *on* his division's objective no less - was apparently cut off from communications with the rear. Therefore, at 2:45 p.m. he again called General Johnson for a report and was told pretty much what he had been earlier. The only addendum was that Colonel Stacey had his elements then in attack, though they had so far managed little. Captain Blagden's attack on the left of the 307th's lines had disintegrated in dismal failure relatively soon after it had been launched, with the Captain apparently having been wounded for the effort.

There was a pause and then General Alexander exploded, aids later saying that they had never seen the General so mad before. His instructions to General Johnson, which were never recorded verbatim, were loud, short, and precise; get the line up to Major Whittlesey as soon as possible - or else.

Colonel Houghton was up on the line with Major McKinney when the remnants of Captain Blagden's attack, which had gone over about 1:00 p.m., came dragging back to support positions. They had accomplished nothing. The Germans definitely still occupied the ridge of Hill 198, strung seemingly miles of new wire, and if there had ever been an 'open door' to the Charlevaux Ravine on the left of the 307th's line, it was gone now. Slowly, the remnants of the 3rd Battalion crept back into their holes, while the first strong contingents of the 1st Battalion began to filter past them on their way to the line. (31, 43, 103, 109, 116, 131, 139, 150, 235)

By about 2:30 p.m., it was strangely quiet in the Pocket. There were the sounds of battle emanating from the other side of Hill 198, but the trench mortar had again gone silent shortly after Major Whittlesey's general instruction had gone out. Most of the snipers and machine-guns were silent too. With care, the tired, ragged men found themselves free to move around through the brush of the hillside with little fear. The break in action was something of a relief, but it was also regarded with suspicion. Why had the Germans let up? What were they planning? Some men took the risk of crawling carefully down to the creek or spring and filled a few canteens, something the machine-guns had prevented all morning. Most had been working on deepening their holes or on the latrine pits, which Major Whittlesey had ordered dug the night before, when word had come concerning their situation.

The news had spread like wildfire among the troops as they drifted back to their holes, unconsciously seeking shelter. Above, the clouds continued to roll, heightening the tense, dark mood that was slowly enveloping the hillside. Those who could, nibbled the last of whatever precious food they might have saved over from lunch while others, remembering the all-compass-points attacks on l'Homme Mort, cleaned their weapons, readying themselves for any heavy work that might come. The last of the cigarettes burned everywhere, steadying nerves. There was still no panic, only a strained watchfulness that was strangely familiar to men who had fought in the mess of the Argonne for eight days. When word passed to Pvt. Nell, he heard it with a subconscious nod. He had already suspected something was amiss, as they had not moved out at dawn as he expected:

"A little later in the day it became apparent we were cut off and completely surrounded with machine guns set up on all sides. It was understood by all the men to keep quiet and be alert for any possible attack. We were told we had to hold our position until the rear troops could move up. Scouts were sent out to find an open way back for communication to our regimental headquarters, but no way could be found and many of the scouts never returned. Those who did return reported they could only go a short distance before they were blocked by the enemy... Many efforts were made on the first day, but to no avail." (40)

In fact, Major Whittlesey had sent a patrol out only a short time earlier, to the northwest this time. They were just hurriedly coming back in as the clock tipped toward 3:00 p.m. and the news was gut tightening, but not unexpected by any means. There was a mass of enemy troops gathering on the left, up the hill and beyond the road ahead. It looked like, at any time, the expected counterattack was about to be launched. Major Whittlesey and Captain McMurtry were then just passing the word around when a couple Doughboys that had been in an outpost up above the road came tearing back down into the bivouac, yelling that the Germans were right behind them. Moments later the attack burst forth, against the left flank first. (29, 51, 135, 148, 149, 150)

There was a 'crackling' of something passing through the tree cover above, which was immediately followed by a rapid series of explosions among Lt. Cullen's men. Grenade attack! Bodies in khaki rolled in the mud and screamed in pain and Lt. Cullen was immediately yelling in his booming voice for everyone to remain calm. Then, all at once, an absolute eruption of German machine-gun and rifle fire burst from both flanks, above the road ahead and across the ravine behind, well organized and well aimed. More explosions followed the first series, all along the line now, as the enemy began to rain grenades down from above the road in earnest. The trench mortar over at La Palette renewed its assault with deadly accuracy; the morning barrage having only been for ranging the fall of shot apparently. From the little limestone escarpment close to the rear of Captain Holderman's Company K, came another shower of grenades to add to the rain from the front, along with searching machine-gun fire from a well-concealed emplacement just to the right of the cliff. Carefully, the Captain directed his fire where it would do the most good, and the figures advancing through the trees around them were brought to a standstill – and then slowly driven back. (I)

Stunned at first by the sheer ferocity of the grenade attack, the Doughboys manning the line just under the lip of the road fell back down the hill some before reorganizing again. There, the brush covering the hillside dampened the concussive effect of the potato mashers a bit, so the second round did not have the same heavy effect as along the more sparsely covered roadside. Recovering their wits, the Doughboys laid down the first volleys of return fire, under direction of the officers, and were rewarded by a few howls and yelps. Major Whittlesey was immediately up, cooling directing the Headquarters men and those of G and A across the middle with, "Take it easy, take it easy. Do not get excited. Hold for clear fields of fire; make it count." He moved all along the hillside with that strange grace that only truly tall people have, appearing from out of the brush behind them and seeming to be everywhere at once. For the men just fallen back from the road, that brush was really the saving grace. They all knew that without it they would have been sitting ducks.

When the second round of grenades struck on the left flank, where the attack seemed heaviest, Lt. Cullen's men first began firing indiscriminately into the brush around them until the lieutenant finally went crouching through the position, red faced and yelling for them to hold their fire. He had been in the Small Pocket, as had most of his men, and well remembered the value that ammunition had had there. They were taking heavy, solid fire as a third, heavy rain of grenades and some damned accurate mortar fire poured in. Huddled into their holes as low as possible, the men of H and their ring of machine-gunners waited for Lt. Cullen to give the order to fire, but 'Red' saw no reason to jump the gun (so to speak). In a rather disjointed letter to some former legal associates soon after relief came to the Pocket, the one-time lawyer relayed,

"*Under cover of (the) machine gun fire from our rear they came in close and bombed us with potato mashers. They just gave us hell, but our orders were to "hold to the last man," and hold we would. Consequently, we could not go out after them. A couple of nervous fingers pulled their triggers but I steadied them until the Boche got sufficiently close to be annoying, and then I gave the order "Commence firing." The crack of those rifles was certainly music to me…*" (109)

A few howls and yells met Lt. Cullen's first volley of fire and quickly the Hotchkiss gunners were up and at their weapons, chugging their big 8mm slugs out into the brush around them at 400 rounds a minute, matching the German Maxim guns almost note for note. Another round of grenades came in; another American volley went out. Company H's fire discipline was in excellent form under Cullen's tutelage, and soon, the men began to calm down a bit. (29, 40, 51, 135, 148, 149, 150, 218, 233, 234, 239, 245, 267)

Then suddenly, after about 25 minutes of pure hell, all the firing died off, grenades stopped and the trench mortar fell silent. A strange stillness blanketed the afternoon forest under a thin pall of smoke; neither a bird nor the crack of a stick breaking underfoot was heard. Each Doughboy eyed their surroundings warily over the lip of their funk hole. Someone in H broke the tense repose by starting to cheer, and Lt. Cullen sharply yelled out, "Shut up!" and all was silent again. Then a loud, authoritative, and definitely Teutonic, voice echoed across the ravine.

"*Rudolph!*" it called.

From somewhere near the left flank a disembodied voice answered.

"*Hier!*"

"*Heinrich!*" (Came another call.)

"*Ich bin hier!*" (From somewhere up above and toward the middle.)

Now what in hell was this?

"*Adolph!*"

"*Ja. Hier!*" (The other side of the ravine.)

It appeared as if the Germans were calling the long roll.

"*Eitel!*"

"*Hier!*"

The Doughboys exchanged uneasy glances as more and more names were called out and answered, from seemingly all around them. How many of them could there be?

"*Hans!*"

"*Jawohl! Hier!*"

It was psychological warfare. "*Schrecklichkiet*" in German - "*frightfulness*" - and it appeared to be working as the Doughboys looked around uneasily and fingers twitched nervously on triggers.

At first, that is.

"*Werner!*"

"*Hier!*"

Wait, wasn't that the same voice that just answered a moment ago? Could be…

The faceless Hun voice called out another name, but before any German could answer, a Doughboy yelled back instead.

"He fucked off!" and a ripple of laughter wiggled through the Pocket.

"Shut up!" some American officer yelled again (probably Lt. Cullen once more). Then...

"Sind deiner menschen da?" ("Is everyone ready?")

A chorus of *"Ja! Ja!"* echoed out and then,

"Nun, alle zusammen! Ein, und zwie, und drie!" ("Now, all together! One, and two, and three!")

As the German called out the number "three," there was a heavy pounding of boots in the forest and the crashing of bodies through the brush. Once again, the gates of hell flung wide as another round of potato mashers came down, heavier than all the three previous combined. Immediately, the Maxims started up their stuttering chant. That was apparently the signal to the trench mortar, which started dumping rounds in faster than any of the Americans believed possible, almost seeming like there were *two* mortars firing instead of one. The Doughboys merely hunkered lower in their funk holes and took the initial volley, then rose and before any officer could give the order, began to lay down their own solid pattern and the firing became general, well aimed, and effective. Trained or not, the replacements were veterans now after a week of Argonne fighting, and it told as they matched the well-seasoned New Yorkers for skill in dropping the enemy.

But Americans were dropping too and one of the first to fall was little Lt. Griffin of Company H. He took two machine-gun bullets through the left shoulder and now lay rolling on the ground, his boyish face pinched in pain. It was not the last brush with German (or American for that matter) steel he would have in the Pocket either. Writing to his wife from an evacuation hospital two weeks later, he described:

"The picture I have of you has a hole in it from a piece of shell. I have four bullet holes in my overcoat and my trousers were torn to pieces by a grenade, but I only have my knees cut besides the bullets in my shoulder. The strap to my field glasses was cut by a bullet, my gas mask was cut in half by shrapnel, and my helmet has a dent from a bullet. But they did not get me..." (20, 106)

Then, just before 4:00 p.m., the trouble on the left with the machine-guns started. The trench mortar found the range on one of the Company D/306th MG Bn. guns there, commanded by Sgt. Robert Graham, and scored a direct hit, killing the entire crew. Private Stanley Sobaszkiewicz of H saw it and later remarked:

"A little ways down from (my hole) I ran into something I'll remember the rest of my life. There in a little open spot, was a machine gun that looked to be out of order, but the whole spot looked to me like a wagon wheel composed of dead American soldiers, with the machine gun as the hub. I can still draw a picture of it in a short time because it is fresh in my mind..." (44)

Then, on the right flank, with a rush, a party of Germans drove off the crew of one of the heavy guns there and made off with it. Said the adjutant of the 7th Company/122nd, more simply, "Sergeant Eppler ran into an enemy machine-gun... aimed at the servers, which made them run off, and we captured the enemy automatic." Rushing about the machine-gun perimeter line that afternoon and watching all this was their commander, Lt. Marshall Peabody, who now had great holes to cover in his defensive echelon, with two guns missing. The left was the more serious of the two and to which he initially directed his attentions. Quickly trying to rearrange a couple of the guns to fill the gap, the powerfully built lieutenant showed himself through an opening in the brush just a bit too much, for a bit too long and took a nasty, ripping enemy machine-gun burst down one leg below the knee, falling to the dirt in almost immediate shock. His second in command in D, Lt. Maurice Revnes, rushed over to the spot and taking stock of the situation, found to his horror that at least two other guns were also unmanned due to enemy fire. Dashing off a runner to tell Lt. Cullen that, without reinforcement, the Hotchkiss line was in danger of folding on the left, he sent a man to drag the badly bleeding Lt. Peabody off to the wounded area and then promptly took hold of a gun himself. But he was not seated on the tripod long before an enemy bullet tore apart his calf and another shattered his ankle, nearly severing his foot and sending him out of the position to the wounded area as well. Company 1st Sergeant George E. Hauck now took over, just as a small force of H men sent from Lt. Cullen arrived to help. Nearly half of the Company D machine-gunners on the left flank were already dead or wounded, leaving the precious Hotchkiss guns in largely inexperienced hands - and this was just the first day in the Pocket. Luckily, the Hotchkiss is a very forgiving weapon, with little propensity to jam. Even in inexperienced hands, it can still be relied upon to get the job done. (29, 40, 51, 128, 135, 147, 148, 149, 150, 213, 218, 233, 234, 239, 245, 267, 280, 338)

Facing forward up the hill Lt. Cullen's Company H Chauchat gunners and rifle-men continued to beat back the strong resistance from above and duck the potato mashers that relentlessly came down on them, sometimes tied two and three together. Again, from Lt. Cullen's letter:

"We couldn't, of course, see them due to the heavy brush and waited for them to rush us. During a lull, their leader called out "Kamerad, vill you?" He thought we were ready to surrender! That was about the last straw for me. "Come in and get us, you Dutch bastard!" I yelled at him, with a few additional cuss words that I knew of in his own damn language, and we opened fire on where we thought they might be and gave them hell…" (109)

The lull in the attack Lt. Cullen described came about just after 4:00 p.m. By that time, Major Whittlesey was down where the four terribly overworked medics were busily plying their trade, trying to get a count of the wounded and taking reports from various company commanders of their strength totals. Though the troop assaults slacked off during the lull, the trench mortar and machine-gun fire continued almost unabated. Meanwhile, a couple able-bodied men worked desperately on their stomachs at deepening and lengthening the shallow trench that the wounded were laid out in. The ground around them was soaked with blood and frequently pattered by bullets. It had been a mauling, vicious attack, stronger than anyone had expected and very costly on the U.S. side. Those losses seriously concerned Major Whittlesey since he had not had a particularly strong force to begin with, as far as Argonne standards went, and judging from the number of men piling up there around him, he guessed they would soon no longer be able to continue the fight unless reinforcements arrived. Still, more men were continuing to pour into the wounded area when Private Frank Erickson, Lt. Cullen's prime runner, came tearing up with a salute and a message from the lieutenant:

From: C.O. Co. H Left Flank   At: Left Flank
Hour: 4pm   To: C.O. Red Battalion
The Boche attacked on the left flank and were driven off by our rifle fire. They attacked me in front with trench mortars and caused a number of casualties. Lt. Griffin is injured. Please send a machine gun to help out on this flank and some more men, also one officer or good non-com.
Cullen, Lt. (135, 246)

Major Whittlesey had to wonder two things about this message. First, had Lt. Cullen really been hit from the *front* by a trench mortar? So far, all the mortar fire had been from

315

the rear, or so he thought. (This was not actually so, but the fire that Lt. Cullen here reports would be the first indication of that and Major Whittlesey would not really explore the situation until some time later.) Second, just how many machine-guns did the lieutenant need on the left? He already had the vast majority of them over there and another could certainly not be spared from the right, as there were few there to begin with. Nor was there any other officer then available to help out on the left.

Instead, Captain McMurtry himself decided to go. Telling the Major that he would explain to Lt. Cullen why there was no extra machine-gun available, the pugnacious Irishman gathered up 15 men or so, all that could be spared from the companies immediately around the PC funk hole, and then led them crawling off through the brush. Private Gust Dahlgren of Company G was one of them:

"Later the same day after we had dug pretty fair holes 15 of us were taken at intervals and detailed to follow a captain. He sent us out to find the location of our machine guns. We took over and a good many of the fellows were lying around, having been killed. They looked fairly natural, not torn up. However, about the next day the artillery and mortar fire tore things up and the unburied bodies got badly mangled." (44)

With the lull in troop attacks, Captain McMurtry crawled left with his group. The line of Doughboys that had fallen back from the lip of the road began moving up into their original positions again, but a particularly pesky Boche machine-gun, overlooking the Pocket from above and near dead center, kept everyone's heads down and made it slow going. A few rifle grenades were gathered, passed up the hillside and then shot the relatively short distance across the road and up against it, but to no good end. They largely missed and the damned gun went on chewing at the lip of the road. And, that was the end of the grenades… (29, 40, 51, 128, 135, 147, 148, 149, 150, 213, 218, 233, 234, 239, 245, 267, 280, 338)

It was just after 4:00 p.m. and Captain McMurtry was crawling off toward the left when Major Whittlesey called up the hill for Private Richards to bring a pigeon. Sitting down in a fresh funk hole near the bottom with a pigeon message book on his knee, he wrote:

Germans on cliff north of us in small numbers and have tried to envelop both flanks. Situation on left very serious. Broke through two of our runner posts today near 294.7-275.7. I have not been able to reestablish posts today. Need 8000 rounds rifle ammunition, 7500 Chauchat, 25 boxes machine gun ammunition, 250 offensive grenades. Casualties yesterday in Co.'s A, B, C, E, G, H, 8 killed 80 wounded. In same Co.'s today 1 killed, 60 wounded. Present effective strength of companies here 245. Situation serious. Place 294.6-276.3.

Whittlesey Major 308 (131, 246)

If anything in this message is misleading, it is the numbers the Major gives as "present effective strength" and casualties. In regard to casualties, he repeats the previous day's figure of 88, which he had already once given in the 7:30 a.m. message (the one that never made it through). This really has no bearing on what he had to work with as of that morning. However, he then lists, "1 killed, 60 wounded" so far that day, which was incorrect. The 60 wounded may have been something close to accurate as far as how many were then in the wounded collection point when Major Whittlesey wrote this message, but even as he was writing, there were others limping in. While this figure, no doubt, also included those who were wounded the night before, it most assuredly does not include those who had been carried back both the previous night as well as early that morning. Nor can the "1 killed" possibly be, since Private Hollingshead alone saw two men killed that morning, and there was at least one machine-gun crew wiped out, and possibly more; admittedly, all casualties Major Whittlesey would not likely know about for some time, but casualties none-the-same. Nor is there any mention made of the men of Company E who failed to come back from the morning link-up, or any of the missing members of the ration party, or from the various patrols that had gone out; all of which detracted from the command's over-all strength as well.

Adding the casualty (killed, wounded, or missing) totals then, we start with the number Whittlesey reported, 61, and then add, as a low estimate, Pvt. Hollingshead's two dead and the dead four-man machine-gun crew, as well as the known number of missing and wounded from the morning expedition - perhaps 30 men of Company E, 15 of the ration party, and at least four runners. This gives a *very* conservative total of at least 116 casualties thus far, or a casualty rate against a beginning total of 687 (see Appendix A) of about 17 percent in the first 20 hours.

Major Whittlesey's listing of the number of "present effectives," he had to work with as 245, is also very unusual, for it apparently only counts the six companies of the 308th he listed and leaves out the whole host of the other elements - the 306th machine-gunners, Company K/307th, the three liaison men from 305th F.A., the four remaining medics and both groups of Battalion PC men. The Major then actually had a much stronger force than he was reporting. So why mislead the number? He certainly must have had a better grasp on his total than he was letting on, for in the report he filed after the episode was all over, he specifically states that by the morning of October 4, he still had 520 total effectives. Perhaps, under the great pressure of the intense German attack, some figures merely slipped his mind. After all, this last had happened before, when he sent out the ration request earlier that day. This would be indicative of the extreme stress that the Major was almost constantly under and the toll it was beginning to take on him. On the other hand, it may also have been a clever attempt to sway Colonel Stacey into sending out orders for him to effect a fighting retreat and withdraw all his forces out of that damned ravine, or perhaps to 'con' him into sending more troops up. Either way, the totals that the Major gave are very strange indeed.

Meanwhile, as Major Whittlesey's message was winging its way back, Captain McMurtry and his little band of support men for the gunners around H had been spotted moving by the enemy and were being chewed to pieces by machine-gun fire as they crawled along. Half were killed or wounded before they had even got half way over, including Captain McMurtry, who got a slug through the knee just below the kneecap. This forced the rest to seek better cover along the hillside and delayed their arrival on the left flank considerably. During the lull, Lt. Cullen was in his funk hole waiting for the reinforcements and heard German voices, just beyond the little nipple of hillside that marked the end of his perimeter and close enough for him to understand what they were saying, making plans for a renewal of the attack. When Captain McMurtry finally did lead his surviving reinforcements into the lieutenant's position, Cullen quickly detailed them out to relieve his men at the Hotchkiss guns - just in time for the enemy to begin a renewed round of attacks all along the line. Once more, the damned potato mashers were coming down in bundles and the trench mortar started blowing big chunks out of the hillside, as the machine-guns stepped up their pace. (29, 40, 51, 128, 135, 147, 148, 149, 150, 213, 218, 233, 234, 239, 245, 267, 280, 338)

The Germans made their last all-out assaults against the entire perimeter line again at just about 5:00 p.m., charging forward, yelling, going to ground, charging again and getting bolder with each round of grenades thrown. The disembodied voice called out at least once more during this attack, *"Alle zusammen!"* which was again followed by the heavy pounding of boots. When, as before, the Doughboys could clearly see the field gray of the German uniforms through the trees, they aimed and fired straight volleys. No officer needed direct them; the instinct of days of killing had taken over. Yowls of pain, followed by explosions on the surrounding hills told the men that they had nailed Germans about to throw live grenades who, having been hit, dropped them and had them explode at their feet. For the first time, hunks of German bodies and blood rained down disgustingly on some of the Doughboys, particularly from the little cliff behind Captain Holderman's position on the right. Some cheered the gruesome spectacle.

On the left flank, as the attack progressively grew more furious Captain McMurtry, nursing his wounded knee in Lt. Cullen's funk hole, watched as the lieutenant necessarily rearranged his forces for better control, as the situation warranted. The left flank was taking the heavier pounding again, close as it was to the manpower storage points of the Moulin d'Charlevaux position and Hill 205, and Lt. Cullen was not letting anyone slack off in the least, yelling and threatening his men relentlessly. Despite all the boom and bluster, Captain McMurtry could not help but notice the lieutenant's general coolness under fire; even if gaining it in a somewhat bullying way, the red-faced man had total control over the situation. He also noted how the lieutenant never really got up to the line where the shooting was, even though he did have his .45 out and continually pumped rounds in the German's direction. Still, Lt. Cullen's defensive perimeter was both strong and effective and when he barked, his men jumped. No doubt about it; the Germans were definitely going to have a tough time getting through here.

Down at the foot of the hill, Private Roland Judd of Company A was killed. Seeing that the medics desperately needed water, and figuring the Hun gunners had other things to do besides watch the brook and spring, as they had been all that morning, Pvt. Judd slithered down to the edge of the stream through the weeds during the attack. He was just filling a canteen when a German sniper spotted him in the bushes and plugged him through the head. No one had seen him go down there, and he was not missed for a couple days. By the time anyone reached his body, he was virtually unrecognizable and his date of death is officially, and mistakenly, listed as October 5. (29, 40, 51, 128, 135, 147, 148, 149, 150, 213, 218, 233, 234, 239, 245, 267, 280, 338, 351, 357, 358, 359)

Captain Stromee of Company C also went down during that second big assault, with the first of two wounds he would receive in the Pocket. Catching the brunt of a grenade blast across his back and one shoulder, he crawled over, got bandaged and stretched out among the wounded, taking a spot near Lt. Peabody, whose tourniqueted leg had swelled enormously and was covered in sticky, clotted blood and dirt. Dragging out his field diary, Captain Stromee merely scrawled, *"October 3rd; Very heavy barrage. Am wounded 5pm"* and left it at that. (233, 239)

The second attack lasted for about 45 minutes and by about a quarter to six, the Hun machine-guns were starting to wind down. Thankfully, the trench mortar also began to slow its fire and finally stopped altogether as darkness fell. Off in the bushes the Doughboys could hear the groans and wails of the German wounded and the crunching of the forest floor as their buddies came to carry them off. No one fired at them, however. Ammunition supplies had dropped throughout the afternoon and with no resupply, few thought of wasting even a single shot. Additionally, no one really had the strength or ambition left to bother about them; the afternoon attacks had pretty well tired everyone out. (29, 40, 51, 135, 148, 149, 150, 218, 233, 234, 239, 245, 267)

There were plenty of American wails and groans echoing through the ravine that evening as well. Major Whittlesey was in the wounded area again as night came on, getting the word from Private Jack Gehris, who had unofficially taken on the duties of chief medic, as to the status of their supplies. "Gone," Pvt. Gehris told him quietly and chillingly off to one side. "All gone. We have nothing left to work with." Any sterile bandages had run out about half an hour ago, the Dakin-Carrell solution they used to clean out wounds had not even lasted out the morning and virtually all the men's personal field dressing packets, which they carried on their cartridge belts, had been used up already. They were scavenging the dead for unused bandages and shoelaces to tie up wounds with now, they had nothing for pain - not even cigarettes - and water was running out. Without immediate care, some of the more seriously wounded would likely not last the night and others would be in just as bad of shape by morning. (29, 51, 109, 118, 135, 143, 148, 149, 150, 196, 204, 206)

Captain McMurtry had limped back over from the left as the silence fell, a bandage wrapped tightly around his broken knee and singing Lt. Cullen's praises. As the darkness deepened, he and Major Whittlesey talked in low tones about what to do next. Though there had been some little fire from the left rear that day, obviously Lt. Knight had not been able to drive forward anymore than they had been able to drive back. With better than half of Company E already gone from the initial attempt, it looked as if trying again to get a line back the way they had come would prove a useless gamble. And they both unhesitatingly agreed that the French seemed a certain write-off. What about on the right then? There had been a certain level of activity in the distance over there, had there not? Maybe Captain Holderman's buddies were not that far back after all and could yet be reached. A small unit might be able to work through the line up on Hill 198 in the darkness and get through to them. While Captain McMurtry set outposts and began to arrange local patrols, Major Whittlesey made his way along the hillside to see the Company K commander about sending out a patrol from his right flank.

Again, Lt. Pool did not like the idea of sending any men out in a small force. They had already taken a large force up that hill once that day, and gotten only casualties for it. What chance would a small force have? However, Major Whittlesey insisted that the risk was worth taking, since something had to be done for the wounded and therefore Captain Holderman picked a small patrol and sent them out. The night stillness of the ravine had only been broken by the infrequent German flares that went up and the occasional playing of machine-gun fire, when the patrol returned several hours later and reported to Holderman, who took them to see the Major. They had not been able to get through the Boche defenses up on the hill; there were even more troops and barbed wire up there now than when the whole company had tried to get through earlier that afternoon. Only a major effort was going to drive that line, they predicted. The Major dismissed them tiredly and in the darkness, they snaked back to the right flank to get some well-earned rest, their nerves shot. After the patrol had gone, he held a short conference with McMurtry and Holderman. The truth was obvious; there was nothing to do anymore that night but sit and wait for the rest of the line to catch up. Either that, or wait for fresh orders to come through. Either way, it was all in Colonel Stacey's hands now and the Regimental Commander had better hurry his ass up, or else there would be nothing left for orders to direct or to drive the line up to, if the attacks of the day were any indication of how tomorrow would go.

It was that night that Major Whittlesey sent the first of the forage parties out to scavenge what they could from the German dead that lay too close to American lines to be carried off by their comrades. (29, 30, 44, 109, 135, 148, 149, 150, 239, 245)

General Alexander returned from his 5:00 p.m. Division Commander's meeting later that night with his temper again restored to sane levels, and the new plan in hand to break the deadlock of the Argonne Forest. There had been much activity along the Muese-Argonne front since September 26, generally successful, but certainly not coming up to the expectations of 1st Army Command, and certainly not in the Argonne Forest, where the 77th had stalled out, along with the left regiment of the 28th. There, the main sticking points were obviously the La Palette Pavilion on the left, and Le Chene Tondu on the right. General Pershing's staff, having studied the situation, recognized that if there was to be any impetus to the offensive in that quarter, further assistance was going to be needed. It was a fact that the American command had never initially planned to take the forest by direct assault; only the extreme circumstances there had made the attempt necessary. Now, it was those very same extreme circumstances that demanded a return to that original plan.

To the east of the 28th, the 35th Division had battled forward valiantly ever since jump-off, and in the days since had driven past the Giselher strongpoint of the Butte de Vauquois, and on to a line about even with the little town of Exermont. They arrived there late on the afternoon of September 29, an exhausted and used-up division, only to be hit with a fresh German replacement division that kicked them squarely in the teeth. Worn down (they had taken some 6,000 casualties already in the offensive), and unable to resist the fresh German onslaught, their line broke. Falling back through the dark that night, every man who could be mustered stood the line; even the division's cooks and wagoneers wielded rifles. In the emergency, General Pershing then ordered up his favorite division, the mighty 1st Division, from his reserves to relieve the badly hurting Kansas and Missouri National Guardsmen of the 35th. They hurried up to the 35th's line, sometimes finding it only by advancing to contact with the enemy, and by the night of October 1, the situation was again mostly under control. The wrecked 35th was on its way to reserve positions below the forest, and the 1st spent the next 24 hours organizing and consolidating its new front before pushing on.

The new plan to break the deadlock of the Argonne was to incorporate the 1st Division, having them drive on a northwest angle toward the little town of Fleville, striking the enemy from the side and above the stalled action further south in the forest. (By the evening of October 6 however, it would also prove necessary to move portions of the 82nd "All American" Division into the line between the 28th and the 1st, in order to assist the 28th in breaking past Le Chene Tondu. The 82nd would then push forward as well, before then swinging to the west and also slamming into the Argonne from the side, just below the 1st, and adding to the incredible pressure being applied to the German left flank above the 77th Division.) At the same time, the French, west of the 77th, would move to strike the Germans from the north by northeast in a similar fashion, thus enclosing the Germans in a salient between the two divisions. The weight of these two forces pressing intolerably at their sides, coupled with renewed pressure to be applied from below by the 77th and 28th Divisions, would then force any German resistance within that salient to either quickly withdraw or face collapse. The stalemate would thus be broken.

The 28th Division would of course focus most of its attention on driving past Le Chene Tondu, attacking from both the south and east simultaneously, while the 1st Division pushed north and westward up and around the 28th's right flank. As for the 77th Division, General Alexander decided that the main effort needed to be thrown against the more difficult left flank, where La Palette Pavilion loomed from up on Hill 205, and where Major Whittlesey had already actually punched through the Giselher line and was then on the assigned objective. What made the plan additionally attractive was that the French 1st D.C.D, to the left, had since agreed to assume responsibility for at least *most* of the 800-meter gap between their right flank and the 77th's left flank. That action, in turn, made it all the easier for collaborative attacks to be launched against Hill 205 by two forces instead of one, which then greatly increased the chances for success. The natural outcome of the destruction of enemy resistance on Hill 205 would then be the relief of Major Whittlesey's beleaguered command, simply by breaking the main line through the Giselher, and moving it up to the Major's position.

The overall renewal of the main drive of the Muese-Argonne Offensive was now scheduled to begin all along the 1st Army front at 5:30 a.m. of October 4, the next day, during which the new plan for the Argonne utilizing the 1st Division would be brought to play. With that fact in mind, General Alexander then meant to end that first day of the renewed drive by having taken out the La Palette Pavilion and driving his whole line up to Major Whittlesey's, come hell or high water. (II) (2, 8, 10, 20, 24, 30, 31, 36, 42, 43, 88, 91, 109, 111, 116, 131, 144)

The Division Commander then called his Brigade Commanders that night in turn, explaining what needed to be done. While the 153rd Brigade would push ahead as hard as it could, its primary job in the attacks for October 4 was to act as a 'containing force' and keep the enemy away from the right flank of the 154th as it pushed on. They would also do the same for the left of the 28th Division, until the line was broken there before Le Chene Tondu. Then, once the 154th and the left of the 28th had broken out, the brigade was to move forward *en masse*, overwhelming any remaining enemy forces left before it. The 154th, Alexander told General Johnson, needed to break Hill 205 and the La Palette Pavilion at all costs and push up to the objective line where Major Whittlesey's command was stalled out. If need be, elements of the 307th that were then in reserve would be directed to assist that remainder of the 308th that was pushing up the Ravin d'Argonne. At the same time, the French had orders to begin organizing in Binarville for a simultaneous assault the following morning, and were in the process of moving a battalion of the 4th C.a.P up from support behind the 9th and into the area to handle the attack. The French were said to have an advanced line along their left flank well beyond Binarville, General Alexander said, and were going to attack all along their line as well tomorrow. Where was their *right* though, General Johnson wanted to know. Communications were mixed on that, General Alexander admitted, but he had just received word following his staff meeting, at about 6:00 p.m., that they were then near Tranchee de La Palette, above the town. However, nearer in toward the 308th's left, it was unclear. He had also passed along word of Major Whittlesey's situation to them and they were enthusiastic about helping. Elements of the 3rd/308th had liaison with them closer to the 308th's lines, did they not, General Alexander asked. The Brigadier allowed that they had *some*, but it appeared to be only with outposts. Colonel Stacey had already been sending one company forward to face left and protect that flank. Perhaps they could do something about it from over there. (2, 91, 103, 109, 116, 138, 139)

General Johnson then checked with Colonel Stacey as to the dispositions of his troops, who also gave him an earful of bad temper and bad nerves, and he then called General Alexander back. The 3rd/308th had some liaison with the French at outposts just north of Binarville and along the Binarville-Moulin de l'Homme Mort road, the Brigadier said. The French had been forced that morning to evacuate most of their troops in the immediate vicinity of Hill 205 to the entrenchments 500 meters *south* of town due to heavy shelling. As of this evening, it was unclear whether they had moved back into the town yet or not. Two other 3rd/308th companies (K and M) had since been sent forward to support the front line companies (D and F) who then only had about 70 men each. Further, according to Colonel Stacey the regiment had had over 500 casualties just in the last couple days and was in sorry shape. General Alexander remained unimpressed however; a simultaneous attack with the French needed to go forth with all possible speed and vigor the following morning. They were going to break past Hill 205 tomorrow and that was that. There were plenty of grenades and ammunition available and rations were on the way too. If anything else was needed, all General Johnson had to do was call.

General Johnson knew that to argue further was futile. The line, obviously, needed to be broken and, equally as obvious, the division commander had decided they would do that by eliminating the great obstacle of Hill 205, which he apparently saw as the main impediment keeping them from reaching Major Whittlesey. What General Johnson apparently failed to realize at the time however, was that Hill 205 was seen not so much by General Alexander as the main sticking point on the left as it was by General Pershing's 1st Army staff, and that the Division Commander really had not had Major Whittlesey in mind when considering the local plan for taking it out - only the breaking of the line. Major Whittlesey's predicament was still only an abstract bit of the larger picture at that point (and would remain so until the end of the next day). If there was any real significance to the Major's position to General Alexander at all this point, it was that he was through the Giselher. The next natural step was to bring the rest of the line up to him; not in rescue, but in attack to push the advance of the offensive and save his division's - and thus by proxy, his own - reputation. (91, 131, 144, 238)

However General Johnson, we must remember, was mostly looking at the situation from a local standpoint - he had a Battalion Commander and nearly 700 men stranded behind enemy lines with no communication and it had been General Alexander's orders that had dictated General Johnson's plan that had put them there in the first place. Now, there were aspects of the orders (and thus plan) to get them out that apparently bothered the Brigadier nearly as much as had the plan that got them in. In some ways, it seemed more perhaps as if the simultaneous attack was aimed not so much at getting the Major's forces out, as at showing the French how to get the job done against the strong point of La Palette. However, orders were orders, and war was war, and General Johnson already knew how far arguing with the Division Commander was likely to get him. Therefore, at 8:10 p.m., he then sent the initial attack order up to Colonel Stacey:

On receipt of orders for this division to advance October 4th you will continue your advance toward the objective after liaison has been established with the French on your left and the 307th Inf. on your right. The exact hour at which you will move will be designated later. Organize your command with this purpose in view. Your advance will be covered by artillery fire which will search out the ravine in your front. (131)

The time designated for the attack was telephoned up to l'Homme Mort at around 10:30 p.m. There would be a massive artillery preparation along the front of the 154th beginning at 6:00 a.m. and lasting until 7:30 a.m., after which he was to push the company D/F combination up the ravine again. By that time, the line of the 307th, set to attack at 7:00 a.m., should have come abreast and the line of the French would be even as well. Colonel Stacey, with whom the orders to attack Hill 205 again did not sit well, in turn called the information up to Captain Scott, the commander of the 3rd Battalion, and then also to Lt. Knight, whom he spoke to at Sgt. Cahill's telephone station. Asking if the lieutenant had all he needed for the attack, Paul Knight answered sourly that he did indeed (all the while thinking "everything but men"). His nerves frayed, Colonel Stacey burned bright at Lt. Knight's tone of voice. Acidly, he made the comment that the lieutenant did not sound "very enthusiastic" about the attack and informed him, in his best Regular Army manner, that it was absolutely imperative that they break through to Major Whittlesey the next morning. Lieutenant Knight, exhausted and pretty well convinced that his two decimated companies did not stand a chance in hell of success in the coming attack, no matter how many 3rd Battalion men were behind him nor how many grenades he might have, simply said offhandedly that he would do his best. He then dropped the phone and walked off into the night to find Captain Scott and make further plans. His footsteps across the fall leaves and shrapnel clinkers were drowned out when a machine-gun chattered in the dark distance on the other side of Hill 198 and a trench mortar shell burst uncomfortably close. (29, 51, 109, 116, 238)

After he had Colonel Stacey squared away, General Johnson called the orders over to Colonel Houghton, whom he no doubt viewed as his only hope at breaking through to Major Whittlesey, since the 308th would be tied up before Hill 205. By that time, the 1st/307th had largely relieved the 2nd Battalion from the line, with their companies D and C up front (l to r), supported by companies B and A, respectively. The 2nd Battalion, meanwhile, slipped back and took up support positions behind the 1st, and then sent its men down by company to the Depot des Machines to get a hot meal, water and fresh, lice-free uniforms and underwear. Of the battered companies from the past eight days fighting, only companies I, F, and M of the 3rd Battalion were still up close to the line, remaining up on the left in support near where L had made some progress the two days previous. General Johnson told Colonel Houghton that he wanted those "three" companies to again

322

attack that same point of Hill 198 to try and further exploit that earlier break, similar to the plan that Captain Blagden had already tried that midday. Meanwhile the 1st Battalion, now manning the line and in much better shape than the 2nd to support the attack, would drive hard forward. The three companies on the left were to flank the Germans who, thus attacked squarely from two sides, would be quick - and smart - to pull back. The 1st Battalion would then drive up to an even line with the 308th's advance element on the Binarville-La Viergette road, form liaison left and then refuse their right flank back to the 305th and drag them up as well. Colonel Stacey would, at the same time, support the attack from the left, driving hard ahead and breaking the enemy line on his front as well. Meeting Colonel Houghton's men on the objective, they would then relieve Major Whittlesey's force.

Colonel Houghton, however, scoffed openly at the plan. He had just been up to inspect conditions on the line, concerned by the rising tide of casualties and lack of progress for their cost. He had seen the heights of Hill 198 and its well-wired approaches for himself. He would need twice his current number of troops to force a gap there, he said. And the Germans were not likely to collapse just because a hole had been punched in their line by two or three companies on their flank. After all, it had not happened with Major Whittlesey's six. Well, there was no choice, General Johnson said. The attack would go forward at 7:00 a.m. behind the artillery barrage. The line must be brought up to Major Whittlesey's line as quickly as possible. Those were the direct orders from General Alexander himself.

After getting off the phone with General Johnson, Colonel Houghton, never one to simply sit back and accept stupidity, called General Alexander himself and as tactfully as he could told his Division Commander that he thought the plan stood no chance of success. While he well understood what was at stake, there just had to be another way. General Alexander, who knew, respected and understood Colonel Houghton, told him nevertheless that the orders were cut and that he was to proceed with them. The line must be broken, this was how it was going to be done, and that was that.

Later that night, Colonel Houghton however, gathered as many of his company officers together as he had left and told them of the orders personally, adding that he himself did not see any way that they could succeed - only that they would produce more casualties. He then instructed them, in a left-handed sort of way, not to press the attack if they saw no clear way through, only to come to contact with the enemy and then report that they had been stopped by the wire and heavy machine-gun fire. "I don't want any more lives lost in that damned wire needlessly," he told them before dismissing them and then meeting privately with Major McKinney. General Johnson had told him during their telephone conversation that they were likely to lose all or part of their 2nd Battalion to assist whatever was left of the 308th tomorrow in their drive up that damned ravine to try and get through to Major Whittlesey, he said. In fact, their own assaults on Hill 198 also had as much to do with reaching the Major as breaking up the German defenses for further advance of the offensive, if the Colonel had read the Brigadier's tone right. What they needed to do then, he told Major McKinney, was think up a way to use what they were going to have left, break the line, and get through to Major Whittlesey as quickly as possible. That or face more of these maniac, pointless assaults at the wire and slopes of Hill 198. (29, 51, 103, 116, 138, 139, 235)

Meanwhile, in the German line, Major Hunicken was forced to call Hauptmann Von Sybel that evening and admit that the assault on the American position in the Charlevaux Ravine had been something of a failure, though by no means a complete one. They had hurt the enemy; that was certain. However, they had been hurt as well, and the Americans were stubbornly refusing to either surrender or pull back. He had spoken a short time ago to both Lt. Col. Schmidt and Hauptmann Von Wiedenbach of the 122nd and had gotten a report form them concerning the activities of their two companies involved in the action on the eastern side of the ravine and had learned that they had suffered as had the 254th. There had been a number of German casualties in the attack, which had actually played out into two phases. The first phase had been the initial assault, strong and disciplined, which had beaten the Doughboys back some at every point. They had caught them by complete surprise and had made some progress by the left flank at first. But the Americans were well armed with both light and heavy machine-guns that had made all the difference; though now with one less heavy gun, which sat in the dugout PC of the 122nd, Major Hunicken made a point of stating.

Thus, they had met intense fire from the strong American force, which was heavy enough to drive them back into safer positions. There they had quickly regrouped and soon made another try. The second phase had, admittedly, been ragged and mostly uncoordinated between the units. Driven largely by rage at the thrashing they had taken at the hands of what they considered to be a force of inferior quality, it had gone nowhere fast and by 6:00 p.m. was all been but over. Afterward, the men had returned to their positions, dragging with them what wounded and dead they could. There were, he said, still quite a few dead left behind that lay too close to the enemy position to bring back. Losses? The 7th and 12th companies of the 122nd had suffered the loss of three officers and about a dozen enlisted dead, with perhaps 18 wounded. The 254th had suffered about as equally, perhaps a little more. Reports were still coming in.

Hauptmann Von Sybel listened to all this with a pained ear. He was not in a position to neither question nor kibitz Major Hunicken, even if he was the Divisional Operations Officer, since he was only a Captain and Hunicken a Major, but there would likely have been little he would have questioned anyway. He was well aware of the difficulties facing those brave units crawling around in the brush around the Americans, as well as Major Hunicken's own bravery and intelligence. Manfred Hunicken had served long and well in the peacetime army, having risen to the rank of captain long before the war due to his innate abilities (which in itself was a feat outside of wartime). The 76th Reserve Division had served virtually all of its war in Russia, up until the Argonne, and there Hunicken, as a Major, had been a star in the ascendant in command of the 254th. Trying to find fault then was a useless exercise. What the Hauptmann could do, however, was to gather the information and pass it on to General Quadt-Wykradt-Huchtenbruck, who would then likely give him *carte blanche* to do what he thought was necessary to win the battle. Hauptmann Von Sybel had previously served well for General Quadt-Wykradt-Huchtenbruck, as well as their Corps commander General Wellmann (on whose staff the Hauptmann had been for a short time) earlier in the war and both had implicit trust in the experienced, intelligent and innovative young man. Therefore, it was little more than a formality when the Hauptmann called both the Division and Corps commanders to inform them of the progress made that day and his plans for the next day, which amounted to little more than continued concerted attack against the *Americanernest* in as much force as could be mustered. Tomorrow, he was sure, would be the decisive day of the assault and would prove to be the impudent American's undoing. (29, 51, 120, 123, 124, 128, 307)

(I) There is also the possibility that Company K was at that moment somewhat understrength. Captain Holderman later wrote that part of his men were still trying to work their way back across the ravine from the earlier disastrous breakthrough attempt about the time that the German afternoon attack hit. Holderman's report states that he had split the company in two at the wire and had left Lt. Pool in charge of one contingent to fight a rear guard action that had enabled Holderman to return to the bivouac with a second contingent to alert Major Whittlesey that they had been unable to get through. He further states that Pool and his men did not get back over to the right flank until 5:00 p.m. The Captain, writing three years after the event, must have confused his times however, for eye witnesses place both he *and* Lt. Pool at the 1:00 p.m. meeting with Major Whittlesey and Captain McMurtry. It is very likely then that the lieutenant indeed returned with the majority of his contingent in time for the meeting and that any missing men were, at most, a last, late returning squad under a sergeant or corporal that was caught out beyond the creek when the attack hit.

(11) Though he may have appeared outwardly nonplussed by the situation in the Charlevaux ravine, the truth was that the loss of Major Whittlesey's command - either by complete annihilation or capture - would leave a stain on General Alexander's record that could never be sponged away. Therefore, the Major was heavy on his mind, if just for that reason alone. However, additionally, General Liggett, the 1st Corps Commander, had asked about the matter at the meeting, something that had greatly embarrassed the Division Commander. Almost immediately, according to several that were there, General Alexander began 'dancing' around the facts, complaining about his Brigadiers and making excuses for the situation in the Charlevaux. Never all that popular to begin with, this did little to endear him to his fellow Division Commanders or the 1st Corps staff, General Liggett in particular. Alexander apparently left the meeting more than a little chagrinned at having had to 'have his ass saved' in the Argonne, as it were, as well as being questioned as to the reasons for the current situation in the Charlevaux. His actions over the next few days bear this out.

Ancillary sources used in this chapter include: 21, 25, 29, 30, 47, 49, 51, 148, 150, Various 152-216, 250-254, 257, 260, 261, 262, 268, 269, 272, 273, 278-283, 285, 286, 292, 296-306, 309, 310, 314-319, 323, 326-330, 338.

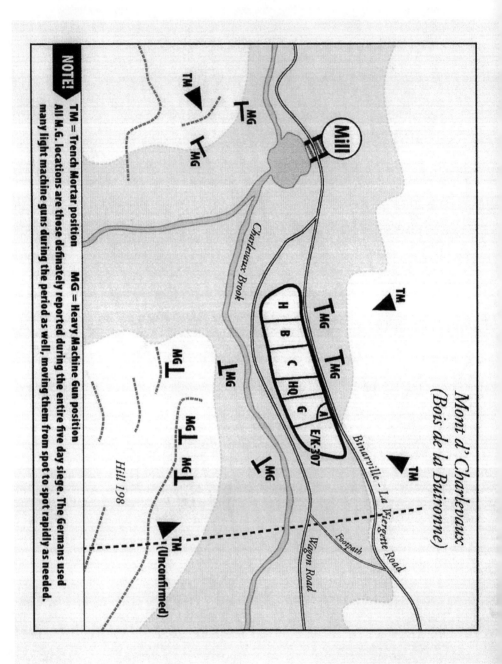

Mont d' Charlevaux
(Bois de la Buironne)

NOTE! TM = Trench Mortar position   MG = Heavy Machine Gun position

All M.G. locations are those definately reported during the entire five day siege. The Germans used many light machine guns during the period as well, moving them from spot to spot rapidly as needed.

Mill

Charlevaux Brook

Hill 198

H B C HQ G A E/K-307

Binarville - La Viergette Road

Wagon Road

Footpath

TM (Unconfirmed)

October 4, 1918 A.M.
"Take it easy. This cannot go on much longer…"
Major Charles Whittlesey.

By dawn, the 1st Battalion had full control of the 307th's zone of advance, and companies I, F, and M were positioning themselves for the drive against the regimental left flank. Meanwhile, Company L of the 308th had shifted over to the east ridge of the Ravin d'Argonne in order to help exploit the break through when, or if, a break came. There were few clouds to obscure things and for the first time during the drive through the Argonne, the men clearly saw the stars through the trees and did not have to curse the rain. Companies E, G, H, and L of the 307th (for all intents and purposes now the regiment's 2nd Battalion), had drawn back around Depot des Machines and were enjoying some rest and a hot meal - their first in nine days - little realizing the large part they would play in the coming day's events. By nightfall, in fact, two of their commanders would be out of action for good; Captain Grant of H, dead in the mud of the Ravin d'Argonne, and Captain Rainsford of L, seriously wounded.

The latter, Walter Kerr-Rainsford, whose observations and quotes continually pepper this text, was born in Toronto, Canada, on February 19, 1883, though he grew up in Massachusetts and Connecticut. He attended Harvard University, graduating with a B.A. in architecture in the class of 1904, alongside another young up and coming American hopeful, Franklin Delano Roosevelt. From there Rainsford went to France and attended the prestigious 'Ecole National des Beaux Arts of Paris', from which he graduated in 1911. A tall, unassuming, sensitive and caring man by nature, when the war broke out, he joined the American Field Service as an ambulance driver, in January 1916, as part of the Harvard contingent. He served in 'Section Sanitaire (Americaine) No. 3', driving his ambulance for a time around the hellish nightmare of the Verdun sector and around Alsace before opting out of the program that August and returning home. When America declared war that following April, Rainsford applied to the 1st Plattsburg camp of 1917, graduated as a 1st Lieutenant, and was given command of a platoon in Company M of the 307th. It was with them that he went to France, eventually commanding the whole company and was wounded for the first time (in the face) in August 1918, during a battle before the ruined Chateau Diable in the "fist-fight on the Vesle."

When he returned to duty, he caught up with his regiment during the build-up for the Muese-Argonne Offensive and was placed at the head of Company L, which he then lead into the hell of the Argonne at the front of his regiment for the next six days. Having made it through the wire to the top of Hill 198 and back down again on the afternoon of October 2 (and having been mauled in the process), the company was drawn back into safer positions to lick its wounds. Throughout that night, its outposts listened to the sounds of German activity up on the ridge of Hill 198 with apprehension, knowing that it could only mean trouble, but also that there was nothing at all they could do about it. The morning of October 3 found them pulled back well behind the line, charged with maintaining routes of communication forward as the 1st Battalion took over the line, cleaning out infiltrators and fending off German machine-guns playing on the regiment's right flank. It proved a daunting task and their day was a long one. (17, 72, 84, 99, 103, 104, 119, 138, 235, 347)

Now, standing in the mud of Depot des Machines nine mornings after the first one of the battle, Captain Rainsford took stock of what he had left out of his original 230 men and found that there were now less than 100. By noon the next day they would be half even that, and what was left would be under the command of a sergeant. (103)

Dawn comes late that time of year in the section of the Charlevaux Ravine where the Pocket is. About 400 meters east of Captain Holderman's right flank outpost positions, the track of the ravine dips southeastward, behind a large spur of ground jutting out from the northern slope of Hill 198. This spur and the woods along the heights of the Bois de la Buironne opposite it, serves to effectively block any direct light from the rising sun until rather late morning. Combined with that fact, the rain and clouds had so far only added to the gloom Major Whittlesey's men already felt every morning. By the morning of Friday October 4, 1918 however, the rain had stopped just after midnight and the clouds had actually rolled away. It looked like it just might be a nice day for once.

Under the morning stars, Major Whittlesey and Captain McMurtry were already up and organizing some early morning patrols. The night patrols, which the Major had purposely kept on a short leash to avoid trouble, had already come in and made their reports. It had been a quiet night, only a very few of their opposite numbers out there, mirroring their own actions and sending up parachute flares and Very lights, but nothing more. In fact, the later it got, the more the patrols were not even sure that they were still surrounded, as they had encountered less and less of the enemy. Additionally, they had not come across any armed and manned machine-gun nests nor any observation posts keeping watch over the Pocket as they figured there would be, considering the ferocity of the previous afternoon's attacks. If the Germans were still out there, watching them, then it was from a distance. (29, 51, 135, 148, 149)

Overall, the reports were encouraging. It had indeed been relatively quiet ever since the last attacks had been broken up the previous evening. Only a few stray shells that had fallen into the position just after midnight and some sparse sniper activity and distant machine-gun bursts had intruded to disturb the men's rest. And since it had been a little warmer and not rained for once, some sleep had actually been possible. The thought then occurred: perhaps the situation had relieved itself. Maybe the Germans had withdrawn after all, under the realization that there was no way that the U.S. forces would ever allow the command in the ravine to remain long out of contact with their main line, no matter how many enemy troops separated them. Then too, Major Whittlesey's men had also given as bad as they had gotten during yesterday's intense afternoon attacks. The Germans might be thinking that it would be better to simply pull back, bide their time and husband their lives and resources, similar to what they had done on l'Homme Mort when they pulled out just as it seemed that the tide had been turning in their favor. Better that, than to fight a loosing battle against a force determined to reunite. That might be one possible explanation for the curious lack of enemy troops out there overnight. It was certainly an attractive one.

But all this speculation needed confirmation. Therefore, the Major was up early under the stars and decided to send out three patrols with two main objectives. First, it was imperative that someone get back to the main line and appeal directly for relief of the command in the Charlevaux, whose general condition was rapidly deteriorating. Besides the obvious lack of food and water, the wounded in particular were suffering badly from the lack of proper medical care and exposure. Many had already died, their wounds just too severe for the medics to bind together with shoelaces and sweat stained undershirts. There was also a developing ammunition situation, something that had been pressing to begin with and was growing more serious. Grenades were gone, machine-gun and Chauchat ammo was relatively low and the rifle supply was getting down to just what the men carried in their rifle belts and just a few dozen precious bandoliers.

On top of all that, there was a morale issue; nothing serious, but certainly something to contend with. Overall, the men's spirits were still relatively high. However, walking around the position the night before, after the heavy attacks had been repulsed, the Major had heard several dispirited comments being muttered by some of the men when they did not know he was listening. It had happened during his rounds that morning too. No food, no water, low ammunition, no help for the wounded, cut off... all these things were starting to drag on the already well-used men. What hope was there, some were asking? What did any of it matter when it looked like soon they all would be like those poor pathetic bastards in that bloody hole down by the wagon road, or worse - like those under the little mounds beginning to dot the hillside. Some of the other company officers reported hearing such as well, and this was a bad sign. If the men's general fighting spirit was allowed to drop too low, it would only be a matter of time before the situation would collapse in on itself. Then, if it came down to sacrifice or surrender, which would they choose? Without morale, the answer seemed inevitable. All of this, the pain, the suffering and the sacrifice of battling forward and holding on to the advanced position in order to accomplish the greater goal of breaking the Giselher line would have been for nothing. And that would have been unacceptable to Charles Whittlesey; above all, the sacrifice could not have been for nothing. Therefore, the position must be resupplied in order to hold out.

The answer to all of these difficulties was based, of course, around the issue of whether those in charge back at regimental truly understood how desperate the situation in the Charlevaux Ravine was becoming. Major Whittlesey was not at all sure that the pigeon messages were even making their way through. His only way of knowing that would have been a reply message, of which he had none.

His second objective with the patrols was simply to comply with the last orders he had received, which he believed still stood - to organize along his objective line and hold the position, forming liaison to the left and right, being prepared to resume the advance upon receipt of further orders. While he was holding his line as ordered, he still had no liaison right or left, something that would also have been almost as good as reaching the rear. If the Germans had pulled out, that would mean that the flanks were open and he could easily comply with his orders. The patrols needed to see if this was possible.

However, those orders concerning his flanks also had to be viewed with regard to his current situation. They were, after all, three days old and much had changed. Since the main effort of the German attacks had been against Lt. Cullen's left flank positions the previous day, it seemed pretty obvious that to send men farther up that valley between Hill 205 and the Binarville-La Viergette road looking for a liaison there would simply be a waste of precious lives. The French were not there, the Germans were. That was a fact undeniable. Looking for liaison directly west then was pretty much a dead issue. Nor had anyone from companies D and F managed to break through, despite the spirited fighting they had heard from back there the previous afternoon. With Hill 205 yet so obviously well occupied, it was not a stretch to figure that the main line must still be south of that damned hill on the U.S., as well as on the French, side. In fact, it was probably exactly where it had been when the advanced force had left it behind on the afternoon of the 2nd.

Possibilities from the right flank were much brighter. Since they had also heard the sounds of battle emanating from the other side of Hill 198 the afternoon before, there seemed little doubt but that the 307th's main line was at least even with that of the 308th. And from what Captain Holderman had said the morning of October 3 when he had came into the Pocket, they might well even be forward of the 308th's line. (Remember also that Major Whittlesey had even reported 307th men operating within his right flank zone.) Further, outside of the grenade throwers on the cliffs forward and behind that flank's position and one machine-gun to the rear, there had been little enemy activity on the right. This might be an indication that the Germans were not as well established there, possibly because the 307th was now closer than Major Whittlesey and Captain Holderman initially thought. Perhaps because the rest of the 307th's 3rd Battalion was now catching up with Captain Holderman? Maybe… In any case, it certainly deserved a look.

One patrol was to go out to the south/southwest, generally following the original route taken into the ravine and again attempt to make contact with D and F companies. However, Company E movement of the morning before, along that same route, had drawn about as much fire as one company could draw. Therefore, Major Whittlesey decided to send a smaller force, squad strength, and assembled one from Company G men under Corporal (acting Sergeant) Holger Peterson, a tall skinny blond Swede from New York who had been a garage mechanic before being drafted. On the right, he had Captain Holderman assemble two small patrols of Company K men and gave instructions for each to work opposite sides of the Charlevaux Ravine down for at least three-quarters of a kilometer and report back the results. It was just going on 5:30 a.m. - still dark - when the three patrols set out on their respective journeys. (29, 40, 51, 135, 148, 149, 150, 220, 239)

About the same time that Corporal Peterson was crawling down through the swampy bottom of the Charlevaux, the entire 1st Army line exploded with artillery fire. While not as destructive as the initial bombardment of September 26th had been, it nevertheless blasted the hell out of the German lines and momentarily sent them reeling. Once the barrage lifted forward, the infantry then stormed out ahead in a solid mass, plowing on to their objectives everywhere - everywhere but in the zone of the 154th Brigade, 77th Division that is.

There, General Johnson had decided to delay his general attack until 8:00 a.m., instead of going over at 7:30 a.m. as had been the original plan, in order to insure firm liaison between the 308th the slightly lagging 307th. The barrage on his front began at 6:00 a.m. and played the front well for an hour, laid to cut as much of the enemy wire as possible, before moving forward for another 20 minutes or so and then slowly dying out. The heavy Stokes mortars of the 302nd Trench Mortar Battalion then followed the barrage, carefully laid so as to allow the enemy little quarter, and by the time the attack came off, they had already tossed in nearly a hundred rounds. Once their fire lifted, the 307th was up and attacking. (103, 116, 131, 132, 139, 144)

The coordinates used for the heavy barrage that morning were ones based upon those sent back by pigeon out of the Charlevaux Ravine by Lt. Teichmoeller the morning previous; which had then been adjusted from the reports of the short firing from that same day's noon shoot. Lengthened by at least 100 meters, they should have then been right on the mark. To insure this, a liaison man was sent forward, Lt. George Putnam of the 152nd F.A. staff, to observe a few ranging shots overnight. It all went well. From a former German observation post in a tall tree, the lieutenant watched the first few shots go well over the ridgeline ahead of the 308th's main line and saw the smoke from the ravine beyond. By bringing the fire back just a few degrees then, the shots would necessarily fall directly on the ridge and, more importantly, the wire before it. (93, 140)

With the 307th up and attacking soon after 7:00 a.m. and making strong connections over on the right, liaison with the French would be the next most important thing before Colonel Stacey had the 308th move down the ravine. The question then was, just where was the liaison with the French on the left - back in Binarville, or not? Captain Scott, the 3rd/308th commander, who was taking an increasingly important role in the proceedings within the ill-fated ravine, sent out patrols again on Colonel Stacey's orders to find out. The 'firm line' that had been reported the day before was not so firm as they had thought, nor was contact with outposts truly firm contact at all, at least in the Colonel's mind.

Nevertheless, at 7:10 a.m. he received a message from the liaison force - they had found what went for liaison in the areas just east of Binarville and passed the information back to Stacey:

Have mixed liaison group, one patrol at 5.30am at point 294.25-275.05 at junction of road running east and west from Binarville with road running north and south. 307th at 295.1-275.4, trench N.E. (131, 136)

Flanks apparently covered then, the 308th's attack went over just before 8:00 a.m., now parallel with the 307th to the right, but without receiving any real benefits from the artillery barrage. Lieutenant Putnam had ranged the artillery in well and it had fallen squarely onto Hill 198 and the tremendous wire belt before it, but still had had little effect. (Nor did the Stokes shells, for that matter.) There was simply too much wire to deal with. Then the Germans came out from underground following the bombardment's cessation and trained their machine-guns. If there had not been many of the damned death dealers on Hill 198 on the afternoon of October 2, when Major Whittlesey's force had walked over it, there sure as hell were plenty there now. (109, 116, 131, 132, 136)

While the 307th was battling against Hill 198 in much the same places they had been for two days now, Lt. Knight meanwhile rammed D and F forward down the Ravin d'Argonne again. Barely 80 men remained to a company now and they trailed a line of casualties under the intense German counter-artillery fire that met them as they struggled along, hammering their way desperately forward. The lieutenant would launch four separate and vicious attacks against the German defenses along Hills 198 and 205 that morning, backed solidly by companies K and M. Each time however, they were stopped cold. All the while, to his right, men of 1st/307th, with the three companies of 3rd/307th on their left, slammed uselessly at the German wire as well, desperate to attempt the flanking maneuver that would bring Major Whittlesey relief. They too remained halted firmly; any progress they made through the few gaps in the wire was rapidly beaten back down by swift German counter attacks from above.

As the attack pressed forward - and before it came to its ultimate stand still - a sergeant, leading a single, understrength squad from Company K/308th, was making his own bit of history there in the Ravin d'Argonne. First Sergeant Benjamin Kaufman was advancing on the left of Lt. Knight's men, when his squad came under fire from a German machine-gun nest well hidden in the brush ahead. Two of his men, out front as scouts, went down with wounds at the first stutter of the gun, while the rest took cover. Flanking attacks on the nest only brought a hail of additional gunfire. No doubt about it; these Huns were *good*, and the advance was stopped cold.

Organizing a gang among the remaining men he had, Sgt. Kaufman went up the middle of the formation with grenades and led the assault in. Before they could get anywhere near the nest however, a bullet shattered the sergeant's right arm. Nevertheless, he was up again in a flash, anger seething, and rushed the machine-gun nest *alone*, throwing grenades in with his left hand as he moved through the forest murk. Upon reaching the nest, he found all but one of the crew either dead or scattered, and drawing his *empty* pistol from its holster, he took the last remaining German as prisoner, then forcing the Hun to carry his own machine-gun back behind U.S. lines. There, shattered arm bleeding profusely, Sgt. Kaufman passed out at the first aid station which had been set up at the l'Homme Mort bunker. Kaufman lived however, and later received *nine* separate awards for bravery in recognition of his actions that day – one of those being the Medal of Honor. (105, 132, 350, 356, 360)

German versions of the morning attack tell a tale of shell fire, more shell fire, and still more shell fire before a violent wave of American troops surged forward and were repelled, despite the American's use of gas. A "Battalion-sized" attack slammed into Hill 205 and tried to break through to their stranded comrades beyond in the Charlevaux, while an attack "three companies strong" went up Hill 198 at the 122nd Regiment. By the time the assault died out, there had been more than a few German casualties, which they could ill afford, and a call was being placed by Major Hunicken to division for the 76th Pioneer Reserve Company to be brought up. He had wanted yet more troops besides these, but there were no more to be had. The French were making another of their fruitless pushes well to the west, near Lancon, and all spare manpower reserves had been sent that way. Instead, the division staff officer to whom Major Hunicken had spoken suggested that Hauptmann Von Sybel's program of attack using trench mortars, machine-guns, and hand grenades continue – indeed, perhaps even increase. In other words, simply batter the enemy into submission. Hauptmann Bickel also suggested that the enemy be encouraged to surrender. There were several English speakers among the 254th and he was sure that at least a few of the Americans in the ravine were of German parentage. Perhaps if shown the hopelessness of their situation and offered the chance, they might just give up.

Hauptmann Von Sybel too had made several calls rearward, ordering up more light machine-guns, ammunition and hand grenades for his coming assaults that day, meant to either kill or capture the entire American command in the ravine. He was sure that this operation was going to be a success, as all night long troops up on Hill 198 had listened to the most pitiful wailing moans and screams from the wounded down in the *Americanernest*. That was a sure indicator that the khaki force was in sorry shape. Also, the filthy dead body of one of the Americans killed while out on patrol early that morning seemed to support that the beleaguered force was in a bad way. Brought in and searched, he was found to have no food with him, no water in his canteen, no personal bandage pack and, most interestingly, his cartridge belt was nearly empty – all surely indications that the Americans were near the end of their rope. Apparently, the attacks of the day before had done more than a little good. Now for the final blow. (I)

More than anything however, what Hauptmann Von Sybel wanted before the final attack was launched was an officer prisoner to be taken from the force there in the Charlevaux. Enlisted prisoners were fine and good for basic information, but a private soldier was unlikely to know actual troops strengths, military plans and dispositions, and supply actualities. An officer, on the other hand, could provide any number of details with the right man talking to him and not even realize it. This was particularly important because Hauptmann Von Sybel was still relatively unsure as to the actual number of Americans down in that damned ravine. Several more prisoners had been taken since the first one and all had given varying answers when asked about troop strength. It appeared that there were more than a few of the "peasant" class in the American force, uneducated and slow to military practices. These particularly could not be expected to know anything worthwhile. Was it possible that there were really two full battalions down there? If their casualties had been as heavy as reports (and the screams and cries coming from the ravine all night) seemed to indicate, there certainly were not two full battalions of fighting strength down there anymore. Still, their force might yet be strong, perhaps strong enough even to reverse direction and batter their way out. Again, an officer would know, but so far, the Hauptmann had no officer. For now at least, he realized he would be forced to accept that it was still likely they were out numbered by the men in the ravine and would need to work fast to effect their destruction - before they effected his.

At that same time, General Wellmann at the 1st Corps PC had awoken very early to alarming reports that the French were attempting a massive assault along the Valley of the Aisne. Shortly after, reports came in stating that the Americans were also making another bid to push up the Aire Valley, in the east of the Argonne Forest. It was a grim situation, for it was obvious that the Allied forces were trying to pinch out the greater Argonne Forest, since they were having great difficulties getting through it. And General Wellmann knew that the enemy must not be permitted to simply pass the forest but instead must be held in place on either side of it, just as in its middle, in order for the line to stand in his sector.

For the French, his answer to that problem was to order Major Ditfurth to commit the last Corps reserves left, an infantry regiment and two artillery batteries of the 45th Reserve Division, against them. (Which, arriving just in time, eventually did drive the French attack to ground). In the east, he counted on General Von Kliest to drive the Americans back with the units of his Army Group Argonnen already there; that, or at least to continue to hold them in check. If both sides held, that section of the Giselher running through the greater Argonne would still remain intact, and damn the enemy that tried it! (29, 30, 51, 123, 128)

Corporal Peterson and his patrol were back within an hour. By the light of the U.S. barrage lighting up the early morning sky, they had crawled carefully through the swampy mess that the German shelling of the day before had made of the banks of the Charlevaux Brook, almost to the other side. After getting as far as the tall grass and brush opposite the creek, one of Cpl. Peterson's men spotted movement ahead and alerted him to it. Peering carefully into the rising grayness of the morning, he could just make out the familiar shape of a German helmet moving stealthily a short distance ahead. Corporal Peterson let him get closer and then, rising suddenly, brought his rifle up and shot him down point blank. Other shots rang out, from both sides. Then, the Germans sent up a flare, lighting the whole scene up like day, and the sharp stutter of a machine-gun began rapping out. Corporal Peterson yelled to his men for a withdrawal, fighting all the way, and made it back with only one casualty, Private Oscar Wallen, who was shot in the back. (29, 30, 51)

The other two patrols came in soon after to report as well. There was nothing out to the east. They had carefully worked their way up the ravine, going slightly beyond the spur jutting out from Hill 198 on the map, and had neither seen nor heard anything outside of the sounds of battle coming from the other side of Hill 198. As far as they could tell of both ridgelines along the Charlevaux, there did not seem to be anyone out there. (29, 30, 135, 148)

Major Whittlesey and Captain McMurtry considered this an encouraging turn of events. Obviously, there were still Germans between the Charlevaux Ravine and the 307th, enough to keep that regiment at bay anyway. Otherwise, there would be 307th men coming up the ravine from the east. However, the apparent lack of German troops along the route the patrol had taken might indicate that the command was not necessarily totally surrounded anymore. It might indicate a withdrawal deeper into German lines had begun and the resistance that the 307th's forces to the south were facing was nothing more than a rear guard effort. This might also be true of the trouble Corporal Peterson's patrol had run into. Perhaps they had been nothing more than enemy patrols scouting routes backward. Was a similar situation to what had happened the night of September 29th-30th repeating then, and the Germans actually freeing up the Pocket by a voluntary withdrawal as they had hoped when they sent patrols out? Indications were good, and the two battalion commanders started organizing more patrols. If the Germans were loosening their grip and there was a way starting to open up to the rear, then they certainly must find it, exploit it and establish a secure route so that the wounded might be evacuated and supplies be brought up as soon as was possible. (II)

With patrols readying themselves to scout for possible good news then, Major Whittlesey again sat down, pulled out a pigeon message book, and started to scrawl a report to Colonel Stacey. Calling for Private Richards, the Major's first message of the day took flight minutes later.

Time: 7.25am

All quiet during the night. Our patrols indicate Germans withdrew during this night. Sending further patrols now to verify this. At 12.30 and 1.10am, six shells from our own light artillery fell on us. Many wounded here whom we cannot evacuate. Need rations badly. No word from D or F companies. (246)

There were now only three pigeons left.

Major Whittlesey's message arrived at the divisional message center 35 minutes later, and within the hour, General Alexander's chief of staff, Colonel Hannay, had seen it and was on the phone directly to General Johnson.

"A report has come in by pigeon from your first battalion," Colonel Hannay began. "Is that a fact that he needs rations badly and cannot get his food up?"

General Johnson allowed that Major Whittlesey was still cut off as of last reports, but that they were doing everything possible to drive the line up to him. Colonel Stacey had told him that a rations dump had been established 1,200 meters back of the main line, with more coming up by rail. Wounded were also being carried out on the rail. It was all *very* efficient, the Colonel had said, sourly.

Back and forth, General Johnson and Colonel Hannay went, rehashing much the same as had been for the two day's previous; the Germans were well ensconced and had no intentions of giving up their main line, while U.S. forces were equally determined to drive them out, though success had thus far eluded them. There had been some give on the left of the 307th, had there not, Colonel Hannay asked? Yes, the Brigadier said, but it had only been slight - a few men shallowly through the wire, nothing more. Nor would it likely last without something to back them up. What reserves were there? Just the 2nd/307th down at Depot de Machines and Company L/308th, supporting the 3rd/307th's drive to get through on their left, General Johnson said. Worse however, was that the French were apparently nowhere to be found on the left... (109, 116, 131, 138, 150)

But this was not entirely true.

The French closest to Hill 205 were, by then, in attack (as they were all along their line). The attack had actually gone over uncoordinated with their American counterparts however, though not through lack of trying. Throughout the night of October 3, Captain Klotz and Lt. de Coppet, the 77th's U.S. and French liaison men respectively, had been going back and forth between the PC's of the 1st D.C.D, the 9th C.a.P and the 77th in order to coordinate the attack. The French, having moved back into Binarville after the German shelling had let up late that afternoon, began to build a base of advance in anticipation. Their next step was to move in elements of the 4th C.a.P, which was to bring off the attack there, who then began patrolling the open space between the 77th's left and Binarville. The majority of the 9th would need as many troops as it could muster to launch a simultaneous attack to reclaim the Tranchee d'Charlevaux during the general attack. By 7:15 a.m. on October 4, Klotz and de Coppet's work had paid off and the 1st D.C.D received, and was distributing, orders to secure a firm liaison with the 77th Division's left flank in anticipation of conjoined attacks on Hill 205 that were meant to eradicate the position altogether. While the 4th C.a.P moved against one side of the damned hill, Colonel Stacey was to drive what was left of the 308th against the opposite side, thus crushing the defenders.

The problem was that the French had already launched a push at 6:30 a.m., in accordance with their previous orders to force a way through to the Charlevaux Ravine and then drive down to meet up with Major Whittlesey's force; orders which they believed, at attack time, had still stood. The attack was a fierce and determined one, with the 4th C.a.P driving hard against the foot of Hill 205 and heading toward the trenches of the La Palette Pavilion beyond. By mid-morning, the battalion had managed to claw their way forward of the devastated no-man's-land between the Binarville-Autry road and the enemy trench line there and then up the slope of the hill. In one spot, they even actually got *into* a portion of the La Palette Pavilion trenches, but the victory was short lived. The German counterattack came on strong and they were repelled after but a few brief minutes, not only out of the trench line and off the hill but also all along the French right flank as far up as Tranchee d'Charlevaux. Without a coordinated attack across the area between the two great armies and support by the U.S. forces to their right, they once again realized the impossibility of the situation and began to fall back. Before 11:30 a.m., the French line was again in place where it had begun the attack from, along the Binarville-Autry road and within the town of Binarville itself. Outposts were sent back out, the closest to the 308th being again in the orchard 500 meters west of the 308th's left flank and just north of the Binarville-Moulin de l'Homme Mort road, where the liaison platoon of Company I/308 had found them on the morning of the 3rd. By noon then, nearly everything along the French right flank was as it had been at 6:00 a.m. that morning - except the casualty totals.

It was about that time that General Alexander received a call from Colonel Malin Craig at 1st Army PC with news that the French left had reached and retaken Lancon again; certainly exciting, but hardly beneficial to the local situation. There, General Alexander had a recent message from Colonel Stacey, relayed through General Johnson, which said that the Colonel's liaison men had sent word of only some lonely French outpost's above Binarville. Their actual line, they thought, still remained back *south* of the town about 500 meters, with only an outpost line actually occupying the town. This had Colonel Stacey worried about further infiltration if he was going to push on to the Charlevaux that afternoon, since his reserves would now only be enough to support the attack - not guard a flank that was supposed to be covered by an ally. All this was certainly a confusing state of affairs, especially from a command that had only the afternoon before explicitly promised General Alexander cooperative attacks. So just where were the French? Finally, General Alexander decided to send out Captain Klotz and Lt. de Coppet once again, to the PC of the 9th C.a.P. and have the Regimental Commander there mark on the map the *exact* line of the French front locally. It would not do to have a similar situation as was then in play ahead of the 308th break out someplace else on his line at the same time, especially further back. Then, turning his attention back to what was going on in the Ravin d'Argonne, he sent word to General Johnson to be passed forward that the afternoon attack, which he was then planning, had better succeed that day or he would have the hide of the person responsible for the failure. (2, 10, 91, 92, 109, 116, 131, 132, 144, 146, 148, 150)

Burial details were out that morning in the Pocket, tiredly trying to scrape open graves for the many dead of October 3 in the rocky, root-filled earth of the hillside. But it was slow and painful work and therefore many of the men on the detail contented themselves with simply placing the bodies in shallow excavations and then throwing a few shovel-fulls of earth over them; just enough to cover them from sight. There were bodies and body parts everywhere and the hillside was beginning to look like a Lower East Side New York butcher shop to the men trapped there. The worst spot was where the wounded were. There, the four medics tied the torn flesh of wounds together using everything from rifle slings and bits of underwear, to spiral puttee leggings and leaving any maggots found on the wounds there, to eat out the rot and infection. (29, 40, 135, 206, 236)

Elsewhere around the Pocket, men had started working on deepening their funk holes or brushing off what mud they could from their cloths, while dreaming and talking in low tones of food, a bath, fresh underwear, and home. Private Larney, over near the Battalion

PC hole, rubbed his two-days beard and looked longingly at his razor, but there was not enough water for that. Even Major Whittlesey, who had shaved everyday without fail since the jump-off into the Argonne, now skipped one this morning as well for much the same reason and the stubble gave him a mournful look. (It would not do to appear clean-shaven when other men, especially the wounded, could not be so, and when water was at an even higher premium than it had ever been.) Most failed to notice initially, however. One of Pvt. Larney's last precious cigarettes made the rounds of the Headquarters Company men for breakfast, shared so that as many men as possible got at least a puff. Then, with the light, the German machine-guns and snipers started up again and the men scraping out the shallow graves were forced to do so on their empty, growling stomachs, virtually one handful of dirt at a time. The rest hunkered deep in their holes again, waiting and watching for an attack. Waiting and watching... (29, 51, 245)

It was about 8:30 a.m. when the first trench mortar shells started to dump into the position, sending everyone scrambling for cover. At first there did not seem to be any extraordinary difference from the day before in their fast whine and loud, cracking explosions, until someone noted that they were coming in far too fast and far too scattered to all be from one gun. They seemed to be searching the complete width and breadth of the Pocket all at once. Careful observation revealed that there were at least two more guns firing away at them, in addition to the one on Hill 205. Except these new guns seemed to be tossing their shells in from *forward* of the ravine on a high, arcing course. So Lt. Cullen had been right the day before; he *had* been getting nailed from the front. Major Whittlesey immediately sent several scouts to find the locations of these new guns and they were back in about an hour, reporting that the guns were ahead and well above the road. There was one about 200 meters down off each flank.

One gun had been bad enough, but three could cause terrible carnage across the hillside. Though their aim into the ravine was bad, making the barrage of shells not nearly as terrible as it might have been, even if they were not hitting anything right then that did not mean that they would not correct their fire in the future. In the meantime, the sheer weight and number of explosions were enough to tear at anyone's nerves, much less men who were already sick, exhausted, and starved. Attacking them would be difficult at best however, due to the steep, up-hill slope and the clear field of vision down hill that they commanded, not to mention the likely-hood of the usual protective machine-gun cordon. In addition, after the shellacking that Lt. Rogers' men had taken going after that one across the ravine, Major Whittlesey did not think it prudent to send men off after these two, especially when he had such limited manpower at his disposal. Therefore, in the end, Major Whittlesey decided there was really nothing that could be done about the guns just then and adopted a 'wait and see' attitude. If they corrected their poor aim, then perhaps they might try taking them out. But, for now, better to let them alone. (29, 51, 135, 148, 149, 150, 245)

There were other reasons for letting them be as well, which Captain Holderman later noted in his monograph on the whole episode:

"His... trench mortar shells would appear at a high angle, descending upon the position or upon the road at the foot of the position. (Only) about fifteen percent of (these) trench mortar shells fell on the position, but many of those failed to explode... a great deal of the enemy trench mortar ammunition was defective, which rendered many of his shells "duds". Many of his shells (also) passed over the occupied reverse slope and struck along the road to the rear of the position and in the ravine to the rear. Had all of the trench mortar shells fired by the enemy fallen onto the position, then there would have really been a Lost Battalion!"
(149)

The scouts had also reported that they had seen plenty of Germans crawling around above the road. Disturbingly, Major Whittlesey was also getting other reports from all over the Pocket of Germans occasionally being seen again up on Hill 198 across the ravine and moving in the weeds of the ravine. With harassing sniper and machine-gun fire continuing, along with the trench mortar shells, it certainly looked like the two Battalion Commander's earlier hopes of a German withdrawal were just so many wasted thoughts.

Then, the potato masher grenades started coming again, first tentatively from the little cliff behind the right flank and then again in a veritable shower of them from the heights above the road in front. The German method of attack had gone unchanged from the day before. Round after round of the death dealing cylinders rained down on the hillside. They were again followed by a long stutter from the machine-guns. Raking the Pocket from stem to stern, fire was coming from behind down in the ravine and up on Hills 198 and 205, as well as from both flanks and at least two guns above the road ahead now. A hell of a lot of American rifle fire came in return, and the occasional German body tumbled down the hill to the road as a result. Then, another round of the grenades, sometimes two or three again coming down tied together with rope. Still the men set themselves, wishing that they had some grenades of their own, particularly the tough little French VB rifle grenades, but there were none.

When next he had a chance to look at the time, it was 10:15 a.m. and the patrols that Captain McMurtry had sent out to verify what the early morning patrols had found off the right flank were still not back. Since they had been gone some two hours now, the implication was clear. (Many of their bodies were found days later by the relieving troops of the 307th.) What was more, the firing was dying out to the south of Hill 198 as the last gasps of the attacks made there by the remainder of 308th faded into the mid-morning sunlight. Neither companies D and F, nor any of Captain Holderman's comrades were anywhere to be seen in the Charlevaux Ravine. Instead, all the Doughboys saw were more Germans, all they heard was more stutter from the machine-guns and all they took was the blasts of more potato mashers. Despite the sunlight, it was not turning out to be a nice day after all. (109, 116, 135, 148, 149, 150, 234, 236, 239, 245)

Major Whittlesey had no choice but to face the bitter facts; there had been no breakthrough and there was going to be no relief that morning. The likely reason why the earlier eastern patrol had found no Germans on the right was because they had all been up on the line beating off the initial morning advance of the 307th. Everything he had warned Colonel Stacey about was now coming to pass. His command was still surrounded in the Charlevaux and certainly looked to stay that way; at least until they reached the point when the men were simply too hunger-wracked, sick, and fatigued to pull a trigger, or when all the ammunition had run out.

Sitting down, he began to scrawl another message to Colonel Stacey; one that laid out just exactly how bad off the command really was, leaving no room for doubt:

Time: 10.35am
Germans are still around us, though in smaller numbers. We have been heavily shelled by mortar this morning. Present effective strength (A,B,C,E,G,H, Co's) 175; K Co 307th, 45; MG Detachment, 17; total here about 235. Officers wounded: Lt. Harrington A (sic), Capt. Stromee C, Lts. Peabody and Revnes MG, Lt. Wilhelm Co E missing. Cover bad if we advance up the hill and very difficult to move the wounded if we change position. Situation is cutting into our strength rapidly. Men are suffering from hunger and exposure and the wounded are in very bad condition. Cannot support be sent at once? (246)

No other communication that Major Whittlesey had yet sent out from the field during the drive thus far through the Argonne had expressed as much of a message of sheer desperation and hopelessness. None other had been so shortly plaintive in its request for relief, nor had any other been as brutally honest in assessing his situation. One can almost feel the contrition and bitter chagrin the Major must have felt in laying out on paper exactly how damaged his command was, in brusque and horrific frankness. (General Alexander would later say of it (2) that never before had he heard a message so couched in "extreme pessimism.") Out of an estimated original strength of 700 or so officers and men from the seven depleted companies of infantry and two sections of machine-gunners under his command (including Captain Holderman's men), by his own count, he now had just 235 effectives left. The rest in killed, wounded, and missing, if taken at face value, represented a mean loss of just over 65 percent in slightly under 40 hours. (III)

Omer Richards tossed the pigeon in the air and silently watched as Major Whittlesey's sad missive winged its way out of the ravine. Then he turned and crawled back to his hole next to the combined Battalion PC hole, while the German machine-guns and trench mortars continued to play along the Pocket's perimeter. (29, 51, 109, 116)

Now, there were only two birds left.

Morning had broken across the aerodrome at Remicourt with a ground fog that covered the field in a thick dewy mist, despite the fact that the sun was actually making an appearance. Mechanics of the 50th Aero Squadron shivered as they readied the DH-4s for the first patrols of the day and watched fellow 'mechs' of the 1st and 12th Aero Squadrons, sharing the Remicourt field with the 50th, doing the same. There had been a rash of problems with blown spark plugs in the big 12-cylinder Liberty engines that powered the DH's lately and this had kept the men extremely busy most of the night. No crew wanted to lose "their" plane, or "their" officers manning it, to engine failure on the wrong side of the lines.

The first line patrols went out not long after dawn, but were quickly back. The ground was still shrouded in a blanket of white; there was nothing to be seen yet. Though the sky above showed its promise of a fine day, this in itself could be a mixed blessing. Lately, the Germans had been pestering the 50th's planes quite a bit, with their Fokker fighters jumping them from out of the piled cloud-banks above while observers were busy looking for the line below, leading to some tense moments. It had reached the point that now no one plane went out on patrol without another flying above for protection. There was safety in numbers. While the threat would be minimized considerably if the day did turn out clear for once, it also meant however that the Fokkers would likely be up in larger numbers, flying in bigger formations to contend with.

At about 1:30 p.m., a 50th squadron DH with a big red number '2' painted on the sides took off headed for the Argonne Forest, with a protection plane leaving a few minutes behind. Pilot of the mission plane was 2nd Lt. Harold E. Goettler, and his back-seater was 1st Lt. Erwin R. Bleckley. Lieutenant's Goettler and Bleckley were a regular team and old hands in the squadron, having been with it almost since its formation and working together all through the St. Mihiel affair. Therefore, they knew well what they were up against as they gathered height over the field and then turned toward the lines. (110, 241)

Harold Ernest Goettler was born on July 21, 1890 in Chicago, Illinois. He was a big, handsome man, weighing around 220 lbs. and standing 6'3" tall, with close-cropped blond hair, blue eyes and a ready, winning smile. He had been a football and basketball star at the University of Chicago, from whence he had graduated in 1913 as member of the Delta Kappa Epsilon fraternity and the Class Honors Society. Born of German immigrant parents, it was of little surprise to those who knew him when he immediately went to the German consulate's office in Chicago and offered his services to his parent's country of birth when war broke out in August 1914. However, the consulate dissuaded him, stating the war would doubtless be a short one and it was unlikely he would see any action. Goettler, somewhat dejected, went back home and got into the real estate business. Yet, after Germany's U-boat attacks against U.S. shipping at the beginning of 1917, followed by the 'national slap' of the Zimmermann telegram, it became clear where his loyalties lay. He enlisted in the U.S. Army Air Service, through the University of Illinois, in August 1917. Just before leaving for training in Texas, at a luncheon he told a friend he had chosen the aviation service because there would be "no slogging through the mud. It's you against the other fellow, just like any football game. And if things go wrong you don't come back home without an arm or a leg – you just don't come back home."

Goettler was among a contingent of men who were sent from Texas, to Canada and finally to England for training by the Royal Flying Corps, where he proved an adept pilot, but far too large for the diminutive fighter planes of the time. Therefore, his training centered on bomber and observation aircraft and his logbook and war diary describe the wide variety types that he flew. At 28, Goettler was older than most of the other pilots and a careful, cautious and mature flyer. He rarely went in for aerobatics or stunts and was noted for his steady hand on the control stick. He quickly earned himself the nickname of 'Dad' and due to his meticulous flying, spent considerable time teaching new pilots. Posted to the 50th Aero (Observation) Squadron in August of 1918, he quickly settled in. An outgoing and likable extrovert, his best friend in the 50th was a fellow pilot, Lt. David Beebe, with whom he helped organize squadron baseball games. His regular observer/gunner was Lt. Erwin R. Bleckley, with whom he had flown the 50th's first mission of the war, during the St. Mihiel offensive, and so they took off that October 4 as a familiar team. (15, 47, 110, 241)

Erwin Russell Bleckley was born in Wichita, Kansas on December 30, 1894. He never went to college, instead working in his father's bank, The Fourth National Bank of Wichita. When war broke out that April of 1917, he was the second Witchitan to volunteer for service, enlisting in the 1st Kansas Field Artillery. Federalized that July, the 1st Kansas F.A. became the 130th Field Artillery Regiment/35th (N.G.) Division and went to Camp Doniphan in Oklahoma for training that fall. In March 1918, Erwin answered a call for aerial observers and was detached from the 130th for immediate overseas duty with the U.S. Army Signal Corps (then the parent organization of the Air Service). In France, 'Bleck', as he was known universally while in the army, attended the 5th Artillery Aerial Observation School at Le Valdahon airfield, down near the Swiss border, before joining the 50th Aero Squadron that August, where he paired up with Harold Goettler. Accurate and particular in his observational skills and a terrific shot with the Lewis machine-gun, Erwin was quickly considered one of the most dependable 'back-seaters' in the squadron and was a particularly good match for the equally careful and precise Lt. Goettler. Short and stocky, with brown eyes, a generous mop of dark hair and a serious nature far beyond his young years, he was a friendly but quiet man, hard to get to know and a Mason who attended the Episcopalian Church. (15, 47, 110, 241)

Their mission that early afternoon was a contact patrol to find the 77th Division's front, as usual. The fog had long since burned off and it looked as if the mission stood a very good chance of success in the bright weather. Their instructions were to fly an east-to-west route along a line running south of and parallel to the towns of Fleville-Cornay-Marq. They were to keep as low as possible in order to get an accurate 'fix' on the line. Things in the forest were reportedly very confused, especially on the far left of the 77th's front, and the excellent weather that they now were quickly climbing into would afford them a splendid opportunity to decipher some of that chaos. (110, 248, 249, 255, 277)

Captain Klotz and Lt. de Coppet had not been gone long on their mission to the French, when General Alexander called back to General Johnson and issued his instructions for the afternoon attack, in which he had allowed a certain amount of room for local variation as needed. General Johnson, in turn, using the Division Commander's instructions, then composed orders for a modified plan of re-attack along the brigade line for that afternoon, and at 12:15 p.m., passed them up to Colonel's Houghton and Stacey.

The latter was, by then, making ready to move up to the line, from where he planned to direct the attack personally. When Colonel Stacey received the plan, he quickly recognized that it was both a long shot, as well as perhaps a desperate attempt to accomplish the seemingly insurmountable task before them. Further, it seemed almost tailor made to ruin what was left of the regiment: (2, 131, 132, 144)

You will proceed at once, taking with you the divisional reserve (2nd battalion of the 307th Inf.) to the relief of the troops of your regiment under command of Major Whittlesey, now occupying the front line of your regimental sector. On the way up, you will pick up the three companies now under the command of Captain McDougall, 308th Inf. (Companies M, L, and K, though Captain Scott was already using L to supplant the 3rd/307th, battling to the right of the 308th. – author) *When this relief has been made you will occupy the position now held by the six companies in the front line, your flank refused toward the left (enemy).*

At 2.30pm fire of destruction will be placed on the wire covering enemy trenches in the sector of the 307th Inf. (This also included the sector about to be occupied within the 308th's zone by the 2nd/307th, along the right side of the ravine. – author) *This fire will play for two hours and on its closing the 307th Inf. will advance through the gaps, coming up on a line abreast of your advanced troops. This movement must be energetically pushed on your part to relieve the situation in your sector of the front.* (131)

Though the plan gave him the manpower support he needed to wage another attack, Colonel Stacey did not like the odds and told General Johnson as much, again restating his belief that pushing ahead down the ravine was likely operational suicide. A short and decidedly heated debate followed, which did not fall in Colonel Stacey's favor. Hanging up on the Brigadier, the Colonel then whipped off the orders for the 2nd/307th to come forward. Those orders arrived by runner at Depot des Machines about 1:00 p.m., and the battalion immediately set out for l'Homme Mort. Once there, Captain Scott and Colonel Stacey put them in the line to the right of what remained of the 308th. Looking at the map, none of the 307th Company Commanders had any idea what would be involved in moving up the ravine they saw marked thereon, only that it was apparently the one down which their own Company K had gone and where I/F and M had been turned back by machine-gun fire a couple mornings ago. They also noted that their suspected course of attack would take them up against Hill 198 again, and that, they knew, could not be good. Setting out through the mud and shellfire up the Ravin d'Argonne, a sense of foreboding must have filled the air. Hopefully the slopes of 198 would be more approachable over in the 308th's zone than they had been in the 307th's. It was a vain hope. (103, 109, 131, 139, 235, 238)

After getting Colonel Stacey squared away on the details of his attack (and cooling off some), General Johnson next set to providing artillery coverage for it. The 152nd F.A. had provided admirable cover for the morning assault, after having corrected their fall of shot following the 'trouble' they had earlier had. By using those corrected coordinates then, (based originally on those sent by Lt. Teichmoeller the morning of October 3, remember) and then merely adding the distance the attack had progressed down the ravine that morning - about 125-150 meters worth - they should be right on target again, as further evidenced by Lt. Putnam's overnight ranging. (No one would ever think to connect Lt. Putnam's ranging shots with the six rounds that fell on Major Whittlesey overnight however.) Additionally, by 11:30 a.m., Major Whittlesey's 10:35 a.m. pigeon message had made its way through the message center and up to General Johnson's PC. "Still surrounded... being heavily trench mortared... needing support,' the Major had written. Well, perhaps some support could be given. Since the artillery was already going to be laying a barrage on Major Whittlesey's near side (along the ridgeline of Hill 198), why not have them run a barrage line along his *far* side as well - say, along the Binarville-La Viergette road - and keep the Germans off his back while Colonel Stacey broke through? That would be a really good idea, General Johnson figured as he picked up the phone and asked the operator to connect him with the 152nd F.A. Brigade PC.

Lieutenant Putnam, still up at l'Homme Mort after his liaison mission of the previous night, received word from Major Harry Wanvig, his commanding officer at 152nd F.A. PC, ordering him forward to the main line to find someone from the 308th Infantry that could verify the location of the contingent of men they had cut off up ahead of them. Making his way then up the shell-battered ravine, Lt. Putnam eventually came upon a small group of dirty line officers and asked if they could show him on the map the location of Major Whittlesey's command. A captain looked at the lieutenant's map for a moment and then stabbed a dirty finger at a spur of hill near the Charlevaux Mill, where the Binarville-La Viergette road made a shallow dip - but not the spur of hill that marked Major Whittlesey's left flank though, where the road also dipped a little. (IV)

"Right there," the Captain said.

Lieutenant Putnam fished a piece of emergency toilet paper out of his pocket and marked down the coordinates the captain indicated - 294.2 by 276.4 - which were actually about 500 meters west of Major Whittlesey's true position, though along about the same horizontal line. He then wrote a brief message in his field message book indicating that the coordinates contained therein were for Major Whittlesey's position in the Charlevaux Ravine, and then sent his runner out to take it back to Major Wanvig. Therefore, around the time that the 2nd/307th was reading its orders in the Depot des Machines (near 1:00 p.m.), the 152nd F.A. PC had calculated their coordinates and were sending them out to batteries of the 305th and 306th F.A. And with that, the fire mission was laid out to begin at 2:30 p.m. (29, 51, 93, 97, 98, 109, 116, 131, 132, 140, 144)

When the dust finally began to settle in the Ravin d'Argonne that noon hour, little had been accomplished for the high price the remainder of the 308th had paid that morning. Outposts to the line, after four desperate and headlong attacks, had been driven forward only about 100 meters, perhaps a little more, but that was all that could be achieved. The troops lay exhaustedly in the muddy holes they occupied and stared blankly at the sunlight poking through the trees, as if it were something they had never seen before. Casualties dotted the area, gas settled into the bigger of the funk holes and hollows and many men were manning the line with dirty bandages wrapping various parts of their bodies. The German artillery and trench mortars continued to drop without let up as parties of men came up with rations - cold corned beef and hardtack again - which the gas-sickened men largely declined. Lieutenant Knight's men had shot their bolt and just then had no more to give.

Captain Scott therefore slid D and F left along the main line, placing them on the far left flank in liaison with the French, where he figured there would be little action come the afternoon attack (he figured wrong). He replaced them with 3rd Battalion's companies K and M, coming up from behind. In support, he shifted Company L (which had been on the right of the ravine supporting the three 307th companies trying to drive through the wire from atop the east ridge) over behind K and M and then called back for more heavy machine-guns. As a result, portions of Company B/306th M.G. Bn. and a gun or two from the Machine Gun Company/308th came up. About that time, word arrived from Colonel Stacey; on General Johnson's orders he would be coming up, along with his perpetual bad mood, to supervise the afternoon attack and would also be bringing what remained of the brigade's reserves with him from Depot des Machines - a beat up battalion from the 307th. The afternoon attack looked like it was going to be a real S.O.B. of a drive, and Captain Scott was sure that he would be leading the lion's share of it in. At least he hoped so. The last person the largely inexperienced Battalion Commander wanted to have to deal with face to face during a difficult push was Colonel Stacey and his sour attitude.

Lieutenant Paul Knight, wounded twice now in the heavy action and most probably in shock, returned limping to Sgt. Cahill's telephone station to find a message for him from General Alexander. If he did not have his men (Men? What men? He hardly had any left.) through the German wire by the end of the day, he would be facing a court marshal for dereliction of duty. It was too much. Lieutenant Knight read the message again - red faced, bleeding, his uniform torn to shreds - simply threw the paper in the mud, turned and limped off in the direction of the first aid station to get bandaged up. He had done his share; no, more than his share. Fuck the bastards... let them court martial him.

But instead of a court martial, they later gave him the Distinguished Service Cross for his share. (29, 51, 109, 116, 131, 132, 144)

(I) Interestingly, the records of the 122nd seem to indicate that they themselves had installed a trench mortar on the back side of Hill 198 that morning, referred to by the regimental historian as being a "Priest Mortar", and began to shell the Pocket's right flank with it. However, there is no mention of fire coming from this weapon in any of the statements left behind by men that were over there that I have been able to find, save for one. In a monograph that Captain Holderman later wrote for the army on his experiences in the Pocket (see Appendix B), the Captain states that the command was bombed by "French" artillery on October 5th, which he equates to the terrible U.S. barrage that the force in the Charlevaux would suffer through on the afternoon of the 4th (though this later barrage was considerably smaller). Since there is no mention made anywhere of a second allied barrage falling on the men in the ravine, and no supporting official record of it either, it is safe to assume that the Captain must be referring to a heavy barrage made by this mortar of the 122nd in conjunction with the one operating from his right front. Certainly this combined fire, along with that of the one firing from Hill 205, would seem to be coming in from a generally correct direction, and if the pace was quick enough it might be mistaken by a tired and wounded man (and Captain Holderman was certainly both by the 5th) for another barrage.
(II) Upon hearing the story, many have wondered at this point why Major Whittlesey would not have considered breaking back through to the rear in force if indeed the Germans had been pulling out, as he apparently believed. (It was an act he also had intimated he might favor in his last message of the day previous.) After all, the rear attack certainly would seem an easy one to have accomplished and the results far more beneficial to his men than staying there in the ravine. The answer is Whittlesey simply did not have orders to withdraw. Sending back a strong force to reconnect with the main line would be the proper next step, but only after recon patrols had told him the chance of success of such a move. After all, he certainly did not want another Company E fiasco on his hands, for he lacked the men to spare.
Another point to consider is that what Major Whittlesey's command was going through in the Charlevaux Ravine was not much worse than anything they had gone through during the preceding days of the Argonne drive, save for the inability to evacuate the wounded. Hunger, thirst, low ammunition, cold, wet, extreme danger—all were part of the "business as usual" of daily life in the offensive. The only addition was that now they had no real way to communicate with the main force, a situation that might, and could reasonably be expected at any given moment to be, rectified by proper and timely advance of that main force. While the Major realized what could happen if their present situation continued (and he was apparently very nervous that it would), none of that had happened yet. There was little point in anticipating it and pulling out, because he might be wrong. And if he was, the unique advantage of his advanced position would be lost. He could not bring himself to compromise his morals and principles nor his military duties (which may also have led to a court marshal).
(III) The lion's share of the dead and wounded that Major Whittlesey's command was to suffer during their five-day siege in the ravine occurred within the first 48 hours, before they had fully realized that help would not likely be forthcoming. Many of those dead were men who, not being able to get treatment, succumbed to early wounds, dying pitiful, pain-wracked deaths from tetanus or gangrene or shock as they lay in their own filth in the cold mud, listening as their buddies behind tried desperately to reach them. Many of the lightly or less-severely wounded simply returned to the firing line after whatever initial treatment the could get, which further clouds accurate counts somewhat. But certainly more than half of the force under Major Whittlesey's command was, by the morning of October 4, some kind of casualty. This time, in his message the Major was not 'fudging' the numbers with some ulterior motive in mind either; they were true and accurate, much as it must have bothered him to admit such. See Appendix A for a full accounting of the men in the Charlevaux Ravine.
(IV) Lieutenant Putnam was never later able to actually identify who the captain was that pointed out the position on his map - or so he told author Tom Johnson for his 1938 book, The Lost Battalion, but this may have simply been a 'smoke screen' (see the chapter, 'Creating the Legend'). There were few captains left on the line however, and this severely narrows down the likely candidates. In this case, it may very well have been Captain Alan McDougall, the then assistant 3rd Battalion Commander to Captain Scott, who was definitely in the area. The only two other possible candidates would be Captain Scott, who was likely with Colonel Stacey at the time, or perhaps Captain Lucien Breckenridge, who might possibly have been at l'Homme Mort around then.

Ancillary sources used in this chapter include: 21, 25, 29, 30, 47, 49, 51, 148, 150, Various 152-216, 250-254, 257,

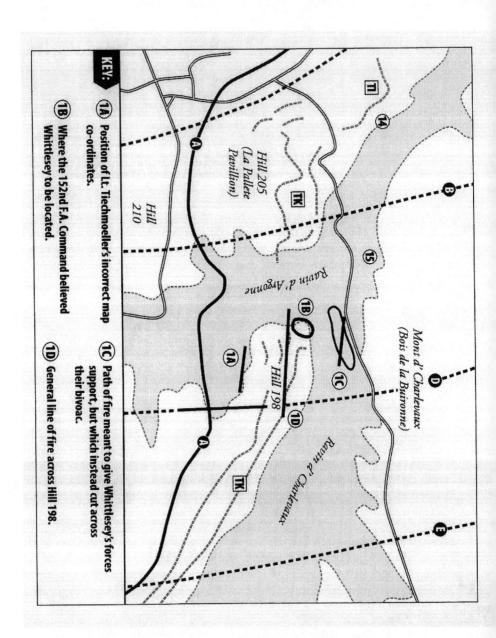

October 4, 1918 P.M.

"…For heaven's sake, stop it…"
Last message out of the Pocket, 3:00 p.m., October 4, 1918.

The 2nd/307th arrived on the 308th's line at about 2:00 p.m. and reported to Colonel Stacey, who in turn handed them to Captain Scott, who then started them down the ravine. He set Company G to the far right and on up the east slope backed by E and put L to G's left, down on the ravine floor and backed by H. Captain Rainsford was to advance Company L forward behind G to where the ravine bottle necked and then turn slightly left and assault the southeastern slopes of Hill 205 in conjunction with the 308th's K and M, which were directly to his left. Left of K and M, guarding the left flank of the division, was what remained of D and F, now under the command of a lone sergeant until Lt. Knight came back from the first aid station (which he would shortly before the attack). Company I/308th still provided link with the French, as well as support for D and F. Right of Captain Rainsford, Company G's orders were to move its right forward over the shoulder of Hill 198 and its left straight down the ravine ahead. On the map, it seemed a not too difficult plan as Captain Scott went through the details with the grim little group of officers who stood at a narrow crossroads of sorts on the bottom of the ravine, half way up to the line from l'Homme Mort. However, none had ever been up that far into the Ravin d'Argonne and almost all the officers who had were either dead or wounded by then. Therefore, they had no first-hand knowledge of what lay ahead. Captain Rainsford later wrote of their first glimpse down the ravine:

"A steep and narrow ravine, its sides choked with brush and wire, the crests to the right and left held with machine guns, rifle and hand grenades, a long distance machine gun fire sweeping down its length from the north and the first ranging shells wailing in from across the hills. Roncesvalles or Thermopylae may have looked so to their assaulting columns, grim in the sunset light; and the thought rose unbidden to the mind — what a place chosen for men to die." (103)

The clock was tipping 2:30 p.m. as the company commanders trudged up through the shellfire to their waiting men, formed them in platoon skirmish lines as per orders, and then went to ground. Soon after, the prepatory barrage started whistling overhead. (103, 109, 131, 235)

Company B/306th M.G. Bn., from comfortable support positions in the heights of Le Quatre Chenes, first found itself that day lending heavy fire support to the 1st/307th's morning attack, which had amounted to little. Then, as the morning passed to afternoon, they too received orders moving them to the 308th's zone of advance, just behind the 307th contingent, to support the afternoon attack. As they arrived, they could see infantry officers setting their men into attack formations and taking to the ground. They were themselves just getting their guns into position when, from above, the familiar whistle of passing shell fire began to cut the air, coming from behind them on a line center, and just off to the left of center. Private Charles Minder, manning his gun there in the dreary forest, welcomed the "entertainment" the barrage offered and wrote his mother later that night:

"Our artillery has been exceptionally active today and it did my heart good to see the beautiful accuracy of our boys. The shells were dropping right on the crest of the hill in front of us..." (37)

For the next hour and a half, before they had to get under way with their support firing, Pvt. Minder and his crew watched the shells dance along the crest of Hill 198 with great interest. He would likely have changed his tune, however, had he but known where the rest of the barrage was dropping.

Above the lines, but just barely (for 1,000 feet of altitude was not really height), Lt. Goettler steered the big DH-4 to give Lt. Bleckley the best chance of finding the line as they flew across into the zone of the 305th Infantry, turned west and slowly began their afternoon line run. Before long, several little puckered holes began to appear in their wings as German anti-aircraft fire blasted away at them from the forest below. Their guardian ship hovered protectively several thousand feet above in the cold sunshine. For the better part of an hour, they patrolled up and down each infantry regiment's advance zone, in ascending order, dropping flares, and Lt. Bleckley dutifully marked his map when he could. The requests for panels or answering flares was getting little response.

It was just about 2:45 p.m. when they came over the 308th's advance zone, the last area to check before heading home. Lieutenant Bleckley dropped flares on what he thought was the correct line (it had been the line on the day before anyway) and got answering flares from within a north/south ravine in the forest. Marking his map while Lt. Goettler swung around just north of Rome Farm (a little above Binarville) in order to make another pass east, Lt. Bleckley again then called for the line. They were tearing through the sky along a narrow east/west valley now, just a little to the north of where the flares of the last pass had come from. Shortly into their second pass, they began to take small arms fire from the ridge of a hill to their right, which was being heavily shelled. The line was obviously not up that far. Also, to the left, the artillery was really plastering something on the far hillside of the narrow valley. The plane rocked in the eddies of the passing shells. Neither flyer was looking however. Lieutenant Bleckley was instead intent on finding the line and Lt. Goettler was too busy trying to keep the plane on an even keel in the rough air. In a moment, they had sped well beyond the area. Both had seen plenty of artillery barrages from the air before and they had long since ceased to fascinate, so the bursting shells below them went largely unnoticed.

Swinging around to the west again, over the 307th's zone, Lt. Bleckley signaled that he had seen all that he needed to and they could head home after the next pass. Lieutenant Goettler raced down the narrow ravine again, which was marked "Charlevaux" on Bleckley's map, gaining altitude and rocking through the backwash of those passing shells one more time. Turning south over the outskirts of Binarville, he then made straight for Remicourt. Both men relaxed as they left the line well behind. They had been over the 308th's area a bare 10 minutes perhaps and as their plane faded into the distance, the artillery continued pounding that something down in that ravine... (241, 249, 276, 277)

Only sparse activity had been evident down in the Pocket as the clock ticked past 2:00 p.m. and made its way relentlessly toward 2.30 p.m. The attacks of the morning had finally faded and the trench mortar had knocked off for a time just after lunch, giving Major Whittlesey's men a welcome break. An order had gone out about the same time to curtail all unnecessary movement, but it was hardly needed. The startling amount of dead and wounded thus far had been inducement enough to keep the men in their holes. Only occasionally might a man venture out to try to fetch some water from the spring on the left flank, which the Germans were watching sporadically or maybe from one of the closer shell craters, seeping with dirty ground water. Later Lt. Cullen would write of the crater water, "Though we could feel the solid substances in the water… we were nevertheless thankful that we had that much." Otherwise, the men either lay still and bled or waited apprehensively for the expected afternoon Hun attack, all the time thinking of food or home.

The hardest part now was the waiting. Waiting for relief, waiting to die, waiting for a respite in machine-gun fire to be able to get out of a funk and use the latrine holes. Earlier, the Major had caught a man squatting down behind a convenient tree to relieve himself and had not been happy. "What do you think I had those latrines dug for?" he had yelled at the soldier and sent a firm order out that the latrine holes be used without fail. Getting to them now however was difficult at best and the safe chances to do so were few. Therefore, men were now, more often than not, doing what they had to do simply where it looked the safest. (29, 51, 109)

Down at the foot of the hill where the four medics had set up the wounded collection area, Privates Gehris, Bragg, Sirota and Walker had taken to sending the more lightly wounded back to their funk holes. They were running out of room in the long trench, though they were constantly widening and deepening it due to the need to make way for the most seriously wounded who required more attentive care. Not that it did much good, as spiral puttees and under shirts were among the only bandages they could muster now; they had no medicines of any kind. Still, Pvt. Gehris and the other three well knew the effect that a comforting hand could have on a hurt soldier's morale, especially under such adverse conditions. As added protection, Pvt. Gehris had had some of the more able men dig deep and low into the side of the hill, then gather up some logs, sticks and branches and build a long, low lean-to sort of shelter over the excavation, and cover it with a layer of dirt and leaves. Into it, he placed the worst cases, to not only shelter them from the elements and give them a false sense of security, but also to keep them out of sight of the rest of the men. Private Gehris well knew that it was no good for morale to display for the others what could - and in all likelihood, would - happen to the rest. (206)

When it came to the wounded, Major Whittlesey had not questioned what the medics, and Jack Gehris in particular, had asked or reported. The Major liked Pvt. Gehris and his straight forward way of dealing with both the wounded and the other medics and relied on him as being sort of 'in charge' at the foot of the hill. The tall Battalion Commander spent a certain amount of time visiting the wounded every day, usually making a stop during each inspection he made of the position and constantly encouraged the officers under him to do the same whenever possible. He always offered a firm handshake, that sideways smile and sometimes a small joke delivered in his quiet lawyer voice and positive attitude. (I) (29, 51, 148, 150, 206)

However, about one thing Major Whittlesey was most adamant - the dead were to be buried as quickly as possible. Like Pvt. Gehris, he realized the terrible impact that their sight could have on morale. Therefore, he and Captain McMurtry kept men on a constant rotating basis, never the same men, burying the dead, just off to one side of the wounded area at first and then later wherever they could. It was a hard job in the rocky, rooted soil under fire and it was a particularly repulsive job, especially when the body was all torn up by shellfire or multiple machine-gun bursts and had been out in the elements for a while.

Yet, there were two minor bright spots down there in that terrible place of suffering. The first was the constant antics of Captain Stromee and Lt. Peabody. Stromee, with his great tearing wound down his side, deserved his spot there with the wounded, as did Peabody, with his horribly mangled leg. The captain, who was in terrible pain, nevertheless still insisted in issuing orders to his men in Company C and tried very hard to remain as in command of them as possible through Lt. Schenck, demanding updates and reports on a regular basis. For this, Lt. Peabody would sometimes needle him good-naturedly. Then, the game would be on, and back and forth they would go at each other. Both were old National Guardsmen who had been on the border and therefore spoke the same language, foul as it was, and each took great delight in bating the other. Their joking around, stories from the 1916 expedition, and general tomfoolery relieved some of the intense suffering down there, proving that while laughter might not be the best medicine in all situations, it sure as hell helped in most. When nobody was watching, however, both were locked in their own worlds of pain, with great grimaces playing upon their pale faces. They were extraordinary men. (29, 51, 226, 239, 245)

The other bright spot was Pvt. Gerhis's little mixed rat terrier dog, Billy. Private Gehris had picked up the dog somewhere along his travels in France and the two had since become inseparable companions. So much so, that when Major Whittlesey had found out about him, he had allowed Pvt. Gehris to keep the dog, and Billy had soon become just 'one of the boys', even going over the top into the Argonne with them. Gehris shared his scanty rations with him, making sure the dog ate even if he did not, kept him free of cooties as best as he could and huddled the little dog in his tunic when it was cold. In return, Billy was completely devoted to Pvt. Gehris and lent an added dimension to the medic's work, for few things are as comforting as the unfettered care shown by a dog. There in the Pocket, Billy made his rounds with Pvt. Gehris from one wounded man to the next, almost as if he considered himself a medic as well, nuzzling a hand or licking a face and nearly always bringing forth a smile. (206)

Above, the sky in the west was just beginning to show the threatening look of rain again when, just as the clock was passing onto 2:30 p.m., there was the familiar, far-off 'whump' of artillery firing in the south. The big guns had been fairly quiet all day since the usual "hate" that had preceded the failed morning attack. As the whistle of incoming shells drew closer, all eyes peered upward into the leaden sky. The shells were definitely coming in from the south-southwest. That meant they were American. And an American barrage out of the blue usually signaled the start of a push. Another breakthrough drive had begun!

The first shells burst up on the opposite ridge line along Hill 198, followed by two or three that burst out across the ravine near the foot of the slope over there, blowing tall geysers of mud, brush, and water into the air. Then came a regular barrage above and below 198, the explosions dancing along the ridge and down the slope, followed almost at once by the reports from a multitude of guns thumping in the distance. The air was soon filled with incoming whistles and every man's heart beat high in his chest. Those who could, got up on their feet, shouting and cheering. The barrage was laid well for once and if the artillery cleared the ridge behind, then the rest of the boys in the regiment would have no more problems getting up and over Hill 198 than they themselves had had the afternoon of the 2nd! It certainly seemed like help might finally be on the way; their hell was almost over. (29, 51, 109, 135)

Up there on the ridge of Hill 198, it was hell all right. There, once the shells started to come in, Lt. Hopf and his 10th Company/122nd hunkered down and prepared to ride it out, but by far it was one of the most intense barrages they had yet endured. Wrote Lt. Hopf later:

"The afternoon of October 4th offered the usual sights: incessant patrol combat all along the front. My company was (then) violently shelled from 2.30pm to 5.20pm (sic) in the afternoon. At 3.45pm my (staff adjutant) commented, "I don't think much will be left of the company!" The men from the unit, and those attached to it, were encouraged by the sterling example of the leaders... concentrating on their duty to maintain the position at all cost, they remained faithfully at their posts, letting a shower of projectiles rain down on them without the slightest protection..."

Also on the ridge were Lt. Fritz and his 6th Company, who also observed:

"On October 4th, there was the usual scenario: cautious advance of enemy patrols, which we brought down. However, the heavy shelling that occurred between 2.30 and 4.30pm (sic) really put our nerves to the test. In particular all hell broke loose on the right (flank) and it wasn't surprising that it was shaken..."

As it rained steel, the Germans hunkered down in their dug outs to ride it out... (128)

For the next few minutes all seemed well to the Doughboys in the Pocket as they enjoyed watching the Huns get the shellacking they deserved. The barrage of shells continued in rounds. A series of bursts mushroomed out all along the ridgeline. Then, far off, the reports of the guns again. Down the opposite slope and to the bottom, more mud and water sailed through the air. Soon there were too many explosions to distinctly hear the distant reports. Then, slowly, deliberately, the part of the barrage falling at the foot of Hill 198 began creeping across the ravine, seemingly 10 meters at a time while other flashes still continued to dance along the ridgeline.

Across?

Another round of shells made their way closer to the outpost line.

Slowly, the shouts and cheers began to die out.

Still, the barrage crept relentlessly forward.

Oh, Lord... it looked like it wasn't going to stop.

Now, the men on the hillside began running and shouting, but in a different vein. They were jumping into whatever funk hole was nearest. Peering nervously over the edge or curled up shaking in the bottom, bracing themselves as the line of shells drew closer, until finally...

The next round of shells came in directly on the perimeter line, skipped yet another few meters forward and settled dead square onto the hillside that Major Whittlesey's tortured command occupied. There it stayed put, not moving another meter forward.

It was a terrible, relentless dam of whizzing steel and ear popping explosions, much as the men had been through several times before in the Argonne, extending from the ridge of Hill 198, and then skipping over the majority of the ravine to fall squarely onto the Pocket. What made this particular barrage all the more terrible though, besides the obvious perpetrators, was not only its incredible accuracy (no doubt about it; those 77th gunners were good all right), but the men's own inability to escape from under it. Being surrounded, there was no way the companies could effectively shift from out of the fire. They were forced to simply sit there and take it. Brush, earth, and wood torn from trees sailed through the air every which way. Flesh ripped and bones shattered as the spent iron of the shells found soft home. Private Bill Johnson of Company A was killed, as was Pvt. Paul Andrews and his sergeant, Mike Greally, both of G. Private Bill Cavanaugh, one of the pigeon handlers, was badly wounded along with medic George Walker, who now lay face down in the dirt with some 50 pieces of shrapnel littering his back. Lieutenant Griffin of H was hit again a couple of times, though not seriously, while the second hit Captain Stromee took *was* serious. (20, 29, 44, 109, 118)

The main track of the barrage seemed to be a 200-meter or so strip, not quite directly cutting through the middle of the Pocket, with a slight angle to it. On the left, the heaviest fire seemed to be more up toward the road, while farther to the right it was practically down below the hill. The cadence was fast; most seemed to recall up to 25 rounds a minute, but the Germans were not simply sitting idly by all this time however. For them, the barrage was a dream come true and they gladly joined in, gleefully throwing trench mortar shells, hand grenades, and copious amounts of machine-gun fire into the fray as fast as they could, adding to the American's misery.

Yet there are different aspects to the explosions of different shells and the men who had been under fire before could tell the difference between an exploding French model 75 or 155 and a German trench mortar shell. That, and the direction from which the fire came, left no doubt in their minds - the main barrage was all American. Private Nell, in Company G and right in the main path of the onslaught later remembered:

"(The) barrage came plowing its way down the hill directly towards us. It blew dirt high in the air as it moved on across the valley. There was absolutely nothing we could do. We had to just take what came, knowing without a doubt that it was our own artillery. It stopped right on our position and continued well over an hour…Everyone was expecting the next shell to get him. There were many direct hits blowing men to pieces and wounding dozens more…. And this shelling blasted away a good part of our bushes and timber, making it easier for us to be seen by the enemy." (40)

Private Emil Peterson in Company H had dug in right next to a tree upon entering the ravine the evening of the 2nd. Now he realized exactly how advantageous this move had been:

"Big shells would burst among us (and) this made some of the boys hunt for better cover. One came running up and lay in the hole next to me. (When) I told him that the Germans must have moved some of their artillery in the back of us, he informed me that it was our own artillery shelling us. Soon a shell came and destroyed his cartridge belt, which he had laid outside his hole. That made him move in a hurry!" (224)

Privates Magnus Krogh and Roland Thorbone, both of Company B, were sharing a hole up near the road not far from a tree, with which they had their own adventure:

"Sand, rocks, trees (and) brush flew all around and a shell landed about the length of my gun away from us. It must have stunned us, as when we woke up in the morning, Roland told me to look and see what had happened. We were all covered with dirt and a tree had fallen on us. We dug ourselves out from under the best we could and saw legs, arms and bodies lying all around. My rifle was shot to pieces and I lost my mess kit, razor etc…" (44)

Two other Company B men dug in near a tree were Privates Leonard Glenn and Ray Hammond, who were inseparable companions. Said Pvt. Glenn remembered:

"Ray and I dug in at the foot of a big tree about half way up the hill. Everyday we dug a little deeper. One of our six-inch shells struck our big tree. The concussion knocked me down and when I recovered I found that a piece of the shell, about ten inches long, had struck my rifle, ruining it. Of course, another one was not hard to find…" (44)

Glenn and Hammond would be two of the lucky ones; they both not only survived the barrage, but were also able to walk out of the Pocket four days later.

Private Max Lesnick of Company C found himself wounded and helplessly buried in his funk hole by one of the close landing shells. With only his lower legs sticking out and unable to move, he began to realize that it was likely all over for him and he began to make his peace. All of a sudden, a pair of unknown hands yanked him out and set him up on his feet before then disappearing into the powder smoke. Private Lesnick never got a good look at the man and it would not be until they met at a 1957 Lost Battalion survivor's reunion that he would find out that it had been Pvt. Stephan Honas from Company B who saved his life. (166, 219)

Privates John McNearney and William Burns of H were sharing a hole together when a direct hit by a 75 wiped out the hole next to them shared by Private Richard Hyde and

Corporal George Nies, also of H. Months later, McNearney handed Hyde's wristwatch back to his mother in St. Paul, Minnesota; all that had remained of her son. It was still ticking. (44)

Private Ralph John and a buddy were lying in their hole, listening to the shells coming over and trying to guess where they would land as a way of alleviating some of the terror they both felt. One finally came too close and the two were buried, with only one of Pvt. John's arms sticking out free. Fortunately, he was able to reach his shovel and dig himself and his partner out. Getting into another hole, with a death grip on the shovel now, the same thing happened. Again, they dug themselves out. When it happened a third time, they decided to take up a position further down the line when Pvt. John…

"…stepped on something that wasn't too solid and felt it roll under my feet. I looked down and there were three men lying on the ground covered up with dirt until you couldn't see them. They were still alive but stunned. I would not have known they were there if I hadn't stepped on the leg of one of them." (220)

After digging them out, Pvt. John and his partner crawled on through the rain of shells.

Farther along, one unidentified soldier hunkered down terrified in his funk hole peered out just in time to see Captain McMurtry stumping his way toward him as fast as his wounded knee would carry him. Coming upon the frightened private, the Captain turned and winked at him. "Just like the 4th of July, isn't it soldier?" he said loudly, yet very calmly, above the din, before passing on. "After that," the man later reported, "I wasn't so much afraid. Instead, I got mad at those damned gunners who couldn't tell us from the krauts…" (51, 245)

The scene down at the foot of the hill where the wounded were laid out was perhaps the worst and best described as one of unremitting terror. Many of the more seriously wounded could not move and found themselves forced to simply lie still and take the punishment around them, when every instinct they had told them to run and hide. Many cried and screamed in turn. The three remaining medics now went along trying to their best to calm them. Private Gehris in particular was running all around the position, collecting and carrying in wounded men with absolutely no regard for his own safety, an act for which he would later be awarded the Distinguished Service Cross. He had just brought a man in and was laying him out in the low covered 'dugout' when all at once, there was a blinding flash and a roar, then all noise was muffled and the world went dark. He could not see, move, or breathe and a strange weight seemed to be holding him down. Buried alive! Frantically he struggled and pushed. Then, he felt a scratching at his arms, hands, and head, and with the help from whoever was digging above him, soon managed to drag himself mostly clear. Looking around, Pvt. Gehris found little Billy, just "one of the boys," digging furiously to free his friend Jack - pay back for all the corn willy and hard tack.

The low shelter, and most of its occupants, had been completely destroyed. (109, 206)

Lieutenant Eager was trying to keep the Company G men together and shift them over to the left, out of the heaviest of the fire, when he came upon the one sight during the whole siege that struck him the deepest:

"It was during this time when the barrage was on (and) I was going down the line there (when) I saw this boy who carried the pigeon cage on his back. Although (with) the shells falling over there and the noise and all that, the pigeons were cooing and it was the most mournful sound I believe that I had heard in a long time; those pigeons cooing while the barrage was going on…" (234)

When the first of the shells burst within the command's position, Major Whittlesey was immediately up and stalking all over the hillside, trying his best to assuage the terrified men around him. And though he himself gave every outward appearance of being calm, a sharp, high pitch in his voice betrayed a general nervousness. *"Take it easy, take it easy! This cannot last long. Stay calm; they shall realize their mistake any time now…"* However, when some 20 terrifying, shell-packed minutes had gone by, and "they" still had not realized the mistake, the Major finally decided that something, anything, needed to be done, and fast. While a man was obviously not going to get through the cordon around them, a bird certainly might and, for once, he was running crouched over. Coming from the direction of the right flank through the barrage, he grabbed Pvt. Omer Richards by the arm, who he found down near the wagon road, and half dragged him along behind him up the hill to the command hole. Private Larney, in his own hole just across from the Battalion PC funk, later remembered:

> *"The barrage arrived directly upon us from the rear. It crossed the swamp behind us and settled upon us and stopped there, ripping the sky apart… I saw Major Whittlesey come running along in a stooping position, as was every man who was moving. Following him was Omer Richards, who was lugging a wicker pigeon coop… He and Omer were ducking over to what appeared to be a quieter spot to send a message…"*
> (218, 245)

Right near the Battalion PC hole, Major Whittlesey stopped and crouched down, while the shells continued to batter the hillside and Pvt. Richards squatted next to him. Bill Cavanaugh was lying in a hole nearby, already wounded after having had a tree fall on him a few minutes before, while Teddy Tollefson and another fellow were in a hole somewhere farther down the slope with the empty 2nd Battalion pigeon basket. Major Whittlesey already had one of Pvt. Cavanaugh's pigeon message books in his breast pocket. He whipped it out now and began scribbling carefully, in plain block letters and with a look of intense concentration on his face.

Private Larney, watching the scene intently, noticed that there was a very thin ribbon of blood trailing slowly down one side of Major Whittlesey's nose, mixing with the sweat that was now flowing freely from his brow. Spying it, Larney yelled, "Major, are you alright?"

Whittlesey did not even look up.

Private Larney yelled the question again, struggling to be heard over the roar of explosions all around him and dragging himself closer toward the edge of the command hole.

Again, Major Whittlesey did not answer, and again Pvt. Larney yelled the question, now close enough to almost shout directly in Whittlesey's ear. At that, the Major seemed to snap out of the intense concentration that held him and dabbed a finger to the bridge of his nose, just above the cross-wire of his glasses, where there was a small diagonal cut. It came away with a little blot of blood on it from where a piece of shrapnel had obviously only narrowly missed finishing him off. Major Whittlesey simply stared at it for a moment or two, as though unsure as to what it was, then shook his head as if to clear it of unnecessary thoughts and turned his attention back to the little message book. (29, 51, 135, 218, 245)

Tearing the message out of the book, he thrust it over to Pvt. Richards, tossing Cavanaugh's book aside, which Cavanaugh then reached over and retrieved…

CO. 1st Bn 308
To CO. 308 Infty
3pm
We are along the road parallel 276.4.
Our own artillery is dropping a barrage directly on us.
For Heavens sake, stop it.

Whittlesey
Major 308 (246)

Private Cavanaugh heard Major Whittlesey yell, "This is our only hope. Get it out right away!" (44) as the nervous Pvt. Richards wrapped the message into the little aluminum tube. He reached deep into the cage, grabbing one of the last two remaining birds, but just as he was pulling it out a shell went off close by, startling him. The terrified bird slipped from his grasp and took to the air. Private Richards swore shortly and lunged half out of the hole after it, but the horribly frightened bird had already fluttered quickly away beyond his reach. (29, 51, 245)

Richards, Whittlesey and the rest of the Headquarters men stared up at it with sinking hearts for a moment and Pvt. Richards swore aloud to himself again, but the expletive was lost in the roar around them. Major Whittlesey looked sternly at Pvt. Richards and then up at the sky again before then uttering an extremely rude, and out of character, one-syllable word of his own. Turning to the Major, Pvt. Richards yelled into the din, "I'm sorry, Sir," and then immediately reached back into the cage for the last bird; a 2-year-old black and gray checkered English National Union Racing Pigeon Association cock #615 named "Cher Ami." Though his head was buzzing steadily from all the noise and shock of the explosions all around him, this time Pvt. Richards managed a firm grasp of this last bird and, with gritted teeth, carefully clipped the message to the pigeon's leg before lifting his hands skyward. (13, 21, 29, 109, 265, 353)

Cher Ami ("dear friend" in French), U.S. Army serial number 43678 of the Signal Corp's 1st Pigeon Division, was an experienced messenger that had already carried some 12 missives back since the start of the Argonne offensive. His home loft was Mobile #9, then stationed at the 77th Division message center down at Rampont and he knew the way very well. Now, however, the air must have been too full of flying German scrap steel for his tastes. Private Richards thrust Cher Ami in the air and the bird flew up, but then only circled around two or three times in the eddies created by the shell blasts before landing again, slightly farther down the hill in what remained of a shrapnel twisted tree. There he perched and all eyes below fixed on the errant, frightened pigeon on which so much depended.

Turning to Pvt. Richards, the Major exclaimed excitedly above the blasts, "Can't you do something?"

Richards picked up a stick and tossed it up. "Hey! Hey! Go on there!" he yelled, and quickly Major Whittlesey and several others joined in. Cher Ami however, simply jumped up to a higher branch and remained fixed, too frightened to fly. Private Nell, crouching deep within his nearby hole, saw:

"…Major Whittlesey turned our last homing pigeon loose with what seemed to be our last message… We knew without a doubt that this was our last chance. If that one lonely, scared pigeon failed to find its loft… we would go just like the others who were being mangled and blown to pieces.

When he let this last pigeon loose it flew up and landed in a tree near my position. We all started throwing rocks and sticks at the bird so it would continue on its way…" (40)

Still, Cher Ami would not budge though. Something had to be done, and quickly. Making up his mind for better or worse, Pvt. Richards swore heartily and then suddenly jumped up, darted down the hill and began to shimmy up the tree, shaking it as he went. All around him, the shells continued to scream down and bullets pinked the bark by his hands. Cher Ami, above, remained firmly on the branch, preening his feathers in fear and eyeing Richards with cocked head.

"Come on you goddamn bird!" he yelled into the roar. *"Fly!"*

Richards climbed still farther up the tree until he could at last reach the branch, shook it firmly and finally Cher Ami took off, circled around a couple times again to get his bearings and then headed back over the ravine in the direction of the 77th's main line, gaining height as he went. Below, a hundred open-mouthed faces followed his line of flight.

A few feeble cheers, muffled by the explosions, went up around him as Omer Richards dropped down from the tree, miraculously unhurt, and scampered back up the hill. Major Whittlesey, Pvt. Larney, Cpl. Baldwin, and Sgt. Mjr. Gaedeke were already half way down the hill by the time Pvt. Richards dropped into a hole next to the Battalion PC funk. "Anyway, at least I got something to eat," he later remarked. (Over the next couple of days, he rationed out for himself the last two remaining packages of pigeon food.) Suddenly, there was an explosion and half the Battalion PC funk hole next to him disappeared into a shell crater. Private Richards, although covered by dirt, went untouched and was down the hill and in another hole nearer the bottom in nothing flat. (29, 40, 51, 109, 218, 245)

Rifles cracked from the German lines as Cher Ami winged his way back across the ravine, rising in height with every foot of forward progress. The enemy knew well what the bird was for and meant to stop it. Private Fred Evermann of Company B watched Cher Ami take off and head out and then:

"...A shell exploded directly below the bird, killing five of our men and stunning the pigeon so that it fluttered to the ground midway between the spring... and the bridge we crossed to get into the Pocket." (44)

That last pigeon, the last hope, the last means of communication, appeared to have failed his final mission and the shelling went on.

Major Whittlesey was already down the hill by that time, directing efforts to move the wounded farther to the left, into a position below Company B where a few fallen logs offered at least a bit more protection and the shelling was a bit less. Additional protection was provided by the bodies of the dead. Some of those that had not yet been buried, or torn to pieces by the shells, were now being piled up in a rude wall between where the wounded were now being laid out against the base of the hill, and the machine-gun fire coming from the other side of the wagon road. Privates Gehris, Bragg and Sirota tried to keep everyone and everything as calm and orderly as possible, but the move was a chaos of hurt men screaming as broken bones ground together and the corrupt flesh of infected wounds ripped even further. The machine-gun bullets from across the brook thumped sickeningly into the 'corpse wall' as the wounded hunkered down behind it. (29, 51, 109, 145, 196, 204, 236)

Overhead, the noise of an aeroplane engine caught Major Whittlesey's attention. Looking up through a break in the trees, a plane with U.S. markings was buzzing over the ravine. Turning to Pvt. Larney, who was right on his heels, the Major yelled above the roar, his thin voice almost lost, "Can you get the panels out?" Private Larney turned and was off like a rabbit without even a nod for a salute, yanking the cloths out of his pack and laying them across the bushes and ground of the first open spot he found, unashamedly ducking at each shell burst. He could not tell for sure if the plane saw them or not as it sailed over and out across the ravine again a short while later, gaining altitude, but it seemed as though it had rocked its wings. When it did not come back for another pass after a few more minutes had passed, Pvt. Larney gathered up the panels again and began heading back up the hill towards his hole near the Battalion PC. Hopefully, they had been seen. (29, 51, 109, 218, 245)

Lieutenant Cullen, over on the left, had also heard the airplane and called to a man who was cowering in a nearby hole, threw a dirty white towel at him and yelled for him to crawl out and try to signal the plane. The man, Private Joseph Shanz of Company G, scrambled out into a small open area, lay on his back and began to draw the towel back and forth across his chest. A burst of machine-gun bullets nearby convinced him that this was something less than a good idea. He too could not be sure that the plane had seen anything either, but again it had seemed to rock its wings some. (44, 109)

Meanwhile, back at the wounded area along the bottom edge of the hill, Captain McMurtry came limping through the mess of wounded men and explosions over to where Major Whittlesey was standing, wondering if it might not be better to shift position some to get out of the heaviest of the shell fire.

"No," yelled the Major. "That would be out of the frying pan and into the fire. At least the German artillery cannot get at us here, nor their trench mortars very much. We have already sent out our coordinates so our own guns cannot keep this up forever."

However, the idea of relocating the now destroyed command hole and tightening up the company dispositions some more might not be such a bad idea. The two discussed it briefly and decided to move the Battalion PC down to just right of the wounded, about a quarter way up the hill, and then have the command generally shift left and right out of the path of the greater majority of the shellfire until it was over. Once it stopped, then they could spread out again. Turning to Sgt. Maj. Gaedeke, the Major told him to go spread the word where the new command hole would be located and then sent along Cpl. Baldwin as well, to help get the men in the main lane of the shellfire shifting out of it. (29, 51, 245)

To the right of Company A's tiny position, Lt.'s Leak and Harrington were trying desperately to keep what remained of E together, sandwiched between Leak on the left and Harrington on the right. A man to the left of Lt. Leak (probably Cpl. Baldwin) crawled up and yelled, "The Major says to move to the right out of the barrage."

The lieutenant, dazed by the noise and concussion of the explosions all around him, simply asked, "Where did that order come from?"

"Well, from the Major!" the man replied, but already men were pressing right all along the hill, jumping from hole to hole between bursts.

Lieutenant Leak got what remained of E moving right and more down toward the wagon road, thinking the cover might be better there. They had gone only a short distance and had seemed to have escaped the brunt of the shelling, when Leak passed the word to dig in. He himself was digging on the edge of the road, kneeling down with a knot of men on the hillside just above him and Harrington farther over to the right, when he took a piece of shrapnel in the left leg, just above the knee. The digging was then forgotten as he fell forward flat, his screaming into the dirt lost in all the noise around him. (154, 236)

After getting his orders, Sergeant-Major Gaedeke had quickly jogged off through the rain of shells, his helmet pulled well down and letting every Headquarters Company man and officer he came to know about the change in PC location and the order to shift out of the fire if they could. Corporal Baldwin was only a short distance behind. However, they did not get far, as Cpl. Baldwin later remembered:

"We started along the slope, about ten feet apart, with Ben in front. We had gone only a little way, when there came a blinding flash and a terrific roar, and everything went black in a cloud of dirt thrown up by the shell. Ben (had been) at the exact spot where the shell burst. He disappeared as completely as the flame of a candle you would blow out. We never found any part of his body, nor even a piece of his uniform..." (283)

So passed 25-year-old 1st Battalion Sergeant-Major Benjamin Gaedeke of up state New York, who had joined the Army in emulation of his lieutenant older brother, William, and then served on the Mexican border with distinction; in the blinding flash and heaving earth of an exploding American shell. Private Bob Manson, Major Whittlesey's 1st Battalion interpreter, later said, "We could only find his hat and his gat." (His helmet and pistol, in the slang of the day.) Corporal Baldwin, once he had shaken off the shock of the explosion, got up and continued on, miraculously unharmed. (29, 51, 172, 245, 283)

After he pulled the signal panels back in, Pvt. Larney looked around and saw Pvt.

Manson, alone and still up in his hole just below the lip of the road and scrambled up to tell him of the Battalion PC move. The shelling was not so bad up there, and across the road, where they could see a man had sprawled out just below the cliff, there was no shelling at all. They decided to go over there too, but when the two got up and began across the open road, Manson hot on Larney's tail, a German machine-gun opened up, cutting away at the weed cover, and the place lost all its attraction.

"We've got to get out of here! Let's go!" shouted Manson and ran through a hail of bullets to tumble down the hill with one finger nearly severed by a bullet. Private Larney nearly made it unhurt but, at the last moment, he drew a shot through his left thigh, just above the knee. The third man (a "big fella", according to Larney) came running after them, drew a shot through the chest and went tumbling down the hill. There he lay at the bottom for a while, apparently getting his breath back, before then amazingly getting up and making his way into the nearest hole to ride out the rest of the storm. Private Larney stumbled a short way down the hill too before stopping to rest near an auto rifle team, loosing shots up the hill toward the road. Down below him, he then saw Corporal Baldwin, who was dragging a wounded man along, headed for the medical area.

"Hello, Jim! This is Sam Feuerlicht of C Company," Cpl. Baldwin yelled above the roar, indicating the man he was carrying. "He's wounded."

Private Larney got on the other side of Feuerlicht to help, figuring it might be a good idea to have his own wound looked at, and together, the three stumbled forward but only made it a few meters before there was a roar and the flash and Cpl. Baldwin found himself again in the immediate midst of yet another exploding American shell. Feuerlicht sagged from Baldwin's grasp, one side of his chest gone now and Larney was on the ground with a piece of iron in his right elbow. Corporal Baldwin, again amazingly unhurt except for a torn sleeve on his tunic, reached into Larney's pack and grabbed a signal panel, tore part of it up, and used the pieces to bind up his buddy's wounds. Then, the two struggled on through the hailstorm of lead and steel toward the new command hole down by the first aid. (29, 51, 109, 152, 153, 157, 218, 245)

Major Whittlesey watched the wounded Pvt. Larney stumble in. How much time had passed since he had sent out that pigeon? He could not really say, but one thing was certain - the shelling was not stopping, and if it continued much longer, there would be no one left on their feet. Spying Pvt. Richards again, the Major ran over to the hole he was crouching down with in.

"Go find Tollefson and get me another pigeon!" he yelled and Pvt. Richards took off running across the hill toward the old command funk.

When he reached Pvt. Tollefson's hole though, all he found was a smoking crater, a smashed pigeon crate and two bodies, one with half its head gone that *might* have, at one time, been Teddy Tollefson. (Tollefson would have had no pigeons left anyway.) Private Richards crawled back to his own hole near the new Battalion PC, where he figured he would find Major Whittlesey, but he was not there. By that time however, the shelling was starting to slack off anyway and so Richards figured that Cher Ami must have gotten through and any extra pigeon would not have been needed. Therefore, Pvt. Tollefson went unreported as dead for the time being. It was now nearly 4:00 p.m. (29, 51, 44, 218, 219, 245)

Around 3:45 p.m., 2nd Lt. Leon Hattemer of Battery E/305th F.A. dropped into the 308th Regimental PC at the l'Homme Mort bunker to use the telephone, on his way back from a liaison mission to the line checking the fall of shot of that afternoon's barrage. There, he found a muddy Colonel Cromwell Stacey, looking very tired and poorly, his eyes sunken and rimmed in dark circles, talking with Captain Bradley Delehanty, the 308th Regimental Intelligence Officer. The infantry attack for that afternoon was set to go off soon and the Colonel was just getting set to go out ahead and lead it in. Of course, the talk was all about Major Whittlesey and the great need to get him and his command out of the Charlevaux. Foot and pigeon messages had been coming in over the past couple days from the Major, though in hardly a cohesive order, and they had painted a very dark picture indeed of what was going on in that ravine. General Johnson had made it clear to Colonel Stacey that afternoon that division wanted the line advanced up to the Major's command, but it sounded more like General Alexander was more worried about a breakthrough of the line than he was about Major Whittlesey's situation. Lieutenant Hattemer remarked on the barrage then falling just up the ravine preparing the line for the breakthrough advance, which was also providing, he said, "harassing and neutralizing fire" around Major Whittlesey to keep the Germans "off of his back". Captain Delehanty looked especially interested at that, since brigade had told him nothing about any 'protective barrage' meant for Whittlesey's command, and asked casually, "Where's your line of fire?"

Lieutenant Hattemer whipped out his map and pointed out a line along the far slope of the Charlevaux Ravine. "Right along this line here, where the Boche must be," he said. Captain Delehanty and Colonel Stacey both started in shock and then looked directly at Lt. Hattemer, dumfounded.

"Those are the coordinates of Whittlesey's position!" Colonel Stacey exclaimed.

"Good God, man! Support them?" Captain Delehanty cried. "You're firing to destroy them! That's exactly the line Whittlesey is occupying!"

Lieutenant Hattemer just stared now, horror-struck, at the map. "Are you sure?" he asked anxiously, but Captain Delehanty was already on the phone yelling, desperately trying to get connected through to the 152nd Field Artillery PC. (29, 93, 131, 140, 238)

It was just going past 3:30 p.m. when the little bell of Mobil Loft #9 rang, signaling that a messenger pigeon had just landed and passed through the gate into the coop. Lieutenant Pelham Bissell and Corporal George Gault were the signals men on duty that day and Gault wandered over to fetch the message. What he found in the cage was a blood stained gray and black checked cock squatting unsteadily and leaning to one side. The pigeon collapsed entirely as he reached in. Retrieving it, he saw the bird was bleeding badly from a gaping wound in the chest and missing an eye, barely alive. Then turning the hurt bird over to get the message, he found the little aluminum tube scarcely hanging on to what remained of the torn tendons of a missing leg. The poor little guy had gone through hell to get the message through, that was for sure. Opening the tube and extracting the message, Cpl. Gault first froze at what he read and then ran immediately for the lieutenant and the telephone.

Corporal Gault and Lt. Bissell got Major Milliken, their C.O. in the 302nd Field Signal Battalion, on the line at the 77th Division PC nearby. "Major, listen to this one," Cpl. Gault said anxiously and read the message to him in code.

"You can't mean that! Give it to me in clear, no matter who may be listening," Major Milliken said and the corporal repeated the message.

"We are along the road parallel 276.4.
Our own artillery is dropping a barrage directly on us.
For Heavens sake, stop it."

Major Milliken told Cpl. Gault to get the original of the message to him right away and the corporal rushed it off to a motorcycle messenger waiting just outside and watched him speed away. He then turned his attentions to the hurt, brave pigeon, Cher Ami. He and Lt. Bissell then largely ignored their duties for the better part of the next hour until the divisional veterinarian arrived to take the barely alive bird away. In the meantime, Major Milliken had gotten on the phone with the 152nd F.A. Headquarters, nearly screaming the message to them. It was five minutes to 4:00 p.m. when the artilleryman on the other end of the line told the Major that they had already finished what "little shooting" they had done that afternoon. Hanging up and going outside, Major Milliken stared up into the dead gray sky to the north and listened. In the distance, he could make out a few scattered booms as the guns were just then falling silent. Shortly thereafter, the messenger arrived bearing Major Whittlesey's missive and he officially clocked it into the 77th Division message center at 4:22 p.m. - approximately one hour and twenty-two minutes after the Major had sent it… (13, 21, 29, 51, 245, 265, 353)

The clock was just ticking toward 4:00 p.m. when the shelling in the Charlevaux Ravine first slacked off and then stopped almost as quickly as it had begun, leaving behind only a thick pall of powder smoke rising from the hillside. Then, strangely, the German machine-guns and trench mortars died out as well and an utter stillness enveloped the ravine. Dust and leaves swirled in the light breeze and an unusual grayness seemed to hang in the air, like a funereal shadow, but stark and clear. All around the dead screamed out silently. At first, no one moved. Then, a few wounded began to wail loudly and pitifully and several dazed men scrambled out to try to help them.

It was just what the Germans had been waiting for and the clatter of a single machine-gun began again, chopping those few men down, including Corporal Holgar Peterson, who had done such a good job on patrol just that morning. Then, the German fire began again in earnest; first one, then two, then perhaps as many as a dozen guns, raking the hillside from every corner along its width and breadth, cutting off branches and bushes as neatly as if trimmed, barely a foot above the ground. There was no answering U.S. fire at first. So intense was the rate and amount of machine-gun fire that the men hunkered as deep into any hole available as they could. Enemy rifle fire could be discerned within the storm as well, snipers trying desperately to score the moment even the tiniest bit of khaki showed itself. (29, 51, 109, 135, 148, 149, 150)

The wicked machine-gun barrage continued unremitting for approximately 15 minutes. Then came a rain of potato masher grenades, again sailing through the air over the road to the front to explode on the torn hillside. Private Arthur Shepard in Company B had one land directly in front of him. Thinking fast, and with few other options open to him, he jumped directly on it with both feet, squashing it into the mud and heaved a tremendous sigh of relief when it failed to go off. Years later he would remark, "Boy, I saw St. Peter crooking his finger at me that time!" Private Hubert Esch of Company C had his pack destroyed by a grenade so thoroughly that all he could later find was his spare pair of socks. Meanwhile, from behind came a similar shower of the lethal packages from up on the little cliff jutting out near Company K on the right flank. Private Joseph Lehmeier and two others were in their hole and found themselves on the receiving end:

"John J. Knettel and Joseph Materna… and myself were in a dugout and a German grenade lit on Joe's back. I grabbed it and threw it back and about 20 feet away from us, it went off. Joe got his ear cut and I got my head full of small particles from it, which made my head bleed considerably. If I had not thrown it back, the three of us would have been killed." (44)

From the left and front, another round of trench mortar shells began to sail into the position, adding to the already devastated scene. The German afternoon attack was beginning, perfectly timed. (29, 51, 109, 198)

A fusillade of rifle and machine-gun fire followed the explosions and then another round of grenades before German troops came pouring down the hill and across the road to its edge to put fire into the Pocket from within mere meters of the stunned Doughboys. The brunt of the furious assault from above fell against the front of Lt. Gordon Schenck's

Company C position where the men were forced to give ground slightly, falling back down the hill. To the right of C, Company B began to shift right and reoccupy the smoking swath that had been cut across the center of the Pocket by the barrage and from there they raked the attacking enemy from the flank of their charge. Quickly the two companies drove the attackers back, who left at least two bodies riddled by U.S. bullets lying on the road. After darkness, the bodies were searched for food but none was found. (29, 51, 109, 116)

Below the hill, following the initial machine-gun barrage, Lt. Eager also began to move his men back into the wasteland that had been Company G's positions. There, the men immediately encountered the enemy moving across the marshy ravine behind and pushing in past what had been the outpost line at the bottom of the hill. The enemy line extended over as far as the Company H positions and a general firefight began, with men immediately taking cover in shell craters, behind fallen trees and bodies, anywhere at hand. Soon, some Company K men joined in from that flank. Here, the grenade assaults were not as heavy as farther up the hillside, but by contrast there was also less cover and the machine-guns had relatively straight lines of fire from across the creek and up on Hill 198 behind, making things very hot indeed. Private Emil Peterson, of Company H, later remembered the German push: (29, 51, 148, 149, 234)

"One evening the Germans started a drive from the rear. It was foggy (actually the powder smoke was still hanging in the air from the barrage – author) *but we could see them moving from tree to tree. They would shout, "We are coming, we are coming!" Our rifles and machine guns soon put a stop to their drive, (but) a buddy next to me who had a shallow hole was killed…"* (44, 224)

At the base of the hill lay what was left of Company E, dug into the shallow, improvised holes that had shielded them from the barrage. It was their position that the Germans overran first as they pushed into the perimeter of the Pocket. Gathering up prisoners among the frightened, rattled Doughboys, they quickly sent them back as they continued the assault. However, the resistance they met was tougher than anticipated and they were eventually driven back across the ravine, taking most of their casualties with them. Private Rangitsch, now just nine weeks on from his induction into the Army, was one of the few in Company E who escaped capture and later said:

"The Germans came on a mopping up expedition to finish the work, made a counter attack and captured our lieutenant and 17 privates… With dead men all around the only cover afforded was by those same dead… When the Germans came "over the top," the biggest part of us jumped under the dead ones… (The) commanding officer tried to burrow under the cold bodies too; did so in fact, but because he had St. Vitas' dance he was detected and captured…Finally the Germans left with the prisoners in a hurry. Then we came crawling out from all the holes and from under the bodies. It seems to me that only 5 or 6 came out alive." (225)

Private Arnold Morem was another Company E man who escaped, though he was to be wounded on October 7 and would have to be carried out of the Pocket. "The Germans tried to rush us," he said. "We let them get close and then cut loose. A lot of Germans got killed and quite a number were wounded." (44)

The commanding officer that Rangitsch referred to as having "St. Vitas' dance" (an old country saying meaning that a man was shaking too much to remain still) was the new Lt. Harrington, his nerves all but shot on this, his fourth day of combat. An officer was definitely a valuable prize, and so quickly he was drug back across the ravine and into German lines atop Hill 198.

The wounded Lt. Leak, still sprawled out at the base of the hill just left of K's position, was also taken and later described the experience:

"I stayed there the remainder of the barrage and then attempted to crawl back to the left, when I observed several Germans. On seeing them I turned on my stomach again and lay still, hoping that they would pass me by. But one of them stuck me with his bayonet and I jumped and they then told me in English to come along. Having no choice, I went." (236)

The bayonet wound Lt. Leak received in his right hip was minor, more a surprise than a wound, but his left leg, truly wounded, was now starting to swell alarmingly as the German soldiers jerked him to his feet. He was relieved of his .45, and then helped to limp away from the Pocket and back over the broken ground of the ravine, while the German attack against the perimeter continued to rage behind him. Through the brush, he could see a small herd of enlisted men, now also prisoners, likewise being lead back. (11)

Fighting savagely, the hollow-eyed bundles of raw nerves occupying that blighted hillside slowly drove the Germans back beyond the creek again and the enemy attacks petered out. Up ahead and on top, as Lieutenant's Schenck and Rogers' men pushed the enemy back beyond the road, all the while the machine-gun sitting in the nest directly above the Pocket continuing to pour withering covering fire down the hill, forcing Doughboy heads as low as possible. Then it too finally fell silent, with only the 'tink' of its cooling barrel just faintly being heard for a while by the men dug in close to the road. Captain Holderman immediately called for volunteers to hunt some snipers bothering his flank and Privates Bob Yoder, George Newcom, and "Indian" Frank Martinez crawled off to "have some fun." (They would stay out there late into the night, but have little success at the dangerous game of sniping the snipers.) Soon, however, the Germans were gone, the machine-gun barrage was over and it was quiet in the Pocket again. It was about 6:00 p.m.

Once again, Captain McMurtry found Major Whittlesey and broached the subject of not so much 'moving' the position *per se*, as perhaps 'shifting' it some, away from the left flank. The main target of the German attacks seemed to be falling around that hillside spur and by drawing back east off it some, they might make the job of defense on that flank easier for what men remained there. There were only two or three operational Hotchkiss guns left there now and the Chauchats were also one by one falling silent as they either jammed hopelessly or just simply quit, with no one left who knew how to fix them. The Major thought for a moment and then agreed. A shift might indeed be beneficial, as long as they all stayed in the same basic area, since their coordinates had already gone out several times. That had not seemed to matter much at first, but since the shelling had stopped that last bird must have gotten through. He would have liked to have had another now, but they were all gone, and communications were now *really* cut off. Still, they had to try. As Captain McMurtry went limping out to direct Lt. Cullen to draw in his left flank a bit, the Major stalked off through what meager cover remained on the hillside to again ask for volunteers to try to get back to the main line, and to set guards and outposts in the rapidly fading light. (29, 44, 51, 109, 135, 148, 149, 150, 223, 245)

Four men stumbled back through the tangle and shellfire of the ravine unsteadily, each with a corner of the stretcher on his shoulder. The figure reposed atop was Captain Walter Kerr-Rainsford, late Commanding Officer of Company L/307th Infantry Regiment. Stunned, hurt and bleeding, he watched interestedly, but totally detached, as things he knew or remembered slipped by him, almost as if in a dream. The Battalion Commander limped by, out of action and moving painfully with the aid of a big stick. His face was a knot of filth and pain as he said that the battalion was soon to be in the hands of Captain Grant of H, but that he had sent for the Regimental Commander to take his place. The words only floated and seemed to mean little to the figure on the litter. Then, a little further on, they passed the body of Captain Grant; his friend, commander of Company H, who had played baseball before the war and who had amused them all with his big league stories, lying in a tangled, bloody heap in the mud next to the rail line, stone dead, and with an equally bleeding lieutenant by his side as good as dead. The body faded into the dreamy distance...

The men carrying Captain Rainsford rested a moment, set him down. Then, there was his Company 1st Sergeant, looking at his wounds and telling him he would be all right. He joked with the sergeant about how the man never seemed to get hit, though he was always in the thick of it. The sergeant, a serious fellow, allowed that he could never figure that out either - and then was killed three days later. The stretcher-bearers picked up Captain Rainsford again and the journey continued.

A surgeon at Depot des Machines bandaged his legs, shoulder, and face and the captain simply let him, largely uninterested in the whole affair. Funny thing about that shoulder. They had worked their way part way up the slope of Hill 205 through incredibly heavy fire, when all at once he noticed his shoulder was acting funny but paid it little attention at the time, too busy to notice he had been shot and never feeling any pain. Then, he had been standing talking to the Battalion Commander, holding his map between them, when there was a roar and a sledgehammer blow across his knees, a swipe of smoke between them, and he had had the sensation of floating through the air. Next thing he knew, he was writhing in the leaves and then being drug onto a litter and lifted high in the air as men around him shouted. It had been a rifle grenade that had gotten them, he finally decided. Just then, the surgeon finished his bandages and the men picked up the stretcher again and continued the journey further back.

Slowly on they went, as the night drew down. There was the German blanket he had left behind that morning; still lying on the side of the trail where he had tossed it, along with a half empty can of bully beef. No need for either now! The trail continued until eventually they placed him onto a narrow gauge rail car, which his long frame overlapped, pulled by a horse and driven by an old, French soldier; a long campaigner of the Argonne no doubt. Every time the horse jerked to a halt, he took the impetus of the stopping car on his hurt legs against the horse's hindquarters, which neither of them much cared for, and he would let out a sharp yelp. Finally, just as the last of the light was fading, they came out of the forest and into an open area (Croix Gentin) populated by Ford motor ambulances (he had almost forgotten that there was a world without forest). For Captain Walter Kerr Rainsford, late Commanding Officer of Company L/307th Infantry Regiment, the war was finally, and most decidedly, over. (58, 103)

The attack up the Ravin d'Argonne behind the 2:30 p.m. barrage had not gone well. Moving out once the guns had fallen silent around 4:00 p.m. in the platoon skirmish lines ordered by Captain Scott, G Company had quickly fallen into disorganization as it moved past the bottleneck of the ravine and up against the slope of Hill 198. The Germans were definitely waiting and opened up through the smoking, ruined trees with their machine-guns. Captain Rainsford's Company L, meanwhile, came past the bottleneck slightly behind G, turned half left as ordered and began to storm the slopes of Hill 205. They had nearly overrun the trenches at its foot when they were driven back by the intense machine-gun fire that hit the company directly in the face. Elements of 3rd/308th on their left, companies K and M, were also slamming at the hillside from another direction and the effect was almost enough. They managed to get up a portion of the slope (where Captain Rainsford, one of his lieutenants, and Captain Scott received their package of a German rifle grenade) before they were violently driven off. Company L had lost all of its officers and came under the command of another 307th platoon leader, Lt. Goodwin of E, who was in turn wounded before the end of the next day. Captain Scott, bleeding badly, had sent a message for Colonel Stacey to come and take command of things. He had not realized what they would have faced in that ravine when he took command that morning, but now understood well: the ravine was a death factory. Sending for Captain Grant to take over until Colonel Stacey arrived, Captain Scott limped off, using a tree branch as a crutch and leaving a trail of blood in the mud behind him.

Captain Grant had led H into battle just behind L and had been drawn into the fray as well, and within a half-hour of the battle's start was the senior officer still on his feet in the ravine. Getting the message from Captain Scott, he and a lieutenant started forward but had not gone far before a German shell burst on the railroad track just beside them. The Captain was killed instantly, and the lieutenant mortally wounded. Command then passed to virtually the only remaining officer still on his feet in 2nd/307th, Lt. Weston Jenkins of Company E, who in turn shared command with Captain Breckenridge (then in command of what remained of the 3rd/308th), until Colonel Stacey could arrive. Far off to the left, Lt. Knight had made it back to the line in time to command D and F through the battle along that flank, which disintegrated into muddled confusion without French cooperation. They had largely given up assault along their right flank for the day, preferring instead to wait for the cooperative attacks to come the next morning.

Studying the situation, Lt. Jenkins found that by 5:00 p.m. any reserves that might have been available had already been chewed up. Tactical control was all but impossible since there were no officers left to guide the men. Therefore, the meager hold gained on Hills 205 and 198, which had been bought with so much blood that afternoon, could not last nor would there likely be any further success to come that day. Drawing the conclusion that continuance of the advance would be useless under those conditions, Lt. Jenkins made the tactically sound decision near nightfall to suspend operations in the ravine, draw everyone back past a line even with the bottleneck and dig in. Their fare-thee-well from the Germans was a terrible, blasting barrage of shells and gas that searched the width and breadth of the ravine all night as they huddled into their holes. Once again, the heavens opened up, drenching the exhausted, bedraggled Doughboys.

Colonel Stacey, heavily unnerved and agitated by all he had seen once he had gotten forward during the last gasps of the battle, stumbled back to l'Homme Mort to phone General Johnson. The push had been a complete and utter failure. (29, 51, 103, 109, 131, 138, 139, 144, 238)

Lieutenant Leak, his ears still ringing from the barrage and his leg aching terribly, was dragged up Hill 198 and soon found himself sitting next to the narrow road running close behind the German trenches up there. It had quieted down considerably in the ravine by then and German troops were straggling back up the hill. Incredibly, within a short time a sour-faced Lt. Harrington and a small batch of sorry looking enlisted were brought up and placed beside the road as well, quite near him. Whispering in low, hasty tones, the two bedraggled officers conferred. The Germans must not find out how bad off the men in the ravine actually were or there would be a bloodbath. Quickly, setting up the basics of what he hoped would be a believable story with Lt. Harrington, Leak then passed it on to the few enlisted men by them before some German troops came up and separated them. Lieutenant Leak was taken down a deep passageway in the earth to an enormous dugout, where his leg was dressed with a fresh bandage before he was placed in a small room alone. There, he found a small deal table, two chairs, and blessed warmth. (154, 236)

Meanwhile, in the Charlevaux Ravine, profound silence filled the air, except for the ringing in men's ears and the shrieks and wails of the wounded and dying. Much cover had been stripped from the hillside, and a wide swath across the position was studded not with funk holes and trees, but smoking, shallow shell craters and blackened stumps. Pieces of cadaver littered the scene, along with bloody heaps of rag that had once been a uniform, or a bandage, or part of a man. Entrails were scattered everywhere. Men peered over the edge of funk holes with terrified tears coursing through the dirt on their cheeks. Some breathed a silent prayer of thanks while others were more noticeably audible in prayer. All kept an eye cocked toward the rapidly graying sky or the German positions, not fully convinced that it was truly over. Nobody was yet willing to move out into the open.

Except for Major Whittlesey and Captain McMurtry, that is. Almost immediately, they were up and stalking over the hillside, the Captain's wounded knee now swollen to nearly twice its normal size and the Major having little choice but to hutch into what meager cover was left. While McMurtry supervised the tightening of the position, Whittlesey took stock over the wounded and got together small parties which he sent out to gather and bury what bodies and body parts could be safely reached. Then turning to Corporal Baldwin he said, "Go around and make a check on how many killed and wounded we have taken. See the officer commanding each company and report back to me as quickly as you can."

The corporal crawled off to do so, his torn sleeve flapping as he slithered across the broken ground. He was back within the hour and the results were far from encouraging; as near as the Baldwin was able to figure, there had been 30 killed outright by friendly fire and at least another 80 or so wounded, many of them severely. Captain Stromee had taken another hit and would not be doing any commanding of Company C anymore. Private Frank DiGiacomo, an Upton man with G, had had his nose clipped and Pvt. Bill Cavanaugh, the pigeon handler, had had first a tree drop on him, then some shrapnel. Captain Holderman had taken at least four separate wounds - one in each leg, one to his face, and one to his right foot. He was bleeding rather badly from them all but remained on his feet with K. Lieutenant Griffin was slightly wounded again and Lt. Fred Buehler of G had been hit several times and gone down, leaving the company in command of a sergeant. Private Paul Andrews of G was dead, as was Pvt. Bill Johnson of A, Sgt. Mike Greally of G and Pvt. Arthur Beske of B. Lieutenants Leak and Harrington were missing, along with a great majority of their remaining men and so were Sergeant-Major Gaedeke and Private Tollefson.(IV) (44, 27, 29, 51, 74, 106, 109, 135, 148, 149, 150, 168, 245, 218, 232, 233, 239)

Private Alfred Simonson of Company B was one of the wounded:

"I was wounded two times; first in the right cheek and then again in my right knee. I would like to find the fellow who saw me when I got wounded. He is, or was, some place in Minnesota, but I do not recall his name. I was bleeding so bad from the wound in my cheek, that somebody wrapped a piece from an old underwear around my head… It was plenty tough… I, for one, later woke up in the hospital." (44)

Down at the wounded area at the bottom of the hill, Gehris, Bragg, and Sirota sorted the living from the dead while the sky opened up, letting a slow, cold rainfall. The low, long dug out and its covering had been almost completely wiped out, along with most of the men in it and the scene there was particularly grisly. More so because of the low wall of dead bodies that had been set up between the hillside and the wagon road to protect the wounded sheltered in the shallow trench from machine-gun fire. Major Whittlesey quickly set men to cover those corpses with the muddy churned up earth and some fallen brush, while others carried still more seriously wounded down the hill. Web belt tourniquets and shirt strip bandages were now all that the medics had left to offer, as well as used bandages now being scavenged from the many bodies already littering the scene. (152, 204, 206, 236, 245)

Lieutenant Cullen, supervising the redisposition of men on the left flank and beyond, due to the increasingly critical officer shortage, shortly came across Pvt. Sidney Smith, who had been wounded. Said Smith:

"It was on the 2nd day of October (sic) I got shot in the back. I seen the hole through the front of my blouse and it looked like I got shot straight through the heart." (256)

Lieutenant Cullen, however, remembers Pvt. Smith as being hit during the machine-gun barrage of the 4th:

"Sidney Smith was shot through the stomach (sic). I told him he could go over to Battalion Headquarters and get a safer place, but he answered "Hell I ain't hurt much and I can still shoot this gun, so here I stay." I have cited him for bravery. He stuck alright and then refused medical attention until the rest had been treated and walked back to the first aid station." (109)

Private Smith had actually been hit on the left side, a shot that had broken two ribs. Nevertheless, Lt. Cullen's word bore weight, for Pvt. Smith later got the Distinguished Service Cross based upon the lieutenant's recommendation. (80, 109)

In the near silence following the last sputters of machine-gun fire, Pvt. Robert Pou uncurled himself from the bottom of his funk hole and peeked up over the edge. Something had dropped down during the artillery barrage right next to his hole and he was anxious to see what it was, for if it was a dud shell that meant he would be forced to abandon his current 'grave' and go dig another, just to be on the safe side. However, when he peered over the edge, what he found was no dud shell. It was what was left of 1st Battalion Sergeant-Major Ben Gaedeke - still alive.

What remained of Sgt. Mjr. Gaedeke, after the shell that had landed directly next to him exploded, had been blown through the air, to land where Pvt. Pou now found him, little more than a bleeding, moaning hulk. A good portion of the boy was gone. It was a wonder that he had any life left in him at all and Pvt. Pou knew that there was no hope. Despite that, he spent what remained of that afternoon and on into the night making Gaedeke as comfortable as possible. Once, after dark, he even risked everything to slither down to the brook and bring the dying boy back a drink of water. (Disgustingly, while he was gone, someone had rifled the young man's body and took his money belt.) It was in that vein that Robert Pou sat with Ben Gaedeke's horribly mutilated form until finally, sometime in the early morning hours of October 5, 1918, the young man from Upstate New York mercifully slipped into oblivion. (152)

Hauptmann Von Sybel and his cohort, Hauptmann Bickel, were just sitting down to dinner in a big dugout drilled deep into Hill 198 just west of the dividing line with the 122nd Regiment, when an orderly arrived and announced that two officer prisoners had been taken in the last attack on the *Americanernest*. The news so surprised and pleased Hauptmann Von Sybel that he stood up too quickly from the table and his thigh nearly upset a gramophone wheezing out a German tune on the little deal table next to him. There had been a great barrage into the ravine that afternoon, one that had extended from the barrage that had battered the troops up on Hill 198 endlessly for a couple hours. Apparently, one, or perhaps more, of the American guns had the wrong range and had accidentally and unknowingly plastered their own men. Of course, the German troops had been only too willing to help in the destruction and had poured trench mortar and machine-gun fire into the area as quickly and thickly as they could as well.

So, he was to have his officer prisoner that he had wished for. Not one, but two! Perhaps a little late, but certainly still useful. After such a barrage as the Americans had taken that day from their own guns, as well as that meted out by his own valiant men, there could be little left of the troops in the ravine. They must be ready to surrender! The information he wanted was at hand, but he realized that that information was not going anywhere, so there was no need to rush his meal. Any information they might get tonight would be useless in the rain-swept darkness on the forest anyway and could not be acted upon until tomorrow at least. Therefore, sitting back down again and calming himself, the

Hauptmann turned to the orderly that had brought the message and ordered, "Take the usual steps with the soldiers. With the officers give them a meal and make them comfortable. Hauptmann Bickel and I will see them shortly."

After they had finished their meal, the two officers then strolled over to the two rooms where the prisoners were being held separately. The most important question that Hauptmann Von Sybel wanted answered was exactly how many American troops were in the Charlevaux Ravine. Were there two *battalions*, or two *companies*? Reports from his men's attacks indicated that they had met heavy rifle and machine-gun fire. If only two companies had indeed gone into the ravine originally, as some of the captured enlisted had said, and there were now as many U.S. casualties as he figured, then who was doing all the shooting at his men?

The first officer they tried was a big, surly looking man who said his name was Harrington, Lieutenant Victor Harrington, from Company E of the 308th. "And the regulations of the Hague Convention do not require me to give you any further information," he said in a rough, displeased tone, concluding the interview as far as he was concerned.

Hauptmann Bickel translated to Von Sybel what the Lt. Harrington had said, as the prisoner sat stock still in his chair and stared straight ahead, a bowl of potato soup cold and untouched on the table before him.

Bickel produced a cigarette case, snapped it open, and offered it to Harrington.

"Have one and we shall talk as gentlemen," he said in a passable accent. Victor Harrington merely looked up at him and scowled.

The two Germans exchanged knowing glances and a few German words. Filled with a relaxing dinner, neither felt up to the task of wearing down the resistance of the prisoner. Perhaps the other officer would be more talkative. They left Lt. Harrington alone again.

The other prisoner was just finishing his bowl of thick soup when the two Germans entered the small room. Hauptmann Bickel pulled up a chair and sat down at the little table with him. This one was a thinner man than the other and had a leg wound with a fresh bandage on it. Bickel again offered up the open cigarette box and the prisoner took one with a nod.

"Your name?" the Hauptmann started.

"Lieutenant James V. Leak."

"The 'V' is for 'Von' perhaps?"

"No. Vestal." Lt. Leak answered. A brief look of displeasure passed across his face that Hauptmann Von Sybel picked up on.

"You are of the 308th Jaeger Regiment," Bickel said. "Commanded by Major Whitsley. A very good troop, but it must be bad for your wounded. From our front lines, we can hear them cry out."

Lieutenant Leak let his spoon drop, relaxed and shifted in the chair to relieve pressure on his wounded leg. James Leak as a lawyer was a very skilled one; a fact belied somewhat by his thick, slow Texas drawl, which lead some back home to believe that they were dealing with a simple back-woods hick. Yet that drawl could be a very disarming combination and he had learned from it.

Smiling inside, and letting the crafty lawyer side now take over, the thick drawl came slow with a Texan's natural self-assurance.

"Yes that is unpleasant. But for being wounded and seeing others wounded we will learn to put up with war," he said.

"You are a philosopher, lieutenant? That is rare, but do men like yours - surrounded and without food - find war so comfortable?" Hauptmann Bickel continued.

Lieutenant Leak painted an expression of blank amazement on his face.

"But we have plenty of food," he said and then stopped, as if he had given away a military secret.

Bickel leaned forward. "Ach, so?" And Leak then allowed how they had gotten a big issue of rations and ammunition before starting out on the 1st.

Bickel translated and Hauptmann Von Sybel, standing behind him, nodded slowly, looking directly at the American.

"Enough rations for all two companies?" Hauptmann Bickel began slyly, but Lt. Leak interrupted and corrected him.

"Battalions. Two battalions."

There was a pause.

"So? We have other informations." Bickel said, relaxed, and muttered something to Von Sybel, who looked anxious.

"Then it is wrong. We have the 1st and 2nd battalions of the regiment. Of course there have been some losses, but I do not think there are less than 1,200 now," he replied easily. "New Yorkers. The gangster type; very ruthless and good shots. They will never give up."

He glanced up at Hauptmann Von Sybel and caught his eye.

"Never," he concluded and looked back at Bickel.

Bickel leaned back slightly in surprise and Von Sybel, seeing this, shot something at him in German. Back and forth they went again as Lt. Leak smoked the cigarette. His ruse seemed to be having some little effect. Then, abruptly, he was shuffled out of the room and Lt. Harrington was sent for.

If what the prisoner said was true, Hauptmann Von Sybel argued, then his own force keeping the Americans bottled up in the Charlevaux Ravine truly *was* well out-numbered. That would explain the tremendous amounts of withering fire his men had been taking. With that large of a nest of Americans sitting pretty just beyond their own lines, they only needed to wait for the rest of their forces to catch them up, which they were already trying desperately to do. Then, this whole stretch of the line would likely crumble. Moreover, if the nest of Americans did rally and counter attack in force to one direction or the other - it did not really matter which - then there would be little his thin line of troops surrounding the ravine could do to stop them. However, before any further decisions could be made about what to do concerning the situation, the information must be corroborated for truth's sake.

Lieutenant Harrington was brought in and sat down, the sour look still on his face. Hauptmann Bickel started, "We have to inform you, we know the true strength of your battalions."

Harrington tensed for a moment, almost let a smile slip across his lips, but then caught himself and forced an angry expression onto his face.

"So Leak has been giving things away, has he?" he snapped, staring hard at Bickel.

"Then you confirm his statement?" the German queried.

"What statement?"

"How many has your Major in the ravine?"

The dirty American officer now paused, pursed his lips and then said tightly, "Two battalions. Twelve hundred and fifty, with plenty of machine-gun ammunition. And be damned to you!"

Hauptmann Von Sybel was out the door instantly the moment that Bickel had translated the statement and was soon on the phone to General Quadt-Wykradt-Huchtenbruck, who suggested that if the information were true, then close-in attacks against such a large force would only use up men uselessly. Therefore, the attacks should be kept long range, since there were no reinforcements yet available to send. In any case, the Americans might simply be telling stories too. Thereupon the prisoners would be taken at the earliest opportunity to be interrogated by the 254th's Regimental Intelligence Officer, Lieutenant Prinz, who was then in Buzancy. He would know if they were lying. In the meantime, keep the pressure on and wear the Americans down. They might pull out of their own accord once they started to loose a number of men and see that they cannot break the line.

Hauptmann Von Sybel, somewhat less than convinced that was likely to happen, hung up to confer with Hauptmann Bickel, who had been interrogating some of the captured enlisted Americans. They also had confirmed what Lieutenant's Leak and Harrington had said. But, orders were orders, so Hauptmann Von Sybel sent a message out to Major Hunicken and then out along the cordon surrounding the ravine: All direct, uncoordinated, close-in attacks against the *Americanernest* must immediately cease. Instead, long-range attacks were to increase in intensity using snipers, trench mortars, machine-guns and hand grenades if possible. Starting tomorrow, all direct attacks must be carefully orchestrated for effect.

General Quadt-Wykradt-Huchtenbruck, in the meantime, called up his Corps Commander, General Wellmann, to ask for the non-existent reinforcements that would be needed to eliminate the Pocket of Americans. General Wellmann seemed irritated that more than an entire German regiment, plus ancillary units, had not been able to eradicate two simple American battalions. The general allowed that it was not as simple as that, due mainly to the very size of American battalions and the weaknesses of his own weary troops. The Corps Commander seemed to think this over and then conceded that perhaps there was something to that after all and agreed to call someone at *Army Group Argonnen* to see what could be done to obtain some fresh troops, perhaps even storm troops. (29, 51, 123, 124, 154, 184, 236, 307)

Lieutenant Leak's lie seemed to be working.

Just before 5:00 p.m., Captain Klotz and Lieutenant de Coppett returned to General Alexander's PC with a map showing that the French main line had again actually fallen back to the southern edge of Binarville locally, but also that it was well outposted ahead of the town, particularly in the orchard just off the 308th's left flank. Then, not long after, word was received from Lt. de la Chapelle, the French Signal Officer at the 1st D.C.D's PC. Their line had stabilized and halted for the night, he reported, once again resting on the road running northwest to Autry from the fork above Binarville, then down to just above town, where it swung east and ran along the outpost line 100 meters or so above the Binarville-Moulin de l'Homme Mort road. There, full liaison (or what passed for it in that open space) had been reestablished with the Company I/308th again. Lieutenant de la Chapelle also mentioned two other interesting facts. First, that there had been a report from a French line officer that evening who had said that he had been in the Charlevaux Ravine that afternoon and talked personally to Major Whittlesey (something Klotz and de Coppet had mentioned as well, but which General Alexander immediately dismissed as just plain bull, which it was). Second, and a far more significant fact that General Alexander did not dismiss, was that the French had received reports of a considerable artillery barrage having dropped down into the Charlevaux ravine, supposedly directly on the spot where Major Whittlesey's command was reported to be. The General, somewhat alarmed at the news, said nothing but resolved to look into the matter at his first opportunity. (2, 10, 29, 51, 91, 131, 140, 144, 146)

The Division Commander then called General Johnson and issued out his basic instructions for the next morning's attack, which he again assured the Brigade Commander would most definitely be a coordinated effort with the French, and in which he had every confidence of success, always providing that everyone did their job well. The fine details of the attack he again left to the Brigadier, but the usual prepatory barrage would begin at 6:30 a.m. For his part, it appears that General Johnson may have also believed that General Alexander's plan had success written all over it, for it finally allowed for almost the numbers that he figured would be needed to get the job done. In any case, there is no record of his having argued with General Alexander over the instructions, as had been the case. Then, General Alexander sent Captain Klotz and Lt. de Coppet out again around 10:30 p.m. to finalize plans with the French for the morning's cooperative attacks, in order to leave as absolutely little to chance as possible. They returned about 2:30 a.m. with everything arranged, the French fully aware of the situation and ready to go. Unfortunately, fate would again intervene, and yet one more time derail General Alexander's carefully laid plans. (2, 10, 29, 51, 91, 131)

Meanwhile, as General Alexander was arranging with General Johnson to send his troops down the Ravin d'Argonne, a phone call came in about 9:00 p.m. to the office of the Chief of Air Service for the 1st Corps, Colonel Frank Lahm, from Colonel John Hannay, General Alexander's Chief of Staff. The 77th Division had had a situation develop on its front where a fair-sized infantry unit had advanced ahead of the lines and become cut off from rearward communications. All attempts at delivering a message by foot to the Major in command had so far failed. It was also believed that the Major had no more carrier pigeons with which to communicate rearward. It was imperative, Colonel Hannay said, that communications be reestablished to the battalion commander, a Major Whittlesey, as quickly as possible so that he could understand the situation around him. To that end, the General commanding the 77th Division was requesting that messages be dropped to Major Whittlesey's command, situated at the bottom of a narrow ravine, from the air at the earliest possible moment after daybreak the next day. The messages, four of them so as to insure that the Major got at least one, needed to be dropped as close to the Major's PC as possible, of course, to avoid them falling into enemy hands. Coordinates of his PC would be provided from the last messages the Major had sent out, thus providing for extreme accuracy. Assistant Chief of Staff to the 77th Division, Lt. Col. Howze, would be arriving there shortly with the messages. Once he had, Colonel Lahm was further requested to phone Colonel Hannay back acknowledging their receipt and then send them off immediately to the 77th's contact squadron, the 50th Observation Squadron, by officer courier.

Colonel Lahm recognized an earnestness in Colonel Hannay's voice over the situation that could not be ignored. This Major Whittlesey and his battalion must be in a really bad way for the division to go to all this fuss. When Lt. Col. Howze arrived, grave and concerned, with the messages it was already 2:00 a.m. on the 5th, and he too greatly impressed upon Colonel Lahm the extreme importance of at least *one* of the messages getting into the Major's hands. He also handed the Colonel a basket of pigeons, asking that they be dropped to the Major as well, along with the first message next morning. Colonel Lahm, now truly understanding that the situation was indeed a serious one, decided that he would deliver the messages to the 50th Aero personally, so that there could be no misunderstanding about what needed to be done. Therefore, he set out in the pre-dawn darkness for Remicourt and once there awoke Lt. Morse. The two then had a long discussion over the situation and a look at the map, Colonel Lahm giving the Squadron Commander the coordinates that had been provided to him by Lt. Col. Howze and taken directly from Major Whittlesey's pigeon messages - 294.6-276.3.

Lieutenant Morse studied the situation carefully. The ravine certainly was narrow; it would be a tricky thing to hit the mark accurately, but certainly not impossible. As for the pigeons, they would wrap the basket well in a few sandbags and then attach several of the little parachutes from the parachute flares. Place the first of the messages in the basket where it could not be missed, while a second plane making multiple passes over the same spot could drop the other three:

From: Old Dreadnought
Date: 4th October
To: Detroit Red
Defend yourself in your present position. Help is coming to you. (131)

As daylight started to break, Lt. Morse picked his pilots and observers for the mission, got them together in the operations shack and briefed them over a large-scale map of the Argonne. It was the perfect chance to show what good they could actually do for the 'gravel crushers' and he intended to make full use of the opportunity on what would be the first aerial resupply attempt in history. (47, 110, 141, 248, 249, 276, 277)

It was near 8:00 p.m. when, from the other side of Hill 198, the men in the Pocket heard the first volleys of rifle fire and the cough of Chauchats echoing over to them through the darkness. Soon, the sound of grenade and heavy machine-gun fire added to the din. No doubt about it, there was something serious going on back over the other side of the ridge behind and for a couple minutes, everyone's hopes of a breakthrough rose. Private Minder, firing in support of the attack from down in the Ravin d'Argonne, described the action in one of his letters home:

"We all had to go up and help the infantry on a raiding party... (so) we went over to the left about a hundred yards... mounted our guns a little higher up on the side of the hill and were told to shoot over there heads whenever we saw a flash from the other side of the valley. That was where the Germans were and also on top of the hill.
The infantry started off and in about five minutes little red flashes like fireflies could be seen all over the place. They even seemed to come from the top of the trees... (and) every time we saw a flash, we sent a few shots over in that general direction (and) were very busy changing the gun from one point to another. (But) in a half hour it was all over..." (37)

The attack - never actually meant to be one at all - was a squad of men under Sgt. George Russell of Company B/307th, sent out to try to break through to Major Whittlesey with a copy of General Alexander's message. They were headed out to follow the approximate course that the men in the Charlevaux had taken in to the ravine two days before, when they were spotted by German outposts. Soon, a barrage of machine-gun fire was upon them and Pvt. Minder's gun crew was throwing shots across the ravine ahead of them. Eventually however, they were turned back and withdrew into the 307th's lines once again - but the raid had cost them the life of Sgt. Russell. Meanwhile, the men in the Charlevaux listened as the fire behind them first began to fade and then died away all together, taking with it once again their hopes of rescue. Then, for a time, all was relatively still again. (242, 338)

Not long after that, the Germans started down a new track against the surrounded command. It was about 9:00 p.m. when all of a sudden a multitude of parachute flares and Very lights began to shoot up over the ravine. The flares, weird things giving off a ghostly, shadow-throwing light as they swung back and forth drifting down slowly through the misty rain, discomfited Major Whittlesey's exhausted, nervous men. German voices again calling across and echoing down the valley only served to amplify the surreal situation and the men looked at each other, wide eyed in the night. There was movement out there, but exactly where from, was impossible to tell. Tensions rose further as another round of flares sailed up and another round of German calls echoed out. In the bushes of the high ground, and out in the ravine itself, the Germans used the Doughboy's unease to their advantage and crept quietly closer. A few wild American shots rang out and an officer calmly called, "Steady there." Then came the first round of potato masher grenades, coming from all sides at once and exploding with brilliant flashes and sounds that seemed so much more stark and defined in the dark. Yells and screams filled the gloom and a round of U.S. rifle fire sang out. Another round of grenades followed. The Germans were now on the road above, against the edge of the wagon road below and creeping in from the sides. The Americans fell to the firing line in force and gave a clean volley that was answered by howls and cries of pain and death beyond them. The Germans pushed again; again American rifles answered in the dark. (29, 51, 109, 135, 148, 149, 150)

It was all over relatively quickly. Finally driven back, the Germans fled in confusion, leaving behind their dead. They would return for them later, creeping back up once all had settled down again, but not before ravenous Doughboys had again rifled the bodies for food and water. Slowly, the rest of the rainy night passed without further event.

Well... not quite. Late that night, Private John of A Company was down at a guard post toward the right flank, just above the wagon road. Suddenly, he heard a suspicious noise very near his hole. Visions of the terrifying night attack of late danced through his head:

"I was in a crouched position with my rifle at my side... Stealthily, (the noise) came nearer and nearer to me. When I thought the object was close enough, I sprang to my feet ready to fire away at the spot and umph, umph, umph in quick succession came the grunts of a wild pig as it scooted off through the forest! You have heard the expression of people's hearts coming into their mouths? Well, I had to swallow mine several times before it would stay down. If the whole German army had stepped out in front of me I wouldn't have been nearly so scared, because that was about what I was expecting... anything but a wild pig." (220)

Farther down the line, Pvt. Albert Kaempfer and a couple buddies of his in Company K were slipping along through the mud down toward a muddy shell hole with seeping water in the bottom, when they thought they heard something coming toward them. None of them had rifles and, terrified that the end had come, they drew back into what cover they could find and set themselves for a fight. Then, with a rush, Private John's wild pig tore past them.

Once they got their breath back, the thought of the running pork chops danced through their minds as they continued down to get their muddy drink. It was delicious. (29, 51)

Shortly after Colonel Hannay got off the phone with Colonel Lahm at 1st Corps Air Service PC, he called General Johnson, instructing that the same message ("Defend yourself in your present position. Help is coming to you.") be attempted delivery on foot if possible, as well as by air. (III) General Johnson immediately had the message delivered to Colonel Stacey. The Colonel in turn got it up to Company B/307th, still out on the line along the eastern ridge of the Ravin d'Argonne, which then sent out a squad to try to deliver it. Stacey also sent it up to Lt. Knight, out on the left, who received it about 11:00 p.m. The lieutenant, though he could hardly afford the men, was willing to try almost anything by that time to help relieve the situation ahead and assigned the task to Corporal/acting Sergeant Mike Davis, telling him to gather up a strong patrol to take with him. "Don't go straight down this hell-hole of a ravine," he told him. "Circle around to the left, through the French sector. You just may squeak through." Sergeant Davis collected 11 other men and just before 1:00 a.m. set out on the long journey to circle around above Binarville and attempt entry into the Charlevaux Ravine from west of Hill 205. Enemy shells and machine-gun fire were ripping the ravine to shreds in the dark and before they had climbed up onto the western ridge and passed through the woods to the French outposts, they had already taken one killed. This did not portend well for the rest of their mission. (29, 105, 109, 131, 238)

Once the missive was on its way to Major Whittlesey, General Johnson then called Colonel Houghton, in order to issue his morning orders which were basically unchanged from those of that previous morning. The only difference was that, this time, the flank-turning effort was to be attempted on the right flank, at the joint with the 153rd Brigade, instead of on the regimental left, which would constitute the main portion of the attack. What remained of the 3rd Battalion, now merged almost beyond definition with the units of the 1st, would provide support. Jump-off was to be at 7:00 a.m., behind a half hour artillery barrage, in conjunction with the 308th, who would merely hold their portion of the line east of the ravine while, at the same time, attempting to eradicate the Hun defenses on Hill 205 in conjunction with the French. Colonel Houghton, as could be expected, blanched at the orders of course. They had certainly done no good once already; what would lead anyone to believe that they would do any during a second attempt? Nor, however, was he able to offer a better plan and so, in the end, he had no choice but to acquiesce to what General Johnson wanted. (29, 109, 116, 131, 138, 139)

General Johnson next set himself to phone the orders up to Colonel Stacey, a call he knew would be difficult at best and which he, quite frankly, was dreading. Colonel Stacey's every answer to every question or order the past few days had been insolent, aggressive, and filtered through a general bad attitude and poor disposition that angered the Brigadier greatly. It had been obvious from the start that the Colonel had not been happy with his reassignment to the 77th, but had at first accepted it as a good soldier does. He was, after all, a well-experienced, respected and decorated member of the Regular Army. However, things had quickly gone down hill as the battle progressed and it certainly appeared as if the Colonel were on the verge of some kind of break down. Yes, he was under great pressure. But then, so were all who sent men into battle to face possible death or mutilation.

There was also the matter of the last message that Colonel Stacey had sent back to General Johnson late that afternoon following the final collapse of the attack in the ravine, a message couched in terms of infinite defeat. "Am making every effort but believe it is impossible to push through with these tired, disorganized men," it had said in part. "Fresh troops will have to do the job. Request I be relieved." General Johnson, reading the message, had sent one back, informing the Colonel that no such action could then be taken and that there were no more troops left for him to flesh out the 308th with, other than those that had already been sent up. The Brigadier had then told no one of the message, most especially General Alexander, for even if Colonel Stacey no longer felt up to the responsibility of leading the regiment, there was little that General Johnson could do. No one was then available to take the Colonel's place. There was also the possibility that Colonel Stacey had since cooled off and had time to get a grip on his nerves again since the message had come through. It was very late that night then when General Johnson called Colonel Stacey to fill him in on the morning attack that he was to lead. (29, 131, 144, 238)

Strangely, when Colonel Stacey heard the orders he did not immediately rail or argue. Instead, General Johnson first listened to the cold and slightly chilling rasp of the Colonel's still gas-affected breathing over the phone line for a moment. Then, the nerve-wracked Regimental Commander simply exploded. The situation was impossible, he ranted. He had no experienced men, no materials, no officers who knew how to perform their duties. The regiment, such as there was of it, was filled with inefficiency and incompetence and was then down to maybe, *maybe*, 75 men per company. There was simply no hope of driving them through those enemy defenses ahead, no matter how many Frenchmen there were said to be on the left. They were too worn out and had given all they had already. The Brigadier obviously did not understand the difficulties his command was facing and, in light of that, the Colonel felt he had no choice but to refuse acceptance of the responsibility for any further attacks. He again officially requested to be relieved of command, as he felt the responsibility too great for him, and asked to be reassigned to the rear where he felt his efforts would be better served, perhaps in the Service of Supply.

General Johnson was appalled. Colonel Stacey was self-destructing right before him, but there was little he could do. The man had all but lost his nerve and definitely needed to be relieved of his command, of that there was no possible doubt. But since there was no one left of comparable, or even near, rank in the regiment to take the Colonel's place (he did not even have any battalion commanders - Whittlesey and McMurtry were in the Charlevaux, Scott and the 307th's Blagden had been wounded, and McKinney was needed by Houghton), General Johnson was stuck. Finally, he settled on calling Division PC; General Alexander had assigned the Colonel to the 308th. Let General Alexander figure out what to do with him.

Hanging up on Colonel Stacey, Brigadier Johnson next got the Commanding General on the phone then and came clean on the whole affair. Telling General Alexander that he believed Colonel Stacey's actions on both occasions that day had been "weak in the extreme," and that the Colonel's "will-power and nerve had completely forsaken him," he finished by telling him that Stacey was now refusing to accept responsibility of any forthcoming attacks…

(29, 51, 131, 144, 238)

(I) Some retellings of the Lost Battalion tale over the years have suggested that Private Gehris was, in fact, not in the Pocket, but this is simply not true. The reason behind this erroneous idea stems from Pvt. Gehris's citation for the DSC, which describes his 'first aid shack' in such a way as to seem that it was a real shack built farther behind the lines. What the citation is describing, of course, is the rough lean-to that Gehris had put together there at the foot of the hill. The citation goes on to describe the 'shack' being destroyed by artillery fire; which indeed it will be, as we shall soon see. Conversations with members of the Gehris family served to clear this matter up, as well as visits to the actual site of the action in France to check the details of the story. There, it is still possible to see where the lean-to had once been set up, and then destroyed.

(II) It was the last stand for Captain McMurtry's beloved Company E. Private Rangitsch was correct; besides Lieutenants Leak and Harrington, the Germans took 17 other Americans out of the Pocket with them that terrible afternoon, mostly Company E men but also several from Company G and at least one from Company K. Four days later, when what remained of Major Whittlesey's force was relieved, only Pvt. Rangitsch and four others from E would walk out of the Pocket; the rest of those who had originally come into the Charlevaux Ravine had by then been either wounded, killed, or captured. Two, whose remains were never found, are still listed as "Missing" today.

(III) General Johnson had actually been the first to suggest that supplies be dropped to Major Whittlesey from the air, on October 3, but it seems that no one had been listening when he suggested it.

(IV) Upon hearing that Sgt. Mjr. Gaedeke was missing, Major Whittlesey was reportedly very silent and pensive for a long moment. He was very fond of the young man, as were most of those that knew him and as the Pocket was not very large and the barrage had been so heavy, Whittlesey likely realized that the dependable NCO was probably dead. When Baldwin had finished his report, the Major then turned to him and said simply, "You will take his stripes," and said nothing more.

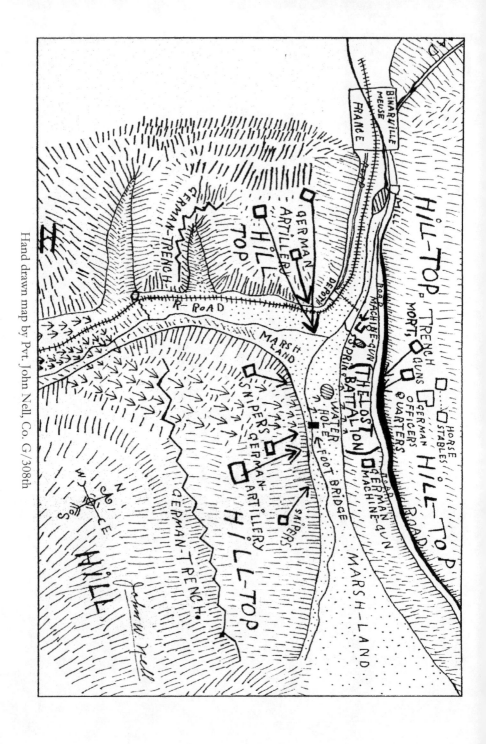

Hand drawn map by Pvt. John Nell, Co. G/308th

October 5, 1918 A.M.
"No relief. Conditions growing worse…"
Diary of Pvt. Jim Larney.

"Relieve him!" General Alexander stormed over the phone. "You should have done that without reporting to me! The responsibility for this attack is not on Stacey, but on me; I'm ordering it! Relieve him at once and send him down to the 2nd echelon!"

General Johnson was slightly taken aback, but continued. There was no one to take the Colonel's place, he said. Relieving him would put the regiment in the hands of an 'emergency' Captain (meaning a drafted officer), since any other line officers he had in the brigade of higher rank were all either dead, wounded, or then unreachable.

"I don't care if it leaves the regiment in the hands of an emergency corporal, as long as he'll fight!" General Alexander continued. "Relieve that man at once and send him back to headquarters and relieve any other officer who talks that way! You, will take personal command of the attack."

After another slight pause, General Johnson then reminded the Division Commander that Colonel Stacey was also a Regular Army man, with hash marks to the ground and was well connected. This would certainly put a black mark on the Colonel's record and he would no doubt seek out as many favors as his 20 years' service afforded him to try to get back against General Alexander. Perhaps it might be better for the General in the long run if he thought up another, more clandestine, way of removing the Colonel. General Alexander calmed some and thanked the Brigade Commander for his concern, but said he was willing to take the chance. The attack was more important and needed to come first. Colonel Stacey was to be relieved immediately.

General Johnson and his small staff arrived at the l'Homme Mort bunker just before dawn and there found Colonel Stacey, sleepless, irritable, and extremely nervous. Little had been done with the regiment since they had drawn back from the previous afternoon's last attack. Nor did he have much to say about the operations in the ravine; neither could he give an accurate headcount of then available troops to the man General Johnson had chosen to 'succeed' him at the head of the regiment, Captain Lucien Breckenridge. "Breck" was the son of a prominent New York family and a Plattsburg graduate who had served various rolls in the regiment since its inception but had little actual combat leadership experience. Showing no signs of redress to his poor attitude, even at getting what he wanted, Colonel Stacey gathered his few things together and hopped aboard one of the little horse-drawn, narrow-gauge flat cars taking the wounded out and went back to the aid station. He was never in combat again. (I) (131, 144, 238)

Sergeant Davis's patrol from Company D had moved very stealthily through the dark, the experience of a hundred patrols in the Argonne Forest under their belts. Whether they had actually passed through French-held territory or not when they moved northeast of Binarville is anybody's guess. Nor did it made much difference. For it was just before dawn, probably no more than four hours later, when the patrol returned and handed back to Lt.

Knight his now sweat and blood stained message. They had not quite been able to make it into Whittlesey's position in the Charlevaux he said, though he believed that they had come very close before one man had been spotted. After that, nothing had gone right. One unnamed member of the patrol left behind this somewhat disjointed version of events:

"Mike had a message for the men in the trap (and) Major Whittlesey who were cut off from the rest of us. Mike told us that if he was bumped off, one of us must take the message through. When we started, it was horrible dark night and snipers were everywhere… well, we twisted around through the brush and wound down a canyon, making no noise scarcely, (when) we passed by some Jerry dugouts. I was the last man in the column and I seen a Jerry in the door of the dugout with his back to us… Then we went up a hill, which I afterwards found was right near where the boys were that were cut off and our destination. But here we met with horrible gunfire (and) one of the boys was killed instantly there with a bullet through his head. The rest of us took cover… and there was no chance for our little party to move about because Jerry was everywhere… Well, (then) Jerry threw over a barrage and the shells sure busted close. One busted so close to me that it put me out of business. When I woke, my friend Bacon was with me (and) he gave me a drink. The world didn't seem right to me, but… I didn't say anything to anyone about it; I just followed the boys around not knowing where I was going (until) we finally got back to the good old company."

Of the 12 that set out (Davis included), only five returned. (105)

General Johnson and Captain Breckenridge poured over the details for the advance into the early dawn. The plan, as laid out by General Alexander, was simple; the Division Commander had definitely arranged for a combined assault against Hill 205 with the French, who were going to send two companies of the 4th C.a.P in attack supported by another pair to the left of the 308th. Captain Breckenridge, meanwhile, would have D/F and K, supported by L and M, in line next to them left to right. (The 2nd/307th had been ordered back to Depot, again into reserve.) A half-hour long veritable storm of artillery was set to begin at 6:00 a.m. and General Johnson had instructions to draw all the troops back to the Binarville-Moulin de l'Homme Mort road, some 500 meters behind the intended line of fire. Having had a brief talk with General McCloskey (commander of the 152nd F.A. Brigade) concerning the reported firing into the Charlevaux the afternoon before, and not being particularly satisfied with the answers he got, General Alexander was taking no chances. Following the lifting of the barrage at 6:30 a.m., all troops were to advance together in assault and break the line ahead. No excuses for failure would be accepted.

Following the initial advance at 6:30 a.m., the plan was all General Johnson's. The stronger elements of Company K, backed by M, were to slam forward on the right of the ravine in yet another attempt to drive through the line at the point where Major Whittlesey had gone through three days earlier. Meanwhile, the chewed up D/F combination would plow into the front of the German trench line ahead. The French then would come in on an oblique from the left, hitting the Huns hard and pushing up the widest section of the hill. From there, with Hill 205 occupied on the left by the French and Lt. Knight's men from the ravine, elements of 3rd Battalion would be free to go through the wire right of the Haupt-Widerstands-Lienie on the ravine floor. (If they had not already broken the enemy defenses of Hill 198, that is.) From there, they could move hard and fast into the Charlevaux with impunity.

To the east of the ravine, the 1st/307th was to keep the Germans occupied along the main line of their regiment's sector (now extended somewhat west, almost to the ravine), while elements of the 3rd/307th would assist them. Together, they were to force a break in the German defenses at the point where the 153rd and 154th Brigades joined. While elements of the 305th and 306th pounded the German line at that point on an oblique from the right, elements of the 307th would then force the line from the direct front at the corner. Surely, one of these massive movements was likely to succeed in creating a breakthrough to Major Whittlesey's position, General Johnson felt. At 5:30 a.m. then, he left Captain Breckenridge to arrange his men on the line of departure assigned by General Alexander and made his way over to Colonel Houghton's PC, in order to see to the situation there.

At 6:00 a.m., the first shells started screaming overhead toward the Boche lines, and by 7:00 a.m., the 307th's attack was well underway. Pressing forward into the wire, it was again met by fierce resistance. General Johnson arrived just as the artillery started and then spent the next hour with Colonel Houghton at his PC (little more than a hole in the ground behind a big tree), discussing what needed to be done to get into the Charlevaux Ravine. Colonel Houghton was then suffering from a mild malaria attack and, pumped full of Lee's Jamaican rum to tolerate its effects, he was in no mood for another wasted effort. He had talked to his company officers the night before and said that they were going to take elements of B and M companies to probe a spot in the wire on the right that they thought might show some promise.

Meanwhile, disaster had befallen the combined effort with the French in the zone of the 308th. The artillery had gone over at 6:00 a.m. as planned, but part of it had fallen short. In fact, the troops of the regiment had been forced to scatter by the fall of shot, much of which was not falling on the German trenches at all but instead on the line along which the regiment had drawn back to for safety. The French to the left broke liaison and shifted farther left, waited out the barrage, and then moved forward in attack at 6:30 a.m. as per orders. The 308th however, was spread out by the shelling and took several wounded and at least one killed. With the inexperienced Captain Breckenridge at their helm, it had taken some time to pull together, and they had not attacked until more than an hour after the barrage had lifted. The element of surprise against the enemy ahead (and cooperation with the French on the left) was long gone when they started forward in attack - and hit a solid wall of waiting German counter fire. (II) (10, 17, 29, 51, 91, 99, 104, 109, 116, 119, 131, 138, 139, 140, 144)

The messages and the basket of pigeons meant to be dropped to Major Whittlesey by the 50th Aero Squadron, left the ground at Remicourt at just before 6:00 a.m. on a nasty, October 5 morning, blanketed by a thick fog and local, scattered rain showers. The two flyers with the basket, Lieutenants Robert Anderson, pilot, and Woodville Rogers, observer, had a hell of a time seeing anything on the ground at all though. If the mission had not been impressed upon them as one of dire emergency by Lt. Morse, they likely would have turned back. Flying as low as they were being forced to in that fog was tantamount to suicide in a forest composed of tall hills, topped with even taller trees, that concealed enemy territory. Additionally, air navigation at that time was very rudimentary, so without ground marks to double check positions, the disorienting effects of the fog made it that much easier to get lost. In fact, they had already lost the second plane that had taken off just minutes after they had. Therefore, the two aviators winged their way through the white blanket very carefully.

Finally, through the dense bank, Lt. Rogers spotted what looked like the spur of hill shown on the map as being just east of the Moulin d'Charlevaux and pointed it out to Lt. Anderson, who circled back. Lieutenant Rogers then dumped the pigeon basket over the side just as they passed over the spur, judging that their forward momentum would 'float' the basket on its little parachutes the remaining 500 meters or so into Major Whittlesey's last reported position, if the parachutes worked. (Nothing like this had ever been tried before.) And the little parachutes indeed did the trick, as the lieutenant saw them open and the package begin to float gently down, before it was swallowed up in the blankness behind the speeding, climbing plane. (Just what good the package might actually have done however is anyone's guess, since it did not come down in Major Whittlesey's position but instead some 8 kilometers to the south.)

About that same time, the lost second plane, piloted by Lt. Samuel Fitzsimmons with Lt. Charles Pursley as observer and carrying the three other messages, buzzed down through the rainy mist above the Charlevaux Ravine. They had lost their companion plane long before and had only, by some miracle, found themselves above what they believed was Major Whittlesey's position. They started to circle, attempting to get their bearings, and after a moment, Lt. Pursley gave the sign that this was the right spot. Lieutenant Fitzsimmons wheeled and made three separate passes over the ravine on an east/west line and a rather high altitude, while the observer tossed out a streamered message container each time. Woken up in the sloppy weather by the DH's big Liberty 12 engine, the Germans along the ridge of Hill 198 watched the containers come down - and fall squarely into their hands, after which the plane wheeled and disappeared into the mist southward. (110, 141, 241, 249, 276, 277)

Late on the night of October 4, the Germans received orders to transfer the officer prisoners from the *Americanernest*, Lieutenant's Leak and Harrington, along with the enlisted captured at Charlevaux to the headquarters of the 76th Reserve Division at the town of Buzancy. There, they were to be interrogated by the 254th's Regimental Intelligence Officer, Lieutenant Fritz Heinrich Prinz, a tall, dark blond officer from Stettin. Lieutenant Prinz, 34, knew America and Americans well. He had spent eight years in the United States as the German representative for a worldwide tungsten-mining firm, living in first Spokane and then Seattle in Washington State. It had only been out of duty as a German subject that he and his wife, Auguste, had left America at the outbreak of war in Europe in 1914. Thus, he was well versed in American customs and mannerisms and had a firm grasp on the English language (including current slang and profanities). Only a passing accent gave away his European heritage and a very winning, persuasive personality made him very good at his job. Apparently never firmly behind the Kaiser's politics in the first place, now in 1918 he was even less so. Besides, he liked America and Americans and the fact that he was forced to now fight them appalled him. The French he could not have cared less about. But the Americans; now that was different.

Division had warned Lt. Prinz that the prisoners were on their way and to be ready to do his utmost with them. There has been a serious break in the 254th Regiment's line at the Giselher Stellung and a group of Americans was firmly lodged in a ravine just beyond it, near Binarville. Initial interrogations had revealed that there might be as many as some 1,200 men there. However, Hauptmann Bickel had done the session and he was not as well versed in Americanisms, as was Lt. Prinz. He had to definitely find out if the report was true, for if it was then the reinforcements Hauptmann Von Sybel was asking for must be scraped together at once.

On the morning of October 5 then, the prisoners were hustled out of their relatively warm enemy dugout billets on Hill 198 and marched a short distance to a road behind Hill 205, where motor trucks were waiting. Incredibly, Lieutenant's Leak and Harrington were left alone with the enlisted men for the briefest of moments again and they were able to whisper encouragement to them. (*The lie seems to be working, you fellows. Keep it up.*) The ride to Buzancy was an uneventful, uncomfortably cold one and they arrived at a big chateau well before mid-morning. There, the enlisted were carted off in a different direction and Lt. Leak never saw them again. He and Lt. Harrington were hustled into the building and separated. Led down a long hallway to a room with big ornate oak doors, when they opened Lt. Leak saw a tall officer in a spotless uniform with smooth, greased-back blond hair walking toward him, already smiling and with outstretched hand.

"Do come in lieutenant and have some coffee," he was saying, while the mud-covered, wounded American adjusted to the warmth. "I am Lt. Prinz and I used to live in Seattle for many years. You fellows sure have given us a bit of trouble there in that ravine, haven't you? How many do you have down there anyway?" (123, 154, 163, 222, 236)

Meanwhile, with the collapse of the French efforts west of Hill 205 once again on October 4, and considering the situation at Charlevaux Ravine, Major Ditfurth made the decision to again reshuffle his dispositions slightly. Figuring that the 9th Ldwr and the troops of the 45th Reserve Division that had been sent west should be enough to handle the ever-weakening French, he had then sent orders for the 254th to again slide east. The 252nd would move into occupation of Hill 205, the 253rd would go mostly into reserve and the majority of the 254th could then concentrate on the eradication of the *Americanernest*. This meant that the regiment would again have the strength to take some of the pressure off the damaged 7th and 12th companies of the 122nd down in the ravine, who had each taken a severe beating at the hands of the surrounded Americans over the past two days. With the majority of the 254th, as well as those elements of the 376th Pioneer Battalion and the 76 Pioneer Reserve Company already on the task, Major Ditfurth held every confidence that they would be enough to do the job. Perhaps even without the addition of the storm troops that had been requested.

However, Hauptmann Von Sybel had his doubts. If what the American officer prisoners had said was true and there really were 1,200 men still in that ravine, then even a full regiment and ancillary units would likely not be enough to stop them if they decided to move. (An American enlisted man had even further clarified the question by stating that there were still between 600 and 1,000 effectives left, but this was still awaiting Lt. Prinz's conformation.) Thus, Hauptmann Von Sybel had presented Major Hunicken with the information, as well as a warning that only coordinated attacks, designed to wear the American force down through attrition, were the only solution.

Nor did Major Hunicken ignore this advice, for the attrition that Hauptmann Von Sybel so blithely spoke of was having its effect on his troops as well. The men of his regiment were already worn out by the last 10 days of hard fighting, short rations and rough conditions. A constant pummeling of the larger American force in the Charlevaux would be almost as hard on them as it would be to the Americans. Yet they must continue their efforts if the battle was to be won, which it *must* be. And the easiest way, was to crush the American force outright. With that in mind, the Major then began enacting a plan of attack against the *Americanernest* that was specifically designed to damage the American force, while giving his own troops as much protection as possible.

In the early morning fog, it was useless to mount any large-scale operations. There was far too much chance of firing into one's own troops, no matter how tempting the use of the excellent fog cover might seem. However, *moving* troops through the fog into place for a later, major attack was a different matter all together. Therefore, early that morning, Major Hunicken began to move one full battalion of the 254th into position within the prepared defensive areas above the Binarville-La Viergette road, ahead and above the American position in the ravine. From there, once the fog had broken, he would launch a heavy wave attack, proceeded by concentrated machine-gun fire and grenades, from directly in front of the Americans, falling on them hard from above. Meanwhile, down below and around the surrounded force, the sporadic 'harassment attacks' would continue until the major attack was launched. Once that major operation was underway, additional coordinated attacks by another full battalion, moving against other strategic points of the American perimeter, would be initiated. (29, 51, 120, 123, 128)

One of these 'harassment squads' also kicked up more than they had bargained for that morning. While moving into position, the Germans accidentally stumbled across three ragged Doughboys, tucked into a exceptionally thick area of the hillside behind the Pocket.

There, Corporal Irving Goldberg had thus far succeeded in secreting away his wounded sergeant, Harold Kaplan, and the equally wounded medic Pvt. Saul Marshallcowitz, ever since they had been ambushed as part of Lt. Wilhelm's ill-fated 'link up' patrol on the morning of the 3rd. Biding their time, they had been determined to wait the Germans out. Now however, they were quickly and quietly collared up and dragged off to be interrogated by Hauptmann Bickel.

The fog in the Charlevaux Ravine that morning seemed to be lasting longer than usual; a very fortunate thing for the troops heading for Mont d'Charlevaux, as they then found themselves with plenty of time to cross the ravine some distance from the American flank, climb up the hill and prepare for the attack. There, they waited. It was not quite 10:00 a.m., with the fog starting to burning off and Major Hunicken's men just setting out for their initial assault, when an American observation plane flew over the position… (110, 123, 356)

That morning found the German-speaking Doughboys in the Pocket not lacking for anyone to talk to. The preceding day's bombardment had emboldened the enemy, to the point where an almost constant battle of words was raging, in addition to the conventional warfare raining death upon Major Whittlesey's men. Said Private Julius Langer of Company H:

"From where I was dug in I could both see and hear the Germans and as I am of German parentage, I could understand what they said. I talked to them and they tried to talk us into surrendering, which was laughable…" (44)

Others who spoke German frequently answered back. Both the bilingual Corporal George Speich, of Company K, and Lt. Cullen, who knew just enough German to be dangerous, recalled later that they enjoyed calling the Germans around them "Wint-betreben," which, literally translated means "wind-bag experts" or, more loosely, "stink experts." It also had the slang connotation of meaning "horse's ass, farting," which was highly offensive to the Germans. Private Harry Melvin, a stray Company F man who was several times placed on guard duty up near the road, could plainly hear the enemy on the cliff above him calling for the Doughboys to "come up". Charley Meyers, a private in Company B who was, often times, stationed up there with Pvt. Melvin, would holler back in German, daring the enemy to come and get them. Private Meyers was also one of the few in the Pocket that would pay any attention to Ernst Brahn, the poor German boy they had taken prisoner the first morning in the Pocket. The little kraut had originally been put in Lt. Cullen's big funk hole under a bush on the far left flank for safekeeping (apparently since Major Whittlesey and Captain McMurtry were seldom in the main command hole). There he stayed until the morning of October 5. However, when the trench mortar started up about 9:00 a.m., Lt. Cullen ordered the boy back to the command hole. Fire seemed again centered on the left flank and it would be a shame if the little prisoner were killed by his own comrades. (29, 44, 51)

Another who conversed with the young German was Sergeant Lionel Bendheim of Company C. A trench mortar shell had badly smashed Sgt. Bendheim's leg the day before, and it was now filling with gangrene and puss. Initially situating himself in the wounded area close to the command hole, the sergeant found the little prisoner cowering there. In as rough shape as any of the Doughboys, and more often than not terrified out of his mind, Brahn would sit and gab openly in German with Bendheim. It helped them both keep their minds off their enormous difficulties. (II) (29, 145, 338)

The English-speaking Germans on the hills around also took particular amusement in frequently calling out fake orders of movement to see if anyone would do what they were "told." If a Doughboy were to show himself however, it often meant death and so they quickly learned that it was wisest to wait for orders brought to them by a known officer or NCO, or passed along by one of their buddies. Private Emil Peterson says he was fooled once by a very real sounding order and started to climb out of his hole, "But when a bullet just missed my head, I got back down in a hurry!" Another boy was seen by his officer getting up out of his hole and gathering his gear. When asked just what in hell he thought he was doing, the boy responded that he had heard the word passed that they had been relieved. (29, 44, 51, 338)

The Germans also delighted greatly in flinging an almost steady rattle of taunts down from the hills. The Doughboys below usually ignored them for as long as they could, but more often than not, would end up cursing them soundly.

'Kamerad... vill you?' came the usual German request to surrender.

'Go fuck yourself, Heinie bastard,' was the familiar American response, then followed closely by a rattle of enemy machine-gun fire and perhaps a few grenades from above.

Then:

'Order your coffins, Americans, ve are coming!' draped in heavy Germanic laughter that echoed across the ravine, usually followed by something like:

'Up yours, you kraut sons of bitches.'

After the war, when asked about the behavior of the men under him during this "Shreklichtkiet" (German for "frightfulness"), Major Whittlesey was apt to simply reply, rather dryly, "The men swore a good deal." (29, 44, 51, 135)

The thick layer of fog that had rolled down across the valley during the night would again cover everything in its dewy blanket until well after 8:30 a.m. The rain that had fallen all night long had tapered off into an irritating mist just after dawn. Taking advantage of the fog, Major Whittlesey got the burial details out and working, though it was mostly a wasted effort. The ground was just too tough and the men's strength failing too fast for that anymore. Besides, German snipers and machine-gunners were well on guard now and popped off at the sounds of the digging. Major Whittlesey then went and had a quiet word with McMurtry and the Captain slipped over and had the burial details give up the digging and just put the bodies (or parts) in the nearest unused funk or shell hole and cover them with whatever brush was at hand. Down below the hill, men crawled carefully along the wounded line and did what they could with mud and brush to cover the low wall of corpses shielding the wounded. (29, 109, 135)

While the machine-gun and sniper fire continued to search the blankness in the ravine, the trench mortars had not yet woken up and that was at least some relief. The scene that greeted the beleaguered command's third day in the Pocket was no longer one of simple grim determination, but one of a more grisly tenacity. For the living unwounded, the almost constant machine-gun and trench mortar fire, not to mention the disastrous barrage of the previous day, was beginning to take a toll on morale and physical endurance. Those hardships of body proved the most difficult to codify, recalled Pvt. Arthur R. Looker of Company B:

"Our little plot of ground was not a pretty sight. Graves everywhere, but necessarily so shallow that limbs of our comrades would show through the bit of soil we had been able to scoop over them. And wounded in almost every funk hole. Hunger was gnawing and thirst parching us all, especially those of us who had been gassed during the strenuous drive preceding our present adventure." (267)

Many men were sick, though illness could be a weird sort of blessing, for it brought on quicker exhaustion and, as on l'Homme Mort six days prior, exhaustion brought blessed sleep, which was almost impossible otherwise. Some, who had not been out of their muddy holes in two or three days, were starting to have trouble with their feet as well, another similarity to what had happened on l'Homme Mort. Dry socks had long ago disappeared and boots stayed wet through almost constant immersion in the wet slime that lined the bottom of most all funk holes. Since they could rarely get up and walk around to keep blood circulating through their extremities, men often developed trench foot, a horrible flesh rotting disease similar to gangrene. A few who did take their boots off to try to dry their socks and rub their feet were horrified to discover that their feet immediately swelled up alarmingly. Then, they suffered the agonizing process to trying to force their feet back into their boots - if they could get them back in at all.

Fingers were also affected. Skin - filthy, wrinkled and tender from the constant exposure to moisture, cold and gas - split at the slightest blow or brush with a sharp stick or rock. With nothing to tie up wounds or keep them clean, infection quickly set in. In addition, pleurisy, bad colds, some influenza and the makings of pneumonia from constant exposure to the elements for 10 days and no hot anything (food or otherwise) were also beginning to seriously affect some men, as was dehydration. The constant wet weather was wreaking real havoc with the gassed men as well, and their wheezing and snuffling just to get breath was a disgusting and discouraging sound. Most men also had body lice, as well as nervous stomachs that, combined with the scarcity of water that made brushing teeth impossible, left many with a mouth full of painful sores. It was getting to be an effort just to wake up – when one could sleep. (142, 143)

As usual, Major Whittlesey was up well before most everyone else on that October 5 and once again working his way around the Pocket. He was forced to crawl and crouch more than usual now, since there was little remaining brush cover and though perhaps a fatalist in combat, he was also no fool. He was still sending patrols out every morning, noon and evening to try and find a way through, though they were now smaller two or three man efforts. Some never came back, while those that did, unable to find a break, brought information, so that the Major and Captain McMurtry at least had some idea of what was going on immediately around them. A late patrol of the night before, for instance, returned around dawn with a couple of men wounded. They reported no way out but did confirm a new enemy machine-gun position. Dismissing them, Major Whittlesey then sent out his morning patrols.

The patrol that went forward to the road that morning was not out long before returning with news. From the road, they had watched across the valley as a large body of Germans, perhaps 200 in number, had moved east along the ridge of Hill 198 and then down the hill off the right of the commands bivouac. Major Whittlesey probably speculated that it was likely the makings of the typical morning attack, but said nothing. No use riling the men until it happened and their was nothing to do about it anyway. Then, off in the distance, the artillery again started booming and from toward the French sector came the distinctive chug of Hotchkiss guns, the crack of rifles and the echoing explosions of hand grenades. An attack was on over there…

As Major Whittlesey made his way around the Pocket that morning, checking dispositions and strengths, he was approached for the first time directly by several individual soldiers, all with the same question: "Major, do you think we are gonna make it out of here?"

"Did you not hear those Sho-Sho's in the distance yesterday and last night?" he answered, voice full of confidence. "Don't you worry; there are two million Doughboys working behind us to get us out. The rest of the regiment will fight the devil himself to get through to us. We will be all right; it will not be long now."

He might then offer a bit of advice as to adding surface cover to their funk holes or clearing a better field of fire before moving along, as calm and seemingly unconcerned about their situation as ever. (IV)

Yet, the very act of the questioning began to worry the Major that morning, and rightly so. Never before had private soldiers approached him so boldly and directly with such questions as they had yesterday after the barrage and now this morning. He was well aware that, as a Major and Battalion Commander, he generally seemed a figure so far above the ordinary soldier as to seem almost unapproachable. He also went to some length to achieve and maintain this level of separation; which is, in reality, a good military leadership tactic. By being the overall commanding figure, he was then able to create an unquestionability about his words. Ordinarily, this would then build a high level of confidence in his command structure under situations of duress. Now however, the dire situation seemed to be stripping away a certain level of that confidence, and morale appeared to be dropping because of it. He had heard men talking as he went his rounds and it seemed few believed that they were going to get out of the ravine. What he had heard the other day had only been the start. Now, it seemed as if the talk was approaching some sort of culmination; he did not want to think of the possible consequences. (29, 51, 109)

Some of this, of course, should have been expected. After all, the situation was far worse than anything they could have imagined and the command structure, which traditionally counters this sort of effect, was slowly being whittled away. A surviving, handwritten message by Major Whittlesey from this morning - the latest known surviving Pocket message from during the siege - is very revealing. It is sent to Lt. Rogers of Company B and is one simple line, *"What is the approximate strength of 'B' Co. this morning including patrols and outposts?"* and is signed "C.W.W." Scrawled across the bottom is Lt. Rogers' answer, *"About 20 men. Will have count made right away."* and signed simply "HR." On the back, the Major has scribbled several columns of figures, and in his scratches we see the true attrition of both officers and men in full color.

Under "Off. Casualties" he lists: A - Lt. Harrington (which should be Lt. Williamson; Harrington was with E - author); C - Capt. Stromee; E - Lt. Wilhelm (missing); G - Lt. Buhler; H - Griffin, and Lieutenant's Peabody and Revnes of the machine-guns. To this however, we must also add the missing and captured Lieutenant's Leak and Harrington, the wounded but still active Captain's McMurtry and Holderman, and Lt. Trainor of C who, though wounded, remained in his hole helping Sgt. Raymond Blackburn control his platoon. That left only Lieutenant's Pool of K, Rogers of B, Eager of G, Cullen of H, Schenck of C, Noon of the machine-guns, and Teichmoeller of the artillery, besides Major Whittlesey himself, as the only unwounded officers in the Pocket. The officer loss then stood at about 60 percent. (By the end of the siege however, when Major Whittlesey and Lieutenant's Eager and Cullen were the only officers standing and unwounded, that total would have climbed to 85 percent.) By October 5 then, these losses had thus changed the command dynamic considerably. What remained of E (not much), was now under the command of Sgt. Fredrick A. Baldwin. Company A's meager numbers were under Sgt. Herman Anderson. Company D of the machine-guns had gone to Sgt. George Hauck (who would soon take over C as well, after Lt. Noon was killed). Sergeant Patrick Landers commanded a platoon of H, beside Lt. Cullen. Company 1st Sergeant Amos Todisco had a platoon of G, beside Lt. Eager; and Sgt. Samuel Marcus had first a platoon of B and then the whole company, after Lt. Rogers was killed. Though Captain Holderman would stay in command of Company K right until the end, despite his many wounds, after Lt. Pool was later shot in the back, the Captain would then largely rely on Sgt. James Carroll to help run things. "Cream-puff" Carroll his men jokingly called him, since he had been a drapery salesman in New York before the war. However there was very little soft about the man. For his excellent work in the Pocket, Captain Holderman would later lobby a battlefield commission for him and the sergeant would end the war as 2nd Lt. James Carroll.

Other figures on the back of Major Whittlesey's message from that morning show the command's official strength, which the Major listed as: A – 10, B – 22, C – 45, E – 12, G – 20, H – 50, and 307 K – 45. Next to that column, another list adds: Bn Hqs 1st – 10, 2nd – 15, MG C – 8 (2 guns), and MG D – 9 (4 guns). Adding all these together - and believing in their accuracy - totals a grim picture of 246 effectives, which almost certainly includes wounded who returned to the line to keep fighting. This still leaves a mean loss of just over 64 percent of the force either killed, missing, or too badly wounded to fight when they woke up to their third day in the ravine. Combining these losses with the realities that those "effectives" had to endure (such as the complete lack of medical resources, which then forced them to have to watch their wounded buddies literally rot), it is small wonder that most men were physically and psychologically nearing the end of their rope. (Keep in mind also the two weeks of Argonne hell they had already gone through before they landed in the Pocket as well.) (109, 245, 246)

In truth, it had been the bombardment by their own troops the afternoon before that had been the real kick to morale. Many figured that if regiment did not know enough than to put their shells right on top of them, then how could they be trusted to fight through and relieve them? They would probably drive the line right past them and never even realize it, the stupid bastards. Yet Major Whittlesey could not afford to let their morale sink to the bottom, and so he made his rounds and passed out words of encouragement in his most convincing, unquestionable tone. And, for the most part, it *did* have the desired effect, though maybe not to quite the extent as has generally been written, nor for as long as has been believed either. Did the Major believe any of it himself? That is hard to say. Nor does it matter. The point is that no matter how he might look, old "Galloping Charlie" was sure "full of the old pepper" as far as they were concerned and even if the situation looked doomed, as long as the Major's encouragement was there, the men would fight like furies. It was only later, when his words had a chance to fade from the front of their minds, and time had a chance to work on their hungry and dehydrated souls, that they would begin to doubt him. Then...

Then, the German trench mortars started spreading their morning hate and discontent and the hungry Doughboys watched the pretty pink and red flashes through the ground fog.

However, for all of Major Whittlesey's encouragement, even he knew that there were not two million Doughboys in what remained of the 308th. In fact, there were barely 300 rifles available in what remained of the 1st, 2nd, and 3rd battalions back in Ravin d'Argonne, and they were about to attack behind a new regimental commander.

At 8:00 a.m., another patrol from the 50th Aero, this one with Lt. William Frayne as pilot and Lt. Howard French as observer, took off for the lines on a contact patrol, two hours after Anderson and Rogers had dropped their message to Major Whittlesey some 8 kilometers too far south of his position, and Fitzsimmons and Pursley had tossed the others to the Germans. Most of the line was still shrouded from aerial view, but as the time slowly passed, the fog started to break up and they were able to make some real progress as they beetled back and forth over the 77th's advance zones. With him, Lt. French had brought along several small bundles of chocolate and smokes to drop to the men below and as they repeatedly roared over the forest and called for the line, he threw the bundles out where he got signals.

The end of their line run found them headed west over the confused area of the 308th Infantry. At about 9:20 a.m., Lt. Frayne circled back around, north of Binarville, to make another pass. Lieutenant Morse had warned the two flyers to be extra watchful for the group of 308th Infantrymen that the 77th Division reported was advanced well out ahead of the main line and were without liaison down in the Charlevaux Ravine. If the rest of the regiment did not break through and reach them that day, then the 50th would likely be detailed to try to drop supplies to them on the next. Although the flyers saw that mission as a new and interesting challenge, they also were well aware that it meant low flying, which brought the high risk of ground fire. Thus, it would be better to know today all the where's and what's that faced them in the area, then to have to go in blind tomorrow. Therefore, Lt. Frayne dipped the plane back around again and prepared for another pass just north of the line as Lt. French brought his field glasses up and began scanning the ground.

That second pass brought them over what had to be the ravine Lt. Morse had been talking about. South of it, Lt. French could see smoke drifting and just make out through the foliage that a serious battle was going forth toward the ravine. The effort to reach that stranded command had obviously started. Looking off to the north, through a break in the trees the Lieutenant's glasses caught sight of enemy troops massing in trenches near the top of a large hill and starting down toward a road cut into the side of it. Just below the road, light shells were falling on the hillside that looked to be coming from the direction of the U.S. line. Obviously, these were reinforcements getting ready to hustle up to the battlefront on the other side of the ravine. Then, from farther up the hillside, a few Germans emerged from a dugout with fresh soil ringing its entrance and began to fire a machine-gun at the plane. Lieutenant French pointed them out to his pilot, as well as the massing troops. With the enemy troops just starting down the hill to cross the ravine, Lt. French realized that they needed to do something to help out "their boys" on the line, and fast!

Lieutenant Frayne pulled the big DH up and gave her the gas, gaining altitude as he turned back over the 307th's zone to make another pass. Lieutenant French, meanwhile, readied his Very pistol. Once they were over the approximate spot where the German troops were on top of the big hill, the lieutenant began to loose off several colored shots in a specific pattern, meant to communicate with any artillery observers further to the south the message, "Fire on me."

Behind, up on the heights of Hill 210, Lt. Leon Hattemer was out spotting again for Battery E/305th F.A., standing on a little bench jutting out near the top of a half dead tree, with his field glasses up. Soon thereafter, the phone rang at 152nd F.A. Brigade PC near La Harazee. There was a barrage request being made by a U.S. plane, along a longitudinal line approximately 276.55, with the lateral along 294.8 or so. Before too long then, the thump of the artillery rang out behind Lt. Hattemer and several bursts appeared down in the ravine below the high circling plane of Lieutenant's French and Frayne. Lieutenant French sent up some additional lights for correction of the shots, did so at least one more time, and then finally called "Fire for effect" when he was satisfied that the shots were falling "on target". He was quickly rewarded with a multitude of bursts directly where he had wanted them - up near the hilltop and along the road cut into its side.

Satisfied that they had done their part to help prevent an enemy reinforcement to the attack then going on along the line, Lt. Frayne turned the plane back toward Remicourt. Other sorties would be flown by the 50th that day, but none would come as close to Major Whittlesey's command as had Lieutenant's French and Frayne, who actually did more good than they knew.

And, as far as the artillery batteries to the south then firing that barrage the two flyers had just directed in were concerned, it was simply further proof that Major Whittlesey's command could not possibly be where they had been firing their barrage the previous afternoon. After all, that U.S. plane had just directed them to fire onto virtually the same piece of real estate. (93, 110, 140, 141, 227, 249)

By 9:15 a.m., things had woken up around the Pocket. Enemy machine-guns that had started up with the daylight were whipping lead around at an alarming rate and around 8:30 a.m. that damned trench mortar on Hill 205 had started to dump its rounds in again, fast, with most fire concentrated on the left flank up near the road. Heavy machine-gun and mortar fire, everyone knew, usually presaged an enemy attack. Coupled with the information that the scouts had brought in that morning of the troops hustling along Hill 198, it was not hard to figure where this one was going to come from or where it was going to strike. Therefore, the two Battalion Commanders crawled out to the flanks to make sure all was set. Over at Lt. Cullen's hole, they found the lieutenant about as ready as he could be, even up and moving about his position despite the machine-gun fire. The previous night, he had heard Germans talking quietly up on the road and in the brush on the other side of the nipple of hillside that they had pulled off, not more than 10 or 15 meters away. Only understanding bits and pieces of what they had been saying, he nevertheless had gotten the gist of it - they were planning the American's annihilation. (Other Company H men had reported the German voices too. If ammunition had been more plentiful, the Doughboys swore, there would be more dead German bodies out in the woods this morning.) The trench mortar fire, Lt. Cullen agreed, was just preliminary; the main event could not be far behind. (29, 51, 109, 148, 149, 150)

On the right flank, where all had been relatively quiet in the misty dawn, a morning patrol that had been out slowly snaked back in and reported to Captain Holderman as the two Commanding Officers arrived to warn the Captain of the expected attack. The Captain sent the exhausted men back to their holes while, stealthily, a couple other of his men wormed their way down to the wounded area with mess gear containing rainwater that they had caught overnight for Gehris, Sirota, and Bragg to use. There, a precious remaining cigarette was making the rounds among the shivering wounded in lieu breakfast. Hollow eyes stared a thousand yards off into the gloomy forest. Some men dozed, while others quietly died. Tension, hung over a blanket of hungry exhaustion, enveloped everyone in khaki. A plane buzzed overhead and sent up a call for ground signals. Were the panels out? Yes sir, what was left of them. Most had been ripped down to make bandages and the plane was awfully high up; the tiny squares would likely be missed from such an altitude and they were not very white anymore. Still, a few men risked a bullet and crawled out into open areas again with grimy towels and waved them about. It was around 9:45 a.m.

Off in the distance, to the southwest, there was a dull report, then another, and soon came the familiar whistling of falling shells. All faces turned skyward with anxious expressions, eyes scanning the sky behind the ravine. A shell crashed down, exploded at the foot of Hill 198, and sent a geyser of muddy water towering into the air, as had happened yesterday. A second, then a third burst in the same vicinity, then came a series of the distant reports and a line of a dozen exploding shells drew out along the ravine behind the Pocket.

'Son of a bitch! Not again...'

Suddenly, the Pocket was again alive with activity, much of it pointless, as the enemy machine-guns chattered diligently. Some men began digging with anything they could find, flinging dirt in all directions, as if they were going to dig deep enough in the next few seconds to protect them from an exploding 75 or 155. Others, with eyes clamped shut tightly and rifles forgotten, simply curled up in the bottom of their hole and waited for the shocks to begin, a scream just barely contained behind their lips. Down at the foot of the hill, those wounded able to move huddled closer to the line of mud and brush covered corpses behind, or deeper into what remained of the long, shallow hole they were in. Others who could not move, and some who had scarcely been able to keep themselves under control and out of shock thus far, wailed pitifully and fouled themselves where they lay.

Major Whittlesey and Captain McMurtry were up and yelling for everyone to stay calm, the Major's voice rising and thinning against the explosions. Captain Holderman was doing the same except that, over there, a few shells had apparently already fallen on his position. Shrapnel whizzed around, mixing high-pitched whirring noises in with the heavy bursts. Could they take another beating like yesterday, or would this finish the command, mentally as well as physically? Major Whittlesey stalked along the hillside, bolt upright again and with a terribly apprehensive look across his dirty, beard-fringed face. Another round of explosions, again creeping across the ravine bottom, same as yesterday, came closer to the position. Again, mud and water rained down through the rush grass and tree cover; again, the dull 'tunk' of steel meeting thick tree trunks echoed shortly in the morning air. The advancing line of shells continued to just outside of the south perimeter line, only one or two falling into the position near the center. Everyone out there unconsciously held their breath. And it was there, strangely, that the barrage seemed to pause for a moment... (29, 51, 135, 148, 149)

Then, all the men's fervent prayers were answered with the next round of explosions, which appeared all over the hill *above* the road ahead, dancing wildly among the trees up there. German wails and screams followed, as dismembered limbs and bits of flesh and bone again rained down on the hillside. All at once, a mighty cheer went up from the Pocket. So, the goddammed artillery had finally found the range! Said Lt. Eager:

"(When) they started another barrage, I remember thinking or at least saying to myself, "If they put this barrage down like the other one, there will not be any of us that survive!" And I don't believe we would have, but when they came up to where we were they put the barrage around us in what is called a box barrage. When they put it around us, evidently we knew then that the pigeon had gotten through, which was the first indication we had that it had..." (234)

However, there was much more behind that barrage than Lt. Eager would ever realize. Sometime over night, General Alexander had indeed looked into the situation that French Lieutenant de la Chapelle had reported the prior evening, of an artillery barrage falling into the Charlevaux Ravine. General Johnson, with whom he first spoke, admitted that firing to support Major Whittlesey had been his idea - and a good one, General Alexander was forced to agree - but that he had no idea how the barrage could have gone so wrong. Major Whittlesey had sent several messages out from his position, all clearly marked with his correct map coordinates. Therefore, what had happened was a complete mystery to the Brigade Commander.

General Alexander's next call then had been to General McCloskey, who commanded the 152nd F.A., and General McCloskey had assured his Division Commander that it could not have been U.S. guns that had fired onto Major Whittlesey's men, then suggesting that perhaps a French battery was responsible. General McCloskey's men had fired by corrected coordinates sent out by their own man there with the Major's force in the ravine. Additionally, one of his own liaison men had ranged that fire mission himself, right from the front, that day. Therefore, any problems regarding 'short firing' should likely be taken up with the French. (V) (2, 131, 140, 144)

Absolutely none of which, however, mattered to Major Whittlesey's men in the Pocket just then, who were regarding the current barrage as a Godsend and for a change praising the artillery. And as the barrage continued for the next 50 minutes or so, blowing the Germans ahead all to hell, the Doughboys' flagging morale took a tremendous boost. More so, when it was realized that one of the guns firing had dropped a few rounds wildly short and, by chance, took out the trench mortar on the northeastern slope of Hill 205 that had been giving them such fits since the beginning. True, that still left the two to the front, but few of *their* shells were actually landing on the hillside. The one to the southwest had been the real son of a bitch since the start. Therefore, when the damned thing went silent for good, the news spread fast and another great cheer went up.

As the barrage slowed and finally ground to a halt just before 11:00 a.m., Major Whittlesey realized that the midday enemy attack would likely be a wash. There certainly seemed to be considerably less than the average amount of machine-gun fire now, in any case. Perhaps the enemy had pulled out of the ravine for the time being in fear that a repeat of yesterday's terrible barrage might be in the offing. There would be a short chance to get the men out and get things done then, if they hurried. Seizing the narrow window of opportunity then, in the near silence that followed the barrage (all that could be heard was the terrible battle raging in the Ravin d'Argonne and from the French zone around Hill 205), the Major got some men cautiously up and out of their holes to gather in the dead. Others stumbled out to simply stretch - it was too good an opportunity to miss.

Sergeant Martin Tuite of Company C was out, and glad of it, when he happened to glance over and saw Lt. Schenck sitting upright on the edge of his funk hole too, reading from a little 3-inch by 5-inch leather bound book. Seeing Sgt. Tuite eyeing him questioningly, Lt. Schenck closed it and held it up for the sergeant to see the title, *Science and Health*, by Mary Baker Eddy (Lt. Schenck was Christian Scientist by faith).

"This is like food and drink to me," the young lieutenant said, smiling. "A wonderful comfort."

Sergeant Tuite nodded and then brought out a rosary.

"This is my comfort."

Many others there were in the Pocket also holding their charms and symbols of faith and strength under the gray, leaden French sky.

Then, the machine-guns started to chatter raggedly again and everyone quickly scurried back into their holes.

It had been a nice break while it lasted though. (29, 40, 51, 109, 116, 135)

In direct correlation to that barrage of October 4, neither would General McCloskey ever admit that it was his artillery that had broken up the American attack up the Ravin d'Argonne that morning of October 5 either. But broken it up it had, and up there, things were going particularly badly for the 308th because of it. After liaison with the 308th had been broken by that shelling, the French had gone ahead and sent two companies of the 4th C.a.P into the attack on time, storming forward in assault under the assumption that the 308th would be doing the same. They did not realize however, exactly how badly the shelling had disorganized the 308th's companies, nor how much trouble Captain Breckenridge had in getting them back together for the assault. It was not until 7:30 a.m. that the 308th moved out, with all surprise lost, against an enemy that had not only shaken off the effects of what shells had found them, but had set themselves to meet the American assault with heavy machine-gun and counter battery fire. While the 308th was still some 200 meters away from their objective line then, to their left the French were well ahead of them and already crawling up the side of Hill 205 to the La Palette Pavilion on top by 9:45 a.m. that murky morning. (10, 29, 51, 91, 131, 140, 144)

Meanwhile, General Johnson was over in the sector of the 307th, where there appeared to be a development on the regiments far right. There, Company B, with M in support, had found what looked to be a 'seam' in the thick wire ahead, which they were then exploring. Then, at 9:20 a.m., the Brigadier received a report with dispositions of the 1st and 3rd Battalion/307th companies that looked good at first. Company D had led a holding attack while Company C had thrown a platoon and a half against the spot where Company L had driven through four days before. It eventually failed however; the breaks had been wired shut tight again. Additional messages flew back and forth after that, stating that enemy machine-guns buried deep in the heavy wire and dense forest were preventing further movement and that the line had stalled. Without the 307th moving forward farther, General Johnson knew, there was little point to the 308th's attack farther left, for even if they did manage to get through to Major Whittlesey, they were not enough in numbers to exploit the break and make good use of the advanced position. With no flank support, the push would likely leave them cut off too, only adding to the number of troops then unreachable (and orders to 'forget the flanks' could be damned). It had to be the 307th that drove through on Major Whittlesey's right then, no matter what General Alexander thought. Perhaps on the overall scale of the offensive Hill 205 was indeed the hold up that needed to be broken past. However, on a more local, brigade scale, where the obstacle was simply reaching Major Whittlesey any way possible, it would be accomplished easiest in the zone of the 307th. (91, 103, 104, 131, 138, 139)

Shortly before 10:00 a.m., a call came in to the 307th Regimental PC from General Alexander for General Johnson. Captain Klotz and Lt. de Coppet, over at the 1st D.C.D's PC had rung him a short time before. The French, they said, had taken and were holding La Palette Pavilion, well in advance of the line of the 308th, which, they were complaining, had not participated in the attack on Hill 205 at all. Where in hell was the 308th? General Johnson, in response, was very frank about the attack, stating that reports were that the 308th had indeed not progressed much, apparently due mostly to delays caused first by Colonel Stacey's departure (since the Colonel had made no dispositions for further attack in his last hours) and then by the disaster of a misplaced artillery barrage (further details of which had been trickling over to him periodically). Adding to this, they had gotten no support from their right, where the 307th had gone forward but still was not far enough to support the attack down the ravine. General Alexander then informed the Brigadier, in no uncertain terms, that he was to immediately take the 2nd/307th and proceed to the 308th's zone, take direct charge of the situation personally, support the French on Hill 205, and drive through that line ahead without delay! General Johnson replied that in doing so he would be out of direct contact not only with the Division Commander but with the general situation as well, and would be forced to communicate exclusively by runner. General Alexander said that he understood that, but that it did not matter. The French needed to be supported and that line needed to be broken at once! The Brigadier was to proceed with the attack as ordered, again advancing without regard for his flanks or losses. (2, 10, 91, 131, 132, 138, 146)

Hanging up, and no doubt smarting again from the verbal shellacking, General Johnson gathered his meager staff and set out for Depot des Machines to get the 2nd/307th. He found them morosely ensconced not far into the ravine from Defsauer Platz, trying to scrape the mud out of their weapons under a light rain shower. Assembling them and marching back to the very spot they had bled so much over the day before, the Brigadier arrived about noon and found what remained of the 308th already falling back. A message arrived from a Company I liaison team on the left; the French, after having held the La Palette Pavilion and the western approaches of Hill 205 for barely a quarter of an hour, had been beaten back by a tremendous counter assault made by troops coming up from the Moulin d'Charlevaux behind the hill. The 1st D.C.D's line then (such as it was), had already drawn back well behind the general line occupied by the 308th (such as it was). The French commander sent a message up as well, stating that he had every intention of falling back still farther. Whereas the French main line was again on the Binarville-Autry road to the left and above Binarville, immediately west of the 77th their line would fall once again back in the old enemy entrenchments south of town and along the Binarville-Moulin de l'Homme Mort road. The 4th C.a.P, a broken unit by the fierce attacks of the last two days, was being removed from the line to go into support positions behind the 9th, who were then extending to take their place. By 1:30 p.m., as the U.S. barrage for the afternoon attack was already starting to go over, everything about the French line was as it had been that morning - except for their casualty totals.

Meanwhile, that noon hour General Johnson took quick stock of what he had to work with while they waited for an artillery preparation that he had called for from Defsauer Platz. In companies D, F, and K of the 308th, he found barely 60 men each and those who remained were tired, and in some cases already wounded. He also had several stragglers from the companies then up in the Charlevaux; men who, for whatever reason, had not been up with Major Whittlesey's force on the evening of the 2nd. There was at least one 30 man platoon of Company G, a strong squad or two of E (perhaps 14 or 15 men), the larger majority of what was left of A (about 40 men), and a couple under strength squads from B and C (about 10 or 15 men each). A few replacements had shown up now as well, perhaps as many as two dozen, this time from the 41st (Depot) Division. Companies L and M were not in much better shape than K, and I had most of its men out on liaison duty with the French. As for the 2nd/307th, he counted a mere 250 men, which constituted the whole of that battalion… (29, 51, 91, 105, 109, 116, 131, 138, 144, 146, 150)

While he busily prepared these meager numbers to move forward, collecting mud on his uniform and boots just as any common private soldier might and with a grimy Eddystone slung over his shoulder, in the last moments Captain Breckenridge came up with a fresh batch of officer replacements, just assigned to the regiment. These men had never seen an actual day of combat before and they were now meant to take the decimated units into full-fledged battle. The shells had, by then, started flying overhead when General Johnson gathered them around. Ripping the General's rank from his shoulder straps to avoid making himself a target in the coming fight, the Brigadier shortly gave what direction and advice he could before sending them off into that valley, where reined the shadow of death. General Johnson then moved down into the fray himself to the head of the attack - his first time under direct enemy fire since 1899.

(I) From there Stacey was passed through at least two other hospitals, where he was diagnosed with a bad case of neurasthenia - the army's polite term for "shell-shock" - before being evacuated to the big American hospital center at Savenay-Loire-Inferieure, and from there eventually sent home. His mother died before he got there. General Johnson later remarked at the generally haggard appearance of the Colonel when he arrived that night at l'Homme Mort. He appeared as if he had not slept in days, his eyes had taken on a dark, sunken appearance and he was extremely nervous and fidgety. Under questioning, in a bad temper he told General Johnson little of what had been happening and did not seem to remember details from the recent past, most particularly the afternoon attacks. The Brigadier had been truly appalled by his appearance.

(II) As one of the machine-gun officers was killed by this friendly fire, an investigation was later launched to find out 'what had happened'. The investigation was decidedly short however, and the artillery was quickly relieved of all responsibility for the faux pas, the blame for the machine-gun lieutenant's death going to "enemy artillery fire". In all reality however, available evidence would seem to indicate that it actually was American fire that had killed the man.

(III) Ernst Brahn had been wounded during the U.S. barrage on October 4 and would later die while in captivity, near the end of the month, from effects of the wound. Lieutenant Cullen had sent him over to the command hole that afternoon as well, and the German, a big young man, had helped move the wounded out of some of the heavier fire. Otherwise, he spent all of his time hunkered down in the bottom of a funk hole, just like everyone else.

(IV) It was this confidence and willingness to expose himself to fire that made Charles Whittlesey legend with his men. Most of them knew that few leaders would risk what he and Captain McMurtry did simply to pass along words of encouragement and, at the time, several thought he was crazy for it. It was only after everything was all over and they were back in the states as "Heroes of the Lost Battalion" that the legend grew larger than life, then increased in size again after Whittlesey's death. While it is true that the Major was willing to remain above ground more often than below it, in direct opposition to some other officers, he did so simply because he felt it was his duty to do so to try to keep morale as high as possible. Many men also assumed that Major Whittlesey himself believed every word he spoke to them. His voice to them seemed to carry the words on a carpet of finality – if the Major said it, then by God it was the truth. His simple faith in rescue (at least outwardly) buoyed their flagging spirits continually.

(V) Later on October 5 however, General McCloskey issued a brigade memorandum, which seemed specifically designed to prevent exactly the sort of situation Major Whittlesey's men had been forced to endure for an hour and a half the day before:

Hereafter, when a barrage is called for by the infantry for protection, the rate of fire will be four per gun per minute for four minutes, two shots per gun per minute for two minutes. The barrage will then cease, and will not be repeated unless called for again by the infantry, either by signal or by telephone.

While nowhere near an admission of guilt, this highly interesting memorandum certainly begs more than a few questions. Even more so when the shoot directed by Lt.'s French and Frayne, which truly *was* dropping in support of the Pocket (though they never realized it), was reported later that day to be firing on virtually the same coordinates that the guns either had or had not - depending on who was answering the questions - fired onto on the afternoon before.

Ancillary sources used in this chapter include: 21, 25, 30, 47, 49, Various 152-216, 250-254, 257, 260, 261, 262, 268, 269, 272, 273, 278-283, 285, 286, 292, 296-306, 309, 310, 314-319, 323, 326-330, 338.

October 5, 1918 P.M.
"Send more on Lost Battalion"
Cable dispatch to reporter Damon Runyon.

The barrage against the German positions in the ravine, laid squarely and true on the Hun alone this time, continued until 2:30 p.m. Then, General Johnson's formations moved out into the German counter fire, where they promptly fragmented under the control of the inexperienced officers at their helm, into squad sections led mostly by sergeants and corporals. With the remains of companies D and F/308th moving as one on the left, the 2nd/307th moved as it had the day before. This time however, L and H merged as one and went down the right bottom of the ravine and along the eastern slope and ridge, while behind them a merged G and E moved in support, liaisoned to the rest of the 307th. Meanwhile, General Johnson himself led the 3rd/308th into the ravine between Company L/307th and the remains of the 308th, with K and M working together as one company along the ravine floor and west ridge, supported by L/308th. (29, 51, 109, 116, 131, 144)

A little after 3:00 p.m. General Johnson, celebrating his 57th birthday in the mud by fighting as ferociously as any one of his privates, sent back his first reports from the point of attack to be called in to General Alexander. His coordinates put him directly at the bottom of the ravine and just slightly to the left, before the Haupt-Widerstands-Lienie. The message laid out his intentions, also showing that some progress was actually being made:

Attack started from this point at 2.45pm. One company deployed on each side of ravine. (1 Co. = 2 Cos. Consolidated) Following as support. Line about 300 yards in advance of this point. (Obviously a scout line, otherwise the main line would be only some 200 meters away from the opening to the Charlevaux and well beyond the German main line, which it was not yet – author) *Left against wired entanglements. Right advancing slowly. Have given orders to pass support companies through bottom of ravine with view to outflanking the Germans. Meeting heavy machine gun fire from both sides of the ravine; also infantry and artillery fire. Pushing for all I am worth. Personally directing.* (131)

The effort to get around the German flank of their main line by moving down the bottom of the ravine between the heights on either side immediately took its toll. New officers paid the highest price, some as they tried to move their men in textbook formations without taking into account the true conditions of the battlefield, others as they stood frozen in fear and shock by the ferocity of the attack and enemy counter fire. Lieutenant Jenkins, commanding Company E/307th and also at that time for all intents and purposes still the 2nd/307th's 'Battalion Commander', later said of what he saw during the movement:

Lt. Goodwin and I, in passing two companies forward with the idea of passing around the flank of the enemy's trench line, had to stand and personally move small groups of men, under heavy artillery and machine gun fire, from cover to cover, in order to insure their not being killed before reaching the point from which they could approach the flank of the trench line. (103)

By 3:35 p.m., when General Johnson sent his second message back, the attack had barely progressed beyond the line mentioned in the first message, if at all:

I am being held on a general line 275.5, heavy artillery, machine gun and rifle fire. French upon our immediate left or slightly to our rear. Two of their liaison group are with me. I am attempting to advance and passed company through interval in wire which exists in bottom of ravine. I am myself with the company which is attempting to pass through and who in the last few minutes have lost over 20 killed and wounded out of 85. (131)

The French liaison men were actually Captain Klotz and Lt. de Coppet, sent by General Alexander to try and arrange for continued cooperative attacks on the 6th and most interested in seeing if the 308th would be up to it. General Johnson had little time for questions though because if the French were on the immediate left they were not attacking. (Actually, they were attacking, but it was farther up the line.) Once again, the 308th's left was wide open, with only the trusty Company I men beating off German assaults against that flank, in conjunction with only a thin French outpost line. Meanwhile, the flanking action at the bottom of the ravine was beginning to 'head south' fast, as evidenced by this account given by 2nd Lt. Clarence Davis, a platoon commander in one of the 3rd/308th's companies:

"We were subjected to terrific machine gun fire. The fire of our own artillery did not seem to damage the wire much. They could not find it among the trees. The green men fought remarkably well; you never saw such bravery. But unfortunately, their lack of knowledge of automatic rifles soon exhausted our supply of ammunition as they fired whole clips at a burst and we were soon within ten feet of the German's strongly entrenched position with our ammunition gone. We took what we could from our fallen comrades and looked in vain for supporting platoons. (But) instead of supporting platoons, Germans came around behind us as well as in front. My knowledge of the Argonne drive from here on is hearsay, for I was captured and sent to a German hospital..." (29)

The attack was then in desperate straights by as early as 3:45 p.m., when General Johnson whipped off a message to a Captain Whelply, the 152nd F.A. liaison officer on his now meager staff, asking if some counter battery fire could be called in against some German positions. The idea was apparently advised against, however, as the General's next message, timed at 3:51 p.m., asked that Lt. John Fitch of the Headquarters Company (now in charge of the Stokes mortar teams) report to the General with his weapons at once. (2, 10, 91, 109, 131, 144)

Major Whittlesey had figured correctly about the noon attack, for it had never come. The only thing bothering the Doughboys in the Pocket then between 11:00 am and just before 3:00 p.m., besides their basic sufferings, were a few trench mortar shells and some uncoordinated machine-gun and sniper fire. Most men simply sat in their holes and waited for something to happen, fighting that other enemy that was almost as bad as the Germans - boredom. Some dug their funk holes deeper, some prayed harder and others chewed roots or leaves to get some moisture back into their dehydrated mouths. A few munched on candles and wet bark to relieve some hunger pangs. It was a gloomy day and after the excitement of watching the Hienies get the crap kicked out of them earlier, harsh reality had once more taken hold. Grim determination blanketed the Pocket, as did a rainy mist that lasted all afternoon and well into the night. (29, 40, 44, 51, 135, 148, 149, 150, 220, 256)

That afternoon of October 5 was a particularly long and tiring one, made so by the general inactivity and tremendous strain. At least during an attack the time seemed to pass speedily. Sitting idly, however, time dragged endlessly and left too much room for thought.

Over on the left, even Lt. Cullen well remembered the strain and later wrote of it:

"The men were beginning to get restless and were constantly popping out of their meager shelters on one mission or another (but) observation of the Boche was so close that a branch could not move without a stream of machine gun bullets being poured at that point… My job consequently grew more and more dangerous (as) I had to visit my posts and encourage the men. I had no discretion in the matter and I talked with them, gave them the few cigarettes that remained and distributed a little tobacco that I had stowed in my knapsack… (But) the strain was beginning to tell on the men and their eyes took on an abnormal and peculiar hue." (109)

Down in the wounded area, the medics worked diligently to bring as much comfort and relief as they could. They were improvising greatly now; cloth waist belts and sticks made functional splints for broken limbs, as well as tourniquets. They were scavenging more used bandages from the dead, folded so the nasty mess from a previous wound would come into as little contact as possible with a new wound. Other bandages were rinsed in a bit of water first, though the dirt in the water helped the wounds little. Another excellent bandage turned out to be the men's long, woolen, spiral puttees, once the mud had been washed off them. Even web cartridge belts were being used to bind wounds, though overall it was getting increasingly difficult to find anything clean to put next to an open wound to keep the dirt and filth out and tetanus at bay. Water helped, but most of what little there was went for drinking, not washing wounds.

And water *was* available, both from the brook and the spring, but more often than not men were too frightened to try and get any. German snipers kept careful watch over the choice spots to retrieve water, primarily those without much brush and there were machine-guns sighted all along the brook as well. Trying different locations was no help, as the Germans could tell men were on the move toward the brook by movement in the tall rush grass near the waters' edge and they would then quickly pepper the area with machine-gun fire. In spots, the water was as little as *10 meters* away from the parched men.

Still, there were those who regularly made the attempt to get it, both officially and unofficially. The most notable of these was Private Philip "Zip" Cepaglia, an Upton man in the 1st Battalion Headquarters platoon and Major Whittlesey's favorite personal runner. Well liked, "Zip" Cepaglia has been lovingly described as "a pint sized, greasy little wop" and the most courageous man in the Lost Battalion. He was barely five feet six inches tall, might have weighed near a hundred pounds at some point - though certainly not while in the Pocket - and was, quite possibly, the fastest man alive; at least as far as anyone in the 308th was concerned. "Zip" was one of the very few that had Major Whittlesey's official permission to get water, simply because he seemed able to, and he took the job very seriously. Sharing a hole with Pvt. Larney and Cpl. Baldwin next to the command funk, "Zip" made repeated trips to the brook, usually at night, and never failed to bring in the goods. This provided all the headquarters officers and men a bit of water on a fairly regular basis and provided a decent amount of what the wounded received. He took an enormous risk doing this, pressing his luck further with each trip, yet he escaped unhurt every time, though not without one or two close calls. It was these many risky trips to the brook that was no doubt uppermost in Major Whittlesey's mind when he later recommended Pvt. Cepaglia for the Distinguished Service Cross. Few, in fact, deserved it more. (29, 51, 109, 152, 153, 192, 219)

Private Emil Peterson in Company H also made the trip for water a few times, though he does not mention whether Major Whittlesey was aware of it or not:

"There was some muddy water to be had down below the hillside. This was in the open and very dangerous to get to as the German snipers would fire at anyone who would attempt to reach it. I made two

393

or three trips with several canteens and got them filled for myself and for some of the boys near me. Each time I was lucky enough to get back safely." (224)

So was Private Hubert Esch, a Company C replacement from Minnesota:

"I took five canteens down to the water hole located below us and filled them with water. The next night I filled five more, and got back safely. Major Whittlesey found out about this in some way and he ordered me not to go anymore as I might get hit. The Germans had snipers located around the water hole and it was a dangerous place to be in and many got killed near it." (44, 198)

Others were not so lucky, as described by Private Roy Lightfoot of Oregon, also a Company C man. "Comrades all shot up and lying around under trees and every place," he later said and remembered:

"It was worse when you crawled down to the foot of the hill after water; dead bodies all around the water hole and the water had lots of blood in it. But it tasted good anyway..." (44)

Private Arthur Swanbeck of Company K had his own close call getting water:

"One morning I went down to a shell hole to get water, but a German sniper spied me and he started punching holes in the water. So, that was the end to the filling of the canteens..." (44)

Others recalled a man that went down to the brook and came back with a canteen leaking from several bullet holes; certainly a close call. Rainwater too, collected in helmets, mess pans, or shell holes, relieved the situation to a degree, but there was only a relatively small amount of that available. In fact, so many had already died attempting to get water that the Major ended up sending out a general order that no one was to try and get water without first getting permission from either he or Captain McMurtry. The Major then posted several guards, mostly taken from Lt. Schenck's Company C, along the edge of the hillside to keep an eye out for those sneaking down to get water unofficially, particularly at the spring over to the left. He then gave them orders to shoot anyone they saw doing so (all the while knowing that just having the men on guard would likely be deterrent enough.) (29, 51, 135, 239)

Despite the failure of the Germans to launch a morning attack, the afternoon nevertheless brought one on at about 3:00 p.m., beginning with the usual ranging bursts of machine-gun fire into different points of the Pocket. NCO's called out to their men to get down, but it was a useless order as everyone had ducked low at the first shots. Then, all at once, all the German machine-guns opened up with everything they had - which was a lot. Apparently, the midday lull had less to do with the artillery barrage that morning than it had to do with the Germans setting up more machine-guns aimed into the perimeter. A veritable barrage of bullets, thousands of them, pelted the Pocket from one end to the other in terrible, whipping streams, just about a foot off the ground. Everyone stayed hunkered as low as they could, those who had spent some of their precious, remaining energy at deepening their funk holes ever grateful for having done so now. What little brush cover remained on the blighted hillside was slowly being eliminated as wave after wave of bullets swept across the position. Sapling trees and ground brush continued to litter the area, cut as cleanly as if by a scythe, while the higher of the funk hole parapets were slowly whittled down to ground level. One man, in Company G, just *had* to put his hat on the end of his bayonet and stick it up out of his hole. He was rewarded with a virulent hail of lead. Some, surprised by the suddenness of the attack, failed to get down quickly enough and paid for it dearly. One unnamed writer left behind these impressions of being under fire:

"Bullets flayed the soil in straight streaks, breaking the stiffened limbs of corpses, perforating and ripping the bodies, plunging into the vacant faces, bespattering the dried out eyes. We feel the heavens burst over our heads and the earth opening under our feet. Everything is swept away by the blasts of a tornado of projectiles." (21)

The suddenness and viciousness of the machine-gun fire seemed even to startle the ostensibly imperturbable Major Whittlesey. As the first shots raked the ground around him, he leapt up like a frightened hare from where he had been crouching talking to some soldiers and took off like lightning for the hole he shared with McMurtry, which was nearby. He long jumped into it, nearly landing on the wounded Captain, as bullets zinged past. He slid to a stop in the bottom, head tucked well in. Quickly regaining his composure, he looked around at McMurtry and, with an indignant expression exclaimed, "Most unpleasant!" The Major may have been commenting on the weather for the amount of emotion he emitted. Captain McMurtry merely looked sideways at him with a rye smile. (29, 51, 109, 135, 148, 149)

Lieutenant Cullen was shouting orders to his men above the din, as was Captain Holderman on the right, when, after about 20 minutes, the first blasting eruption from a potato masher rent the hillside. It was followed in quick succession by several more and then a hail of rifle fire as the Germans launched their first wave of direct attacks on the Pocket for the afternoon, coming at the men from the front yet again. At the first sign of movement following the initial round of grenades, everyone stationed below the road was at its edge, leveling a volley of Eddystone and Chauchat fire at the attacking Germans. A few shrieks from up on the hillside were followed by another round of grenades sailing down through what remained of the leaves above the Doughboys, some exploding in the air just above their heads with a stunning effect. Another round of rifle fire burst forth and the Germans came on again. Another line of Doughboys behind the first rank under the road poured fire over the heads of their stunned comrades and into the line of enemy soldiers, again holding them in check. Even Lt. Revnes of the machine-guns was there, popping off with his .45 automatic and dragging his wounded, swollen leg behind him.

For once, the attack was not as strong against the left as it had been and for that Lt. Cullen was grateful. He directed some men up to the road to pour fire in from that flank against any attackers that may have made it down to road level while at the same time maintaining a vigilant watch all along his now modified left flank position. On the right flank, Captain Holderman was instead getting the belly full of attack that was usually Lt. Cullen's fare. There, from the little cliff behind his position, came round after round of grenades, in bundles and in singles, while the machine-gun off to one side prevented any of his men from scaling the steep hill to stop the grenade attacks. Then, from the heavy brush at the foot just east of the cliff, came a round of rifle fire. The Germans had scooted down the hillside from farther off the flank and come in under cover of the grenade attack to nail the Doughboys from the side. Captain McMurtry, who had drug his wounded self over there to see what support he could lend Captain Holderman's men, was blazing away with his .45 not more than 10 feet from Lt. Pool when the young Texan officer took a shot directly in the back. Seeing this, a few men fell back and Captain McMurtry yelled out for them to get back into position, and then for first aid for the lieutenant. Shortly, medic Pvt. Irving Sirota came tearing down the wagon path, jumping from remaining bush to funk hole to shell hole between grenade blasts, scooped up the wounded Lt. Pool and quickly made his way back to the wounded area with him. Both Lt. Pool and Captain McMurtry remembered the brave act too, and Sirota, the little 31-year-old ex-druggists clerk who had been born in Minsk, Russia and enlisted in good faith to serve his new country, later got the

Distinguished Service Cross on their behest.

Captain Holderman, meanwhile, had gathered up several men and rushed to help plug the hole that Lt. Pool's wounding had caused. The limping, multiply wounded Captain had already taken the brunt of a German grenade blast only shortly before, which had left him with his face cut above the bridge of his nose and his right wrist badly wounded. Nevertheless, he set his men in a small semi-circle and in almost no time they had the Germans pushed back outside the perimeter line again. (29, 51, 109, 131, 135, 144, 148, 149, 150, 204, 218, 234, 245)

The afternoon attack on the Pocket continued in this vein for the better part of an hour and a half, vicious and intense and with the center of the position taking the main brunt of the push toward the end, admirably defended by Lt. Schenck and his men. They, along with what remained of the auto rifles and Lt. Cullen's telling flanking fire off the left, were enough to keep the enemy at bay, until the attack apparently lost its appeal and finally broke up. By a little after 6:00 p.m., everything was mostly quiet again and the men were settling down for another night of misery as the darkness, rain, and the last of the trench mortar shells relentlessly fell. There had, luckily, been only a few casualties, which was surprising considering the very violence of the machine-gun barrage that had opened the attack. (Major Whittlesey, ever the master of understatement, would later say in his official report on the days spent in the Pocket that the machine-guns during this particular attack fired "with an intensity difficult to exaggerate," and that it was "one of the most unpleasant features of our entire experience.") However, Lt. Pool's loss was especially hard hitting, for even though he was still alive, he was too bad off to continue leading his men. Another officer gone; another gap in the chain of command. Captain Holderman, wounded in various places of his body as well as both legs, was now hobbling around on a discarded rifle, refusing to stay put. Instead, he had his dressings wrapped tighter and continued at the head of Company K. With Sgt. 'Jimmy' Carroll assisting him even more now (indeed, even calling many of the shots), the Captain never once wavered. Each round of attacks saw him right up front, .45 in hand and a grim smile on his bloodstained face. (27, 29, 30, 109, 116, 149, 245)

Captain McMurtry came crawling back to the command hole about a half-hour after everything fell quiet and slid in next to Major Whittlesey. The attack on the right had been very trying and a lot of grenades had come down on the Company K men, all of whom the Captain had nothing but praise for, most especially the wounded Holderman. A natural soldier, that one. He had even lead a force up the hill ahead during the attack to try and flank the Hun flankers from above, dragging his wounded legs painfully along as they crawled up to the muddy embankment at the road. And though they were beaten back down by machine-gun fire from up on the hill across the road before they could do any good, something like that took a lot of pepper to do, wounded as he was. (44)

As McMurtry sang a song of Holderman, the Major examined the wounded Captain carefully. He looked very tired and his knee was terribly swollen and... "What have you got there?" Major Whittlesey asked suddenly. Captain McMurtry just looked at him uncomprehendingly.

"Turn around." There was something sticking out of the little officer's back, up near his shoulders and toward the center, almost at a right angle. The Captain turned sideways in the hole, Major Whittlesey grabbed it and gave a slight tug and the mystery object came easily free - with a tremendous yelp from McMurtry. The Major held it out for the Captain to see. It was a small part of the wooden handle from a German potato masher grenade.

Turning back around, Captain McMurtry, his face screwed up with pain and his shoulders hitched up high, looked at Major Whittlesey severely.

"Murder!" he exclaimed. "If you do that again I'll wring your neck!"

The Major grinned into the darkness and chuckled softly.

"Go get it dressed. I won't do it again; there was only the one. Did you not know that you were wounded?" he said, still chuckling.

As the Captain crawled off to see one of the medics, it began to dawn on him just why he had gotten so many strange looks and heard some men snickering behind his back as he had crawled over to the command hole just a short time before. At the time, he had neither understood what it was all about, nor cared; he'd been too tired. Now, as he crawled along, he thought that somebody might have said something to him. After all, it wasn't all *that* funny, was it? (29, 51)

Early that afternoon, General Hunter Liggett, commander of the 1st Corps, personally paid a visit to General Alexander at 77th Division PC. General Liggett was a straightforward man and wasted no time getting down to business. He asked how the attack was progressing and if there had been any headway in General Alexander's zone of advance. The Division Commander was forced to admit that there had not been, knowing all along that the information could not be good for the visit. And, what of Major Whittlesey's situation, General Liggett asked? Again, General Alexander was forced to admit no change, but pointed out that he was driving the 154th Brigade as hard as he dared, in order to elicit the necessary line rupture. General Liggett listened stonily and then again got right to the point. General Pershing had heard of the situation, not only with the 77th Division as a whole but also with Major Whittlesey's command in particular, and was not happy about any of it. Not only was the 77th holding back the line in the Argonne (and thus the whole of the left flank of the offensive), but if the Major's force in the ravine were to be wiped out, or captured en masse, that would create a public relations nightmare for the AEF when the folks back home got wind of it. Therefore, the Commander of the AEF himself was passing along specific orders for the relief of Major Whittlesey's command at once:

Direct that a vigorous attack be made this afternoon to relieve the companies on the left of the 77th Division that are cut off. Suggest that they be notified by airplane of the attack so that the action of the people cut off will be coordinated. (131)

General Alexander read the message over and then inquired if he understood correctly - he was to suspend his own General Order #27, which actually had been, in its own way, merely an extension of General Pershing's own General Orders of Battle for the 1st Army itself. General Liggett made it clear that, under these extreme circumstances, the orders for no retirement of captured ground might be set aside and the focus of operations shifted from rupture of the line for the sake of advancement of the offensive, to instead rupture for the relief of Major Whittlesey's forces. The situation demanded it, as did their overall commander. The force in the Charlevaux Ravine *must* be relieved. 2, 31, 43, 131, 144)

General Johnson had by this time (around 4:00 p.m.), already reached something of an impasse in the Ravin d'Argonne. He had gone as far as he was likely to go and called up the mortars to prepare the way for one last try. He sent his current report of situational information back to be called in to General Alexander and runners out to the l'Homme Mort bunker to fetch his blankets, as he had decided he would stay with the men in the ravine that night rather than back at the bunker. The coordinates that he sent back were the same erroneous ones that he had been giving ever since the start of the attack:

Have not been able to advance my line more than 300 yards beyond this point and am up against wire and trenches on both sides of the valley. I am still trying to push my men forward and pass between ends of trenches. The Boche has machine guns in bottom of valley which commands this interval. I am putting

Stokes mortars on the point I believe these guns to be located. Shall continue to push and have directed Captain Breckenridge, who is in immediate command, to push his troops forward. (131)

Lieutenant Fitch and his mortar crews arrived around the time the message was being phoned to General Alexander and began to throw rounds down the ravine again, now almost denuded of any under foliage in that area. They had, so far during the push up the Ravin d'Argonne alone, already expended well over 400 rounds trying to move the infantry just the distance from the l'Homme Mort bunker to the Giselher trenches south of the Charlevaux Ravine (about a kilometer and a half). Even as General Johnson had them begin laying in shells against the gap between the hills, there would be little prospect that they could accomplish what the General hoped for in this one last gamble and, in fact, they did not. When Captain Breckenridge took his men forward and tried to slam them through the gap some 45 minutes later, they were stopped cold again by enemy troops that had survived the shelling . By just after 5:30 p.m. then, General Johnson was sending back word that the ball game was over, his men had lost the inning and they were then pulling back into more secure positions again. He had contact with the French commander on his left, who he found had orders to maintain his position behind the 308th's line, and had asked him to advance at least even again along the Binarville-Moulin de l'Homme Mort road. By dark, Company I had liaison with them but it did not really matter, for everything was eerily quiet except for the standard shelling and machine-gun annoyances of an Argonne night. It seemed as if the Germans were just as exhausted as the Doughboys. (29, 91, 131, 144)

General Alexander, meanwhile, after having gotten the last messages from General Johnson concerning the attacks' failure, immediately began making plans for another try on the line for October 6. This time, though, the attack was aimed at relieving Major Whittlesey, as per General Pershing's orders. If the situation had made little impression on the division commander on October 3, and his primary concerns of October 4 and the morning of October 5 had been the breaking of his line first and foremost, then General Liggett's visit had definitely changed all that. Orders from General Pershing were as orders from God himself, and if General Pershing deemed Major Whittlesey's relief necessary enough to give up ground, then it must be made so. They would airdrop another message to Major Whittlesey specifically ordering him to retreat, while committing the rest of the 154th Brigade over there to a massive cooperative assault with the French aimed at driving through the line and meeting up with the Major's forces. With pressure from both sides, the Huns would surely give up the ghost and there could at last be the longed-for reconnection.

But were the Major and his forces still there holding on? No one had yet heard directly from him, despite the insistence of a certain French 9th C.a.P officer that obviously did not know what he was talking about. They had definitely heard some ammunition being expended late that day on the other side of Hill 198 though, and that gave at least some hope. In any case the orders were to try and so try they would. With that in mind then, at about 6:00 p.m. General Alexander sent Colonel Hannay over to personally see Colonel Lahm at 1st Army Air Service Headquarters. At the same time, Captain Klotz and Lt. de Coppet went back west to see the French and further coordinate arrangements for the morning's cooperative attack.

The two liaison officers brought back the answer to the question of whether the Major's force in the ravine was still there hanging on about 9:30 p.m. that night. The French had taken a prisoner sometime that day who had stated that the group of Americans surrounded out ahead of their main line were indeed still there in the Charlevaux Ravine, and still holding out defiantly.

Colonel Hannay, meanwhile, brought the order to be airdropped to Major Whittlesey over to Colonel Lahm with instructions that it be dropped at once that evening, as well as the next morning, by orders of General Pershing himself. The patrols of the next day, along with the message, were to drop a generous supply of food, ammunition, medical supplies, and another basket of pigeons. The entire attention of the 50th Aero Squadron was to be directed at bringing relief to Major Whittlesey's men. There should be no misunderstanding of the importance of these missions - lives were depending on them.

From: Old Dreadnought
Date: 5th Oct.
To: Detroit Red
Retire with your forces to Regimental PC. The attention of the enemy in your rear is being held by our rifle and machine gun fire. This should enable you to locate the enemy by his fire and strike him in the rear and flank. (131)

Colonel Lahm once more recognized the deadly seriousness in the situation, not the least indicator of which was General Pershing's own personal interest. Therefore, the Colonel again personally took the message over to Lt. Morse at Remicourt. Arriving around dusk, Colonel Lahm stayed until the two planes, sent immediately out with copies of the message, got back later that evening. He then called Colonel Hannay direct with the news. Meanwhile, plans were made on the aerodrome to drop supplies into the ravine. The bundles themselves were made up by the mechanics, who worked all throughout the night on them. The pilots to carry out the first missions the next morning were thoroughly briefed on the matter. Coordinates given by Colonel Hannay, through Colonel Lahm, were double-checked against the maps. There could be no mistakes; this time they must be on target, without fail. It was 10:30 p.m. before Colonel Lahm left Remicourt in the midst of all this activity.

Though they did not yet know it, the two planes that had gone out that evening with the messages (the crews of which still remain unidentified with any exactitude) had already widely missed their mark. Still unaccustomed as they were to that sort of work over the featureless landscape of an evening shrouded woodland, they actually dropped the two messages just within the edge of the French zone west of the Charlevaux Mill, some 800-900 meters off the mark from Major Whittlesey's left flank. (2, 10, 91, 131, 132, 138, 139, 141, 144, 146)

About the time that the two planes of the 50th were winging their way out with the messages, in the Pocket the Major was again contemplating how best to get word back to Colonel Stacey at regimental (whom he had no way of knowing had by then been replaced). With the wounded in a very sorry state, it had become imperative that something be done quickly, the medics had said, or else they were likely to loose a good many very soon. Sergeant Lionel Bendheim, of Company C, was in particularly sorry shape. With a leg that had been shattered by a mortar shell quickly filling with puss, he was obviously not only in very great pain, but would need to have the smashed appendage taken off soon, if he was to live beyond the infection then corrupting it. Nevertheless, Sgt. Bendheim had since given up his spot in the wounded area and was now sharing a funk farther to the right with his officer, Lt. Schenck. Captain Holderman's wounds were also beginning to look gangrenous, further exacerbated by the fact that he refused to sit still for any length of time. (29, 338)

Yet despite all that, many men (in particular the New Yorkers) remained in fairly good spirits, even though few now believed that they would ever see anything beyond the ravine again. Many of these were also resolved to bring down as many Boche as possible before the end came; if they had to sell them, then they wanted to sell their lives for as dear a price as they could command. Some of the replacements were another story though. Stunned initially by a battle that they had been wholly unprepared for, and more non-reliant in the Major's abilities than the regimental originals, their bonds of duty were not nearly as strong. In fact, Major Whittlesey had overheard talk among some of possible avenues of exit from the ravine - with or without the rest of the regiment. This was talk of out and out desertion in the face of the enemy and particularly disheartening, as it spoke of a breakdown of spirit at an individual level, which in turn then destroyed the team effort so necessary to bring about success, or even survival. That would mean that the command, in some corners at least, was beginning to break down in basic structural determination. The next step would be a collapse of morale, followed by annihilation of the position. However, if they just had some sign of coming relief, or even of resupply, that might boost the flagging morale in those corners the critical few degrees necessary to induce a sustained fight.(I)

Therefore, it was imperative that they get word back of their plight and let Colonel Stacey or General Johnson, or even General Alexander, decide their next move. A runner successfully through might also be able to lead medical help or carrying parties back the way he had gone, which would in turn provide the morale boost then so desperately needed. In any case, they had to try *something*, even if there was little chance of success.

Therefore, not long after Captain McMurtry crawled away to get his back taken care of, Major Whittlesey called softly into the falling darkness to the remaining scouts and runners in the holes around him asking for volunteers to again try to make it back. The smaller the numbers, perhaps the better the chance, so he only wanted two or three. There was a distinctly pregnant silence. Everyone knew the chances were slim. Many had gone out to try and many had not come back. Then, a voice spoke up.

"I'll try, sir." It was Private Joseph Friel, a New Yorker and one of the few Company A men still on his feet.

"Anyone else?" the Major asked, wanting at least a second man. Two could keep each other's morale and alertness up. Then, he caught an eye not far from him.

"What about you, Botelle?" Runner Private George Botelle had already been a major asset in the Pocket, carrying messages all over that barren hillside and never failing in his mission. Now however, he apparently felt that he had already done his bit, hemming and hawing some at the Major's inquiry.

There was a short, whispered exchange between the Battalion Commander and the Company C runner, the Major laying the situation out on the line to the Upton man plainly. Somebody had to get back and let them know what was what, or else it would be curtains for them all. Private Botelle heard him out and then thought hard for a minute before,

"All right. I'll go."

The Major gathered the two together and, in deadly earnest, told them to demand to be taken to Regimental PC as soon as they got through the line. He gave them a verbal report to give once they got back - what the conditions were like in the ravine, the need for food, water, medical evacuation and fresh orders - and made them repeat the message. Then they dropped their rifles, helmets, gas masks and rifle belts, each arming themselves with just a .45 pistol and two clips of ammunition, before then crawling through the brush toward the creek. As they crawled out past where some of the outposts had been playing at the dangerous sport of sniping back at German snipers in the dark, they passed the body of Pvt. Frank Martinez of Company G along the way. He had lost his round of the game when he had been nailed in the head from so close a range that the impact had popped both of his eyeballs out of their sockets. At the brook, they stopped a moment and carefully drank their fill before moving off again through the brush. It was not long after they had gone that the men in the Pocket heard the heavy rattle of a German machine-gun off in the direction the two had been going and so figured they were done for... (29, 51, 109)

With Friel and Botelle on their way, Major Whittlesey again started his rounds, inspecting positions and lending encouraging words. He was out on the right flank with Captain's McMurtry and Holderman, when off in the distance they heard the distinctive cough of a Chauchat from over on the other side of Hill 198. It was not the sound of the beginning of a full-fledged battle, just a lone gun in the misty gloaming, which fired intermittently and was soon answered briefly by a German machine-gun. Somebody was pestering the Hun over there, no more. Yet, it set the Major to thinking.

"Listen," Whittlesey said and they all strained to hear as the Chauchat coughed again. "Does it not remind of the bag-pipes of Lucknow?" he continued softly and wistfully, referring to the old, Irish tale of another, long ago, surrounded command. The gun again chugged in the distance and as they all listened, Major Whittlesey suddenly ventured that if they all could hear that gun firing on this side of the hill, then perhaps *they* might be heard on the opposite side as well. If that were perhaps so, they might loose off a few rounds from a Chauchat as a signal to let them know over there that they were indeed still holding out in the ravine. Captain Holderman called softly into the darkness and a few moments later, a young replacement crawled carefully over to them with a Sho-Sho in tow. Major Whittlesey whispered what he wanted done and the man then aimed up the hill and let off 5 shots, paused, let off 5 more, paused and then let off 5 more; clearly a signal. It was all too clear, apparently, for after about the fourth round, enemy machine-gun fire came into the immediate vicinity and several Very lights lit up the rain-swept ravine like daylight for a few minutes. The signaling abruptly came to an end. (II) (29, 51, 109, 148, 149, 150, 245)

As far as Major Hunicken and the 245th were concerned, the day had definitely not worked out as planned. The artillery bombardment that had hit his men up above the Binarville-La Viergette road on Mont d'Charlevaux had been especially devastating and he had lost a great deal of them. Many that had escaped had only done so by crawling into some dugouts up there and riding out the storm. He had hesitated that afternoon about mounting any further assaults but had been persuaded, largely at Hauptmann Von Sybel's urging, to keep the pressure on the surrounded Americans. The Hauptmann had then settled for an intense machine-gun barrage and strong 'nibbling' attacks on the fringes of the position, mostly with grenades. During these, they had captured six more American soldiers, but the 122nd Regiment's companies had again lost their share of men and now their Regimental Commander was begging for them to be relieved before they were completely destroyed. Unfortunately, and in spite of the reshuffled dispositions of the 76th Division, they were still needed however, in light of the losses the 254th had suffered that morning on Mont d'Charlevaux.

There were problems elsewhere as well. The American drive up the Aire Valley was making far more headway than the German High Command could tolerate. Troops there had been worn out beyond effective usefulness against the huge American divisions, and there was now considerable shifting of units occurring within Army Group Argonnen (known hereafter as A.G.A.) General Wellmann had been informed that he would be losing the troops of the 45th Reserve Division that had only recently been given to him to fight the French and would be replaced by the 1st Prussian Guards, a unit that had been badly hammered in the Aire Valley. Army Group Argonnen General Staff felt that their strength, though not up to holding off the large American divisions, would be sufficient to hold the battered French at bay in the areas around Lancon and Autry. General Wellmann was not pleased by the news, but what followed was even more unpleasant.

A.G.A. also informed him that the situation had become so serious in the Aire Valley that, if further retreat there were warranted then those units yet holding out on any remaining sections of the Giselher Stellung within the Argonne Forest would be forced to evacuate and draw still further back to the Kriemhilde. To this, General Wellmann voiced his strong objection. His 76th Reserve Division was still holding out and would likely continue to do so. Why would the whole of the line need to be evacuated because certain divisions could not hang on? A.G.A. replied that the army could not risk having large pockets of its troops left to fight it out in salients of resistance and risk having them get cut off from the main body. Troop strength was too precious. Therefore, the 76th's Chief of Staff was to draw up plans for evacuation. These were not orders for evacuation, just the warning that such an order might be likely.

General Wellmann again broached the subject of the Pocket of Americans currently trapped just behind the 254th Regiment's line near the La Palette Pavilion. It might be possible to thwart some of the heavy attacks being made against the main line there - attacks apparently designed largely to reach this stranded band of soldiers - if he were given the storm troops he had earlier requested to simply destroy that damned nest of Americans. This would save lives that could better be used elsewhere on the line. According to Hauptmann Von Sybel, the 76th Divisions Operations Officer, the 254th's commander, Major Hunicken, had been doing everything and anything to get rid of the problem, but his troops needed help. There were, according to several statements made and verified by prisoners captured there, somewhere between 600 and 1,000 troops surrounded in that ravine, along with many wounded. This far outweighed what Major Hunicken had to turn against them. Additionally, eradication of such a large body of the enemy's men in one fell swoop would likely deal a serious blow to their morale, besides being a tremendous boost to the morale of his own troops in the immediate area. Elimination of the *Americanernest* could only do good, but storm troops would be needed.

The voice of A.G.A. on the other end of the phone paused for the briefest of time before finally agreeing to send a battalion of storm troops, complete with heavy equipment and flame-throwers, first thing in the morning. General Wellmann, pleased, then telephoned Hauptmann Von Sybel - the storm troops were on their way, a whole battalion of them, and would arrive in the morning. Hauptmann Von Sybel then passed the information on to Major Hunicken. Hopefully, it would not already be too late. (20, 29, 30, 35, 48, 51, 122, 123, 307)

Lieutenant Kidder Mead, who was the Press Officer for General Liggett's 1st Corps, had been watching with some interest the progress of the 77th Division through the Argonne Forest right from the start. During the First World War, the Army, for the most part, was the ultimate decision maker in what news from the front was released to the public and how it was framed. Therefore, Lt. Mead's main responsibility was to sift through a day's newsworthy events within his sector and send off daily, and sometimes twice daily, bulletins to the local civilian press headquarters, then located at the little town of Bar-le-Duc. (Another press station, located in Paris, was primarily concerned with what the French and British were accomplishing.) There, the civilian reporters poured over the bulletins and decided what was worth following up on and what was not. There was certainly a definite rivalry among the Associated Press correspondents and those of the Universal Press Services stationed at Bar-le-Duc to get the coveted "scoop". Nevertheless, they had all also entered into a sort of 'cooperative collective' with each other (though definitely not with the Paris office) and tried to share stories to a certain degree. After all, they were a rather small, intimate group in a rather dangerous position and it was a big war; there were plenty of stories to go around.

It helped that Lt. Mead of the 1st Corps had a nose for hard news, having worked for the New York World before the war and therefore usually only included decent story tips in his bulletins. This particularly endeared him to the Bar le Duc pressmen, who appreciated his candor and knew they could rely on him. Lieutenant Mead also knew a good human-interest story when he saw one, and, from September 29, he had been keeping one eye on a developing situation within the 308th Infantry Regiment of the 77th

Division, then on the far left of his front. His attention had first been drawn there by the replacement of the 308th's commander - an unusual event only two days into a battle. Then, following directly on the heels of that information, came word that the Assistant Regimental Commander had been killed trying to rescue a battalion of the regiment's men under a Major Whittlesey who had gotten too far advanced and had their communications line cut. Sensing a definite story, he included it in his daily bulletin that evening. The next day, a couple of reporters, one AP and one UP, showed up to get more information on what they thought could potentially be a good scoop. They were somewhat disappointed to learn that the situation was already rapidly clearing itself up and Major Whittlesey's men were no longer in very difficult straights. They gathered the few meager details there were and, in the next couple of days, a few short, one-paragraph items appeared in a couple newspapers back in the United States about the incident. The greatest significance to the event was that now it was more than just Lt. Mead who was keeping an eye on the story. One of those reporters, the UP man as it happened, figured that where there was smoke, there was bound to eventually be a little fire and remained on watch of Lt. Mead's bulletins for any further information on the situation of the 308th Infantry.

It was the news bulletin that Lt. Mead sent out on October 4 that originally spawned the legend of the Lost Battalion then, and the UP reporter was the catalyst. Lieutenant Mead had also kept an eye on the 308th. Being on the 'inside track', he had been able to make an educated guess as to what was likely to happen to Major Whittlesey's unit if it stayed the course it was headed which, of course, it had. The October 4 bulletin sparked the interest of the young Universal Press service correspondent Damon Runyon, who had earlier laid his 'claim', according to the pressman's gentleman's agreement, on any further 308th business following that initial episode on l'Homme Mort. (This was followed by a series of his buddies at Bar-le-Duc laying in their stakes for second and third rights on any story.) Smelling definite smoke the day he read in the bulletin Lt. Mead's first official mention of Major Whittlesey's predicament in the Charlevaux Ravine (October 4), he included the 'bite' on a list of developing stories he then sent to the UP cable editor in the states, Harold D. Jacobs. Then, immediately after the cable had gone, Runyon and fellow UP man Fred S. Ferguson hurried up to 1st Corps PC to get more details - just in case. There, Lt. Mead did not disappoint them and returning to Bar-le-Duc late that night, they found that their cable editor in the U.S. had already cabled back just a single, short message: "Send more on Lost Battalion." By the next day, October 5, Runyon was back at 1st Corps, this time with several more buddies, getting the latest on Major Whittlesey's predicament. And it was therefore on October 6 - a Sunday, the biggest newspaper day of the week - that America first woke to the news that Major Whittlesey and his 'Lost Battalion' were trapped behind enemy lines in the Charlevaux Ravine. (14, 29, 30, 246)

It was very late that night, according to Pvt. Jim Larney, when Pvt. Botelle surprisingly came crawling back, alone, through the perimeter line, with his head bleeding badly from where a bullet had laid half his scalp open across one side and cracked his skull. Private John, of Company A and then on outpost duty, saw him come in:

"That night the Major sent two volunteers back to see if they could get through now. In a short time one of them came back and was so badly shot he just made it. The other never returned..." (220)

He and Pvt. Friel had been ambushed by a machine-gun and Friel had been killed outright, Pvt. Botelle told Captain McMurtry. He was unsure where it had all happened or how he had actually gotten back; only that they had done their best and that the ravine was literally crawling with Germans. As he gave the report, medic Pvt. Jim Bragg wrapped a spiral puttee around a filthy bandage that was holding Botelle's torn flesh in place and then sent him back to his hole. There was no room left at the foot of the hill, nor any cover to safely dig the wounded pit any longer or wider, so Pvt. Botelle was better off on his own. Captain McMurtry, meanwhile, had crawled off to give the news to Major Whittlesey, whom he found curled up in the bottom of the command hole sound asleep and, reportedly, crying. (29, 51, 109, 135, 218, 245)

(I) It is possible – and most likely probable - that even Major Whittlesey's personal resolve was beginning to falter somewhat by this time. He too had listened all day to the breakthrough efforts being perpetrated on the other side of Hill 198 and had heard the eventual fading of the fire as the attacks over there first fell off in intensity and then ceased altogether near sundown. It was beginning to look like they would never break through from the rear on their own. Logic, then, might have dictated that Major Whittlesey would consider what had been suggested during the meeting on the afternoon of the 3rd; that of taking their own initiative and drawing their remaining forces back in attack against the Germans from behind, while at the same time the forces attacking up Hill 198 hit the Germans from their front. Though it would certainly be a risk, it would be no greater risk than they were taking by staying put and being slowly battered to pieces there in the ravine. Yet, that logic still did not marry with the Major's last orders, which remained firmly committed to, believing them to still be in full effect. And therein lay the quandary that no doubt haunted the Major (indeed, even after the war) and perhaps kept his own resolve in doubt. Common sense telling him to get out any way he could to save his men from ultimate destruction, countered by his almost inhuman resolve to adhere to his given orders.

(II) 'Three dashes' is a seldom used 'responsatory' code signal, of very old and misty origins, that means exactly what Major Whittlesey was using it for – 'We are here' or 'We are still holding on'. It is an easy enough signal to remember, can be perpetrated by any useful instrument to hand and was meant to convey its meaning over great distances of battlefield, or where line of sight between units or organizations was blocked. Its 'call' signal was 'three dots' and there is some speculation that this might be where the distress signal 'SOS' (which is three dots, three dashes and three dots) might have originated from. It is unknown whether Major Whittlesey realized the significance of the signal he was sending, but in light of his general intelligence, it would be more than likely that he did, even if no one over on the other side of Hill 198 did.

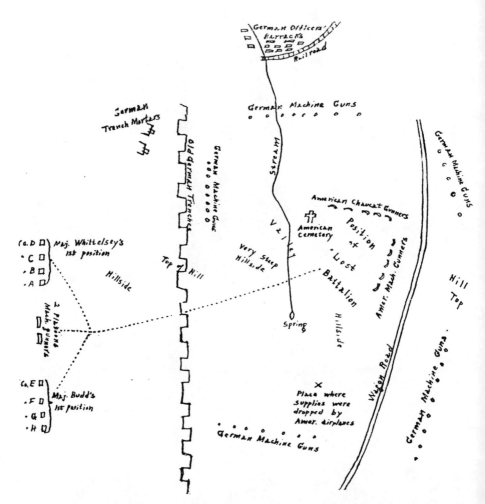

Hand drawn map by Pvt. Arthur Looker Co. B/308th

October 6, 1918 A.M.

"Direct that a vigorous effort be made this afternoon to relieve the companies on the left of the
77th Division that are cut off…"
General Hunter Liggett, commanding 1st Corps.

Dawn of October 6 revealed a truly ghastly sight in the Pocket as the casualty total pushed closer to the 70 percent mark. Little good, thick cover remained, many funk holes were now half caved in by the heavy fire and most contained a wounded Doughboy - if not a dead one. Most wounded were not even bothering to go down to see the medics now, since everyone realized there was next to nothing that they could do anyway. Instead, they tried to bandage themselves using anything at hand, with help from a buddy if needed. Many were not even reporting getting wounded anymore either, especially those good few who had been wounded more than once (in some cases even three or four times). As men dug into the hillside that first evening of October 2, they had joked between them about how often they had been forced to 'dig their own graves' in the Argonne so far and at how many times they escaped having to use them. Now however, the joke seemed to be becoming a horrifying reality. Said Pvt. John Nell:

"The number of dead was rapidly increasing, as was the count of the wounded. It was a deplorable and dismal sight to witness the poor fellows who were suffering with immense pain and bleeding terribly. The seriously wounded knew their time was limited. Every once in a while you could see a wounded man pass out and then see another get shot and wounded, as if to take his place… I well remember one poor fellow lay on top of the ground close to the hole I was in. He had a large (piece of) shrapnel about six inches long buried in his upper leg and a bullet in his stomach. He lay there two days before he passed out… Another man not far from him had shrapnel in his head. He suffered from the afternoon until almost daybreak. Both men suffered tremendously before the reprieve of death overtook them." (40)

Private Stanley Sobaszkiewicz, of Company H, also remembered a man hit in the head by shrapnel:

"There was one buddy that made me feel bad. He was just a short distance up the hill and to the right of my funk hole. He got hit in the head and was suffering for three days and three nights before he (finally) died. It was a relief to us all…" (44)

For many of the wounded that lay down behind the low wall of mud covered, rotting corpses, infections and gangrene were taking firm hold, and the death rate was climbing because of it. One of Captain Holderman's leg wounds had medic Jack Gehris very worried. Yet, the Captain ignored the medic's worries, staying instead in command of Company K and remaining unendingly cheerful. Many others, like Captain Stromee, carefully watched their own limbs for the telltale streaks of red just under the skin that told of the blood poisoning which shortly preceded tetanus; a ghastly, painful way to die. One delirious Company K man cried out incessantly, "Lieutenant Pool! Lieutenant Pool! For God's sake bring me some water!" A drink only stifled his cries for the briefest of time.

Over and over again, another called for a nameless lieutenant to come and roll him over, while many called for their mothers. A few quietly cried and shook with simple pain and fear while others had neither moved nor spoken in days, wrapped in a deep blanket of shock. A rain shower overnight had only added to their misery, but the temperature had finally gone up some, so at least it was not as cold. (29, 51, 109, 135, 245)

Crawling exhaustedly back and forth among the hurt men, long completely out of supplies Sirota, Bragg, and Gehris could do nothing but offer comforting words and perhaps hold a hand. Even many of the used bandages were now just too bloody and puss-soaked to use any more and everyone had already given what they could spare as far as underwear, shirts, and puttees went. The less appalling bandages, saved for men who at least had a decent chance at survival once relief arrived, were rinsed in what precious, muddy water could be spared and then reused again. Private John well remembered the scene at the bottom of the hill:

"The most terrible thing… was the fact that we could do nothing for the wounded… What little supplies each of us carried had long since been used. Even shirts, socks and underwear had been torn into bandages…Many wounded men would almost rot before they died (and) the stink was almost unbearable. They surely were brave though, knowing that we didn't have any food or water to give them, they didn't ask for much and didn't complain much either for the intense pain they must have been in. At night sometimes we would be able to bury a few of them in shallow graves or just throw dirt over them in their dugout (but) whenever (we) would stand up in sight, the German would open up… full blast." (220)

One man, who was brought in early that morning by an outpost, had been hit while crawling around searching German corpses for food the previous night. The Germans, who only came out after it was well dark to collect the bodies of their dead, had spotted the man in his search and wounded him. Advancing on him, they immediately bandaged his wounds up clean and tight. Telling him that since they had discovered the Americans in the ravine had honored their dead in the first couple of days by buying them (actually, Major Whittlesey had ordered it to keep morale up and the smell down), they would give the man a choice. He could, if he wished, return to the Pocket to stick it out with his buddies, or be taken back with them as a prisoner. The man chose to go back to the hillside and was let alone as he crawled off toward an outpost. Back at the wounded area, the medics found him to be the most well bandaged man among them and allowed him to return to the line. It was the single most decent act perpetrated by either side during the whole five-day siege. (29, 109, 118, 148, 149)

Major Whittlesey continued to move about the hillside, exhaustedly crawling through what cover remained and still visiting the wounded often. The strain was now apparent on his unwashed and unshaven face, but he simply still could not pass a wounded boy without lending what he could in the way of comfort. And while he continually encouraged others to visit the wounded, most preferred to stay away. Each man already had his own brand of misery to contend with and in any case, the smell of rotting corpses and infected wounds was far too revolting.

Captain McMurtry also continued to visit the charnel house at the foot of the hill, trying to be cheerful and give a degree of hope. His shattered knee was getting infected, as was the wound from where Major Whittlesey had pulled the piece of grenade handle out of his back the evening before. One boy, hit through the stomach, kept howling in a low, continuous and mournful way. McMurtry sat with him, stroking his hair and calming him until he promised, "It pains like hell, Captain, but I'll keep as quiet as I can." He died a half-hour later, never having made a further sound. (29, 51)

Private Larney, sharing a funk hole near the Battalion PC hole with Cpl. Baldwin and Pvt. Cepaglia, though wounded too refused to go the short distance over and join the others, so pathetic and repulsive was the scene. Instead, he made notes in his diary of the death and misery surrounding him. Major Whittlesey had seen him at it earlier and continued to encourage him to do so, despite it being strictly against regulations. He told Larney that he wanted a record of what had happened there, "just in case". It was the only time during the whole engagement that the Major reportedly showed a hint of loss in his seemingly limitless faith in front of the men, and then only privately to Jim Larney. (218, 152, 153)

The Major also continued to ask for volunteers to bury the dead, but few that morning had the strength to spare. Therefore, they remained lying for the most part where they fell, perhaps with a little meager brush covering their faces. Grotesque, twisted forms littered the hillside, as did bits of flesh and body parts, American and German alike, which blackened under the meager morning sun. Clotted blood sat in small pools on the ground or in the hollows of a corpses' exposed dead flesh. Many of the living noticed, much to their utmost horror, that the blood seemed to give off an unearthly glow at night, when the moonlight broke through the clouds and showed on it. Many dead were unrecognizable, such as the remains of Ben Gaedeke. After dying by Pvt. Pou's funk hole in the early morning hours of October 5, Pvt. Pou had since buried what had remained of the young Sergeant Major's body. However, the shallow grave was later hit almost direct by a German trench mortar shell, mangling the corpse further and sending it flying. What was later found was not positively identified until October 9, the date given on his grave marker in the huge Romagne American War Cemetery as his date of death. (29, 51, 152, 218, 245)

Private Arthur R. Looker, a Company B replacement from Viola, Wisconsin who had already suffered through the Small Pocket, now found himself forced to share his hole with the dead body of his best buddy, Private Marvin B. Long, a Montana boy, killed the night before:

"I shall never forget that night… That night "Marvie" and I were shivering in the same funk hole, the bottom of which was oozing mud so deep as nearly to go over our shoe tops. And the rain kept pelting us. Finally, shortly after midnight, we got up to find a little relief and being very wet and cold we tried to get warm by holding each other tightly embraced. But after standing thus for about two hours a machine gun bullet came along and killed my buddy right there. I know I was not the only one losing his buddy that night, but that doesn't take away the hurt of my loss — nor that of the other fellow for that matter." (267)

Private Nell also remembered the dead:

"It was a strenuous effort to bury the dead. But it was necessary because they were stinking terribly. So, you tried your best to cover up a mutilated corpse, which had previously been your buddy, your hole mate or someone close to you…" (40)

Lack of food was next on the list of miseries that continued to rapidly reduce the effectiveness of command. While the atrocious smell of the polluted corpses and rotting, infected, wounds actually helped drive away the appetites of those closest to them, for those farther away the ravenous hunger pains lead to radical steps. Many tried eating the occasional handful of cleaner looking grass or weeds and some chewed tree bark, while others tried eating leaves or twigs. However, the after effects were less than desirable - terrible stomach cramps and uncontrollable bowels. Many had entered the ravine already with a case of diarrhea, brought on by the strain and poor diet of those initial days of the advance. Now, this desperate diet, combined with the almost unending nervous strain of the first days in the Pocket (most especially the shelling on October 4), had only exacerbated the situation. The lack of accessibility to the latrine holes added greatly to the misery of that sickness. With no other choice, men were forced to remain in their funk holes and simply urinate or defecate into their breeches, thus adding to the already putrid smell of the hillside and the slime lining the bottom of most funk holes. Along the bottom of the hill, the wounded, many too hurt to move, also had no choice and were thus forced to lie in there own filth, as well as the filth of those around them. (This included dying men, who had a tendency to relax their bowels and bladder as they slipped away.) All of this led to an increase in the serious infections that the three impotent medics were powerless to treat.

For some, however, the lack of food seemed to have little effect. Private "Zip" Cepaglia, whose water forays certainly helped keep both the men in Headquarters Company and the wounded somewhat well supplied, later remarked that after the first day, he "got used to it. Didn't get all worked up; just took things as they came." Lieutenant Eager, who admittedly had not had to face the initial first food-barren week of the Argonne push, was even more matter of fact:

"Some people ask me if being without food didn't bother me or bother us a great deal. Speaking for myself, I can say that it didn't bother me too much after the first day. The first day was the hardest, but after that I did not seem to mind it so much. We were able to get water because there was a big shell hole at the bottom of the hill and the stream running down there kept it filled up all the time with fresh water. We would go down at night and come up with water enough to do us during the day time." (243)

The German dead that had fallen too close to U.S. positions for their comrades to retrieve were thoroughly searched for food as quickly as possible, but usually there was little to be found. What there was, was sent to the wounded in most cases. (I) (29, 109, 116, 135)

In Company H, Pvt. Lowell Hollingshead had been having cruel dreams of food. In his dream, he would wake in his hole to find everyone gone. Wandering back down the hill the way they had come in, he saw the company mess sergeant, standing near a field kitchen and beckoning to him. Visions of steak, with mountains of mashed potatoes and lakes of brown gravy danced in his head and he ran toward the kitchen, mouth watering. But he was racing the whistle of a shell and before he could reach his bounty, the field kitchen and all its food disappeared in a great explosion. Waking up abruptly with rumbling stomach, Pvt. Hollingshead looked around at the familiar sight of the torn hillside around him as another echoing whine approached. One of the trench mortars had woken up and was dropping in its shells at a slow cadence. There was a hot chip of aluminum on his shoulder - the remains of the mess kit of the man in the hole next to him. The man and the hole had taken a direct hit and almost completely disappeared; almost, but not quite and Holly's appetite rapidly diminished under a wave of nausea. And that was how Pvt. Hollingshead's fourth day in the Pocket began. (29, 33, 163, 222)

Ammunition too was beginning to run dangerously low in some spots of the Pocket, so the dead were being searched for more than bandages and food now. A few managed to drag in a couple German rifles and some ammunition for them, along with a few precious potato masher grenades and were able to keep fighting that way. One man even nabbed a fine sniper rifle with scope. But for the machine-gunners there was nothing that could be done, as German ammunition was not even close to the 8mm rimmed stuff that the Hotchkiss's and Chauchats fired. Only three of the heavy guns now remained functional and there were virtually no trained gunners to handle them. However, the forays grew fewer and fewer as strength dwindled and the odds grew seemingly too great. Private John later remembered:

"We soon started to search the dead men for… ammunition. There were a lot of men lying just outside the woods in the clear space. Once I tried it out there to search (for) ammunition but the bullets were flying too thick for me. It seems they were coming from all sides… close enough to clip the leaves off the trees and

low brush so that they would sting the devil out of my face. Yet none of them hit me..." (220)

Yet, despite the danger, many of the stronger men continued volunteering to go out at night and search the enemy dead, though sometimes with dubious results. One Company K boy, his head swathed in a filthy bandage and just back in from a food search mission the night of October 5, pleaded for permission from Captain Holderman to go back out again. Permission was duly granted and the young man slid off through the moonlit brush with pistol in hand. He was gone for hours and all feared the worst when he suddenly showed back up just before dawn of October 6, dirty, bedraggled, and all smiles, presenting Captain Holderman a fine, enormous and elaborately ordained German pipe. *'Here you go, Cap. The previous owner wasn't using it anymore.'* The food search mission had actually turned into a souvenir search mission, and the boy was loaded down like a camel with pipes, precious German tobacco, watches, belt buckles, buttons, notebooks, pens, and generally anything else he could safely and quickly stow in his pockets and tote back. And the moral? Never underestimate the American desire for souvenirs. Captain Holderman also took it as a sign that morale, at least among his men, was still rock solid and if the Boche did overrun the position, they would likely have to kill every damn one of the Doughboys to do it. (29, 109, 149)

However, general morale, that fourth morning in the Pocket had taken a new, different turn downward. No longer was the anger and frustration of the men directed exclusively against the enemy. Instead, some were directing it toward each other. Many men seemed to have run out of patience almost completely with virtually everything, their tempers flared and harsh words were spoken all across the Pocket. Men who were the best of friends under normal circumstances were shooting smart-assed answers at each other over the simplest of questions and bickering over otherwise long-forgotten details. "We got to where we hated each other more than we did the Germans," one man remembered years later. Cohesion of the command against the common enemy seemed to be dissolving. (29, 219, 245, 338)

Up before the dawn again, Major Whittlesey made his normal rounds, took reports from scouts and outposts and visited the wounded to see how many had died over night. Along the way, a few more ragged scarecrows approached him with fear in their eyes, asking the Major when they would ever get out of there. And despite the Major's continued assurances that there were "two million Doughboys working to get us out", some of the men must have whispered to themselves, "Two million ... yeah... right," after he had passed them by.

It was just too bad that those "two million Doughboys" could simply not seem to get beyond that damned hill back there, while here in this damned ravine men were bleeding to death...

It was 5:30 a.m. when the crash of artillery began in the zone of the 153rd Brigade, and around 6:00 a.m. when troops began to once again battle forward against the German wire. Soon thereafter, General Alexander and his small entourage of staff showed up to inspect the goings on. He was already in perhaps more trouble than he knew over the affair in the Charlevaux and was most certainly going to see General Johnson about the matter today. However, he still had another brigade fighting the war to keep an eye as well and he had been ignoring them the past few days. In that sector of the line, the brigade commander, General Whittenmeyer, had the 2nd and 3rd battalions of the 306th Infantry holding across his whole front, with the 305th in support. They were slamming forward with reckless abandon as he and General Alexander walked along well back of the line. Their mission, outside of advancing the line of course, was mainly to assist the left flank of the 28th Division, on their right, in breaking past the sticking point of le Chene Tondu. There had been a little forward progress over there in the last day or two, General Whittenmeyer said, by way of encouragement.

However on the critical left, at the junction of the 153rd and 154th, they had been met by some serious resistance and the stall continued, the line yet dragging quite a few meters behind. General Alexander asked what steps were being taken to correct this and the Brigade Commander said that since there was full and solid liaison there, he had his left most company poised to give containing fire against the line on a slightly northwestern angle. This would likely assist units of the 307th that Colonel Houghton had detailed to try to break through at the joint from their side of the brigade dividing line. How it was going over there though, General Alexander would have to ask Colonel Houghton, since General Whittenmeyer had not heard anything about it yet that day. (2, 90, 91, 113, 131, 138, 139, 148, 150)

Strangely, by that time the main line of the 307th was following the track of the Ravin d'Charlevaux (though some 400-500 meters south of it) beginning just before the point where it took a southeastward bend, some 400 meters off Major Whittlesey's right flank. From there, both the line and ravine continued southeastward until a point just ahead of the junction between the 153rd and 154th brigades. Here, the Charlevaux was fed into by the Ravin de la Fountaine aux Charmes and its creek (though a different one from the one at the start of the battle), which ran down on a slightly southern angle from the east. After that point, where the two ravines and ribbons of creek met, the Charlevaux continued on its southeastward angle, crossing the main battle line on an oblique just to the right of the brigade dividing line and from there on into the back areas of the 153rd Brigade. The 153rd had, by then, moved into the heights of the Bois de la Naza where they faced the Ravin de la Fountaine aux Charmes, running parallel to their front line 300 meters ahead, and the Bois d'Apremont beyond that, standing between them and the Binarville-La Virgette road. Thus, the line from the 307th's left flank, on over to the right flank of the 153rd Brigade, resembled a shallow "V" shape that mirrored the track of the Charlevaux Ravine from a point 400 meters off Whittlesey's left flank, over to the junction point with the Fountaine aux Charmes, and then along that ravine over to the divisional dividing line with the 28th Division. The apex of the "V" in the line stood some 500 meters almost due south of the apex of the "V" formed by the junction of the two ravines and creeks ahead, and it was that joint that was proving to be the critical scene of action on that morning of October 6. (368, 370, 371, 374)

Seeing that all was well in hand with General Whittenmeyer's command, General Alexander then hightailed it over to see Colonel Houghton. As with General Johnson, there was no love lost between Colonel Houghton and General Alexander at all. (The Colonel obviously felt that the Division Commander was out of touch with the realities and difficulties facing his troops.) Therefore, when General Alexander found Colonel Houghton's advanced Regimental PC, set up in a hole dug under the roots of a large tree not far back from the firing line, with Lee taking care of his malaria-ridden charge, the Colonel greeted the Division Commander genially, if somewhat coolly. Ahead, the battle blasted forward and runners occasionally came in with field messages as the two officers discussed the situation. Colonel Houghton had his 1st Battalion on the line, Company D on the left and A on the right, supported by what remained of most of 3rd Battalion. Company D had already met with some serious resistance and A was withdrawing slightly by the time General Alexander arrived, but the line on the right had moved forward some. Colonel Houghton wasted no time or words letting General Alexander know his exact assessment, telling him that the German troops ahead were not the main problem; they were not class A troops by any means, nor particularly strong in numbers. The main difficulty in this section of the line - as it was in nearly all sectors of the Argonne - were the positions themselves that the Germans had taken up behind a thick girdle of wire. This wire belt was an average of 30 meters deep and in places 5-6 feet high. Nor was the belt laid out in straight paths, but instead kinked at intervals, giving German gunners good fields of fire around the corners. Factoring in the brush and weeds that had grown up around the tangles and a blockade of the first order had been created, making it almost impossible to get through. None of the artillery barrages on October 4 or 5 had done much damage, since nearly all the shells seemed to land well beyond the belt, or dangerously short of it. Though they were working at it on virtually a constant basis, Colonel Houghton said, they had no Bangalore torpedoes or wire grenades to blast their way through, since supplies were still well jammed up in the rear. Thus, they were forced to carve holes in the barrier by hand, always a slow and laborious process and costly in lives. Further, it seemed any progress made was quickly repaired by the Germans at night. In the morning, they were faced with the same barrier as before, if not stronger.

There was, however, one possible bright spot, the Colonel continued. One of his men, Lt. Fredrick Tillman, a New Yorker who had gone through Plattsburg and now commanded Company B, thought that he had found a 'weak seam' at the end of a switchback in the wire before the hill facing the regimental right flank. So far, this weakness appeared to have gone unobserved by the Huns. Early that morning, in the pre-dawn, some of his scouts had gotten through it and crawled all the way up to the junction of the Charlevaux Brook and the Fontaine aux Charmes Brook before sliding back. Still undiscovered as the watery sun started to rise, Lt. Tillman now had men working on slowly and unobtrusively cutting larger the gap in the wire there. If successful, they might be able to discreetly infiltrate a body of men directly into the German line, to there lie until such time as enough had built up to make movement profitable (not unlike the German tactics of infiltration). Then, they might move up the Ravin d'Charlevaux and come up to Major Whittlesey's right flank from that direction. However, it was going to take time and restraint to pull off the delicate maneuver right under the very nose of the Germans. In the meantime, Colonel Houghton had every intention of keeping the pressure up all along the rest of his front, in order to steer attention away from what was happening on the right. He requested that General Whittenmeyer direct his left-most company, then facing slightly northwest, to keep up an oblique covering fire from there, which he was doing. 2, 91, 104, 131, 138, 139, 144, 367, 371)

General Alexander was pleased with what he heard and directed that Colonel Houghton should continue his endeavors to drive up the Ravin d'Charlevaux to Major Whittlesey's right. Then the Division Commander set out to see General Johnson concerning his activities in trying to get through to Major Whittlesey's left flank from the bottom of the Ravin d'Argonne. It appears then that General Alexander was still determined to get through to Whittlesey by driving the line up to his flanks.

The morning had started badly for the Germans. General Wellmann was at breakfast when he received a typed report from Major Ditfurth concerning the order to prepare evacuation procedures. If he were to do such a thing, he would need to have back the Pioneers that Major Hunicken was using against the surrounded American troops in the Charlevaux Ravine. General Wellmann, with no other reserves to give, could do nothing more than sigh and agree to release the men, should the time come for such a measure. In the meantime, breakfast forgotten, he rang up A.G.A. and asked that they release some additional machine-gun detachments to him, along with the storm troops already coming, explaining Major Ditfurth's dilemma. A.G.A. promised him not only the machine-gun sections, but also another Pioneer company for Major Ditfurth. This willingness by Command to give forth with troops, when just a few hours before he had been told there were none to be had, did not sit well with the Corps Commander. There was obviously something up, he speculated.

Then came the call from Hauptmann Von Sybel at La Palette. It had been necessary, he said, for General Quadt-Wykradt-Huchtenbruck to release the soldiers of the 122nd from duty in the Charlevaux Ravine, since their two companies were down below 30 men apiece - and those 60 men were needed to bolster the faltering main line companies. With no choice, Major Hunicken requested two companies from the 253rd down to take their place. Additionally, the 254th's casualty totals had risen considerably in the last two days. If they kept on their present course, the regiment would likely cease to be a functional unit within as little as a week. Hand in hand, the promised storm troops - supposed to be the regiment's 'saving grace' - had indeed arrived that morning and reported to Major Hunicken. However, rather than a battalion of them, a mere 16 had shown up; 16 men from the 376th Pioneer Battalion, equipped with storm equipment, all that could be spared, they said, while the battle up the Aire Valley raged. Hauptmann Von Sybel asked, rather dejectedly, just what he was to do with a mere 16 largely untrained storm troops against an American contingent that numbered in the hundreds. True, they had brought flame-throwers, but he still had to wonder about the wisdom of using them without heavier back up.

General Wellmann was taken aback. A.G.A. had obviously played him for a fool and, all at once, he realized there would be no additional machine-gunners and no Pioneers. Without a doubt, things were much worse off than he had anticipated, and suddenly he understood that the order to prepare for a possible draw back to the Kriemhilde had been a red herring. The real order would no doubt come down from A.G.A. soon, meaning that all this determination to save the Giselher had been for nothing. And if they were beaten in the Argonne, one of the single toughest positions along the whole of the 480-mile Western Front, then the war was very likely lost. Angry at this, he told Hauptmann Von Sybel that he must do his best with what he had. That den of Americans must be cleared out, no matter what! The 254th already had too much time and blood invested in the operation to let it go, nor could it be allowed to continue to drag out endlessly. The whole damned affair was tying up troops that could be better served elsewhere. Therefore, that *Americanernest* must be destroyed! (33, 123)

It was a damp, misty morning again at Remicourt as Lt. Morse's flyers prepared for the day's heavy work. The mechanics had again been busy overnight and there were small bundles of supplies stacked all over the squadron's operations shack, many well wrapped in blankets. Ammunition for both rifle and pistol, as well as for machine-gun and auto-rifle, hand and rifle grenades, food, medicine and bandages, a couple crates of pigeons with little flare parachutes attached … everything Major Whittlesey and whatever men he might have left would need. All the 50th men needed to do was deliver the goods.

But, there arose the question of just where the Major and his command were… Several flyers had been over that ravine now, and not one had seen an American uniform or a U.S. ground panel there. How could they be sure that they were dropping on the correct spot? So far, the only troops that had been spotted down there had been the Germans that Lieutenants French and Frayne had called the barrage down upon. The PC of the 77th Division was reporting Major Whittlesey's command as "down on the bottom of the ravine" and had passed along coordinates sent back by the Major himself, including those from the "For heaven's sake stop it" message of October 4. However, these did not ring true with where the artillery thought he was; *they* stated that those were the coordinates on which they had fired the afternoon previous, as directed by Lieutenants Frayne and French. So where then was the cut off battalion, if they were still there at all?

They were last known to be at 294.6-276.3, Lt. Morse told his men firmly and therefore that was to be their aiming point. The Squadron Commander had been provided with copies of almost all of Major Whittlesey's pigeon messages by the 77th's Assistant Chief of Staff, Lt. Col. Howze, who was by then on the aerodrome to watch operations and report on their efforts to General Alexander. Lieutenant Morse had also studied the map with Colonel Lahm the previous night. However, *knowing* where the spot was on the map was not the tricky part, Lt. Morse told his flyers as they gathered around an infantry map spread out on a large table. The tricky part was going to be *finding* that correct spot over the featureless and fog hidden landscape below them as they sped along at 70 miles per hour or more. Additionally, wind speed and direction, prop blast, weight of the object being dropped, and speed of the aircraft would all figure in to make the assignment all the more difficult. And as if that was not enough, they would also need to fly very low, thus exposing themselves to what would likely be very heavy ground fire.

It was very quiet then in the operations shack as the crews waited for dawn to break at least a little, and the mechanics loaded bundles into the observers' cockpits.

The first of the DH's roared off the field toward the Charlevaux at a little before 6:00 a.m. with Lt. Harold Goettler at the controls and Lt. Erwin Bleckley, in the back seat, surrounded by so many food parcels (and a crate of pigeons) that he could hardly squeeze in. The heavily laden No. 2 plane lumbered into the air and over St. Menehould, where Lt. Goettler turned toward the forest. They had never gained any real altitude and were at slightly less that 1,000 feet, sweeping blindly through the haze, with the ground coming only occasionally into view. Finding anything in that ravine at that height would be almost impossible. As they neared the forest, they eyed the pink flashes of the firing artillery through the mist warily

At Vienne le Chateau, Lt. Goettler turned the plane true north, dropped still lower and followed the road into Binarville. It was a quick trip and over the battered little village where he steered northeast, signaled for Lt. Bleckley to get ready, dropped the nose of the plane and headed toward the slot of the Charlevaux Ravine in a shallow dive. They came out of the heaviest of the fog at about 300 feet up in a sweeping turn that pointed them almost due east. 'Dad' Goettler then leveled off at about 200 feet and they began a run over the ravine while 'Bleck' quickly double-checked his map. They were in the right spot, no doubt about it…

A hail of enemy gunfire met them as they roared down the valley, engine running full out and haze swirling behind them. A glance to both sides showed that the heights of the hills on either side had risen above their top wings. They were actually *in* the valley! He pulled up a bit over some trees and 'Bleck' fired a Very light, hoping that Major Whittlesey's men would fire one in return. There was no answer, nor had the observer seen anyone below that might be U.S. troops. They raced on down the valley (it was curving off to the southeast now) and 'Dad' pulled up to make a sweeping turn well over the 307th's zone. Lieutenant Bleckley looked back and down. Everything was just a whitewashed sea of green and brown trees with a thin ribbon of silver - the brook - snaking down the center and only occasionally visible through the foliage. It seemed hopeless.

Goettler swung around and dived down for another pass, again at less than 300 feet of altitude and the Germans opened fire again, heavier. Little holes appeared in the wings and they could make out the rattle of machine-guns above the roar of the engine. Bleck loaded his Very pistol again and when they were almost out of the valley, toward the west end, fired another round, all the while scanning the slopes of the valley on either side and the ravine floor. The very top of the northern slope he largely ignored; that was where Lt. French had seen the Germans yesterday and called in the artillery. The top of the southern slope was covered with little flashes of light (German machine-gun muzzle flashes) and certainly was not the spot they needed. However, it was easy to see the road along the side of the northern hill clearly and that was a good sign, as they could match it up with the map and thus tell that they were definitely over the right spot. As Dad again pulled the big plane up in a sweeping turn, this time just north of Binarville, Bleck looked back into the mist again. No answering flare, no small white ground panels, no one to be seen on the ravine floor.

Swinging around one more time, Lt. Goettler angled in and came into the ravine full tilt, again just above the treetops. Bleckley again scanned the ground; those men should be down there somewhere. A bullet suddenly smacked into the cabane strut right by Goettler's head and another ricocheted off one of Bleckley's Lewis guns. Then, looking ahead and over the left side of the plane Bleck squinted through the mist and something caught his eye, down near the bottom of the northern slope, just east of a little hillock sticking out of the hillside. Movement! A waving white something! Another bullet thumped into the plane somewhere close by. The ground fire was getting worse. Grabbing the bundles, Lt. Bleckley waited until he reckoned Dad had them over the spot near the movement he had seen and started heaving them over the side, watching them fall shortly to the ground. Another bullet slammed into the fuselage ahead of Goettler, but in a few moments they were up and out of the ravine and turning back for home. Bleckley tapped Goettler on the back excitedly as they swung around; he had seen something, and when they passed over the ridge of Hill 198, gaining height, he turned his guns down and peppered the Huns from above, giving back some of what they had gotten.

Back at Remicourt a few minutes later, the other pilots gazed in awe at Dad and Bleck's plane No. 2, which had more than 40 holes punched into it. The flight sergeant looked it over and pronounced it down for the day at least and the two intrepid flyers went to make out their report. Fog almost down to the ground and very heavy enemy fire had made the mission difficult. However, Lt. Bleckley was fairly confident that he gotten the bundles on target according to the map and, though he could not be absolutely sure, he had thought he'd seen some U.S. uniforms along the northern hillside of the ravine, between the road and the ravine bottom. He was sure he had seen some movement down there in any case. The artillery had fallen on that road half way up and above, correct? Maybe they were still there on the hillside then, just lower then where the artillery thought them to be. All that would be needed was a few more passes down the ravine to confirm it. Lieutenant Morse gave it some thought. However, with the fog almost down to the ground, he ultimately decided that there was no point in sending out any more patrols until the weather had softened up some. That battalion was not going anywhere. (47, 110, 141, 241, 249, 276, 277)

The sound of an approaching airplane had attracted some attention among the Doughboys in the Pocket, but not enough to cause anyone to jump up, run out, and signal to it in the open. There just was not enough cover left and the German machine-guns had started up at about 6:15 a.m. By now, they were well in tune, as were the two forward trench mortars. (The Germans had not yet replaced the one to the rear that the barrage had taken out the day before. That was something at least.) Yet, something had to be attempted, or so thought Lt. Cullen as the plane made a very low pass through the ravine and fired a Very light as it headed east. It was so low, in fact, that one could almost see the nervous pilot's face as the German machine-guns quickened their pace. Shouting to one of his men, this time Corporal John J. Bowden, Lt. Cullen tossed out a dirty white towel and yelled for the man to try to signal the plane if it flew by again. Corporal Bowden scrambled onto a little clear knoll and began dragging the towel back and forth across his chest as the plane wheeled and indeed came around for a second pass. Then, Lt. Cullen himself ran out into another nearby clear spot, lay down, and began doing the same. Down the hillside to the east, Pvt. Larney already had what was left of his panels out across some bushes, placed in the same spot as when the plane had come over the day before. The plane roared by again and let off another Very light. (29, 44, 109)

Then, a curious thing happened. As the plane turned and began another pass down the ravine, the observer leaned out and started to throw packages to the ground. Lieutenant Cullen and Cpl. Bowden continued their signaling as all eyes watched the bundles land and bounce once, twice and then roll through the weeds and brush - and right into German held territory. Further to the west, the first package that had been dropped floated down on the ends of several little parachutes and also landed out of reach. Obviously, the flyers were trying to drop supplies to them, but their aim was off by a couple dozen meters. The Doughboys watched as the packages came down so tantalizingly close, and then cursed the errant flyers. The bundles, like the water in the brook, were so near and yet so far. It would have been funny were it not so very cruel.

The plane wheeled and came for another pass down the ravine, Cullen and Bowden waving their towels like mad now, hoping above hope that they had been seen. However, this time the plane was gaining altitude and angling over Hill 198 and a moment later, they heard the observer's guns chatter. A few feeble cheers went up in the Pocket; if the flyers could not hit the mark with their stuff, at least they seemed to be with their guns and every little bit helped. Lieutenant Cullen and Cpl. Bowden each crawled back into their holes and all was again quiet on the hillside, except for the trench mortar shelling, the machine-guns playing and the wounded dying. (109, 135, 245)

When General Alexander got over to the Ravin d'Argonne, he found a muddy General Johnson and an equally dirty Captain Breckenridge surrounded by a motley collection of troops about a half kilometer north up the ravine from l'Homme Mort, setting plans to head into battle again. Though a barrage had fallen ahead and the Germans were in the process of giving back all they had gotten, there had so far been no attempt at advance in the zone of the 308th, only holding actions. What remained of the companies of the 308th were merged and mixed almost beyond recognition after the disastrous efforts of the previous day and a good many of the replacement lieutenants who had led them in had gone down quickly. Even General Johnson had taken a slight bullet wound to the calf, but had refused to be sent down. Discussing the situation with General Alexander, the Brigadier wasted no time in making the observation that there seemed little hope of a breakthrough up the ravine and the two generals quickly walked off alone. (2, 109, 116, 131, 144)

What was actually said between them was never recorded, but, considering their mutual dislike for one another, it was likely neither cordial nor quiet. General Johnson had now seen first hand what they were up against and might well have told General Alexander that the task of overrunning the German positions by simple frontal assault was virtually an impossibility. Perhaps he might have even explained that being as short of men and material as they were, there was simply no sound plan likely to carry those German positions. It appeared that Colonel Stacey and Major Whittlesey had been right; the positions were untenable.

What is known about the meeting however, is that General Alexander simply told General Johnson about Colonel Houghton's coming attempt to drive up to Major Whittlesey's right flank. He also reminded the Brigadier that he had the 2nd/307th - an entire battalion, mind you (such as it was) - at his disposal to attempt a drive up to the Major's middle, along the route that Whittlesey himself had taken in. He also had the remainder of the 1st & 2nd/308th, as well as all of the 3rd/308th, to get up to the Major's left with, as well as explicit orders to do so. Therefore, there would be no more argument; an attack would be made up the ravine that afternoon and Major Whittlesey would be reached if at all possible that afternoon.

Taking his leave, General Alexander went first to Depot des Machines to check on supplies for the attack and then set to arranging for a further attack to be made against Hill 205 on the morning of October 7, again in cooperation with the French on the left. Apparently then, his belief that the afternoon attacks by the 308th would amount to anything was a pretty thin belief. Besides, if there was any real chance of relieving Major

Whittlesey's situation, he later stated that he knew it was Colonel Houghton's plan that would accomplish the task, and not anything General Johnson might attempt. (2, 131, 144)

'Hey Yanks! Good stuff in the boxes. We thank you for it!' came the calls across the ravine from up on Hill 198. The Germans had retrieved the bundles dropped from the plane and one of their English speakers was now describing, in excruciating detail, exactly what each contained.

'Well…what have we here? Bully beef, hard bread, and canned stew? Whatever will we do with all this food? It is much more than we need. Are you hungry, Yanks? Perhaps you might care to come up here and join us?'

German laughter and a machine-gun rattle echoed simultaneously.

'Bandages and medicines? What ever is the matter? You hurting Yanks?' - another voice, viciously.

The Doughboys, hunkered in their funk holes, licked their lips at the mention of the food, exchanging glances, and then scanned the ravine behind them for any bundles they might have missed in their previous 100 examinations of the area. Meanwhile, the three remaining able medics could only bow their heads and close their eyes to avoid the faces of their crestfallen charges at the mention of the much-needed medical supplies.

'Aw, go piss up a rope ya goddamned Hienie prick!' followed by a few rifle shots into the bushes.

'Knock it off!' (severely) Ammunition was worth its weight in gold by then.

'What is this? More food? It is too much, simply too much. It looks as if we will have to throw some of it away!'

At that, the Pocket simply exploded in uncontrollable vile Doughboy language. In fact, Captain Holderman would later remark that he "had never before known that the American soldier's vocabulary contained so much 'enlightening information' and so many 'endearing terms'…" Major Whittlesey, also listening to the vulgar epithets being thrown across the ravine, mused that perhaps the men were not so beaten down after all. (29, 51, 109, 135, 148, 149, 150)

The one bright spot to the whole affair was that there was no morning attack at 9:00 a.m.; the Germans apparently were too busy taunting the Doughboys and eating their newfound bounty to get one together. In any case, the torturous descriptions being hurled into the ravine were, in many ways, worse than any conventional attack and the effects far more demoralizing. Nevertheless, the Doughboys figured that the usual German mid-day 'hate' would not be skipped however and as time slowly passed toward noon, they began to prepare themselves for another onslaught.

Meanwhile, much farther to the northeast of the 77th Division, the 1st Division was pushing solidly opposite and above the right flank of the 28th and driving hard away from the outskirts of the little town of Fleville (taken on the 4th), after having again broken past Exermont and beyond the armed stud of dirt known simply and innocently as Hill 240. Their casualties had been tremendous and unrelenting in the Argonne operations so far, totaling by day's end something in the neighborhood of 6,000 over the previous days of fighting, and they were tiring. Once well beyond Fleville however, they, along with the right flank of the 28th just below, faced almost due west and had orders to begin a drive against the German side from above the 77th's line. However the 28th was tired and worn as well, still with its left flank entangled some distance below at le Chene Tondu ('The Twisted Oak') and was unlikely to do much more. It was then that a brigade from the 82nd Division, fresh, strong and ready for a fight, entered the battle. Colonel Malin Craig, General Liggett's Chief of Staff over at 1st Corps, had sent them, their job being to give the drive westward that little extra 'vim' it needed off the 28th's flank. That afternoon of

October 6 then found them arriving between the 28th and the 1st Divisions and getting into position for what would be their real test of fire.

Meanwhile, to the left of the 77th Division, the French (still on a forward line of Autry-Lancon that then dived southward to Binarville) struggled to maintain their positions in the immediate Binarville district against fierce German opposition and counterattacks. Plans for demonstrations against Hill 205 had not come about, first postponed and then cancelled all together that morning, and the 9th C.a.P thus held their positions in and around Binarville. Their general line now ran ahead of the town and from there eastward about 500 meters above and parallel with the Binarville-Moulin de l'Homme Mort road once again. General Johnson had liaison with them along the track of the road somewhere, through Company I/308th, and sent an inquiry as to whether they intended to cooperate in the afternoon attack that General Alexander had ordered. They replied that they did not, and therefore General Johnson prepared to attack the Ravin d'Argonne wide open to his left once again. (8, 10, 35, 36, 42, 88, 109, 111, 116, 131, 146)

(1) Private Sidney Smith, in an interview given in 1980, made the statement that what food that was brought in, was confiscated by the officers and "kept for themselves", but this is hardly the truth. Virtually all food that was found was immediately given to the wounded, there being very few exceptions. Yet, at one point during the siege, Major Whittlesey came upon a boy munching on a big, dark, loaf of German bread. "Where on earth did you get that?" he asked him, to which the boy replied, "Off'n a dead Hienie. Have some, Sir?" Whittlesey declined the offer with, "No, thank you. You earned it; you eat it." But it must have been hard to turn down, and if Sidney Smith's assessments had been right, then surely the Major would have accepted it.

Ancillary sources used in this chapter include:20, 24, 27, 31, 34, 43, 49, Various 152-216, 225-229, 232, 233, 238, 239, 243, 250-254, 257, 260-264, 268, 269, 273, 278, Various 282-330

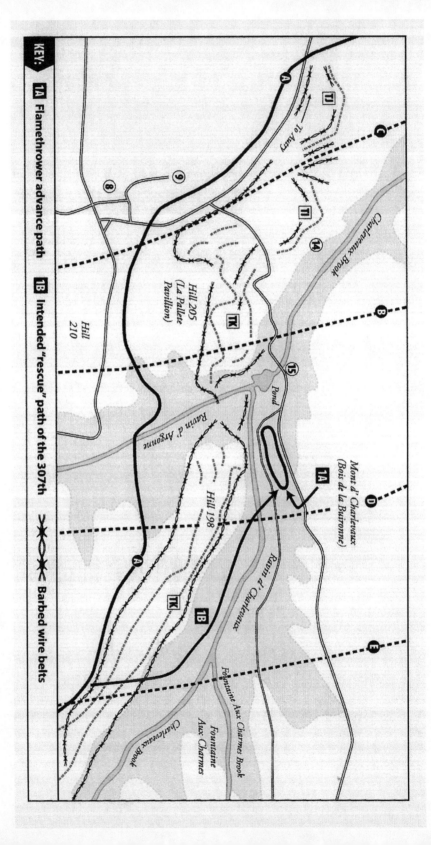

1A Flamethrower advance path   1B Intended "rescue" path of the 307th   ✳━✳ Barbed wire belts

October 6, 1918 P. M.
"We'll find 'em, or we won't come back."
Lt. Erwin R. Bleckley, 50th Aero Squadron.

It was 11:30 a.m. before Lt. Morse decided that the fog had burned off enough to begin the resupply relays into the Charlevaux. Just before noon the second flight of the day, plane No. 6 carrying Lt. Floyd Pickrell as pilot and Lt. Alfred George as observer, started out with a load of ammunition and food. The weather had indeed cleared, at least enough to see the ground from 1,000 feet and the team was soon swooping over Binarville and heading toward the Charlevaux Ravine at something near 400 feet. Two passes brought them nothing to show for their efforts however, only holes in the wings and fuselage. The enemy fire had gotten worse with the better visibility and Lt. George quickly realized what Lt. Bleckley had; it was very difficult to see anything clearly in that ravine at any real speed. Another pass closer to the ground brought intensified fire. Then, on a final pass, Lt. George rechecked his map and decided that they had to be in the right place. It was now or never. He heaved the packages out, signaled to Lt. Pickrell and the team zoomed out of the ravine and headed back to Remicourt.

There, the two flyers reported on the heavy ground fire as mechanics studied plane No. 6. Though it had absorbed a copious amount of fire, it was still not as bad as Lt. Goettler's No. 2 from that morning and they pronounced that it could quickly be made ready again. One thing was certain though; the Germans did not want those men in the ravine resupplied. As further proof of that, plane No. 12 carrying Lieutenant's Francis Slater and Shelby Batson, which had left about 35 minutes behind Lieutenant's Pickrell and George, landed and rumbled up to the hangers a short time later. It was shot to hell and Lt. Slater had taken a slug through the foot. Their report made clear that the ground fire was worse yet when they arrived over the ravine. The previous team had sure stirred up a hornet's nest for them! It would then likely be even worse for the team that had left after them, they speculated. (110, 241, 249)

Down in the Charlevaux Ravine, as the clock moved relentlessly on through another hungry day, Major Whittlesey's men watched as the planes started coming over again and the Germans turned their machine-guns skyward against them. None of these planes were calling for panels however, so it seemed obvious that the previous flight that morning over the Pocket had spotted their panels, or the waved towels at least. Still, the Major kept the battalion panels out, such as they were now, and Captain Holderman too put out some company panels he had found which had not yet been completely used for bandages, though by then they were rather small. Also, while most of the German guns were being kept occupied with 'things aerial', Major Whittlesey had a few men make use of the rare opportunity and crawl down to the creek with a few canteens. Blessed water! All too quickly the flyers were gone though and again not one single package made it into the perimeter, though a few had gotten close. 29, 149)

The team sent out after Lieutenant's Slater and Batson was that of Lt. George Phillips, pilot, and Lt. Mitchell Brown, observer, in plane No. 8. They had took off at about 1:15 p.m. or so and, sweeping down over Binarville only minutes after Lt. Slater had been nailed in the foot, they tore down the ravine at top speed and low altitude just as the others had. Almost immediately, they began dumping their supplies while ground fire ripped at them from all sides and the plane shuddered in Lt. Phillips' hands. East they traveled, the lieutenant pulling the big ship in a wide sweeping turn over the 307th's zone and then nosing down for another pass, still lower than before. Lieutenant Brown scanned the ground below and saw nothing but the flashes of enemy ground fire and Lt. Phillips dropped lower still, to a mere 300 feet, and Lt. Brown tossed the last of the packages over blindly. The small windshield shattered right in front of Lt. Phillips' face, followed shortly after by the altimeter on the dashboard exploding in a shower of little parts as holes appearing in the fabric at his side. One of the German guns had the range and wind good, that was for sure! Then came a dull 'thump' under the engine cowling ahead and the motor began to first miss and then slow, before finally coming to a stop altogether.

It was only the speed they were traveling at that carried them as far as they went - which was just far enough to fall out of German hands. Lieutenant Phillips held the nose of the rapidly sinking plane up and stretched the glide out as long as he could, but with only 300 feet of altitude that was not long. They barely skimmed over the trees out of the ravine and just managed to pass over Hill 205 and a heavily wired field in front of the German lines, before coming to a rapid, rending end. The plane hit, bounced and hit again, coming to rest in a shell hole in no-man's-land amidst a storm of enemy fire, right in the middle of a French afternoon attack. In a flash, Lieutenant's Philips and Brown were up and out of the plane and sprinting for the nearest cover (another shell hole), with enemy machine-gun bullets kicking up the dirt all around them and peppering their wrecked plane. There, French troops found them a short time later and brought them back to their headquarters at Binarville while German artillery quickly reduced their DH to matchwood. (110, 241, 249)

Around noon, General Wellmann received the expected, dreaded message that the situation in the Aire Valley had reached the critical stage. The Americans had advanced beyond the limits of General Von Kliest's exhausted troops' endurance to resist. The U.S. artillery was laying down impenetrable barrages of fire and the whole section of Army Group Argonnen over there, already bent well back beyond its limits, was beginning to collapse from the east. The order had then been issued by A.G.A. that all line units were to begin preparations to withdraw to the prepared positions of the Kriemhilde Stellung. The movement was to begin in 36 hours.

General Wellmann immediately, if futilely, called A.G.A. and offered protest, asking for more time. Just two more days he said, for his men of the 76th Division to destroy the nest of Americans then lodged behind his front (the only thing that apparently mattered to him anymore, since all else was lost).

The answer came back: You have 36 hours.

But the storm troops he had requested had only just arrived, and Major Hunicken and Hauptmann Von Sybel, orchestral conductors of the operations, still felt that they had a chance at eradication of the surrounded force. The situation was still in hand.

Answer: You have 36 hours. After that, evacuation will begin as scheduled.

Then, calling Hauptmann Von Sybel shortly after to give him the news of the orders for evacuation, he was heartened to learn that the regiment had brought down two U.S. planes already that day had been trying to drop supplies to the beleaguered force in the ravine. Major Hunicken currently had the pioneer/storm troops readying to push against the Americanernest and before the evening was up, the Hauptmann hoped to have good news for the General. The Corps Commander listened and then announced the gut wrenching order he had just received.

"…Therefore Herr Hauptmann, you have just 36 hours to complete the operation. After that evacuation will begin as scheduled…" (30, 122, 123)

Back at Remicourt, Lt. Col. Howze sent a message back to General Alexander at Division PC just before he started out for the 308th PC to check on further progress up the Ravin d'Argonne. By his estimation, the relays of planes seemed to be doing some good and General Alexander would likely be pleased. It was at least some good news:

Date: Oct. 6, '18
Hour: 1.20pm
Six planes working to carry out the supplies. Two of them had come back before I left the field, the first one returning claimed that he saw some movement around the point. The second plane did not see anything at all, dropped the supplies at point designated. The 1st plane dropped pigeons and says that he dropped the cage overboard in good shape and that the parachute opened so he thinks the pigeons were delivered alright.

With the supplies apparently getting to Major Whittlesey, General Alexander believed that there should be no problem in his attempting to break back through from the rear and meet up with General Johnson's forces somewhere over Hill 198, as per orders. (The Division Commander of course had no way of knowing that the Major had never actually received the instructions to do this.) By 3:00 p.m. or so, there were reports coming in that there was apparently a hell of a lot of shooting going on over on the other side of that hill in Major Whittlesey's arena, so he was evidently trying to make the link. Believing then that the ammunition and medical supplies had helped, the General immediately sent word to the 50th to continue with the resupply until he told them to stop. If General Johnson and Captain Breckenridge could get through that damned wire over there on their side, the terrible ordeal might finally end and they could get on with winning the war. (131, 141, 144)

However, the attacks that General Johnson and Captain Breckenridge perpetrated in the Ravin d'Argonne that afternoon were not anything like General Alexander expected. Instead, all they provided was a waste of time and another pile of casualties. The five companies of the 308th - if companies were what they could be called now - started out at just after 2:00 p.m. in the usual, loose assault formations under the usual, heavy German artillery fire. By about 3:00 p.m. they had managed to make it to within about 300 meters of the German main line, once again trying like hell to plow directly down the valley between Hills 198 and 205, where they were confronted by more fresh barbed wire. By 4:00 p.m. they had been stopped cold, were being plastered soundly and General Johnson was launching counter strokes against Hill 205 itself. Swinging far out to the left and looking for the French liaison forces that were supposed to be there, the General had no way of knowing that what French that *had* attacked, had already been stopped by German machine-gun fire and artillery 300 meters behind his left flank. By 5:00 p.m. then, the assault was a palpable failure (much as he had expected it to be) and the Brigadier reluctantly reported such to an unhappy General Alexander. Exhaustion blanketed the scene; even the mortar crews were tired of wasting their shells so fruitlessly. Most of what remained of the 306th Machine Gun Battalion, and that was not much, was now over backing the 308th and their associates in the afternoon debacle once again, the 2nd/307th. Private Charles Minder wrote that night of the area around the ravine:

"The infantry units are cut to pieces. There doesn't seem to be any way to get them out. It's impossible to get an ambulance into this jungle and we haven't any stretchers here and haven't seen any medical fellows for a long time. The wounded are lying out there groaning and suffering and all they get is first aid… the whole

section here sounded like a shooting gallery. The rifle shots were popping constantly. It's a queer sound when they whistle through the air..." (37)

The 2nd/307th, at the same time coming up again on the 308th's immediate right that afternoon, slammed forward against Hill 198 and was again stopped with virtually nothing to show for the effort. As usual, the preliminary half-hour artillery barrage that had led in the attack had done little damage. And though they continued, with Pvt. Minder and his compatriot's throwing copious amounts of lead over their heads and up to the ridge of the hill, by 6:00 p.m. they were pulling back, as were the remains of the 308th on their left. The fall of the deadly afternoon towards night's darkness found them again taking up muddy positions along a line extending eastward from the Binarville-Moulin de l'Homme Mort road. There had been a light rain falling intermittently nearly all day and now for a short time a true downpour let loose. Nobody however, had the strength left to care.

As for Colonel Houghton's 307th forces, the artillery barrage led off an assault made by his 1st Battalion on line, still supported by the remains of his 3rd Battalion, however no gain was made in this sector during the afternoon assaults either. When he heard about that, soon after getting the failure report from Brigadier Johnson, General Alexander called Colonel Houghton immediately and the two had a rather acrimonious conversation, only calmed by the Colonel's mention again of the seam in the wire to the front of his right flank. There, Lt. Tillman had been slowly working elements of his Company B through all afternoon and piling them up in holes, carefully and artfully carved out of the brush covered ground in inconspicuous spots behind the wire. If their luck held, they would gain an upper hand for sure. How long before they might be counted on to make a difference in things, the Commanding General asked. That depended, Colonel Houghton replied. It was a delicate operation that must not be rushed. General Alexander then demanded that he must have success by the morning of the following day and it was then that Colonel Houghton, malaria flaring and angry to boot, hung up on his Division Commander. (2, 10, 29, 91, 109, 116, 131, 138, 139, 144)

By 2:00 p.m., the air above the Charlevaux Ravine was again alive with machine-gun and rifle fire as yet another DH-4, this one with No. 14 painted on the side, began spilling packages out over the ravine floor - all of which again bounced right into waiting German arms. The pilot, Lt. Allen "Tracy" Bird, came in over the 307th's sector at a somewhat higher altitude than the others had and swung around while the observer, Lt. William "Billy" Bolt, looked back and fired a call for signal panels into the air. From somewhere behind, a few answering lights streamed into the air, but in no coded order that he understood. Maybe the infantry did not have the correct flares anymore. Lieutenant Bird steered the plane back down the ravine again and now Lt. Bolt brought his field glasses up and scanned both the valley bottom and the slope of Hill 198, but saw no sign of a U.S. presence; only the flashes from enemy guns, all over the place, firing up at them. He then turned his attention to the opposite side of the ravine as well and saw nothing there either except more trees and the slopes of the hill above them - on which plainly stood the enemy, also firing at them. As they raced along taking fire, it certainly looked to the lieutenant as if the stranded force in the ravine – if they indeed were where they were supposed to have been – had been overrun...

They were just reaching the western end of the ravine, when Lt. Bird distinctly heard a sharp 'whap' come from the front of the plane and the motor started to vibrate terribly. Alarmed, and immediately turning for home, the lieutenant gave her the gun and climbed as quickly as he could. If there was going to be a problem and he was going to have to make an emergency landing, he wanted height to buy some time with which to search out a safe spot. However, they never even made it to 1,000 feet. Just turning south over

Binarville, there was a loud 'crack', followed by another and then pieces of the propeller sailing out into air. A bullet had apparently hit the prop while they were over the ravine, upsetting the feather balance it required and the resulting vibration tore the laminated wood apart. The Charlevaux Ravine had claimed another victory over the 50th Aero Squadron.

They came down safely in a relatively level field between Vienne le Chateau and La Harazee, climbed down out of the now useless plane, answered the function of nature that their nerves had called up and then started walking toward Vienne le Chateau. Lieutenant Bolt was sure of what he had seen and the information needed to get back as quickly as it could.

Lieutenant David C. Beebe landed back at Remicourt with his observer, Lt. Daniel Brill, at about 2:20 p.m. He had been high escort for Lieutenant's Bird and Bolt and was surprised when he found that they had not yet returned. Immediately, he ordered his plane refueled and rearmed and more supplies for Major Whittlesey packed into Lt. Brill's cockpit. He would go out, search for the missing plane, and drop a load of supplies while at it. Standing by, he nervously chain-smoked and watched the mechanics work over the plane.

Lieutenant Beebe's mind was a thousand miles away then, when his best friend in the squadron, Lt. Harold Goettler, approached him. Since the morning patrol had put their No. 2 plane out of commission, Dad and Bleck had had plenty of time to analyze their early morning mission and believed that they had figured a few things out. So far, no one but Lt. Bleckley had actually seen anything definite in the ravine, in large part because of the intense ground fire, which was making it too hot to stick around for any good, long looks. Therefore, nobody had any real way of knowing for sure that the drops had landed where they were intended. Reason also deduced that the command, which according to coordinates was occupying a low spot between the road running along the side of Mont d'Charlevaux and the ravine bottom, were probably afraid to send up Very lights or to lay out their panels for fear of drawing enemy fire. In short, another reason that they had not been seen was because they did not *want* to be seen. Therefore, the only thing to do was root out their position by direct observation from a very low altitude and at a very slow speed. It was a lot of ground to look over, as well as a big risk against the ground fire, but what else was there to do? Additionally, by giving the Germans a target to shoot at and then marking down on a map where that fire came from, they could then deduce precisely where the Doughboys definitely were *not*, and thus increase the accuracy of the drops. They might then strafe the German positions from above as well, in order to further assist the ground pounders. And since Bleck was the only one who had yet seen anything at all, he and Goettler had discussed it and were willing to lead someone else in on a run to show them where he had seen the movement and begin the process. Was Beebe up for the adventure?

Lieutenant Beebe looked at Dad stiffly. With two planes and crews as yet unreturned already and every other crew that had returned reporting the ground fire steadily growing more stubborn, it was a gutsy plan. Stooge over the same spot and *let* the Germans shoot at you… it seemed madness. Yet, it was probably the only plan with any real chance of success, and taking the idea to Lt. Morse found the squadron commander agreeing with them, if apprehensively. With Goettler and Bleckley's No. 2 machine down for the day at least, Pickrell and George's No. 6 machine was quickly wheeled out and more bundles were packed into the observer's cockpit for Bleck to toss out as they scanned the ravine. Since the plane had already been filled with gas and oil to make a second flight that day, Dad and Bleck were ready to go shortly before Lt. Beebe was. Telling Beebe they would head out and get a jump on marking out the enemy gun positions, Lt. Goettler quickly clumped out to No. 6 and got in, anxious to get started. Once Beebe and Brill caught up to them, they could then begin their package runs together.

It was sometime around 2:30 p.m., and the big Liberty 12-cylinder was already ticking over when Bleck climbed up, squeezed into his cockpit around the packages and unlocked the twin Lewis guns from their hold-downs. With Lt. Morse calling out, "Good luck and be careful" in his ear above the exhaust roar, Lt. Bleckley turned and called back, "Don't worry lieutenant. We'll find 'em or we won't come back!" Then Dad waved away the wheel chocks, turned into the wind as he gave the DH the gas and took off toward the lines one last time... (110, 241, 248, 249, 255, 259, 277)

Noon had come and gone in the Pocket and the Germans still had not made a real attack that day. There, the Doughboys had listened to the sounds of battle coming from the other side of Hill 198 all morning, but the effort seemed not nearly as furious as on previous days. In fact, the only thing that had caused the men in the Pocket any stirring at all had been the relays of planes passing down the ravine - some of them at incredibly low heights - and the resultant ground fire thrown against them. More packages fell into enemy hands with each pass, followed shortly by the Germans announcing the contents of each and taunting the Doughboys unmercifully. Yet, even that did not bother the Americans as much as the lack of an attack. Most likely, the Germans were planning something big, and the longer the wait, the worse the thought of an attack became. When the afternoon attack finally did come - early; shortly before 2:30 p.m. instead of the usual 3:00 p.m. - with the typical heavy machine-gun barrage and the increased cadence of the trench mortars announcing its impending start, everyone was well on edge for it. (29, 148, 149)

Major Hunicken himself had taken charge of the German attack that was to go over against the Pocket of Americans that afternoon. He had positioned his men with a large contingent set to roll down the hillside from the front, and a second large contingent down in the ravine ready to set out against the American's left. A third was situated around the meager storm troops and a couple of flame throwers they had brought with them, gathered in an open spot above the Binarville-La Virgette road, well to the east of the American right flank. Hauptmann Von Sybel had not as yet been able to pass along to the Major the orders concerning the withdrawal that he had been given. Therefore, the Regimental Commander was operating under the assumption that the withdrawal was still only a 'possibility' and was completely unaware of the deadly earnestness that the operation had taken on. Therefore, he apparently had designed this attack to be simply a predict to a final, murderous assault, to be launched at a later time and meant only to 'compress' the remaining American force into a smaller area, thus making them easier to eliminate. The few participating pioneer/storm troops, big, tough, grim looking men, handled their deadly weapons carefully as they sat in the fall leaves of a shallow spot above the Pocket, waiting for the word to go and not worried much about the prospect of battle. They had seen it all before. Then, the machine-guns started up all around the hillside below, followed shortly by the first grenade bursts. With that, the men got to their feet, lit the pilot flames in the nozzles of their weapons and stepped down the narrow path on the hillside in the direction of Captain Holderman's right flank. (123)

At the presage, everyone in the Pocket immediately hunkered down and set themselves to meet what they knew was coming next. First, the rain of potato mashers; then a rush of Boche troops either from the road, against the flanks, or across the valley to the rear; followed by another round of grenades. It was as bad as the attacks had been a thousand years ago on l'Homme Mort, in that a man could never be sure from which direction they would come and were therefore unable make plans to beat it off. Except now, the men who had been out there were thinking of the l'Homme Mort incident as mere child's play compared to the Charlevaux Ravine. Those few that were still alive anyway.

Private Larney and Cpl. Baldwin were sharing a hole near the Command funk when the mortar fire started to get particularly bad. Private Larney, stiff and sore from his wounds, was genuinely glad for the company that Walter Baldwin presented for it helped keep his mind off his hurts. (The two were among the very few friends in the Pocket still able to talk for any length of time without getting on each other's nerves and would remain life long friends in fact.) And despite all that he had gone through so far in the Pocket, Cpl. Baldwin had still not received a single scratch. He certainly seemed to live a charmed existence and Major Whittlesey had recently named him acting 1st Battalion Sergeant Major in place of the still missing Ben Gaedeke, a responsibility he took very seriously. Suddenly, there was a roar and the two were showered in dirt and debris as a mortar shell exploded nearby and virtually buried them. Quickly, they scooped the loose dirt out of their hole and hunkered down again. (218, 245)

Lieutenant Marshal Peabody was in a hole just a little way up the hill from Cpl. Baldwin and Pvt. Larney when the attack announced itself with ranging shots of machine-gun fire. The little lieutenant, whose ripped up leg was filling with gangrene and puss and would no doubt require amputation once they got out if he were to live, had given up his spot in the wounded area for someone he considered more injured. Neither he nor Captain Stromee had the strength to verbally wrangle anymore anyway, so he merely sat in his hole, only speaking when spoken to, but otherwise locked within a world of intense pain. He occasionally might manage a twisted grin or perhaps ask if someone or another were still alive, but overall it was plainly obvious that if relief did not come soon, he would succumb to his wounds, perhaps within a day; two at the most.

Yet, Lt. Peabody never once complained or whined. Instead, he consistently thought only of the others around him and always shared out what water was passed to him with whomever had not had a drink recently. In light of his gallantry and plumb, he had been given the one single overcoat that there was in the Pocket to wear for a little while. It had been brought in by Lt. Griffin of H, who himself lay in a nearby hole with a stunned, "This can't be happening to me" look on his wounded, boyish face. Lieutenant Peabody was no doubt grateful for the chance to warm up a bit, since blood loss makes a body very cold and it may be assumed that the unselfish lieutenant had no thoughts of keeping the coat for very long. Not when there were others waiting for a turn too, after all. (29, 51, 245)

Whether it was a machine-gun bullet or a sniper bullet that got him no one could ever say for sure. Nor does it really matter. Major Whittlesey and Captain McMurtry had scrambled into the Battalion PC hole below him when the guns started to chatter, but it was obvious the hole would be little protection. Lieutenant Peabody made a comment that they had "picked out a rather exposed position" and the two Battalion Commanders, agreeing, then skipped over behind a little rise in the ground instead. All of a sudden, the wounded lieutenant came tumbling down the hillside, flopped over the top of Pvt. Larney and Cpl. Baldwin and rolled through their hole before stopping at the foot of the hill, without ever having uttered a sound. He had taken a bullet straight through the head and he had come to rest with his lifeless limbs flung wide and the precious overcoat now lay in the mud between the body and Larney and Baldwin's hole. Part of the story always had it afterwards that Pvt. Larney snaked out of the hole and grabbed the coat and that he and Cpl. Baldwin wore it in turn until nightfall, however Pvt. Larney stringently denied that. "Not so; pure invention!" he later wrote, adding:

"Pure invention about taking that coat! Peabody fell out of the coat all right, and it lay untouched by Baldwin and myself. Though we were tempted to use it, we didn't. (We) thought it bad luck…"

The coat was still there two days later when they were relieved from the Pocket too -

and still untouched. (29, 51, 147, 218, 245)

Then, the trench mortar suddenly ceased, meaning only one thing - the push was coming next. "Hang on, everybody!" someone in charge yelled out as the first round of potato mashers came down from above and the explosions ripped the air. Captain McMurtry had wiggled his way over to Captain Holderman's flank again once the machine-guns had slowed a little and Major Whittlesey was gathering a group of Company C men to meet the probable frontal attack, when suddenly a veritable wave of German troops came pouring over the hill ahead and down onto the road's edge. A wall of enemy rifle fire then slammed down the hillside, followed closely by a second round of grenades, this time from a closer angle and much more effective. The flanks too were being pounded with rifle fire and grenades, while from the rear the box was completed by the heavy machine-gun fire. It was the most coordinated attack yet and stunningly effective. Most notably, in the first or second round of grenades (no one remembered which for sure), one (or more likely several tied together) landed right at the gun that Lt. Noon of Company C/306th MG, the last machine-gun officer still standing, was operating on the left flank. In a blinding flash, it blew him, the gun, and his loader to pieces. Now, there were only two of the heavy Hotchkiss guns left, one on either flank. Private Jim Strickland of H was hit on the left flank as was Private Bill Armstrong of C, who almost had his head taken clean off by a piece of shrapnel from one of the last trench mortar shells. Meanwhile, down at the bottom of the hill a sniper killed Cpl. John Hinchman of C, and Pvt. Stanislaw Kozikowski killed the sniper in turn. (29, 44, 51, 148, 149, 150, 351)

As the first wave of Germans came on and the grenade volleys grew astonishingly heavy, Major Whittlesey directed some of the more mobile wounded out of their holes in the threatened area and sent them farther over toward the left, nearer the wounded area. At the same time, he had the more able of those wounded set up a defensive interior perimeter around the wounded area and the men who could not be moved. Private Larney later wrote in his diary, "I had great difficulty in scrambling out on account of being stiff and lame from the wounds," but move he did, right up to that new perimeter line with a rifle in his hands and Cpl. Baldwin by his side. (29, 218, 245)

Major Whittlesey already had the men just under the road's edge pulled back some and firing good, aimed volleys when all at once a second German wave came, spilling down the embankment and actually advancing into the edge of the Pocket. With yells and a roar of close-range rifle and grenade fire, the Boche hammered at the men in the funk holes. Barely *10 meters* separated some of the Doughboys from the Germans as they fought a little way further down the hill, until something in the Doughboy troops seemed to snap. Now, some of Major Whittlesey's ragged men stood fully upright in their holes, all caution gone, wide-eyed, intense, and screaming and began literally pouring fire up into the wall of onrushing attackers. The line of Germans wavered, rallied, wavered at a second furious U.S. volley (accompanied in one or two spots by a rush with the bayonet) and then began to fall back in some disorder. Then the Doughboys, still yelling like maddened demons, but picking their shots carefully and calmly, climbed out of their holes and actually began to give chase up to the edge of the road. Some stood on the road and fired up into the backs of the Germans as they scrambled up Mont d'Charlevaux ahead, while a very few climbed up after them and stood above the road and fired. Down on the left, Lt. Cullen watched a similar phenomenon from his quarter with some measure of internal disquiet. The fury with which the attack was being beaten back was almost scary to watch. None of the men had ever acted like that before and when it was all over, some of them came back down off the road still shaking with rage and shouting obscenities and epithets back at the Germans. It took some of them a long time to calm back down, while others, exhausted by the whole ordeal, immediately dropped off to blessed sleep once the attack had ended. (109, 116, 147, 148, 149, 150)

Major Whittlesey, watching from down below, continued to direct the defensive efforts and level his own revolver up the hill from time to time. Despite the breech of the line at the road, they seemed to be holding their own. Lieutenant Cullen had the left flank sowed up pretty tightly and Captain McMurtry had gone over to help Captain Holderman on the right, which also seemed to be holding. As long as the Huns did not come across the ravine from behind as well, they looked to be all right then, although the amount of U.S. fire had gotten smaller due to a general lack of ammunition. Yet that might also simply be an indication that the men were picking their shots much more carefully now, which would be a good thing. However, the report of Lt. Noon's death, and with him the loss of another machine-gun, was particularly bad news. Still, there was not much Hotchkiss ammo left to begin with so they were eventually going to lose the heavy guns anyway. Yet, the loss of the lieutenant himself was a hard blow; another officer gone, another chip taken out of the rock of control. Then came another potential blow to control as a man came running through the position from the direction of the right flank, terror filling his eyes and shouting, "Liquid Fire!" at every step.(I) (29, 44, 245)

"Liquid Hell!" shouted Whittlesey back. "Get back where you belong, damn it!" and the man turned back. But from the wagon road, looking down in the direction of the right flank, one could see the plumes of oily black smoke rising. Through what remained of the trees, came the glow of long pennons of living flame. (29, 245)

Over there, Captain's Holderman and McMurtry, both in little shape to be moving around, were yelling out orders to Sgt. Jim Carroll, who was largely directing the men's movements as the attack raged against the right. Then, coming down the wagon path came something different. There was a strange hissing sound that caused some men to pause and exchange puzzled glances just before, through the remaining trees, they watched the waning sunlight suddenly augmented by a sheet of living flame. The German flame-throwers had arrived.

Suddenly, the Company K position came alive with dirty, pale faces poking over the rims of funk holes. A couple men jumped up and took off west toward the Battalion PC funk shouting, while most others stared wide-eyed at the unearthly spectacle advancing toward them, their weapons hanging limply in their hands momentarily forgotten. Only a desultory rifle fire crackled as the stunned Doughboys sat frozen. Slowly, the demonic weapons advanced. Then, Captain Holderman rose full from his hole, two broken rifles holding his terribly hurt frame upright and began yelling commands to defend the position, his automatic in his outstretched right hand blazing away. With that, the spell was broken and the hillside burst again with rifle fire. Private's Vincent Witschen and Joseph Lehmeier, both Company K men, were being led to an outpost position by an officer (most possibly Sgt. Carroll) when the attack began:

"He took us to the right a little ways, but the Germans watched every move and the officer had not gone very far when they shot liquid fire at Lehmeier and myself. They missed us, but it was too close for comfort". (44)

The Germans did not miss everyone with the infernal machines. Private William Johnson recalled that he saw, "One of the boys got badly burned." It might have been Private Ludwig Blomseth, a Company G man:

"The Germans shot liquid fire over and I was forced to leave my guard post. My coat was on fire and as I ran to safety, I turned to see if my partner was coming and fell into a hole and decided to stay there. We tried to extinguish the fire by rolling on the ground, however some of the men were so badly burned they died." (44)

More potato mashers sailed over the heads of the men with the flame-throwers, to explode violently in front of the Doughboys who, fighting through their terror, were still holding a solid line of defense. Then, what was happening up at the road began repeating itself on the right. Carroll, Holderman, and McMurtry needed not give commands, for the men were control unto themselves, or rather controlled furies. Shouting and swearing, some of them between long, moaning sobs, they stood up in their holes as had Captain Holderman, drew beads on the onrushing Boche and let fly with deadly accuracy before themselves rushing the oncoming enemy line with the bayonet. A couple Doughboys immediately dropped and in a flash the terribly hurt Captain Holderman was up, out of his hole and dragging them back in; a superhuman effort for someone who could barely walk unaided by that time. Earlier that day, the Captain had taken a piece of trench mortar along his pelvic arch and had had trouble moving steadily upright ever since - until his men's lives were on the line that is. Then, the incredible officer's truly remarkable devotion to his men showed, in spades.

A Chauchat coughed into the bushes toward one of the flame-throwers and the jet of fire suddenly stopped. The Germans stumbled backward in the face of the furious assault and the grenades stopped coming. Sergeant Carroll himself ran forward and dropped to a knee, took aim at the remaining flame-thrower and fired. The big German carrying it dropped to the ground and a moment later was engulfed in a wall of his own flame. Meanwhile, the lone Hotchkiss gun and the Chauchat barked again above the sound of another solid fusillade of U.S. rifle fire. German fire had all but ceased now and the first flame-thrower had disappeared from evidence within the confusion. Doughboys were standing and firing, running and firing, kneeling and firing, and all were shouting and yelling like maddened beasts. Then, the Germans finally broke and ran all together with a few Doughboys giving chase down the wagon road shortly.

There, as abruptly as it had begun, the afternoon attack ended at around 4:00 p.m., again leaving behind in the silence only the groans and wails of the wounded. It had been the most furious attack to date and one that left many German bodies behind, but few American. It had also been one of the scariest attacks in many ways, flame-throwers aside. The reckless actions of some of the men had seemed almost ferociously inhuman and this bespoke of their extreme duress, which could only next lead to a complete end to personal caution altogether and from there the wholesale wasting of life. In plain English, many men simply did not care anymore. Some, now firmly convinced that they were never going to see themselves out of the ravine had, in their minds, therefore nothing left to risk. If that sort of attitude spread, as it was very likely to once the meager amounts of ammunition quickly exhausted, it would not be long before either wholesale desertion or mass suicidal attacks would begin, until the position became either simply too weak to hold, or self decimated altogether. (29, 40, 51, 109, 116, 148, 149, 150, 224, 246, 256, 267)

Major Whittlesey must have worried over that as he sat in the Battalion PC funk near the wounded once the firing had stopped. The loss of Lt. Noon and his Hotchkiss presented yet another problem, for without the two guns out on the left, that flank could not be kept secure in its current position. Consolidating the position further, as they had done once already, might relieve that problem some. However, doing so also increased their vulnerability to an attack against all four points of the compass. So far, the Germans had refrained from doing that and the two Battalion Commanders could only guess that perhaps the enemy's numbers would not allow for strong attacks from all four sides at once. Yet, if the Pocket shrunk much further, the enemy would surely find the task of an all around attack much easier. On the other hand, they themselves no longer had the numbers left to maintain the perimeter of the full position that they now occupied, even in its slightly shrunken form from what it had been on the evening of October 2. The breech that the Germans had been able to make in the center of the position from the road above during the recent attack was evidence of that. There were barely more than 275 men left to man the line now, and that was not nearly enough to maintain a firm perimeter of this size.

Another consideration was that they had already sent their coordinates back and to leave where they had said they were at might later cause problems for any relieving force. That bird had obviously gotten through a couple days ago and airplanes had been over nearly all day trying to drop them supplies. Even during the attack they had watched a couple wheel back and forth, thankfully drawing some of the fire. However, even though Captain Holderman had put out his company panels, as had Pvt. Larney the battalion ones, it did not seem as if they had been seen, since none of the dropped packages had even come close to the Pocket. Yet another point to be made, in the same vein as the misdrops of the air packages, was that a consolidation was not actually a move, *per se*. They would still be in the same space, just occupying a little less of it and that should not affect things all that much. Particularly if they kept their outpost line along the former perimeter line.

In the end, the decision was a short one, since the benefits well out-weighed the detriments. They had no choice but to consolidate further for safety's sake and Major Whittlesey sent Pvt. Cepaglia out to fetch Captain McMurtry while he began making the plans. (29, 51)

Lieutenant Goettler steered the DH out toward the lines from Remicourt and in a very few minutes, he and Lt. Bleckley were again turning beyond Binarville toward the Charlevaux Ravine in the gray afternoon light at about 2:45 p.m. Getting the ready signal from Bleck, Dad banked around Hill 205 and brought the plane down into the ravine below 200 feet, lower than they had ever been before - lower than any 50th plane had been in fact - and throttled back the Liberty until they were flying just above the critical stall speed. Then they began to pass back and forth and live the longest minutes of their lives as ground fire immediately slammed up at them in a violent storm. Some distance away, over in the French sector above Binarville at Rome Farm, William Ettinger, a New York-born ambulance driver with the American Field Service driving for the French, stood in the doorway of the farm's destroyed main house's cellar, now being used as a French advanced dressing station, and watched all that happened next:

"The afternoon of October 6th, 1918, I was standing in the doorway of a dug-out... watching a plane which was flying parallel to the lines at about 100 meters above them (or even less) at what looked to be a particularly unsafe and low altitude. Standing with me were a couple of Frenchmen — stretcher-bearers — and we were discussing the probable identity of the plane as none of us had ever seen an American plane before. Neither evidently had the French anti-aircraft gunners around there because both the French and German... machine guns were giving him a great reception. Although subject to a constant and terrific firing from all sides he continued, undisturbed, to fly up and down the line without (to us) any apparent objective as he was not shooting up the Boche trenches and did not seem to be directing artillery fire, but on the contrary was drawing everybody's fire for some distance around. He seemed to be patrolling a sort of beat... He then dropped some day signals (a row of smoke balls of some sort) which had the effect of decreasing the French fire but redoubling the Hienies efforts. He continued that patrol... certainly a cool customer (until) finally the plane, still at a very low altitude, dove head first to the ground. Three or four Frenchmen and myself reached him a couple minutes after he hit..." (241)

Lieutenant Goettler had been dead before the plane hit the ground, with a German machine-gun bullet in his head, and his body had become entangled in the wreckage and badly mutilated in the crash. Lieutenant Bleckley, thrown some distance from the badly mangled plane by the impact, was found to be just barely alive with massive internal injuries. Ettinger and his pals immediately carried the wounded flyer back to the first aid post at the farm, where the doctor on duty worked on getting him stable for slightly over half an hour. Finally he told Ettinger to get his ambulance and take Bleckley to the 110th American Evacuation Hospital at Villers-Daucourt, still some 18 kilometers from St. Menehould, since the wounded man needed much more care than he could get at a mere first aid post. However, the doctor also made it clear that he did not think Bleckley's chances of surviving the trip were particularly good.

Ettinger carefully bundled the badly injured flyer into his ambulance and took off at top speed. Bleckley was the first of his own countrymen that he had hauled in France and he was determined to give him at least a fighting chance. "All I could think of was, 'God, help me to get this boy back in time to be saved' over and over again," he said later, "and cursed everything and everybody that got in my way." However, right outside Villers-Daucourt, he was held up by a French train and, for nearly 20 minutes, he was forced to argue with the engineer until he finally moved the train enough to let Ettinger through. By then, it was too late; Bleckley had died by the time they unloaded him at the hospital just a couple minutes later. (241)

Lieutenant's Beebe and Brill came swooping in low over the ravine only a few minutes after Goettler and Bleckley had made their final pass. There they met a terrific web of ground fire from all sides. It was hotter than they had expected in the ravine, and Lt. Beebe searched the sky all around for the No. 6 plane while Lt. Brill sat nervously in the rear cockpit, marking ground fire hot spots on his map. Slowly, they circled above the ravine, slightly higher than had Dad and Bleck, at about 300 feet. The plane was taking a serious pounding and it seemed as if every gun in the world was firing up at them. Another pass - where in hell was Dad? Lieutenant Brill gave the signal he was going to drop his stuff; it was just too damned hot in that ravine to stay. Beebe nodded understanding and the observer quickly tossed the load out and they turned for home, bullet holes piercing the fabric of the plane everywhere. Goettler must have found it too hot for the plan as well, Beebe thought.

Back at Remicourt, a few minutes later, the mechanics gathered in another silent circle around another shot up DH after it had rumbled to a stop in front of one of the canvas hangers. It was a wonder that the thing had managed to make it back for the amount of holes it had collected and even more of a wonder that neither of the crew had been hit. Lieutenant Beebe, unfolding himself from the cramped cockpit and standing stiffly up, quickly scanned the field all around him. Plane No. 6 was nowhere in sight. *"Where's Dad?"* he asked Lt. Morse anxiously as he climbed down from the sieved plane. "Didn't you meet up with him?" the Squadron Commander answered and the two officers simply stared at each other wide-eyed and silent for a moment before then turning and hurrying for the telephone in the operations shack. (110, 248, 249, 255, 259, 277)

As Major Whittlesey and Captain McMurtry crouched in their hole near the wounded area, all around them men were dragging back into their original positions tiredly. The perimeter had held - this time. However, the men were tiring faster these days as the lack of food, water and decent rest took more of a toll. What would happen tomorrow if such a determined attack again came over, as it was likely to?

It was then that Sgt. Hauck of Company D/306th MG (who was now in charge of the machine-guns) came up to report on the flame-thrower attack. This was the first Major Whittlesey had heard of it, recalled Pvt. Larney, since the soldier that had run over to him screaming about it earlier. They had been pretty successful in driving them off, Sgt. Hauck said. Out of the bushes they had come, two, maybe three of the damned things. They had turned their gun and a Chauchat in there and that had seemed to do the trick. The sergeant was dirty and looked drawn and tired and Major Whittlesey listened with growing concern. Anyone hurt? No one the sergeant knew of (although two bodies would be found later that night by Company K's Private Sam Altiera while he was out on patrol, burned nearly beyond recognition). "Okay," said the Major. "Then that's what you have to do if they try it again," and he thanked and then dismissed the sergeant. (245)

Darkness was rapidly descending when another man crawled over to see the Major right as Sgt. Hauck slipped away. It was Pvt. Sidney Foss, of Company K, and in the gloaming, he slipped Major Whittlesey a note sent over by Lt. Maurice Revnes, the wounded machine-gun officer – the only one left alive now from the 306th MG, as a matter of fact. The lieutenant had been a tower of courage ever since he had been wounded early in the siege and had gone to the battle line for every single German push that had been made, using first his pistol and then, after ammo for the .45 gave out, grabbing up a rifle and more than doing his bit with that. All the while, he was in tremendous pain from his own, now half infected, half gone foot. Yet, helping in the defense of the perimeter had seemed to ease some of the distress he felt over the general situation, and for that reason, he had hung on just as long as he could.

Now however, he seemed to have come to the end of his endurance. Having sat among some of the most severely wounded for some time, before then moving in to a hole with Sgt. Anderson of Company A and Pvt. Foss of K, he had seen first hand the unending suffering and misery that accompanied the worst imaginable of deaths. And since he was the only machine-gun officer still alive and in possession of most of his faculties, technically he was still in charge of what remained of both C and D of the 306th MG's. Therefore, Sgt. Hauck (actively in command and in control of the guns on the left) had been keeping him updated on things – and recently, they did not look good. The sergeant had reported after this last attack that only enough 8mm ammunition remained for the guns to sustain about 12 more minutes' worth of fire for all three guns combined. Sergeant Anderson (helping Sgt. Hauck out and in control of the lone gun on the right), had also corroborated that fact. The next attack then would likely spell the end for the automatic weapons, and without them, it was just a matter of time before the flanks were overrun. (147, 245)

Therefore, the wounded lieutenant had recently come to the conclusion that there simply had to be some relief of the situation attempted, if only for the sake of those whom death had yet to overtake. To that end, he had sent the note to Major Whittlesey, in which he suggested, if not exactly surrender, at least the arrangement of a truce with the Germans to allow the more severely wounded to be gotten back through the line to receive the medical care they so desperately needed. It seemed an eminently plausible proposition, one that the Germans could hardly refuse, especially since they had even bandaged and allowed to return to the position that wounded Doughboy a short while ago:

Major W.

If our people do not get here by noon, it is useless for us to keep up against these great odds. It's a horrible thing to think of, but I can see nothing else for us to do but give up - The men are starving - the wounded, like myself, have not only had no nourishment, but a great loss of blood. If the same thought may be in your mind, perhaps the enemy may permit the wounded to return to their own lines. I only say this because I, for one, cannot hold out (much) longer (and) when cornered as we are, it strikes me that it is not a dishonorable deed to give up.

Revnes (147)

Major Whittlesey read the note with growing dismay, passed it to Captain McMurtry to read and after that put it in his pocket. Concern creased his tired, dirty face and he murmured something to no one in particular about Lt. Revnes "being a little scared." Asking Pvt. Foss where the lieutenant was, the private pointed over to the right and offered to show the way. Telling Captain McMurtry to continue with the consolidation of the perimeter while he went to look into the note, the Major then slipped down the hillside in the darkness behind Pvt. Foss. In a couple minutes, he was sitting down next to Lt. Revnes, talking with the hurting man and quickly saw just how poorly the past few days had affected his resolve.

Silently at first, the Major heard Lt. Revnes out and then firmly explained in his low voiced, positive way just why the proposition was not feasible. Never mind that fraternization with the enemy was illegal under U.S. military law. To make a deal such as had been suggested would be tantamount to tipping their hand to the Germans. So far, the Huns really had no idea how many they had in the ravine, or just how bad off they really were. If they were to start offering to make bargains with the enemy, then the Germans would be able to make a fair assessment of the true strength and condition of the command in the Pocket. (There was no reason for the Major to be coy with Lt. Revnes about how bad off the beleaguered force was by then; anyone with eyes could see it.) Then, once they had that morsel of information, it would not be long before the curtain would be lowered on that hillside. The next time the Boche attacked, it would be without any guesswork, but instead precise and direct.

There were also the men to think about. The command structure had asked them to hold out all this time against terrible odds and under horrible conditions, telling them that they had no choice but to do so, as their duty demanded it. To give ground now – no matter in what arena, even for the sake of the wounded – would be like slapping them in the face and dismissing all their hard efforts and sacrifice. How then could they ever be asked to make any further sacrifice, let alone be expected to make it? Besides, the remainder of the regiment could clearly be heard trying to break through from behind, so it would likely not be long until help would be there. All they needed to do was hang on just a bit longer. Men had held out under much worse conditions than they had so far and so they could do so as well. It would likely not be long now...

They talked a long time, Major Whittlesey continuing to expand on his ideas of duty, and doing his utmost to prop up the flagging resolve and discipline of the hurt officer, until Lt. Revnes began to feel a little better about things. "There will be no surrender," was the Major's last, firm, statement as he moved to go and, turning to Sgt. Anderson, he then gave specific and direct orders that if the sergeant saw "any signs of anybody surrendering," or if he saw "a white flag or anything," that the sergeant should shoot the man perpetrating such an act. Then the tall Battalion Commander made his way back to the command funk and slumped down next to Captain McMurtry. The lieutenant was not a coward; everyone had seen him drag his wounded self to the line and fight like a tiger there on several occasions. However, the note spoke to a defeatism that heretofore had relegated itself strictly to the enlisted, replacements in particular. Both Battalion Commander's knew that sort of talk had grown worse over the last few days and that if the Germans came on again in force with those flame-throwers, some form of major breakdown might occur. Now, it had seemingly spread to the officer class as well, and with little control at the top as it was (only Lieutenants Schenck, Cullen, and Eager; Captains Holderman and McMurtry; and Major Whittlesey were left to command), any sort of mass hysteria could not be checked if the controlling element was just as defeated as the controlled. Lieutenant Revnes was all right for now, but a few more days of watching rotting men die might drive him to a point where no words from any higher authority would make a difference. He would likely not be alone either. (II) (147, 245)

They talked about the situation for a little while before Captain McMurtry apparently again tactfully suggested a fighting withdrawal. Major Whittlesey again flatly refused the suggestion however. Their last orders had bid them stay where they were, and stay there they would. Besides, movement would mean leaving the many wounded behind since there were not enough hands to both carry them and fight their way through now. In any case, there were many wounded too badly hurt to be carried without litters, of which they had none. The consolidation he had left Captain McMurtry to enact, by then just about complete, was okay; indeed necessary. However, the Major made it clear that there would be no withdrawal, and from this point on the subject was reportedly never broached again. (29, 218, 245)

That settled, the two officers only had two avenues still open to them then - continue to maintain the security of the position and get word back of their plight as soon as possible. In regards to their position, local control had to be maintained by a strictly limited command structure now; hence the reduced size of the Pocket. By the time everything settled that night, the consolidation movement had brought the slender oval, which had started life the evening of October 2 at about 350 meters long, down to just over 200 meters. One Hotchkiss still guarded the right flank, while there were still two out on the left, though the ammunition for both was down to less than five boxes total – about 4 minutes firing for each. Auto rifles were again disbursed just below the road's edge and at the foot of the hill to the rear, but they too were few, three working at the most and virtually exhausted of their ammunition as well.

Redispersion of the men had revealed a previously unforeseen problem though; moving them had proven unexpectedly difficult, since exhaustion was the worst enemy by now. No one had the strength to bury the dead anymore (even the much respected Lt. Peabody lay exactly where he had fallen, untouched) let alone do anything else, except perhaps for fighting off the enemy. But what would happen when they no longer had the strength to do even that? The ferocious displays during the afternoon's attack could not continue. Some men afterward had barely drug back to the position and then simply collapsed into their holes, completely used up. At some point then, it seemed eminently likely that the unremitting Germans would overpower the limited capacities of the remaining men and the position would then be effectively crushed.

At the same time, outposts still needed to be set, no matter how tired or weak the men were. With the consolidation complete, the Major had officers call for volunteers instead of simply assigning men to the task, in order to give the men at least the illusion of choice over their fate. It was a simple stratagem designed as a morale booster and it worked well since a volunteer soon filled most outposts. These posts were now taken up along the former perimeter line, in existing holes, so the men heading out there were at least spared the task of digging new positions.

Next, the Major and Captain McMurtry set to the task of getting someone through the lines and back to regimental with a desperate plea for help. Many had already approached each of the Battalion Commanders that day requesting permission to make the attempt, but they had refused them all. Daylight attempts were pure suicide - there were just too many of the enemy out there and any movement of even just the tall grass brought a stutter of machine-gun fire. However, in the now beginning rain and the descended darkness (it was nearing 8:00 p.m.) an attempt might fare much better. There had to be a seam in the fabric of the German line to work a way out through somewhere. If someone could find that seam, then they could lead relief back in through it.

Evidence had also shown that large parties moving anywhere in the ravine only invited trouble. Thus, it was decided that only smaller groups of two or three would go out, along non-established routes, staying off main trails and only moving where they might get through with little trouble from the foliage. Whatever the method however, they simply had to get somebody back. The Major then asked Captain McMurtry if he thought he could get a few men to try and shortly the Captain crawled away into the darkness to do so. (29, 51, 109, 148, 149, 150)

Just after 4:30 p.m. a DH took off from Remicourt, this one marked with a big No. 20 on the side and carrying Lt. Maurice Graham as pilot and Lt. James McCurdy in the back seat, and headed for the Charlevaux Ravine. At the same time, Lt. Beebe stood next to Lt.

Morse as the latter spent over a half-hour on the phone trying to raise anyone in the 308th that might have seen at least one of his three missing planes come down. Earlier, Lt. Beebe had explained to Lieutenant's Graham and McCurdy the plan he and Lt. Goettler had been working on and now the two were off on their own accord to try to complete that work and bringing yet another load of supplies for Major Whittlesey's men.

As had the others, they came in wide over the ravine, dropped down to just above treetop level and began to sweep back and forth, with Lt. McCurdy peering intently over the side to identify the correct spot by uniform recognition. The ground fire, showing plainly now in the rapidly falling evening gloom, was horrible and bullets peppered the fabric. Frantically, they searched the ground below, in hopes that they might find their charges and get the hell out of there. Still there was no sight below of U.S. troops. Lieutenant McCurdy, methodically marking the German gun positions on the map, made sure of their position again. Yes, they were over the correct spot, just where Major Whittlesey had said he was. Then, there! From a fresh looking dugout, several men suddenly appeared and Lt. McCurdy got ready to drop the supplies. Another look below as the bundle balanced on the cockpit coaming. Wait… they were shooting at him, and the uniforms were all wrong. Bullets popped and sang around his ears and then one found home in the observer's neck. Flopping back in the cockpit, his blood spattered into the wind behind…

Lieutenant Graham immediately wheeled the DH for home, landing several minutes later as the blood continued to pour from the wounded observers' neck. The squadron surgeon, Dr. L.G. Feinier, got to work immediately on the flyer right there on the field, getting him on a stretcher and stabilizing him for the ambulance. Lieutenant McCurdy however, insisted on giving Lt. Morse a full report, even as Dr. Fienier was bandaging him up. There were Germans on the coordinates they had gotten from the 77th, he said, and he had seen no U.S. troops at all. It looked as if the position Major Whittlesey and his men had occupied had probably been wiped out and the Germans were mopping up the area. (110, 241, 248, 249, 255, 259)

With Captain McMurtry off arranging patrols of his own, Major Whittlesey crawled down the hillside and again called for volunteers, this time a group of them, to break off into pairs and also try and work a way back. Since moving out to the left rear of the Pocket seemed a dead end, the Major had set on a plan to have them first move east down the road above, find a clearer spot if they could, and then work back to the south. The Major quickly succeeded in gathering up the men for the attempt and led them up the hill to see them off. Private John was one of the volunteers, although as he put it, "Our backbones and our stomachs were rubbing."

"I was so weak I could hardly make it and the hill was pretty steep. The major passed me and said, "Come on Jack, this may be our last battle." I looked up at him and said, "I'm a game son of a bitch!" When we got to the road, we sat on the edge of the bank, scouting the woods across and above the road. I didn't know it at the time, but Major Whittlesey was sitting behind me about three feet. I saw a German running crouched over and wheeling around with my rifle, fired at him. When I had fired, the end of the barrel was very close to the major's shoulder and he almost shouted, "What the hell is coming off?" I just pointed to the German who was then rolling over the bank and he said, "Good work boy." (220)

Off they went by groups of two, quietly and nervously skipping from one clump of fall-tinged bushes to another down the sides of the road in the dark. However, all of them found that they could not get through and eventually the survivors worked there way back into the Pocket late that night, bleeding and battered, after encountering enemy machine-guns in the inky blackness. Of the 20, only three came back alive and unwounded; the rest told the tale by their hurts or absence. One man had a finger shot off and Sergeant Anderson of A, whom Major Whittlesey had put in charge, had a bullet run across the bridge of his nose, burning a brown furrow along his brow. It knocked him down but he was otherwise all right. (29, 51, 137)

Captain McMurtry's adventurers did not fare much better. Asking for volunteers between the command hole and the right, he had no trouble gathering a group either, since the men would do just about anything the gregarious and popular officer asked. Sergeant Jeremiah Healey was the first to volunteer, along with Privates Bill Begley, Ed Johnson, and the wounded George Newcom, all of Company G. He also got Pvt. Bob Yoder of E, just back from another successful sniping expedition, as well as the little New York Italian firecracker Pvt. Frank Lipasti of K and two other last-minute converts, Privates Walter Domrose of E and Isadore Willinger of K. Once paired up, Captain McMurtry explained the seriousness of the situation to them all; someone had to get through and alert regimental to just how bad the situation was in the ravine and then lead relief back in along their same exit route. Therefore, they needed to pay close attention to where they were going. He instructed them to bring back as much medical supply as they could and then food and ammunition, in that order. The rain would likely help mask any noise some, but they still needed to be extremely careful, since the Germans had taken up patrolling the Doughboy perimeter closer than ever. The Major already had men moving out to the road up front, heading off to the right. Therefore, the best plan might be to head off down to the brook and then out to the right as well, since heading out to the left had only brought casualties every time it had been tried before.

The little party slipped off into the darkness to the edge of the perimeter, crouching down and silently slinking off into the pitch dark, trying to maintain contact with each other for as long as possible. They had not gone far however, when the Germans suddenly shot up a parachute flare, which popped brightly and began to shed its weird, shadowed light across the rainy ravine. Instantly, the party dropped - but not before there was a stutter of machine-gun fire and Privates Begley and Lipasti were riddled.

Two down, six to go.

Scattering into the brush, everyone hunkered down to wait out the excitement. When they moved out again, this time sliding along on bellies devoid of the cushion of food, Privates Newcom and Yoder found themselves together and crawling down near the creek. Silently, they drank their fill and then froze as the action of a machine-gun clicked in the dark, very close by. Suddenly, from right above their heads, a machine-gun barked out, spitting its stream of lead. Private Newcom later marveled at how the Germans could miss seeing the two in the muzzle flashes, lying there almost directly below the barrel of the weapon. But miss them they did and after the gun again fell silent, they spent a great deal of time very carefully inching their way out of the area and eventually back to the Pocket, while German rifle and machine-gun fire continued to crackle all around them in the hours that it took. Then, a short time later, Pvt. Johnson came back in dragging a badly wounded Pvt. Healey.

Privates Domrose and Willinger were never heard from again and are still listed as missing to this day. (29, 44, 51, 109, 148, 149, 150, 351)

Lieutenant Dan Morse was not a content man as he watched the wounded observer, Lt. McCurdy, being loaded into the ambulance and driven off the field. Three of his planes and their crews were missing for the day's work, two men that had gotten back were wounded and at least two other planes were so badly shot up as to be unserviceable for days. Still, the squadron had no way of knowing if any of this sacrifice had lead to any good whatsoever for the men trapped in that damned ravine. Nor did the situation sit well with Lt. Beebe, nervous for news of his missing friend, Lt. Goettler. Therefore, just after 5:00

p.m., two planes were rolled out and started up: Lieutenant's Beebe and Brill's badly shot up No. 4 and Lt. Morse's No. 3. With Beebe and Brill leading Morse and his back seater, Lt. Stewart "Jay" Bird, the two DH's lumbered into the air from Remicourt and headed out on a search mission around the Charlevaux area in the gray, dissolving light.

Once beyond Binarville, Lt. Beebe dropped down to the treetops and began a run toward the ravine, hopping over the southern ridge just east of the little pond, Etang de Poligny. Lieutenant Morse, following some distance behind, did the same and the two planes raced down the valley, over and past the Moulin d'Charlevaux and on toward the Pocket, drawing massive amounts of fire all the way and scanning the ground in every direction for any sign of the three missing planes. Nothing. Making a wide turn over the Bois de la Buironne, they came down again, dropped supplies where they thought Major Whittlesey's force was and continued down the ravine, hopping back out and patrolling the French area above Binarville. Still nothing, and nothing yet a half-hour later when they finally gave up and went home, discouraged and with both planes battered almost as badly as the two already grounded.

There, they were heartened to learn that word had come through from the 77th Division message center at 5:50 p.m. that Lieutenant's Phillips and Brown were alive and okay. After coming down just north of Binarville, they had been brought by some French liaison troops to the 154th Brigade PC (now at l'Homme Mort), given a complete report to a Captain Delehanty of the 308th and were on their way back to Remicourt in Brigadier General Johnson's car. That was something at least, and Lt. Morse could breathe a bit easier. Then at 7:30 p.m., word came from Lieutenant's Bird and Bolt and the situation brightened yet again. Forced down by their shattered propeller between Vienne le Chateau and la Harazee, they had walked seemingly forever before coming upon American troops. They sent word of having seen flares along what they referred to as the "Binarville-Apremont road" and troops around the area, but the coordinates they gave were confusing. If read correctly, they place them well over toward the right flank of the division. They, too, were on their way back to Remicourt, none the worse for their adventures.

Lieutenant Morse was greatly relieved. Now, if only they would get some word from Dad and Bleck, all would be right. However, by full dark he and Lt. Beebe were still waiting anxiously, Lt. Bleckley was already in the ground at the Villers-Daucourt U.S. Medical military cemetery and Lt. Goettler's mangled body was still lying with the wreckage of DH-4 No. 6 within the French zone somewhere northeast of Binarville. (110, 241, 248, 249)

The French attacks that day had been confused and poorly controlled affairs made at great cost and for no gain. They had wanted to move up on the 308th's left, but the area to which they intended their troops (the disputed zone between Binarville and the 77th's left) had been so heavily blasted by enemy artillery and machine-gun fire that no move had been possible. Even farther over, where their line skirted northwest around Binarville along the Binarville-Autry road, they had made an assault aimed at breaking between the Tranchee de Charlevaux and Hill 205 to get into the Charlevaux Ravine, but had been soundly beaten back there as well. Two U.S. observation planes had also reportedly crashed in that area. By 7:45 p.m., General Alexander's liaison men were again trying to arrange for a cooperative attack to be made on the 7th when Lt. de la Chapelle, at 1st D.C.D. PC, sent them word of French intentions for that day. They were going to shell the enemy works on the southwestern side of Hill 205 and its approaches, followed by a strong assault aimed at eradicating the La Palette Pavilion altogether once and for all. Further, should there be a strong counterattack by the Germans, the plan then called for a rolling barrage to be thrown out that would reach at least to the Moulin d'Charlevaux and possibly beyond, behind which the French troops would again advance. Lieutenant de la Chapelle also made it clear that the French no longer believed that Major Whittlesey and his men were still holding out in the Charlevaux Ravine - their observers had earlier reported Germans occupying the spot where 1st D.C.D command thought the beleaguered Americans were. (2, 10, 91, 131, 144)

General Alexander did not trust the accuracy of the French gunners and believed that Major Whittlesey was indeed still holding out (even despite the report from Lt. McCurdy of the 50th, which he had by then seen). Therefore, he immediately sent word back that he wanted Lt. de la Chapelle to have the French postpone the risky artillery plan. The thought no doubt flashed through his mind again: Could it have been French guns that had dropped the barrage on Major Whittlesey the afternoon of October 4? The idea certainly seemed more than probable if they thought Germans were in the area. However, the French had believed the Major still holding out until apparently changing their minds just today. Indeed, even a French soldier had claimed to have talked to Major Whittlesey just the other day. No matter, for in any case such an operation as Lt. de la Chapelle was presenting would likely be detrimental to his own plan of driving the 308th along the ridges of the Ravin d'Argonne and up into the Charlevaux Ravine. There, the attacking force of the 308th would likely be open to at least some of that French artillery fire along the way. Since there would most definitely be an enemy counterattack following the French attack (as there always was), he could not risk either General Johnson's, nor Major Whittlesey's, troops getting fall-out from any rolling barrage meant to deal with any counterattack. (2, 10, 144)

On the other hand, General Alexander's plan also called for a massive barrage, this one to fall along some of the same trenches the French wanted to clobber, as well as those in the U.S. sector some 800 meters south of the La Palette positions, beginning at midnight and only lifting at 6:00 a.m. This was an absolutely monumental weight of fire, not seen in the Argonne for days and meant to eradicate all traces of enemy defenses along those trenches. It would then move forward from 6:00 a.m. to 7:00 a.m., then settling on an east/west axis line running right through Hills 205 (where it was meant to drop directly on the pavilion complex) and 198. Following behind this rolling barrage would be two companies of the 308th on the eastern ridge of the ravine, three companies on the western ridge, and the French forces to their left. Supporting the 308th would be the 2nd/307th, equally divided between the two mutually supportive 308th columns, along with all of the available brigade mortars and machine-guns that could be mustered. Once the massive barrage reached the east/west line, it was to pause a moment and then lift as the troops went into full headlong assault against the decimated enemy positions. If all went well, French and U.S. forces attacking in a connected "V" along two sides of a triangle that was Hill 205 would successfully take the La Palette Pavilion and the whole position would only be a bad memory by no later than 9:00 a.m. that morning. This is basically the same plan that had been tried under Colonel Stacey's direction and failed, which itself had then been replaced by General Johnson's plan of driving up the center bottom of the ravine after he took over from the Colonel - virtually the same plan that Major Whittlesey was to have originally followed on October 1. (It was certainly a vicious circle, as well as a very costly one.)

Meanwhile, the 307th was to attack as well, but would concentrate its main efforts around the hole in the enemy wire they had found facing their right flank. The rolling artillery barrage in that sector would begin at 6:00 a.m. and cease at 7:00 a.m. along with that of the 308th, though the line along Hill 198 was not to receive quite the same amount of attention as in the Ravin d'Argonne. Once General Johnson had forced a gap in the wire with his troops in the Ravin d'Argonne, driven through and gotten into the Charlevaux, then Colonel Houghton was to follow up that advance from his own sector. After forming a defensive line back to his main line, they all would meet opposite Major Whittlesey's much-relieved forces along the Binarville-La Viergette road, along which they could organize a solid offensive line and prepare for an afternoon assault up Mont d'Charlevaux. (2, 10, 29, 91, 93, 97, 98, 116, 131, 138, 139, 140, 144)

General Johnson got these orders from General Alexander at about 9:30 p.m., and though they must have made him uneasy, immediately began setting his companies for the coming assault. For Pvt. Minder's machine-gun crew, this meant taking up a line in a shallow, muddy trench near the railroad running alongside the Binarville-Moulin de l'Homme Mort road, while artillery ranging shots whistled over in the dark:

"About ten o'clock, just as we were settling down for the night, we received orders to pick up our equipment and we started off... parallel to the front lines. There weren't any stars out, but the sky was kind of light and we saw fairly well. We didn't hike very far and stopped and stretched out our machine guns about 25 yards apart. It was fairly open in front of us and we put over a barrage, all taking turns at the gun, firing a clip a minute all night long until day broke. The lieutenant was there and checked up every so often with the prismatic compass... Our artillery has been firing over our heads... we can hear them going over and exploding off in the distance. The German artillery (too) is still laying them down nicely in this valley. They have the range down fine..." (131)

At midnight, the massive barrage began, putting some men in mind of the night of September 25-26 by its intensity - and of how ineffective that barrage had been against the German wire. "Probably not be much better this time either," some likely muttered in the rain.

And they were right.

(I) So began what has arguably become one of the most famous actions of the whole ordeal in the Charlevaux Ravine - the use of flame-throwers by the Germans against the Pocket - though there remains considerable debate concerning whether it actually happened on this date or not. It is a well-known part of the Lost Battalion legend that the Germans used flame-throwers at the last against the command in the Charlevaux, and that the sight of the hissing jets of living flame so infuriated the men that the Germans gave up trying to eliminate the position and pulled out. The truth is actually quite different, and as confusing then as now.

When Tom Johnson did his interviews for his 1938 book, The Lost Battalion (see Appendix B), he was assured without a doubt that the flame-thrower attack had variously taken place on October 5, 6, or 7, depending upon whose memory he was plying just then. The Germans however, who one would think would know best, seemed pretty clear as to the date of the actual attack in what writings there are from their side. As far as they were concerned, an initial attack had been made on October 6, and a second on October 7. Yet, Jim Larney debated this stringently, for according to his diary, the attack happened only on October 7. Still other, only recently discovered, evidence (including more eyewitness reports), support the German claim of attacks on both days. Tom Johnson eventually solved the problem in his book by placing a first attack on the afternoon of October 6 and then merely mentioning that flame-throwers were again used during the final attack of October 7 as well, but it really seems more of a guess than anything else.

By using Tom Johnson's information and deductions, as well as testimony of men and information he did not have access to in 1938, the truth is that there were most definitely two attacks made involving flame-throwers; a small one initially on October 6 and then a larger one on October 7, which seems to be the one upon which the legend is based. Indications are that there were only two of the death-dealers used on October 6 and that their handlers were quickly driven off toward the end of the attack, which was by about 4:00 p.m. Although they had elicited much terror, no damage had seemingly been done. On October 7, reports point to at least four of the weapons coming at the men, though one source says five, again from the same direction off the right flank and that on that occasion, all German soldiers handling them were killed. Further evidence of this came from the bodies of those German soldiers, and some of their accompanying equipment, found just off the right flank perimeter in the morning light of October 8. German reports however, indicate that not all of the men carrying the flame-throwers were killed though.

(II) Born in New York in 1889, Maurice Revnes was a successful stage manager and play producer in the City before signing up for the Plattsburg camp in September 1917. Upon completion of the course, he was assigned to a machine-gun section in the newly formed 78th Division, though as time passed he actually did nothing with the guns, but instead filled ancillary roles within his unit. Transferred to the 77th Division just before they sailed to France, overseas he was first made a transportation officer in the 2nd Corps before going back to the 77th and forming the enormously popular divisional vaudeville troupe eventually known as, 'The Argonne Players'. However, unsatisfied with his 'supportive' role in the division, he requested a combat assignment and was sent to the 306th Machine Gun Battalion, ostensibly on his "experience" with machine-guns in the 78th Division - which he did not actually have, though he did attend an AEF machine-gun school for a couple weeks and there gained some rudimentary knowledge. Nevertheless, given command of a platoon in Company D under Lt. Peabody, he went into combat on September 26 almost as inexperienced as any of the 40th Division replacements under him. Considering that general inexperience, as well as his complete lack of any real knowledge concerning Major Whittlesey and his strict ways (and by the same token, also a general lack of loyalty toward him) it is no wonder that his resolve would falter much more quickly than any of the other officers in the Pocket, even despite his Plattsburg training. In truth, Revnes had no business leading front line troops and probably should have had his request for a combat role turned down in favor of his being able to use his true talents on the stage (much as Major Whittlesey's best role in the division had actually been in charge of the Headquarters Company).

October 7, 1918 A.M.
"I have a message for the Major..."
Pvt. Lowell Hollingshead.

Some hope of relief was again revived in the Pocket with the distant booming that heralded the opening of the barrage back in the Ravin d'Argonne that night. Optimism, largely lost over the past few days, seemed to swell briefly; sleep held no better dream than that which the barrage seemed to offer. From their position on that bloody hillside, Major Whittlesey's men looked back across the Charlevaux Ravine and watched the flashes beyond the ridge of Hill 198. While the dancing bursts of pink and white filled the night sky seductively, they also led to increased German machine-gun and sniper fire within the ravine, aided considerably by a multitude of flares and Very lights thrown into the air to better silhouette targets. U.S. fire in return was virtually nonexistent from the Pocket. Ammunition supply was reaching the bottom.

"On the morning of October 7, and the fifth day of the siege," wrote Captain Holderman in 1925, "it was almost impossible to find men who had strength enough to go to the slopes as scouts." He continued,

"There was no change as far as the situation was concerned, for as fast as patrols would venture out they were immediately driven in by the enemy. The position by now was in a bad state, for the dead of three day's fighting had not been buried, nor was it possible to accomplish this. The wounded were suffering intensely, as gangrene had set in on most of them and many men were dying. Every bit of strength had to be conserved in order to repel attacks of the enemy from the ridge above the position..." (149)

About this day, both the toughest and last day for the cut off command, Whittlesey later wrote in his after-action report that he only had a total effective strength of 275 men. This figure certainly includes a great many lightly wounded who had returned to the line, so the actual figure of those unwounded probably hovered closer down around the 200 mark. (Even among the 194 survivors who eventually walked out of the Pocket, a good deal were lightly wounded.) It would be an eventful day, because the fifth day would be marked not only by some of the Pocket's toughest fighting but by the most famous event of the Lost Battalion legend - the delivery of the German request for Major Whittlesey to surrender his forces and the Major's famed supposed reply of "Go to Hell!" (135)

The clouds above the ravine were just starting to lighten that morning, as rifle and machine-gun fire mixed with the artillery booms started coming from behind the Pocket. Private Emil Peterson slithered his way toward a muddy shell hole below Company H's position with some dirty dregs of water in its bottom. It was a bit late to be sneaking down there and orders forbade it, but since he was the only one willing to try and the morning mist made for good cover, piss on orders. He was desperately thirsty, despite the tapering rain. With him, he also carried the canteen of a boy who promised him tobacco if Pvt. Peterson would fill it for him. Sliding silently, he took his time, all went well and he soon crawled back up the hill with the water, and retrieved his tobacco. Settling down in his hole, it was about 8:00 a.m.

God he was hungry! Though the water and tobacco helped some, Pvt. Peterson could not help but think about a bundle that he had seen tossed out by one of the airplanes the evening before. They had all watched it come down, the closest bundle tossed yet. Though it had bounced into German-held territory, it had nevertheless seemed to come to rest not too far off the company's left flank. However, since it actually lay out of sight, no one could say for sure just where in the bushes it was. Usually, the Germans would let them know, crowing and making a big production out of calling out the contents of the stray packages, laughing and tempting them to "come on over and eat – we now have plenty."

This time though, there had been not a sound from the Hienies and that was certainly strange. Maybe the package had not been discovered and was still out there. Now there was a nice thought. In any case, Pvt. Peterson was too tired from the water run to do much of anything about that package just now except dream about it. He called to the boy in the hole nearest him and said he was going to rest for a while, since the barrage had kept him up for most of the night.

"If anything should happen, say, if the rest of the boys break through, call me now," he joked and tipped back into his 'grave'. (183, 224)

Most men had been some 90 hours now without food and with little or no water. Private Jim Larney remembered that for almost four days all he and Cpl. Baldwin had between them was part of a can of corned beef, half a package of crackers and a single pack of cigarettes. "We would debate whether to eat half a cracker or a whole one, whether to smoke half a cigarette or a whole one… the crackers didn't last." Near Pvt. Larney in the fog that morning, a little Italian boy from the Bowery suddenly jumped to his feet out of the hole he was occupying and started galloping madly in a circle. Swearing viciously in Italian the whole time and completely out of control, he raged for several minutes, seemingly sure to draw a sniper bullet, until several men calling out to him managed to get him calmed back down enough to get underground again. Even at that early hour, the tension across the hillside was already mounting. (29, 33, 51, 245)

Over on the right flank, barely half the distance than what it had been two days ago, Major Whittlesey slipped over to Captain Holderman's funk and asked him if he thought he had anyone who might try to get through the lines before the sun got too high. Most runners so far had seemingly gotten lost in the darkness and had been killed or captured for it. He and Captain McMurtry thought there might be a better chance of success for one man in the early light with the misty weather. Captain Holderman is said to have thought for a moment and then offered up his best man. However, according to Pvt. Larney, Sgt. James Deahan of Company K later told him that Captain Holderman was reluctant to offer any men for such an obviously dangerous and virtually suicidal mission. It was only after the Major irritably insisted and pulled rank that the Captain relented. Calling half-heartedly for volunteers and getting none, Captain Holderman then apparently picked those who first caught his eye, which turned out to be Private Abraham Krotoshinsky; a small, slope-shouldered Jew from New York and two others who were never identified. (After the war, "Krot", who never considered himself a hero, would say of the event, "The Major called for volunteers and I was picked...") (29, 51, 33, 245)

Major Whittlesey pulled the men aside and gave them the usual instructions, impressing upon them the seriousness of the situation and telling them to maintain their distance from one another so as to increase the chances of at least one getting through. He was pulling no punches now; no one had made it through and many had not come back, so they needed to be careful and alert. Stay off the main trails and ask to be taken to see Colonel Stacey immediately when they got back. Wishing them all good luck, the officers watched them drop all their excess equipment and crawl off tiredly down the hill in the direction of the creek. As they disappeared into the brush near one of the water holes, a machine-gun opened up almost immediately and Major Whittlesey and Captain Holderman watched the bushes waggle in three different directions as the men scattered from its fire. Captain Holderman, smoking a homemade cigarette given to him by one of his men, laconically commented, without any apparent conviction, that he hoped they would make it.

Meanwhile, Private Peterson was not the only one in Company H thinking about that airplane package off the left flank that morning. There was apparently much whispering traveling between holes about the possibilities that it held and how close it might be. Nearly everyone had seen it come down, bouncing through the rush grass, and had watched it with the eyes only a truly hungry man had.

They bantered back and forth between holes in deep whispers, someone suggesting that they might consider searching for it, and that perhaps Pvt. Rainwater could lead them. Private James B. Rainwater sat silently and hungrily in his hole nearby. He was a half-breed American Indian 40th Division replacement from Mt. Morrison, Colorado that had been a miner before being drafted and there was little – if anything – that he did not know about the forest. (I) (116, 347, 351)

The conversation dragged, as they listened to the attack in the distance starting to fall off behind them. And as the firing and sounds of battle dropped, so too did hopes of relief in the Pocket again and one by one the men fell into a hungry, morose silence. Then, the talk of the package picked up again and developed into determination.

'No hope... nothing to lose.' someone must have pointed out.

'But we don't have orders.'

'Fuck orders. I'm hungry and these bastard officers are gonna get us all killed. If I gotta die, I want to do it with something in my stomach.'

A pause; what they were contemplating was desertion. That was what leaving your post in the presence of the enemy was, after all, and they could be shot for that. (As if it was not likely to happen anyway.)

Slow starvation, or desertion then.

It was some choice.

'All right. I'm with you.'

Several other figures rose from their funk holes.

It was just after 10:00 a.m.

Artillery fire echoed down the Ravin d'Argonne through the rainy dawn, painting its vivid bursts across the darkened forest backdrop. It was a terrible barrage, though few around Hills 205 and 198 had much confidence in it. There, General Johnson was stretching himself far too thin in both the roles of 308th Regimental Commander (since Captain Breckenridge, lacking experience, could only do so much) and Brigade Commander. Luckily for him, Colonel Houghton needed little supervision. Behind the barrage, General Johnson slowly moved his men into attack formations. Two 308th companies - letter designations of which were largely useless now; each company being no more than a polyglot of whatever men were to hand - took position along the east side of the ravine and three along the west side, with one liaisoned firmly to the French. Meanwhile, the 2nd/307th, such as it was, moved up and fanned across the ravine in strong support 300 meters behind. Then, at 5:00 a.m., the barrage lifted to the German main line and stepped up in tempo. This raised at least a glimmer of hope that it may at last blow the long awaited hole through the wire, thus bringing the nightmare in the ravine to an end. Much to General Johnson's overworked credit (and despite reports he had seen from a certain Lt. McCurdy, a flyer who had been working to drop supplies to Major Whittlesey's men the day before, as well as a similar French report), he simply would not believe that the command was no longer there in the Charlevaux Ravine. He knew Major Whittlesey's character, both through his dealings with him through Colonel Stacey as well as when he had been a Captain in charge of the 308th Headquarters Company, and knew him to be dedicated to duty far beyond nearly anyone he had seen during his entire military carrier. If his presumptions were correct, and there was no reason to doubt that they were, then Major Whittlesey would never surrender his hard-won position, no matter how many wounded they had taken or how badly off the command was. That was how it had been out on l'Homme Mort too. As for the only other option to those reports - complete annihilation - General Johnson dismissed these as unthinkable. No… After all this, Major Whittlesey still had to be there. (10, 29, 51, 91, 109, 131, 141, 144)

Therefore, when the attack went off promptly at 6:00 a.m., a mud-stained General Johnson was right there at the head of the front line along the west side of the ravine leading it in again. His first message went back to Sgt. Cahill's telephone head shortly thereafter and was telephoned directly through to General Alexander:

Movement started at 6.00am. Our troops moving forward intermingled with the French. Understand the French state their objective to be trench at 294.2-275.6. Upon reaching this point, our troops will move straight on to the Moulin de Charlevaux (sic) and establish themselves along the general line 276.3. I am working in close cooperation with the French. (131)

So far, so good. The trench the French were aiming for was that of the La Palette system along the southwestern top of Hill 205, where they had been on at least two other occasions, but driven out. General Johnson's intention of moving beyond them by their right and into the Charlevaux seemed eminently plausible then - at first. Yet, it was not long after this message went out that functional difficulties began to set in. Captain Breckenridge, back at the telephone head (now 308th Advanced Regimental PC instead of a Battalion PC, since battalions were now largely a thing of the past) with the support 2nd/307th, sent a runner back to General Johnson with a message timed at 6:17 a.m., stating that the phone was already out. Additionally, the two support companies that the Captain had sent forward had received no heavy U.S. machine-gun fire as planned and by 7:00 a.m., the German counter artillery fire had again increased such that no one was moving in support at all. By 7:30 a.m., General Johnson had sent a runner back with his own ominous message, which went back to the 154th Brigade's Operations Officer at l'Homme Mort, Captain F.H. McKnight, and was telephoned directly in to General Alexander:

At this hour the French had not moved forward, but my troops had attacked the position from which the assault on the trenches could be made. I could not see or locate the French at this hour and have therefore ordered my troops to assault without them. We are meeting M.G. and rifle fire. I shall be beyond wire communication for a while, but shall return later. (131)

The Brigadier's next message, timed at 8:00 a.m., reiterates that the French had not moved, but also adds that the artillery, as all feared, had not had any effect whatsoever on the German wire. The command forward was now taking particularly heavy shell and machine-gun fire as was the support. Yet, the real trouble was clearly indicated in General Johnson's next message, originally timed at 8:15 a.m. but not arriving until almost an hour later since the General wrote the disjointed tome over the space of a half an hour as the fighting raged around him. This one was again brought by runner back to l'Homme Mort:

Meeting heavy opposition; machine gun and high explosive shells. French line on our left held up and state unable to advance. Have sent word that I am pushing forward and asked them to try and advance with me. Wire not cut and artillery fire has been without effect. My line now immediately in front of wire.

French not attacking trenches but lying in sunken road to my left.

Word just received that the French have been ordered to fall back and give artillery a chance to prepare before renewal of the attack. (131)

Accompanying this message was the note sent to General Johnson from Lt. de la Chapelle at French 1st D.C.D PC, concerning the French artillery intentions and translated as:

Let me know exactly where is your left because I want to make fire of the 75's and 37mm guns. The whole left wing is stopped by machine gun fire and the trench must be fired by the right. On account of this, I must know exactly where you are. (2, 131)

(Note that by "left wing" Lt. de la Chapelle means the left flank of the French company attacking just west of General Johnson. Their one held up flank had effectively halted the entire company and thus the entire French advance against Hill 205.) (10, 29, 91, 131, 142, 144, 146)

General Alexander read the messages with grim foreboding, particularly the request for coordinates from the French. He had already passed instructions to the French the night before stating that he did not want them firing in the direction of his troops, no matter what the circumstances! Since the French had made it clear the day before that they no longer believed Major Whittlesey and his troops were holding out anywhere in the Charlevaux Ravine, they now seemed determined to blanket Hill 205 and the area beyond it in heavy artillery fire to pave the way for another attack. This, even though

General Johnson was reporting that the six-hour U.S. barrage of that morning had done virtually no good. What good then would a mere hour-long French one do?

Nor was General Alexander, like Brigadier Johnson, willing to admit that Major Whittlesey and his men were no longer holding out either, if for no other reason than it was his orders that put them there, it was his division that they belonged to and it was therefore his responsibility if they *were* wiped out. Such a terrible event would likely leave a deep and permanent scar on his career. In fact, there had been an investigating officer, a Captain Rich, sent down from 1st Corps only the day before, collecting statements concerning the whole affair from not only himself, but General Johnson, Colonel Houghton, and even one or two junior officers as well. All three commanding officers had been very frank in their statements, given out of earshot of one another, and the affair had been wrapped up rather quickly - with the lions' share of the blame landing squarely on Colonel Stacey's shoulders. It had all been done on the "Q.T." of course, since General Liggett was no more anxious than was General Alexander for the press to get wind of it. In fact, there had already been several news stories run in the States about what people were starting to call the "Lost Battalion" and General Pershing was not happy over it all. (31, 150)

Nor could General Alexander, according to his own later statements, understand why the command in the ravine had not been yet reached, even though he had himself seen the terrain and spoken with men of his own experience and background who were fighting across it (namely General Johnson). If Major Whittlesey, an emergency officer leading draft men, had been able to get through the German line, then by God should not a Regular Army officer leading the same stripe of men be able to get through? That said, if an emergency officer could get through a line a Regular Army officer could not, then surely that emergency officer was of some great caliber and would be still holding out.

With this belief coupled to the memory of the disaster that had apparently befallen the men in the ravine on October 4, General Alexander then did not want the French firing at *anything* in or around the U.S. zone. Therefore, once again, he sent Captain Klotz and Lt. de Coppett over to French 1st D.C.D. to stop the planned barrage. Then, he got on the phone with General McCloskey, at the 152nd F.A. PC, and arranged for some U.S. counter fire to fall on some of the more stubborn pockets of resistance being reported by General Johnson. It was by then 9:45 a.m. however, and General Johnson's attack was already well on its way to falling apart. (2, 10, 29, 91, 109, 116, 140, 144, 146, 150)

The Brigadier meanwhile, leaving the already faltering attack in Captain Breckenridge's hands temporarily, had gone over to make a quick check on the progress of Colonel Houghton's assault. There, he found most of 1st/307th working on the right of the regimental zone, around the seam in the wire at the joint with the 153rd Brigade. The majority of the 3rd/307th was working along the left of the regimental front, against the wire belt before Hill 198 proper. While there was good and firm liaison on both flanks for once, progress was nevertheless slow and deliberate, with the Boche putting up everything they had, Colonel Houghton reported. If there was going to be any actual movement in his zone that day, then it would not be until later that afternoon and then likely only on the right, through the break in the wire they were exploiting. Yet, men were still not through the wire seam in enough numbers to do any real damage and to rush the operation would only ruin its chances for success. How soon in the afternoon, General Johnson wanted to know. If they were to reach Major Whittlesey that day, it would probably be more toward evening, the Colonel figured, and only as part of a general assault that could initially draw as much attention away from the spot as possible.

As for the left of the 307th's zone, where there was contact with elements of the 308th moving along the east ridge of the ravine, no progress had been made there at all, nor would there likely be since the wire had not been cut by the artillery. Hold then, was all they could do. (103, 104, 131, 138, 139, 144)

With this information, along with that of the French situation and the failure of the morning barrage to be of any real effect, General Johnson had decided by about 9:30 a.m. that the 308th was unlikely to do much more in the Ravin d'Argonne that morning other than increase their casualty count. Coupled with the nerve wracking French plan to possibly fire a barrage against their own right flank area, which would necessarily jeopardize the 308th's left flank units, General Johnson decided to err on the side of caution upon his return to l'Homme Mort and sent a message by runner up to Captain Breckenridge on the line, stating:

You will conform to the movements of the French. Should their right fall back, you will return to the position occupied this morning, giving the artillery chance for additional preparation before advancing to attack. We will conform in our advance to the French and for this purpose the left flank company must maintain the closest contact in all your movements. (131)

It was a bold move, one which the Brigadier felt would likely bring down the wrath of General Alexander, but one necessary nonetheless, primarily because of the French artillery plan - which he had no way of knowing General Alexander was then trying to stifle himself as well. But until that artillery preparation had been put down against the wire, which would then provide for the flank support General Johnson needed on his left to move forward, there seemed little point in continuing a general attack that was most certain to fail on its own. Further, if plans could be drawn up to support a late afternoon attack in Colonel Houghton's sector, then they might get Major Whittlesey out yet that day, since the promise of the break on Colonel Houghton's right seemed to hold much hope. In that case, wisdom spoke to husbanding as many troops as possible then. Therefore, once Captain Breckenridge, up at what went for Advanced Regimental PC in the devastated ravine, got the order from General Johnson, he immediately began a withdrawal that conformed to the French right and just after 10:10 a.m. was reporting it complete and solid liaison gained. For all intents and purposes then, the carefully prepared morning assault of October 7 was over by 10:15 a.m.; another effort in futility that resulted only in a portion of that late morning afterward being spent in fighting off a German counter attack.

Around 10:20 a.m., a message arrived at l'Homme Mort from Captain McKnight, who General Johnson had earlier sent over to French 1st D.C.D PC to find out just what the French were planning. Beaten back soundly by heavy shell and machine-gun fire all along their line facing Hill 205, they had suffered heavily and now felt that they could do no more for the day without the artillery preparations that they wanted and for which General Alexander refused to agree to. General Johnson then found the he had erred correctly - the French were giving up the attack, not going to shell anything and his troops would have been waiting for flank support that would have never come. Calling up Colonel Hannay at General Alexander's PC shortly before 10:30 a.m. then (a shrewd move, since the Colonel was much easier to deal with than was General Alexander, especially when failure was involved), General Johnson reported:

"My line withdrew in compliance with my instructions at 10:10 a.m. to a line approximately 275.1 in regimental sector. This with the idea of preparation for attack in conjunction with the French this afternoon, they having informed me that they were retiring with the idea of making another attack. I have just heard from my staff officer, who is with French headquarters, that for reasons which he will let me know later, the French will not attack again today. I am therefore sending two companies to hold the line from which I fell back until I learn when the French are going to attack, if ever. My casualties so far as reported are about 68 wounded and many dead. Only a partial report.

Now, Hannay, this is a complete change of plan. First, the French said they were reforming for attack, and now they do not know. I consider it almost murder, Hannay, to send these men up against this wire and these trenches." (10, 91, 131, 144)

General Johnson then braced himself for a storm as Colonel Hannay relayed the report to General Alexander, especially the last part. But the Commanding General was already well ahead of the situation, and Colonel Hannay let General Johnson know that it had been General Alexander who had prevented the French barrage. Plans for a concerted American only attack, to come off that afternoon, were then being put together. There had also been some big doings farther down the line to the east and the Division Commander had just gotten off the phone with 1st Corps PC, as well as Colonel Houghton. General Johnson needed to have all of his troops pulled back 500 meters from the main line by no later than 2:00 p.m., for it was then that General McCloskey had orders to blow that whole goddamned German line back to Hell. They were *going* to get Major Whittlesey out that day, and that was all there was to it. (2, 29, 131, 138, 139, 144)

The two other men who had gone out with Pvt. Krotoshinsky were back in the Pocket by around 10:30 a.m., one wounded terribly in the shoulder and neither having any news of their third. The Major sent them back to their funk holes and after some brief thought called for Lt. Schenck, asking him to get two men from Company C together who might be willing to make the attempt next. Lieutenant Schenck, as one of the last officers standing, was being counted on more and more by both Battalion Commanders and was thus gaining even more respect in their eyes. Carrying out the multitude of tasks the two assigned him, never complaining and always positive, if not downright cheerful, both commanders had already decided that he would be rewarded with whatever medals and promotions they could recommend once they had gotten out of the Pocket. After a short appeal, Lt. Schenck got Privates Stanislaw Kozikowski, a Polish immigrant auto-rifleman, and Clifford Brown, a very religious farmer from up state New York, who both agreed to try.

Lieutenant Schenck gave them much the same speech that Major Whittlesey had given the three others earlier. It was imperative that someone get back to regimental, he told them, and let them know just how bad things were up in the ravine and that they could not hold out much longer. He then had them to strip off their helmets and all their excess equipment, for noise discipline, and gave them his pocket compass before sending them down the hill through the brush. (II) After watching them slither off into the brush. Lt. Schenck then crawled off toward the hole he was sharing now with the wounded Sgt. Bendheim. Just as he skirted around a rock in his path, a trench mortar shell landed nearby and a ragged piece of shrapnel ripped most of the young lieutenant's face away and others peppered his back. He had been a handsome youth, strong and dependable, and Pvt. Larney later remarked, "Poor Gordon Schenck! He worked his heart out all through this period. I could see his uniform tattering to shreds and the exhaustion piling on him. Captain Stromee was down with his wounds all this time..." Now, the young lieutenant from Brooklyn merely lay a faceless, distorted form in the mud, having made not a sound as the life was torn from him. His death left only Major Whittlesey, and Lieutenants Cullen and Eager as the only unwounded officers in the Pocket now. (III) (29, 54, 218, 245)

Private Krotoshinsky, meanwhile, had slipped off across the creek and was still slowly making his way southeastward toward the U.S. lines, keeping the brook to his left and Hill 198 on his right:

"I started at sun up on a gray, gloomy day already weak from lack of food and already convinced that death would be the only outcome. I didn't care. After five days of being fired at all hope was gone and all I wanted was peace. Yet there must have been a spark of hope that kept me going.

My worst experience of the day came early in the morning. I was lying just behind the German lines, concealed beneath some bushes, when a German officer walked by and accidentally stepped on my fingers. I managed to stay quiet but it took a great deal of effort. It was several hours before I could leave my place of concealment..." (33)

Quietly, he continued to work his way back as the hours passed and his nerves stretched tighter...

While the attack with the flamethrowers the evening before had failed to clear the nest of Americans out of the Charlevaux Ravine, Major Hunicken had nevertheless gotten reports that it *had* succeeded in compressing them into a smaller area, which was something after all. They had lost one of the flamethrowers, and the man carrying the other one had been severely wounded though and this was a serious blow to the meager assault force; one that the Major could not replace. Then, once back at the Regimental PC at La Palette that evening, Major Hunicken had been greeted by Hauptmann Von Sybel with the grim news of the imminent withdrawal. Time was almost out. Therefore, they had one last chance to try again to eliminate the *Americanernest* that next day and if they failed, then everything the regiment had suffered through these last two weeks would have all been largely for nothing...

Then, the next morning, the first good news in days arrived - the appearance of 20 more pioneer/storm troops, under command of an officer, who had brought more flame equipment. Immediately, Major Hunicken and Hauptmann Von Sybel began making plans for a serious assault against the American position; an all out "do or die," last-ditch effort. The usual harassment of the nest would continue all day (despite the loss of the No. 1 trench mortar), and several small attacks might be made, just to keep abreast of the American outpost positions and to keep their nerves stretched tight. However, the real effort would come toward late afternoon, when the storm troops would lead the main body into the attack, which would again come at the Americans from three sides. Behind, into the ravine, would fall what trench mortar shells could be sent from above the road ahead, along with a barrage of machine-gun fire. The attack would then further compress the remaining American force back down the hill and inward from the flanks, toward the Charlevaux Brook where, blocked from escape across the ravine by the machine-gun fire and mortars, the Americans would face two choices - complete annihilation or surrender.

Certainly, the idea was not new. However, many additional factors seemed to be now on the German side, not the least of which was the larger body of storm troops and their flamethrowers. There were also indications that the American force was falling apart internally, as evidenced in statements both Hauptmann Bickel and the recently arrived Lt. Prinz had taken from several more prisoners lately captured while out on patrol in the ravine. These allowed that losses in the Pocket were "tremendous," that they could no longer bury their dead and that rations and ammunition, despite the attempted airdrops, were "tight," since they had received none of the packages that had been dropped. A good many of these captured troops were ragged and disheveled, with their spirit mostly gone. Some had even apparently wandered off from the position on their own. With conditions that bad within the American perimeter, the two German officers figured, the odds might have tipped in their favor now by just enough to parlay any attack into victory.

Therefore, Major Hunicken and Hauptmann Von Sybel gathered the remaining officers of the regiment together (including Hauptmann Bickel and Lt. Prinz) for a final briefing that noon hour before deploying them to take their men into attack positions against the surrounded Americans. One way or the other, either through surrender or death, the enemy force in the ravine was not to be allowed to remain a single night more. Further, the withdrawal to the Kriemhilde Stellung had been ordered and the enemy, if at all possible, should not be allowed to realize that another withdrawal was in progress, meaning no movements were to be made by open road or in the daylight. Therefore, following eradication of the *Americanernest* then, once darkness had well fallen the officers were to lead their men back to the Kriemhilde positions along prescribed routes laid out in orders that Hauptmann Von Sybel distributed. Certain units would act as rear guards, while others would leave immediately. The eastern flank of the Army Group Argonnen along the Aire Valley had already virtually collapsed by then - and along with it had gone the 36-hour time frame. The effects of the collapse were rapidly beginning to be felt up the line even then, coming straight toward them. It would not be long before their flank support in the 2nd Landwehr would disintegrate and this portion of the line would then be forced to fold as well. The only blot on the record of the 76th Division during their time in the Argonne had been the piercing of their line by this impudent band of Americans. Otherwise, the La Palette Pavilion region of the Argonne, defended primarily by the 254th Regiment for the last six hard days, had stood like a rock, resisting all assaults made on its section of the line. Therefore, eliminating the Americans in the ravine would likely be their last chance at redeeming their one dishonor in the Argonne fight.

Therefore, the officers and men of Infantry Regiment 254/76th Reserve Division of Hesse dispersed one last time into the Charlevaux Ravine. Not to win the war, or stop the American advance, but instead to try to avenge their regimental honor, each man preparing to do his utmost to settle the stalemate in the regiment's favor - including their intelligence officer, Lt. Heinrich Prinz. (51, 123, 124, 307)

Private Lowell Hollingshead had been reposed in his funk and having yet another dream about the rolling kitchens, but had woken up in time to hear the ragged ends of the conversation concerning the airplane bundle. It was a chance at some grub and his stomach certainly ached for something - anything - and so the ragged 18-year-old rose up out of his hole with the others. Seven others rose out of their holes alongside 'Holly' that misty morning, all of them privates; Jack Recko, Jim Rainwater, Cecil Duryea, James Ilardo, Robert Christian, Henry Chinn, and Raymond Clark. Quickly, they started down the hillside. Private Peterson had been dozing when he heard Duryea softly call to him to come along. Thinking that perhaps there had been a breakthrough, Peterson got up, grabbed his rifle and crawled tiredly behind. Of the group of nine, only Privates Chinn and Ilardo were original Upton men, the rest were replacements. Says Peterson:

"I got out, then I saw around me there were probably nine men running slowly towards the ravine we had crossed when we first came. When I got to the ravine, the boys were already across. The Germans were firing at us all this time. On the other side we stopped and talked things over." (224)

The mist had helped mask some of their initial movements across, and as they crouched in the brush next to the brook getting their wind back, Pvt. Rainwater crept to the head of the column to take the point. At length, everyone set themselves to move out. So far, so good. (IV) (33, 158, 163, 222, 224, 280, 290, 291)

Lieutenant Cullen was reclined stiffly in his hole, disappointedly listening to the lessening fire coming from beyond Hill 198, when a tense Company H soldier crawled up and told the lieutenant he'd better 'come see this for himself'. Crawling down the hill a bit, he was just in time to see the end of a small party of Doughboys disappear into the rush grass. What in hell was this all about, he asked? The soldier told him that he thought they were going out after one of the airplane packages. Lieutenant Cullen, face brightening with anger, swore heartily.

A short time later, when Major Whittlesey came through on one of his frequent inspections, the lieutenant pulled him aside, telling him what had happened. Most of the men were replacements, he said, but that at least one had been identified as an Upton man.

Major Whittlesey was terribly concerned, as it was another sign that discipline and morale were failing fast. From the replacements, he might have reasonably expected a certain amount of this, but from an Upton man - that was something different. It showed a complete loss of faith in the command structure that had led him for more than a year; a loss of faith that might only spread once word got around of what had happened. It was, in effect, the beginning of the infection of the true, unadulterated, hopelessness and indiscipline that both Battalion Commanders had feared might begin. (29, 51)

Little was Major Whittlesey aware but that the situation had progressed even farther, By that time, several men in pairs and singly had already simply dropped off into the bushes and headed out on their own, New Yorkers and replacements alike, and none of them with orders to do so. (158, 222)

Down at the bottom of the ravine, after a short rest and a long drink from the brook, the errant little party pushed forward along a narrow trail in single file, rifles ready and alternating between moving on their hands and knees and a creeping crouch. They moved exhaustedly, with frequent halts to either rest or let Pvt. Rainwater get his bearings. "We were so weak from hunger, we could hardly move," Pvt. Peterson said later. Yet, they pushed on, eyes bulging from their sockets with hunger and nervousness, looking desperately all around for the package. They were well into German-held territory now, where any moment might bring rapid death and they could see nothing through the heavy brush. Where was the damn thing? They plunged ahead, moving sluggishly through the tangle. Still nothing. (224)

They had managed perhaps 400 meters beyond the brook when Pvt. Rainwater suddenly stopped the column with raised hand. All at once, the sharp stutter of machine-guns rang out and all hell broke loose. The fire came from both in front as well as behind. They had walked into a trap. Private Rainwater, out ahead and half-crouched over, took the first blast across the stomach and immediately went down without a sound, nearly torn in two. Of the three directly behind, Pvt. Chinn was also killed outright, while Private's Christian and Clark lay screaming and bleeding from horrible wounds for a short time, until death overtook them as well. The rest dropped to the ground, also wounded. Private Duryea, the fifth in line, took a couple slugs high in the right leg. Private Hollingshead took a bullet in the lower left thigh, one of the two that had passed through Private Peterson's left knee, who had been the man in front of him. Private Recko, behind Hollingshead, got a ripping wound up one side. The last in line, Private Ilardo, was seriously wounded in the right leg as well. Immediately, all who could, rolled into whatever cover there was as the chattering bursts continued. Then, after a short while, the firing stopped and the forest was mostly silent again, except for the bark of the trench mortar shells behind and sporadic machine-gun fire into the Pocket. (163, 222, 224)

Back in the Pocket, the firing of a machine-gun in the distance off the left flank cut the early morning air, followed by the moans and wails of wounded men. Those in Company H in the know, exchanged glances over the edges of the crumbling funk holes. It looked as if the food gathering expedition had been a dismal failure, simply adding nine more names to the casualty list. The firing beyond Hill 198 had almost completely dried up, except for the incessant artillery fire and by then trench mortars and machine-guns had been working over the Pocket for some time as well. It was about 10:45 a.m.

All at once, there was a mighty explosion, followed closely by another, and then another; all of them well out in the ravine but startling nonetheless. They were not trench mortar shells - the size of the burst was too big – but instead regular artillery rounds. But whose? A few more fell, closer in toward the position. They were coming in from behind, again! Several more dropped in, closer than before and some of the men now began to panic, one even jumping up as if to take off running across the ravine until stopped by his officer. Major Whittlesey was up and crouching his way around through the brush, again shouting in his thinnest voice for them all to take it easy. Yet, he knew full well that if it was another barrage as had occurred on October 4, the ball game was likely over and all control would certainly dissolve. On the right, filthy bandages seemed to be all that was holding Captain Holderman's terribly wounded body together and he was now up and stumping around that flank on two broken rifles, yelling for his men to hang tight. Meanwhile, Captain McMurtry had slithered down to the wounded area in the first few bursts, to try to help keep the men there calm.

However, the note of the bursts was all wrong to be a 75 and not big enough for a 155 either. What then? Major Whittlesey crawled to some brush near the bottom by the wagon road where he could take a good, long look through his field glasses unmolested. A report echoed again, there was a whistling in the air and the burst hit just short of the Pocket. Up towards the top of Hill 205, he saw a smoke curl. No wonder the bursts did not sound quite right. They were not French model 75's, but instead German 77's. So,

Lt. Teichmoeller's earlier prediction had come true; the Germans had finally moved a field gun up near the top of Hill 205 behind them and were now taking ranging shots.

Major Whittlesey crawled over and quietly let Captain McMurtry know what it was. There was no further alarm, for both knew what a field piece well ranged from behind meant - hell, after October 4 everyone would. While the hillside slope protected them from what might come down from in front of them, it did not protect them from behind. Since Major Whittlesey had feared that something along those lines would happen on l'Homme Mort, when they moved into this ravine he had carefully picked the spot they now occupied in part because of the protection it offered from shelling. However, with a gun behind them it would not be long before the Pocket was wiped out. However, since there was absolutely nothing anyone could do about it except hunker down and wait for the end, the Major did not tell anyone else.

Yet just as suddenly as it had started, the shellfire stopped after only about a dozen shots. When it did not begin again after about a half an hour, wristwatches were showing nearly noon, but that really meant nothing. The Germans had seemingly abandoned their normal schedule the day before, so an all out attack could conceivably come at any time, besides the usual 'nibbling' of the perimeter. Were the Germans out of ammunition? Or, having ranged the gun, were they merely biding their time, waiting for a concerted effort, such as the previous afternoon's furious assault? In a scenario such as that, artillery would make all the difference. For a time after, it was deathly quiet in the ravine. (29, 51, 109, 135, 148, 149, 150)

Then, the machine-guns started to chatter again, trench mortars barked out once more, and the day in the Pocket picked up where it had left off before the strange interlude.

It was also about that time that Sgt. Tuite, crawling across the Pocket on some errand, was stopped by Sgt. Bendheim, alone in his greasy funk now that Lt. Schenck was dead, with his poisoned leg well beyond help and the pain virtually beyond description. "Shoot me, please… for God's sake shoot me…" he begged Sgt. Tuite. However, the faithful sergeant instead sat with and quieted the wounded man, giving him the comfort of God's constancy until he again accepted his situation, despite the incredible pain. Only then, once Lionel Bendheim was back in a place of approbation, did Martin Tuite move on. It was an incredible act of charity by one with virtually nothing to give to one with virtually nothing left. (V) (29, 245)

Meanwhile, across the ravine bottom, near the foot of Hill 198, Pvt. Peterson rolled into a convenient shell hole close by and attempted to bandage his wounded leg with a muddy spiral puttee, while the machine-gun fire continued over his head. When it stopped, he peeked over the edge and saw:

"(The Germans) came out and covered up our dead and some who were still moaning with brush and sticks. Those who were not severely wounded, they carried away. Then they broke up their rifles. This I could see from where I was laying. They did not see me when they were doing this, but when they did one of them threw a hand grenade at me that flew over my head. I then threw up my rifle. They then came over and carried me over to where the rest of the American wounded were laying. I helped dress my buddy's wounds (Pvt. Duryea) with bandages I asked the German Red Cross boys to take from the dead Americans, as the Germans had none.

Hollingshead and one buddy were able to walk (probably Pvt. Ilardo) and they were taken away. My buddy, Cecil Duryea, and myself were not able to walk, so we were left there. One German saw I had a wristwatch and came over and tore it from my wrist. He also took the tobacco I had received... We sat here only a few minutes, then they carried us over to their machine gun and placed us one on each side of the barrel. In case more of our boys should come along, they were prepared to give them the same reception that they gave us. We were to be used as shields... (44, 224)

Private Hollingshead lay on his back on the ground in the brush into which he had rolled for several minutes staring up at the cloudy, gray sky through the trees following the barrage of lead, stunned but alert. "This can't really be happening to me - this is just a dream" kept repeating in his mind as he lay there. Still as death, a twinge of guilt bit into him for the first time and he wished he were back among his buddies and the comparative safety of that muddy hillside. He closed his eyes tight against his fear. After the machine-gun died out, he decided to take a chance and half rolled over to peek through the brush, anxious to see what had become of his buddies. There he was met with the horrible sight of Pvt. Rainwater's virtually sawed-through form just a short distance ahead. Then, twigs cracked and he felt rather than heard a presence near him. Looking up and off to one side slowly, he saw a German looming over him out of the brush about six feet away and leveling a Luger pistol at his head. Terrified, Pvt. Hollingshead slowly rolled back over onto his back again, raising his hands above his head. At length, "Kamerad" was all he could manage to squeak out through his terror. Then, much to his surprise, the German lowered his gun and smiled. In one of many interviews he would give over the years, 'Holly' later said:

"The kraut pointed to my left leg. I looked down and for the first time realized I had been hit. Of my seven buddies, I found four were dead and the other three seriously injured. We four survivors were helped over to a machine gun nest. Pretty soon a German runner motioned for me to go back through the forest with him. After we had gone a short distance I was turned over to another guide. This happened several times until we reached the German headquarters. Each new guide would go through my pockets, but none took any of my belongings. One thing that interested them was my safety razor; they all wanted that. Two offered to buy it and one wanted to trade his straight razor for it, but when I refused it was put back in my pocket.

Quite a distance from the headquarters, I was blindfolded and the bandage was not taken from my eyes until I arrived there. I was taken into a dugout and when my eyes were uncovered, I was surprised to see how enormous and well furnished it was, being divided into small rooms having board floors and walls...On a beautifully carved table was an old typewriter and a phonograph. Several chairs and a comfortable couch in the room all went to make the place as cozy and homelike as a front line dugout could be made. I was then greeted by a handsome, well-dressed German officer, Lt. Fritz Prinz..." (33, 222)

Back down in the ravine, Private's Duryea and Peterson were being used as terrified human shields at the machine-gun position, but no more Doughboys had come along the path. After a time, the Germans finally carted the two wounded Americans up the slope of Hill 198 and left them lying near the same deep dugout entrance Pvt. Hollingshead had been taken to. Again, Pvt. Peterson:

"A German officer (apparently Lt. Prinz) was standing in the dug out doorway. The first thing we asked him for was something to eat and he gave us a slice of dark bread and a cigarette. This man could

speak English well (and) was smoking cigarettes all the time and seemed to be very excited… He asked how many were left on the hillside and if they had much ammunition left. I told him they had plenty of ammunition and would never surrender. He asked about a German we had captured and what we had done with him. I told him he was okay, although I did not know anything about him…" (224)

Lieutenant Prinz, who had been called back to the front of the 254th from Buzancy after he had interrogated Lieutenant's Leak and Harrington in order to handle the other captives from the Pocket, continued to interrogate the two wounded Doughboys for some time, asking seemingly innocuous questions. He even allowed once or twice how he himself was tired of the war. After a while, he went back into the dugout and Pvt. Peterson took the opportunity to furtively bury some letters he was carrying that he remembered had derogatory statements about Germany in them. A short time later, a middle-aged German came along, examined his wounded leg and stabbing a dirty finger at Peterson's forehead, said in perfect English, "This is where you should have gotten it." He then showed the two wounded men his nice rifle and bragged about shooting one of the officers in the ravine in the head. (Probably Lt. Peabody.) Eventually the two wounded Doughboys were left alone, seemingly forgotten as the Germans went about the daily business of making war on the Pocket. Since there was little chance of escape, they made themselves as comfortable as possible. (VI)

Down in the dugout, some minutes before he would leave to speak with Private's Peterson and Duryea, Lt. Prinz first greeted a terrified Pvt. Hollingshead, standing stiffly at attention before him. Lieutenant Prinz stood up from the table, walked forward with a smile and outstretched hand, and introduced himself.

"Oh how do you do? I am Lt. Prinz."

"Private Hollingshead, sir. Lowell Hollingshead."

"How long since you've eaten?" the German asked, pumping Holly's hand. His English was almost faultless, but with more than a hint of accent. His speech pattern was very Continental, much as was Major Whittlesey's.

"Five days," Hollingshead answered.

He let Holly's hand go.

"You poor devil. You must be starved."

"I certainly am."

The German officer turned to an orderly, rattled off some quick German, and the man disappeared deeper into the dugout. It was wonderfully warm in the room. Seeing the wound on Pvt. Hollingshead's leg, Lt. Prinz led him over to the couch and had him sit down. Pulling a gold tipped cigarette from a box on the table he stuck it between the errant private's lips, lit it, and soon thereafter, a German doctor expertly bandaged his wounded leg. Not long after, the orderly reappeared with a small pail full of vegetables, meat and whatnot, all swimming in vinegar and accompanied by a large loaf of dark bread, which he put on the table. Private Hollingshead simply stared at it, then back at Lt. Prinz.

"Go ahead." The German smiled and gestured to the food. "Dig in."

Holly needed no second invitation.

As he set to eating with a vengeance, two other German officers (most likely Hauptmann's Von Sybel and Bickel) came in, spoke briefly with Lt. Prinz in German and then, after lighting cigarettes, one of them began to question the dirty, disheveled Doughboy in rather poorer English than had Lt. Prinz. What was the ammunition supply like in the ravine? What outfit was he with and their troop strength? What was the morale like among his comrades? Private Hollingshead largely ignored them, continuing to jam the food into his mouth. He only paused once for a short moment, long enough to say, "Sorry, too busy to talk right now," without even looking up before continuing his feeding frenzy.

Exchanging glances and hiding smiles, the three Germans let him eat and held a low, long conversation among themselves before Lt. Prinz slipped from the room to talk to prisoners Peterson and Duryea. They were prepared to provide one last chance for the American commander in the ravine to save the lives of what remained of his command (and, unknowingly, the honor of the 254th regiment) and this famished prisoner might just be the one to help them do it. (33, 123, 163, 222, 263, 280, 290, 291, 292, 329)

It was not until 10:00 a.m. that Lt. Morse decided to fly a patrol over the Charlevaux Ravine again. By then, the morning fog had mostly cleared, making clearer surveillance of the ground possible. They had no real way of knowing whether they had gotten the supplies on target the day before, since the heavy ground fire had prevented them from making the long observations needed to insure success. Hopefully, the sacrifices made the day before had not been in vein. All night they had waited for some firm word of Lieutenant's Goettler and Bleckley, but none had come. The only intimation of what had happened was when Lt. Bleckley's map case and map, marked with the few positions he and Dad had had time to scout the afternoon before, arrived late that night by courier, with word that Bleck had been taken to a hospital. Other than that there had been no news and Lt. Morse had not been able to find out anything more. In light of Lt. McCurdy's report that Major Whittlesey was not where he had said he was then, Lt. Morse called up the 77th Division earlier that morning to double check the coordinates again and find out the latest information. He was given the same set of map numbers and told that nothing had yet changed. Further, the squadron was requested to continue dropping supplies. All right, fine. But where, since the command in the ravine was obviously not where they had said?

Yet, since they could hardly ignore the order for the missions to continue, and if that command really *was* still out there, then the squadron would have to try and locate them first. Orders or not however, it was a fool's errand to risk losing any more planes or men carelessly. Attention then turned to Lt. Bleckley's map, showing at least a few of the spots to stay away from. Perhaps if they were to follow that map from a higher altitude than before, a crew *might* have a fighting chance of getting in and out of the ravine without being all shot to hell. The team would need to scout the entire ravine thoroughly however and thus develop a fairly accurate idea of where to drop the supplies. Once Major Whittlesey's true position was located, then they could send out more planes, but not before.

Lieutenant Beebe immediately volunteered for the patrol, but Lt. Morse turned him down. Dave Beebe was Dad Goettler's best friend in the squadron and much too close to the situation and Lt. Morse figured that he would likely take wide chances in his efforts to not only find Major Whittlesey and his men, but also some sign, any sign, of his pal. Therefore, Lt. Morse unofficially grounded the pilot; something Lt. Beebe only bitterly accepted.(VII) Instead, just before 10:30 a.m., Lieutenant's Robert M. Anderson, pilot, and Woodville J. Rogers, observer, took off on the contact patrol in a DH marked No. 16 and with the name "Shy-Ann" painted on the engine cowling. Though they had flown high protective cover the day before for a couple of the planes dropping supplies into the ravine, they had not gotten that low themselves and therefore had only a general idea of exactly where in the long ravine to look. Heading in over Binarville, they came to the valley from near Etang de Poligny, but well up around 600 meters or so, in order to avoid the heaviest of the fire from the 'hot spots' on the map. As Lt. Rogers scanned the ground through a pair of good binoculars, they started to make a thorough sweep. Lieutenant Anderson calmly swung back and forth, all the while slowly working his way east. Occasionally, hits from ground fire pierced parts of the plane; the generator for the wireless set was smashed, a control wire cut, a thud as a bullet sunk into a strut. It was a slow, nerve jangling process.

About 11:30 a.m., Lt. Rogers signaled to his pilot that he had seen something when they were just about three-quarters of a kilometer east of the Moulin d'Charlevaux and Lt. Anderson swung around as the observer scanned the area again. Yes, there they were - two small, dirty company-infantry panels, near the foot of the northern hillside of the ravine, almost indistinguishable from the earth beneath them, but definitely there. He grabbed his Very pistol and fired the call for more panels. Nothing. Lieutenant Anderson swung around again and Rogers fired another light. The enemy ground fire increased from below. Then, just as Lt. Anderson was swinging around for yet another pass, his observer let out a 'whoop'; he now had seen not only the two little panels, but a larger, battalion one near some brush, that he had missed before just to the west of (and equally as dirty as) the other two. He marked the coordinates - 294.9-276.3 - noted the time and gave Lt. Anderson the signal that he had what they wanted, who immediately swung the DH south toward Remicourt, success riding the air with them. (110, 248, 249, 259, 276)

It was the great pain in his leg that finally stopped Private Hollingshead's feeding frenzy. Lieutenant Prinz laid him down on the couch again and called the doctor back into the room, who unbandaged Holly's knee, spread something on the wound and wrapped it up tight again. Then, Lt. Prinz and the other two German officers started the questions in earnest.

"No sir. I will not tell you a word," Hollingshead simply repeated again and again. His leg throbbed and he could tell that the other two Germans were starting to lose patience.

"What state do you hail from?" Lt. Prinz suddenly asked off handedly. This was a different track and Hollingshead told himself to be careful.

"Ohio, sir."

"Oh yes, I have been there. To Cincinnati. In fact, I was in business in your country for six years before the war. Washington State. Beautiful country up there."

The German looked tired, Private Hollingshead thought.

"We already know all about your command there in the ravine, you know. Even that the French have dropped the Honor Cross award to your commander by airplane," Lt. Prinz said slightly smugly. (VIII) Then he said, "I admire the courage of those men on the hill and I feel sorry for them. Look here."

Leading Private Hollingshead out of the dugout and a short distance across the top of Hill 198, he handed him a pair of field glasses and pointed through the trees across the ravine to the hillside opposite. There, Holly saw the terribly piteous sight of what remained of the American position he had crawled away from that morning. He was surprised to see it so clearly. The brush and tree cover was far more decimated than they had realized in their anxiousness for any kind of concealment. The low wall of mud covered, rotting corpses shielded the wounded, though just barely, and listening closely he could hear their moans and wails in the distance, while a faint, yet pungent stink tickled his nostrils on the slight wind. Horror struck and deeply affected, Pvt. Hollingshead pretended to be mixed up in his directions and said he could see nothing.

"Oh, I see. As you Americans say, you are a little entangled," Lt. Prinz said and let out a small chuckle at the pun before then leading Holly back inside. He had to have been sure that the wounded American had seen what he was intended to, since one could hardly miss it.

Once back down in the warm dugout, Pvt. Hollingshead felt faint. The loss of blood and shock was obviously catching up, as was the sudden big meal, and Lt. Prinz had him lie down on the couch again. Sitting down at the typewriter and inserting a clean piece of white paper, the German worked the keys swiftly and briefly before he pulled up a chair next to the couch and sat down with the results of his labors in his hand. Private Hollingshead immediately sat up - too fast and almost vomited his lunch at Lt. Prinz's feet.

Lieutenant Prinz looked at him steadily.

"I can hear the screams of your wounded clear over here. I know they are dying," he said. "It is a terrible thing."

Hollingshead allowed that it was much worse when they were your friends and you were right up beside the screaming and dying.

The German now looked Holly in the eye uncomfortably.

"I am your enemy. But can we not act like human beings?"

"I guess we could," Hollingshead replied warily after a short pause.

Prinz paused briefly, still stared intently at the boy and then leaned in as if in earnest.

"I've written a letter to your commanding officer, asking him to surrender," he began, handing Private Hollingshead the note he had typed. "He has no means of escape anyway and it seems horrible to kill so many brave men. I offer him this one chance. I want you to take it back to him."

Holly looked at the paper and thought a moment, unsure he could even make the decision. Everything still seemed dream-like just then, maybe from the blood loss, maybe from the shock and excitement, he could not tell which. Could he do this thing his enemy asked of him? On one hand, to carry the message was to admit abandoning his position on the hillside, which was, in effect, desertion and another great twinge of guilt washed over him. He might also be considered an agent of the enemy and shot for that. After all, he would be delivering a letter from the enemy - of his own free will - that requested of the American commander their unconditional *surrender*. That smacked of treason of some sort.

On the other hand, he had no desire to spend the rest of the war, however long that might be, as a prisoner held by the Germans. Who knew how he would be treated? Sure, they had been good to him so far, but right now they wanted something from him. It would probably be a different story in a prison camp inside Germany. Better to try his luck being rescued back with the command. At least there, he had a chance of freedom. Then again, he might be killed out there...

There was also the pitiable sight he had seen through the binoculars. Something had to be done for the men he left behind; perhaps this was it. Maybe the Major would see this as an opportunity to save the rest of them from becoming what Pvt. Rainwater, Pvt. Clark and the hundreds of others on the hillside had become. Possibly, an offer of surrender presented *to* him might be just the face-saving measure the Major wanted, rather than having to make the offer himself. But then again, delivery of just such a note might paint him as some sort of collaborator with the Germans.

"If I do this, you must put in the letter that I do so strictly against my will," he said finally.

"Done," Prinz said, and took the paper back.

"I'd still like some time to think about it. Could I tell you after I've had some time to rest?" Pvt. Hollingshead asked.

"But of course." The German lieutenant smiled and stood up.

Holly then lay back down and dozed on the couch as the ancient typewriter again clicked in his ears, this time from seemingly far, far away. It was about 2:00 p.m. (33, 163, 222, 280, 290)

Back at Remicourt, Lieutenant's Anderson and Rogers landed about 12:30 p.m. and rumbled to a stop in front of the hangers. They had the location, Lt. Rogers exultantly yelled to Lt. Morse, and they quickly got on the phone to the 77th Division. However, a pall hung over the field, for definite word had just come in shortly before that Lt. Goettler was dead and that Lt. Bleckley had been wounded and died of his wounds.

Ambulance driver Bill Ettinger, having delivered Lt. Bleckley's body to Villers-Daucourt, had reported there that Lt. Goettler's body was still entangled in the wreckage, before then heading back to his first aid post at Rome Farm above Binarville. Shortly before midday of October 7 another ambulance driver, New York native Lt. Martin Owens, commanding Ambulance Section 517, went out to retrieve Lt. Goettler's body. Arriving at the crash scene, he found that Ettinger's stretcher-bearers had already extracted the Chicago lieutenant from the wreck the day before, wrapping his terribly mutilated body in some of the fabric of the plane in order to keep it together and laid him out on the grass beside it. Loading the body onto a litter and sliding it into his ambulance, Lt. Owens then searched Lt. Goettler's pockets, finding his pay book, wallet, home address, a few pictures and some other things. He then unhooked one of the winged propeller devices from his collar and ripped a small piece of fabric from the plane, all of which he later sent home to Goettler's mother. Driving the body to Villers-Daucourt, Lt. Goettler was buried late that afternoon in grave number 69, right next to Lt. Bleckley's number 70, with Chaplain W. Stuart Rule of Kentucky giving the last rights. (110, 241, 249)

East of the valley of the Aire River, the right flank of the 28th Division had moved up some, pulled along by elements of the 82nd Division and the 1st Division in line, moving above it to the northeast beyond the towns of Fleville and Chatel-Chehery. Up there, the German line seemed to be cracking and letting go a bit at a time. There were pockets of American troops battling forward and backward almost hourly and the front was a shifting mess. However, the efforts seemed to be paying off, and progress was rippling all down the line. As the 28th's right advanced behind and below the 82nd's onslaught (themselves below the 1st), it was necessarily dragging along its left as well, which was ever so slowly beginning to batter their way past le Chene Tondu. As they did, it allowed the 153rd Brigade of the 77th to advance their right flank as well. The 306th, which was manning the entire brigade front with the 305th now behind in support pending a rupture of the German line, found its line stretching tighter by the hour. Reports had their advanced scouts nearly to the cross roads of La Viergette, or at least nearing the Binarville-La Viergette road (though well east of the Pocket) and this caused General Whittenmeyer to make preparations to slip some of the 305th back into his line along the right, in order to exploit the anticipated break there. Meanwhile, on the left of his front, the 306th had already been working with the right elements of the 307th at an opening in a wire angle, through which several dozen 1st/307th men were working to get through. It looked as if there might be a break coming from that direction as well very soon. (35, 42, 88, 90, 111, 113, 138, 139)

General Alexander heard all this from both General Whittenmeyer, and 1st Corps chief of staff Colonel Malin Craig through phone conversations late that morning. It was good news. If the 82nd and the 1st Divisions were actually putting their pincer pressure on the forest from their side and it was causing ripple effects on down to his line by that morning, then perhaps the French side of the plan would not be needed. If what appeared to be happening in General Whittenmeyer's zone were any indication as to what might continue, it would not be long before that section of the line in the 154th Brigade sector would start to open as well. With their flank threatened in the east by the pincer pressure, combined with the steady hammering of General's Johnson and Whittenmeyer from the south, the Germans were unlikely to hang on to what little they still possessed of the Giselher line in the forest and instead pull back to the Kriemhilde. Then why not help it along all he could? And again, the best way to advance the line was to simply move it up to where Major Whittlesey was - opposite the Giselher. With the 153rd Brigade already on the ball and moving and General Johnson with the 308th holding steady pressure against, but unable to advance beyond, Hills 198 and 205, Colonel Houghton and his 307th would be the key then. And since they already had a good chance at getting through that wire seam over there, General Alexander thought he smelled success at hand. (2, 91, 131, 139, 144)

Getting Colonel Houghton on the phone, the Division Commander laid out the situation farther down the line and demanded to know how soon before the Colonel thought he would be ready to move his men forward, as everything to his right was well ahead of him. (True - this time.) Colonel Houghton explained the situation to General Alexander just as he had to General Johnson; to rush the operation would take away the element of surprise required and would send the whole enterprise down in flames. It would be that afternoon before he would be ready, considering his present strength. If the General wanted it any sooner, then Colonel Houghton would need more troops. He asked for his 2nd Battalion back, saying that with them he could bust the line quicker, and then head west hard and fast down the Binarville-La Viergette road ahead of Major Whittlesey, relieving him and likely meeting up with the French down near the Charlevaux Mill. They would then effectively cut off all of both Hills 198 and that bastard Hill 205 from any support, eliminating the problem and grabbing up a nice bag of prisoners to boot. Nevertheless, General Alexander refused, telling Colonel Houghton that those men were needed to back up the decimated 308th in their holding campaign in the Ravin d'Argonne. Then let the 306th slide down west and cover more of the line, which would allow his 1st/307th to concentrate its remaining troops for the operation at the wire, Houghton asked. That was impossible, General Alexander replied, as both the 305th and 306th had pulled ahead of the 307th, which was the point of the call in the first place; when was Colonel Houghton going to move his line along with them? *They* seemed to be progressing with what *they* had.

The Colonel knew full well that the left elements of the 153rd were not really much farther ahead than his own right, since they were working in conjunction with each other there just to the right of the wire seam (though the *right* of the 153rd was climbing ahead). This he told General Alexander, in no uncertain terms, but the Division Commander merely replied that General Whittenmeyer had personally confirmed their positions; troops of the 153rd were pushing toward the Binarville-La Viergette road.

"Then for Christ's sake tell them to stop machine-gunning and bombing my men," the fever-wracked Colonel Houghton finally exclaimed. "All the fire we're getting is coming from that direction!" he yelled, slamming the phone down.

Slowly, the filtering at the wire continued. (2, 10, 91, 131, 132, 138, 139, 142, 144)

However, General Alexander was now determined to drive his line through the German resistance that day at almost any cost. He next contacted General McCloskey concerning the lack of damage to the wire done by the morning barrage in the sector of the 154th and the need for a second barrage that afternoon; they *had* to get through *this afternoon* and that was that! General McCloskey wanted ranging shots this time, observed for accuracy. How about a barrage from about noon until 2:00 p.m., directed from the air? The attack could go over after that. Pull the troop's well back then, General Alexander was told. This barrage would include everything they could muster - some 155's, some 75's from both the 305th and the 304th, 302nd Trench Mortars, 37mm guns... everything but the kitchen sink. Get 'em back at least 500 meters to the rear of the line. Never mind the area around the French this time, General Alexander said, just concentrate along the 307th's front, the bottom of the Ravin d'Argonne and the slopes at the opening to the Charlevaux. He would call the 50th Aero Squadron and arrange everything.

However, Lt. Morse beat the Division Commander to the punch, calling first with news of Major Whittlesey's apparent location, for they had seen his panels on the ground. Therefore, they must still be holding on. It was just what General Alexander wanted to hear and he passed the good news on to General Johnson personally - Major Whittlesey's force was still holding there in the Charlevaux, *confirmed*. By 1:00 p.m. that afternoon then, the planes were out and the first ranging shells were flying in sharp and accurate into the German main line.

Meanwhile, as the tremendous shellfire came down, the Germans on the line between the Pocket and the remainder of the battered 308th grew more nervous. They were already losing their grip on the line farther up to the east and it now looked as if there was to be another major push made by the enemy to relieve the *Americanernest*, very soon. Therefore, the final attack then being planned for that afternoon against the surrounded American force definitely needed to succeed, for there would be no more chances after.

Without even realizing it then, both sides of the ravine were building up toward a final effort... (2, 93, 94, 97, 98, 100, 110, 114, 131, 138, 139, 140, 141, 144)

Major Whittlesey's men watched the planes wheel around above them on their artillery missions. What was the point, they wondered? The rest of the regiment was never going to break through, and every man-jack in the ravine was already just as good as dead... At the creek edge, someone again tried for a full canteen and accidentally let the cap on its little keeper chain bang against the dented aluminum body of the vessel, making a sharp 'tink' that rang out. A machine-gun barked briefly from somewhere out among the weedy ravine bottom and another thick rivulet of blood ran across the sodden ground and into the brook.

(I) Private James B Rainwater was one of the Company D men that had gotten mixed in with the 1st Battalion runners just before the Small Pocket that Major Whittlesey had hung onto after; something of a habit with the Major all through the battle. He was however, no relation to Pvt. Carl A. Rainwater, a Company G/2nd Battalion Scout from Cascade County, Montana then also in the Pocket and starving up near the Combined Battalion PC funk.

(II) Major Whittlesey came over and gave them a talking to as well, impressing upon the two the great importance of their mission. "If you get through," he told them, "tell them that we have not surrendered and that we need help at once." It seemed almost an "impassioned plea", to which Cliff Brown replied to the effect that they would make it back, because "God would lead them through." According to an unprovenanced newspaper clipping in the author's files, as they were stripping off their excess equipment just before they set off, a replacement lieutenant (most probably the wounded Lt. Trainor) gave them hell for attempting to go back without proper uniform and made to stop them. Brown pitched a bitch at this, and he and 'Koz' then appealed to the Major, who told them to go out as they saw fit.

(III) Other reports have Lt. Schenck as being killed by the shell after he had gotten back to his hole with Sgt. Bendheim, who apparently took a piece of shrapnel from it in his unwounded leg. However, James Larney's later descriptions, as well as those given to author's Tom Johnson and Fletcher Pratt for their 1938 book, agree with the version given in the text. Gordon Lockwood Schenck's body still lies in France with his men, at the big American cemetery at Romagne sous Montfaucon.

(IV). After the war ended and he was home starting to give interviews about his experiences, Pvt. Hollingshead would relay a story about how a mystery sergeant, whom he did not know and could never again name, crawled over to the Company H position that morning. "The Major has asked for volunteers to try and work their way back to one of those fallen packages," the sergeant is supposed to have said, and Hollingshead was but one of those volunteers. None of the others who would survive the expedition they undertook along side of him ever contradicted the story either, ostensibly as it effectively absolved them all of the crime of desertion. Indeed, the story may have even been cooked up before they left the bivouac, but either way is pure bunk. Had the Major truly sought volunteers for such a mission, it would have been among his experienced men and not the replacements, nor would he have sent a sergeant over to Company H looking for said volunteers when Lt. Cullen was perfectly capable of doing so himself, and likely would have. Further, there has always been some speculation as to who was actually in his party, but available evidence now indicates the individuals named in this text. More to the point is the speculation as to who the American Indian was that led the party out, most often thought in previous years to have been Pvt. Robert Dodd, a Nevada replacement and a full blooded member of the Paiute tribe. However, once again, available evidence disputes this and points instead to Pvt. Rainwater, not the least of which will be the later testimonial by Pvt. Hollingshead of seeing the Indian leader of the group nearly cut in two by machine-gun fire when they are ambushed. Private Dodd however, survived the war and returned to Nevada.

(V) In their 1938 book The Lost Battalion, Tom Johnson and Fletcher Pratt refused to name Bendheim who, though he did lose his leg afterward, nevertheless lived a long and happy family life after the war, for fear of embarrassing him. They further named the sergeant he had stopped as Walter Baldwin instead of Martin Tuite in order to keep people off the trail. However, Jim Larney, close enough to hear the exchange and best friends with Walter Baldwin for years anyway, corrects the story by naming both Tuite and Bendheim. Here, Lionel Bendheim is only mentioned in honor of his true courage and very real humanity.

(VI) One interesting thing that Pvt. Peterson also mentioned is that besides seeing several other prisoners from the ravine up on the hill, he also recalled seeing a German dressed in an American uniform "running around," as he put it, with the other German troops. This is significant, when considered alongside Pvt. Hollingshead's story about the mystery sergeant who had gathered up the party on the Major's orders to go out looking for the airplane package. Private Peterson's statement then begs the question - could there have really been a "mystery" sergeant? Was he a German, who crawled into the position in a U.S. uniform to create some sort of nefarious trap to capture or kill more Doughboys?

Probably not. There is plenty of evidence indicating that the men who went out looking for the food did so of their own accord. Again, as previously stated, the most damning evidence against the story is that Major Whittlesey would not have sent a sergeant to do the job of gathering together the party in Company H when its officer, Lt. Cullen, was still alive and unwounded and perfectly capable of performing the task, or of even delegating it. Nor did any surviving sergeant (few though they were) who had been in the ravine that day ever step forward and claim to be the one who sent the party out, as he almost certainly would have once Pvt. Hollingshead started to gain fame after the war, and few NCOs were killed on October 7. Additionally, Lt. Cullen knew nothing about the party until it was already well on its way across the brook, and it was he who reported it to Major Whittlesey, who, according to the lieutenant himself, knew nothing at all about it. The final and most condemnatory piece of evidence reveals itself in the next chapter, when Pvt. Hollingshead actually admits to his "indiscretion" – desertion - and to none other than Major Whittlesey himself.

As for the man Pvt. Peterson saw "running around" with the Germans on Hill 198, he never said whether the man sounded like a German when he spoke. However, among the many different languages and dialects spoken by men the 308th, there were more than a few German speakers. Even if the man did sound German, it certainly would not mean that he was not just another Doughboy prisoner being hustled around by German captors.

(VII) He was closely watched by other members of the squadron for several days afterwards as well, having fallen in to a deep depression. Then, three weeks after Lt. Goettler's death, Beebe was shot down and captured, spending 10 days as a prisoner of war.

(VIII) The Germans genuinely seem to have believed this fantastic yarn. Exactly how this ridiculous part of the legend actually got started is unknown. However, it seems to have been a purely German invention since no mention of it has ever been found in any other documented source other than those from the German side. The 'Honor Cross' is obviously a reference to the Croix de Guerre, something that Major Whittlesey did get, but not until much later.

Ancillary sources used in this chapter include: 1, 20, 24, 30 , 31, 32, 36, 43, 50, Various 52-86, 147, Various 152-216, 218, 219, 225, 227, 228, 230, 235, 240, 243, 246, 250, 251, 254, 257, 260-264, 268, 272, 273, 278, Various 282-338, 339, 347, 349, 350, 354-360, 362, 364, 370, 371, 374

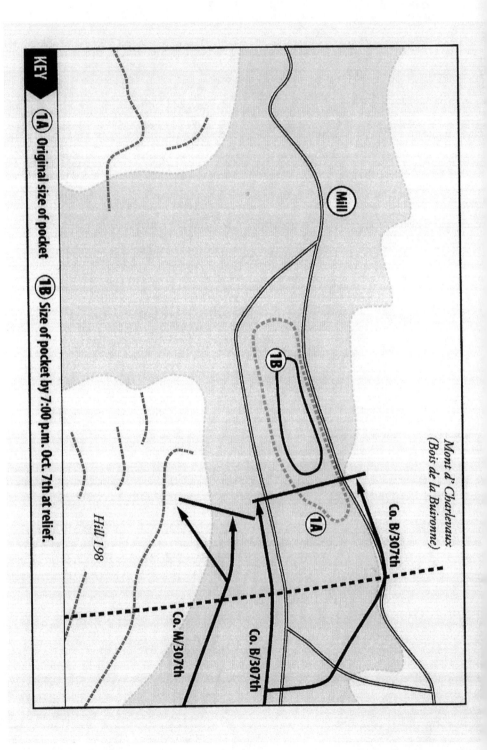

KEY

1A Original size of pocket   **1B** Size of pocket by 7:00 p.m. Oct. 7th at relief.

Mont d' Charlevaux
(Bois de la Buironne)

Mill

1B

1A

Co. B/307th

Co. B/307th

Co. M/307th

Hill 198

466

October 7, 1918 P.M.
"…He is quite a soldier, we envy you."
Lt. Prinz, referring to Pvt. Hollingshead in the "surrender letter."

The barrage that afternoon was largely a wasted effort and without flank support from the French, the attack of the 308th quickly fell apart under the fire from Hill 205 again. In fact it all had happened so quickly that it had hardly given the men in the Pocket pause, so rapid was the crescendo, peak, and fade. Barely a half an hour after it began, most of the heavy fighting had died away already and both sides exhaustedly settled down to the normal afternoon bickering that usually filled the line. General Johnson, surprised at the lack of duration, if not general malaise to the attack, passed word of its broad lack of success on to General Alexander. The remaining men of the 308th seemed to have come to the end of their rope; it was to be all on Colonel Houghton's head after all.

On the far northeast line of 1st Corps though, the 28th, 82nd and 1st Divisions that afternoon were finding still more successes even beyond those of the morning. The Germans seemed to definitely be pulling out. Le Chene Tondu was evacuated of German troops at around 2:00 p.m. and after that, the left of the 28th had started moving in earnest. Enemy troops were seen evacuating the Bois de la Naza and suddenly the 153rd was pressing well ahead too, their right connected firmly to the 28th Division's flank. Like a garden gate, the line was beginning to swing wide and clear against the German's left flank within the greater Argonne forest, driving them back.

Then, a message arrived at 77th Division PC from Colonel Houghton; the filtering plan of the past two days had begun to pay dividends. His Major McKinney, the only battalion commander left in the regiment (besides Colonel Houghton himself, who was wearing whatever hat fit by that time) had sent men from his Company B, under Lt. Fredrick Tillman, into attack through that gap in the wire to follow up the successes farther to his right. The Germans had been caught completely by surprise at the results of the infiltration and though Lt. Tillman, assisted by his only surviving lieutenant, Stuart Hamblin, was running into heavy machine-gun fire from his left, slightly below where Major Whittlesey was, he was working his way around it and making good, if slow, progress. "Expect to get them out today…" Colonel Houghton sent back to General Johnson and General Alexander both around the time General Johnson was reporting the failure of the general attack in the 308th's sector. General Johnson then sent orders up to Colonel Houghton for Major McKinney to have Lt. Tillman press on to Major Whittlesey's position at all cost and immediately began issuing directions to get large quantities of food, water, clothing and medical supplies up into the Ravin d'Argonne by rail as soon as possible. The 307th was getting close; time was of the essence. However, already by that time - about 3:00 p.m. - Lt. Tillman and B, with elements of companies A, D, and M in the vanguard, were closer than any of them realized. (103, 104, 138, 139, 235)

In fact, it was just past 3:00 p.m. and only about a kilometer and a half away from Lt. Tillman's position, that Lt. Prinz gently shook Private Lowell Hollingshead's shoulder, rousing him. "If you are to get the message back before dark, you must start now," Lt. Prinz said mildly.

Swinging his legs to the floor, Pvt. Hollingshead thought again for a moment and asked to read the letter. Lieutenant Prinz showed it to him, indicating where the private needed to sign his name, as he had not known how to spell it. The letter seemed to exonerate him of all wrongdoing, Holly thought, the German having made it abundantly clear that he was delivering the message against his will. Yet only nervously did Pvt. Hollingshead sign the letter in both spots Lt. Prinz indicted, then:

"All right, I'm ready, sir," he said, which was a lie. He was still as unsure as ever about the situation.

"Splendid!" Lt. Prinz boomed and straightened up.

Holly stood up and immediately almost fell back over. His leg hurt terribly and had grown horribly stiff. Lieutenant Prinz quickly reached back into a corner and handed over a wooden cane, which Pvt. Hollingshead took with appreciation, and then helped the boy to his feet. Folding the letter into an envelope and sealing it, Lt. Prinz then stuffed it into the breast pocket of the Doughboy's filthy service coat, pulled two full packs of cigarettes from his own pocket and put them in another of Holly's pockets, and then stuffed what remained of the bread from the table into yet another. Disappearing from the room for a moment, the lieutenant returned with a small white flag with an instructional stencil on it showing how it could be used as either a sling or tourniquet (a common item in the German army at the time), tied it to a stick, and handed it to Holly.

"This will give you protection crossing no-man's-land. As good as a flag of truce," he said confidently, but Pvt. Hollingshead did not feel at all so confident.

Lieutenant Prinz then wrapped a blindfold carefully back across the nervous Doughboy's eyes, telling him he would be given a guide to take him to within 100 meters of the American position. His own men in their outposts would all be instructed that he was coming so they would not fire as he made his way back to his commanding officer and delivered the letter. Private Hollingshead however, was growing uneasy, sure he was being set up for murder and silently cursed himself for ever agreeing to go on this fool's errand.

"Good luck, my friend," Lt. Prinz said from somewhere beyond the blindfold and shook the private's sweaty hand. "Your guide's name is Adolph."

Turning to Adolph, Prinz rattled a string of German and whisked him and Private Hollingshead out the door and up the steps of the dugout, where Privates Duryea and Peterson watched them walk off.

Back down in the dugout, Lt. Prinz picked up the telephone and let his commander know the situation. Major Hunicken, with mixed feelings, recognized it was a final attempt at saving lives on both sides and he had already agreed earlier to send out word to his officers to hold off the attack for another hour or so and await the results of the letter. They in turn passed orders to all their outposts: there was an American prisoner with a German escort coming toward the *Americanernest*; the American was *not* to be fired upon, but let back into the position... (33, 163, 222, 263)

"Just heard from Houghton; his advanced elements are now on the line 95.4-75.9," General Johnson said, calling General Alexander around 3:15 p.m. "He is probably on 76.0 now. He is moving toward Whittlesey and taking rations and medical supplies. I have given him orders to take over the entire line of the brigade sector on arrival and the 308th will constitute the second line regiment. On the left I have sent out a company on each side to try out what's on the front (of the Ravin d'Argonne), particularly those trenches on the left (meaning those of Hill 198, on the left of the brigade – author) and given orders for rations and medical supplies to be rushed up on the railroad."

Those map coordinates put the 307th just over a half a kilometer away from Major Whittlesey's bivouac; close, but still no cigar. Yet everything was now being prepared in the Ravin d'Argonne for the Majors ultimate relief. Most particularly the 307th and 308th ambulance companies had been alerted for the eventuality of the Binarville-La Viergette road being secured, and the men of the 308th Regimental Band to be prepared to act as stretcher bearers back to l'Homme Mort if needed (part of which was being used as a first aid station). General Johnson then set about having Captain Breckenridge send probing patrols out from the main line on the 308th's right using the only available man power 'reserve' he still had available to him – the decimated 2nd/307th. These patrols were met with heavy fire, primarily coming from German troops falling back along the line from the east. Still, the Brigadier kept up the harassing tactics, if only to draw some additional pressure away from the successes of the 307th. However, as far as another possible general attack up the Ravin d'Argonne, after the fiasco that the midday attack had been, it was simply out of the question. Therefore, the Brigadier sent a message to Colonel Hannay later that afternoon stating that he thought it "would be murder to send his men back against that wire again" that day and if ordered to, he "would not do so."

Colonel Houghton, meanwhile, had Major McKinney driving his men forward as hard as possible. Parts of his main line were now over the headland of Hill 198, due in large part to the filtering tactic, and were beginning to slowly progress down the hill's reverse slope. This put his advance elements only about 400 meters south and 400 east of what had been the right flank perimeter line of the Pocket up until the evening before. Now however, that flank was perhaps 450-475 meters away to the west ahead of them; a small difference on paper, but a big one in the tangle of the Argonne. There was still a strong line of German troops separating Lt. Tillman and his Company B from the Pocket, dug in along a line that had only started bending back just east of about vertical 295.3 or so on the map - still too damned far away from Major Whittlesey yet. (The Major's position may be described as generally being along a line 294.9; with the numbers descending on the map from east to west). Yet even farther west, the French on the other side of the 308th had again taken up residence no farther forward than Binarville and were effectively out of the fighting for the day, being unable to move forward at all. (103, 109, 131, 138, 139, 140, 370)

The German, Adolph, was very careful to ensure that the blindfolded Private Hollingshead did not fall as they moved through the forest toward the Charlevaux Ravine, something that Hollingshead always later remembered with fondness. The little German babbled in his native tongue to him for a short time, but Holly, who did not understand at all, remained unable to answer. Soon, the German went silent too and after a while, they stopped and Hollingshead, sensing himself alone, took the opportunity to lie down and rest. Despite the cane, his leg ached acutely, his stomach was upset and he was very tired and terribly scared, now *really* beginning to think the whole adventure was a bad idea. Surprisingly, someone threw an overcoat over him, but he could not tell if it was to make him comfortable or to conceal him from an aircraft that he could hear buzzing around somewhere above. After a few minutes of comparative peace, he heard German voices talking excitedly very close at hand and the sound of a machine-gun's action being worked. All of a sudden, a long, chattering burst tore out very nearby, startling the daylights out of him and convincing him almost beyond persuasion that his own murder was imminent. Just as suddenly as it had begun though, the firing stopped. A short time later, Adolph reappeared, gently helping him up and directing him forward.

For the first time in minutes, Hollingshead breathed normally and they continued on their way.

They stumbled on for what seemed to the wounded private an eternity, before proceeding down a steep incline. At the bottom and a little way on again, the German soldier removed the blindfold. To Hollingshead's surprise, he found himself on what appeared to be the wagon road below the Pocket, but just where he did not know. He looked both left and right, blinking in the gloom of the misty afternoon but recognized only the road bank above the hillside on his right. He felt very vulnerable and naked standing out in the woods - a woods he had come to fear being out of cover in over the last 12 days - and had to fight down the urge to take off running for the nearest hole. Fat lot of good it would have done to try though, as his leg had started bleeding and throbbing again. Adolph handed him the stick with the white kerchief on it and then, again much to Hollingshead's surprise, grabbed his hand and shook it with a slight smile. Then gently turning him to his left, he pointed the direction down the wagon path, gave the errant Doughboy a slight push in the small of the back, and said, "goodbye and good luck" in German. Private Hollingshead slowly took a step and then another, raised the flag, and started forward on the longest walk of his life. He was headed west, that much he guessed, but could he really be all the way over beyond the *right* flank? Had they really traveled that far today? It seemed so far from where they had been captured that morning - God, *that* morning! It seemed so long ago…

Stumbling forward, waving the flag in front of him, he fell in the brush despite the cane, got up, and fell again. It was imperative he kept the flag waving for all to see. He was still terrified that one side or the other was going to open fire on him at any minute. Thankfully, the wagon road was infinitely easier to walk on than had been the forest floor. Once, he turned to see if the German was still on the road, but he had gone quickly back to his own position. A few stray shots rang out ahead from the slope on his right, but toward what direction he could not say. He listened for the tell tale 'swish' through the leaves that would indicate the shot had come close, but heard nothing. He kept moving, fell again, and this time was slower in getting up. He felt weak and faint and his knees shook. His legs and feet seemed to weigh a ton each and the food that he had eaten in the dug out was once more threatening to show itself. His thigh throbbed horribly and a stain of thick, sticky blood had soaked through the clean bandage. Struggling upright again, he staggered a few more yards and dropped to the muddy ground, still holding the flag high and giving it the occasional twirl.

Yet, his mind seemed fresh, alert and alive, with thought. How far had he come? More importantly, how far had he still to go? It was agony to get back up. Perhaps he should have refused to deliver the letter and stayed with the Germans. They had not treated him all that badly. Perhaps prison camp would not have been such a bad place to be. At least, he would be out of danger. It was taking all of his energy just to take one step. The flag waggled lower and still lower in front of him, until…

"Halt!"

He had gone about 100 meters, perhaps a little more, when the command came sharply from somewhere in front of him. It was distinctly American.

Hollingshead froze in his tracks and suddenly his body tensed with alertness, all the tiredness seemingly drained from his being in a burst of pure adrenaline.

"I've just come from the German lines, and I have a message for the Major!" he finally managed to call out to the unseen voice, his eyes wide.

"Who are you?" The Yankee accent was definitely unmistakable now.

"Private Hollingshead, Company H," he answered.

"Let's see that message!" the voice demanded.

"I can't. It's for Major Whittlesey."

There was a rustling and muttering of voices in the brush ahead on the right. Peering hard, Hollingshead could just make out the shape of American helmets and faceless heads through the meager foliage in the descending afternoon shadows.

"Wait there! Don't you move!" warned the unseen voice. There was more rustling on the hill. Hollingshead shifted slightly, but otherwise did not move, the flag hanging out in front of him motionless.

Shortly, a second voice, he supposed an officer, called to him demanding to see the message. Hollingshead again refused, repeating that it was for the Major and no one else, and once more identified himself.

"Bring him in and we'll take him to the Major," he heard the second voice order.

Hollingshead stumbled another yard or two forward and a ragged Doughboy hopped out of the brush and into the openness of the wagon road, crouched down, rifle ready, scanning all around for a possible trap. He advanced the few yards toward him, grabbed Hollingshead roughly by the arm, and practically dragged the wounded boy back into the brush at the foot of the slope on the right. Swiftly, Hollingshead was moved down across the base of the hill toward the center of the position, taking as much advantage of what little cover remained. The second voice, that of Sgt. Carroll of K, led the way. Hollingshead moved as well as he could with his wounded leg, but had little choice over the speed at which they traveled. They had him by one arm, while the other still clung to the cane and flag tightly. It did not take long to get to the middle of the shrunken Pocket where Sgt. Carroll shortly reported, "Major? We found this man wandering in from the right flank. Says he's got a message from the Hienies for you…"
(29, 33, 51, 163, 222, 263, 280, 292, 329)

What happened next has been the subject of much speculation and debate over the years. Most popular versions have been very 'watered down,' apparently in order to prevent any embarrassment for both Major Whittlesey's reputation, as well as Private Hollingshead's and probably designed to enhance Whittlesey's status as a hero. In the standard version, used by Johnson and Pratt for their 1938 book *The Lost Battalion*, which is the most accepted, Major Whittlesey and Captain McMurtry were sitting together in the headquarters funk, engaged in conversation as to whom to put in charge of the various units now that most officers were either killed or too badly shot up to continue, when Hollingshead suddenly showed up. The letter was presented to Captain McMurtry (Hollingshead's own Battalion Commander and to whom the letter was actually addressed), who then began berating the private for leaving his position. Major Whittlesey, however, stopped him, read the letter, and then passed it to McMurtry, who also read it, before passing it to Holderman, who appeared seemingly out of nowhere. Major Whittlesey then chastised the private before sending him back to his position with H and then ordered the signal panels taken in, in order to prevent their being confused as a sign of surrender. (29, 51)

That version of the story does not stand up in the light of at least two main eyewitness accounts, or other known facts. First, Major Whittlesey and Captain McMurtry had long before assigned the more capable sergeants and corporals to replace the missing officers (the only possible exception being a replacement for Lt. Gordon Schenck, who had only been killed a short time before). Therefore, any meeting was more likely to discuss who would lead Company C, or perhaps to arrange another patrol. Nor was any other officer but Major Whittlesey present when Private Hollingshead and his escort arrived on the scene - this according to Pvt. Larney, lying wounded near the Major's side in the next funk hole. Major Whittlesey, said Pvt. Larney, was most definitely alone in the headquarters funk and any meeting already over when Sgt. Carroll (usually described simply as "an officer") and the unnamed escort soldier arrived with Pvt. Hollingshead. Captain McMurtry was a short distance away, already sliding out on some errand, and Captain Holderman was off somewhere. (Exactly where remains unclear, but he was definitely not out on the left flank or else he would have likely brought Pvt. Hollingshead in himself, as well as having written about it in one of the several descriptions he left behind concerning the event.) In fact, he was most probably having one of his many bandages tightened just a short distance away, since the PC funk was very near the wounded area. He arrived on the spot too quickly to likely be anywhere else. Besides Major Whittlesey, apparently only Cpl. (now Sgt. Mjr.) Baldwin and Privates Larney, Cepaglia, Richards and Manson and perhaps a runner or two were immediately close to hand when Pvt. Hollingshead was brought in and it was very quiet in the Charlevaux Ravine at the time.

A second eyewitness to the next few minutes who left behind what he saw was Private Fred Evermann of Company B. He had been on guard duty near the edge of the wagon road down off the right flank and from his position he had seen the German and Pvt. Hollingshead as they came down the slope of Hill 198 to the road. Having watched as the wounded private stumbled forward and was dragged in, Pvt. Evermann then left his post (one wonders what Major Whittlesey would have done had he been aware of that) and followed the private escort that brought Hollingshead "over to Whittlesey"; where again, no mention is made of any other officer being present. Therefore, with these several pairs of eyes watching the drama unfold, the errant Pvt. Hollingshead had now arrived on the spot. (44)

Private Hollingshead crawled forward to Major Whittlesey's hole (not "walked up" as is so often stated, nor were any of them standing at any time, which would have been pure suicide), dropped the cane and the flag, but did not salute as this would have singled Major Whittlesey out as an officer to the snipers. It was shortly after 4:00 p.m.

"Sir, I am Private Hollingshead of Company H. I have been captured and sent in by the Germans with a message for the commanding officer," the nervous private managed to stammer out. His fear of being thought a traitor at this particular juncture seemed a very important detail, and Holly's face was a mass of worry while his stomach continued to turn somersaults.

He pulled the envelope from his pocket and presented it to the Major, who glanced at it and then back at Hollingshead before he took it. Major Whittlesey tore the end of the envelope open, extracted the letter - still having said nothing - unfolded it and silently read it as Hollingshead remained nervously watchful. All eyes were now on Major Whittlesey. Private Evermann says he saw the Major shake his head as he read the note and heard him utter, very low of voice, "No sir, by God! Never!" but if Major Whittlesey did say it, no one else heard it. The text of the letter, reproduced here verbatim, complete with spelling mistakes and grammatical errors, was straightforward enough:

To the Commanding Officer of the 2nd Batl.J.R. 308
of the 77th American Division

Sir

The Bearer of the present, (here Hollingshead signed his name)
has been taken prisoner by us on October (the date was left blank)
He refused to the German Intelligence Officer every answer to his
questiones and is quite an honourable fellow, doing honour to his fatherland in the strictest sense of the
word.
He has been charged against his will, believing in doing wrong to his country, in carrying
forward this present letter to the Officer in charge of the 2nd Batl.J.R.308 of the 77th Div. with the

purpose to recommend this Commander to surrender with his forces as it would be quite useless to resist any more in view of the present conditions.

The suffering of your wounded man can be heared over here in the German lines and we are appealing to your human sentiments.

A withe Flag shown by one of your man will tell us that you agree with these conditions.

Please treat the (again, here Holly had signed his name) *as an honorable man. He is quite a soldier we envy you.*

The German commanding officer. (246)

When he finished reading, Major Whittlesey simply folded the letter, replaced it in the envelope with a thoughtful look stretched across his pinched, dirty features. It would have been then that he asked Hollingshead about his wound and if the Germans had treated him all right. Hollingshead apparently answered with much enthusiasm that his treatment had been very good indeed, showed the clean bandage and brought forth the bread and cigarettes that he had stuffed into his pocket. No doubt the wounded around them gasped at these delicacies. Major Whittlesey, who was feeling the strain as much, if not more so, than anyone in the Pocket, bristled. Seeing the looks on the faces of the wounded within earshot, he sharply ordered the young man to, "Shut up with that now." (29, 33, 44, 51, 109, 116, 152, 153, 163, 218, 222, 245, 280, 283)

By this time, a small crowd was gathering. Sergeant Major Baldwin leaned in closer to the command hole, next to the ever-faithful "Zip" Cepaglia and Captain McMurtry, who had overheard some of the exchange, had crawled back and slouched down into the hole as well. Major Whittlesey then handed the note over to him and the Captain, his face reddening at the sight of Hollingshead, apparently turned the envelope between his two index fingers a few times, looked at it a moment, then sideways at Hollingshead again and finally asked sharply, "Why did you leave your post?" (29, 245)

Pvt. Hollingshead, face now flushed with fear, replied honestly, "I crawled out with some other men of the company this morning to try and get a basket dropped by an airplane yesterday, and we were captured by the Germans, sir."

"How many of you were there?"

"Nine, sir. The ones who were leading were killed by machine-gun fire. Me and some others were wounded and taken prisoner."

(This is a correct and corroborated quote and is precisely what Pvt. Hollingshead said according to both Jim Larney and an interview given by Hollingshead himself early on.) (29, 163, 222, 245, 280, 309)

Then Captain McMurtry's face really flushed hot. He was just about to let fly at the wayward private when Major Whittlesey interrupted with, "George, you had better look at the letter." (29)

As the Captain took the letter out of the envelope and began to scan it, Major Whittlesey, barely controlling his own anger, admonished Pvt. Hollingshead. "You," he pointed at the boy, "had no business leaving your post, under any circumstances, without direct orders from your officer - which you did not have," he said tightly. And from there Pvt. Larney says, Major Whittlesey went on and "really gave Hollingshead hell!" "Now, go over and lay down with the wounded," Major Whittlesey ended a minute later and it was a very chagrinned Hollingshead who, with Sgt. Carroll helping, crawled the few yards over to the pile of wretched creatures occupying the long hole and lay down. It was not until later that the story about the unknown sergeant and the orders to try and break through to the rear would appear - nor that sympathetic fellows in the command would, while not confirming the story, not publicly dispute it either. Even Major Whittlesey, bothered apparently by what would be his own actions to come in the next few moments, never publicly disputed the story. (29, 245)

About the time Captain McMurtry finished the note and looked up at the Major's schoolmaster-like face, Captain Holderman had drug himself over and joined them, apparently alerted to the doings by one of the wounded. Captain McMurtry handed the note to him to read and he and Major Whittlesey studied the hurt captain's dirty features as he read it. Slowly, they saw a smile begin to steel across his filthy, beard-fringed face. When he finished, he looked up and glanced at the two officers, his eyes dancing and a grin spreading wide. "They're begging us to quit," he said. "They're more worried than we are." Both Captain McMurtry and Major Whittlesey now let smiles crease their dirty faces as well. That part about "appealing to your humane sentiments" - this from the man who had been sending grenades, trench mortar bombs, and flamethrowers in on them for a week now. It would be funny if it weren't so ludicrous - or so tragic.

Captain McMurtry pulled himself as upright in the hole as his wounds and safety would allow and boomed, "This means we've got 'em licked! They wouldn't have sent this if they weren't slipping!" (29, 109, 149, 245)

Captain Holderman handed the note back to Major Whittlesey, who glanced at it one more time. Nodding, he folded it back into the envelope and once more placed it in his gas mask bag. It would be at this point - if the legend had any truth to it - that Major Whittlesey turned in the direction of the German lines and yelled for them to "GO TO HELL!" at the top of his lungs. However, in actuality Major Whittlesey simply turned to Sgt. Major Baldwin and Pvt. Larney and said, "I want you to go out there and get those signal panels taken in as quickly as you can. We do not want 'those people' thinking they are a sign of surrender. Get moving." (29, 218, 245, 283)

As Baldwin crawled off, the Major passed an order that all signal apparatus be brought to him and sent word to Lt. Cullen to have Private Bill Powers take in the 2nd Battalion panels, which were laid out on the left. Private Evermann, who had actually carted a field size heliograph (with stand, mind you) into the Pocket, then hustled off to his hole to fetch it. To the right, Captain Holderman sent word for Sgt. Jim Deahan to drag in the Company K panel laid out there and hide the small towel he had laying next to it. There was to be NO signaling of any kind and no white *ANYTHING* allowed in the open. (Not terribly difficult by this stage of the game, as most anything that had once been white was now a grimy dirt color.) (29, 44, 135, 148, 149, 150, 219, 245)

Then, again according to eyewitness Pvt. Larney, Major Whittlesey overheard Pvt. Hollingshead behind him "bragging" to the wounded about his decent treatment at the hands of the Germans again and it proved too much for the overstrained commander to take. Could not the damn kid see that he was just torturing those poor men? Major Whittlesey's normally even temper flashed uncharacteristically and he managed to catch Sgt. Major Baldwin just before he crawled away. With Baldwin by the arm and pointing over in Holly's direction, according to Larney, in a voice loud enough for Hollingshead and all around him to hear plainly, Major Whittlesey said sharply, "If that son of a bitch doesn't shut up, I want you to take Larney's .45 and shoot him!" (152, 245)

A blanket of utter silence descended. Major Whittlesey glared at the wounded Hollingshead and snapped angrily, "Go back to where you belong!" Private Hollingshead slowly turned and limp-crawled off toward the left flank like a scolded puppy, his stomach turning worse than ever now. (152, 245)

Recovering his temper with some effort in the awkward moment, the Major turned to the other two officers and said, "Well, we better warn off everybody to fix bayonets, because we're sure to be in for it now!" As the three officers crawled to do so, Baldwin crawled out to retrieve the panels with the help of Private Irving Liner, since Jim Larney was too stiffened by his wounds to move much now. (29, 109, 148, 218, 245)

It must have been near 4:30 p.m. or so that afternoon, when a figure tottered into the position that Company B/306th MG Bn. had taken up down on the western slope of the Ravin d'Argonne. Private Charles Minder described the incident in a letter to his mother later that night:

"An infantry runner came over late this afternoon. He looked like a skeleton. He asked us the way back to headquarters and we told him. He said they were all shot to pieces and that the wounded were suffering terribly. We gave him something to eat and then he kept on going." (37)

Also about that same time, though further down the line, another thin, filthy man rambled through the brush and into a 307th company outpost area babbling almost incomprehensibly, "Stop the artillery! Bring doctors and medicine, but for God's sake stop the artillery!" Once they got some food into him he was sent back with a guide, but he never really had calmed down enough to make much sense to anyone and no one had ever bothered to get his name. (29, 51)

Private Krotoshinsky had taken much time to work his way back so far, crawling in little rushes through areas alive with German troops one minute and deserted the next. There was considerable activity and sounds of combat seemingly all around him and he redoubled his efforts to be as careful as possible. While Kozikowski and Brown had angled more straight down to the southwest from the Pocket, 'Krot' had merely skirted that direction in order to get across the creek bottom before then shifting to a truer southeasterly course. The mist and general sogginess of the day helped greatly, especially when the German had stepped his fingers into the mud, but he was tiring quickly, his reserve of strength about gone. If something was to happen, it needed to be soon.

"All day I was under heavy fire. Every minute I thought they would get me, I expected death, but I thought of it only as a physical thing, nothing more. I thought of nothing but the necessity of getting that message through... I was kept busy (constantly) retracing my route and making detours in the effort to throw the Germans off the track..." (33)

The light was starting to fade (though what time it was he could only guess as his wristwatch had stopped long ago) when he suddenly stumbled silently onto a German machine-gun nest, well hidden in the brush along the hillside before him. Lying flat under the nearest mess of bramble and not moving at all, he could just make out the barrel and flash suppressor of the heavy Maxim gun sticking out from a well-assembled false wall of brush, almost indistinguishable from the rest of the brush around it. Listening intently, he could hear the Germans manning the gun talking in low tones. They obviously had not seen nor heard him, Krot knew, since there was no note of alarm in their voices at all and he realized his luck had taken a turn for the good. Still, there was no way around it; he was going to have to pass by the nest's front in order to move ahead. Alert as a cat now, Krot inched his way past the position, taking an extraordinary amount of time. By the time he had made his way and paused to rest his fraying nerves, night was almost upon him. (33, 356)

Meanwhile, Private's Kozikowski and Brown, armed only with pistols, had moved across the creek bottom that morning and angled up the hillside opposite, keeping their distance but always remaining within easy sight of each other, or at least making the effort. When separated, the lead man would wait for the follower, since neither felt they could make it alone. Early in the journey, they had been startled when two figures came crashing in upon them from behind; deserters who had heard they were trying to get back and decided to tag along. 'Koz' and Brown saw the intense fear in their eyes and could tell by their out of control movements and actions that they would get all of them killed if they were to stay together. Brown, ever the patient man, told the two fugitives that he and Koz would take the lead and instructed them to follow, but only after they had gotten a half hour's start. Then, he and his Polish companion set out again - merely to be almost immediately overtaken by the thunderous approach through the brush of the other two.

What kept the Germans from hearing the commotion was anybody's guess and Brown, religious or not, cursed them soundly and again reiterated the plan. It was clear that the fear the other two felt was far too great to be overcome. Starting out again, Koz and Brown immediately dove into the thick brush when they heard the other two coming and simply let them pass by before moving on. What became of the errant runaways or who they were no one knows. After all had been quiet again for at least a half an hour, Koz and Brown continued on, as the rain started to fall more heavily. (29, 33, 51)

The field message, when it came through, was like a streak of lightning across the murky afternoon. It arrived at l'Homme Mort, brought in by a mud-covered runner, for General Johnson from Colonel Houghton and had initially come from Lt. Tillman, timed at 4:35 p.m., stating simply:

295.0-276.3 – about 40 minutes ago. That's your left. (139)

They were damned near there, and General Johnson excitedly called General Alexander's PC at once with the news. Surprisingly, General Johnson got the Division Commander himself, then back collecting some of his things in anticipation of moving his PC forward. Those coordinates were *very* near Major Whittlesey's advanced position, he said, and it looked like they were definitely going to get through to him yet that afternoon, unless the Huns pulled off something big. Nothing doing, General Alexander told him; the Germans were in full retreat all along the 1st Corps line - all except at Hill 205 apparently. By taking up Major Whittlesey's position and then pushing down the road toward Charlevaux Mill and beyond however, working along the road into Binarville they could likely rectify that in no time. What plans had General Johnson made for Major Whittlesey's relief? Again, General Johnson explained what he had earlier told Colonel Hannay: there was water and medical supplies on the way up by rail, along with hundreds of pounds of food and the first aid stations and divisional surgeon were all standing by, as were the ambulances. He had also had Colonel Houghton's men carry extra rations up with them, for when they broke through. (General Alexander had himself already ordered an additional first aid station be set up at Depot des Machines as well, to deal with some of the wounded carried out of the ravine by rail since l'Homme Mort would likely not be able to handle them all. There was also to be a large supply of fresh uniforms on hand, as well as shower baths.) And casualties so far in the relief effort, General Alexander wanted to know? Not as bad as expected, the Brigadier told him. Yes, the German defenses certainly appeared to be collapsing. It should be little problem to move that last, short distance to where Major Whittlesey was. But even as the two Generals spoke, and the men along the advancing main line faced the final challenge between them and Major Whittlesey, the men in the Pocket were just a short time away from their own last, furious challenge. (29, 103, 109, 116, 131, 138, 139, 144, 150)

Word of the surrender letter flew around the Pocket like greased lightning, and the effect was not only electrifying, but stunning. A queer sort of tenacity of spirit combined with rage seemed to seep from the very ground. Men who had been on the verge of despair moments before, convinced that their deaths would be for naught, now became grimly determined to make those deaths stand for something, and a desire for vengeance swept across the hillside. No American command had ever surrendered all at once, that anyone could remember just then, and nearly to a man they became determined not to be the first ones to do it, if just on principle. If those Hienie bastards wanted that useless hillside, they were going to have to come down and get it by force - and pay the price for it. There was simply no way in hell that any single U.S. soldier there was going to freely give an inch of that rotten, death-plagued plot of dirt simply because the enemy had demanded it! If they were to die in the resulting defense of that God forsaken piece of woodland, then they would be selling their lives for one simple, yet sacred, principal: No surrender.

Major Whittlesey took the news himself over to the left to tell Lt. Cullen, who asked to see the letter. The Major brought it out from where he had put it in his gas mask bag and watched the lieutenant's eyes narrow and his lips tighten as he read it. Looking up at the Major, he handed the note back silently. There was little he needed to say, for what he thought was plain across his face. "You need to be ready," Major Whittlesey said simply in a low, calm voice. "Don't worry, Major," was all Lt. Cullen said just before he turned and slithered off into the brush to set his men and hand out what ammunition he still had. (109)

Captains McMurtry and Holderman crawled across the pitch of the hill to the center and right respectively, warning men to be on the ready for the attack that they all now felt sure would be coming and evenly distributing whatever ammunition they could scrounge. At every hole, it was the same; they all wanted to know of it were true that the Hienies had asked them to surrender. Enraged by the affirmative answer their officers gave, the Doughboys made sure that the Germans did, in turn, get their response - though a lot quicker and more direct than the meager American command had anticipated (or had the Germans themselves for that matter). It was even a little frightening to the remaining officers as, loudly and clearly, the individual soldiers began sending the wrath of their answers skyward:

Why those dirty, rotten sons of bitches!' (turning toward the ravine and yelling) *'I'd just like to see them try to make us! Just let me near one of those Dutch bastards!'*

(Then a grimy, helmeted head popped up farther down the hillside.)

'What was that you said over there?'

'Didn't you hear? The Germans sent a message in demanding that the Major surrender.'

(A pause as an incensed look roiled through the filth and beard stubble below the helmet.)

'Surrender, eh? (menacingly) *What did the Major say?'*

'What the hell do you think he said? He probably told 'em to go to hell.'

'Yeah? Damn right! (then toward the ravine, yelling) *Come try and get us, you Hienie fucks!'*

In the wounded area, the scene was almost unbearable. Horribly wounded men, who had been barely strong enough to lift a rifle only that morning, now became incensed with rage, finding a reserve of vigor they never knew they had. Getting up in the long hole as far as torn flesh and broken bones would allow, they too let the Germans know their answer, in no uncertain terms.

'Somebody give me a rifle goddamnit! You Dutch prick! You want surrender? Well, you can kiss my wounded American ass!'

'Come on down here you kraut son of a bitch! Wounded or not, I'll fight you man to man and piss on your dead face when I'm through!'

By about a quarter to five that afternoon, the rain was falling off and on, the mist was almost constant, and the air above the ravine was blue with epithets and choice oaths in a multitude of accents.

'You-a no good-a Boche! I'm-a cutta you balls off an' I'm-a feed 'em to you!'

Everywhere, the three officers crawled it was the same. Wounded or exhausted men who had not moved in two or three days, wracked by hunger and sickness, fatigued almost beyond description, pulled themselves out of their holes and dragged up to the firing line, begging for a rifle and cartridges. Even the wounded Lieutenant's Griffin and Revnes were there, manning the interior line around the wounded. Others, too badly wounded to hold themselves upright or steady a heavy service rifle (like Sgt. Bendheim, Captain Stromee, Private's Otto Volz, Arnold Morem, Lee Harkleroad and a host of others), crawled into positions from which to load rifles and pass them on for those who could still pull a trigger. Other men, now without cartridges, pulled out their bayonets and began to sharpen them against pieces of limestone, giving them a jagged, evil edge while they eyed the ravine intensely. (29, 51, 109, 135, 148, 149, 150, 245)

For good or bad, the Germans were getting their answer.

On the hills above, Major Hunicken and his men listened to the tirades coming from below and with the English speakers translating, quickly realized that the Americans were not going to surrender as Lt. Prinz hoped. Hauptmann Petri, commander of the 2nd/254th, had himself expected as much and had already been getting his men prepared for what he was sure would be a difficult afternoon attack, even before Corporal Hollingshead had been released on the wagon road barely an hour before. Being Major Whittlesey and Captain McMurtry's immediate opposite number, the Hauptmann had been the instrument on the ground directing the attacks against the Pocket for the better part of four days now. And as the Doughboys insolently tossed Lt. Prinz's surrender offer aside and let it be known that they preferred death, he sent his men in, led once again by that contingent of storm troopers that Major Hunicken, and Hauptmann Von Sybel had begged for. With the tumbling of the first grenades through the air ahead of them, the attack was on. It was just a little before 5:00 p.m. (51, 123, 307)

The German attack hit the perimeter line of the isolated command hard, coming like a hurricane from all four points of the compass at once. As usual, heavy machine-gun fire and round after round of grenades spearheaded the assault, followed by waves of advancing field gray, firing as they came. The only thing missing was the trench mortars, which had been strangely quiet for the past couple hours. Still, it was an onslaught pushed forward with a ferocity that *might* have broken the Doughboy line - certainly it was the most ferocious attack yet - had it not been for the response brought about by the surrender letter, which initiated a repeat of the odd furor that had marked the frenzied Doughboy reaction to the attacks of the previous afternoon. Except that the furor was almost a controlled sort of 'raging response' this time, much as a cool and calculated murder might be, which somehow made it even more eerie and frightening than it had been the day before, when all semblance of control had seemingly vanished. There was no crying or wailing this time, but instead only a peculiar, low, almost animal-like growling mixed in among the many shouts of encouragement and orders being flung about. It was as if a grim sort of single-minded 'meanness' had taken on human form.

In the center, where the attack was most furious and came solidly from both across the road above and across the ravine behind simultaneously, Major Whittlesey and Captain McMurtry massed the men as best they could, shifting small groups one way or the other to check the rapid enemy rushes. They were buying time but it seemed it would not be long before it would all be over. Rifle ammunition was about gone, there were no operating auto rifles left at all, and it seemed pretty clear that they would soon have no recourse left but to fall to the bayonet; something tantamount to suicide against the enemy automatic weapons. Yet, at this most critical of moments, the men seemed to be working together better than either officer had ever seen before. Camp Upton or 40th Division man; there was no longer a distinction between the two. Wounded or unwounded, it did not matter. They had finally been reduced to the point where each had equal experience of the situation, equal accoutrements and equal chances of survival. It was the hard, rock bottom of their lives, where all of them lay invariant and could only depend upon each other, without worldly discrimination or distinction. This was their longest and most distinctive hour and no one would be the same after it. All across the Pocket, a unity of thought and deed prevailed: No matter what, the Germans would not take that hillside from them. Not *this* time.

Over in his sector, Lt. Cullen had his men grouped in a solid semi-circle along the now shrunken left flank, tight and evenly spaced and extending from either side of the single operating machine-gun located in the center. The weapon had a good field of fire before it and held every advantage it could, save for two - it was now in the hands of the only man willing to take the chance at running it, an inexperienced private, and it was almost out of ammunition. Yet, the Doughboy line was strong and as the time ticked slowly and relentlessly by, they held the Germans solidly in check. Again, the enemy tried his 'calling the roll' trick, but each response this time was met by accurate U.S. rifle fire in the direction from which it had come, bringing many yelps and cries. Then, once the German assault managed to overwhelm his perimeter, washing over the road and down the embankment of the flank slightly, Lt. Cullen's men could not be bothered to fall back at all. Instead, they *stood and advanced* directly up the slope into the German muzzles - by then only a bare few meters in front of them - with wild, unearthly shouts and yells that terrified the Germans. Before long, they had driven the field gray line back beyond the road through sheer tenacity and brute force. One small group, once they had reached the road, even hastily organized a bit of a counterattack, again climbing up above the far embankment to chase the retreating enemy until their lack of ammunition and own exhaustion forced them back into their hillside positions. (29, 51, 109, 116, 148, 149, 150, 218, 234, 239, 245, 254, 257, 263)

From down near the edge of the wagon road on the left, Pvt. Hollingshead awoke in his funk hole in the middle of the attack. Crawling back to his position with Company H like a scolded puppy after Major Whittlesey had ordered him away, he had been telling Pvt. Harold Neptune near him of his morning adventure when Lt. Cullen, overhearing the tale, also threatened to shoot him if he did not keep quiet. Sickened then, by fear, excitement, all the food he had eaten and the loss of blood from his wound, Hollingshead had passed out, only to awaken during the afternoon battle. Now, looking down the wagon road toward the right flank, he could see a strange glow through the dim forest and realizing what it was, the great fear welled up in him again. "Oh my God," he exclaimed, before turning his head out of his hole and finally throwing up all the German food. "What the hell are you crying about?" the wounded Pvt. Neptune asked him testily while he fired his rifle at the coming onslaught. "At least you had something to eat. I ain't got nothin' in me to puke." However, Holly did not hear him since he had passed out again. (163, 222, 280, 309)

The glow off the right flank was the reappearance of the German flamethrowers, except, there were twice as many this time; spitting their long jets of flame and leaving little dropped pools of burning liquid on the ground behind them from their fiery nozzles. Sergeant Hauck turned the last working Hotchkiss gun on the right in the direction of the demonic weapons and let fly, following Major Whittlesey's instructions of the previous afternoon. Ammunition was almost exhausted for the heavy weapon now, and there was none at all left to be spared for the Chauchats, so he tried to make every shot count. Captain Holderman and Sgt. Carroll already had the men set in a tight semi-circular line, *a la* Lt. Cullen, but other than that, there was little else for them to do except encourage the men now, who were already up and driving the Germans hard of their own accord. Legend holds that Captain Holderman, as usual, was right there at the front of the line, his hurt frame leaning on a broken rifle for support, blazing away with his .45 and letting out with a terrific 'whoop' every time he scored a hit, which was often. At least that much of the story is true, since the Captain *was* then in the final stages of clinching his nomination for the Medal of Honor as, unknown to him, Major Whittlesey watched from a short distance away in no small measure of awe. The legend continues that the intrepid Captain also killed his fifth German about the time he got his fifth wound, but that aspect of the tale is more fantasy than reality; Holderman was already *well* beyond his fifth wound by then. (27, 29, 51, 103, 109, 149)

Lack of 8mm Hotchkiss ammunition or not, the flame-throwing storm troops were eventually and successfully stopped and the fear that they brought, stemmed. Ever so slowly, as the clock tipped its way toward 6:00 p.m., the ragged Doughboys on the right also doggedly pushed the Germans back away from their perimeter. In the distance - and not really all that far - if any of them had been listening in the midst of the Germans' attack, they might have heard the distinctive cough of Chauchats and the sharp bark of grenades. However, it is unlikely anyone was paying any attention to anything but driving off the attacking gray waves and their accompanying surges of flame.

Yet, noticed or not, the 307th was getting closer. (103)

Back up on Hill 198, Private's Emil Peterson and Cecil Duryea had been carried down into the enormous German dugout late that afternoon and placed against the wall near the entrance. They were then given a pail of water and two German overcoats and told to sit tight. When he asked if they would be taken to a hospital anytime soon, Pvt. Peterson was told that the Red Cross would be coming for them shortly and not to worry. Privately, they both wondered about Hollingshead, but declined to ask after him, for fear of the answer. Outside, there was much activity as evening came, with plenty of shooting in the distance and shells dropping all over. It looked as if the Germans were planning a major attack, for from where he was, Pvt. Peterson could see the enemy taking down machine-guns and carrying them in the direction of the Pocket. It did not look good for the men they had left behind.

They had been left completely alone for some time and when it eventually became quiet, except for some sporadic shelling, Pvt. Peterson scouted the dugout for food. Finding none, he contemplated escape, but Pvt. Duryea was far too wounded to drag through the forest and begged him not to leave him. Off in the distance to the east, they could hear the dull cough of Chauchats and the rattle and whine of machine-gun and rifle fire, but were unsure if it was just a German attack against the weakened right flank. With no options available, the two wounded Doughboys wrapped up in their German overcoats and drifted off into an exhausted sleep as darkness began to fall. (224, 291)

The filtering through the wire seam in the 1st/307th's sector was quickly turning into a veritable breach of the whole enemy line. Company A, supported by elements of Company D (advanced of the main line that they held slightly further to the rear) and most of C broke past the German positions on Hill 198 along a rather wide base, leading the attack from the right. Leading on their left was Lt. Tillman's Company B, supported by what remained of Company M from their rear. Company A, emerging from the wire, soon came under heavy machine-gun fire which D, behind, swung out to assist with and their gangs went into action. Messages were flying between PCs at top speed as everyone realized the significance of the break in the German line and moved quickly to exploit it. Perhaps the most representative of those messages is one Major McKinney must have sent back somewhere between 3.00-3:30 p.m., though it is actually untimed:

M.G. fire from junction of creeks and in front. Been following wire, which goes down slope to the north. 'D' to push forward and think they will get it strong. 'A' slowly moving forward, pushing out small combat groups and coming up to them. Seem to have run into an organized position on their right front. M.G. and rifle fire from front and right. Wizz-bangs (a kind of fast artillery shell - author) on 'D' and 'A'. (Lt.) Hastings (D co.) has sent for one pounder and is placing Stokes... Have cut through at turn. 'D' is 150 yards (sic) in advance of this turn and will swing N.W. following wire as soon as MG's on our front are disposed of. They have just had two killed trying to cross the path there. We are attacking what I believe is the left of their organized position. (139)

Then, a little later:

D has been stopped. Patrols report large force 200 yards (sic) to the north. M.G. fire from front and right. Rifle fire from north apparently very close. Some fire from left... (139)

It was that fire from the left that was proving the most significant. There, Major McKinney had Lt. Tillman working under orders to push along an oblique angle down the ravine directly toward Major Whittlesey's last known right flank position. Lieutenant Tillman, first to move his meager numbers cleanly through the wire and against the collapsing German line in the woods, slid down the far slope of Hill 198 and into the lower Charlevaux Ravine, only to be met by a belt of stubborn machine-gun and rifle fire blocking his push up the ravine. Strangely, however, not all of it seemed to be directed at their advance. It was around the time that Private Hollingshead was delivering the surrender message to Major Whittlesey in the Pocket that Lt. Tillman sent his own message back to Major McKinney concerning the blockage of his main force:

Have developed a Boche post at 295.7-275.8 and M.G. at 296.1-275.7. We are getting M.G. fire from ravine on our right front. Just lost 4 men from it. Am trying to envelop. (139)

Some of Lt. Tillman's men swung out farther to the right and drove against the Hun machine-gun nest, while others kept up fire from the front and left, all trying to force a way past. It was getting on toward late afternoon by the time they had the nest eliminated and Lt. Tillman sent a message back to Major McKinney that they were nearly at horizontal 276.3, very close to Major Whittlesey's stated line of 276.4, and that it should not be long. Almost immediately after that message went out however, they ran into a German bombing party of eight or nine troops, some heavily laden with hand grenades and some with sniper equipment, hurrying up the ravine obviously on some mission of importance. The resulting firefight was sharp and stiff, yet it was not particularly long before Lt. Tillman's men were moving again. So far, by Argonne Forest standards, their progress was nothing short of spectacular. They found less and less heavy resistance barring their way as they pushed on, yet moved with careful deliberateness nonetheless. Rifle fire punctuated the rapidly falling darkness; shadowy shapes flitted about in the forest around them and machine-gun fire fell off. Were the Germans actually retreating, or just regrouping? No one could be sure, so caution was the word.

They discovered a wagon path along the right side of the heavily wooded ravine bottom that they were now spread out across and working along. There was a meandering brook down the middle and sporadic machine-gun fire coming from Hill

198 to their left, which was rapidly diminishing as the rest of the 307th did their work. Tillman had his scouts out, carefully developing both sides of the ravine and was also getting reports that other scouts on the right had reached the Binarville-La Viergette road. Apparently it was a lot closer than they originally thought, only about 150 meters north up the sharp embankment from the wagon road. Up there, things seemed to be progressing well - almost too well perhaps. It was too quiet. Where in hell was Major Whittlesey's command? They should be coming up on them any time. It was around 6:00 p.m. and the cloud cover above had it dark already, but at least the rain had let up into a simple, irritating mist.

Then, the slight wind shifted a bit, carrying forward a putrid odor reminiscent of rotting, spoiled meat and excrement and Lt. Tillman and his signalman, working along through the brush to one side of the wagon road, looked at each other with wrinkled noses.

'Christ almighty... what is that stink?' (103, 104, 138, 139)

Private Krotoshinsky slithered forward through the mud and thick brush an inch at a time in the growing darkness. There was firing everywhere around him and he had nearly been discovered a hundred times by passing bands of German troops, all of them loaded with equipment and rushing about in some measure of urgency. Pure, 100 percent adrenaline was the only thing keeping him going now. His wide eyes alone might have been enough to get him discovered had any enemy soldiers been looking down. However, none were, being otherwise occupied with some great movement, and Krot wondered if they had finally succeeded in over running the hillside.

He was looking back at a passing band of Boche troops, praying hard that they had not heard him creeping through the falling drizzle, when his hand dropped off into nothingness. He froze as his heart practically stopped. He had come upon an enemy position! Retreating as quietly as he could behind a nearby tree, he waited for signs of movement or noise, convinced it was all over. When there was neither after a short while, he figured that he had not been spotted and decided to investigate, finding the position to be an empty trench, well built but scarred by artillery. The trench line atop Hill 198! He was close! Crossing over, there was firing in the distance behind, but in front only silence, and on the opposite side he started darting from tree to tree to bush and around the wire. Taking whatever cover he could, more alert than ever now, he crossed the second trench line. It was empty; not a German soldier about. Still very much on the alert (for it simply would not do to cash it in so close to the finish line) he crept up to another tree crouched down. Then, voices. Dear God, it was English!

Krot jumped up and started walking forward. "Hello! Hello!" he called out. There was a rustling in the brush in front. In moments, he had half a dozen bayoneted Eddystones pointed at him, their owners nervous and fidgety. Who was he? Private Krotoshinsky of Company K/307th the grinning, filthy little man said, hiding his Polish accent as best he could. Just coming in from Major Whittlesey's surrounded command in the ravine ahead with a message. Then, from out of the crowd around him:

"Abe?" a familiar voice asked incredibly.

"Do you know this man?" Captain Hastings, commander of CompanyD/307th, asked Private William Bergen, one of the Company K men that Captain Holderman had sent back for rations the night of the 2nd and who was then working with D.

"Yes, sir. That's Abe Krotoshinsky, from my company. Where the hell you guys been Abe?" Pvt. Bergen asked.

The rifles came down and Pvt. Krotoshinsky was quickly fed and given coffee, telling his tale behind huge mouthfuls. The news was sent back to Major McKinney, who passed it on to Colonel Houghton, who in turn sent orders up for Pvt. Krotoshinsky to lead a batch of D men up with rations and medical, as the front seemed to be stabilizing by that point (about 6:15 p.m.). Private Krotoshinsky, not at all sure that anything up there was stabilized, nonetheless felt a million times better for the food and drink and soon set out with a group of men back up to that little corner of hell in the Charlevaux. It would not be over until they were *all* relieved. (29, 33, 109, 116, 135, 356)

The German attack fell off and broke apart at just about 10 minutes before 6:00 p.m., with the remaining German troops drifting off northwards toward prearranged collection points on their officer's orders. From those points, they would head out for the Kriemhilde Stellung. Their attack had failed, and the *Americanernest* still stood. Dejected, the handwriting was now on the wall. If they could not beat off a mere handful of Americans, how could they expect to pound back their entire army? For many of them, the agony of that question still had 34 more days to fester before the final, bitter answer slapped them in the face.

Darkness had descended by the time the attack faded, and in the gloaming, Major Whittlesey and Captain McMurtry moved through the shrunken position, taking casualty reports and checking up on the men. Miraculously, there had been few casualties and for that, they were grateful. The twist was that the afternoon defense had marked the absolute end to the Doughboy's abilities to hold the position. Everywhere the two commanders went, they were met with the same story: ammunition was virtually or totally gone, strength all but played out, resolve all but faded. Sleeping Doughboys littered the hillside, some having dropped right where the end of the attack had found them, above ground without cover, too tired and used up to even crawl back to a hole, or to care. Others sat and stared straight ahead vacantly, seeing nothing, feeling nothing, realizing nothing. Some hardly seemed to be able to answer direct questions anymore, instead giving simply a blank look and perhaps an unintelligible murmur. The Doughboys had nothing left to give at all. For good or bad, it was over.

The two Battalion Commanders realized this even before they were back in the collapsing command funk. The drizzle was not even noticed. A blanket of hopeless despair had now enveloped the hillside and it seemed only a matter of time before its choking effects would be felt. Without any words needing be spoken, everyone instinctively knew that the next morning's attack would likely be the last.

Meanwhile, the Doughboys on the perimeter line - the only ones with any ammunition now - listened to movement through the brush coming from all around them. A hell of a lot of it there was too, along with some general rifle and Chauchat fire off to the east and south, accompanied by shouts and calls, most of them too muffled by the wet forest to hear with any real clarity. It seemed clear that an attack of some sort was then in the making. The Doughboys looked nervously at each other, some with tears of fear coursing down their cheeks as the mist dripped from their helmets. It would not be a long fight when it came, certainly terrifying in the darkness and a damned shame that they had lasted this long only to die dirty, hungry and exhausted, never actually having had any real chance to survive... (29, 51, 109, 116, 135, 148, 149, 150)

Lieutenant Tillman, at the head of Company B's advance, was moving stealthily through the brush along the side of the wagon road with his .45 in his hand and the hillside on his right. The putrid smell of decay was getting stronger the farther up the ravine they went and he had to fight to keep from putting his gas mask on. It did not smell like any gas he had ever encountered before, but what if the Germans had something new in their bag of tricks?

Then, the lieutenant stumbled in the dark, tripping through a hole from which a sharp yelp of pain emitted. There was a rustling lunge and a barely discernable sheen in the misty darkness, from which the lieutenant was just able to roll away from, as a bayonet flashed by and into the dirt at his side with a metallic ring. Behind the lethal weapon, Lt. Tillman could just make out an American helmet rising from the hole to make another attempt.

"What's the matter with you?" the lieutenant cried into the darkness and the dun form paused. "I'm looking for Major Whittlesey's command."

"I don't give a damn who you are and what you want," the shape said menacingly. "You step on my buddy again and I'll kill you." It was Private Robert Pou of Company E, whose outpost hole was now the farthest to the right and closest to the road following the consolidation of the bivouac.

Lieutenant Tillman leaned in closer to better see the ragged form before him. His odor was simply atrocious and he began to realize just what part of the terrible tang was that he had been smelling.

"I didn't mean to step on your friend," the lieutenant said, arching back a little, "I just fell in this hole in the dark. Where is Major Whittlesey? I am Lieutenant Tillman of the 307th. You're relieved and we'll have food up to you right away."

A pause, then "I'm sorry, sir," Pvt. Pou said into the dark. "I didn't see. Do you have a cigarette, sir?" Private Pou could see several other dark forms hurrying up behind Lt. Tillman now, as well as other soldiers moving along the hill and through the brush of the ravine. Yet, other than the rustle of bodies pushing through the rush grass and fallen branches, everything had gotten eerily quiet. A few of the 307th men could be seen advancing into the position along the hillside and then back out again, some gagging. Private Pou leaned down into his hole and gently shifted his wounded comrade into a better sitting position to see the relief coming in as Lt. Tillman fished for the cigarette that the shabby Doughboy had requested.

"See? We're relieved," Pvt. Pou said to the wounded man in the hole. "I told you we would be all right," to which the filthy form gave a small cheer and a weak smile.

As an enlisted medic - one *with* supplies - stepped up to take a look at the wounded man, Lt. Tillman quickly scribbled a message to Major McKinney stating that they had reached Major Whittlesey's position and sent the runner, an ex-Northwood's lumberman, off with it under orders to hurry. Watching the man disappear, only sporadic rifle fire echoed in the distance. It was about 6:20 p.m. (21, 29, 51, 131, 135, 138, 139, 245)

Back somewhere along the 308th's main line in the Ravin d'Argonne, a figure appeared out of the dark, limping through the brush in a German overcoat and headed directly toward an American position with one hand outstretched. By some miracle, no outpost guard along the sparsely manned line fired at the dirty, disheveled figure, though it called out with a thick accent. He was quickly grabbed up and taken to the nearest Company PC, little more than a hole in the ground, and just as quickly sized up for what he was - the wounded Private Jimmy Ilardo, Italian immigrant from New York, whose real name was Pasquale but who had taken the name James in order to sound more American. He had been carried to the big dugout on Hill 198 too, along with the rest of the survivors of the Hollingshead party, though to another entrance and left with an overcoat the same as had Private's Peterson and Duryea. Forgotten in the German evacuation, he had simply climbed out of the hole and made for the U.S. lines as fast as his wound would allow at his earliest opportunity. He was getting his leg looked at and his first bite to eat in five days about the same time advanced elements of the 307th were sharing out their scanty rations with the men off the right flank of Major Whittlesey's position. (158)

Lieutenant Tillman's runner was standing in front of Major McKinney barely 10 minutes after he had left the position in the Charlevaux Ravine with the news of the breakthrough. Already however, Captain Thomas A. Stone, the Regimental Intelligence Officer, had arrived from Colonel Houghton's PC and was then assembling enough men to post a double-strength runner line back up to the Pocket. Word had come through to Colonel Houghton about Pvt. Krotoshinsky just a few minutes before Lt. Tillman's runner, and Krot was to have led the group up. Now, the plan changed since Lt. Tillman's runner was able to lead them back along a more direct and safer route that he had marked on his way out. Loaded down like camels, with as much food and medical supplies as they all could carry (which was not really much), they started toward the ravine barely five minutes later, Private Krotoshinsky just behind the Northwood's runner and Captain Stone just behind Krot. (29, 138, 139, 245)

Meanwhile, Major McKinney sent definite word of the breakthrough back to Colonel Houghton, who in turn passed it to General Johnson, and by 6:35 p.m., the Brigadier was on the phone with Colonel Hannay at General Alexander's PC. "Houghton's command has reached Whittlesey's command and is getting up supplies, food, etc. to them," the Brigade Commander announced. "A great many wounded. I have directed Houghton to take over the entire front and organize for the night." It was what they had been waiting to hear all afternoon, expecting it really. However, now that it had come, the moment seemed almost an anticlimax that far behind the line. (139)

Not so in the Charlevaux Ravine, though. There, the initial 'rescue group' got back to Lt. Tillman on the wagon road just before the clock showed 7:00 p.m. Behind them, they had dropped runner posts every 50 meters and had moved with great care, despite the urgency they felt, since there were still many dark shadows moving around them off among the trees, which they took to be German infantry. (And Germans they were too. Captain Stone and his men were then still hours beyond realizing the full extent of the German evacuation, so their care was warranted.) By the time they reached them on the wagon road below the Pocket, many of Lt. Tillman's men were already moving along the edge of the position's right flank and sharing out what 'iron rats' and smokes they had.(1) Private Nell well recalled when he received word that relief had come up:

"Sometime after dark I heard someone moving and passing close by. Several were moving from my right... then someone came back by going in the other direction... I thought to myself, "What is up now? Another attack by the enemy?"... I heard someone moving and talking in a low voice to my right... Nervously waiting... when they got up close I whispered to him, "What's up?" He replied in a low whisper, "Relief has come in on our right and more is coming in behind them." Well, I could hardly believe that it was true (and) it was not long until everyone was whispering it to each other... It was like being reborn... It was not long until the incoming boys were sharing what little rations they had with us. It felt like we had been saved from death, hanging on by our last string of hope." (40)

Lt. Eager also remembered the tremendous moment:

"We could hear the Germans pulling out about an hour before they got up to us. They were making a lot of noise pulling out and they were going around us... While in there I got a bullet through my helmet. That is how close they came to getting me...That night when the outfit came in they had some iron rations with them and they did pass out to the men what they had, which was very, very little... it didn't go very far; about a taste was all you got." (234)

Private John, one of the last of the men left from hard luck Company A on the hillside, later wrote of the moment they had all been waiting for:

485

"Shortly after dark, following terrible fighting and shooting to the rear of us that didn't let up even when dark came, a bunch of our boys broke through. They said they could smell us a long way off... It wasn't safe yet for us to try to go back during the night, so we settled down with happy hearts and thoughts of what the next day would bring to spend the last night in that hell hole Pocket." (220)

Lieutenant Tillman had sent orders to the road above for his officer there, Lt. Hamblin, to hold along the edge of the bivouac until he had spoken with Major Whittlesey, and the scouts had a chance to develop the situation ahead and to the west. Logic dictated that they would be outposting the position thoroughly, but firm orders from Major McKinney would be needed before they could slow the advance. In the meantime, the lieutenant had been talking with Pvt. Pou and sharing cigarettes with some of the other men in holes around him. Later, deeply moved by what he saw, Tillman would say:

"My God, it was pitiable! Those fellows had been through a hell that made our drive through to relieve them seem like a pleasure excursion... It was evening of the sixth day (sic) they had been there and they were madmen... Their surgical supplies had run out the second day and we found their wounded all gangrened. The men sat and stared with drawn faces, burning eyes, tense jaws... We sent runners for dressings and food but couldn't get (any appreciable amount) through till morning. My men had been marching on iron rations and had precious little left in food or tobacco, but they gave it all to the other fellows... The sheer horror of that strip of hillside is unimaginable. The stench was unbearable; bits of flesh, legs and arms, parts of bodies, were all about. The hillside in their position had been literally blown to pieces. (There was) hardly a spot that had not been struck..." (21)

Captain Stone and his little party arrived faster than Lt. Tillman had figured and brought with them a few rations and bandages, as well as outposting instructions. Sending a runner up to Lt. Hamblin to carefully move down the road and secure the position from ahead, Lt. Tillman then sent Pvt. Pou, nerves now well calmed by his first tobacco in five days, over to fetch Major Whittlesey. (Lieutenant Tillman apparently was not able to stand the stench or sight of the position and had no desire to advance deeper into it to search out the Major himself.)

Over near the command hole, there was already some whispering going on, but nobody had yet dared get out of his hole to see if the story of relief was true, nor to ask the Major. Captain Holderman too, just a few meters to the right of the command hole, plainly heard Lt. Tillman's men moving up on the road above, as well as through the brush below, but thought it might very well be more Germans preparing for another attack. He sent word out among his men to be ready, although he was well aware that no one likely had much ammunition left and any further Hun assault would merely end in a successful slaughter of the Americans. As for Major Whittlesey and Captain McMurtry, they were hunkered down and conversing in low tones (though about what is unknown) in the command funk. The Captain was carefully rubbing his wounded leg to keep the circulation going in order to prevent the infection then eating away at it from getting worse. Nearby the artillery lieutenant, John Teichmoeller, was in a hole nursing the constant, blinding headache from a severe concussion he had received during the barrage on October 4. His hearing was still much effected, as was his balance, and quite literally he had felt like shit ever since and had not been able to do much for the command.(II) Scattered around the command hole was all that remained of the two Battalion PC platoons, mostly wounded runners and scouts, perhaps a dozen men in all. That was it.

Private Pou slouched tiredly up to the command hole, half crouched over in the dark, and approached the two dirty Commanding Officers. Since he could not be readily seen in the dark, he gave a rather sloppy, quick salute.

"Sir?" he said quietly, "There's a Captain Stone on the road with a patrol and he wants to see you, sir." Private Pou's statement was almost a mumble, largely lost in the great void of fatigue that had enveloped the scene. Therefore, neither Major Whittlesey nor Captain McMurtry caught the mystery captain's name clearly.

Major Whittlesey, himself well worn out and apparently somewhat disoriented by the languor of the hillside, paused for a moment, stared at Pvt. Pou almost blankly, and then said simply, "All right." Turning to Captain McMurtry he said, "George, you stay here and I'll see what this is all about," before he motioned to Pvt. Cepaglia in the next hole over.

"Come on, Cepaglia."

Private Larney and Sgt. Mjr. Baldwin, in the hole with him, shifted to let 'Zip' climb out. "Is it safe now on the road?" Zip asked warily, in his strange Brooklyn/Italian accent.

"I guess so," Major Whittlesey said. His voice sounded drained and distracted as he slowly unfolded his length stiffly up out of the command hole. He and Pvt. Cepaglia then disappeared into the misty darkness behind Pvt. Pou, all three walking fully upright down the hill to the wagon road.

Captain McMurtry, watching them go, continued to massage his leg and let his exhausted mind wander at its own tempo absently.

"Sir? There's a Captain so-and-so on the road with a patrol…"

Wait a minute… A *Captain*? His mind asked the question. The only Captains, besides himself of course, were Stromee, down with the wounded and half paralyzed on one side, and Holderman, who was in a hole perhaps a dozen meters away and barely able to walk upright on his own as it was. Yet Pvt. Pou had said there was "a Captain" on the road…

"…with a patrol…" his mind finished.

"Is it safe now on the road?"

"I guess so."

Slowly the truth began to steal its way across McMurtry's brain. Listening, there was no firing anywhere at all around him - and there was *"A Captain on the road with a patrol!"*

Relief! It had to be!

In a flash, the hurting ex-Rough Rider was up and jogging in the same direction that Whittlesey, Cepaglia, and Pou had gone, making toward the right flank as fast as his wounds would allow. (10, 29, 51, 91, 103, 104, 109, 116, 131, 135, 138, 139, 144, 148, 149, 150, 234, 245, 246)

Crouching low and moving slow, Privates Brown and Kozikowski crept along through the German-held territory as alert as a pair of Lynx in the descended darkness. Prior to this point, they had not dared move anywhere near upright, the number of roaming German soldiers and the amount of gunfire being far too great. They, like Pvt. Krotoshinsky, had also come upon a German machine-gun nest, only discovering the fact as they were inching through the brush just in front of it in the murky darkness when they heard the action of the weapon being pulled back. The next moment brought a veritable stream of hot lead flying just above their backs; had their asses been any fatter, they would have lost them. It was a long, nerve-wracking hour before they had managed to completely move past the dangerous area and then begin snaking exhaustedly around in a safer stand of thicker brush, their chests hurting from holding their breath so much.

But the quiet now was almost as unnerving as had been the machine-gun fire then. Where were the Germans? They seemed to have abandoned the hillside, but that could hardly be. It was all very curious. 'Koz' kicked something with his foot - a dead pigeon. Picking it up and showing it to Brown, the same thought ran through both of their minds, but Koz smelled the dead bird and then pinched his nose offensively. What was that there though, tied around the bird's neck? A small message tube dangled. American message tubes fitted on the bird's leg; only the Germans tied them around the neck. Private Brown folded the fragile message paper out of the tube, looked at it, though he did not speak German and then shoved it into his pocket before they dropped the limp, lifeless bird and the two moved on, alert as ever.

It was very late, perhaps 10 or 11:00 p.m., when they finally made the top of the hill and nervously worked their way across the German trench lines and through the wire, prying up one strand at a time. Where were the Germans, damn it? Surely, they had to be watching their line. Yet, they hadn't been on the afternoon of October 2 either, so *maybe* the two wet, dirty Doughboys were okay yet. They traversed the slope, passing through more wire and by empty machine-gun nests, skirting shell holes and the occasional body and then finally down the other side of the hill. The sky was beginning to lighten and they did not want to be caught out in the daylight on that damned hill. They just *had* to be getting close! The answer came a short while later as Pvt. Brown fell into a well camouflaged hole in the dark - and recognized it as the very one he had dug for himself on the evening of October 1! Amazed, he crawled out of the muddy funk, stood up and began talking to Koz in a normal voice, trusting that the line had not been pushed back since they had left it so many days ago.

It was not long before a Company M/308th outpost heard them, picked them up and took them to their Company PC in a muddy funk along the bottom of the Ravin d'Argonne. There, a lieutenant they did not know gave them a can of beans, a canteen of water and the news that the Pocket had been relieved a few hours hence, before then sending them back to talk to Captain Breckenridge at l'Homme Mort. As the guide led them further back down the rail line through an early morning mist and fog, they could see what a pounding the ravine had taken in the last five days, even in the weak, watery light. For the first time, they began to understand just why the rest of the regiment had not been able to break through to them sooner. (29, 131, 144, 338)

Captain McMurtry found Major Whittlesey standing on the wagon road just beyond the right flank, in among a group of enlisted men and officers, with half of a huge steak sandwich in his hand and the other half in his mouth, which still held a strange, grim look of earnestness. He was notable among the others not simply because of his towering height, but mostly because he was so much more spectacularly dirty and unkempt than they were, even though all were obviously combat men.

"For God's sake," the limping Captain cried to Major Whittlesey as he stumped up, "Give me a bite of that!" As the grinning Major did, Captain Stone pulled another out of a mussette bag he was carrying. They had been shoved in there by Colonel Houghton's 'striker', Chinese Lee, just before the Captain went forward to Major McKinney's Advanced Battalion PC that afternoon, once it had become obvious that they were going to get through to Major Whittlesey. Now, the two starved officers finished them off in nothing flat and drained whatever was in the nearest canteen offered. Elements of companies A and M of the 307th were starting to show up by then and were equally appalled at the sights they found. Yet, most still made their way through the bivouac, sharing out what food, tobacco and drink they had, trying hard not to break down in front of the wreckage of humanity they found in the holes around them and not in any hurry to eat again any too soon for it. It was hardest for the relieving force at the wounded area, where they found the dead laying thick, every imaginable kind of horrible wound, many blackened, rotting and oozing puss, and where the rain had washed the mud from the 'corpse wall' to expose the horror that lay beneath. Many relieving men, though long hardened to the horrors of combat, turned away and vomited. (21, 29, 51, 103, 104, 109, 116, 139)

Yet, the relieving men were met at every corner by a dazed smile appearing tentatively above the rim of a filthy funk hole, sometimes with tear tracks coursing through the dirt staining the face attached to the smile. Relief had come and soon they would get the care they needed. Though there was not much carried into the Pocket that night, most men got at least a taste of food and many relieving men were kept busy running back and forth to the brook with canteens until late. Major Whittlesey walked gingerly through the Pocket until well past midnight, again fully upright, hands behind his back and as seemingly unconcerned as ever, lending what words of encouragement he could, laughing quietly with them (when they could find something funny), and giving them the feeling that they had all come through together because of each other, and telling each one how proud he was of him. It was the one and only time during the war that he allowed himself to be seen on an even and level plane with them. Captain McMurtry followed suit, though it was less of a stretch for him. They were all the same that night, commander and commanded alike. For the time being, Major Whittlesey let Lt. Tillman be in charge and became 'just one of the boys'.

There was one point when the state of the Major's mind showed best that night however, at least when the relief first came in. He and Captain McMurtry both had initially strongly insisted that Lt. Tillman place his men along the hillside within the perimeter itself, so as to not only reinforce the position, but also to increase the feeling of security among their men. The two commanders felt that there needed to be proof positive of the relief to restore some semblance of spirit. Major Whittlesey may have also wanted Lt. Tillman's men there to try and keep any of his command from perhaps thinking the area secure and inadvertently slipping out of the position to make their way back further in search of food, as had Pvt. Hollingshead and company. (By that time, the Major was probably aware of others that had skipped out as well.) The area was far from secure however, and to lose men at this late stage would be too cruel.

Lieutenant Tillman however, managed to talk the commanders out of that plan from two standpoints. First, since the immediate area *was* far from secure, vigilance needed to be maintained between the southern slope of Hill 198 and the advanced line that had been established along the heights above the Binarville-La Viergette road ahead. This was in order to prevent the possibility of a larger entrapment of not only the rescued command, but the relieving force as well. It certainly looked as though the Germans had evacuated the area (though Hill 205 was still securely in their hands and maintaining a narrow supply line back between the French to the west and the 307 outposts on the road to the east), but one could not be sure. If they were simply regrouping for a solid morning attack, then it would be much better for his men to be in the open, above and ready, to meet any assault head on from level ground. The forward line would also hold the Binarville-La Viergette road itself securely, in order to allow ambulances to come up right away the next morning. Overall then, spreading the relieving force in a protective cordon *around* Major Whittlesey's position, instead of in *among* it, made good tactical sense and the Major eventually agreed to the plan and then let Lt. Tillman control everything as he and Captain McMurtry turned their attentions to the care of their men.

The second reason Lt. Tillman was reluctant to place his men among Major Whittlesey's troops, despite the latter's insistence, was the atrocious smell and profound ghastliness of the position. The hillside literally looked like a cemetery of recently deceased that had been badly shelled and whose bodies had been disinterred and mutilated. It smelled like an abandoned, formerly busy, slaughterhouse that had never been cleaned up and left to stand for days in the summer heat. While Major Whittlesey's men had gotten used to the hideous smell and abominable sights over the past five days, it was still far beyond anything the 307th men had ever seen and Lt. Tillman simply could not bring himself to force his men to take up positions in holes lined in blood, filth, or pieces of human flesh. He was never compelled to tell Major Whittlesey or Captain McMurtry this terrible truth however, since they both eventually agreed that it was perhaps better tactically the other way. Therefore, Lt. Tillman's men simply outposted the position then and waited for the dawn, talking in low tones of the horrible sight they surrounded. (10, 21, 29, 33, 51, 91, 103, 104, 109, 131, 138, 139, 148, 149, 150, 225, 234, 239, 245)

Once word was received that elements of the 1st/307th were definitely on Major Whittlesey's position early that evening, General Johnson had Captain Breckenridge begin arrangements to advance into the Charlevaux Ravine and reconnect with the Major's command from the left and behind. What yet remained of the 2nd/307th, still under his control, would advance over Hill 198, establish a line behind Major Whittlesey's Pocket, form liaison with their brethren from the 307th to the right and then extend left as far as they could. Meanwhile, those remaining 1st and 2nd Battalion/308th troops (about 26 men out of the original 214 in Company D and a like sum from F, along with the strays from the other companies that were up with Major Whittlesey) were to move down the ravine bottom and cross through the gap between Hills 198 and 205. Beyond, they were to connect with the Major's troops, and extend a line back to the 3rd/308th. The 3rd Battalion would then maintain control of the rear areas until the situations of the 1st and 2nd battalions could be assessed in the morning. Since there was so little remaining of D and F, again Lt. Taylor and Company K of the 3rd Battalion received orders to accompany them forward into the Charlevaux in order to help carry supplies and man runner posts up to the beleaguered command. They were all to set out at once, darkness and mist notwithstanding. General Johnson, having lost the initiative once already (on the evening of October 2, when Major Whittlesey had failed to establish the line rearward in the dark to begin with) was not about to let the situation repeat itself. It was later then, about 9:30 p.m., when he had gathered enough information to phone Colonel Hannay again with an update:

"I am at the command post of the 308th Infantry on the right of the ravine. Two companies have advanced and are now in contact with Whittlesey. (These were B, as already explained, and F, see text below, of the 307th - author) On the left, they (companies D, F and K/308th) are pushing up the trench line with the French on their left and are advancing to the front line. I have given orders that on arriving at the front line they are to halt and reorganize. Supplies are now being pushed forward, including medical aid and attendants. I have given orders for Houghton to take over and reorganize the entire front and as soon as reorganized to push forward. The 308th Infantry is to reorganize and hold its present position. I'm going to advance my own post tomorrow."

"Can you give us an idea of just where the 308th will be?" Colonel Hannay asked, relaying the information to General Alexander who was apparently then too busy with details of the breakthrough to come to the phone himself.

"I have sent officers up to find out exactly the coordinates of the 308th, as the coordinates previously given were wrong. They are more to the right," General Johnson finished. (III) (29, 103, 105, 109, 116, 131, 144, 148)

Earlier that evening of October 7, Lt. Knight had led his little band slowly down the ravine through the rainy darkness in a loose combat formation. No one knew for sure just what the Germans actually still had control of ahead and what they did not, so caution was the word and they moved with great care. There were occasional and sporadic rifle arguments and machine-gun rattles, along with Very lights and parachute flares coming down from Hill 205, all of which kept the tired, wet men on their toes. On their toes was apparently not enough though, for while they managed to establish that the Germans still held Hill 205 (obviously) and a stretch of ground south of it up on the west ridge of the ravine, they failed to find a way in the dark through the thick wire at the ravine head up to Major Whittlesey's position. Eventually deciding, after several hours of fruitless search and hard work with the wire cutters to give up until they had better light, Lt. Knight then led his little group back to l'Homme Mort. Lieutenant Taylor, bringing up the rear with his Company K, had fared no better and showed up at the bunker a short time later. By that time, it was past midnight. (105, 131, 144)

By contrast, portions of 2nd/307th, still working up on the eastern heights of the ravine, carefully labored toward Hill 198 from the south at about the same time lieutenants Knight and Taylor were setting out down the ravine. Moving carefully through the brush and wire filled darkness over an unfamiliar route, they made their way largely unmolested up the hillside, passing old machine-gun positions that had previously chewed them to pieces and around shell holes and fallen trees from a week's worth of bombardment. Once on top, they found the dual trench lines of the *Haupt-Widerstands-Lienie* abandoned all the way west to their termination at the Ravine d'Argonne, as well as to the east, where they found some 3rd/307th men forming defensive lines within the German positions themselves. Moving ahead and down the north slope of Hill 198 into the Charlevaux Ravine, a foul odor began to waft back at them out of the darkness as they neared the bottom. They would have put on gas masks, except it did not smell like any gas they had ever encountered. Then, a few scouts came back through the night with sick, sour looks and reports of reaching Major Whittlesey's position. All realized then what the reek was. The unofficial history of Company F/307th, then in the lead of 2nd's advance into the ravine states, in part, "That evening we finally succeeded in getting through and establishing liaison posts along the road. Instructions were given not to take any German prisoners. After receiving this message, we met and killed some Germans…"

Yet, once across the ravine proper, Company F took position in a thin Cossack line along the south side of the wagon road below the Pocket, connected on their right to elements of Company M, behind Lt. Tillman's B, and on their left to the remainder of their own 2nd Battalion. The rest of that battalion extended in a southwestward curve back along the narrow gauge line running down the bottom of the Ravine d'Argonne between Hills 198 and 205. Patrols had shown that the Germans still had control over the stubborn La Palette complex and the Moulin d'Charlevaux (and Lord only knew what else), both of which lay between the U.S. and the French forces farther west, and which were still keeping the two great armies apart. Fortunately, there was little combat activity in the confusing zone, other than some German light shelling into the Ravin d'Argonne. The men outposting the Charlevaux Ravine position went largely unmolested then, as long as they stayed off Hill 205 and kept a distance from a rough German outpost line that their scouts found slightly farther west. (91, 103, 104, 138, 139, 235)

By midnight of October 7 then, General Johnson saw the situation of his 154th Brigade standing thus: On the far right, elements of the 1st/307th (mostly Company A backed by C) were on the Binarville-La Viergette road, well above the curve of the Charlevaux Ravine and in firm liaison with the left of the 306th, whose line swept sharply north as it progressed east. Then, as the 307th's line extended west, it continued along the road running above the Pocket, now firmly occupied by Company B from a point about directly in line with what had once been the right flank perimeter of the Pocket, on over to a point about 500 to 600 meters east toward the Moulin d'Charlevaux. Security of the road was specifically ordered to be maintained by General Johnson himself, in order that the ambulances could be brought up at first light. Company B also dropped elements down the hillside along either flank of the Pocket to the wagon road below.

Beneath the Pocket, Company F/307th extended along the far edge of the wagon road from just about Major Whittlesey's former left flank position, on over to Company M/307th, who were somewhere just off the Pocket's former right flank perimeter. With F connected on their flanks to those elements of B spread down the hillside, Major Whittlesey's command within the cordon was well buttoned for the night. Then, from Company F's left, the main line (the remainder of 2nd/307th) continued south, its troops actually facing west instead of north, down into the gap between Hills 205 and 198. There they had no actual connection through the wire with elements of the 3rd/308th within the Ravin d'Argonne, but instead had a runner line over the shoulder of Hill 198 to them. The 3rd, in turn, continued the line down to just about 500 meters above the Binarville-Moulin de l'Homme Mort road, and then westward over to the French outposts in the orchards just east of Binarville. The line that had originally been ordered occupied by the evening of October 2 had finally been completed then, though only after five of the most grueling days that the men of the 154th Brigade had ever seen, or would ever see, and at the near complete destruction of two regiments of infantry. (10, 17, 91, 103, 104, 109, 235, 245)

General Alexander, busily following the rapid progress of General Whittenmeyer's rapidly advancing brigade as they headily pursued the German retreat, received the news of Major Whittlesey's relief at about the same time General Johnson was sending his troops forward into the Charlevaux Ravine, which was around 9:00 p.m. The advance of the afternoon by the division's right had been spectacular after a stall of six long days and therefore the situation in the Charlevaux Ravine had taken a bit of a back seat with the General as the breakout rapidly progressed. In any case, the splitting of the German line would undoubtedly have been the catalyst for an advance up to Major Whittlesey's position anyway, which is, in essence, just what happened. The tearing of the divisional right flank, progressing westward down the line as the entire left flank of the 1st Corps ripped loose, had provided the leverage needed for Colonel Houghton's filtering tactic to pay off handsomely on a local basis, thus freeing Major Whittlesey and his men. Nor did the event apparently make that big an impression upon General Alexander when he was finally told of the success in the Charlevaux either. When Colonel Hannay gave him the news that night, his only remark (as stated in his autobiography) was simply that the information was "most welcome."(IV) (2, 20, 35, 91, 103, 109)

It was over.

With most of the pressure relieved, once the initial burst of tired excitement wore off, the men in the Pocket settled back into their funk holes to wait for morning and the rest of the help that would then arrive. Food, water, medical aid, clean cloths, a shave and a bath would all come with the impending morning sun. The totals, if anybody bothered to figure them that night, might have made them even more anxious for the dawn. If one counted, from the time Major Whittlesey had actually realized they were surrounded on October 3 (about 10:30 a.m., though he would not admit it to himself until near noon of that day), until their relief at about 7:00 p.m. of October 7, they had been bottled up in the Charlevaux Ravine for about 104.5 hours. Counting from the approximate time that the Germans had actually closed the ring (about 5:00 a.m. of October 3) brought the total up to 109.5 hours. Counting total time actually occupying the ravine, from the time they had taken up residence until relief came in (from about 7:00 p.m. of October 2 to 7:00 p.m. of October 7), gave 120 hours. Food and medical supplies had mostly been exhausted by noon of October 3, making for some 103 long hours without either and most of the heavy casualties had been taken within the first 48 hours. Further, it had rained for at least a portion of virtually every one of the five days and nights, the majority of October 4 being the only exception. A full counting of dead and wounded enlisted men would wait for the next day, and, in fact, never really be made. (The most accurate one ever compiled is included in this book. See Appendix A.) For the officers though, the numbers were all too clear - of the 19 that had commanded in the ravine only three, Major Whittlesey, Lt. Cullen and Lt. Eager, still remained on their feet largely untouched. The rest were either killed, wounded, or missing, making up a grand total of 84 percent officerial casualties, or one for every 7.5 hours of occupation.

However, none of that would be realized (or cared about) until much later. On the night of October 7, all that mattered was that the Pocket was secured. A line of outposts surrounded them securely instead of the Germans, and runners traipsed back and forth in a constant stream, bringing up supplies while Major Whittlesey's men lay quiet and unmolested for the first time in days. Their relief was a real, tactile thing that could be felt in the air and as the night wore on, a strange peace descended across the Charlevaux Ravine; a peace that has remained largely unbroken to this very day. Off to the right, some distance away, a Stokes mortar started, there was the bark of Chauchat fire off to the left rear and some stray enemy shells fell far out into the Ravine d'Argonne, but none of that meant anything now. Secure in the knowledge that someone else was 'watching the door' Major Whittlesey's men were at last able to drift off to their first real sleep ever in that stinking ravine and by midnight, all was mostly calm and quiet in the Pocket. A few blankets had magically appeared to cover the most severely wounded. How many were there yet lying in the mud at the foot of that hillside that night that closed their eyes in relief and tragically never opened them to the sunrise the next morning? No one can ever say, but certainly a few must have. The rest, however, would soon at last be finally free of the appalling suffering and anguish that had increasingly surrounded them for the last five long days and nights.

Then, sometime after midnight, a shriek filled the air as a survivor tossed in nightmare and already the second fight of the Charlevaux Ravine had begun - that of living the ordeal over again in their dreams...

(I) Some of Lt. Tillman's men had actually been detailed to carry sand bags full of rations along with them as they moved up, so sure was General Johnson that they would reach Major Whittlesey's position that afternoon. Reports of "60 sacks of food" are no doubt an error however, since that would have entailed most of Lt. Tillman's men at that time. The likelihood of 60 cans of corned willy is more probably correct, along with several tins of hard bread. Company M, which was working behind and to the left of Company B, likely carried some in as well. The initial group of troops that came up with Private Krotoshinsky and company brought more but certainly no one got more than a few bites that night, though Major Whittlesey was careful to see that everyone got at least a little. At one point along the perimeter, an unnamed man later recalled finding out about the relief when a Doughboy appeared through the brush with a sand bag containing a few cans of food hanging from his bayonet.

(II) John P. Teichmoeller would continue to be plagued by problems stemming from that ill-placed barrage even after the war. Headaches and an inability to concentrate on anything for very long had left him unable to return to his studies and kept him in almost constant misery. In 1921, doctors finally discovered what they described as 'swelling on the brain' that was figured to be a direct result from what he had experienced in the Pocket on October 4, 1918. He underwent surgery to correct the problem but, sadly, died from complications of the operation not long after – one of the several late victims of the episode in the Charlevaux.

(III) Herein lay the impetus of the falsehood that Major Whittlesey gave the wrong coordinates for his position in the Charlevaux Ravine, which would be held as the most damning evidence of his incompetence when other officers later privately passed judgment on his actions. However, the coordinates Major Whittlesey gave all along had been *absolutely correct* for a position just east of the left flank perimeter. His coordinates then, had been correct up until the command had been forced to evacuate the flanks and consolidate the whole hillside position, which had only occurred in the last two days. Only then did the coordinates become 'wrong' - long after all contact rearward had been severed, and it was that which was reported to General Johnson by an advance company that had reached Major Whittlesey from the left rear, which was Company F/307th. (See further text.) Colonel Houghton, too, was reporting erroneously to the Brigadier that Major Whittlesey was not where he had said he was, which would then come to General Alexander's attention on October 8, and so the bogie had been laid.

(IV) In all likelihood, the filtering tactic would have worked anyway – although probably not before Major Whittlesey's position would have been either annihilated or overrun, the way things were going. While it was definitely, the attacks of the 1st and 82nd Divisions farther north that forced the Germans to finally abandon the entire line in the Argonne Forest, the men of the 154th Brigade would no doubt have eventually reached the position in the Charlevaux Ravine, since the German forces there were close to the breaking point by then. Out of reserves, and having to deal with both the incessant French attacks making tremendous headway farther west, as well as the repeated American attacks up the Ravin d'Argonne and against Hill 198, would have likely proven too much. The line would have been broken then (though on a much more limited basis than as effected by the 1st and 82nd's efforts), primarily because Major Whittlesey's men had held out in the Charlevaux Ravine – though they almost certainly would not have been around to see it.

Ancillary sources used in this chapter include: 12, 14, 21, 24, 25, 27, 31-36, 42, 43, 48, 49, Various 52-86, Various 152-216, 219, 221, 223, 225, 227-233, 235, 239, 243, 244, Various 247-280, Various 282-338, 339, 340, 347, 349, 350, 352, 356, 362, 364, 368, 370, 372, 373, 374

Above:
The beginning of
the Giselher
Stellung on Hill 198
in early 1915

Inset:
Approximately the
same stretch of the
line on Hill 198 in
2001 (Taylor V. Beattie)

The prisoners captured during the afternoon attack of October 2nd;
(Sgt. Owens - far right)   Photo taken near l'Homme Mort bunker. (109)

The Pocket, as seen from across the Charlevaux Ravine near the crest of Hill 198 - Careful examination shows the cutting of the road above, the wagon road below, and the funk holes along the slope. Taken in February of 1919, the photo is somewhat misleading; the foliage of the previous October was much thicker. (109)

Official AEF shots of the Pocket: Left, the path leading to the spur of the hill on the left flank; above right, the remains of the foot bridge; below right, water-filled shell hole near the center section (116)

The cliff just behind the right flank looking north down into the Pocket
(Taylor V. Beattie)

The reburied bodies of the Lost Battalion dead just west of the left flank in early 1919
(Gilles Lagin)

Above: The left flank
of the Pocket as seen
from across the
German drill field,
April 1919 (Gilles Lagin)

Right: The same view
in 2001, showing the
flooding of the creek
done in the 1920's
(Taylor V. Beattie)

Center section of the Pocket in 2002 (Taylor V. Beattie)

Above: October 8th, the "Lucky 194" walk out by the left flank
2nd Battalion on ground in front; 1st Battalion behind (38)

Below: About 15 minutes later; the official photograph.
The new Lt. Col. Charles Whittlesey stands on the far left (109)

Lieutenant Colonel Charles White Whittlesey (344)
Above right: Receiving the Medal of Honor (130)
Above left: his medals-part of the Williams College collection
Below left: The only known photo of Whittlesey with his Medal of Honor

Major George Gibson McMurtry Jr. (101)
Inset: Receiving the Medal of Honor from General John J. Pershing (48)

Private Lowell Hollingshead
Above right: The surrender letter as it appears today in the Whittlesey Collection at Williams College
Center: Holding the cane given to him by Lt. Prinz, photo taken sometime in the late 1950's (Becky Henn)
Below left: Before the Charlevaux episode, in 1918 (Becky Henn)

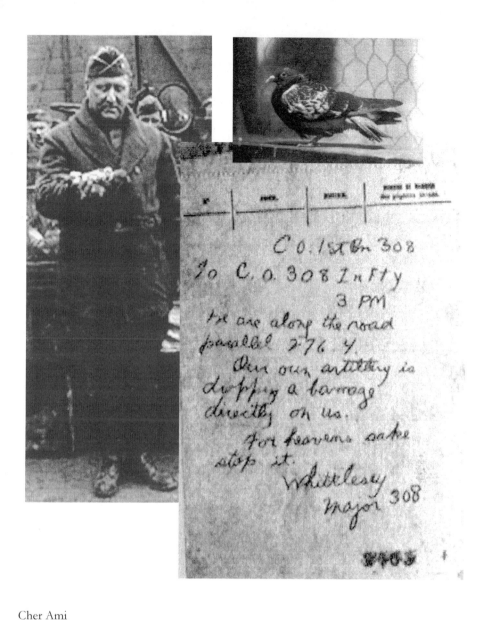

Cher Ami
Above right: Cher Ami shortly before his death in 1919 (353)
Above left: Lt. Pelham Bissell holding Cher Ami before the pigeon left France
Center: The final pigeon message that Cher Ami carried on October 4, 1918 (44)

Lt. Paul Knight

Lt. Karl Wilhelm
(101)

Lt. William Cullen
(344)

Lt. James V. Leak
(Frances Bingham)

Capt. Leo Stromee
(Rick Lytle)

Lt. Victor Harrington
(Samuel Steele)

Lt. Sherman Eager
(Ruth Eager Moran)

Lt. Marshall Peabody
(Marshall P. Hoke)

Pvt. Robert E. Pou
(44)

Bn. Sgt. Mjr. Benjamin Gaedeke
(David Gaedeke)

Pvt. Jack Gehris
(David Gehris)

Pvt. Irving Sirotta
(Marvin Edwards)

Pvt. James Bragg
(Tommy Bragg)

Billy, in the States postwar
(David Gehris)

Depot des Machines, post event

Standing at left, Walter Baldwin; standing right rear with helmet, Sgt. Charlie Cahill; standing right front with helmet, 'Zip' Cepaglia

Pvt. James Larney
(John Larney)

Cpl. Walter Baldwin
(Thomas Baldwin)

Pvt. Omer Richards

Lt. Maurice Griffin and the overcoat he wore in the Pocket (44)

Pvt. John Nell
(40)

Pvt. Sidney Smith
(Victor Fritch)

Pvt. Emil Peterson
(Orvin Perterson)

Staff of the 308th Regiment in late October 1918
Front row, far left: Lt. Col. Charles W. Whittlesey (38)

Pvt. Lee McCollum
(33)

Pvt. Abraham Krotoshinksy
(344)

The Company A survivors
Front row center: Lt. Henry Williamson; front row second from left, Sgt. Herman
Anderson; rear row second from right, Pvt. Ralph John (108)

Capt. Nelson Holderman
(33)

Col. Eugene Houghton
(38)

Lt. Thomas Pool

Sgt. James Carroll

Major Carl McKinney
(109)

Lt. Frederick Tillman
(279)

Capt. Walter Kerr-Rainsford

Lt. Harold Goettler
Upper right: his grave in early 1919
Bottom left: his grave (boxed) at the family plot in Graceland Cemetery, Chicago, IL

Lt. Erwin R. Bleckley and his grave in the American cemetery at Romagne-sous-Montfaucon, France

Goettler and Bleckley's regular DH-4, which was severely shot up the morning of October 6th, 1918, the day they died.

"Shy-Ann", the plane that Lt.'s Anderson and Rogers were flying when they confirmed the Lost Battalion's location.

General Freiherr
Quadt-Wykradt-Huchtenbruck,
Cmdg. 76th Rsv. Div.

General Karl Wellman,
Cmdg. 1st Rsv. Corps.

Major Manfred Hunicken,
Cmdg. 254th Inf. Reg.

3rd from right: Lt. Fritz Prinz;
3rd from left: Major Hunicken

Capt. Herman Petri,
Cmdg. 2nd Bn./254th

Entrance to the German camp
at the Charlevaux Mill (Gill Lagin)

The German bunker at the Charlevaux Mill

Note: All photos on this page, except noted,
are derived from source 123. See appendix B.

Part 4:
The Postscript of Time

October 8, 1918

"Do not write about me; write about these men…"
Major Charles Whittlesey, afternoon of the 8th.

As Tuesday, October 8, 1918, dawned - the last October 8 of a war that eventually claimed 13 million lives - activity began in earnest within the Charlevaux Ravine and beyond once again. Elements of the 307th and 308th began to stir within the Ravine d'Argonne and make for the Charlevaux and other points north. German artillery started falling out well beyond the Pocket's left flank, to protect their rear guard units in retreat that were being hassled by a French attack launched at dawn on the other side of Hill 205. Some shells were also falling up beyond the road above the Pocket, with a few strays even landing down in the ravine itself, which Major Whittlesey's men largely ignored. While elements of the 308th moved up toward the Pocket, Lt. Tillman took some of his men off down the road to the west to push along the left flank of the division, which was now facing Northwest, above the French right. Though the attacks of the day before had made terrific gains within the 153rd Brigade and everything east of them, and in the 154th Brigade's area of operations they had finally reached Major Whittlesey and the objective line intended for October 2, there was still much work to be done. Hill 205 was still a sticking point, along the slopes of which a small portion of those 13 million lost lives would be claimed that day in the last efforts of driving those few remaining German troops out of the position. (10, 91, 104, 109, 116)

General Johnson began the day by sending 308th companies D and F, backed up by K, down the Ravine d'Argonne at first light to try to find the way through to Major Whittlesey that they had been unable to locate the night before. He realized he was in the last throws of his command at the regimental level and was determined to finish the job in that damned ravine, come what may. Word had come the night before that Lieutenant Colonel (later General) Gordon Johnston, a friend and personal favorite of General Alexander's, would be arriving around mid-morning to take the reins of the 308th. This would leave General Johnson again at the head of the 154th Brigade, where he should have been all along. (I) (105, 247)

The patrols General Johnson sent out met little resistance as they moved carefully up the ravine, for there was little resistance to meet. Some sporadic rifle and machine-gun fire came down from an observatory on the southeastern corner of La Palette Pavilion and its trenches near the top, but that was about all. On the other hand, there was a hell of a racket coming from the other side of Hill 205 by then, where the French were pushing up the Binarville-La Viergette road from the fork just north of Binarville and were again meeting resistance near the La Palette and Charlevaux trenches. With the Americans on the road beyond the hill and the Germans in general retreat, the task of eliminating the blockade of Hill 205 should have been relatively easy but instead, they were running into the same old hornet's nest, still plenty active, despite the handwriting on the Germans' wall. Damned Boche.

No matter to Lt. Knight's band of the 308th as they moved forward along the Ravin d'Argonne however. They broke or bypassed what little resistance they came upon, carefully crossing through some light shellfire falling into the ravine, before finally passing between the two hills and out into the Charlevaux Ravine. There, they found the field off Major Whittlesey's left flank being nailed by trench mortars from the northwest, while light, long range, machine-gun fire from La Palette pinged the ground around them as they moved forward into the ravine. These annoyances were nothing however, after the last six days of hell they had just endured in the Argonne ravine. Meeting some 1st/307th outposts, who brought them into Major Whittlesey's position, Lt. Knight then made his way to the Major and reported that the link that was meant for the night of October 2 was finally complete. Company K, in support of Lt. Knight, quickly came forward with what rations they had been hauling and word was sent back to General Johnson that the route was now thoroughly open and to send food and medical up at once, in large quantities. It was about that time that Lt. Col. Johnston arrived at l'Homme Mort and General Johnson began filling him in on the preparations made for his move to relieve Captain Breckenridge, then up on the line, from command of the 308th regiment. (10, 91, 105, 109, 116)

It was at 8:30 a.m. when Colonel Houghton telephoned General Alexander with a first, full indication of just how things along his section of the front were going. While General Johnson wrestled with sorting out and reassembling what he had left of the 308th and Lt. Col. Johnston's apparent arrogance (for indications are that he *was* arrogant with General Johnson), Colonel Houghton reported: "My front line is at 294.7–276.35 and extends to the right to 295.05-276.45. I am trying to establish contact with the 306th. Have patrols out to the front and flanks and will push to the left. Ration details have not yet arrived but medical officers have and are attending the 308th wounded. A great many of these men will be difficult to get out. Lieutenant Flynn is locating 306th M.G. to take charge."

"What is the condition of the line?" General Alexander wanted to know.

"The left of the line reports being fired on from the northwest by trench mortars. We will develop the position. Lieutenant Tillman's patrol killed several Germans last night when taking Company B into position. It was a bombing party that had attacked (sic) the 308th. Lieutenant Tillman arrived in advance with companies A, B, and M and did excellent work in handling the situation. A patrol just returned reports an officer of the 305th acting as advanced guard for the 306th and reports the 306th about a 1,000 yards to the right of our position at 294.85-276.55 and also reports that they have not received word to extend left. Instructing Company A to establish liaison with the 306th as A is on the right. I am going to put 3rd Battalion on the right in contact with the 306th with two companies of the 305th as a liaison group in between.

"The 1st Battalion will be on the left with instructions to extend out a 'feeler' for the French and develop any resistance that may be there. I have also ordered MG's which are already there to push well to the left to assist the French, who are apparently now attacking La Palette and meeting with resistance. We hear considerable M.G. fire, rifle fire, and bombing in that direction.

"I have placed the 2nd Battalion, which was the divisional reserve and turned over to me last night by General Johnson, in support along the old position which we advanced from yesterday. Its center will be at a point at about 275.5-295.55. They will extend in a westerly direction with that point as a center. They will have instructions to move forward when we have formed our line and advanced."

The news Colonel Houghton reported represented all that General Alexander had been wanting since the evening of October 2, the only remaining obstacle still being Hill 205 but General Johnson and the French were then taking that on. However, with all the casualties they had suffered in the last five days, how secure were the lines? Every indication was that the Germans were in retreat all along the line, but that did not mean small, local counterattacks might not break through yet. (II)

"How about your communications with your line? How about Boche in between you?" the General asked.

"That ravine with the railroad track in it, running north to Le Charlevaux?" Colonel Houghton answered. "You swept that out at daylight this morning."

That would have been General Johnson's men, General Alexander knew, but from whom he had not yet heard.

"Do you believe there are any Germans east of that, on your side?" The general was being very thorough now.

"There are no Germans in there," the Colonel answered shortly. "I have gotten them out."

"Have you anything up near the corner where 76 and 94 meet?" (These are map lines – author)

"We are pushing that way now, but we will be above 76. We are pushing along the road."

"Be very sure to clean out everything in those trenches and dugouts," General Alexander warned. A couple days before, when he had been up to the front, he and Lt. de Coppett had been shot at by a couple snipers for the second time during the battle. "Have you heard anything definite from Whittlesey?"

"He is definitely all right."

"How about his losses; do you know anything?"

"We have no definite report, but we found him on the coordinates about where we have given our front line. The reason he was fired into by our friendly artillery was because he had given us the wrong coordinates of his position." General Alexander ignored this last statement, which he knew to be most probably untrue and hanging up, began to arrange for trucks to bring Major Whittlesey's men back to Depot des Machines. Then, he set out for the front. It was time to see the situation for himself. (III) (2, 138, 139, 144, 148, 149, 150)

Slowly, the Pocket stirred as the first morning of comparative freedom broke under another foggy blanket. A stiff breeze blew out of the east, keeping the temperature floating in the mid-50s Fahrenheit where it would remain for most of the day. At the first indication of light, several men made a beeline for the brook to try to clean the accumulated mud from their bodies and tattered uniforms. Razors were one of the first things to appear, along with a few precious bars of soap. Both were indiscriminately shared out. A single tattered, filthy shirt that had escaped being used for bandages made the rounds of one small group as a towel. Sergeant John Colasacco of Company C, a big, strong man who had tipped the scales at over 200 pounds before the fight in the Argonne, found that he had only the strength to crawl on his hands and knees over to the brook. Once there, he had little left over, without a short rest, to drink and wash. Others were in little better condition, stiff and sore from being cramped into funk holes for so long, their feet and ankles horribly swollen. The lightly wounded made their way as best they could down to the foot of the hill to try to find some attention from the few doctors and medics that had come up over night. Most found they had to wait, as the more seriously wounded received attention first. No one bitched about it though. (21)

The men gathered, helping each other when they could. There were few uniforms that were anything more than filthy rags, most torn, muddy, and as often as not encrusted with blood or feces. Many were missing their puttees, given up as bandages. Those who had been runners or who had gone out on patrol had scratched and bloody hands and faces from crawling through the brush and brambles. There was very little conversation at the brook, and what there was, the men carried on unconsciously in low, whispered tones. Cautiously and quickly they cleaned up, looking around them as they did so, still uncomfortable about being out in the open. The occasional shell dropped closer in towards the perimeter, but it did not bother them, since they had been through so much more than that. Private Nell was one of the first who went down to fill his canteen at the spring near the left flank:

"The next morning... I took a look at the spring. About 50 feet (away) there were several railroad ties stacked up in a square with the rear opened. By the side of this pile of ties lay a pile of empty machine gun shells, enough to fill a wagon box with sideboards... It is presumed that there were about as many at the other end on our right flank, as well as at the other machine gun nests set up around us... I learned that our rifle ammunition was almost gone and no one seemed to have any grenades at all." (40)

Private Nell was right - the rifle ammunition was very nearly completely exhausted. As for the Hotchkiss guns, only two of the nine that had gone into the ravine were still operational, one on each ragged flank, though there were no trained gunners left to operate them (save for Sgt. Hauck) and only two half-empty boxes of ammunition remained, one for each weapon; enough for about 15 to 20 seconds of conservative fire. Of the numerous Chauchat auto rifles that had been so important in guarding the front of the Pocket, none remained in functional order and there was no ammunition left for them at all. Grenades had long since become nothing more than wishes and the perimeter of the position had been almost completely denuded of cover, as had sections of the hillside. In fact, defenses were such that had the Germans attacked just *one more time* the previous evening, the position in the Charlevaux Ravine would most definitely have collapsed, probably right from the outset. That was how close the situation had come to a far worse ending. (10, 103, 109, 116, 129, 147)

For the troops of the 307th and 308th making their way slowly into and around that section of the Charlevaux Ravine, the terrible truth of the situation endured by Major Whittlesey's force over the last five days quickly became obvious. The hillside was a horrifying mess. Trees were down everywhere and funk holes had been blown in, leaving only a trace of the former occupant. Even some of the medics, who were used to combat wounds and their accompanying odors, had to hold handkerchiefs over their noses and mouths the closer they got to the Pocket and some still gagged. There remained pools of clotted, congealed blood standing in spots. Several men were too afraid to come out of their holes, not yet able to convince themselves that it was all over. There were, in fact, still a number of bullets pinging around, though it was nothing compared to what they had been through. Yet for some, there were enough stray shells on the left to compound any neurosis they might have remaining. But these were the few. Most of Major Whittlesey's survivors simply sat at the foot of the hillside, or on the edge of their holes and either stared off into the distance blankly or grinned back at their relievers with a wide-eyed, shocky, yellow-toothed grin, which was horrifying to look at.

The first among the relieving troops into the ravine that morning, were detailed to move through the position and gather up those more seriously wounded and move them to a better collection point, away from the terrible, long wounded hole behind the corpse wall. This in itself was a horrid and repugnant task. Many of these men had lain there for days and their wounds were infected, rotting messes. Several had lain next to corpses, while most lay in a terrible filth of mud, blood, puss, urine and excrement. Slightly later, that same group of relievers, along with some of the survivors, would get an even worse task; collecting the corpses and whatever stray, blackened and rotting body parts they could find. Private John, walking around the Pocket solemnly, later described what he saw and what they would be up against:

"Such a mess you never did see. Some of our men were dead, others were dying and moaning for help. Some were already buried and others just in pieces... Everybody living was like a living scarecrow. It didn't

seem so terrible then, as it was a sight that was before our eyes every minute of the day and to each of us it seemed so evident that it would only be a short time until we would take our place along side of them, that we became reconciled to it. But now, it seems so terrible and inhumane..." (220)

A salvaged weapons and equipment pile was started off to one side and those men who had been forced to arm themselves with captured German rifles now gladly abandoned them. Battered helmets, broken Eddystones and bayonets, torn and bloodstained web equipment and uniforms, ruined packs - the pile slowly grew. Then the flamethrower tanks were brought out of the woods off the right flank, along with their dead operators, a few of which had roasted alive when their tanks were hit by U.S. fire and thus flamed. Other German corpses were brought in from the ravine bottom, close to what had been the perimeter line up until two days before. Some of them were in as bad of shape as any of those in the Pocket and were now laid out next to the remains of those they had earlier been trying to destroy, including that of the formally popular Lt. Marshall Peabody and the as yet unidentified remnants of Sergeant-Major Gaedeke. Father James Halligan, the 308th's chief spiritual advisor, came up and roamed among them administering the Last Rights to all; Jew or Gentile, German or American, it did not matter. They were all the same now...

Dud shells littered the ravine, some half-buried, others lying right atop the ground, a few definitely of the French 75mm and 155mm variety while many others were of the German trench mortar type. (By contrast, no shells from the German 77mm that had opened up for a short time were ever reported found.) Off in the not so distant battle zone ahead and ahead left, the men of the 307th struggled to get up Mont d'Charlevaux and rifle and grenade fire echoed back through the wet trees. There was some shelling into the field nearer the Charlevaux Mill and beyond the other side of Hill 205 as the French tried to move up the road from Binarville again, along with some light, long-range machine-gun fire pinging the ground off the left flank. A few shells were even dropping along the road above the Pocket, farther off to the left. Down in the Pocket itself though, it was largely quiet just then, beyond a few of the closer explosions from over on the left, which were little more than largely unnoticed background noise. Otherwise, there was only the moaning and crying of the wounded, some coughing by the relievers, the clatter of equipment being thrown on piles and an occasional call for assistance. (21, 29, 51, 103, 109, 116, 148, 149, 150, 245)

Major Whittlesey was up well before any of the others, shaving and cleaning himself and his uniform at the creek, before going to help distribute rations that had come up over night and assisting in moving the wounded. The sky had lightened considerably when some men from the 308th behind began to come around Hill 198. One of the first officers into the Pocket, after Lt. Knight had come up, was Lt. John Taylor of Company K/308th. They had been the first up to the bivouac on l'Homme Mort too, and there they had seen the results of the Small Pocket. Now, they simply stared in disbelief at what they found in the Pocket of the Charlevaux. Lieutenant Taylor later remembered Major Whittlesey as looking tired, quiet and drawn but washed and clean-shaven, asking mainly for medical help. Some of Lt. Taylor's men moved in to do what they could, while others from the 308th coming in behind them went up to the road above to take a place with Lt. Tillman's advancing men. (29, 109)

Standing in a small circle, discussing what needed to be done and while awaiting orders, someone among Lt. Taylor's men offered Major Whittlesey a small glass flask of fine brandy, which he gladly accepted. However, it slipped from the Major's uncharacteristically shaking hand and broke on the rocky ground. Torn with apology, Major Whittlesey was mortified. Shortly after that, one of Lt. Taylor's platoon leaders who had surveyed the scene, a young and relatively new 2nd lieutenant, stepped forward toward the Major with his hand extended. Lieutenant Cullen, standing there among the little group as well, described the uncomfortable scene that played out:

"He said something to the Major about having been glad to have been one of them who helped "rescue" us. There was a pause then, "Rescue hell!" said the Major. "If you had come up when we did, you would not have put us in that fix!" (109)

Glancing around angrily for a moment at the faces in the small group standing around him and Lt. Taylor, Major Whittlesey quickly turned on a heel and stalked off, to again begin going down a line of wounded with a can of corn willy and a "ten cent mess spoon." (29, 109, 116, 245)

That was where General Alexander found him when he finally arrived. With the news of the breakthrough and the Major's relief definitely confirmed by both General Johnson and Colonel Houghton, General Alexander had decided to see the situation up in the Charlevaux Ravine for himself. He and Lt. de Coppett then set out in his car that morning headed for the Pocket from the recently established Divisional PC at Abri du Crochet. Nearing the little crossroads of La Viergette, they ran across General Whittenmeyer, then directing the move of his 153rd Brigade PC into a marvelous bunker system that reportedly at one time had been used by the Crown Prince of Bavaria, and where in the coming days General Alexander would eventually set up Division PC as the battle line moved up. Orders for the 153rd that day called for a general reorganization of the front in their zone while the 154th caught up on the left, so no fast attacks were scheduled until October 9. Finding all well in hand, General Alexander corralled General Whittenmeyer and the three officers set off west down the road toward La Viergette.

There was now considerable shellfire coming in along certain parts of the road as the Germans were well aware that it was an excellent supply and artillery movement route, Therefore, they were determined to do as much damage to it as they could as their troops brought off the fighting retreat back into the Kriemhilde Stellung. This shellfire kept everything using the road mostly to the east toward La Viergette (about a kilometer east of the Pocket) and the three 77th officers were no exception. Passing through the crossroads, they were about a half kilometer from the Pocket when the shellfire forced the three officers to abandon the car along the roadside and proceed on foot. This was right about at the point where a narrow path from the wagon road running along below the Pocket came up the hillside and intersected with the Binarville-La Viergette road above it. Heading down the muddy hillside and then following along the wagon road (still strewn with dead Germans), the smell was already upon them when, but a few minute's walking later, they came to the quiet hive of activity that was the Pocket. All around them lay the wounded, the tired and the worn out, with relievers scurrying among them with bandages, cans of food and canteens of water. General Alexander and company moved along about them quietly, the Division Commander appearing as unconcerned as if he were taking a stroll back home, with a cigarette in his hand instead of his usual cigar and swinging a walking stick that had been given to him years before, during his days in the Philippines. However, it was not unconcern that had its hold on him that day, as he would later state that:

"It was with great relief and equal pride that I saluted the remnant of that heroic command. I offer no apology for the use of that traffic worn word and I was reminded by their demeanor of a phrase in what is probably the greatest prose poem in our language, Napier's "Peninsular War." In his account of the battle of Albuera he uses these words: "The enemy rolled backward down the slope, the rain followed after in torrents stained with blood and fifteen hundred unwounded men, the remnant of six thousand unconquerable British soldiers, stood triumphant on that fatal hill." Here too, two hundred and twenty-five (sic) unwounded men, the remnant of six hundred and fifty (sic) unconquerable American soldiers still held with

firm grip the position from which all efforts of the enemy, backed by hunger and thirst, could not drive them..." (2)

Passing along, General Alexander stopped frequently to talk with those men he came upon, still reclined in their holes, exchanging words of encouragement and gaining a much better understanding of what had happened. When he finally asked for Major Whittlesey, it was near where Pvt. Manson was sitting on the edge of a hole with a spoon and a can of corned willy. Swinging around, the Private said, irritably, "Who in hell wants the Major *now?*" Seeing the dual two-stars advancing on him, he jumped to his feet with a salute, explaining that the Major was over with Captain Holderman (apparently at the new wounded area, farther to the left). "Shall I call him over for you sir?" Manson asked tiredly, but the Major General said no, he would find the Major on his own. A little farther on, Alexander came to Captain McMurtry, his wounds now preventing him much movement at all, ensconced on the edge of the old command hole discussing things with Sgt. Mjr. Baldwin, the hurting Pvt. Larney, and little Zip Cepaglia. As he walked coolly up, the men caught the General's rank flash in the meager sunlight and they started to get tiredly to their feet, but General Alexander motioned them to remain seated and saluted them shortly.

"Well, you men have sat heavy on my chest for a week," he began quietly and looked around at the filthy figures reclined all around him. "I guess we lost more men trying to get you out than you had in here, but never mind that. Where's Major Whittlesey?" he finished, looking straight and hard at Baldwin, evidently more than a little shaken by the scene around him.

"Down the foot of the hill, sir," the new Sgt. Mjr. answered and pointed indifferently toward the left flank. There, a little farther down the wagon road, Major Whittlesey could be seen moving along a line of wounded men with the open can of corn willy and a tin of hard tack, a dirty overseas cap crushed onto his head. Several doctors then in the Pocket were urging the starved men not to eat too much at first, to avoid any internal distress caused by such large quantities of food introduced to a shrunken stomach, and Major Whittlesey was trying to help with that as much as he could.

"Shall I go get him for you, sir?" Baldwin asked flatly after a moment.

"By no means," the General said quietly. "I'll go to him."

With Baldwin and Cepaglia trailing slightly behind Lt. de Coppett and the two Generals, they came up to Major Whittlesey unexpectedly, giving the latter no time to react. General Alexander grabbed for his hand before it could swing into a salute as the tall man pulled himself erect, towering over his Division Commander.

"How do you do? From now on you're Lieutenant Colonel Whittlesey," he said quietly, giving the Major's hand a firm squeeze and looking him in the eye.

Major Whittlesey averted the General's gaze momentarily and murmured something apropos but so indistinct that nobody really heard, or remembered in any case, (including General Alexander it seems) and then said nothing more. General Alexander dropped Whittlesey's hand limply and there was an uncomfortable pause while he studied the Battalion Commander and waited for a reaction, any reaction, to the promotion. None was forthcoming. Major-cum-Lieutenant Colonel Whittlesey, relatively clean or not, looked beaten and nearly all in. His pistol belt, gas mask and helmet were back in the command hole and he stood before the division commander in only his dirty, stained uniform and an overseas cap, with a set of dull Captain's bars on it, on his head; out of uniform for front line duty. No one wanted the General there - he did not belong - and an awkward silence followed the initial retort.

Then General Alexander, seeking a way to relieve the discomfited moment of unease enveloping them all, quickly glanced up at the remaining tree cover above them.

"Well," he said, "I can certainly see why the airplanes couldn't find this place."

Then from behind him came Pvt. Cepaglia's sharply accented voice and the General turned a little to look at the little Italian runner.

"Well, General, the artillery certainly found it, sir," he said dryly but with feeling.

"Oh no," General Alexander answered without missing a beat, and taking a long pull from his cigarette he fixed Cepaglia in a firm stare. "That was French artillery." Another uncomfortable pause descended until, finally, Major Whittlesey explained about the surrender request the Germans had sent in with Pvt. Hollingshead and then walked the General back to the command hole to get it, since it was still in his gas mask bag. After reading it briefly, General Alexander folded it back in the envelope and stuffed it in his pocket. With all that he had heard so far, he had already thought about recommending Whittlesey, McMurtry, and several of the others there for the Distinguished Service Cross. However, with the surrender letter as evidence, the situation was rapidly moving into the realm of the Congressional Medal of Honor. Along with Lt. de Coppett, General Whittenmeyer, and Lt. Col. Whittlesey tagging along behind, the General then spent the better part of the next hour talking to men along the hillside about what had happened there, including Lieutenant's Cullen and Eager and Captain Holderman. When he finally left, he had made up his mind; his new Lieutenant Colonel was a bonafide hero. (2, 29, 51, 109, 245, 338, 356)

It was just before 10:30 a.m. that morning when Colonel Hannay received the first official word at advanced 77th Division PC from Lt. Col. Morey, the Divisional Intelligence Officer, concerning the condition of Whittlesey's detachment in the Charlevaux ravine:

After conversation with someone at Denver-1, who was talking with the Sgt. Maj. of Whittlesey's Bn. I phoned as follows to Corps:
"Whittlesey's Bn. rec'd nothing from air men. Whittlesey is O.K. Men are weak."
He further estimated effective strength of Bn. as 125 men and 50 wounded coming out." (138, 150)

General Alexander was returning to Division PC about that time and upon hearing the information, immediately called General Whittenmeyer, whom he had just left off at his new Brigade PC. A temporary ambulance station needed to be immediately set up where the wagon road below the Pocket came up the hill to the Binarville-La Viergette road, in order to deal with some of Major Whittlesey's wounded. Any closer and the shelling would be too much for the little ambulances to get through safely. General Whittenmeyer in turn ordered the ambulance station set up at the La Viergette crossroads, where ambulances of the 307th and 308th Ambulance Companies could work in conjunction with Ambulance Company 306, then sending its Ford ambulances up from Abri du Crochet. Colonel Hannay had also fielded a confusing phone call about that time from General Johnson about bringing supplies up to the Pocket along that road from either the direction of Binarville, which was base for the French attack then in progress, or through the shellfire along the road coming in from La Viergette. The Brigadier had stated that "the whole front is more or less under shell fire. The men in Whittlesey's battalion who have been lying along the road up there are constantly under shellfire. By bringing transport along that road it would expose these men up there to shellfire…" Nevertheless, General Alexander not only ordered the ambulances up, but ordered 10 trucks up to the ambulance station as well, to pick up Whittlesey's survivors and bring them to Depot des Machines. Just who the "someone" was that Colonel Morey talked to at Colonel Houghton's PC has never been established, but the Sergeant Major was obviously Walter Baldwin, whom the new Lt. Col. Whittlesey had permanently assigned to the post just that morning. The initial troop strength information, bleak as it must have sounded, is actually very close to what might be considered an actual number, depending upon how one looked at it overall, and certainly illustrated the lengths to which Whittlesey's men had gone during the last five days to defend the position. (See Appendix A.)(IV) (2, 118, 131, 139, 142, 143, 148, 140)

As another foggy dawn broke across Hill 198, Privates Emil Peterson and Cecil Duryea, still down in the entrance to the German dugout where the retreating Germans had left them, heard lots of activity outside and figured that their captors had returned. They sat tight, not sure what to do, but aware that they might have been forgotten there and shot if they showed themselves. Finally, however, around 10:00 a.m., Pvt. Peterson risked taking a peek and saw American leggings outside the entrance. Telling Duryea what he saw, the two decided that it might be all right to come out. Peterson called out to an American officer he could see standing about 40 feet away, who immediately drew a bead on the German overcoat before him with his automatic. Yelling for the two wounded Doughboys to come out, Pvt. Peterson emerged first, hands aloft, before throwing off the overcoat and shouting, "We're Americans! Don't shoot!" Within a half an hour, he and Duryea had been taken down to the Ravin d'Argonne and were both atop a narrow gauge rail car being pushed back to the aid station at l'Homme Mort. (224, 291)

The ambulances General Alexander had ordered started to roll about 10:30 a.m., even despite the shellfire coming in along parts of the Binarville-La Viergette road. A message sent to the Division Commander by Colonel Houghton late that morning, using information from someone among his staff who was up at the ambulance station at La Viergette, well illustrates just what a big job the evacuation was. (Again, these numbers are wildly inaccurate; the situation was actually far worse yet. See Appendix A.)

The 308th, when they went in with Whittlesey, had 375 men, inclusive C and D Cos. of the 306th M.G. Bn., of which we have 321 men and officers left. Co. K 307th, went in with 88, of which we have 73 remaining, a total of 394, all ranks. Of these 156 are wounded, 51 stretcher cases. Killed and missing: 9 officers, of which four are known to be killed; of the five missing officers, 2 known to be wounded. 3 other officers wounded now in our hands. 50 enlisted men killed and missing... (138, 139)

By that time, there had already been medical men crawling all over the Pocket for several hours, washing out infected wounds with Dakin-Carroll solution and tying them together with fresh bandages, in order to get some of the most serious cases ready for transport. Then, they carefully and, with some difficulty, passed the wounded up the hill on stretchers to the waiting Model T ambulances on the road above. Others were sent back on the light gauge rail system to a first aid station at the l'Homme Mort bunker, and then on to a field hospital at Abri du Crochet, farther to the south. Many from these two places would then end up back at La Chalade, where an even bigger field hospital, with better facilities, had been set up in the church there. Nevertheless, even as used to combat casualties as they were, what the ambulance drivers found waiting at the Pocket appalled many of them. Private Fred Wadsworth was one of the ambulance drivers from the 308th Ambulance Company who came up on the road that morning and still elicited obvious signs of repugnance when, as an old man in his late 80's, he was interviewed about the subject:

"They legs was blowed off, they arms... (Here he paused for a moment as a far away look of unbridled revulsion crossed his face) The maggots was crawlin' all through them. It was the terriblest sight you ever witnessed. There wasn't very many of them what was alive 'cause the Germans had piled so many big shells in on 'em that they'd kilt (sic) most of them (sic)." (341)

Another medical man who had come up, though sometime during the night, was

Private Henry Grossman assigned to the 307th who later said:

"We were ordered to go to the rescue of the 308th Infantry, the "Lost Battalion," and when we reached there it was an awful sight. We had a tough fight getting to the men... Of (company 'K' of) the 307th Infantry, I had the honor of burying almost all the dead boys of that (company) and saw to it that they had a decent burial." (21)

From the Pocket, the ambulances then whisked down the road toward La Viergette, where the aid station had been established that could stabilize them for further transport, and from there on to Abri du Crochet, to a large field hospital set up in one of the old German dug outs, while others went directly back to La Chalade. The wounded Pvt. Sidney Smith gave one example of the trip to La Chalade. He had lain in his hole all night, mostly unconscious, after the last attack of October 7 and was one of the few unaware that relief had broken through. He woke, he said, when someone kicked him in the ribs. That turned out to be a doctor tagging the wounded to be sent back - the first he knew of their relief. He also had a hell of a time being treated that next morning:

"I said, "Ain't you gonna give me a tag?" He (the doctor) got all excited and said, "Why? You're going to die before too long." (But) he still put a tag on me. Then he says, "There's a boy, 18 years, old who had his hand shot off... You take care of this boy." A first aid man was coming towards us on this trail. He looked at this boy and he knew he had blood poison in his hand. You could smell it. He said to the boy, "You're going to have to go." Then he said to me, "Where are you shot?" I said "Down in the chest." He smelled down my collar and he said, "You don't have to go." (256)

After spending most of the afternoon in the Pocket and watching nearly everyone else go, Pvt. Smith eventually went as well, later that night on one of the rail cars:

"After it got dark, they moved us and loaded four of us into railroad cars. It was a small narrow gauge train...We finally stopped at this Catholic Church that was an aid station. There was this lieutenant with me who had been shot (It was Lt. Griffin of Company H - author) and we were put in this ambulance, in the front seat with the driver... It was four days before I got to this hospital (where) they had sheets drawn up around trees and there were thousands of us laid on the ground..." (256)

Privates Emil Peterson and Cecil Duryea were rolled out of the Charlevaux area down the Ravin d'Argonne on the narrow gauge system after their rescue from the dugout on Hill 198, stopping first at the aid station in the l'Homme Mort bunker, then back to the 1st Corps triage set up back at La Croix Gentin. After being stabilized there, they also traveled by ambulance to the church at La Chalade. Private Peterson later wrote:

"This was an old church which had been ruined by shells. Here our wounds were partly dressed and we were taken to a Red Cross base hospital where I was operated on and the bullet removed... I still have the bullet." (224)

Another wounded man who knew nothing about the relief until that morning was Pvt. Joseph Giefer, one of the handful of Company D men in the Pocket. He went out by ambulance:

"I got hit on October 6th; several pieces of shrapnel in the head and my chest was splattered. One of my fingers was also injured. I do not remember when we were released as I must have been unconscious at the time, due to the pain and loss of blood. The first I remember was when they were cutting off my shoes at the first aid station. It was not until the Armistice was signed that I was able to rejoin my company." (44)

As the day dragged toward afternoon, the wounded Pvt. Larney, together with 1st Battalion Sergeant Major Walter Baldwin, watched while the more seriously wounded (read: nearly dead) got carted out ahead of him. When Pvt. Larney's turn finally came however, at around 5:00 or 6:00 p.m., Sgt. Mjr. Baldwin had already been marched out with the rest of the survivors and Pvt. Larney was leaning against the side of his funk hole, "very weak and very sick," as he put it. In his diary, he later wrote:

"Captain Breckenridge saw me swinging from tree to tree as my legs were weak as I tried to get to the ambulance up the hill. He got behind me and took twist in my belt and said, "Keep your legs going Bud, and I will push you up there," and he did. At the division field hospital, in an empty church somewhere, I got soup and cigarettes. Vomited the soup. Couldn't keep it down." (218)

After a short stay at the La Chalade church, a couple more days passing found Pvt. Larney settled into Base Hospital No. 10 at Chaumont, sunk into a real bed, between clean, white sheets and doing his best to forget the whole ordeal. There, someone shoved a week old American newspaper in his hands and before him, front page, was an article about something called the "Lost Battalion," which he read with some interest, learning that he and the others were all heroes. "That was the first I knew of it," he later remarked offhandedly. (118, 131, 138, 139, 142, 143, 144, 369)

Around the time Pvt. Larney was being carted off in the ambulance, Lt. Paul Knight and several of his men were making their way around the Pocket, surveying the carnage. Author Tom Johnson later said that Paul Knight had told him that his conscience hurt him as he walked the broken ground, and that he felt he had not done his job by having not been able to bring his company (Company? What company?) up even with Major Whittlesey's left. As he walked the area in a blue funk, turning down toward the brook, he heard a faint voice calling, coming weakly from under a clump of broken brush, "Take me… Take me…" Looking around, he found Sgt. Lionel Bendheim. His leg was a tangled, infected, gangrenous mess (it was later amputated), and he had either been missed by the medics or simply passed on as dead. Lieutenant Knight quickly turned back up the hill and summoned an ambulance and a crew of men to carry the wounded soldier out. Again, according to Tom Johnson, the sergeant was supposedly the last of the wounded taken out from Major Whittlesey's scarred and battered little corner of hell. (29)

As the wounded were being carted out, so too were the dead being gathered for burial. Whittlesey had put Lieutenant Eager onto the task, and he in turn got together what few men he could from the ranks of the survivors, along with a number of disquieted helpers from among the relieving force, and set to the revolting task of identifying and burying in temporary graves what they could find. Identifying the remains of the dead proved one of the most daunting tasks. Some of the corpses had been exposed to the elements for as long as five days and were well polluted by then, with blackened, swollen features. Others had little left to identify. In many cases, positive identification was made only through items found in their pockets or by their dog tags, if those remained. Where such was the case, one of the two little aluminum discs was taken from the remains to later be turned in to regimental as proof of death, along with a description of the temporary grave's location. The other was attached to a piece of wood or a reversed rifle firmly stuck into the ground above the temporary grave by the cord that it was worn with, to mark the remains for those units sent out later to excavate the graves to a permanent (or semi-permanent) location at a more convenient time. Where no tags remained, or nothing among the personal effects found on the body, if there were any, could give clue to the corpse's identity, the grave was left as 'unknown'. (V) (50, 349)

There might have been many more 'unknowns' from the episode, had not Major

Whittlesey's men done the majority of the job. It was truly a nauseous and abhorrent task, with bodies literally coming to pieces in their hands and rotted skin readily sloughing off. While many would have found this sort of work particularly revolting any other time (as many of the relieving force did), Whittlesey's men had been surrounded by such grisly scenes for the last week, that the job lacked the truly horrifying flavor it normally would have. Private Clyde Hintz of Company B was one of those given burial detail and later said, "In most cases they were buried where they had fallen, usually in the hole where they dug in." John McNearney, who had watched his buddies Richard Hyde and George Nies killed by a direct hit during the barrage of October 4, scrapped their remains back into their hole with a shovel and threw a few scoops of dirt over them. (44)

Private Herbert Tiederman of the 2nd Battalion H.Q. platoon did the same for what remained of his friend, Pvt. Theodore Tollefson. "(He) had been with me most of the time since we started on Sept. 26," Pvt. Tiederman later remembered. Then, dug in just a few feet away to the left of him, Tiederman had seen the shell burst on the 4th that had killed the young Hayfield, Minnesota lad. He would stay in the Pocket with the rest of the Lost Battalion dead until February of 1919, when members of the 805th Pioneer Infantry disinterred their remains and temporarily reburied them in straight, clean rows in the German drill field just off the left flank, under little white crosses. They remained there until the big U.S. military cemetery at Romagne sous Montfaucon would be ready to accept them in May of 1919. There, most of them rest to this day. (44, 50)

The evacuation of the Charlevaux Ravine by the survivors of the ordeal continued into the afternoon. Lieutenant Colonel Whittlesey spent nearly all of his time that morning down at the bottom of the hill supervising the removal of the wounded, along with Captain McMurtry who, having refused to be evacuated until all the other wounded were gone, was helping out. His knee, now the approximate size of a football, pained him terribly and his back was bleeding again, but he still would not budge, even when Major Whittlesey himself half-assed ordered him to go. Legend says that the indomitable Captain merely smiled at the new Lt. Col. and said, "Surest thing you know, Charles. Just as soon as the men are all gone," before then stumping over to another hurt lad to give a little comfort. That certainly sounds like something McMurtry would have said, and it is true that he did not leave the Pocket until all the rest of the wounded had gone. Yet another part of the legend then states that as they were watching some of the wounded being carried out, Whittlesey turned to Captain McMurtry and said, thoughtfully, "George, we will never again be in finer company than we are right now," to which Captain McMurtry firmly agreed. And forever after, McMurtry insisted that that was exactly what Charles Whittlesey had said. (29, 51, 109, 116, 218, 245)

Certainly a better authority could not found…

Nor would Captain Nelson Holderman leave until all of his men had been well cared for and evacuated either. Possessed of seven separate wounds by the end of the siege, as well as a plethora of minor ones (most of which were either already infected or well on their way to becoming so), he alternately sat in a bloody heap or leaned on his two broken rifles at the bottom of the hill, directing efforts on what remained of his right flank position. It is doubtful that after the rebuff from Captain McMurtry, who would ordinarily have listened to him, that Lt. Col. Whittlesey ever even attempted to say anything to Captain Holderman about leaving, since it was unlikely that the Captain would pay any attention to him anyway, especially without orders from higher up. At least the wounded officer, whose actions over the five previous days had been nothing short of spectacular, had allowed his wounds to be properly cleaned and dressed along with his men. But that was only par for the course; if it was good enough for the men, it was good enough for him. Lieutenant Colonel Whittlesey simply added that fact to the already enormous pile of Captain Holderman praises grouped in his mind. The Captain certainly deserved recognition for the great sacrifices he had made there in that ravine, and Whittlesey would see to it that it would be delivered, if at all possible. Captain McMurtry, equally impressed with the young officer, readily agreed. (27, 195, 350, 355)

It was around 1:30 p.m., after most of the more seriously wounded were gone, that Major Whittlesey corralled Lieutenant's Cullen and Eager (the only two unwounded officers left of the original group that had gone in on October 2, besides himself) and issued orders for the march out of the ravine. Those orders had come by runner shortly before from General Johnson, then directing efforts back at l'Homme Mort. They were to take the survivors back down the Ravine d'Argonne to Depot des Machines, where fresh clothes, food, water, and bathing facilities had been established. The trucks General Alexander had already dispatched to the aid station near La Viergette had since been recalled due to revived intense shelling along the road, attracted by the stream of ambulances. Instead, the General had sent orders for those trucks to divert and pick up the clothing and supplies needed for Major Whittlesey and his men and deliver the stuff to Depot. He then sent the orders to General Johnson for Major Whittlesey to walk his men back, which was thought to be a safer route than the shell-filled road. However, he could hardly have been more wrong...

It was also important that the marchers look as good as they could, since the Signal Corps had sent up a still photographer and a cinematographer crew to record the event. Therefore, the men must be checked over to see that everyone was as clean and soldierly as possible and anyone with any obvious wounds weeded out, so that the folks back home could be proud. All along the wagon road at the foot of the hill were spread the band of survivors, those either lucky enough to remain unwounded or those who considered themselves not wounded seriously enough to go out by ambulance or rail. Lieutenant Colonel Whittlesey put Lt. Cullen in charge of what remained of the 1st Battalion, while Lt. Eager, his burial details just finishing up their grisly job, took charge of 2nd Battalion's remnants.

Immediately, the two officers began to organize those men assigned to them for the march out, weeding out those they felt would be better served to wait for an ambulance or rail car and then getting the remainder to clean up as best as they could before taking a final count. It was a disturbing number. There had been, by best count available, 687 men in the ravine at around 7:00 p.m. of October 2. As of about 2:30 p.m. on the afternoon of October 8, there were about 243 men left sitting or lying along the hillside as the three officers began working their way through the survivors. This is a mean loss in killed, wounded, missing and sick of 444 initially, or about 65 percent of Whittlesey's command. Then, when survivors actually began their march out at just about 3:00 p.m. that afternoon, the actual number selected, or able, had dropped to 194 officers and men both, and even among those there were still more than a few lightly wounded. (This well illustrates just how far off the figures that Colonel Houghton had earlier sent General Alexander actually were.) The total included Lt. Eager's Company G, which contained only 24 men, beside himself - two noncoms and 22 privates - out of a beginning total of 75. Company B had only 25 men left out of 74 and Lt. Cullen's Company H, which had been the largest of the companies to walk into the ravine on the evening of October 2 with 124, now had only 21 men walking out, less him. Hardest hit, by far, were companies A and E. Of the 19 men A had settled into the Pocket with on October 2, only three remained able to walk back. Of Company E's original 74, only eight were able to go and they left behind two officers in captivity. (For more on the totals, again see Appendix A.) (29, 44, 51, 109, 116, 131, 144, 148, 149, 150, 234, 239, 245)

About 3:00 p.m., Lt. Col. Whittlesey blew his whistle and the other two officers got the men up onto their feet and ambled them into position. Turning to the west, they shouldered arms and tiredly set out, passing first around the spur of hill that had been the left flank's perimeter edge at one time, and all the while filing past the graves of their comrades visible through the remaining brush cover. One dispatch from the time recalls,

"At the foot of the hill the men who had defended the position stopped to look back on the scarred battlefield, on which so much suffering had been concentrated. The hillside was strewn with bandages, broken pistols, shells and equipment of every sort. Here and there were rotting limbs of men who had died and whose bodies had been torn again by the frenzy of German shells and hurled from their burying place. Saplings that had been cut in two by machine gun fire and gnarled bushes and stumps of shattered trees stuck their twisted forms out of the hill, like crippled men showing their scars.

(And yet) there was no paean of thanksgiving, as there might have been, from those who had been taken from the maw of death. (Instead) there were low curses and a burning hatred for all things, which quickly passed as the sense of safety and relief came over the men..." (21)

Off to one side, down near a bend in the brook, the cinema crew with their heavy, tripod-mounted camera carefully followed their progress, the cinematographer's arm steadily cranking the machine at an even pace. Except for the sounds of battle in the distance, all was relatively quiet as members of the relieving force stood by and watched the survivors meander past them, a steady light wind blowing. The surviving film of the event belies the truth, as their faces bore the obvious signs of all they had been through. One man among the relieving force watching them file past later remarked, "When I looked into those eyes, there was nothing I could say to them. Their faces were just blank. There was nothing there." (29, 51, 109, 246, 342)

Some distance around the left flank spur Lt. Col. Whittlesey brought them to a halt. A picture snapped at the time - and usually misdated to Oct. 29 - shows the 1st battalion remnants scattered in a group on the ground with the 2nd coming up behind them. A Signal Corps man wanted a better group picture of the survivors and so, with no little effort, Lt. Col. Whittlesey, Lt. Eager and Lt. Cullen grouped everyone into a semicircle at the foot of the hill just west of the Pocket. As the picture was about to be snapped, the sun came out briefly and bathed the scene in fresh light. Some men even managed a smile. In the picture, Whittlesey stands on the far left, hands clasped behind his back, with Lt. Cullen next to him and Sgt. Mjr. Walter Baldwin immediately to Lt. Cullen's left. Then once the picture had been snapped, the cinematographer handed the Lt. Col. a newspaper with an article about him and his men and then had the enlisted group in a tighter semicircle around Whittlesey as he looked at the article. One can only wonder what his thoughts were, since the camera was set up too far away to see his face with any clarity in the grainy film. (VI) (38, 342)

Once the photo session was over and the weak men had rested a few minutes, the officers lined them up and turned them south toward the mouth of the Ravine d'Argonne and then sent them moving down the rail line at the bottom. French elements had reached beyond the Binarville-La Viergette road and were up as far as Etang de Poligny by late morning, and therefore Hill 205 and the area directly behind it had now been evacuated by the Germans. This would make the trip back down the ravine relatively safe from small arms fire. However, the Germans were still dropping shells along the Binarville-La Viergette road and around the Moulin d'Charlevaux. Then, just as the men set out toward the Ravin d'Argonne, the Germans inexplicably lengthened their fire. Now the survivors of the hell in the Charlevaux were faced with one last challenge in getting out of the ravine, as evidenced by this account from Pvt. Nell:

"We were in line single file, standing in the middle of the track and the enemy, who was on top of the hill (Mont d'Charlevaux to the north – author), began dropping shells directly in front of us. Many of the shells hit fifty to seventy-five feet in front of us on the track. We were hemmed in again, with no place to

march except on the track. It was hard to face after our ordeal of the past five days. We were all nervous and afraid, but we had to keep moving. The officers kept yelling to move out before we were all blown to pieces, but the ones who were in the lead seemed as if they could not move. I was some distance back, but I went forward and kept going. This got the men started, but by this time the shells were landing right in front of us, many hitting the track. One hit under the ties, raising the ties and rails up on end... (The) shells were coming over one right after the other, with a loud, screaming whistle and a loud, blasting explosion. It was a dreadful feeling, facing these shells and explosions at such close range..." (40)

Private Nell kept up at the head of the column as long as his strength would carry him, but he eventually was forced to fall out, simply too weak to go on. He would later catch up to the rest of his unit at Depot des Machines by staggering 100 meters at a time, all that he could manage before again needing rest. Certainly, he would not have been the only one whose weakened condition would force such a scenario; others must have had trouble keeping up as they made their way down that shell-ravaged ravine, but just how many can never be known for sure.

Yet the column went on through the shelling, with Lt. Col. Whittlesey and the other two officers desperately driving the men forward. It was the last effort and everyone knew it, so they gave all that they had left, until they finally came out of the shellfire, which again included gas and had reached nearly as far back as l'Homme Mort. All the way down the devastated ravine, the haggard men looked around them, somewhat aghast at the destruction that had been wrought there during the last five days and they began to understand just why they had not been rescued sooner. Once at l'Homme Mort, they stopped at some YMCA and Red Cross canteen wagons there, dropped a few more men at the aid station who simply could not go on, and then trudged on through the ravine around the hill and into Depot des Machines. Lieutenant Colonel Whittlesey, Lt. Eager and the 1st Battalion arrived there sometime just before 5:00 p.m. and there they found four rolling kitchens going full tilt, plenty of fresh, clean water for drinking and bathing and new uniforms and underclothing. Lieutenant Cullen and the 2nd Battalion pulled in shortly thereafter. For all the men, it had been a long walk back... (10, 38, 44, 91, 109, 116, 131, 246, 342)

General Alexander was back at his PC that afternoon and the evacuation of Lt. Col. Whittlesey's wounded men was just wrapping up, when the first of the reporters showed up for details. Damon Runyon, the lad from the Universal News Service that had been following the Lost Battalion story from l'Homme Mort on, had been up with the 307th for the last two days waiting for them to get to Whittlesey and then had watched the survivors march out, along side Tom Johnson and a couple other reporters. Immediately after, they had apparently jumped into a car, along with the Saturday Evening Post reporter, Will Irwin, and made a beeline over to General Alexander's PC at Abri du Crochet. Finding General Alexander in a better mood than any of them had seen him in a long time, they began to scribble away as the Division Commander told them what he knew. It had been a heroic stand, equal to the Alamo. Major Whittlesey was now a Lieutenant Colonel and all of the men had accounted for themselves bravely. At the part about the surrender letter, General Alexander pulled the one-page message out and they all passed it around, marveling at the fantastic story they now had to send out, which was getting better by the minute. It was then that Irwin, while reading the letter a second time, in a flash asked General Alexander plainly, "And what did Whittlesey tell them?"

General Alexander, reigning high above the situation, boomed back, "What *would* he tell them? He told them to go to hell!"

And so the makings of yet another legend was born of the situation in the Charlevaux Ravine. (2, 14, 246)

Lieutenant Colonel Whittlesey and his men had drug into the Depot des Machines right around the same time that the three reporters were heading there to search out an interview. It had been a tough march, yet once at the Depot they found that the four field kitchens set up were under General Alexander's personal orders to run all day and all night if necessary. No man of Lt. Col. Whittlesey's command was to be denied any meal at any time over the next 36 hours. Fresh underwear, socks, and uniforms waited, showers and delousers had been set up, medical personnel were on hand and billeting provided in the German buildings, the floors of which were now covered thickly with fresh straw and there were piles of clean blankets and overcoats. (21, 29, 51, 109, 132, 135, 144, 234)

Most men simply wanted something to eat more than anything else. Private John's first real food in six days was a bite of a "big, white onion, and boy did I bite into it!" But he, like many of the others, soon found. "I would eat a few bites and then run aside and lose it… I'll bet I made forty trips to the bushes (that night) - with both ends operating." Private Sidney Smith, coming through on his way to Abri du Crochet, described seeing "One big fella on all fours, pulling himself along with two sticks. When he spotted another fella with a loaf of bread he threw away his sticks, crawled over to this boy and took (it) away and wolfed it down." A few men could hardly force anything down without either gagging on the food, or simply bringing it back up again right away. Again, medical personnel did what they could to prevent the men from over doing it, but more than a few were forced to be evacuated to the hospitals later that night and early the next morning for having eaten too much. Others stuck it out better, but were sick for days nonetheless. Even after the event was over, the command was still taking casualties. (143, 220, 256)

The reporters, of course, were all over the story from the get-go. There had been a number of them - Runyon, Johnson, Fred Ferguson, John Gilder, Will Irwin, and several others - that had managed to make it up to the Charlevaux Ravine and see some of it for themselves. There, all marveled at the wonderful spirit that the survivors showed. Those on their feet and marching out, though generally tired and short on patience and nerves, after having had a chance to relax and a bite to eat showed a great pride in what they had done in holding out. Captain Holderman was later of the opinion that by the afternoon of the 8th, most of his men were ready for another six days' worth of fighting, such was their spirit. Many in the crowd watching them march westward from that hillside had tears in their eyes as the men passed them holding their heads high, despite their exhaustion. And around the aid station at l'Homme Mort and the field hospital in the church at La Chalade, it was the same. At those places, the medical personnel, in addition to the reporters, were also equally astonished at the general chipperness and pluck of their charges, no matter how terribly wounded. Filthy men, ravaged by the situation and in terrible pain from rotting, infected wounds, still flashed broad smiles, told built up lies about their adventure, traded the most outrageous quips among each other and flirted unashamedly with the Red Cross nurses. They were boys that had been thrown into a difficult and terrifying situation who had come out as men; perhaps bloodied and scarred but, at least for the time being, emotionally unaffected and still possessed by their youthful outlook. They were not heroes - not in their own eyes anyway - but they knew they were survivors, and that meant more to them than anything else.

And the reporters wrote about them - a lot. In fact, the story of the Lost Battalion would eventually become the most over reported story of the war, at least from the U.S. participation anyway. When several reporters found Lt. Col. Whittlesey late that afternoon at Depot des Machines, he was sitting alone on a tree stump off to one side in a clearing. He saw them coming and, guessing who they were by their attire, got tiredly to his feet. Tom Johnson later remembered that before they could even get really started with their questions, Whittlesey held up a hand and said in his low, authoritative lawyer voice, "Please do not write about me. Write about these men." The interview that followed was not a very long one. Obviously quite tired, he was not entirely forthcoming with information, merely answering questions automatically, though politely, but rarely offering anything more than raw answers. Contrarily, he introduced any enlisted man that might be wandering by, constantly steering the conversation in their general direction and elicited much enthusiasm over their actions during the whole episode. When Pvt. Irving Liner happened to amble by on his way to taking in a nice, hot shower bath, but still stunningly filthy just then, Lt. Col. Whittlesey introduced him as "one of my finest was a New York Jew, a runner named Liner." Private Liner simply blushed and said, "Just to think; a year ago I was studying law and I had every comfort too. Now, I have been lousy for two weeks!" Then he wandered off again.

Yet, steadfastly, Whittlesey refused to speak about his own accomplishments, but continually directed the conversation toward the others. He commented especially on the replacements, praising them for their fine spirit and the good job they had done, and included those who had worked so hard to get them out of the Charlevaux as well: "The real story is not here," he said. "The real story is with the men who, day and night, fought for our relief." The hardest part, he said, was not being able to wash and hearing the gunfire of those so close to them just beyond the hill behind not being able to reach them. When one reporter asked about the surrender letter, Whittlesey simply related the story, shortly and with little detail, which was obviously not going to be enough for the news dogs.

It was Will Irwin that asked, "And what was your answer, Major?"

The commander merely looked pensive for a moment and then simply told the young reporter, "We said nothing."

Soon after that, Whittlesey ended the interview and went back to be with his men, leaving the news reporters largely unsatisfied. They then fanned out among the other survivors to try for more detail. It was indicative of how Lt. Col. Whittlesey would conduct nearly all his interviews concerning the subject for the next three years that remained of his life.

Later, back at 1st Corps headquarters, dispatches began to come in to Lt. Kidder Meade from Bar le Duc containing the complete text of the surrender letter, one of which had scrawled across the bottom of it, "The reply to the above was, Go to Hell!" Lieutenant Meade then issued an official Army statement to the press on the incident in his morning dispatch of October 9, which included this little bit of exciting fantasy. By then, other reporters were clamoring to interview Lost Battalion survivors, mostly the wounded, access to which was relatively easy, as well as Lt. Col. Whittlesey. However, it was Damon Runyon, Will Irwin, and Tom Johnson who had really landed the first scoop on the story and so the morning of October 9 found their readers waking up to the first news concerning the relief of now Lt. Colonel Whittlesey and his men. By that afternoon then, all of America had been told the final chapter in the Lost Battalion story.

Or so they thought.

(12, 14, 21, 29, 48, 51, 109, 131, 132, 133, 135, 144, 245, 246, 283, 285, 286, 320, 321, 352, 356)

(I) General Evan Johnson would leave the 77th altogether around mid-October, having quarreled once too often with General Alexander, and finish the war with the 78th Division. To his discredit, General Alexander gave no thanks, nor any other recognition, for all the good work General Johnson had done. Lieutenant Colonel Gordon Johnston would eventually gain fame as the most decorated man in the U.S. Army below the rank of General. He had served in Roosevelt's Rough Riders, in the Philippines (where he won a Medal of Honor) and on the Mexican Border. He would only lead the 308th for a short time, before going over to the 82nd Division. He was killed in 1934 while playing polo when his horse fell on him.

(II) Indications are that the 308th Infantry had something just over 1200 casualties between September 26 and October 8. If true – and the total is likely somewhat higher, for reasons already discussed in the text – that would indicate that the regiment had lost a full battalion's worth of troops in just 13 days of fighting; an incredible total.

(III) This last sentence of Colonel Houghton's report merely added to General Johnson's earlier one, from which many later accusations of coordinational inaccuracies on Major Whittlesey's part would be based, beginning a firestorm of controversy that has raged to this day. General Alexander, however, had already made a determination in that direction, at least as far as the artillery was concerned, and declined initial comment.

(IV) The information concerning the airdrops was quickly passed along to Colonel Lahm and from him on to Lt. Morse at Remicourt. Lieutenant Morse in turn, refused to believe his men had done no good at all at such a great cost and proceeded to gather as much information as he could find that pointed in the opposite direction. Over the next few weeks, he amassed a credible amount of certain evidence, while discounting or just plain ignoring certain other evidence that did not, or seemed not to, fit what he and the rest of the squadron were convinced was the truth. He would later write the squadron history using some of that evidence and help muddy the Lost Battalion story waters because of it, although shortly afterwards the great courage and ultimate sacrifices of Lieutenant's Goettler and Bleckley would clearly be recognized and stand on their own merits.

(V) As an interesting aside, in 2005 the author received a WW1 dog tag from a collector in France that had reportedly turned up in the Pocket in 2001. The name on the tag was that of Pvt. Eugene M. McGrath, a member of Company C/308th who had reportedly been killed while with Whittlesey's men, on October 5, 1918. However, his name appears on the roll of those listed as 'Missing in Action' from the Pocket. Research turned up that McGrath had been drafted out of Armour, South Dakota in late May, 1918; went to Camp Kearney in June; to Camp Upton in July; across to France in August; into the Argonne with the 308th in September; was dead in October; and his parents notified in November. The tag, meanwhile, has been verified as definitely being original. Obviously, the tag somehow became separated from either the body when it was moved into its temporary grave, or when it was moved from the temporary grave into a permanent one. The tag now resides safely in the author's personal Lost Battalion collection, which is the largest privately owned Lost Battalion collection in the world.

(VI) For years, the rumor went around about a group of pictures that were said to have been actually taken in the Pocket during the five-day episode by one of the men there using a vest pocket sized camera, including one apparently snapped at the moment Major Whittlesey read the surrender letter. However, no one had ever claimed to have been the photographer, and the only supposed photographs of the set that have ever been known to have surfaced publicly turned out to be a still shot taken during filming of the 1921 movie, a picture of some 1st Division soldiers on a hillside near the town of Exermont and a grainy black and white newspaper photo of a painting done for the *Ladies Home Journal* in 1919. The author has spent considerable time and effort in trying to track down even *one* of the other rumored photographs that might then be authenticated from faces in other pictures contained in his extensive Lost Battalion photo collection or other means, but to no avail. In the thousands of photos from the war that have been sifted through, both public and private, no photo that even *might* have been taken during those five days of hell has ever been uncovered, nor has the author ever found any further mention of them in any of the numerous personal accounts he has used in preparing this volume. The conclusion currently stands now that there were no photos taken during the siege.

Ancillary sources used in this chapter include: Various 152-216, Various 282-338, 339, 340, 351, 374

Survivors and Casualties
"When you come back, and you will come back…"
Another popular song of the day.

The 77th Division's war continued in earnest on October 9 – not, however, with the 308th in the lead on the left of the divisional front. The events up the Ravin d'Argonne and in the Charlevaux Ravine had obviously left them a hurting, broken regiment. Casualties, as were discovered in horrifying detail in the days following the event, had far exceeded anything anyone had anticipated; especially Lt. Col. Whittlesey's virtually decimated 1st Battalion. It was then that General Alexander fully realized the need to rest and refit them - if the war in their area of operations was to continue - and he therefore ordered the 307th to take over the whole front of the 154th Brigade's zone of advance for the time being. With the 305th taking a similar stance across the 153rd's front, this placed most of the hurting 306th and 308th in divisional reserve. The morning of October 9 then saw the push up the Mont d'Charlevaux resumed, but with completely revamped dispositions for the first time in 14 days.

As for the 308th, internally they faced changes as well. The newly made Lt. Col. Charles Whittlesey still retained command of the 1st Battalion, but would soon be accepting additional responsibilities too. George McMurtry later remembered that although Whittlesey had gone into the fight on September 26 so very ill, he came out of the Pocket in the Charlevaux perhaps a little bit weak, but otherwise reasonably well physically. "He turned in and slept the better part of two nights and a day," he added, "and came up smiling the morning of the second day." Sometime during that period, Whittlesey had also sat down and composed his official report of the incident, which was, to this author's mind at least, largely one of understatement and incredible modesty. Much later, he also chronicled some of his and the battalion's adventures in those immediate post-Pocket days in a letter to the regimental historian, L. Wardlaw Miles:

"Gordon Schenck had been killed in the Pocket, and Stromee and Williamson were wounded, so there were none of the original officers left with the 1st battalion; but when we got out we were rejoined by Knight and 'D' company. There weren't many men left in the 1st battalion, but what there were, were fine and cheerful, and we sat around for two days cleaning up and resting. In the afternoon of the 1st day (the 9th), they sent me about 20 second lieutenants just out of training school who had been sergeants in the draft; all 2nd Lt.'s and most of them a corking lot of fellows. I whisked them around somehow into companies, trying to guess which would be the best company commanders.

And after that rest of two days they told me I was to take command of the Division Reserves (being a Lt. Col. by that time, just made) and that the 1st battalion would be part of that reserve. Here I lost sight of the 2nd battalion… Along about October (11th) I… finally joined up with the rest of the Division Reserve – a Battalion of the 306th and an M.C. battalion, and we got set in the heart of the

forest… and there in a charming little ravine running east and west the war practically ended for me…"
(109)

Meanwhile, as the 1st Battalion rested, the rest of the regiment, once rested, fed, re-clothed and re-equipped, was already on the move up to the front line again within 12 hours of the relief Pocket. The 3rd Battalion - battered, but not nearly as bad as the 1st or 2nd - moved up into support positions behind the 307th around mid-afternoon of the 9th. In that stance they would largely remain and take the brunt of what continued fighting the 308th was to see during the next 7 days, after which the division would be relieved. Command of the 3rd battalion was officially handed over on October 10 to Captain Breckenridge and on that same day, Colonel Hannay succeeded Lt. Col. Gordon Johnston as the 308th's Regimental Commander. Lieutenant Colonel Johnston then went to the 82nd Division to take a promotion and a brigade there.

As for the 2nd Battalion, in only slightly better shape than the 1st, and with Captain McMurtry in the hospital, they found themselves leaderless. With no one else then immediately available at the time, the job was handed over to Captain John H. Prentice from the 307th. After cleaning up and stuffing themselves at the four rolling kitchens at their disposal, most of the 2nd Battalion men had finally turned into what billets were provided about 8:00 p.m. on the night of October 8 for what one reporter referred to as "the first sleep they had had in six days that was not haunted by fear that the Germans would attack." Then word came through late that night that the 2nd/308th was to lend support for the 3rd/308th, who would themselves be working behind the 307th. In other words, they would be going back to the Charlevaux Ravine again, at least for a little while, and Lt. Prentice was then faced with the unenviable task of getting his new command up and moving forward again. He later wrote of the incident:

"I was ordered to wake these men (and) I felt I was taking my life in my hands to give them the news of the hike ahead of them. As I looked at them asleep, one on top of another, on mud and stone, comfortable despite all this because safe, I hesitated. It seemed a heartless thing to do. (But) they were soldiers, and I an officer, and orders were orders. So I roused them at 2.00am, after they had slept about six hours, and we made ready for the march. The men did not grumble, nor was there the suspicion of refusal. They donned their heavy packs and hiked further into the "Forest of Terrors." And I noticed that, heavy though their marching equipment was, the men who had been cut off had loaded into them as much corn willy and hardtack as their packs could hold…" (21)

The 2nd Battalion had as its initial task to clean up the Charlevaux Ravine west of the Pocket over to where the Binarville-La Viergette road turned south toward Binarville and also to establish firm liaison with the French. Both operations were successfully completed by the afternoon of the 10th with "that damned ravine" claiming no further loss of life or injury. One enemy prisoner was even taken; a large German police dog found resting on the grave of his former master, a German officer. Eventually, the dog returned to New York with a mess sergeant of the 2nd/308th, where one of its sires would later become the world famous canine movie star Rin-Tin-Tin.

And so the war rolled on as the drive to the Muese River ground forward. The target towns of St. Juvin and Grand Pre beckoned in the distance to the 77th, and the Kriemhilde Stellung was almost close enough to taste. There was hard fighting for the men of the 308th through the towns and at a loop of the Aire River. Casualties again rose as the 3rd/2nd Battalion combo found themselves slipping in and out of the line left of the hurting 307th, and German tenacity increased the closer the U.S. forces moved to the Kriemhilde *Haupt-Widerstands-Lienie*. By October 13, the 3rd Battalion strength total had tumbled to a mere 147 operational effectives *for the entire battalion*, while the 2nd could count only about 200. Finally, on October 15, word was received that the division was to be relieved, and at 3:30 a.m. of the 16th, the 311th Infantry of the 78th "White Lightning" Division arrived to take the place of the 308th in the line. The two battered battalions then picked up their gear and marched out for Abri du Crochet, thirteen kilometers well behind the lines to the south now, and arrived there about 11:00 p.m. that night, where they found that the 1st Battalion had just moved out for La Chalade, still further to the south.

Meanwhile, Lt. Col. Whittlesey and 1st Battalion had been languishing among comfortable dug outs, having had very little asked of what was left of them and enjoying a certain amount of general freedom rarely heard of in the army at that time. Lieutenant Williamson, who had not been too terribly wounded in the Pocket to begin with (he lost part of a finger), returned from the hospital a few days afterward, going back to Lt. Knight and D Company. Lieutenant Colonel Whittlesey sent a few of the new officers over to rebuild Company A just as some of the replacement enlisted started to roll in and put a Lt. Barclay McFadden in command there, who would complete the company's record of adventures that Lt. Whiting had earlier started. More replacements arrived, and slowly the command started to come to life again.

After a few days at Abri du Crochet, the 2nd and 3rd Battalions then made their way down to La Chalade as well. There they too began to rest, rebuild, and refit. From time to time individual companies would go up to the front in support roles, mainly in order to provide some experience for the replacements since everyone well recognized what a disaster it had been sending some of the 40th Division men in back on the morning of September 26. There were more pictures and interviews; the Lost Battalion, as the men were finding out, was still a big story in the states and there were rumors that Whittlesey, and perhaps McMurtry, would be getting the Medal of Honor. The regimental band performed concerts and the 'Argonne Players' (an amateur vaudeville group formed from men in the division before the offensive by none other than Lt. Maurice Revnes) gave a wonderful, and memorable, performance in the huge German underground theater near Le Chene Tondu. It was the hit of the season, at least as far as the men of the 77th were concerned anyway.

However, all too soon, the war again intruded and orders were received to go back to the front. The 77th was to take up a position between the 78th Division, on their left, and the 80th Division, on their right, in what was thought might yet be the final war-winning push. Therefore, on the morning of October 31, the 308th again set out to take their place on the left of the line; a regiment full of replacements and behind yet another set of leaders. After overseeing the rebuild of his battalion, Lt. Col. Whittlesey had received orders to return to the states; his combat experience was needed to help in the formation of a new line regiment of the National Army then being assembled for duty in France. Therefore, his place had been taken at the head of 1st/308th by Captain Snowden A. Fahnestock, yet another old Plattsburg hand from Headquarters Company/308th. Lieutenant Prentice was sent back to the 307th, and Major Francis Weld came up from Regimental HQ and took 2nd Battalion. Captain (soon to be Major) Breckenridge still held sway over 3rd, and in that configuration, they marched off.

The fighting had not slacked off either. On the contrary, it had intensified as the allied armies reached closer to Germany. The Kriemhilde had been pierced, despite desperate resistance and high casualties taken. The 154th Brigade shifted itself as needed; sometimes placing the 308th ahead, sometimes behind. Captain Weld was wounded on November 4 – what turned out to be the last day of heavy combat the regiment was to see – and George McMurtry, now a Major, returned, still limping heavily, from the hospital to take his place. The 5th, 6th, and 7th found the regiment once again in support of the 307th and were days of rapid advance for little cost. Everyone felt the Huns were beat and therefore waited impatiently for the end. Rumors of a peace settlement circulated freely, but no one really believed them. Still, a fever pitch was being reached and it was like something in the air; some of the new replacements dared hope that they just might actually be done with it all by Christmas! By November 8, they were bivouacked in and around the little town of Angecourt, an incredible 38 kilometers north from the bunker at l'Homme Mort, and with only 3 wounded officers, 17 wounded enlisted and 5 killed in action to show for it since the 4th of November – a marked difference from the same time period the month before!

And it was there, poised on the banks of the Muese to relieve elements of the 5th Marine Regiment for an attack being planned for the morning of November 15, that the Armistice was signed on the 11th hour of the 11th day of that 11th month and the whole shootin' match was over...

A cold, wet winter yet lay ahead of the 77th Division however. Rumors that as the first National Army division to arrive on French soil they would be one of the first to go home failed to materialize. Instead, combat training again began; the armistice was a cease-fire, not a peace agreement, and the war could resume at any time so they needed to be prepared. The veterans of Baccarat - and the Vesle - and the Argonne - bitched irritably and endlessly while yet another batch of replacements, sent to again fill the companies to full strength, took it in stride. One last batch of new officers also arrived, since few original combat tested company commanders now remained in the 308th – Lieutenant's Knight of D and Taylor of K were among some of the only ones that had come from Camp Upton. So was 'Red' Cullen, by this time a Captain and revered by the new men as incredibly tough for what he had gone through in the Pocket – and all without receiving a single scratch. On the 25th of November, General Alexander validated that reputation during a review of the regiment by pinning the Distinguished Service Cross to his breast (the first officer of the 308th to get it) for his service in the Charlevaux, swelling his chest to at least twice its normal size.

Time passed; 1918 died and 1919 presented itself. More men – officers and enlisted alike – got the DSC and there were many of the Charlevaux men among them, living and dead. On February 24, the great General Pershing arrived and reviewed the division, liking what he saw very much. A couple days earlier, the AEF commander had had the privilege of bestowing the Medal of Honor upon Major McMurtry; the award of his country's highest decoration for valor being based largely on the statements and testimonial provided by none other than his friend and comrade, Lt. Col. Charles Whittlesey. Now, as Major McMurtry stood at the head of his battalion while General Pershing handed out the plethora of medals he had brought, all in the regiment looked on the short, barrel-chested officer with pride, heartily approving of the award and agreeing to a man that few ever deserved it more.(I)

The march of time into 1919 passed mostly uneventfully for the 308th, excepting a court of inquiry held into the matter of the note Lt. Revnes had sent to then Major Whittlesey in the Pocket (of which more in a moment). By February it had become obvious that the division was not going to Germany to do Army of Occupation duty (thank God!) as they had been moving in stages closer to the coast ever since the beginning of December. In March divisional shoulder patches were authorized and handed out, which featured a golden Statue of Liberty embroidered on a blue field. The same insignia was painted on the front of everyone's helmets and overseas chevrons were handed out – one gold stripe for each 6 full months of overseas duty, or a blue one for less than six. Those with only a blue looked on with envy at those few Upton men who sported the two gold of a year in France. Those Upton men with two gold could not have cared less about stripes and only wanted to catch that big boat home; now rumored to be only a short wait away, perhaps as soon as the end of the month. (91, 109, 116, 147, 199)

Wound stripes were also handed out at the same time to those men that had returned to their unit from the hospital; a single gold chevron sewn above the right cuff of the tunic for each wound received. (The famed 'Purple Heart' was not yet available at that time.) And there were a lot of wound stripes to be seen among the veterans of the 308th, particularly among the men who had been in the Charlevaux Ravine. However, not all of the wounded from the Pocket returned to their units. Laurence Stallings, a young Marine Corps lieutenant who lost a foot near Belleau Wood, tells in his book, *The Doughboys*, about meeting up with an unnamed member of the Lost Battalion while in the hospital:

"*We were soon visited by an ambassador from the Lost Battalion. He had lain some days on Whittlesey's 'bench' with two broken arms, two broken legs, shot through jaws. Now his plastered arms were folded as in prayer, his legs in plaster, his jaws wired, with two front teeth extracted so that he could suck nourishment through a tube. He soon began to send many 'to the cleaners' in dice games; he could wiggle the toes on one foot, another lieutenant holding a mirror so that he might 'read 'em and weep'. The fiery Rhum Negrito was too painful for his mouth wounds, and so I extracted a rubber tube from the very fiber of my being and someone flushed it (out)... Then someone filched a small funnel and with the tube thrust through his nostril well past the fractured area, a brother officer slowly pouring, he could get drunk along with the rest. He showed no emotion until the night a crap shooter mentioned that his toes were not giving enough rattle to the bones; then he wept because he was unable to get to his feet and fight the critic...*" (48)

For some wounded members of the Lost Battalion the wait to go home was a long one, depending largely on the wound received. Private Sidney Smith did not return to the States until June of 1919, already 8 months after the armistice and 9 since he had been wounded. Still others, luckier than most, were home before the division was, such as Pvt. John Nell. Private Nell, though unwounded, was one of the men too physically drained to keep up with the others when they walked out of the Pocket and eventually wound up in the hospital - but not before he had been returned to the lines to fight with the 2nd Battalion some more. He came home on a hospital ship in December 1918, went back to Colorado and then eventually on to Texas where he spent the rest of his life, dying in 1955. He was active in both the Texas VFW and a Lost Battalion Survivors Association set up on the West Coast by Captain's Holderman and Stromee (usually referred to as the 'Last Man Standing Club'). He was also one of the few 40th Division men who frequently sent his greetings along to the New York Lost Battalion Survivors Association that was later set up in New York. Greatly bothered by all he had seen in 1918, Nell sat down and typed out his memoirs in the late 30's, a poignant, straight forward tome that gave no glory to the drive in the Argonne at all, ending with:

"Although the war is over, the memories still go on in my dreams. I still see the desperate fighting and hear the groans of the wounded... The politicians pay hypocritical homage to the dead, saying: "They died gloriously for their country." Like hell. The ones I saw died pitifully, just doing their duty." (40)

In 2000, the manuscript was found and brought to Texas publisher/editor Ron Lammert's attention by Nell's son, C.W. Nell, and finally published in April 2001. (40, 162)

For other members of the Lost Battalion, remaining in France, home had been sort of an abstract thing from the war zone to begin with, like Pvt. Joseph Dyrdal of Company B. The grandson of a Minnesota Civil War veteran, he wrote to his family on September 24, 1918:

"Whatever you do, don't worry. I am getting along fine. Don't expect letters too often because it sometimes is pretty hard to get a chance to write as we do a lot of moving around. But (I) will write whenever I get the chance..." (44)

That chance never came; Pvt. Dyrdal was killed in the Pocket on October 6. This last letter was found in his pocket and mailed later.

For PFC Harold V. Arnold however, the opposite was true. Seriously wounded in the Pocket, he was evacuated and shuffled from hospital to hospital – while back in the States, his family had been mistakenly notified he had been killed. They were quite surprised then to receive a letter from him, written from the safety of a bed in a base hospital and more than a little pleased when he returned home several months later. He went on to father 11 children before his death in 1958. (214)

Early in April of 1919, members of the McManus Film Corporation arrived in France to begin filming a Lost Battalion movie with the cooperation of the U.S. Army's Signal Corps. Getting permission from AEF command, they gathered up several survivors of the incident and trucked them back to the Pocket for a couple days worth of filming and – for the men at least – mixed emotions. George McMurtry even made a cameo in one scene, carrying his pistol and stumping across the broken ground once again. If only the actual incident had been as tame as the filmed version... (152, 153, 344)

Then on April 14, the 308th boarded trains that took them to the port city of Brest where, by the next afternoon, they were settled into the great embarkation (oh that sweet, sweet word!) center of Camp Pontanazen. The next four days were a flurry of activity as final inspections were made, unauthorized equipment turned in and all the myriad of details made ready to send the regiment home. Then, finally, came the 'day of days' when they began the final round on their 'trip of trips', which can be told no better than in this description taken from *The History of the 308th Infantry*:

"They are inspected as they pass down the road. Embarkation lists are checked up, and the men are conveyed to the S.S. America on lighters. And now – all together incredible and yet somehow actual fact – now, at five minutes past six, on the afternoon of April 19th, the America has weighed her anchor and, together with 3,160 others, each individual on board has really started for home... It is said that the trip was uneventful, which in the circumstances seems a curious word to describe days which brought men hourly nearer and nearer that which they had so long desired. Surely it was eventful to arrive off Ambrose Channel Lightship at midnight of April 28th. Surely it was yet more eventful to reach New York harbor at 8.00am the next morning, and then – surely most eventful of all – to land at Hoboken. The troops proceeded by ferry boat to Long Island City, and then on to Camp Mills... (109)

It was almost over. They remained at Camp Mills attending to details for a final parade and the mustering out process until May 5, when they reported to the 8th Coastal Artillery Armory on Kingsbridge Road in the Bronx early on the morning of May 6. That day the entire 'Metropolitan Division' paraded up 5th Avenue before the city they had gone to war representing. Colonel H.K. Averill, who had originally commanded the 308th during its formation at Camp Upton well over a year ago, was back in command again and led the regiment from the head with pride; a regiment he now hardly recognized but of whose record he was keenly aware. Then, back at Camp Upton where it had all began, two days later he issued his final farewell to the regiment he had helped train, stating in part, "You have rendered magnificent service. You have earned the eternal gratitude of your country. You are the finest body of men any officer ever commanded. I wish you all God-speed."

Following the parade, two days' leave was granted to some of the city men, while most of the mid-states men were given their travel warrants and turned out to the railroad station to begin their journeys to camps closer to their homes for official separation from the army. On the morning of May 9, for the remaining men final company musters were held, rifles were turned in, and final pay issued. Then they were turned out on the company streets of Camp Upton for a final time and marched off to the train station themselves, through a driving rain that lasted all day – one final reminder of the Argonne perhaps. There was a final call on the station platform of "Dismissed!" and at that moment the last of the 77th Division men were officially separated from all their associations with the army of the United States of America and the AEF. Their war was over. (33, 109, 116)

They were finally home.

For Lost Battalion Private Harold Brennan, of Company E, home was a little brown stone in Brooklyn, N.Y. where, upon his return from France, his parents threw him quite a welcome home party, described by his daughter Patricia as "Probably an all night, good old fashioned Irish drinking binge". In keeping with the times, the local paper even did a story on it. However, for Brennan the war had lasting effects; he was later diagnosed with Tuberculosis, a holdover from a dose of gas he got in the Argonne. (Unfortunately, this would not be an uncommon thing for the returning vets.) A quiet man throughout his life, he rarely spoke of the war, or the Lost Battalion, and despite the TB went on to have a large family. He died in 1966 at the age of 71. *(165)*

Private Ralph John of A Company went home to South Dakota and tried to get on with life, but those days of fighting in the Argonne had left a deep imprint with him. Returned to the lines after the episode in the Charlevaux he was gassed, the effects of which, like Private Brennan, stayed with him long after the war both in short breath and terrible stomach problems. He also had continual and severe trouble with his feet; his army boots, as he put it, having broken the arches in them through being the wrong size.

His most difficult disability though, was the mental one of dealing with what had happened and all he had seen in the Charlevaux Ravine. On the eve of WW2, he sat down and wrote out the memoir of his short war, a 17-page personal and affecting description of his experiences as a soldier in 1918. "At the time," he wrote, "it all seemed like another big battle we had all pulled through," *"(but) I write awhile and my eyes get so full of tears at the memory of it all that I just have to quit... If, after exhaustion, I do sleep it is only to live it all over again in dreams, seemingly more real than when I'm awake. Now, after more than 20 years, the memory carries an indelible copy of those miserable days in the Pocket that will never be blotted by good times or other troubles I may have."* (220)

Ralph Edmun John died in South Dakota, sometime in the mid-1960's. (153, 220)

It took Private Sidney Smith a long time to recover from his wound. He bounced from hospital to hospital in France until June 1919, when he was finally sent home and discharged. At the time he was just a week shy of having been in the service a year and had spent a mere 13 days of that time actually in combat. Still, it was enough to leave deep emotional scars. Settled down on a homestead back in Montana, he got married, but...

"My wife was afraid to sleep with me for a long time. We lived close to the railroad where the trains would come screaming by and I'd wake up in the night thrashing. I was awful nervous." (256)

Nonetheless, Smith became a local hero due to his having won the DSC with the Lost Battalion and always marched in the local Armistice Day parade, but rarely spoke of the episode. He finally gave a revealing interview to noted WWI historian Hayes Otoupalick and reporter Dennis Gordon in 1980 and died just a couple years later. His family remains very proud of his wartime accomplishments, even after 86 years. (207, 256)

Private Jacob Rangitsch of Company E, who had gone into battle in the Argonne just 7 weeks after his induction and luckily escaped getting captured in the German raid that had taken Lt.'s Leak and Harrington, survived the war unwounded to go back to Montana, get married and raise a family. He worked most of his life for the Montana State University as a grounds custodian and truck driver, being extremely popular with the student body, and finally retired in April of 1960. From time to time he moodily gave an interview concerning his experiences in the Pocket to a local paper, but never embellished the part he played. Instead, he seemed to prefer to forget the whole thing in favor of the better life he had afterward. Jake died in the late 1970's. At the time of this writing his grandson, Zach, is a proud Captain of artillery in the 1st Division. (182, 225)

Jake's commanding officer, Lt. James Vestal Leak, was one of only a handful of Lost Battalion men that the Germans actually took the trouble to move back to the prison camp at Grand Pre. It was initially reported back home that he had been killed in the Argonne, but the tangle was soon cleared up when his first letter arrived from Germany. After he was released, in December 1918, he spent the rest of his time in the army with Company G/308th, not being given any real assignments, but just putting in time. (George McMurtry, back in charge of 2nd battalion by then, recognized that Lt. Leak had more than done enough, and therefore asked little of the war-weary officer.) He came home with the division in April 1919, went back to Texas and again picked up his law practice, even serving as a judge for a short while, before getting married and raising his family. He too, occasionally gave an interview concerning his experiences, but otherwise the only connection to the Lost Battalion he kept was by staying in contact with ex-lieutenant Tom Pool of Company K/307th, who became a Sheriff in nearby Beaumont, Texas. After the 1938 book came out however, he did make the trip to New York for at least one of the reunion dinners, and just after the start of WW2, gave a moving talk at a local college. But the episode in the Charlevaux was not the life altering experience for him that it was for so many of the others, nor was prison camp for that matter. To Jim Leak it was all just an interlude - albeit one of the most memorable - in a full life lived well. He died young, in 1942. (154, 236)

Lieutenant Victor Harrington also spent the remainder of the war in a prison camp and was also reported missing, presumed dead. Except that from him, no contradicting letters ever made it back home. Therefore it was quite a surprise when he showed up back in Detroit, Michigan in late May of 1919 and there found that his young wife had already remarried; an awkward situation to be sure! Nevertheless, the second marriage was quickly annulled, and the Harringtons spent many long years together raising a family. Proving he was no coward by a long shot, Victor went to work for the FBI, became a prohibition agent and even occasionally worked with the great Elliot Ness. A private man, he never spoke of his short war experiences or of the Lost Battalion to anyone but his wife and is never known to have attended any of the reunions. (184)

Lieutenant Sherman Eager, one of the three lucky officers not wounded in the Pocket, stayed on the front with the 308th and fought right through the drive to the River Meuse and the Armistice, all without receiving a single scratch. After the end of hostilities, he was transferred to the 1st Division, doing some duty with the Army of Occupation before again being transferred, this time to the 88th Division. With them he sailed for home in June of 1919, and went on to teach a physics class at Oklahoma Agricultural and Mechanical College, making a fine life for himself and a family. Once, on a visit years later to the Smithsonian Museum in Washington D.C. with his wife and children, they came across Cher Ami on display there in his glass case and for a few minutes the old soldier was back in the Charlevaux Ravine again. With a distant look he quietly relived the tale one more time as a small crowd gathered around him, in the end telling his children, "Outside of your mother, you all owe your lives to that pigeon." Sherman Eager died in the late 1970's. (161, 234)

Lieutenant Eager's assistant in running G Company toward the end of the siege, Company 1st Sergeant Amos Todisco, only spent a short time in the hospital recovering from his relatively minor wounds and soon after the war was discharged to return home to Boston. However, civilian life for Amos, who had been a soldier before the war as well, was not his cup of tea and he immediately made every effort he could to get back into the army after a short reunion with his family. He was quickly accepted and while waiting for orders to his new duty station, took a temporary job with the Boston transit system driving a trolley car to fill in his remaining civilian time. Just a couple of days before he was to report for duty again, at the end of his last shift driving, Amos climbed down off his car in the trolley barn with his cash box in hand. Another driver, backing a trolley in and not looking where he was going, backed his car into Amos', pinned the Charlevaux survivor in between the two, and crushed him to death. (194)

Private Emil Peterson of Company H bounced around from hospital to hospital with his wounded leg until returning to America at the end of December 1918. At home in Iowa, he raised a family and somewhere along the way also wrote out a fascinating account of his adventures in the Argonne. His brother, Carl Peterson, also an AEF veteran, later wrote a small 50-page pamphlet on the Lost Battalion in the late 1930's which featured parts of Emil's story. However, Emil was destined never to see the kind of popularity gained by his fellow short time POW, Lowell Hollingshead. (183, 224, 315)

After the relief of the Pocket on the night of October 7, Holly was evacuated by ambulance early the next morning, first to the ambulance stop at La Viergette and then on to the church at La Chalade. (All the while, unknown to both of them, Hollingshead's brother David was among the relieving troops down in the Charlevaux Ravine with the 307th.) Overwhelmed by the casualties coming in from the ravine and seeing the seriousness of his wound and the very real possibility of gangrene therein, a triage doctor at La Chalade moved him off to one side and tagged him as an amputation case. While he was lying there, another doctor happened to strike up a conversation with the young man. It turned out that the doctor was from Dayton, Ohio and had done some fishing around Hollingshead's hometown of Mt. Sterling. 'Kicking things around', as it were, made the doctor feel sorry for Holly, a fellow Ohioan, and looking over the wound he decided to instead give it a few good cleanings and wait for the morning to see what it looked like then. Throughout the night, the doctor kept coming by with his bottles of Dakin-Carroll solution, continually bathing the wound, and, sure enough, in the morning light was pleased to announce that Lowell could keep his leg after all - all largely because he was from Mt. Sterling, Ohio!

Holly came home that spring of 1919 to wide acclaim as the 'Hero of the Lost Battalion' and soon had almost as many speaking requests as Charles Whittlesey himself. His parents largely took over his 'bookings' and soon he was making a fine income at $100.00 a pop to tell his story – which had changed almost immediately the minute he hit the states again. Suddenly, there had been a sergeant that had crawled over to him and his friends on that fateful morning, stating that the Major was asking for volunteers to go out and try to find an airplane package that had recently fallen close off their left flank. He had also been quoted as saying however that the sergeant had said that the Major had wanted volunteers to try and "work their way back to American lines", and in still another interview stated that they had gone out on their own to "look for the (field) kitchens". Luckily for the young man, few at the time seemed too worried about the details of his experience and were only concerned with who he was and hearing about what had generally happened, since Lt. Col. Whittlesey himself had so very little to say about it. Already then, the facts of the story were holding little importance to an American public fascinated by its heroes…

As the years passed on toward and into the Depression, Hollingshead's story settled down however and the generally accepted version he usually told concerned the mystery sergeant and the airplane package. Meanwhile, no one who had been in the Charlevaux Ravine ever really came forward to contradict the story either, since first off, no matter how mad the false story made them, it just did not matter much to them anymore after all those years. (As one of them later put it, "To tell the truth, we had the subject chewed to death long ago.") Secondly, and most importantly, they did not wish to tell what really had happened in order to protect Charles Whittlesey's memory. By that time Whittlesey was dead and had already been almost lionized by the public, and even Hollingshead never said an unkind thing about him. To have the truth come out then would be to expose Charles Whittlesey's flaws – something that virtually all of the men that had served under him were not willing to do. Those who had seen him strutting around that hillside, heard his positive mutterings ("Remember, there are two million doughboys working to get us out. It will not be long now!"), and saw his determination, were not about to let anything bad be said about the man that had 'pulled them all through'. One veteran of the incident summed up the general feeling towards Whittlesey in one simple sentence: "We held on because he did." (219, 323)

Then there had also been Lt. Col. Whittlesey's own discreet requests made immediately afterward to many of those in his headquarters 'group' that had been there to refrain from making any statements about the event that might cast a bad light on an already difficult situation. They were in the public eye and he obviously realized that they could not afford to do anything that might tarnish an image that helped the all important 'Cause'. Nor, as far as was know, had the Battalion Commander ever preferred charges of desertion or collaboration against the boy for what he had done either; something they all realized that he might well have done. If the Major had been willing to let it go then, shouldn't they? (245)

Therefore they simply just seethed about the subject, wishing they could 'get the damned kid to shut up', but never really being able to do so. In any case, most of the New York men considered him little more than "a deserter" and "a coward" anyway and would have nothing at all to do with him. And so the years passed and Hollingshead continued to remain a period pop figure; loved by the public and hated by the men he had endured the episode with. In 1941 Bob Manson, Whittlesey's one time interpreter, who had less animosity toward Holly than any of the others, brought him to one of the Survivor's Association meetings in New York, where he was completely shunned, nearly to a man, by everyone there. It had not helped any that there had been a letter from Hollingshead to the association not long before, concerning plans he had been working on for a vaudeville circuit 'reenactment' type show of the event, asking if anyone was interested in participating. The men in the association considered it a most contemptible suggestion and their hatred grew because of it. Further, when Fritz Prinz, on a one-time trip to the states a few years after the war, had hoped to see the boy again and been unable to, Holly had publicly said that he had not been aware that the German had been in the country, but would have "walked all day" to see him. It was yet another example, the New York men said, of his apparent 'collaboration'.

And yet, on the other hand, once, upon hearing that someone had said that they would give a million dollars to have experienced what he had, Holly very quickly replied, "Hell, I'll take the million," proving that even he apparently was haunted by the experience, despite his outward appearances.

His fame diminished greatly with the coming of WW2, and afterwards Holly's life played out a normal and pleasant one. He married, had a passel of kids, and ended up as a prison guard at the local penitentiary in Ohio until his retirement. Occasionally the subject of the battalion would come up, and he would give another radio or newspaper interview. In 1962, he again took a trip to France and paid a visit to the spots where he had served during his youth. Accompanied by a reporter, a photographer, and the cane he had gotten from Lt. Prinz, he made his way back to the Charlevaux Ravine. Standing on the roadside above, looking down the still funk studded hillside into the Pocket, he spoke quietly of the events that had happened there almost 50 years before, but he did not go down the hill. He then capped the trip off with a visit to the huge Romagne American military cemetery, where he visited the graves of some of those killed in the Pocket, among them Marshall Peabody and Ben Gaedeke. It was also around that time that he made an effort to locate Fritz Prinz, who he occasionally had corresponded with in the 1930's and found, through the West German government that Prinz and his wife and son had "disappeared" during Hitler's maniac last years.

After the trip, and following the death of his wife, both of which had occurred within a relatively short span of each other, Holly began to go downhill. He was a lonely man, and some of his last interviews seemed to hint tantalizingly at what had really happened in the Charlevaux, almost as if he were trying to make peace with his past. (When letters he had written home from France after the event, as well as an interview with fellow POW Cecil Duryea, surfaced during the writing of this book, all the pieces fell into place and the mystery cleared.) Toward the end, he impulsively, and without apparent reason, gave away the cane that Lt. Prinz had given to him that long ago day in the Argonne, to a little boy in the neighborhood sometime in the late 1960's. His family, horrified, tried desperately to get it back, (he had always said, "That cane saved my life and I'd risk mine to save it.") but the boy's mother, recognizing it for what it was, refused to give it back, and the cane has long since disappeared from the scene, as did Holly himself not long after, peacefully in his sleep. His adventure in the Argonne had made Lowell Hollingshead an icon within the pop culture of his day, right along side Charles Whittlesey, and his decision there in the Argonne that October afternoon was truly the turning point, and defining moment, of his life. (33, 152, 153, 163, 218, 219, 222, 245, 292, 309, 329, 338)

The episode in the Charlevaux Ravine was also the turning point in the lives of many of the others that were there as well. Unfortunately however, that turning point left some of the men far more deeply affected, the greater majority of them among the virtually untrained 40th Division replacements. Totally unprepared for what they were sent to do in the Argonne in the first place, it proved too much for many of them in the end, while most of the New York men, whose full training and prior combat experience had prepared them to a much greater degree for the Argonne, remained relatively more unaffected. Private Arthur Looker, of B Company, eventually wound up in the hospital at Fort Snelling, Minnesota; one of the many places that the army sent those suffering from 'nervous disorders'. The popular name for the condition at the time was of course 'shell shock' and is the condition we now know as 'post traumatic stress disorder'. But no matter what you call it, the effects are still the same and the cure was slow. It took some time before Looker could function in normal society again. After giving initial statements to the army and then a couple very cohesive interviews early on, his memory began to fail and he later remembered only fragmented pieces from his time in both of the Pockets, all jumbled together until the story made little sense. He eventually went back to his parents' home in Wisconsin, then on to a farm in Missouri, where he died in the 1970's. His family there said he never talked about the war. (208, 267)

Others found the Pocket creeping into everyday life at the most surprising of moments. One man recalled how years after the war he had been forced to leave a movie theater because of his experience in the Charlevaux. "In Topeka I was watching a war picture," he said. "There was a hill like where we were surrounded and it give me the creeps so I had to go out." (44)

In a letter written around the mid 1930's, Private Arnold Morem, wounded in the Pocket with E Company, wrote, "It seems to me that at times I can still smell the awful odor that came from the dead bodies lying around." (44)

Another wrote to the Lost Battalion Survivors Association in New York, soon after it was formed in 1938, "We just do not have the control we should have. I went through without a visible wound, but have spent many months in hospitals and dollars for medical treatment as a result of those terrible experiences." (219)

And yet another example was Private Lars Olson, a native of Denmark who had been in the Pocket with Company C. Sometime after he came home from France, he began to suffer violent episodes and was eventually taken to the hospital at St. Peter, Minnesota for observation. Upon his release, he immediately returned to Denmark and was never heard from again. His buddies claimed that what he had gone through in the Pocket, coupled with reading of Major Whittlesey's suicide, are what finally drove him over the edge. Corporal Wilber C. Whiting, of Company H, also killed himself and Pvt. Chester Lysen, of C Company, was, as late as 1938, still being treated full time at a veteran's hospital in Minnesota for non-physically related reasons. (44, 138, 315)

The episode had definitely taken a 'nervous toll'…

Yet the most well known case of 'war nerves' to come out of the whole Lost Battalion incident is undoubtedly that of Charles W. Whittlesey himself, whose life was undeniably forever altered by the events in the Pocket. His became a classic case of several different psychosis' all wrapped into one pitiful life, contained only frailly, and but for the briefest of time, by an enormous sense of responsibility that eventually ended up working against itself. It is virtually impossible then to view the episode in the Charlevaux Ravine, Charles Whittlesey's short life after the event, and his eventual – and perhaps inevitable – death as separate events. They are all married into an almost unbreakable chain of cause and effect that led him into the dark waters of the ocean of grief that eventually engulfed him. While we can never truly know what was going on in

Charles Whittlesey's mind between October 8, 1918 and November 26, 1921, we can make fairly accurate summations from available evidence and base credible theories on those, all of which we will explore in more detail shortly.

Initially however one might start with his own sense of right and wrong and the high values he carried, both of which had always served him so well as a soldier earlier, but which would also actually seem to bring about the very troubles he and his men would face (or so his critics would say). Is it possible he might have felt the same way? One cannot say absolutely. But what one can say is that in following his orders so closely – even when others would not, and did not – that he paid a higher and more terrible price for upholding a value system that apparently knew no limitations. His suicide to one side then, while it is certainly true that the war destroyed Charles Whittlesey, it is equally true that so did Charles Whittlesey's very character destroy him as well.

(Sources used to create the following section on Charles Whittlesey, post-Charlevaux, include: 2, 12, 27, 29, 30, 32, 33, 40, 48, 65, 69, 72, 76, 78, 87, 96, 109, 116, 131, 132, 135, 144, 147, 148, 149, 150, 152, 153, 157, 161, 162, 163, 192, 194, 195, 199, 204, 218, 219, 220, 222, 233, 234, 236, 238, 239, 245, 246, 257, 258, 264, 266, 274, Various 282-338, 346, 349, 350, 352, 353, 357, 358, 359, 360)

By the morning of October 10 – two days after walking out of the Charlevaux Ravine - Lt. Col. Whittlesey seemed to have it all together again and was well on the way to rebuilding his battalion. What men he had remaining were back in better spirits than they had been in a long time and were enjoying the break from action while a new batch of junior officers arrived and the Battalion Commander interviewed each to find the best, then putting those in the company commander slots. In the distance, they could hear the war progressing ahead of them and the shells still flew overhead toward 'Hunland' with regularity, but overall the men did not care. All that mattered was that they had survived that week in hell and were thankful for a chance to rest. Pack rolls appeared, the first time the men had seen them since the night before the jump-off, a million years or so ago, and the men got back their overcoats, blankets and shelter tent half's; too late for the stay in the Charlevaux, but welcome nonetheless.

During this time, Lt. Col. Whittlesey also began to file recommendations for decorations of valor for his and Major McMurtry's men – lots of them. He was determined that these men that had shown themselves to be much better soldiers, and people, than even he had thought they were, and should be recognized for what they had done. He had done what he had considered the only right thing to do by staying put in the ravine and had asked his soldiers to do the same. Most had. This was surely worth recognition then, he felt, since he clearly understood that many did not hold the same high standards and values he did regarding the orders they had received. The few that he was aware of that had not obeyed his command and snuck off without permission, he apparently preferred to simply dismiss as beneath contempt and therefore largely ignored them, rather than put up any fuss over them. There was probably a part of him that even understood their actions – whether he agreed with them or not – and this would be particularly true where Lowell Hollingshead was concerned, since the boy had shown that he had guts by coming back. Yet, he was also aware that many men from the battalion did not see it that way about the 'runaways', and most especially about Holly, and held a great deal of animosity toward them. In that instance the Lieutenant Colonel even ostensibly asked some of his men to refrain from commenting negatively on Holly and the others, at least publicly, since such prognosticating would do no good for the regiment. And they listened to him too, since there was nothing they would not do for him.

In the end, nearly all the men Lt. Col. Whittlesey recommended ended up getting some sort of recognition for what they had done; some the DSC, and others perhaps a mention in the final few General Orders of the division (which in itself was a high honor). He also had gone to the hospital where Major McMurtry was recovering and collaborated on a few of the recommendations, not the least of which included doing what they could to get Captain Holderman the Medal of Honor. Both had been more than suitably impressed by not only the officer's courage and determination, but his ability to follow orders – even ones he did not agree with – to the letter and try his best to carry them out. Charles Whittlesey, who had himself walked in Captain Holderman's shoes in that respect, could especially appreciate this last.

As previously discussed, Lt. Cullen did not receive such high honors, as some might believe he should have. This would certainly seem a slap in the face to the man that had not only done good duty in the Small Pocket, but then also directed the defense of the difficult left flank in the Charlevaux Ravine, from whence a majority of the heavy attacks had come. And though reasons why he might have received such higher laudits may be argued, we can never really know just why 'Red' Cullen was either not recommended by his Battalion Commanders, or was turned down by 'the powers that be' for decoration with the MoH. In any case, he was forced to settle for the DSC, which one might also argue better compensation than nothing at all. Then too, one must consider that the army barely recognized the event in the Charlevaux Ravine as little more than just another day at the front in the first place. And yet, there were still plenty of others that Whittlesey and McMurtry had recommended that received their just due as well - in fact virtually all of them - so the truth concerning Lt. Cullen's being skipped on the decoration will probably never be known. Lieutenant Cullen's situation aside however, Lt. Col. Whittlesey's hope that his men should be recognized for all they had done would, over time, be well recognized and one could never afterwards argue that the men from the Charlevaux Ravine did not receive their fair share of the laudits.

Whittlesey was also in some indecision during this same time on what action he might take concerning Lt. Revnes in regards to the note that the wounded officer had passed to him urging that an honorable surrender of a sort be arranged with the Germans for the sake of the wounded. On the one hand, the very fact of the note went against Alexander's G.O. #27, in that any man suggesting to give ground - no matter what the circumstances - might be shot for it, and certainly what Lt. Revnes had suggested fell within the parameter of that unusual order's boundaries. Yet on the other hand, even though his duty demanded that action be taken against the officer for the suggestion even being made, Lt. Col. Whittlesey remained undecided as to whether he should go forward and prefer charges against Lt. Revnes or not. After all, by the time Lt. Revnes had passed along the note he had initially lain among the human wreckage of the wounded area for several days, before moving into the hole near the right flank. And Whittlesey had seen for himself how bad that could be during the frequent visits he paid there. The hurt officer could therefore hardly be blamed for taking the view that he had. There was also the fact to be considered that after the Battalion Commander had gone over and spoken with the wounded officer, he had seen Lt. Revnes's spirits revive somewhat. In fact, so much so, that in the final two defenses of the Pocket, Revnes, who had definitely already more than done his share, had voluntarily crawled to the perimeter line with a rifle. There being so many very good arguments against it then, how could he, in good conscience, then charge the officer with anything?

In the end, the situation seems to have been wrenched from Charles Whittlesey's very grasp. Having shared the dilemma with several other officers in the regiment (including Major McMurtry and Captain Holderman, who both urged the Lieutenant Colonel to file the charges), Charles Whittlesey somewhat reluctantly filed a full report on Lt. Revnes's actions, whereupon the recuperating officer would eventually be charged with a violation of the 75th Article of War, "Misbehavior in the Field". It was the first in a long line of tumultuous indecision's Charles Whittlesey would face while trying to reconcile what had happened during the war, but unfortunately it would not be the last.

However, by that time courts-martial were backed up considerably within the AEF, and so therefore the case was placed on the back burner for the time being. (147)

The 1st Battalion moved out of Depot des Machines for Abri du Crochet on the morning of October 11 and as they did so, in the distance they could hear the noise of war, something they largely ignored as it faded behind them. (It was also on this day that Whittlesey received official confirmation of his Lieutenant Colonel-cy.) Abri was a hive of restful activity and for the first time in nearly a month they settled back into a life of relative ease, except for a training schedule designed to prepare a recent batch of replacements fresh from the States for the realities of war. The newly made Lieutenant Colonel even made a trip or two over to see the wounded that still remained in nearby field hospitals. Meanwhile, mail – a luxury long forgotten – had finally caught up with them and they all had a chance to write back. In a letter to one of his old Williams College class mates, dated October 13, Charles Whittlesey could only touch on what had happened:

"I appreciated your last letter: If I said it any other way I'd be trying to put into words what I cannot write... Believe me, I felt you right at my side with your cheery voice when that letter reached me at the end of a day that had been – oh well, "some digging". It's a great life. Finest thing in the world, and we'll never have the same small outlook on men when it's over. Some of these fellows are just finer than anyone can say..." (246)

Life at Abri continued in a relatively easy vein for a couple days more, as did a few reporters again and another cinematographer, and Whittlesey had 'moving pictures' taken with Major McKinney. He even smiled. Then the battalion picked up and moved down to La Chalade, and there they were joined by the rest of the regiment a few days later. Then, on October 31, they received orders to go back into the line again for what would turn out to be the final drive of the war - but they would be doing it without Lt. Col. Whittlesey.

The new Lieutenant Colonel had received orders that same day sending him home. As a now experienced combat veteran, he was to be detailed in helping to raise and train a new National Army regiment to bring to France, in anticipation of the great offensive planned for the spring of 1919. Leaving La Chalade on November 1, he sailed from the port at Brest on the 4th aboard (appropriately enough) the *S.S. Plattsburg* and while he was at sea, seven days later, the Armistice was signed and it was all over but the singing.

He landed at Hoboken on November 14 amid the initial jubilation of peace and there found reporters already waiting for him on the dock. Apparently somewhat flattered by the continued attention the story seemed to yet be enjoying, he made his few first general statements in America about the episode, mostly praising of the enlisted men, and then let it go, not yet realizing that the story was as big as it already was. The next day however, the newspapers spread the word of his return from coast to coast and he first began to truly realize his budding new celebrity status. The 'Lost Battalion', he found, was already legend, as was he himself as their commander, if only for his supposed answer of "Go to hell" to the German request for his command's surrender. It was a status that apparently filled him with an initial foreboding.

Upon landing, he had reported to Camp Dix and was assigned to the 153rd Depot Brigade, pending final orders concerning the new regiment. However with the Armistice apparently going to hold, all plans for further expansion of the army were scrapped, and Lt. Col. Whittlesey was granted extended leave to Pittsfield. The next few days then found him virtually hounded by reporters as he went home to visit his family for the first time in almost a year, and the full, tragic magnitude of his celebrity finally hit home. It was in Pittsfield that he was further appalled to find the newspapers now referring to him directly as "Go to hell Whittlesey", and the beginning of the end of Charles Whittlesey had begun.

However, it initially appears, at least to some small degree, that Whittlesey accepted the new status of 'war hero' that had been thrust upon him, recognizing that it was his duty as a soldier and winner of his country's highest honor to accept the responsibility that came as a result of those actions taken in the Charlevaux Ravine. This, even though he merely saw those actions as his only recourse under the circumstances. Therefore, those first few months following his return from France found Charles Whittlesey initially more willing to obligingly answer questions put to him, though at no time did he ever actually come right out and volunteer the entire story of what all had happened in that ravine. Mostly, his statements were so worded so as to paint the enlisted in the best possible light, or to advance his own political beliefs (for Charles Whittlesey the returning veteran became twice as political after the war as he had been beforehand). Even privately, to family and close friends, he was equally reluctant to discuss intimate details of the episode.

Yet, details were what everyone was curious about. Consequently, he was consistently badgered, mainly by outside sources, to tell what he knew, and under this almost constant pressure to be what the country thought a hero should be, he slowly began to revile the role he was forced to play. Trying then to withdraw from under it (something which was, in truth, probably never in his power to do to begin with), within six months of his return it became apparent that his fame already had him trapped. Therefore, as time passed, his motives for granting interviews appeared to change, and he did so simply to try and appease the many chasing after him in a vain effort to find a little peace for himself. Yet these 'scoops' increasingly fell far short of what the press actually wanted, for instead of telling the story of what had happened blow by blow, Charles Whittlesey continued to spend most of the time talking up the individual soldiers under him. (Though he never really admitted as much, it certainly seems apparent that the Harvard educated Whittlesey had come to realize that it was not the trappings of the world that made a man a success, so much as it was the make up of the man himself, and that success itself was also a very subjective thing. To a man who had held Socialist ideals nearly all of his adult life, it was a self-effacing line of thought, indicative of the growth of person he had undergone in France.) This vicious cycle would continue right up until his death, unabated. It is safe to say then that being a hero, in part, ruined Charles Whittlesey's life.

As his leave continued, he found himself being bombarded by speaking requests, few of which he initially refused. The first larger one was to a meeting of the Williams Club on November 21. There, before 300 of his fellow classmen, Lt. Col. Whittlesey again gave a slightly disappointing rendition of events, steadfastly refusing all night to actually detail what had happened, but instead again devoting most of his time to the enlisted under him. "Remember", he said, in part, "that those who have been picked out for special praise are but the symbols of the men behind them. No man ever does anything alone. It's the chaps you do not hear about that make possible the deed you do hear about." He also praised the French for the training they had received at their hands and spoke of his fellow Williams-ites and their fine record in the war, most particularly 'Winnie' Dobson, shot in the shoulder in the Ravin d'Argonne, and Bell Brooks, killed on the Vesle. However the night did not end before a guest Cornell man finally shouted out in exasperation, "But did you tell them to go to hell?" to which Lt. Col. Whittlesey (so the news report says) "modestly nodded his head". (Curious, since Whittlesey steadfastly maintained right from day one that he never said it – and as we have seen, he did not. Was it a nod then, or a mistaken gesture of exasperation?) The crowd, the report continues, then went wild. (321)

The next important occasion came on the 1st of December, when he was invited, along with resigned Secretary of the Treasury William G. McAdoo, to speak at the Episcopal Peace Jubilee, held in the "Fighting" 69th Regiment, New York National Guard's old armory, and it proved indicative of speeches to come. Described as a "slender and somewhat stoop shouldered young man", he was at first not recognized when he slipped into the hall and took his seat, for he had laid aside his uniform for the occasion and was dressed in civilian cloths. But when he was introduced, he initially "stood uneasily, shifting his weight from one foot to the other" as he received a standing ovation, which was followed by three solid minutes of cheering. But from there the situation rapidly deteriorated as he delivered a mostly pacifistic view of the current post-war period as he saw it that centered around tolerance. "Germany after the war," he said, "it must be remembered, is going to be part of our world community." The assessment was not taken too well by a crowd of people that had largely never experienced the dirty side of warfare and held only malice in their hearts for the Germans. By the end of the speech, few were cheering. (246, 338)

Then on December 5, the same date he received his official discharge from the armed forces of the United States, the announcement came out in the papers that both he and Major McMurtry (then still in France with the 308th) would be getting the Medal of Honor. The decision had actually been made on November 22, with Whittlesey having been notified soon thereafter, and his instructions for the presentation ceremony had come on the 3rd. However, not wanting any more notoriety than he already had, he had wisely not said anything to any of the reporters that still frequented his parent's house on Pomeroy Avenue in Pittsfield. Instead, they had to wait like everyone else until, on December 24, 1918, Lieutenant Colonel Charles White Whittlesey, United States Army Reserve, received one hell of a Christmas present on Boston Commons in Massachusetts from Major General Clarence Edwards.

Moving pictures and still shots of the ceremony show an unemotional Lt. Col. Whittlesey standing almost tiredly at attention, towering over the General and his cortege, while family, friends and on-lookers stand off at a respectful distance. Surrounding them were an estimated 10,000 spectators. General Edwards had opened the proceedings with a congratulatory speech to all award recipients present (there were several others getting awards after Whittlesey), which was then followed by the playing of the 'Star Spangled Banner' by the Naval Aviation School band. A battalion of Coastal Artillery was on hand and they presented arms, Lt. Col. Whittlesey was called forward and Colonel Edwin Landon, Adjutant General for the army's Department of the Northeast, stepped up and the award citation was read aloud. General Edwards then stepped forward and pinned the medal to Whittlesey's breast saying as he did so, "I am directed by the War Department to bestow upon you this medal for extreme bravery in battle. I was in France at the time your act thrilled the entire AEF, and it gives me great pleasure to present this medal." The General then smiled and shook the stiff Lieutenant Colonel's hand as the latter replied quietly, "This is the greatest honor in my life, and doubly so because General Edwards is conferring this decoration." General Edwards then saluted Whittlesey and Whittlesey returned the salute, was dismissed and, turning, stalked off across the frozen ground on his long legs - the first man of the World War to be awarded the coveted medal. After the other awards had been given, he stood to the right of General Edwards on the reviewing stand as the Coastal Artillery battalion passed in review. Behind him stood his family, beaming. Afterwards, posing for pictures, Charles again disappointed reporters by refusing to lend detail to the story or play up his part in it. Instead, he steadfastly insisted on again only praising the enlisted men, the other officers under him, and making a political statement or two. Then he went home to celebrate Christmas.

Christmas 1918 was only marginally happy for the Whittlesey household. Of course, all were excited to have Charles home, and the Medal of Honor certainly made a fine Christmas present. But Charles was not quite the same man as he had been when he had sailed for France the previous April. Somehow, friends and family later remembered, he now seemed 'edgier' and more aloof, less patient and calm. There was also Elisha; suffering from the gas he had taken driving his camion in and out of the hell of Soissons and Verdun in 1916. Yet the family was together again and that was the main thing.

After the first of the year, Charles Whittlesey finally laid his uniform aside, returned to his practice with Bayard Pruyn on Rector Street and began taking cases. It was good to get back into the old groove again, and even though he still had to field questions from reporters and admirers almost everywhere he went, it was getting better. The troops were starting to return from France now and that greatly helped to divert attention away from him. With a lot of the pressure off then, he started to relax and settle down, seeming a little more like his old self again. He got back into his old digs at the bachelor's apartment on East 44th Street and eventually it seemed almost as if he had never left.

Except that his cough had worsened.

The cough was apparently the result of the gas he had taken on the Vesle when the Regimental PC had been thoroughly shelled into the ground the previous summer, and he had never received treatment for it. By the time they had gone into the Argonne that fall, the cough still had not subsided, but since he had had such a terrible 'cold' at the time, it would have been easy to mistake it as simply a by-product of that illness (although in all reality it was probably not a 'cold' at all, but effects of the poison in his system). In any case, the hard living in the forest had seemingly cured him of most symptoms of sickness and he emerged from the Charlevaux a relatively well man physically, despite the hunger and thirst all had felt. Yet somewhere between then and his return to the states, the cough had returned. One might picture him trying hard to hide it (or ignore it perhaps) at Christmas that year while watching Elisha struggle with similar symptoms. Might the pragmatic Charles have recognized the similarities and gone to see a doctor around the beginning of 1919? The answer is unknown. All that is known is that by the time the regiment returned to the states in May of that year, the cough was back.

Meanwhile, in France, the regiment had anxiously been waiting to go home and, unbeknownst to him, trouble for Charles Whittlesey had been brewing. Many regular army officers, largely ignorant of the truly unique circumstances that had lead Whittlesey and his command into the Charlevaux Ravine, resented his award of the Medal of Honor and the fame he received for an event they contemptuously referred to as 'a joke', and 'a travesty'. Rumors started to circulate and, of course, snowball, that Whittlesey had been 'glory hunting', that he had 'rushed out ahead without orders', that he had played free and wild with his men's lives through inexperience and ineptitude. It was the pressure of the press that had created the fame, they said; not his actions. For without them the event would have gained no public notoriety, then releasing the army to deal with the then Major as they should have been able to - with a court-martial for 'his mistake'. Yet there should still be an investigation some railed, mostly behind closed doors. How could an inexpert, unsuited 'emergency officer' that had gotten himself into such an 'absurd situation' ever be awarded the country's highest decoration for valor? Or be allowed to keep it?

The charges that Whittlesey had filed against Lt. Revnes gave the perfect opportunity that his naysayers needed to question the situation. On December 27, the case finally came up for a hearing and shortly seemed to morph into almost an 'inquisition' of Whittlesey's action alone. Almost 40 of the enlisted men and several of the officers, including Major McMurtry and Captain Holderman, were called out and testimony dragged on for two long days as the situation was described repeatedly in frank detail. Word surfaced that General Johnson had even briefly considered preferring charges against Whittlesey – that is, until he had gotten 'down in the dirt' himself and seen the actual conditions that had lead to the situation. The General was then ordered to give a statement and with that memory of those days still fresh (as well as a minor leg wound he had received in the Ravin d'Argonne at the time), Evan Johnson had only praise for his former Battalion Commander. The court then polled AEF Headquarters for permission to bring the Lieutenant Colonel himself back to France to testify as to his own actions. Common sense, however, won out; permission was refused and the matter was rapidly wrapped up toward the middle of January 1919. Charles Whittlesey had the award, the war was over and things were going to simply be left to rest as they were; the country still needed its heroes. As for Maurice Revnes, the catalyst of it all, he was convicted and sentenced. However, the conviction was brought up for appeal that February and almost immediately overturned in light of the wounded lieutenant's gallant defense of the Pocket's perimeter in the last German attacks. Lieutenant Revnes was then dismissed of all the charges against him, his record expunged and the whole matter was forgotten – officially anyway. (147)

There was also held, around that same time, a court of inquiry into the matter of the artillery barrage of October 4, and oddly enough at the behest of General Alexander himself. Nor did this, in similarity to the Maurice Revnes affair, amount to much either, the investigators having apparently had it been made clear to them beforehand - though in a decidedly 'left handed' way and strictly unofficially of course - that they were not to find anything. The inquiries, made almost exclusively among only certain officers they could find that had been with the regiment at the time (and of course this included very few that had actually been in the Charlevaux Ravine, since few of Whittlesey's officers remained) were over in just a day or two, with the final conclusion that the barrage had indeed been one of French origin. Satisfied that the AEF had been spared from public embarrassment and shame over the mistake, this matter too was then left to fade into the fabric of the general success of the war. (II)

In uniform again for the parade up 5th Avenue on May 6, after the regiment had landed, Lt. Col. Whittlesey marched with the 308th and he and the regiment got the loudest cheers of all at every point at which he was recognized along the route. Major McMurtry, who had turned down a chance to go home early in a regimental staff role to prepare things for the 308th's return in order to stay with his battalion, marched beside him for a time. Afterwards, there were more interviews during which he again disappointed all by, as usual, refusing to talk about the Charlevaux episode. If the role of celebrity had not sat well with him before, it was in the days that immediately followed the parade that he apparently began to really realize that the relative 'break' from the public and press over the first few months of the year caused by the troops' return had merely been the calm before the storm. The return of the regiment would then prove to be a catalyst for more intrusions into his life and it appears that about this time he began to seriously revile his status as 'hero'.

Then the other awards started coming, and with them, more unwelcome notoriety. First, he was made, by Presidential decree, a member of The Legion of Honor of France – and there were more reporters and interviews, all demanding details of those five terrible days. Then he got the French Croix de Guere with Palm, awarded by Colonel Averill – and there were still more reporters and interviews wanting the same. He received the Montenegrin Ordre Du Prince Danilo I ("For what?" he must have wondered, since he'd never even been to Montenegro), a very pretty affair, with a ribbon – and there were still more reporters and interviews. All along he gave none of the coveted details they wanted. Each award brought with it more requests to speak at social functions; Rotary Clubs, Lions organizations, The 308th Infantry Association, and always about the same thing – what had happened in that damned ravine – when all he wanted to do was forget the whole deal and just live his normal life. Except that what had happened in ravine denied him just that, and there was little he could do about it. He accepted more requests than he turned down as 1919 wore on into 1920, not wanting to be singled out yet realizing that he had a responsibility to not only his country, but to the men as well. They must not be forgotten.

Except that they were largely forgotten as the year wore on into a deep, immediate post war economic slump, which by Christmas 1919 was looking more and more like a real depression. It is thought that it was around then that the first of the 'visits' started. There were three types of visits that Whittlesey would experience as the remaining days of his life wore on. The first type occurred when men from the 1st and 2nd battalions began to appear at his office, at first waiting on the sidewalk out front for him to come out after work. Later, others, bolder, went right on in and asked to speak to him. (There were telephone calls as well.) All were looking for work, looking for direction, looking for guidance, looking for a hand out – looking for help of some kind or another, usually with some hard luck story to tell. Some of them had been drafted so young that they had never even had a chance to experience the working world before they went off to war and now they were returning from France sans any marketable skills and scarred by what they had seen; old men in boys bodies. Was there anything that the Colonel (though they usually referred to him as Major) could do? A job lead? A few bucks perhaps – just until they could get back on their feet? Others returned to the same nothing they had had before the war, caused by their own laziness or poor work habits, and were simply looking for a 'free ride'. Still others truly had legitimate hard-luck stories to share. Yet all were, in some form or another, in 'need'.

Not that it mattered. There was little Charles Whittlesey could actually do for them as far as employment went. He was not a job broker after all. But what he could do, and apparently frequently did, was hand out money. As a successful lawyer, unmarried and living alone in a bachelor's apartment with few expenses hanging over his head, he was certainly not hurting for that. Quite soon then, it seems that the former Battalion Commander became known as something of a 'soft touch' and by the spring of 1920, there was a veritable parade of 'his men' alongside the reporters passing through his office on almost a daily basis.

The second brand of 'visits' was made by the mothers, widows, and other family members of those men under him that had died while in France, all seeking details of their loved one's last days or moments. It no doubt pained Charles Whittlesey immensely to face them, but to turn them away was something he seemingly could not do either; to deny them some sort of peace of mind would have been far too cruel. Therefore, he would be forced to again and again relive each moment that he had seen a boy killed outright, or been wounded and slowly rotted to death in the mud of the Charlevaux, or watched as tetanus slowly and painfully squeezed the life out of a young body… and more often than not, then lie to the weeping figure before him, assuring them that their loved one had 'gone quickly' and 'felt no pain'. It was a melancholy fact that few men at the front in the Argonne died peacefully. This was especially true in the Ravin d'Charlevaux, but how could such horrors be revealed to someone already so bereaved? Quite simply, they could not, and as far as anyone can tell, he then gave what comfort he could offer; comfort he himself was denied by the very knowledge that he hid away of all that he had seen.

'He felt no pain ma'am.'

(Like hell; he screamed horribly for hours.)

'It was all over in an instant and he was quickly at peace.'

(Except that it took him two days to die.)

'He was very courageous.'
(He cried out for you, over and over again.)
'You may be very proud of him.'
(I am so very sorry I could not bring him home to you...)

Yet, he would have hated himself for having to lie too. And then, at night when he closed his eyes, he was forced to relive it all again, which was made all the worse because he then knew how powerless he was over it all.

The third type of 'visits' were the ones that Charles Whittlesey himself made to local veterans hospitals, where he would tour the wards and talk to the patients. He was already doing volunteer work with the Red Cross Role Call organization - chairing meetings, attending veteran's funerals (sometimes two or three a week) and helping in their charity drives anyway - so these visits seemed merely an extension of those activities. Many in the wards recognized him and felt honored to meet him. Others did not know him, or if they did, did not care who he was and had little to say. But little needed to be said; he was among men who he understood and who understood him, even without words. Yet coming to the hospitals and seeing the wounded and, in some cases, dying men, would have produced intense conflict within him. He did not want to be there necessarily, yet he would have felt a strange compulsion to be among men who 'understood'. Therefore he was entering a vicious cycle where the hospitals reminded him of all he wanted to forget, and yet were the only place he felt truly at home because there, they all remembered as he did. Consequently, by about the middle of 1920 we see Whittlesey already beginning to exhibit some of the classic signs of what we now know as post traumatic stress disorder, but which was then completely unknown. (III)

Another aspect to his visits may have had something to do with seeking treatment for the cough that had been brought about by his gassing on the Vesle, which was reportedly bothering him more and more. Treatment by the government was free to ex-AEF personnel and would have produced no actual paper trail for anyone to discover what was happening to him or what he was doing about it, as a private doctor's records – and bills for payment – might (though no official records have ever been found). Gas poisoning was a strange thing and affected different men in different ways. Few were actually killed by gas during the war, the number equaling something like one-half percent of all combat deaths. (In fact, more died following the war from its after effects. See IV below.) However, there are many, many cases of its long-term effects lasting for years after the war was over. Others ended up going to different extremes to try and correct their problems, such as relocating to different, dryer parts of the country in order to relieve the most common problem that men who had suffered from gas during the war afterwards faced – tuberculosis.

In the early 1900's tuberculosis was not the almost unheard of disease that it is today in the U.S., and sanatoriums abounded. Then, later on after the war, they served a vital function in treating men that had attained a form of the disease through having been gassed. Gas related tuberculosis was not an uncommon thing then in the early to mid 1920's. Nor was it untreatable by any means, but on the contrary; in some forms, depending largely on the severity, it could be completely cured and frequently was. First indications of the disease in its infant form were wheezing and coughing spells, shortness of breath and a tightness around the chest. In the simplest explanation, left untreated it produced, at best, a death that lasted perhaps a couple years as the victim slowly lost use of failing lungs, until one day there was simply no breath left to be had. In its worst form, death might take a decade or more of symptoms that went beyond the above and then on to producing suppurating open sores on the outside of the chest as the disease literally ate at the body. In either case, it would not be a preferred way to die.

Gas related tuberculosis - Charles Whittlesey was faced with it every time he went home to Pittsfield and visited with Elisha, who it appears undoubtedly had it from his gassing with the French around Verdun. Gas related tuberculosis - Charles had never been treated for his gassing on the Vesle and had had a deep, rattling cough ever since then that would not let go for more than a few weeks at a time. Gas related tuberculosis - The Major had been suffering from a terrible 'cold' as they jumped off into the Argonne, although it was late summer and nearly everyone else was fine. Then, as everyone else around him sickened, he seemed to get better – except for that damned cough. Gas related tuberculosis - Charles Whittlesey was a perfect candidate.

By June 1920, when he was a guest of honor for the Williams College commencement ceremonies, Whittlesey was faltering some at work, most probably due to the many and varied distractions his fame brought to the office he shared with John Bayard Pruyn. Therefore, in all fairness, Charles Whittlesey dissolved his partnership with his old friend and took a position with the firm of White and Case, at 14 Wall Street in the City, though Pruyn would still remain his closest friend. At White and Case he took up banking law; as complex and mind absorbing as any form of law might be, no doubt in an attempt to occupy his thoughts as completely as was possible. Absorbed in work, he perhaps thought he might finally be able to settle down some again, a state of mind that nevertheless continued to elude him as 1920 wore on towards 1921. The Williams Club, once a personal haven, was now apparently more of a distraction than anything else and he visited less frequently than before. Home in Pittsfield was, as always, home - both warm and welcoming. But Elisha was there, wheezing his life away, providing a constant reminder of the war. Christmas 1920 had been a typical family affair at the Pomeroy Street house, but he was even farther detached than he had been during the previous holiday, even though he had been back from France for two years now. He tried to hide how he was feeling, but it appears that it was all too obvious; friends and family describe him from this period as moody and prone to uncharacteristic outbursts of temper. His patience, always seemingly infinite before, had ostensibly eroded, and he would lash out acidly if pressed on nearly any issue. His health went wildly up and down from week to week and concentration was a chore. "Charles," brother Melzar later said, "was not the same when he came back from France. The war had changed him."

His personal appearances and speeches continued. He enthusiastically backed America's entry into the League of Nations, attended the first New York State American Legion Convention and backed losing presidential candidate Ohio governor James M. Cox for the ticket in 1920. He continued to speak out for peace and tolerance (though he also was no advocate of letting the Germans off the hook completely), yet few cared to hear about any of his political or social views. He was nervous, brittle, impatient, and strained as 1921 dawned. At lunch with a friend one afternoon early in the New Year he complained, "They are always after me about the war. I've got to help some soldier or make some speech or something. I used to think I was a lawyer. Now I don't know what I am." The visits had not stopped with his move to White and Case either; before long his office was again the center of a myriad of requests from his ex-soldiers and their families. His new associates, recognizing who he was, tried their best to take the distractions in stride and ignored the intrusions, but Whittlesey was purportedly angered and embarrassed by them.

In February of 1921, he was a guest of honor, along with George McMurtry, at a dance given by New York men that had been in Company K/307th to raise money for a soldiers fund, something he was actually glad to do if only for the chance to visit with his former 2nd battalion counterpart and to see some of the men again, with whom he felt that special bond. His speech that night was indicative of that bond, and several had tears in their eyes when he had finished.

That bond, however, received a serious blow when, in July, John "Jack" Monson, one of the heroes that had broken out of the Small Pocket with Arthur McKeogh, died penniless and a pauper, and his body laid unclaimed for several days in the morgue of the Bellevue Hospital. Monson had been on the verge of occupying a spot on 'Potters Field' when someone discovered a box in his personal effects with his medals in it and, realizing just who he was, got hold of his sister. Then the newspapers got wind of the situation and really wound it up. Charles was terribly sick at the time, bed ridden and feverish as he had been for better than a week, when he read the news and was instantly taken aback. It was appalling that someone from the war, one of his men – and a DSC winner, mind you – could be forgotten like that, and he immediately went to speak at the funeral, which through public conscription turned into an affair fitting for the man. He followed the casket out of the church and at the cemetery stood next to Arthur McKeogh, with whom he had stayed in sporadic contact since the latter had written a book on the 77th in 1919, before returning home and going back to bed.

His sickness during Monson's funeral was not out of the ordinary by then for Charles Whittlesey. While his health had been up and down since his return from the war, lately the 'down' part had mostly characterized it and by the spring of 1921, others in his bachelor's rooming house were complaining to the landlady, Miss Sullivan, about his wracking cough and incessant nightmares, both of which were keeping them awake at night. She was apparently forced to speak to him several times about it, but what Whittlesey's reaction was, is unknown. Embarrassment at the least, to be sure. Others around him remarked later on his generally poor health and discernible sadness during this time, but there seemed little they could do. Truly, Charles was greatly bothered, but by what?

As the year dragged on, he continued his personal appearances and in the late summer took on a particularly difficult case at work, one that required lots of effort and concentration and kept him alone and out of public view for great lengths of time. He had virtually stopped going to the Williams Club by then and few saw him outside of his office. As summer gave way to an early fall, he allowed himself to be wrangled into chairing the Red Cross Roll Call for the next year, and was offered command of the 308th Infantry Organized Reserves. Both were positions which he did not really want but also did not feel he could decently turn down. Anything having to do with veterans of the war took precedence. On the 23rd of September, he was officially commissioned Lieutenant Colonel of the reserves and another floodgate of bad memories, the retention of which had never been anything more than conditional at best, was thrown open wide.

October of that year found a Charles Whittlesey few recognized. He still paid regular visits home, but they were uncharacteristically shorter now and much of the happiness had seemingly been drained from the family.(V) The case he had taken at work was keeping him thoroughly occupied for longer and longer stretches. He was pale and seemed desperately unhappy. After giving a speech at a Red Cross fund raising dinner toward the end of the month, which he attended in the company of Marguerite Babcock, John Pruyn's sister-in-law and a dear close friend, he hinted at how he felt, saying, "Raking over the ashes like this revives all the horrible memories. I'll hear the wounded screaming again. I have nightmares about them. I cannot remember when I had a good night's sleep."

Then came the invitation to attend the interment of America's Unknown Soldier on November 11, 1921. As a Medal of Honor winner, he was instructed to act as an honorary pallbearer, along with George McMurtry, Nelson Holderman, and 27 other MoH holders. He did not want to do it and apparently told McMurtry as much, but having no choice in the matter, steeled himself as best as he could for the difficult event. Two weeks before the day, Frank Weld, the then Captain who had delivered the orders that put him and his men into the Charlevaux Ravine, and with whom he and McMurtry were to travel to Washington, stopped by Whittlesey's office to finalize travel arrangements. Appalled at the steady flow of people in and out of the office of his former fellow officer, Weld asked in amazement, "With all these distractions, how do you get through the day?" Charles, looking up tiredly, is said to have responded, "Not a day goes by but that I hear from some of my old outfit, usually about some sorrow or misfortune. I wish they would leave me alone." Then, after a short pause adding, "I cannot bear much more." (Some stories have Whittlesey telling this to former Captain Lewis Scott of the 308th during the ceremony two weeks later. It seems more likely however that he actually told this to Weld.) During the last weekend in October, he went back to Pittsfield to visit with his family for what would be the last time. They thought him to be rather ill looking and depressed.

The ceremony at Arlington National Cemetery went off virtually without a hitch. Whittlesey was not well; not exactly sick, but definitely not healthy. Before the ceremony, in front of the flag draped casket he fidgeted in his seat uncomfortably, telling McMurtry, "I should not have come here. I cannot help but wonder if that may not be one of my men from the Pocket. I shall have nightmares tonight and hear the wounded screaming once again." During the ceremony however, Whittlesey, sitting right next to George McMurtry and Nelson Holderman (the latter whom he had not seen since France) and a short distance away from Alvin York, remained pale and stock still, barely moving and starring straight ahead. Afterwards though, he seemed to again regain his composure, and on the trip back to New York, he and McMurtry stopped off in Atlantic City, where McMurtry says the two had a good time and Charles seemed very relaxed and at ease. They parted with a handshake upon return to the city and that was the last time that McMurtry ever saw him.

At lunchtime, on Friday, November 18, Whittlesey walked into the American Express office located just around the corner from his firm on Wall Street and inquired about passenger trips to Cuba. Shown availability, he booked passage on the United Fruit Company owned liner *S.S. Toloa*, bound for Havana on the 24th and from a chart picked a starboard side cabin with easy access to a staircase leading to the upper promenade deck. He paid the bill in cash and signed simply 'C.W. Whittlesey' to the register, not volunteering anything more in order to avoid any recognition or fuss. Then, ticket in hand, he went back to his office.

His father showed up that weekend, concerned by his son's pallid and distracted appearance during his last visit. But Frank Russell instead found Charles in high spirits and the two had a good visit together; in fact the best in a long time. That Saturday, the 19th, Frank was treated to watching his hero son sit on stage with other war veterans and give honor to visiting former Overall Allied Commander during the war, Marshal Ferdinand Foch. (VI) When Frank asked about his son's plans for the coming Thursday (Thanksgiving), Charles said that he had accepted an offer from John Pruyn and his wife Edith to dine with them and their new baby and then had plans to go to the Army/Navy game that weekend. However, to a fellow boarder at his bachelor's apartment building inquiring the same thing later that night, he mentioned the possibility of a sea trip, "To get away from things."

Monday the 21st and Tuesday the 22nd Whittlesey spent buried deep in the case he had been working so industriously on for so long. On the 23rd, he dictated a new will to a stenographer, had it witnessed, and placed it in his safety deposit box at the Corn Exchange Bank along with some other important papers. No one involved thought the new will unusual, as lawyers frequently made out fresh ones the more successful – or well known – they became. And by then, Charles Whittlesey was obviously very well known.

Thanksgiving Day was indeed spent in the company of the Pruyn's and their one-year-old baby girl. Charles showed up early and spent a great deal of time playing with the baby, for whom he had brought the present of some pretty hairpins. He was unusually happy and cheerful, more so than anyone had seen him in recent memory, and seemed virtually completely relaxed and at ease. Asked about his weekend plans, he mentioned going to see his family in Pittsfield.

The next day, Friday the 25th, he lunched with Fitzhugh McGrew, a fellow lawyer at White and Case and someone for whom Whittlesey had a great deal of respect. Charles seemed well relaxed and at ease then too, more like his old self than ever, and he and McGrew talked of Egyptian funerals, though the subject was not of Whittlesey's choosing. Late that afternoon, he placed a large envelope in the top left hand drawer of his desk, did not lock it, made sure his work area was neat and tidy and walked out of his office for the last time. He had made it known to his co-workers that day that he was going to Pittsfield for the weekend.

That evening he dressed, went out for dinner, and saw a movie in the company of Marguerite Babcock. (Legend has it that they went to see the 1921 silent "The Lost Battalion", which Whittlesey and others from the 308th had donated some time for in 1919, but it seems highly unlikely that this is truly so. Other reports say they saw a theater presentation.) Miss Babcock found him relaxed and jovial; quite a difference from his usual somber attitude of late. Afterwards, he returned to his bachelor's apartment and just before turning in asked Miss Sullivan to please have his breakfast ready by 8:00 a.m., telling her, "I am going to be alone for a few days. I am tired." That next morning, the 26th, after breakfast he wrote out a check for his December rent and gave it to her just as he was leaving, saying cryptically, "You had better cash this right away." Then he left.

The S.S. Toloa hoisted anchor about noon that Saturday and for the third and last time in his life, Charles Whittlesey sailed out over the ocean. He was quite quickly recognized and for once let it be known who he was, not at all trying to hide from his celebrity status. When the master of the ship, Captain Farquhar Grant, learned who he was, Charles was immediately invited to dine that evening at the Captain's Table, an offer he could hardly refuse. At dinner, he was the convivial conversationalist, willingly and of his own accord discussing the war and what had happened in the Charlevaux Ravine. His only request was that he asked if Captain Grant would to be so kind as to wireless ashore for the outcome of the Army/Navy game that had been played that day. No one thought him out of sorts; nothing seemed apparently amiss.

As the cloudy night wore on, Charles wound up sitting at a table sharing drinks with one Mr. Maloret, a Puerto Rican exporter working out of Havana who had been in the Spanish-American War and dealt with the AEF during the Great War. Sitting in the smoky atmosphere, Charles politely answered the man's questions about the Charlevaux episode. He had grown progressively quieter as time passed, but otherwise still seemed fine. All at once, just after 11:15 p.m. or so, Whittlesey abruptly stood up and excused himself, saying he was going to turn in and then strode out the saloon door into the black of the fog shrouded night beyond. There were a number of people on deck outside.

Despite that, he was never seen again.

The next day, Sunday the 27th, rough seas and rain were encountered and few left their cabins. Consequently, Charles Whittlesey was not missed at meals or in the saloon that night. The next day however, Monday the 28th, in the afternoon Mr. Maloret asked the ships purser about him and the two went to Whittlesey's stateroom to check on him. Finding the room unlocked and apparently empty, the purser fetched an assistant chief steward, who in turn fetched Captain Grant, and Whittlesey's stateroom was entered just after 4:00 p.m. There his bed was found unused, his luggage neatly placed at the foot and on the desk a note to the Captain on ship's stationary with instructions for the disposition of his luggage and specifics that telegrams be sent to his parents, John Pruyn, and his brother Elisha (who had only recently taken a room in the same bachelor house as Charles). He also wished a telegram sent to attorney Robert Little, of White and Case, stating, "Look in upper left hand drawer of my desk for memorandum of law matters I have been attending to. I shall not return."

Captain Grant immediately commenced a search of the ship, which turned up nothing, before then sending a message to the United Fruit Company offices in New York:

4:45pm Nov. 28th
Charles Whittlesey, passenger to Havana, disappeared yesterday. Left several letters here. Request notification to relatives.
   Grant (246)

John Pruyn, who was legal council to the United Fruit Company, just happened to be in the company office that day – the same one from which Whittlesey had procured his ticket some days previous – when the message came in and was thus the first to hear the terrible news. Other messages from the Toloa followed (which would eventually arrive some 12 hours late in Havana; Captain Grant having back-tracked part of his sea route without telling anyone in order to search for a body, of which no trace was ever found). Returning to the office on Rector Street later that afternoon in shock, Pruyn there found another message from Captain Grant, this time sent directly to him, asking that he notify Whittlesey's family himself. It also stated that the Captain would be "sending papers" via a ship bound for New York that they would meet up with in the Canal Zone. Pruyn, heartsick, sat down at his desk and picked up the telephone…

The papers carried the story for some months afterward, getting as much mileage out of the tragedy as was possible and labeling Charles Whittlesey as a latent victim of the war. Those friends and family he had left behind banded together against the reporters almost immediately after the letters Charles had left behind arrived in New York a week or so later, and merely issued the statement that they also considered Charles to be a "war casualty". An address given that December during a memorial service in Pittsfield also painted him as such, as did one given by Colonel Averill at the armory used by the 308th Reserves, and there were many others to follow that were conducted along those lines as well. The family and friends also did their best to keep Marguerite Babcock's name out of everything, stating that she and Charles were "merely old and dear friends", though at one point early on she did issue a statement of her own, before then fading into the background.

Of the many letters Whittlesey had left behind for various family members and friends only one of the sad missives, that to John Bayard Pruyn himself, has ever come to light and that was only many years later, after Whittlesey had been largely forgotten. None of the other letters Charles had written were ever made public or even hinted at as to their contents. In fact, when asked about his in 1937 by author Tom Johnson, Charles's brother Melzar stated that he had never even opened it; that if his brother had not been able to tell him himself why he had done it, then he did not want to know. "No," he said sadly, to Johnson, "now that you have reminded me of it, I think I'll destroy it tonight." (29)

It was Pruyn that Whittlesey had assigned as executor of his estate; not a difficult job as most of his things he had left to his family. The 'surrender letter' from Lt. Prinz (which he had been allowed to keep after the war) he left to George McMurtry, who in turn almost immediately gave it to Charles's father Frank. Frank also was left the Medal of Honor, which had held some significance to Charles, despite the cost associated with it. He also forgave his brother Elisha of a debt that was owed, but beyond that had little else to give. In the end, Pruyn found a mere $680.00 in liquid assets and in his room at the bachelor's apartment a gold watch and several suits. That was all, besides his uniforms and other military items then in storage at the Pomeroy Avenue home in Pittsfield. (Interestingly Whittlesey's service revolver, which he brought home from France, has never been found, which some had said he had a habit of keeping close by at times, though this is unsubstantiated.) Charles Whittlesey, war hero and successful lawyer that lead a rather austere lifestyle and should have had much more to show for his career then, instead strangely died leaving little behind in the way of material goods or monetary gain.

Why did he do it? This is the classic question of all those left behind by a suicide. At this distance of time there can never be an accurate answer (as with all suicides, really). However we can speculate, and in doing so draw some very likely conclusions through the evidence at hand. Initially, we may safely assume that Charles Whittlesey was suffering terribly from a severe case (can there be a non-severe case?) of Post-Traumatic Stress Disorder. He did display many of the classic symptoms: grim nightmares in which the event is relived, trouble concentrating, altered moods and personality contrary to the normal, an aversion to discussing what had happened, violent revulsion to reminders of the event – yet sometimes followed by an apparent uncontrollable compulsion to associate ones self with certain aspects of those reminders. Certainly he must have suffered from a fair amount of 'survivors guilt'; feelings that he should have died instead of many of those men under him – especially the untrained replacements that had never really stood much of a chance in the first place. "Why should I be allowed to remain? Why not them?" are not uncommon questions one asks themselves when suffering with PTSD. Perhaps this feeling was then increased by some of the widows and mothers that had visited him. It certainly must have been when he visited the veteran's hospitals.

Then, too, he may have felt some blame for what all had happened, since he had been in command and given the orders that had lead to many deaths; whether they had been his decisions initially or not was inconsequential. Further, he had been the one to hold them in that ravine – even when all prudence and common sense said to fall back, as had others. There is also every possibility that Whittlesey had heard all the whispering behind his back from the jealous army officers grinding axe's with his name on them, who did not really know all the facts but thought they did. About how it had been his fault somehow, that he was responsible, that he had been 'glory seeking', that he was taking the credit for the sacrifices made by those under him, etc... Whether he believed any of this claptrap or not remains beside the point. The point would be that he was hearing it, and it likely created at least some question in his mind – perhaps if he had argued with Colonel Stacey more strenuously, or maybe even refused altogether to lead those men into the Charlevaux things might have been different. After all, he had known what was likely to result, had he not? However, to do so would have gone against his stringent moral code, something he could not allow himself to do and in any case the war had to be fought; he had to look at the 'big picture'. But that did not stop the whispering, or the questions his tortured mind likely raised.

Adding to this was Charles Whittlesey's sensitive and idealistic nature. The intense political troubles the world went through right after the war during the peace negotiations lead many to believe that those who had fought and sacrificed in it had done so basically for nothing, since it had apparently solved nothing. President Wilson's '14 Points for Peace' had been pretty much cast aside by the French and the British in their desire for revenge against Germany, and Wilson was apparently proving to be a weak leader. Why then had all these poor boys gone so far away and died so tragically?

This author is also of the opinion that Whittlesey was further suffering physically as well as mentally and emotionally. The wracking cough he was consistently plagued by for well over three years was very likely a case of the previously discussed disease, gas related tuberculosis. Perhaps on one of his many veterans' hospital visits he sought medical treatment. Perhaps he was told at one late point that the disease in him would be terminal, likely within a short period of time. Adding a drawn, painful death then to the mental and emotional tortures he already faced would likely have been too much. With all peace of mind gone then and physical health also in a rapid downward spiral, the future would have taken on a very black hue indeed. What then was there to be lost, except a broken life?

As previously stated, in the end we can never know for sure what was going through Charles Whittlesey's mind as he walked out of that saloon aboard the Toloa that last night of his life. Yet whatever it was, the decision had been made long before; one of the possible indicators of a coming suicide is a sudden upswing in an individual's mood and personality from an extended downturn or disturbance for no apparent reason. His mood toward the end had certainly been an improvement over what it had been ever since he had come home from France. And he had been in good spirits up until about a half an hour before he left the saloon, when he quieted down, apparently steeling himself for what he was about to do. Then, he simply walked out of the picture. Perhaps he went back to his cabin and got his revolver; perhaps he had it with him already. Maybe he threw it in the ocean and then jumped in after it; maybe he jumped in and tread water until the ship had faded into the darkness and then put a bullet in his head. Perhaps he had gotten rid of the gun long before and simply jumped in and let the sea take him. Rumors circulated for a short time in the mid 1930's that he may have hidden on the ship, his pockets stuffed with all the money he should have had left behind due to his position in life and later simply walked off in Havana to live out the remainder of his life in peace, away from the rumors, myths and legend of who he was and what had happened in that ravine. But that was definitely not something that would have been in Charles Whittlesey to do. His family, friends and commitments meant far too much to him and his high moral code would have prevented any such cowardly act. Also, the suicide note left to John Pruyn makes clear in the first lines his intentions:

S.S. Toloa

Dear Bayard,
Just a note to say goodbye. I'm a misfit by nature and by training, and there's an end of it. I'm sorry to wish upon you the job of executor; but there is very little to do…" (246)

And with that, Charles Whittlesey's war was over.

In 1938, at the instigation of none other than reporter Thomas Johnson, the Lost Battalion Survivors Association was organized in New York. The first 'official' meeting was held on September 26, 1938, the 20th anniversary of the jump off into the Argonne, and all subsequent meetings, held once a year, were planned as close to that date as possible. (There had been 'unofficial' meetings going on for years before however.) Held at several different locals in New York City throughout the years over a lunch, Walter Baldwin was elected president for life of the association and the meetings were completely funded by George McMurtry, who was also permanent master of ceremonies. Each year Baldwin would arrange everything and at the end present McMurtry with the bill. The old 2nd Battalion commander would then promptly write out a check, without fail and without question, no matter how much it cost. John Larney, long healed of his wounds and none the worse for wear, was usually right at Baldwin's side helping out. Meetings would generally start off in the bar, the men drifting into the hotel from all over the city (and, on more than a few occasions, from all over the country) and before long the camaraderie was thick enough to cut with a knife. Conversation however rarely concerned itself with what had happened in the Charlevaux Ravine, but instead centering on what the men had been doing in the last year (or more, depending on the case). Sometimes though, it did waft back toward the ravine and the stories then were extraordinary.

Later, they would enter the dining hall and all take their seats at the tables with the low light glinting off the blue and gold silk of the survivor's meeting ribbons bedecking the men's chests. At the front of the room would be a lone chair, empty but for a beautiful spray of Dahlias lay delicately upon it. Sent each and every year by the former Miss Anita Degoll, they were in honor of the man she was to have married, but had been denied the chance to by the Charlevaux – Marshall Peabody. She never personally attended a meeting and had long since married another. But for at least one day a year anyway, her heart was obviously again his. So when the flowers stopped coming sometime in the mid 1960's, everyone knew why. Lunch would be served, but before anyone was allowed to eat George McMurtry would rise, glass in hand, at exactly 1:00 p.m. and the room would quickly fall silent. All eyes on him, he would raise his glass to the chair full of flowers and announce solemnly, "Gentlemen, to the dead of the Lost Battalion." All would then raise their glasses in toast, turn toward the chair and repeat McMurtry's words, drink, and then the luncheon would begin.

The meetings, which had seldom seen more than 50 or 60 attend in any given year after the first (which was attended by 125 men), lasted until sometime in the late 1960's, George McMurtry's estate even continuing to pay for them well after his death in 1958. Eventually though, they simply petered out when there were not enough of the men left to make a meeting. After that, a few 'old timers' met every now and then at the 77th Division club house in the city, but by the early 1980's – sixty some years after they had beaten back the Hun in the Argonne – it was all over and the living memories of the Lost Battalion faded into history. As near as this author has been able to discover, Sergeant Robert Hitlin, from the Small Pocket, was the last to go, in 1989. (4, 152, 153, 166, 192, 219, 221)

Nelson Holderman never saw action again, though one might argue that he had gotten a belly full of it anyway. Promoted Major after the evacuation of the Pocket was complete, he stayed in the hospital into 1919 and, amazingly, eventually recovered fully from all of his injuries, with nothing but an occasional limp when it rained and some scars to show for the episode. Charles Whittlesey, on hearing that his and George McMurtry's recommendation that the young, fire-eating officer be awarded the Medal of Honor was going to be acted upon, wrote him just before the award was made in 1921, *"To my great delight I have just received a notification of the award to you of the Medal of Honor... This is the finest news in the world and I am looking forward with eagerness to passing it on to George (McMurtry). I wish I could be on hand to see you decorated."* Charles Whittlesey was also later heard to comment that he thought no one had ever deserved the coveted medal more than did Nelson. (246)

In 1924, Holderman wrote a treatise on the Charlevaux incident as he saw it for the army's Infantry School at Ft. Benning and then went back to California with his Medal of Honor, accepting a full, permanent commission in the California National Guard. In 1926 he was promoted to full Colonel and appointed by the governor of California to run the state's veterans hospital at Yountville, which he quickly brought up to then modern day standards from the Civil War era wreck it had been. It was there, among the men he most admired, that he served out the rest of his life, remaining very active in veteran's affairs and constantly down playing anything that he had done in the war and his wounds. He also got together with former Captain Leo Stromee (who oddly enough, though wounded far less severely than Holderman, failed to recover fully, and was left with a partially paralyzed face for the rest of his life) and helped promote a West Coast version of the Lost Battalion Survivors Association. With them, Holderman never missed a single meeting or parade where he could always be found marching proudly under the blue and gold banner of the association.

At about 4:00 p.m. on September 3, 1953, the 67-year-old campaigner was found dead in the bathroom of his home on the Yountville grounds from a massive heart attack. He left behind a wife, Margarite, a daughter, Myra, and two sons, Nelson Jr. and Armand, a successful Air Force jet pilot that had recently returned from the war in Korea. (27, 44, 162, 195, 233, 239, 205, 338, 350, 355)

The Lost Battalion episode ruined Cromwell Stacey's stellar army career. Once he had 'removed himself' from the impossible situation in the Ravin d'Argonne, he slowly made his way through the system of hospitals and doctors back to the States, where he had been diagnosed with NDNYD (Nervous Disorder Not Yet Diagnosed or, in modern terms, PTSD). Meanwhile, back in the 77th Division, all the blame for Major Whittlesey's situation had been dumped squarely and unfairly into his lap, largely due to the investigation conducted during the episode, which, if one examines it carefully and knows the details, can be seen as a pretty straight forward screw job. Somebody had to be the goat and he was picked, probably by General Alexander, though no hard evidence of such has ever been found. It took two courts of inquiry in the 1920's, in the process of which Stacey called in every debt, threat, and favor he ever had out there, to clear his name and record as far as the army was concerned. Even General Leonard Wood and Alexander's own Chief of Staff, Colonel John Hannay, gave testimony as to his excellent leadership skills and proper course of action in the Argonne. Nevertheless, though eventually cleared and his record expunged, the stigma of fault for the episode remained and he was to live with a black mark following him around for the rest of his life. Despite that, he stayed in the army until retirement, as might well be expected (it was his only home), and held a variety of decent posts and commands throughout the rest of his career, but he was never promoted beyond Colonel – just as his father had never been. He died at his home in Riverside, California, in 1963. (238)

General Evan Johnson took a fair amount of the blame for the episode as well in its immediate aftermath. Transferred out of the division at his own request not long after Whittlesey's relief (actually 'pushed out' by Alexander is more the term for it, if truth be told), he ended the war with the 79th Division. After the war, he wound up a military attaché in Rome, but since he died from complications from surgery he underwent there in 1923, he has remained a largely forgotten figure of the whole episode and was therefore spared much of the same criticisms that Stacey always faced. And of all the officers involved in the incident, outside of those in the Lost Battalion itself, it was probably he that afterwards most understood and appreciated what all had happened and tried to make sure that Charles Whittlesey and his men received the best possible care because of it. He was truly a 'soldier's soldier'. (29, 116, 238, 347)

General Robert Alexander also stayed in the service after the war, and defended the decisions he had made in the Argonne right up to his death in 1941. His fame was a divided one, for there were certainly those who loved him as a commander, particularly those who had known him during his days with both the 32nd and 41st Divisions. But there were also just as many that did not think much of him at all. In that regard, he has been accused of being everything from merely unfeeling, to being nothing short of a butcher with his men. Yet judged solely on his record he must be considered among the best of the war's division commanders, since the 77th under him racked up more kilometers of advance against the enemy than any other division in France. As stiff and aloof as always, his autobiography did not sell well and he never received the laudits other combat commanders later did, despite his division's stellar record. To his credit however, he always later accepted full responsibility for the entire Lost Battalion episode – for the good it did anyway – and stood by his principals, always insisting that he had been right in giving the orders that he did, which he arguably had. It is hard to dispute his line of reasoning too, for the reality is he was in a very hard place to be; the line had to move, men had to die to do it, and he had to give the orders for that to happen. Then, he had to live with it. (VII) (2, 116, 238, 338)

Harold Goettler and Erwin Bleckley were each also posthumously awarded first the DSC, and then the Medal of Honor, after the war for their tremendous show of bravery in attempting to locate exactly where Major Whittlesey's mud covered command was in the ravine. Harold Goettler's body came home in 1922, and Major General Clarence Edwards, who had presented Charles Whittlesey with his MoH, also presented Goettler's mother with his. She barely moved and did not speak as he pinned the medal to her blouse, while Harold's former fiancée looked on silently as well. 'Dad' lies under a stone in the family plot in Graceland Cemetery in Chicago today. (15, 47, 241, 284, 287)

Erwin Bleckley, on the other hand, still lies under a gold-edged government 'Medal of Honor stone' in the enormous American war cemetery at Romagne-sous-Montfaucon, France. His MoH was pinned on his father's lapel by Major General C.B. Duncan, then commander of the 7th Corps, on March 23, 1923 at the Forum in Wichita, Kansas. Afterwards, a tearful E.E. Bleckley said, "It is beyond my power for me to say anything in appreciation of the honor bestowed by this nation upon my son. The award is more expressive of the deed, the memory of which we commemorate more then any words by me on behalf of my family. A young life given to his country makes my heartstrings vibrate with the memory of his service." (15, 47, 241, 331-337)

Indeed…

'Red' Cullen was bumped up to Captain after he left the Charlevaux and returned to his law practice following the war, having never received a single wound. He was at most of the Survivors Association meetings, and had earlier spoken at one of the memorial services for Whittlesey, but still never quite seemed to 'fit in' with the rest of the men that had been in the ravine. His greatest post war veteran related accomplishment was his being instrumental in getting "Lost Battalion Hall" built in the Rego Park area of Queens, a large building meant to be used by various veterans' organizations and to which he had hoped the survivors association would move their meetings. They never did however, rumor holding that he had alienated too many of the men involved in the decision years before. Today, it is used as a neighborhood recreation hall, and few of the kids that frequent it have ever even heard the story of the Lost Battalion. (33, 109, 152, 153, 219, 245, 246, 353)

Cher Ami recovered from his wounds to come home to a hero's welcome, crossing the ocean to the states in an officer's berth on the USS Ohioan and having a full honor guard when the ship docked in Hoboken, well ahead of the 77th Division. His story, perhaps more than any other, filled the public imagination, though it was frequently confused with the story of 'The Mocker', another pigeon hero from the Argonne days. During what remained of the little pigeon's life, he received the Croix de Guere with palm from the French government and a full pension (!) from the U.S. government, as well as a wooden leg, hand carved by the men of the Signals Platoon of the 308th Infantry (which he politely refused to wear). Rumors also held for years that he had been awarded the DSC for his actions during the Charlevaux incident, but they are nothing more than that. Retired to the Signal Corp's 'old pigeons home' (yes, a real place) after he had gone all over the country on a Liberty Loan tour following the Armistice, he died there in June of 1919 and was immediately stuffed. He can be seen to this day still on display at the Smithsonian Museum of American History – virtually the only World War One artifact on display. If one looks very close, one can still see where the wound in his chest was... (13, 21, 265, 353)

The episode in the Charlevaux Ravine all those years ago has always meant different things to different people. For some who had been there, it was a turning point, after which nothing would ever be the same again. For others, it was just a passing event that they had endured and then did not think much about afterwards. To the public at large of the day, it was an exciting example of courage and determination, of American fortitude and might, brought to bear against an unequal enemy. To General John Pershing, it was one of the three greatest epics of the whole war, and it lent even further validation to his AEF. For some, it was the tragic end to the possibilities that life had to offer.

For me, it has been an exciting journey of discovery – sometimes frighteningly repulsive, at other times sad or terrifying, only very occasionally funny, but at all times one hell of a good story to tell. (And you can't miss if you've got good material.) I believe that we are all put on earth to accomplish certain tasks and that I did not pick this story to tell. Instead, I believe I was picked to tell it, and I have now fulfilled a task which I was *meant* to do. It is a story that I have enjoyed telling. I hope you have enjoyed hearing it.

(I) Charles Whittlesey had already gotten his MoH by then and Captain Holderman, still in the hospital, would get his in 1921, largely on the word of Whittlesey and McMurtry both. All this left 'Red' Cullen feeling somewhat left out, as one might imagine. After all, had not his actions on the left flank been at least as courageous as Captain Holderman's over on the right? Apparently not, possibly due to his not having been wounded. One might expect the commander of the battalion to have stayed mostly out of harms' way – Charles Whittlesey excluded of course, but then again he was not the average Battalion Commander either – but with all but one other of the officers having been hit, that must have spoke volumes to Whittlesey and McMurtry. All the more so since Lt. Eager's escape from a wound appeared to have been more pure luck than anything else, since he was just as active in the Pocket as any other officer. Then too, perhaps the two battalion commanders' had heard some of the rumblings among the men that had been over there on the left flank, some of which was not particularly flattering of the generally unpopular Lt. Cullen's character. In any case, he never got the MoH and as far as is known never really raised a fuss over it either.

(II) Yet on the morning of the 8th, just after General Alexander had left the Pocket, Baldwin, Cepaglia, Monson, Richards and Larney had all come forward and offered to Whittlesey to sign sworn documents that were in direct contradiction to the General's statement before them all that the barrage of the 4th had been French - when it had quite obviously been American. The Major, however, had affected little interest. He was already wise to the ways of 'higher authority' and knew no good could come of it, and so had never made waves over the matter in any official capacity.

(III) Whittlesey is also thought to have started making large cash donations to the Red Cross and various veteran's organizations around this time as well, perhaps out of some sense of 'survivor's guilt', though no conclusive evidence has ever been found to support this since he apparently never left a paper trail.

(IV) Of the hundreds of veterans families I talked to during preparation for this book, nearly all mentioned that their relative suffered respiratory or digestive troubles to one degree or another all their lives which had been attributed to their having taken in some gas during the war. The degree of suffering varied widely depending on how much actual action the man had seen and how much gas he had taken in, ranging from relatively light troubles, such as merely being more susceptible to colds and 'flu, all the way on up to larger issues such as serious lung, throat, stomach and heart problems, as well as blindness and mental issues. In many cases the men that had suffered the most gas ended up having repeated operations to try and correct the problems, something which rarely worked, and were permanently disabled by their ailments. After all, one cannot work if one cannot breath.

(V) Russell had taken ill and died in 1911, and Elisha would eventually succumb to his illnesses in 1922, not long after Charles had gone. This would leave only Melzar remaining of the six children that had been born in Wisconsin.

(VI) This event is usually described as occurring on the 20th. However, a program from the proceedings in the author's personal collection proves otherwise.

(VII) Interestingly, the 32nd Division had initially been slated to be made a Depot Division when it first reached France. When that decision was changed and it ultimately was allowed to remain a combat division, Alexander was then transferred to the 41st, which would remain a Depot Division, and under his command, the best one in France and so win him a combat commander's slot. Is it not likely then that the apparent attempt to keep him a 'depot commander' might not have been a strategic move against him, since he was not a West Point officer? Or did the other regular army officers know something more about Alexander's character that might cause them to think he might be unsuitable to lead an actual combat division?

Creating a Legend
In the beginning…

The 'story' (as opposed to the epic) of the Lost Battalion started out as nothing more than a newspaper story. However, it is perhaps a fantastic example of what power the media actually has; then as well as now. Charles Whittlesey and his men would perhaps not have been the heroes they were to became without the press pumping up the story; we already know that the army did not see them as heroes at first, nor later either, really. But, by the time those men crawled out of their muddy holes in the Charlevaux Ravine on that morning of October 8, 1918, the press had already built them up as one hell of a band of men – which they were – and the makings of the legend were then in place. All it needed for a true legend to be born then was a further catalyst. And it was the voice of one man, Lt. Arthur McKeogh, Major Whittlesey's diminutive former adjutant in 1st Battalion and escaped hero of the Small Pocket, that initially got that ball rolling. Sent home on September 30, which was the day that the 2nd/308th broke through to the 1st on l'Homme Mort and relieved the situation there, while Lt. McKeogh was at sea Major Whittlesey's command then went through the hell of the second, more famous, Pocket. The day that Lt. McKeogh landed in New York was October 8, the day of Major Whittlesey's rescue from the Pocket in the Charlevaux Ravine –which Arthur McKeogh, having been at sea, knew nothing about. However, by that time Whittlesey and his Lost Battalion were already on their way into the history books and *anything* concerning them was solid gold as far as the press was concerned.

When a disembarkation officer at the dock in Hoboken noticed on the personnel roster the magical number '*308th*' and that Lt. McKeogh had been 1st *Battalion* adjutant, he put two and two together, got five, and began to pump McKeogh for details concerning what he referred to as "The Lost Battalion Story". Lieutenant McKeogh, having no clear idea of what the man was talking about, initially figured he meant the tangle that he, Monson, and Herschkowitz had worked their way out of on l'Homme Mort. Wondering how news of his adventure could have gotten around the States so quick, but flattered nonetheless, he told his tale. There was a reporter hanging around nearby who wandered over about then and soon another 'Lost Battalion Story' appeared in the papers - only this one being touted as "first hand". And so, the original confusion of details from the two stories being mixed together was born and first began to muddy the 'Legend of the Lost Battalion' waters.

Further confounding the matter, a short time later Lt. McKeogh was hired by *Collier's Magazine* to write his story, which then ran it under the bold heading "The Lost Battalion" (*Colliers Magazine, November 16th, 1918*). This became the very first full length 'anything' having to do with the Lost Battalion, rather than the shorter newspaper articles. Since Arthur McKeogh had been a newspaperman before the war, and therefore had a flair for the dramatic writing style of the time, his story became a very popular version of events with the public at large - which continued to combine the two stories, even though McKeogh, by then fully aware of all the facts, had made it clear that his story had nothing to do with the Charlevaux Ravine. When Whittlesey came home that next month (December), he himself had little ambition to say anything concerning either affair – in truth he simply wanted to forget the whole war – and therefore didn't ever really bother to straighten out the story either, despite the myriad of newspaper interviews he was forced to give. Then, by the time the rest of the 308th came home, in May 1919, most of them could not have cared less either and were just glad to be home. Therefore, the story in the public's mind remained a mixed up, convoluted, combination of the two tales rolled into one for the next few years, despite several magazine articles and short stories in popular books that alluded to the contrary.

Arguably, the first of these book stories was written by Arthur McKeogh. The little ex-officer had always felt a certain amount of guilt over his having missed the second, more famous, episode in the Charlevaux Ravine and would then become the first true 'historian' of the Lost Battalion. He did some of the first interviews with several of the returning survivors and then used them to piece together the tale for a little book he wrote quite soon after the war entitled, *The Victorious 77th Division in the Argonne Fight (1919 - John H. Eggers & Co., New York)*. In it, was given a short, glazed over account of the first entrapment (in which McKeogh never even mentions his own part) and the very first cohesive description of the second, Charlevaux, entrapment in a fairly correct sequence of events. However, the book did not sell very well and was therefore not very widely read. Consequently, like everything else written about the event, it had little impact of the story in the public mind.

Also, just about the time McKeogh's book was coming out, another appeared which contained an equally cohesive, if minorly flawed, description of the Lost Battalion episode called, *Americans Defending Democracy (1919 – World's War Stories Inc., New York)*. Interestingly, the editor of the book, one John Franklin Gilder, wrote the story based mostly on an interview with one of Whittlesey's wounded men, Sergeant John Colasacco of Company 'C', done when Gilder himself was an AEF reporter. There is also a supposed 'interview' (though again factually flawed and very inane) with Cher Ami, and one with a medic from the 307th that helped clean out the Pocket on October 8. Nor did this book sell well either however, though it is a fascinating read.

Finally, perhaps the biggest blob of mud in the Lost Battalion waters came in the form of a cinema production. Early in 1919, the McManus Film Corporation began shooting a movie in cooperation with the U.S. Army Signal Corps about the Lost Battalion, which was ultimately released to the general public in early 1921 as *The Lost Battalion*. (It was used extensively before that with veterans groups and was originally released in the fall of 1919.) The most fascinating thing about the film is that parts of it were actually shot in France, there in the Pocket where it had all happened, and in it several of the men that had been in both entrapments played themselves, including Charles Whittlesey, George McMurtry, Walter Baldwin, Zip Cepaglia and William Cullen. Arthur McKeogh, by then noted as someone knowledgeable on the subject, was brought in as a technical advisor, along with Herschkowitz and Monson (the first time they had all seen each other in nearly a year), and several other LB men from both Pockets were also given cameos in the opening sequences. The story line to the film however was itself a combination of the two entrapments, and this served to further cement the incorrect story in the public mind and build upon the legend and myths already beginning to spring up around the episode, as the flick was very well received by the public. (Most Lost Battalion men themselves however dismissed the film as "ridiculous" which, in large part, it is.) By the mid 1920's, then, about the only people who really knew what had actually happened in the Charlevaux Ravine in early October 1918 were the men who had actually been there (who did not want to talk about it), Arthur McKeogh (who had cared enough, or rather felt guilty enough, to ask), and an ex-AEF reporter from the New York Sun, Thomas M. Johnson.

It is largely due to Tom Johnson's efforts that the story of the Lost Battalion did not fade into obscurity following Charles Whittlesey's suicide, or its truth completely disappear beneath the myths. He had been one of the first to interview Whittlesey on October 8, and since that moment had been fascinated with the story. Throughout the 1920's then, he turned the tale into something of a cottage industry for himself, seeking out as many of the survivors and major players for interviews as he could and writing numerous newspaper and magazine articles on them and the subject. Then, in 1927, Johnson wrote his first book, *Without Censor: New Light on our Greatest World War Battles (1927 – The Bobbs-Merrill Co., Indianapolis)*. In it, he basically admitted that during the war he and his news-hound cohorts had been officially sanctioned by the AEF to lie in their dispatches home and cast a much brighter light on things than there had been at the time. The book then was supposed to be what *really* happened, and even though it is now obvious that Johnson still held back quite a bit, it was a fascinating read for the time. The book also contained - not surprisingly - a chapter called "Finding the Lost Battalion", which really turned out to be little more than a teaser for his next book, first published in 1938 (also by Bobbs-Merrill/Indianapolis) and entitled, *The Lost Battalion*, which he co-wrote with a man by the name of Fletcher Pratt. Pratt was a military historian who knew a great deal about what we had done in France during the last year of the war (some said even more than the Generals leading the battles had known). It was a good partnership, and the two men devoted a lot of time to the project and conducted even more interviews with survivors. All the while, Johnson continued writing a series of newspaper articles throughout the project that helped keep public interest piqued for the story. When the book was finally released then, it became an instant hit, big enough to remain almost constantly in print ever since and be regarded as the only true comprehensive study on the Lost Battalion, until now.

However, the book was apparently not entirely their own work – or accurate. A great deal of it was based on the diary kept by Major Whittlesey's signal-man in the 1st/308th, Pvt. James Larney; information that Johnson, who did most of the actual writing, took a great deal of 'poetic license' with. Legend also holds that an original short manuscript for the book was actually written by Battalion Sergeant Major Walter Baldwin soon after the war and bought by Johnson in the 1920's for $200.00 (a story that this author, despite much effort, has never been able to neither prove nor discount.) The book also contains some serious flaws. Besides the obvious omission of virtually anything having to do with the Small Pocket or the battle before they entered the Charlevaux Ravine, there was also much information that was not available to the two authors then that has since become available, particularly governmental documents that were not declassified until after WW2. There was also a great deal written by the men, particularly the Midwestern men, after the book came out as well, much of it meant to counter some of the more 'questionable' aspects of Johnson and Pratt's work, which was told primarily from the New York men's perspective. Therefore, the story, to the replacements anyway, came from a rather narrow viewpoint. However, few of the refusions ever saw the light of day.

It also appears, according to information left behind by James Larney (who was himself little impressed by the book and let his feelings be known in the margins of his own copy – See Appendix B) and several others that Johnson purposely left out many details that he very likely knew. This was apparently in an effort to spare certain survivors or their families any embarrassment, shock, or shame over some of the more unsavory acts committed, or not committed, in the Pocket, as well as the details concerning their relative's deaths. Additionally, some details apparently were 'twisted' (to put it politely) to fit a scene or purpose, while others were just plain wrong. Private Larney also pointed out large parts of the book were apparently 'dramatized', while other parts were simply nothing more than just pure fiction. The book is also not nearly as in depth or as fully descriptive as it might have been either, though to be fair this probably has more to do with the writing style of the time than anything else. Additionally, though Johnson had been reporting in France during the war, his descriptions in the book of areas and places as told from 20 years down the road suffer for that reason and contain many critical errors.

Another reason for some of the 'creative writing' may have been legal. Many of the men whom Johnson and Pratt apparently had this 'dirt' on were still alive at the time the book was published, and could reasonably have brought suit against the two writers for defamation of character or slander, whether the information was true or not. In addition, neither writer wanted to slam anybody's reputation and a lot of the information could have been potentially very damaging to some, particularly Whittlesey and Hollingshead. Therefore, many facts have remained hidden lo these many years.

Yet for all its flaws, Johnson and Pratt's book did tell the story in a general way and brought down a few of the more persistent falsehoods and rumors usually associated with the tale. It also kept Charles Whittlesey's memory alive and kept the story from entirely disappearing under the shadow of the 'Sergeant York Legend', and for that it must be commended. It has been a guide – *the* guide really – for the Lost Battalion for the last 67 years, until now.

Interest in the Lost Battalion was revived again in the 21st century with the release of the A&E channel's motion picture, *The Lost Battalion*, starring Rick Schroeder and Phil McKee. Unfortunately, despite the information that has been out there for these many years, the movie again persisted in perpetuating many of the rumors, myths and legends associated with the story. That said, it is nonetheless a very entertaining film to watch, and it served a greater purpose in that it brought Major Whittlesey and his men back into the public conscience after 80+ years - where they arguably should have been all along.

We live in a time and a culture that can little understand, or appreciate, the brand of warfare that the men of the Lost Battalion knew. However, if we are to grow and learn as a people and successfully chart a steady course ahead through what is to be, we need to remember where we have been, and what we have done. And few finer examples of courage and fortitude from that long ago era can be found than those displayed on that muddy, battered hillside of northeastern France in the early fall of 1918.

In The Ravin d'Charlevaux

"Goodbye..."

October 10th, 2002 – Argonne Forest, France

Time changes everything. Indeed, hardly a truer statement can be found in life. And, as I clump my way through the Argonne Forest, so I find it also to be with the sights attributed to the 308th's advance path of so long ago. Once places of pain and death, they now belay what happened there with peaceful forest scenes. Only if one looks closely will they see the evidence of the past – and evidence there is. Trees have healed around shrapnel wounds and there is still much indication of the German occupation. The remains of trenches dip there way along ridgelines, barbed wire remains hidden within clumps of brush and weeds, funk holes still dot the forest, unexploded ordinance can still be turned up, sometimes with surprisingly little effort. Kicking around the leaves and grub along the edge of an old funk hole I spy something familiar, bend down and discover an unspent bullet. Carefully cleaning off the base, I examine the markings. American. "What Whittlesey's men would not have given for this," I think. Farther on in my walk I kick up a piece of shrapnel – a big, jagged piece.

War has been here.

I begin the most important part of my journey starting at the Small Pocket, a portion of which remains on public land - the portion on the hillside. The rest of it (up toward the rear of l'Homme Mort) is now a farmer's land, wired off for the pleasure of his cows. Shell holes and funk holes dot the hillside; the trench across the top is still there, though softened by age; and left over barbed wire now sprouts from either side of several trees that have grown around and engulfed it. If one follows the rail bed around the eastern side of the hill from the bottom toward Depot des Machines, there is to be found a concrete fountain at a spring sitting against the hillside, slowly being taken over by moss. It was built in 1915 when the 9th Landwehr occupied the area. Of the bunker complex in the cutting of the hillside, only the concrete one used by Whittlesey, and later by Stacey and Johnson as a PC is still there. At the base of the hill is a sign announcing that you are in the 'Communal Forest of Binarville'. The mill complex is gone, as is the pond largely, and the whole area is heavily grown over. The Binarville - Moulin de l'Homme Mort road, running before the clearing in front of the Small Pocket is still unpaved limestone, exactly as it was in 1918. Yet, despite the changes that the years have brought, if any of the survivor's came down the road today, I would be willing to bet that any of the men that fought there so long ago would easily recognize the area.

Following the Ravin d'Argonne north along the 2 kilometers toward the Charlevaux Ravine, one can see just what a massively difficult job the Major and those men had before them there. The ridges on either side loom above and the flats of former machine gun nests dot the slopes. The wagon path down the middle is still there, as is the rail bed next to it for a time, though in some places one sinks almost knee deep in the mud. Spent bullet casings can be found under foot just inches below the soil, as well as the occasional pile of unused grenades and a few mortar shells. The ditch that is all that remains of the Giselher Stellung line at the foot of Hill 205 still winds up the wash toward the top of the hill and has a few barbed wire picket stakes adorning the edge, in some places camouflaged in the brush and sticking up just enough to find an unprotected ankle. On top of Hill 205, the roofs of concrete bunkers stick out of the ground and the outline of connecting trenches is evident. Climbing the hill is an arduous task even for those in shape and well rested from a night spent in a comfortable Verdun hotel - let alone half-starved, sick, sleepless and wet men being fired at with automatic weapons. At the top, for a moment my companion, Lt. Col. Beattie, and I stop, close our eyes and listen. That far off rapping sound... is it a woodpecker, or the faint vestiges of an automatic weapon firing? And those shouts and calls... members of our research party finally catching up to us, or the ghostly echoes from so long ago? We simply look at one another, say nothing and start back down the slope.

The bottom of the wide ravine on the eastern side is still marshy and very difficult to cross, though one can follow Whittlesey's approximate path with care. The hole on the side of Hill 198 where Lt. Rogers and Company B captured their prisoners the afternoon of October 2 is still there, though mostly filled with leaves and forest debris. Hill 198 can also be a treacherous climb; a big windstorm that tore across France in 1999 left a litter of downed trees that makes passage to some of the more desirable spots up there almost inaccessible along certain routes. The main trench line of the Giselher Stellung, now only a fairly deep ditch, zigzags its way along the wide top of the hill and is still very commanding. Mind that bit of barbed wire there... The second, smaller, 'back-up' trench line is barely a ditch now and if you don't know where to look for it you'll likely miss it, though the narrow road where Major Whittlesey came upon Lt. Rogers standing on the afternoon of October 2nd is still recognizable. The big German dug out where Lt. Prinz composed the now famous 'surrender letter' has long ago collapsed, and all that remains are the two entrances, one of which Pvt. Hollingshead left out of, letter in pocket, on the afternoon of October 7. Farther down the ridge, the little cliff behind Captain Holderman's position on the right flank of the Pocket is still there, though the tree and brush cover have receded somewhat. Nevertheless, it is still an excellent offensive spot, with a grand view of nearly the whole rear of the right flank and a beautiful machine-gun position just west of it covers the flank.

Retracing the Major's steps down the hill into the Charlevaux Ravine one comes to the point where they crossed the brook. It is even possible to locate where the footbridge was if one has the panoramic photo of the ravine taken in 1919 with them - and he is not afraid to get boot leather wet as they must have in 1918. So too can be found some of the former German machine gun nests down there. Then, once across the marshy ravine bottom one reaches the wagon road at the foot of Mont d'Charlevaux, still recognizable, and stands looking obliquely at the spot where the great episode all happened. Here, one cannot help but be moved.

The Pocket itself today presents a contradiction. Once a place of such suffering and tragedy, the hillside now exudes a peace and tranquility that almost deny the blood-soaked memories of those five terrible days in October 1918 that remain stored within its earth. Above, birds sing happy melodies and the wind sighs through the boughs of trees grown post-war, while below the brook bubbles merrily by. Damming in the 1920's has increased the size of the mill pond below where the Charlevaux Mill once stood (there is a house there now) so that the nipple of hill extruding from the left flank is very near the water now; the very same water that once tempted the thirsty men of the 308th, but for which an attempted drink could spell death. That water also mostly covers the German drill field and open spaces off the left flank now, where just a short couple of months after the event, the pioneer infantry troops came back and temporarily reburied Major Whittlesey's dead in straight rows there, until the big American war cemetery at Romagne was ready for them. Along one side of the expanded pond are camping spaces for tents and mobile campers alike, about where the wagon path once ran on toward the mill. Following just north of the bank of the brook east, is the old wagon path itself. In 1918 it wasn't much, nor is it now. However, it still makes lateral travel along the bottom of the Pocket fairly easy in dry weather, though in wet weather it is a quagmire toward the left flank. Also near the left flank can be found the natural spring that so tempted the men in 1918, but again one must actually look for it. (Note: In November 2005, the author returned to the Pocket again and discovered that the spring has now been well tapped for the use of the camping area.)

It is also interesting to note that besides the wagon path, all main department (read: county) roads that cut across France in 1918 are still there today – they are simply paved now. This goes for the Binarville-La Virgette Road that runs along the upper edge of the Pocket as well. When Pvt. Larney dived across it on October 4, 1918 it was simply a hard bed of crushed limestone carved out of the hillside. Today it is still a hard bed of limestone, but with a coating of black top and a fairly regular stream of cars flowing down it. Each one passes a 5-foot tall triangular marble marker standing on the south side of the road. On the two sides that more or less face the road, are carved arrows that point down the hill, and the words 'Lost Battalion'. The eastern side also lists the dates of the action and the units involved. However, few stop to look, and fewer still know what it means anymore.

There remain on the hillside itself the signs of what happened there. The funk holes dug by the men are still very much in evidence and prolific, except where the American barrage of October 4 did its main work. There, an oblique strip along the hill shows the inundations of ground caused by heavy overlapping shellfire. Again, if one knows what to look for, it is easy to locate where the long and deep 'wounded hole' was. Elsewhere, trees damaged by shellfire or torn down all together by the shells have left their mark behind too. A battered, rotted stump still angles ponderously over one of the funk holes. Several men had the experience of the tree they dug next to for protection being up rooted and thrown over them. Who occupied this one? At this late date, we can never know.

Across and above the Binarville - La Virgette Road, German machine-gun positions still loom with awesome fields of fire right down into the Pocket. It is no wonder that some of the doughboys were driven back well below the lip of the road. It is astonishing to note exactly how close the German and American troops actually were to each other. In some places not more than 15 or 20 meters separated them and during an attack even less would have. The individual slit trenches farther behind the machine-guns on Mont d'Charlevaux are still there, though they are not much more than wide depressions in the ground now. But perhaps the most moving section of all the German positions above the Pocket remains the area where the German troops assembled just before the flame-thrower attacks. From there, one can then easily follow the path down the hill beyond the right flank that the crews took on the afternoons of October 6 and 7, all the way down to the wagon path below the hill. Again, Lt. Col. Beattie and I stop to ponder all we have seen along our long path to this point. War has been here.

We start back up the hill.

It is the afternoon of my last day here, and I am sitting next to Major Whittleseys' second command hole just above the Charlevaux brook, overlooking the spot where so many men fell to sniper fire just for a drink of muddy water. Somehow, I cannot seem to shake a peculiar feeling that I can only describe as one of 'significance' that I have felt on my every visit to this place. The hillside is a landmark of some consequence for what happened here and I feel honored to have been allowed to move along this steep ground and among these holes and to know their true meaning as I did so. Back in America, the Pocket had become a mystical place for me - a sort of 'Holy Grail', if you will - after having had the ghosts of all these men haunting me for all these years. Now, having been to this place, I have felt the presence of those ghosts here, and having seen it, smelled it, and touched it, have now have been touched by it as well. I close my eyes and again try to imagine myself back in time. Once more, I strain to hear, strive to see: the gunfire echoes, the trench mortar bombs explode; the cries of the wounded fill the chilled night air; Major Whittlesey struts from hole to hole, emerging through a morning fog, *"Remember, there are two million Americans behind you fighting to get through."*; A pigeon flutters skyward amongst vivid ground flashes; 'Zip' Cepaglia slinks to the brook in the dim half-light of dusk for water; Pvt. Hollingshead appears waving his small white flag – *"I have a message for the Major…"*; Haggard men are rising up and shouting…*'Come and get as you Dutch bastards!'*; Shapes in the dark along the wagon road below…; *"Major? There's a Captain Stone on the road…"*

I begin to realize that in telling the story of what has happened here, the Pocket has inadvertently become a part of me.

Opening my eyes, I see that the sun is beginning to sink.

It is time.

Rising from my seat in the dirt, I finally turn and slowly make my way back up the steep hillside one last time. The leaves crunch, a breeze blows gently through the trees and the Charlevaux bubbles softly behind me. I reach down and finger the dirt; one last long look from above down into the place that affected so many men's lives so long ago, and has filled my own thoughts for so long now - and will always continue to do so, I know. Then I turn to go. Goodbye 'Pocket'… goodbye ghosts of the Lost Battalion. I have tried to tell your story as completely and as honestly as I could.

I hope I have done it justice.

(Mike Jetzer)

Appendix: A
Lists of Individuals Known to Have Been
in the Charlevaux Ravine, October 2 – 7, 1918

No complete and accurate list of who was in the Charlevaux Ravine during those five days of the episode has ever existed. Therefore, in wanting to include one in this volume, over my eight years of research I was forced to reconstruct one, which I believe to be about as accurate a compilation as will ever likely be put together. There were several lists to start from, as well as odd bits and pieces of lists in books, official records and personal remembrances but none were anything like complete.

A perfect example of this incompleteness, albeit one with an explanation, is the list of Lost Battalion men that appears in the back of *The History of the 308th Infantry*. Nobody had paid much attention when they were carting the wounded out of the ravine on October 8 as to who was going and who was staying. Nor had the official reports filed later by those survivors in command of the companies there during the time been anything like accurate either, although Whittlesey did record approximate numbers that he was aware of at the end (as did Captain Holderman). And as far as medical records went, there were so many wounded flowing out of the Charlevaux Ravine, as well as those that were the result of the day's normal action along the front of the 154th Brigade, that no one was asking where on the battlefield a soldier had been hit – or caring, for that matter. The medical personnel were too busy hurrying to take care of everyone to worry about filling out much paperwork in that respect, although there were a few records kept. (These, in the form of a list that is supposed to contain the names of all the men pulled out of the Charlevaux, turned up in the files of the 77th Division some time in the mid 1930's. It is wildly inaccurate however.)

And when the army tried to reconstruct a list of who had been there and who had not, in March and April of 1919, they were forced then to rely largely on the memories of surviving men that had been there, and those left that had rescued them. Officers - in most cases replacements far removed from the event - simply went around the companies involved and asked what and who these men remembered. The results, as might be guessed, were somewhat sporadic and far from precise, yet hardly surprising considering the extreme conditions and pressures under which the men had been during those times. Equally not surprising is that a large number of the replacements that had been killed and wounded in the Pocket were forgotten; men that few had known in the first place, or had had time to get to know under the almost constant combat and atrocious conditions of the week proceeding the event. Still, it was a start.

The list was then published with a disclaimer, stating much of what has just been explained and further stating that of the 194 men who actually walked out of the ravine that afternoon of October 8, even some of those were wounded as well, and that the list was known to be incomplete. The *approximate* 'official' figures given, then ran thus:

Number given as the original force..554
Number of men listed as killed during the action.......................107
Number of men listed as wounded during the action..................190

If one adds up the numbers given of the killed (107), wounded (190) and the number that apparently walked out (194), one only gets 491; a far cry from 554. Additionally, if one actually adds up all the names then given in the book, one arrives at the total of 561, not 554. Then too there was even question as to the actual number of men that had walked into the ravine to begin with. The lowest reported estimates I have found sink to 463, which is ridiculous, as even the army obviously knew at the time that there were at least 550. (Yet this is a number that might only include certain members of the command, while excluding others.) The number however, varies wildly upward from there, but a total that turns up with regularity in AEF files is the number 679, which is the base number that was used to reconstruct the list contained in this book. Yet it appears that that particular number was meant to list only 'combat effectives' and excluded the five medics and three artillerymen there in the Pocket. Therefore, a working total of 687 was settled upon; a number that has been reached.

The time frame used here to set parameters for accuracy is from 7:00 p.m. of October 2, through 7:00 p.m. of October 8. This time frame allows for the inclusion of Lt. Wilhelm and his men of Company E that went out to try and reach Lt. Knight's force back on the other side of Hill 198 on the morning of the 3rd, which is an important group of men usually left off other lists.

Each name on this list has been verified against official records, unit histories and other records in the author's files and then crosschecked for as much accuracy as possible. It was very fashionable in the 1920's and 30's to have been one of the heroes of the Lost Battalion and many men who were not there in the Charlevaux Ravine claimed that they were just for the attention. (As an example, even Al Capone is rumored to have said he received his famous scar as a member of the Lost Battalion!) Family legends also had a tendency to place a relative, who had been in one of the *units* of the Lost Battalion, there in the Charlevaux Ravine - even if the man had been wounded days, weeks, or in one case I found, months, before Whittlesey and his command became trapped. Additionally, not *all* the men from the units listed as being in the Charlevaux Ravine were there, as explained in the text. Take for instance companies A and G, who both left men back along the runner line. The men along that line are not included in the list, nor should they be; only the contingents from those companies that actually toughed it out in the Ravine are.

On the other hand, companies D and F, the bulk of which were left back on the west ridge as a containing force (and virtually destroyed themselves attempting to get Whittlesey out) both had 15 men each in the ravine, as runners and scouts. Many of these men have been left off previous lists as well, as have the great many men that were taken prisoner during the event.

Perhaps no one, not ever Major Whittlesey, could ever say for sure how many walked into that ravine on the afternoon of October 2. Yet what follows may be considered to be the most definitive list to date. Following the Lost Battalion list, is the only complete listing of those men from the 'Lost Platoon' of Company D ever assembled as well. (1, 29, 32, 33, 36, 38, 44, 51, Various 52-86, 87, 96, 101, 105, 108, 109, 115, 116, 118, 130, 131, 133, 134, 135, 136, 137, 138, 139, 142, 143, 144, 147, 148, 149, 150, Various 152-216, Various 218-246, 347, 351, 352, 353, 356, 357, 358, 359, 360, 362)

Key: W=Wounded; K=Killed; POW=Prisoner of War; S=Sickness; W/S=Wounded or Sickness, condition not specified; DOW=Died of Wounds. (Notes: Sickness includes those simply too weak to walk out of the Pocket. Those listed as W/DOW with a date following, died of their wounds after the event.)

The Lost Battalion

Name	Rank	Reg./Bn.	Company	Disp.
Adams, Charles F.	Pvt.	307/3rd	K	W/S
Adams, Charles I.	Pvt.	307/3rd	K	W
Ahlstedt, Rueben H.	PFC	308/2nd	G (2nd Bn. Runner)	W
Albis, Stanislaus	Pvt.	308/1st	B	W
Altiera, Samuel A.	Pvt.	307/3rd	K	W/S
Amatetti, Bart	Pvt.	308/1st	B	W/S
Anastasia, Anthony	Pvt.	308/2nd	F (2nd Bn. Scout)	W
Anderson, Carl A.	Pvt.	307/3rd	K	W/DOW 1/24/19
Anderson, Gus	Pvt.	307/3rd	K	K
Anderson, Herman G.	Sgt.	308/1st	A	W
Anderson, Joseph A.	Pvt.	308/1st	D	W
Andrews, Paul F.	PFC	308/2nd	G	K
Armstrong, William W.	PFC	308/1st	C	W
Arnold, Harold V.	PFC	308/2nd	F (2nd Bn. Scout)	W
Baker, David H.	Pvt.	308/1st	B	W
Baker, Edward	Pvt.	307/3rd	K	W
Bakka, Richard W.	Pvt.	308/2nd	E	K
Baldwin, Frederick W.	Sgt.	308/2nd	E	
Baldwin, Joseph K.	Cpl.	308/1st	C	
Baldwin, Walter J.	Cpl.	308/1st	Hq.1stBn.	
Bang, John	Pvt.	307/3rd	K	K

Baskin, Louis	Pvt.	308/1st	C	S
Becker, Gustav A.	Pvt.	306th M.G. Bn.	C	K
Becker, Martin	Cpl.	306th M.G. Bn.	D	K
Bedrna, William	Pvt.	308/2nd	2nd Bn. Scout	
Beebe, Leonard	Pvt.	307/3rd	K	W
Beeson, Leonard R.	Pvt.	307/3rd	K	W
Begley, William A.	PFC	308/2nd	G	K
Bejnarowicz, Joseph	Cpl.	308/1st	C	
Bell, Morris C.	Pvt.	308/1st	1st Bn. Runner	
Bendheim, Lionel	Sgt.	308/1st	C	W
Benson, Arthur E.	Pvt.	308/1st	C	
Bent, Elmer E.	Pvt.	308/2nd	H	
Benthagen, George M.	Pvt.	308/2nd	G	K
Berg, Louis	Pvt.	307/3rd	K	
Berlev, Floyd	Pvt.	307/3rd	K	W
Beske, Arthur A.	Pvt.	308/1st	B	K
Bickers, Everett	Pvt.	308/1st	C	W
Bickmore, Harold	Pvt.	308/1st	B	
Bivalace, Giovanni	Pvt.	307/3rd	K	W
Blackburn, Raymond	Sgt.	308/1st	C	
Blanchard, Alonzo D.	Cpl.	307/3rd	K	
Bland, Charles J.	Pvt.	308/2nd	E	K
Blevins, George	Pvt.	308/2nd	G	
Blomseth, Ludwig	Pvt.	308/2nd	G	W
Blowers, Bert L.	Pvt.	307/3rd	K	W/DOW 12/18/18
Boden, John	Cpl.	308/2nd	G	K
Bolvig, Eiler V.	Cpl.	308/2nd	H	K
Bonaventura, Pistoria	PFC	308/1st	B	W
Botelle, George W.	Pvt.	308/1st	C (Hq. 1st Bn.)	W
Bowden, John	Pvt.	308/2nd	H	W
Bradford, Robert F.	Cpl.	307/3rd	K	
Bradshaw, Stanley O.	Pvt.	308/1st	B	W
Bragg, James M.	Pvt.	308/Med. Det.	G	W/S
Brennan, George H.	Pvt.	306th M.G. Bn.	D	
Brennan, Harold	Pvt.	308/2nd	E	
Brennen, Thomas J.	Cpl.	308/1st	C	W
Brew, William F.	Pvt.	307/3rd	K	W
Brice, James E.	Pvt.	308/2nd	E (Hq. 2nd Bn.)	W/S
Bringham, Victor L.	Pvt.	307/3rd	K	W
Brinkoma, Ralph	Pvt.	307/3rd	K	W
Brody, Irving	Pvt.	308/1st	B	W
Bronson, Emery	Pvt.	308/1st	B	W
Bronstein, Benjamin	Pvt.	308/2nd	E	POW/DOW
Brown, Clifford R.	Pvt.	308/1st	C	
Brown, Edwin C.	Sgt.	308/2nd	H	W
Brown, Gilbert E.	Pvt.	307/3rd	K	W/DOW 10/15/18
Bruton, James	Pvt.	308/2nd	G	K
Bueskins, Herbert	Pvt.	307/3rd	K	W
Buhler, Frederick	2nd Lt.	308/2nd	G	W
Burns, William C.	Pvt.	308/2nd	H	
Buth, Henry C.	Pvt.	308/2nd	H	K
Cadieux, Henry J.	Pvt.	308/1st	B	W
Caldwell, Louis B.	Pvt.	308/2nd	H	
Callahan, William	Sgt.	308/2nd	E	
Callwell, Samuel H.	Pvt.	308/2nd	H	K
Cappiello, Savino	Pvt.	308/1st	C	W/S

Name	Rank	Unit	Company	Status
Carnebucci, Catino	PFC	308/1st	C	K
Carroll, James B.	1st Sgt.	307/3rd	K	
Cassidy, Henry C.	Pvt.	308/1st	C	W
Castrogiovanne, Samuel	Pvt.	308/1st	C	K
Cathcart, Joseph E.	Pvt.	308/2nd	H	
Cavallo, Thomas	Pvt.	308/2nd	H	K
Cavanaugh, William M.	Pvt.	308/2nd	Hq. 2nd Bn.	W
Cella, Innocenzo	Pvt.	308/1st	A	W/S
Cepeglia, Philip	Pvt.	308/1st	C (Hq. 1st Bn.)	
Chamberlain, James	Cpl.	307/3rd	K	
Chambers, Joseph H.	Pvt.	308/2nd	H	W
Charlesworth, Percy	Pvt.	308/1st	C	W
Chavelle, Charles H.	PFC	308/1st	B	W
Chinn, Henry	Pvt.	308/2nd	H	K
Chiswell, George H.	Pvt.	308/2nd	E	W
Christ, Charles F.	Pvt.	307/3rd	K	
Christensen, Hans W.	Pvt.	307/3rd	K	
Christenson, Phillip	Pvt.	307/3rd	K	W
Christian, Robert E.	Pvt.	308/2nd	H	K
Christopher, Joseph J.	Pvt.	307/3rd	K	W/DOW 10/28/18
Chupp, Ammon	Pvt.	308/2nd	2nd Bn. Runner	W
Church, Roscoe G.	Pvt.	307/3rd	K	K
Clark, Raymond O.	Pvt.	308/2nd	E	K
Clarke, Nathan	Pvt.	306th M.G. Bn.	D	K
Clay, Thomas H.	Pvt.	308/2nd	H	W
Clemons, Melvin E.	Pvt.	308/2nd	G	
Coatney, Arthur F.	Pvt.	308/2nd	H	W
Coe, Richard R.	Pvt.	308/2nd	H	W
Cohen, Morris	Pvt.	306th M.G. Bn.	D	W
Colan, James	Cpl.	308/2nd	G	W
Colasacco, John	Sgt.	308/1st	C	S
Cole, Harvey R.	Pvt.	307/3rd	K	K
Collins, John	Pvt.	308/1st	A	W
Condon, James T.	Pvt.	308/1st	C	W/S
Conneally, John	Pvt.	308/2nd	G	
Connelly, John	Pvt.	308/2nd	E	W
Connelly, Timothy	Pvt.	307/3rd	K	
Conrad, James M.	Pvt.	306th M.G. Bn.	D	W/DOW 10/9/18
Copsey, Albert V.	Cpl.	308/1st	B	
Cornell, Charles B.	Cpl.	308/2nd	H	
Cornell, Henry C.	Pvt.	306th M.G. Bn.	C	W
Covert, Parley J.	Pvt.	308/2nd	E	POW
Crosby, John A.	Pvt.	308/1st	C	W
Crotly, Martin J.	Pvt.	306th M.G. Bn.	D	W
Crouse, William P.	Pvt.	307/3rd	K	K
Cullen, William J.	1st Lt.	308/2nd	H	
Cummings, Roy	Pvt.	308/2nd	H	
Cunningham, Niles F.	Pvt.	308/1st	C	W/S
Curley, Edward T.	Pvt.	308/1st	C	W
Dahlgren, Gust A.	Pvt.	308/2nd	G	W
D'Amato, Patrick	Pvt.	308/1st	C	
Damcott, John F.	PFC	308/1st	C	K
Damon, Harold P.	Pvt.	308/2nd	H	
Daomi, Patrick	Pvt.	308/2nd	E	K
Dayo, Harrison	Pvt.	308/2nd	2nd Bn. Scout	
Deaderick, Osro	Pvt.	308/2nd	G	

Deahan, James A.	Sgt.	307/3rd	K		
Del Sasso, John L.	Pvt.	308/2nd	E		W/DOW 10/20/18
Delgrosso, Frank	PFC	308/2nd	G		W
Delmont, John	Pvt.	308/2nd	H (2nd Bn. Scout)		W/S
Delserone, John	Pvt.	308/2nd	H		W
Demmick, Frank C.	Pvt.	306th M.G. Bn.	D		K
Devanney, Patrick	Pvt.	308/2nd	E		W/DOW 10/11/18
DeWitt, Roy	Pvt.	308/2nd	E		K
Diesel, Louis	PFC	306th M.G. Bn.	D		K
DiGiacomo, Frank	Pvt.	308/2nd	G		W
Dingledine, Elliot N.	Pvt.	306th M.G. Bn.	D		W/DOW 10/9/18
Dodd, Robert	Pvt.	308/2nd	H		W
Doherty, Arthur A.	Cpl.	308/2nd	E (2nd Bn. Runner)		W
Domrose, Walter L.	Pvt.	308/2nd	E		M
Donato, Thomas F.	Pvt.	308/1st	D		
Dorr, Donald E.	Pvt.	308/2nd	H		K
Downs, Lee H.	PFC	308/1st	C		S
Drake, Herbert M.	Pvt.	308/2nd	H		
Duffy, George W.	Cpl.	308/1st	B		W
Dunham, Ralph O.	Pvt.	308/2nd	F (2nd Bn. Runner)		
Dunnigan, Thomas	Pvt.	308/1st	B		
Duryea, Cecil L.	Pvt.	308/2nd	H		W/POW
Dyrdal, Joseph B.	Pvt.	308/1st	B		K
Eager, Sherman W.	2nd Lt.	308/2nd	G		
Edlund, Herman D.	Pvt.	308/2nd	G		
Edwards, Lyle J.	Pvt.	308/2nd	H		
Eggleston, George	Pvt.	306th M.G. Bn.	D		
Eichorn, John	Pvt.	308/2nd	2nd Bn. Runner		W
Eifert, Otto	Pvt.	308/2nd	E		POW
Elkin, Gabriel	Pvt.	308/2nd	H		
Ellbogen, Martin	Pvt.	308/2nd	F (2nd Bn. Scout)		W
Elliott, Frederick	Pvt.	308/2nd	G		W
Engen, Conrad	Pvt.	308/2nd	H		W
Englander, George M.	Bugler	308/2nd	G		W
Erdahl, Olaf	Pvt.	308/2nd	H		
Erickson, Alfred E.	Pvt.	308/2nd	H		W/DOW 10/16/18
Erickson, Arthur	Pvt.	308/2nd	G		
Erickson, Frank G. S.	Pvt.	308/2nd	H		
Erickson, Henry	Pvt.	308/1st	A		W
Esch, Hubert V.	Pvt.	308/1st	C		
Estes, Frank R.	Pvt.	308/2nd	H		
Etenauer, Albert A.	Pvt.	307/3rd	K		W
Evans, Peter	Pvt.	308/2nd	B		W
Evermann, Frederick	Pvt./Signalman	308/1st	B (Hq. 1st Bn.)		
Fairbanks, Truman P.	Pvt.	308/2nd	G		W
Fare, John	Pvt.	307/3rd	K		W
Farncomb, Harvey M.	Pvt.	308/1st	D (1st Bn. Scout)		W
Fassett, Ancel E.	Pvt.	308/2nd	H		K
Feeney, Francis	Pvt.	308/1st	B		
Fein, Arthur E.	Pvt.	307/3rd	K		W
Felton, James P.	Pvt.	307/3rd	K		W
Feuerlicht, Samuel	Pvt.	308/1st	C		K
Fitzgerald, Peter A.	Pvt.	308/2nd	G		W
Flack, Earl A.	Pvt.	308/2nd	H		
Flaming, Henry P.	Pvt.	308/2nd	H		

Flower, Leo A.	Pvt.	306th M.G. Bn.	C		W/S
Flynn, John T.	Pvt.	308/1st	B		W/S
Flynn, Raymond E.	Pvt.	308/2nd	E		S
Fortunato, Joseph C.	Mech.	308/1st	C		
Foss, Sidney J.	Pvt.	307/3rd	K		
Francis, William E.	Pvt.	308/2nd	H		W
Fredette, Frank D.S.	Pvt.	308/2nd	2nd Bn. Runner		
Freeman, Harold	Sgt.	308/2nd		G	W
Friel, Joseph	Pvt.	308/1st	A		K
Frink, Charles W.	Pvt.	308/1st	C		W
Gaedeke, Benjamin F.	1st Bn. Sgt. Mjr.	308/1st	Hq. 1st Bn.		K
Gafanowitz, Robert	PFC	308/2nd		G	W
Gallagher, Dennis A.	Pvt.	308/2nd	G		W
Gallob, Hyman	PFC	308/1st	B		K
Gaupset, Sigaurd	Pvt.	308/2nd	H		W
Gavin, George M.	Pvt.	308/1st	B		K
Geanekos, Angel	Pvt.	308/1st	B		
Gehris, John D.	PFC	308/Med. Det.	G		W
Gibbons, Peter	Pvt.	307/3rd	K		
Gibson, Frederick	Pvt.	308/1st	B		K
Gibson, Herbert B.	Pvt.	308/2nd	H		W
Giefer, Joseph	Pvt.	308/1st	D		W
Giganti, Joseph A.	Pvt.	308/1st	C		S
Gilkey, Ralph	Pvt.	308/1st	Hq. 1st Bn.		W
Gill, Thomas H.	Pvt.	307/3rd	K		
Gillece, Bernard	Cpl.	308/2nd	E (2nd Bn. Scout)		
Gilley, George	Cpl.	307/3rd	K		
Gitchell, Leonard C.	Pvt.	308/2nd	H		K
Gladd, David E.	PFC	308/1st	C		K
Glenn, Leonard N.	Pvt.	308/1st	B		W
Goldberg, Irving R.	Cpl.	308/2nd	E		POW
Goldhorn, Henry W.	Pvt.	308/2nd	H (2nd Bn. Scout)		W/S
Graham, Robert J.	Sgt.	306th M.G. Bn.	D		K
Greally, Michael J.	Sgt.	308/2nd	G		K
Green, Bert M.	Cpl.	307/3rd	K		W/S
Greenfield, Barney	Pvt.	308/1st	B		S
Greenwald, Irving W.	PFC	308/2nd	E (2nd Bn. Scout)		W
Griffin, Maurice V.	1st Lt.	308/2nd	H		W
Griswold, Lester	Pvt.	308/1st	C		W
Gross, Herbert	Pvt.	308/2nd	E (2nd Bn. Runner)		
Grossberg, Percy	Pvt.	308/2nd	G (2nd Bn. Scout)		
Gudis, Peter C.	Cpl.	308/2nd	E		
Habeck, Frank	PFC	308/2nd	E		W
Hagerman, Mark C.	Sgt.	308/2nd	G		
Halligan, William C.	Pvt.	308/1st	B		M
Hamilton, John R.	Pvt.	308/2nd	2nd Bn. Runner		
Hammond, Raymond E.	Pvt.	308/1st	B		
Hanson, Theodore	Pvt.	308/2nd	H		K
Hanson, Walter	Pvt.	308/1st	B		
Harkleroad, Lee C.	Pvt.	306th M.G. Bn.	C		W
Harlin, Albert D.	Pvt.	308/1st	D (Hq. 1st Bn.)		
Harrington, Victor A.	2nd Lt.	308/2nd	E		W/POW
Harris, Thomas	Pvt.	308/1st	B		
Hatch, Boyd S.	Cpl.	307/3rd	K		

Hatcher, Otto R.	Pvt.	308/1st	C	
Hauck, George E.	Sgt.	306th M.G. Bn.	D	
Havens, George E.	PFC	308/2nd	E	K
Hazen, Louis N.	Pvt.	308/1st	C	W
Healey, Jeremiah	Sgt.	308/2nd	G	W
Hearty, James B.	Pvt.	308/1st	B	W
Hecker, Arthur J.	Pvt.	308/2nd	H	
Held, Jacob	Cpl.	308/1st	C	
Hendrickson, Alfred	Pvt.	307/3rd	K	W/DOW 10/19/18
Hepworth, Clyde	Pvt.	308/2nd	H	S
Hermsdorf, Harold J.	Sgt.	308/1st	B	
Heuer, Joseph P.	Sgt.	307/3rd	K	
Hicks, Arthur	Pvt.	307/3rd	K	W
Hicks, Stacy M.	Pvt.	308/1st	C	
Hiduck, Anthony	Pvt.	308/1st	A	W
Hildebrand, Carl	Pvt.	308/1st	B	K
Hinchman, John A.	Cpl.	308/1st	C	K
Hintz, Clyde A.	Pvt.	308/1st	B	
Hission, William	Pvt.	308/1st	C	
Hoadley, George	Pvt.	307/3rd	K	
Hoff, Henry	Pvt.	308th/1st	D	
Hofstetter, Benjamin J.	Pvt.	308/2nd	H	K
Hogue, Frank D.	Pvt.	307/3rd	K	W
Holbert, Edward	Pvt.	308/2nd	H	
Holden, Wyatt L.	Pvt.	308/1st	C	
Holderman, Nelson M.	Capt.	307/3rd	K	W
Holen, George G.	Pvt.	308/1st	D	
Holliday, William M.	Pvt.	308/1st	B	K
Hollingshead, Lowell R.	Pvt.	308/2nd	H	W/POW
Holt, James M.	Pvt.	306th M.G. Bn.	D	
Holt, John	Pvt.	308/1st	B	W/DOW 10/13/18
Holzer, William	Pvt.	308/2nd	G	W
Honas, Stephan M.	Pvt.	308/1st	B	W
Hoven, Sylvester	Pvt.	308/1st	B	K
Hudlow, Rubin	Pvt.	308/1st	A	W
Huff, George	Pvt.	307/3rd	K	
Huntington, Loyd A.	Pvt.	308/2nd	H	W
Hurd, Irwin C.	Pvt.	308/2nd	E	K
Hutt, Thomas	Pvt.	308/2nd	E	POW
Hyde, Richard W.	Pvt.	308/2nd	H	K
Ilardo, James P.	Pvt.	308/1st	Hq. 1st Bn.	W/POW
Iltz, Henry	Pvt.	306th M.G. Bn.	C	W/S
Indiana, Dominick	Pvt.	308/1st	C	
Ingraham, Theodore	Pvt.	308/2nd	F (2nd Bn. Scout)	
Iraci, Alfio	Pvt.	308/2nd	E	K
Irwin, James	Pvt.	308/1st	B	
Jacob, William	Sgt.	308/1st	C	
Jacobson, Charles	Pvt.	308/2nd	E	
Jacoby, Leo J.	Pvt.	308/1st	C	
Jammaron, Victor	Pvt.	308/3rd	I (att: Hq. 1st Bn.)	W
Jeffries, Charles B.	Pvt.	305th F.A.	Batt. D	M
Jepson, Earl F.	Pvt.	308/1st	B	K
John, Ralph E.	Pvt.	308/1st	A	
Johnson, Charles J.	Pvt.	307/3rd	K	K
Johnson, Edward	Pvt.	308/2nd	G	K
Johnson, Frank L.	Pvt.	308/1st	D (1st Bn. Runner)	K

Johnson, Louis N.	PFC	306th M.G. Bn.	C	W/DOW 10/12/18
Johnson, Maurice E.	Sgt.	306th M.G. Bn.	D	
Johnson, Raymond	Pvt.	308/1st	C	W
Johnson, William F.	Pvt.	307/3rd	K	W
Johnson, William J.	Pvt.	308/1st	A	K
Jolly, Samuel	Pvt.	308/2nd	H	K
Jones, Arthur H.	PFC	308/1st	B	M
Jones, David O.	Pvt.	307/3rd	K	W
Jorgenson, Arthur F.	Pvt.	308/2nd	F (2nd Bn. Scout)	
Jorgenson, Eric F.	Pvt.	308/1st	A	K
Jorgenson, Herbert	Pvt.	308/2nd	G (2nd Bn. Scout)	W
Joyce, Joseph	Pvt.	308/2nd	H	W
Judd, Roland P.	Pvt.	308/1st	A	K
Kaempfer, Albert O.	Pvt.	307/3rd	K	W
Kandel, Benjamin	Pvt.	308/2nd	E	K
Kaplan, Harold	1st Sgt.	308/2nd	E	W/POW
Karaluinas, John	Pvt.	307/3rd	K	W
Karpinsky, Frank	Pvt.	308/1st	B	W
Kaspirovitch, Jacob	Pvt.	308/2nd	E	W
Kaufman, Emil	Pvt.	308/1st	C	
Keegan, James A.	Pvt.	308/1st	B	S
Keenan, Joseph C.	Cpl.	306th M.G. Bn.	D	
Keeney, Jesse	Pvt.	306th M.G. Bn.	C	
Keim, George	Pvt.	308/1st	C	
Kellog, Ernest	Pvt.	308/2nd	E	K
Kelly, Joseph D.	Pvt.	306th M.G. Bn.	D	W
Kelly, Michael	Pvt.	308/2nd	E (2nd Bn. Scout)	
Kelmel, William	Pvt.	307/3rd	K	
Kennedy, Edward A.	Pvt.	306th M.G. Bn.	D	W
Kennedy, Frank	Pvt.	308/1st	D	W
Kennedy, Joseph C.	Cpl.	308/2nd	G	
Kiernan, Joseph	Pvt.	308/2nd	E (2nd Bn. Scout)	W/S
King, Joseph R.	Pvt.	308/1st	C	W
Kirchner, Gerard	Sgt.	308/2nd	H (Hq. 2nd Bn.)	
Klein, Irving	Cpl.	308/1st	A	W
Knabe, William H.	PFC	307/3rd	K	W
Knapp, John	Pvt.	308/2nd	E	K
Knauss, Daniel M.	Pvt.	308/2nd	H	
Knettel, John J.	Pvt.	307/3rd	K	
Knifsund, Otto M.	Pvt.	308/1st	C	
Knott, Carlton V.	Pvt.	308/1st	B	K
Koebler, George	PFC	308/2nd	H (2nd Bn. Scout)	K
Koernig, George C.	Pvt.	308/2nd	H	K
Kolbe, Charles A.	Pvt.	306th M.G. Bn.	C	W
Kornelly, Phillip	PFC	308/1st	B	W
Kostinen, Frank J.	Pvt.	308/1st	C	
Kozikowski, Stanislaw	Pvt.	308/1st	C	
Krantz, Walter J.	Pvt.	308/1st	C	
Krogh, Magnus B.	Pvt.	308/1st	B	W
Kronenberg, Max	Pvt.	308/2nd	E	POW
Krotoschinsky, Abraham	Pvt.	307/3rd	K	
Kurtz, Nicholas	Pvt.	308/2nd	H	W
Landers, Patrick J.	Sgt.	308/2nd	H	
Langer, Julius	Pvt.	308/2nd	H	
Larkin, Archibald F.	Pvt.	308/1st	C	

Name	Rank	Unit	Company	Status
Larney, James F.	Pvt./Signalman	308/1st	Hq. 1st Bn.	W
Larson, Erik	Pvt.	308/1st	C	
LaSalle, Erhart	Pvt.	307/3rd	K	
Lauder, Frank N.	Pvt.	308/1st	C	
Layman, Raymond E.	Pvt.	308/2nd	G	
Leak, James V.	1st Lt.	308/2nd	E	W/POW
Lee, Bernard J.	Pvt.	308/1st	C	K
Leflaer, Len L.	Pvt.	308/2nd	H	
Lehmeier, Joseph	Pvt.	307/3rd	K	W
Lekan, Michael	Wagoner	307/3rd	K	K
LeMay, Adlare J.	Pvt.	308/1st	D (1st Bn. Runner)	W/POW
Leonard, William J.	Bugler	308/2nd	H	
Lesley, James E.	Pvt.	308/2nd	H	
Lesnick, Maxwell	Pvt.	308/1st	C	W
Levine, Joseph	Pvt.	308/2nd	E (2nd Bn. Scout)	
Lightfoot, Roy H.	Pvt.	308/2nd	H	
Liner, Irving L.	Pvt.	308/1st	D (1st Bn. Runner)	
Lipacher, Isaac	Pvt.	307/3rd	K	W
Lipasti, Frank	Pvt.	307/3rd	K	K
Little, Robert G.	Pvt.	308/2nd	H	K
Loendorf, Jacob	Pvt.	308/1st	C	W
Loering, George C.	Pvt.	308/2nd	F (2nd Bn. Runner)	
Lokken, Martin O.	Pvt.	308/1st	B	
Lonergan, James E.	Pvt.	306th M.G. Bn.	D	W
Long, Marvin E.	Pvt.	308/1st	B	K
Long, Patrick	Pvt.	307/3rd	K	
Looker, Arthur R.	Pvt.	308/2nd	B	W
Looslie, Daniel H.	Pvt.	308/1st	B	K
Lovell, Arthur, R.	Pvt.	308/2nd	G	
Lowman, Cecil O.	Pvt.	308/1st	C	
Luckett, Henry C.	Pvt.	308/2nd	H	K
Lucy, William J.	Pvt.	308/2nd	H	
Lukas, Michael J.	Pvt.	308/2nd	E (2nd Bn. Runner)	
Lund, Engval	Pvt.	308/2nd	F (2nd Bn. Runner)	W/S
Lynch, James A.	Pvt.	308/2nd	H	K
Lyons, Frank John	Pvt.	307/3rd	K	W
Lyons, Thomas J.	Pvt.	308/2nd	H	K
Lysen, Chester	Pvt.	308/1st	C	W
Macali, Joseph	Pvt.	308/1st	B	W
Mace, Daniel B.	Pvt.	308/1st	B	W
Magnusson, David	PFC	308/2nd	F (2nd Bn. Scout)	W
Mahony, Marion E.	Pvt.	308/1st	B	
Main, Frederick T.	Sgt.	308/1st	C	
Mandell, Frederick A.	Pvt.	308/1st	C	W
Mann, Sydney C.	Pvt.	308/2nd	H	S
Mannion, Thomas J.	Pvt.	307/3rd	K	W/S
Manson, Robert	Pvt.	308/1st	B (Hq. 1st Bn.)	W
Marchelewski, Stephan	Pvt.	308/1st	C	
Marcus, Samuel	Sgt.	308/1st	B	S
Marcy, Leon W.	Cpl.	306th M.G. Bn.	D	K
Mares, Rito	Pvt.	308/2nd	G	
Marion, Roy L.	Pvt.	308/1st	C	W
Marshallcowitz, Saul	Pvt.	308/Med. Det.	H	W/POW
Martin, Albert E.	Pvt.	307/3rd	K	W
Martin, Wayne W.	Pvt.	308/1st	A	

Martin, William H.	Pvt.	308/2nd	G	W/DOW 10/24/18
Martinez, Frank	Pvt.	308/2nd	G	K
Materna, Joseph	Pvt.	307/3rd	K	W
Mathews, Andrew	Pvt.	308/2nd	H	
Mathews, Richard W.	Cpl.	308/1st	B	W/S
Mauro, Frank	Pvt.	308/2nd	H	W
Mayhew, George	Pvt.	308/1st	C	
McCabe, John	Pvt.	308/1st	C	
McCallion, John J.	Pvt.	308/2nd	E (2nd Bn. Runner)	
McCauley, Jesse J.	Pvt.	308/2nd	G	
McCoy, Bert C.	Pvt.	308/1st	A	W
McDade, Daniel S.	Pvt.	308/1st	Hq.1stBn.	K
McElroy, Joseph A.	Pvt.	306th M.G. Bn.	C	W
McFeron, Olin	Pvt.	308/1st	C	
McGowen, Joseph L.	Pvt.	308/1st	C	
McGrath, Eugene M.	Pvt.	308/1st	C	M
McMahon, Martin	Cpl.	308/1st	B	W
McMullin, William	Pvt.	308/2nd	E	POW
McMurtry, George G.	Capt.	308/2nd	2ndBn.Cmdr	W
McNearney, John A.	Pvt.	308/2nd	H	
Mead, Joseph P.	Pvt.	308/1st	C	K
Mears, Robert L.	Pvt.	308/1st	C	
Medboe, Joseph	Pvt.	308/1st	B	W
Medesker, Peter L.	Pvt.	308/1st	D (1st Bn. Runner)	K
Mele, Michael	Pvt.	308/2nd	G	W
Meltam, Nicholas B.	Pvt.	308/1st	A	W/S
Melvin, Harold J.	Pvt.	308/2nd	F (2nd Bn. Scout)	
Mendenhall, Jesse J.	Pvt.	308/2nd	H	K
Merry, Earnest S.	Cpl.	308/2nd	E	W
Meyerowitz, Tobias	Pvt.	307/3rd	K	
Meyers, Charles	Pvt.	308/1st	B	W
Mikulewicz, F.M.	Pvt.	308/3rd	I (att: Hq. 2nd Bn.)	
Miller, Fernnau	Pvt.	308/2nd	H	
Miller, Henry	Mech.	308/2nd	H	K
Miller, Henry I.	Pvt.	308/2nd	E	M
Miller, Nathaniel	Pvt.	308/2nd	G	W
Miney, Patrick	Pvt.	308/2nd	E	W
Monan, Robert F.	Pvt.	307/3rd	K	
Monk, William	Pvt.	308/1st	C	W
Mooney, James E.	Pvt.	308/1st	D (1st Bn. Runner)	
Morem, Arnold M.	Pvt.	308/2nd	E	W
Morris, Albert	Pvt.	308/1st	C	
Morris, Louis	PFC	308/1st	B	W
Morrow, Bert B.	Sgt.	308/1st	C	W/S
Munson, Gustave	Pvt.	308/2nd	H	W
Murphy, James J.	Sgt.	307/3rd	K	W
Murphy, John	Pvt.	308/1st	C	
Murray, Frederick	Pvt.	308/2nd	F (2nd Bn. Runner)	W
Murray, Kenneth	Pvt.	307/3rd	K	
Murray, Thomas	Pvt.	307/3rd	K	W
Mynard, Edwin S.	Sgt.	306th M.G. Bn.	D	
Nauheim, Alfred P.	Cpl.	308/1st	A	W
Nell, John W.	Pvt.	308/2nd	G	
Nelson, Arthur G.	Pvt.	308/2nd	H (2nd Bn. Scout)	W
Nelson, Olaf	Cpl.	308/2nd	H	S
Neptune, Harold B.	Pvt.	308/2nd	H	W

Name	Rank	Unit	Co./Notes	Status
Newcom, George H.	Pvt.	308/2nd	G	W
Nies, George W.	Pvt.	308/2nd	H	K
Noon, Alfred R.	2nd Lt.	306th M.G. Bn.	C	K
Norton, Grant S.	PFC	308/1st	B	M
Novotny, Otto	Pvt.	308/2nd	F (2nd Bn. Runner)	
O'Connell, John	Pvt.	308/2nd	E	POW
O'Brien, Lewis	Pvt.	308/1st	C	
O'Connell, James P.	Cpl.	306th M.G. Bn.	D	
O'Conner, Patrick J.	Pvt.	308/2nd	G	K
Officer, Arthur E.	Pvt.	308/2nd	H	
Ofstad, Gile	Pvt.	307/3rd	K	W
O'Keefe, John	Pvt.	308/2nd	E (2nd Bn. Scout)	W
O'Keefe, Thomas C.	Bugler	306th M.G. Bn.	D	K
Oliver, Walter T.	Pvt.	306th M.G. Bn.	D	W
Olson, Frederick	Pvt.	308/1st	C	
Olson, Lars	Pvt.	308/1st	C	
Olstren, Andrew	Pvt.	307/3rd	K	
Orlando, Angel	Pvt.	308/2nd	H	W
Osborne, Lawrence M.	Sup.Sgt.	308/1st	B	M
Ostrovsky, Isadore	Pvt.	308/2nd	H	
Oxman, Charles	Pvt.	308/1st	C	
Pagliaro, Benjamin	Pvt.	308/2nd	G	S
Pardue, Robert M.	Pvt.	308/2nd	E	W
Parker, George W.	Pvt.	306th M.G. Bn.	C	W
Patterson, Clarence	Pvt.	308/2nd	2nd Bn. Runner	
Payne, Andrew G.	Pvt.	308/1st	C	W
Peabody, Marshall G.	2nd Lt.	306th M.G. Bn.	D	K
Pennington, Joseph R.	Pvt.	308/2nd	E	W
Perea, Enrique	Pvt.	308/2nd	H	
Perrigo, Myron D.	Pvt.	308/2nd	G	W
Pesetti, Salvatore	Pvt.	307/3rd	K	
Peters, Clarence	Pvt.	308/1st	B	W
Peterson, Emil A.	Pvt.	308/2nd	H	W/POW
Peterson, Holgar	Cpl.	308/2nd	G	K
Peterson, Walter S.	Pvt.	308/1st	B	W
Peterson. William L.	Pvt.	308/2nd	E	K
Petti, Alfred J.	Pvt.	308/2nd	H (2nd Bn. Scout)	
Phelps, Harold L.	Pvt.	308/1st	C	K
Phelps, Jacob C.	Pvt.	307/3rd	K	W
Phillips, Henry	Pvt.	308/3rd	E	POW
Pierson, John L.	Pvt.	307/3rd	K	W
Pinkstone, Charles W.	Cpl.	308/1st	C	W
Pollinger, Frank J.	Pvt.	308/2nd	G	W
Pomeroy, Lawrence	Pvt.	308/1st	B	
Pool, Thomas G.	1st Lt.	307/3rd	K	W
Pope, Calgere	Pvt.	307/3rd	K	
Potter, Oscar	Pvt.	308/2nd	G	S
Pou, Robert E.	Pvt.	308/2nd	E	
Powell, Josephus	Pvt.	308/2nd	H	W
Powers, William J.	Pvt./Sign alman	308/2nd	Hq. 2nd Bn.	
Probst, Louis M.	Mech.	308/2nd	E (2nd Bn. Scout)	W/S
Prusek, Joseph	Pvt.	307/3rd	K	
Pugh, Charles J.	Pvt.	308/2nd	E (2nd Bn. Runner)	
Puniskis, Joseph H.	Pvt.	308/1st	C	
Raidant, Silas L.	Pvt.	308/2nd	G	W

Name	Rank	Unit	Company	Status
Rainwater, Carl A.	Pvt.	308/1st	G	
Rainwater, James B.	Pvt.	308/1st	D (1st Bn. Scout)	K
Rangitsch, Jacob	Pvt.	308/2nd	E	
Rank. Lloyd	Pvt.	3081st	B	
Ratonda, Herman E.	Pvt.	308/1st	D (1st Bn. Scout)	W
Ratto, Vito	Pvt.	308/2nd	E	
Rauchle, Frank	Cpl.	306th M.G. Bn.	C	W/S
Ray, Guy W.	Pvt.	308th/1st	C	
Raygor, Earnest E.	Pvt.	308/2nd	E	K
Rayony, Spiro	Pvt.	308/2nd	2nd Bn. Runner	
Rayson, Homer	Pvt.	308/2nd	2nd Bn. Scout	W/DOW 10/19/18
Recko, Jack	Pvt.	308/2nd	H	W/POW
Rector, Frank C.	Cpl.	306th M.G. Bn.	D	
Regan, William	Pvt.	308/2nd	G	
Reid, Lauren G.	Pvt.	308/2nd	G	K
Reiger, John	Pvt.	308/1st	B	W
Renda, John	Pvt.	308/2nd	H	W
Revnes, Maurice P.	2nd Lt.	306th M.G. Bn.	D	W
Reynolds, John	PFC.	308/1st	C	K
Rhoads, Solomon E.	Pvt.	308/2nd	H	
Rice, Chauncey I.	Cpl.	306th M.G. Bn.	D	
Richards, Omer	Pvt.	308/1st	Hq. 1st Bn.	
Richardson,	Pvt.	306th M.G. Bn.	C	
Richter, Morris	Pvt.	308/1st	C	W/S
Ridlon, Earnest J.	Pvt.	308/2nd	G	W
Rissi, Bernard	PFC	308/2nd	G	K
Ritter, Charles	Pvt.	308/2nd	H	W
Roberts, Benjamin	PFC	307/3rd	K	W
Robertson, Arch	Pvt.	308/2nd	H	
Rochester, Nathaniel N.	PFC	308/2nd	E	K
Rodriquez, Alfred	Pvt.	308/2nd	2nd Bn. Scout	
Roesch, Clarence R.	2nd Bn. Sgt. Mjr.	308/2nd	Hq. 2nd Bn.	
Rogers, Harold M.	2nd Lt.	308/1st	B	W/DOW 10/9/18
Ronan, Maurice H.	Pvt.	306th M.G. Bn.	C	
Rosby, Thornweld	Pvt.	307/3rd	K	W
Rose, Sidney	Pvt.	308/2nd	E	W
Rosenberg, Samuel	PFC	308/2nd	H	W/DOW 10/12/18
Ross, Albert A.	Pvt.	308/2nd	G	K
Rossum, Haakon A.	Cpl.	308/2nd	G	W
Royall, Joseph	Pvt.	308/2nd	H	
Rudolph, Aloysius J.	Pvt.	308/2nd	E	K
Rugg, Hiram M.	Pvt.	308/2nd	H	W
Rumsey, Wilbert F.	Pvt.	307/3rd	K	K
Ruppe, John	Pvt.	308/2nd	H (2nd Bn. Scout)	K
Ryan John F.	Cpl.	306th M.G. Bn.	D	K
Sackman, Julius	Sgt.	306th M.G. Bn.	D	W
Sadler, Thomas G.	Pvt.	305th F.A.	Batt. D	W
Sands, Lester T.	Pvt.	308/2nd	H (2nd Bn. Scout)	
Santillo, Anthony	Pvt.	306th M.G. Bn.	D	K
Santini, Guiseppe	Pvt.	308/2nd	G	
Scanlon, John H.	Pvt.	306th M.G. Bn.	D	W
Schaffer, Harold L.	Cpl.	308/2nd	H	W
Schanz, Joseph A.	Pvt.	308/2nd	G	
Schenck, Gordon Lockwood	2nd Lt.	308/1st	C	K

Schettino, Lememe	Pvt.	307/3rd	K	
Schmidt, John H.	Mech.	308/2nd	G	W
Schmitz, Joseph J.	PFC	306th M.G. Bn.	D	W
Schultz, Otto J.	Pvt.	308/2nd	E	W/DOW 11/7/18
Schultz, William	Pvt.	308/2nd	G	
Schwartz, Paul A.	Cpl.	307/3rd	K	W/S
Scialdono, Guiseppe	Pvt.	307/3rd	K	W
Segal, Paul	Pvt.	308/1st	B	
Selg, Eugene	Pvt.	308/2nd	G	
Semenuk, Harold	Pvt.	308/1st	C	
Senter, Henry H.	Pvt.	308/2nd	H	W
Shaffer, Harold L.	Cpl.	308/2nd	H	W
Shea, James E.	PFC	308/2nd	H	K
Shepard, Arthur H.	Pvt.	308/1st	B	W
Sica, Rocco	Pvt.	308/2nd	E	K
Simonson, Alfred	Pvt.	308/1st	C	W
Sims, George P.	Cpl.	307/3rd	K	
Sirota, Irving	Pvt.	308/Med. Det.	D	S
Sketson, Orlander	Pvt.	308/1st	B	K
Slingerland, James E.	Pvt.	308/2nd	G	
Smith, Sidney	Pvt.	308/2nd	H	W
Sobaszkiewicz, Stanley	Pvt.	308/2nd	H	W
Solomon, Arthur	Pvt.	308/2nd	F (2nd Bn. Scout)	
Spallina, Joseph	Pvt.	307/3rd	K	W
Speich, George F.	Cpl.	307/3rd	K	W
Speigel, Isidore	Pvt.	308/2nd	H	
St.Cartier, Lucien	PFC	308/1st	C	K
Stamboni, Joseph	Pvt.	306th M.G. Bn.	D	W
Stanfield, John A.	Pvt.	308/2nd	H	
Steichen, Albert N.	Pvt.	308/2nd	H	S
Stenger, William	Pvt.	308/2nd	H	
Stingle, Frank	Pvt.	307/3rd	K	W
Stoianoff, Blaze	Pvt.	308/2nd	H	
Strickland, James R.	Pvt.	308/2nd	H	W
Stringer, Edward	Pvt.	308/2nd	E (2nd Bn. Runner)	W
Stromee, Leo A.	Capt.	308/1st	C	W
Stumbo, Leroy A.	Pvt.	307/3rd	K	W
Sugro, Benedetto	Pvt.	308/1st	C	
Sullivan, Jerry	Pvt.	308/2nd	E	POW
Summers, Alfred E.	Pvt.	308/2nd	G (2nd Bn. Scout)	
Sundby, Melvin G.	Pvt.	308/2nd	H	W/DOW 10/15/18
Swanbeck, Arthur	Pvt.	307/3rd	K	W
Swanson, Edward	Pvt.	308/2nd	H	
Swanson, Olaf W.	Pvt.	308/2nd	E	K
Swanson, Sigurd V.	Pvt.	308/1st	B	W/S
Swartz, John B.	Pvt.	308/2nd	H	W
Sweeney, Bernard J.	Pvt.	306th M.G. Bn.	D	W
Swenson, Oscar A.	Pvt.	308/2nd	G	K
Taasaas, Andrew J.	Pvt.	308/2nd	H	
Talbot, William R.	Pvt.	308/2nd	E	K
Tallon, Daniel B.	Cpl/2nd Bn. Clk.	308/2nd	E (Hq. 2nd Bn.)	W/DOW 10/9/18
Teichmoeller, John G.	1st Lt.	305th F.A.	Batt. D	W
Test, Pietro	Pvt.	307/3rd	K	W
Thatcher, Lee C.	Pvt.	308/1st	B (1st Bn. Runner)	
Thomas, Clifford	Pvt.	307/3rd	K	W

Thomas, Harold H.	Pvt.	308/2nd	H	M
Thompson, Arthur A.	Cpl.	306th M.G. Bn.	D	W
Thorbone, Roland	Pvt.	308/1st	B	
Thorsen, Harold	Pvt.	308/2nd	G (2nd Bn. Runner)	W
Tiederman, Herbert	Pvt.	308/2nd	Hq. 2nd Bn.	
Todisco, Amos	1st Sgt.	308/2nd	G	W
Tollefson, Theodore	Pvt.	308/2nd	Hq. 2nd Bn.	K
Tolley, Courtney W.	Pvt.	306th M.G. Bn.	D	
Torpey, Leslie C.	Pvt.	306th M.G. Bn.	D	
Trainor, Leo W.	2nd Lt.	308/1st	C	W
Travers, John H.	Pvt.	306th M.G. Bn.	D	W/DOW 10/17/18
Treadwell, Raymond	Pvt.	307/3rd	K	W/S
Trekan, Anton	PFC	308/1st	C	K
Trigani, Antonio	Pvt.	308/2nd	G	
Tronson, Melvin C.	Pvt.	308/2nd	E	POW
Tucker, Jack	Cpl.	308/1st	C	
Tuite, Martin F.	Sgt.	308/1st	C	
Tulchin, David	Pvt.	308/1st	C (Hq. 1st Bn.)	
Tumm, Charles G.	Cpl.	308/2nd	H	K
Turnquist, Benjamin E.	Pvt.	307/3rd	K	
Underhill, Lester	Mech.	308/2nd	K	
Untereiner, Hugo E.	Pvt.	308/2nd	H	
Van Fleet, Albert V.	Pvt.	308/1st	A	K
Vitkus, Joseph	Pvt.	308/2nd	E	
Vittulli, Constantine	Pvt.	308/1st	C	W
Voelker, Alphonsus F.	Cpl.	308/1st	C	W
Volz, Otto M.	Pvt.	307/3rd	K	W
Voorheis, John L.	Pvt.	308/1st	C	W/S
Wade, Farland F.	Pvt.	308/2nd	G (2nd Bn. Scout)	W
Walker, George	PFC	308/Med. Det.	G	W
Wallen, Oscar	Pvt.	308/2nd	G	W
Wallenstein, Charles	Pvt.	308/1st	C	W/S
Weaver, Glenn H.	Pvt.	308/2nd	G	W
Weiner, Walter	Pvt.	308/2nd	2nd Bn. Scout	
Weinhold, Frederick	Pvt.	308/2nd	E	POW
Weinmann, George J.	Pvt.	308/2nd	F	W
Wenzel, Edward L.	Pvt.	308/2nd	H (2nd Bn. Scout)	POW
Wheeler, Otto	Pvt.	308/2nd	H	K
White, Peter H.	Pvt.	308/2nd	F (2nd Bn. Runner)	
White, Scott R.	Pvt.	308/2nd	H	S
Whiting, Wilbur C.	Cpl.	308/2nd	H	
Whittlesey, Charles W.	Major	308/1st	1st Bn. Cmdr	
Wilber, Frederick L.	PFC	308/2nd	G	W
Wilhelm, Karl E.	1st Lt.	308/2nd	E	W
Williamson, Henry J.	2nd Lt.	308/1st	A	W
Willinger, Isadore	Pvt.	307/3rd	K	POW
Willis, Oscar	Pvt.	308/2nd	H	W
Witschen, Vincent	Pvt.	307/3rd	K	
Witthaus, Albert R.	Pvt.	308/2nd	H	W
Wolf, Samuel	Pvt.	308/1st	B	
Wolfe, Earl I.	Pvt.	308/1st	C	
Wondowlesky, Stephen	Pvt.	308/1st	A	
Woods, James R.	Pvt.	308/2nd	G	
Workman, William J.	Pvt.	308/2nd	H	K
Wornek, Ernest	Pvt.	308/2nd	G	W
Wright, William J.	Pvt.	306th M.G. Bn.	D	

Yoder, Robert	Pvt.	308/2nd	E	W
Zeman, Louis	Pvt.	308/2nd	H	K
Ziegenbalg, William	Pvt.	308/1st	B	

The total number listed as killed during the episode comes to 118, while the total number listed as wounded equals 252. Additionally, there are also 9 men listed as missing, 24 that were taken prisoner, 16 evacuated as sick and 25 evacuated for an undetermined malady. Added up then, this gives a total number of casualties of 444, or a casualty rate of just about 65 percent, against a total strength of 687. Yet this does not reflect those losses due to hunger, general weakness and the process of 'weeding out' that the three remaining officers went through just before the march out from the Charlevaux Ravine. These further detracted from Whittlesey's remaining force, and figuring again from an original strength of 687, less the 194 that walked out of the ravine, we then get a loss total of 493. This then gives an aggregate loss of 72 percent, or in other words, 2 out of 3 men became a casualty of some kind during the five days of the siege...

Below are the names of the men from the 'Lost Platoon' of Company D/308th, under Lt. Charles Turner, that was almost completely wiped out, along with the names of the four lone survivors that managed to make it back to the 308th's lines during the night.

Arrigo, Ciro	Pvt.	308/1st	D	K
Brenner, Louis	Pvt.	308/1st	D	K
Eckersley, Frank M.	Pvt.	308/1st	D	K
Fellito, Carmine	Cpl.	308/1st	D	Escaped
Fetting, Arthur H.	Pvt.	308/1st	D	Escaped
Hawkins, Earl W.	Pvt.	308/1st	D	Escaped W
Holcomb, Everett M	Pvt.	308/1st	D	Escaped
Lundquist, August W.	Pvt.	308/1st	D	K
Mainwaring, William	Pvt.	308/1st	D	K
Matejcek, Hugo W.	Pvt.	308/1st	D	K
McLauchlin, Charles A.	Pvt.	308/1st	D	K
Miller, Elmer	Pvt.	308/1st	D	K
Morehouse, Walter E.	Pvt.	308/1st	D	K
Turner, Charles W.	1st. Lt.	308/1st	D	K
Zapke, William	Pvt.	308/1st	D	K

On top of these men listed above, scores of others were involved in the battles fought to get through to Whittlesey, perpetrating further brave acts along side Lt. Turner's men; far too many, in fact, to all be included here or for their full stories to be told in the main text. Nevertheless, let the names of *all* those above - Lost Battalion or not - stand in representation of those many others who gave so much in the mud of that foreign forest so long ago, and let their deeds be never forgotten.

They truly were heroes, one and all.

Appendix: B
Bibliography
And Other
Consulted Sources

General Books:

1. 71st Congress, 2nd Session. *List of Mothers and Widows of American Soldiers, Sailors and Marines Entitled to Make a Pilgrimage to the War Cemeteries in Europe* - United States Government Printing Office, Washington D.C. 1930
2. Alexander, Robert *Memories of the World War* - The MacMillan Company, New York. 1931
3. American Battle Monuments Commission. *A Guide to the American Battle Fields in Europe* - United States Government Printing Office, Washington D.C. 1927
4. Berry, Henry *Make the Kaiser Dance* - Doubleday & Co., Garden City, New York. 1978
5. Braim, Paul F. *The Test of Battle* - White Mane Books, Shippensburg, PA. 1987
6. Capart, G.P. *A Blue Devil of France* - W.J. Watt & Co., New York. 1918
7. Clifford, John G. *The Citizen Soldiers: The Plattsburg Training Camp Movement 1913-1920* - The University Press of Kentucky, Lexington. KY. 1972
8. Coffman, Edward M. *The War to End All Wars* - Oxford University Press, New York. 1968
9. Comite Commemoratif De l'Argonne. *La Guerre en Argonne 1914-1918, Fascicule No. 4* - C.C.P., Paris. April 1974
10. Comite Commemoratif De l'Argonne. *La Guerre en Argonne 1914-1918, Fascicule No. 9* - C.C.P., Paris. June 1975
11. Conroy, J.W. *Landing Force Manual* - The United States Naval Institute, Annapolis, MD. 1918
12. Cooke, Donald E. *For Conspicuous Gallantry: Winners of the Medal of Honor* - C.S. Hammond & Co., Maplewood, NJ. 1966
13. Cothren, Marion B. *Cher Ami: The Story of a Carrier Pigeon* - Little, Brown, and Co., Boston, MA. 1934
14. Crozier, Emmett *American Reporters on the Western Front 1917-1918* - Oxford University Press, New York. 1959
15. Durkota, Alan E. *Medal of Honor Aviators of World War One: Volume 1* - Flying Machine Press, Stratford, CT. 1998
16. Eisenhower, John S.D. *Yanks* - The Free Press, New York. 2001
17. Eisenstein, Douglas R. *Whispers in the Wind* - Xlibris Corp., Xlibris.com 2001
18. Ellis, John *Eye Deep in Hell* - Pantheon Books, New York. 1976
19. Ellis, O.O. and Garey, E.B. *The Plattsburg Manual: A Handbook for Military Training* - The Century Co., New York. 1917
20. Freidel, Frank. *Over There* - Little, Brown, and Co., New York. 1964
21. Gilder, John Franklin, Editor. *Americans Defending Democracy* - World's War Stories Inc., New York, 1919
22. Gregory, Barry *Argonne: 1918* - Ballantine Books Inc., New York. 1972
23. Hallas, James H. *Squandered Victory* - Praeger Publishers, Westport, CN. 1995
24. Harbord, James G. *The American Army in France 1917-1919* - Little, Brown and Co., Boston, MA. 1936
25. Hartwell, E.C. *Story Time Readings – Eighth Year* - American Book Company, New York, 1921

26. Haulsee, W. M., Howe, F.G., and Doyle, A.C. *Soldiers of the Great War, In Three Volumes* - Soldiers Record Publishing Assoc., Washington D.C. 1920

27. Hopper, James *Medals of Honor* - The Johns Day Company, New York. 1929

28. Hunt, Frazier. *Blown In by the Draft* - Doubleday, Page and Co., Garden City, New York. 1918

29. Johnson, Thomas M. *The Lost Battalion* - The Bobbs-Merrill Co., Indianapolis, IN. 1938

30. Johnson, Thomas M. *Without Censor: New Light on our Greatest World War Battles* - The Bobbs-Merrill Co., Indianapolis, IN. 1927

31. Liggett, Hunter *Commanding an American Army* - Houghton Mifflin Company, New York. 1925

32. McCollum, Lee C. *Our Sons at War* - McLee Publishing Co., Battle Creek, MI.1940 and 1941

33. McCollum, Lee C. *Rhymes of a Lost Battalion Doughboy/History and Rhymes of the Lost Battalion* - Various/Bucklee Publishing (1939), Cedar Rapids, IA. 1919-1939

34. McKeogh, Arthur. *The Victorious 77th Division in the Argonne Fight* - Johns H. Eggers & Co. New York, 1919

35. Mead, Gary *The Doughboys: America and the First World War* - The Overlook Press, New York. 2000

36. Michelin & Cie. *The Americans in the Great War, Volume 3 – The Muese-Argonne Battle* - Michelin & Cie, Clermont-Ferrand, France.1920

37. Minder, Charles F. *This Man's War* - William Farquhar Payson Inc., New York. 1931

38. Moore, William E. and Russell, James C. *U.S. Official Pictures of the World War, Volumes 2, 3, and 4* - Pictorial Bureau, Washington D.C. 1921

39. Mosier, John *The Myth of the Great War* - Harper Collins Publishers, New York. 2001

40. Nell, John W. *The Lost Battalion: A Private's Story* - Historical Publishing Network/Lammert Publications Inc., San Antonio TX. 2001

41. P.L. Crosby, P.L. *Between Shots with the 77th Division in France* - Harper & Brothers, New York. 1919

42. Palmer, Frederick. *Our Greatest Battle* - Dodd, Mead and Co., New York. 1919

43. Pershing, John J. *My Experiences in the World War* - Da Capo Press edition, Da Capo Press, New York. 1931/1995

44. Peterson, Carl J. *Lost Battalion Survivors of Minnesota and the Northwest* - Self-Published, Hayfield MN. 1939

45. Ranlett, Louis F. *Let's Go!* - Houghton Mifflin Co., New York. 1927

46. Scott, Emmett J. *Scott's Official History of the American Negro in the Great War* - Houghton Mifflin Company, New York. 1919

47. Sloan, James J. *Wings of Honor: American Airmen in World War 1* - Schiffer Military/Aviation History, Atglen, PA. 1994

48. Stallings, Lawrence *The Doughboys: The Story of the AEF* - Harper & Row Publishers, New York. 1963

49. The Army Times, Editors of *The Daring Regiments: Adventures of the AEF in World War 1* - Dodd, Mead & Co., New York. 1967

50. Thisted, Moses N. *Pershing's Pioneers* - Alphabet Printers, Hemet, CA. 1982

51. Werstein, Irving *The Lost Battalion: A Saga of American Courage* - W.W. Norton & Co. Inc., New York. 1966

College, County and State Histories:

52. Adams, Arthur (Editor) *Harvard College Class of 1899 Fortieth Anniversary Report* - Harvard University Press, Cambridge, MA. 1939

53. American Legion Post #39 *Service Record of Rosebud County, Montana* - Forsyth, MT. 1949

54. Brooklyn Daily Eagle *Brooklyn and Long Island in the World War* - Brooklyn, New York. 1918

55. Burt County Herald *Victory! Burt County Nebraska in the World War* - Burt County Herald, NE. 1919

56. Cascade County War Council *History and Roster of Cascade County (Montana) Soldiers and Sailors* - War Book Publishing Co., Great Falls, MT. 1919

57. Chreiman, W.W. *In the World War: Saunders County, Neb.* - Wahoo Democrat Publishing, Wahoo, NE. 1920

58. City of Rochester *War Service Record Rochester and Monroe County, New York: Vol. 1* - The Dubois Press, New York. 1924

59. Gail, W.W. *Yellowstone County Montana in the World War* - War Book Publishing Co., Great Falls, MT. 1919

60. Haight, Walter L. *Racine County in the World War* - Haight Publishing, Racine, WI. 1920

61. Hanson, Joseph M. *South Dakota in the World War 1917-19* - State Historical Society, S.D. 1940

62. Hassell, Clarence L. *Grand Forks County (North Dakota) in the World War* - The Page Printerie Inc., Grand Forks, N.D. 1920

63. Holbrook, F.F. and Appel, L. *Minnesota in the War With Germany, Vol. I-II* - Minn. Historical Society, St. Paul, MN. 1928

64. Holbrook, Franklin F. *St. Paul and Ramsey County (Minn.) in the World War* - Ramsey County War Records Commission, St. Paul, MN. 1929

65. Howe, Herbert B. (Editor) *Dicennial Record, Class of 1905, Williams College* - Tuttle, Morehouse and Taylor Press, Waterhouse, CN. 1915

66. Ipswich Tribune *In the World War: Edmunds County, S.D.* - C.L. Jackson, Ipswich, S.D. 1919

67. Kern County Board of Supervisors *Veterans of WW1, Kern County, CA.* - Kern County Library, Kern County, CA. 1984

68. Kingsbury County War Society *In the World War: Kingsbury County, S.D.* - Buckbee-Mears Co., St. Paul, MN. 1920

69. Lehman, E.P. and Park, Julian *A Williams Anthology: 1910* - Williamstown, MA. 1910

70. Mason, William H. *Snohomish County (Washington) in the War* - Mason Publishing Co., Everett, WA. 1920

71. McNamee, Daniel V. *Columbia County in the World War* - J.B. Lyon Co., Albany, New York. 1924

72. Mead, Frederick S. (Editor) *Harvard's Military Record in the World War* - Harvard Alumni Assoc., Boston, MA. 1921

73. Nelson, Arthur M. *In the World War: Martin County, Minn.* - Sentinel Publishing Co., Fairmont, MN. 1920

74. Olivia Times *In the World War: Renville County, Minn.* - Olivia Times Publishing, Olivia, MN. 1920

75. Pipestone County War Council *In the World War: Pipestone County, Minn.* - The Leader Publishing Co., Pipestone, MN. 1919

76. President and Trustees of Williams College, *Williams College in the World War* - The Schilling Press, New York. 1926

77. Reeves, George W. *Jefferson County (New York) in the World War* - Hungerford-Holbrook Press, Watertown, New York. 1920

78. Resch, Tyler *Berkshire: The First 300 Years 1676-1976* - Eagle Publishing Co., Pittsfield, MA. 1076

79. Sawtell, Frank M. (Editor) *Harvard College Class of 1902 Twenty-Fifth Anniversary Report* - The University Press, Cambridge, MA. 1927

80. Shore, Chester K. *Montana in the Wars* - Star Printing Company, Miles City, MT. 1977
81. Smith, Park *Lewis and Clark County Montana War Record* - Lewis and Clark Post #2 of the American Legion of Montana, Helena, MT. 1919
82. Sullivan, Maurice J. *Nevada's Golden Stars* - A. Carlisle Pub., Reno, NV. 1924
83. Sweeney, Daniel J. *Buffalo and Erie County New York in the World War* - The Committee of One Hundred, Buffalo, New York. 1919
84. Taft, Edward A. (Editor) *Harvard College Class of 1904 Twenty-Fifth Anniversary Report* - The Plimpton Press, Norwood, MA. 1929
85. Whitman County War Commission *With the Colors from Whitman County, Washington* - Lou E. Wenham, Pullman, WA. 1920
86. Yakima Independent *Honor Roll of Yakima County Washington* - F.C. Whitney and Sons, Yakima, WA. 1919

Unit Histories:
U.S.
87. Brooklyn Daily Eagle. *Atta Boy! The Story of New York's 77th Division* - Brooklyn, New York. 1919
88. 1st Division Society. *History of the 1st Division During the World War 1917-19* - Winston Publishing, Washington D.C. 1922
89. 50th Aero Squadron Assoc. *Roll Call: 50th Squadron, A.E.F.* - Private Printing, J. Howard Hill. 1938
90. Adler, Julius O. *History of the 306th Infantry* - 306th Infantry Association, New York. 1935
91. American Battle Monuments Commission. *77th Division Summary of Operations in the World War* - United States Government Printing Office, Washington D.C. 1944
92. American Battle Monuments Commission. *92nd Division Summary of Operations in the World War* - United States Government Printing Office, Washington D.C. 1944
93. Camp, Charles W. *History of the 305th Field Artillery* - The Country Life Press, Garden City, New York. 1919
94. Compiled by the men. *Regimental History of the 306th F.A., 77th Division 1917-1919* - The Knickerbocker Press, New York. 1920
95. Compiled by the Regiment. *History of the 26th Engineers (Water Supply) in the World War 1917-1919* - The New England Water Works Assoc. 1919
96. Demaree, Joseph P. *History of Company A/308th Infantry of the Lost Battalion* - Harvey Publishing, New York. 1920
97. Foster, John *The 'C' Battery Book, 306th F.A., 77th Division 1917-1919* - Privately Published. 1920
98. Headquarters Company. *Hickoxy's Army: Being a Sort of History of Headquarters Company, 306th Field Artillery* - Headquarters Company, 306th F.A. Book Fund. 1920
99. Headquarters Platoon *Company C, 307th Infantry, 77th Division, A.E.F.* - Imprimerie V. Hureau, 21 rue Carnot, Sable-Sur-Sarthe, France. 1919
100. Howard, James M. *The Autobiography of a Regiment: A History of the 304th Field Artillery in the World War* - Private printing in New York. 1920
101. Hussey, Alexander and Flynn, Raymond. *The History of Company E, 308th Infantry* - The Knickerbocker Press, New York. 1919
102. Kenamore, Clair. *From Vauquois Hill to Exermont: A History of the 35th Division* - Guard Publishing Co., St. Louis, MO. 1919
103. Kerr-Rainsford, W. *From Upton to the Muese with the 307th* - D. Appleton & Co., New York. 1920

104. Klausner, Julius *The History of Company B, 307th Infantry* - Privately printed in France. 1919

105. Knight, Paul R. *History of Company D, 308th Infantry, 77th Division, A.E.F.* - No publishing data. 1919

106. Lavine, A. Lincoln *Circuits of Victory* - Country Life Press, Garden City, New York. 1921

107. MacLean, W.P. *My Story of the 130th Field Artillery* - The Boy's Industrial School, Topeka, KS. 1920

108. McCollum, Lee C. *Our Company: Company A, 308th Infantry* - Lumberman Printing Co., Seattle, WA. 1919

109. Miles, L. Wardlaw. *History of the 308th Infantry* - The Knickerbocker Press, New York. 1927

110. Morse, Daniel P. *The History of the 50th Aero Squadron* - The Blanchard Press, New York. 1920

111. Proctor, Harry G. *The Iron Division: P.A. N.G. in the World War* - John C. Winston Co., Philadelphia, PA.. 1919

112. Smith, Henry W. *A Story of the 305th Machine Gun Battalion, 77th Division, A.E.F.* - The Modern Composing Room, New York. 1941

113. Tiebout, Frank B. *A History of the 305th Infantry* - The 305th Infantry Auxiliary, New York. 1919

114. Unattributed. *History of Battery C, 304th Field Artillery* - No publishing data.

115. Unattributed. *History of the 40th (Sunshine) Division 1917-1919* - C.S. Huston & Co., Los Angeles, CA. 1920

116. Unattributed. *History of the 77th Division in the World War 1917-1919* - 77th Division Association, New York. 1919

117. Unattributed. *The 302nd Engineers: A History* - No publishing data.

118. Unattributed. *The History of the 308th Ambulance Company/302nd Sanitary Train/77th Division* - New York. 1919

119. Unattributed. *Through the War with Company D, 307th Infantry* - New York. 1919

German

120. Frante, A. *History of the 2nd Landwehr Division of Wurttemberg* - Berlag Berger's Literarisches Buro, Stuttgart, Germany. 1921

121. General Headquarters Intelligence Staff, A.E.F. *Histories of 251 Divisions of the German Army Which Participated in the War 1914-1918* - Chaumont, France. 1919/London Stamp Exchange LTD. 1989

122. General Headquarters Staff (2nd Section) A.E.F. *German Manpower Employed Against the American Muese-Argonne Offensive 26 September-11 November 1918* - Army War College Compilation. 1919 (Note that the original of this document is in the author's own personal collection.)

123. Regimental Staff. *Battle History of Reserve Infantry Regiment Number 254 in the World War* - Bernhard-Sporn, Berlin, Germany. 1925

124. Roll, Hans. *History of the 76th Reserve Infantry Division Vol. 2* - Berlag von Karl Siegismund, Berlin, Germany. 1918

125. Schmidt, A.D. *Reichsarchiv: Argonnen* - Gerhard Stalling, Oldenburg, Germany. 1927

126. Strohm, Gustav. *The Wurttemberg Landwehr Infantry Regiment Number 120 in the World War 1914-1918* - H.G. Belfer Berlagbuchhandlung, Stuttgart, Germany. 1922

127. Von Elster, Elstermann. *History of the 76th Reserve Infantry Division Vol. 1* - Drud der Buchdruderei, Darmstadt, Germany. 1924

128. Von Kleftor-Kling, G. *The Wurttemberg Landwehr Infantry Regiment Number 122 in the World War 1914-1918* - H.G. Belfer Berlagbuchhandlung, Stuttgart Germany. 1923

129.Wadsworth, James E. *Behind the German Lines in the Argonne* - Privately Printed and Distributed.1919

Official governmental documents:

130.Note: Most of these records are to be found in Records Group #120, National Archive Records Storage Facility at College Park, Maryland. There are also several statements and questionnaires filled out in the 1970's by men of the 77th Division to be found in the Archives of Carlisle Military Barracks in Pennsylvania, which detail their experiences in the Argonne. Other information, such as muster roll records and reports on Americans taken prisoner by the Germans, can be found at the NARA storage facility in St. Louis.

131.*154th Infantry Brigade Messages and Reports* - Memoranda, field messages, etc., and transcripts of telephone conversations taken down verbatim, pertaining to the operation initiated by Field Order # 43, Hdqrs 77th Division, 24th September 1918. All paper of records at Hdqrs 154th Brigade.

132.*Report on Battles # 4: Muese-Argonne Offensive, Sept. 26 to Nov. 11 1918 (308th Infantry Regiment)* - Prepared by Captain E. N. Lewis, post war Operations Officer of the 308th.

133.*Report on the Activities of the Headquarters Company, 308th Infantry, in the Muese-Argonne Offensive* - Prepared by Captain G.J. Stockly, C.O. Headquarters Company/308th.

134.*Report of Operations of the 306th Machine Gun Battalion - Sept.26th to Nov. 10th, 1918* - Prepared by Captain Lewis Scott and Major Douglas Campbell, Officers Commanding 306th MG Bn.

135.*Report of 1st and 2nd Battalions, 308th Infantry from Oct. 2nd to Oct. 8th 1918 prepared October 9th 1918* - Prepared by Major Charles W. Whittlesey, Officer Commanding 1st/308th

136.*308th Infantry Regiment Report of Operations, Sept. 26th – Oct. 16, 1918* – Unatributed. Note: the dates on this document from 1 October on are in error and off by one day.

137.*Report of Operations of Company 'A'/308th Infantry, Sept. 26 to Oct. 9, 1918* - Prepared by Captain Barclay McFadden and Lt. Clinton Whiting.

138.*Grouping of Operations and Intelligence Reports of the 307th Infantry* - Unofficial grouping of day to day material, containing stray operations reports, field messages, telephone logs and transcriptions, field and operations orders found astray in the government's files. Compiled by author.

139.*Report of Operation of the 307th Infantry, Sept. 26th – Nov. 8th, 1918* - by Colonel Eugene M. Houghton, Officer Commanding 307th Infantry Regiment

140.*Grouping of Reports of the 305th and 306th Field Artillery and related papers* - Unofficial grouping of stray items pertaining to the actions of the above units, found astray in the governmental files. Much of this material was only declassified in 1947 and 1948 and then apparently simply placed in any 77th Division records box that was to hand. Compiled by author.

141.*Report on Use of the 50th Aero Squadron in Operations to Assist the Lost Battalion* - Prepared by Lt. Col. M.W. Howze, Assistant Chief of Staff 77th Div.

142.*Overall Report of Medical Department Activities of the U.S. 1st Army, AEF – Section #4, The Muese-Argonne Operation: Chapter 20. (Partially Abstracted From "Major Operations of the AEF in France, 1917-1918")* - Prepared by the Historical Section, Army War College.

143. *Medical Reports for the 154th Brigade* - Records for the period Oct. 1-9 - including a flawed "mystery" 1930's list of purportedly Lost Battalion names. Assembled by the division surgeons.

144. *Loose Field Orders, General Orders, Field Messages, Telephone Logs and Conversational Transcriptions, Section Reports, Individual Reports, etc...* - Unofficial grouping of a myriad of stray paperwork that was found well out of order in the government files. Compiled by the author.

145. *'Prisoners Captured' Reports/Enemy Unit Reports* - Includes interrogation reports, lists of names of the men captured, where they were captured and where they were sent, troop movements, etc... Unattributed.

146. *Items Relating to Liaison With and Movements of the French 38th Corps, September 26th through October 9th 1918* - Unattributed.

147. *Records of the Judge Advocate General: Court Martial of Lt. Maurice S. Revnes* - Judge Advocate General's Office, 1919.

Monographs:

148. *The Operations of the So-Called Lost Battalion, October 2nd to October 8th, 1918* - Prepared by the Historical Section, Army War College, August 1928.

149. *Operations of the Force Known as the Lost Battalion, From October 2nd to October 7th, 1918 Northeast of Binarville, In the Forest of Argonne, France* - Prepared by Captain Nelson M. Holderman for the Company Officers' Class, 1924-1925, The Infantry School Fourth Section, Committee 'H' at Fort Benning, Georgia.

150. *Personal File of Major Hugh A. Drum, Reports-Statements-Etc. Papers Relating to Lost Battalion, 77th Division* - Colonel Hugh A. Drum (post war report).

Family Archives, Private Collections and Interviews

151. These individuals provided a bulk of information, making available their private family archives, including letters, diaries, memoirs, newspaper and magazine articles, official records and photos, as well as relating stories and remembrances that their relative passed on. Most of this information has been previously unpublished. Interviews were conducted through e-mail or letter, by telephone and in person. In some instances these contributions were huge; in others, less so. In a few instances where the present day contact is not related, they are the owner of that historical individual's paperwork, records or wartime grouping, access to which was made fully available.

Historical Individual – Present Day Contact

152. Private James F. Larney, Headquarters Company/308th – John Larney

153. Battalion Sergeant-Major Walter Baldwin, 1st/308th – Tom Baldwin

154. Lt. James V. Leak, Company E/308th – Frances Bingham

155. Private Victor Jammaron, Company I/308th (attached HQ Co/308th) – Leo Jammaron

156. Pvt. Lee Downs, Company C/308th – Jim Downs

157. Pvt. Morris C. Bell, H.Q.Co./308th – Thomas O. Bell

158. Pvt. James P. Ilardo, Company H/308th – Jeannie Hughes

159. Sgt. Carmen Calbi, Company I/308th – Carmen Calbi Jr.

160. Sgt. Benjamin H. Von Pentz, Company F/307th – Robert Von Pentz

161. Lt. Sherman Eager, Company G/308th – Ruth Eager Moran

162. Captain Leo Stromee, Company C/308th – Rick Lytle

163. Pvt. Lowell Hollingshead, Company H/308th – Becky Henn/Richard Amick

164. Pvt. Otto Utt, Company A/308th – Joyce Bromm
165. Pvt. Harold Brennan, Company E/308th – Patricia Nirmaire
166. Pvt. Steve Honas, Company B/308th – Julie Girard
167. Pvt. Edward Kilkenny, Company E/302nd Engineers – Thomas Kilkenny
168. Pvt. Franklin DiGiacomo, Company G/308th – Alfred DiGiacomo
169. Pvt. Roy Lightfoot, Company H/308th – Don Wilkinson
170. Pvt. George Quinn, Company D/308th – Brian Quinn
171. Pvt. Paul Sluk, Machine Gun Co./308th – James Wickman
172. 1st Bn. Sgt.-Major Benjamin Gaedeke, 308th – George and David Gaedeke
173. Pvt. Thomas Donata, Company D/308th – Susan Carr
174. Cpl. Domenico Levi, Company A/308th – Angelo Levi
175. Pvt. Herman A. Ratande, Company D/308th – Maricarol Miller
176. Pvt. Charles Wilfahrt, Company K/308th – Jeff Wilfahrt
177. Pvt. Marion Mahoney, Company B/308th – April Young
178. Pvt. Luther Ficklin, Company B/308th – Billie Hendricks
179. Pvt. John F. Drinkwater, Company D/306th MG Bn. – Willy Drinkwater
180. Pvt. Andrew Taasaas, Company H/308th – Julie Nelson
181. Lt. Marshall Peabody, Company D/306th MG Bn. – Marshall P. Hoke
182. Pvt. Jacob Rangitsch, Company E/308th – Zachary Allen
183. Pvt. Emil Peterson, Company H/308th – Orvin Peterson
184. Lt. Victor Harrington, Company E/308th – Samuel Steele
185. Pvt. Henry Cassidy, Company C/308th – anonymous
186. Pvt. Sabas McGuire, Company K/308th – Robert Collins
187. Pvt. Benjamin Pagliaro, Company G/308th – Joseph Pagliaro
188. Pvt. John Foster, Company K/307th – Robert Conner
189. Pvt. Charles Pinkstone, Company C/308th – John Lanning
190. Pvt. Louis Goncher, Company A/308th – Marc Goncher
191. Pvt. Robert Yoder, Company E/308th – Chris Yoder
192. Pvt. Phillip Cepaglia, HQ Co./308th – Tony Cepaglia
193. Pvt. Joseph Dyrdal, Company B/308th – Rhonda Walker
194. Sgt. Amos Todesco, Company G/308th – Martha Young
195. Captain Nelson Holderman, CO, Company K/307th – Gene Holderman
196. Pvt. James Bragg, Med. Det. (Co. G)/308th – Tommy Bragg
197. Pvt. Jacob Loendorf, Company C/308th – Boyd Leuenberger
198. Pvt. Hubert Esch, Company C/308th – The Esch Family
199. Lt. Dewitt Morgan, Company A/308th – Kathy Morgan
200. Pvt. Erhard Lissell, Company A/308th – Dan Olson
201. Pvt. Guiseppe Scialdone, Company K/307th – George Ryan
202. Pvt. Joseph Joyce, Company H/308th – Kevin McDonough
203. Pvt. George Weinmann and Pvt. George Parker, both of Company F/308th – George Weinmann
204. Pvt. Irving Sirotta, Med. Det. (Co. D)/308th – Marvin Edwards
205. Sgt. Martin Tuite, Company C/308th – Richard Tuite
206. Pvt. John Gehris, Med. Det. (Co. G)/308th – David Gehris
207. Pvt. Sidney Smith, Company H/308th – Victor Fritch
208. Pvt. Arthur Looker, Company B/308th – Steve Ray
209. Pvt. Louis Rickler/Pvt. Samuel Chester, Med. Det. (Co E)/308th – Perry Haberman
210. Pvt. Joseph Giganti, Company C/308th – Marylou Weber
211. Sgt. (?) Frank Robinson and Pvt. (?)Martin Humphreys, Company D (?)/306th MG Bn. – John Culleeny
212. Sgt. Harrison Hicks, Company K/307th – John Hicks
213. Pvt. Frank G.S. Erickson, Company H/308th – Mark Erickson

214.PFC Harold V. Arnold, Company F/308th – Robert Simpson
215.Pvt. Eugene M. McGrath, CompanyC/308th – Mr. and Mrs. Lowell McFarland/Francis Kopel
216.Pvt. Joseph McElroy, Company C/306th MG. Bn. – anonymous (Excerpts from a set of letters Pvt. McElroy sent home were provided by their one time private owner. However, the letter collection has since been broken up and sold into private collections, and for that reason I have refrained from using but a small quote from one of them.)

Unpublished materials

217.(In addition to information related to the above, listed below are larger assemblages of previously unseen material. As above, in all cases below at least a copy of the item is in the author's files, if not the original document.)
218.*Diary of Private James F. Larney.* (Note: portions of this diary were published in a serialized form in several newspapers during the early 1930's, however the entire diary has never been seen by the general public. Additionally, Pvt. Larney kept adding to the diary long after the event, 'fleshing out' details. Also made available was Pvt. Larney's copy of *History of the 308th Infantry*, in which he wrote detailed notes in the margins concerning the events described.)
219.*Newsletters of the Lost Battalion Survivors Association.* Courtesy Thomas Baldwin. Issues for the 1955, 1956, 1957 and 1958 meetings. (The Walter Baldwin collection.)
220.*'I Was One of the Lost Battalion' by Pvt. Ralph Edmun John.* Private memoir, courtesy Thomas Baldwin. (The Walter Baldwin collection.)
221.*Roster for the Lost Battalion Survivors Association Meeting – September, 1941.* Courtesy Julie Girard.
222.*Transcripts of a Radio Interview with Pvt. Lowell Hollingshead.* Part of the enormous Hollingshead family collection. Courtesy Becky Henn and Peter Amick.
223.*War Diary of Pvt. Robert Yoder.* Courtesy of his daughter, Eileen M. Schneiter, with the help of Jack M. Fosmark and Chris Yoder.
224.*Memoirs of Pvt. Emil Peterson.* Courtesy Orvin Peterson.
225.*Memoirs of Pvt. Jacob Rangitsch.* Courtesy Zachary Allen.
226.*Memoirs of Marshall G. Peabody.* Courtesy Marshall P. Hoke.
227.*Memoirs of Pvt. Charles Wilfahrt.* Courtesy Jeff Wilfahrt.
228.*Private Papers of Pvt. Herman A. Ratande.* Courtesy Maricarol Miller.
229.*Private Papers of Pvt. Thomas Donata.* Courtesy Susan Carr.
230.*War Diary of Pvt. Paul Sluk.* Courtesy James Wickman.
231.*Private Papers Relating to Pvt. George Quinn.* Courtesy Brian Quinn.
232.*Private Papers of Pvt. Franklin DiGiacomo.* Courtesy Alfred DiGiacomo.
233.*War Diary of Captain Leo Stromee.* Courtesy Rick Lytle.
234.*Interviews with and Private Papers of Lt. Sherman Eager.* Courtesy Ruth Eager Moran.
235.*'A History of Company F/307th Infantry' by Sgt. Jean Grosjean and Sgt. Benjamin H. Von Pentz.* Courtesy Robert Von Pentz.
236.*Private Papers of and Lectures by Lt. James V. Leak.* Courtesy Frances Bingham.
237.*Letters of Privates Harold Wiltse and Harold Young.* Courtesy Paul Infranco.
238.*The Wartime Papers of Colonel Cromwell Stacey.* Author's own personal collection
239.*The Truth About the Lost Battalion' by Captain Leo A. Stromee.* Monograph, author's own personal collection.
240.*Private Papers of Sgt. David Jolley.* Authors own personal collection.

241. *The Lt. Harold Goettler Collection, including items pertaining to Lt. Erwin Bleckley, 50th Aero Squadron.* Author's own personal collection.

242. *Private Papers Pertaining to Sgt. George Russell, KIA.* Authors own personal collection.

243. *Letters of Pvt. Solomon Weil.* Author's own personal collection.

244. *Letters of Reverend C. Greenway pertaining to the Lost Battalion.* Author's own personal collection.

245. *Annotated Version of Johnson and Pratt's 1938 book, 'The Lost Battalion'.* Courtesy Andrew Berkowitz. (This copy of the 1938 book had once belonged to Private James Larney, who had at one time gone through it with a fine toothed comb and written in the margins – heavily – what was wrong with it, all the mistakes and inaccuracies, and then what *really* had happened. Most of what he wrote dovetailed perfectly with other information discovered from other sources. A full copy of this book now resides in the author's own personal collection.)

246. *Papers and Ephemera Pertaining to Major Charles W. Whittlesey* – Various. Virtually everything military that Charles Whittlesey left behind was eventually donated to Williams College by both his parents and fellow associates and is now held as the Charles White Whittlesey Collection there. This includes his uniforms (including the uniform and glasses he wore in the Pocket), equipment, footlockers, personal effects, letters, medals, etc… George McMurtry also later donated the surrender letter, which is there as well, now sealed in plastic. The collection also contains Whittlesey's field message books and a hoard of other important and pertinent paperwork, among which can even be found his suicide note to John Bayard Pruyn. Copies of all now reside in the author's own personal collection. Williams College also holds the Thomas Johnson collection; papers relating to the former AEF reporter among the first to interview Whittlesey following the relief of the Pocket. With the help of the Florence County Historical Society in Florence Wisconsin, I was also able to track down the former location of the house in which Whittlesey was born (and pictures of it before it was torn down) as well as the church he belonged to, where there are records of his family in the church register. While no direct associates of Whittlesey's from his Wisconsin days are yet alive, their decedents are, and consequently so are a few stories concerning him. There are also some letters from his mother back to friends in town after they had moved East, invitations his parents had been sent to social functions in town and finally some rare newspaper articles concerning the family's departure from town, in the only known examples left of the local paper from that time period. Here is also located the only known photo of Whittlesey's little sister that had died so young.

Selected Magazine Articles:

247. Allen, Stookie. "Men of Daring – Col. Gordon Johnston, Rescuer of the Lost Battalion" *Argosy*, February 8th, 1936

248. Bamford, Hal. "Airdrop to Immortality" *The Airman, The official Magazine of the U.S. Airforce*, December 1958

249. Barrett, William E. "The Squadron the World Forgot" *Cavalier*, March 1961

250. Baumgartner, Richard. "Strong Force Encircled" *Military History*, April 1988

251. Beattie, Taylor V. "Ghosts of the Lost Battalion" *Military History*, August 2002

252. Bullard, Robert L. "The American Negro as a Soldier" *The Literary Digest*, June 27th 1925

253. Craig, John. "Lost Battalion" *Two Fisted Tales*, April 1952

254. Eager, Sherman W. "The Lost Battalion" *Scabbard and Blade*, April 1936

255. Frisbee, John L. "Valley of the Shadow" *Air Force Magazine*, December 1984

256. Gordon, Dennis and Otoupalik, Hayes. "Interview with Sidney Smith of the Lost Battalion" *The Doughboy*, Winter 1980-81

257. Hanser, R. and Stockton, H. "Alamo of the Argonne" *True: The Men's Magazine*, December 1960

258. Holman, John. "Lt. Col. Charles W. Whittlesey: Something About the Leader of the Intrepid Lost Battalion" *National Service with the International Military Digest*, Volume 5 - #1, January 1919

259. Hucker, Robert. "Save the Lost Battalion" *Air Classics*, May 1978

260. Johnson, Thomas M. "Lost Battalion of the 77th Division" *Infantry Journal*, June 1926

261. Johnson, Thomas M. "The Lost Battalion" *Readers Digest*, November 1938

262. Johnson, Thomas M. "The Lost Battalion" *The American Magazine*, November 1929

263. Johnson, Thomas M. and Pratt, Fletcher. "The Lost Battalion's Last Day" *Infantry Journal*, June 1941

264. Kubert, Joseph. "Medal of Honor for Unflinching Courage" *G.I. Combat*, May 1972

265. Lane, Rose W. "A Bit of Gray in a Blue Sky" *Ladies' Home Journal*, August 1919

266. Lewis, Edwin N. "In the Argonne's Mist and Mystery" *The American Legion Weekly*, September 26th 1919

267. Looker, Arthur R. "The Story of the Lost Battalion" *Reveille: The Call to a New Life*, May 15th 1919

268. Maddox, Robert. "Ordeal of the Lost Battalion" *American History Illustrated*, December 1975

269. McCarthy, Joseph. "The Lost Battalion: The Epic Tale of World War 1" *American Heritage #4*, October 1977

270. McKeogh, Arthur. "Runner Quinn" *The Saturday Evening Post*, August 16th 1919

271. McKeogh, Arthur. "The Lost Battalion" *Collier's Magazine*, November 16th 1918

272. Moore, William E. "How the Lost Battalion Was Lost" *The American Legion Weekly*, December 23rd 1921

273. New York Times (Editors). "The Epic of the Lost Battalion" *The New York Times Magazine*, September 30th, 1928

274. Pratt, Fletcher. "To Hold it High" *American Legion Magazine*, February 1940

275. Ray, T. Bill. "Rescuers Remember a Lost Battalion" *Life*, February 23rd 1959

276. Richardson, James M. "The Rescue of the Lost Battalion" *Popular Aviation*, May 1931

277. Ruffin, Steven A. "They Found the Lost Battalion" *Air Power History*, Fall 1989

278. Swindler, Henry O. "The So Called Lost Battalion" *The American Mercury*, November 1928

279. Unattributed. "The Legion and the Lost Battalion" *Click: The National Picture Monthly*, September 1939

280. Waldron, Robert. "Survivor of the Lost Battalion" *The Columbus Dispatch Magazine*, March 31 1963

Selected Newspaper Articles:

281. Note: In addition to these listed below, the author has also collected several dozen stray newspaper clippings that contained a certain amount of useful information, but which had no provenance to them. These, when used, were listed in the text under 'Unattributed.'

282. Boston Sunday Advertiser   12/22/35
283. Brooklyn Sunday News   10/2/38
284. Chicago Daily News   9/3/21
285. Chicago Herald Examiner   11/10/18
286. Chicago Herald Examiner   12/25/18
287. Chicago Tribune   3/3/23
288. Chicago Tribune   5/8/39
289. Chicago Tribune   9/3/21
290. Cincinnati Dispatch   6/8/58
291. Circleville Union Herald   2/20/19
292. Columbus Sunday Star   9/10/39
293. Des Moines Register   2/26/28
294. Des Moines Register   8/31/71
295. Des Moines Tribune-Capital   3/24/31
296. Indiana News Record   3/14/29
297. Longview Daily News   5/30/35
298. Longview Daily News   7/16/42
299. Mason City Globe-Gazette   6/12/42
300. Nassau-Suffolk Daily News   12/30/65
301. New York Times Magazine   4/4/19
302. New York Times Magazine   9/25/38
303. New York Times Magazine   9/30/28
304. Palatka Daily News   11/12/2001
305. Pasadena Star News   9/27/48
306. Rochester Post-Bulletin   8/23/72
307. The Austin Monitor   4/9/38
308. The Camp Upton News   1/12/18
309. The Cincinnati Enquirer   3/20/30
310. The Daily Missoulian   3/31/60
311. The Florence Mining News   12/?/1894
312. The Florence Mining News   8/18/1894
313. The Florence Mining News   8/26/80
314. The Hartford Courant   2/4/70
315. The Hayfield Herald   9/7/39
316. The Montana Kaimin   3/7/41
317. The New York Times   1/26/22
318. The New York Times   1/7/32
319. The New York Times   10/13/32
320. The New York Times   11/15/18
321. The New York Times   11/22/18
322. The New York Times   11/29/21
323. The New York Times   11/5/53
324. The New York Times   2/4/21
325. The New York Times   7/16/21
326. The New York Times   9/24/51
327. The New York Times   9/27/54
328. The New York Times   9/4/53

329. The Springfield News-Sun	2/18/40	
330. Times News Weekly (NY)	12/6/2001	
331. Wichita Beacon	11/11/23	
332. Wichita Beacon	11/30/31	
333. Wichita Eagle	10/13/2003	
334. Wichita Eagle	10/30/31	
335. Wichita Eagle	6/25/32	
336. Wichita Eagle	8/26/31	
337. Wichita Eagle	8/8/44	
338. Unattributed	-/-/-	

339. Editors. *The Stars and Stripes (Official Newspaper of the AEF)* - Printed in France. The six weekly issues spanning from the last week of September 1918, through the first week of November 1918.

340. Woollcott, Alexander *The Command is Forward* - The Century Co., New York. 1919

Additional Sources

341. PBS video *The Great War – 1918* - WBGH, Boston, MA.1990
342. *The 77th Division in the War.* Video from the National Archives in Washington D.C., a full copy of which is in the author's own collection.
343. George Gibson McMurtry's Spanish-American War service record, which is available on the National Archives website (see below).
344. *The Lost Battalion*, a film by the McManus Corporation, Copywrite 1921.
345. *The Lost Battalion*, a David Gerber film for A&E, Copywrite 2001.
346. "Missing in Action" a monograph on Charles Whittlesey by Martin C. Langeveld, Copywrite 2000. Courtesy William Whittlesey.
347. 'Statement of Service' cards, which for many of the men that served in WW1 are available from most county or state governmental sources. College records also provided much personal information on those who attended.
348. Additional information on Pvt. Earl Jepson came from the PBS special *The Nevada Experience – The Great War*, a KNPB – Channel 5 Public Broadcasting production.

Internet

349. www.worldwar1.com
350. www.homeofheroes.com
351. www.ABMC.gov
352. www.longwood.k12.ny.us
353. www.homestead.com/prosites-johncotter/lost_battalion.html
354. www.scuttlebuttsmallchow.com/bwmuseum.htm
355. www.militarymuseum.org
356. www.jewishvirtuallibrary.org
357. www.genform.genealogy.com
358. www.webfamilytree.com
359. www.ancestry.com
360. www.freepages.military.rootsweb.com
361. www.geddys.com
362. www.carlisle.army.mil
363. www.knpb.org

Maps

364. Forty, Simon *Historical Maps of World War 1* - PRC Publishing, London, U.K. 2002

365. Grieves, Loren C. Capt. *Military Sketching and Map Reading* - Copywrite 1917

366. Michelin Co. *Michelin's Atlas Routier et Touristique* Clermont-Ferrand, France.2002

367. General map of German dispositions in the Argonne Forest 1916-18. Courtesy Lt. Col. Taylor V. Beattie

368. Artillery Map, showing the zone of the 56th Reserve Field Artillery Regiment within the Argonne Forest, including a complete accounting for all German positions therein. Courtesy Gilles Lagin.

369. Ambulance driver's map/308th Ambulance Company (Unattributed). Author's own personal collection.

370. French 'Binarville 1:20,000' military map. Author's own personal collection.

371. Captured German map of the Argonne Forest, hand sketched by a 308th Infantry officer with all centers of German machine gun resistance. Author's own personal collection.

372. Hand drawn map of the Pocket. Contained in John Nell's accounting (see above).

373. Hand drawn map of the Pocket. Contained in Arthur Looker's accounting (see above).

374. Some other maps referred during the research for this text came from the publications, *77th Division Summary of Operations*; the *92nd Division Summary of Operations*; the *History of the 26th Engineers*; the *Medical Activities of the US 1st Army-Section #4*; and also from *A Guide to the American Battlefields in Europe*.

The author's personal collection is now believed to be the largest privately owned collection of Lost Battalion artifacts, paperwork and related ephemera in the world.

General Index

609

Nell, 78, 79, 84, 87, 94, 118, 121, 122, 139, 187, 201, 272, 312, 350, 353, 407, 409, 485, 506, 518, 528, 529, 537, 538, 584, 592, 604
Newcom, 263, 275, 360, 437, 585
Nies, 351, 526, 585

Peabody, 32, 33, 34, 263, 314, 318, 337, 347, 383, 427, 435, 441, 457, 504, 519, 543, 561, 585, 598, 599
Pershing, 22, 35, 56, 62, 63, 64, 67, 68, 74, 80, 88, 106, 108, 112, 128, 179, 213, 214, 221, 239, 319, 320, 321, 397, 398, 399, 448, 501, 536, 564, 592
Peterson, 10, 158, 159, 160, 161, 162, 163, 177, 301, 330, 333, 350, 358, 359, 381, 393, 443, 444, 445, 452, 453, 454, 455, 456, 457, 458, 465, 468, 480, 484, 506, 523, 524, 541, 585, 592, 598, 599
Petri, 186, 284, 478, 512
Phillips, 421, 422, 438, 585
Pool, 78, 108, 210, 211, 270, 279, 280, 281, 291, 299, 300, 305, 309, 310, 319, 324, 383, 395, 396, 407, 508, 540, 585
Pou, 298, 299, 305, 364, 409, 484, 486, 487, 504, 585
Prescott, 60, 83, 94, 96, 97, 101, 105, 106, 114, 115, 116, 117, 118, 123, 125, 231, 246
Prinz, 366, 378, 379, 452, 456, 457, 458, 459, 460, 461, 467, 468, 478, 502, 512, 543, 559, 572
Probst, 49, 294, 585
Putnam, 330, 331, 340, 341, 342
Pvt. Brown, 488
Pvt. Johnson, 437
Pvt. Powers, 302

Quadt-Wykradt-Huchtenbruck, 75, 271, 272, 324, 366, 367, 414, 512
Quinn, 9, 160, 166, 177, 598, 599, 601

Rainsford, 71, 85, 93, 94, 108, 141, 145, 169, 189, 193, 211, 229, 235, 236, 237, 254, 255, 256, 270, 276, 327, 328, 345, 360, 361, 508, 595
Rainwater, 262, 394, 445, 452, 453, 454, 456, 461, 464, 586
Rangitsch, 95, 359, 372, 540, 586, 598, 599
Recko, 452, 454, 586
Revnes, 9, 263, 315, 337, 383, 395, 433, 434, 440, 478, 535, 536, 546, 547, 550, 551, 586, 597
Richards, 144, 292, 304, 316, 333, 338, 352, 353, 354, 356, 472, 506, 564, 586
Roesch, 275, 309, 586
Rogers, 184, 252, 253, 254, 256, 259, 262, 264, 297, 298, 300, 302, 336, 360, 377, 383, 384, 459, 461, 511, 572, 586
Russell, 38, 39, 40, 45, 339, 369, 556, 565, 592, 600

Sadler, 259, 586
Schenck, 80, 132, 254, 258, 264, 347, 358, 360, 383, 388, 394, 396, 399, 434, 450, 455, 464, 471, 533, 586
Sgt. Anderson, 433, 434
Sgt. Robert Graham, 314
Shelata, 270, 279, 280, 287
Shepard, 358, 587
Simonson, 363, 587
Sirota, 265, 347, 354, 363, 386, 395, 408, 587
Slater, 421
Sluk, 598, 599
Smith, 58, 78, 85, 86, 94, 95, 97, 100, 119, 123, 125, 126, 132, 148, 149, 157, 158, 161, 163, 164, 172, 174, 180, 194, 195, 200, 225, 302, 363, 364, 419, 506, 524, 530, 537, 540, 587, 594, 595, 598, 601
Speich, 380, 587
Stacey, 62, 116, 117, 118, 123, 125, 127, 128, 135, 148, 149, 157, 158, 167, 172, 174, 180, 183, 184, 188, 190, 193, 194, 204, 205, 215, 216, 217, 218, 219, 220, 221, 225, 229, 232, 233, 234, 235, 239, 240, 241, 242, 245, 246, 247, 251, 252, 254, 258, 259, 260, 262, 266, 269, 274, 275, 282, 287, 288, 289, 290, 291, 296, 299, 300, 308, 309, 311, 317, 319, 321, 322, 330, 333, 334, 335, 337, 339, 340, 341, 342, 345, 356, 357, 361, 362, 370, 371, 372, 375, 389, 390, 399, 400, 417, 439, 445, 446, 448, 559, 562, 571, 599
Stallings, 177, 537, 592

1651243

Made in the USA